A

PRACTICAL GRAMMAR

OF THE

LATIN LANGUAGE;

WITH PERPETUAL EXERCISES IN

SPEAKING AND WRITING.

FOR THE

USE OF SCHOOLS, COLLEGES, AND PRIVATE LEARNERS.

BY

George

G. J. ADLER, A.M.,

LATE PROFESSOR OF THE GERMAN LANGUAGE AND LITERATURE IN THE UNIVERSITY OF
THE CITY OF NEW YORK.

"Iter autem per experientiae et rerum particularium silvas perpetuo faciendum est."

FRANCISCUS DE VERULAMIO.

BOSTON:
SANBORN, CARTER, BAZIN, & CO.
M DCCC LVIII.

Entered according to Act of Congress, in the year 1857, by

G. J. ADLER,

in the Clerk's Office of the District Court of the District of Massachusetts.

" Atque hoc modo inter empiricam et rationalem facultatem (quarum morosa et inauspicata divortia et repudia omnia in humana familia turbavere) conjugium verum et legitimum in perpetuum nos firmasse existimamus."

" Iter autem . . . . . per experientiae et rerum particularium silvas perpetuo faciendum est."

FRANCISCUS DE VERULAMIO, *Instaur. Magn. Praef.*

☞ A Key to the exercises of this Grammar, by the author, is in preparation, and will soon be published.

CAMBRIDGE:

ELECTROTYPED BY METCALF AND COMPANY.

NOTICE.

The author of this Grammar gives practical instruction in the Latin and German languages and literatures. Circulars containing terms, &c., may be obtained of the Publishers, and also at the bookstore of Ticknor & Fields, 135 Washington St., Boston. Applications may be addressed per Post Office.

PREFACE.

THE preparation of a text-book for the study of the Latin, similar to that edited by me, some twelve years ago, on the German, has since that time been repeatedly suggested to me by various persons interested in the progress of education. Years however elapsed before I could even think of entering on such a task, partly on account of other time-absorbing occupations, partly because I felt, in common with many others, some hesitation to undertake the somewhat delicate part of treating a so-called dead language like a living organism, yet in vogue as an element of national existence. It was not until after I had completed what I considered myself bound to render, as professor of a modern language in the city of New York, that I could give the question a serious consideration; and in the winter of 1854, after my secession from the University of that city, some of my leisure hours were devoted to the collection and construction of exercises similar to those contained in my edition of Ollendorff's German Method.

These tentatives, which were commenced for recreation merely, and without any direct reference to publication, were some months after again suspended and postponed indefinitely. I had, however, proceeded far enough to convince myself perfectly of the feasibility of the plan, and felt assured, that, if the student in this practical pursuit of a new language would find a pleasure at all commensurate with the satisfaction I myself experienced in my attempts to explore and point out the road to him, my task would prove a promising and successful one.

It was under this conviction, that, in the spring of 1856, I again took up my papers, and resolved to begin the work in earnest. I accordingly revised and enlarged upon what I had already collected, until my materials amounted to ten fascicles of phrases and exercises, of about the extent of those contained in my edition of Ollendorff's German Method. Soon after, I concluded an arrangement for the publication of a complete practical Grammar of the Latin upon the basis of these preliminary studies, and after many months of new researches both into the theory and practice of the language, the final result has been the volume now offered to the inspection of the public.

But although it was intended that the book should upon the whole pursue the course indicated by the methods on modern languages now almost exclusively in vogue, and to make constant repetition and the perpetual construction of connected sentences and phrases from English into the language to be acquired the chief exercise of the student, yet I could not make up my mind to surrender system to mere empirical practice to the extent to which this is done by Mr. Ollendorff. My aim was rather to sacrifice nothing of the theory, to leave no point of grammar unexplained or unconnected, but to make the student advance with equal pace from practice to theory, and from theory to practice, until he makes himself the master and conscious possessor of the entire structure of the language, as far at least as this can be effected by a Grammar.

I have therefore commenced with the simplest elements, and with exercises which a child even could comprehend and learn from repetition or dictation. As the course advances, and the rules of construction come gradually more and more into requisition, the syntax commences, of which I have prefixed connected portions to each lesson, to be committed either entirely or in part, as the student progresses with his exercises. I have thus succeeded in incorporating by degrees a complete syntax of the language, to the rules of which perpetual reference is made in subsequent parts of the book, and with which the student must become familiar before he can reach the end of the volume. In regard to the etymology, I have naturally treated the declension of substantives, adjectives, and pronouns in the first lessons. These, with the practice given, are soon completely in the power of the learner. But the doctrine of the gender of substantives, the declension of Greek nouns, the derivation of adjectives and adverbs, &c., which would only have embarrassed and retarded the student in the beginning, are deferred until nearly the close of the book. With the verbs I have proceeded in a similar manner. I first give only the present tense active, then in another lesson the passive, and in a third the present of deponent verbs. A general outline of the formation of tenses follows, in Lesson XXVIII., from which the student is referred to the paradigms of conjugation on pages 664–665, which may be read and committed, as in ordinary Grammars; but in the regular order of the book, he learns and applies only one tense at a time, on which he practises until he is fit for another, and so on to the end.

I have retained the division into Lessons, as the most suitable arrangement for a book of this description. A strict separation of the etymology and syntax, and a connected scientific treatment of the principles of grammar, however desirable in themselves, would have destroyed the characteristic feature of the method, which begins with sentences instead of isolated vocables, and thus applies the simpler principles of construction at the very outset. It is however by no means intended that those divisions called Lessons should be the task invariably assigned to the student. The judgment of the teacher must in all cases determine the proper *pensum* of the learner, according to the capacity or proficiency of the latter, and that may sometimes be more, and perhaps oftener less, than the *pensum* of the book, which is not unfrequently considerably longer than the average lessons in similar manuals on modern languages.

In the use of the book care should be taken to keep the main design steadily in view, which is the writing and memorizing of the exercises appended to each lesson. In these the student applies directly the principles already acquired, and undergoes as it were a daily self-examination on what has gone before. Hence it is much more important that he should properly attend to those, than that he should be kept too long upon the mere mechanical committing of barren lists of words, or of rules which, without application, always remain a dead letter in the memory.

Much benefit can be derived from the guidance of the instructor, whose aid in reading over the advance lesson, in explaining and removing difficulties, in separating the essential points from those of minor importance, will not fail to contribute greatly to the encouragement and rapid progress of his *studiosi*. As in many lessons of the book the principles advanced are far from being exhausted in the exercises at the end, the teacher or scholar can easily expand them by adding others similar to those given, — a practice which cannot be too strongly recommended.

To insure a correct pronunciation, I give directions at the very beginning for the accentuation of Latin words, and in the examples preceding the exercises, as well as in those given under the principal rules, the use of the accent is practically exhibited. To enable the student to accent according to the rules set forth in the first lesson, the quantity of all the words given in the vocabularies, as well as of those declined or conjugated, is indicated with almost lexicographical minuteness. In this respect I have rendered what I think is found in no other Grammar of the Latin, and am persuaded that this system, without which we can scarcely conceive of a correct pronunciation, will commend itself to the approbation of all competent to judge upon the subject.

As many of the exercises relate to the familiar talk of daily intercourse, it has sometimes become necessary to designate objects either entirely unknown to the Ancients, or known under a different form. The words employed for this purpose are either modern, as *coffea, tabacum, bibliopegus* (bookbinder), or else genuine Latin terms, but employed in a sense somewhat different from that in which they occur in classical Latinity, as, for example, *calceus* for our " shoe," *pileus* for our " hat," *speculum* for our " looking-glass," &c. To prevent misunderstanding or confusion on this subject, all the words of this description are marked, as modern or applied to objects of modern life, with an asterisk before them ; e. g. *coffea, *pileus, &c.

I have one word to add with reference to the syntax. This important part of grammar has been treated much more comprehensively than one might suppose from its somewhat disjointed appearance. The subject of agreement, the syntax of the oblique cases, the use of the infinitive, the somewhat complicated doctrine of the subjunctive, and other equally important topics, are developed as fully as in many Grammars of larger size or greater pretensions, and it is hoped that on this point nothing of any moment will be found omitted. All the rules and remarks are illustrated by numerous examples carefully selected from the classical authors of antiquity. The examples under the rules are separated from the rest of the book by a different arrangement, the Latin on the right and the English on the left, while in the general oral exercises this order is inverted. The book is thus expected to carry its own authority in itself, and to justify the imitative combinations and constructions adopted in the exercises. The doctrine of questions is fully developed and elucidated in Lesson LXXXV.; the order or arrangement of words and sentences, in Lesson XCVII. Both these lessons the teacher will do well to consult before he sets his students to work.

In the elaboration of this volume, I have availed myself of the best authorities which a long acquaintance with the philology of modern Germany had made familiar to me. On the etymology I have freely used Zumpt; on the syntax, the somewhat larger and completer manuals of Ramshorn and Krüger. On the orthography of words, and on the subject of quantity, I am chiefly indebted to the last edition of Dr. Georges' *Lateinisch-Deutsches Hand-Wörterbuch* (Leipsic, 1855). On the use of the particles I have, besides the authorities already mentioned, examined a number of other sources, especially the original treatise of Tursellinus. For correct Latin equivalents for the English terms and constructions employed in the book, I have diligently consulted the German-Latin Lexicons of Scheller, Kraft, and especially the more recent work of Georges. On doubtful or difficult points I have also had an opportunity to consult the more comprehensive works of Freund, Facciolati and Forcellini, and several others. From these authorities I have, however, adopted nothing but what I could justify by classical examples and analogics, and I have given no Latin equivalents for English terms or phrases, without testing them by comparing all the connections in which they are recorded as occurring in the classical writers. The subject of questions and answers I myself examined by a careful reading of the comedies of Terence, from which I had made numerous extracts before I was in possession of the sources from which I afterwards derived what I have advanced upon this point in Lesson LXXXV.

I have thus had rather a redundancy than a lack of materials on the majority of topics connected with the theory of grammar, while on the practical application of many principles, I was more than once forced to the reading of my Terence or my Cicero in order to obtain the desired light. — In this connection I have publicly to express my obligations to several gentlemen of Cambridge for their politeness in extending to me the privileges of their valuable University Library, to which I am indebted for several of my authorities.

I submit now the result of my somewhat protracted and by no means trivial labors to the candor and enlightened judgment of the classical scholars of America. As to the plan I have pursued, although it aims at nothing short of a radical change in the teaching of the language, I scarcely feel as if it needed an apology. The plan of learning a language by writing it, is not only the surest, but the only, road to its complete acquisition. Methods analogous to this, though unrecorded, must have been employed by those who have used, and who to some extent still use, the Latin as a medium of written communication, and not unfrequently with an elegance that reminds us of the Ancients. Let the reader think of an Erasmus, of Ficinus, of the learned family Stephanus, of Calvin, and other luminaries of the age of the revival of letters and of the Reformation, of others who have since reflected light and strength from the manly literature of ancient Rome. I think experience will prove, that the labor of acquisition, if not easier, will at any rate be more attractive and remunerative, with the method here proposed, which makes the student assist as it were in the production of his Latin, instead of forcing him to lay up barren lists of words or unproductive rules.

I have in conclusion to add, however, that the course here pointed out does not by any means pretend to be the ultimate goal of the journey to be pursued. No method in the shape of grammar, or manual of any kind, can teach completely any language, ancient or modern. It can only be acquired by familiarity with those written monuments, which are at once the flowers and conservatories of the idioms, in which they breathe a life immortal. Of these the Romans have left us many of imperishable excellence, to which we must ever point as the most perfect exponents of their language, as the armories of the Roman mind. And these are yet to add wholesome vigor to the intellect of youth, and consolation to the failing strength of age.

G. J. ADLER.

Boston, February, 1858.

ABBREVIATIONS.

Cf.   *stands for* confer, *compare.*

Compos.   "   "   compositum, *compound,* or composita, *compounds.*

e. g.   "   "   exempli gratiâ, *for example.*

i. e.   "   "   id est, *that is to say.*

The asterisk (*) before a word shows it to be of modern origin, or applied to a modern object.

ADLER'S

NEW LATIN METHOD.

Lesson I. — PENSUM PRIMUM.

INTRODUCTION.

A. LATIN GRAMMAR, considered as a science, has for its object the investigation of the laws which govern the forms and the construction of the language. When destined for the practical purposes of instruction, it becomes the art of learning to read, write, and speak the Latin language with correctness.

OF THE ALPHABET.

B. The letters of the Latin alphabet are twenty-five:— A, a; B, b; C, c; D, d; E, e; F, f; G, g; H, h; I, i; J, j; K, k; L, l; M, m; N, n; O, o; P, p; Q, q; R, r; S, s; T, t; U, u; V, v; X, x; Y, y; Z, z.

Letters are divided into vowels (*litterae vocales*) and consonants (*litterae consonantes*).

The sound of vowels is complete in itself, whereas that of consonants becomes distinct only in conjunction with a vowel.

OF VOWELS AND DIPHTHONGS.

C. The simple vowels of the Latin alphabet are six: *a, e, i, o, u, y.* To these may be added the double vowels or diphthongs *ae (æ), ai, au, ei, eu, oe (œ), oi,* and *ui.*

1. The vowel *y* (*ypsilon*) is only found in words adopted from the Greek, as *Cyrus, tyrannus, syngraphus.*
2. The diphthongs *ei, oi,* and *ui* occur only in a few interjections,

1

such as *hei*, *eia*, *viei*, *hui*, and in *dein*, *proin*, *huic*, and *cui*, when these words are contracted into one syllable.

3. The diphthong *eu* is found in words originally Greek, and in the Latin *ceu*, *seu*, *heu*, *heus*, *neu*, and *neuter*.

4. Respecting the proper sounds of these vowels, there is at present no uniformity of usage, the common custom in vogue among the different nations of Europe being that of following the analogy of their respective vernacular idioms. This has given rise to a diversity of pronunciations, among which the English and the Continental are the most conspicuous. The following table exhibits the difference between the English and the German sounds of each of the vowels, both long (‒) and short (˘) :—

	ENGLISH SOUND.	GERMAN SOUND.
a	māter, mannă*	*ā* always *ăh*, *ă* as in *am*.
e	dēlĕo, fessus	*ē* like *a* in *fate*, *ĕ* as in *fre*
i, y,	fīnis, mīrābĭlĭs	*ī* like *ee* in *keen*, *ĭ* as in *fin*.
o	corōnă, dŏmĭnus	*ō* as in *bōne*, *ŏ* as in *shone*.
u	ūsŭs, dŭumvir	*ū* like *oo* in *moon*, *ŭ* the same sound short.
ae	Caesar, caestus†	like *ā* in *fate*.
ai	Măĭa,‡ aio	broader, with the sound of both vowels.
au	aurum, causa	like *ou* in *house*.
ei	eia, omneis	like *i* in *shine*.
eu	Orpheus,§ neuter	nearly like *oi* in *foil*.
oe	poena, foedus	like the French *eu* in *feu*.
ui	huic, cui ‖	like *ooi* rapidly sounded.

REMARK. — In the above examples, the learner is expected to sound the vowels as he would under similar circumstances in English words.

OF THE CONSONANTS.

D. The consonants are divided into *liquids*, *mutes*, and *double consonants*.

The liquids are *l*, *m*, *n*, *r*.

The mutes comprise the remaining simple consonants of the alphabet, with the exception of the sibilant *s*.

The mutes are again subdivided, with reference to the organ by which they are pronounced, into *labials* (*v*, *b*, *p*, *f*), *gutturals* (*g*, *c*, *k*, *qu*), and *linguals* (*d*, *t*).

---

* *A* final is generally sounded broad, like *ah*; but this is not prolonged unless the vowel is long, as *Musa* = *Musăh*, but *Musā* = *Musāh*.

† In the diphthongs *ae* and *oe* (which are also printed *æ*, *œ*) the sound of *e* (long) only is heard.

‡ But *ai* is also written *aj*, as *Achaja*, *Maja*, &c.

§ This may become, by diæresis, *Orphĕus*, gen. *Orphĕi*. The same is true of other vowels usually treated as diphthongs, as *Laïus*, *Laërtes*, &c.

‖ Pronounced in English *hike*, *ki*.

The double consonants are *x* and *z* (called *zeta*). The former combines the sounds *cs*, the latter *ds*.

E. The power of these consonants is upon the whole the same as that of the corresponding English letters. Nor are there as many international discrepancies of pronunciation as in the vowels. The following remarks will illustrate their force more particularly : —

1. *C* before *a, o, u*, or a consonant has the hard sound of *k*, as *caput, cultus, clavis;* and before *e, i, y, ae, ei, eu,* and *oe* the soft sound of *s*, as *Ceres, civis, caelebs, coelum.**

2. *Ch* has the force of *k*, as *pulcher, machīna*.

3. *G* before *a, o, u*, or another consonant is likewise hard, as in English, e. g. *garrŭlus, guttus, gleba;* but it is soft before *e, i, y*, or another *g*, e. g. *gener, gingīva, gypsum, agger.†*

4. *H* is a mere aspiration, and not regarded as a consonant. In some words it is either expressed or omitted, e. g. *have* or *ave, ahenum* or *aënum, mihi* or *mi*.

5. The ancient Romans made no distinction of form between the consonants *j, v* and the vowels *i, u;* but the same characters *I* and *V* had sometimes the power of vowels and sometimes of consonants.

6. *K* has now become a superfluous letter, and is only used in certain abbreviations, as *K.* for *Kaeso ; Kal.* for *Calendae*.

7. *M* at the beginning or in the middle of a word is sounded as in English. But *m* final, when preceded by a vowel, was not so distinctly pronounced by the Ancients. Hence, when the following word commenced with a vowel, the *m* final was either entirely silent (in poetry always so) or regarded as a mere connecting link between the vowels.

8. *Q* occurs only in connection with *u* followed by another vowel, as *quum, qui, coquus*.

9. *S* has upon the whole the same power as in English. Among the older Latin writers, however, it seems to have had the stronger sound of *ss*, as they wrote *cassus, caussa, accusso*, &c., instead of the later *casus, causa, accuso*.

10. *Ti* and *ci* short, when followed by another vowel, are generally sounded like *shee*, as in *Horatius, nuntius, justitia ; Fabricius, novicius,* &c. But *ti* retains its proper sound, *a)* when the *i* is long, as in *istīus, totīus ; b)* when the *t* is preceded by an *s, x*, or another *t*, as in *ostium, mixtio, Bruttii ; c)* in words originally Greek, as *Miltiades, Aegyptius ; d)* before the *er* of the infinitive passive, as *nitier, flectier,* &c.; *e)* at the beginning of a word, as in *tiara*.

---

* It is, however, probable that the Romans once sounded the letter *c* always like *k*, as the Greeks did. But the above distinction is too old and general to be disregarded.

† But in words of Greek origin it retains the hard sound of the original *γ*, as *gigas, gigno*, &c.

OF THE HIATUS.

F. The concurrence of two vowels, either in the middle of a word or at the close of one and the beginning of another, gives rise to what is called an *hiatus.* This the Romans avoided, especially in poetry, *a*) by the contraction of the two vowels into one long one, as in *audīsti* for *audiisti*, *deprēndo* for *deprehendo*,* &c.; *b*) by *Synaeresis*, i. e. by pronouncing the two vowels rapidly like a diphthong, as *deïnde, huïc, omnia ;* and *c*), when the hiatus occurred between two words, by the *elision* (i. e. by the suppression in reading) of the final vowel of the first word, as in *atque ego, sapere aude,* which as thus elided read *atqu' ego, saper' aude.*

OF SYLLABLES.

G. A syllable may consist either of a single vowel or diphthong, or of the union of a vowel or diphthong with one or more consonants, e. g. *o-vum, du-o, i-ste, con-stans.*

1. The Latin language generally tolerates no more than two consonants at the end of a syllable or word; when there are three, the last is always an *s*, as in *stirps.*

2. Nor does a syllable commonly commence with more than two consonants, except where at the beginning of a word *sc*, *sp*, and *st* are followed by an *r*, or where in the middle of a word one of the letters *c, p,* or *s* is followed by a mute and liquid, as *scri-ptor, spre-tus, stri-ctim ; do-ctrina, clau-strum, i-sthmus, magi-stri, corru-ptrix.*

3. The division of words into syllables may be regulated by the following laws : —

a) A consonant between two vowels belongs to the last, as *e-go, pa-ter, so-ror.*

b) The consonants which may begin a Greek or Latin word (according to Remark 2) belong together in the division of a word into its component syllables, as *pa-tris, i-gnis, a-ctus, o-mnis, i-psi, pa-stor, po-sco, fau-stus, sce-ptrum, ca-strum,* &c.

c) Combinations of consonants which never occur at the beginning

---

* The *h*, not being regarded as a consonant, does not prevent the hiatus. In verse this is equally true of *m* final, so that *multum ille et* is pronounced *mult' ill' et*, &c. In a similar manner the older Latin poets elided the final *s* of the terminations *us* and *is*, but only before consonants, as *nuntiu' mortis* for *nuntius mortis*, &c.

of a word are treated according to the analogy of the rest, e. g. *Daphne, rhy-thmus, smara-gdus,* &c.

d) Compounds are usually divided according to the parts of which they are composed, as *ab-est, abs-condo, inter-sum, ob-tuli, red-eo,* &c. But where the composition is uncertain or obscure, or when the first component has lost a part of its original termination, the division is effected as in simple words, e. g. *am-bages, ani-madverto* (contracted for *animum adverto*), *long-aevus, po-tes* (for *potis* + *es*), &c.

4. Words consisting of one syllable are called *monosyllables;* those of two, *dissyllables;* and those of more than two, *polysyllables.*

OF THE QUANTITY OF SYLLABLES.

H. The quantity of a syllable is the relative time occupied in its pronunciation. It is upon this principle that the entire fabric of Latin versification depends.

Every syllable is either *long* (–), or *short* (⌣),* or *common* (≃), i. e. sometimes long and sometimes short, as *amāvi, legĕrĕ, volŭcris.*

1. A syllable is long *by nature,* when its vowel is naturally long, as *causa, concĭdo;* it is long *by position,* when its vowel is followed by two consonants or a double consonant, as *stirpis, sermo, discessit.*

2. All diphthongs and such simple vowels as have originated in a contraction are by nature long, as *caedo, proelium, audax; cōgo* (from *coăgo*), *bōbus* (for *bovibus*).

3. A vowel before another vowel is commonly short, as *mĕus, dĕa, pĭus, vĕho.*

4. A vowel before a mute and liquid is common, as *lŭcrum, tenĕbra, tonĭtrus.*

5. The quantity of the simple vowels under other circumstances can only be determined by the authority of the poets, and is commonly given in the Lexicon. The rules respecting the quantity of final syllables, &c. belong to Prosody.

OF THE ACCENT.

I. Accent is the peculiar tone or emphasis with which a particular syllable of a word is uttered.

Every Latin word has one principal or leading accent, and only one.

The leading accent is either the *circumflex* (^) or the *acute* (').

---

* The short syllable being taken as the unit of measure, the pronunciation of a long syllable would occupy double the time of a short one.

1*

There is also a subordinate accent called the *grave* (` ` `).
But this denotes rather the absence of the principal accent, and
is scarcely used. In words of several syllables, the last syllable but one is called the *penult* or *penultĭma* (sc. *syllăba*), and
the last but two, the *antepenult* or *antepenultĭma.*

The place of the accent is determined by the following
laws: —

1. Monosyllables have the circumflex, when their vowel is long by
nature, and the acute, when their vowel is short by nature or long by
position, as *flôs, spês, môns, fûns,* but *árs, dúx, fáx, párs.*

2. In words of two syllables the accent is always on the penult, and
it is *a*) circumflex, when the penult is long by nature and the last
syllable short, as *jûrĭs, lûcĕ, mûsă, spînă;* but *b*) acute under all
other circumstances,* as *fócŭs, hómŏ, villă, áxĭs, deös, músā.*

3. Words of three or more syllables are accented either on the
penult or on the antepenult: —

   a) When the penult is short, the antepenult has invariably the
acute, as *accéndĕre, caédĕre, hómĭnēs.*

   b) When the penult is long by nature and the last syllable short,
the former has the circumflex, as *humânŭs, amâssĕ, audîsse.*

   c) When the penult is long by position, or when the last syllable
is likewise long, it has the acute, as *modéstŭs, edúctus, humánĭs.*

4. The antepenult is the limit of the accent, and polysyllables are
all treated like words of three, e. g. *poëmátĭbus, Constantinópŏlis,
sollicitudinĭbus.*

5. Some words are entirely unaccented, as *ne, que, ve, ce.* But
these never appear alone, being always appended to other words, of
which they often change the place of the accent,† e. g. *musáque, musáque, habêsne, pleráque,* &c.

6. The quantity of a word being given (as it commonly is in Lexicons), its accent can be easily determined according to one of the
above rules. — The beginner should carefully distinguish between
quantity and accent, which in Latin are not only distinct, but often
apparently at variance. The former is the principle of versification,
the latter the indispensable condition of a correct pronunciation and
the very soul of living discourse.

OF THE PARTS OF SPEECH.

J. The words of the Latin language, arranged according to their signification, may be reduced to nine
classes, usually called *parts of speech*, of which five are
inflected, and four invariable.

---

* That is, 1) when both syllables are short (*fócŭs, hómŏ*) ; 2) when the first
is short and the second long (*deös, meös*) ; 3) when the first is long by position
only (*áxĭs, villă*) ; 4) when both are long (*mûsā*).

† This is generally thrown back upon the next syllable preceding them.

1. The declinable parts of speech are: *Substantives* or *Nouns*, *Adjectives*, *Pronouns*, *Verbs*, and *Participles*.

2. The indeclinable are: *Adverbs, Prepositions, Conjunctions*, and *Interjections.* All these are termed *Particulae* or *Particles.*

3. To these classes may be added the *Gerunds* and *Supines*, two forms of verbal substantives peculiar to the Latin.

OF DECLENSION.

K. Nouns and adjectives are said to be *declined*, and their inflection is called *Declension.* Verbs are said to be *conjugated*, and their inflection is called *Conjugation.*

In the declension of substantives and adjectives, the relations of *Gender, Number*, and *Case* are indicated by certain changes of termination.

Latin nouns have three genders, the *Masculine, Feminine*, and *Neuter ;* and two numbers, the *Singular* and the *Plural.*

They have six cases: the *Nominative, Genitive, Dative, Accusative, Vocative*, and *Ablative.*

The Nominative is, as in English, employed as the subject of a finite verb.

The Accusative corresponds upon the whole to the English Objective.

The remaining cases serve to express various relations, which in English are usually denoted by such prepositions as *of, to, for, with, by*, &c.

There are five different modes of inflecting substantives, called the *first, second, third, fourth*, and *fifth declensions.* These are distinguished from each other by the termination of the genitive singular, which in the first declension is *ae*, in the second *i*, in the third *is*, in the fourth *ūs*, and in the fifth *ëi*.

Lesson II. — PENSUM ALTĔRUM.

OF THE FIRST DECLENSION.

A. The first declension comprises all substantives and adjectives which form their genitive in *ae.* The nominative of such of these words as are of purely Roman origin ends in *ă*, that of a few Greek words in *ē, ēs*, and *ās.* Those in *ă* and *ē* are mostly feminine, the rest are masculine. The singular of a noun in *ă* in connection with *mĕa*, "my," and *tŭa*, "thy" or "your," is thus inflected : —

Nom.	*my paper*	mĕă chartă
Gen.	*of my paper*	mĕae chartae
Dat.	*to or for my paper*	mĕae chartae
Acc.	*my paper*	mĕăm chartăm
Voc.	*O my paper*	mĕă chartă
Abl.	*with or by my paper*	mĕā chartā.

Nom.	*your table*	tŭă mensă
Gen.	*of your table*	tŭae mensae
Dat.	*to or for your table*	tŭae mensae
Acc.	*your table*	tŭăm mensăm
Voc.	*O your table*	tŭă mensă
Abl.	*with, from, or by your table*	tŭā mensā.

So decline *taenĭa, fascĭa, hŏra, penna.*

REMARK. — The *a* of the ablative of the first declension is always long, and sometimes printed *â*. — But in all other cases of words declined, the final *a* is generally short, as *chartă* (Nom.); *candelabră,* candlesticks; *templă,* temples.

N. B. — In the vocabularies of this Grammar the quantity of every Latin word will be given, and the paradigms of inflection will show the quantity of the different case-terminations. From these data the student will accent according to the Rules of Lesson I., page 6. Examples of the application of these principles of accentuation are furnished in the phrases of each Lesson.

Have you?	{ Habêsne ? * Num hábēs ? { Éstne tíbĭ ? An húbēs ?
Yes, Sir, I have.	{ Íta ést,† dómĭne, hábĕo. { Sánē quídem, dómĭne, ést.
Have you the hat?	{ Habêsne (tû) pílĕum ?‡ { Éstne tíbĭ pílĕus ?

---

* In asking questions, the Romans usually employed certain signs of interrogation, of which the most common are the enclitic *ne* (always affixed either to the verb or to some other word of the sentence), the particles *num, ăn, ecquid, numquid, utrum, nonnĕ,* &c. — The enclitic *ne* and *ecquid* can be used in questions *of every description,* whether the expected answer be affirmative or negative; *num* and *numquid,* only when it is expected to be "no"; *nonne,* only when it is to be "yes"; *an* and *utrum* chiefly in double questions.

† The most current Latin adverbs corresponding to our English "yes" are : *ĕtĭam* (= even, even so), *vĕrŏ* (indeed), *rectē* (you are right), *certē* (certainly), *ĭtă, ĭtă est, sic est* (it is so), *sānē* or *sānē quídem* (indeed, surely), *immo* or *immo vĕrŏ* (yes, yes). But the Romans frequently reply by a simple repetition of the verb or of the emphatic word of the inquiry, e. g. here with a simple *Hábĕo* and *Est.* — The ceremonious use of a word like our "Sir" was unknown to the ancients. To *dómĭne,* however, the vocative of *dominus* (master, lord), there can be no objection.

‡ The Romans have no article. Its place is in certain cases supplied by a

| Yes, Sir, I have the hat. | { Sic ést, dómine, hábeo pílĕum. |
| | { Étiam, dómine, ést míhi pílĕus. |

B. *Obs.* The verb *hăbĕo*, being transitive, is followed by the accusative of the object, and the neuter verb *est* by the nominative.

The pen.	*Penna, ae, *f.*
The ribbon.	Taenia, ae, *f.* ; fascia, ae, *f.*
The table.	Mensa, ae, *f.*
The paper.	*Charta, ae, *f.*
The hat.	{ *Pílĕus, i, *m.*, *Acc.* pílĕum, *or*
	{ *Pílĕum, i, *n.* (*Nom.* & *Acc.*)
The sugar	Sacchărum, i, *n.* (*Nom.* & *Acc.*) .
The salt.	{ Säl,* *gen.* sälis, *m.*, *acc.* sälem.
	{ Säl, *gen.* sälis, *n.*, *acc.* säl.

C. *Obs.* Words of the neuter gender have the nominative, accusative, and vocative, singular and plural, always alike.

		Masc.	Fem.	Neut.
My.	{ Nom.	*mĕŭs*	*mĕă*	*mĕŭm.*
	{ Acc.	*mĕŭm*	*mĕăm*	*mĕŭm.*

		Masc.	Fem.	Neut.
Thy (your).	{ Nom.	*tŭŭs*	*tŭă*	*tŭŭm.*
	{ Acc.	*tŭŭm*	*tŭăm*	*tŭŭm.*

D. RULE. Adjectives and adjective pronouns agree with their substantives in gender, number, and case. Thus:—

My sugar.	Méum sácchărum (*Nom.* & *Acc.*).
My hat.	{ Nom. pílĕus méus (*m.*), pílĕum méum (*n.*).
	{ Acc. pílĕum méum, *or* méum pílĕum.
My pen.	{ Nom. méa pénna, *or* pénna méa.
	{ Acc. méam pénnam, *or* pénnam méam.
Your salt.	{ Nom. säl túum (*or m.* túus).
	{ Acc. säl túum, *or* túum säl.

Have you my hat?	Habêsne méum pílĕum?
Yes, Sir, I have your hat.	{ Véro, dómine, pílĕum túum hábĕo.
Have you my ribbon?	Habêsne taéniam méam?
I have your ribbon.	Hábeo túam taéniam.

---

demonstrative pronoun, by *unus*, one, *aliquis*, some one, &c. But ordinarily the distinctions expressed by our articles must be mentally supplied from the context.—The learner will also notice the omission of the pronouns *ĕgŏ*, *tŭ*, which the Latin language employs only for the sake of emphasis or contrast.

* The substantives *pílĕus* and *säl* have two forms, i. e. the masculine and neuter, without any difference of signification.

Have you the pen?	{ Éstne tíbí pénnă? { Habêsne pénnam?
I have the pen.	{ Ést míhí pénnă. { Hábĕo pénnam.

EXERCISE 1.

Have you the table? — Yes, Sir, I have the table. — Have you my table? — I have your table. — Have you your pen? — I have my pen. — Have you the sugar? — I have the sugar. — Have you my sugar? — I have your sugar — Have you the paper? — I have the paper. — Have you your paper? — I have my paper. — Have you the salt? — I have the salt. — Have you my salt? — I have your salt.

Lesson III. — PENSUM TERTIUM.

OF THE SECOND DECLENSION.

A. The second declension comprises all substantives and adjectives which form their genitive in **ĭ**. The terminations of the nominative are **ŭs** (generally masculine, sometimes feminine), **ĕr**, **ĭr** (masculine),* and **ŭm** (neuter). Examples: —

Mĕus dŏmĭnus, *m., my master.*   Lĭber tŭus, *m., your book.*

Nom.	*my master*	mĕŭs dŏmĭnŭs	*your book*	lĭbĕr tŭŭs
Gen.	*of my master*	mĕĭ dŏmĭnĭ	*of your book*	librī tŭĭ
Dat.	*to my master*	mĕō dŏmĭnō	*to your book*	librō tŭō
Acc.	*my master*	mĕŭm dŏmĭnŭm	*your book*	librŭm tŭŭm
Voc.	*O my master*	mĭ† dŏmĭnĕ	*O your book*	lĭbĕr tŭe
Abl.	*with my master*	mĕō dŏmĭnō.	*with your book*	librō tŭō.

Săcchărum bŏnum, *n., good sugar.*

Nom.	*the good sugar*	sacchărŭm bŏnŭm
Gen.	*of the good sugar*	sacchărī bŏnī
Dat.	*to the good sugar*	sacchărō bŏnō
Acc.	*the good sugar*	sacchărŭm bŏnŭm
Voc.	*O good sugar*	sacchărŭm bŏnŭm
Abl.	*with the good sugar*	sacchărō bŏnō.

---

* To these must be added one adjective in *ur*, viz. *satur, satŭra, satŭrum,* sated, satisfied.

† This vocative is sometimes *mĕus* and sometimes *mĭ,* after the analogy of proper names in *ius,* which have always *i,* as, *Virgĭlius, Virgĭli; Horātĭus, Horāti;* so also *filĭus, fĭli; gĕnĭus, gĕni.*

Like *domǐnus* decline *pǐlĕus, pannus, ĕquus, calcĕus*, and all nouns and adjectives of this declension which end in *ǔs*. After the manner of *lǐber*, decline *ǎger, culter, fǎber, mǎgister*, &c.;* like *sacchǎrum*, all neuters in *ǔm*, as *aurum, cǒrǐum, lignum, plumbum*, &c. (Cf. Lesson IV.)

REMARK 1. The final *i* of the genitive of this declension, and of Latin words generally, is *long*; except in *mǐhi, tǐbi, sǐbi*, where it is common (ǐ).

2. The final *o* of the dative and ablative singular of this declension is always long. But in Latin words generally it is common, as *sermǒ, amǒ, hǎbĕǒ*.

		Masc.	Fem.	Neut.
Which (of many)?	Nom.	Qui(s),	quae,	quǒd or qulǐd.
	Acc.	Quĕm,	quǎm,	quǒd or qulǐd.
Which (of two)?	Nom.	Ūtĕr,	utrǎ,	utrǔm.
	Acc.	Utrǔm,	utrǎm,	utrǔm.
Good.	Nom.	Bǒnus,	ǎ,	ǔm.
	Acc.	Bǒnǔm,	ǎm,	ǔm.
Great, large, big.	Nom.	Magnǔs,	ǎ,	ǔm.
	Acc.	Magnǔm,	ǎm,	ǔm.
Bad.	Nom.	Mǎlus,	ǎ,	ǔm.
	Acc.	Mǎlum,	ǎm,	ǔm.
Bad, i. e. worthless.	Nom.	Vīlǐs,	vīlǐs,	vīlĕ.
	Acc.	Vīlĕm,	vīlĕm,	vīlĕ.
	Or :	— Nēquǎm (*indeclinable*).†		
Beautiful, fine.	Nom.	Pulchĕr,	pulchrǎ,	pulchrǔm.
	Acc.	Pulchrǔm,	pulchrǎm,	pulchrǔm.
	Also :	— Formōsǔs,	ǎ,	ǔm
Ugly.	Nom.	Turpǐs,	turpǐs,	turpĕ,
	Acc.	Turpĕm,	turpĕm,	turpĕ.

My good sugar.   Sácchǎrum méum bónum (*Nom. & Acc.*)
Your bad sugar.   Sáccharum túum vǐlĕ (nĕquam).

The fine table (paper, ribbon).	Nom.	Ménsa (chárta, taénǐa) pǔlchra.
	Acc.	Ménsam (chártam, taénǐam) pǔlchram.
The ugly hat (book, salt).	Nom.	Pǐlĕus (liber, sǎl) túrpis.
	Acc.	Pǐlĕum (lǐbrum, sǎlem) túrpem.
Which hat? Which paper?	Nom.	Quís pǐlĕus? Quaé‡ chárta?
	Acc.	Quém pǐlĕum? Quǎm chártam?
Which sugar?		Quód sácchǎrum? (*Nom. & Acc.*)
		Quíd sácchǎri? (*Nom. & Acc.*)

---

* Some nouns (and adjectives) in *er* retain the *e* in the genitive, and have *ĕri* instead of *ri*, as *gĕner, gĕnĕri.* a son-in-law ; *púer, -ĕri*, a boy ; *liber, -ĕri*, free, &c. — *Vǐr*, a man, has *vǐri*, and so its compounds, as *decemvǐr, -vǐri; ĕvǐr, -vǐri.*

† *Mǎlus* is said of persons, and is *morally bad; vǐlis* chiefly of things *worthless*; *nĕquam* of persons and things both.

‡ Diphthongs receive the accent upon the second vowel.

B. Obs. The interrogative *quod* is always used adjectively, and agrees with its noun in gender, number, and case; *quid* is more like the English *what?* and is either used independently or has its noun in the genitive. — The masculine *which?* is more commonly *qui* than *quis* when a substantive is expressed with it.

Have you good sugar?	Éstne tíbĭ sácchărum bónum?
Yes, Sir, I have good sugar.	{ Sánē, dómĭne, ést mĭhĭ sáccharum bónum.
Have you the fine ribbon?	Habêsne taénĭam púlchrŭm?
I have the fine ribbon.	Hábĕo taénĭam púlchram.
Which hat have you?	{ Quĭ ést tíbĭ pílĕus? { Quém pílĕum hábēs?
I have my ugly hat.	Pílĕum méum túrpem hábĕo.
Which ribbon have you?	{ Quaē ést tíbĭ taénĭa? { Quăm hábēs taénĭam?
I have your fine ribbon.	Taénĭam túam púlchram * hábĕo.

EXERCISE 2.

Have you the fine hat? — Yes, Sir, I have the fine hat. — Have you my bad hat? — I have your bad hat. — Have you the bad salt? — I have the bad salt. — Have you your good salt? — I have my good salt. — Which salt have you? — I have your good salt. — Which sugar have you? — I have my good sugar. — Have you my good sugar? — I have your good sugar. — Which table have you? — I have the fine table. — Have you my fine table? — I have your fine table. — Which paper have you? — I have the bad paper. — Have you my ugly paper? — I have your ugly paper. — Which bad hat have you? — I have my bad hat. — Which fine ribbon have you? — I have your fine ribbon. — Have you my fine pen? — I have your fine pen.

Lesson IV. — PENSUM QUARTUM.

OF THE THIRD DECLENSION.

A. Substantives and adjectives of the third declension have their genitive in *ĭs*. The terminations of the nominative are numerous, some ending in one of the vowels *a, e, i, o, y,* and others in one of the consonants *c, (d), l, n, r, s, t, x.* This declension comprises nouns of every gender.

---

* In writing his exercises, the learner should be careful to select the proper case and gender of the adjectives, which must always correspond with that of the nouns with which they are to be connected. In this and the following lessons, the nominative and accusative are the only cases used.

Nouns ending in *a, e, i, y, c, l,** and *t* are neuter.

Nouns in *o, or, os,* and *eus* are generally masculine, but sometimes of other genders.

Those in *as, aus, es, is, ys, bs, ns,* and *ps* are generally feminine, sometimes masculine.

Those in *er* and *n* are masculine and neuter.

	Lăpĭs, *m., a stone.*		
Nom.	*a stone*	lăpĭs	
Gen.	*of a stone*	lăpĭdĭs	
Dat.	*to a stone*	lăpĭdĭ	
Acc.	*a stone*	lăpĭdĕm	
Voc.	*O stone*	lăpĭs	
Abl.	*with a stone*	lăpĭdĕ.	

	Vestĭs, *f., a garment.*	
the garment	vestĭs	
of the garment	vestĭs	
to the garment	vestĭ	
the garment	vestĕm	
O the garment	vestĭs	
with the garment	vestĕ.	

	Cănis, *m. & f.,*† *the dog.*	
Nom.	*the dog*	cănĭs
Gen.	*of the dog*	cănĭs
Dat.	*to the dog*	cănĭ
Acc.	*the dog*	cănĕm
Voc.	*O dog*	cănĭs
Abl.	*with the dog*	cănĕ.

	*Tĭbĭālĕ, *n., the stocking.*	
the stocking	tĭbĭālĕ
of the stocking	tĭbĭālĭs
to the stocking	tĭbĭālĭ
the stocking	tĭbĭālĕ
O stocking	tĭbĭālĕ
with the stocking	tĭbĭālĭ.‡

	Sartŏr, *m., the tailor.*	
Nom.	*the tailor*	sartŏr
Gen.	*of the tailor*	sartōrĭs
Dat.	*to the tailor*	sartōrĭ
Acc.	*the tailor*	sartōrĕm
Voc.	*O tailor*	sartŏr
Abl.	*with the tailor*	sartōrĕ.

	Căpŭt, *n., the head.*	
the head	căpŭt
of the head	căpĭtĭs
to the head	căpĭtĭ
the head	căpŭt
O the head	căpŭt
with the head	căpĭtĕ.

	Frătĕr, *m., the brother.*	
Nom.	*the brother*	frătĕr
Gen.	*of the brother*	frătrĭs
Dat.	*to the brother*	frătrĭ
Acc.	*the brother*	frătrĕm
Voc.	*O brother*	frătĕr
Abl.	*with the brother*	frătrĕ.

	Săl, *m. & n., the salt.*	
the salt	săl	*neut.*
of the salt	sălĭs	
to the salt	sălĭ	
the salt	sălĕm, săl	
O salt	săl	
with the salt	sălĕ *or* -ĭ.	

---

* Nouns in *l* are generally neuter, but sometimes masculine.

† Nouns which are sometimes masculine and sometimes feminine, according to the context, are said to be of the *common gender.* So *adolescens* and *juvĕnis,* m. & f., a young man or woman ; *conjux,* m. & f., a husband or a wife ; *infans,* m. & f., an infant ; and a number of others. Nouns of which the gender is unsettled are said to be of the *doubtful gender ;* as *dies,* m. & f., a day ; *penus,* m., f., & n., provisions.

‡ Neuters ending in *ĕ, ăl,* and *ăr* have ĭ in the ablative instead of *ĕ ;* as

REMARK. The final *e* of the ablative of the third declension is always short, and the final *i* long.

		Masc.	Fem.	Neut.
It.	{ Nom.	Is	ĕā	id.
	{ Acc.	Eŭm	ĕăm	id.

B. Obs. The pronoun *is, ea, id* must be put in the same case and gender as the substantive for which it stands.

Not; no.	*Nŏn; nōn vĕrō, mĭnĭmĕ.*
I have not.	Nôn hábĕo.
No, Sir.	Nôn (mínĭme) véro, dómĭne.
Have you the table?	Habêsne ménsam?
No, Sir, I have it not.	{ Mínĭme, dómĭne; (éam) nôn hábĕo.
	{ Nôn hábĕo, dómĭne, nôn.
Have you the hat?	An hábēs pílĕum?
No, Sir, I have it not.	Mínĭme, dómĭne; (éum) nôn hábĕo.
Have you the sugar?	Num hábēs sácchărum?
I have it not.	Nòn hábĕo.

D. Obs. The English idiom requires here *id non habeo*. In Latin, however, the pronoun *is, ea, id* is frequently omitted, when it would have to stand in the same case as the noun to which it relates.

The coat.	*Tŏga, ae, *f.*
The cloth.	Pannus, i, *m.*
The horse.	Equus, i, *m.*
The shoe.	*Calcĕus, i, *m.*
The thread.	Fīlum, i, *n.*
The candlestick.	Candēlăbrum, i, *n.*
The wood.	Lignum, i, *n.*
The leather.	Cŏrĭum, i, *n.*
The lead.	Plumbum, i, *n.*
The gold.	Aurum, i, *n.*

| *Of.* | *E, ex.* |

E. Obs. The preposition *e* or *ex* is followed by the ablative. *E* can be put before consonants only, *ex* before vowels and consonants both.

Of gold.	Ex aúrō, aúrĕus, a, um.
Of cloth.	E pánnō.

---

mărĕ, mărĭ; ănĭmăl, ănĭmălĭ; calcăr, calcărĭ. Except săl, făr, baccăr, jŭbăr, hĕpăr, and *nectăr*, which retain the *ĕ*.

F. Obs. The material of which anything is made may either be expressed by the ablative of a substantive with *e* or *ex*, or by means of an adjective in *ĕus*. Thus:—

Wooden *or* of wood.	Lignĕus, a, um.
Paper — of paper.	Chartācĕus, a, um.
Leather — of leather.	Scortĕus, a, um, *or* e cŏrio.
Leaden — of lead.	Plumbĕus, a, um, *or* e plumbo.
Linen — of linen.	Lintĕus, a, um.
Stone — of stone.	{ Lapĭdĕus, a, um. { Saxĕus, a, um.
Pretty.	{ Bellus, a, um. { Venustus, a, um.
The paper hat.	{ Nom. Pílĕus chartácĕus. { Acc. Pílĕum chartácĕum.
The wooden table.	{ Nom. Ménsa lígnĕa. { Acc. Ménsam lígnĕam.
The linen (thread) stocking.	Nom. & Acc. Tíbĭále líntĕuṃ.
The golden candlestick.	Nom. & Acc. Candēlábrum aúrĕum *or* ex aúro.
The horse of stone.	{ Nom. Équus lapídĕus. { Acc. Équum lapídĕum.
The golden ribbon.	{ Nom. Taénĭa aúrĕa. { Acc. Taénĭam aúrĕam.
The cloth coat.	{ Nom. Tóga e * pánno. { Acc. Tógam e pánno.
Have you the paper hat?	Núm hábēs pílĕum chartácĕum?
No, Sir, I have it not.	{ Éum nôn hábĕo, dómĭne, nôn. { Nôn, dómĭne; éum nôn hábĕo.
Have you the stone table?	An hábēs ménsam lapídĕam?
I have it not.	(Éam) nôn hábĕo.

OF THE GENITIVE OF THE THIRD DECLENSION.

G. From the paradigms of this lesson it will be perceived, that substantives of this declension vary considerably as to the manner, in which they assume the characteristic termination of the genitive. The following rules are intended to give the learner some insight into the extent of this variation.†

1. Nouns in *a* change *a* into *ătĭs*, as *pŏēma*, *pŏēmătis*, n., a poem.
2. Nouns in *e* change *e* into *ĭs*, as *cŭbĭlĕ*, *cŭbĭlis*, n., a couch.

---

* Prepositions before their cases are not accented.
† These rules, though not directly connected with the exercises of this lesson, are yet recommended to the careful attention of the student.

3. Those in *i** are generally indeclinable, but sometimes have *ĭtos*, as *hydrŏmĕli, hydromĕllĭtos*, n., mead.

4. Those in *y* add *ŏs*, as *mĭsў, mĭsўos*, n., vitriol.

5. *O* commonly becomes *ŏnĭs*, as *sermo, sermōnĭs*, m., speech. But *do* and *go* become *dĭnĭs* and *gĭnĭs*, as *grando, grandĭnĭs*, f., hail; *origo, orĭgĭnĭs*, f., origin.†

6. Nouns in *c, d, l, n* simply add *ĭs*, as *hālĕc, hālēcĭs*, n. & f., a sort of pickle; *Davĭd, Davĭdĭs*, m., a man's name; *cŭbĭtal, cŭbĭtālĭs*, n., a cushion; *ren, rēnĭs*, m., the reins.‡

7. Those in *ar, er, or*, and *ur* commonly add likewise *ĭs*, as *nectar, nectārĭs*, n., nectar; *ansĕr, ansĕrĭs*, m., a goose; *lector, lectōrĭs*, m., a reader; *sulphŭr, sulphŭrĭs*, n., sulphur.§

8. Those in *as* generally change *as* into *ātĭs*, as *vērĭtas, vērĭtātĭs*, f., truth.‖

9. The only nouns in *aes* are *aes*, n., brass, and *praes*, m., bondsman, which have *aerĭs* and *praedĭs*.

10. Nouns in *aus* have *audĭs*, as *laus, laudĭs*, f., praise; *fraus, fraudĭs*, f., fraud.

11. Those in *es* generally change *es* into *ĭs*, as *fūmes, fūmĭs*, f., hunger; *rūpes, rūpĭs*, f., a rock; but sometimes into *ēdĭs, ĭtĭs*, or *erĭs*, as *haeres, haerēdis*, m., an heir; *miles, mīlĭtĭs*, m., a soldier; *Cĕres, Cĕrĕrĭs*, f., the goddess Ceres.

12. Nouns in *is* have commonly *is*, as *apis, is*, f., a bee; *ovis, is*, f., a sheep; but sometimes also *ĕris, ĭnis, ĭtis*, or *ŭdis*, as *pulvis, pulvĕris*, m., dust; *sanguis, sanguĭnis*, m., blood; *lăpis, lăpĭdis*, m., a stone; *Quĭris, Quĭrītis*, m., a Roman. — *Sēmis*, m., one half, has *sēmissis*.

13. Those in *os* change *os* into *ōtis*, as *săcerdos, -ōtis*, m., a priest; *nĕpos, -ōtis*, m., a grandson; but also into *ōdis, ōis*, and *ŏris*, as *custos, -ōdis*, m., a keeper; *hēros, -ōis*, m., a hero; *rōs, rōris*, m., dew.¶

14. The termination *us* becomes *ŏris, ĕris, ŭris, ūdis (ŭtis)*, or *ŏdis*, as *corpus, -ŏris*, n., a body; *ŏpus, -ĕris*, n., a work; *crūs, crūris*, n.,

---

* Nouns in *i* and *y* are Greek, and so are their genitives *ĭtos* and *yos*.

† A number of other nouns in *o* have likewise *ĭnis*, as *hŏmo*, a man; *nēmo*, nobody; *Apollo*, &c. — *Căro*, flesh, f., has *carnis*, and *Anĭo*, m., the name of a river, *Anĭĕnis*.

‡ But *lac*, n., milk, has *lactis*, and those in *men* have *mĭnis*, as *nūmĕn, nūmĭnis*, n., the deity. Greek nouns in *on* have *onis* and *ontis*, as *icŏn, icōnis*, f., an image; *Achĕrōn, -ontis*, m., name of a river.

§ But those in *ber* and *ter* have *brĭs* and *trĭs*, as *Octōber, Octōbrĭs; păter, patris*, m., a father. Some in *ur* have *ŏris*, as *ebur, ebŏrĭs*, n., ivory, &c. — *Jĕcur*, n., the liver, has *jĕcŭrĭs* or *jĕcĭnōris*, and *hĕpar*, n., the liver, *hēpătĭs* or *hĕpătos; cŏr*, n., the heart, has *cordis; ĭter*, n., a journey, *ĭtĭnĕris*, and *Jŭpĭter*, m., *Jŏvis*.

‖ Greek nouns in *as* have *antis* and *ădis* (or *ădos*), as *gĭgas, gĭgantis*, m., a giant; *lampas, lampădis* or *lampădos*, f., a lamp. Other exceptions are: *ăs, assis*. m., a coin; *măs, măris*, m., a male; *văs, vădis*, m., a surety, and *vās, vāsis*, m., a vessel.

¶ *Ōs*. n., the mouth, has *ŏris*, but *ŏs*, n., a bone, has *ossis*. The genitive of *bŏs*, m. & f., an ox *or* cow, is *bŏvis*.

the leg; *incus, -ŭdis,* f., an anvil; *sălus, -ūtis,* f., safety; *trĭpŭs, -ŏdis,* m., a tripod.

15. Greek nouns in *eus* have *ĕos,* as *Orpheus, Orphĕos,* &c

16. Nouns in *ls, ns,* and *rs* change *s* into *tis* or *dis,* as *puls, -tis,* f., a sort of pap; *pars, -tis,* f., a part; *glans, -dis,* f., any kernel-fruit; *serpens, -tis,* f., a serpent

17. Those in *bs, ps,* and *ms* have *bis, pis,* and *mis,* as *urbs, -bis,* f., a city; *stirps, -pis,* m. & f., offspring; *hiems, hiĕmis,* f , winter.*

18. The only nouns in *t* are *căput, căpĭtis,* m., the head, and its compounds, *occĭput, -ĭtis,* &c.

19. Nouns in *x* change this letter into *cis* or *gis,* as *vox, vōcis,* f., the voice; *călix, călĭcis,* m., a cup; *rex, rēgis,* m., a king; *codex, codĭcis,* m., a book. — But *nix,* f., snow, has *nĭvis; nox,* f., night, *noctis; sĕnex,* adj , old, *sĕnis* or *sĕnĭcis;* and *sŭpellex,* f., furniture, *sŭpellectĭlis.*

EXERCISE 3.

Have you the wooden table? — No, Sir, I have it not. — Which table have you? — I have the stone table. — Have you my golden candlestick? — I have it not. — Which stocking have you? — I have the thread stocking. — Have you my thread stocking? — I have not your thread stocking. — Which coat have you? — I have my cloth coat. — Which horse have you? — I have the wooden horse. — Have you my leathern shoe? — I have it not. — Have you the leaden horse? — I have it not. — Have you your good wooden horse? — I have it not. — Which wood have you? — I have your good wood. — Have you my good gold? — I have it not. — Which gold have you? — I have the good gold. — Which stone have you? — I have your fine stone. — Which ribbon have you? — I have your golden ribbon. — Have you my fine dog? — I have it. — Have you my ugly horse? — I have it not.

Lesson V. — PENSUM QUINTUM.

OF THE DECLENSION OF ADJECTIVES.

A. Adjectives are inflected like substantives of the first, second, and third declensions. Those in *ŭs, ă, ŭm* and *ĕr, ă, ŭm* belong to the first and second declension; those in *ĕr, ĭs, ĕ,* those in *ĭs, ĭs, ĕ,* and all the adjectives of one termination, to the third.

---

* But the adjective *caelebs,* single, has *caelĭbis,* and the compounds of *ceps* have *ĭpis,* as *princeps, -ĭpis,* the foremost. The genitive of *anceps,* doubtful, is *ancĭpĭtis.*

B   2*

B. Some adjectives have a special termination for each of the three genders (e. g. *bŏnŭs, ă, ŭm, ācĕr, ācrĭs, ācrĕ*), some have one common form for the masculine and feminine (e. g. *vīlĭs,* m. & f., *vilĕ,* n.), and others have but one ending (in the nominative singular) for every gender (e. g. *fēlĭx, dīvĕs,* &c.). The following paradigms exhibit the declension of *bonus, pulcher,* and *turpis,* in the singular.

Bŏnus, bŏnă, bŏnŭm, good.

		Masc.	Fem.	Neut.
Nom.	the good	bŏnŭs	bŏnă	bŏnŭm
Gen.	of the good	bŏnī	bŏnae	bonī
Dat.	to the good	bŏnō	bŏnae	bŏnō
Acc.	the good	bŏnŭm	bŏnăm	bŏnŭm
Voc.	O the good	bŏnĕ	bŏnă	bŏnŭm
Abl.	with the good	bŏnō	bŏnā	bŏnō.

Pulchĕr, pulchră, pulchrŭm,* beautiful.

		Masc.	Fem.	Neut.
Nom.	the beautiful	pulchĕr	pulchră	pulchrŭm
Gen.	of the beautiful	pulchrī	pulchrae	pulchrī
Dat.	to the beautiful	pulchrō	pulchrae	pulchrō
Acc.	the beautiful	pulchrŭm	pulchrăm	pulchrŭm
Voc.	O the beautiful	pulchĕr	pulchră	pulchrŭm
Abl.	by the beautiful	pulchrō	pulchrā	pulchrō.

Turpĭs, turpĭs, tŭrpĕ, ugly.

		Masc.	Fem.	Neut.
Nom.	the ugly	turpĭs	turpĭs	turpĕ
Gen.	of the ugly	turpĭs	turpĭs	turpĭs
Dat.	to the ugly	turpī	turpī	turpī
Acc.	the ugly	turpĕm	turpĕm	turpĕ
Voc.	O the ugly	turpĭs	turpĭs	turpĕ
Abl.	with the ugly.	turpī †	turpī	turpī.

Like *bŏnŭs* decline *mălŭs, ă, ŭm; mĕŭs, ă, ŭm; formōsŭs, ă, ŭm,* &c. — Like *pulchĕr:* *aegĕr,* sick; *intĕgĕr,* entire; *nĭgĕr,* black; *pĭgĕr,* slow, &c. — Like *turpĭs: brĕvĭs,* short; *dēformĭs,* deformed; *dulcĭs,* sweet; *omnĭs,* all; *ūtĭlĭs,* useful, &c.

---

* Some adjectives of this declension *retain* the *e* of the root-termination, e. g. *tĕnĕr, tĕnĕra, tĕnĕrum; mĭser, mĭsĕra, mĭsĕrum.* But the majority reject it.
† Adjectives of the third declension have *e* or *i* in the ablative singular, but those whose neuter ends in *e* have *i* only.

The trunk.	*Riscus, i, *m.*, arca, ae, *f*.
The button.	*Orbĭcŭlus fibulatŏrĭus, ĭ, *m*.
The money.	Pĕcūnĭa, ae, *f*.
The cheese.	Cāsĕus, i, *m*.
The silver.	Argentum, ĭ, *n*.
Of silver.	Argentĕus, a, um (Adj.).
The baker.	Pistŏr, ōris, *m*.
The neighbor.	{ Vīcīnus, i, *m*. { Proxĭmus, i, *m*

Anything, something.	*Ălĭquid, quidquăm, nonnĭhĭl.*
Nothing.	*Nĭhĭl* (indecl.), *nĭhĭlum, i,* n.
Have you anything?	{ Éstne tíbĭ álĭquid ? { Habêsne (tû) álĭquid ?
I have something.	{ Ést mihĭ nónnihĭl. { Hábĕo álĭquĭd.
Have you anything?	{ Núm quídquam * hábēs ? { Núm ést tíbĭ quídquam ?
I have nothing.	{ Ést míhĭ níhil. { Níhil réi hábĕo.

Hungry.	Esŭrĭens, tis.
Thirsty.	Sĭtĭens,† tis. (Vide Lesson VI. *B.*)
Sleepy.	{ Somnĭcŭlōsŭs, ă, ŭm. { Cupĭdŭs (ă, ŭm) somnī.
Tired.	Fessŭs (defessus), ă, ŭm.
Are you hungry?	Esŭrisne ?
I am hungry.	(Égo vérō) ēsúrĭo.
Are you thirsty	Sĭtisne ?
I am thirsty.	(Égo vérō) sítĭo.
I am not thirsty.	Nôn sítio.
Are you sleepy?	{ Ésne tû somnĭcŭlôsus ? { Án és cúpĭdus sómnī ?
I am sleepy.	Súm cúpĭdus sómnī.
I am not sleepy.	{ Nôn súm cúpĭdus sómnī. { Égo somniculôsus nôn súm.
Are you tired?	{ Ésne tû féssus ? { Núm és féssus ?
I am tired.	Súm féssus.
I am not tired.	Nôn súm féssus.

C. Rule. When a substantive expresses the relation of property or possession, it is put in the genitive; as,

---

* *Quidquam* is generally put, when the sentence contains a *négation* (either expressed or implied), a condition, comparison, &c., and also in connection with the particles *vix*, scarcely, and *sine*, without. (Compare Lesson VI. *C.*)

† *Esuriens* and *sitiens*, properly the present participles of the verbs *ĕsúrĭo*, I am hungry, and *sĭtĭo*, I am thirsty. When *hungry* and *thirsty* are in the predicate of the sentence, it is necessary to use the verbs, and not the participles.

The dog of the baker.	Cánis pistôris (*Nom.*).
The baker's dog.	Pistôris cánem (*Acc.*).*
The coat of the tailor.	Tógam sartôris (*Acc.*).
The tailor's coat.	Sartôris tóga (*Nom.*).
My brother's paper.	{ Chárta méi frâtris† (*Nom.*). { Frâtris méi chártam (*Acc.*).
My neighbor's good salt.	{ Méi vicíni sâl bónum. { Sâl bónum vicíni méi.
The old bread.	{ Nom. Pânis vétŭlus. { Acc. Pânem vétŭlum.
The pretty dog.	Cánem béllum (venústum).
The silver ribbon.	Taéniam argénteam (*Acc.*).

D. Rule. Adjectives (and the adjective pronouns *meus, tuus,* &c.) may stand either before or after their substantives; but when the substantive is a monosyllable, the adjective comes always last.

Have you the neighbor's good salt?	Núm hábēs sâl bónum vicíni?
I have it not.	Nôn hábĕo.
Have you my brother's silver candlestick?	Án hábēs frâtris méi candēlâbrum argénteum?

EXERCISE 4.

Have you the leathern trunk? — I have not the leathern trunk? — Have you my pretty trunk? — I have not your pretty trunk. — Which trunk have you? — I have the wooden trunk. — Have you my old button? — I have it not. — Which money have you? — I have the good money. — Which cheese have you? — I have the old cheese. — Have you anything? — I have something. — Have you my large dog? — I have it not. — Have you your good gold? — I have it. — Which dog have you? — I have the tailor's dog? — Have you the neighbor's large dog? — I have it not. — Have you the dog's golden ribbon? — No, Sir, I have it not. — Which coat have you? — I have the tailor's good coat. — Have you the neighbor's good bread? — I have it not. — Have you my tailor's golden ribbon? — I have it. — Have you my pretty dog's ribbon? — I have it not. — Have you the good baker's good horse? — I have it. — Have you the good tailor's horse? — I have it not. — Are you hungry? — I am hungry. — Are you sleepy? — I am not sleepy. — Which candlestick have you? — I have the golden candlestick of my good baker.

---

* The common rule is that the *genitive* (and in general *every word governed*) should be put *before* the word governing it. This, however, is by no means invariable, and the learner may safely use either of the formulas in the sense of their English equivalents.

† Instead of the possessive genitive, the Romans sometimes employ an adjective; as, *dŏmus păterna* for *dŏmus patris,* the father's house; *hŏmo ingĕniŏsus* for *hŏmo ingĕnti,* a man of talent, &c.

Lesson VI. — PENSUM SEXTUM.

A. The adjectives in *ĕr*, *ĭs*, *ĕ* are but few in number. The nominative masculine has sometimes *ĭs* instead of *ĕr*.

Ācĕr *or* ācris, ācris, ācrĕ, *sharp.*

	Masc.	*Fem.*	*Neut.*
Nom.	ācĕr *or* ācris	ācris	ācrĕ
Gen.	ācris	ācris	ācris
Dat.	ācrī	ācrī	ācrī
Acc.	ācrĕm	ācrĕm	ācrĕ
Voc.	ācĕr *or* ācris	ācris	ācrĕ
Abl.	ācrī	ācrī	ācrī.

So decline *alăcĕr* or *alacris*, cheerful ; *cĕlĕber* or *cĕlĕbris*, famous ; *cĕler* or *cĕlĕris*, swift ; *sălūbĕr* or *sălūbris*, wholesome.

ADJECTIVES OF ONE TERMINATION.

B. Adjectives of one termination do not differ essentially from other words of the third declension, except that they may have either *ĕ* or *ī* in the ablative. The present participle in *ns* is included in this class. Examples : —

	Dīvĕs, -vĭtĭs, *rich.*		Vĕtŭs, -tĕris, *old.*		Sĭtĭens, -ntĭs, *thirsty.*	
	Masc. & Fem.	*Neut.*	*Masc. & Fem.*	*Neut.*	*Masc. & Fem.*	*Neut.*
Nom.	dīvĕs		vĕtŭs		sĭtĭens	
Gen.	dīvĭtĭs		vĕtĕris		sĭtĭentĭs	
Dat.	dīvĭtī		vĕtĕrī		sĭtĭentī	
Acc.	dīvĭtĕm	dīvĕs	vĕtĕrĕm	vĕtŭs	sĭtĭentĕm	sĭtĭens
Voc.	dīvĕs		vĕtŭs		sĭtĭens	
Abl.	dīvĭtĕ.*		vĕtĕrĕ *or* I.		sĭtĭentĕ *or* I.	

So decline *fēlix, fēlĭcĭs,* happy ; *paupĕr, paupĕrĭs,* poor ; *anceps, ancĭpĭtĭs,* doubtful ; *sollers, sollertĭs,* clever ; *prūdens, prūdentĭs,* wise ; *ămans, ămantĭs,* loving, &c.

REMARKS ON THE ABLATIVE.

1. Participles in *ans* or *ens* have always *ĕ* in the ablative, when they are used as participles proper or as substantives ; as, *sole oriente,* when the sun rises ; *infans,* abl. *infantĕ,* the infant. But when used as adjectives, they have rather *ĭ* than *ĕ*.

---

* See Remark 5.

2. Comparatives have rather ĕ than ĭ, as *mājŏr, mājŏrĕ*, greater, &c.

3. *Praesens*, present, when said of things, has ĭ; when said of persons, ĕ.

4. Proper names derived from adjectives have always ĕ, as *Clēmens, Clēmentĕ.*

5. Those that have ĕ exclusively are *paupĕr, sĭnex, princeps*, and the majority of those in *es*, as *dĭves, sospes, dēses, pūbĭs, impūbĕs*, and *superstes.*

Anything or something good.	⎰ Ālĭquĭd (quĭdquăm, nonnĭhĭl) bŏnŭm. ⎱ Alĭquĭd (quĭdquăm, nonnĭhĭl) bŏnī.
Nothing or not anything good.	⎰ Nĭhĭl bŏnŭm. ⎱ Nĭhĭl bŏnī.
Something bad (worthless).	Ālĭquĭd vīlĕ (nēquăm).
Nothing bad (worthless).	Nĭhil vīlĕ (nēquăm).

C. Obs. The partitive genitive of neuter adjectives after *alĭquid, nĭhil*, &c. can only be used when the adjective is of the second declension. . Thús we can only say *alĭquid vīlĕ, turpĕ*, &c., and not *alĭquid turpĭs;* but indifferently either *alĭquid bŏnŭm* or *alĭquid bŏnī.*

Have you anything good?	⎰ Éstne tíbi álĭquid bónī ? ⎱ Habêsne álĭquid bónum ?
I have nothing bad.	⎰ Nòn ést míhi quídquam vīlĕ. ⎱ Níhil néquam hábeo.
Have you anything ugly ?	⎰ Núm ést tíbĭ quídquam túrpĕ ? ⎱ Án hábēs álĭquid túrpĕ ?
I have nothing ugly.	⎰ Nòn ést míhĭ quídquam túrpĕ. ⎱ Níhil túrpe hábĕo.
What! .	*Quid !*
What have you ?	⎰ Quíd tíbĭ ést ? ⎱ Quíd hábēs ?
What have you good ?	⎰ Quíd ést tíbi bónī ? ⎱ Quíd hábēs bónŭm ?
I have the good bread.	⎰ Hábeo bónum pânem. ⎱ Bónum pânem hábĕo.

		Masc.	Fem.	Neut.
That or the one.	Nom.	*illĕ*	*illă*	*illŭd.*
	Acc.	*illŭm*	*illăm*	*illŭd.*

D. Obs. The English *that*, or *the one*, is, among the later Latin authors, expressed by the demonstrative *illĕ, illă, illŭd.* By the earlier classical writers, however, the noun is either itself repeated or to be supplied from the context.

Which book have you?	Quém líbrum hábēs?
I have that of the baker.	{ Hábeo íllum pistôris. { Pistôris líbrum hábĕo.
Which sugar have you?	{ Quód sácchărum hábēs? { Quíd ést tíbi sácchari?
I have that of my brother.	{ Hábĕo íllud méi frắtris. { Ést míhi sácchărum frắtris.

Or.	Ăn.

E. Obs. In double questions, the first member is introduced by *utrŭm* (whether) or by the enclitic *-nĕ*, and the second member by *an* (or). Thus:—

Are you tired or sleepy?	{ Útrum és féssus *án* somnĭcŭlôsus? { Ésne tû féssus *án* somnĭcŭlôsus?
I am sleepy.	Somnĭcŭlôsus súm.
Have you my book or that of the neighbor?	{ Éstne tíbi líber méus *án* vicíni? { Útrum hábes librum méum *án* vi- cíni?
I have that of the neighbor.	{ Ést míhi líber vicíni. { Hábeo íllum vicíni.
Have you your hat or the baker's?	{ Útrum tíbi ést líber túus *án* pistô- ris? { Tuúmne líbrum hábĕs *án* pistôris?
Are you hungry or thirsty?	{ Útrum ésŭris *án* sítis? { Esurisne *án* sítis?
I am hungry.	Esúrĭo.

EXERCISE 5.

Have you my book? — I have it not. — Which book have you? — I have my good book. — Have you anything ugly? — I have nothing ugly? — I have something pretty. — Which table have you? — I have the baker's. — Have you the baker's dog or the neighbor's? — I have the neighbor's. — What have you? — I have nothing. — Have you the good or bad sugar? — I have the good — Have you the neighbor's good or bad horse? — I have the good (one).* — Have you the golden or the silver candlestick? — I have the silver candlestick. — Have you my neighbor's paper, or that of my tailor? — I have that of your tailor. — Are you hungry or thirsty? — I am hungry. — Are you sleepy or tired? — I am tired. — What have you pretty? — I have nothing pretty. — Have you anything ugly? — I have nothing ugly. — Have you the leather shoe? — I have it not. — What have you good? — I have the good sugar.

---

* The words included in parentheses are not to be translated in these exercises.

Lesson VII. — PENSUM SEPTIMUM.

OF THE FOURTH DECLENSION.

A. The fourth declension comprises all substantives which form their genitive in *ŭs.* The nominative singular has two terminations, viz. *ŭs* for masculine and feminine nouns, and *ŭ* for neuters. Examples: —

Fructŭs, *m., the fruit.*	Cornū, *n., the horn.*	Dŏmŭs, *f., the house.*
Nom. fructŭs	cornū	dŏmŭs
Gen. fructūs	cornūs	dŏmūs *or* domī *
Dat. fructŭī	cornū (cornŭī)	dŏmŭī *or* domō
Acc. fructŭm	cornū	dŏmŭm
Voc. fructŭs	cornū	dŏmŭs
Abl. fructū.	cornū.	dŏmō.

Like *fructus* decline *adĭtus*, access; *cantŭs*, a song; *currŭs*, a chariot; *ictŭs*, a stroke; *mōtŭs*, motion; *risus*, laughter; *sĕnātŭs*, the senate; *sumptŭs*, expense; *victŭs*, living. Also the feminines *ăcŭs*, a needle; *mănŭs*, a hand; *trĭbŭs*, a tribe, &c. — Like *cornū* decline *gĕlū*, ice; *gĕnū*, the knee; *vĕrū*, a spear; *tŏnĭtrū*, thunder.

REMARK. — The final *u* of Latin words generally is long.

Have you my coat or the tailor's ? $\begin{cases} \text{Éstne tíbĭ tóga méa án sartôris ?} \\ \text{Útrum hábēs tógam méam án (íl-} \\ \text{lam) sartôris ?} \end{cases}$

I have yours. $\begin{cases} \text{Ést míhĭ túa.} \\ \text{Túam hábĕo.} \end{cases}$

		Masc.	Fem.	Neut.
Mine.	Nom.	mĕŭs	mĕă	mĕŭm.
	Acc.	mĕŭm	mĕăm	mĕŭm.
Yours.	Nom.	tŭŭs	tŭă	tŭŭm.
	Acc.	tŭŭm	tŭăm	tŭŭm.

B. Obs. The possessive pronouns *mĕus, tŭus, sŭus,* &c. may either be joined to nouns in the sense of the conjunctive *my, your (thy), his,* &c., or they may stand absolutely, like the English *mine, yours (thine), his,* &c. They are inflected like *bŏnus, a, um.* (Cf. Lesson V.)

		Masc.	Fem.	Neut.
This.	Nom.	hĭc	haec	hŏc.
	Acc.	hunc	hanc	hŏc.

---

* The genitive *domi* is only used in the sense of *at home.* The dative *domui* is the more usual form; but the ablative of this irregular noun is always *domo.*

Is this your hat?	Éstne híc pílĕus túus?
No, Sir, it is not mine, but yours.	Mínĭme, dómĭne, nôn ést méus, séd túus.
Is this my ribbon?	Núm haêc ést taénĭa méa?
No, it is not yours, but mine.	Nôn ést túa, séd méa.
Is this your sugar?	Án hóc ést sácchărum túum?
It is not mine, but that of my brother.	Nôn ést méum, séd méi fràtris.

The man.	{ Vǐr,* *gen.* vǐri, *m.* { Hōmo, ǐnis, *m. & f.*
The stick, cane.	{ Băcŭlum, i, *n.* { Scĭpĭo, ōnis, *m.*
My brother.	Frăter mĕus, *gen.* frātris mĕi.
The shoemaker.	Sŭtor, ōris, *m.*
The merchant.	Mercātor, ōris, *m.*
The friend.	{ Amĭcus, i, *m.* { Fāmĭlĭāris, is, *m.*
Neither — nor.	{ Nĕc — nĕc. { Nĕque — nĕque. { Nĕque — nĕc.

C. Obs. The disjunctive conjunctions *nec* and *nĕque* are used in the same sense, except that the former more frequently stands before consonants and the latter before vowels.

Have you the merchant's stick or yours?	Tĕnêsnĕ† bácŭlum mercātôris án túum?
I have neither the merchant's stick nor yours.	Néc mercatôris bácŭlum néc túum ténĕo.
Are you hungry or thirsty?	{ Útrum ésŭris án sítis? { Esŭrisne án sítis?
I am neither hungry nor thirsty.	Égo néque ēsúrĭo néc sítĭo.

EXERCISE 6.

Have you your cloth or mine? — I have neither yours nor mine. — I have neither my bread nor the tailor's. — Have you my stick or yours? — I have mine. — Have you the shoemaker's shoe or the merchant's? — I have neither the shoemaker's nor the merchant's. — Have you my brother's coat? — I have it not. — Which paper have you? — I have your friend's. — Have you my dog or my friend's? — I have your friend's. — Have you my thread stocking or

---

* *Vir* is used with reference to the sex, and *homo* with reference to the species.

† *Tĕnĕo* is properly "I hold," and may be used in these exercises for variety, especially where "to have" may signify "to hold in one's hand," or "to retain, keep."

3

my brother's ? — I have neither yours nor your brother's. — Have
you my good baker's good bread or that of my friend ? — I have
neither your good baker's nor that of your friend. — Which bread
have you ? — I have mine. — Which ribbon have you ? — I have
yours. — Have you the good or the bad cheese ? — I have neither
the good nor the bad. — Have you anything ? — I have nothing. —
Have you my pretty or my ugly dog ? — I have neither your pretty
nor your ugly dog. — Have you my friend's stick ? — I have it not.
— Are you sleepy or hungry ? — I am neither sleepy nor hungry. —
Have you the good or the bad salt ? — I have neither the good nor
the bad. — Have you my horse or the man's ? — I have neither yours
nor the man's. — What have you ? — I have nothing fine. — Are you
tired ? — I am not tired.

Lesson VIII. — PENSUM OCTAVUM.

OF THE FIFTH DECLENSION.

A. Nouns of the fifth declension have their genitive
in *ei* and the nominative in *ēs*. The fifth declension
differs but slightly from the third, and is a mere modi-
fication of it. Dĭēs, *m. & f., the day,* rēs, *f., a thing,*
and spĕcĭēs, *f., the appearance,* are thus inflected : —

Nom.	dĭēs	rēs	spĕcĭēs
Gen.	dĭēī	rĕī *	spĕcĭēī
Dat.	dĭēī	rĕī	spĕcĭēī
Acc.	dĭĕm	rĕm	spĕcĭĕm
Voc.	dĭēs	rēs	spĕcĭēs
Abl.	dĭē.	rē.	spĕcĭē.

So decline *ăcĭēs,* f., the edge *or* point ; *făcĭēs,* f , the face ; *effĭgĭēs,*
f., the image, effigy ; *mĕrīdĭēs,* m., midday, noon ; *spēs,* f., hope ; *sĕrĭēs,*
f., the series.

REMARK. — The *e* of the ablative of the fifth declension is always
long.

B. Obs. Nouns of this declension are feminine, except *dĭēs,*
which in the singular is generally masculine and sometimes
feminine,† but in the plural always masculine. Its compound,
mĕrīdĭēs, is masculine, and used in the singular only.

---

* The *e* of the genitive and dative is long when a vowel precedes, but short
after a consonant, e. g. *acĭēī, facĭēī,* &c., but *spēi, rēi, fĭdēi,* &c.
† It is feminine when it denotes, 1) *duration* of time, e. g. *diem perexiguam,
integram,* (for) a very short day, an entire day ; 2) an *appointed day,* e. g.
certā (constitutā, dictā, &c.) *die,* on the appointed day.

The cork.	*Embŏlus, i, m.
The corkscrew.	*Instrumentum* (i, n.) embŏlis extrahendis.
The umbrella.	*Mūnimentum (i, n.) capĭtis pluviāle; umbrācŭlum,† i, n.
The boy.	Pŭer, ĕri, m.
The Frenchman.	*Francogallus, i, m.
The carpenter.	Făber (ri, m.) tignārĭus.
The hammer.	Mǎllĕus, i, m.
The iron.	Ferrum, i, n.
Of iron, iron.	Ferrĕus, a, um.
The nail.	Clāvŭs, i, m.
The pencil.	*Stĭlus cerussātus, i, m.
The thimble.	*Mūnimentum (i, n.) dĭgĭti.
The coffee.	*Coffĕa, ae, f.
The honey.	Mĕl, gen. mellis, n.
The (sea) biscuit.	Pānis nautĭcus (castrensis).
The sweet biscuit.	{ Pānis dulcĭārĭus, m. { Buccellātum, i, n.

Have I?	{ Habeône? Ecquĭd égo hábĕo? { Án (égo) hábĕo? Éstne mĭhĭ?
You have.	Hábēs. Ténēs. Tĭbĭ ést.
What have I?	{ Quíd (égo) hábĕo (ténĕo)? { Quíd ést mĭhĭ?
You have the carpenter's hammer.	{ Mǎllĕum fábri tignárii hábes (ténes). { Ést tíbi málleus fábri tignárii.
Have I the nail?	{ Habeône clâvum? { Éstne míhi clâvus?
You have it.	Hábes. Ést.
Have I (the) biscuit?	{ Án égo hábĕo pânem castrénsem (nautĭcum)? { Éstne míhi pánis (ĭlle) castrénsis?
You have it.	Hábes. Tĭbĭ ést.
I am right (correct).	Vérē (réctē) lóquŏr.
I am wrong (incorrect).	Érro.
You are correct, wrong.	Récte lóquĕris, érras.
I am right (i. e. morally in doing so).	Ést míhi făs.
I am wrong (morally in doing so).	Ést míhi néfăs.‡

---

* The Ancients having no term for such an instrument, it must be expressed by circumlocution. On the dative embŏlis extrahendis, "for extracting corks,". compare Lesson XXV., Obs. — The same remark applies to munimentum capitis pluviale (where pluviale is an adjective in e), to munimentum digiti, and to a host of other names of modern objects. In all the cases, we can only approximate by description.

† The word umbrăcŭlum (from umbra, shade) was used by the Ancients in the sense of our "parasol."

‡ The expressions vĕrē or rectĕ lŏquŏr and erro have reference to language or opinions simply; whereas făs and nĕfăs involve the moral distinction of right and wrong in action or in speech. The latter phrases are often followed by an infinitive, as, Estne mihi fas (or licetne mihi) hoc facere? Is it right for

Am I right (i. e. correct) or wrong?	Rectêne lóquor án érro?
You are neither right nor wrong.	Néque réctē lóquĕris, néque érras.
Am I right (correct)?	Loquórne récte?
You are correct.	Vérē (réctē) lóquĕris.
Am I right (correct)?	Núm lóquor vérē?
No, you are wrong.	Ímmo vérō* érras.
Am I right (morally)? } Is it right for me? }	Éstne míhi fâs?
It is wrong.	Ést tíbi néfâs.
Which biscuit have I?	Quód buccellâtum hábĕo?
You have that of my brother.	Frâtris méi buccellâtum hábes.

EXERCISE 7.

Which dog have you? — I have neither the baker's dog nor that of my friend. — Are you sleepy? — I am not sleepy. — I am hungry. — You are not hungry. — Am I thirsty? — You are not thirsty. — Have I the cork? — No, sir, you have it not. — Have I the carpenter's wood? — You have it not. — Have I the Frenchman's good umbrella? — You have it.· — Have I the carpenter's iron nails or yours? — You have mine. — You have neither the carpenter's nor mine. — Which pencil have I? — You have that of the Frenchman. — Have I your thimble or that of the tailor? — You have neither mine nor that of the tailor. — Which umbrella have I? — You have my good umbrella. — Have I the Frenchman's good honey? — You have it not. — Which biscuit have I? — You have that of my good neighbor. — Have you my coffee or that of my boy? — I have that of your good boy. — Have you your cork or mine? — I have neither yours nor mine. — What have you? — I have my good brother's good pencil. — Am I right (correct)? — You are right (correct). — Am I wrong (morally)? — You are wrong. — You are not wrong. — Am I right or wrong? — You are neither right nor wrong. — Am I hungry? — You are hungry. — You are not sleepy. — You are neither hungry nor thirsty. — What have I good? — You have neither the good coffee nor the good sugar. — What have I? — You have nothing. — What have you? — I have something beautiful.

Lesson IX. — PENSUM NONUM.

OF PRONOUNS.

A. The pronouns of the Latin language are divided into the following classes: — 1. PERSONAL: *ĕgŏ, tŭ,*

---

me to do so? Am I right in doing so? *Illud dicere tibi nefas est,* It is wrong for you to say so, You are wrong in saying so. *Fas* and *nefas* are both indeclinable, like *nihil.*

  * *Immo vero* corresponds to the English "nay, rather," "nay, on the contrary."

sŭī (and *ipse*).   2. DEMONSTRATIVES : *hĭc, iste, ille, ĭs*. 3. RELATIVES : *quī, quae, quŏd*.   4. POSSESSIVES : *mĕus, tŭus, sŭus, noster, vester*.   5. INTERROGATIVES : *quĭs? quĭd? quī, quae, quŏd?*   6. INDEFINITE : *ălīquĭs, quĭs, quisquam*.   7. PATRIALS : *nostrās, vestrās, cūjās*.

B. The personal pronouns *ĕgŏ*, I, *tū*, thou, *sŭī*, of himself, of herself, of itself, are thus inflected : —

NOM.	*I*	ĕgŏ	*thou*	tū	——	—
GEN.	*of me*	mĕī	*of thee*	tŭī	*of himself, &c.*	sŭī
DAT.	*to me*	mĭhī *or* mī	*to thee*	tĭbī	*to himself, &c.*	sĭbī
ACC.	*me*	mē	*thee*	tē	*himself, &c.*	sē
VOC.	——	ĕgŏ	*O thou*	tū	——	—
ABL.	*with me*	mē.	*with thee*	tē.	*with himself, &c.*	sē.

REMARK. — The suffix *tĕ* is sometimes emphatically added to the nominative *tu;* as *tūtĕ*, thou *thyself;* and the suffix *mĕt* in the same sense to all the cases of *ego, tu,* and *sui;* as *egŏmĕt, tŭtĕmĕt, sŭĭmĕt*, I myself, &c. — So also *mēmĕ, tētĕ, sēsĕ*, for *me, te, se*, in the accusative and ablative singular.

C. The Latin language has no pronoun of the third person corresponding in every respect to the English *he, she, it*, the termination of the verb being commonly deemed sufficient to indicate the relation of personality. But when perspicuity or emphasis requires a pronoun, one of the demonstratives *hic, iste, ille* (most commonly the latter) is used for the nominative, and the oblique cases of *ĭs, ĕă, ĭd* for the remaining cases. The pronoun of the third person would thus be something like the following : —

		Masc.	*Fem.*	*Neut.*
NOM.	*he, she, it*	illĕ	illă	illŭd
GEN.	*of him, of her, of it*	ējŭs	ējŭs	ējŭs (rei)*
DAT.	*to him, to her, to it*	ĕī	ĕī	ĕī (rei)
ACC.	*him, her, it*	ĕŭm	ĕăm	ĭd (illŭd)
VOC.	— — —			
ABL.	*with him, with her, with it*	ĕō	ĕā	ĕō (eā re).

D. The pronoun *ipsĕ, ipsă, ipsŭm* may be joined to

---

* The Romans are fond of employing the word *res*, "thing." instead of the neuter of adjectives and pronouns. This becomes necessary in cases where ambiguity as to gender would otherwise arise, as here in the genitive, dative, and ablative. So also *cujus rei, cui rei, quā re*, for *cujus*, &c.

every case of *ego*, *tu*, and *sui*, with the force of the English *self* (*myself*, *thyself*, *himself*, &c.).   Its singular is thus declined:—

	Masc.	*Fem.*	*Neut.*
Nom.	ipsĕ	ipsă	ipsŭm
Gen.		ipsīus *	
Dat.		ipsī	
Acc.	ipsŭm	ipsŭm	ipsŭm
Voc.	ipsĕ	ipsă	ipsŭm
Abl.	ipsō	ipsā	ipsŏ.

Thus: *ego ipse* (*ipsa*), I myself; *tu ipse* (*ipsa*), thou thyself; (*ille*) *ipse*, he himself; *mihimet ipsi*, to myself; *temet ipsum*, thyself; *sui ipsius*, of himself.

Have I the iron or the golden nail?	Ferreúmne clâvum hábĕo, án aúrĕum?
You have neither the iron nor the golden nail.	Néque férrĕum hábēs clâvum, néque aúreum.

The sheep.	Ŏvĭs, ĭs, *f.*
The ram.	Vervĕx, ēcĭs, *m.*
The hen.	Gallīna, ae, *f.*
The chicken.	Pullus gallīnācĕus (*gen.* i), *m.*
The ship.	Nāvĭs, ĭs, *f.*
The bag (sack).	Saccŭs, i, *m.*
The painter.	Pictor, ōris, *m.*
The young man.	Jŭvĕnĭs, ĭs, *m.*
The youth (lad).	{ Adŏlescens, tĭs, *m.* { Adŏlescentŭlus, i, *m.*

E. The substantives *ŏvĭs*, *nāvĭs*, and *jŭvĕnĭs* are thus inflected:—

Nom. ŏvĭs	nāvĭs		jŭvĕnĭs
Gen. ŏvĭs	nāvĭs		jŭvĕnĭs
Dat. ŏvī	nāvī		jŭvĕnī
Acc. ŏvĕm	nāvĕm	*or* nāvim	jŭvĕnĕm
Voc. ŏvĭs	nāvĭs		jŭvĕnĭs
Abl. ŏvĕ.	nāvī	*or* nāvĕ.	jŭvĕnĕ.

F. Obs. The words *navis*, *messis*, and *clavis* have usually *em* in the accusative, sometimes *im*.   The nouns *febris*, *pelvis*, *puppis*, *vestis*, *securis*, and *turris* have oftener *im* than *em*.   Those which have regularly *im* are: a) the substantives *amussis*, *ravis*, *sitis*, *tussis*, and *vis*;

---

* The genitive *ipsius* and the dative *ipsi* are here intended for all the genders.   The same applies to all the subsequent paradigms.

b) a variety of nouns and proper names derived from the Greek, as *basis, poësis, paraphrasis, Osiris, Zeuxis, Charybdis,* &c.

Who ?	*Quis ? Cui* (with *est*) ?
Who has ?	{ *Quis habet ?* { *Cui est ?*
Who has the trunk ?	{ Quis húbĕt árcam ? { Cui ést ríscus ?
The man has the trunk.	Vír ríscum hábet (ténet).
The man has *not* the trunk.	Vír ríscum *nôn* hábet (ténet).
Who has it ?	Quis éŭm hábet ?
The youth has it.	Adoléscens éum hábet.
The youth has it *not*.	Adolescéntŭlus éum *nôn* hábet (té- net).
He has.	{ *Hăbĕt, tĕnĕt* (is, hic, ille).* { *Est ei.*
He has the knife.	Ís (ílle) cúltrum hábet.
He has *not* the knife.	Cúltrum *nôn* hábet.
Has the man ?	Habétne vír ? Écquid hábet hó- mo ? Án hábet hómo ?
Has the painter ?	{ Habétne píctor ? Núm hábet pí- { ctor ? Éstne (án, núm ést) pi- { ctóri ?
Has the friend ?	{ Habétne amícus ? Án hábet amí- { cus ? Éstne (écquid, án ést) { amíco ? (Cf. Lesson II. note *.)
Has the boy the carpenter's ham- mer ?	Tenétne púĕr mállĕum fábri tigná- rĭi ?
He has it.	Véro (éum) ténet.
Has the youth it ?	Eúmne ténet adoléscens ?
He has it not.	(Éum) nôn ténet.
Is he thirsty ?	Sitítne ? Án (écquid) ís sítit ?
He is thirsty.	Íta ést, sítit.
Is he tired ?	{ Núm (númquid) féssus ést ? { Án ést féssus ?
He is not tired ?	Nôn ést féssus.
Is he right or wrong ?	{ Rectêne lóquĭtŭr, án érrat ? { Útrum vérĕ lóquĭtur, án érrat ?
He is right (correct).	Vérĕ lóquĭtur.
He is not wrong.	Nôn érrat.
Is he hungry ?	Esurítne ? Núm ésŭrit ?
He is not hungry.	Nôn ésŭrit.

EXERCISE 8.

Is he thirsty or hungry ? — He is neither thirsty nor hungry. — Has the friend my hat ? — He has it. — He has it not. — Who has

---

* The pronoun of the third person, like that of the second and first, is commonly omitted, except where perspicuity requires it.

my sheep? — Your friend has it. — Who has my large sack? —
The baker has it. — Has the youth my book? — He has it not. —
What has he? — He has nothing. — Has he the hammer or the nail?
— He has neither the hammer nor the nail. — Has he my umbrella
or my stick? — He has neither your umbrella nor your stick. — Has
he my coffee or my sugar? — He has neither your coffee nor your
sugar; he has your honey. — Has he my brother's biscuit or that of
the Frenchman? — He has neither your brother's nor that of the
Frenchman; he has that of the good boy. — Which ship has he? —
He has my good ship. — Has he the old sheep or the ram?

EXERCISE 9.

Has the young man my knife or that of the painter? — He has
neither yours nor that of the painter. — Who has my brother's fine
dog? — Your friend has it. — What has my friend? — He has the
baker's good bread. — He has the good neighbor's good chicken. —
What have you? — I have nothing. — Have you my bag or yours?
— I have that of your friend. — Have I your good knife? — You
have it. — You have it not. — Has the youth it? — He has it not.
— What has he? — He has something good. — He has nothing bad.
— Has he anything? — He has nothing. — Is he sleepy? — He is
not sleepy. — He is hungry. — Who is hungry? — The young man
is hungry. — Your friend is hungry. — Your brother's boy is hungry.
— My shoemaker's brother is hungry. — My good tailor's boy is
thirsty. — Which man has my book? — The big (*procērus*) man has
it. — Which man has my horse? — Your friend has it. — He has
your good cheese. — Has he it? — Yes, sir, he has it.

Lesson X. — PENSUM DECIMUM.

The husbandman.	Agrīcŏla, ae, *m.*
The peasant, rustic.	Rustĭcus, i, *m.*; homo agrestis.
The ox.	{ Bōs, *gen.* bŏvis, *m.* & *f.* { Taurus, i, *m.* (a bull).
The cook.	Cŏquŭs, i, *m.*; cŏquă, ae, *f.*
The servant.	{ Minister, ri, *m.*; fămŭlus, i, *m.* { Ministra, fŭmŭla, ae, *f.*
The bird.	{ Ăvis, is, *f.* { Vŏlūcris, is, *m.* & *f.*
The broom.	Scōpae, ārum,* *f. pl.*
The eye.	Ŏcŭlus, i, *m.*
The foot.	Pēs, *gen.* pĕdĭs, *m.*
The rice.	Ŏrȳza, ae, *f.*

---

* Many nouns in Latin are never used in the singular, as *angustiae,* difficulties ; *divitiae,* riches ; *feriae,* holidays ; *liberi,* children, &c. Compare Lesson
XVII. *B.*

His (conjunctive).	{ *Sŭŭs, sŭă, sŭŭm.* { *Ejŭs, illŭs.*

A. Obs. The possessive pronoun *sŭus* is declined like *mĕus* and *tŭus.* It corresponds to the English "his" when, in the reflexive sense of "his own," the subject of the sentence is meant; but when another person is referred to, *ējus* (of him) or *illŭus* (of that man) must be employed. As:—

Has he his (own) hat?	Tenétne pĭlĕum súum?
Have you his (the other man's) hat?	Tenêsne tû pĭlĕum éjus (illĭŭs)?
Has the servant his broom?	Habétne minĭster scópas súas? (Cf. Lesson XIII. *B.*)
He has his broom.	{ Hábet scópas súas. { Scópas súas hábet.
Has the cook his (own) chicken or that of the rustic?	Habétne cóquus gallĭnam súam, an (íllam) rústĭci?
He has his own.	{ Súam hábet. { Hábet súam próprĭam.
His or *his own* (absolute).	{ *Sŭus, sŭa, sŭum.* * { *Proprĭus, a, um.*† { *Ejus, illĭus (ipsĭus).*

B. Obs. The absolute possessive pronoun *suus* is declined like the conjunctive. Instead of it, *proprĭus* is sometimes used. There is here the same distinction between *sŭus* (*proprĭus*) and *ejus* (*illŭus*) as in *Obs. A.*

Has the servant his (own) trunk, or mine?	{ Habétne fámŭlus rísc̆um súum (pró- prĭum), án méum? { Suímne rísc̆um hábet fámŭlus, án méum?
He has his own.	{ Súum próprĭum hábet. { Hábet suúmmet.
Have you your (own) shoe, or his (that man's)?	{ Útrum túum hábes cálcĕum, án éjus (illĭŭs)? { Tuúmne hábes cálceum, án éjus (illĭŭs)?

---

* The suffix *met* is sometimes added to all the cases of *suus,* in the sense of the English "own," and commonly in connection with *ipse,* himself; e. g. *Suummet librum ipse tenet,* He himself has his own book. To the ablative singular *suo, sua* (and also to *meo, mea, tuo, tua,* &c.) the syllable *ptĕ* máy be annexed in the same sense; as *suaptĕ manu,* with his own hand; *meoptĕ ingenio,* by my own genius; *nostraptĕ culpâ,* by our own fault.

† Both these words are sometimes put together, in order to render the notion of possession still more prominent: *suus proprius,* precisely like the English "his own."   C

| I have his (that man's) | { Éjus (hábĕo).
{ Hábeo (cálcĕum) éjus (illiŭs). |
| *Somebody* or *anybody, some one*
or *any one.* (Indefinite Pro-
nouns.) | { Ălĭquĭs ; quĭs ; quispĭam.
{ Quisquam, ullus ; non nēmo.
{ Num quĭs ? Ecquis ? |

C. Obs. The indefinite pronouns *ălĭquis, quis,* and *quispĭam* are always *positive,* and differ but little from each other, except that *quispĭam* is more general (= "some one or another"). *Quisquam* (like *quidquam* of Lesson VI., q. v.) and *nullus,* on the other hand, are only used where the sentence contains a *negation,* either expressed or implied. *Quis* may stand for *ălĭquis,* but only after particles like *si* (if), *nisi* (unless), *num* (whether), and *ne* (lest). *Ecquis ?* and *num quis ?* are inter-rogative.

Has any one ? (Yes.)	{ Habétne álĭquis (quíspiam) ? { Ecquis hábet ?
Has any one ? (No.)	{ Núm quís (quísquam) hábet ? { Habétne quísquam (úllus) ?
Some one has.	{ Álĭquis (quíspĭam) hábet. { Nôn némo hábet.
Nor has any one.	Néque quísquam hábet.
If (unless, whether) any one has.	Sí (nísi, núm) quís *or* álĭquis há-bet.

D. The indefinite *quis,* and its compounds *aliquis, ecquis, quisquam,* and *quispiam* are thus inflected :—

Nom.	quĭs	ălĭquĭs	ecquĭs	quisquam	quispĭam
Gen.	cūjus	ălĭcūjus	eccūjus	cūjusquam	cūjuspĭam
Dat.	cuĭ	ălĭcuĭ	eccuĭ	cuĭquam	cuĭpĭam
Acc.	quem	ălĭquem	ecquem	quemquam	quempĭam
Voc.	——	——	——	——	——
Abl.	quō.	ălĭquō.	ecquō.	quōquam.	quōpĭam.

Has any one my hat ?	{ Habétne álĭquis méum pílĕum ? { Ecquis hábet pílĕum méum ? { Núm quís hábet pílĕum méum ?
Somebody has it.	Hábet éum álĭquĭs (quíspĭam, nôn némo).
Who has my stick ?	{ Quís ténet scipĭónem méum ? { Cuĭ ést bácŭlum méum ?
Nobody has it.	{ Némo (núllus) éum ténet. { Némĭnĭ (núlli) ést.
No one, nobody, or not anybody.	{ Němo, nullus. { Němo hŏmo, nullus homo. { Nec quisquam, neque ullus.*

---

* The Romans frequently employ *quisquam* or *ullus* in connection with *nec* or

E. Obs. The indefinite *nēmo* is seldom used in the genitive, *nullīus* being employed in its stead. The word *homo* is sometimes added to *nēmo* as well as to *nullus.* These words are thus inflected: —

Nom.	nēmo	ullŭs	nullŭs
Gen.	nēmĭnis	ullīus	nullīus *
Dat.	nemīnĭ	ullī	nullī
Acc.	nemĭnem	ullum	nullum
Voc.	nēmo	——	——
Abl.	nēmĭnĕ.	ullō.	nullō.

Who has my ribbon ? { Quís hábet taénĭam méam ?
{ Cuí ést taénĭa méa ?

Nobody has it. { Némo (núllus) éam hábet.
{ (Éa) némini (núlli) ést.

Who is right ? { Cuí ést fās ?
{ Quís lóquĭtur vére ?

No one is right. { Fås ést nemĭnĭ (núllĭ).
{ Némo vére lóquĭtur.

Is any one hungry ? Esurítne álĭquis ? Núm quís ésurit ? Écquis ésurit ? Án quís-quam ésŭrit ?

No one is hungry. { Némo ésŭrit.
{ Ésŭrit núllus.

Nor is any one hungry. Néc quísquam (néque úllus) hómo ésŭrit.

EXERCISE 10.

Have you the ox of the peasant or that of the cook? — I have neither that of the peasant nor that of the cook. — Has the peasant his rice? — He has it. — Have you it? — I have it not. — Has his boy the servant's broom? — He has it. — Who has the boy's pencil? — Nobody has it. — Has your brother my stick or that of the painter? — He has neither yours nor that of the painter; he has his own. — Has he the good or bad money? — He has neither the good nor the bad. — Has he the wooden or the leaden horse? — He has neither the wooden nor the leaden horse. — What has he good? — He has my good honey. — Has my neighbor's boy my book? — He has it not. — Which book has he? — He has his fine book. — Has he my book or his own? — He has his own? — Who has my gold button? — Nobody has it. — Has anybody my thread stocking? — Nobody has it.

---

nunquam, instead of *nemo,* as in English we likewise say, "nor was there ever any one," instead of "no one ever was," &c.

* *Ullus* and *nullus* are properly adjectives in *us, a, um.* But they deviate from the inflection of adjectives by having their genitive in *ius* (instead of *i, ae, i*) for every gender, and their dative in *i* (instead of *o, ae, o*). Compare *unus* of Lesson XVIII.

Which ship has the merchant? — He has his own? — Which horse has my friend? — He has mine. — Has he his dog? — He has it not. — Who has his dog? — Nobody has it. — Who has my brother's umbrella? — Somebody has it. — Which (*quas*) broom has the servant? — He has his own. — Is anybody hungry? — Nobody is hungry. — Is anybody sleepy? — Nobody is sleepy. — Is any one tired? — No one is tired. — Who is right? — Nobody is right. — Have I his biscuit? — You have it not. — Have I his good brother's ox? — You have it not. — Which chicken have I? — You have his. — Is anybody wrong? — Nobody is wrong.

Lesson XI. — PENSUM UNDECIMUM.

OF DEMONSTRATIVE PRONOUNS.

A. The Latin language has three demonstrative pronouns, with special reference to each of the three persons, viz.: *hĭc, haec, hŏc,* this (of mine); *istĕ, istă, istŭd,* that (of yours); *illĕ, illă, illŭd,* that (of his). To these must be added the determinative *ĭs, ĕă, ĭd,* which sometimes has the demonstrative force of *this* or *that.* These words are thus inflected: —

	Hic, *this (of mine).*				Ille, *that (of his).*		
	Masc.	*Fem.*	*Neut.*		*Masc.*	*Fem.*	*Neut.*
NOM.	hĭc	haec	hŏc		illĕ	illă	illŭd
GEN.		hūjus				illĭus	
DAT.		huĭc				illĭ	
ACC.	hunc	hanc	hŏc		illŭm	illăm	illŭd
VOC.	hĭc	haec	hŏc		illĕ	illă	illŭd
ABL.	hōc	hāc	hōc.		illō	illā	illō.

	Iste, *that (of yours).*				Is, *that, this.*		
	Masc.	*Fem.*	*Neut.*		*Masc.*	*Fem.*	*Neut.*
NOM.	istĕ	istă	istŭd		ĭs	ĕa	ĭd
GEN.		istĭus				ējŭs	
DAT.		istĭ				ĕĭ	
ACC.	istŭm	istăm	istŭd		ĕŭm	ĕăm	ĭd
VOC.	istĕ	istă	istŭd		ĭs	ĕă	ĭd
ABL.	istō	istā	istō.		ĕō	ĕā	ĕō.

REMARKS.

1. The demonstrative force of *hic*, &c. is often increased by the addition of the syllable *ce*, as *hicce*, *haecce*, *hocce*, *hujusce*, &c. — With the interrogative particle *ne*, the pronouns become *hiccine* (or with one *c*, *hicine*)? *haeccine*? *hoccine*? &c.

2. In composition with *ecce* and *en* (= lo! see! here!), these pronouns have given rise to the following forms, frequently used in common discourse: *eccum*, *eccam* (pl. *eccos*, *eccas*); *eccillum* or *ellum*, *ellam* (pl. *ellos*, *ellas*), and *eccistam*, "there he (she) is," "there they come," "see there," &c. — *Ea*, in connection with *re* and the affix *pse*, gives rise to *reapse*, "indeed."

3. *Hic* implies *proximity*, either of space or of time, to the person speaking. *Ille*, on the other hand, refers to something *remote*, and also to something *well known*, *already mentioned*, or *distinguished*. When directly opposed to each other, *ille* signifies "the former," and *hic*, "the latter."

4. *Iste* has always reference to the person spoken to, and is hence called the pronoun of the second person; as *iste liber*, *istud saccharum*, this book, that sugar (of yours or mentioned by you). It sometimes conveys the notion of disapprobation or contempt, as *ille* does that of honor; as *iste homo*, this fellow; *ille Socrates*, the well-known (illustrious) Socrates.

5. *Is*, when used as a demonstrative, points to a person or thing already mentioned, in the sense of the English "this man," "that thing" (of which I am speaking or have just spoken), or of an emphatic "he, she, it"; e. g. *Is est, an non est?* Is it *he* (is this the man) or not? In the oblique cases it is the pronoun of the third person (*his*, *him*, *hers*, *her*, &c.). See Lesson IX. *C.*

6. The pronoun *hic*, in connection with *ille* and *iste*, gives rise to the compounds *istic* (or *isthic*), *istaec*, *istoc* or *istuc*, and *illic*, *illaec*, *illoc* or *illuc*, both of which are declined like *hic*, *haec*, *hoc*.

The sailor.	{ Hŏmo nautĭcus.
	{ Nauta, ae, *m.*
The chair.	Sella, ae, *f.*
The seat (of honor).	Sŏlĭum, i, *n.*; sēdēs, ĭs, *f.*
The looking-glass.	*Spĕcŭlum, i, *n.*
The light.	Lux, lūcis, *f.*; lūmĕn, ĭnis, *n.*
The light, candle.	Lūmĕn, ĭnis, *n.*; candēla, ae, *f.*
The lamp.	Lūcerna, ae, *f.*; lampăs, ădis, *f.**
The tree.	Arbŏr, *or* arbōs, ŏris, *f.*
The garden.	Hortus, i, *m.*
The foreigner.	Pĕregrīnus, i, *m.*; advĕna, ae, *m.* (just arrived).
The stranger (guest).	Hospĕs, ĭtis, *m.*

* *Lampas* is a word of Greek origin, and sometimes retains its original inflection. Thus: N. *lampas*, G. *lampădis* or *-ădos*, D. *lampădi*, Acc. *lampădem* or *-ăda*, V. *lampas*, Abl. *lampăde*.

The glove.	*Digitabŭlum, i, n.
The ass.	Asínus, i, m.
The hay.	Foenum, i, n.
The grain (seed).	Gränum, i, n.
The corn (grain generally).	Frümentum, i, n.; annōna, ae, f. (one year's produce).
The letter.	Epistŏla, ae, f.; littĕrae, ārum, f. pl. (Cf. Lesson XIII.)
The note (billet).	Schĕdŭla or scĭdŭla, ae, f.
The horse-shoe.	*Sŏlĕa ferrĕa (ae, f.) ĕqui.
This book — that book.	{ Nom. híc líber — ílle líber. { Acc. húnc líbrum — íllum líbrum.
This note — that note.	{ Nom. haêc scídŭla — ílla scídŭla. { Acc. hánc scídŭlam — íllam scí- { dulam.
This hay — that hay.	Hóc foênum — íllud foênum.
This (that) hay (of yours).	Ístud foênum.
That worthless man.	Hómo íste nêquam.
That great man.	Vír ílle mágnus.
Is he (this) the man ?	Án ést ís hómo ?
That is the cause.	Éă ést caûsa.
Have you this hat or that one ?	Habêsne húnc pílĕum án íllum ?
I have not this, but that one.	{ Nôn húnc, séd íllum hábĕo. { Nôn húnc hábeo, séd íllum.
But.	*Sĕd, vērŭm; autĕm.*

B. Obs. The adversative conjunctions *sed* and *verum** are nearly synonymous, and are always placed at the beginning of the clause introduced by them. *Autem*, like the English " however," generally stands after the first, second, or third word.   Examples : —

Not I, but you.	Nôn égo, séd (vêrum) tû.
You are neither right nor wrong, but (however) your brother is wrong.	Tú néque réctē lóquĕris, néque érras, érrat aùtem fràter túius.
Has the youth this book or that one ?	Tenétne adolescéntŭlus húnc líbrum án íllum ?
He has this, but not that one.	Húnc quídem ténet, íllum aùtem nôn.
He has not this, but that one.	Ténet nôn húnc, séd (vêrum) íllum.
Have you this looking-glass or that one ?	{ Útrum hóc spécŭlum hábēs án illud ? { Hoccíne spécŭlum hábēs, án íllud ?

* *Verum* gives preponderance to the second member of the sentence, and may be rendered by "but rather," " but in reality."

I have neither this nor that one.	{ Néque hóc hábeo néque íllud.
	Hábeo néque hóc néque íllud.

Have you this man's light or that one ? — Tenêsne lûmen hújus hómǐnis ǎn illǐŭs ?

I have neither this man's nor that ˙one's. — Téneo néque lûmen hújus hómǐnis néque illius.

I have not this man's, but that one's. — Égo nôn hújus víri lûmen téneo, séd (vêrum) illius.

EXERCISE 12.

Which hay has the foreigner ? — He has that of the peasant. — Has the sailor my looking-glass ? — He has it not. — Have you this candle or that one ? — I have this one. — Have you the hay of my garden, or that of yours ? — I have neither that of your garden nor that of mine, but that of the foreigner. — Which glove have you ? — I have his glove. — Which chair has the foreigner ? — He has his own. — Who has my good candle ? — This man has it. — Who has that looking-glass ? — That foreigner has it. — What has your servant ? — He has the tree of this garden. — Has he that man's book ? — He has not the book of that man, but that of this boy. — Which ox has this peasant ? — He has that of your neighbor. — Have I your letter or his ? — You have neither mine nor his, but that of your friend. — Have you this horse's hay ? — I have not its hay, but its shoe. — Has your brother my note or his own ? — He has that of the sailor. — Has this foreigner my glove or his own ? — He has neither yours nor his own, but that of his friend. — Are you hungry or thirsty ? — I am neither hungry nor thirsty, but sleepy. — Is he sleepy or hungry ? — He is neither sleepy nor hungry, but tired. — Am I right or wrong ? — You are neither right nor wrong, but your good boy is wrong. — Have I the good or the bad knife ? — You have neither the good nor the bad, but the ugly (one). — What have I ? — You have nothing good, but something bad. — Who has my ass ? — The peasant has it.

Lesson XII. — PENSUM DUODECIMUM.

OF INTERROGATIVE PRONOUNS.

A. There are three interrogative pronouns in Latin, viz.: 1) the substantive *quĭs?* (masc. & fem.) "who?" *quĭd?* "what?" 2) the adjective *quī, quae, quŏd?* "which?" and 3) *ŭtĕr, utră, utrŭm?* "which of the two?" They are thus inflected: —

Quis? quĭd?   *Who? what?*

NOM.	*who? what?*	quĭs?	quĭd?
GEN.	*whose? of what?*	cūjŭs?	cūjŭs rei?*
DAT.	*to whom? to what?*	cuĭ?	cuĭ rei?
ACC.	*whom? what?*	quĕm?	quĭd? .
VOC.	———	———	———
ABL.	*with whom? with what?*	quō?	quā rē?

Quī, quae, quod?   *Which? what?*

NOM.	*which? what?*	quī	quae	quŏd?
GEN.	*of which* or *what?*		cūjŭs?	
DAT.	*to which* or *what?*		cuĭ?	
ACC.	*which? what?* ·	quĕm	quăm	quŏd?
VOC.	———	———	———	———
ABL.	*with which* or *what?*	quō	quā	quō? †

Utĕr, utră, utrŭm?   *Which of the two?*

NOM.	ŭt	utră	utrŭm?
GEN.		utrĭus? ‡	
DAT.		utrĭ?	
ACC.	utrŭm	utrăm	utrŭm?
VOC.	———	———	———
ABL.	utrō	utrā	utrō?

REMARKS.

1. The emphatic *năm* affixed to either of these pronouns gives animation to the inquiry; as *quisnăm?* who, pray? *quidnăm?* what then? *quinăm, quaenăm, quodnăm?* which, pray?

2. The general rule is that *quis* should stand substantively for both genders, and *qui, quae* adjectively; as, *quis?* who? *qui vir?* which (or what) man? *quae femina?* what woman? But this distinction is frequently disregarded, especially for the sake of euphony; e. g. *qui* (for *quis*) *sis considera*, consider who you are; *quis* (for *qui*) *iste tantus casus?* what is this great calamity of yours?

3. Instead of *quod* in the same case with its substantive, we may

---

* On this use of *rei*, see note, page 29.

† There is an obsolete ablative *qui* for every gender, yet in use in forms like *quicum* (= *quōcum* or *quācum*, with whom, with which), and adverbially in the sense of *how?* e. g. *Qui fit?* How comes it? *Qui tibi id facere licuit?* How could that have been lawful for you?

‡ The following nine adjectives are pronominals, and their compounds form the genitive in *ĭus*, and the dative in *ĭ: ūnŭs, sōlŭs, tōtŭs, ullŭs; ŭt̬r. neutĕr, altĕr, nullŭs,* and *ăllŭs.* Of these, *alter* alone has *alterius*, the rest have *ĭus* in prose and sometimes *ĭus* in poetry.

use *quid* partitively with the genitive; as *quod saccharum?* or *quid sacchari?*

4. Instead of the genitive *cujus*, "whose" (both interrogative and relative), the adjective *cujus, a, um* is sometimes employed; as *cujus liber? cuja mensa? cujum foenum?* whose book, &c.   But this mode of expression is antiquated, and scarcely used except in law.

5. To *quis?* correspond in the answer the pronominal adjectives *alius*, another (one); *ullus*, any one; and *nullus*, no one.   To *uter?* we reply with *alter*, the one of two, the other; *neuter*, neither of (the) two; *alteruter*, the one or the other; *utervis* and *uterlibet*, each of the two; and the compound relative *utercunque*, whichever of the two.

6. These pronouns are used precisely in the same manner when the question becomes *indirect*, in which case, however, the verb must be in the subjunctive; e. g. *Quis est?* who is it? *nescio quis sit*, I do not know who it is (may be); *dic mihi, uter habeat*, tell me who has; *uter habeat, nescio*, I know not who has (lit. may have).   (Vide Lesson XXX. *C.*)

OF RELATIVE PRONOUNS.

B. The relative *quī, quae, quŏd*, "who," "that *or* which," is inflected like the interrogative of the same form.   Relatives always agree with their antecedents in gender and number: —

The man, who, whose, to whom, whom, by whom.

Vír, quī, cújus, cuí, quém, quô.

The woman, who, whose, to whom, whom, by whom.

Fémĭna, quaê, cújus, cuí, quám, quâ.

The affair, which, of which, to which, which, with which.

Negótĭum, quód, cújus, cuí, quód, quô.

Have you the hat which my brother has?

Habêsne tû pĭleum, quem fráter méus hábet?

I have not the hat which your brother has.

{ Nôn hábeo pĭleum, quém fráter túus hábet.

Quém hábet fráter túus pĭleum nôn hábeo.*

Have you the gold which I have?

Án hábes aûrum, quód égo hábeo?

I have the gold which you have.

{ Hábeo aûrum, quód tû hábes.

Quód tû aûrum hábes, íd et égo hábeo.*

C. Obs. Of the relative *qui, quae, quod* there are two compounds, *quicunque* and *quisquis*, "whoever," "every one who," of which the

---

* The general rule is that *the Relative should be placed after its antecedent, and as near as possible to it.*   The clauses, however, are frequently inverted; as, *Terra, quod accepit*, (*id*) *nunquam sine usurâ reddit*, The earth never returns without usury what it has received.

former is declined like the simple pronoun (with the syllable *cunque* affixed to each case); as, *quicunque, quaecunque, quodcunque,* gen. *cujuscunque,* &c. — The latter has a double inflection: *quisquis* (masc. & fem.), *quidquid* or *quicquid* (neut.). E. g. *Quisquis ille est,* "whoever he is (may be)." *Quicunque* is est, *ei* me profiteor inimicum, " *Whoever* he may be, I profess myself an enemy *to him.*"

OF DETERMINATIVE PRONOUNS.

D. Determinative pronouns are such as serve to point out the antecedent of a relative. They are in Latin: *is, ea, id,* "he, she, or it," "that *or* the one"; the demonstrative *ille, illa, illud,* "the," "that *or* the one"; and the compound *idem, eadem, idem,* "the same." They are thus inflected:—

Is, ille — qui, &c., *that or the one, which.*

	Masculine.			*Feminine.*			*Neuter.*		
Nom.	Is,	illĕ —	quī	ĕă,	illă —	quae	Id,	illŭd —	quŏd
Gen.	ējus,	illīŭs —	cūjŭs	ējŭs,	illīŭs —	cūjŭs	ējŭs,	illīŭs —	cūjŭs
Dat.	ĕī,	illī —	cuī	ĕī,	illī —	cuī	ĕī,	illī —	cuī
Acc.	ĕŭm,	illăm —	quĕm	ĕăm,	illăm —	quăm	Id,	illŭd —	quŏd
Voc.	—	—	—	—	—	—	—	—	—
Abl.	ĕō,	illō —	quō.	ĕā,	illă —	quā.	ŏ̆,	illō —	quō.

I have that *or* the one which you have (*masc. & fem.*).	Hábeo éum *or* íllum (éam *or* íllam), quém (quám) tû hábes. Ést míhi ís *or* ílle (éa *or* ílla), quí (quae) tíbi ést.
I have that *or* the one which you have (*neut.*).	Hábeo íd (íllud), quód tû hábes. Ést míhi íd (íllud), quód tíbi ést.
Which horse have you?	Quém équum hábes ? Quís ést tíbi équus ?
I have that which your friend has.	Hábeo éum (íllum), quém amícus túus hábet.
Have you not the light which I have?	Nònne hábes lúmen, quód égo hábeo ?
I have that (the one) which you have.	Hábeo íd (íllud), quód tû hábes.

E. The determinative *idem, ĕădem, idem,* "the same," "the very one," is a compound of *is, ea, id* and the syllable *dem.* It is thus inflected:—

Idem, eădem, Idem, *the same* — quī, *which.*

Nom.	*the same*	ĭdĕm,	ĕădĕm,	Idĕm	—quī,	quae,	quŏd
Gen.	*of the same*	ējusdĕm			— cūjŭs		
Dat.	*to the same*	ĕīdĕm			— cuī		
Acc.	*the same*	ĕundĕm,	ĕandĕm,	Idĕm	—quĕm,	quăm,	quŏd
Voc.	*O the same*	ĭdĕm,	eădĕm,	Idĕm	—quī,	quae,	quŏd
Abl.	*with the same.*	eōdĕm,	eădĕm,	eōdĕm	—quō,	quă,	quō.

Have you the same horse which I have ?	Habêsne tû eúndem équum, quém égo hábeo ? Éstne tíbi idem équus, qui míhi (ést) ?
I have the same.	Hábeo eúndem. Ést míhi idem.
Which coat has the man ?	Quám tógam hábet vír ílle ? Quaê ést vírō ílli tóga ?
He has the same which you have.	Eándem hábet, quám tû (hábes). Ést éi eúdem ác tíbi.

F. Obs. The pronoun *idem* serves to express the identity of two things, and is followed either by the relative *qui, quae, quŏd,* or by one of the particles *ăc, atque, ŭt, quăm* (= the English " as "), *cŭm* (= " with "), *quăsĭ* (= " as if"), &c.

Has he the same corn which you have ? Has he the same corn *as* you (*with* you) ?	Habétne ílle *idem* fruméntum, *quŏd* tû hábes ? Éstne éi *idem* fruméntum *ác* (or *átque, quám*) tíbi (or *têcum **) ?
He has not the same which I have. He has not the same as I (with me).	Nôn idem hábet, quŏd égo hábeo. Éi nôn ést idem átque míhi (mê-cum).
The carriage.	Currŭs, ūs, *m.*; pilentum, i, *n.*
The house.	Dŏmŭs, ūs, *f.*; aedēs, ium, *pl. f.* (Vide Lesson XVII. *D.*)
Which carriage have you ?	Quém hábes cúrrum ? Quŏd ést tíbi pílentum ?
I have that which your friend has.	Éum húbeo, quém amícus túius há-bet. Míhi ést íd, quŏd ést amíco túo.
Has he the same house which I have ?	Núm hábet ílle eándem dómum, quám et égo hábeo ?
He has not the same.	(Eándem) nôn hábet.

EXERCISE 13.

Have you the garden which I have ? — I have not the one that you have. — Which looking-glass have you ? — I have the one which your brother has. — Has he the book that your friend has ? — He has not the one which my friend has. — Which candle has he ? — He has that of his neighbor. — He has the one that I have. — Has he this tree or that one ? — He has neither this nor that, but the one which I have. — Which ass has the man ? — He has the

---

* The preposition *cum*, "with," generally stands *before* the case governed by it; but it is suffixed to the pronominal ablatives *me, te, nob´s, vobis,* which are always *mēcum, tēcum, nōbiscum, vōbiscum.*

one that his boy has. — Has the stranger your chair or mine ? — He
has neither yours nor mine ; but he has his friend's good chair. —
Have you the glove which I have, or the one that my tailor has ? —
I have neither the one which you have, nor the one which your
tailor has, but my own. — Has your shoemaker my fine shoe, or that
of his boy ? — He has neither yours nor that of his boy, but that of
the good stranger. — Which house has the baker ? — He has neither
yours nor mine, but that of his good brother. — Which carriage have
I ? — Have I mine or that of the peasant ? — You have neither
yours nor that of the peasant ; you have the one which I have. —
Have you my fine carriage ? — I have it not ; but the Frenchman
has it ? — What has the Frenchman ? — He has nothing. — What
has the shoemaker ? — He has something fine. — What has he fine ?
— He has his fine shoe. — Is the shoemaker right ? — He is not
wrong ; but this neighbor, the baker, is right. — Is your horse hungry ?
— It is not hungry, but thirsty. — Have you my ass's hay, or yours ?
— I have that which my brother has. — Has your friend the same
horse that my brother has ? — He has not the same horse, but the
same coat. — Has he my umbrella ? — He has it not.

Lesson XIII. — PENSUM TERTIUM DECIMUM.

OF THE PLURAL OF SUBSTANTIVES AND ADJECTIVES.

A. The nominative plural of the five declensions is
characterized by the following terminations : —

1. Substantives and adjectives of the first declension have
the nominative in *ae*, and the genitive in *ārŭm ;* as *mensae, men-
sārŭm ; bŏnae, bŏnārŭm.*

2. Masculines (and feminines) of the second declension form
their plural in *ī,* neuters in *ă.* The genitive of both is *ōrŭm.*
E. g. *dŏmĭnī, dŏmĭnōrum ; pŭĕrī, pŭĕrōrŭm ; fĭlă, fĭlōrŭm ;
bŏnī,* neut. *bŏnă, bŏnōrŭm.*

3. Masculines and feminines of the third declension change
the *ĭs* of the genitive singular into *ēs ,* neuters, into *ă* or *ĭă.*
The genitive of this declension is *ŭm* or *ĭŭm.* E. g. *lăpĭdĭs,*
pl. *lăpĭdēs, lăpĭdŭm ; vestĭs,* pl. *vestēs, vestĭŭm ; pistōrĭs,* pl. *pistōrēs, pistōrŭm ; căpĭtĭs,* pl. *căpĭtă, căpĭtŭm ; turpĭs,* pl. *turpēs,*
neut. *turpĭă,* gen. *turpĭŭm.*

4. Masculines and feminines of the fourth declension retain
the *ūs* of the genitive singular, and neuters (in *ū*) assume the
termination *ŭa.* The genitive plural of this declension is uni-
formly *ŭum.* E. g. *fructūs, fructŭum ; cornŭa, cornŭum.*

5. Nouns of the fifth declension form their plural in *ēs*, and their genitive in *ērŭm* ; as *rēs, rērŭm* ; *dĭēs, dĭērŭm.*

The following list exhibits the nominative and genitive plural of the majority of substantives thus far used in this book, according to their respective declensions : —

FIRST DECLENSION.

The husbandmen.	Agrĭcŏlae,	ārum.
The candles.	Candēlae,	"
The letters.	Epistŏlae,	"
The hens.	Gallĭnae,	"
The lamps.	Lūcernae,	"
The grains.	Mĭcae,	"
The pens.	*Pennae,	"
The notes.	Schĕdŭlae,	"
The brooms.	Scōpae,	"
The chairs.	Sellae,	"
The horse-shoes.	*Sŏlĕae ferrĕae,	"

SECOND DECLENSION.

The friends.	Amĭci,	ōrum.
The asses.	Asĭni,	"
The cheeses.	Cāsĕi,	"
The nails.	Clāvi,	"
The cooks.	Cŏqui,	"
The knives.	Cultri,	"
The corks.	*Embŏli,	"
The carpenters.	Făbri tignārĭi,	"
The servants.	{ Fămŭli, Mĭnistri,	" "
The Frenchmen.	Francogalli,	"
The gardens.	Horti,	"
The books.	Libri,	"
The hammers.	Mallĕi,	"
The eyes.	Ŏcŭli,	"
The buttons.	*Orbĭcŭli fibulatōrĭi,	"
The strangers.	Pĕregrīni,	"
The hats.	*Pĭlĕi, m.	"
The chickens.	Pulli gallĭnācĕi,	"
The bags.	Sacci,	"
The pencils.	*Stĭli cerussāti,	"
The men.	Vĭri,	"
The neighbors.	Vĭcĭni,	"
The canes.	Bacŭla,	"
The gloves.	Digitābŭla,	"
The threads.	Fĭla,	"
The grains.	Grāna,	"
The carriages.	Pilenta,	"
The knives.	Scalpra,	"

The looking-glasses.	*Spĕcŭla, ōrum.
The umbrellas.	*Umbrăcŭla, "

THIRD DECLENSION.

The youths.	Adŏlescentes, ĭum, *m.*
The trees.	Arbŏres, um, *f.*
The birds.	·Āves, ĭum, *f.*
The oxen.	Bŏves, bŏum, *m.* & *f.*
The dogs.	Cănes, um, *m.* & *f.*
The brothers.	Frātres, um, *m.*
The men.	Hŏmĭnes, um, *m.*
The strangers.	Hospĭtes, um, *m.*
The young men.	Jŭvĕnes, um, *m.*
The lamps.	Lampŭdes,* um, *f.*
The merchants.	Mercātŏres, um, *m.*
The ships.	Nāves, ĭum, *f.* ·
The sheep.	Ŏves, ĭum, *f.*
The (different sorts of) bread.	Pānes, um, *m.*
The feet.	Pĕdes, um, *m.*
The bakers.	Pistōres, um, *m.*
The (different sorts of) salt	{ Săles, ĭum, *m.* { Sălĭa, " *n.*
The tailors.	Sartōres, um, *m.*
The canes.	Scīpĭōnes, um, *m.*
The shoemakers.	Sūtōres, um, *m.*
The rams.	Vervēccs, um, *m.*
The garments.	Vestes, ĭum, *f.*
The birds.	Volucres, um, *m.* & *f.*
The heads.	Căpĭta, um, *n.*
The lights.	Lūmĭna, um, *n.*
The stockings.	*Tibĭālĭa, ĭum, *n.*

FOURTH DECLENSION.

The carriages.	Currus, ŭum, *m.*
The houses.	Dŏmus, ŭum, *f.*

B. The following paradigms may serve as examples of the declension of the plural number.

1. PLURAL OF THE FIRST DECLENSION.

Mensae, *tables;* fĭlĭae, *the daughters;* nautae, *sailors.*

Nom.	mensae	fĭlĭae	nautae
Gen.	mensārum	fĭlĭārum	nautārum
Dat.	mensīs	fĭlĭābŭs	nautīs
Acc.	mensās	fĭlĭās	nautās
Voc.	mensae	fĭlĭae	nautae
Abl.	mensīs.	fĭlĭābŭs.†	nautīs.

---

* The plural of this noun is likewise partly Greek : N. *lampădes,* G. *-ddum,* D. *-ĭdĭbus.* Acc. *-ddes* or *-ădns,* V. *-ădes,* Abl. *-dĭbus.*

† This form of the dative and ablative is the best for *dea* and *filia,* in order

REMARK. — In the plural of every declension the nominative and vocative, and the dative and ablative, end always alike.

2. PLURAL OF THE SECOND DECLENSION.

Ĕquī, *the horses ;* librī, *the books ;* candēlābră, *the candlesticks.*

NOM. ĕquī	librī	candēlābră
GEN. ĕquōrŭn	librōrŭm	candēlābrōrŭm
DAT. ĕquīs	librīs	candēlābrīs
ACC. ĕquōs	librōs	candēlābră
VOC. ĕquī	librī	candēlābră
ABL. ĕquīs.	librīs.	candēlābrīs.

The *pl.* lĭbĕrī, *children,* and the plural of dĕus, *a god,* are thus declined : —

NOM. lĭbĕrī	dĕī, dĭī *or* dī
GEN. lĭberōrum *or* liberum*	dĕōrum *or* dĕum *
DAT. lĭbĕrīs	dĕīs, dĭīs *or* dīs,
ACC. lĭbĕrōs	dĕōs
VOC. lĭbĕrī	dĕī, dĭī *or* dī
ABL. lĭbĕrīs.	dĕīs, dĭīs *or* dīs.

3. PLURAL OF THE THIRD DECLENSION.

Hŏmĭnēs, *men ;* pistōrēs, *bakers ;* vestēs, *garments ;* nāvēs, *the ships.*

NOM. hŏmĭnēs	pistōrēs	vestēs	nāvēs
GEN. hŏmĭnŭm	pistōrum	vestĭŭm	nāvĭŭm
DAT. hŏmĭnĭbŭs	pistōrĭbŭs	vestĭbŭs	nāvĭbŭs
ACC. hŏmĭnēs	pistōrēs	vestēs	nāvēs
VOC. hŏmĭnēs	pistōrēs	vestēs	nāvēs
ABL. hŏmĭnĭbŭs.	pistōrĭbŭs.	vestĭbŭs.	nāvĭbŭs.

Lūmĭnă, *lights ;* tĭbĭālĭă, *stockings ;* poëmăta, n., *poems.*

NOM. lūmĭnă	tĭbĭālĭă	poëmătă
GEN. lūmĭnŭm	tĭbĭālĭŭm	poëmătŭm
DAT. lūmĭnĭbŭs	tĭbĭālĭbŭs	poëmătĭs
ACC. lūmĭnă	tĭbĭālĭă	poëmătă
VOC. lūmĭnă	tĭbĭālĭă	poëmătă
ABL. lūmĭnĭbŭs.	tĭbĭālĭbŭs.	poëmătĭs.

to distinguish them from the same cases of *dĕus* and *fīlĭus* of the second declension. So the words *anĭma,* the soul ; *lĭberta,* a freed-woman ; *nāta,* daughter ; *mula,* a she-mule ; *ĕqua,* a mare ; *asĭna,* a she-ass. — may have *ăbus* instead of *is,* and for the same reason. The numerals *dŭŏ,* two, and *ambŏ,* both, have *dŭābus* and *ambābus* regularly.

 * So also *fabrum, socium, decemvirum,* instead of *fabrorum,* &c. This con-

Adolescentēs, *young men ;* cănēs, *dogs ;* bŏvēs, *oxen.*

Nom.	ădŏlescentēs	cănēs	bŏvēs
Gen.	ădŏlescentĭūm	cănūm	bŏŭm
Dat.	ădŏlescentĭbŭs	cănĭbŭs	būbŭs *or* bŏbŭs
Acc.	ădŏlescentēs	cănēs	bŏvēs
Voc.	ădŏlescentēs	cănēs	bŏvēs
Abl.	ădŏlescentĭbŭs.	cănĭbŭs.	būbŭs *or* bŏbŭs.

Remarks.

1. The normal termination for the Nom., Acc., and Voc. *pl.* of neuters is *ă.* Some, however, have always *ĭa.* They are: 1.) Those ending in *e, al, ar,* as *măria, sălia, calcāria,* from *măre,* the sea, *săl,* salt, and *calcār,* a spur; 2.) All participles in *ns* and such adjectives as have either *ĭ* or else *ĕ* or *ĭ* in the ablative singular, comparatives excepted, as *ămantĭa, ēsŭrĭentĭa, părĭa, făcĭlĭa, turpĭa,* from *ămans, ēsŭriens, pār, făcĭle, turpe.* But we say *mājŏra, doctĭŏra,* from the comp. *mājor,* greater, *doctĭor,* more learned.

2. The general termination of the genitive plural is *ŭm ;* but the following have *ĭŭm : —*

a) All those which have *ĭa* in the nominative plural, as *mărĭum, calcārĭum, ămantĭum, făcĭlĭum, turpĭum.*

b) Words in *ēs* and *ĭs* which do not increase in the genitive singular (i. e. which receive no additional syllable), as *năvis, năvĭum ; vestis, vestĭum ; nūbēs, nūbĭum ;* except *vātēs, strŭes, cănis, pănis,* and *jŭvĕnis,* which have *vātum, strŭum, cănum,* &c.

c) Of nouns in *er* some have *ĭum,* as *imber, imbrĭum ; linter, lintrĭum ; venter, ventrĭum ; ūtĕr, ūtrĭum ;* others again have *ŭm,* as *pătrum, matrum, fratrum, accĭpĭtrum,* from *păter, măter,* &c. — *Căro* has *carnĭum,* and *sĕnex, sĕnum.*

d) Many monosyllables, especially those ending in *s* and *x* with a consonant preceding; as *dens, dentĭum ; mons, montĭum ; merx, mercĭum ; lis, lĭtĭum ; ŏs, ossĭum ; nox, noctĭum ; vis, virĭum,* &c.

e) Dissyllables and polysyllables in *ns* and *rs* have generally *ium* and sometimes *um ;* as *còhors, còhortĭum ; cliens, clientĭum ; ădŏlescens, ădŏlescentĭum ;* but *parentes, parentum.*

3. In the dative and ablative plural, Greek nouns in *ma* have usually *ĭs,* sometimes however *ĭbŭs ;* as *poēma, poëmătis* or *poëmătĭbus ; diploma, diplomătis* or *diplomătĭbŭs,* &c.

4. The accusative plural of those words which have *ium* in the genitive is among some writers *ĭs* or *eis,* instead of *ēs ;* as *artĭs, civĭs, omnĭs,* instead of *artēs, civēs,* &c.

---

tracted genitive (commonly but incorrectly printed *ŭm*) is the common form of names of measures, weights, and coins, as *nummum, sestertium, denarium, cadum, medimnum, modium, jugerum, talentum,* the regular genitive plural of *nummus, sestertius,* &c. The poets extend this form to names of nations, and say *Argĭum, Danaum,* &c., in lieu of *Argivŏrum,* &c.

4. Plural of the Fourth and Fifth Declensions.

Fructŭs, *m.*, *fruits*; cornŭă, *n.*, *horns*; dŏmŭs, *f.*, *houses*; dĭēs, *m.*, *days*; rēs, *f.*, *things*.

Nom.	fructūs	cornŭă	dŏmūs	dĭēs	rēs
Gen.	fructŭŭm	cornŭum	dŏmŭŭm	dĭērŭm	rērum
Dat.	fructĭbŭs	cornĭbŭs	dŏmĭbŭs	dĭēbŭs	rēbus
Acc.	fructūs	cornŭă	dŏmōs	dĭēs	rēs
Voc.	fructūs	cornŭă	dŏmūs	dĭēs	rē
Abl.	fructĭbŭs.	cornĭbŭs.	dŏmĭbŭs.	dĭēbŭs.	rēbus.

Rem. 1. Some nouns of the fourth declension have *ŭbus* instead of *ĭbus* in the dat. and abl. *pl.*; as *arcŭs, arcŭbŭs; vērŭ, verŭbŭs*, &c.

2. The plural of the fifth declension is regular throughout.

5. The Plural of Adjectives.

The plural of adjectives is subject to the same laws as that of substantives. Those in *us, a, um*, and *er, ra, rum*, follow the inflection of the first and second declensions, and the rest that of the third. Examples: —

1. Bŏnĭ, bŏnae, bŏnă, *the good;* pulchrĭ, pulchrae, pulchră, *the beautiful.*

	Masc.	*Fem.*	*Neut.*
Nom.	bŏnī	bŏnae	bŏnă
Gen.	bŏnōrum	bŏnārum	bŏnōrum
Dat.	bŏnīs	bŏnīs	bŏnīs
Acc.	bŏnōs	bŏnās	bŏnă
Voc.	bŏnī	bŏnae	bŏnă
Abl.	bŏnīs	bŏnīs	bŏnīs.
Nom.	pulchrī	pulchrae	pulchră
Gen.	pulchrōrum	pulchrārŭm	pulchrōrŭm
Dat.	pulchrīs	pulchrīs	pulchrīs
Acc.	pulchrōs	pulchrās	pulchră
Voc.	pulchrī	pulchrae	pulchră
Abl.	pulchrīs	pulchrīs	pulchrīs.

Like *bŏnĭ, ae, a*, decline *mĕĭ, mĕae, mĕă*, my, mine; *tŭĭ, tŭae, tŭă*, thy (your), thine (yours), &c. Like *pulchrĭ, rae, ra: mĭsĕrĭ, mĭsĕrae, mĭsĕră*, the miserable, &c.

2. Dēformēs, dēformĭă, *the ugly;* ācrĕs, ācrĭă, *the fierce.*

	Masc. & Fem.	*Neut.*	*Masc. & Fem.*	*Neut.*
Nom.	dēformēs	dēformĭă	ācrēs	ācrĭă
Gen.	dēformĭŭm	dēformĭum	ācrĭŭm	ācrĭŭm
Dat.	dēformĭbŭs	dēformĭbŭs	ācrĭbŭs	ācrĭbŭs

D   5

Acc.	deformēs	deformĭă	ācrēs	ācrĭă
Voc.	deformēs	deformĭă	ācrēs	ācrĭă
Abl.	deformĭbŭs	deformĭbŭs.	ācrĭbŭs	ācrĭbŭs.

REMARK. — The general rule is that all adjectives of the third declension have *ĭa* in the neuter plural and *ĭum* in the genitive. — Like *deformes* are inflected *vĭlēs, turpēs*, and all adjectives in *is, e ;* like *ācrēs*, all those ending in *er, ris, re.*

3. Fēlīcēs, fĕlīcĭă, *happy ;* vĕtĕrēs, vĕtĕră, *old ;* sapĭentēs, sapĭentĭa, *wise.*

Nom.	felĭces	felĭcĭă	vĕtĕrēs	vĕtĕră	sapĭentēs -tĭa
Gen.	felĭcĭŭm	felĭcĭum	vĕtĕrŭm	vĕtĕrŭm	sapĭentĭŭm *or* -um
Dat.	felĭcĭbŭs	felĭcĭbŭs	vĕtĕrĭbŭs	vĕtĕrĭbŭs	sapĭentĭbŭs
Acc.	felĭces	felĭcĭă	vĕtĕrēs	vĕtĕră	sapĭentēs -tĭa
Voc.	felĭces	felĭcĭă	vĕtĕrēs	vĕtĕră	sapĭentēs -tĭa
Abl.	felĭcĭbŭs	felĭcĭbŭs.	vĕtĕrĭbŭs	vĕtĕrĭbŭs.	sapĭentĭbŭs.

REMARK. — Adjectives of one termination, including participles in *ns*, generally have *ĭă* in the neuter plural and *ĭŭm* in the genitive. Some, however, have *ă* instead of *ĭă* in the nominative and accusative, as *vĕtĕră, plūra*, and comparatives generally; e. g. *felĭcĭŏră, majŏră*, &c. — Exceptions to the genitive in *ium* are: 1) such as have *e* only in the abl. sing., as *paupĕrum, superstĭtum ;* 2) compounds of *facio* and *capio*, or of such nouns as have *ŭm* in the gen. pl., as *ancĭpĭtum, inŏpum, quadrŭpĕdum*, &c. ; 3) the following adjectives have likewise *ŭm : caelebs, cĕlĕr, cĭcŭr, compŏs, impŏs, dĭvĕs, mĕmŏr, immĕmŏr, supplex, ūbĕr, vĕtŭs*, and *vĭgĭl ;* 4) participles in *ns* sometimes have *um* among the poets.

C. The following table exhibits the terminations of the five declensions through all the cases, singular and plural.

1. TERMINATIONS OF THE SINGULAR.

	I.	II.		III.	IV.		V.
			Neut.			Neut.	
Nom.	ă (ē, ās, ēs)*	ŭs, ĕr,	ŭm (os, on)	a, e, o, c, l, n, r, s, t, x	ŭs,	ū	ēs
Gen.	ae† (ēs)	ī		ĭs	ūs		ĕī
Dat.	ae	ō		ī	ŭī		ĕī
Acc.	ăm (ēn)	ŭm		ĕm, ĭm	ŭm, ū		ĕm
Voc.	ă (ē)	ĕ, ĕr,	ŭm	Like Nom.	ŭs,	ū	ēs
Abl.	ā (ē).*	ō.		ĕ (ī).	ū.		ē.

* Of the nouns in *e, as, es* of this declension no examples have as yet been given. They are mostly of Greek origin, and will be considered hereafter.

† Of this there is also an ancient form in *āī*, as *aulāī*, for *aulae*, from *aula* a hall. But this is not used except in poetry.

2. TERMINATIONS OF THE PLURAL.

	I.	II.	Neut.	III.	Neut.	IV.	Neut.	V.
NOM.	ae	ī,	ă	ēs,	ă (ĭă)	ŭs, ŭă		ēs
GEN.	ārŭm	ōrŭm		ŭm (ĭŭm)		ŭŭm		ērŭm
DAT.	īs (ābŭs)	īs		ĭbŭs		ĭbŭs		ēbŭs
ACC.	ās	ōs,	ă	ēs,	ă (ĭă)	ŭs, ŭă		ēs
VOC.	ae	ī,	ă	ēs,	ă (ĭă)	ŭs, ŭă		ēs
ABL.	īs (ābŭs).	īs.		ĭbŭs.		ĭbŭs.		ēbŭs.

REMARK. — With respect to the quantity of the terminations of the plural number, the following rules may serve to guide the learner : —

1. *I* final is always long, and *a* final always short, as *dómĭnĭ, lĭbrī, bónă, fĭlă.*

2. The *is* of the dative and ablative plural of the first and second declensions is long, as *taénĭīs, dómĭnīs, candelábrīs.*

3. The terminations *es* and *os* are long, as *cánēs, lápĭdēs, dómĭnōs, lĭbrōs.*

4. The vowel before the *m* final in all Latin words is generally considered short, as *lápĭdĕm, cánĕm, pânĕm, dómĭnôrŭm.*

5. The *us* of the plural of the fourth declension is long, but in *ăbus, ĕbus, ĭbus* it is short ; as *frúctŭs, mánŭs ; frúctĭbŭs, diēbŭs, homĭnĭbŭs.*

EXAMPLES.

The good boys.	{ NOM. Púĕrī bónī. { ACC. Púĕrōs bónōs.
The fine tables.	{ NOM. Ménsae púlchrae. { ACC. Ménsās púlchrās.
The bad boys.	{ NOM. Púĕrī nêquăm. { ACC. Púĕrōs nêquăm.
The pretty dogs.	{ NOM. Cánēs venústī. { ACC. Cánēs venústōs.
The ugly dogs.	NOM. & ACC. Cánēs defórmēs.
The old stockings.	NOM. & ACC. Tĭbĭálĭă vétĕră.
My silver candlesticks.	NOM. & ACC. Candelábră méă ar-géntĕă.
Your good books.	{ NOM. Lĭbrī túī bónī. { ACC. Lĭbrōs túōs bónōs.
Have you those fine tables ?	Núm hábes ménsas íllas púlchras ?
I have them not.	Nôn hábeo.
Have you pretty dogs ?	{ Écquid tíbi súnt * cánes venústi ? { Habêsne cánes venústos ?

* When the noun is in the plural, *sunt,* "there are," must take the place of the singular *est.*

I have pretty dogs.	{ Súnt míhï cánes venústi.
	{ Hábeo (cánes venústos).
Have you my good books?	Tenêsne tû líbros méos bónos?
I have your good books.	Téneo (líbros túos bónos).
Have you my silver candlesticks?	Habêsne candēlábra méa argéntĕa?
I have them not.	Nôn hábeo.
Have I them?	Án égo hábeo?
You have them not.	Nôn hábes.

Exercise 14.

Have you the tables? — Yes, sir, I have the tables? — Have you my tables? — No, sir, I have not your tables. — Have I your buttons? — You have my buttons. — Have I your fine houses? — You have my fine houses? — Has the tailor the buttons? — He has not the buttons, but the threads. — Has your tailor my good buttons? — My tailor has your good gold buttons. — What has the boy? — He has the gold threads. — Has he my gold or my silver threads? — He has neither your gold nor your silver threads. — Has the Frenchman the fine houses or the good notes? — He has neither the fine houses nor the good notes. — What has he? — He has his good friends. — Has this man my fine umbrellas? — He has not your fine umbrellas, but your good coats. — Has any one my good letters? — No one has your good letters. — Has the tailor's son my good knives or my good thimbles? — He has neither your good knives nor your good thimbles, but the ugly coats of the stranger. — Have I your friend's good ribbons? — You have not my friend's good ribbons, but my neighbor's fine carriage. — Has your friend the shoemaker's pretty sticks, or my good tailor's pretty dogs? — My friend has my good shoemaker's fine books; but he has neither the shoemaker's pretty sticks nor your good tailor's pretty dogs. — Is your neighbor right or wrong? — He is neither right nor wrong. — Is he thirsty or hungry? — He is neither thirsty nor hungry. — Is he tired or sleepy? — He is sleepy. — Am I sleepy? — You are not sleepy. — What have I? — You have my fine notes. — You have the chairs of my neighbor. — Have you the knives of my friend? — I have not the knives of your friend, but the dogs of my neighbor.

Lesson XIV. — PENSUM QUARTUM DECIMUM.

OF THE PLURAL OF PRONOUNS.

A. The plural of the personal pronouns *ego* and *tu* is *nōs*, "we," and *vōs*, "you." The remaining cases are : —

		Masc. & Fem.			*Masc. & Fem.*
Nom.	*we*	nōs	*ye* or *you*		vōs
Gen.	*of us*	nostrum *or* nostrī	*of you*		vestrum *or* vestrī
Dat.	*to us*	nōbīs	*to you*		vōbīs
Acc.	*us*	nōs	*you*		vōs
Voc.	——	nōs	*O ye* or *you*		vōs
Abl.	*with us*	nōbīs.	*with you*		vōbīs.

REMARK. — The difference between *nostrī, vestrī* and *nostrum, vestrum* consists in this: that the latter are chiefly used as partitive genitives after interrogatives, numerals, comparatives, and superlatives, and the former after other words; e. g. *uter nostrum?* which of us two? *nemo vestrum,* no one of you; *vestrum primus,* the first of you; but *miserēre nostri,* pity us; *amor nostri,* love of (towards) us; *vestri similes,* your like (those like you).

B. The pronoun of the third person is *illī, illae, illă,* "they," of which the remaining cases are:—

		Masc.	*Fem.*	*Neut.*
Nom.	*they*	illī	illae	illă
Gen.	*of them*	ĕōrŭm	ĕārŭm	ĕōrŭm
Dat.	*to them*		īis *or* ĕīs	
Acc.	*them*	ĕōs	ĕās	ĕă
Voc.	——	illī	illae	illă
Abl.	*by them.*		īis *or* ĕīs.	

C. The reflexive *sui* is the same in the plural as in the singular. The intensive *ipse* has *ipsī, ipsae, ipsă.* Thus:—

Sŭī, *of themselves.*			Ipsī, ipsae, ipsă, *ourselves, yourselves, themselves.*		
		For every gender.	*Masc.*	*Fem.*	*Neut.*
Nom.	——		ipsī	ipsae	ipsă
Gen.	*of themselves*	sŭī	ipsōrŭm	ipsārŭm	ipsōrŭm
Dat.	*to themselves*	sĭbi		ipsīs	
Acc.	*themselves*	sē	ipsōs	ipsās	ipsă
Voc.	——		ipsī	ipsae	ipsă
Abl.	*by themselves*	sē.		ipsīs.	

REMARK. — We thus say, as in the singular, *nos ipsi* (or fem. *ipsae*), we ourselves; *vos ipsi* (or fem. *ipsae*), you yourselves; and *illi ipsi* (or fem. *illae ipsae*) or simply *ipsi,* they themselves; *ea ipsa,* these things themselves, &c.

5 *

D. The plurals of the demonstrative pronouns *hĭc,
ille, iste,* and *is,* are *hĭ, illī, istī,* and *ĭĭ.* The remaining
genders and cases are as follows : —

	Hĭ, hae, haec, *these.*				Illī, illae, illă, *those (of his).*		
	Masc.	*Fem.*	*Neut.*		*Masc.*	*Fem.*	*Neut.*
Nom.	hĭ	hae	haec		illī	illae	illă
Gen.	hōrŭm	hārŭm	hōrŭm		illōrŭm	illārŭm	illōrŭm
Dat.		hīs				illīs	
Acc.	hōs	hās	haec		illōs	illās	illă
Voc.	hĭ	hae	haec		illī	illae	illă
Abl.		hīs.				illīs.	

	Istĭ, istae, istă, *these (of yours).*				Iĭ, ĕae, ĕă, *these, those.*		
	Masc.	*Fem.*	*Neut.*		*Masc.*	*Fem.*	*Neut.*
Nom.	istĭ	istae	istă		iĭ (ĕĭ)	ĕae	ĕă
Gen.	istōrŭm,	istārŭm,	istōrŭm		ĕōrum	ĕārum	ĕōrŭm
Dat.		istīs				iĭs *or* ĕĭs	
Acc.	istōs	istās	istă		ĕōs	ĕās	ĕă
Voc.	istĭ	istae	istă		iĭ (ĕĭ)	ĕae	ĕă
Abl.		istīs.				iĭs *or* ĕĭs.	

E. The relative *quī, quae, quŏd* (and also the interrogatives of the same form) makes its plural in *quī,
quae, quae,* "who, which, *or* that," or interrogatively
"which? .what?" Thus: —

Quī, quae, quae, *which, that ; which? what?*

		Masc.	*Fem.*	*Neut.*
Nom.	*which*	quī	quae	quae
Gen.	*of which*	quōrŭm	quārŭm	quōrŭm
Dat.	*to which*		quībŭs	
Acc.	*which*	quōs	quās	quae
Voc.	———	———	———	———
Abl.	*by which.*		quībŭs.	

Remark. — For *quĭbus,* in the relative sense, there is an antiquated form *quīs* or *quéis,* which is not unfrequently employed by
prose-writers of a later period.

F. The plural of the determinative *is, ea, id* is the
same as that of the demonstrative; that of *idem* is as
follows : —

Iidem, eaedem, eädem, *the same.*

		Masc.	*Fem.*	*Neut.*
Nom.	*the same*	īdĕm	ĕaedĕm	ĕädĕm
Gen.	*of the same*	ĕōrundĕm	ĕärundĕm	ĕōrundĕm
Dat.	*to the same*		iisdĕm *or* ĕisdĕm	
Acc.	*the same*	ĕosdĕm	ĕasdĕm	ĕädĕm
Voc.	*O the same*	īdĕm	ĕaedĕm	ĕädĕm
Abl.	*by the same.*		iisdĕm *or* ĕisdĕm.	

REMARK.— The form *iisdem* is more common than *eisdem.* The same is true of *iis, ii, eis,* and *ei.*

G. The plural of the relative in connection with the determinative *is, ea, id* (vide Lesson XII. *D.*) is as follows:—

Ii, eae, ea — qui, quae, quae, *those which.*

	Masculine.		*Feminine.*		*Neuter.*	
Nom.	iī	— quī	ĕae	— quae	ĕä	— quae
Gen.	ĕōrŭm	— quōrŭm	ĕärŭm	— quärŭm	ĕōrŭm	— quōrŭm
Dat.	iīs	— quībŭs	iīs	— quībŭs	iīs	— quībŭs
Acc.	ĕōs	— quōs	ĕïs	— quäs	ĕä	— quae
Voc.	—		—		—	
Abl.	iīs	— quībŭs	iīs	— quībŭs	iīs	— quībŭs.

In the same manner decline *illī — quī, illae — quae, illä — quae,* "those which"; and *īdĕm — quī, ĕaedĕm — quae, ĕädĕm — quae,* "the same which."

I have those which you have. (Masc.)	Hábĕo ĕōs (íllōs, &c.), quôs tû hábēs.
	Súnt míhi iī (íllī, &c.), quī tíbī súnt.
I have those which you have. (Fem.)	Hábĕo ĕäs (ílläs, &c.), quäs tû hábēs.
	Súnt míhi ĕac (íllae, &c.), quae tíbī súnt.
I have those (things) which you have. (Neut.)	Hábĕo ĕa (ílla, &c.). quac tû hábēs.
	Súnt míhi ĕä, quae tíbī súnt.

The Roman.	Rōmănus, i, *m.*
The German.	Germānus, Theodiscus, i, *m.*
The Turk.	*Turca, ae, *m.*
The Italian.	Itălus, i, *m.*
The Spaniard.	Hispănus, i, *m.* Hispaniensis, is, *m.*
Large (tall, big).	Grandis, is, e. Procērus, a, um.
Tall, high.	Altus, a, um.

Small, little.	{ Parvus, a, um. { Parvŭlus, a, um. { Pusillus, a, um.
Long.	Longus, a, um.
The small books.	Libri parvi, libelli.*
The large horses.	Ĕqui grandes (*or* procēri).
They have.	{ *Hábent* { *Súnt íis.*
Have the English the fine horses of the French?	Habéntne Ángli púlchrŏs Francogallôrum équōs?
They have not those of the French, but those of the Romans.	Nòn Francogallôrum séd Romanôrum équōs hábent.
Have you the books which the men have?	Habêsne tû (íllos líbros), quôs líbros hómĭnes hábent? †

G. *Obs.* The antecedent of the relative is sometimes repeated in connection with the pronoun of the second clause. Sometimes it is expressed with the relative only, and sometimes (though rarely) it is entirely omitted.

I have not the books which the men have, but those which you have.	Nòn hábeo (íllos líbros), quôs (líbros) hómĭnes hábent, éos aútem hábeo, quôs tû hábes.
Have you not the same books which I have?	Nónne tú eósdem líbrŏs hábes, quôs égo hábeo?
I have the same.	{ Eósdem (hábeo). { Égo véro eósdem hábeo.
Which books have you?	{ Quôs líbrŏs hábēs? { Quíd librôrum hábēs?
I have those of the Romans.	Líbros Romanôrum hábeo. (*Vide Less.* VI. *C*)
Have you these books or those?	{ Útrum hôs líbrŏs hábēs án íllōs? { Hoscíne líbrŏs hábēs án íllōs? { (*Vide Less.* XI. *A. Rem.* 1.)
I have neither these nor those.	{ Hábĕo néque hôs néque íllōs. { (Égo) néque hôs néque íllōs hábĕo.
I have neither those of the Spaniards nor those of the Turks.	Néque Hispanôrum néc Turcârum líbrŏs hábĕo. (*Cf. Less.* VI. *C.*)
Have you *what* I have?	Án hábēs (íd), *quód* égo hábĕo?

---

* From the diminutive *libellus*, *i*, m., a little book, a pamphlet. (Compare Lesson XX. *E.* 7.)

† The question, "Have you the books which the men have?" may thus be expressed in several ways: 1) *Habesne tu* illos libros, *quos homines habent?* 2) *Habesne tu* illos libros, quos libros *homines habent?* 3) *Habesne tu* quos libros *homines habent?* The first of these is the most general. The antecedent is entirely suppressed in: 4) *Sunt qui* (or *quos*), for *Sunt homines qui* (or *quos*), "There are those who," "There are men whom."

H. RULE. Adjectives and pronouns of the neuter gender, both singular and plural, are frequently employed substantively, as *hoc*, " this (thing)," *illud*, " that (thing,)" *haec*, " these things," *illa*, " those things," *triste*, " a sad thing," *multa*, " many things," *omnia*, " all things," *summum bonum*, " the chief good."

I have not what you have.	Nôn hábĕo (íd), *quód* tû hábēs.
Have the men those things which you have ?	Habéntne hómines *eã, quae* tû hábés ?
They have the same things which I myself have (the same things with myself).	{ *Eãdem* hábent, *quae* égo ípse hábĕo. Eãdem hábent *átque* égo ípse. (*Cf. Less.* XII. *F.*)

EXERCISE 15.

Have you these horses or those ? — I have not these, but those. — Have you the coats of the French or those of the English ? — I have not those of the French, but those of the English. — Have you the pretty sheep of the Turks or those of the Spaniards ? — I have neither those of the Turks nor those of the Spaniards, but those of my brother. — Has your brother the fine asses of the Spaniards or those of the Italians ? — He has neither those of the Spaniards nor those of the Italians, but he has the fine asses of the French. — Which oxen has your brother ? — He has those of the Germans. — Has your friend my large letters or those of the Germans ? — He has neither the one nor the other (*neque has neque illas*, or *neque illas neque alteras*). — Which letters has he ? — He has the small letters which you have. — Have I these houses or those ? — You have neither these nor those. — Which houses have I ? — You have those of the English. — Has any one the tall tailor's gold buttons ? — Nobody has the tailor's gold buttons, but somebody has those of your friend.

EXERCISE 16.

Have I the notes of the foreigners or those of my boy. — You have neither those of the foreigners nor those of your boy, but those of the great Turks. — Has the Turk my fine horse ? — He has it not. — Which horse has he ? — He has his own. — Has your neighbor my chicken or my sheep ? — My neighbor has neither your chicken nor your sheep. — What has he ? — He has nothing good. — Have you nothing fine ? — I have nothing fine. — Are you tired ? — I am not tired. — Which rice has your friend ? — He has that of his merchant. — Which sugar has he ? — He has that which I have. — Has he your merchant's good coffee or that of mine ? — He has neither that of yours nor that of mine; he has his own. — Which ships has the Frenchman ? — He has the ships of the English. — Which houses has the Spaniard ? — He has the same which you have. — Has he my good knives ? — He has your good knives. —

Has he the linen stockings which I have?— He has not the same that you have, but those of his brother.— Which books have you?— I have those of the Romans. — Are those men hungry?— They are not hungry, but thirsty. — They are neither tired nor sleepy.

Lesson XV.—PENSUM QUINTUM DECIMUM.

The glass.	{ Vās (gen. vāsis)* vitrĕum, n. { Scȳphus, i, m. (wine-glass).
The goblet.	Pōcŭlum, i, n.
The comb.	{ Pectĕn, ĭnis, m. { Pectuncŭlus, i, m. (small comb).
Have you my small combs?	Habêsne mĕōs pectúncŭlōs?
I have them.	(Éōs) hábeo.
I have them not.	(Éōs) nôn hábeo.
Them (those).	{ Nom. ĭi, ĕae, ĕă. { Acc. ĕŏs, ĕās, ĕă.

A. Obs. The pronoun *them* is commonly not put in Latin, when it would have to stand in the same case as the substantive to which it relates. (Cf. page 14, *D.*)

My or *mine* (plural).	Mĕī, mĕae, mĕă.
Your (*thy*) or *yours.*	Tŭī, tŭae, tŭă.
His (*own*).	Sŭī, sŭae, sŭă.
His (*another man's*).	Ējŭs, illĭŭs (gen. sing).
Their (*own*) or *theirs.*	{ Sing. Sŭŭs, sŭă, sŭŭm. { Plur. Sŭī, sŭae, sŭă.†
Their or *theirs* (of a third person).	{ Masc. Ĕōrŭm, illōrŭm (gen. pl.). { Fem. Ĕārŭm, illārŭm "

B. The plural of the possessive pronouns *mĕus, tŭus, sŭus* is inflected like that of the adjective *bonus.* Thus:—

		Masc.	Fem.	Neut.
Nom.	*my* or *mine*	mĕī	mĕae	mĕă
Gen.	*of my* or *mine*	mĕōrŭm	mĕārŭm	mĕōrŭm
Dat.	*to my* or *mine*		mĕīs	
Acc.	*my* or *mine*	mĕōs	mĕās	mĕă
Voc.	*O my* or *mine*	mĕī	mĕae	mĕă
Abl.	*with my* or *mine.*		mĕīs.	

* The plural of *vās* is *vāsa*, from another singular, *vāsum.* (See Lesson XIX. *D.* 2.)

† The reflexive adjective pronoun *suus* is equivalent to the English "his,"

Have you my fine glass ?	Ecquĭd hábēs vâs vítrĕum méum púlchrum ?
Has he my fine glasses ?	Án ílle hábet vâsa vítrĕa méa púlchra ?
He has them.	Hábet.
He has them not.	(Éă) nôn hábet.
Those men have them.	Vírĭ íllĭ éă hábent.
Have those men them ?	Númquid éă vírĭ íllĭ hábent ?
They have them not.	Éă nôn hábent.
Have you my books or his (i. e. that man's) ?	Habêsne líbrōs méōs án éjus (illĭus) ?
I have neither yours nor his (books).	Égo néque túōs néque illíus líbrōs hábeo.
Has he his (own) book, his (own) books ?	Habétne líbrum súum, líbrōs súōs ?
He has them.	(Éōs) hábet.
Have they their (own) house, their (own) houses ?	Habéntne dómum súam, dómōs súās ?
They have them not.	(Éās) nôn hábent.
Have you yourself their (i. e. those people's) good comb, good combs ?	Án tû ípse hábes péctĭnem ĕórum bónum, péctĭnēs illórum bónōs ?
I have myself their good little combs.	Égo ípse pectúncŭlōs ĕórum bónōs hábeo.
Which carriages have you ?	{ Quôs hábes cúrrus ? { Quae piléntă hábes ?
I have my own.	{ Hábeo méōs próprĭōs, { Méă próprĭa hábeo.
They (those).	*Íllĭ, íllae, íllă.*

C. Obs. The pronoun *they* is in Latin commonly omitted with the verb. But when the verb *sum* is employed to denote possession, the dative *iis* or *illis* must be put. E. g. :—

They have.	{ Habent (*with the Acc.*). { Est iis (illis) (*with the Nom. Sing.*). { Sunt iis (illis) (*with the Nom. Pl.*).
Have they the good book ?	{ Habéntne (íllĭ) líbrum bónum ? { Éstne íis (íllis) líber bónus ?
They have the good book.	{ Hábent líbrum bónum. { Ést íis líber bónus.
Are they hungry ? thirsty ?	Esurĭúntne ? Sitĭúntne ?
They are not hungry (thirsty).	Nôn ēsúrĭunt (sítĭunt).

when the subject of the sentence is in the *singular*, and to "their" when it is in the plural. E. g. Has *he his* book, *his* books ? *Habetne librum* SUUM, *libros* SUOS ? — Have *they their* book, *their* books ? *Habentne librum* SUUM, *libros* SUOS ?

Are they tired, sleepy ?	Súntne féssī (*fem.* féssae), somnĭ-cŭlósi (*fem.* ae) ?
They are sleepy.	Cúpĭdī (*fem.* ae) sómnĭ súnt.
Are they right ? wrong ?	Loquuntúrne récte ? Errántne ?
They are neither right nor wrong.	Néque récte loquúntur néque ér-rant.
Are they right (morally) ?	Éstne ĭis fâs ? Licétne ĭis ?

OF COMPOUND SUBSTANTIVES.

D. The compound or double substantives of the Latin language are comparatively few,* and of these even, many are most commonly treated as separate words. With respect to their declension, they are divided into two classes.

1. Those of which the last component alone is inflected, as *juris-dictio* (= *jūris* + *dictio*), *ōnis*, f., the administration of justice ; *jūris-consultus*, or *jūrĕconsultus*, *i*, m., a lawyer ; *plēbiscĭtum*, *i*, n., a vote of the people ; *sĕnātŭsconsultum*, *i*, n., a decree of the senate.

2. Those of which both components are inflected, either separately or combined. Such are : —

a) Jusjūrandŭm, *n.*, *an oath.*

	SINGULAR.	PLURAL.
Nom.	jusjūrandŭm	jūrajūrandă
Gen.	jūrisjūrandī	jūrumjūrandōrŭm
Dat.	jūrijūrandō	jūribusjūrandīs.
Acc.	jusjūrandŭm	jūrajūrandă
Voc.	jusjūrandŭm	jūrajūrandă
Abl.	jūrejūrandō	jūribusjūrandīs.†

b) Pătĕr fămĭlĭăs, *or* fămĭlĭae, *m.*, *the master of a family.*

	SINGULAR.		PLURAL.	
Nom.	pătĕr fămĭlĭăs	*or* -ae	patrēs fămĭlĭăs	*or* -ārŭm
Gen.	patris fămĭlĭăs	" "	patrŭm fămĭlĭăs	" "
Dat.	patrī fămĭlĭăs	" "	patrĭbŭs fămĭlĭăs	" "
Acc.	patrem fămĭlĭăs	" "	patrēs fămĭlĭăs	" "
Voc.	pătĕr fămĭlĭăs	" "	patrēs fămĭlĭăs	" "
Abl.	patrĕ fămĭlĭăs	" "	patrĭbŭs fămĭlĭăs	" "

In the same manner decline *māter fămĭlĭăs*, f., the mistress of a family ; *fĭlĭus fămĭlĭăs*, m., and *fĭlĭa fămĭlĭăs*, f., the son, the daughter, of a family or house.

---

* This remark applies only to such compounds as are formed by the union of a noun with another or with an adjective. Compounds with particles (i. e. prepositions and adverbs) are quite numerous.

† The Genitive, Dative, and Ablative plural do not occur.

c) Rēs publĭca, *f.*, *a commonwealth.*

	SINGULAR.	PLURAL.
NOM.	rēs publĭca	rēs publĭcae
GEN.	rŭī publĭcae	rērŭm publĭcārŭm
DAT.	rĕī publĭcae	rēbús publĭcis
ACC.	rĕm publĭcam	rēs publĭcās
VOC.	rēs publĭcă	rēs publĭcae
ABL.	rē publĭcă	rēbús publĭcis.

OF IRREGULAR NOUNS.*

E. The irregular nouns of the Latin language may be divided into three general classes: — the *Indeclinable,* the *Defective,* and the *Redundant.*

Those which do not admit of any inflection, i. e. are altogether *indeclinable,* are: —

1. Greek and Latin names of the letters of the alphabet, as *alphă, bētă, gammă, deltă,* &c.

2. A number of substantives adopted from foreign languages, as *mannă, paschă, gummĭ,* &c.

3. Greek neuters in *ŏs* and plurals in *ē,* as *Argŏs, chăŏs, cētŏs* or *cētē,* a sea-monster, *Tempē,* &c.

4. Many Hebrew proper names, as *Bethlehem, Gabriel, Jerusalem, Ruth,* &c. — *Jēsŭs* has *Jēsum* in the Acc. and *Jēsū* in the remaining cases.

5. The following Latin neuters: *fās,* right; *nĕfās,* wrong; *instar,* likeness; *mănĕ,* morning; *nĭhĭl,* nothing; *părum,* too little; *pondō,* a pound (or pounds); *sĕcŭs,* sex; *sēmĭs,* half. These are generally used in the Nom. and Acc. only, except *mănĕ,* which occurs also in the ablative.

6. Infinitives, adverbs, and other particles, used substantively, as SCIRE *tŭum,* your knowing (knowledge); *ultĭmum* VALE, the last farewell; *hoc ipsum* DIU, the very word "a long time"; *istud* CRAS, that to-morrow of yours, &c.

7 To these may be added the indeclinable *adjectives: frūgĭ* (the obsolete dative of *frux,* which is not used), useful, fit, honest; *nēquăm,* bad; *praestō,* present, ready; *pŏtis* or *pŏtĕ* (obsolete, and only with *esse,* to be), able, capable; *sēmĭs,* and a half; and *damnus* (only in law), guilty.

F. Nouns are *defective* in case or in number. Those defective in case are: —

1. Those which want the nominative, as *dăpĭs,* of food; *dĭcĭōnĭs,*

---

* This examination of the irregular nouns in this and the following lessons has no necessary connection with the exercises, but is nevertheless recommended to the attention of the learner.

of dominion ; *fĕmĭnĭs*, of the thigh ; *frŭgĭs*, of fruit ; *internĕcĭōnis*, of carnage ; *ŏpis*, of power ; *pollĭnis*, of meal-dust ; *vĭcis*, of alternation ; *verbĕris*, of a lash (stripe).   Many of these genitives occur in the remaining cases of both numbers.

2. A number of monosyllables which want the *genitive plural*, as *ōs, ōris*, the mouth ; *vās, vādis*, bail ; *glōs, glōris*, the husband's sister ; *pax, pācis*, a treaty, &c.

3. Those which occur in the *Nom.* and *Acc. only*, as the indeclinable *fās, nĕfās*, &c., to which may be added the plurals *colla*, the neck ; *flamĭna*, breezes ; *grātēs*, thanks ; *murmŭra*, murmurs, &c.

4. A number of substantives, which occur only in certain cases, as *astūs*, cunning, Abl. *astū*, Nom. & Acc. Pl. *astūs ; fors*, chance, Abl. *forte*, by chance ; *lŭēs*, disease, Acc. *lŭĕm*, Abl. *lŭĕ ; prĕces*, pl., prayers, Abl. Sing. *prĕce ; sătĭās* for *sătĭĕtās*, satiety, occurs only in the Nom. Sing. — *Vis*, might, power, wants the dative ; in the remaining cases it has G. *vis*, A. *vim*, V. *vis*, A. *vi ;* Pl. N. *vires*, G. *virium*, &c.

5. A number of words used in certain connections are always in a particular case, as : —

a) The Genitives *dĭcis* and *nauci* in *dicis causā*, for form's sake ; *non nauci facere*, not to value a straw.

b) Certain Datives with the verb *esse*, to be, as *despĭcātui*, *dīvĭsui, ostentui, dŭci esse*, to be an object of contempt, to serve for division, for display, as a guide, &c.

c) The Accusatives *infĭtĭas* with *ĭre*, to deny ; *suppĕtĭas* with *ferre*, to bring help ; *vēnum* with *ĭre* (*or* dăre), to be offered for sale (to offer for sale).

d) The Ablatives *nātū* (by birth) in connection with *mājor, mĭnor, maxĭmus*, &c., the elder, younger, oldest, &c. (by birth) ; *sponte*, with *mĕā, tŭā, sŭā*, of my, thy, his own accord ; *in promptu* and *in procinctu* with *esse* and *stāre*, to be ready, to stand prepared.

e) Verbal substantives in Abl. Sing. with one of the possessives *mĕō, tŭō, sŭō*, &c., as *admonitu, concessu* or *permissu, mandatu, jussu* (and *injussu*, &c.) *meo, tuo, suo*, at my, thy, his own request, with my, thy, his own permission, command, order, &c.

f) The Abl. Pl. *grātīs* (from *grātīī*), without reward, gratis ; *ingrātīs*, against one's will ; *fŏrīs*, out of doors (to the question *where ?*), which to the question *whither ?* becomes *fŏrās*, Acc.

6. Many nouns do not admit of the *Vocative* from the nature of their signification.

7. The *adjectives* defective in case are : —

a) Those which do not occur in the nominative ; as (*sons*) *sontis*, " hurtful " ; (*sēmĭnex*) *sēmĭnĭcis*, " half dead " ; and a few other similar compounds.   To these add (*cetĕrus*), *a, um* and *ludĭcrus, a, um*, of which the Nom. Masc. does not occur.

b) The genitive *prīmōris*, " the fore," " first," which wants the Nom. and neuter forms, and the plural *plērĭque*, " most," which borrows the genitive of *plurĭmi*.

c) *Necesse* and the obsolete *necessum*, "necessary," which are used only in the neuter and in connection with *est*, *erat*, or some other verb; and the obsolete *volupe*, "agreeable," likewise used only with *est*, &c.

d) The vocatives *macte*, pl. *macti*, which occur as the only forms of an obsolete *mactus, a, um,* and commonly with an imperative of *esse*, in the sense of "honored," "praised," "prosperous."

EXERCISE 17.

Have you my good combs ? — I have them. — Have you the good horses of the English ? — I have them not. — Which brooms have you ? — I have those of the foreigners. — Have you my coats or those of my friends ? — I have neither yours nor those (*illas*) of your friends. — Have you mine or his ? — I have his. — Has the Italian the good cheeses which you have ? — He has not those which I have, but those which you have. — Has your boy my good pencils ? — He has them. — Has he the carpenter's nails ? — He has them not. — What has he ? — He has his iron nails. — Has anybody the thimbles of the tailors ? — Nobody has them. — Who has the ships of the Spaniards ? — The English have them. — Have the English these ships or those ? — The English have their ships. — Have your brothers my knives or theirs. — My brothers have neither your knives nor theirs. — Have I your chickens or those of your cooks ? — You have neither mine nor those of my cooks. — Which chickens have I ? — You have those of the good peasant. — Who has my oxen ? — Your servants have them. — Have the Germans them ? — The Germans have them not, but the Turks have them. — Who has my wooden table ? — Your boys have it. — Who has my good bread ? — Your friends have it. — Have those Italians my good letters ? — They have not your good letters, but your good books. — Are they hungry or thirsty ? — They are neither hungry nor thirsty, but (they are) sleepy. — Are they right or wrong ? — They are wrong. — They are neither right nor wrong. — Have they your knives or those (*illos*) of the English ? — They have neither mine nor those of the English. — Have I his looking-glasses or those (*illa*) of his cook ? — You have neither the one nor the other (neither these nor those).*

Lesson XVI. — PENSUM SEXTUM DECIMUM.

Some, any (some one, any one).	*Aliquis, -quă, -quŏd* or *-quĭd.* *Quidăm, quaedăm, quoddăm* or *quiddăm.* *Ullŭs, ă, ŭm.* *Nonnullŭs, ă, ŭm.* *Aliquŏt* (pl. indeclinable).

---

* The English "the former — the latter" is *ille* — *hic*, and "the one — the other," *alter* (or *unus*) — *alter* (or *ille*). See page 103, note ‡.

Does any?   Whether any?   *Ecquis, ecquae, ecquŏd or ecquĭd?*
If any (if any one).   *Sĭ quĭs, sĭ quă, sĭ quŏd or quĭd.*
Lest any (= that no).   *Nē quĭs, nē quă, nē quŏd or quĭd.*

A. The indefinite pronouns *ălĭquĭs, quĭdam, ullŭs,
nonnullŭs, sĭ quĭs, nē quĭs,* and *ecquĭs?* are used either
as substantives in the sense of *some one, any one, something, anything,* or as adjectives in the sense of *some* or
any. They are thus inflected:—

Alĭquĭs, -quă, -quŏd or -quĭd, *some, any* (generally).

	SINGULAR.				PLURAL.		
Nom.	ălĭquĭs	ălĭquă	{ ălĭquŏd ălĭquĭd }	ălĭquī	ălĭquae	ălĭquă
Gen.		ălĭcūjŭs		ălĭquōrŭm	-ārŭm	-ōrŭm
Dat.		ălĭcuī		ălĭquĭbŭs		
Acc.	ălĭquĕm	ălĭquăm	{ ălĭquŏd ălĭquĭd }	ălĭquōs	ălĭquās	ălĭquă
Voc.	Like Nom.			Like Nom.		
Abl.	ălĭquō	ălĭquā	ălĭquō	ălĭquĭbŭs.		

Quĭdam, quaedam, quoddam *or* quiddam, *a certain one.*

SINGULAR.

Nom.	quĭdăm	quaedăm	{ quoddăm quiddăm
Gen.		cūjusdăm	
Dat.		cuĭdăm	
Acc.	quendăm *	quandăm	{ quoddăm quiddăm
Voc.	Like Nom.		
Abl.	quŏdăm	quădăm	quŏdăm.

PLURAL.

Nom.	quĭdăm	quaedăm	quaedăm
Gen.	quōrundăm	quārundăm	quōrundăm
Dat.		quĭbusdăm	
Acc.	quŏsdăm	quăsdăm	quaedăm
Voc.	Like Nom.		
Abl.		quĭbusdam.	

Ecquis, ecquae *or* ecqua, ecquod *or* -quid? *any one* (interrogatively).

	SINGULAR.				PLURAL.		
Nom.	{ ecquĭs ecquī	ecquae ecqua	ecquŏd ecquĭd }	ecquī	ecquae	{ ecquae ecquă

———————
* The *n* instead of *m* in *quendam, quandam, quorundam,* and *quarundam* is
euphonic.

GEN.	eccŭjŭs			ecquōrŭm -ārŭm , -ōrŭm		
DAT.	eccuĭ			ecquībŭs		
ACC.	ecquĕm	ecquăm	{ ecquŏd }{ ecquĭd }	ecquōs	ecquās	{ ecquae }{ ecquă }
VOC.	——	——	——	——	——	——
ABL.	ecquō	ecquā	ecquō.		ecquībŭs.	

Ullŭs, ullă, ullŭm, *any* (negatively).

	SINGULAR.			PLURAL.		
NOM.	ullŭs	ullă	ullŭm	ullī	ullae	ullă
GEN.		ullīŭs		ullōrŭm	ullārum	ullōrŭm
DAT.		ullī			ullīs	
ACC.	ullŭm	ullăm	ullŭm	ullōs	ullās	ullă
VOC.	——	——	——	——	——	——
ABL.	ullō	ullā	ullō.		ullīs.	

REMARKS.

1. The neuter *alĭquod* is always used adjectively in agreement with its noun, whereas *alĭquid* generally stands substantively; as *alĭquod detrimentum*, some detriment; but *aliquid*, something; *aliquid boni*, something (of) good, &c. — *Aliquis* is both substantive and adjective, and is sometimes joined with *unus;* as (*unus*) *aliquis*, some one; *liber aliquis*, some book.

2. *Quĭdam* is said of individuals or objects, of the nature of which we are either ignorant, or which we do not wish to specify: "a certain (one)," "a sort of," "a certain degree of." E. g. *Quidam de meis amicis*, a certain one (some one) of my friends; *quŏdam tempŏre*, at a certain time; *quoddam commune vincŭlum*, a certain (a sort of) common bond; *quiddam boni*, (a certain) something good, a certain degree of good. — This pronoun may stand either substantively or adjectively, and *quiddam* differs from *quoddam*, like *aliquid* from *aliquod*. — The plural *quidam*, *quaedam*, *quaedam* is often used simply with the sense of *aliquot* or *nonnulli*, "some," "several."

3. Between the forms *ecquis* and *ecqui*, *ecquae* and *ecqua*, there is no appreciable difference, *ecquĭs* and *ecquī* being both used either independently in the sense of "any one," "some one," or adjectively in the sense of "any"; as *Ecquĭs* (or *ecquī*) *hic est?* Is there *any one* here? *Ecquis* (or *ecqui*) *est tibi liber?* Have you any book? The same may be said of the neuters *ecquod* and *ecquid*. The latter, however, (*ecquid*,) frequently loses all pronominal force, and serves merely to introduce a question.

4. *Ullus* is generally an adjective, and is only used in sentences involving a *negation* or *uncertainty.* Hence it is frequently preceded by *nōn*, *nĕc*, *sĭnĕ*, *si*, *nŭm* or *numquĭd;* as *sine ullā spê*, without any hope; *si tibi est ullus amīcus*, if you have any friend; *nego tibi esse ullum amicum*, I deny that you have any friend, &c. —*Ullus*, how-

E   6 *

ever, becomes *positive* by a double negation in *nonnullus, a, um,*
"some," as does also *nihil* in *nonnĭhĭl,* "something."

5. *Quis* is commonly put instead of *aliquis* in all sentences involving a condition, a negation, or comparison. When thus employed in
the sense of *any* or *any one,* it is preceded by *si, nisi, ne, num, quo,
quanto,* or *quum;* as *si quâ ratione,* if in any way; *si quid est tibi
bonum,* if you have anything good; *ne quod pericŭlum incidĕret,* lest
(= that no) danger might occur; *quanto quis est doctior, eo modesti-
or,* the more learned any one is, the more modest he will be. — *Si-
quis* and *nēquis* are declined exactly like *ecquis,* i. e. the fem. sing.
is *siqua* or *siquae,* and the neut. *siquod* or *siquid.*

6. When the substantive denotes a *quantity* or *mass* in the singular,
the English "some" or "any" may be expressed by *ălĭquantum* or
ălĭquantŭlum (with the genitive), and when it denotes *number* in the
plural, by the indeclinable *ălĭquŏt* (in the same case with the noun).
E. g. *alĭquantum* sacchari, some sugar; *aliquot* libri *or* libros, some
books.

7. The English word "any" is often *entirely suppressed* in Latin.
Thus: —

The wine.	Vīnum, i, *n.* ; mērum, i, *n.* (*pure wine*).
Some (any) wine.	Vīnum *or* alĭquántum víni.
Some (any) bread.	Pânem *or* aliquántum pânis.
Some (any) paper.	Chártam *or* aliquántum chártae.
Some (any) books.	Líbros *or* álĭquot (nonnúllos) líbros.
Some good cheese.	{ Cásĕum bónum. { Aliquántum cásĕi bōni.
Have you any wine ?	{ Écquid ést tíbi vínum ? { Habêsne vīnum (alĭquántum víni)?
I have some.	{ Ést (míhi nonnúllum): { (Alĭquántum) hábeo.
Have you any water ?	{ Écqua (écquid) ést tíbi áqua ? { Habêsne áquam (*or* aliquántum áquae) ?
I have some.	{ Ést (míhi nonnúlla). { (Alĭquántum) hábeo.
Have you any good wine ?	{ Ecquid ést tíbi vínum bónum ? { Habêsne aliquántum víni bóni ?
I have some.	{ Ést (míhi aliquántum). { (Nonnúllum) hábeo.
Has he any good cloth ?	{ Écqui(s) ést éi bónus pánnus ? { Habétne bónum pánnum ?
He has some.	Ést. Hábet.
Have you any shoes ?	{ Écqui súnt tíbi cálcei ? { Habêsne cálceos álĭquot (álĭquos) ?
I have some.	{ Súnt míhi álĭquot (álĭqui). { Nonnúllos (quôsdam) hábeo.

Have you some good or bad horses ?	Écqui tíbi súnt équi bóni án nê-quam ? Habêsne équos bónos án nêquam ?
I have some good ones.	Súnt míhi (áliqui) bóni. Hábeo (nonnúllos or quôsdam) bónos.
Have you good or bad water ?	Écquae ést tíbi áqua bóna án nê-quam ? Útrum áquam hábes bónam án ví-lem ?
I have some good.	(Ést míhi) bóna. Bónam hábeo.
Have you good or bad wine ?	Éstne tíbi vinum bónum án vílĕ ? Útrum vínum hábes bónum án vílĕ?
I have some bad.	(Ést míhi) vílĕ. Víle (nêquam) hábeo.

OF NOUNS DEFECTIVE IN NUMBER.

B. Words defective in number are either such as have *no plural*, or such as have *no singular*.

Those which do not admit of a plural are called *singŭlārĭa tantum*. They are:—

1. Abstract nouns, or such as denote a quality or intellectual exist-ence considered as general or indivisible; as *justĭtĭa, pĭĕtas, tempĕran-tĭa, sĕnectus, fămēs, sĭtĭs,* &c., justice, piety, temperance, old age, hun-ger, thirst,* &c.

2. Names of materials or of a mass without subdivision; as *aurum,* gold; *argentum,* silver; *argilla,* white clay; *coenum,* mire, mud; *săbŭ-lum,* sand; *sanguis,* blood, &c.

3. Collectives, i. e. such as denote a totality or mass of individuals or things; as *plebs* and *vulgus,* the vulgar; *pŏpŭlus,* the people; *su-pellex,* furniture; *victus,* food, support; *vīrŭs,* poison (of every kind). So also *indŏlēs,* natural parts; and *scientĭa,* the totality of a man's knowledge, &c.

4. Proper names, except when they are common to several indi-viduals; as *Virgĭlĭus, Cĭcĕro, Plautus,* &c.   But *Caesar, Caesăres.*

5. The following words: *justĭtĭum,* suspension of business (in courts, &c.); *lētum,* death; *mĕrĭdĭes,* noon; *spĕcĭmen,* example; *vēr,* spring; *vespĕr* and *vespĕra,* evening.

___

* Abstract terms, however, frequently do occur in the plural, *a*) when they denote *different kinds* of the same quality, as *excellentiae, quiĕtes, irăcundiae, fortĭtūdĭnes, mortes, mĕtŭs,* different kinds of excellence, rest, anger, bravery, death, fear, &c. ; and *b*) to express *a repetition* of the same thing in different subjects, as *adventūs, effūsĭōnēs,* arrivals, eruptions ; *intĕrĭtūs, exĭtūs, ŏdĭa, ănĭmi,* destruction, exit, odium, courage, as experienced or incurred by differ-ent men. — To these may be added the idiomatic Latin plurals *nĭvēs, grandĭnēs, imbrēs, plŭvĭae,* falls of snow, hail, rain, and *soles,* spells of sunshine.

6. To these may be added the peculiar use of names of vegetables and fruits, where in English we employ the plural; as *fābam, lentem, răpum* serĕre, to sow beans, lentils, turnips; *cĭcĕris* cătinus, a bowl of peas; *nux, ūva,* the nut, grape, i. e. nuts, grapes, &c.

EXERCISE 18.

Have you any sugar? — I have some. — Have you any good coffee? — I have some. — Have you any salt? — I have some. — Have I any good salt? — You have some. — Have I any shoes? — You have some. — Have I any pretty dogs? — You have some. — Has the man any good honey? — He has some. — What has the man? — He has some good bread. — What has the shoemaker? — He has some pretty shoes. — Has the sailor any biscuits? — He has some. — Has your friend any good pencils? — He has some. — Have you good or bad coffee? — I have some good. — Have you good or bad wood? — I have some good. — Have I good or bad oxen? — You have some bad (ones). — Has your brother good or bad cheese? — He has neither good nor bad. — What has he good? — He has some good friends. — Who has some cloth? — My neighbor has some. — Who has some money? — The French have some. — Who has some gold? — The English have some. — Who has some good horses? — The Germans have some. — Who has some good hay? — This ass has some. — Who has some good bread? — That Spaniard has some. — Who has some good books? — These Frenchmen have some. — Who has some good ships? — Those Englishmen have some. — Has anybody wine? — Nobody has any. — Has the Italian fine or ugly horses? — He has some ugly (ones). — Have you wooden or stone tables? — I have neither wooden nor stone (ones). — Has your boy the fine books of mine? — He has not those of your boy, but his own. — Has he any good thread stockings? — He has some. — What has the Turk? — He has nothing. — He has (a certain) something bad (*quiddam mali*). — Who has something good? — A certain stranger has something good. — Has any one hay? — Certain husbandmen have some hay and (*et*) corn.

Lesson XVII. — PENSUM SEPTIMUM DECIMUM.

No, not any, none.	*Nullŭs, nullă, nullŭm.* *Nĭhĭl* (with the gen.). *Numquĭs, -quae, -quŏd* or *-quĭd?* Sometimes simply *Nŏn.*

A. Obs. The pronominal adjective *nullus* is declined like *ullus.* (Vide Lesson XVI.) Its masculine singular is also employed substantively in the place of *nemo,* "no one, nobody" (Lesson X. *C.*) *Numquis* is declined like *ecquis,* and is used in questions to which *nullus* is expected in the answer. Instead of the adjective *nullus*, *nihil* is frequently put partitively with the genitive, singular and plural. Sometimes the English " no," " none," is expressed by a simple *non*. Examples: —

Have you any book ?	{ Númquis ést tíbi líber ? { Habêsne líbrum áliquem ?
I have none.	{ Nôn ést. { Núllum hábeo.
Have you any wine ?	{ Númquid ést tíbi vínum (víni) ? { Núm hábes aliquántum víni ?
I have none.	{ Nôn (núllum) ést. { Núllum hábeo.
Have you no bread ?	{ Án ést tíbi níhil pânis ? { Án núllum pânem hábes ?
I have none.	{ Níhil. { Núllum (hábeo).
Have I no paper ?	{ Númquid ést míhi níhil chártae ? { Núm chártam núllam hábeo ?
You have some.	{ Ést tíbi nónníhil. { Nonnúllam véro hábes.
Have you no shoes ?	{ Nôn tíbi súnt úlli cálcéi ? { Án níhil calcéôrum hábes ?
I have none.	{ Núlli. { Níhil (núllos, nôn úllos) hábeo.
Have you any ?	{ Númqui tíbi súnt ? { Núm áliquos (úllos) hábes ?
I have none.	{ Nôn súnt. { Núllos hábeo.
Has the man any ?	{ Núm quí súnt víro íllī ? { Núm vír ílle úllos hábet ?
He has none.	{ Nôn súnt. { Núllos hábet.
Has he any good books ?	{ Écqui súnt éi líbri bóni ? { Habétne líbros áliquos bónos ?
He has some.	{ Súnt éi áliqui (nonnúlli). { Nonnúllos (áliquot) hábet.
I have no money, no books.	Níhil pecúniae, nihil librôrum hábeo.

The American	*Americānus, i, *m.*
The Irishman.	Hibernus, i, *m.*
The Scotchman.	Scōtus, i, *m.*
The Dutchman.	Batāvus, i, *m.*
The Russian.	*Russus, i, *m.*
Are you an American ?	Ésne tû Americânus ?
I am (one). I am not.	Súm. Nôn súm.
Have you the books of the Dutch or those of the Russians ?	{ Útrum líbros ténes Batavôrum án Russôrum ? { Batavorúmne líbros ténes án Russôrum ?

B. The substantives which are *pluralia tantum*, i. e. used in the plural number only, are : —

1. The names of certain determinate days of the Roman month, as *Calendae*, the Calends ; *Nōnae*, the nones ; *Idūs*, the ides. To these add *nundīnae*, a fair (held every ninth day) ; and *fērīae*, holidays.

2. The names of festivals and public games, as *Bacchānālīa*, *Flōrālīa*, *Sāturnālīa*, &c., festivals in honor of Bacchus, Flora, Saturn, &c., *Olympīa*, the Olympic games, and *lūdi*, public games generally. So also *nātālītīa*, birthday festival ; *rĕpōtīa*, drinking-bout after a feast ; *sponsālīa*, espousals.

3. Many names of towns and countries, including such as are properly names of nations, e. g. *Arbēlă* (*orum*), Erbil ; *Athēnae*, Athens ; *Gādēs*, Cadiz ; *Leuctră* (*orum*) ; *Delphī ; Trēvīrī*, the country of the Treviri ; *Pārīsīi*, Paris ; *Syrācūsae*, Syracuse ; *Persae*, Persia.

4. The following substantives, which, with a plural form, commonly preserve a *plural signification :* —

Alpes, *the Alps.*
ambāges, *quibbles, subterfuges.*
argūtīae, *subtleties, wit.*
arma, *arms.*
artus, *limbs.*
bellāria, *dainties.*
cāni, *gray hairs.*
coelītes, *the celestials.*
consentes, *the twelve highest gods.*
crepundia, *toys.*
dēlicīae, *delight ; darling.*
divitīae, *riches.*
donāria, } *presents.*
lautia, }
excūbiae, *watches.*
exta, }
intestīna, } *the intestines.*
viscĕra, }
exūvīae, } *spoils.*
spōlia, }
facētīae, *pleasantry.*
fōri, } *book-cases.*
forūli, }
fōria, *excrements.*
grātes, *thanks.*
gemīni, *twins.*
gerrae, } *nonsense.*
quisquilīae, }
ilia, *the entrails.*
impedimenta, *baggage.*
indūvīae, *articles of clothing.*

infĕrīae, } *funeral rites.*
justa, }
infĕri, *the gods below.*
insidīae, *snares.*
lamenta, *complaints.*
lĕmŭrēs, *departed spirits.*
libĕri, *children.*
majōres, *ancestors.*
mānes, *shades (of the dead).*
mĭnae, *menaces.*
moenīa, *walls.*
parietīnae, *dilapidated walls.*
pĕnātes, *household-gods.*
postĕri, *descendants.*
praestigīae, *jugglers' tricks.*
prĕces, *prayers.*
primōres, } *nobles, leaders.*
procĕres, }
rēlĭquīae, *the remains.*
salēbrae, *impediments.*
sentes, } *thorns.*
vĕpres, }
serta, *garlands.*
sŭpĕri, *the upper gods.*
tormĭna, *the gripes.*
tricae, *fooleries, gewgaws.*
utensīlia, *necessaries (of life).*
valvae, } *door-folds.*
fōres, }
vērbĕra, *blows.*

5. The following substantives, which, though plural in form, have more or less a *singular signification :* —

altāria, *the high altar.*
cancelli,
clāthri, } *lattice-work, grating.*
casses,
plăgae, } *hunter's net.*
clitellae, *pack-saddle.*
clūnes,
nătes, } *the buttocks.*
cūnae,
cunābŭla, } *the cradle.*
incunābŭla,
exsĕquiae, *the funeral.*
fauces, *the throat.*
fĭdēs, *the lyre.*
indūciae, *armistice.*

inimicĭtiae, *enmity.*
lŏcŭli, *a casket.*
mănūbiae, *booty.*
nuptiae, *a wedding.*
ŏbĭces, *a bolt, bar.*
pantĭces, *the paunch.*
praecordĭa, *the diaphragm.*
pugillāres,
tăbŭlae, } *writing-tablets.*
cērae,
scālae, *the ladder.*
scōpae, *the broom.*
sordes, *the dirt.*
tenĕbrae, *darkness.*
virgulta, *the brushwood.*

C. Some substantives assume a different signification in the plural, and sometimes also a different gender. Thus : —

Singular.	Plural.
fastus, *pride.*	fastus, } *the calendar.*
	fasti,
fŏrum, *the market-place.*	fŏri, *the gangways.*
lustrum, *a period of five years.*	lustra, *dens of wild beasts.*
tempus, *time.*	tempŏra, *the temples (of the head).*

D. Others modify their signification in the plural without abandoning that of the singular : —

Singular.	Plural.
aedes, is, *a temple.*	aedes, ium, *a house.*
ăqua, *water.*	ăquae, *mineral springs.*
auxĭlĭum, *help.*	auxĭlĭa, *auxiliary troops.*
bŏnum, *something good.*	bŏna, *property.*
carcer, *a prison.*	carcĕres, *the lists (barrier).*
castrum, *a castle.*	castra, *a camp.*
cŏmĭtĭum, *a part of the Roman forum.*	cŏmĭtĭa, *an election-meeting.*
cōpĭa, *abundance.*	cōpĭae, *military forces.*
cŭpēdĭa, *daintiness.*	cŭpēdĭae *or* } *dainty bits.*
	cŭpēdĭa, *n.*
ĕpŭlum, *a banquet.*	ĕpŭlae, *the food, meal.*
făcultas, *ability, power.*	făcultātes, *property, means.*
fortūna, *fortune, luck.*	fortūnae, *gifts of fortune.*
hortus, i, *a common garden.*	horti, } *a garden for pleasure.*
	hortŭli,
littĕra (or lĭtĕra), *a letter of the alphabet.*	littĕrae (lĭtĕrae), *a letter, writings.*
lūdus, *pastime, school.*	lūdi, *a public spectacle.*

nāris, *the nostril.* — nāres, Ium, *the nostrils,* or *the nose.*
nātālis (*i. e.* dies), *birthday.* — nātūles, *the birth (with respect to rank).*
(ops), *help.* — ŏpes, *power; property.*
ŏpĕra, *trouble, pains.* — ŏpĕrae, *operatives.*
pars, *the part.* — partes, *a party; rôle.*
rostrum, *a beak, bill.* — rostra, *the orator's stage.**
sāl, *salt.* — sāles, *witty sayings, repartee.*

E. The *Adjectives* defective in number are *pauci*, a few, and *plē-rīque*, most, which in ordinary language want the singular. Of *paucus*, the neuter diminutive *pauxillum* or *pauxillūlum* only occurs in the sense of "some little." The singular *plerusque* was anciently used in the sense of "the greater part of," but is now only put in the neuter (*plerumque*), and adverbially, "for the most part."

EXERCISE 19.

Has the American good money? — He has some. — Have the Dutch good cheese? — Yes, sir, the Dutch have some. — Has the Russian no cheese? — He has none. — Have you good stockings? — I have some. — Have you good or bad honey? — I have some good. — Have you some good coffee? — I have none. — Have you some bad coffee? — I have some. — Has the Irishman good wine? — He has none. — Has he good water? — He has some. — Has the Scotchman some good salt? — He has none. — What has the Dutchman? — He has good ships. — Have I some bread? — You have none. — Have I some good friends? — You have none. — Who has good friends? — The Frenchman has some. — Has your servant any coats or brooms? — He has some good brooms, but no coats. — Has any one hay? — Some one has some. — Who has some? — My servant has some. — Has this man any bread? — He has none. — Who has good shoes? — My good shoemaker has some. — Have you the good hats of the Russians, or those of the Dutch? — I have neither those of the Russians nor those of the Dutch, I have those of the Irish. — Which sacks has your friend? — He has the good sacks of the merchants. — Has your boy the good hammers of the carpenters? — No, sir, he has them not. — Has this little boy some sugar? — He has none? — Has the brother of your friend good combs? — The brother of my friend has none, but I have some? — Who has good wooden chairs? — Nobody has any.

Lesson XVIII. — PENSUM DUODEVICESIMUM.

OF NUMERALS.

A. The numerals of the Latin language are either adjectives or adverbs.

---

* The platform or desk from which the ancient Romans spoke, so called from its having been adorned with the *beaks* of captured ships.

Numeral adjectives are divided into five classes: *Cardinal,*
Ordinal, Distributive, Multiplicative, and *Proportional.*

Of adverbial numerals there is but one class, which answer
to the question *how many times?* as *sĕmĕl,* once, *tĕr,* thrice.

B. Cardinals contain the answer to the question *quŏt?* how
many? as *ūnus,* one, *dŭo,* two, *centum,* a hundred. Of these
the first three are susceptible of declension, and those from
quattuor (four) to *centum* (a hundred), inclusive of both, are
invariable. The multiples of 100, as far as *mille* (a thousand), are declined like the plural of *bonus;* as *dŭcenti, ae, a,*
two hundred, &c. — *Unus, dŭo,* and *trēs* are thus inflected: —

Unus, a, um, *one.*

	SINGULAR.			PLURAL.		
	Masc.	*Fem.*	*Neut.*	*Masc.*	*Fem.*	*Neut.*
Nom.	ūnŭs	ūnă	ūnŭm	ūnī	ūnae	ūnă
Gen.		ūnīus		ūnōrŭm	ūnārŭm	ūnōrŭm
Dat.		ūnī			ūnīs	
Acc.	ūnŭm	ūnăm	ūnŭm	ūnōs	ūnăs	ūnă
Voc.	ūnĕ	ūnă	ūnŭm	ūnī	ūnae	ūnă
Abl.	ūnō	ūnā	ūnō.		ūnīs.	

	Dŭo, dŭae, dŭo, *two.*			Trēs, trĭa, *three.*	
	Masc.	*Fem.*	*Neut.*	*Masc. & Fem.*	*Neut.*
Nom.	dŭŏ	dŭae	dŭŏ	Nom. trēs	trĭă
Gen.	dŭōrŭm	dŭārŭm	dŭōrŭm	Gen. trĭŭm	
Dat.	dŭōbŭs	dŭābŭs	dŭōbŭs	Dat. trĭbŭs	
Acc.	dŭōs *or* dŭo	dŭăs	dŭŏ	Acc. trēs	trĭă
Voc.	dŭŏ	dŭae	dŭŏ	Voc. trēs	trĭă
Abl.	dŭōbŭs	dŭābŭs	dŭōbŭs.	Abl. trĭbŭs.	

REMARK 1. The plural *ūnī, ūnae, ūnă,* can only be used, *a)* when
joined with substantives that are *pluralia tantum,* i. e. used in the
plural only; as *ūnae scōpae,* one broom; *ūnae litterae,* one letter; *ūnă
castra,* one camp; *in ūnīs aedĭbus,* in one house; *b)* when it assumes
the sense of "only," "alone," "one and the same," "like," &c.; as
tres uni passus, only three steps; *unis morĭbus,* with one and the
same kind of manners, &c.

2. Like *dŭŏ* is inflected *ambō, ambae, ambō,* "both." — Instead of
the genitives *dŭōrum, dŭārum,* the contracted form *dŭum* is frequently
employed, especially with *millĭum,* thousand.

C. Obs. The numeral *mille,* thousand, is indeclinable in the singular, but is regularly inflected in the plural, e. g. *mīlĭa, mīlĭum, mīlĭbus,*
&c. It is generally followed by the genitive (sometimes by an appo-
sitional case) of the objects enumerated, as *mille homĭnum, duo (tria,*

7

quattuor,* &c.) *milia homĭnum* (more rarely *homĭnes*), &c. — This is its construction as a *substantive;* but *mille* is *far more frequently* used as an *indeclinable adjective* in all the cases, singular and plural; e. g. *mille equĭtes*, a thousand knights; *mille hominum numero*, a thousand men in number; *mille modis*, in a thousand ways.

D. The Romans have a separate class of numerals in answer to the question, *How many each (apiece)?* or *How many each time?* (*Quŏtēni, ae, a?*) These are always in the plural, and are called *Distributives.* E. g. *bini (terni, quăterni*, &c.), "two (three, four) each," or "two (three, four) *each time*," "two by two"; *singŭli*, "one each," "one by one," "one at a time." Examples: —

Boys of sixteen or seventeen years each.	Púĕri *sênum septenŭmve dênum†* annôrum.
They met with one interpreter each.	Cúm *singŭlis* interprétĭbus congrés-si súnt.
He gave us three books apiece.	Dédit nóbis *térnos* líbros.
His daughters have each a son.	Fíliae éjus *singŭlos* fílios hábent.
He does not know how much twice two is.	Nôn dídĭcit, bís bina quót éssent.

E. Obs. These distributives are employed instead of the cardinals, *a)* in connection with such substantives as are used in the plural only,‡ as *binae* (not *duae*) *scopae*, two brooms, *quaternae nuptiae*, four weddings, &c.; *b*) with substantives whose plural assumes a simple signification different from the singular, as *castrum*, a castle, *duo castra*, two castles; but *una castra* (*pl.* peculiar), a camp, *bina castra*, two camps; *aedes*, a temple, *tres aedes*, three temples; but *aedes* (a *pl.* with singular signification), a house, *unae aedes*, one house, *trinae*§ *aedes*, three houses; *littera*, a letter (of the alphabet), *quattuor litterae*, four letters (of the alphabet); but *litterae (pl.*), a letter (epistle), *unae litterae*, one letter, *quaternae litterae*, four letters, &c.

The hatter.	*Opĭfĕx (*gen.* -ĭcis) pīlĕōrum, *m.*
The joiner.	Făbĕr (rī, *m.*) scrīnĭārius.
Round.	Rotundus, a, um.
A or an (one).	{ Ūnŭs, ă, ŭm. { Alĭquĭs, -quă, -quŏd.

---

* It is also customary to use the distributives instead of the cardinal numerals, and to say *bina* (*terna, quaterna*, &c.) *milia* for *duo milia*, &c. — The *accusative* of the objects enumerated becomes necessary when one of the declinable numerals *dŭcenti*, &c. is added; as, *habet tria milia trecentos milites*, he has three thousand three hundred soldiers.

† The plural in *um* is the *regular* form for this class of numerals, instead of the *orum, arum, orum* of other adjectives.

‡ This applies only to such nouns as have a singular signification with this plural form. Plurals like *liberi*, children, follow the general law.

§ In all these cases, where the distributive is thus used for the cardinal numeral with nouns of a plural form, the English "one" must be expressed by *uni, ae, a*, and "three" by *trini, ae, a. Singŭli* and *terni* remain distributive always.

F. Obs. The indefinite article *a* or *an* is generally omitted in Latin. When expressed, however, it is *ŭnŭs, ă, ŭm,* "one," or *ălĭquĭs, quă, quŏd,* "some one." Examples:—

Have you a looking-glass?	Éstne tíbi (únum) spécŭlum? Habêsne (únum) spécŭlum?
I have one.	Ést míhi únum. Hábeo únum.
Have you a book?	Éstne tíbi (únus) líber? Habêsne (únum) líbrum?
I have one.	Ést míhi únus. Hábeo únum (álíquem).
I have none.	Ést míhi núllus (*or* Non est). Núllum hábeo.
Have you a good round hat?	Éstne tíbi bónum únum pílĕum rotúndum? Án hábes bónum únum pílĕum rotúndum?
I have one.	Ést míhi únus. Únum hábeo.
Has he a beautiful house (home)?	Núm ést éi dómus púlchra? Númquid ílle hábet dómum únam púlchram?
I have none.	Ést éi núlla (*or* Nôn ést). Núllam hábet (*or* Nôn hábet).
I have two of them.	Míhi súnt dúae. Égo (eárum) dúas hábeo.
He has three of them.	Súnt éi três. Hábet (eárum) três.

G. Obs. The partitive genitive after numerals is commonly omitted in Latin, when the quantity denoted by them is equal to the whole. But the relative pronoun may stand in the same case with the numeral.

You have four of them.	Súnt tíbi quáttŭor. Quáttŭor (eârum*) hábes.
Of which you have five.	Quae tíbi quínque sunt. Quâs† quínque hábes.
Have you five good horses?	Súntne tíbi quínque équi bóni? Núm quínque hábes équos bónos?
Nay rather, I have six of them.	Ímmo véro míhi súnt séx. Hábeo (eôrum) séx.

---

* *Eârum* can only be correctly put when it refers to a larger number already alluded to.
† *Quae* and *quas,* because the numeral *quinque* denotes the entire number possessed ; but *quârum* if a larger number is meant.

I have six good and seven bad ones.	Súnt míhi séx bóni *ét* séptem víles. Égo séx bónos septémque víles hábeo.
And. (Copulative conjunction.)	Et, ăc, atque, -que.

H. Obs. The conjunction *ac* cannot be used when the next word begins with a vowel or the letter *h*. *Et* and *atque* stand before vowels and consonants both. The enclitic *que*, like the interrogative *ne*, is always suffixed to the word which it serves to connect.

Have you a (one) letter?	Éstne tíbi úna epístŏla? Habêsne únas líteras?
I have ten of them.	Súnt míhi décem. Hábeo (eârum) dénas.
I have ten letters and five notes.	Súnt míhi décem epístŏlae *ét* (*ác, átque **) quínque schédŭlae. (Égo) dénas lítteras *ét* (*ác, átque*) quínque schédŭlas hábeo. (See *Obs. E.*)
Titus and Cajus have each of them a book.	Títus ét Cájus líbros síngulos hábent.
They have five looking-glasses apiece.	Súnt íis quína spécŭla. Quína spécŭla hábent.
I have three houses and a thousand pens.	Súnt míhi aédes trínae ét mílle pennârum. Égo aédes trínas *átque* mílle pénnas hábeo.

I. The following Table exhibits a list of the cardinal and distributive numerals of the Latin language: —

CARDINAL.			DISTRIBUTIVE.	
1. ūnus, a, um,	*one.*	I.	singŭli, ae, a,	*one each.*
2. dŭŏ, ae, o,	*two.*	II.	bīni, ae, a,	*two each.*
3. trēs, trĭa,	*three.*	III.	terni (or trīni), ae, a,	*three each.*
4. quattuor,	*four.*	IV.	quaterni, ae, a,	*four each.*
5. quinque,	*five.*	V.	quīni, ae, a,	*five each.*
6. sex,	*six,* &c.	VI.	sēni, ae, a,	*six each,* &c.
7. septem		VII.	septēni, ae, a.	
8. octo		VIII.	octōni, ae, a.	
9. nŏvem		IX.	novēni, ae, a.	
10. dĕcem		X.	dēni, ae, a.	

* *Atque* (= ad + que) is emphatic, and may be rendered by "and besides." *Et* connects objects considered as *distinct*, *que* things *belonging to*, or *resulting from*, each other. *Ac* has upon the whole the same force as *atque*, but it is often employed instead of a simple *et*, to prevent a repetition of the latter.

	CARDINAL.		DISTRIBUTIVE.
11.	undĕcim	XI.	undēni, ae, a.
12.	dŭŏdĕcim	XII.	dŭŏdēni, ae, a.
13.	{ trĕdĕcim *or* dĕcem et tres }	XIII.	terni dēni, ae, a.
14.	quattuordĕcim	XIV.	quaterni dēni, ae, a.
15.	quindĕcim	XV.	quini dēni, ae, a.
16.	{ sēdĕcim (sexdecim) *or* dĕcem et sex }	XVI.	sēni dēni, ae, a.
17.	{ septendĕcim *or* dĕcem et septem }	XVII.	septēni dēni, ae, a.
18.	{ dĕcem et octo *or* dŭŏdēviginti * }	XVIII.	{ octōni dēni, ae, a. duodevīceni, ae, a.
19.	{ dĕcem et nŏvem *or* undēviginti }	XIX.	{ novēni dēni, ae, a. undēvīceni, ae, a.
20.	viginti	XX.	vīcēni, ae, a.
21.	{ unus et viginti viginti ūnus † }	XXI.	vīcēni singŭli, ae, a.
22.	{ dŭo et viginti viginti dŭo }	XXII.	vīcēni bīni, ae, a.
23.	tres et viginti	XXIII.	vīcēni terni, ae, a.
28.	{ octo et viginti dŭŏdētriginta }	XXVIII.	vīcēni octōni, ae, a.
29.	{ nŏvem et viginti undētriginta }	XXIX.	vīcēni nŏvēni, ae, a.
30.	triginta	XXX.	trīcēni, ae, a.
40.	quădrāginta	XL.	quădrāgēni, ae, a.
50.	quinquāginta	L.	quinquāgēni, ae, a.
60.	sexāginta	LX.	sexāgēni, ae, a.
70.	septuāginta	LXX.	septuāgēni, ae, a.
80.	octōginta	LXXX.	octōgēni, ae, a.
90.	nōnāginta	XC.	nonāgēni, ae, a.
99.	{ nōnāginta nŏvem undĕcentum }	IC.	{ nonāgēni nŏvēni, ae, a. undēceni, ae, a.
100.	centum	C.	centēni, ae, a.
109.	{ centum et nŏvem centum nŏvem }	CIX.	centēni nŏvēni, ae,
200.	dŭcenti, ae, a	CC.	dŭcēni, ae, a.
300.	trĕcenti, ae, a	CCC.	trĕcēni, ae, a.
400.	quădringenti, ae, a	CCCC.	quădringēni, ae, a.
500.	quingenti, ae, a	IↃ *or* D.	quingēni, ae, a.

---

* For 18, 28, 38, &c. and for 19, 29, 39, &c. the subtractive expressions *dŭŏdeviginti, dŭŏdētriginta, undēviginta,* &c., as far as *undĕcentum,* are more common than the compounds *dĕcem et octo,* &c., and neither the *dŭo* nor the *un* of these words is inflected.

† The rule for the juxtaposition of the *intermediate* numbers is, that *from 20 to 100 either the smaller may precede* WITH *et, or the larger* WITHOUT *et,* as in the case of 21. But beyond 100, *the larger always comes first,* with or without *et;* e. g. *dŭcenti quadrāginta sex,* or *dŭcenti et quadrāginta sex,* 246.

7 *

CARDINAL.		DISTRIBUTIVE.
600. sexcenti, ae, a	DC.	sexcēni, ae, a.
700. septingenti, ae, a	DCC.	septingēni, ae, a.
800. octingenti, ae, a	DCCC.	octingēni, ae, a.
900. { nongenti, ae, a ⎫ { noningenti, ae, a ⎬	DCCCC.	nonagēni, ae, a.
1,000. mille	CIɔ or M.	singŭla milĭa.
2,000. dŭo (or bina)* milĭa	MM.	bina milĭa.
5,000. quinque (or quina) milĭa	Iɔɔ.	quina milĭa.
10,000. dĕcem milĭa	CCIɔɔ.	dĕna milĭa.
100,000. centum milĭa	CCCIɔɔɔ.	centēna milĭa.

EXERCISE 20.

Have you a good letter ? — I have a good letter and a good book. — Has your servant a broom ? — He has six brooms and five chickens. — Has your friend any houses ? — He has some. — He has ten houses (aedes) and five gardens. — What has the youth ? — He has a thousand books and two thousand notes. — Who has a beautiful round table ? — The hatter has one. — The friend of our tailor has ten round tables and twenty chairs. — Have you a good servant ? — I have one. — Has your hatmaker a beautiful house ? — He has two (of them). — Have I a pretty gold ribbon ? — You have one. — What has the joiner ? — He has beautiful tables. — Has he a beautiful round table ? — He has one. — Has the baker a large looking-glass ? — He has one. — Has the Scotchman the friends that I have ? — He has not the same that you have, but he has good friends. — Has he your good books ? — He has them. — Have I their good hammers ? — You have them not, but you have your good iron nails. — Has that hatter my good hat ? — He has not yours, but his own. — Have I my good shoes ? — You have not yours ; you have his. — Who has mine ? — Somebody has them. — Has anybody two letters ? — The brother of my neighbor has three. — Has your cook two sheep ? — He has four. — Has he six good chickens ? — He has three good and seven bad. — Has the merchant good wine ? — He has some. — Has the tailor good coats ? — He has none. — Has the baker good bread ? — He has some. — What has the carpenter ? — He has good nails. — What has your merchant ? — He has good pencils, good coffee, good honey, and good biscuits. — Who has good iron ? — My good friend has some. — Am I right or wrong ? — You are wrong. — Is anybody sleepy ? — The shoemaker is sleepy and thirsty. — Is he tired ? — He is not tired. — Has your servant the glasses of our (nostrorum, vide next Lesson) friends ? — He has not those of your friends, but those of his great merchants. — Has he my wooden chair ? — He has not yours, but that of his boy. — Are you thirsty ? — I am not thirsty, but very hungry (vehementer esurio).

---

* Vide page 74, note * .

Lesson XIX. — PENSUM UNDEVICESIMUM.

How much?	*Quăm multŭm? quantŭm?* (with the gen.).
How many?	{ *Quăm multi, ae, ă?* { *Quŏt?* (indeclinable).
How much bread, wine, water?	{ *Quám múltum pânis, víni, áquae?* { *Quántum pânis, vini, áquae?*
How many knives?	{ *Quót (quám múlti) cúltri?* { *Quám múlti cultrôrum?*
How many tables?	{ *Quót (quám múltae) ménsae?* { *Quám múltae mensârum?*
How many looking-glasses?	{ *Quót (quám múlta) spécŭla?* { *Quám múlta speculôrum?*
Only, but. (Adv.)	{ *Tantum, sŏlŭm,* non nisĭ, dun- { taxăt.
How many tables have you?	{ *Quót tíbi ménsae súnt?* { *Quám múltas ménsas hábes?*
I have only two.	{ *Míhi nôn súnt nísi dúae.* { *Dúas tántum hábeo.*
How many knives have you?	{ *Quót súnt tíbi cúltri?* { *Quúim múltos cúltros hábes?*
I have but one good one.	{ *Ést míhi únus sŏlus bónus.* { *Únum sŏlum bónum hábeo.*
How many glasses have you?	{ *Quót súnt tíbi vâsa vítrĕa?* { *Quám múlta vâsa vítrĕa hábes?*
I have but six.	{ *Súnt míhi duntáxat séx.* { *Séx tántum hábeo.*
I have ten, *and those* (*and indeed*) good ones.	*Décem míhi súnt, éaque (ét éa, át-que éa) bóna.*

A. Obs. The demonstrative *is, ea, id* is often put with the conjunctions *et, atque, que, et — quĭdem,* and *nec* by way of explanation of something that precedes, in the sense of the English "and that," "and indeed," "nor indeed," "and not indeed" (*nec is*).

I have a hundred books, and those good ones.	*Céntum líbros (librôrum) hábeo, ét éos bónos.*
I have but one table, and that a poor one.	*Únam tántum ménsam hábeo, eúm-que ténŭem.*
What? What kind of? What sort of?	{ *Quĭs, quae, quŏd or quĭd.* { *Qui(s)năm, quaenăm, quodnăm or quidnăm?* { *Quālĭs, quālĭs, quālĕ?*

---

* In connection with a substantive, and especially with one denoting a person, the English "only" is frequently expressed by the adjective *solus* or *unus* ("alone"); as, *ego solus habeo,* I only (alone) have ; *solos poëtas legit,* he reads only poets.

B. Obs. The pronominal adjective *quālis* denotes the nature or quality of a person or object, and is the correlative of *tālis*, " such," " so constituted." It is inflected like *turpis* (Lessons IV. and XIII.). The pronoun *quī, quae, quŏd* agrees with its noun in gender, number, and case, but *quĭd* stands substantively, and is followed by the genitive.

What (sort of a) book have you?	Quâlis (quís) ést tíbi líber ? Quâlem líbrum (quíd líbri) habes ?
I have a fine book.	Ést míhi líber púlcher. Líbrum púlchrum hábeo.
What (kind of a) table has he ?	Quâlis (quaênam) ést éi ménsa ? Quíd ménsae hábet ? Quám *or* quâlem ménsam hábet ?
He has a wooden table.	Ést éi ménsa lígnĕa. Ménsam lígneam hábet.
What (sort of) sugar has your friend ?	Quâle (quód) ést amíco túo sácchărum ? Quídnam ést amíco túo sácchări ? Quâle (quód) hábet amicus túus sáccharum ?
He has good sugar.	Ést éi sáccharum bónum. Bónum sácchărum hábet.
What (sort of) knives has he ?	Quáles (quí) súnt éi líbri ? Quíd librôrum hábet ? Quáles (quôsnam) líbros hábet ?
He has bad books.	Súnt éi líbri víles (nêquam). Líbros hábet nêquam (víles).
What paper have you ?	Quâlis (quaê) ést tíbi chárta ? Quídnam chártae hábes ? Quâlem (quám) chártam hábes ?
I have beautiful paper.	Ést míhi chárta púlchra. Púlchram chártam hábeo.

Our, ours.	*Nostĕr, nostră, nostrŭm.*
Your, yours (plural).	*Vestĕr, vestră, vestrŭm.*

C. The possessive pronouns *noster* and *vester* are declined like *pulcher.* Thus: —

Nostĕr, nostră, nostrŭm, *our, ours.*

	SINGULAR.			PLURAL.		
NOM.	nostĕr	nostră*	nostrŭm	nostrī	nostrae	nostră
GEN.	nostrī	nostrae	nostrī	nostrôrŭm	-ārŭm	-ōrŭm
DAT.	nostrō	nostrae	nostrō		nostrīs	
ACC.	nostrŭm	nostrăm	nostrŭm	nostrōs	nostrăs	nostră
VOC.	Like Nom.				Like Nom.	
ABL.	nostrō	nostrā	nostrō		nostrīs.	

Have you our candlestick or his ?	Nostrúmne candēlábrum hábes án éjus (íllius) ?
I have his.	Éjus (hábeo).
Has he his own hats or ours ?	Útrum ílle ténet píleos suósmet án nóstros ?
He has ours.	Nóstros (ténet).
Which paper have you ?	Quám chártam hábes ?
I have that of our friends.	Familiáriüm nostrórum chártam hábeo.
How many are there of us ?	Quót (quám múlti) súmus ?

D. Obs. When *quot* or *quam multi* denotes the entire number, they do not admit the partitive genitive after them. The latter can only be put where in English we use *among*.

How many are there of you ?	Quót éstis ?
How many are there of them ?	Quót sunt ílli ?
There are twenty of us, of you, of them.	Vigínti súmus, éstis, súnt.
How many are there *among* us, *among* you, *among* them ?	Quót sunt nóstrum, véstrum, illórum ?
There are twelve among us, you, them.	Duódēcim súnt nóstrum, véstrum, illórum.

OF REDUNDANT NOUNS.

E. Redundant nouns are such as exhibit a superfluity of forms. This may take place in several ways :—

1. There may be two forms for the nominative and one only for the remaining cases ; as *arbŏr* or *arbŏs*, gen. *arbŏris*, f., a tree ; *hŏnŏr* or *hŏnŏs*, gen. *hŏnŏris*, m., honor, &c., &c.

2. There may be one form for the nominative, and two forms of different declensions for the genitive and remaining cases ; as *laurŭs*, gen. *i* & *ūs*, f., the laurel-tree * ; *cupressŭs*, *i* & *ūs*, f., the cypress ; *ficŭs*, *i* & *ūs*, f., the fig-tree ; *pinŭs*, *i* & *ūs*, f., the pine ; and *cŏlŭs*, *i* & *ūs*, f., a distaff. Among these may be included *jūgĕrum*, *i*, n., a Roman acre, which has a redundant ablative : sing. *jūgĕrō* & *jūgĕre*, pl. *jūgĕris* & *jūgĕribŭs* † ; and the plural *ilĭa*, the entrails, which in the gen. has *ilĭum* & *ilĭōrum*, and in the dat. and abl. *ilĭbŭs* & *ilĭis*. *Vās*, gen. *vāsis*, n., a vessel, has its plural from the secondary form *vāsum*, *i*, n. :— *vāsa*, *vasōrum*, &c.

---

* The remaining cases are, Dat. *laurō*, Acc. *laurŭm*, Voc. *laurĕ*, Abl. *laurō* and *laurŭ*; Pl. Nom. *lauri* and *laurūs*, Gen. *laurōrum*, Dat. and Abl. *lauris*, Acc. *laurōs*, Voc. *lauri*. Other names of trees prefer the second declension, except *quercus*, which is entirely of the fourth.

† The forms of the second declension are to be preferred in prose.

F

3. One and the same noun may have two forms of different genders, but of the same declension.   Such are:—

băcŭlum,* i, n.	*and* băcŭlus, i, m.	*a staff, stick.*
baltĕus, i, m.	" baltĕum, i, n.	*girdle, belt.*
callus, i, m.	" callum, i, n.	*hard flesh, callus.*
cătillus, i, m.	" cătillum, i, n.	*a small dish.*
cătinus, i, m.	" cătinum, i, n.	*a dish, platter.*
clĭpĕus, i, m.	" clĭpĕum, i, n.	*a shield.*
cŭbĭtus, i. m.	" cŭbĭtum, i, n.	*the fore-arm; a cubit.†*
intŭbus, i, m.	" intŭbum, i, n.	*succory (a plant).*
jŭgŭlum, i, n.	" jŭgŭlus, i, m.	*the collar-bone.*
lŭpinus, i, m.	" lŭpinum, i, n.	*lupine (a plant).*
pălātum, i, n.	" pălātus, i, m.	*the palate.*
păpȳrus, i, m. & f.	" păpȳrum, i, n.	*the papyrus (reed).*
pīlĕum, i, n.	" pīlĕus, i, m.	*sort of hat.*
porrum, i, n.	" porrus, i, m.	*leek.*

4. One and the same substantive may have two forms of different declensions, as:—

ălĭmōnĭa, ae, f.	*and* ălĭmōnĭum, i, n.	*aliment.*
angĭportus, ūs, m.	" angĭportum, i, n.	*alley, lane.*
arcus, ūs, m.	" arcus,‡ i, m.	*a bow; an arch.*
buccĭna, ae, f.	" buccĭnum, i, n.	*a horn, trumpet.*
cingŭlum, i, m.	" cingŭla, ae, f.	*a girdle, belt.*
consortĭo, ōnis, f.	" consortĭum, i. n.	*partnership.*
delphĭnus, i, m.	" delphīn, īnis, m.	*a dolphin.*
ĕlĕphantus, i, m.	" ĕlĕphās, antis, m.	*an elephant.*
essĕdum, i, n.	" essĕda, ae, f.	*a war-chariot.*
hebdŏmăs, ădis, f.	" hebdŏmăda, ae, f.	*a week.*
jŭventus, ūtis, f.	" { jŭventa, ae, f. / jŭventās,§ ātis, f. }	*(the age of) youth.*
mendum, i, n.	" menda, ae, f.	*a fault, error.*
pălumbēs, is, m. & f.	{ pălumbus, i, m. / pălumba, ae, f. }	*the ring-dove.*
paupertās, ātis, f.	" paupĕrĭēs, ‖ ēi, f.	*poverty.*
pāvō, ōnis, m.	" pāvus, i, m.	*a peacock.*
pĕnum, i, n.	" { pĕnus, ūs & i, m. & f. / pĕnus, ŏris, n. }	*provisions.*
plebs, gen. plēbis, f.	" plēbēs, ēi, f.	*the common people.*
senectus, ūtis, f.	" senecta,¶ ae, f.	*old age.*
tăpētĕ, is, n.	" { tăpētum, i, n. / (tăpēs,) ētis, m. }	*tapestry; carpet.*

---

* In this list the form most generally in use is put first, without reference to gender.

† The measure is commonly denoted by *cubitum*, especially in the plural.

‡ The latter chiefly of the rainbow.   But this noun may also be referred to case 2.

§ Chiefly in poetry:—youth personified.

‖ The poetical form.

¶ This latter is poetical.

tŏnĭtrus, ūs, *m.* } *and* tŏnĭtrŭum, i. *n.*   *thunder.*
tŏnĭtrū, ūs, *n.* }

vespĕra, ae, *f.*   " { vesper(us), ĕri,* *m.* } *evening.*
                       { vesper, ĕris, *m.* }

5. A number of feminine nouns have two forms, one of the first, the other of the fifth declension † : —

barbărĭa, ae,   *and* barbărĭēs, ēi, *f.*   *barbarity.*
dūrĭtĭa, ae,   "   dūrĭtĭēs, ēi, *f.*   *hardness.*
luxŭrĭa, ae,   "   luxŭrĭēs, ēi, *f.*   *profusion, luxury.*
mācĕrĭa, ae,   "   mācĕrĭēs, ēi, *f.*   *a garden-wall.*
mātĕrĭa, ae,   "   mātĕrĭēs, ēi, *f.*   *matter, materials.*
mollĭtĭa, ae,   "   mollĭtĭēs, ēi, *f.*   *suppleness, softness.*
mŭrĭa, ae,   "   mŭrĭēs, ēi, *f.*   *salt liquor, brine.*
segnĭtĭa, ae,   "   segnĭtĭēs, ēi, *f.*   *sluggishness.*

6. Verbal substantives of the fourth declension with a secondary form in *um* : —

cōnātus, ūs, *m.*   *and* cōnātum, i, *n.*   *an effort, attempt.*
eventus, ūs, *m.*   "   eventum, i, *n.*   *an issue, event.*
praetextus, ūs, *m*   "   praetextum, i, *n.*   *an ornament, a pretext.*
rictus, ūs, *m.*   "   rictum, i, *n.*   *the jaws, open mouth.*

F. Among redundant nouns we must include those which, in the plural, assume another gender and another form, partly in addition to the regular form. Such are : —

1. MASCULINES, which in the plural havé an additional NEUTER form : —

jŏcus, i, *m.*   *a jest, joke ;*   *pl.* jŏci   *and* jŏca.
lŏcus, i, *m.*   *a place ;*   "   lŏci ‡   "   lŏca.
sĭbĭlus, i, *m.*   *a whistling sound ;*   "   sĭbĭli   "   sĭbĭla.§
Tartărus, i, *m.*   *the infernal region ;* "   Tartăra (*only*).

2. FEMININES with an additional NEUTER form in the plural : —

carbăsus, i, *f.*   *a curtain, sail ;*   *pl.* carbăsi *and* carbăsa.
margărīta, ăe, *f.* *a pearl ;*   " margărītae " margărīta, -orum.
ostrĕa, ae, *f.*   *an oyster ;*   " ostrĕae   " ostrĕa, -orum.

3. NEUTERS with plurals of different genders : —

balnĕum, i, *n.*   *a bath ;*   *pl.* balnĕa, *n. and* balnĕae,‖ *f.*
coelum, i, *n.*   *the sky, heavens ;* " coeli (*only*), *m.*

---

* Of this form there is only the Acc. *vespĕrum* and the Nom. commonly *vesper*, sometimes *vespĕrus*. The ablative is *vespĕre* and *vesperi*. But *vesper, ĕri*, m., the evening-star, is regular.
† But this form of the fifth declension is commonly used only in the Nom., Acc., and Abl.
‡ The masculine, chiefly of *places* or *passages* in books ; the neuter, of localities proper.
§ *Sibĭli* denotes single or isolated whistling or hissing sounds, and *sibĭla* continued hissing (chiefly in poetry).
‖ The latter more frequent, and in the sense of "public baths."

dēlīcium, i, *n.*	*delight ;*	*pl.* dēlīciae (*only*), *f.*
ēpŭlum, i, *n.*	*a public banquet ;*	" epŭlae (*only*), *f.*
frēnum, i, *n.*	*the bridle, rein ;*	" frēni, *m. and* frēna, *n.*
porrum,* i, *n.*	*leek ;*	" porri (*only*), *m.*
rastrum, i, *n.*	*a rake, harrow ;*	" rastri, *m. and* rastra, *n.*
sisĕr, ĕris, *n.*	*skirwort (a plant) ;*	" sisĕres (*only*), *m.*

EXERCISE 21.

How many friends have you ? — I have two good friends. — Have you eight good trunks ? — I have nine. — Has your friend ten good brooms ? — He has only three. — Has he two good ships ? — He has only one ? — How many hammers has the carpenter ? — He has only four. — How many shoes has the shoemaker ? — He has ten. — Has the young man ten good books ? — He has only five. — Has the painter seven good umbrellas ? — He has not seven, but one ? — How many corks have I ? — You have only three. — Has your neighbor our good bread ? — He has not ours, but that of his brother. — Has our horse any hay ? — It has some. — Has the friend of our tailor good buttons ? — He has some. — Has he gold buttons ? — He has no gold (buttons), but silver (ones). — How many oxen has our brother ? — He has no oxen. — How many coats has the young man of our neighbors ? — The young man of our neighbor has only one good coat, but that of your friend has three of them. — Has he our good rams ? — He has them. — Have I his ? — You have not his, but ours. — How many good rams have I ? — You have nine.

EXERCISE 22.

Who has our silver candlesticks ? — Our merchant's boy has them. — Has he our large birds ? — He has not ours, but those of the great Irishman. — Has the Italian great eyes or great feet ? — He has great eyes and great feet. — Who has great thread stockings ? — The Spaniard has some. — Has he any cheese ? — He has none ? — Has he corn ? — He has some. — What kind of corn has he ? — He has good corn. — What kind of rice has our cook ? — He has good rice. — What kind of pencils has our merchant ? — He has good pencils. — Has our baker good bread ? — He has good bread and wine. — Who has good cheese ? — Our neighbor has some. — Has our tailor's friend some cloth ? — He has some. — He has none. — What has he ? — He has our bad coats. — Who is thirsty ? — Nobody is thirsty; but the friend of our neighbor is sleepy. — Who has our iron knives ? — The Scotchman has them. — Has he them ? — He has them. — What kind of friends have you ? — I have good friends. — Is the friend of our Englishman right ? — He is neither right nor wrong. — Has he good little birds, and good little sheep ? — He has neither birds nor sheep. — What has the Italian ? — He has nothing.

---

* The singular *porrus*, m. is rarely used.

— Has our tailor's boy anything beautiful? — He has nothing beautiful, but something ugly. — What has he ugly? — He has an ugly dog. — Has he an ugly horse? — He has no horse. — What has our young friend? — He has nothing. — Has he a good book? — He has one? — Has he good salt? — He has none. — How many are there of us? — There are fifty of us. — How many are there among them? — There are a thousand among them. — How many are there of you? — There are twenty-five of us. — What sort of combs have you? — I have good combs.

Lesson XX. — PENSUM VICESIMUM.

Much, a good deal.	{ *Multŭm* (with the gen.). *Multŭs, ă, ŭm.* *Permultŭm* (a good deal).
Many, a large number.	{ *Multi, ae, ă.* *Multŭm* (with the gen. pl.). *Non pauci, ae, ă.** *Cōpĭa magna, ae, f.* (with the gen.).

A. Obs. The indefinite numeral *multus* is declined like *bonus,* and has the construction of adjectives. But instead of *multus* in agreement with its substantive, the neuter *multum* is often put partitively, and followed by the genitive, either singular in the sense of "much," or plural in the sense of "many." As

Much bread, money, sugar.	Múltum pánis, pecúniae, sácchări.
Many books, letters, candlesticks.	{ Múlti líbri, múltae epístŏlae, múlta candelábra. Múltum librórum, epistŏlárum, candelabrórum.
Many men.	{ Múlti hómĭnes (or hómĭnum).† Cópĭa (hómĭnum) mágna.
Many (i. e. men); many things.	Múlti; múlta (*neut. pl.*) = rês múltae.
Have you much good wine?	Éstne tíbi (habêsne) múltum víni bóni?
I have a good deal.	{ Ést míbi permúltum. Permúltum habeo.

---

* *Non pauci* is negative: "not a few." — *Copia* or *multĭtŭdo* (gen. *-dĭnis*) *magna,* "a large force, body, or multitude." Besides these, *frequentes* is also used in the sense of "numerous."

† *Multi hominum* is the same as the English "many among men," "many of the human family."

8

Have you much of the money?	Éstne tíbǐ (habêsne) múltum éjus pecúniae?
I have a good deal of it.	{ Ést mǐhi éjus sátis múltum. { Sátis múltum éjus hábeo.
Too much.	{ Nǐmǐus, ǎ, ǔm. { Nǐmǐs multǔm, nǐmǐum (with the 　gen.).
Too many.	{ Nǐmǐs multǐ, ae, ǎ. { Nǐmǐs multǔm or nǐmǐum (with the 　gen. pl.).
Too much bread, money, wine.	Nímis múltum (nímǐum) pânis, pe-cúnǐae, víni.
Too many men.	{ Nímis múlti hómǐnes (hómǐnum). { Nímǐum hómǐnum.
We.	Nōs. (Lesson IX. B.)
We have.	{ Nóbis ést (pl. súnt). { Nôs habêmus (tenêmus).
We are.	Nôs súmus.
We are hungry, thirsty.	(Nôs) ēsúrǐmus, sitǐmus.

B. Obs. The pronoun *nos*, like *ego, tu, ille*, &c., is commonly not expressed before the verb.

We are right (correct), wrong.	(Nôs) récte lóquǐmur, (nôs) errâ-mus.
We have not much money.	{ Nóbis nôn ést múltum pecúnǐae. { Nôn múltum pecúnǐae habêmus.
Ye or you (pl.).	Vōs. (Lesson IX. B.)
Ye (or you) have.	{ Vóbis ést (pl. súnt). { Vôs habêtis.
Ye (or you) are.	Vôs éstis.
Ye (or you) are hungry, thirsty.	(Vôs) ēsúrǐtis, sitǐtis.
Ye (or you) are right, wrong.	{ (Vôs) récte lŏquímǐni. { (Vôs) errâtis.
Ye (or you) are tired, sleepy.	(Vôs) éstis féssi, somnǐcǔlósi.
Enough.	{ Sǎtǐs, sǎt, adsǎtǐm (with the 　gen.); pl. sǎtǐs multǐ, ae, ǎ.

C. Obs. The adverb *sǎtǐs* is often employed substantively, like the pronouns *nǐhǐl, quǐd, quantum, multum*, &c., and is followed by the genitive singular or plural. E. g.

Enough bread, money, sugar.	Sátis (sát) pânis, pecúnǐae, sác-chari.*

---

* *Sǎtǐs* may, however, also stand adjectively; as *sǎtis ōtǐum, sǎtis consǐlǐum*, leisure, advice enough; so that we may likewise say, *Sǎtǐs pecúnǐa, sacchǎ-rum, homǐnes*, &c. — In questions, *satin'* for *satisne* is very common; as *Satin' salre?* Is all quite well? *Satin' plane audǐo?* Do I hear with sufficient dis-tinctness?

Men enough.
{ Sát (sátis) hóminum.
{ Sátis múlti hómines.

Looking-glasses enough.
{ Sátis speculôrum.
{ Sátis múlta spécula.

Have you money enough?
{ Éstne tíbi sátis pecúniae?
{ Habêsne sátis pecúniae?

I have only a little, but (yet) enough.
Párum tántum hábeo, séd (támen) sátis.

Little.
{ *Părŭm, paulŭm* (with the gen.).
{ *Pauxillum, pauxillŭlum.*

D. Obs. The construction of the adverb *parum* (*paulum*) is the same as that of *satis. Parum* is frequently used in the sense of " too little."

(But) little bread, money, sugar.
Párum (paúlum) pânis, pecúniae, sácchari.

Only a little, not much, but little.
{ *Nonnísī părŭm* (*paulŭm*).
{ *Paulŭm* (*părŭm*) *tantŭm.*
{ *Nŏn multum.* (All with the gen.)

A little (a small quantity).
Paulŭm, paulŭlŭm, ălĭquantŭlŭm, pauxillŭm.

A little wine, salt, bread.
Aliquántŭlum (paúlŭlum) víni, sá- lis, pânis.

Have you a little sugar?
{ Éstne tíbi aliquántŭlum sácchari?
{ Habêsne paúlŭlum sácchari?

I have.
Ést. — Hábeo.

You have but little courage.
{ Nôn ést tíbi múltum ánimi.
{ Párum tántum hábes fortitúdinis.

The courage (spirit, gallantry).
Ánimus, i, *m.*; fortitūdo, inis, *f.*; virtus, ūtis, *f.*

A few, few.
{ *Pauci, ae, ă* (pl.).
{ *Perpauci, ae, ă* (quite few).

(A) few men.
{ Paúci hómines (hóminum).
{ Paúci (*without* homines).

(A) few things.
Paúcae rês *or* paúcă (*neut. pl.*)

Few men have money enough.
Paúci (hómines) sátis pecúniae há- bent.

I have only a few things.
Paúca tántum hábeo.

Have you (ye) many friends?
Hăbētísne múltos amícos?

We have but few (of them).
{ Paúcos tántum (eôrum) habêmus.
{ Habêmus nôn nísi paúcos.

Of them.
Eôrum, eărum, eôrum.

Has the stranger much money?
Habétne peregrínus múltum pecú- niae?

He has but little (of it).
{ Párum tántum (éjus) hábet.
{ Nôn hábet (éjus) nísi párum (pauxíllum).

OF THE CLASSIFICATION OF SUBSTANTIVES.

E. Latin substantives are commonly divided into a number of general classes, of which some are peculiar to the language. The principle of division depends partly on their signification and partly on their derivation. These classes are: —

1. *Common Nouns,* or such as denote a genus or species comprehending a plurality of individuals or parts; as *hŏmo,* a man; *ĕquus,* a horse; *dŏmus,* a house.

Among common nouns may be included the *names of materials*: as *aurum,* gold; *sāl,* salt; *argentum,* silver.

2. *Collectives,* or those which, though singular in form, are plural in signification; as *pŏpŭlus,* a people; *sĕnātus,* a senate.

3. *Abstract Nouns,* or such as denote some *quality, activity,* or *mode of existence;* as *pulchritūdo, -ĭnis,* beauty; *pĭĕtas, -ātis,* f., piety; *infantia, ae,* f., infancy; *cursus, -ūs,* m., a course; *fămes, -is,* f., hunger.

The majority of these substantives are formed from adjectives or verbs. Those derived from adjectives commonly end in *ĭtas* (*ietas*), *ĭa, tūdo, ĭtĭa,* or *ēdo;* as *bŏnus — bŏnĭtas,* goodness; *vĕtus — vĕtustas,* oldness, age; *ēlĕgans — ēlĕgantia,* elegance; *mĭsĕr — mĭsĕrĭa,* misery; *longus — longĭtūdo,* length; *justus — justĭtĭa,* justice; *dulcis — dulcēdo,* sweetness.

4. *Proper Nouns,* or names of individuals, countries, and places; as *Cæsăr, Cĭcĕro, Virgĭlĭus; Itălĭa, Rōma.*

5. *Patronymics,* derived from proper names of persons, and indicative of extraction. These generally end in *ĭdes* (*īdes, ădes, iădes*) masculine, and in *is* (*ēis, ias*), *īne,* or *ione* * feminine. E. g. *Prĭămĭdēs,* a son of Priam; *Lāërtĭădēs,* a son of Laertes; *Nērĕis,* a daughter of Nereus; *Neptūnīnē,* a daughter of Neptune.

6. *Patrials* or *Gentiles,* derived from proper names of countries or places, and indicative of nationality; as *Anglus,* an Englishman; *Arabs,* an Arab; *Celta,* a Celt; *Trōs* (gen. *Trōis*), a native of Troy; *Trōăs, -ădis,* f., a woman born at Troy; *Arpīnās, -ātis,* a native of Arpinum.

The majority of Patrials are originally adjectives; as *Romānus, a, um; Syracusānus, a, um; Antĭŏchensis, is, e; Athēnĭensis, is, e,* &c.

---

* Patronymics in *dēs* and *nē* are of the first declension; as *Prĭamĭdēs, -dae, -dne, -den, -ĭle, -ĭā* (*dī*); *Neptunĭnē, -ēs, -ē, -en, -ē, -ī.* Those in *is* and *as,* of the third; as *Nērĭis, -ĭdis* or *-ĭdos,* &c.; *Thestĭas, -ĭdis,* f., &c.

7. *Diminutives*, or such as convey the idea of littleness, and sometimes of endearment; as *fraterculus*, a little brother; *litterlŭla*, a little (short) letter.

This class of substantives is very numerous in Latin. They are formed from other substantives, and end (according to the gender of their primitives) most commonly in *ŭlus, ŭla, ŭlum*, or *cŭlus, cŭla, cŭlum*; sometimes also in *ŏlus, a, um*; *ellus (illus), a, um*, or *uncŭlus, a, um*. The following, formed from words already known to the learner, may serve as examples:—

servŭlus, i, *m.*	*a little servant;*	*from*	servus.
hortŭlus, i, *m.*	" *garden;*	"	hortus.
pŭerlŭlus, ⎫			
puellus, ⎬ i, *m.*	" *boy;*	"	puer.
puellŭlus, ⎭			
infantŭlus, i, *m.*	" *infant;*	"	infans.
căpĭtŭlum, i, *n.*	" *head;*	"	caput.
opuscŭlum, i, *n.*	" *work;*	"	opus.
chartŭla, ae, f.	" *paper;*	"	charta.
aedicŭla, ae, *f.*	" *house;*	"	aedes.
diēcŭla, ae, *f.*	" *while;*	"	dies.
currĭcŭlum, i, *n.*	" *chariot;*	"	currus.
corcŭlum, i, *n.*	" *heart;*	"	cor.
cornĭcŭlum, i, *n.*	" *horn;*	"	cornu.
ocellus, i, *m.*	" *eye;*	"	oculus.
lĭbellus, i, *m.*	" *book;*	"	liber.
cultellus, i, *m.*	" *knife;*	"	culter.
cătellus, ⎫ i, *m.*	" *dog;*	"	canis.
cătŭlus, ⎭			
filiŏlus, i, *m.*	" *son;*	"	filius.
filiŏla, ae, *f.*	" *daughter;*	"	filia.
pileŏlus, i, *m.* ⎫	" *hat;*	"	pileus (um).
pileŏlum, i, *n.* ⎭			
băcillum, i, *n.*	" *stick;*	"	baculum.
villum, i, *n.*	" *wine;*	"	vinum.
lăpillus, i, *m.*	" *stone;*	"	lapis.
hŏmuncŭlus, i, *m.*	" *man:*	"	homo.
dŏmuncŭla, ae, *f.*	" *house;*	"	domus.
equŭlěus, i, *m.*	" *horse;*	"	equus.

8. *Amplificatives* (usually in *o*), which convey the notion of largeness and contempt; as *bucco, ōnis, m.* (from *bucca*, the cheek), a blubber-head; *nāso, ōnis, m.* (from *nāsus*, the nose), a man with a large nose.

9. *Verbal Nouns*, or such as are derived from verbs. These are either common or abstract; as *lector, ōris, m.*, a reader; *audītor, ōris, m.*, a hearer; *ămor, ōris, m.*, love; *clămor, ōris, m.*, a clamor; *contemptĭo, ōnis, f.*, and *contemptus, ūs, m.*, contempt; *gaudĭum, i, n.*, joy; *ornāmentum, i, n.*, an ornament.

EXERCISE 23.

Have you much coffee ? — I have only a little. — Has your friend much water ? — He has a great deal. — Has the foreigner much corn ? — He has not much. — What has the American ? — He has much sugar. — What has the Russian ? — He has much salt.— Have we much rice ? — We have but little. — What have we ? — We have much wine, much water, and many friends. — Have we much gold ? — We have only a little, but enough. — Have you many boys ? — We have only a few. — Has our neighbor much hay ? — He has enough. — Has the Dutchman much cheese ? — He has a great deal. — Has this man courage ? — He has none. — Has that foreigner money ? — He has not a great deal, but enough. — Has the painter's boy candles ? — He has some. — Have we good letters ? — We have some. — We have none. — Has the joiner good bread ? — He has some. — He has none. — Has he good honey ? — He has none. — Has the Englishman a good horse ? — He has one. — What have we ? — We have good horses. — Who has a beautiful house ? — The German has one. — Has the Italian many pretty looking-glasses ? — He has a great many; but he has only a little corn. — Has my good neighbor the same horse which you have ? — He has not the same horse, but the same carriage. — Has the Turk the same ships that we have ? — He has not the same ; he has those of the Russians.

EXERCISE 24.

How many servants have we ? — We have only one, but our brothers have three of them. — What knives have you ? — We have iron knives. — What bag has the peasant ? — He has a thread bag. — Has the young man our long (*longas*) letters ? — He has them not. — Who has our pretty notes ? — The father of the sailor has them. — Has the carpenter his nails ? — The carpenter has his iron nails, and the hatmaker his paper hats. — Has the painter beautiful gardens ? — He has some, but his brother has none. — Have you many glasses ? — We have only a few. — Have you enough wine ? — We have enough of it. — Has anybody my brooms ? — Nobody has them. — Has the friend of your hatmaker our combs or yours ? — He has neither yours nor ours ; he has his. — Has your boy my note or yours ? — He has that of his brother. — Have you my stick ? — I have not yours, but that of the merchant. — Have you my gloves ? — I have not yours, but those of my good neighbor.

EXERCISE 25.

Has your little servant my broom ? — He has it not. — Who has my little paper ? — Our neighbor's little son has it. — Has any one my little daughter's little book ? — Nobody has your little daughter's little book, but somebody has her little carriage. — What has the little boy ? — He has the little work of his friend. — Have you any little houses ? — I have ten little houses, and six young (little) horses. — Who has my little stick ? — Your little brother has it. — Is any one sleepy? — The little daughter of the tailor is sleepy. — What has that little man? — He has his little gardens, and his little knives. — Is he a Roman? — No, sir, he is not a Roman, but an Arab. — Are you a Celt? — I am not a Celt, but a German. — How many little eyes has that child (*infantŭlus*)? — It has two. — How many little hats have you? — I have but one. — Who is right (correct)? — My little son is right. — Is any one wrong? — The young man (*adolescentŭlus*) is wrong.

Lesson XXI. — PENSUM UNUM ET VICESIMUM.

The pepper.	Pīpĕr, ĕris, *n.*
The meat (flesh).	Căro, *gen.* carnis, *f.*
The meat (food).	Cĭbŭs, i, *m.*; esca, ae, *f.*
The vinegar.	Ăcētum, i, *n.*; vīnum ăcĭdum, i, *n.*
The beer.	Cerevisĭa (cervisĭa), ae, *f.*
The shirt.	*Indŭsĭum, i, *n.*; tŭnĭca lintĕa, ae, *f.*
The leg.	Crūs, *gen.* crūris, *n.*; pēs, pĕdis, *m.* (the foot).
The head.	Căpŭt, ĭtis, *n.*
The head (i. e. natural talent).	Ingĕnĭum, i, *n.*; indŏles, is, *f.*
The arm.	Bracchĭum, i, *n.*
The heart.	Cŏr, *gen.* cordis, *n.*
The heart (i. e. soul).	Pectŭs, ŏris, *n.*; ănĭmus, i, *m.*
The month.	Mensis, is, *m.*
The work.	Ŏpŭs,* ĕris, *n.*
The volume.	Vŏlūmĕn, ĭnis, *n.*; tŏmus, i, *n.*
The florin.	*Flōrēnus, i, *m.*
The dollar (crown).	*Thălērus, i, *m.*
The kreutzer (a coin).	*Kreutzērus,† i. *m.*
The shilling.	*Schillingus, i, *m.*
A few, some few.	{ Alĭquŏt (indeclinable). Nonnullī, ae, ă. Paucī, ae, ă; perpaucī, ae, ă (very few).

A. Obs. The proper equivalent for the English "few" is *paucī, ae, ă,* and is opposed to "many." — Instead of this, *nonnulli* and *alĭquŏt* may be used in the sense of "some, some few, several."

---

* This word, like the English, signifies both *work* or *labor* in general, and also a literary production.
† I put these modern coins with a Latin termination, instead of the more incouvenient circumlocution *nummus nomen gerens kreutzer, schilling.*

Have you a few books ?	{ Súntne tíbi áliquot líbri ? { Habêsne áliquot líbros ?
I have a few (some few).	{ Súnt míhi áliquot. { Nonnúllos hábeo.
He has a few.	{ Súnt éi áliquot (nonnúlli). { Nonnúllos (áliquot) hábet.
I have only (but) a few knives.	{ Pauci tántum cúltri míhi súnt. { Cúltros hábeo nôn nísi paúcos.
You have only a few.	{ Paúci modo (tántum) tíbi súnt. { Hábes nôn nísi paúcos.
Few men.	Paúci hómines, paúci.
Few things.	Paúcae res, paúca (*n. pl.*).
Very few (men), things.	Perpaúci, perpaúca.
Other, the other, another.	{ *Altĕr, ĕra, ĕrŭm* (of two). { *Álĭŭs, ă, ŭd* (of several).

B. Obs. Altĕr is opposed to *ūnus* or another *alter*, and signifies *the other of two. Alīus,* on the other hand, is applied to several or many, and is *another* (of many). These words are thus inflected:—

S. altĕr, *the other.*   P. altĕrī, *the others.*

Nom. altĕr	altĕră	altĕrŭm	altĕrī,	altĕrae,	altĕră
Gen.	altĕríus		altĕrōrŭm	altĕrārŭm	-ōrŭm
Dat.	altĕrī			altĕrīs	
Acc. altĕrŭm	altĕrăm	altĕrŭm	altĕrōs	altĕrās	ultĕră
Voc. altĕr	altĕră	altĕrŭm	altĕrī	altĕrae	altĕră
Abl. altĕrō	altĕrā	altĕrō.		altĕrīs.	

S. ălĭŭs, *another.*   P. ălĭi, *others.*

Nom. ălĭŭs	ălĭă	ălĭŭd	ălĭī	ălíae	ălĭă
Gen.	ălíŭs		ălĭōrŭm	-ūrŭm	-ōrŭm
Dat.	ălĭī			ălĭīs	
Acc. ălĭŭm	ălĭăm	ălĭŭd	ălĭōs	ălĭŭs	ălĭă
Voc. ălĭŭs	ălĭă	ălĭŭd	ălĭī	ălíae	ălĭă
Abl. ălĭō	ălĭā	ălĭō.		alĭīs	

The other horse (of two).	{ Álter équus. { Álter equôrum *or* ex équis.
The other horses (of two troops).	Équi áltĕri.
Another horse.	Álĭus équus.
Other horses.	Álĭi équi.
Another thing.	Rês álĭa, (*or simply*) álĭud. (Lesson XV. *H.*)
Other things.	Rês álĭae, (*or simply*) álĭa.
Have you another horse ?	{ Éstne tíbi álĭus équus ? { Habêsne állum équum ?
I have another.	{ Ést míhi álĭus. { Hábeo álĭum.

Have you the other horse ?	{ Éstne tíbi álter equôrum ?
	{ Habêsne áltĕrum éx équis ?
I have it not.	Nôn ést. Nôn hábeo.

		Nom.	Acc.
	Masc.	nullíus álíus	nullúm álíum.
No (none) other.	Fem.	nullá álíǎ	nullǎm álíǎm.
	Neut.	nullúm álíúd	nullúm álíúd.
	Masc.	nulli álíi	nullós álíos.
No other.	Fem.	nullae álíae	nullás álíás.
	Neut.	nullá álíǎ	nullá álíǎ.

I have no other horse.	{ Ést míhi núllus équus álíus (or
	álíôrum equôrum).
	Álíum équum núllum hábeo.
I have no other.	Míhi ést álíus (álíôrum) núllus.
	Álíum núllum hábeo.
Have you other horses ?	Núm tíbi súnt équi álti ?
	Númquid hábes équos álíos ?
I have no others.	Súnt míhi álti núlli.
	Núllos álíos hábeo.
I have some others.	Súnt míhi álti quídam.
	Nonnúllos álíos hábeo.
Has he another shirt ?	Éstne éi indúsíum álíud ?
	Habétne (ílle) indúsíum álíud ?
He has another.	Ést (éi álíud).
	Hábet álíud.
He has no other.	Ést éi álíud núllum.
	Núllum álíud hábet.

C. Obs. When the words *alter* and *alius* are repeated in opposition to each other, the first *alter* signifies " the one," and the second " the other"; and the first *alius* " one," and the second " the other."

The one hates the other.	Álter (or ûnus) áltĕrum ôdít.
One (of many or of two parties) hates the other.	Álíus álíum ôdít.
They hate each other.	Álti álíos odérunt.
It is one thing to asperse and another to accuse.	Álíud ést maledícĕre álíud accusâre.

The rest (the others).	{ *Rèlíqui, ae, ǎ.*
	{ *Cētēri, ae, ǎ.*
Have you the other (the rest of the) horses ?	{ Súntne tíbi équi cétĕri ?
	{ Habêsne équos cétĕros (rélíquos) ?
I have them not.	Nôn súnt. Nôn hábeo.
What have the rest (the others) ?	{ Quíd hábent cétĕri ?
	{ Quíd ést cétĕris (rélíquis) ?
They have nothing.	Níhil hábent.
Has he the other things (i. e. the rest, remainder) ?	Án hábet cétĕra (rélíqua) ? (Vide Lesson XV. *H.*)
He has them not.	(Éa) nôn hábet.

OF ORDINAL NUMERALS.

D. Ordinal numerals contain the answer to the question *Quŏtŭs, ă, ŭm?* " Which of a certain number, rank, or place?" as *prīmus*, the first; *sĕcundŭs*, the second; *dēcĭmŭs*, the tenth. They are all of them adjectives of the first and second declensions, and inflected like *bŏnus, a, um.* Examples:—

Have you the first or the second book?	Éstne tíbi líber primus án sĕcúndus? Útrum líbrum hábes primum ín sĕcúndum?
I have the third.	Ést míhi tértíus. Tértium hábeo.
Which volume have you?	Quótum ést tíbi volúmĕn? Quótum volúmĕn hábes?
I have the fifth.	Ést míhi quíntum. Quíntum hábeo.
Which note have you?	Quóta ést tíbi schédŭla? Quótam schédŭlam hábes?
I have the fifth.	Ést míhi quínta. Hábeo quíntam.
Which is the hour (of the day)?	Quóta hôra ést?
It is ten o'clock (the tenth).	Hôra décima ést.*
What day of the month is it?	Quótus ést díes ménsis?
It is the sixth.	Séxtus ést. Díes ést ménsis séxtus.

E. Adverbial numerals correspond to the question *Quŏtĭens?* or *Quŏtĭēs?* " How many times?" The answer then is either, generally, *tŏtĭens* (or *tŏtĭēs*), so many times; *ălĭquŏtĭens* (or *-ēs*), several times; or definitely, *sĕmĕl,* once; *bĭs,* twice; *dēcĭēs,* ten times, &c.

F. The following table exhibits a list of the ordinals of the Latin language, and of the corresponding adverbial numerals:—

ORDINALS.		NUMERAL ADVERBS.	
1.	primŭs, ă, ŭm, *the first.* prĭor, prĭus, ōris, (of two).	sĕmĕl,	*once.*
2.	sĕcundus, a, um, *the second.* alter, ĕra, ĕrum (of two).	bĭs,	*twice.*

---

* Among the ancient Romans the tenth hour was *four* o'clock, P. M., the first being our six, A. M. The division of the days of the month was likewise different from ours (as will be shown hereafter). In writing and speaking the Latin, however, it is now customary to follow the modern method. It is necessary to add here, that " *at* an hour," " *on* a day " (or, more generally, " time when "), must be put in the ablative; as *horā primā,* at one o'clock; *tertio Aprilis,* on the third of April. A date may be written thus:— *Romae, tertio Octobris, a. p. Chr.* MDCCCLVI.; Rome, October 8d, 1856.

	ORDINALS.		NUMERAL ADVERBS.	
3.	tertius, a, um,	the third.	tĕr,	thrice.
4.	quartus, a, um,	the fourth.	quătĕr,	four times.
5.	quintus, a, um,	the fifth.	quinquĭĕs,	five times.
6.	sextus, a, um,	the sixth, &c.	sexĭēs,	six times, &c.
7.	septĭmus, a, um.		septĭēs.	
8.	octāvus, a, um.		octĭēs.	
9.	nōnus, a, um.		nŏvĭēs.	
10.	dĕcĭmus, a, um.		dĕcĭēs.	
11.	undĕcĭmus, a, um.		undĕcĭēs.	
12.	dŭŏdĕcĭmus, a, um.		dŭŏdĕcĭēs.	
13.	tertĭus dĕcĭmus, a, um.		terdĕcĭēs or trĕdĕcĭēs.	
14.	quartus dĕcĭmus, a, um.		quaterdĕcĭēs or quattuordĕcĭēs.	
15.	quintus dĕcĭmus, a, um.		quinquĭesdĕcĭes or quindĕcĭēs.	
16.	sextus dĕcĭmus, a, um.		sexĭesdĕcĭēs or sēdĕcĭēs.	
17.	septĭmus dĕcĭmus, a, um.		septĭesdĕcĭēs.	
18.	{ octāvus dĕcĭmus, a, um. { dŭŏdevicēsĭmus, a, um.		octĭēsdĕcĭēs. dŭŏdĕvicĭēs.	
19.	{ nōnus dĕcĭmus, a, um. { undēvicēsĭmus, a, um.		nŏvĭēsdĕcĭēs. undēvicĭēs.	
20.	{ vicēsĭmus, a, um. } { vigēsĭmus, a, um. }		vicĭēs.	
21.	{ vicēsĭmus primus,* a, um. { ūnus et vicēsĭmus, a, um.		sĕmĕl et vicĭēs. vicĭēs (et) sĕmĕl.	
22.	{ alter et vicēsĭmus, a, um. { vicēsĭmus et alter, a, um.		bĭs et vicĭēs. vicĭēs (et) bĭs.	
23.	{ tertĭus et vicēsĭmus, a, um { vicēsĭmus tertĭŭs, a, um.		tĕr et vicĭēs. vicĭēs (et) tĕr.	
28.	{ vicēsĭmus octavus, a, um. { dŭŏdētricēsĭmus,† a, um.		octĭēs et vicĭēs. vicĭēs (et) octĭēs.	
29.	{ nōnus et vicēsĭmus, a, um. { undētricēsĭmus, a, um.		nŏvĭēs et vicĭēs. vicĭēs (et) nŏvĭēs.	
30.	{ tricēsĭmus, a, um. } { trigēsĭmus, a, um. }		tricĭes.	
40.	quădrāgēsĭmus, a, um.		quadrāgĭes.	
50.	quinquāgēsĭmus, a, um.		quinquāgĭes.	
60.	sexāgēsĭmus, a, um.		sexāgĭes.	
70.	septuāgēsĭmus, a, um.		septuāgĭes.	
80.	octōgēsĭmus, a, um.		octōgĭes.	

* The rule respecting the juxtaposition of ordinals is, that *either the smaller numeral should precede the greater* WITH "*et*," or *the greater the smaller* WITHOUT "*et*," as in this instance. To this, however, those from 13 to 19 must be regarded as exceptions, *tertius decimus* or *tertius et decimus*, &c. being here the only admissible forms. For 21st, ŪNUS *et vicēsĭmus*, fem. ŪNA *et vicēsĭma* (or, contracted, *unetvicēsĭma*), are more common than PRĪMUS *et vicēsĭmus*, &c. So also ALTER *et vicēsĭmus* (*tricēsĭmus*, *quădrāgēsĭmus*, &c.) better than SĒCUNDUS *et vicēsĭmus*, &c.

† For 28, 38, &c., 29, 39, 99, &c., the subtractive expressions *dŭŏdētricēsĭmus*, *dŭŏdĕquădrāgēsĭmus*, &c., *undētricēsĭmus*, *undĕquădrāgēsĭmus*, *undĕcentēsĭmus*, &c., are used, without any change of *duo* or *un*, precisely as in cardinals.

	ORDINALS.	NUMERAL ADVERBS.
90.	nōnāgēsĭmus, ă, ŭm.	nongĭēs, *ninety times.*
100.	centēsĭmus, a, um.	centĭes.
200.	dŭcentēsĭmus, a, um.	dŭcentĭes.
300.	trĕcentēsĭmus, a, um.	trĕcentĭes.
400.	quădringentēsĭmus, a, um.	quădringentĭes.
500.	quingentēsĭmus, a, um.	quingentĭes.
600.	sexcentēsĭmus, a, um.	sexcentĭes.
700.	septingentēsĭmus, a, um.	septingentĭes.
800.	octingentēsĭmus, a, um.	octingentĭes.
900.	nongentēsĭmus, a, um.	nongentĭes.
1,000.	millēsĭmus, a, um.	millĭes.
2,000.	bis millēsĭmus, a, um.	bis millĭes.
3,000.	tĕr millēsĭmus, a, um.	tĕr millĭes.
10,000.	dĕcĭēs millēsĭmus, a, um.	dĕcĭes millĭes.
100,000.	centĭēs millēsĭmus, a, um.	centĭes millĭes.
1,000,000.	dĕcĭēs centĭēs millēsĭmus, a, um.	millĭes millĭes.

EXERCISE 26.

Have you a few knives? — I have a few. — Have you many rams?
— I have only a few. — Has the friend of the great painter many
looking-glasses? —He has only a few. — Have you a few florins? —
I have a few. — How many florins have you? — I have ten. — How
many kreutzers has your servant? — He has not many, he has only
two. — Have the men the beautiful glasses of the Italians? — The
men have them not, but we have them. — What have we? — We
have much money. — Have you the carriage of the Dutchman or that
of the German? — I have neither the one nor the other. — Has the
peasant's boy the fine or the ugly letter? — He has neither the one
nor the other. — Has he the gloves of the merchant or those of his
brother? — He has neither the one nor the other. — Which gloves
has he? — He has his own. — Have we the horses of the English or
those of the Germans? — We have neither the one nor the other. —
Have we the umbrellas of the Spaniards? — We have them not; the
Americans have them. — Have you much pepper? — I have only a
little, but enough. — Have you much vinegar? — I have only a little.
— Have the Russians much meat? — The Russians have a great deal,
but the Turks have only a little. — Have you no other pepper? — I
have no other. — Have I no other beer? — You have no other. —
Have we no other good friends? — We have no others. — Has the
sailor many shirts? — He has not many; he has only two. — Have
you a wooden leg? — I have not a wooden leg, but a good heart. —
Has this man a good head? — He has a good head and a good heart.
— How many arms has that boy? — He has only one; the other is
of wood. — What kind of head (i. e. talents) has your boy? — He
has a good head.

EXERCISE 27.

Which volume have you? — I have the first. — Have you the second volume of my work? — I have it. — Have you the third or the

fourth book ? — I have neither the one nor the other. — Have we the
fifth or sixth volume ? — We have neither the one nor the other. —
Which volume have we ? — We have the seventh. — What day of
the month is it ? — It is the eighth. — Is it not (*nonne*) the eleventh ?
— No, sir, it is the tenth. — Have the Spaniards many crowns ? —
The Spaniards have only a few; but the English have a great many.
— Who has our crowns ? — The French have them. — Has the youth
much head (i. e. talent) ? — He has not much head, but much courage.
— How many arms has the man ? — He has two. — How many shirts
has he ? — He has only two. — He has six good and ten bad (ones).

EXERCISE 28.

Have you the crowns of the French or those o. the English ? — I
have neither those of the French nor those of the English, but those
of the Americans. — Has the German a few kreutzers ? — He has a
few. — Has he a few florins ? — He has six of them. — Have you
another stick ? — I have another. — What other stick have you ? — I
have another iron stick. — Have you a few gold candlesticks ? — We
have a few. — Have these men vinegar ? — These men have none,
but their friends have some. — Have our boys candles ? — Our boys
have none, but the friends of our boys have some. — Have you some
other bags ? — I have no others. — Have you any other cheeses ? —
I have some others. — Have you other meat ? — I have no other.
— Has your friend many other books ? — He has but very few
others. — How many shillings has that boy ? — He has only five. —
Have you the other horse ? — I have it not. — Have they the other
(the rest) of the books ? — They have them. — Have you the other
things (the remainder) ? — I have it not. — What is the hour ? — It
is twelve o'clock. — Is it not five ? — No, sir, it is only four.

Lesson XXII. — PENSUM ALTERUM ET VICE-SIMUM.

The part, portion.	Pars, *gen.* partis, *f.*
The volume, tome.	{ Völümĕn, Inis, *n.* { Tŏmŭs, i, *m.*
Have you the first or third tome of my work ?	Útrum óperis méi tómum hábes primum án tértium ?
I have both.	Ámbos (utrúmque) hábeo.
Both.	{ Ambō, ambae, ambŏ. { Uterquĕ, utrăquĕ, utrumquĕ.

A. Obs. Ambō is "both," considered as united; *uterque*,
"both" in the sense of "each of the two," "the one as well as
the other." The former is inflected like *duo*, and the latter like
uter. (Cf. Lesson XII. A.) Thus : —

G   9

		Masc.	Fem.	Neut.
Nom.	both	ambō	ambae	ambō
Gen.	of both	ambōrŭm	ambārŭm	ambōrŭm
Dat.	to both	ambōbŭs	ambābŭs	ambōbŭs
Acc.	both	ambōs (ambō)	ambās	ambō
Voc.	O both	ambō	ambae	ambō
L.	with both	ambōbŭs	ambābŭs	ambōbŭs.

SINGULAR.

	Masc.	Fem.	Neut.
Nom.	ŭterquĕ	utrăque	utrumquĕ
Gen.		utrīusquĕ	
Dat.		utrīquĕ	
Acc.	utrumquĕ	utramque	utrumquĕ
Voc.	uterquĕ	utrăquĕ	utrumquĕ
Abl.	utrōquĕ	utrāquĕ	ntrōquĕ.

PLURAL.

	Masc.	Fem.	Neut.
Nom.	utrīquĕ	utraequĕ	utrăquĕ
Gen.	utrōrumquĕ	utrārumquĕ	utrōrumquĕ
Dat.		utrīsquĕ	
Acc.	utrosquĕ	utrasquĕ	utrăquĕ
Voc.	utrīquĕ	utraequĕ	utrăquĕ
Abl.		utrīsquĕ.	

REMARKS.

1. *Ambō*, like *duŏ, trēs, dŭcenti*, &c., is a natural plural, and consequently wants the singular.

2. *Uterque*, although involving a plural signification, is commonly put in the singular; as *uterque polus*, both poles; *utrăque fortūna*, both good and bad fortune; *uterque părens*, both parents. Sometimes, however, also in the plural; as *utrīque Dionysii*, both the Dionysiuses; *utrăque oppĭda*, both towns.

3. The plural *utrīque* is regularly used, when two parties or collective bodies are spoken of; as *Utrīque* (i. e. plebs et senatus) *victorĭam crudelĭter exercebant*, They both (i.e. the people and the senate) made a cruel use of their (respective) victories.

4. The remaining correlatives of *ŭtĕr*, "which of (the) two?" are: *altĕr*, "the one of two." *or* "the other" (Lesson XXI. *B.*); *altĕrŭter*, "one or other of two," "the one or the other"; *neuter*, "neither of the two"; *ŭtervis* and *uterlĭbet*, "any one of the two you please," "either of the two." All these compounds of *uter* are inflected like the simple pronoun, except *altĕrŭter*, of which either both components are declined separately, as *alter ŭter, altĕra utra, altĕrum utrum*, gen. *altĕrīus utrīus*, &c., or the last only, as *altĕrŭter, altĕrutra, altĕrutrum*, gen. *altĕrutrĭus*, &c.

Have you my book or my paper?	Útrum hábes méum lībrum án méam chártam ?
I have both.	Ámbō (utrúmque) hábeo.

B. RULE. — An adjective, participle, or pronoun, belonging to two or more nouns, is generally put in the plural. Its gender is determined according to the following rules : —

1. When the substantives are of *the same gender*, the adjective, participle, or pronoun agrees with them in gender. E. g. *Pater mihi et frater mortui sunt*, My father and brother are dead. *Soror ejus et mater mortuae sunt*, His sister and mother are dead.

2. When substantives denoting *living beings* are of *different genders*, the adjective is masculine rather than feminine, and feminine rather than neuter. E. g. *Pater mihi et mater mortui sunt*, My father and mother are dead. *Soror tua et ejus mancipium (neut.) inventae sunt*, Your sister and her slave have been found.*

3. When substantives denoting *inanimate objects* are of different genders, the adjective is neuter. E. g. *Libros atque mensas multa pulchraque habeo*, I have many fine books and tables. *Labor voluptasque dissimilia naturā sunt*, Labor and pleasure are naturally unlike.

4. When there is a *mixture* of animate and inanimate objects, the adjective either assumes the gender of the animate object, or is put into the neuter. E. g. *Famulos et domos bonos multosque habeo*, I have good servants and houses, and many of them. *Canes mihi et cornua venatica multa eaque bona sunt*, I have many dogs and hunting-horns, and those good ones.

5. The adjective, however, frequently agrees (in gender, number, and case) with the nearest noun, and is understood with the rest. E. g. *Amor tuus ac judicium (sc. tuum) de me*, Your affection and (your) opinion of me. *Libros atque mensas multas easque pulchras habeo.*

Which of us (of you, of them) two has that book ?	Úter nóstrum (véstrum, eórum) líbrum íllum hábet ?
Neither of us (of you, of them) has it.	Neúter nóstrum (véstrum, eórum) éum hábet.
One or the other of us (of you, of them) has it.	Álterúter nóstrum (véstrum, eórum) éum hábet.
Both of us (of you, of them) have it.	Utérque nóstrum (véstrum, eórum) éum hábet. Nôs (vôs, ílli) ámbo éum hábent.
Which of the two books have you ?	Útrum† líbrum (librôrum) hábes ?
I have either, neither, both, of them.	Alterútrum, neútrum, utrúmque eórum (éos ámbos) hábeo.
Which of the two pens has your brother ?	Útram hábet fráter túus pénnam (pennârum) ?

---

* *Inventae*, if the slave is a female, but *inventi* if a male.

† From this we must distinguish the interrogative *útrum*, which has no influence upon the construction of other words, except as the sign of a double question.

He has both.	{ Utrámque (utrásque) hábet. { Ámbas hábet.
Have you my light or my stick ?	Utrúmne hábes méum lúmen án báculum ?
I have them both ?	{ Utrúmque (útraque) hábeo. { Hábeo éa ámbo.
Which of the two sets of books have you ?	Útri súnt tíbi líbri (librôrum) ?
I have both.	Utríque. (Vide *A*. Rem. 3.)
Still, yet.	*Etïamnŭm, adhŭc* * (adverbs).
Some or *any more.*	{ SING. *Etïamnŭm (adhŭc) ălĭquantŭm.* { PLUR. *Etïamnŭm (adhŭc) ălĭquŏ (or* *ălĭquōs, -quās, -quŏ).*
Left, remaining.	*Rĕlĭquŭs, ă, ŭm.*
Some *or* any more bread, money, wine.	{ Etiámnum (ádhuc) aliquántum pânis, pecúnïae, víni. { Aliquántum pânis, pecúnïae, víni réliquum.

Some or any more books, letters, glasses.	{ Ádhuc (etïámnum) áliquot líbros, epístolas, vâsa vítrëa.
	 { Áliquos líbros réliquos.
	  Áliquas epístolas réliquas.
	  Áliqua vâsa vítrëa réliqua.

Have you any more wine, water, bread (left) ?	{ Éstne tíbi ádhuc aliquántum víni, áquae, pânis ? { Habêsne aliquántum víni, áquae, pânis réliquum ?
I have some more (left).	{ Ést míhi ádhuc aliquántum. { Hábeo nonnúllum réliquum.
Has he any more books ?	{ Écqui tíbi súnt ádhuc (etiámnum) líbri ? { Habêsne áliquos (áliquot) líbros réliquos ?
I have some more (left).	{ Súnt míhi ádhuc áliquot. { Hábeo nonnúllos réliquos.
Have I any more candlesticks ?	{ Écqua (númqua) míhi súnt ádhuc candēlábra ? { Án égo áliquot candēlábra réliqua hábeo ?
You have no more (left).	{ Núlla (nôn) súnt. { Núlla réliqua hábes.
Not any more, no more.	{ *Nĭhĭl amplĭus* (with the gen.). { *Nullŭs (ă, ŭm) rĕlĭquŭs (ă, ŭm).*

---

* The primary signification of *adhuc* (= *ad* + *huc*) is "hitherto," "thus far," "as yet." There is good authority, however, for its secondary senses of *praetérëa,* "besides," and *etïámnum,* "yet," "as yet," "still."

Has he any more bread, water, vinegar?	Númquid ést éi ádhuc pânis, áquae, acéti? Núm ílle aliquántum pânis, áquac, acéti réliquum hábet?
He has no more (left).	Ést éi níhil réliquum. Níhil éjus ámplius hábet.
I have no more books.	Líbri míhi núlli réliqui súnt. Níhil ámplius librôrum hábeo
I have no more letters.	Epístŏlae míhi núllae réliquae súnt. Níhil ámplius epistolárum hábeo.
I have no more looking-glasses.	Spécŭla míhi núlla réliqua sunt. Níhil speculôrum ámplius hábeo.
Not much more (left).	*Părum (paulum) rĕlĭquum.* *Non (haud) multum amplĭus* (with the gen. sing. and pl.)
Not many more (left). *(Only a few left).*	*Non multĭ (ae, ă) rĕlĭquĭ (ae, ă).* *Nŏnnĭsi paucĭ (ae, ă) rĕlĭquĭ (ae, ă).*
Have you much more wine?	Númquid ést tíbi ádhuc múltum víni? Núm múltum hábes víni réliquum?
I have not much more.	Ést míhi éjus réliquum nôn nísi párum. Haûd múltum ámplius hábeo.
Have you many more books?	Núm tíbi etiámnum múlti líbri súnt? Núm líbros múltos ádhuc hábes réliquos?
I have not many more.	Paúci tántum míhi réliqui súnt. Nôn múltos réliquos hábeo.
Has he one more book?	Éstne éi ádhuc únus líber réliquus? Habétne etiámnum únum líbrum?
He has one more good book.	Ést éi ádhuc únus líber bónus réliquus. Hábet etiámnum únum líbrum bónum.
Have we a few more knives?	Habemúsne ádhuc áliquot líbros (réliquos)?
We have a few more.	Habêmus (ádhuc) nonnúllos réliquos.
Have they any more letters?	Écquae íis ádhuc súnt epístŏlae?
They have a few (some) more.	Súnt íis ádhuc áliquot. Hábent nonnúllas réliquas.
Has he a few good goblets (left)?	Súntne éi ádhuc áliquot bóna pócŭla? Habétne nonnúlla bóna pócŭla réliqua?

9*

He has a few more (left).   { Súnt éi ádhuc áliquot.
                                 { Hábet nonnúlla réliqua.*

EXERCISE 29.

Which volume of his work have you? — I have the second. — How
many tomes has this work? — It has three. — Have you my work, or
that of my brother? — I have both. — Has the foreigner my comb or
my knife? — He has both. — Have you our bread or our cheese? —
I have both. — Have you my glass or that of my friend? — I have
neither the one nor the other. — Have we any more hay? — We
have some more. — Has our merchant any more pepper? — He has
some more. — Has he any more candles? — He has some more. —
Have you any more coffee? — We have no more coffee, but we have
some more vinegar. — Has the German any more water? — He has
no more water, but he has some more meat. — Have we any more
gold ribbons? — We have no more gold ribbons, but we have some
more silver (ribbons). — Has our friend any more sugar? — He
has no more. — Have I any more beer? — You have no more. —
Has your young man any more friends? — He has no more.

EXERCISE 30.

Has your brother one more horse? — He has one more. — Have
you one more? — I have one more. — Has the peasant one more ox?
— He has one more. — Have you a few more gardens? — We have
a few more. — What have you more? — We have a few good ships,
and a few good sailors more. — Has our brother a few more friends?
— He has a few more. — Have I a little more money? — You have a
little more. — Have you any more courage? — I have no more. —
Have you much more money? — I have much more, but my brother
has no more. — Has he enough salt? — He has not enough. — Have
we buttons enough? — We have not enough. — Has the good son of
your good tailor buttons enough? — He has not enough. — Which of
you two has some money left? — Neither of us has any left. — One
or the other of us has a good deal of it left. — Has the sailor my stick
or my sack? — He has neither (*neutrum*) of the two. — Have you my
hat or my coat? — I have both. — Which of you (three) has my
paper? — I have it not. — Has the youth anything left? — He has
nothing left. — Have you many more candles? — I have not many
more.

---

* Instead of *reliquus* (*a, um*) *est,* and *reliqui* (*ae, a*) *sunt,* the compounds of
sum, superest and *supersunt,* may be employed in a similar sense. E. g. *Super-
estne tibi aliquantum aquae, vini, pecuniae?* — *Superest.* — *Non superest.* — *Libri
mihi multi iique boni supersunt,* &c.

Lesson XXIII. — PENSUM TÉRTIUM ET VICE-SIMUM.

As much — as.	Tăm mŭltam — quăm (mŭltŭm). Tantŭm — quantŭm* (quăm), (with the gen.).
As many — as.	Tăm multĭ, ae, a — quăm multĭ, ae, a. Tŏt (indecl.) — quŏt (indecl.).
As much bread as wine.	Tántum (tám múltum) pânis, quántum (quám múltum *or* quám) víni.
As many men as children.	Tót hómĭnes quót† lĭbĕri. Tám múlti hómĭnes, quám (múlti) lĭberi.
Have you as much gold as silver?	Habêsne tántum aúri, quántum (quám) argénti?
I have as much of the former as of the latter.	Hábeo tántum illĭus, quántum (quám) hújus.
I have as much of the one as of the other.	Tántum ex (de) áltĕro (úno), quám éx (de) áltĕro hábeo.

A. Obs. The partitive relation denoted by the English "of" is in Latin expressed either by the genitive or by the prepositions *e*, *ex*, or *de* with the ablative.

Have you as many hats as coats?	Habêsne tót pílĕos quót tógas?
I have as many of these as of those.	Tót (tám múltas) illôrum, quót (quám múltas) hârum hábeo.
I have as many of the one as the other.	Hábeo tám múltas (tót) ex únis, quám múltos (quót) ex áltĕris. ‡
Have you as many (wine-) glasses as goblets?	Súntne tíbi tót (tám múlti) scýphi, quót (quám múlta *or* quám) pó-cŭla?

---

* In a similar manner the Romans say, *tantus — quantus*, as great — as ; *tālis — quālis*, such — as; *tŏtĭes — quŏtĭes*, as many times — as, &c. Words thus corresponding with each other are called *correlatives*.

† *Tot — quot*, *tantum — quantum* are more frequent than *tam multi*, &c. The Romans are fond of inverting the logical order of these clauses, and of saying *quot — tot*, *quantum — tantum*, &c., and sometimes the *tot, tantum,* &c. is entirely suppressed; as *Cras et quot dies* (= *tot dies, quot*) *erimus in Tusculano*, To-morrow and *as many days as* we shall be in Tusculanum.

‡ "The former" of two persons or things is commonly expressed by *ille*, and sometimes also (especially when two persons are spoken of) by *prior*, m. & f., *prius*, gen. *priōris*. "The latter" may then be either *hic* or *posterior*, m. & f., *posterius*, n., gen. *posteriōris*. "The one" may be expressed by *alter* or *unus*, "the other," by *alter* or *ille*. The words may thus be used in every gender and in any of their cases, singular and plural. The plural *úni — altĕri* is here employed precisely like *utrique* of Lesson XXI. *A.* Rem. 8.

I have quite as many of the one as of the other.	Súnt míhi tótĭdem ex álteris, quót ex álteris *or* íllis.
Quite (or *just*) *as many — as.*	*Tŏ́tĭdĕm* (indecl.) — *quŏ́t.*
Quite (or *just*) *as much — as.*	*Tantumdĕm* (or *tantundĕm*) — *quantŭm.*

B. Obs. *Tŏ́tĭden* is a compound of *tot* and *ĭ́dĭdem*, and *tantumdem* of *tantum* and *ĭ́dĭdem* (= likewise). The construction of these words is the same as that of *tot* and *tantum*.

I have just as much of this as of that.	Ést míhi tantúndem hújus, quántum illíus.
I have just as many of these as of those.	Súnt míhi tótĭdem hôrum, quót illôrum.
I have just as much wine as water.	Ést míhi tantúndem víni, quántum áquae.
You have just as many hats as letters.	Tíbi súnt tótĭdem pílĕi, quót epístŏlae.
More.	*Plŭ̄s*, pl. *plŭ̄res, plŭ̄ra.*

C. Obs. The comparative *plŭ̄s* has only the neuter in the singular, but a double form in the plural. It is thus inflected : —

	SINGULAR. Neut.	PLURAL. Masc. & Fem.	Neut.
NOM.	plŭ̄s	plŭ̄rēs	plŭră (plŭrĭă)
GEN.	plŭrĭs	plŭrĭŭm	
DAT.	———	plŭrĭbŭs	
ACC.	plŭ̄s	plŭ̄rēs	plŭră (plŭrĭă)
VOC.	———	———	———
ABL.	plŭrĕ *or* ĭ.	plŭrĭbŭs.	

REMARKS.

1. The dative singular of *plus* is wanting.

2. The form *plūrĭa* for *plŭ̄ra* is obsolete, but still in use in the compound *complurĭa*, several.

3. *Plŭ̄res* and *complūres* are the only comparatives which have their genitives in *ĭum*. All others have *um*. (Cf. Less. XIII.).

4. The neuters *plus* and *plura* are often used substantively,* and then the former signifies "more" (in the abstract), the latter "more things."

D. Obs. The neuter singular *plus* stands partitively, and is followed by the genitive of the noun, which may be either sin-

---

* And *plus* also adverbially; as *plus formosus* (= *formosior*), more beautiful; *plus plusque diligere*, to cherish more and more.

gular or plural. *Plures* and *plura* have the agreement of regular adjectives, but they are frequently employed in the sense of "more than one," or "several." Thus : —

More bread, water, wine.	Plûs pânis, áquae, víni.
More men.	Plûs hóminum, plúrēs hóminēs.
More letters.	Plûs epistŏlârŭm, plúrēs epístŏlae.
More goblets.	Plûs pōcŭlôrum, plûră pócŭlă.
Than.	Quam ; * quam quod, quam quantum ; quam quot.
More water than wine.	Plûs áquae quám (quantum) víni.
More men than children.	{ Plûs hóminum quám (quot) líbĕrum (= liberôrum). Plúres hómĭnes quám (quot) liberi.
More of this than of that.	{ Plûs hujúsce quam illíus. Plûs de (ex) bôc quám de (ex) íllo.
More of the one than of the other.	Plûs ex (de) áltero (úno),quám ex (de) áltĕro *or* íllo.
More of these than of those.	{ Plûs hôrum (hârum, hôrum) quám illôrum (illârum, illôrum). Plûs (plúres, plûra) ex (de) hís quám ex (de) íllis.
More of the one than of the other.	Plûs (plúres, plûra) de álteris (únis), quam de álteris *or* íllis.
I have more of your sugar than of mine.	{ Ést -míhi plûs túi sácchări quám quantum méi. Égo plûs de sácchăro túo hábeo, quám quod de méo.
I have more books than letters.	Súnt míhi plúres librôrum quám quot epistolârum.
Less.	Mínŭs (neut. with the gen.).
Less water than wine.	Mínus áquae quám (quam quantum) víni.
Less bread than sugar.	Mínus pânis quám (quod) sácchări.
How many books have you ?	{ Quót súnt tíbi líbri ? Quót líbros hábes ?
I have more than five hundred.	{ Súnt míhi plûs quingénti. Plûs quingéntos hábeo.

E. Obs. When the comparatives *plus, amplius,* and *minus* are followed by a numeral, the particle *quam* is often omitted.

---

* With reference to this *quam,* and the construction of comparatives generally, see Lesson XLII. The student will notice here the idiomatic use of *quantum, quod,* and *quot.*

I have less than twenty.	{ Súnt míhi mínus vigínti. { Mínus vigínti hábeo.
How much money have you ?	Quántam pecúniam hábes ?
I have less than ten dollars (crowns).	Mínus décem thaléros hábeo.
I have more than twenty thousand dollars.	Súnt míhi ámplius vígínti míllia thalêrum (= thalerórum).
Less (i. e. fewer) men than children.	Paucióres hómines quám (quam quot) líberi.
Fewer (less).	*Paucĭōres*, m. & f., *paucĭŏra*, n.

F. Obs. The neuter singular *mĭnus,* "less," is construed like *plus,** and the plural *paucĭōres, a,* "fewer," like *plures.* They are thus inflected : —

Nom.	mĭnŭs	paucĭōrēs	paucĭŏră
Gen.	mĭnōrĭs	paucĭōrŭm	
Dat.	mĭnōrī	paucĭōrĭbŭs	
Acc.	mĭnŭs	paucĭōrēs	paucĭŏră
Voc.	————	————	————
Abl.	mĭnōrĕ *or* ī.	paucĭōrĭbŭs.	

Less of this than of that.	{ Mínus hujúsce quám illíus. { Mínus de (ex) hôc quám de (ex) íllo.
Fewer of these than of those.	Paucióres ex (de) his quám ex (de) íllis.
Fewer of the one than of the other.	Paucióres de álteris (únis), quam de álteris *or* íllis.
Fewer of us than of you.	Paucióres nóstrum quám (quam quot) véstrum.
More than I, than you, than he.	Plûs (plúrēs, plûră) quám† égo, quám tû, quám ílle.
Less than I, than you, than he.	Mínus quám égo, quám tû, quám ílle.
More than we, than you, than they.	Plûs (plúrēs, plûră) quám nôs, quám vôs, quám íllí.
Fewer than I, than you, than he.	Paucĭōrēs quám égo, quám tû, quám ílle.
Fewer things (less) than we, than you, than they.	Pauciŏră quám nôs, quám vôs, quám ílli.
As much as I, you, he.	Tántum (tám múltum), quántum (quám) égo, tû, ílle.

---

* With this difference, however, that *mĭnus* is followed by the genitive singular only. In the plural, *paucĭōres,* fewer, becomes necessary.
† Or *quam quantum, quam quod, quam quot,* according to the context.

As many as we, you, they.	Tót (tám múltos), quót (quám) nós, rós, ílli.
Have you more books than I ?	Tenêsne tû plûs librôrum, quám égo ? Súntne tíbi plúres librôrum, quám míhi ?
I have more of them than you.	Téneo eórum plûs quám tû. Súnt míhi plúres quám tíbi.
Have I less sugar than they ?	Núm ést míhî mínus sácchări quám íllis ?
Nay (on the contrary), you have more.	Ímmo véro tíbî plûs ést.
Has the young man fewer friends than we ?	Habétne júvěnis pauclóres amícos, quám nôs (habêmus) ? Súntne júvěni pauclóres amíci, quám nóbis (súnt) ?
He has less (fewer).	Pauclóres hábet. (Súnt éi) pauclóres.
Have we as much bread as they ?	Habemúsne tántum pànis, quántum ílli (hábent) ? Éstne nóbis tám múltum pànis quám íllis ?
We have just as much as they.	Tantúndem habêmus, quántum (quám) ílli. Nóbis ést tantúndem, quántum (quám) íllis.
Have you as many children as they ?	Écquid vôs tót líbĕros habêtis, quót ílli (hábent) ? Súntne vóbis tót líbĕri quót íllis ?
We have just as many as they.	Tótĭdem habêmus, quót ílli (hábent). Nóbis súnt tótĭdem quót íllis.
Several.	Plúrēs, m. & f., plūră, n. Complúrēs, m. & f., complúrĭa,* n. Nonnúlli, ae, ă.
Several different (diverse).	Divérsi, ae, ă. Várĭi, ae, ă.
Several men, women, children.	Plúres (complúres) víri, muliéres, líbĕri.
Several lights, looking-glasses, candlesticks.	Plûra (complúrĭa) lúmĭna, spécŭla, candelábra.
Several (different) houses, books, horses.	Dómūs, líbri, équi divérsi (várii).†
The father.	Pătĕr, *gen.* patris, *m.*
The son.	Filĭús, i, *m.*
The woman.	Mŭlĭĕr, ĕris, *f.*

---

* Compare *C. Obs.* and Remarks of this Lesson.
† Compare Lesson XXII. *B. Obs.*

The daughter.	Fīlĭa, ae, *f.*; nāta, ae, *f.*
The child (infant).	Infâns, tis, *m.* & *f.*
The children.	Libĕrī, ōrum, *m. pl.**
The captain (of the army).	Centŭrĭo, ōnis, *m.*
The sea-captain.	{ Praefectus (i, *m.*) nāvis. { Navarchus, i, *m.*
The tea.	Thēa, ae, *f.*; infūsum (i, *n.*) thēae.†
The cake.	Plăcenta, ae, *f.*
Cakes (of every kind).	Pānĭfĭcĭa, ōrum, *n. pl.*
The enemy.	Inĭmīcus, i, *m.*; hostis, is, *m.*
The finger.	Dĭgĭtus, i, *m.*‡
The boot.	Călĭga, ae, *f.*

EXERCISE 31.

Have you a coat ? — I have several. — Has he a looking-glass ? — He has several. — What kind of looking-glasses has he ? — He has beautiful looking-glasses. — Who has my good cakes ? — Several men have them. — Has your brother a child ? — He has several. — Have you as much coffee as honey ? — I have as much of the one as of the other. — Has he as much tea as beer ? — He has as much of the one as of the other. — Has this man as many friends as enemies ? — He has as many of the one as of the other. — Has the son of your friend as many coats as shirts ? — He has as many of the one as of the other. — Have we as many boots as shoes ? — We have as many of the one as of the other. — We have more of the one than of the other. — Have we less hay than he ? — We have just as much as he.

EXERCISE 32.

Has your father as much gold as silver ? — He has more of the latter than of the former. — Has he as much tea as coffee ? — He has more of the latter than of the former. — Has the captain as many sailors as ships ? — He has more of the one than of the other. — Have you as many rams as I ? — I have just as many. — Has the foreigner as much courage as we ? — He has quite as much. — Have we as much good as bad paper ? — We have as much of the one as of the other. — Have we as much cheese as bread ? — We have more of the latter than of the former. — Has your son as many cakes as books ? — He has more of the latter than of the former; more of the one than of the other. — How many books has he ? — He has more than five thousand. — Has he more than twenty ships ? — He has less than twenty; he has only fifteen. — Has this little boy more than ten fingers ? — He has no more than ten.

---

* On this *plŭrāle tantum*, see Lesson XVII. *B.* 4.
† *Thea* is the Linnæan name of the plant; *infŭsum*, an infusion generally.
‡ This is the general name. The special names are: *pollex, ĭcis,* m. (the thumb); *index, ĭcis,* m.; *mĕdĭus, i,* m. (the middle finger); *annŭlāris, is,* m. (ring-finger); *mĭnĭmus, i,* m. (little finger).

EXERCISE 33.

How many children have you ? — I have only one, but my brother
has more than I; he has five. — Has your son as much head as
mine ? — He has less head than yours, but he has more courage. —
My children have more courage than yours. — Have I as much
money as you ? — You have less than I. — Have you as many books
as I ? — I have less than you. — Have I as many enemies as your
father ? — You have fewer than he. — Have the Americans more
children than we ? — They have fewer than we. — Have we as many
ships as the English ? — We have less than they. — Have we fewer
knives than the children of our friends ? — We have fewer than they.
— How many have they ? — They have more than eighty. — How
many have we ? — We have less than twelve.

EXERCISE 34.

Who has fewer friends than we ? — Nobody has fewer. — Have
you as much of my tea as of yours ? — I have as much of yours as
of mine. — Have I as many of your books as of mine ? — You have
fewer of mine than of yours. — Has the Spaniard as much of your
money as of his own ? — He has less of his own than of ours. —
Has your baker less bread than money ? — He has less of the latter
than of the former. — Has our merchant fewer dogs than horses ?
He has fewer of the latter than of the former ; fewer of the one than
of the other. — He has fewer horses than we, and we have less bread
than he. — Have our neighbors as many carriages as we ? — We have
fewer than they. — We have less corn and less meat than they. —
We have but little corn, but meat enough. — How many houses have
you ? — I have more than thirty of them. — How many horses has
the brother of our friend ? — He has more than a hundred horses,
and less than fifty books. — How much money have we ? — We have
less than ten shillings. — Has your young man less (fewer) mirrors
than we ? — He has more than you ; he has more than a thousand.

Lesson XXIV. — PENSUM VICESIMUM QUARTUM.

OF THE LATIN VERBS.

A. Latin verbs are divided into three principal
classes : — 1. *Transitive verbs ;* 2. *Intransitive* or *neuter
verbs ;* 3. *Deponent verbs.*

1. Transitive verbs are active verbs, the sense of which is
not complete without the addition of an object, which is gener-

ally in the accusative; as *ămo*, I love, sc. *amīcum*, my friend ; *scrībo*, I write, sc. *epistŏlam*, a letter.

2. Intransitive or neuter verbs are those which denote either a simple mode of existence, or such an activity as does not terminate in any object; as *dormĭo*, I sleep, *curro*, I run.

3. The class of deponent verbs is peculiar to the Latin. They have a passive form with an active (or reflexive) signification; as *lŏquor*, I speak, *sĕquor*, I follow.

4. Transitive verbs have two forms, called the *Active* and the *Passive Voices*; as *mŏnĕo*, I remind, *mŏnĕor*, I am reminded ; *audĭo*, I hear, *audĭor*, I am heard.

5. Latin verbs have four Moods, viz.: — 1. the *Indicative* ; 2. the *Subjunctive*; 3. the *Imperative*; and 4. the *Infinitive* ; as, 1. *ămo*, I love; 2. *amārem*, I might love; 3. *amāto*, let him love; 4. *amāre*, to love.

6. They have *six* Tenses: — 1. the *Present*; 2. the *Imperfect*; 3. the *Perfect*; 4. the *Pluperfect*; 5. the *First Future* ; and 6. the *Future Perfect*. E. g. 1. *audĭo*, I hear; 2. *audĭēbam*, I heard ; 3. *audīvi*, I have heard; 4. *audīvĕram*, I had heard ; 5. *audĭam*, I shall hear ; 6. *audīvĕro*, I shall have heard.

7. The Latin verb has *four* Participles: — The *present active* in *ns*; the *future active*, in *tūrus*; the *perfect passive*, in *tus*; and the *future passive*, in *ndus*; e. g. *ămans*, loving; *amātūrus*, about to love; *amātus*, loved; *amandus*, to be loved.

8. Among the forms of the Latin verb are usually included the *Gerund* (vide Lesson XXV.), the active *Supine* in *um*, and the passive Supine in *ū*; e. g. *amātum*, to love ; *amātū*, to be loved.

OF THE CONJUGATION OF VERBS.

B. There are in Latin *four Conjugations*, distinguished from each other by the termination of the *Infinitive Present*, which ends as follows: —

1. āre; 2. ēre; 3. ĕre; 4. īre.

Examples: — *amāre*, to love ; *monēre*, to remind; *legĕre*, to read; *audīre*, to hear.

The characteristic terminations of the Present Indicative in the first and second persons are: —

1. o, ās; 2. ĕo, ēs; 3. o (ĭo), ĭs; 4. ĭo, īs.

Examples: — *ămo*, *ămās*, I love, thou lovest; *mŏneō*, *mŏnēs*, I remind, thou remindest; *lĕgo*, *lĕgĭs*, I read, thou readest; *audĭo*, *audĭs*, I hear, thou hearest.

C. To the full conjugation of Latin verbs, it is essential to know *four principal parts*, from which the rest are derived. These parts are : — *a*) *the Present Indicative ; b*) the *Present Infinitive ; c*) the *Perfect Indicative ; d*) the *Supine* in *um.* The terminations of these parts are : —

1st conj.	o,	ārĕ,	āvī,	ātŭm,
2d conj.	ĕo,	ērĕ,	ŭī,	ītŭm,
3d conj.	o (ĭo),	ĕrĕ,	ī,	tŭm,
4th conj.	ĭo,	īrĕ,	īvī,	ītŭm.

Examples : — 1. amo, amāre, amāvi, amātum ; 2. monĕo monēre, monūi, monītum ; 3. lego, legĕre, lēgī, lectum ; facĭo, facĕre, fēci, factum ; 4. audĭo, audīre, audivi, auditum.

REMARK 1. — The invariable or permanent part of the present (indicative and infinitive) is called the first or general *root* of the verb (*am, mon, lĕg, aud*) ; that of the perfect, the second root (*amāv, monū, lēg, audīv*) ; and that of the supine in *um,* the third root (*amāt, monīt, lect, audīt*).*

REMARK 2. — Many verbs are irregular in the formation of these principal parts, which frequently follow the analogy of two different conjugations (e. g. the verb *do* below). In these cases the infinitive present determines to which of the conjugations the verb is to be referred. Some verbs again are defective, the supine, or the perfect and the supine both, being wanting.

To love, cherish.	Ămo, āre, āvi, ātum, Dĭlĭgo, ĕre, lexi, lectum. (ALIQUEM, ALIQUID).†
To set in order, arrange.	Dispōno, ĕre, pŏsui, pŏsitum (ALIQUID).
To open.	Ăpĕrĭo, ire, pĕrŭi, pertum (ALIQUID).
To do.	Ago, ĕre, ēgī, actum (ALIQUID).
To do (make).	Făcĭo, ĕre, fēci, factum (ALIQUID).
To give.	Dō, dăre, dĕdi, dătum ‡ (ALICUI ALIQUID).
To see.	Vĭdĕo, ēre, vīdi, vīsum (ALIQUEM, ALIQUID).
To say, speak.	Dico, ĕre, dixi, dictum (ALIQUID).
To carry.	Porto, āre, āvi, ātum (ALIQUID).
To wash.	Lăvo, āre, āvi (or lāvi), ātum (lautum or lōtum) (ALIQUEM, ALIQUID).
To want, need.	Ĕgĕo, ĕre, ŭi, — (ALIQUĀ RE). Indĭgĕo, ĕre, ŭi, — (ALICŪJUS).

---

* The manner in which the different tenses, &c. are formed from these primary parts is explained in Lesson XXVIII., which see. The student should make himself familiar with the formula of every verb, as it occurs in this and in subsequent lessons.

† See Rules *F.* and *G.* of this Lesson.

‡ The verb *do* has the syllable *dă* short ; as *dăre, dămus.* The monosyllabic forms *dā* and *dās* are the only exceptions.

OF THE PRESENT INDICATIVE.

D. The present indicative of Latin verbs corresponds in general to that of the English. The distinctions, however, indicated by the English *I love, do love, am loving*, are not expressed by any separate forms in Latin. The present indicative of the respective conjugations is thus inflected: —

1. Amo, *I love.*

SING.	*I love*	ămŏ *
	Thou lovest	ămās
	He loves,	ămăt,
PLUR.	*We love*	ămāmŭs
	Ye love	ămātĭs
	They love.	ămant.

2. Mŏnĕo, *I remind.*

I remind	mŏnĕŏ
Thou remindest	mŏnēs
He reminds,	mŏnĕt,
We remind	mŏnēmŭs
Ye remind	mŏnētĭs
They remind.	mŏnent.

3. Lĕgo, *I read.*

SING.	*I read*	lĕgŏ
	Thou readest	lĕgĭs
	He reads,	lĕgĭt,
PLUR.	*We read*	lĕgĭmŭs
	Ye read	lĕgĭtĭs
	They read.	lĕgunt.

4. Audĭo, *I hear.*

I hear	audĭŏ
Thou hearest	audĭs
He hears,	audĭt,
We hear	audĭmŭs
Ye hear	audītĭs
They hear.	audĭunt.

Like *ămo* inflect: do, porto, lăvo, &c. — Like *moneo* : hăbĕo, vĭdeo, ĕgĕo, and indĭgĕo, &c. — Like *lĕgo* : dĭlĭgo, dispōno, dīco, &c. — Like *audĭo* : ăpĕrĭo, ēsŭrĭo, sĭtĭo, &c.

E. Obs. Verbs of the third conjugation in *io* are inflected like *audio*, except that the *i* of the different persons is short. The verb *sum*, I am, is irregular. The present indicative of *făcĭo*, I make, do, and *sŭm* runs thus:

SING.	*I do*	făcĭŏ	*I am*	sŭm
	Thou dos	făcĭs	*Thou art*	ĕs
	He does,	făcĭt,	*He is,*	est,
PLUR.	*We do*	făcĭmŭs	*We are*	sŭmŭs
	Ye do	făcĭtĭs	*Ye are*	estĭs
	They do.	făcĭunt.	*They are.*	sunt.

Do you love your brother ?	Amâsne tû frâtrem túum ?
I do love him.	Véro, éum ámo.

F. RULE. — The object of an active transitive verb is put in the Accusative. This accusative may be either a person (*aliquem*) or a thing (*aliquid*). As

---

* The *o* final of the present tense of all verbs is commonly long, but in poetry sometimes short.

Púer líbrum légit.	*The boy reads the book.*
Vídĕo hómĭnem.	*I see the man.*
Ápĕri fenéstram.	*Open the window.*

Does your brother arrange his books?	Dispŏnítne frắter túus líbros súos?
He does arrange them.	Dispônit.
He does not arrange them.	Éos nôn dispônit.
Do ye see anything beautiful?	Vidétísne áliquid púlchri?
We do see something beautiful.	Vidêmus véro quíddam púlchri.
What is that little boy doing?	Quíd ágit ílle puércŭlus?
He is doing something bad.	Ágit áliquid nĕquam (máli).
Do you open the window?	Apĕrísne fenéstram?
I am opening it.	Apério.
Who is washing his stockings?	Quis lávat tibiália súa?
The sailors are washing them.	Lávant éa naútae.
What do the men say?	Quid dícunt hómĭnes?
They say nothing.	Níhil dícunt.
Does your father give you a good book?	Dátne tíbi páter líbrum bónum?
He gives me a good book.	Dát míhi líbrum bónum.

G. Obs. In Latin, as in English, the *immediate* object of transitive verbs (whether they be active or deponent) is put in the *Accusative* (*álĭquem* or *álĭquid*), and the *remote* object (i. e. that *for* or *with reference to which* anything is done) in the *Dative* (*álĭcui*).* As

Dá míhi líbrum.	*Give me the book.*
Mítto tíbi epístolam.	*I send you the letter.*
Cómmŏdat nóbis cúltrum.	*He lends us the knife.*
Nón schólae, sed vítae díscĭmus.	*We learn not for school, but for life.*

Dost thou love him?	{ Eúmne ámas? { Númquid éum ámas?
I do not love him.	Éum nôn ámo (nôn díligo).
Do you want your money?	{ Egêsne tû pecúniã túã? { Indígêsne pecúniae túae?

H. Obs. The verb *ĕgĕo* and its compound *indĭgĕo* are intransitive, and are generally followed† by the Ablative, but sometimes by the Genitive of the object needed. (Cf. Lesson XXVI. *B.*)

---

* In connection with this rule it is necessary to remark, that many verbs in Latin are neuter, while their English equivalents are transitive. No details can at present be given, but the construction of every verb will be pointed out as it is needed by the student of this method. Of Latin verbs generally, some are followed by the *Nominative*, others govern the *Genitive, Dative, Accusative,* or *Ablative.*

† I. e. they *govern* the Ablative and Genitive. In Latin the object commonly precedes the verb, and can only be said to follow in *logical order.*

H   10 *

I really do need it.	{ Égo véro éã égěo. { Sáne, éjus indígěo.
What do you stand in need of?	Quâ rê índiges?
I do not need anything.	Níhil égěo.
Do you want any one (anything)?	Egêsne áliquo (áliquã rê)?
I need my father.	Pátris* indígěo.

EXERCISE 35.

Does your brother love you? — He does love me. — Do you love him? — I do love him. — Does your father love him? — He does not love him. — Dost thou love me, my good child? — I love thee. — Dost thou love this ugly man? — I do not love him. — Does the servant open the window? — He does open it. — Dost thou open it? — I do not open it. — Does he open the book? — He does not open it. — Dost thou set my books in order? — I set them in order. — Does the servant arrange our boots and shoes? — He sets both the one and the other in order. — Do our children love us? — They do love us. — Do we love our enemies? — We do not love them. — What do you give me? — I do not give thee anything (I give thee nothing). — Do you give my brother the book? — I do give it to him. — Do you give him a hat? — I do give him one. — What do you give him? — I give him something beautiful. — What does he give you? — He gives me nothing.

EXERCISE 36.

Does the sailor wash his stockings? — He does wash them. — Do you wash your hands (manus tuas)? — I do wash them. — Does your brother wash as many shirts as stockings? — He washes more of the one than of the other. — Do you wash your shirts? — I do not wash them. — Do your brothers wash their stockings or ours? — They neither wash yours nor theirs; they wash those (i.e. the stockings) of their children. — What does your servant carry? — He carries a large table. — What do these men carry? — They carry their wooden chairs. — What books does the young man carry? — He carries good books. — Does he read them? — He does not read them? — What do you read? — I am reading nothing. — What do the men say? — They are saying something good. — What dost thou say? — I do not say anything. — What are you doing? — I am doing nothing. — What are the boys doing? — They are doing something bad. — They are reading good books. — Are these men hungry or thirsty? — They are neither hungry nor thirsty.

EXERCISE 37.

Dost thou hear anything? — I hear nothing. — Does your father hear anything? — He neither hears nor sees anything. — Dost thou

---

* The genitive (especially of the person) is quite frequent after indigeo.

see anything? — I see nothing. — Do you.see my large garden? — I do see it. — Does your father see our ship? — He does not see it, but we see it. — How many ships do you see? — We see a good many; we see more than thirty (*plus triginta*). — Do you give me books? — I do give thee some. — Does your father give you money? — He does not give us any. — Does he give you hats? — He does not give us any. — Do you see many sailors? — We see more soldiers than sailors (*quam nautarum*). — Do the soldiers see many storehouses? — They see more gardens than storehouses. — Do the English give you good cakes? — They do give us some. — Do you give me as much wine as beer? — I give thee as much of the one as of the other. — Do you give me some more cakes (*panificia aliquot amplius*)? — I do not give you any more. — Do you give me the horse which you have? — I do not give you that which I have? — Which horse do you give me? — I give you that of my brother. — Do you want (need) your money? — I do want it. — Does your father want his servant? — He does want him. — Dost thou need anything (*aliquā re*)? — I need nothing (*nihil*). — Do we want our carriage? — We do want it. — Do our friends want their clothes? — They do want them,

---

Lesson **XXV.** — PENSUM VICESIMUM QUINTUM.

OF THE GERUND.

A. The gerund is a verbal substantive of the second declension neuter gender. It is formed from the present indicative by changing the 1. *o*, 2. *eo*, 3. *o* (*io*), 4. *io* of the respective conjugations into 1. *andi*, 2. *endi*, 3. *endi* (*iendi*), 4. *iendi*; as, ămo, *amandi*; mŏnĕo, *mŏnendi*; lĕgo, *lĕgendi* (făcĭo, *făcĭendi*); audĭo, *audĭendi*. Its nominative is wanting, the present infinitive being commonly used in its stead. The gerund is thus declined: —

GEN.	*of loving*	ămandĭ	GEN.	*of seeing*	vĭdendĭ
DAT.	*to loving*	ămandō	DAT.	*for seeing*	vĭdendō
ACC.	*loving*	ămandŭm	ACC.	*seeing*	vĭdendŭm
ABL.	*by loving*	ămandō.	ABL.	*by seeing*	vĭdendō.

So decline: apĕrĭendi, dandi, dīcendi, făcĭendi, lăvandi, lĕgendi, mŏnendi, portandi, &c.

B. Gerunds generally govern the same cases as their verbs. They are in other respects construed like substantives, according to the following rules: —

a) The Genitive is used : 1. After certain adjectives implying an operation of the mind ; as *cupĭdus, dilĭgens, gnārus, ignārus, mĕmor, immĕmor, perĭtus, studĭōsus,* &c. 2. After many substantives, especially after *ars, causa, consilium, cupidĭtas, facultas, occasio, potestas, spes, studium, tempus, voluntas,* and the ablatives *causā* and *gratiā,* " for the sake of." E. g. *cupĭdus dicendi,* desirous of speaking ; *studiosus audiendi,* fond of hearing ; *ars pingendi,* the art of painting ; *tempus abeundi,* the time of leaving (to leave) ; *discendi causâ,* for the sake of learning.

b) The Dative of the gerund is employed after verbs and adjectives, especially after *intentum esse, opĕram dare, tempus impendere,* and after *utĭlis, inutĭlis, noxĭus, par, aptus, indoneus,* &c.; as, *operam dat studendo,* he applies himself to study ; *intentus est legendo,* he is bent on reading ; *aptus discendo,* apt to learn ; *utilis bibendo,* useful to drink.

c) The Accusative of the gerund always depends on prepositions, especially on *ad* (to, for) and *inter* (during, while) ; sometimes also on *ante* (before), *circa,* and *ob.* E. g. *paratus ad videndum,* ready to see ; *inter ludendum,* while playing, &c.

d) The Ablative of the gerund is either used, 1. to denote the instrument in answer to the question *whereby ? wherewith ?* or, 2. it is dependent on one of the prepositions *ab, de, ex,* or *in ;* as, *defessus sum scribendo,* I am wearied with writing ; *justitia in suo cuique tribuendo,* justice in giving every man his own.

EXAMPLES : —

The desire of living well.	Cŭpídĭtas bénĕ vivéndi.
The science of avoiding unnecessary expenses.	Scléntĭa vitándi súmptus supervácŭos.
Desirous, fond of hearing.	Cúpĭdus, studĭôsus audĭéndi.
Sulphur water is useful for drinking (to drink).	Áqua nitrôsa útĭlis ést bibéndo.
He is not solvent (able to pay).	Nôn (par) ést solvéndo (*dat.*).
They were present at the registration.	Scribéndo (*dat.*) adfŭérunt. (A law term.)
He came for the purpose of seeing (to see).	Vênĭt ad vidéndum.
He keeps dogs for hunting purposes.	Álit cánes ad venándum.
Easy to take (to be taken).	Fácĭlis ad capléndum.
While walking, drinking, playing.	Inter eúndum (ambulándum), bibéndum, ludéndum.
The mind of man is nourished by learning and thinking.	Hómĭnis méns discéndo álĭtur ét cogĭtándo.
He spends his leisure in reading and writing.	Ótĭum súum in legéndo consûmĭt ínque scribéndo.

OF THE FUTURE PASSIVE PARTICIPLE.

C. The future passive participle is formed according

to the analogy of the gerund. Its terminations for the respective conjugations are:—

1. *andus, a, um;* 2. *endus, a, um;* 3. *endus, a, um* (*iendus, a, um*); 4. *iendus, a, um.* As, *ămandus, a, um,* to be loved; *vĭdendus, a, um,* to be seen; *lĕgendus, a, um,* to be read; *făcĭendus, a, um,* to be done; *audĭendus, a, um,* to be heard. This participle is regularly inflected like *bonus, a, um;* it is used in all the cases, both singular and plural, and agrees with its substantive in gender, number, and case.

REMARK.— Verbs of the third and fourth conjugations may also have *undus* instead of *endus,* especially when *i* precedes; as *dicundus, faciundus, audiundus,* &c. Thus, regularly, *potiundus,* from *potior,* I possess. In other verbs this form occurs chiefly in certain standard expressions, such as *In jure dicundo,* In administering justice; *In finibus dividundis,* In determining the boundaries, &c.

OF THE NOMINATIVE OF THE PARTICIPLE IN "DUS."

D. The nominative (and sometimes the accusative) of the future passive participle has generally the signification of *necessity* or of *propriety,* more rarely also of *possibility;* as *amandus,* "one that must be loved, is to be loved, ought to be loved"; *legendus,* "that must be read, is required to be read," &c. The construction of this participle has the peculiarity of requiring the agent (*by* whom the action is to be performed) in *the dative case,* instead of in the ablative with *ab.* (Cf. Lesson XXXIV.)   Examples:—

I, thou, he, must love.	Amándum ést míhi, tíbi, ílli.
We, you, they, must see.	Vidéndum ést nóbis, vóbis, íllis.
I, you, they, must read.	Légéndum ést míhi, tíbi, íis.
I (thou, he) must write a letter (I have a letter to write).	Epístŏla míhi (tíbi, éi) scribénda * ést.
We (ye, they) must write letters (have to write letters).	Epístolae (nóbis, vóbis, éis) scribéndae súnt.
I (you, they) have to read the book.	Libér ést míhi (tíbi, íllis) lĕgéndus.
We (you, he) have to read books.	Líbri súnt míhi (tíbi, ílli) legéndi.

---

* It was customary among the earlier Latin writers (and also among the later poets) to employ the object *accusative* after the neuter form of the participle of transitive verbs, and to say, *epistolam* (or *epistolas*) mihi scribendum est; as, for example, Lucretius: *Quoniam aeternas poenas in morte timendum est,* instead of *Quoniam aeternae poenae in morte timendae sunt* (Since we must dread eternal punishment in death). But this construction is rarely used by Cicero, and the rule should be to employ the nominative and the participle in the same case.

I, thou, he, must rest (go, sleep), &c.	Quiescéndum (ëúndum,* dormiéndum) ést míhi, tíbi, éi, &c.
We ought especially to cherish diligence, and to practise it always.	Diligéntia praecípüe colénda ést nóbis, et sémper adhibénda.
One must venture (risk), one must die.	Audéndum ést, moriéndum ést.
Every one must (should) use his own judgment.	Súo cuique judícïo (*abl.*) uténdum ést.
I know that I must write a letter.	Scío epístolam míhi ésse scribéndam.

OF THE OBLIQUE CASES OF THE PARTICIPLE IN "DUS," OR OF THE GERUNDIVE.

E. The future passive participle rarely retains its original signification of necessity or propriety in the oblique cases (i. e. in the genitive, dative, &c.), but is commonly employed in the sense of a present participle or of the gerund. When thus used, it is called the *Gerundive.* Thus we say :—

The design of writing a letter (*lit.* of a letter to be written).	Consílium epístolae scribéndae, *instead of* consílium scribéndi epístolam.†
The design of writing letters (*lit.* of letters to be written).	Consílium epistolárum scribendárum, *instead of* consílium epístolas scribéndi.
A committee of ten on legislation (*lit.* for the writing of laws).	Decémviri légibus scribéndis (*dat.*).
One of the committee of three on grants of public lands.	Triúmvir ágro dándo (*dat.*).
He is born for the endurance of miseries.	Nâtus ést misériis feréndis (*dat.*).
He was sent to procure ships.	Míssus ést ad náves comparándas (*for* ad comparándum náves).
He comes to defend the city.	Vénit ad úrbem defendéndam (*for* ad defendéndum úrbem).

* In intransitive verbs this neuter form of the participle with *est, erat,* &c. is the only one in use.   The dative of the agent is often left indeterminate.

† This conversion of the object accusative of the gerund into the passive construction of the gerundive may always take place, unless in those cases where perspicuity would suffer from the change.   When the accusative after the gerund is a pronoun or adjective of the *neuter* gender, the conversion usually does not take place, to prevent ambiguity respecting the gender of these words.   Thus always: Stúdium *illud efficiéndi* (the desire of accomplishing that), and never *illius efficiéndi; Cúpidus plúra cognoscéndi* (desirous of knowing more), and never *plúrium cognoscendórum.*   Thus also: In *súum* cuique *tribuéndo* (in giving every one his own), more commonly than, In *súo* cuique *tribuéndo.*   In general, however, the rule is, that, *when the verb governs the accusative, the passive construction with the participle is to be preferred to the gerund with the accusative.*

Fortitude in the endurance of hardships and dangers.	Fortĭtúdo in labórĭbus periculísque subĕúndis (*for* in subĕúndo labóres, &c.).
I am engaged in writing a letter.	Occupâtus súm in epístŏlā scribéndā (*for* in scribéndo epístŏlam).
I am engaged in writing letters.	Occupâtus súm in epístŏlis scribéndis (*for* in scribéndo epístolas).
The plan has been formed of destroying the city, of murdering the inhabitants, of blotting out the Roman name.	Ĭnĭta sŭnt consílĭa úrbis deléndae, cívĭum trucidandórum, nómĭnis Románi extinguéndi.

F. Obs. From the above examples, it will be perceived that the gerundive agrees with its substantive in gender, number, and case. Violations of this general rule, however, both with respect to gender and to number, are not unfrequent in the genitive of substantives, and especially of pronouns. E. g. :—

Since there is an opportunity of seeing you (*fem.*).	Quónĭam *tui* (fem.) *vidéndi* (for *videndae*) ést cópĭa.
For the sake of exhorting you.	Véstri *exhortándi* (for *exhortandórum*) caúsā.
The liberty of plundering fruit.	Licéntĭa diripĭéndi pomórum (*for* poma).
The power of selecting examples.	Exemplórnm (*for* exémpla) eligéndi potéstas.

EXERCISE 38.

Are you fond of reading? — I am fond of reading. — Are your brothers fond of reading? — They are not fond of reading. — Who is fond of hearing? — The merchants are fond of hearing. — Does he come for the purpose of seeing? — He does come for the purpose of seeing. — They come (*veniunt*) for the purpose of hearing. — Is it useful to drink wine? — It is useful. — It is not useful to drink wine. — Are you (*esne tu*) solvent (i. e. can you pay your debts)? — I am solvent. — I cannot pay my debts. — Is the place easy to take (easily taken)? — It is difficult (*difficilis*) to be taken. — Do you read while you are playing? — I do not read while I am playing. — By what (*quā re*) is the mind of man nourished? — It is nourished by learning and thinking. — Does he spend his leisure in reading? — No, sir, he spends it in playing. — Does he read for the sake of learning (*discendi gratiâ*)? — He reads for the sake of writing.

EXERCISE 39.

Must you read? — I am not obliged to read. — Must they sleep? — They must sleep. — Must your brother go? — He must go. — Who must go (*cui*)? — The sailor must go. — The boys must go. — Must the captains go? — They must go. — Must one venture? — One must

venture. — One must not venture. — What must (should) one do
(*quid est faciendum*) ? — Every one must (should) use his own judgment. — Do you keep (*alisne tu*) dogs for hunting ? — I do not keep
any. — Must you write a letter (Have you a letter to write) ? — I
must write one (I have one to write). — Have I any letters to write?
— You have some to write. — Who has (*cui sunt*) many letters to
write ? — The merchant has many to write. — I have none to write.
— Who should practise diligence? — We all (*nobis omnibus*) should
practise and cherish it.

EXERCISE 40.

Have you (*estne tibi*) the design of writing a letter ? — I have the
design of writing several. — Has your father the design of writing
letters ? — He has the design of writing letters and notes. — Is the
time of departure at hand (*adestne tempus abeundi*) ? — It is at
hand. — The time of departure is not yet (*nondum*) at hand. — Is it
time to speak ? — It is time to speak. — Are you (*esne tu*) engaged
(*occupatus*) in writing a letter ? — I am not engaged in writing a
letter, but in writing notes. — Is your son fond of writing letters ? —
He is not fond of writing, but of reading them. — Is paper useful for
writing letters ? — It is. — Have you an opportunity to speak ? — I
have an opportunity to speak. — Who has an opportunity to read ?
— Your son has an opportunity to read and to write ? — Who comes
to see ? — I come (*ego venio*) to see. — Who was (*quis missus est*) sent
to procure ships ? — The captain was sent. — Have you the desire to
accomplish (i. e. of accomplishing) that ? — I have (*est*). — What
must we do ? — We must give every man his own.

Lesson XXVI. — PENSUM VICESIMUM SEXTUM.

A wish, a mind, desire.	Cŭpĭdĭtas, voluntas, ātis, f. ; stŭdĭ-um, i, n.
Time, leisure.	Tempus, ŏris, n. ; spătĭum, ŏtĭum,* i, n.
A mind (desire) to work.	{ Volúntas opĕrándi. { Stúdĭum ópĕris facĭéndi.
Time to work.	{ Spátĭum ad laborándum. { Ótĭum (témpus) ad ópus facĭén-dum.
I have a mind (wish, desire) to do anything.	{ Ést míhi volúntas (cupídĭtas, stú-dĭum) álĭquid facĭéndi. { Cúpĭdus súm álĭquid facĭéndi. { Cúpĭo álĭquid fácĕre.

---

* *Tempus* is the proper word for "time" generally. *Otium* is "leisure."
Spatium is properly "space," "room," i. e. a certain portion of time, an allot-
ment or allowance of time for doing anything.

A. Obs. The preposition *to,* which in English is always the sign of the infinitive, is not always so in Latin. It is sometimes rendered by the infinitive, sometimes by the supine in *um,* and sometimes by one of the oblique cases of the gerund or gerundive. The shade of difference in these expressions will readily be perceived by the learner.

I have time to work (for working).	{ Est mǐhi spátǐum ad lābōrándum. { Hábeo ótǐum ad ópus fǎciéndum.
I have a mind (desire) to work.	{ Cúpǐdus súm laborándi. { Cúpǐo ópus fǎcĕre.
I have the courage to speak.	{ Est mǐhi ánǐmus loquéndi. { Aúdĕo lóqui (dícere).
To work.	{ *Lǎbōro, āre, āvi, ātum.* { *Ōpus fǎcĕre* (to do work).
To speak.	{ Lǒquor, lǒqui, lǒcūtus sum.* { Dīco, ĕre, xi, ctum.
To desire.	Cǔpio, ĕre, īvi (ǐi), ǐtum (ALIQUID FACERE).
To venture, dare.	Audĕo, ĕre, ausus sum † (ALIQUID FACERE).
To cut.	Sĕco, āre, secǔi, sectum (ALIQUEM, ALIQUID).
To buy.	Ēmo, ĕre, ēmi, emptum (ALIQUEM, ALIQUID).
To lack (want, to be without).	Cărĕo, ĕre, ǔi, ǐtum (ALIQUA RE).

B. RULE. Verbs signifying plenty or want are generally followed by the Ablative, sometimes by the Genitive. As : —

Égĕo pecúnǐā.	*I want (am in want of) money.*
Cáret ánǐmo.	*He lacks (has not) the courage.*
Liber scátet vítǐis.	*The book abounds in errors.*
Índǐget pátris.	*He needs his father.*
I have not, I lack.	{ Nòn hábeo (*with the acc.*). { Mǐhi déest (*with the nom.*). { Cáreo (*with the abl.*).

---

* *Loquor* is a deponent verb of the third conjugation. The principal parts of verbs of the passive form are only *three,* viz. : — 1. the Present Indicative (*loquor*); 2. the Present Infinitive (*loqui*); and 3. the Perfect Indicative (*locutus sum*). With respect to the signification, *loqui* is properly "to speak," "to talk," e. g. Latin, English; and *dicere,* "to say," or "to speak," in connected or formal discourse.

† On this deponent perfect, see Lesson XXXIII. *A.* Rem. 4.

11

I have not (I lack) the courage to speak.	Déest* míhi ánĭmus loquéndi. Cáreo ánĭmo loquéndi. Nôn aúdĕo lóqui (fắri).
To cut it (of cutting, for cutting it).	Éum, éam, íd secâre (secándi). Ad éum, íd secándum. Ad éam secándam (fem.).
To cut them (of cutting, for cutting them).	Éos, éas, éa secâre (secándi). Ad éos secándos (masc.). Ad éas secándas (fem.). Ad éa secánda (neut.).
To cut some (sing.).	Alĭquid secâre (secándi). Ad nonnúllum secándum. Ad nonnúllam secándam (fem.).
To cut some (plur.).	Aliquot (nonnúllos, &c.) secàre (secándi). Ad nonnúllos secándos, &c. Ad álĭquot secánda.
Have you time to cut trees?	Habêsne ótĭum ad secándum arbóres? Éstne tíbi spátium ad arbóres álĭquas secándas?
I have time to cut some.	Hábeo ótĭum ad secándum álĭquas. Ést míhi spátium ad álĭquot secándas.
Have you a mind to cut the bread?	Cupidúsne es pânis ín frústa secándi? Cupísne pânem ín frústa secâre?
I have no mind (desire) to cut it.	Nôn súm cúpidus éjus in frústa secándi. Éum in frústa secâre nôn cúpĭo.
To buy some more.	Plûs (ámplĭus) émĕre or eméndi. Ad ámplĭus (plûs) eméndum.
To buy one.	Ûnum (-am, -um) émĕre or eméndi. Ad únum (-am, -um) eméndum.
To buy one more.	Úno (-a, -o) ámplĭus (plûs)† émĕre or eméndi. Ad eméndum úno (-a, -o) plûs (ámplĭus).

* *Deest* is compounded of *de* + *sum*, and is inflected precisely like the simple verb. It is construed with the dative of the person:— *Deest mihi, tibi, hominibus*, &c., " There is wanting to me, to you, to the men "; i. e. " I have not, lack, want."

† *Plus* and *amplius* are here used substantively, like *aliquid, nihil*, and may like them be followed by a partitive genitive; e. g. *plus equorum*, more horses; *amplius librorum*, more books. *Uno* is the ablative of excess: " more by one." We thus can say either *uno equo amplius*, or *uno amplius equorum*, one more horse.

To buy two.

> Dúos (dúas, dúo) émĕre *or* eméndi.
> Ad eméndum dúos (dúas, dúo).

To buy two more.

> Duôbus (-âbus, -ôbus) ámplius (plûs) émere *or* eméndi.
> Ad eméndum duôbus (-âbus, -ôbus) plûs (ámplius).*

Have you a mind to buy one more horse?

> Cupísne émere úno plûs equôrum?
> Ésne cúpídus eméndi úno ámplius equôrum?

I have a mind to buy one more.

> Cúpĭo émere úno plûs.
> Súm cúpídus eméndi úno ámplĭus.

Have you a mind to buy some books?

> Cupísne émere líbros álíquos?
> Cupídúsne és librôrum áliquot eméndi?

I have a mind to buy some, but I have no time.

> Cúpĭo áliquot (nonnúllos) émere, séd cáreo ótĭo (déest míhi spátĭum).

Am I right in doing so? (Is it right for me to do so?)

> Éstne míhi fãs (*or* licétne míhi) hóc fácĕre?

You are not right. (It is wrong for you.)

> Nôn ést tíbi fãs (nôn lícet).
> Ést tíbi néfas.

EXERCISE 41.

Have you still a mind to buy the house of my friend?—I have still a mind to buy it, but I have no more money.— Have you time to work?—I have time, but no mind to work.— Has he time to cut some sticks?—He has time to cut some.—Have you a mind to cut some bread?—I have a mind to cut some, but I have no knife.— Have you time to cut some cheese?—I have time to cut some.— Has he a desire to cut the tree?—He has a desire to cut it, but he has no time.—Has he time to cut the cloth?—He has time to cut it. —Have I time to cut the trees?—You have time to cut them?— Has the painter a mind to buy a horse?—He has a mind to buy two.—Has your captain of the navy time to speak (*ad loquendum*)? —He has time, but no desire to speak.—Have you a mind to buy a carriage?—I have a mind to buy one.—Have I a mind to buy a house?—You have a mind to buy one.—Has your brother a mind to buy a great ox?—He has a mind to buy a little one.—We have a mind to buy little oxen.—How many horses have you a mind to buy?—I have a mind to buy four.—Has any one a mind to buy a broom?—This man has a mind to buy one.—What has that man a mind to buy?—He has a mind to buy a beautiful carriage, three beautiful horses, good tea, and good meat.

---

* The learner must bear in mind that, although these formulas are arranged with special reference to the expressions *cupio, cupidus sum,* and *otium ad* of this Lesson, they are of general importance, as these same constructions will perpetually recur with other words in different parts of the book.

EXERCISE 42.

Have you a desire to speak ? — I have a desire, but no time to speak. — Have you the courage to cut your arm ? — I have not the courage to cut it. — Am I right in speaking? — You are not wrong in speaking; but you are wrong in cutting my trees. — Has the son of your friend a desire to buy one more bird ? — He has a desire to buy one more. — Have you a mind to buy one more beautiful coat ? — I have a mind to buy one more. — Have we a mind to buy a few more horses ? — We have a mind to buy a few more, but we have no more money. — What have you a mind to buy ? — We have a mind to buy something good, and our neighbors have a mind to buy something beautiful. — Have their children a desire to buy any birds ? — Their children have no desire to buy any. — Have you the courage to buy the trunk of the captain ? — I have a desire to buy it, but I have no more money. — Who has a mind to buy my beautiful dog ? — Nobody has a mind to buy it. — Have you a mind to buy my beautiful birds, or those of the Frenchman ? — I have a mind to buy those of the Frenchman. — Which book has he a mind to buy ? — He has a mind to buy that which you have, that which your son has, and that which mine has. — Have you two horses ? — I have only one, but I have a wish to buy one more.

Lesson XXVII. — PENSUM VICESIMUM SEPTIMUM.

OF COMPOUND VERBS.

A. The majority of Latin compound verbs are formed by prefixing certain particles to simple verbs. These particles are either the separable prepositions *a* (*ab* or *abs*), *ad, ante, circum, cum, de, e* or *ex, in, inter, ob, per, post, prae, praeter, pro, sub, super, supter,* and *trans,* or one of the inseparable prefixes *amb* (*an*), *dis* (or *di*), *re,* and *se.*

REMARKS.

1. It is frequently the case that the radical vowel or diphthong of the simple verb is changed in the compound ; as *frango, diffringo ; laedo, collīdo,* &c.

2. The final consonant of many of the above prepositions is often *assimilated,* i. e. changed, into the initial of the verb. The notes to the following list of compound verbs will show to what extent this is done.

EXAMPLES OF COMPOUND VERBS.

A[1] — āmitto, *I lose.*
Ab — ăbĕo, *I go away.*
" — aufŭgio, *I escape.*
Abs — abscondo, *I conceal.*
Ad[2] — addo, *I add (to).*
" — affĕro, *I bring (to).*
" — assŭmo, *I take, assume.*
Ante[3] — antĕpōno, *I prefer.*
" — antĭcĭpo, *I anticipate.*
Circum — circŭmĕo, *I go around.*
Cum[4] — combūro, *I burn up.*
" — compōno, *I compose.*
" — collĭgo, *I collect.*
" — corrĭpio, *I seize.*
" — conservo, *I preserve.*
" — cŏălesco, *I blend with.*
" — cŏmĕdo, *I eat up.*
" — cōgĭto (= co-agito), *I think, reflect.*
De — descendo, *I descend.*
E[5] — ējĭcĭo, *I cast out.*
" — escendo, *I disembark.*
Ex — exaudĭo, *I hear.*
" — expōno, *I expound.*
In[6] — intro, *I enter.*

In — illido, *I strike against.*
" — immūto, *I change.*
" — irrumpo, *I burst into.*
Inter[7] — interpōno, *I put between.*
" — intellĭgo, *I comprehend.*
Ob[8] — obsto, *I stand against.*
" — oppōno, *I place against.*
" — ostendo, *I show.*
Per[9] — perlĕgo, *I read through.*
" — pellĭcĭo, *I allure.*
Post — postpōno, *I value less.*
Prae — praefĕro, *I prefer.*
Praeter — praetermitto, *I omit.*
Pro — prōcurro, *I run forward.*
" — prōdĕo,[10] *I go forth.*
Sub[11] — subjĭcĭo, *I subject.*
" — succēdo, *I follow.*
" — suspendo, *I suspend.*
Super — supĕrimpōno, *I place upon.*
Supter — suptĕrăgo, *I drive under.*
Trans[12] — transĕo, *I pass over (beyond).*
" — tradūco, *I lead over.*
" — transcribo, *I transcribe.*

B. The particle *amb* (*am, an*) has the sense of *around, about, concerning.* *Dis* or *di* denotes separation or dispersion, sometimes also

---

[1] *A* is put before m and v; *ab* before vowels and the majority of consonants; *abs* only before c and t. In the verbs *aufĕro, aufŭgio,* the *ab* is changed into *av = au.*

[2] *Ad* remains unchanged before vowels, and before d, j, v, m; but before the remaining consonants it is assimilated.

[3] *Ante* changes its *e* into *i* only in the verbs *antĭcĭpāre* and *antĭstāre.*

[4] *Cum* in composition never appears without a change of form. Before b, p, m, it becomes *com*; before l, n, r, it is assimilated into *col, con, cor*; before the remaining consonants it is always *con*; before vowels it is generally *co*, but sometimes *com.*

[5] Before vowels, and before c, p, q, s, t, generally *ex*; before the rest of the consonants, *e*; before *f*, assimilation.

[6] *In*, before m, b, p, becomes *im*; before l and r it is assimilated; in all other cases it remains unchanged.

[7] *Inter* remains unaltered, except in *intellĭgo.*

[8] *Ob* is assimilated only before f, g, p. The form *ostendo* is from the obsolete *obs* and *tendo.*

[9] *Per* generally remains unaltered, except sometimes before r.

[10] The letter *d* is sometimes inserted between the prefix and the verb, to prevent a hiatus; as *pro-d-ĕo, re-d-ĕo,* &c.

[11] *Sub* before vowels remains unchanged; it is assimilated before the consonants c. f. g, m, p, and sometimes also before r.

[12] *Trans* rejects the final *s*, when the verb begins with one; it sometimes becomes *tra* before consonants.

11 *

intensity. *Re* is generally *back*, *again*, but it sometimes likewise denotes separation. Its form before a vowel is *red*. *Se* is equivalent to the English *aside*, *apart*. These particles are called inseparable, because they are never used as independent words. Examples:—

Amb— ambĭo, *I go about.*
  " — ambĭgo, *I quarrel (about).*
  " — ampŭto, *I cut off.*
  " — anquĭro, *I investigate.*
Dis— disjĭcĭo, *I scatter.*
  " — dispōno, *I arrange*
  " — dīmitto, *I dismiss.*
  " — diffĕro, *I put off.*

Re — rĕmitto, *I send back.*
  " — rĕlĕgo, *I read again.*
  " — reclūdo, *I unlock.*
  " — rĕdĕo, *I return.*
Se — sēvŏco, *I call aside.*
  " — sēdūco, *I lead aside.*
  " — sējungo, *I separate.*

C. Obs. Verbs are also compounded with nouns, adjectives, and with other verbs and adverbs; as *vēnumdăre*, from *vēnum* + *dăre*; *călĕfăcĕre*, from *calĭdus* + *făcĕre*; *obstŭpĕfăcĕre*, from *ob* + *stŭpĕo* + *făcĕre*, &c. But the great majority are compounds with prepositions.

To break, to break into pieces.	Frango, ĕre, frēgi, fractum (ALIQUID and NEUTER). Confringo, ĕre, frēgi, fractum. Diffringo (ALIQUID).
To keep, take care of.	Servo, āre, āvi, ātum. Rĕpōno, ĕre, pŏsuī, posĭtum. (ALIQUID).
To pick up.	Tollo, ĕre, sustŭli, sublātum (ALIQUID).
To mend, repair.	Rĕpăro, āre, āvi, ātum. Rĕfĭcĭo, ĕre, fēci, fectum. (ALIQUID).
To light, kindle.	Accendo, ĕre, di, sum (ALIQUID).
To make (*or* light) a fire.	Ignem (*m.*) accendĕre (făcĕre).
To burn (be on fire).	Ūro, ĕre, ussi, ustum. Ardĕo, ĕre, arsi, arsum.
To burn up, destroy by burning.	Combūro, ĕre, bussi, bustum. Concrĕmo, āre, āvi, ātum. (ALIQUEM, ALIQUID).
To seek, look for.	Quaero, ĕre, quaesīvi, quaesītum. Conquiro, ĕre, isīvi, isītum. (ALIQUEM, ALIQUID).
To warm.	Călĕfăcĭo, ĕre, fēci, factum (ALIQUID).
To make.	Făcio, făcĕre, fēci, factum. Confĭcĭo, ĕre, fēci, fectum. (ALIQUID).
To do.	Ăgo, ăgĕre, ēgi, actum. Făcĭo, făcĕre, fēci, factum. (ALIQUID).

To be willing, to wish.   *Vŏlo, velle, vŏlŭi* (ALIQUID FA-
CĔRE).

D. Obs. The present indicative of the verb *vŏlo*, which is irregular,
is thus inflected.

SING.	*I will, am willing, or wish*	ĕgo vŏlo
	Thou wilt (you will), &c.	tū vīs
	He will, is willing, &c.	ille vult,
PLUR.	*We will, wish,* &c.	nōs vŏlŭmŭs
	Ye will, wish, &c.	vōs vultĭs
	They will, wish, &c.	hī, ĭi, illi vŏlunt.

REMARK. — The forms *volt* and *voltis* occur in ancient authors instead of *vult* and *vultis.*

Will you? Do you wish? Are you willing?	{ Vīsne? Écquid vīs?	An (tū) vīs? Núm vīs?
Will he? Is he willing? Does he wish?	{ Vúltne? Équid (ís) vúlt?	An (ílle) vúlt? Núm vúlt?
Do you wish to make my fire?	Vīsne tū mĭhi accéndĕre (fŭcĕre) ígnem?	
I am willing to make it.	{ Vŏlo éum accéndĕre.	Égo éum făcere nôn nŏlo.
I do not wish to make it.	Nŏlo éum accéndere.	
Does he wish to buy your horse?	Vúltne équum túum émere?	
He wishes to buy it.	Vúlt éum émere.	
He does not wish to buy it.	{ Nôn vúlt éum émĕre.	Éum émĕre nôn vúlt.

To be unwilling.   *Nŏlo, nollĕ, nŏlŭi* (ALIQUID FA-
CĔRE).

E. Obs. The verb *vŏlo* is compounded of *nōn* and *vŏlo*, and follows
the inflection of the simple verb. Thus:—

SING.	*I am unwilling,* &c.	nōlo
	Thou art unwilling, &c.	nōn vīs
	He is unwilling, &c.	nōn vult,
PLUR.	*We are unwilling*	nōlŭmŭs
	Ye are unwilling	nōn vultĭs
	They are unwilling.	nōlunt.

REMARK. — *Nevis* and *nevolt* occur in the older Latin writers instead of *nonvis* and *nonvult.*

F. RULE. The verbs *vŏlo, nŏlo, mālo, cŭpĭo, sŏlĕo,
audeo,* and others expressing willingness, desire, ability,
custom, duty, and the like, are followed by the infinitive; as,

Vólo fíéri dóctus.*	*I wish to become learned.*
Nôn vúlt abíre.	*He is unwilling to go.*
Débes ésse díligens.	*You ought to be diligent.*
Sólet trístis ésse.	*He is wont to be sad.*
Pótest líber ésse.	*He can be free.*

Has the tailor time to mend my coat.	Habétne sártor spátium ad reparándum méam tógam ? Éstne sartóri ótium ad tógam méam reficiéndam ?
He has time to mend it.	Ést éi ótium ad éam reficiéndam. .
Has the shoemaker time to mend my boots ?	Éstne sutóri spátium ad cáligas méas reficiéndas ?
He has time to mend them.	Ést éi spátium ad éas reficiéndas.
Am I right in keeping (is it right for me to keep) your money ?	Éstne míhi fás pecúniam túam servâre (repónĕre) ?
You are not right in keeping it.	Nôn ést tíbi fás (tíbi néfas est) éam servâre (repónĕre).
Who has to mend (who must mend) our coats ?	Cui súnt tógae nóstrae reparándae ?
The tailor has to mend them.	Reparándae súnt sartóri.
What have I to do ? ·	Quíd ést míhi faciéndum ?
You have to warm our coffee.	Coffĕa nóstra tíbi calefaciénda ést.

EXERCISE 43.

Have you a desire to keep my letter ? — I have a desire to keep it. — Am I right in keeping your money ? — You are right in keeping it. — Has the tailor a desire to make my coat ? — He has a desire to make it, but he has no time. — Has your tailor time to mend my coats ? — He has time to mend them. — Have you courage to burn my hat ? — I have not the courage to burn it ; I have a mind to keep it ? — Has the shoemaker's boy a mind to mend my boots ? — He has no time to mend them. — What has our friend's tailor to mend ? — He has to mend our old coats. — Who has to mend our boots ? — Our shoemaker has to mend them. — What has our hatmaker to do ? — He has to mend your great hats. — Has your brother's joiner anything to do ? — He has to mend our great tables and our little chairs. — Do you wish to keep my twenty-seven crowns ? — I wish to keep them. — Will you pick up that crown or that florin ? — I will pick up both. — Do you wish to cut his finger ? — I do not wish to cut it. — Does the painter wish to burn vinegar ? — He wishes to burn some.

---

* After verbs expressing a desire or wish (such as *rólo, nôlo, málo, cúpio, opto, studĕo*), the noun, adjective, or participle of the predicate is in the *Nominative, when the subject* of the sentence *remains the same*, but in the *Accusative* when *a new subject is introduced*, or the pronoun of the same person repeated. Thus : *Cupio esse clemens*, I desire to be clement ; but *Cupio te esse clementem*, I desire you to be clement ; and also *Cupio me esse clementem*, instead of *Cupio esse clemens*. And in the same way : *Volo eum fiĕri doctum*, I wish him to become learned ; and *Volo me fiĕri doctum*, instead of *Volo fiĕri doctus*.

— Is the peasant willing to burn his bread? — He is not willing to burn his own, but that of his neighbor. — Have you anything to do? — I have nothing to do. — Have we anything to do? — We have to warm our coffee. — Do you wish to speak? — I wish to speak. — Is your son willing to work? — He is not willing to work.

EXERCISE 44.

Do you wish to buy anything? — I wish to buy something. — What do you wish to buy? — I wish to buy some good books. — What has he to buy? — He has to buy a good horse. — Will you buy this or that table? — I will buy neither this nor that. — Which house does your friend wish to buy? — He wishes to buy your brother's great house. — Is your servant willing to make my fire? — He is willing to make it. — Will your father buy these rams or these oxen? He will buy neither the one nor the other. — Does he wish to buy my umbrella or my cane? — He wishes to buy both. — Do you wish to make a fire? — We do not wish to make any. — What do you wish to make? — I wish to make vinegar. — Will you seek my knife? — I will seek it. — Have you to look for anything? — I have nothing to look for. — Has he time to seek my son? — He has time, but he will not seek him. — What has he to do? — He has to make a fire, to wash my thread stockings, to buy good coffee, good sugar, good water, and good meat. — Will he buy your good trunk? — He will buy it. — Will you buy my great or my little house? — I will buy neither your great nor your little house; I wish to buy that of our friend. — Will you buy my beautiful horses? — I will not buy them. — How many rams will you buy? — I will buy twenty-two. — Does the foreigner wish to buy much corn? — He wishes to buy but little. — Do you wish to buy a great many gloves? — We wish to buy only a few, but our children wish to buy a great many. — Will they seek the same boots which we have? — They will not seek those which you have, but those which my father has. — Will you look for my coats, or those of the good Frenchman. — I will look neither for yours nor for those of the good Frenchman; I will look for mine and for those of my good son.

Lesson XXVIII. — PENSUM DUODETRICE-SIMUM.

OF THE DERIVATION OF TENSES.

It has already been said (Lesson XXIV.) that the different tenses and other parts of the Latin verbs are all formed from four principal parts; namely, from the Present Indicative, the Present Infinitive, the Perfect Indicative, and the Supine in *um*. This formation takes place according to the following laws: —

I

A. From the PRESENT INFINITIVE (*ămāre, mŏnēre, lĕgĕre, audīre*) are derived : —

1. The *Imperative Passive*, which has invariably the same form ; as *amāre, mŏnēre, lĕgĕre, audīre*, be thou loved, admonished, read, heard.

2. The *Imperative Active*, by dropping the final *re* ; as *ămā, mŏnē, lĕgĕ, audī*, love, admonish, read, hear thou.

3. The *Present Infinitive Passive*, by changing, 1. *āre*, 2. *ēre*, 4. *īre*, into, 1. *āri*, 2. *ēri*, 4. *īri*, and 3. *ĕre* into *i* ; as *amārī, monērī, lĕgī, audīrī*, to be loved, admonished, read, heard.

4. The *Imperfect Subjunctive Active*, by adding *m* ; as *amārĕm, monērĕm, legĕrĕm, audīrĕm*, that I might be loved, admonished, read, heard.

5. The *Imperfect Subjunctive Passive*, by adding *r* ; as *amārĕr, monērĕr, legĕrĕr, audīrĕr*, that I might be loved, admonished, read, heard.

B. From the PRESENT INDICATIVE (*ămo, mŏnĕo, lĕgo, audĭo*) are derived : —

1. The *Present Indicative Passive*, by adding *r* ; as *ămor, mŏnĕor, lĕgor, audĭor*, I am loved, admonished, read, heard.

2. The *Present Subjunctive Active*, by changing the terminations of the Present Indicative (1. *o*, 2. *ĕo*, 3. *o* (*ĭo*), 4. *ĭo*) into, 1. *em*, 2. *ĕam*, 3. *am* (*ĭam*), 4. *ĭam* ; as *ămem, mŏnĕam, lĕgam* (*capĭam*), *audĭam*, that I may love, admonish, read (take), hear.

3. The *Present Subjunctive Passive*, by changing the final *m* of the Active into *r* ; as *ămer, mŏnĕar, lĕgar* (*capĭar*), *audĭar*, that I may be loved, admonished, read (taken), heard.

4. The *Imperfect Indicative Active*, by changing the terminations of the Present into, 1. *ābam*, 2. *ēbam*, 3. *ēbam* (*iēbam*), 4. *iēbam* ; as *amābam, monēbam, legēbam* (*capiēbam*), *audiēbam*, I loved, admonished, read (took), heard.

5. The *Imperfect Indicative Passive*, by changing the final *m* of the same tense in the Active into *r* ; as *amābar, monēbar, legēbar* (*capiēbar*), *audiēbar*, I was loved, admonished, read (taken), heard.

6. The *First Future Active*, by changing the termination of the Present into, 1. *ābo*, 2. *ēbo*, 3. *am* (*ĭam*), 4. *ĭam* ; as *amābo, monēbo, lĕgam* (*capĭam*), *audĭam*, I shall love, admonish, read (take), hear.

7. The *First Future Passive*, by changing the final *m* of the same tense in the Active into *r* ; as *amābor, monēbor, lĕgar* (*capĭar*), *audĭar*, I shall be loved, admonished, read (taken), heard.

8. The *Present Participle Active*, by changing the terminations of the Present Indicative into, 1. *ans*, 2. *ens*, 3. *ens* (*ĭens*), 4. *ĭens* ; as *ămans, mŏnens, lĕgens* (*capĭens*), *audĭens*, loving, admonishing, reading (taking), hearing.

9. The *Future Passive Participle*, by changing the same terminations into, 1. *andus*, 2. *endus*, 3. *endus* (*ĭendus*), 4. *ĭendus* ; as *aman-*

dus, monendus, legendus (capiendus), audiendus, to be loved, admonished, read (taken), heard.

10. The *Gerund,* in a similar manner; as *amandi, monendi, legendi (capiendi), audiendi,* of loving, admonishing, reading (taking), hearing.

C. From the PERFECT INDICATIVE (*amāvi, monŭi, lēgi, audīvi*) are derived: —

1. The *Pluperfect Indicative,* by changing the final *i* into *ĕram;* as *amāvĕram, monŭĕram, lēgĕram, audīvĕram,* I had loved, admonished, read, heard.

2. The *Future Perfect,* by changing the final *i* into *ĕro;* as *amāvĕro, monŭĕro, lēgĕro, audīvĕro,* I shall have loved, admonished, read, heard.

3. The *Perfect Subjunctive,* by changing *i* into *ĕrim;* as *amāvĕrim, monŭĕrim, lēgĕrim, audīvĕrim,* that I may have loved, admonished, read, heard.

4. The *Pluperfect Subjunctive,* by changing *i* into *issem;* as *amāvissem, monŭissem, lēgissem, audīvissem,* that I might have loved, admonished, read, heard.

5. The *Perfect Infinitive Active,* by changing *i* into *isse;* as *amāvisse, monŭisse, lēgisse, audīvisse,* to have loved, admonished, read, heard.

D. From the SUPINE IN "UM" (*amātum, monĭtum, lectum, audītum*) are derived: —

1. The *Perfect Participle Passive,* by changing the final *um* into *us, a, um;* as *amātus, a, um,* loved; *monĭtus, a, um,* admonished; *lectus, a, um,* read; *audĭtus, a, um,* heard.

2. The *Future Participle Active,* by changing *um* into *ūrus, a, um;* as *amātūrus, a, um,* about to love; *monĭtūrus, a, um,* about to admonish; *lectūrus, a, um,* about to read; *audĭtūrus, a, um,* about to hear.

REMARK. — The Participle in *ūrus* in connection with *esse* serves to form the *Future Infinitive Active;* as *amātūrum (am, um) esse,* to be about to love; *monĭtūrum (am, um) esse,* to be about to admonish, &c. The same Participle, compounded with the different tenses of the verb *sum,* gives rise to a new conjugation, by which the various shades of a future or incipient action are indicated; as *amatūrus sum,* I am about to love; *amatūrus ĕram,* I was about to love; *amatūrus ĕro,* I shall be about to love, &c.

E. In the PASSIVE VOICE several tenses are *periphrastic* or *compound,* and are formed by combining the Perfect Participle with one of the tenses of the verb *sum.* These compound tenses are: —

1. The *Perfect Indicative,* with *sum;* as *amātus (a, um) sum,* I have been loved; *monĭtus (a, um) sum,* I have been admonished, &c.

2. The *Perfect Subjunctive*, with *sim ;* as *amatus* (*a, um*) *sim*, **that** I may have been loved; *audītus* (*a, um*) *sim*, that I may have been heard, &c.

3. The *Pluperfect Indicative*, with *ĕram ;* as *lectus* (*a, um*) *ĕram*, I had been read; *audītus* (*a, um*) *ĕram*, I had been heard, &c.

4. The *Pluperfect Subjunctive*, with *essem ;* as *amātus* (*a, um*) *essem*, that I might have been loved; *monītus* (*a, um*) *essem*, that I might have been admonished, &c.

5. The *Future Perfect*, with *ĕro ;* as *audītus* (*a, um*) *ĕro*, I shall have been heard; *lectus* (*a um*) *ĕro*, I shall have been read, &c.

6. The *Perfect Infinitive*, with *esse ;* as *amātum* (*am, um*) *esse*, to have been loved; *audītum* (*am, um*) *esse*, to have been heard, &c.

7. To these compound or periphrastic parts of the Passive Voice we must add the *Future Infinitive*, which is formed by combining the Supine in *um* with *iri ;* as *amātum iri, lectum iri*, &c., to be about to be loved, read, &c. (See Paradigms, pp. 664, 665.)

To tear, lacerate.	Discindo, *ĕre, ĭdi, issum.* Lăcĕro, *āre, āvi, ātum.* (ALIQUID).
To drink.	Bĭbo, *ĕre, bĭbi, bĭbĭtum.* Pōto, *āre, āvi, ātum or pōtum.* (ALIQUID).
To carry (take).	Fĕro, ferre, tŭli, lātum. Porto, *āre, āvi, ātum.* (ALIQUID).
To bring (carry).	Affĕro, afferre, attŭli, allātum. Apporto, *āre, āvi, ātum.* (ALICUI ALIQUID).
To go.	Ĕo, íre, ívi or íi, ĭtum (NEUTER).

F. Obs. The verbs *fĕro*, I bear, carry, and *ĕo*, I go, are irregular in several tenses. The present indicative is thus inflected : —

SING.	*I carry*	fĕro	SING.	*I go*	ĕo
	Thou carriest	fers		*Thou goest*	ĭs
	He carries,	fert,		*He goes,*	ĭt,
PLUR.	*We carry*	fĕrĭmus	PLUR.	*We go*	ímus
	Ye carry	fertis		*Ye go*	ítis
	They carry.	fĕrunt.		*They go.*	ĕunt.

To be.	Sŭm, esse, fŭi, fūtŭrus.
To be at home.	Dómĭ (gen.) *ésse.*
To go home.	Dómum (acc.) *íre.*

G. Obs. 1. The English " at home " is in Latin expressed by the genitive *dŏmĭ*, to which may be added *meae, tuae, nostrae, vestrae,* and *aliënae,* in the sense of " at my, thy (your), our, your, another man's house or home"; but when another adjective or pronoun follows, the ablative with *in* is required; as *in illā domo*, in that home; *in domo pri-vātā*, in a private house.   When the genitive of the possessor is added, either *domi* or *in domo* may be used; as *domi* or *in domo alicujus*, at some one's house or home; *domi* or *in domo Caesāris*, at the house of Cæsar.

2. The English "home" (after verbs of motion) is expressed by the accusative *domum*, and so also *domum meam, tuam, nostram, ve-stram, aliēnam*, " to my, thy (your), our, your, another man's house or home"; but with any other adjective or pronoun the preposition *in* is required; as *in domum illam*, to that house or home; *in domum novam*, to the new house or home.   When the genitive of the pos-sessor is added, it is either *domum* or *in domum alicujus*, to some one's house or home.

Is your father at home ?	Éstne páter túus dómi ?
He is not at home.	Nòn est (dómi).
Is his brother going home ?	Ítne fráter éjus dómum?
He is going home.	Ít (dómum).
With or *at the house of.*	{ *Apud* (Prep. with the Acc.). *Cum* (Prep. with the Abl.). *Domi* or *in domo* (with the Gen.).
To or *to the house of.*	{ *Ad* (Prep. with the Acc.). *Domum* or *in domum* (with the Gen.).
To be with the man *or* at the man's house.	{ Apud vírum *or* cum víro ésse. Dómi *or* in dómo víri esse.
To go to the man *or* to the man's house.	{ Ad vírum íre. Dómum *or* in dómum víri íre.
To be with one's friend (at the house of one's friend).	{ Apud amícum *or* cum amíco (súo) ésse. Dómi *or* in dómo amíci ésse.
To go to one's friend *or* to the house of one's friend.	{ Ad amícum (súum) íre. Dómum *or* in dómum amíci íre.
To be with me, thee (you), us, you, at my house, &c.	{ Apud mê, tê, nôs, vôs ésse. Mécum, técum, nobíscum,* vobís-cum esse. Dómi méae, túae, nóstrae, véstrae ésse.
To be at one's own, at another man's house.	Dómi súae, aliénae esse.
To go to one's own, to another man's house.	Dómum súam, aliênam íre.
To be with him, with them, with some one.	{ Apud éum, éos, áliquem ésse. Cum éo, íis, áliquo ésse. Dómi *or* in dómo éjus, eórum, ali-cújus ésse.

---

* The preposition *cum* with *mê, tê, sê*, always becomes *mécum, técum, sécum*; with *nôbis, vôbis*, either *nôbiscum, vôbiscum*, or *cum nôbis, cum vôbis*.

12

To go to him, to them, to some one.	Ad éum, éos, áliquem íre. Dómum *or* in dómum éjus, eôrum, alicújus íre.
To be with no one, at no one's house.	Apud néminem (núllum) ésse. Cum núllo (némine) ésse. Dómi *or* in dómo nullius ésse.
To go to no one, to no one's house.	Ad núllum (némlnem) íre. Dómum *or* in dómum nullius íre.
To be with one's father, at one's father's house.	Apud pátrem (cum pátre) ésse. In dómo patérnā ésse.
To go to one's father, to one's father's house.	Ad pátrem íre. In dómum patérnam íre.
Is your little boy at any one's house?	Éstne puérculus túus apud áliquem (in dómo alicújus)?
He is at no one's house (with no one)?	Nôn est apud quénquam. In dómo nullius est.
Do you wish to go to your friend?	Vîsne ad amicum túum (dómum *or* in dómum amíci túi) íre?
I do not wish to go to him.	Nólo ad éum (dómum *or* in dómum éjus) íre.

At whose house? *With whom?*	Cújus in dómo? Apud quém?
To whose house? *To whom?*	Cújus in dómum? Ad quem?
To whom (to whose house) do you wish to go?	Ad quem (cújus in dómum) vis íre?
I do not wish to go to any one (to any one's house).	Nólo ad quénquam (in dómum cujúsquam) íre.
With whom (at whose house) is your brother?	Apud quem (cújus in dómo) est fráter túus?
He is with us (at our house).	Est apud nôs. Dómi nóstrae est.

EXERCISE 45.

Do you wish to tear my coat? — I do not wish to tear it. — Does your brother wish to tear my beautiful book? — He does not wish to tear it. — What does he wish to tear? — He wishes to tear your heart. — With whom is our father? — He is with his friend. — To whom do you wish to go? — I wish to go to you. — Will you go to my house? — I will not go to yours, but to my tailor's. — Does your father wish to go to his friend? — He wishes to go to him. — At whose house is your son? — He is at our house. — Do your children wish to go to our friends? — They wish to go to them. — Is the foreigner at our brother's? — He is there (*apud éum*). — At whose house is the Englishman? — He is at yours. — Is the American at our house? — No, sir, he is not at our house; he is at his friend's. — Is the Italian at his friends'? — He is at their house.

EXERCISE 46.

Do you wish to go home? — I do not wish to go home; I wish to go to the son of my neighbor. — Is your father at home? — No, sir, he is not at home. — With whom is he ? — He is with the good children of our old neighbor. — Will you go to any one's house ? — I will go to no one's house. — At whose house is your son ? — He is at no one's house; he is at home. — What will he do at home ? — He will drink good wine. — Will you carry my letters home ? — I will carry them to my father's. — Who will carry my notes ? — The young man will carry them. — Will he carry them to my house ? — No; he will carry them to his brother's. — Is his father at home ? — He is not at home; he is at the foreigner's. — What have you to drink ? — I have nothing to drink. — Has your son anything to drink ? — He has good wine and good water to drink. — Will your servant carry my books to my brothers' ? — He will carry them to their house. — What will you carry to my house ? — I will carry to your house two chickens, three birds, good bread, and good wine. — Will you carry these chairs to my house ? — I will not carry these, but those. — What will the German do at home ? — He will work and drink good wine.

Exercise 47.

What have you at home ? — I have nothing at home. — Have you anything good to drink at home ? — I have nothing good to drink; I have only bad water. — Has the captain as much coffee as sugar at home ? — He has as much of the one as of the other at home. — Will you carry as many crowns as buttons to my brother's ? — I will carry to his house as many of the one as of the other. — Will you carry great glasses to my house ? — I will carry some to your house. — Has the merchant a desire to buy as many oxen as rams ? — He wishes to buy as many of the one as of the other. — Has the shoemaker as many shoes as boots to mend ? — He has as many of the one as of the other to mend. — Has he as much wine as water to drink ? — He has as much to drink of the one as of the other. — Has the Turk a desire to break some glasses ? — He has a desire to break some. — Has he a mind to drink some wine ? — He has no mind to drink any. — Will you buy anything of me (*de mê*) ? — I will buy nothing of you. — Of whom (*de quô*) * will you buy your corn ? — I will buy it of the great merchant. — Of whom will the English buy their oxen ? — They will buy them of the Dutch. — Will the Spaniards buy anything ? — They will buy nothing.

---

* The person *of whom* any is bought is in Latin put in the Ablative with the preposition *de*; so that the formula is: *aliquid de aliquo emĕre*, to buy any of any one.

Lesson XXIX. — PENSUM UNDETRICESIMUM.

OF THE CLASSIFICATION OF VERBS.

A. Latin verbs in general may be divided into *Primitive* and *Derivative*, and with reference to their composition into *Simple* and *Compound.*

Primitive verbs are those which are not derived from any other word, but are themselves the roots for other parts of speech.

Derivatives are formed either from nouns, adjectives, or other verbs.

Simple verbs may be either primitive or derivative.

Compound verbs are formed by the union of a verb with another verb or with some other part of speech. (See Lesson XXVI.)

B. The verbs derived from other verbs are subdivided into a number of classes. These classes are : —

1. *Frequentatives*, or such as denote a reiteration or frequent repetition of the action expressed by the primitive; as *dictāre* (from *dico*), to say often; *quaeritāre* (from *quaero*), to inquire repeatedly.

These verbs are all of the first conjugation, and are generally formed from the supine of their primitives, by changing the *ātum* of the first conjugation into *ĭto, ĭtāre,* and the *um* of the remaining conjugations into *o, āre;* as *portātum* (the supine of *porto,* I carry) — *portĭto, āre,* I carry often; *dormītum* (the supine of *dormio,* I sleep) — *dormĭto, āre,* I am apt to sleep constantly, I am sleepy. But others again are formed from the present indicative of their primitive, and some even from other frequentatives; as *agĭto, āre* (from *ago,* I drive), to drive up and down; *latĭto, āre* (from *latĕo,* I am concealed), I hide myself; *dictĭto, āre,* I say or tell often; *lectĭto, āre,* I read again and again (from the obsolete frequentatives *dictāre, lectāre*), &c.

2. *Desideratives*, in *ŭrĭo, ŭrīre,* denoting a desire for that which is indicated by the primitive. These verbs are likewise derived from the supine of the primitive, and are always of the fourth conjugation; as *ēsum* (the supine of *edo,* I eat) — *ēsŭrĭo, īre,* I desire to eat, I am hungry; *emptum* (from *emo,* I buy) — *emptŭrĭo, īre,* I desire to buy; *coenātum* (from *coeno,* I dine) — *coenātŭrĭo, īre,* I desire to dine, &c.

But a number of verbs in *ŭrĭo, ŭrīre* (and *ŭrĭo, ŭrĭāre*) are no frequentatives and can readily be distinguished by the long *u;* as *ligū-rīre,* to be dainty; *prūrīre,* to itch; *centurĭāre,* to divide into centuries; *decŭrĭāre,* to divide into companies.

3. *Inchoatives* or *Inceptives* in *sco, scĕre,* which serve to indicate the beginning of an action or state; as *languesco, ĕre,* I

am growing languid (from *languēre*, to be languid) ; *ingemisco*, *ēre*, I begin to sigh (from *gemēre*, to sigh).

The final *sco* of these inchoatives is *asco* from primitives of the first conjugation, *esco* from those of the second, and *isco* from those of the third and fourth.

Inchoatives frequently occur compounded with prepositions, while their primitives are simple verbs; as *pertimesco*, I begin to dread, from *timeo*, I am afraid ; *conticesco*, I become silent, from *tacĕo*, I am silent; *obdormisco*, I fall asleep, from *dormĭo*, I sleep.

Some inchoatives are derived from substantives and adjectives : as *maturesco*, I grow ripe, from *matūrus, a, um ; puĕrasco*, I am becoming a boy, from *puer*, a boy, &c.

A number of verbs in *sco* are no inchoatives, as *cresco*, I grow ; *nosco*, I learn to know ; *posco*, I demand.

4. *Diminutives*, with the termination *illo, illāre*, which is annexed to the root of the primitive without any other change ; as *cantillo*, I sing a little, I trill (from *cantare*, to sing) ; *conscribillo*, I scribble (from *scribĕre*, to write) ; *sorbillo*, I sip (from *sorbēre*, to sup, drink up). The verbs of this class are but few in number.

5. *Intensives* in *sso, ssĕre ;* as *capesso, facesso, petesso* (from *capĭo, facĭo, pĕto*), I seize, perform, seek with earnestness or eagerness.

C. Verbs derived from nouns are called *Denominatives.* E. g. *lucĕo*, I shine ; *fraudo*, I deceive, defraud ; *vulnĕro*, I wound (from *lux, fraus, vulnus*), &c.

A large number of Latin verbs derived from substantives signify *to be* or *to imitate that which is indicated by the noun.* The majority of these verbs are deponents of the first conjugation ; as *domīnus — domīnāri*, to act the lord, to domineer ; *cornix — cornĭcāri*, to chatter like a crow ; *fūr — fūrāri*, to be a thief, to steal ; *Graecŭlus — graecāri*, to live like a Graeculus, to live luxuriously and effeminately ; but also *păter — patrisso, āre*, I take after my father ; *būbo — būbŭlo, āre*, to screech like an owl, &c.

Where?	*Ŭbĭ?*	*Ŭbĭnam?* *	(Adverbs.)
Whither? *Where to?*	*Quō?*	*Quorsŭm?* *Quorsŭs?*	(Adverbs.)

D. Obs. 1. The interrogative adverb *ŭbi?* implies motion or rest in a place, and the noun of the answer generally stands either in the genitive or ablative,† but sometimes in the accusative with one of the prepositions *ad, apud, super,* or *supter.*

---

* This *nam* is affixed with some emphasis. So also *Ŭbi loci? Ŭbi gentium? Ŭbi terrarum?* Where in the world?

† When this ablative is the *name of a town* of the third declension, it stands *without* a preposition; as *Carthagine*, at Carthage; but otherwise it has *in* before it.

12 *

Obs. 2. The interrogative adverb *quŏ?* implies motion or direction towards a place, and the noun of the answer is always in the accusative, either with or without a preposition.

There.	Ĭbĭ, illĭc, ictĭc (rest).
Thither (there).	Ēō, illō, illŭc (motion).
To carry thither.	Ēō (illo, illŭc) portâre (férre).
To carry it thither.	(Éum, éam), íd íllō portâre.
To carry some thither.	{ SING. Aliquántum éō (íllo, ílluc) portâre (férre). PLUR. Áliquot éō (íllō, ílluc) portâre (férre).
To carry them thither.	Éos (éas, éa) éō (íllo, ílluc) portâre *or* férre.
Where is my son ?	Úbi ést fílĭus méus ?
He is at home.	{ Dómi ést. Dómi súae ést.
Is his brother there too ?	Éstne íbi ét * frâter éjus ?
He is not there, but at the neighbor's.	Nôn ést íbi ; apud vicĭnum est.
Will you carry my books to the merchant ?	Vĭsne tû lĭbros méos ad mercatô-rem portâre ?
I do not wish to carry them to him.	Nólo éos ad íllum portâre.
To send.	Mitto, ĕre, mĭsi, missum (ALICŬI ALIQUID, ALIQUID AD ALI-QUEM).
To come.	{ Vĕnĭo, ĕre, vēni, ventum. Pervĕnĭo, ĕre, vĕni, ventum (NEU-TER).
To lead.	{ Dūco, ĕre, duxi, ductum. Dēdūco, ĕre, duxi, ductum. (ALIQUEM AD ALIQUEM).
When? At what time?	*Quandŏ? Quō tempŏre?*

E. RULE. Time *when* is put in the Ablative without a preposition, as : —

Hórā duodécĭmā.	*At twelve o'clock.*
Hŏc témpŏre.	*At this time.*
Dĭĕ constitútā.	*On the appointed day.*
To-morrow.	Crās (*adv.*), crastĭnō tempŏre.
To-day, this day.	{ Hŏdĭē (*adv.*), hŏc dĭē, hodĭernō tempŏre.
Somewhere, anywhere.	Ălĭcŭbĭ, usquăm, uspĭăm (rest).
Somewhither, anywhither.	Ălĭquŏ, quŏquăm, quŏpĭăm (motion).

---

* The conjunction *et* has sometimes the sense of *also, too.*

F. Obs. The adverb *ălĭcŭbi* is compounded of *alĭquis* and *ŭbi*, and is synonymous with *in aliquo loco*, "in some place," or "somewhere," "anywhere," generally. *Uspĭam* may commonly stand in the same sense, but *usquam* can only be employed in clauses involving a condition or negation, as after the conjunctions *si*, *nisi*, *neque* (*nec*), *non*, *nunquam*, &c. The same distinctions apply to the corresponding adverbs of motion, *alĭquo*, *quopiam*, and *quoquam*.

Nowhere, not anywhere.	Nusquăm, nuspĭăm (rest).
Nowhither, not anywhither.	Nusquăm (motion).

Do you desire to go anywhere (anywhither)?	Cupĭsne ire ălĭquo (quópĭam)?
I do desire to go somewhere (somewhither).	Cúpĭo ire ălĭquo.
I desire to go to the house of my father.	In dómum patérnam ire cúpĭo.
I do not desire to go anywhere.	Núsquam ire cúpĭo.
Nor do I desire to go anywhere.	Neque égo quôquam ire cúpĭo.
If he desires to go anywhere.	Si ílle quôquam ire cúpit.
Is your brother anywhere?	Éstne fráter túus alĭcŭbi (úspĭam)?
He is somewhere.	Est alĭcŭbi (in ălĭquo loco).
He is at the house of his father.	In dómo patérnă est.
He is nowhere.	Núsquam (núspĭam) est.
Nor is his friend anywhere.	Néque amícus éjus úsquam est.
Unless your friend is anywhere.	Nísi amícus túus úsquam est.
Will you conduct me to your tailor?	Vísne me ad sartôrem túum dúcĕre?
I will conduct you to him.	Vólo tê ad éum dúcĕre (dedúcere).
When will you lead me to him?	Quándo (quô témpŏre) mê vis ad éum dúcĕre?
I will lead you to him to-morrow.	Égo tê crâs (crástĭno témpore) ad éum dúcĕre vólo.
Who will send me good books?	Quís vúlt míhi míttĕre líbros bónos?
No one will send you any.	Némo tíbi úllos míttĕre vult.
The physician.	Mĕdĭcus, i, *m.*
To write.	Scríbo, ĕre, psi, ptum (ALIQUID ALICUI *or* AD ALIQUEM).
Have you as many letters to write as my father?	Scribendaéne tíbi sunt tam múltae líttĕrae quam pátri méo? Habêsne tót littĕras scribéndas, quót páter méus?
I have more (of them) to write than he.	Scribéndae sunt míhi plûs (plúres) quám éi. Scribéndas égo plúres hábeo quam ílle (ípse).

EXERCISE 48.

Will you go anywhither (anywhere) ? — I will go nowhither (no-where). — Will your good son go to any one ? — He will go to no one. — When will you take your young man to the painter ? — I will take him there (*ad éum*) to-day. — Where will he carry these birds to ? — He will carry them nowhither. — Will you take the physician to this man ? — I will take him there (*ad éum*, to him). — When will you take him there ? — I will take him there to-day. — Will the physicians come to your good brother ? — They will not come to him. — Will you send me a servant ? — I will send you none. — Will you send a child to the physician ? — I will send one to him. — With whom is the physician ? — He is with nobody. — Do you wish to go anywhither ? — I wish to go to the good Americans. — Has he time to come to my house ? — He has no time to come there. — Will the captain write one more letter ? — He will write one more. — Will you write a note ? — I will write one. — Has your friend a mind to write as many letters as I ? — He has a mind to write quite as many.

EXERCISE 49.

Where is your brother ? — He is at home. — Whither do you wish to go ? — I wish to go home. — Whither does your father wish to go ? — He wishes to go to your house. — Whither will you carry this letter ? — I will carry it to my neighbor's. — Is your son at home ? — He is there. — Whither will the shoemaker carry my boots ? — He will carry them to your house ? — Will he carry them home ? — He will carry them thither. — Will you send good sugar home ? — I will send some thither. — Will the baker send good bread home ? — He will send some thither. — Will you come to me ? — I will come to you. — Whither do you wish to go ? — I wish to go to the good French-men. — Will the good Italians go to our house ? — They will go no-whither. — Will you take your son to my house ? — I will not take him to your house, but to the captain's. — When will you take him to the captain's ? — I will take him there to-morrow. — Have you many letters to write ? — I have only a few to write. — How many letters has our old neighbor to write ? — He has as many to write as you. — Who has long letters to write ? — The youth has some to write. — How many more letters has he to write ? — He has six more to write. — How many has he to send ? — He has twenty to send. — Has he as many letters to send as his father ? — He has fewer to send. — Has the hatmaker some more hats to send ? — He has no more to send. — Has your son the courage (*audétne fílius túus*) to write a long letter ? — He has the courage to write one. — Will he write as many letters as mine ? — He will write quite as many. — Will you buy as many carriages as horses ? — I will buy more of the latter than of the former.

Lesson XXX.—PENSUM TRICESIMUM.

OF THE PRESENT SUBJUNCTIVE.

A. The Present Subjunctive is formed from the Present Indicative by changing the terminations of the respective conjugations into, 1. *em*, 2. *ĕam*, 3. *am* (*ĭam*), 4. *ĭam ;* as, amo, *amem ;* monĕo, *monĕam ;* lego, *legam* (facĭo, *facĭam*); audio, *audĭam.** It is inflected as follows :—

FIRST CONJUGATION.

SINGULAR.		PLURAL.	
That I may love	ămĕm	*That we may love*	ămēmŭs
That thou mayst love	ămēs	*That ye may love*	ămētĭs
That he may love,	ămĕt,	*That they may love.*	ăment.

SECOND CONJUGATION.

SINGULAR.		PLURAL.	
That I may remind	mŏnĕăm	*That we may remind*	mŏnĕāmŭs
That thou mayst remind	mŏnĕās	*That ye may remind*	mŏnĕātĭs
That he may remind,	mŏnĕăt,	*That they may remind.*	mŏnĕant.

THIRD CONJUGATION.

SINGULAR.		PLURAL.	
That I may read	lĕgăm	*That we may read*	lĕgāmŭs
That thou mayst read	lĕgās	*That ye may read*	lŏgātĭs
That he may read,	lĕgăt,	*That they may read.*	lĕgant.

FOURTH CONJUGATION.

SINGULAR.		PLURAL.	
That I may hear	audĭăm	*That we may hear*	audĭāmŭs
That thou mayst hear	audĭās	*That ye may hear*	audĭātĭs
That he may hear,	audĭăt,	*That they may hear.*	audĭant.

Like *amem* inflect: *ordinem, dem, portem, laborem, larem,* &c. Like *monĕam : habĕam, vidĕam, fovĕam,* &c. Like *lĕgam : dĭcam, dispōnam, scrĭbam, facĭam,*† &c. Like *audĭam : aperĭam, esŭrĭam, sĭtĭam, vĕnĭam,* &c.

REMARK.—The present subjunctive of the first and third conjugations sometimes has *im* instead of *em* or *am ;* as *edim, commedim ; duim, perduim ;*‡ for *edam, commedam ; dem, perdam.* But this anti-

---

* See Lesson XXVIII. *B.* 2.
† Verbs of the third conjugation in *io* have their present subjunctive in *ĭam.* Thus, also, capio, *capiam,* calefacio, *calefaciam,* &c.
‡ From the obsolete forms *duo, perduo* (= do, *perdo*).

quated form occurs only in a few verbs. It is retained in the irregular verbs *esse* and *velle*, and their compounds; as *velim, nolim, malim; sim, possim, prosim,* &c.

B. The Present Subjunctive of the irregular verbs *sum, vŏlo, nŏlo, ĕo,* and *fĕro (affĕro)* is thus inflected :—

SINGULAR.		PLURAL.	
That I may be	sĭm	*That we may be*	sĭmus
That thou mayst be	sĭs	*That ye may be*	sĭtis
That he may be,	sĭt,*	*That they may be.*	sint.
That I may be willing	vĕlĭm	*That we may be willing*	vĕlĭmŭs
That thou mayst be willing	vĕlĭs	*That ye may be willing*	vĕlītĭs
That he may be willing,	vĕlĭt,	*That they may be willing.*	vĕlint.
That I may go	ĕăm	*That we may go*	ĕămŭs
That thou mayst go	ĕās	*That ye may go*	ĕātĭs
That he may go,	ĕăt,	*That they may go.*	ĕant.
That I may carry	fĕrăm	*That we may carry*	fĕrămŭs
That thou mayst carry	fĕrās	*That ye may carry*	fĕrātĭs
That he may carry,	fĕrăt,	*That they may carry.*	fĕrant.

REMARK.— The compounds of these verbs are all of them inflected in the same way.; as *desim, possim, prōsim,* from *desum, possum, prosum; mālĭm,†* nōlĭm, from *mălo, nōlo; abĕam, prodĕam, transĕam,* from *abeo, prodĕo, transĕo; affĕram, diffĕram, circumfĕram,* from *affĕro, diffĕro, circumfĕro,* &c.

OF THE USE OF THE SUBJUNCTIVE.

C. Obs. The Subjunctive serves to denote various modifications of the action or state expressed by the verb, and is often put in Latin where the English idiom requires the Indicative or Infinitive. It is chiefly employed :—

1st. After certain conjunctions, such as *ut* and *quō,* that, in order that; *nē,* that not, lest; *lĭcet* and *quamvis,* although; *ŭtĭnam,* would that; *quin* and *quomĭnus,* but that, &c. E. g. :—

Vĕnĭo ut vĭdĕam.   *I come to see (in order that I may see).*

---

* Instead of *sim, sis. sit,* the older Latin writers employ the forms *siem, sies, siet;* and also from the obsolete *fŭo,* the forms *fŭam, fŭas, fŭat;* ——, ——, *fŭant.*

† An ancient form of this is *mavĕlim, is, it,* &c. So the Imp. Subj. *mavellem* for *mallem;* the Pres. Ind. *mavŏlo* for *malo;* the Future Indic. *mavŏlam* for *malam,* &c.

Cáve nê scríbas.	*Take care lest you write.*
Útĭnam habêrem.	*Would that I had.*

2d. In indirect or dependent questions, introduced by an interrogative adjective, pronoun, or adverb, such as *quantus, qualis, quotus; quis, qui, cujas; ubi, quo, quorsum, quando, quoties, quomŏdo; an, ne,* &c. E. g. :—

Néscĭo quántum hábĕas.	*I do not know how much you have.*
Dic mĭhi quis (quâlis) sít.	*Tell me who he is.*
Scisne quándo vénĭat !	*Do you know when he comes ?*
Víde án ventúrus sít. *	*See whether he is about to come.*

3d. To denote possĭbility in general, and also an exhortation or command; as

Fórsĭtan témĕre fécĕrim.	*I may possibly have acted rashly.*
Émas quód necésse est.	*Buy what is necessary.*
Eámus. Scribâmus.	*Let us go. Let us write.*

I come in order to see (for the sake of seeing, to see, about to see).	⎧ *Vénĭo ut vídĕam.* ⎪ *Vénĭo ad vidéndum.* ⎨ *Vénĭo vidéndi causâ.* ⎪ *Vénĭo vidêre or visum.* ⎩ *Vénĭo visûrus.*

D. *Obs.* The compound conjunction *in order to, in order that,* is commonly expressed in Latin either by *ut* with the subjunctive, or (after verbs of motion) by the supine in *um;* but it may frequently be likewise rendered by the accusative of the gerund or gerundive with *ad,* by the genitive of the gerund with .the ablative *causâ* or *gratiâ,* " for the sake of," by a mere infinitive, or, lastly, by the future participle in *ûrus.*

Do you wish to go to your brother in order to see him ?	⎧ Vísne ad frâtrem túum íre, ut éum ⎨ vídĕas ? ⎩ Vísne íre visum frâtrem túum ?
I desire to go to him in order to see him (for the sake of seeing him).	⎧ Çúpio ad éum íre, ut éum vídeam. ⎨ Égo éum visum íre cúpio. ⎩ Cúpĭo ad éum íre vidéndi grátĭâ.
Has your brother a knife to cut his bread ?	⎧ Éstne frâtri túo cúlter ad secándum ⎨ pânem súum ? ⎪ Habétne frâter túus cúltrum, quí† ⎩ pânem súum sécet ?
He has one to cut it (wherewith to cut it).	⎧ Ést éi únus ad éum secándum. ⎩ Hábet únum, qui éum secâre póssit.

* The *direct* questions involved in these examples are:— *Quantum habes ?*— *Quis (qualis) est ?*— *Quando (quo tempŏre) venit ?*— *Venturusne est ?*

† This *quí* is an old ablative, and may stand for every gender of that case singular and plural (i. e. for *quó, quâ, quĭbus*). When thus used it represents the *instrument* or *means*, exactly like the English " wherewith," " whereby." Thus Nepos:— *ut, qui efferretur, vix reliquerit*, so that he left scarcely enough, wherewith he might be buried.

I have no money to buy bread (wherewith I may buy bread).	Pecúníam, quí pânem émam, nôn hábeo. Cáréo pecúníā ad eméndum pânem.
Have you paper enough to write a letter (for writing a letter).	Éstne tíbi sátis chártae ad lítteram scribéndam ?
I have not enough.	Nôn est (míhi sátis).
To sweep (out).	Everro, ĕre, erri, ersum. Scopis purgo, āre, āvi, ātum. (ALIQUID, LOCUM ALIQUEM).
To kill, slay.	Occĭdo, ĕre, ĭdi, ĭsum. Interfĭcio, ĕre, fēci, factum. (ALIQUEM).
To slaughter.	Macto, āre, āvi, ātum (ALIQUEM, ANIMAL ALIQUOD).
To salt.	Salio, ĭre, ĭvi or li, ĭtum (ALIQUID).
To lend.	Commodo, āre, āvi, ātum. Credo, ĕre, credĭti, credĭtum. (ALICUI ALIQUID).
To be able. To know how (to be able).	Possum, posse, potui. Scĭo, ĭre, ĭvi or li, ĭtum. (ALIQUID FACĔRE).

E. Obs. *Possum* signifies " to have the power *or* ability," *scio*, " to have the knowledge *or* skill," " to know how." Both these verbs may be followed by the infinitive of another verb. *Possum* is a compound of *pŏtis* and *sum*, and is inflected in the present as follows : —

INDICATIVE.

Singular.		Plural.	
I can (am able)	pŏssŭm	*We can (are able)*	possŭmus
Thou canst (art able)	pŏtĕs	*Ye can (are able)*	pŏtestis
He can (is able),	pŏtest,	*They can (are able).*	possunt.

SUBJUNCTIVE.

Singular.		Plural.	
That I may be able	possĭm	*That we may be able*	possimŭs
That thou mayst be able	possis	*That ye may be able*	possĭtĭs
That he may be able,	possĭt,	*That they may be able.*	possint.*

Can you write a letter ?	Potésne scríbĕre epístŏlam ? Scísne scríbere epístolam ?
I can write one.	Póssum (scío) ûnam scríbĕre.
Can he work ?	Núm ílle laboráre (ópus fácĕre) pótest ?
He cannot work.	Laboráre (ópus fácĕre) non pótest.
Can they come to us ?	Possúntne veníre ad nôs ?
They cannot come to you.	Ad vôs veníre nôn póssunt.

---

* Antiquated forms of this are *possiem, es, et,* &c., or *potessim, is, it,* &c. So also *potestur* for *potest,* and *potesse* for *posse.*

To kill me.	Mê accídere (interfícĕre).
To see me.	Mê vidēre.

F. Obs. In Latin the accusative generally takes its place before the verb on which it depends, and the dative before the accusative.* The verb itself is commonly put at the end of the sentence.

To speak to me (with me).	*Mêcum lóqui, ad mê lóqui.*
To speak to you (with you).	Têcum† lóqui, ad tê lóqui.
To speak to him (with him).	Cum éo lóqui, ad éum lóqui.
To speak to us (with us).	Nobiscum lóqui, ad nôs lóqui.
To speak to you (with you).	Vobiscum lóqui, ad vôs lóqui.
To speak to them (with them).	Cum íllis lóqui, ad íllos lóqui.
To send to him.	Éi míttĕre.
To send to his house.	Ad éum (in dómum éjus) míttĕre.
To send it to me.	Éum (éam, íd) míhi míttĕre.
To send him (them, &c.) to me, to my house.	Éum (éos) ad mê (dómum méam) míttere.
To send it to me to-morrow.	Éum (éam, íd) míhi crástĭno témpŏre míttĕre.
To send him (them) to me (i.e. to my house) to-morrow	Éum (éos) ad mê (dómum méam) crâs míttĕre.
When will you send me the hat?	Quándo vis míhi pílĕum míttere? (Cf. Lesson XXIV. *G.*)
I will send it to you to day.	Ego tíbi éum míttere vólo hódie.
Will you lend me some money?	Vísne míhi crédĕre aliquántum pecúniae?
I will lend you a little.	Vólo tíbi aliquántŭlum crédĕre.
Do you desire to see my brother, in order to speak to him?	Cupísne frâtrem méum vidēre, ut cum éo (ad eum) lŏquâris?
I do desire to see him, in order to speak to him?	Cúpio éum vidêre, ut cum éo (ad éum) lóquar.‡
Has he a broom to sweep my house?	Habétne scópas ad dómum méam everréndam?
He has none.	Nôn habet.
Have you anything to write, to eat, to say?	*Habêsne quod scríbas, quod édas, quod dícas?*
I have something to write, to eat, to say.	Hábeo quod scribam, édam, dícam.
I have nothing to write, to eat, to say.	Nôn hábeo quod scríbam, édam, dícam.
Has he any money to give me?	Habétne quid míhi dét pecúniae?

---

* Unless the accusative be a personal pronoun, which frequently precedes the dative.

† Compare Lesson XXVIII. p. 138, note.

‡ The present subjunctive of the deponent *loquor* is: — Sing. *lóquar, lŏquâris* or *lŏquâre, lŏquâtur*; Plur. *lŏquâmur, lŏquamĭni, lŏquantur.* Compare Lesson XXXV.

J   13

He has no money to give you.	Nôn' hábet quid tíbi dét pecúniae.
Do you lend us books to read?	Commodátísne nóbis líbros legén-
	dos?
We lend you books and letters to read.	Vóbis et líbros legéndos et lítteras commodámus. (Vide Lesson XXII. *B*. 5.)

EXERCISE 50.

Can you cut me some bread? — I can cut you some. — Have you a knife to cut me some? — I have one. — Can you wash your gloves? I can wash them, but have no wish to do it. — Can the tailor make me a coat? — He can make you one. — Will you speak to the physician? — I will speak to him. — Does your son wish to see me in order to speak to me (*ut mécum* or *ad me loquatur*)? — He wishes to see you, in order to give you (*ut tibi det*) a crown. — Does he wish to kill me? — He does not wish to kill you; he only wishes to see you. — Does the son of our old friend wish to kill an ox? — He wishes to kill two. — How much money can you send me? — I can send you thirty crowns. — Will you send me my letter? — I will send it to you. — Will you send the shoemaker anything? — I will send him my boots. — Will you send him your coats? — No, I will send them to my tailor. — Can the tailor send me my coat? — He cannot send it to you. — Are your children able to write letters? — They are able to write some.

EXERCISE 51.

Have you a glass to drink your wine? — I have one, but I have no wine; I have only water. — Will you give me money to buy some? — I will give you some, but I have only a little. — Will you give me that which (*quod*) you have? — I will give it to you. — Can you drink as much wine as water? — I can drink as much of the one as of the other. — Has our poor neighbor any wood to make a fire (*ad ignem accendendum*)? — He has some to make one, but he has no money to buy bread and meat. — Are you willing to lend him some? — I am willing to lend him some. — Do you wish to speak to the German? — I wish to speak to him. — Where is he? — He is with the son of the captain. — Does the German wish to speak to me? — He wishes to speak to you. — Does he wish to speak to my brother or to yours? — He wishes to speak to both. — Can the children of our tailor work? — They can work, but they will not.

EXERCISE 52.

Has the carpenter money to buy a hammer? — He has some to buy one. — Has the captain money to buy a ship? — He has some to buy one. — Has the peasant money to buy sheep? — He has none to buy any. — Have you time to see my father? — I have no time to see him. — Does your father wish to see me? — He does not wish to see you. — Has the servant a broom to sweep the house? — He has one to sweep it. — Is he willing to sweep it? — He is willing to sweep it.

— Have I salt enough to salt my meat? — You have not enough of it to salt it. — Will your friend come to my house in order to see me ? — He will neither come to your house nor see you. — Has our neighbor a desire to kill his horse ? — He has no desire to kill it. — Will you kill your friends ? — I will kill only my enemies. — Do you wish to speak to the children of your shoemaker? — I wish to speak to them. What will you give them ? — I will give them large cakes. — Will you lend them anything ? — I have nothing to lend them (*quod iis commodem*). — Has the cook some more salt to salt the meat ? — He has a little more. — Has he some more rice ? — He has a great deal more. — Will he give me some ? — He will give you some. — Will he give some to my poor children (*liberis meis egenis*) ? — He will give them some. — Will he kill this or that hen ? — He will kill neither (*neutram*). — Will he kill this or that ox ? — He will kill both. — Who will send us biscuits ? — The baker will send you some. — Have you anything good to give me ? — I have nothing good to give you.

Lesson XXXI. — PENSUM UNUM ET TRICESIMUM.

OF THE CONSTRUCTION OF SENTENCES.

A.   A sentence is a thought or concept of the mind expressed in words.   As

Puer légit, the boy reads.   *Arbor flōret,* the tree blossoms.   *Deus est (erat, erit) justus,* God is (was, will be) just.

Every sentence is composed of at least one *subject* and one *predicate.*

The subject of a sentence is the person or object of which anything is affirmed ; as *puer, arbor, Deus.*

The predicate is that which is affirmed of the person or thing called the subject ; as *legit, floret, est (erat, erit) justus.*

The subject is always a substantive, or some other word used substantively, and generally stands in the nominative.

REMARK. — But the subject of a verb in the infinitive mood is put in the accusative.

The predicate is either a finite verb,* or else a noun, adjective, participle, or adverb, with one of the tenses of the copula *sum ;* e. g. *est, erat, erit,* &c.

---

* The term *finite verb* (*verbum finitum*) includes all the verbal forms of every mood, except the infinitive (*verbum infinitum*).

B. The subject nominative may be variously modified or expanded by the addition of other words, which are said to stand in the *attributive relation* to it. This may be done, —

1. By another noun, either in the same case or one of the oblique cases ; as, *Deus, rex coelorum, justus est,* God, the king of heaven, is just ; *amīci nostri puer lĕgit,* the boy of our friend is reading.

2. By an adjective, adjective pronoun, participle, or relative clause ; as, *puer noster studiōsus lĕgit,* our studious boy is reading ; *arbor, quam hĕri in horto vidisti, hodĭe flōret,* the tree which you saw yesterday in the garden blossoms to-day.

C. In a similar manner, the predicate may be modified or expanded by the addition of other words, which are said to stand in the *objective relation* to it. These words may be, —

1. A noun in one of the oblique cases, or an adverb ; as, *puer librum suum bonum lĕgit,* the boy reads his good book ; *arbor in horto nostro flōret,* the tree blossoms in our garden ; *Deus semper erit justus,* God will always be just.

2. An infinitive or another finite verb introduced by a relative, or a conjunction expressed or understood ; as, *cupĭo abīre,* I desire to leave ; *(ille) idōnĕus non est, qui impetret,* he is not fit to obtain ; *cave (ne) cadas,* take care lest you fall.

3. By a noun or adjective in the same case with the subject ; as, *Pompējus imperātor est appellātus,* Pompey was called commander ; *(tu) vidēris vir bonus esse,* you seem to be a good man ; *incēdo regīna,* I walk a queen.

REMARK. — This construction takes place after certain neuter and passive verbs of naming, becoming, remaining, appearing, &c. (Cf. Lesson XXXIV. *C.*)

D. The subject and predicate both are either *simple* or *compound.*

A simple subject consists of one substantive or word used substantively, either alone or modified by attributes ; as *Deus, arbor, puer noster studiōsus.*

A compound subject consists of two or more simple subjects, generally connected by a conjunction, and belonging to one common predicate ; as, *puer et puella lĕgunt,* the boy and girl are reading ; *ego et tu diligentes sumus,* I and you are diligent.

A simple predicate consists of one finite verb, either alone or expanded into the objective relation ; as, *legit, floret, librum suum bonum legit, semper erit justus.*

A compound predicate consists of two or more simple predicates depending on one common subject ; as, *Deus est, fŭit, ĕrit,* God is, was, will be ; *Id et nobis erit perjucundum, et tibi non sane dĕrīum,* This will be extremely pleasant for us, and surely not out of your way.

E. Sentences, like subject and predicate, are also either *simple* or *compound.*

A simple sentence is one which contains a simple predicate, or one finite verb only.

REMARK. — There can be no sentence without a finite verb expressed or understood, and there are as many sentences as there are finite verbs.

A compound sentence contains two or more simple sentences, which are commonly called its *members* or *clauses.*

The members of a compound sentence are either all coördinated as independent, or else one of them assumes the rank of a leading clause, to which the rest are subordinated as dependent.

Independent clauses are such as make complete sense apart from their connection with each other; as, *Ego rēges ejēci, vos tyrannos intrōdūcĭtis; ego libertātem pĕpĕri, vos partam servāre non vultis,* I have expelled the kings, you are introducing tyrants; I have procured liberty, you are unwilling to preserve it.

A subordinate clause can make complete sense only in connection with the main or leading clause, on which it is dependent; as, *Vīta brĕvis est, līcet supra mille annos exĕat,* Life is short, and were it to exceed a thousand years; *Hoc ideo exposui, ut scires,* I have explained this, in order that you might know it.

REMARK 1. — In these sentences the clauses commencing with *līcet* and *ut* are subordinate and dependent on the leading clauses, by which they are preceded.

REMARK 2. — The members of a compound sentence are commonly linked together by conjunctions, relatives, or adverbs.

F. Words are said to agree with each other when they correspond in gender, number, case, or person, and this relation is called *Concord* or *Agreement.*

Agreement may take place under the following circumstances : —

1. Between one substantive and another; as, *Cicĕro orātor,* Cicero the orator; *Augustus impĕrātor,* Augustus the Emperor.

2. Between an adjective or participle and a noun ; as, *vir justus et saptĕns,* a good and wise man ; *vĭri optĭmi,* most excellent men.

3. Between a relative and its antecedent ; as, *puer, qui lĕgit,* the boy who reads ; *puella, quae currit,* the girl who runs.

4. Between a finite verb and its subject nominative ; as, *ego lĕgo, tu ămas, nos sŭmus, homĭnes dīcunt.*

G. One word is said to *govern* another, when it requires it to be put in a determinate case or mood, and this relation is called *Government.*

13*

A word subject to another, according to the laws of concord or government, is said to *depend upon* or *follow* it.

All the oblique cases of Latin nouns, except the vocative, are commonly determined by some other word.

1. The genitive is governed by nouns, adjectives, verbs, participles, and adverbs.

2. The dative is governed by adjectives, verbs, participles, and adverbs.

3. The accusative is governed by active transitive verbs or participles, and by prepositions.

4. The ablative is governed by adjectives, verbs, participles, and prepositions.

To whom ?	Cuī ? Cuĭnăm * ? Ad quĕm ?
Whom ?	Quĕm ? Quemnăm ?
What ?	Quĭd ? Quidnăm ?
To answer, reply.	Respondĕo, ēre, di, sum (ALICUI ALIQUID ; EPISTOLAE *or* AD EPISTOLAM). Rescrībo, ĕre, ipsi, iptum (ALICUI *or* AD ALIQUEM ; LITTERIS *or* AD LITTERAS).
To answer or reply to some one.	Álicuī respondēre.† Álicuī *or* ad áliquem rescríbĕre.
To answer a letter.	Epístŏlae *or* ad epístolam respon-dēre. Lítteris *or* ad líttĕras rescríbĕre.
Do you wish to answer me ?	Núm vis míhi respondēre ? Núm vis míhi (ad mê) rescríbĕre ?
I do not wish to answer you.	Nólo tíbi respondēre. Nólo tíbi (ad tê) rescríbĕre.
To whom do you wish to reply ?	Cuī vis respondēre ? Ad quém (cuī) vis rescríbĕre ?
I wish to reply to my good friend.	Amícō méō bónō respondēre vólo. Égo ad amícum méum bónum re-scríbĕre vólo.
What do you desire to answer him ?	Quíd cúpis éi respondēre (rescrí-bĕre) ?
I desire to answer him only (in) a few words.	Éi nôn nísi paûca rescríbĕre cú-pio.
To whom must we reply ?	Ad quém (cuī) ést nóbis rescri-béndum ?
We must reply to the English-man.	Rescribéndum ést nóbis Ánglo (ad Ánglum).

---

* Compare Lesson XII. *A.* 1 – 6.

† The verb *respondēre* is properly "to answer or reply orally," and is some-times opposed to *rescríbĕre*, which signifies "to write back or to answer in writing." But this distinction is not always observed, and *respondēre* is often used in the sense of *rescríbĕre*.

What have I to do?	Quíd ést míhi faciéndum?
You have to reply to the letter of the Frenchmen.	Rescribéndum ést tíbi líttĕris (úd líttĕras) Francogallôrum.

The place (in general).	Lŏcus, m. pl., lŏci or lŏca.
The garden.	Hortus,* i, m.; hortŭlus, i, m. dim.
The theatre.	Thĕatrum, i, n.
The forest, wood.	Silva, ae, f.
The grove.	Lūcus,† i, m.; nĕmus, ŏris, n.
The warehouse.	Rĕceptăcŭlum (i, n.) mercĭum.‡
The storehouse.	Cella pĕnārĭa, ae, f.
The magazine.	Horrĕum, i, n.
The store, provisions.	Pĕnus, ūs or i, m.; commĕātus, ūs, m. (of an army).
The supply, abundance.	Cōpĭa, ae, f.
The room.	Conclāve, is, n.; dĭaeta, ae, f.
The chamber (sleeping-room).	Cŭbĭcŭlum, i, n.
The butcher.	Lănĭus, i, m.

To go into (an enclosed place).	Inéo, īre, ĭi (īvi), ĭtum. Intrŏĕo, īre, īvi (ĭi), ĭtum.§ (LOCUM or IN LOCUM, AD ALI-QUEM).
In, into (preposition).	In (with the acc. and abl.).
Under (preposition).	Sub (with the acc. and abl.).

H. Obs. The prepositions *in* and *sub*, denoting a tendency or motion towards a place, are followed by the accusative, but when they denote rest or situation in a place, they are followed by the ablative.

To go into the room.	In conclāve inĭre (intrŏīre). Conclāve inĭre (intrŏīre).‖
To be in the room.	In conclāvi ésse.
To go into the garden.	In hórtos inĭre (intrŏīre). Hortos inĭre (intrŏīre).
To be in the garden.	In hórtis ésse.
To go in (i. e. into the house).	Íntrŏ (adv.) íre.
To be within (i. e. in the house).	Íntŭs (adv.) ésse.
To go under the table.	Sub ménsam ire.
To be under the table.	Sub ménsā ésse.

---

* The singular has commonly the sense of a "vegetable garden," and the plural *horti* or the dim. *hortŭlus*, "a garden for pleasure." (Cf. Lesson XVIII. *D.*)

† *Lūcus* is a sacred grove; *nĕmus* a woody landscape laid out for pleasure.

‡ The genitive pl. of *merx*, merchandise.

§ The verbs are compounds of *ĕo* (= *in* + *ĕo, intrŏ* + *ĕo*), and are inflected like the simple verb. (Cf. Lesson XXVIII. *F.*)

‖ The compounds *inĭre* and *introire* have frequently the force of transitive verbs, and then the preposition *in* before the object accusative is omitted.

To go out (i. e. out of the house).	{ Fórās (*adv.*) íre. { Exíre dómo (*abl.*).
To be out (i. e. out of the house).	Fóris (*adv.*) esse.
To go out.	*Exĕo*, íre, ĭĭ (*ivi*), ĭtum.
Where is our son ?	Úbi ést nóster fílius ?
He is in his room.	(Est) in cubícŭlo súo.
Where is the Englishman going to ?	Quô (quórsum) ít Ánglus ?
He is going into the forest.	(Ínĭt) in sílvam.
Do you wish to go into the theatre ?	Núm vís (in) thëátrum iníre ?
I do not wish to go there (thither).	Nólo éo iníre.
Is your father in (in the house) ?	Éstne páter túus íntus ?
He is not in ; he is out.	Nôn ést íntus ; fóris ést.
Does the stranger desire to go in (into the house) ?	Cupítne ádvĕna íre íntrō ?
No, he desires to go out.	Ímmo véro fórās íre (dómo exíre) cúpit.
Where is my dog ?	Úbi ést cánis méus ?
He is under the table.	Sub ménsā (ést).

EXERCISE 53.

Will you answer your friend ? — I will answer him. — But whom will you answer ? — I will answer my good father. — Will you not answer your good friends ? — I will answer them. — Who will answer me ? — The Russian wishes to answer you, but he cannot. — Will the Russian write me a letter ? — He will write you one. — Can the Spaniards answer us ? — They cannot answer us, but we can answer them. — What has the Englishman to do ? — He has to answer a letter. — Which letter has he to answer ? — He has to answer that of the good Frenchman. — Have I to answer a letter ? — You have not to answer a letter, but a note. — Which note have I to answer ? — You have to answer that of the great captain. — Have we to answer the letters of the merchants ? — We have to answer them. — Will you answer the note of your tailor ? — I will answer it. — Will any one answer my great letter ? — No one will answer it. — Will your father answer this or that note ? — He will answer neither this nor that. — Which notes will he answer ? — He will answer only those of his good friends. — Will he answer me my letter ? — He will answer it you. — Will your father go anywhither ? — He will go nowhither. — Where is your brother ? — He is in the garden of our friend. — Where is the Englishman ? — He is in his little garden. — Where do we wish to go to ? — We wish to go into the garden of the French. — Where is your son ? — He is in his room. — Will he go to the magazine ? — He will go thither. — Will you go to the great theatre ? — I will not go thither, but my son has a mind to go thither. — Where is the Irishman ? — He is in the theatre. — Is the American in the forest ? — He is there.

EXERCISE 54.

Will you come to me in order to go to the forest? — I have no wish
to go the forest. — To which theatre do you wish to go? — I wish to
go to the great theatre. — Will you go into my garden, or into that of
the Dutchman? — I will go neither into yours nor into that of the
Dutchman; I will go into the gardens of the French. — Will you go
into those of the Germans? — I will not go thither. — Have the
Americans great warehouses? — They have some. — Have the English great stores? — They have some. — Have the Germans as many
warehouses as stores? — They have as many of the latter as of the
former. — Will you see our great stores? — I will go into your warehouses in order to see them. — Have you much hay in your storehouses? — We have a great deal, but we have not enough corn. —
Do you wish to buy some? — We wish to buy some. — Have we as
much corn as wine in our storehouses? — We have as much of the
one as of the other. — Have the English as much cloth as paper in
their warehouses? — They have more of the one than of the other in
them. — Has your father time to write me a letter? — He wishes to
write you one, but he has no time to-day. — When will he answer
that of my brother? — He will answer it to-morrow. — Will you come
to my house in order to see my great warehouses. — I cannot come to
your house to-day; I have letters to write. — Where is the knife? —
It is under the table. — Is our friend in (the house)? — He is in. —
He is going in. — Do you desire to go out? — No; I desire to go in.
— Is the painter out? — He is not out.

Lesson XXXII. — PENSUM ALTERUM ET TRI-
CESIMUM.

OF THE AGREEMENT OF VERBS.

A. RULE. — The verb must agree with its subject
nominative in number and person. E. g.

Ego ámo.	*I love.*
Tû légis.	*Thou readest.*
Ille scríbit. Púer scríbit.	*He writes. The boy writes.*
Nôs míttǐmus.	*We send.*
Vôs hǎbêtis.	*Ye have.*
Illi dícunt. Hómines dícunt.	*They say. The men say.*

REMARKS.

1. It has already been noticed in several places, that the pronouns
ego, tu, ille, nos, vos, illi are commonly omitted, and only put where
perspicuity or emphasis requires them.

2. The nominative is entirely wanting before impersonal verbs and
verbs used impersonally; as, *Pluit,* it rains. *Pingit,* it snows. *Pudet*

me tui, I am ashamed before you. *Actum est de me,* It is all over with me. *Orandum est nobis,* We must pray.

3. An infinitive, either alone or modified by other words, an adverb, participle, and an entire sentence, may become the subject of a finite verb, which then stands in the third person singular; as, *Mentīri est turpe,* It is disgraceful to lie. *Dulce et decorum est pro patriā mori,* To die for one's country is honorable and sweet. *Docto homīni vivĕre* est *cogitāre,* To a man of letters living is thinking. *Cras istud, quando venit?* When will that "to-morrow" come? *Homīnes errāre non mirum est,* That men should err is not strange.*

4. The infinitive sometimes supplies the place of the finite verb, especially in animated narration; as, *Arma, tela, equi, viri, hostes, cives, permixti* (sc. *sunt*); *nihil consilio, neque imperio* agi; *fors omnia* regĕre, — Arms, weapons, horses, men, enemies, and friends were mixed in promiscuous disorder; nothing is now done by design or in obedience to command; chance controls everything. This is called the *historical infinitive,* and is generally translated by the imperfect.

5. The verb is sometimes entirely omitted; as, *Bona verba* (sc. *loquĕre*), Do not be angry! Softly! *Dii meliŏra* (sc. *dent*)! God forbid! *Quid plūra* (sc. *dicam*)? In short. *Quot homĭnes, tot sententiae* (sc. *sunt*), As many men, so many minds.

B. RULE. — After a collective noun the predicate is either in the singular or the plural. E. g.

Pars mīlĭtum caési, pars cápti sunt.	Part of the soldiers were killed, and a part of them taken prisoners.
Pars stúpet dōnum exitiále, et mólem mirántur équi.	Some are transfixed with amazement at the fatal present, and admire the huge size of the horse.

REMARKS.

1. A verb in the plural is very common, especially among the poets, after *pars, turba, vis, multitudo, exercitus, juventus, nobilitas, gens, plebs,* and *vulgus.*

2. The pronouns *uterque,* each; *quisque,* every one; *alter .... alterum,* and *alius .... alium,* may likewise take a plural verb; as, *Uterque eorum ex castris stativis exercitum* educunt, Each of them leads his army out of the camp. *Quisque suos* patĭmur *manes,* Every one of us suffers the punishment due to him. *Alius alii subsidium* ferebant, One brought help to the other.

C. RULE. — Two or more subject-nominatives in the singular, connected by a copulative conjunction, ex-

---

* The infinitive or an entire clause may also stand as the subject of an impersonal verb; as, Te hilāri animo esse *valde me juvat,* I am delighted (*lit* it delights me) that you are in good spirits. *Juvat me, quod* vigent studia, I am glad that the study of letters is prosperous. This construction is very common.

pressed or understood, generally have a plural verb.
E. g.

Senátus populúsque Románus pâ-cem comprobarérunt.	*The Roman senate and people approved of the peace.*
Vita, mors, divitiae, paupértas ómnes hómines vehementissime permóvent.	*Life, death, wealth, poverty, affect all men most powerfully.*

REMARKS.

1. The verb is in the singular when the compound subject is conceived of as one complex notion or whole; as, *Tempus necessitasque postūlat*, Time and necessity demands. *Senātus populusque Romanus intelligit*, The Roman senate and people understand.

2. When the verb is referred to each of the simple subjects separately, or to the emphatic one, it is likewise in the singular; as, *Conon plurimum Cypri* vixit, *Iphicrates in Thracia, Timotheus Lesbi, Chares in Sigéo*, Conon lived mostly on the island of Cyprus, Iphicrates in Thrace, Timotheus on Lesbos, and Chares in Sigeum. *Aetas et forma et super omnia* Romānum nomen *te ferociōrem* facit, Age and beauty, and, above all, the name of Roman, render thee more warlike.

3. When the sentence contains *et . . . . et, tum . . . . tum* (both . . . . and) or *nec . . . . nec*, the verb is commonly singular; as, *Illam ratiōnem et Pompejus et Flaccus secutus est*, Pompey and Flaccus both pursued that plan.

4. When the nominatives are connected by the disjunctive *aut,* " or," or by *aut . . . . aut,* " either . . . . or," the verb is commonly singular, but sometimes plural; as, *Si Aedcus* aut *Minos* diceret, If Æacus or Minos should say. *Ne Sulpicius* aut *Cotta plus quam ego apud te valēre* vidĕantur, Lest Sulpicius or Cotta should appear to have more influence with you than I have.

5. If an ablative with *cum* is put instead of a second nominative, the predicate is generally plural, but sometimes singular; as, *Demosthenes* cum cetĕris *in exilium* erant expulsi, Demosthenes with the rest had been driven into exile. *Tu ipse* cum Sexto *scire velim, quid cogites.* I should like to know what purpose you yourself and Sextus have in view.

D. RULE. — When the nominatives of a compound subject are of different persons, the predicate agrees with the first person in preference to the second, and with the second in preference to the third.   E. g.

Si tû et Túllia valêtis, égo et Cícĕro valêmus.	*If you and Tullia are well, Cicero and I are well.*

REMARK. — In sentences containing an antithesis or a division (e. g. an *et . . . . et*), the verb assumes the person of the nearest noun; as, Et *tu* et *omnes homĭnes* sciunt, You yourself and all men know.

Postquam in tuto ipse (ego) *et* ille *in periculo esse* coepit, After I my-self began to be safe and he in danger. .

The market (-place).	Fŏrum, i, *n.*
The ball. ·	Saltātĭo, ōnis, *f.*
The country (as opposed to city).	Rūs, rūris, *n.*
The square, public place.	Campus, i. *m.* ; lŏcus publĭcus, i, *m.*
The field.	Ager, *gen.* agri, *m., or in the pl.* agri, ōrum.*
The nobleman.	Hŏmo nōbĭlis ; ĕquĕs, ĭtis, *m.* (a knight).
The boatman.	Nauta, ae, *m.* ; hŏmo nautĭcus, *m.*
The bailiff.	Quaesitor, ōris, *m.*
The judge.	Jūdex, ĭcis, *m.*
People (in general).	Hŏmĭnes, *pl. m.*
To, towards (prep.).	In, ad† (with the acc.).
To go to the market.	In (ad) fŏrum ĭre.
To be at the market.	In fŏro ésse.
To go to the square.	In (ad) lócum públĭcum ĭre.
To be in the square.	In lóco públĭco ésse.
To go into the field.	In ágrum (ágros) ĭre.
To be in the field.	In ágro (ágrĭs) ésse.

E. RULE. — Verbs signifying motion or direction towards a place or object are generally followed by the accusative with *ad* or *in*, or by an adverb of place. As,

Where (in what direction) are these people going ?	Quô (quórsum) éunt hómĭnes ĭlli ?
They are going to (towards) the square.	Éunt ad lócum públĭcum.
Will you lead us into the fields ?	Núm vĭs nôs in ágros dúcĕre ?
I am unwilling to lead you thither.	Nólo vôs éo (ĭlluc) dúcere.
Does your brother come to the market ?	Venítne fráter túus in fórum ?
He does not come there.	Nôn vénit.
Whither do you send your little servant ?	Quô mĭttis sérvŭlnm túum ?
I am sending him to the city to my father.	Mĭtto éum ad pátrem in úrbem.
To go into the country.	Rûs (*acc.*) ĭre.
To be in the country.	Rúri (*or* rûre)‡ ésse.

---

* Often in the plural, especially when opposed to a collection of houses, like the English " fields."

† *Ad* properly implies approximation, and has something of the force of the English " towards." It may thus stand before the names of persons as well as of places; *in* (in this sense), before the latter only.

‡ The form *rŭri* is preferable to *rŭre.*

F. Obs. Rus follows the construction of the names of towns, and rejects the preposition *in* before the accusative and ablative. As,

Do you desire to go anywhere?	Cupísne íre áliquo?
I desire to go into the country.	Égo rûs íre cúpio.
Is the bailiff in the country?	Núm est quaesitor rúri (rûre)?
No; he is at our house.	{ Nôn; apud nôs ést. { Ímmo véro dómi nóstrae est.
To go to the ball.	Saltátum íre.*
To be (present) at the ball.	Saltatióni interésse (adésse).
To dance.	Salto, áre, ávi, átum.
The (act of) dancing.	Saltátio, ōnis, *f.*
To be present at.	{ Adsum, esse, fúi, fūtūrus. { Intersum,† esse, fúi, fūtūrus.
Are the young men going to the ball?	Eúntne adolescéntüli saltátum?
Yes, sir, they are going.	Véro, dómine, éunt.
By no means, sir; they are not going.	Mínime géntium, dómine; nôn éunt.
Is the tailor at the ball?	Adéstne (interéstne) sártor saltatióni?
He is there.	Ádest (ínterest).

G. RULE. — Many verbs compounded with the prepositions *ad, ante, con, in, inter, ob, post, prae, sub,* and *super* are followed by the dative. As,

Praêsum reipúblicae.	*I preside over the commonwealth.*
Antecéllit ómnibus.	*He excels every one.*
Áffer (ádfer) míhi lítteras.	*Bring me the letters.*
Sidera sédibus súis inhaérunt.	*The stars remain fixed in their abodes.*
Objècit sê télibus hóstium.‡	*He exposed himself to the weapons of the enemy.*
At, near (*prep.*).	Ápŭd, juxta, ad (*cum acc.*).
To stand.	Stō, stāre, stĕti, stătum.
To stand by *or* near.	Adsto, áre, stíti, —— (ALICUI REI, APUD, JUXTA).
The window.	Fenestra, ae, *f.*

---

* *Saltātum* is the supine of *salto*, thus put with *íre* to denote the purpose: " to dance," " for the purpose of dancing." Cf. Less. XLVII. *A.*

† *Adsum* is properly " to be near *or* present." *Intersum* conveys the additional notion of " participating in." Both these compounds of *sum* are conjugated like the simple verb.

‡ Intransitive verbs comprehended under this rule are followed by the dative of the d rect object (e. g. *antecellit, inhaerent, praesum*), and transitive verbs by that of the *remote* object (e. g. *affer mihi, objecit telibus*). This rule includes several compounds of *sum*: — *adsum, insum, intersum, praesum, subsum, supersum.*

14

The fire.	Ignis, is, *m.*; carbōnes, *pl. m.* (*the coal fire*).
The fireplace, hearth.	Fŏcus, i, *m.*
To go to the window.	{ Ad fenéstram íre. { Adíre (ad)* fenéstram.
To stand at (near) the window.	{ Apud (juxta, ad) fenéstram stâre. { Adstâre fenéstrae (juxta fenestram).
To go to the fire.	{ Ad fócum íre. { Adíre (ad) fócum.
To stand by the fire.	{ Apud (ad) carbónes stâre. { Adstâre fóco (apud fócum).
Where is the boatman?	Úbinam est naúta?
He is standing by the fire.	{ Stát apud fócum. { Ádstat carbónibus (apud carbónes).
Are we going to the window?	Imúsne (adimúsne) ad fenéstram?
We are not going.	Nôn ímus.
To write to some one (to send one a letter).	{ Littĕras ad alíquem dăre *or* mittĕre (*absolutely*). { Scribĕre alicui *or* ad alíquem † (*with* ut *and the subj.*).
Are you willing to write to me?	Vísne dáre (míttere) littĕras ad mê?
I am unwilling to write to you.	Nólo dáre (míttere) littĕras ad tê.
To whom is you father writing?	Ad quém dát páter túus lítteras?
He is writing to his best friend.	Lítteras dát ad amícum súum óptĭmum.
What is he writing him?	Quíd ei scríbit?
He is writing him to come to the city.	Scríbit éi, ut in úrbem véniăt (Less. XXX. *C.* 1.)

EXERCISE 55.

Where is our friend? — He is at the market. — Where is my brother? — He is in the country. — Do you wish to go into the country? — I do not wish to go there. — Whither do you desire to go? — I desire to go to the market. — Is your brother at home? — No; he is at the ball. — Whither does your son wish to go? — He wishes to go to the great place. — Does the Englishman go into the country in order to see the fields? — He does not wish to go into the country in order to see the fields, but in order to see the forests, the birds, the water, and to drink tea. — Where is the son of the peasant? — He is in the fields to cut corn (cutting corn = *frumentum secans*). — Does the son of the nobleman wish to go anywhither? — He does not wish to go anywhither; he is tired. — Whither does the son of

---

* *Ad* commonly implies motion towards a place; but sometimes also rest or situation in a place. The compound *adíre* of this sentence belongs to Rule *E.*

† The construction *scribĕre alicui* or *ad alíquem* can only be used properly when the contents of the letter are mentioned, or when a command or exhortation is conveyed.

the bailiff wish to carry corn? — He wishes to carry some to the
storehouse of your brother. — Does he wish to carry thither the wine
and the meat? — He wishes to carry both thither.

EXERCISE 56.

Have you time to stand at (*ad standum apud*) the window? — I
have no time to stand at the window. — Is your brother at home? —
He is not at home? — Where is he? — He is in the country. — Has
he anything to do in the country? — He has nothing to do there. —
Whither do you wish to go? — I wish to go to the theatre. — Is the
Turk in the theatre? — He is there. — Who is in the garden? — The
children of the English and those of the Germans are there. — Where
does your father wish to speak to me? — He wishes to speak to you
in his room. — To whom does your brother wish to speak? — He
wishes to speak to the Irishman. — Does he not wish to speak to the
Scotchman? — He wishes to speak to him. — Where will he speak
to him? — He will speak to him at the theatre. — Does the Italian
wish to speak to anybody? — He wishes to speak to the physician. —
Where will he speak to him? — He will speak to him at the ball
(*inter saltandum*, Less. XXV. *B. c.*). — Can you send me some
money? — I can send you some. — How much money can you send
me? — I can send you thirty-two crowns. — When will you send me
that money? — I will send it to you to-day. — Will you send it to
me into the country? — I will send it to you thither. — Will you send
your servant to the market? — I will send him thither. — Have you
anything to buy at the market? — I have to buy good cloth, good
boots, and good shoes.

EXERCISE 57.

What does the butcher wish to do in the country? — He wishes to
buy there oxen and rams in order to kill them. — Do you wish to
buy a chicken in order to kill it? — I wish to buy one, but I have
not the courage to kill it. — Does the boatman wish to kill any one?
— He does not wish to kill any one. — Have you a desire to burn
my letters? — I have not the courage to do it. — Will the servant
seek my knife or my paper? — He will seek both. — Which knife do
you wish (to have)? — I wish (to have) my large knife. — What
oxen does the butcher wish to kill? — He wishes to kill large oxen.
— What provisions does the merchant wish to buy? — He wishes to
buy good provisions. — Where does he wish to buy them? — He
wishes to buy them at the market. — To whom does he wish to send
them? — He wishes to send them to our enemies. — Will you send
me one more book? — I will send you several more. — Are you able
to drink as much as your neighbor? — I am able to drink as much as
he; but our friend the Russian is able to drink more than both of us
(*uterque nostrum*). — Is the Russian able to drink as much of this
wine as of that? — He is able to drink as much of the one as of the
other. — Have you anything good to drink? — I have nothing to
drink.

EXERCISE 58.

Is the friend of the Spaniard able to carry provisions ? — He can carry some. — Whither does he wish to carry provisions ? — He wishes to carry some to our storehouses. — Do you wish to buy provisions in order to carry them to our storehouses ? — I wish to buy some in order to carry them into the country. — Do you wish to go to the window in order to see the youth ? — I have no time to go (*ad eundum*) to the window. — Have you anything to do ? — I have a letter to write. — To whom have you a letter to write ? — I have to write one to my friend. — Do you wish to write to the bailiff ? — I wish to write to him. — What do you wish to write to him ? — I wish to answer (him) his letter. — Are you able to write as many letters as I ? — I am able to write more (of them) than you. — Can you write to your absent friends (*ad amicos absentes*) ? — I can write to them. — Have you paper to write (*ad scribendum*) ? — I have some. — Is the bailiff able to write to anybody ? — He is not able to write to anybody.

Lesson XXXIII. — PENSUM TRICESIMUM TERTIUM.

OF THE PASSIVE VOICE.

A. In the active voice the agent is the nominative of the verb, and is represented as acting upon an object in the accusative; in the passive voice the object becomes the subject of the verb, and is represented as acted upon by the agent in the ablative. E. g.

ACTIVE.	PASSIVE.
Páter ámat fílium.	*Fílius amátur a pátre.*
Sól múndum illústrat.	*Sóle múndus illustrátur.*
Déi providéntia múndum administrat.	*Déi providéntiā múndus administrátur.**

REMARKS.

1. The passive voice in Latin is distinguished from the active by peculiar terminations. It has the same number of moods and tenses, but a number of its tenses are periphrastic. (Cf. Lesson XXVIII. *E.*)

2. Neuter verbs, from the nature of their signification, do not admit of a passive voice. The Romans, however, sometimes employ them passively, but only in the third person singular and impersonally ; as, *Bibitur, curritur, itur, venitur,* There is drinking, running, going,

---

* The father loves the son. PASS. The son is loved by the father. — The sun illumines the world. PASS. The world is illumined by the sun. — God's providence rules the world. PASS. The world is ruled by God's providence.

coming. So also the neuter of the future passive participle: *Eundum est, veniendum est,* There must be going, coming.

3. The verbs *flo,* I become (am made); *vapŭlo,* I am beaten; and *venĕo,* I am sold, have an active form with a passive signification.

4. The neuters *audĕo,* I venture; *fido,* I trust; *gaudĕo,* I rejoice; and *solĕo,* I am accustomed, — assume a passive form in the perfect and the tenses derived from it. Thus: *Ausus, fisus, gavisus, solĭtus sum,* I have ventured, trusted, rejoiced, been accustomed. They are hence called *semi-deponentia.*

5. A numerous class of Latin verbs, both active and neuter, are only passive in form, having an active signification. They are called *Deponent* * *Verbs,* and are of every conjugation.

B. I. The principal parts of the passive voice, from which all the remaining forms are derived, are, 1. *The Present Indicative,* 2. *The Present Infinitive,* and 3. *The Perfect Participle.* Thus: —

	PRES. IND.	PRES. INF.	PERF. PART.
1.	āmŏr,	ămārī,	ămātŭs.
2.	mŏnĕŏr,	mŏnērī,	mŏnĭtŭs.
3.	lĕgŏr,	lĕgī,	lectŭs.
4.	audĭŏr,	audīrī,	audītŭs.

II. The formation of the different tenses of the passive voice has already been explained in Lesson XXVIII. *A – E.* The parts to be considered in this Lesson are, —

1. The Present Indicative Passive, formed from the same tense of the active voice by adding *r;* as,

　　1. ămŏ — ămŏr, *I am loved.*
　　2. mŏnĕŏ — mŏnĕŏr, *I am reminded.*
　　3. lĕgŏ — lĕgŏr, *I am read.*
　　4. audĭŏ — audĭŏr, *I am heard.*

2. The Present Infinitive Passive, formed from the corresponding mood of the active voice, by converting, 1. *ărĕ.* 2. *ērĕ,* 4. *īrĕ,* into, 1. *ārī,* 2. *ērī,* 4. *īrī,* and the *ĕrĕ* of the third conjugation into ĭ only †; as,

　　1. ămārĕ — ămārī, *to be loved.*
　　2. mŏnērĕ — mŏnērī, *to be reminded.*
　　3. lĕgĕrĕ — lĕgī, *to be read.*
　　4. audīrĕ — audīrī, *to be heard.*

3. The Perfect Participle, formed from the supine, by changing *um* into *us, a, um;* as,

　　1. ămātŭm — ămātŭs, ă, ŭm, *loved.*
　　2. mŏnĭtŭm — mŏnĭtŭs, ă, ŭm, *reminded.*

---

* So called from being supposed to have laid aside (*depōno,* I put off, lay aside) the active voice and passive signification.

† In the older monuments of the Latin language, and also among the later poets, the syllable *er* is sometimes appended to the infinitive passive; as *amarier, legier, mittier,* &c.

K　　　14 *

3. lectŭm — lectŭs, ă, ŭm, *read.*
4. audĭtŭm — audĭtŭs, ă, ŭm, *heard.*

4. The Present Subjunctive, formed from the same tense of the active voice, by changing the final *m* into *r*; as,

1. ămĕm — ămĕr, *that I may be loved.*
2. mŏnĕăm — mŏnĕăr, *that I may be reminded.*
3. lĕgăm — lĕgŭr, *that I may be read.*
4. audĭăm — audĭăr, *that I may be heard.*

CONJUGATION OF THE PRESENT PASSIVE.

C. The following paradigms exhibit the inflection of the present tense of the passive voice, indicative and subjunctive:—

FIRST CONJUGATION.

INDICATIVE.	SUBJUNCTIVE.
Amor, *I am loved.*	Amer, *that I may be loved.*
SING. ămŏr	SING. ămĕr
ămārĭs *or* -rĕ *	ămērĕ *or* -rĭs *
ămātŭr,	ămētŭr,
PLUR. ămāmŭr	PLUR. ămēmŭr
ămāmĭnī	ămēmĭnī
ămantŭr.	ămentŭr.

SECOND CONJUGATION.

INDICATIVE.	SUBJUNCTIVE.
Mŏnĕor, *I am reminded.*	Mŏnĕar, *that I may be reminded.*
SING. mŏnĕor	SING. mŏnĕăr
mŏnērĭs *or* -rĕ	mŏnĕārĕ *or* -rĭs
mŏnētŭr,	mŏnĕātŭr,
PLUR. mŏnēmŭr	PLUR. mŏnĕāmŭr
mŏnēmĭnī	mŏnĕāmĭnī
mŏnentŭr.	mŏnĕantŭr.

THIRD CONJUGATION.

INDICATIVE.	SUBJUNCTIVE.
Lĕgor, *I am read.*	Lĕgar, *that I may be read.*
SING. lĕgŏr	SING. lĕgŭr
lĕgĕrĭs *or* -rĕ	lĕgārĕ *or* -rĭs
lĕgĭtŭr,	lĕgātŭr,
PLUR. lĕgĭmŭr	PLUR. lĕgāmŭr
lĕgĭmĭnī	lĕgāmĭnī
lĕguntŭr.	lĕgantŭr.

---

* Of this second person singular the form in *ris* is to be preferred for the indicative and that in *re* for the subjunctive. Thus the student may put Ind. *amàris, monèris, legèris, audìris,* and Subj. *amère, moneàre, legàre, audìàre.*

FOURTH CONJUGATION.

INDICATIVE.	SUBJUNCTIVE.
Audĭor, *I am heard.*	Audĭar, *that I may be heard.*
SING. audĭŏr	SING. audĭăr.
audīrĭs *or* -rĕ	audĭārĕ *or* -rĭs
audītŭr,	audĭātŭr,
PLUR. audīmŭr	PLUR. audĭāmŭr
audīmĭnĭ	audĭāmĭnĭ
audĭuntŭr.	audĭantŭr.

Like *amor*, inflect *commodor, dor,* * *laceror, lavor, portor, reparor, secor, servor,* &c. Like *monĕor: docĕor* (I am taught), *habĕor, jubĕor* (I am commanded), *tenĕor, vidĕor,* &c. Like *legor: dicor, diligor, ducor, emor, frangor, mittor, quæror, scribor, tollor,* &c. Like *audĭor: custodĭor* (I am guarded), *erudĭor* (I am instructed), *munĭor* (I am fortified), *vestĭor* (I am clothed), &c.

D. The Present Passive of *căpĭo*, and of other verbs in *io* of the third conjugation, is thus inflected: —

INDICATIVE.	SUBJUNCTIVE.
Căpĭor, *I am taken.*	Căpĭar, *that I may be taken.*
SING. căpĭŏr	SING. căpĭăr
căpĕrĭs *or* -rĕ	căpĭărĕ *or* -rĭs
căpĭtŭr,	căpĭātŭr,
PLUR. căpĭmŭr	PLUR. căpĭāmŭr
căpĭmĭnĭ	căpĭāmĭnĭ
căpĭuntur.	căpĭantŭr.

Like *capior* are conjugated: 1. All its compounds; as, *accipior, decipior, excipior,* &c. 2. Those compounds of *facio* which change the radical *a* into *i;* as, *afficior, conficior, interficior,* &c. 3. *Jacior,* I am thrown, and its compounds *abjicior, dejicior, rejicior,* &c.

E. The Present Passive of the verb *fĕro,* and its compounds (*affĕro, antefĕro, confĕro, defĕro,* &c.), is irregular. Thus: —

INDICATIVE.	SUBJUNCTIVE.
Fĕror, *I am carried.*	Fĕrar, *that I may be carried.*
SING. fĕrŏr	SING. fĕrăr
ferrĭs	fĕrārĕ *or* -rĭs
fertur,	ferātŭr,
PLUR. fĕrĭmŭr	PLUR. fĕrāmŭr
fĕrĭmĭnĭ	fĕrāmĭnĭ
fĕruntŭr.	fĕrantur.

F. The passive of *facio* is likewise irregular: *fīo, fĭĕrī, factus sum.* The present of *fīo* is inflected as follows: —

---

* The passive of *do* shortens the first *a,* as in the active; as, *dărĭs, dătur; dămur, dămĭni, dantur.* The forms *dor* and *der,* however, are never used.

INDICATIVE.	SUBJUNCTIVE.
Fĭo,* *I am made, I become.*	Fĭăm, *that I may be made, &c.*
SING. fĭo	SING. fĭăm
fĭs	fĭăs
fĭt,	fĭăt,
PLUR. fĭmus	PLUR. fĭămŭs
fĭtĭs	fĭătĭs
fiunt.	fiant.

REMARK. — These compounds of *facio*, which retain the radical *a*, have likewise *fio* in the passive, but those which change the *a* in *i* have *ficior*; e. g. *arefacio — arefio*; *calefacio — calefio*: *labefacio — labefio*, &c.; but *conficio — conficior*, *interficio — interficior*, &c.

G. Obs. The Present Passive always represents the action denoted by the verb as *incomplete* and *still going on.* In this respect it is to be distinguished from the perfect, which exhibits it as already accomplished and complete. E. g.

PRES. *Dómus aedificâtur.*   *The house is being built (is building).*

PERF. *Dómus aedificâta est.*   *The house is built (finished).*

Are you (being) loved?	Amarísne? Ecquid amâris?
Yes, sir, I am loved.	Véro, dómine, ámor.
Is your brother loved?	Fratérne túus amâtur?
He is not loved.	Nôn amâtur.
Which book is read?	Quis líber légitur?
Mine.	Méus.
Are we heard or they?	Útrum audímur nôs an ílli?
They are heard.	Audiúntur ílli.
Are ye reminded?	Monēmínine? Num monémini?
We are reminded.	Monêmur.
We are not reminded.	Non monêmur.
Where is the trunk carried to?	Quô fértur ríscus?
It is carried home.	Dómum (fértur).
Is the coffee (being) warmed?	Calefítne coffĕa?
Yes, it is (being) warmed.	Íta ést, cálĕfit.
Is any one killed?	Núm quis interfícitur?
No one is killed.	Nèmo (núllus) interfícitur.
There are many (being) killed.	Múlti interficiúntur.
Good, well-behaved.	Bĕnĕ† mōrātus, a, um; bŏnus, a, um.
Naughty, bad.	Prāvus, a, um; mālis mōribus.‡
Skilful, clever, diligent.	Pĕritus, a, um; sollers, tis; dílĭgens, tis.
Awkward.	Impĕritus, a, um; ineptus, a, um.

---

* The *i* of the verb *fio* (although preceding another vowel) is long, except when followed by *er*; as, *fiam, fiunt*; but *fieri, fierem.*

† An adverb qualifying *morātus.*

‡ This is called the ablative of *quality*, which must be translated like a genitive: "of bad manners."

Assiduous, sedulous, studious.	Sēdŭlus, a, um; assīdŭus, a, um; stŭdĭōsus, a, um.
Idle, lazy.	Ignāvus, a, um; pĭger, ra, rum; segnis, e.
The idler, lazy fellow.	(Hŏmo) dēsĕs, -ĭdis, m.
To praise.	Laudo, āre, āvi, ātum (ALIQUEM; ALIQUID).
To blame.	⎧ Vĭtŭpero, āre, āvi, ātum. ⎨ Rĕprĕhendo, ĕre, di, sum. ⎩ (ALIQUEM DE ALIQUA RE).
To reward (any one).	⎧ Praemĭum alĭcui dăre or dēferre. ⎨ Praemĭo＊ alĭquem afficĕre or ornāre.
To be rewarded.	⎧ Praemĭo affĭci or ornāri. ⎨ Praemĭum consĕquor,† -sĕqui, -sĕcūtus sum (dep.).
To punish.	⎧ Pūnĭo, īre, ĭvi (ĭi), ītum (ALIQUEM). ⎨ Alĭquem poenā afficĕre.
To esteem.	Alĭquem magni‡ făcĕre or aestĭmāre.
To despise.	⎧ Contemno, ĕre, -tempsi, -temptum. ⎨ Despĭcātŭi§ hăbēre (ALIQUEM).
To hate, to bear hatred towards any one.	Odĭum hăbēre or gĕrĕre (IN ALIQUEM).
To be hated.	⎧ Odĭo (dat.) esse (ALICUI). ⎨ In ŏdĭo esse (APUD ALIQUEM).

By me — by us.	A mê — a nōbis.
By thee — by you.	A tê — a vōbis.
By him — by them.	Ab éo (íllo) — ab íis (íllis).
By the father — by men.	A pátre — ab homínibus.
By fire, heat, by the sword.	Ígni, aéstu, férro (abl.).

H. RULE.— If the agent of a passive verb is a person, it is put in the ablative, with the preposition *a* or *ab*, but if it is an impersonal cause, means, or instrument, it stands in the ablative without a preposition. E. g.

Laudántur a mê, a tê, ab éo (illo).	*They are praised by me, by you, by him.*
Vituperâris a nóbis, ab íllis, a pátre.	*You are blamed by us, by them, by your father.*

＊ The Ablative = " to affect or adorn one *with* a reward."

† Literally, " I obtain (*consequor*, deponent) a reward."

‡ Literally, " to make (or esteem) one of much account." *Magni* is the genitive of price, and agrees with *pretii* understood.

§ The Dative of *despicātus.* Literally, " to have (hold) one for contempt"; like the English " to hold one in contempt."

Térra illa férro ignique perva-   *That land was destroyed by fire and*
stâta est.   *sword.*
Fecunditâte árbŏrum deléctor.   *I am delighted by the fruitfulness of*
    the trees.

Who is punished ?   Quís punĭtur ?
The boy is punished by his father.   Púer punĭtur a pátre.
Why is he punished ?   Quăm ob rém poénā afficĭtur ?
Because he is lazy and bad.   Quía ést ignâvus et nêquam.
Which man is praised, and which   Quís hómo laudâtur, quís vitupe-
one blamed ?   râtur ?
He who is skilful is praised, but   Quicúnque perĭtus est, laudâtur,
he who is awkward is blamed.   qui autem est imperĭtus, is vitu-
    perâtur.

Which boys are rewarded, and   Qui púeri praémiis afficiúntur, qui
which punished ?   puniúntur ?
Those who are clever and studi-   Qui sollértes átque studiósi súnt,
ous are rewarded, but those   praémiis ornántur, qui aûtem
who are awkward and lazy are   inépti ac ségnes súnt, íi puni-
punished.   úntur.
We are loved by our friends,   Nôs ab amícis nóstris amâmur, vôs
and you are despised by every   aûtem ab ómnibus contemnímini.
one.
I am punished, and you are re-   Égo poénā afficĭor, tû ornâris praé-
warded.   mio.
These children are praised be-   Hí líberi laudántur, quía diligéntes
cause they are diligent and   et béne morĭti sunt, íIli aûtem
well-behaved ; but those are   reprehendúntur, quía ignávi át-
reprehended because they are   que mális móribus sunt.
lazy and bad.

Why ?   Cur ? quam ob rem ? (*Conj.*)
Because.   Quia, quod (*Conj.*).
The tutor, master.   Tûtor, ōris, *m.* ; magister, ri, *m.*
The pupil, scholar.   Discipŭlus, i, *m.* ; alumnus, i, *m.*

EXERCISE 59.

Are you loved by your father ? — I am loved by him. — Is your
brother loved by him ? — He is loved by him. — By whom am I
loved ? — Thou art loved by thy parents (*parentes*). — Are we loved ?
— You are loved. — By whom are we loved. — You are loved by
your friends. — Are these men loved ? — They are loved by us and
by their good friends. — By whom is the blind (*caecus*) man led ? —
He is led by me. — Where do you lead him to ? — I am leading him
home. — By whom are we blamed ? — We are blamed by our enemies.
— Why are we blamed by them ? — Because they do not love us. —
Are you punished by your tutor ? — We are not punished by him,
because we are studious and good. — Are we heard ? — We are heard.
— By whom are we heard ? — We are heard by our neighbors. — Is
the master heard by his pupils ? — He is heard by them. — Which

children are praised? — Those that are good. — Which are punished?
— Those that are idle and naughty. — Are you praised or blamed? —
We are neither praised nor blamed. — Is our friend loved by his
masters? — He is loved and praised by them, because he is studious
and good (well-behaved); but his brother is despised by his, because
he is naughty and idle. — Is the letter (being) written? — It is
(being) written. — By whom are those books written? — They are
written by our friends. — To whom is the table (being) sent? — It is
sent to our neighbor. — Where are the knives sent to? — They are
sent to our house. — Are you sent anywhere? — I am sent nowhere.
— Are our shirts washed by any one? — They are washed by no one.
— Is your brother becoming studious? — He is not becoming so. —
Is our coffee (being) warmed? — It is being warmed. — By whom
are our coats (being) mended? — They are mended by the tailor. —
Are our horses (being) bought by any one? — They are bought by
no one. — By whom is the wine drunk? — It is drunk by our friends.
— Is the book read by any one? — It is not read by any one. — By
whom are good books read? — They are read by the wise and the
learned (*a sapientibus doctisque*). — By what (*quā re*) are you delighted? — I am delighted by my new (*nŏvus*) books. — How (*quomodo*) are our enemies killed? — They are killed by the sword.

Lesson XXXIV. — PENSUM TRICESIMUM QUARTUM.

OF THE NOMINATIVE AFTER VERBS.

A. RULE. — After certain neuter and passive verbs,
the noun serving to complete the predicate is put in the
same case as the subject to which it relates. E. g.

Nōs sŭmus amíci.	*We are friends.*
Sérvus fĭt libertīnus.	*The slave is made a freed man.*
Cúpĭo evádĕre orátor.	*I desire to become an orator.*
Camíllus dictátor dícĭtur.	*Camillus is called dictator.*

REMARKS.

1. The noun in the predicate may be of any gender, but if it has
a form of the same gender as the subject, that form is preferred; as,
Amicítia vínculum quoddam *est hominum inter se*, Friendship is a kind
of bond which links men to each other. But, *Licentia* corruptrix *est
morum*, Licentiousness is the corruptrix of morals. *Aquila volucrum*
regina * *est*, The eagle is the queen of birds. *Stilus* optimus *est dicendi* magister, Style is the best teacher of oratory.

2. The noun of the predicate may be of a different number; as,

---

* *Regina*, because the grammatical gender of *aquila* is feminine. But the
masculine *rex* would not be incorrect here.

Captivi milĭtum praeda (*sing.*) *fuerant*, The captives had been booty
of the soldiers. *Omnia Caesar erat*, Cæsar was everything. *Haec
urbs est Thebae*, This city is Thebes.

3. The verb commonly agrees with the subject, but is sometimes
attracted into concord with the nearer noun of the predicate; as,
Loca, quae proxĭma Carthagĭnem Numidia vocatur, The places in the
vicinity of Carthage, which are called Numidia. *Amantĭum irae* (pl.)
amōris integratio est, The quarrels of lovers are the renewal of love.

B. RULE. — An adjective, adjective pronoun, or participle, serving to complete the predicate after verbs
neuter or passive, agrees in gender, number, and case
with the subject to which it relates. E. g.

Ílle púer est modéstus.	That boy is modest.
Hí libri sunt méi.	These books are mine.
Tú vocâris jústus.	You are called just.
Cúpit putâri bélla.	She desires to be considered hand-some.
Scỹthae invícti *mansêre.*	The Scythians remained uncon-quered.

REMARKS.

1. The adjective of the predicate is sometimes put substantively in
the neuter; as, Varĭum et mutabĭle *semper* (*est*) *femĭna*, Woman is
always a fickle and changeable being. Aliud *est actio bona*, aliud
oratio, A good action is one thing, and good talk another. In these
instances we commonly supply in English some general term, like
" thing," " things," " being," &c.

2. The adjective of the predicate sometimes agrees with another
noun *implied* in the subject; as, *Capĭta* (neut.) *conjurationis* caesi *
(*masc.*) *sunt*, The heads of the conspiracy were killed. This is called
the *Constructio ad Synesin.*

3. If the predicate contains a participle with *esse*, it generally agrees
with the nearest noun; as, *Non omnis error* stultitia *est* dicenda, Every
error cannot be called stupidity. *Paupertas mihi* onus (*neut.*) visum
est misĕrum et grave, Poverty seemed to me to be a wretched and a
heavy burden.

4. If the subject is compound, i. e. composed of two or more nominatives, the adjective or participle is generally in the plural, and its
gender is determined by the rules of Lesson XXII. *B.* 1 – 5. Additional examples are: *Rex regiaque classis una* profecti (sc. *sunt*), The
king and the royal fleet departed together. *Murus et porta de coelo*
tacta *sunt*, The wall and gate were struck by lightning. *Filia atque
unus e filiis* captus *est*, The daughter and one of the sons were captured. *Populi provinciaeque* liberatae *sunt*, The nations and provinces
were made free.

---

* In the masculine, because the heads of the conspiracy were considered
men.

5. When the subject is in the accusative, the noun, adjective, or participle of the predicate is in the same case; as, *Cupio* me *esse* clementem,* I desire to be clement. *Scio te haberi doctum,* I know that you are considered a scholar.

6. When the infinitive of a verb neuter or passive is preceded by a dative, the noun or adjective of the predicate may stand in the same case; as, *Natura dedit* omnibus *esse beatis,* Nature has conceded happiness to all men. *Licet mihi esse* beāto,† It is lawful for me to be happy. This construction is frequent with impersonal verbs governing the dative.

7. After the verb *sum* the predicate is frequently an adverb or a noun in an oblique case; as, *Conatus ejus* frustra *fuērunt,* His attempts were in vain. *Recte est aeger,* The patient is doing well. *Esse cum imperio,* To be in command (of an army).

C. The neuter and passive verbs which may thus be followed by nouns, adjectives, or participles, in the same case as the subject, are, —

1. The copula *sum,* and certain neuter verbs denoting motion or situation; as,

cado, *I fall.*	jaceo, *I lie.*
eo, *I go.*	maneo, *I remain.*
evado, *I come off* (*become*).	sedeo, *I sit.*
fīo, *I become.*	sto, *I stand.*
fugio, *I escape.*	venio, *I come.*‡
incedo, *I walk.*	

2. Passive verbs of naming, choosing, constituting, rendering; as,

appellor, *I am called.*	nominor, *I am nominated.*
constituor, *I am constituted.*	nuncupor, *I am named.*
creor, *I am created.*	perhibeor, *I am said.*§
declaror, *I am declared.*	reddor, *I am rendered.*
designor, *I am designated.*	renuntior, *I am proclaimed.*
dicor, *I am said* (*called*).	salutor, *I am saluted.*
eligor, *I am elected.*	vocor, *I am called.*‖

---

* Compare page 128, note.

† This may also be, *Licet mihi esse beatum.* The logical order is, *Me beatum esse mihi licet.* So also, *Mihi* negligenti *esse non licuit,* I was not allowed to be negligent. Vobis *necesse est* fortibus *esse* viris, It is necessary for you to be brave men.

‡ Thus: *In pectus cecidit* prōnus, He fell flat on his chest. *In causam it* praeceps, He goes headlong into the case. *Evadit* victor, He comes off victor. *Incedo* regina, I walk queen. *Manebit* imperator, He will remain commander, &c.

§ Many of these passive verbs, especially those of case 3, are construed with an infinitive of *sum* expressed or understood; as, *Nuntii fuisse perhibentur,* They are said to have been messengers. *Videmini viri boni* esse, Ye seem to be good men, &c.

‖ To these may be added *audio,* which sometimes = *appellor;* as, *Rex paterque* audisti, You heard yourself called king and father.

15

3. Passive verbs of esteeming, numbering, considering, and the like; as,

censeor, *I am supposed.*
credor, *I am believed.*
deprehendor, *I am discovered.*
existimor, *I am esteemed.*
feror, *I am reported.*
habeor, *I am considered.*

judicor, *I am judged.*
memoror, *I am recounted.*
numeror, *I am numbered.*
putor, *I am thought.*
reperior, *I am found.*
videor, *I seem.*

The corner.	Angŭlus, i, *m.* ; lătĭbŭlum, i, *n.* (hiding-place).
The well.	Pŭtĕus, i, *m.*
The fountain.	Fons, tis, *m.*
The hole.	Fŏrāmen, ĭnis, *n.*
To order, command.	Jŭbĕo, ēre, jussi, jussum (ALIQUID FIERI, ALIQUEM FACERE ALIQUID).
I direct, let.	Cūro, āre, āvi, ātum (ALIQUID FACIENDUM).
To go for, fetch (of things).	Affĕro, -ferre, attŭli, allātum. Apporto, āre, āvi, ātum. (ALIQUID ALIQUO).
To go for, fetch, or call (a person).	Arcesso, ĕre, ĭvi, ĭtum (ALIQUEM ALICUNDE* ALIQUO).
To fetch, conduct.	Addūco, ĕre, xi, ctum (ALIQUEM ALIQUO *or* AD ALIQUEM).
To send for (anything).	Jŭbĕo aliquid afferri *or* apportāri. Cūro aliquid apportandum.
To send for (a person).	Jŭbeo aliquem arcessi *or* addūci.†
Does the servant fetch anything for us?	Affértne (apportátne) sérvus áliquid ad nôs?
He does not fetch us anything.	Nĭhil úffert ad nôs. Nóbis nôn áffert quídquam.
Do you go for (call) any one?	Arcessísne áliquem?
I call (go for) no one.	Néminem (núllum) arcésso.
Do you send for anything?	Jubêsne apportári áliquid?
I am sending for some wine.	Vínum apportári júbĕo.
I order my books to be brought (I send for my books).	Líbros méos apportándos cúro.
Will you send for the physician?	Vísne jubêre médĭcum arcessi?
I will send for him.	Vólo jubêre éum arcéssi.
We desire wine to be brought.	Nòs vínum apportári cúpĭmus.
I direct paper to be brought (send for paper).	Égo chártam apportándam cúro.

---

* From some place somewhither.

† The verbs *jubeo* and *curo* are, however, frequently suppressed, and the verb itself is used in a factitive sense; as, *Annulum sibi fecit*, He *had* a ring *made.* *Securi percussit archipiratam*, He *ordered* the chief of the pirates *to be executed.* So *arcessere* may stand in the sense of "to send for" a person, and *apportare* "to send for (cause to be brought)" a thing, &c.

Let us send for a little bread.   Jubeámus aférri aliquántŭlum pâ-
   (Less. XXX. C. 3.)   nis.

We must work (it behooves us to   ⎧ *Laborándum est nóbis.*
work).   ⎨ *Nôs opórtet laborâre.*
     ⎩ *Necésse est laborémus.*

D. Obs. The English phrase *I must, I am obliged,* is expressed in Latin either by the participle in *dus,* or by the
impersonal verbs *oportet,* "it behooves," and *necesse est,* "it is
necessary." The former of the verbs is followed either by the
accusative with an infinitive, or by the subjunctive without *ut;*
the latter is commonly followed by the dative and infinitive, or
by the subjunctive without *ut.*   Thus : —

I must write.	Scribéndum est míhi.
It behooves me to (I must) write.	⎧ Mê opórtet scríbĕre. ⎨ Opórtet (égo) scribam.
It is necessary for me to write (I must write).	⎧ Necésse est mǐhi scríbere. ⎨ Necésse est (égo) scribam.
Must you write a letter to your brother ?	Oportétne tĕ dáre lítteras ad frá- trem ?
I must write one.	⎧ Opórtet mê dáre únas. ⎨ Opórtet dém únas.
Is he obliged to go to the mar- ket ?	⎧ Necesséne est éi in fórum íre ? ⎨ Necesséne est éat in fórum ?
He is obliged to go thither.	Necésse est éat ílluc.
Must you go ?	Eundúmne est tíbi ?
I am not obliged to go.	Míhi nôn ést eúndum.
What has the man to do ?	Quid hómini faciéndum est ?
He is obliged to go into the forest.	Necésse est éat in sílvam.
What have you to do ?	⎧ Quid est tíbi faciéndum ? ⎨ Quid bábes faciéndum ?
I have nothing to do.	⎧ Nôn est míhi quídquam facién- ⎨ dum. ⎩ Níhil faciéndum hábeo.
What have you to drink ?	Quid est tíbi (quid hábes) ad bi- béndum ?
I have nothing to drink.	⎧ Níhil ad bibéndum húbeo. ⎨ Nôn hábeo quód bíbam.
I have nothing but water to drink.	⎧ Áquam sôlam ad bibéndum hábeo. ⎨ Nôn hábeo quod bíbam nísi áquam.
Are you willing to make my fire ?	Visne míhi accéndĕre carbónes ?
I am not unwilling to make it, but I have no time.	Éos accendere nôn nólo, cárĕo au- tem ótio.
This evening.	Hŏdíe vespĕri.
In the evening.	Vespĕri, vespĕre (*abl.*).
This morning.	Hŏdíe mäne (*adv.*).
In the morning.	Mäne (*adv.*).

When must you go into the   Quô témpore te opórtet íre rûs?
  country?
I must absolutely go this morn-   Necésse est éam hódie mâne.
  ing.

EXERCISE 60.

Will you go for some sugar? — I will go for some. — My son (*mi fili*, cf. page 10, note *), wilt thou go for some water? — Yes, father (*mi pater*), I will go for some. — Whither wilt thou go? — I will go to the well, in order to fetch some water. — Where is thy brother? — He is at the well. — Will you send for my son? — I will send for him. — Will the captain send for my child? — He will send for him. — Where is he? — He is in a corner of the ship. — Art thou able to write a letter to me? — I am able to write one to you. — Must I go anywhither? — Thou must go into the garden. — Must I send for anything? — Thou must send for good wine, good cheese, and good bread. — What must I do? — You must write a long letter. — To whom must I write a long letter? — You must write one to your friend. — Is your little boy diligent? — He is both* modest and diligent. — Are these boys awkward and lazy? — They are neither awkward nor lazy. — What are you called? — I am called learned and wise (*doctus et sapiens*). — Are they becoming learned? — They are becoming (so). — Does he come off (*evadúne*) an orator? — He does come off one. — Do they remain good? — They do not remain (so). — Do I walk (as) commander? — You do walk (as one). — Are they considered handsome (*formōsi*)? — They are, on the contrary, considered ugly (*deformes*). — Do they desire to become (*fieri*) clement? — They do desire to become (so). — Is it lawful for me to be happy? — It is lawful. — Do we seem to be just? — You do not seem (to be so).

EXERCISE 61.

What must we do? — You must go into the forest in order to cut some wood. — What has the Englishman to do? — He has nothing to do. — Has the Spaniard anything to do? — He has to work. — Where can he work? — He can work in his room and in mine. — When will you give me some money? — I will give you some this evening. — Must I come to your house? — You must come to my house. — When must I come to your house? — This morning. — Must I come to your house in the morning or in the evening? — You must come in the morning and in the evening. — Whither must I go? — You must go to the great square in order to speak to the merchants. — Where must the peasant go to? — He must go into the field in order to cut some hay. — Must I keep anything for you? — You must keep for me my good gold and my good works. — Must the children of our friends do anything? — They must work in the morning and in the evening. — What must the tailor mend for you? — He must mend my old coat for me. — Which chicken must the cook

---

* " Both . . . . and " is in Latin *et . . . . et*, or *non minus . . . . quam.*

kill? — He must kill this and that. — Must I send you these or those books? — You must send me both these and those. — Have you anything to drink? — I have nothing to drink. — What have they to drink? — They have nothing but water to drink? — Where must you go? — I must go into the garden. — Is it necessary for them to write? — It is not necessary. — Does it behoove us to speak? — It does behoove (you to speak). — Must I send for water? — You must send for some. — Who must send for the book? — Our brother has to send for them. — Do they send for me? — They do not send for you.

Lesson XXXV. — PENSUM TRICESIMUM QUINTUM.

OF DEPONENT VERBS.

A. The deponent verbs of the Latin language are regularly conjugated like the passive voice of other verbs. They are either active or neuter, and belong to every conjugation. E. g.

	PRES. IND.	PRES. INF.	PERF. IND.
1st CONJ.	Hortor,	āri,	ātus sum, *I exhort.*
2d CONJ.	Věrěor,	ēri,	věrĭtus sum, *I fear.*
3d CONJ.	Lŏquor,	lŏqui,	lŏcūtus sum, *I speak.*
4th CONJ.	Blandĭor,	īri,	ĭtus sum, *I flatter.*

THE PRESENT TENSE OF DEPONENT VERBS.

FIRST CONJUGATION.

INDICATIVE.	SUBJUNCTIVE.
Hortor, *I exhort.*	Horter, *that I may exhort.*
SING. hortŏr	SING. hortĕr
hortārĭs *or* -rĕ	hortērĕ *or* -rĭs
hortātŭr,	hortētŭr,
PLUR. hortāmŭr	PLUR. hortēmŭr
hortāmĭnī	hortēmĭnī
hortantŭr.	hortentŭr.

SECOND CONJUGATION.

INDICATIVE.	SUBJUNCTIVE.
Věrěor, *I fear,*	Věrěar, *that I may fear.*
SING. věrěŏr	SING. věrěăr
věrērĭs *or* -rĕ	věrěārĕ *or* -rĭs
věrētŭr,	věrěātŭr,

15 *

PLUR. vĕrēmŭr   PLUR. vĕrĕāmŭr
      vĕrēmĭnī   verĕāmĭnī
      vĕrentŭr.   vĕrĕantŭr.

THIRD CONJUGATION.

INDICATIVE.	SUBJUNCTIVE.
Lŏquor, *I speak.*	Lŏquar, *that I may speak.*

SING. lŏquŏr   SING. lŏquăr
      lŏquĕrīs *or* -rĕ   lŏquārĕ *or* -rīs
      lŏquĭtŭr,   lŏquātŭr,
PLUR. lŏquĭmŭr   PLUR. lŏquāmŭr
      lŏquĭmĭnī   lŏquāmĭnī
      lŏquuntŭr.   lŏquantŭr.

FOURTH CONJUGATION.

INDICATIVE.	SUBJUNCTIVE.
Blandĭor, *I flatter.*	Blandĭar, *that I may flatter.*

SING. blandĭŏr   SING. blandĭăr
      blandĭrīs *or* -rĕ   blandĭārĕ *or* -rīs
      blandītŭr,   blandĭātŭr,
PLUR. blandĭmŭr   PLUR. blandĭāmŭr
      blandĭmĭnī   blandĭāmĭnī
      blandĭuntŭr.   blandĭantŭr.

Like *hortor* are inflected *arbitror*, I think; *comitor*, I escort; *dominor*, I rule; *fatur*, he speaks; *moror*, I delay, stay, &c. — Like *vereor* go *fateor*, I confess; *mereor*, I earn; *misereor*, I pity; *tueor*, I defend, &c. — Like *loquor* go *fungor*, I perform; *labor*, I slip (fall); *obliviscor*, I forget; *sequor*, I follow, &c. — Like *blandior* inflect *experior*, I experience; *mentior*, I lie; *largior*, I lavish; *partior*, I divide, &c.

Do you speak Latin?	Loquĕrísne Latíne?
Yes, sir, I do speak it.	Véro, dómine, lóquor.
No, sir, I am not able to speak it.	Nôn, dómine, lóqui nôn póssum.
Do ye speak it?	Loquiminíne?
We do not speak it.	Nôn lóquimur.
Who speaks Latin?	Quis lóquitur Latíne?
The learned only speak it.	Dócti sóli loquúntur.
Do you flatter any one?	{ Blandirísne álicui.*
	{ Númquid álicui blandíris?
I do not flatter any one.	Némini blándĭor.
Nor do I flatter any one.	Néque égo cuíquam blándior.
Do ye flatter?	Blandiminíne?
We flatter every one.	Blandimur ómnĭbus.
Whom do you exhort?	Quém hortâris?
I exhort my friends.	Amícos méos hórtor.

---

* Verbs of flattering govern the Dative.

What do they exhort us to do?	Quid nôs fácĕre hortántur?
They exhort us to come to them.	Nòs hortántur, ut* ad ípsos veniù- mus.
Do ye exhort us?	Hortaminíne nôs?
We exhort you to send letters.	Vôs hortamur, ut lítteras dêtis
Are ye afraid of anything?	Númquid verémini?
We are afraid of nothing.	Níhil verêmur.
Are you afraid to speak?	Vĕrêrísne lóqui?
I am not afraid to speak, but to write.	Nôn lóqui, sed scríbere véreor.
He is afraid that the enemy might kill him.	Verêtur, ne† hóstis éum interfí- ciat.

As far as.	*Usque ad, usque in* (with the acc.); *tĕnŭs* (prep. with abl. *or* gen.).
How far?	*Quô úsque? Quórsum úsque?*
As far as here.	Hucúsque (*adv*).
As far as there.	Éo úsque; úsque ísthinc.
Thus far, up to this point.	Hactĕnus (*adv.*)
As far as the city.	Úsque ad úrbem.
As far as the fields.	Úsque in ágros.
As far as Rome.	Úsque Rômam.
As far as the end of the road.	Úsque ad términum víae.
As far as (i. e. up to) the chest.	Péctŏre (*or gen.* péctŏris) ténus.

B. Obs. The preposition *tĕnus* is always put after its noun, which may stand either in the ablative or genitive.

To the bottom of the cask.	{ Úsque ad fúndum dólii. Fúndo ténus dólii.
To the bottom of the well.	{ Úsque ad íma pútei. Ímis ténus pútei.
The end (extremity, termi- nation).	{ Fínis, *m. & f.* (*generally*). Extrēmum, i, *n.* (*of time and space*). Termĭnus, i, *m.* (*of space only*).
The way, road.	Vĭa, ae, *f.*
The bottom; ground.	Fundus, i, *m.*; íma, ōrum, *n. pl.*
The garret.	Tabŭlātum, i, *n.*
The cask.	Dŏlĭum, i, *n.*; *dim.* dŏlĭŏlum, i, *n.*
The barrel, hogshead.	Cūpa, ae, *f.*
The purse.	Marsūpĭum, i, *n.*; crŭmēna,‡ ae, *f.*
How far do you wish to go?	Quô úsque vis íre?
I wish to go as far as the square, as the fields, as Rome.	Égo úsque ad cámpum (in ágros, Rômam) íre cúpio.
How far does the water go (i. e. extend)?	Quô úsque exténdĭtur áqua?

---

* This might also be expressed by an Accusative and Infinitive, *nos ad se venire.*

† After verbs of fearing, *ne* == "lest," "that," and *ut,* "that not."

‡ The latter was commonly worn around the neck.

It goes to the bottom of the sea.	Exténditur úsque ad íma máris (ímis ténus máris).
Every day, daily.	{ Síngŭlis diēbus, quŏtídíe, nullo non díe.
Every morning.	Quŏtídíe máne, quot diēbus máne.
Every evening.	{ Quŏtídíe vespĕri. Nullo non vespere.
At what o'clock ? *At what time ?*	*Quŏtā hŏrā ! Quā hŏrā ?* *Quó témpŏre ?*
At one o'clock.	Hórä prímä.*
At twelve o'clock.	Hórä duodécímä.
At half past one.	Médiä hórä post prímam.
At a quarter past three.	Quadránte hórae post tértiam.
At a quarter before four.	Dodránte hórae post quartím.
At noon.	Merídie, témpore merídiáno.
At midnight.	Médiä nócte.
At, i. e. about, towards.	*Circiter, sub (c. Acc. & Abl.).*
About six o'clock.	{ Círciter hórä séxtä. Sub hôram séxtam.
About noon.	{ Círciter merídie (merídiem). Sub merídiem.
.About a quarter before five.	Quadránte círciter hórae ante quíntam.
Towards (*or* about) ten.	Sub hôram décímam.
Noon, midday.	Meridies, ei, *m.*
Night.	Nox, *gen.* noctis, *f.*
The quarter.	Quadrans, tis, *m.*; pars (-tis, *f.*) quarta.
Three fourths.	Dodrans, tis, *m.*
Half.	Dīmídium, i, *n.*
The half part of.	Dīmídius, a, um
The middle part of.	Mĕdius, a, um.
The lowest part of.	Infímus, *or* ímus, a, um.

C. RULE. — The adjectives *prīmus*, *mĕdius*, *extrēmus*, *ultĭmus*, *infĭmus*, *īmus*, *summus*, *relíquus*, and *cetĕrus*, frequently signify *the first part*, *the middle part*, &c. of the object denoted by the noun with which they are connected.† As,

Média nóx (= *médium* or *média*   The middle of the night. *pars nóctis*).

---

* Among the Romans the first hour was from six to seven, A. M. In these exercises, however, the adjectives *prima*, *secunda*, &c. refer to the modern division of the day.

† But when the noun with which these adjectives are connected is compared with other objects of the same kind, they retain their original sense of *the first, middle, last,* &c.; as, *infimo loco,* of the lowest rank.

In primo limine vitae.	*At the very threshold of life.*
Extrémo béllo Peloponnésio.	*During the latter part of the Peloponnesian war.*
Alexándria reliquáque Aegýptus.	*Alexandria and the rest of Egypt.*

To go out (of any place), walk out.	⎰ Excĕo, íre, íi (ivi), ítum. ⎱ Egredíor, di, egressus sum (*dep.*). (EX *or* AB ALIQUO LOCO).
To go out, walk out (in public).	Prŏdĕo, íre, íi, ítum (IN PUBLICUM; EX LOCO).
To remain, stay.	⎰ Mănĕo, ēre, nsi, nsum.* ⎱ Mŏror, āri, ātus sum (*dep.*). (ALIQUO LOCO).
At present, now.	Nunc, hōc tempŏre, in praesentiā.
Here (in this place).	Hic (*adv.*), hōc lŏco.
There (in that place).	Ĭbi, illĭc, isthĭc (*adv.*).
To remain here.	Ilic mănēre.
To remain there.	Ibi (illic, istic) permanēre.
To remain *or* stay at home.	Dŏmi manēre (morári *or* se tenēre).
To be present (to be here).	⎰ *Adsum, esse, fŭi, futurus.* ⎱ Adsto, āre, stĭti, ——.
To be absent (away).	Absum, esse, fŭi, futurus.
Who is here (present)?	Quis ádest?
The young men are here.	Adolescéntes ádsunt.
Is my son here?	Adéstne fílĭus méus?
No, he is absent.	Ímmo véro ábest.
When will you go out?	Quándo vis prodíre in públĭcum?
I wish to go out now.	Prodíre in públicum nunc vólo.
Is any one going out of the house?	Exítne (egreditúrne) áliquis (ex) dómo?
No one is going out.	Némo éxit (egréditur).
Are you going to your brother?	Ísne tû ad frátrem?
I am going to him.	Éo (ad éum).
Do your children remain at home?	Manéntne líberi túi dómi?
They do remain at home.	Mánent (dómi).
They do not remain at home.	Nôn mánent (dómi).
Do you wish to take me to my father?	Cupísne me ad pátrem dúcĕre?
I do wish to take you to him.	Cúpĭo te ad éum dúcere.
Are you willing to give me a knife?	Visne míhi cúltrum dáre?
I am willing to give you one.	Vólo tíbi únum dáre.
Am I going to him?	Egóne ad éum éo?
Thou art going not to him, but to me.	Tû nôn ís ad éum, séd ad mê.

---

* So also the compounds *permanēre*, to remain for a given length of time, and *demorári*, to abide, tarry in a place.

L

Have your friends my books?	Núm amíci túi líbros méos hábent?
They have them not.	(Éos) nôn hábent.
Or have they time to write?	Án est íis spatíum ad scribéndum?
They have.	Est.
When do you go out in the morning?	Quándo pródis in públicum matútino témpore?
I go out every morning about eight o'clock.	Pródëo in públicum quotídie máne hórā círciter octávā.

EXERCISE 62.

Do they speak Latin? — They cannot speak (it). — Do we speak (it)? — We do not speak (it). — Whom do ye flatter? — We flatter no one. — Do they exhort any one? — They exhort their friends. — Do they exhort you to come to them? — They do not exhort me to come to them, but to send them letters. — Art thou afraid of anything? — I am afraid of nothing. — Are they afraid of being killed (*ne interficiantur*)?— They are not afraid. — How far do you wish to go? — I wish to go as far as the end of the forest. — How far does your brother wish to go? — He wishes to go as far as the end of that road. — How far does the wine go? — It goes to the bottom of the cask. — How far does the water go? — It goes to the bottom of the well. — Whither art thou going? — I am going to the market. — Whither are we going? — We are going into the country. — Are you going as far as the square?— I am going as far as the fountain. — When does your cook go to the market? — He goes there every morning. — Can you speak to the nobleman? — I can speak to him every day. — Can I see your father? — You can see him every evening. — At what o'clock can I see him? — You can see him every evening at eight o'clock. — Will you come to me to-day? — I cannot come to you to-day, but to-morrow. — At what o'clock will you come to-morrow? — I will come at half past eight. — Can you not come at a quarter past eight? — I cannot. — At what o'clock does your son go to the captain? — He goes to him at a quarter before one. — At what o'clock is your friend at home? — At midnight.

EXERCISE 63.

Have you a mind to go out? — I have no mind to go out. — When will you go out? — I will go out at half past three. — Does your father wish to go out? — He does not wish to go out; he wishes to remain at home. — Are you willing to remain here, my dear friend (*amice mi carissime*, voc.)? — I cannot remain here; I must go to the warehouse. — Must you go to your brother? — I must go to him. — At what o'clock must you write your letters? — I must write them at midnight. — Do you go to your neighbor in the evening or in the morning? — I go to him (both) in the evening and in the morning. — Where are you going to now? — I am going to the play. — Where are you going to to-night? — I am going nowhither; I must remain at home in order to write letters. — Are your brothers at home? —

They are not there. — Where are they ? — They are in the country.
— Where are your friends going to? — They are going home. —
Has your tailor as many children as your shoemaker ? — He has
quite as many of them. — Have the sons of your shoemaker as many
boots as their father? — They have more than he. — Have the children of our hatter as much bread as wine ? — They have more of the
one than of the other. — Has our carpenter one more son ? — He has
several more. — Are the Italians thirsty? — They are thirsty and
hungry. — Have they anything to do ? — They have nothing to do.
— Are the children of the Irish hungry or thirsty ? — They are
neither hungry nor thirsty, but fatigued.

EXERCISE .64.

Have you time to go out ? — I have no time to go out. — What
have you to do at home ? — I must write letters to my friends. —
Must you sweep your room ? — I must sweep it. — Are you obliged
to lend your brothers money ? — I am obliged to lend them some. —
Must you go into the garden ? — I must go thither. — At what o'clock
must you go thither ? — I must go thither at a quarter past twelve.
— Are you obliged to go to my father at eleven o'clock at night
(*noctis*) ? — I am obliged to go to him at midnight. — Where are
the brothers of our bailiff ? — They are in the great forest in order
to cut great trees. — Have they money to buy bread and wine ? —
They have some. — Does it behoove the children of the French to go
to the children of the English ? — It does behoove them. — Will you
send for some wine and glasses ? — Is it lawful (*licetne*) for the Turk
to remain with the Russian ? — It is lawful for him to remain with
him. — It is not wrong (*non est nefas*) for him to remain there. —
Are you willing to give me some money, so that I may go for some
bread ? — I am willing to give you some, to go for some bread and
beer. — Do your children walk out every day ? — They do walk out
every day at eleven o'clock. — When do you walk out ? — I walk out
every morning. — At what hour does your brother walk out ? — He
walks out at nine. — How far does he desire to go ? — He desires to
go as far as Rome. — How far does he dare (*audeo*) to go into the
water ? — He dares to go (in) up to his chest.

Lesson XXXVI. — PENSUM TRICESIMUM SEXTUM.

OF APPOSITION.

A. RULE. — A noun added to another noun for the
sake of explanation is put in the same case, and, if its
form admits of it, in the same gender and number.
E. g.

Taûrus môns.	*Mount Taurus.*
Tigránes, réx Arménius.	*Tigranes, the king of Armenia.*
Regina pecúnïa.	*Queen money.*
Philosóphïa, invéntrix légum, magístra mórum et disciplínae.	*Philosophy, the inventrix of laws, the mistress of morals and discipline.*
Athénae ómnïum doctrinârum inventríces.	*Athens, the inventrix of all the sciences.*

REMARKS.

1. The noun thus added to another, for the sake of characterizing or describing, is said to be in apposition with it. The explanatory noun is called the *appositum*, and is commonly placed last.*

2. Apposition may take place in the oblique cases as well as in the nominative. E. g. *Apud Herödötum, patrem histörïae,* In Herodotus, the father of history. *Nëro Senëcae, jam tunc senatöri, in disciplïnam tradïtus est,* Nero was put under the tuition of Seneca, then already senator. *Quid enim dïcam de thesauro omnïum, memörïä?* What shall I say in regard to memory, the treasure-house of all things?

3. A pronoun, either expressed or implied in the verb, may stand in place of the first noun; as, *Nös cônsüles dësümus,* We consuls are remiss. *Post me quaestörem,* After my being quaestor. *Hoc tibi juventus Romäna indïcïmus bellum* (sc. *nos*), We, the young men of Rome, declare this war against you. *Philosöphïae multum adolescens tempöris tribüi* (sc. *ego*), In my youth I devoted much time to the study of philosophy.

4. The *appositum* is often of a different gender or number; as, *Tragoedïa Thyestes,* The tragedy Thyestes. *Delïcïae meae, Dicaearchus,* Dicaearchus, my favorite authority. *Aborigïnes, gënus homïnum agreste,* The aborigines, an uncouth race of men.

5. A noun in apposition with two or more nouns is commonly in the plural; as, *Cupïdo atque ïra, pessïmi consultatöres,* Desire and passion, the worst of advisers. *Ennius ferëbat duo, quae maxïma putantur onëra, paupertätem et senectütem,* Ennius bore two burdens, which are deemed the greatest, poverty and old age.

6. Two or more Roman praenomina (of brothers, &c.) are followed by the common family name in the plural; as, *Cn. et P. Scipïönes,* Cneius and Publius Scipio. *Tiberïo Drusöque Nerönibus,* To Tiberius and Drusus Nero.

7. The appositum sometimes agrees with a genitive implied in a possessive pronoun; as, *Studïum tuum, adolescentis, perspexi,* I have witnessed your zeal as a young man. *Tuum, hominis simplïcis, pectus vidïmus,* We have seen the heart of you, simple man.

8. A noun denoting a whole, instead of· being in the genitive, is sometimes put in apposition with its partitive. E. g. *Milïtes* (= milï-

---

* But sometimes emphatically first, as in the last example of Rem. 2.

tum), *pars victoriae fiducĭā, pars ignominĭae dolōre ad omnem licentĭam processĕrant*, The soldiers, some from the confidence of the victory and others from the pain of the disgrace, had plunged themselves into excesses of every kind. *Facĕrent, quod se dignum quisque ducĕrent*, They might do what every one deemed worthy of himself.

9. Adjectives used substantively, especially those of the neuter gender, may likewise stand in apposition; as, *Propinquum nostrum, Crassum, illum divĭtem, laudandum pŭ'o*, Our relative, Crassus, the rich (man), ought in my opinion to be praised. *Batāvi machĭnas etĭam, insŏlĭtum sibi, ausi*, The Batavi even dared (to employ) the war-engine, a thing to which they were unaccustomed.

10. The appositum may have reference to an entire sentence, and *vice versa; e. g. Postrēmo dēsĕrunt tribūnal, mănus intentantes, causam discordĭae et inĭtĭum armōrum*, At last they desert the tribunal, stretching out their hands, the cause of discord and the commencement of hostilities. *Ūnum certāmen erat relictum, sententĭa Vulcātĭi*, There was one subject of dispute left, namely, the opinion of Vulcatius.

11. The genitive is sometimes put instead of the appositum; as, *Arbor fici*, The fig-tree. *Oppĭdum Antiŏchĭae*, The city of Antioch. *Amnis Erĭdāni*, The river Eridanus. *Nōmen Mercŭrĭi*, The name (of) Mercury. But this is not so common as *flūmen Rhēnus, terra Gallia, mons Avenna, oppĭdum Genābum*, &c.

12. The ablatives *urbe, oppĭdo*, &c. are sometimes found in apposition with the name of a town in the genĭtive; as, *Corinthi, Achaĭae urbe*, At Corinth, a city of Achaia.

13. After expressions like *est (dătur, indŭĭtŭr, impōnĭtur) mihi nōmen*, "I am called," "my name is," the proper name is sometimes by attraction put in apposition with the dative of the pronoun (*mihi*, &c.), rather than with *nomen* or *cognomen; as, Scipĭo, cui postĕa Africāno cognōmen ex virtūte fŭit*, Scipio, who afterwards was surnamed Africanus from his valor. *Tĭbi nōmen insāno posuĕre*, They gave you the name of an insane man. But also *Fonti nōmen Arethūsa est*, The fountain's name is Arethusa, &c.

14. The appositum is sometimes introduced by *ut, vĕlŭt, quăsi, tanquam* (= "as," "as if," "like"), *quamvis*, or *ceu; e. g. Aegyptĭi cănem et fĕlem ut dĕos cŏlunt*, The Egyptians worship the dog and cat as divinities. *Herŏdŏtus quăsi sedātus amnis flŭit*, Herodotus flows like a gentle stream. *Filĭum suum, quamvis victōrem, occĭdit*, He killed his own son, although victorious.*

15. The appositum may be modified by an adverb; as, *C. Flamĭnĭus, consul itĕrum*, C. Flaminius a second time consul. *Popŭlum lāte rēgem*, A people ruling (lit. *king*) far and wide.

---

* *Pro victis*, as conquered; *legatōrum numĕro*, as legates; *praedae nomine*, as booty,—occur in the same construction. So also *pro consŭle; as, (Ego) pro consŭle Athēnas venĕram*, I had come as proconsul to Athens.

16

To sell.

{ *Vendo, ĕre, dĭdi, dĭtum.*
{ *Divendo,* &c. (in small quantities).
{ (ALICUI ALIQUID).

To say, affirm.

{ *Dīco, ĕre, xi, ctum.*
{ *Aio ; inquam* (defective).

B. Obs. *Aio* (*ājo*), I say, affirm, and *dīco,* I say, are opposed to *nego,* I deny. *Aio* and *inquam* are defective verbs,
and are chiefly used in citing the language of another. They
are thus inflected in the present :—

PRES. IND.   āio, ăis, ăit ; ——, ——, āiunt.

PRES. SUBJ.   ——, āias, āiat ; ——, ——, āiant.

PRES. IND. { inquam, } inquĭs, inquĭt ; inquĭmus, inquĭtis, inquĭunt.
         { inquĭo, }

PRES. SUBJ.   ——, ——, inquĭat ;   ——, ——. ——.

What do you say (think) ?	Quid áis ?
Do you say so ? Is it possible ?	Ain' (= ăĭsne)* ? Aín' tû ?
What do they say ?	Quid áiunt ?
They say that the city is occu-pied by the enemy.	Áiunt (dícunt), úrbem ab hóstibus tenéri.
I am delighted with Ennius, says one ; and I with Pecuvius, says another.	Énnio deléctor, *áit*† quíspĭam . . . . Pecúvio, *ínquit* álius.

To tell, order, direct.

{ *Jubēre* (with acc. and infin.).
{ *Mando, āre, āvi, ātum.*
{ (ALICUI ALIQUID or UT).

Will you tell the servant to make the fire ?	Vín' jubēre fámŭlum accéndĕre ígnem ?
I will tell him to do it.	{ Jubēre éum vólo fácĕre hoc. { Vólo éi mandâre, ut hoc faciat.
Will you tell the servant to buy a broom ?	{ Vín' jubēre fámŭlum scópas émĕre ? { Vín' mandâre fámŭlo, ut scópas émat ?
I will order him to buy one.	Vólo éi mandâre, ut únas émat.
What do you desire to sell me ?	Quid míhi véndere cúpis ?
I wish to sell you a horse.	Cúpio tíbi véndere équum.
The word.	Vox, vōcis, *f.*; vocabŭlum, i, *n.*; verbum,‡ i, *n.*
The favor.	Officium, i, *n.*; grātum.
The pleasure.	Voluptas, ātis, *f.*; oblectātio, ōnis,*f.*

---

* In familiar discourse the enclitic *ne* often loses its final *e* by Apocope.
If the letter *s* precedes, this is likewise dropped, and the vowel of the syllable,
if long, is shortened ; as, *jussïn', adeón', egon', vĭn* (= *visne*), *jŭbĕn* (= *jubēsne*),
satĭn' (= *satĭsne*), *vĭdĕn'* (= *vidēsne*).

† So also with *ut*; as *ut ait, ut aiunt,* as he says, &c.; *ut Cicero ait, dĭcit, docet.*

‡ *Vox* is a word as spoken and heard ; *vocabŭlum,* an isolated word or term ;
verbum is any part of speech, especially in connected discourse.

To give one pleasure.	{ Voluptātem afferre (ALICUI). { Grātum * esse (ALICUI).
To do one a favor.	(Officium praestāre alicui. { Grātum facĕre alicui. ((ALIQUA RE).

Will you do me a favor?	Visne míhí grātum fácere ?
What one ? In what respect ?	Quā rē ?
This gives me great pleasure.	Hóc est míhi gratíssimum.
To become acquainted with, to learn to know.	{ Nosco, ĕre, nōvi, nōtum. { Cognosco, ĕre, nōvi, nītum. ((ALIQUEM, ALIQUID).
To know, to be acquainted with any one or anything.	Nōsse (= nōvisse) aliquem or aliquid.
I know, thou knowest, he knows.	Nōvi, nōvisti (nōsti), nōvit.
We know, ye know, they know.	Nōvīmus, nōvistis, nōvērunt (nōrunt).
Do you know this man ?	Novistíne hunc hóminem ?
I do not know him.	{ Éum non nóvi. { Nôn est míhi nôtus.
Do you wish to become acquainted with him ?	Vín' éum nóscere (cognóscere) ?
Yes, I desire to become acquainted with him.	Cúpĭo véro éum nóscere (cognóscere).
To want, need.	Ŏpus (n. indecl.) *est mihi* (RES, RE; ALIQUIS, ALIQUO).
To be in want of.	{ *Egĕo alĭquā rē.* { *Indĭgeo alicujus, alĭquā re.* ((Cf. page 113, *Obs. H*)
Do you want (need) this hat?	Éstne tíbi ópus hóc píleo (hícce píleus) ?

C. Obs. The phrase *opus est,* "there is need," is followed either by the nominative or the ablative of the person or object needed.†

I do want (need) it. We are in want of it.	{ Est míhi (éo) ópus. { Éjus indígeo.
We want (need) a teacher. We are in want of a teacher.	{ Ópus est nóbis praecéptor (praeceptôre). { Indigêmus praeceptôris.
Do you want as much coffee as sugar ?	Éstne tíbi ópus túntum colféae, quántum sácchari ?

---

* This is the neuter of *gratus,* agreeable, grateful. In phrases like these, the comparative and superlative, *gratius, gratissimum* (more agreeable, most agreeable), are often used.

† In this rule is usually included *usus est,* which is commonly followed by the ablative, but sometimes by the genitive or accusative; as, *Si quid usus sit,* If anything is wanting. *Spéculo mihi usus est,* I want a looking-glass. *Usus est hóminem astutum.*

I want more of the latter than of the former.	Ópus est míhi plûs* hújus quam illíus.
Do you want oxen (cattle)?	Núm vóbis ópus súnt bóves (ópus est bóbus)?
We do not (want any).	Nôn sunt.
We do need some (a few).	Ópus súnt nóbis nonnúlli (est nonnúllis).
Do you want (need) this money?	{ Éstne tíbi opus hâc pecúniâ? Egêsne hâc pecúniâ?
I do want (am in want of) it.	Est. Égëo.
I do not want it.	{ Non est míhi (éâ) ópus. Éjus nôn indígeo.
Do you want (any) money?	{ Estne tíbi ópus pecúnia? Egêsne pecúniâ.
I do want some (a little).	{ Est míhi ópus aliquántulum. Égeo véro aliquántulâ.
I do not want any.	{ Nôn est míhi ópus úlla. Núllâ égeo.
Do you want (are you in want of) anything?	{ Núm quid est tíbi ópus? Núm áliquâ rê índiges?
I do not want anything.	{ Ópus est míhi níhil quídquam.† Nihil índigeo.
Nor do I want anything.	Néque míhi quídquam ópus est.
What do you want?	Quid (quâ rê) est tibi ópus?
Whom are you in want of?	Cujúsnam índiges?
I am in want of you, of him, of them.	Indígeo túi, éjus, illôrum.
Is he in want of me?	Meíne índiget?
He is not in want of you.	Túi nôn índiget.
Is he in want of his friends?	Indigétne amicôrum suôrum?
He is in want of them.	(Eôrum) índiget.
Do you want these books?	{ Éstne tíbi ópus his líbris? Egêsne (egén') his líbris?
I do want them.	{ Súnt míhi ópus. Égeo ís.
Late (adv.). Too late.	Sērō, sērum. Sērĭus (neut. comp), séro.‡
Is it late?	Éstne séro? Serúmne est?
Is it late in the day, in the night?	Éstne sêrum díeí, nóctis?
It is late.	Est sêrum (séro).
It is too late.	Séro (sérĭus) est.
What time is it?	Quóta hôra est?

---

* Neuter adjectives or pronouns, such as *tantum, quantum, quid, hoc, illud,* &c. are always in the nominative after *opus.* Both *opus* and *usus* are sometimes (though rarely) followed by the genitive or accusative; as, *Temporis, cibum opus (usus) est,* There is need of time, food.

† "Nothing whatever," "nothing at all."

‡ The adverbial ablative *séro* is frequently put for the comparative *serĭus,* too late.

It is three o'clock.	Hôra est tértia.
It is twelve o'clock.	Duodécima est hôra.
It is about noon.	Sub (círciter) merídiem est.
It is midnight.	Média nox est.
It is half past one.	Hôra príma et dimídia est.
It is a quarter past two.	Quádrans hórae post secúndam est.
It wants a quarter to three.	Dódrans hórae post secúndam est.
Have you anything to sell?	Habêsne áliquid, quód véndas (ad vendéndum)?
I have nothing to sell.	Níhil hábeo, quód véndam.
I have these things to sell.	Haêc hábeo, quaê véndam.

Exercise 65.

Will you do me a favor? — Yes, sir; what one? — Will you tell your brother to sell me his horse? — I will tell him to sell it you. — Will you tell my servants to sweep my large rooms? — I will tell them to sweep them. — Will you tell your son to come to my father? — I will tell him to come to him. — Do you wish to tell me anything? (Have you anything to tell me?) — I have nothing to tell you (*Non habeo quod tibi dicam*). — Have you anything to say to my father? — I have a word to say to him. — Do your brothers wish to sell their carriage? — They do not wish to sell it. — John (*Joannes*)! are you here? — Yes, sir, I am here. — Wilt thou go to my hatter to tell him to mend my hat? — I will go to him. — Wilt thou go to the tailor to tell him to mend my coats? — I will go to him. — Art thou willing to go the market? — I am willing to go thither. — What has the merchant to sell? — He has beautiful leather gloves, combs, and good cloth to sell. — Has he any shirts to sell? — He has some to sell. — Does he wish to sell me his horses? — He wishes to sell them to you. — Who can read the tragedy of Thyestes? — I am unable to read it, but my brother desires to read it. — Who is reading my book? — Your scholar, my brother, is reading it. — Who wishes to sell me a knife? — His friend, the baker, wishes to sell you one. — Are you in want of any one? — Yes; I am in want of your father, the merchant. — Whom do they praise? — They praise our enemy, the painter.

Exercise 66.

What are you in want of? — I am in want of a good hat. — Are you in want of this knife? — I am in want of it. — Do you want money? — I want some. — Does your brother want pepper? — He does not want any. — Does he want some boots? — He does not want any. — What does my brother want? — He wants nothing. — Who wants some sugar? — Nobody wants any. — Does anybody want money? — Nobody wants any. — Does your father want anything? — He wants nothing. — What do I want? — You want nothing. — Art thou in want of my book? — I am in want of it. — Is thy father in want of it? — He is not in want of it. — Does your friend want this stick? — He wants it. — Does he want these or those corks? — He wants neither these nor those. — Are you in want of

16 *

me ? — I am in want of thee. — When do you want me ? — At present. — What have you (= do you wish) to say to me ? — I desire to tell you something new (*novum*). — What do you want (*Quid tibi vis*) ? — I wish to speak with you. — Is your son in want of us ? — He is in want of you and your brothers. — Are you in want of my servants ? — I am in want of them. — Does any one want my brother ? — No one wants him.

EXERCISE 67.

Is it late ? — It is not late. — What o'clock is it ? — It is a quarter past twelve. — At what o'clock does your father wish to go out ? — He wishes to go out at a quarter to nine. — Will he sell this or that horse ? — He will sell neither this nor that. — Does he wish to buy this or that coat ? — He wishes to buy both. — Has he one horse more to sell ? — He has one more, but he does not wish to sell it. — Has he one carriage more to sell ? — He has not one more carriage to sell ; but he has a few more oxen to sell. — When will he sell them ? — He will sell them to-day. — Will he sell them in the morning or in the evening ? — He will sell them this evening. — At what o'clock ? — At half past five. — Can you go to the baker ? — I cannot go to him ; it is late. — How late is it ? — It is midnight. — Do you wish to see that man ? — I wish to see him, in order to know him. — Does your father wish to see my brothers ? — He wishes to see them, in order to know them. — Does he wish to see my horse ? — He wishes to see it. — At what o'clock does he wish to see it ? — He wishes to see it at six o'clock. — Where does he wish to see it ? — He wishes to see it in the great square. — Has the German much corn to sell ? — He has but little to sell. — What knives has the merchant to sell ? — He has good knives to sell. — How many more knives has he ? — He has six more. — Has the Irishman much more wine ? — He has not much more. — Hast thou wine enough to drink ? — I have not much, but enough. — Art thou able to drink much wine ? — I am able to drink much. — Canst thou drink some every day ? — I can drink some every morning and every evening. — Can thy brother drink as much as thou ? — He can drink more than I.

Lesson XXXVII. — PENSUM TRICESIMUM SEPTIMUM.

AGREEMENT OF ADJECTIVES.

A. RULE. — An adjective, adjective pronoun, or participle agrees with its substantive in gender, number, and case. E. g.

Amicus cértus.	*A sure friend.*
Spréta glória.	*Disdained glory.*

Gramen vírĭde.	*The green grass.*
Térrae sitiéntis.	*Of the thirsty earth.*
Móntes álti.	*High mountains.*
Colúmnas nítĭdas.	*Shining columns.*
Malórum impendéntium.	*Of impending evils.*
Diébus praetérĭtis.	*In days past.*

REMARKS.

1. All adjectives may generally be employed in two distinct relations. *a)* They are either directly connected with the substantive as its attributes; as, *vir justus, dies praeteritae;* or, *b)* they are linked to it by the copula *sum,* and constitute the predicate; as, *vir est justus, dies praeteritae sunt.* The former of these relations is called the *attributive* and the latter the *predicative.*

2. Adjectives* in the predicative relation have in general the same agreement as those in the attributive. (Cf. Less. XXXIV. *B.*)

3. Personal pronouns may have adjectives in agreement with them, like nouns. The gender of the adjective is determined by that of the substantive represented. E. g. *Ego solus,* or fem. *Ego sola,* I alone. *Tu carus omnibus* expectatusque *venies,* You will be welcomed by all. *Illis absentibus,* They being absent. *Dicitur esse libĕra,* She is said to be free. *Misĕri* (fem. *miserae*) *sumus,* We are wretched.

4. Words not properly substantives, but employed as such (e. g. adverbs, infinitives, or entire clauses), may take an adjective of the neuter gender. Vide examples Less. XXXII. *A.* Rem. 3.

5. The place of the adjective is sometimes supplied by a noun or adverb; as, *Victor exercitus,* A victorious army. *Contemptor animus,* A contemptuous mind. *Minime largitor,* No profuse spender. *Praeclare facta,* Distinguished deeds.

6. The Romans sometimes employ an adjective in agreement with the subject of a sentence, where the English idiom requires an adverb in the predicate. E. g. *Ego primus hanc orationem legi,* I have read this oration first (= am the first that read it). *Hannibal princeps in proelium ibat,* ultimus *conserto proelio excedebat,* Hannibal always was the first that entered into battle and the last that left it. *Nullus dubito* (= *non dubito*), I do not doubt. So chiefly *domesticus* (= *domi*), *matutīnus* (= *māne*), *nocturnus* (= *noctu*), *multus* (= *multum*), *prior, primus, propior, proximus, solus, totus, ultimus, unus,* &c., with many of which the adjective is regularly put instead of the corresponding adverb.

7. When two or more adjectives, regarded as distinct, precede their noun, they are commonly connected by conjunctions; but when they come after it, the conjunction is frequently omitted. E. g. *Multi fortissimi atque optimi viri,* Many brave and excellent men. *Unus et perangustus adĭtus,* One way of approach, and a narrow one. *Oratio*

---

* In these remarks the term "adjective" includes adjective pronouns and participles.

compositta, ornāta, copiōsa, An oration well arranged, elegant, and copious.

8. But when one of the adjectives is so closely allied to the noun as to form one complex notion with it, the remaining adjectives are added without a conjunction. E. g. *Festi dies anniversārii,* Anniversary festivals. *Privāta nāvis onerāria maxǐma,* A private carrying-ship of the largest size. *Externos multos claros viros nominārem,* I might name many foreigners of distinction.

9. A plural noun has sometimes two adjectives in the singular. E. g. *Marǐa supěrum atque infěrum,* The upper and the lower seas (parts of the Mediterranean).

10. An adjective belonging to two or more nouns is generally put in the plural; as, *Veneno absumpti sunt Hannibal et Philopoemen,* Hannibal and Philopœmen were killed by poison. *Liber et Libera Cerere nāti,* Bacchus and Libera born of Ceres. *Natūrā inimica inter se sunt civitas et rex,* The king and state are naturally the enemies of each other. *Injustitiam et intemperantiam dicimus esse fugienda,* We say that injustice and intemperance must be shunned. (On the gender of these adjectives, see Less. XXII. *B.* Compare also Less. XXXIV. *B.* 4.)

11. A collective noun may have an adjective in the plural, which commonly assumes the gender of the individuals denoted by the noun. E. g. *Magna pars vulnerati aut occisi,* A large number killed or wounded. *Cetera multitudo sorte decimus quisque ad supplicium lecti sunt,* Of the remaining multitude every tenth man was doomed to punishment by lot.

12. Adjectives and pronouns are frequently put partitively in the neuter gender and followed by the genitive of their noun, instead of agreeing with it in case; as, *Multum operae,* Much attention (study). *Minus viae,* Less of the journey. *Dimidium pecuniae,* Half the money. *Hoc litterarum,* This letter. *Hoc solatii,* This consolation. *Ad id locorum,* To that time. *Quid causae est?* * What is the reason? Also in the plural: *Subǐta belli,* The surprises of war. *Summa pectǒris,* The upper part of the chest. *Occulta templi,* The recesses of the temple. *Strata viarum saxea,* The stone pavement of the streets. (Compare Lessons XVIII. – XXIII.)

13. An adjective used partitively and followed by the genitive plural of the genus or entire number commonly assumes the gender of that genitive; as, *Animalium alia ratione expertia sunt, alia ratione utentia,* Of animals, some are destitute of reason and others enjoying it. *Multae istārum arbǒrum meā manū sunt sǎtae,* Many of these trees were planted by my hand.

14. When a partitive is followed by the genitive singular of a collective noun, it takes the gender of the individuals implied in it; as,

---

* But this can only be done in the Nom. and Acc. In the remaining cases the adjective *agrees* with the noun; as, *multā operā* (Abl.), *huic solatio, minore viā, harum litterarum.* (Compare Lesson XXXVIII. *A.* 6.)

Priinus Romāni genĕris, The first of the Roman nation. *Ceteri nostri ordĭnis*, The rest of our order. *Nec est quisquam gentis ullius*, Nor is there any one of any nation.

15. Possessive pronouns, being considered the representatives of personal pronouns in the genitive, sometimes take another pronoun, adjective, or participle in the genitive; as, *Nostra* ipsorum *amicitia*, Our own friendship. *In unius mea salute*, On my safety alone. *Nōmen meum absentis*, My name while absent. *Suo solius perīculo*, At his own peril. *Vestrae paucorum laudes*, The praises of you few.

16. In exclamations and addresses the adjective is sometimes in the vocative instead of the nominative, and *vice versa*; as, *Quo moriture ruis !* Where are you rushing to, dying man ? *Rufe, mihi frustra credite amice !* O Rufus! in vain believed my friend. *Projice tela manu, sanguis meus !* Cast away your weapons, my son! *Nove anne, veni !* Come, new year, come !

17. Adjectives of the neuter gender, singular and plural, are sometimes used as adverbs. E. g. *Id* multum *faciebam*, I practised that a good deal. *Qui multa deos venerāti sunt*, Who besought the gods much and earnestly. *Inde Romam, recens condĭtam, commigravit*, He thence emigrated to Rome, then recently founded. *Dormivit altum*, He slept profoundly.

The pain, ache.	Dŏlor, ōris, m., or pl. dolōres.
The violent pain.	Cruciātus, ūs, m.
The evil, misfortune,	Mălum, i, n.
Bad, wicked.	Mălus, prāvus, a, um; nēquam (*indecl.*).
Bad, sad (*of circumstances*).	Mălus, a, um; tristis, e; asper, ĕra, ĕrum.
Bad, sick, sore.	Infirmus, invalĭdus, a, um; aegrotans, tis; ulcerōsus, a, um.
The tooth.	Dens, tis, m.
The ear.	Auris, is, f.
The neck.	Collum, i, n. ; cervix, īcis, f.
The throat (*internally*).	Fauces, ium, f. pl.
The elbow.	Cubĭtum, i, n.
The back.	Dorsum, i, n.
The knee.	Gĕnu, ūs, n.
The headache.	Dŏlor (dolōres) capĭtis.
The toothache.	Dŏlor dentium.
The earache.	Dŏlor aurĭum.
The sore throat.	Dŏlor (dolōres) faucĭum; angĭna, ae, f.
A pain in one's back.	*Notalgĭa, ae, f.
Sore eyes.	Ocŭli invalĭdi *or* aegrotantes.
A sore finger.	Digĭtus ulcerōsus.
The sickness, disease.	Morbus, i, m.

To suffer pain from anything (anywhere).	{ *Dólet * míhi áliqua rês.* { *Dolóríbus labóro, āre, āri,* &c.
To be affected with pain.	*Dolóre* or *dolóríbus áfflci.*
To be sick, infirm (in any respect).	{ *Aegrōto, āre, āvi, ātum.* { *Mínus valĕo, ēre, ŭi, ——.* { (ALIQUA RE).

Are you affected with any pain?   *Afficĕrísne áliquo dolóre?*

I am affected, sir.   *Affícior, véro quídem, dómine.*

Have you a sore finger?   { *Dolétne tíbi dígitus?*
    { *Laborâsne dígito?*

I have (a sore finger).   *Dólet. Labóro.*

Has your little boy a sore throat?   *Laborátne puérculus túus faúcium dolóribus?*

No; he has a sore eye.   *Immo véro áltero óculo aegrótat.*

We have sore eyes (suffer from weak eyes).   *Nòs oculôrum infirmitâte laborámus.*

He has a sore foot.   *Áltero péde aegrótat (mínus válet).*

They have the toothache.   { *Dólent íis déntes.*
    { *Déntium dolóríbus afficiúntur.*

Have you the headache?   { *Habêsne cápitis dolóres?*
    { *Dolétne tíbi cáput?*
    { *Laborâsne cápitis dolóribus?*

I have it.   *Hábeo. Dólet. Labóro.*

Has he a pain in his back?   *Notálgiā afficitur?*

He has none.   *Nôn afficitur.*

To find.   { *Invĕnto, īre, vēni, ventum.*
    { *Reperto, īre, pĕri, pertum.*

B. Obs.   *Invenīre* is to find without any special effort or design; *reperīre*, on the other hand, involves the idea of labor, of difficulty and obscurity.

Do you find what you are looking for?   *Reperísne, quod quaêris?*

I do find what I am looking for.   { *Repério, quod quaéro.*
    { *Rem, quam quaéro, repério.*

He does not find what he is looking for.   *Nôn réperit, quod quaérit.*

Do we find what we are looking for?   *Reperimúsne quod quaérimus?*

You do not find what you are looking for.   *Nôn reperítis, quod quaérítis.*

Have you what you want?   *Habêsne quod tíbi ópus est?*

I have not what I want.   *Nôn hábeo, quod míhi ópus est.*

I find what you are finding.   *Quod ínvenis, id et ego invénio.*

To learn.   { *Dísco, ĕre, dídici, discitūrus* † (ALI-
    QUID AB *or* DE ALIQUO).

---

* From *dólĕo. ĕre, ŭi.*

† The verbs *discĕre* and *studĕre* have no supine, but of the former a participle in *urus* exists.

To study, to apply one's self to, to learn (anything).

{ Stŭdĕo, ēre, ŭi, —— (ALICUI REI).
Ŏpĕram dăre (ALICUI REI).
Discĕre (ALIQUID).

To study letters, apply one's self to literature and the arts.

{ Operam dare litteris.
Studēre optimis disciplīnis atque artibus.

To learn one's letters.
I learn to read, write, speak.
To learn a language.

Primas litteras discĕre.
Dísco légere, scríbere, lóqui.
Línguam áliquam díscere (edíscere*).

To know a language.
    The language.
    Latin.
    French.

Línguam scíre; línguae sciens esse.
Lingua, ae, ƒ.; sermo, ōnis, m.
Latīnus, a, um; adv. Latíne.
Francogallícus, a, um; adv. Francogallíce.

    English.
    German.

Anglícus, a, um; adv. Anglíce.
Germanícus, a, um; adv. Germaníce.

Are you learning Latin?
I am learning it, sir.
How many languages does he know?

Discísne línguam Latínam?
Véro, dómine, dísco.
Quam multas scit linguas?

He knows all the languages.

{ Ómnes línguas scit.
Linguârum ómnium scíens est.

Do you know Latin, Greek, English?
Are you learning to speak Latin?
I am learning to read, write, and speak Latin.

Scísne Latíne, Graéce, Anglíce?
Discísne lóqui Latíne?
Égo Latíne légere, scríbere atque lóqui edísco.

Do they desire to learn English?

Cupiúntne discĕre línguam Anglícam?

They do not desire it.
Who is studying letters?
The young men are studying the liberal arts and sciences.
What are you doing?
I am studying the Latin language and literature.
Can the boy read German?

Nôn cúpiunt.
Quis óperam dat lítteris?
Adolescéntŭli óptimis disciplínis atque ártibus óperam dant.
Quid ágis?
Lítteris Latínis stúdeo (óperam dô).
Potéstne (scítne) púer légere Germáníce?

He cannot do it yet, but he is learning it.

Nóndum pótest, at díscit.

EXERCISE 68.

Where is your father? — He is at home. — Does he not go out? — He is not able to go out; he has the headache. — Hast thou the headache? — I have not the headache, but the earache. — What day of

---

* *Edíscere* is to learn thoroughly, to learn by heart.

the month is it to-day? — It is the twelfth to-day. — What day of the month is to-morrow? — To-morrow is the thirteenth. — What teeth have you? — I have good teeth. — What teeth has your brother? — He has bad teeth. — Has the Englishman the toothache? — He has not the toothache; he has a sore eye. — Has the Italian a sore eye? — He has not a sore eye, but a sore foot. — Have I a sore finger? — You have no sore finger, but a sore knee. — Will you cut me some bread? — I cannot cut you any; I have sore fingers. — Will anybody cut me some cheese? — Nobody will cut you any. — Are you looking for any one? — I am not looking for any one. — Has any one the earache? — No one has the earache. — What is the painter looking for? — He is not looking for anything. — Whom are you looking for? — I am looking for your son. — Who is looking for me? — No one is looking for you. — Dost thou find what thou art looking for? — I do find what I am looking for; but the captain does not find what he is looking for.

EXERCISE 69.

Who has a sore throat? — We have sore throats. — Has any one sore eyes? — The Germans have sore eyes. — Does the tailor make my coat? — He does not make it; he has a pain in his back. — Does the shoemaker make my shoes? — He is unable to make them; he has sore elbows. — Does the merchant bring us beautiful purses (*marsupia*)? — He cannot go out; he has sore feet. — Does the Spaniard find the umbrella which he is looking for? — He does find it. — Do the butchers find the sheep which they are looking for? — They do find them. — Does the tailor find his thimble? — He does not find it. — Dost thou find the paper which thou art looking for? — I do not find it. — Do we find what we are looking for? — We do not find what we are looking for. — What is the nobleman doing? — He does what you are doing. — What is he doing in his room? — He is reading. — How many languages does your brother know? — He knows only one. — Do they find what they are looking for? — They do not find (it). — Does our master suffer from weak eyes? — He does suffer (from them). — Are you troubled with a pain in your back? — I am not troubled.

EXERCISE 70.

Art thou reading? — I am not reading. — Do the sons of the nobleman study? — They do study. — What are they studying? — They are studying German. — Art thou studying English? — I have no time to study it. — Are the Dutch looking for this or that ship? — They are looking for both. — Is the servant looking for this or that broom? — He is neither looking for this nor that. — Who is learning German? — The sons of the captains and those of the noblemen are learning it. — When does your friend study French? — He studies it in the morning. — At what o'clock does he study it? — He studies it at ten o'clock. — Does he study it every day? — He studies it every morning and every evening. What are the children of the carpenter doing? — They are reading. — Are they reading German? — They

are reading French; but we are reading English. — What books does
your son read ? — He reads French books. — What book are you
reading ? — I am reading a German book. — Do you read as much as
I ? — I read more than you. — Does your father read the same book
which I read ? — He is not reading that which you read, but that
which I read. — Does he read as much as I ? — He reads less than
you, but he learns more than you. — Do you lend me a book ? — I
do lend you one. — Do your friends lend you any books ? — They do
lend me some.

Lesson XXXVIII. — PENSUM DUODEQUADRA-GESIMUM.

A. RULE. — Adjectives, adjective pronouns, and participles are often employed independently, especially in
the plural, either with or without a noun understood.
E. g.

Bóni, máli, dócti, dívites, paú-peres; amántes.	*The good, the bad, the learned, the rich, the poor; lovers.*
Méi, túi, súi, nóstri, véstri.	*My, thy, his, our, your friends, men, &c.*
Bónum, málum, vêrum, jústum.	*The good, the bad, the true, the just.*
Bóna, mála, vêra, fálsa, acérba, indigna.	*Good, bad, true, false, bitter, un-worthy things.*

REMARKS.

1. With plurals denoting persons *homines* is commonly supplied.*
So with *omnes, pauci, plerique, nonnulli,* &c. But the possessives *mei,
tui,* &c. have reference to *amici, milìtes* (men, soldiers), *cives* (citizens). With *immortales* the word *dii* is understood.

2. Adjectives of the singular number denoting persons usually have
vir or *homo* expressed with them ; as, *vir doctus, bonus, justus; homo
pauper, dives, improbus,* &c. They sometimes, however, appear alone
in all the cases. E. g. *Sapiens, dives, socius, nupta,* a wise man, a rich
man, an ally, a married woman. *Quid interest inter doctum et rudem ?*
What is the difference between an educated and an ignorant man ?
Quid minus libero dignum ? What can be more unworthy of a free
man ?

3. With adjectives denoting objects, various words are understood ;
as, *Dextra, sinistra* (sc. *manus*), the right hand, left hand. *Ferìna,
agnìna, bubìla, porcìna* (sc. *caro*), Venison, lamb, beef, pork. *Calìda,*

* And not unfrequently expressed, as in *Homines Romăni,* Roman men,
Homines adolescentuli, young men, &c.

M   17

frigida (sc. *aqua*), Warm, cold water. *Tertiāna, quartāna* (sc. *febris*), The tertian, quartan fever. *Decumāna* (sc. *pars*), The tenth part. *Prīmae* (sc. *partes*), The first part or rôle. *Hiberna, aestiva* (sc. *castra*), The winter, summer quarters. *In Tusculāno* (sc. *praedo*), At the country-seat Tusculanum. *Brevi* (sc. *tempore*), In a short time; and also *ex quo, ex eo, ex illo* (sc. *tempore*, which is frequently understood), &c., &c.

4. Of adjectives used substantively, those of the neuter gender are the most common. The singular denotes either an abstract quality or an individual act or object; as, *bonum, malum, vĕrum*, the good, bad, true (or something good, bad, true); *commune, dictum, factum*, something in common, something said, done (= a saying, deed). So the pronouns *hoc, illud, quid, aliquid;* and *quantum, tantum, multum*, &c.

5. The plural of neuter adjectives used substantively indicates a diversity of things of the same quality; as, *bona, mala, vera, falsa, multa, omnia, reliqua*, good, bad, true, false, many, all, the remaining *things* (the rest, remainder). *Dicta, facta*, things said, done, i. e. words uttered, actions. So also *haec, illa, quae, aliqua*, these, those, which, some *things.* ＊

6. Neuter adjectives can thus be used substantively in the nominative and accusative only. In the remaining cases the feminine of the adjective with *res* is commonly employed, to prevent ambiguity. Thus *cujus rei, hac de re, alicui rei, ulla in re, bonarum rerum, omnibus in rebus,*† &c.

7. Adjectives used substantively may have other adjectives in agreement with them; as, *meus natalis* (sc. *dies*), My birthday. *Paternus inimīcus*, A paternal enemy. *Nova nupta*, A newly married woman. *Summum bonum*, The chief good. *Praeclārum responsum*, A famous reply, *Prāva facta,*‡ Depraved actions.

8. A number of words originally adjectives have acquired the rank of substantives; as, *juvenis, adolescens, amīcus, familiaris, comes, vicīnus, statuārius, artifex, index, particeps; summa* (a sum), *confluens* (junction of rivers); *Grammatica, Rhetorica, Statuāria* (sc. *ars*), &c.

9. Additional Examples of adjectives used as substantives are :— *Fortes creantur fortĭbus et bonis*, The brave are made for the brave and good. *Plerĭque* vana *mirantur*, The majority of men are captivated by vanity.§ *Erubescunt* pudĭci *etiam* impudĭca *loqui*, The chaste‖ blush even to utter unchaste things. *Aiunt* multum *legendum*

＊ With many of these neuters the English words *thing, things* may be supplied. Sometimes, however, the sense requires other words, such as *place, part, respect, property,* &c.

† This use of *res* extends to all the cases, and the Romans often say *res ea, nulla res, rem aliquam, rem difficilem, res bonae, malae,* &c.

‡ Participles of the neuter gender sometimes take an adverb instead of an adjective; as, *bene, crudeliter facta, acute responsa, facete dictum,* &c.

§ The plural of these neuter adjectives is frequently rendered by the singular.

‖ In general propositions including both sexes, the adjective is always masculine; as here *fortes, plerĭque, pudĭci,* &c.

esse non multa, They say that we ought to read much, not many things. *Quis rem tam veterem* pro certo *affirmet?* Who can assert a thing so old as a certainty? *Idcirco abestis, ut* in tuto *sitis,* You are absent in order to be safe. *Amicōrum* omnia *sunt communia,* Friends have everything in common. *Ita comprobābis divina* praedicta, Thus you will confirm the divine prediction. *Nihil addo* de meo,* I add nothing of my own.

The Pole:	Polōnus, i, *m.*
The Roman.	Romānus, i, *m.*
The Greek.	Graecus, Grājus, i, *m.*
The Arab.	Arabs, is, *m.*
The Athenian.	Atheniensis, is, *m.*
The Syrian.	Syrus, Syrius, i, *m.*

B. The patrials or gentiles of the Latin language are either derived from the proper names of countries, or else they are themselves the roots for the formation of the latter.

1. The majority of patrials are primitives, from which the name of the country is formed by annexing *ia* to the root; † as, *Arabs — Arabia, Arcas — Arcadia, Gallus — Gallia, Itālus — Italia, Thrax — Thracia.*

2. The patrials derived from names of countries are generally adjectives, with one of the terminations *ānus, as* (gen. *ātis*), *ensis* (*iensis*), *īnus* (*ēnus*), *ĭcus* (*ĭăcus, aicus*), and *ius.* E. g. *Roma — Romānus, Arpinum — Arpinas, Athenae — Atheniensis, Thebae — Thebaicus, Aegyptus — Aegyptiacus, Tarentum — Tarentīnus, Cyprus — Cyprius.*

3. From patrial adjectives in *us, a, um,* adverbs are formed, by changing that termination into *ē.* The following may serve as examples : —

	ADJECTIVE.	ADVERB.
Spanish.	{ Hispaniensis, } { Hispanicus, }	Hispanicē.
Italian.	Italicus,	Italicē.
Polish.	Polonicus,	Polonicē.
Russian.	Russicus,	Russicē.
Latin.	Latinus,	Latinē.
Greek.	Graecus,	Graecē.
Arabic.	Arabicus,	Arabicē.
Syriac.	Syriăcus,	Syriăcē.
Persian.	Persicus,	Persicē.
Egyptian.	Aegyptiăcus,	Aegyptiăcē.

---

* The neuter singular of all the possessives (*meum, tuum, suum, nostrum, vestrum*) is thus employed to denote possession, like the English "mine," "my own," &c.

† The root of a noun is found in the genitive singular by separating the case-termination; as *Arabs,* gen. *Arab-is; Arcas,* gen. *Arcad-is; Gallus,* gen. *Gall-i; Thrax,* gen. *Thrac-is,* &c.

| Sanscrit. | { Sanscrĭtus,
{ Sanscritĭcus, } | Sanscrītē. |
| Turkish. | Turcĭcus, | Turcĭcē. |

Are you a Roman ?	Ésne tû Románus ?
No, indeed, I am an American.	Mínĭme véro ; Americánus sum.
Is he a shoemaker ?	Sutórne est ílle ?
No, he is a tailor.	Nòn véro ; sártor est.
Are you mad ?	Núm és insânus ?
No, surely, no.	Nòn hércle véro.
Do you know Spanish ?	Scìsne Hispánĭce ?
I do know it. I do not.	Scío. Haud scío.

The fool.	(Homo) stultus, fatŭus.
The mouth.	Ōs, *gen.* ōris, *n.* ; *dim.* oscŭlum, i, *n.*
The memory.	Mĕmŏrĭa, ae, *f.*
A good, excellent, weak memory.	Mĕmŏrĭa tenax (-ācis), singulāris, infirma.

To have a good memory.	Vălēre * memoriā.
To have a bad memory.	Părum (mĭnus) valēre memoriā.
To have an excellent memory.	Multum valēre memoriā.

| Blue. | Caerŭlĕus, violācĕus, glaucus, a, um. |

| Black. | Ater, atra, atrum ; nĭger, gra, grum. |

| *To have, to be furnished* or *en-*
dowed with anything. | *Praedĭtum, instructum, ornátum esse*
ALIQUA RE. |

He has an excellent memory.	{ Memóriā singulári praéditus est. { Múltum válet memóriā.
She has blue eyes.	{ Óculis glaúcis ornâta est. { Caerúlea† est.
He has a small mouth (is a man of small mouth).	{ Ore párvŭlo instrúctus est. { Vir est ôris párvi.
Have you a good memory ?	{ Valêsne memóriā ? { Praeditúsne es bónā memóriā ?
I have an excellent memory.	{ Múltum váleo memóriā. { Singulári memóriā instructus sum.
No, I have a bad (weak) memory.	{ Ímmo véro párum váleo memórĭā. { Memóriae infírmae sum.

To play, sport.	Lŭdo, ĕre, ŭsi, ūsum (NEUT.).
To hear, listen.	Audĭre, auscultāre.
Instead of, in place or *in lieu of* *(any one).*	{ Lóco, in lócum ALICUJUS. { Více, in vícem, vícem REI or ALI- CUJUS. { Pro, with the Abl.

---

* From *văleo*, *ĕre*, *ŭi*, —, "I am sound, strong," with the ablative "with respect to."

† *Caeruleus*, used substantively, a blue-eyed man, and the fem. here a woman.

Instead *or* in place of my father.	Lóco pátris, in vícem pátris, pro pátre.
Instead of salt, sugar, &c.	Sális, sácchari více.
Instead of me, thee, us, you.	Méam, túam, nóstram, véstram vícem.
Instead of him, them.	In lócum (vícem) éjus, eórum.

C. Obs. The English *instead of*, when it relates to persons or things in the sense of *in lieu of*, *in the place of*, is in Latin expressed by *loco*, *vice*, or *pro;* but when it limits the meaning of a verb, the formulas *tantum abest ut* . . . . *ut, non modo non* . . . . *sed etiam, magis (potius) quam*, and *quum debeam* * must be employed.

Do you play instead of studying (rather than study, when you ought to study)?	Operámne dâs lúdo mágis (pótius) quam lítteris? Ludísne, quum lítteris studêre débëas?
I study instead of playing.	Óperam dô lítteris, pótius quam lúdo.
So far from playing, I am studying.	Tántum ábest, ut lûdam, ut óperam dém lítteris.
I not only do not play, but I even study.	Nôn módo nôn lúdo, sed lítteris etiam stúdeo.
This boy speaks instead of listening (when he ought to listen).	Púer íste lóquitur, quum auscultâre débeat.
This boy is so far from listening, that he even talks.	Tántum ábest, ut púer íste aúdiat, ut loquâtur. Púer íste nôn módo nôn aûdit, sed étiam lóquitur.
To listen or *attend to any one.*	*Audíre aliquem. Auscultâre alicui.*† *Alicui aures dare.*
To listen or attend to anything.	Audíre aliquid. Observâre aliquid.
Not to listen to (care for) anything.	Non curâre aliquid.
Whom are you hearing (listening to)?	Quém aúdis? Cui dâs aúres?
I am listening to the speaker.	Oratôrem aúdio. Aúres dô oratóri.
Will you listen to (i. e. obey) me?	Vísne míhi auscultâre?

---

* *Tantum abest, ut* . . . . *ut*, I am so far from . . . . that rather. *Non modo non* . . . . *sed etiam*, not only not . . . . but even. *Magis (potius)* . . . . *quam*, rather than. *Quum (cum) debeam*, when I ought. The student should notice that the *ut* of the first formula, and the *quum* of the last, require the subjunctive. See the examples.

† *Auscultare* conveys the secondary notion of deference or obedience.

17 *

Do you listen to what the teacher tells you ?	Audísne (observâsne), quod (quae) praecéptor tíbi dícat (ímpĕret) ?
I do listen to it.	Aúdio (obsérvo).
He listens to what I tell him.	{ Míhi auscúltat. { Ómnia quaê éi dícam, obsérvat.
That which. *What* (= *that which*).	*Id quod, ea quae.* *Quod, quae.*
He does not listen to (observe) what the master tells him.	Quae praecéptor éi ímpĕrat, nôn cûrat.
To correct.	{ Emendo, âre, âvi, âtum. { Corrĭgo, ĕre, rexi, rectum. { (ALIQUID).
To take.	{ Sūmo, ĕre, mpsi, mptum. { Căpĭo, ĕre, cēpi, captum. { (ALIQUID).
To take away.	{ Aufĕro, ferre, abstŭli, ablātum. { Tollo, ĕre, sustŭli, sublātum. { (ALIQUID).
To take off, pull off.	{ Exŭo, ĕre, ŭi, ūtum. { Dĕtrăho, ĕre, xi, ctum.
To take off one's clothes.	{ Exuére sê véstibus. { Detráhĕre síbi véstes.
To take off one's shoes.	{ Detráhĕre pédibus cálceos. { Excalceâre pédes.
To take off one's hat.	{ Detráhĕre cápiti pĭleum. { Nudâre cáput.
Are you correcting your letter ?	Emendâsne (corrigísne) epístolam túam ?
Yes, I am correcting it.	Sáne quídem, éam émendo.
Does he take off his clothes ?	{ Exúitne se véstibus ? { Detrahítne síbi véstes ?
He is taking them off.	Éxŭit. Détrăhit.
We are taking off our clothes.	Exúimus nôs véstibus.
I am taking off my coat.	{ Éxŭo me tógă. { Détrăho míhi tógam.
Are you taking off your shoes ?	{ Detrahísne tíbi cálceos ? { Excalceâsne pédes ?
No; I am taking off my hat.	Nôn véro ; píleum détraho cápiti.
What is the servant taking away ?	Quid aúfert sérvus ?
He is carrying away the chairs.	Séllas (aúfert).
Do you wish me a good morning (good day, good evening).	{ Jubêsne mê sálvum ésse (salvēre) ? { Salutâsne mê máne, vésperi ?
Good morning (day, evening).	Sálve ! * *Plur.* Salvête !
To salute any one, to bid or wish one good morning, &c.	{ Salutâre aliquem. { Aliquem salvum esse (salvēre) jubēre.

---

* This was the common formula for any time of the day.

EXERCISE 71.

Do you speak Spanish? — No, sir, I speak Italian. — Who speaks Polish? — My brother speaks Polish. — Do our neighbors speak Russian? — They do not speak Russian, but Arabic. — Do you speak Arabic? — No, I speak Greek and Latin. — What knife have you? — I have an English knife. — What money have you there? — Is it Italian or Spanish money? — It is Russian money. — Have you an Italian hat? — No, I have a Spanish hat. — Are you a German? — No, I am an Englishman. — Art thou a Greek? — No, I am a Spaniard. — Are these men Poles? — No, they are Russians. — Do the Russians speak Polish? — They do not speak Polish, but Latin, Greek, and Arabic. — Is your brother a merchant? — No, he is a joiner. — Are these men merchants? — No, they are carpenters. — Are we boatmen? — No, we are shoemakers. — Art thou a fool? — I am not a fool. — What is that man? — He is a tailor. — Do you wish* me anything? — I wish you a good morning. — What does the young man wish me? — He wishes you a good evening. — Whither must I go? — Thou must go to our friends to wish them a good day. — Do your children come to me in order to wish me a good evening? — They come to you in order to wish you a good morning.

EXERCISE 72.

Does the man listen to what you are telling him? — He does listen to it. — Do the children of the physician listen to what we tell them? — They do not listen to it. — Dost thou listen to what thy brother tells thee? — I do listen to it. — Do you go to the theatre? — I am going to the storehouse instead of going to the theatre. — Are you willing to listen to me? — I am willing to listen to you, but I cannot; I have the earache. — Does thy father correct my notes or thine? — He corrects neither yours nor mine. — Which notes does he correct? — He corrects those which he writes. — Does he listen to what you tell him? — He does listen to it. — Do you take off your hat in order to speak to my father? — I do take it off in order to speak to him. — Does thy brother listen to what our father tells him? — He does listen to it. — Does our servant go for some beer? — He goes for some vinegar instead of going for some beer. — Do you correct my letter? — I do not correct it; I have sore eyes. — Does the servant take off his coat in order to make a fire? — He does take it off. — Do you take off your gloves in order to give me money? — I do take them off in order to give you some. — Does he take off his shoes in order to go to your house? — He does not take them off. — Who takes away the tables and chairs? — The servants take them away. — Will you take away this glass? — I have no mind to take it away. — Is he wrong to take off his boots? — He is right to take them off. — Dost thou take away anything? — I do not take away anything. — Does anybody take off his hat? — Nobody takes it off.

---

* _Precāri_ (dep.) _alicui aliquid_, to wish any one anything.

EXERCISE 73.

Has the nobleman blue eyes? — He has black eyes and a little mouth. — Hast thou a good memory? — I have not a very good memory (*parum váleo*), but my brother is endowed with an excellent one. — Can he write in place of his father? — He cannot. — Do they send bread instead of salt? — They send salt instead of bread. — Will you go to the ball in my stead? — I cannot go in your stead. — What dost thou (do) instead of playing? — I study instead of playing. — Dost thou learn instead of writing? — I write instead of learning. — What does the son of our bailiff (do)? — He goes into the garden instead of going into the field. — Do the children of our neighbors read? — They write instead of reading. — What does our cook (do)? — He makes a fire instead of going to the market. — Does your father sell his ox? — He sells his horse instead of selling his ox. — Do the physicians go out? — They remain in their rooms instead of going out. — At what o'clock does our physician come to you? — He comes every morning at a quarter to nine. — Does the son of the painter study English? — He studies Greek instead of studying English. — Does the butcher kill oxen? — He kills sheep instead of killing oxen. — Do you listen to me? — I do listen to you. — Does your brother listen to me? — He speaks instead of listening to you. — Do you listen to what I am telling you? — I do listen to what you are telling me.

Lesson XXXIX. — PENSUM UNDEQUADRAGE-SIMUM.

OF THE AGREEMENT OF RELATIVES.

A. The relative *qui, quae, quod* agrees with its antecedent in gender and number, but its case depends upon the construction of the clause introduced by it.   E. g.

Égo, qui (quaê) légo, scribo, lóquor.	*I who read, write, speak.*
Tù, quém (quám) díligo.	*Thou whom I cherish.*
Púer, quém vidísti, dequô audivísti, cújus tutor és.	*The boy whom you saw, of whom you have heard, whose guardian you are.*
Púeri, quôs vidísti, de quíbus audivísti, quôrum tutor és.	*The boys whom you saw, of whom you have heard, whose guardian you are.*
Flúmen, quód appellâtur Támĕsis.	*The river which is called the Thames.*
Ómnia, quaê tíbi díxi, véra sunt.	*All that I have told you is true.*

REMARKS.

1. The word to which the relative refers, and which it serves to limit and explain, is called its *Antecedent.* This may be either a noun, a personal, determinative, demonstrative, or indefinite pronoun, or an entire sentence.

2. The determinatives *is* and *idem,* and the demonstratives *hic, ille, iste,* &c., are called the *correlatives* of *qui.* They are either employed adjectively in agreement with the antecedent, or as substantives constituting the antecedent; e. g. *Loquimur de* iis amicis, quos *novit vita communis,* We are speaking of those friends, which occur in ordinary life. *Nam* cum, qui *palam est adversarius, facile cavendo vitare possis,* For him, who is openly your adversary, you can easily avoid by being on your guard.

3. The construction of the correlative pronominals *tantus . . . . quantus, talis . . . . qualis,* and *tot . . . . quot,* is the same as that of *is . . . . qui,* and the remarks on the latter may in general be applied to them also.

4. The relative *qui* may represent any one of the three persons of either number, and its verb agrees in person with the antecedent; as, *Ego,* qui *te* confirmo, *ipse me non possum,* I, who am consoling you, am unable to console myself. *Tu es is,* qui *me sepissime* ornāsti, You are the man who has honored me the oftenest. *Nobis quidem,* qui *te* amamus, *erit gratum,* To us at any rate, who love you, it will be agreeable. *Etiam is,* qui *omnia* tenet, *favet ingeniis,* Even he, who now has the control of everything, favors genius. *Fere libenter homines* id, quod *volunt, credunt,* Men are always ready to believe what they desire.

5. The clause of the antecedent commonly precedes that of the relative; but this order is frequently inverted in Latin. E. g. *Male se res habet, cum,* quod *virtute effici debet,* id *tentatur pecuniā,* There is a bad state of things, when that which ought to be effected by virtue is attempted with money. *Quam quisque norit artem,* in hāc *se exerceat,* Let every one practise the art he may have learnt. *Hoc non concedo, ut,* quibus rebus *gloriemini in vobis,* easdem *in aliis reprehendatis,* I do not concede to you the right of reprehending in others what you boast of in yourselves.

6. The noun, to which the relative refers, is commonly expressed but once, and in the leading clause. Sometimes, however, it is repeated with the relative, and agrees with it in gender, number, and case; as, *Tantum* bellum, *tam diurnum, tam longe lateque dispersum,* quo bello *omnes gentes premebantur,* So great, so long, so wide-spread a war, by which all nations were oppressed. *Caesar intellexit* diem *instare,* quo die *frumentum militibus metiri oporteret,* Caesar understood that the day was approaching, on which the soldiers were to receive their allowance of corn.

7. The noun is sometimes expressed with the relative only, and understood in the leading clause. This is especially the case when the logical order of the clauses is inverted, as in Rem. 5. E. g. *Accu-*

sător non ferendus est is, *qui*, quod *in altero* vitium *reprehendit*, in eo ipso *deprehenditur*, He cannot be admitted as accuser who is himself caught in the very vice he reprehends in another. *Bestiae*, in quo loco *natae sunt*, ex eo *se non commóvent*, Wild animals do not remove from the locality in which they were born. Quantā vi *civitates libertatem expetunt*, tantā *regna reges defendunt*, Kings defend monarchies with the same vehemence with which states seek their liberty.

8. The antecedent is sometimes entirely suppressed, and the relative *qui, quod* stands in the sense of " he who," " what." E. g. *Qui* (= is, qui) *e nuce nucleum esse vult, frangit nucem*, He who wishes the nut to become a kernel breaks the nut. *Est profecto deus, qui, quae* (= ea quae) *nos gerimus, auditque et videt*, There is certainly a God, who hears and sees whatever we are doing. *Maximum ornamentum amicitiae tollit*, qui (= is, qui) *ex ea tollit verecundiam*, He robs friendship of its greatest ornament who robs it of decorum and respect. So, *Sunt qui dicunt*, There are those who say. *Sunt* quos *juvat*, There are men whom it delights. *Nos imitamur*, quos *cuique visum est*, We imitate whomsoever it pleases us. *Non habeo* quod *scribam*, I have nothing to write.*

9. The antecedent sometimes assumes the case of the relative, and *vice versa*. This is called attraction. E. g. *Naucratem* (= *Naucratis*) *quem convenire volui, in navi non erat*, Naucratis, whom I wanted to find, was not in the ship. *Urbem* (= urbs), *quam statuo, restra est*, The city which I am building is yours. *Hac, quā* (= quam) *diximus, aetate*, At the age (of life) which we have mentioned. *Video me desertum, a quibus* (= ab iis, quibus) *minime conveniebat*, I see myself deserted by those to whom it was least becoming (to desert me). *Judice quo* (= quem) *nösti populo*, With the people, which you know, for a judge.

Wet, moist.	*Humĭdus, ŭlus, madĭdus, a, um.*
To wet, moisten.	{ *Madefăcĭo, ĕre, fēci, factum.* *Humecto, āre, āvi, ātum.* ((ALIQUID).
To show, point out.	Monstro, āre, āvi, ātum (ALICUI ALIQUID).
To show, let see.	Ostendo, ĕre, ndi, nsum (ALICUI ALIQUID).
Will you show me your gold ribbons?	Visne míhi osténdere taénias túas aúreas?
I am willing to show them to you.	Véro, vólo tíbi éas osténdere.
Are ye willing to show us the way?	Vultísne monstrâre nóbis víam?

* So also commonly *quisquis* and *quicunqne*; as, Quidquid *non licet, nefas putare debemus*, We ought to consider wrong whatever is unlawful. *In quascunque partes velint, proficisci licet*, They may go in whatever direction they please.

Certainly we are willing.	Sáne quídem, nôn nólumus.
Is the boy wetting anything ?	Madefacítne púer áliquid ?
He is not wetting anything; he is only moistening the handkerchief.	Nihil madefácit, huméctat duntáxat muccínium.

Brandy.	*Vīnum adustum, i, n.
Tobacco.	*Tābăcum, i, n.; herba nicotiǎna, ae, f.
Smoking tobacco.	*Tābăcum fumārium, i, n.
Snuff.	*Tābăcum sternutatōrium.
Flour.	Farīna, ae, f.
Cider.	Vīnum ex mālis confectum.
The fruit.	Pōmum, i, n.
The apple.	Mălum, i, n., pōmum mālum.
The pear.	Pīrum, i, n.
The gardener.	Hortulānus, i, m.
The relative.	Cognātus, i, m.; propinquus, i, m.
The cousin.	Consobrīnus, i, m.; consobrīna,* ae, f.
The brother-in-law (= husband's brother, wife's brother, sister's husband).	Lēvir, i, m.; marīti frāter;† uxōris frāter; marītus sorōris.
The husband.	Marītus, i, m.; conjux, ŭgis, m.
The wife.	Uxor, ōris. f.; conjux, ŭgis, f.
The handkerchief.	Sudārium, i, n.; muccinium, i, n.
The valet, servant.	Famŭlus, servus, i, m.; minister, ri, m.

Does the servant fetch us some tobacco ?	Apportátne nóbis sérvus tábacum ?
He does fetch us a little.	Appórtat véro nóbis aliquántŭlum.
Will you call (go for) your cousin ?	Visne túum consobrínum arcéssere ?
I am willing (am not unwilling) to go for him.	Arcéssere éum nôn nólo.
Are you desirous of drinking some of my brandy ?	Cupidúsne es bibéndi de víno méo adústo ?
No, I would rather drink pure water.	Ímmo véro cúpidus sum bibéndi áquam pûram.
To intend, think of.	*Cogĭto, āre, āvi, ātum* (ALIQUID FĂCĔRE).
Do you intend to go to the ball to-night ?	Cogitísne hódie vésperi saltātum ire ?
I do intend to go, sir.	Sic est, dómine, cógito.

---

* The Roman subdivisions of cousinship are: *Patruēlis*, m. & f., the son or daughter of a paternal uncle. *Amitīnus*, i, m. (fem. *-a*), maternal uncle's or paternal aunt's child. *Sobrīnus*, i, m. (fem. *-a*), a second-cousin.

† *Lēvir* = *marīti frater*, the husband's brother.

| What do they intend to do ? | Quid fácere cógitant ? |
| They are intending to write letters ? | Epístolas conscríbere cógitant. |

| *To know.* | *Scĭo, ĭre, ĭvi, ĭtum.* |
| *Not to know (to be ignorant).* | *Nescĭre, non (haud) scĭre.* |

To swim.	{ Nō, nāre, nāvi, ——.
	{ Năto, āre, āvi, ātum.
To be able (to have the power or opportunity).	{ Possum, posse, potúi, ——.
	{ Quĕo, ĭre, ĭvi (ĭi), ĭtum.

B. Obs. Possum is to have the physical power, or the means or influence to do anything, and is used in sentences of every kind. *Queo* is to have the ability or qualifications, and is only put in sentences containing a negation (*non queo, nequeo*). *Queo* is anomalous, and its present tense is as follows :—

PRES. INDIC.	PRES. SUBJ.
SING. Quĕo, quĭs, quĭt,	SING. Quĕăm, quĕăs, quĕăt,
PLUR. Quĭmus, quĭtis, quĕunt.	PLUR. Quĕāmus, quĕātis, quĕant.

Does this boy know Latin ?	Num púer íste scit Latíne (línguam Latīnam) ?
He does not know it.	Nôn scit. Haûd scit. Néscit.
Or can he read French ?	An légere pótest Francogállice ?
He cannot.	Non pótest. Néquit.
Can you write an English letter ?	Potésne (scisne) scríbere epístolam Ánglice ?
I can write one.	Póssum. Scío.
I cannot (am not able) to do it.	Fácere nôn póssum (nôn quéo, néqueo).
Can you swim (do you know how to swim) ?	{ Ésne tu perìtus nándi.
	{ Habêsne sciéntiam nándi ?
I do not know how.	{ Nôn sum perìtus.
	{ Sciéntiam nôn hábeo.
Where do you intend to go (think of going) ?	Quo ĭre cógitas ?
I think of going into the country.	Rûs ĭre cógito.
Does your cousin wet his handkerchief ?	Humectátne consobrínus túus sudárium (súum) ?
He does not wet it.	Nôn huméctat.
He does wet it.	Sic est, huméctat.
Can you drink brandy ?	Potésne bíbere vínum adústum ?
I cannot.	Nôn (haûd) póssum.

EXERCISE 74.

Do you intend to study Arabic ? — I intend to study Arabic and Syriac. — Does the Englishman know Polish ? — He does not know it, but he intends learning it. — Do you know how to swim ? — I do not know how to swim, but how to play. — Does your cousin know how to make coats ? — He does not know how to make any ; he is no

tailor. — Is he a merchant ? — He is not one. — What is he ? — He
is a physician. — Whither are you going ? — I am going into my garden, in order to speak to the gardener. — What do you wish to tell
him ? — I wish to tell him to open the window of his room. — Does
your gardener listen to you ? — He does listen to me. — Do you wish
to drink some cider ? — No, I have a mind to drink some beer ; have
you any ? — I have none ; but I will send for some. — When will you
send for some ? — Now. — Do you send for apples ? — I do send for
some. — Have you a good deal of water ? — I have enough to wash
my feet. — Has your brother water enough ? — He has only a little,
but enough to moisten his pocket-handkerchief. — Do you know how
to make tea ? — I know how to make some. — Does your cousin listen
to what you tell him ? — He does listen to it. — Does he know how
to swim ? — He does not know how to swim. — Where is he going to ?
— He is going nowhither ; he remains at home.

EXERCISE 75.

Dost thou go to fetch (*arcessitum*)* thy father ? — I do go to fetch
him. — May I go to fetch my cousin ? — You may go to fetch him. —
Does your valet find the man whom he is looking for ? — He does
find him. — Do your sons find the friends whom they are looking for ?
— They do not find them. — When do you intend going to the ball ?
— I intend going thither this evening. — Do your cousins intend to go
into the country ? — They intend to go thither. — When do they intend to go thither ? — They intend to go thither to-morrow. — At
what o'clock ? — At half past nine. — What does the merchant wish
to sell you ? — He wishes to sell me pocket-handkerchiefs. — Do you
intend to buy some ? — I will not buy any. — Dost thou know anything ? — I do not know anything. — What does thy cousin know ? —
He knows how to read and to write. — Does he know German ? —
He does not know it. — Do you know Spanish ? — I do know it. —
Do your brothers know Greek ? — They do not know it ; but they
intend to learn it. — Do I know English ? — You do not know it ;
but you intend to study it. — Do my children know how to read Italian ? — They know how to read, but not how to speak it.

EXERCISE 76.

Do you desire to drink brandy ? — No, I wish to drink wine. — Do
you sell brandy ? — I do not sell any ; but my neighbor the merchant
sells some. — Will you fetch me some tobacco ? — I will fetch you
some ; what tobacco do you wish (to have) ? — I wish to have some
snuff ; but my friend, the German, wishes to have some smoking-
tobacco. — Does the merchant show you cloth ? — He does not show
me any. — Does your valet go for some cider ? — He does go for
some. — Do you want anything else (*amplius*) ? — I want some flour ;
will you send for some for me ? — Does your friend buy apples ? —
He does buy some. — Does he buy handkerchiefs ? — He buys tobac-

---

* Compare Lesson XLVII. *A.*

18

co instead of buying handkerchiefs. — Do you show me anything? —
I show you my gold and silver clothes. — Whither does your cousin
go? — He goes to the ball. — Do you go to the ball? — I go to the
theatre instead of going to the ball. — Does the gardener go into the
garden? — He goes to the market instead of going into the garden.
— Do you send your servant to the shoemaker? — I send him to the
tailor, instead of sending him to the shoemaker.

Lesson XL. — PENSUM QUADRAGESIMUM.

THE AGREEMENT OF RELATIVES CONTINUED.

A. 1. When the relative refers to two or more nouns, it
stands in the plural, and assumes the gender of an adjective
under similar circumstances (cf. Lesson XXII. *B.*, and Lesson
XXXVII. *A.* 10). E. g.

Pater ejus et mater, qui *mortui sunt*, His father and mother, who are
dead. *Arbitrum habebimus Civilem et Velĕdam, apud* quos *pacta san-
cientur*, We shall have Civilis and Veleda (a woman) as arbitrators,
in whose presence the compact will be ratified. *Favent pietati fideique
dii, per* quae* *populus Romanus ad tantum fastigii venit*, The gods
bestow their favor upon piety and faith, by which the Roman people
has attained such eminent distinction. *Duilius delectabatur crebro fu-
nali et tibicine*, quae *sibi nullo exemplo privatus sumpserat.*

2. When the antecedent is a collective noun, the relative sometimes
assumes the gender and number of the individuals composing it.
E. g. *Caesar* equitatum omnem *praemittit*, qui *videant, quas in partes
hostes iter faciant*, Cæsar sends ahead all his cavalry, to see (*lit.* who
may or might see) in what direction the enemy is pursuing his way.
Academia, a quibus *nunquam dictum est, aut calorem, aut saporem, aut
sonum nullum esse*, The Academy, by which (i. e. by the persons composing it) it was never maintained, that either heat or smell or sound
were nonentities.

3. If the antecedent is a proper name in apposition with a generic
term, the relative may agree with either. E. g. *Helvetii continentur
flumine Rheno*, qui (i. e. *Rhenus*) *agrum Helvetium a Germanis dividit*,
The Helvetii are bounded by the river Rhine, which divides the
Helvetian territory from that of the Germans. *Caesar ad flumen
Scaldem*, quod (sc. *flumen*) *influit in Mosam, ire constituit*, Cæsar re-
solved to advance towards the river Scheldt, which empties into the
Moselle.

---

* Cf. Lesson XXII. *B.* 3.

4. If a noun descriptive of the antecedent is added to the relative, it agrees with that noun in preference to the antecedent.   E. g. *Eodem anno Cumae*, quam *Graeci tum* urbem *tenebant, capiuntur*, Cumæ, a city which the Greeks then occupied, was taken in the same year. *Accidit, ut luna plena esset*, qui dies *maritimos aestus maximos in Oceano efficere consuevit*, It happened to be full moon, which day usually gave rise to the highest tide in the ocean.   *Oppius negotia procurat Egnatii Rufi*, quo *ego* uno equite Romano *familiarissime utor*, Oppius is managing the affairs of Egnatius Rufus, the only Roman knight with whom I am on terms of intimacy.

5. An adjective, qualifying the antecedent, is sometimes joined to the relative, and agrees with it in preference to the antecedent.   E. g. *Verres mittit ad Antiochum regem, rogatum vasa ea* quae pulcherrima *apud eum viderat*, Verres sent to King Antiochus, to ask him for the handsomest vases which he had seen at his residence.   *Themistocles de servis suis* quem *habuit* fidelissimum, *ad Xerxem misit*, Themistocles sent to Xerxes one of his servants, whom he regarded the most faithful.   *Consul*, qui unus *supererat, moritur*, The only surviving consul is on his death-bed.   This is the common construction when the adjective is a superlative, a comparative, or a numeral.

6. When, in connection with the verb *sum*, or a verb of naming, calling, esteeming,* &c., the relative clause contains a noun of a different gender from the antecedent, the relative may agree either with that noun or with the antecedent.   E. g. *Est genus quoddam hominum*, quod *Helotes vocatur*, There is a class of men (which is) called the Helots.   *Domicilia conjuncta*, quas urbes *dicimus*, Assemblages of dwelling-houses, which we call cities.   *Thebae ipsae*, quod *Boeotiae* caput *est*, Thebes itself, which is the capital of Bœotia. *Flumen*, qui *provinciae ejus* finis *erat*, The river, which was the boundary line of that province.

7. The relative sometimes agrees with an antecedent implied in a possessive pronoun, an adjective, or in the context generally.   E. g. *Scauri dicendi genus ad* senatoriam *sententiam*, cujus *ille erat princeps, vel maxime aptum videbatur*, Scaurus's style of oratory seemed to be most admirably adapted to senatorial speaking, of which (i. e. of the senate) he was the princeps.   *Illud quidem* nostrum *consilium jure laudandum est*, qui . . . . *noluerim*, That plan of mine is justly entitled to praise, who was unwilling, &c.   *Veiens bellum exortum*, quibus† *Sabini arma conjunxerant*, The Veian war broke out, with whom the Sabines had united their arms.

8. The neuters *quod* and *quae* sometimes refer to a noun of a different gender, especially to *res*.   E. g. *Sumptu ne parcas* ullā in re, quod *ad valetudinem opus sit*, Do not spare expense in anything which may be necessary for your health.   *Otium et abundantia* earum rerum, quae *prima mortales ducunt*, Leisure and an abundance of those things,

---

* Cf. Lesson XXXIV. C.
† I. e. with the *Veii* implied in the adjective *Veiens*.

which men deem of the first importance. *In sermonibus, quae nec possunt scribi, nec scribenda sunt,* In conversations, which are neither to be written, nor can be written.

9. When the antecedent is an entire sentence, or part of one, the relative is the neuter *quod* or *id quod.* E. g. *Conclamat omnis multitudo Gallorum ....* quod *facere in eo consuerunt, cujus orationem approbant,* All the Gauls shouted, — a thing which they were accustomed to do to one, whose harangue they approved. *Timoleon,* id quod *difficilius putatur, multo sapientius tulit secundam, quam adversam fortunam,* Timoleon (did) what is considered the more difficult of the two, — he bore prosperity with wiser moderation than adversity. *Si nos,* id quod *maxime debet, nostra patria delectat,* If our country, as it especially ought to do, inspires us with delight.

10. The relative is sometimes employed idiomatically to denote a quality or species, in the sense of the English *such, as, in consideration of,* &c. It is thus used either alone or in connection with *is* or *idem.* E. g. Quae *tua est prudentia,* or quā *es prudentiā,* Such is your prudence (in consideration of your prudence).* *Ego* is *in Dionysium sum,* quem *tu me esse vis,* I am towards Dionysius as (or what) you wish me to be. *Nos ii sumus,* qui *esse debemus, id est, studio digni ac litteris nostris,* We are such as (or what) we ought to be, that is, worthy of our zeal and letters. So also, *Quae tua natura est,* In consideration of your natural kindness. Quod *tuum est judicium de hominibus,* Such is your knowledge of human character. Qui *illius in te amor fuit,* In consideration of his regard for you. Quā *est humanitate Caesar,* Such is the humanity of Cæsar.

11. Relative adjectives and adverbs follow the construction of the relative pronoun. E. g. *Non sunt* tanti *ulla merita,* quanta *insolentia hominis,* quantumque *fastidium,* No merits are of so much account as (to counterbalance) the insolence and haughtiness of man. *Nemo orator tam multa scripsit,* quam multa *sunt nostra,* No orator has written as much as I have. Quot *orationum genera esse diximus,* totidem *oratorum reperiuntur,* There are (found) just as many of orators, as we have mentioned styles of oratory. Quales *in republica principes sunt,* tales *reliqui solent esse cives,* As are the leaders of a republic, so are the rest of the citizens wont to be. Quam diu *animus remanet in nobis,* tam diu *sensus et vita remanet,* Sensation and life remain in us as long as the spirit remains. *Crocodilus parit ova,* quanta *anseres,* The crocodile lays eggs as large as geese.

12. The Latin relative frequently assumes the force of a demonstrative, and becomes equivalent to the English *and this (these), since this, although this,* &c.; as, *Quae cum ita sint,* Since these things are so. *Res loquitur ipsa,* quae *semper valet plurimum,* The thing speaks for itself, *and this* is always the most powerful argument. *Magna vis est conscientiae,* quam *qui negligunt, se ipsi indicant,* Great is the power of conscience, *hence those* who disregard it, betray themselves.

* Equivalent to *pro tuā prudentiā,* which also occurs in the same sense.

Oculorum est in nobis sensus acerrimus, quibus *sapientiam non cernĭmus,*
Our eyesight is the keenest of all our senses, *and yet* wisdom is not
discerned *by it.*

The intention, design.	Consilium, i, n.; *propŏsĭtūm,* i, n.
It is my intention, I intend (to do anything).	Propŏsitum est mihi (*fácere áli- quid*).
It is our intention to do this.	Id fácere nóbis est propósitum.
Does your father intend to go out this morning?	Cogitátne páter túus hódie máne in públicum prodire?
It is his intention to do so.	Propósitum est éi fácere hóc.
To receive (anything sent).	{ Accĭpĭo, ĕre, cēpi, ceptum. { Recĭpĕre (ALIQUID AB ALIQUO).
To receive (a guest, &c.).	Excĭpĕre, accĭpĕre (ALIQUEM).
To obtain, get (with effort).	{ Consĕquor, i, cūtus sum. { Assĕquor, &c. (ALIQUID).
Who obtains the preference?	Quis conséquitur principâtum (pri- óres pártes)?
Our friend (obtains it).	Amícus nóster.
Does he receive money, letters, books?	Accipítne pecúniam, epístolas, lí- bros?
He does not (receive any).	Non áccipit.
When do you receive (enter- tain) your friends?	Quó témpore familiáres túos éx- cipis?
I receive them in the evening.	Excípio éos véspere.
The preference.	*Princĭpātus, ūs,* m.; *priŏres partes,* f. pl.
The stable.	Stabŭlum, i, n.
Blind.	Caecus, a, um; ocŭlis captus, a, um.
Sick, ill.	Aeger, ra, rum; aegrōtus, a, um.
To be sick or ill.	Aegrōtum esse, aegrotāre; laborāre morbo (abl.).
Poor, needy.	Inops, is; pauper, ĕris; egēnus, a, um.
To take, conduct.	*Dūco, ĕre, xi, ctum* (ALIQUEM ALI- QUO, AD ALIQUEM).
To guide, lead one by the hand.	{ Mănū dūcĕre aliquem. { Dăre mănūs alicui.
To extinguish, put out.	*Extinguo, ĕre, nxi, nctum.*
To light, kindle.	Accendo, ĕre, i, sum.
To set on fire.	{ Succendĕre (rem). { Ignem inferre (alicui rei).
To depart, set out on a jour- ney.	Proficiscor, i, -fectus sum (dep.).
To go off, leave.	{ Abĕo, íre, ĭi (ívi), Itum. { Discēdo, ĕre, cessi, cessum.

N   18 *

Is any one sick ?	{ Écquis aegrôtus est ? { Num quís mórbo labôrat ?
No one is sick.	{ Némo est aegrótus. { Némo mórbo labôrat.
Do you conduct any one ?	Ducísne áliquem ?
I am conducting my good little daughter.	Dúco véro filíolam méam bónam.
Does the boy guide the blind man ?	{ Ducítne caêcum púer mánu ? (Lesson XXXVIII. A. Rem. 2.) { Dátne púer mánus caéco ?
He does guide him.	Ducit. Dat mánus.
Do you extinguish the candle ?	Extinguísne candêlam ?
No, I am (on the contrary) lighting it.	Ímmo véro (éam) accéndo.
Who sets fire to the house ?	{ Quis succéndit aédes ? { Quis ígnem ínfert aédibus ?
The bad man sets fire to it.	Hómo nêquam éas accéndit.
Do you design to leave ?	Éstne tíbi propósitum abíre (discédere) ?
It is my design.	Est míhi propósitum.
When do you think of setting out ?	Quô témpore cógitas proficísci ?
To-morrow morning.	Crâs mâne.
Do I set out ?	Egóne proficíscor ?
You do not set out.	Nòn proficísceris.

Exercise 77.

Do your brothers intend to go into the country ? — They do intend to go thither. — Do you intend to go to my cousin ? — I do intend to go to him. — Dost thou intend to do anything ? — I intend to do nothing. — Do you intend to go to the theatre this evening ? — I do intend to go thither, but not this evening. — Dost thou receive anything ? — I receive money. — From whom dost thou receive some ? — I receive some from my father, my brother, and my cousin. — Does your son receive books ? — He does receive some. — From whom does he receive some ? — He receives some from me, from his friends and neighbors. — Does the poor man receive money ? — He does receive some ? — From whom does he receive some ? — He receives some from the rich. — Dost thou receive wine ? — I do not receive any. — Do I receive money ? — You do not receive any. — Does your servant receive clothes ? — He does not receive any. — Do you receive the books which our friends receive ? — We do not receive the same which your friends receive ; but we receive others. — Does your friend receive the letters which you write to him ? — He does receive them. — Do you receive the apples which I send you ? — I do not receive them. — Does the American receive as much brandy as cider ? — He receives as much of the one as of the other. — Do the Scotch receive as many books as letters ? — They receive as many of the one as of the other.

EXERCISE 78.

Does the Englishman obtain the preference? — He does obtain it. — Does your cousin receive as much money as I? — He receives more than you. — Does the Frenchman receive his letters? — He does receive them. — When does he receive them? — He receives them in the evening. — When dost thou receive thy letters? — I receive them in the morning. — At what o'clock? — At a quarter to ten. — Dost thou receive as many letters as I? — I receive more of them than thou. — Dost thou receive any to-day? — I receive some to-day and to-morrow. — Does your father receive as many friends as ours (as our father)? — He receives fewer of them than yours (than your father). — Does the Spaniard receive as many enemies as friends? — He receives as many of the one as of the other. — Do you receive one more crown? — I do receive one more. — Does your son receive one more book? — He does receive one more. — What does the physician receive? — He receives good tobacco, good snuff, and good pocket-handkerchiefs. — Does he receive brandy? — He does receive some.

EXERCISE 79.

Do you intend to go to the theatre this evening? — I intend to go there to-morrow. — Do you depart to-day? — I depart now. — When do you intend to write to your friends? — I intend to write to them to-day. — Do your friends answer your letters? — They do answer them. — Do you extinguish the fire? — I do not extinguish it? — Does your servant light the candle? — He does light it. — Does this man intend to set your warehouse on fire? — He does intend to set it on fire. — Does your servant receive shirts? — He does receive some. — Does he receive as many of them as my valet. — He receives quite as many. — Do you receive anything to-day? — I receive something every day. — Dost thou conduct anybody. — I conduct nobody. — Whom do you guide? — I guide my son. — Where are you conducting him to? — I conduct him to my neighbors, in order to wish them a good morning. — What is your son? — He is a physician. — Does your servant guide any one? — He guides my child. — Whom must I guide? — Thou must guide the blind man. — Must he conduct the sick person? — He must conduct him. — Whither must he conduct him? — He must conduct him home. — Whither is he leading the horse? — He is leading it into the stable. — Dost thou guide the child or the blind man? — I guide both. — When does the foreigner intend to depart? — He intends to depart this morning. — At what o'clock? — At half past one. — Does he not wish to remain here? — He does not wish to remain.

Lesson XLI.— PENSUM UNUM ET QUADRAGE-SIMUM.

OF THE COMPARISON OF ADJECTIVES.

A. The property or quality denoted by an adjective may be attributed to an object either absolutely or relatively. This difference has given rise to several distinct forms of one and the same adjective, called its *Degrees of Comparison.*

1. That form of the adjective by which the quality denoted by it is attributed to an object or class of objects, without any reference to other objects possessed of the same quality, is called the *Positive* degree. E. g. Vir *audax*, a bold man; mel *dulce*, the sweet honey; montes *alti*, high mountains. This is to be regarded as its general and fundamental form.

2. When the quality denoted by an adjective is attributed to an object or class of objects in a greater degree than to another or to others, the form of the adjective expressing this relation is called the *Comparative* degree. E. g. Vir *audacior*, a bolder man; mel *dulcius*, the sweeter honey; *montes altiores*, higher mountains.

3. When the quality inherent in a number of objects is attributed to one or more of them in a higher degree than to all the rest, the form of the adjective expressing this relation is said to be in the *Superlative* degree. E. g. Vir *audacissimus*, the boldest man (of a certain number of men); mel *dulcissimum*, the sweetest honey; *montes altissimi*, the highest mountains.

We have thus found three forms of adjectives: — the *Positive*, the *Comparative*, and the *Superlative*.

B. Comparison in its widest sense comprehends the relations of *equality* and of *inequality.* The relation of inequality is subdivided into that of *inferiority* or of *superiority.*

1. The relation of equality is in Latin expressed by the positive with *tam* . . . . *quam, aeque* . . . . *ac* (*atque*), *pariter* . . . . *ac*, &c.; as, *Tam felix, quam bonus*, As happy as good. *Duo montes aeque alti*, Two mountains equally high. *Aeque altus, atque longus*, As high as long.

2. The relation of inferiority is likewise expressed by the positive form of the adjective, which becomes comparative by *minus* . . . . *quam*, less . . . . than, and superlative by *minime*, least. E. g. *Minus felix, quam bonus*, Less happy than good. *Minime felix*, Least happy.

3. The relation of superiority is sometimes indicated by *magis* . . . . *quam*, more . . . . than, and *maxime*, most; as, *Magis idoneus quam tu*, More competent than you. *Maxime idoneus*, The most competent.

But it is more commonly expressed by those peculiar forms of the adjective already known as the Comparative and Superlative.

REGULAR COMPARISON.

C. The comparative degree is formed by adding the terminations *ior*, m. & f., and *ius*, n., to the root of the positive *; and the superlative by adding *issimus, issima, issimum.* Thus: —

POSITIVE.	COMPARATIVE.	SUPERLATIVE.	
Longus,	longior,	longissimus ;	*long, longer, longest.*
Brevis,	brevior,	brevissimus ;	*short, shorter, shortest.*
Audax,	audacior,	audacissimus ;	*bold, bolder, boldest.*
Felix,	felicior,	felicissimus ;	*happy, happier, happiest.*
Iners,	inertior,	inertissimus ;	*sluggish, more sluggish, &c.*
Diligens,	diligentior,	diligentissimus ;	*diligent, more diligent, &c.*
Doctus,	doctior,	doctissimus ;	*learned, more learned, &c.*

ANOMALOUS COMPARISON.

D. Some adjectives are irregular in their mode of comparison.

1. Adjectives in *er* form their superlative by simply adding *rimus.* E. g.

Acer,	acrior,	acerrimus ;	*sharp, sharper, sharpest.*
Celeber,	celebrior,	celeberrimus ;	*distinguished, more d., most dis.*
Pauper,	pauperior,	pauperrimus ;	*poor, poorer, poorest.*
Pulcher,	pulchrior,	pulcherrimus ;	*beautiful, more beautiful, most b.*
Vetus,†	——,	veterrimus ;	*old, older, oldest.*
Nuperus,	——,	nuperrimus ;	*recent, more recent, most recent.*

2. The following in *ilis* form their superlative by adding *limus* to the root: —

Facilis,	facilior,	facillimus ;	*easy, easier, easiest.*
Gracilis,	gracilior,	gracillimus ;	*slender, more slender, most slen.*
Humilis,	humilior,	humillimus ;	*low, lower, lowest.*
Imbecillis,	imbecillior,	imbecillimus ;	*feeble, feebler, feeblest.*
Similis,	similior,	simillimus‡ ;	*like, more like, most like.*

3. Compounds in *dicus, ficus,* and *volus* compare from a participial form in *ens.* As, —

---

* This root is found from the genitive singular by dropping its case-termination; as, *longus — long-i, brevis — brev-is, audax — audac-is, felix — felic-is, iners — inert-is, diligens — diligent-is.*

† The original form of this was *veter;* and the superlative of *nuperus* is derived from the adverb *nuper.*

‡ So the compounds *difficilis* and *dissimilis.* But all other adjectives in *ilis* have *issimus.*

Mălĕdĭcus,	maledĭcentior,	maledicentissimus;	*slanderous.*
Munifĭcus,	munificentior,	munificentissimus;	*munificent.*
Benevŏlus,	benevolentior,	benevolentissimus;	*benevolent.*

So *honorifĭcus, magnifĭcus, malefĭcus, mirifĭcus; malevŏlus.*

4. The following derive their comparatives and superlatives from a different root : —

Bonus,	melior,	optĭmus;	*good, better, best.*
Malus,	pejor,	pessĭmus;	*bad, worse, worst.*
Magnus,	major,	maxĭmus;	*great, greater, greatest.*
Parvus,	minor,	minĭmus;	*small, smaller, smallest.*
Multus,	plūs,*	plurĭmus;	*much, more, most.*

5. Several adjectives have an irregular superlative, and some a double form of the comparative or superlative :

Dexter,	dexterior,	dextĭmus;	*to the right.*
Dives,	{ divĭtior, ditior,	divitissimus; ditĭmus; }	*rich.*
Extera, *f.*	exterior,	{ extĭmus; extrēmus; }	*outward.*
Juvĕnis,	{ juvenior, junior, }	———; †	*young.*
Infĕrus,	inferior,	{ infĭmus; imus; }	*low.*
Postĕra, *f.*	posterior,	{ postrēmus; postŭmus; }	*hind.*
Supĕrus,	superior,	{ suprēmus; summus; }	*high.*

6. The indeclinable *nēquam*, bad, has *nēquior, nēquissĭmus*, and *frugi*, frugal, *frugalior, frugalissĭmus.*

DEFECTIVE COMPARISON.

E. The comparison of some adjectives is defective ; i. e. they occur only in some of the forms of comparison.

1. The following are not used in the positive, which is either entirely obsolete, or only represented by adverbs or prepositions : —

COMPARATIVE.	SUPERLATIVE.		POSITIVE.
Citerior,	citĭmus,	*nearer;*	*citer*, obs. *citra*, this side).
Deterior,	deterrĭmus,	*worse;*	(from *deter*, not used).
Interior,	intĭmus,	*inner;*	(from *intus*, adv., within).
Ocior,	ocissĭmus,	*faster;*	(from the Greek ὠκύς).

* This form is properly the neuter comparative of *multum.*
† This superlative is *minimus natu*, as that of *senex*, old, is *maximus natu* (= the greatest by birth). So the comparatives *minor natu* and *major natu*, instead of *juvenior* and *senior.*

Potior,	potissĭmus,	*preferable ;*	(from *pŏtis*, obsolete).
Prior,	primus,	*former ;*	(from *prae*, prep., before).
Propĭor,	proxĭmus,	*nearer ;*	(from *prope*, adv., near).
Ulterior,	ultĭmus,	*further ;*	(from *ultra*, adv., farther.)

2. The comparative of the following adjectives and participles seldom or never occurs : —

Aprĭcus,	apricissĭmus ;	*sunny.*
Bellus,	bellissĭmus ;	*pretty.*
Comis,	comissĭmus ;	*affable.*
Consultus,	consultissĭmus ;	*proficient.*
Diversus,	diversissĭmus ;	*different.*
Falsus,	falsissĭmus ;	*false.*
Inclytus,	inclytissĭmus ;	*renowned.*
Invictus,	invictissĭmus ;	*unconquerable.*
Invitus,	invitissĭmus ;	*unwilling.*
Novus,	novissĭmus ;	*new.*
Nupĕrus,	nuperrĭmus ;	*recent.*
Par,	parissĭmus ;	*equal.*
Persuāsus,	persuasissĭmus ;	*persuaded*
Sacer,	sacerrĭmus ;	*sacred.*
Vetus,	veterrĭmus ;	*old.*

3. The following want the superlative : —

Adolescens,	adolescentior ·	*young.*
Agrestis,	agrestior ;	*rural.*
Alacer,	alacrior ;	*sprightly.*
Arcānus,	arcānior ;	*secret.*
Caecus,	caecior ;	*blind.*
Declivis,	declivior ;	*steep.*
Dēsĕs,	dēsior ;	*sluggish.*
Diuturnus,	diuturnior,	*long.*
Jejūnus,	jejūnior,	*fasting.*
Juvĕnis,	jūnior ;	*young.*
Longinquus,	longinquior ;	*distant.*
Opimus,	opimior ;	*opulent.*
Proclivis,	proclivior ;	*sloping.*
Prōnus,	prōnior ;	*inclined forward.*
Propinquus,	propinquior ;	*near.*
Salutāris,	salutārior ;	*salutary.*
Satis,	satior ; *	*better.*
Satŭr,	satūrior ;	*sated.*
Sĕnex,	sĕnior ;	*old.*
Secus,	sequior ;	*inferior.*
Silvester,	silvestrior ;	*woody.*
Sinister,	sinisterior ;	*left.*
Supīnus,	supīnior ;	*supine.*

* *Satior* and *sequior* (neut. *sequius* or *secius*) are isolated comparatives, which may be referred to the adverbs *satis* and *secus.*

4. The superlative is likewise wanting in the majority of verbal adjectives in *bilis, ilis, alis,* and in many of those in *ilis.*

F. The form of many adjectives does not admit of simple comparison, and these require *magis, maxime.* Such are:—

1. Those ending in *us* preceded by a vowel; as *idoneus,* fit; *dubius,* doubtful; *vacuus,* empty; Comp. *magis idoneus;* Sup. *maxime idoneus.* *

2. Participles in *dus†* and verbals in *bundus;‡* as *amandus, moribundus,* ready to die.

3. Adjectives ending in *icus, ivus, inus, imus, orus,* and many in *osus* and *entus;§* as, *modicus,* moderate; *fugitivus,* fugitive; *matutinus,* early; *legitimus,* lawful; *canorus,* singing.

4. The following, partly on account of their form, and partly on account of their signification:—

Almus,	*gracious.*	Impos,	*not master of.*
Blaesus,	*lisping.*	Lacer,	*maimed.*
Balbus,	*stammering.*	Mancus,	*crippled.*
Caducus,	*falling.*	Mediocris,	*inferior.*
Calvus,	*bald.*	Memor,	*mindful.*
Canus,	*white.*	Mirus,	*wonderful.*
Cicur,	*tame.*	Mutilus,	*mutilated.*
Claudus,	*lame.*	Mutus,	*mute.*
Curvus,	*crooked.*	Nefastus,	*wrong.*
Compos,	*possessed of.*	Par,	*equal.*
Egenus,	*needy.*	Dispar,	*unequal.*
Ferus,	*wild.*	Sospes,	*safe.*
Gnarus,	*expert.*	Trux,	*grim.*
Jejunus,	*hungry.*	Vulgaris,	*common.*

G. Many adjectives admit of no comparison of any kind, from the nature of their signification. Such are:—

1. Those denoting the material of which anything is made, possession, or descent; e. g. *aureus, ferreus, ligneus; Romanus, Atheniensis; paternus, patrius.*

2. Those denoting a definite quantity or time; e. g. *unicus,*

---

* But not those ending in the monosyllabic *quus* and *quis,* which are regularly compared; as, *antiquus, antiquior, antiquissimus; pinguis, pinguior, pinguissimus.* So also *tenuis, tenuior, tenuissimus,* and a few of those in *uus* and *ius;* e. g. *assiduus, exiguus, pius, strenuus.*

† Of the participles in *ns* and *tus,* many are used adjectively and regularly compared; e. g. *amans, amantior, amantissimus; doctus, doctissimus,* &c. But these are frequently defective.

‡ Except the two superlatives *infandissimus,* abominable; and *nefandissimus,* impious.

§ Except *divinus, festivus, lascivus, rusticus, tempestivus,* and *vicinus,* of which some of the comparative forms occur; e. g. *divinior, divinissimus,* &c.

single; *aestīvus*, of the summer; *hesternus*, of yesterday; *hibernus*, of the winter.

3. Those already involving a comparison, such as compounds of *per, prae* (= very), and *sub* (= somewhat); e. g. *permagnus*, very great; *praedives*, very rich; *subdifficilis*, somewhat difficult.*

4. Diminutives and other adjectives in *lus;* as, *parvŭlus*, very little; *vetŭlus*, a little old; *garrŭlus*, talkative; *anhēlus*, out of breath, &c.

5. Compound adjectives derived from nouns;† as, *versicolor*, of various colors; *dēgĕner*, degenerate.

DECLENSION OF THE COMPARATIVE AND SUPERLATIVE.

H. The superlative is declined like *bonus, a, um*, and the comparative like an adjective of one termination (Lessons V. and XIII.). Thus:—

Altĭor, *m. & f.*, altĭus, *n.*, *higher.*

	SINGULAR.		PLURAL.	
	Masc. & Fem.	*Neut.*	*Masc. & Fem.*	*Neut.*
Nom.	altĭor	altĭŭs	altĭōrēs	altĭōră
Gen.	altĭōrĭs	altĭōrĭs	altĭōrŭm	altĭōrŭm
Dat.	altĭōrĭ	altĭōrĭ	altĭōrĭbŭs	altĭōrĭbŭs
Acc.	altĭōrem	altĭŭs	altĭōrēs	altĭōră
Voc.	altĭŏr	altĭŭs	altĭōrēs	altĭōră
Abl.	altĭōrĕ *or* -ī,	altĭōrĕ *or* -ī,	altĭōrĭbŭs	altĭōrĭbŭs.

So decline *pulchrior, venustior*, handsomer, prettier; *facilior*, easier; *difficilior*, more difficult; *major*, greater; *longior*, longer; *brevior*, shorter; *rotundior*, rounder; *divitior*, richer, &c.

Is your book as good as mine?	Éstne líber túus tám bónus, quám méus (aéque bónus átque méus)?
It is better than yours.	Mélior est, quám túus.
It is not as good as yours.	{ Nòn ést tám bónus, quám túus. { Mínus bónus ést, quám túus.
Are the merchant's children as good (well-behaved) as ours?	Án líberi mercatôris tám béne sunt moráti, quam nostri?
They are better than ours.	Melióres, quám nóstri, súnt.
They are quite as good as ours.	{ Aéque bóni súnt ác nóstri. { Nòn mínus bóni súnt quám nóstri.
Is my table as high as it is long?	Éstne ménsa méa tám álta, quám longa?

---

* Except *praeclārus, -ior, -issimus; praestans, -tior, -tissimus*, eminent; and others derived from verbs, as *praesens*, prompt: *perturbātus*, troubled.

† Except *iners*, inert; *misericors*, compassionate; *perennis*, perennial; and *dēmens*, crazy; which occur in the comparative, though derived from *ars, cor, annus, mens.*

19

It is not as high as it is long.

    { Nôn ést tám álta quám lónga.
    { Mínus lónga ést quám álta.

It is higher than it is long.

Áltior ést quám lóngior.

Is it higher than your tables?

Éstne altiór quam ménsae túae?

It is the highest of them all.

Altíssima ést ómnium.

Whose umbrella is the largest?

Cújus umbráculum ést május?

This (of mine) is large, that (of yours) is larger, but that (of his) is the largest of all.

Hóc ést mágnum, ístud május ést, íllud véro ómnium est máximum.

Which hat is the smallest?

Quís pîleus est mínimus?

Mine is rather small, yours is even smaller, but that of our friend is the smallest of all.

Méus est párvulus, túus étiam minor est, sed amíci nostri pîleus omnium est mínimus.

    Whose?

Cûjus?

    It is.

Est.

Whose book is this?

    { Cújus líber ést hóc?
    { Cújus ést híc líber?

It is the book of my brother.

Líber ést frâtris méi.

It is my brother's.

Frâtris est.

Whose ribbon is the handsomest, yours or mine?

Útra taeniârum pulchrior est, tuáne an méa?

Yours is the handsomest (of the two).

Túa ést púlchrior.

Are the handkerchiefs of the Italians whiter than those of the Dutch?

Écquid muccínia Italôrum candidiôra súnt, quám ílla Batavôrum?

They are not any whiter.

Candidiôra nôn súnt.

They are whiter, but not as good.

Candidiôra súnt véro, at nôn aéque bóna.

Is his coat as black as mine?

Estne tóga éjus tám nígra quám méa (aéque nígra átque méa)?

It is even blacker than yours.

Est etiam nigrior quúm túa est.

Do you read as well as I?

Écquid tú aéque béne légis atque égo?

I read equally well.

Égo non mínus béne légo quám tû.

I read better than you.

Égo mélius légo quám tû.

I do not read as well as you.

Mínus sciénter légo quám tû.

    Well, properly.

Béne, belle; scienter, commŏde (*adv.*).

    Better.

Mĕlius, scientius.

    Light (not heavy).

Lĕvis, e.

    Heavy.

Grăvis, e.

    Easy.

Făcĭlis, e.

    Difficult.

Difficĭlis, e.

    Great, large, big.

    { Magnus, a, um.
    { Grandis, e.

    Huge.

Ingens, tis.

    Long.

Longus, a, um.

    Short.

Brĕvis, e.

Rather short (too short).   Curtus, a, um.
Round.   Rotundus, a, um.
Rich.   Dives, itis.

EXERCISE 80.

Is your brother taller (*grandis*) than mine ? — He is not so tall, but
better than yours. — Is thy hat as bad as that of thy father ? — It is
better, but not so black as his. — Are the shirts of the Italians as white
as those of the Irish ? — They are whiter, but not so good. — Are the
sticks of our friends longer than ours ? — They are not longer, but
heavier. — Who have the most beautiful gloves ? — The French have
them. — Whose horses are the finest ? — Mine are fine, yours are
finer than mine; but those of our friends are the finest of all. — Is
your horse good ? — It is good, but yours is better, and that of the
Englishman is the best of all the horses which we are acquainted with.
— Have you pretty shoes ? — I have very pretty (ones); but my
brother has prettier ones than I. — From whom (*a quo*) does he receive them ? — He receives them from his best friend. — Is your wine
as good as mine ? — It is better. — Does your merchant sell good
handkerchiefs ? — He sells the best handkerchiefs that I know. —
Have we more books than the French ? — We have more of them
than they; but the Germans have more of them than we, and the
English have the most of them. — Hast thou a finer garden than that
of our physician ? — I have a finer (one). — Has the American a
finer house than thou ? — He has a finer (one). — Have we as fine
children as our neighbors ? — We have finer (ones).

EXERCISE 81.

Is your coat as long as mine ? — It is shorter, but prettier than
yours. — Do you go out to-day ? — I do not go out to-day. — When
does your father go out ? — He goes out at a quarter past twelve. —
Is this man older (*grandior natu*) than that (man) ? — He is older,
but that (man) is healthier (*robustus*). — Which of these two children
is the better ? — The one who studies is better than the one who
plays. — Does your servant sweep as well as mine ? — He sweeps
better than yours. — Does the German read as many bad books as
good (ones) ? — He reads more good than bad (ones). — Do the merchants sell more sugar than coffee ? — They sell more of the one than
of the other. — Does your shoemaker make as many boots as shoes ?
— He makes more of the one than of the other. — Can you swim as
well as the son of the nobleman ? — I can swim better than he; but
he can speak German better than I. — Does he read as well as you ?
— He reads better than I. — Have you the headache ? — No, I have
the earache. — Does your cousin listen to what you tell him ? — He
does not listen to it. — Does the son of your bailiff go into the forest ?
— No, he remains at home; he has sore feet. — Do you learn as well
as our gardener's son ? — I learn better than he, but he works better
than I. — Whose carriage is the finest ? — Yours is very fine, but that
of the captain is still finer, and ours is the finest of all. — Has any one
as fine apples as we ? — No one has such fine (ones).

Lesson XLII. — PENSUM ALTERUM ET QUAD-RAGESIMUM.

OF THE COMPARISON OF ADVERBS.

A. Adverbs derived from adjectives or participles, and ending in ē, *ter*, or ō,* are compared like their primitives.

The comparative of the adverb ends in *ius*, like the accusative neuter of the adjective, and the superlative assumes the termination ē. E. g.

POSITIVE.	COMPARATIVE.	SUPERLATIVE.	
Longē,	longius,	longissīmē ;	*far.*
Pulchrē,	pulchrius,	pulcherrīmē ;	*handsomely.*
Fācilē,	fācilīus,	fācillīmē ;	*easily.*
Audacter,	audācius,	audacissīmē ;	*boldly.*
Lēviter,	lēvius,	lēvissīmē ;	*easily.*
Prudenter,	prudentius,	prudentissīmē ;	*prudently.*
Tūtō,	tūtius,	tūtissīmē ;	*safely.*
Rārō,	rārius,	rārissīmē ;	*rarely.*
Honorificē,	honorificentius,†	honorificentissīmē ;	*honorably.*
Saepē,	saepius,	saepissīmē ;	*often.*
Diū,	diūtius,‡	diūtissīmē ;	*long.*

B. Adverbs derived from adjectives of anomalous comparison follow the anomalies of their primitives. E. g.

POSITIVE.	COMPARATIVE.	SUPERLATIVE.	
Bĕnĕ,	melius,	optīmē ;	*well.*
Mălē,	pējus,	pessīmē ;	*bad.*
Părum,	minus,	minīmē ;	*little.*
———,	māgis, §	maximē ;	*more.*
Multum,	plūs,	plūrimum ; ‖	*much.*

C. The following list exhibits the adverbs of defective comparison : —

POSITIVE.	COMPARATIVE.	SUPERLATIVE.	
———,	dētĕrius,	dēterrīmē ;	*worse.*
———,	ōcius,	ōcissīmē ;	*swifter.*

* Many of those in *o*, however, are not compared. On the formation of adverbs generally, see Lesson LXX.

† Compare Lesson XL. *D.* 3.

‡ *Diu* and *saepe* have no corresponding adjectives. The root of the former seems to have been *diutus.*

§ This is properly the comp. of *magnum*, which is not used adverbially. Instead of it, *valde* and *magnopere* are commonly employed.

‖ The superlative of adverbs sometimes ends in *o* or *um.* So *primo* or *primum, potissimum, meritissimo*, &c.

	prĭus,	prīmum ;	*before, sooner.*
——,	ŭbĕrĭus,	ŭberrĭmē ;	*more copiously.*
Nŏvē,	——,	nŏvissĭmē ;	*newly, lately.*
Nŭper,	——,	nŭperrĭmē :	*recently.*
Paenē,	——,	paenissĭmē ;	*almost, entirely.*
Pĕnĭtus,	pĕnĭtĭus,	——;	*inwardly.*
——,	pŏtĭus,	pŏtissĭmum ;*	*rather.*
Mĕrĭto,	——,	mĕrĭtissĭmo ; .	*deservedly.*
Sătis,	sătĭus,	——;	*sufficiently.*
Tempĕrī,	tempĕrĭus,	——;	*seasonably.*
Valdē,	valdĭus,	——;	*greatly.*
Sēcus,	sēcĭus,	——;	*differently.*

The beginning. The end.   In'ĭtĭum, i, n.   Fīnis, m. & f.

To begin, commence.
> Incĭpĭo, ĕre, cēpi, ceptum.
> Exordĭor, īrī, orsus sum (*dep.*)
>   (ALIQUID FACĔRE).
> Initĭum făcere (ALICUJUS REI FA-
>   CIENDAE).

To end, finish, conclude.
> Fīnĭo, ire, ĭvi (ĭi), ĭtum (ALIQUID).
> Fīnem făcĕre (ALICUJUS REI).
> Conclūdo, ĕre, ūsi, ūsum (ALI-
>   QUID).

Will you begin to speak ?	Vīsne incĭpere lóqui ?
	Vīsne initĭum făcĕre loquéndi ?
I am willing to begin.	Incĭpere nôn nôlo.
Is he beginning to speak (= to discourse).	Incipĭtne (exorditúrne) dícere ?
	Facítne initĭum dicéndi ?
He is beginning.	Incĭpit. Fácit initĭum.
No, he is finishing.	Ímmo véro fĭnem făcit (dicéndi).
Are you finishing your letter ?	Concludísne epístolam túam ?
I am not concluding it.	Nôn conclúdo.

Not yet.   Nōndŭm, haud dŭm, adhŭc nōn.
Already.   Jam, jamjam, jam jamque (*adv.*).

Before.
> Prĭus quam (prĭusquam).
> Ante quam (antequam).
> Antĕa quam (anteaquam).
>   (*Conj. with the ind. and subj.*)

Do you speak before you listen ?	Núm lóqueris prĭus quám aúdis (auscúltas) ?
I never speak before I listen.	Égo núnquam lóquor ánte quám aúdio.
Do you take off your stockings before you take off your boots ?	Núm tibiália túa prĭus pédibus détrahis quám cáligas ?
No, I take off my boots first.	Ímmo véro cáligas prĭus détraho.

* Also more rarely *potissime.*
19*

Does your servant sweep the same room which I am sweeping?	Everrítne sérvus túus ipsum conclâve, quód égo evérro ?
He is not sweeping the same.	Ídem nôn evérrit.
Often, frequently.	*Saepĕ, frequenter, crēbro.* *
As often as you.	Tám saépe quám tû.
As many times as you.	Tótíes, quóties tû.
Quite as often as you.	Nôn mínus saépe (frequénter) quám tû.
Oftener than you.	Saépius (frequéntius) quám tû.
Not as often as you.	Nôn tám saépe, quám tû.
Early (in the morning).	Mānĕ (*adv.*), tempŏre matutino.
Early (= in good time).	Matūrē (*comp.* matūrius).
Quite early (in the morning).	Bĕnĕ māne, primā lūce.
Quite early (generally).	Admŏdum matūre.
Late.	Sērō ; tardē.
Quite late.	{ Sērō admŏdum. { Pervespĕri (*in the evening*).
Too.	*Nĭmis, nimium.*
Too late.	{ Sēro,† nĭmis sēro ; post tempus. { Nĭmis tarde, tardĭus. ‡
Too early (in the morning).	Nĭmio māne.
Too early (generally).	{ Nĭmis matūre, maturĭus.‡ { Praematūre.
Too great.	{ Nĭmis magnus (grandis). { Major, grandior (*sc.* aequo).
Too little (small).	Nĭmis parvŭlus ; perparvŭlus.
Too much.	{ Nĭmis, nimĭum (*adv.*). { Nĭmius, a, um. { Plūs aequo, plūs justo.
To breakfast.	{ Jento, āre, āvi, ātum. { Jentācŭlum sumĕre.
The breakfast.	Jentācŭlum, i, *n.*
Do you breakfast as early as I ?	Jentâsne (sumísne jentáculum) tám béne mâne quám égo ?
I breakfast as early as you.	{ Jénto véro tám béne mâne quám tû. { Jentáculum súmo aéque matúre { útque tû.
I breakfast earlier, later than you.	Égo jentáculum súmo matúrius, sérius quám tû.

---

* These are regularly compared : *crebrius, creberrime, frequentius, frequentissime,* &c.

† *Sero* has often the sense of *nimis sero.*

‡ With these neuter comparatives it is necessary to supply *aequo, justo,* or *opinione;* i. e. "later than expected" = "too late," "earlier than usual" = "too early," &c. (Cf. Lesson XLIII. *E.* 2.)

Does he breakfast before he begins to work ?

Sumítne jentáculum, priúsquam ópus fácere íncipit ?

No, indeed, he works before he breakfasts.

Mínime véro ; inítium fácit operándi, antea quam jentat.

Do I come too early ?

Veniône praematúre ?

No, you come rather too late.

Immo véro (nímis) séro vénis.

Do you speak too much ?

Núm lóqueris nímis ?

I do not speak enough.

Immo véro, égo nòn sátis lóquor.

EXERCISE 82.

Do you begin to speak ? — I begin to speak. — Does your brother begin to learn Italian ? — He begins to learn it. — Can you already speak German ? — Not yet, but I am beginning. — Do our friends begin to speak ? — They do not yet begin to speak, but to read. — Does our father already begin his letter ? — He does not yet begin it. — Does the merchant begin to sell ? — He does begin. — Can you swim already ? — Not yet, but I begin to learn. — Does your son speak before he listens ? — He listens before he speaks. — Does your brother listen to you before he speaks ? — He speaks before he listens to me. — Do your children read before they write ? — They write before they read. — Does your servant sweep the warehouse before he sweeps the room ? — He sweeps the room before he sweeps the warehouse. — Dost thou drink before thou goest out ? — I go out before I drink. — Does your cousin wash his hands (*manus*) before he washes his feet ? — He washes his feet before he washes his hands. — Do you extinguish the fire before you extinguish the candle ? — I extinguish neither the fire nor the candle. — Do you intend to go out before you write your letters ? — I intend writing my letters before I go out. — Does your son take off his boots before he takes off his coat ? — My son takes off neither his boots nor his coat.

EXERCISE 83.

Do you intend to depart soon ? — I intend to depart to-morrow. — Do you speak as often as I ? — I do not speak as often, but my brother speaks oftener than you. — Do I go out as often as your father ? — You do not go out as often as he ; but he drinks oftener than you. — Do you begin to know this man ? — I begin to know him. — Do you breakfast early ? — We breakfast at a quarter past nine. — Does your cousin breakfast earlier than you ? — He breakfasts later than I. — At what o'clock does he breakfast ? — He breakfasts at eight o'clock, and I at half past six. — Do you not breakfast too early ? — I breakfast too late. — Does your father breakfast as early as you ? — He breakfasts later than I. — Does he finish his letters before he breakfasts ? — He breakfasts before he finishes them. — Is your hat too large ? — It is neither too large nor too small. — Does our gardener breakfast before he goes into the garden ? — He goes into the garden before he breakfasts. — Do you read French as often as German ? — I read French oftener than German. — Does the physician speak too much ? — He does not speak enough. — Do the Germans drink too

much wine? — They do not drink enough of it. — Do they drink more
beer than cider? — They drink more of the one than of the other. —
Have you much money? — We have not enough of it. — Have your
cousins much corn? — They have only a little, but enough. — Have
you much more brandy? — We have not much more of it. — Have
you as many tables as chairs? — I have as many of the one as of the
other. — Does your friend receive as many letters as notes? — He
receives more of the latter than of the former. — Do you finish before
you begin? — I must begin before I finish.

Lesson XLIII. — PENSUM QUADRAGESIMUM TERTIUM.

THE CONSTRUCTION OF THE COMPARATIVE.

A. Rule. — When two objects are compared with
each other, and the first is the *subject* of the sentence,
the second is frequently put in the ablative without
quam. E. g.

Túllius Hostílius ferócior fúit *Rómulo.**	Tullius Hostilius was more warlike than Romulus.
Vílius ést argéntum *aúro, virtútibus* aûrum.	Silver is inferior to gold, and gold to virtue.
Quíd ést in hómine *ratióne* divínius?	What is there in man diviner than reason?
Quaê figûra, quaê spécies *humánā* pótest ésse púlchrior?	What figure or form can be more beautiful than the human?
Níhil ést laudabílius, níhil mágno et praecláro víro dígnius *placabilitáte* átque *cleméntiā.*	Nothing is more commendable, nothing more worthy of a great and distinguished man, than a forgiving disposition and clemency.
Lácrĭmā níhil cítius† aréscit.	Nothing dries faster than a tear.
Ne lóngius *tríduo* ab cástris ábsit.	Not to be absent from the camp longer than three days.
Fortûna plûs *consíliis humánis* póllet.	Fortune is stronger than human designs.

---

* This = *quam Romŭlus* (*fuit*). So the remaining ablatives of these examples: — *quam aurum* (*est*), — *quam virtutes sunt*, — *quam ratio est.* — *quam humāna* (*figūra* seu *species*) *est*, — *quam placabilitas atque clementia sunt*, &c., and
in general every ablative after a comparative.

† This, and the two following examples, show that the same rule applies also
to the comparative of adverbs. But this is only so when the comparison relates to the *subject* of the sentence.

Néminem* Romanôrum *Ciceróne*   In the opinion of the ancients, no
  eloquentiôrem fuísse véteres   Roman was more eloquent than
  judicárunt.   Cicero.

REMARKS.

1. Among the most common forms of the ablative after comparatives are the neuter adjectives and participles *aequo, necessario, nimio, credibili, vero, solito, justo, dicto,* and the nouns *spe, opinione, expectatione;* as, *plus aequo,* more than is fair; *longius necessario,* further than is necessary; *magis solito,* more than usually; *dicto citius,* sooner than the word was uttered; *opinione celerius,* quicker than was expected; *serius spe,* later than was hoped; *plus nimio,* more than too much. But these ablatives are often omitted. (Compare E. 2.)

2. *Quam* is always put instead of the ablative, where the latter would give rise to ambiguity. E. g. *Hibernia est dimidio minor, ut aestimatur,* quam *Britannia,* Hibernia is supposed to be smaller by one half than Britannia.

3. The ablative after comparatives is the standard by which the object compared is measured with reference to the quality common to both. It may be considered an abridged proposition, and can be resolved into *quam est,* &c. Hence *quam* may always be employed instead of the ablative, but not *vice versa.* E. g.

Mélior tutiórque est cérta páx, *quám sperâta victória.*†   A certain peace is better and safer than an expected victory.

Íta séntio, locupletiôrem esse Latínam linguam,‡ *quám Graêcam.*   It is my opinion, that the Latin language is richer than the Greek.

Núllum ést cértius amicítiae vínculum, *quám consénsus et societas* consiliôrum et voluntâtum.   There is no surer bond of friendship than the harmony and community of plans and wishes.

Páter Tarquínius poténtior Rómae nôn fúit, *quám fílius* Gabiis.§   Tarquin the father was no more powerful at Rome than was the son at Gabii.

B. RULE. — If the object compared with another is in *an oblique case,* and dependent on another word, the conjunction *quam* is used, and the second object is either in the nominative with *est, fuit,*‖ &c., or in the same case with the first. E. g.

---

* *Neminem* is here the subject of the infinitive *fuisse,* and consequently included in the rule.

† In all these examples, *est, fuit, esse* is understood.

‡ The *subject* accusative to *esse.*

§ In this and in the preceding example the ablative is entirely inadmissible, as it would give rise to a confusion of cases.

‖ Or with the verb of the sentence understood.

O

Flagitii mágis nôs púdet, *quám erróris.* *	We are more ashamed of a disgraceful act than of an error.
Némini mágis fáveo, *quám tíbi.*	There is no one whom I favor more than I do you.
Égo hóminem calidiôrem vídi néminem, *quám Phormiônem.*	I have seen no shrewder man than Phormio.
Consílio majóres rês gerúntur, *quám* fortitúdine.	Greater things are accomplished by deliberation, than by valor.
Ab Hanníbale majóres rês géstae súnt, *quám* ab Hamílcare.	Greater exploits have been achieved by Hannibal than by Hamilcar.
Drusum Germánicum minôrem nátu, *quám ípse érat,* frátrem amisit.	He lost Drusus Germanicus, a brother younger than he himself was.
Haêc vérba súnt M. Varrônis, *quám fúit Claúdius,* doctiôris.	These are the words of Marcus Varro, a more learned man than Claudius was.
Longínqua itínera sóla dúcis patiéntiā mitigabántur, eôdem *plûra, quám* gregário mílite, toleránte.	The long marches were mitigated by the patience of the leader alone, — he himself enduring more than a common soldier.

Remarks.

1. Instead of *quam* with an object accusative,† the ablative sometimes occurs in prose and frequently in poetry. E. g. *Est boni consúlis suam salûtem posteriôrem* salûte commúni *ducere,* It is the duty of a consul to consider his own safety secondary to that of the commonwealth. *Neminem* Lycurgo ‡ *aut majorem aut utiliorem virum Lacedaemon genuit,* Lacedæmon produced no man either greater or more useful than Lycurgus. *Quid prius dicam* solitis *parentis* laudibus? What shall I say (sing) before the accustomed praises of our parent?

2. A relative or demonstrative pronoun is commonly in the ablative where we would expect the object accusative with *quam.* E. g. *Hic Attalo,* quo § *graviorem inimíco non habui, sororem suam in matrimonium dedit,* He gave his sister in marriage to Attalus, *than whom* I had no enemy more mortal. *Hōc mihi gratius nihil facere potes,* You could not do me a greater favor *than this.*

3. The comparative *inferior* is occasionally followed by the dative. E. g. *Nullā arte* cuiquam *inferior est,* He is not inferior to any one in any art. But commonly by the ablative or *quam;* as, *Non inferior fuit,* quam *pater,* He was not inferior to his father.

4. The adjective *alius* has sometimes the force of a comparative; as, *Ne putes alium* sapiente bonōque *beatum,* Do not consider any one but a wise and good man happy. *Nec quidquam aliud* libertate

---

* In this and the following examples the ellipsis is *quam nos pudet, quam tibi faveo, quam Phormio est, quam geruntur, quam gestae sunt.*
† After transitive verbs.
‡ Instead of *quam Lycurgum* or *quam Lycurgus fuit.*
§ Better than *quam quem.*

communi *quaesivimus*, Nor did we aim at anything else but our common liberty.

5. The prepositions *ante, prae, praeter,* and *supra* serve to impart a comparative force to the positive, and to enhance that of the comparative or superlative. E. g. *Felix* ante alias *virgo*, A maiden fortunate before (= more fortunate than) others. Praeter alios *doctus*, Learned beyond others. Ante alios *immanior* omnes, More inhuman than all other men. Prae nobis *beatus*, Happier than ourselves.

6. *Magis, minus,* and *potius* are sometimes put emphatically with a comparative, or with *malo, praeopto* (I would rather, I prefer), &c. E. g. *Hoc enim* magis *est dulcius,* This is much sweeter. *Potius maluit,* He preferred. *Non* minus admirabilior *illius exitus belli,* The issue of that war was no less wonderful.

7. *Quam pro* frequently occurs after comparatives, and is equivalent to the English "than in proportion to," "than might be expected from." E. g. *Minor,* quam pro tumultu, *caedes,* Less of a massacre than one might have expected from the bustle. *Species viri majoris,* quam pro humano habitu, *augustiorisque,* The form of a man of greater than human size, and more majestic.

8. The conjunction *atque* occasionally takes the place of *quam.* E. g. *Amicior mihi nullus vivit* atque *is est,* I have no better friend alive than he is. But this does not occur in classical prose.

9. The comparative is often negative, especially in the formulas *non magis* (*non plus*) .... *quam,* no more .... than (but rather less); *non minus* .... *quam,* no less .... than (but rather more); *non melior* .... *quam,* no better .... than (but rather worse); *non deterior* .... *quam,* no worse .... than (but rather better). E. g. *Animus in aliquo morbo* non magis *est sanus,* quam *id corpus, quod in morbo est,* In sickness the mind is no more (= as little) sound, than (as) the body in disease. *Patria hominibus* non minus *cara esse debet,* quam *liberi,* Their country ought to be no less dear (= equally dear) to men than (as) their children. *Luctus non Romae* major, quam *per totam Hispaniam fuit,* There was as great a sorrow throughout entire Spain, as there was at Rome.

C. After the comparatives *plus, amplius, minus,* and *longius,* the conjunction *quam* is frequently omitted without any change of case in the second object.* E. g.

Nôn *amplius* erant *quingenti.*	There were no more than (not over) five hundred.
Plûs *tertia pars* interfecta est.	More than (over) one third of them were killed.
Constâbat *non minus ducentos* Carthaginiensium equites fuisse.	It was manifest, that there were no less than (at least) two hundred horsemen among the Carthaginians.

---

* There is generally a numeral expressed or understood in this construction. The case remains the same which it would be under the same conditions without *plus*, &c.

Quíntus técum *plús ánnum* víxit.	Quintus lived with you more than (over) a year.
Revérsus ést in Ásiam *mínus diébus trigínta.*	He returned into Asia in less than thirty days.
Spátium, quód nôn ést *ámplius pédum sexcentórum.*	A space of no more than (not over) six hundred feet.
Non *longius milia* passuum *octo.*	No farther than eight miles.

REMARKS.

1. *Quam* is likewise omitted after *major* and *minor*, when these words denote a definite age of life. E. g. *Major* (quam) *quinque annis natus*, Older than five years. *Minor* (quam) *decem annos natus*, Younger than ten years.

2. Sometimes, however, these comparatives are regularly construed with *quam* or an ablative. E. g. *Plus quam quattuor milia*, More than four thousand. *Amplius duobus milibus*, More than two thousand. *Minus tribus medimnis*, Less than three medimni. *Plus quam annum*, For more than a year.

D. When two qualities denoted by different adjectives are attributed to the same object in an unequal degree, the adjectives are either both positive with *magis . . . . quam*, or both comparative with *quam* simply. E. g.

Céler túus *disértus mágis* ést, *quám sápiens.*	Your friend Celer is rather eloquent than wise.*
Ártem juris habébitis, *magis magnam* atque úberem, *quam* difficilem atque obscúram.	You will have a science of law more comprehensive and rich than difficult and obscure.
Pestiléntia *minácior quám periculósior.*	A pestilence more menacing than dangerous.
Paúli Aemílii cóncio fúit *rérior, quám grátior* pópulo.	The address of Paulus Æmilius was not so acceptable to the people as it was true.
Ímpetus, nôn *ácrior, quám pertinácior.*	An assault as obstinate as it was fierce.

REMARKS.

1. The construction of adverbs is precisely the same : — *Temere magis, quam satis caute*, Rather rashly than with sufficient caution. *Magis honeste, quam vere*, More for honor's sake than correctly. *Fortius quam felicius*, More bravely than successfully. *Non contumeliosius quam verius*, No more contemptuously than truly, &c.

2. Of these two constructions the double comparative with *quam* is the most common. Sometimes the second adverb is in the positive

---

* I. e. More of an eloquent than of a wise man, — he has less prudence than eloquence. *Disertior est, quam sapientior*, He has considerable prudence, but yet more eloquence.

degree; as, *Vehementius quam caute*, More impetuously than cautiously. But this is an exception to the general rule.

E. The second member of a comparison is frequently suppressed. This happens, —

1. When the comparative serves to distinguish two objects of the same kind. E. g. *Graecia major, Gallia ulterior, ex duobus filiis major* seu *minor* (= the elder or younger of two sons), *major pars hominum.* So, *Uter est melior?* Which is the better of the two? *Respondeo* priori prius, I reply first to the former (of two letters).

2. When it is so general as to be readily understood from the context. E. g. *Quam ceteri, solito, aequo, justo,** &c. In these cases the comparative is commonly rendered by the positive with *somewhat, rather, too,* or *quite.* As,

Si vérsus ést syllabā unā *brévior* aut *lóngior* (sc. justo).	If the verse is a syllable too short or too long.
Senéctus ést natúrā *loquácior* (sc. quám céterae aetátes).	Old age is naturally somewhat loquacious.
Themístocles *libérius* vivêbat (sc. aequo).	Themistocles lived rather too freely.
Ócius ómnes império laéti párent (sc. dicto).†	They all obey the command with alacrity, sooner than it is uttered.
Níhil fére quóndam *majóris réi*, nisi auspicáto, gerebâtur.	Scarcely any matter of importance was formerly undertaken without auspices.
Médici *gravióribus* morbis periculósas curatiónes et ancipites adhibêre sólent.	To the acuter diseases physicians are accustomed to apply dangerous and doubtful remedies.

F. The comparative may be variously modified by other words: —

1. By the intensive *etiam* or *adhuc,* "even," "yet," "still." E. g. *Etiam majores varietates,* A still greater diversity. *Multo* etiam *longius,* Much further even. *Punctum est, quod vivimus, et* adhuc *puncto minus,* Our life is but a moment, and even less than one.

2. By the ablative of the thing, *in respect to which* one object is superior to another. E. g. *Quis Carthaginiensium pluris fuit Hannibale,* consilio, virtute, rebus gestis? What Carthaginian was superior to Hannibal, in sagacity, in valor, or in exploits? *Superior ordine,* Superior in rank. *Inferior fortunā,* Inferior in fortune.

3. By the ablative of the measure or quantity, by which the difference is estimated. E. g. *Dimidio minor,* Smaller by one half. *Decem annis minor,* Younger by ten years. *Uno die longiorem mensem aut biduo,* A month longer by one day or by two days. *Uno digito plus*

---

* Compare *A.* 1.
† So *plures* (sc. *quam unam*) *uxores habere,* to have several wives. *Diutius morari,* to remain too long. *Plura loqui,* to talk too much, &c.

20

habere, To have one finger too many. Altero tanto *longiorem esse*,
To be as long again (twice as long). Sesqui *esse majorem*, To be
greater by one half. *Sol* multis partibus *major atque amplior est, quam
terra universa*, The sun is many times as large as our entire globe.

4. So generally by the neuter ablatives *multo*, by much, much;
paulo, parvo, a little; *aliquanto*, somewhat, considerably; *quanto*, by
as much; *tanto*, by so much; *quo*, the (more, &c.); *hoc, eo*, the (more,
&c.); *altero, tanto*, by as much again; *dimidio*, by one half; *sesqui*,
by one and a half; *nihilo*, by nothing. E. g. *Paulo vehementius*, A
little more violently. *Multo artificiosius*, Much more skilfully. *Aliquanto atrocius*, Considerably more atrocious. *Quanto superiores
sumus*, tanto *nos geramus submissius*, The greater our superiority,
the more humbly let us conduct ourselves. Quo *plures erant*, (hoc)
major caedes fuit, The greater their number, the more bloody was the
massacre. Quo *major est in animis praestantia et divinior*, eo *majore
indigent diligentiā*, The greater and diviner the intellectual superiority, the greater is the necessity of application. *Homines* quo *plura
habent*, eo *cupiunt ampliora*, The more men possess, the more they
desire.

5. Instead of the ablatives *tanto, quanto, aliquanto*, the adverbial
accusatives *tantum, quantum, aliquantum*, are sometimes employed.
E. g. Quantum *domo inferior*, tantum *gloriā superior evasit*, He turned
out as much superior in renown, as he was inferior by birth.

EXERCISE 84.

Is the English language richer than the French ? — It is richer. —
Is it as rich (*locuples*) as the Greek ? — It is not as rich; it is less
rich and less flexible (*flexibilis*) than the Greek. — Which language
is the richest of all ? — There is no language richer than the Greek.
— Is there anything more valuable (*praestantius*) than gold ? — Virtues are far (*multo* or *longe*) more valuable. — Is there anything
diviner in man than reason ? — There is nothing diviner or fairer
(*vel pulchrius*). — Can any form be fairer than the human ? — No figure or form can be fairer. — What is more commendable in a great
man than clemency ? — There is nothing more commendable. — Is
your friend more learned than his brother ? — He is far more learned,
but not as good. — Is he more learned than our neighbor ? — He is
not so learned. — Who of the Romans was (*fuit*) the most eloquent ? —
Cicero was the most eloquent of Roman orators. — Do you favor any
one more than me ? — I favor no one more than you. — Are you
loved as much by your father as by your friend ? — I am loved more
by the former than by the latter. — Is that man inferior to the other ?
— He is not inferior. — Do we seek anything else than liberty. — We
seek nothing else. — Is our neighbor more fortunate than others ? —
He is less fortunate. — Who is happier than we ? — No one. — Ought
our country to be as dear to us as our children ? — It should be no less
dear to us. — How much money have you left ? — I have more than
one third left. — How much has your brother left ? — He has less
than ten dollars left. — How many are there of us ? — There are
more than fifty of us.

Lesson XLIV. — PENSUM QUADRAGESIMUM QUARTUM.

CONSTRUCTION OF THE SUPERLATIVE.

A. The Latin superlative serves to express two distinct relations : —

I. The quality denoted by it may be attributed to one of several objects in a higher degree than to any of the rest. This is called the *Superlative of Comparison*, and is translated by the English superlative, or by *most*. E. g.

Epístolae míhi úno díe três súnt rédditae. Rescrípsi epístolae *máximae*.	Three letters were handed to me in one day. I replied to the longest of them.
Numitóri, qui stírpis *máximus* érat, régnum légat.	He bequeathed his kingdom to Numitor, the eldest of the line.
Miltíades et glóriā majórum et súā modéstiā *únus ómnium máxime* florébat.	Miltiades enjoyed the very highest distinction, both for the glory of his ancestors and for his own modesty.
Péssima sít, núlli nôn súa fórma plácet.	Every one likes his own appearance, be it never so bad.
Míser homo est, qui ipsi quod edit* quaerit, et id aegre ínvenit ; sed ílle ést *misérior*, qui et aégre quaêrit, et níhil ínvenit ; ílle *misérrimus* est, qui, cum êsse† cupit, quod edit non habet.	The man is a wretched one, who has himself to seek his livelihood, and scarcely finds it ; but he is more wretched, who seeks it hard and finds none ; the most wretched (of all) is he, who, when he desires to eat, has nothing.

II. The quality denoted by the superlative may be attributed to an object simply in an eminent or uncommon degree. This is called the *Superlative of Eminence*, and is usually rendered by *very, uncommonly, extremely, most,* &c. As,

Gratíssimae míhi túae lítterae fuérunt.	Your letter was most (— extremely) welcome to me.
Jactátur dómi súae vír *primus* et hómo honestíssimus.‡	He is boasted of as the first man of his family, and a most (highly) honorable man.
Si Aurélios honorífice liberalitérque tractúris, et tíbi *gratíssimos*	If you treat the Aurelii honorably and liberally, you will oblige

---

* For *edat,* "what he may eat."   † For *edére,* to eat.

‡ The superlative of eminence thus commonly occurs in titles and superscriptions. E. g. *Viro* fortissimo *atque* innocentissimo *Sext. Peducaeo praetori. De viro* fortissimo *et* clarissimo *L. Sullā, quem honoris causā nomino,* &c.

optimásque adolescéntes ad- | most agreeable and excellent
júnxeris, et míhi *gratíssimum* | young men, and do me a very
féceris. | great favor.
Égo misérior súm, quám tú, quaê | I am more miserable than your-
és *misérrima.* * | self, who are extremely miser-
| erable.

B. The superlative singular frequently occurs with *quisque*, every one, and the plural with *quīque*, all. But here the singular is commonly translated by the plural. E. g.

Doctíssimus quisque. — Every one of the most learned.
Óptimi quique.† — The best men all (as a class).
Excellentíssima quaêque. — The most excellent things all (as a class).

Márs ípse ex ácie *fortíssimum quémque* pignerári sólet. — Mars himself is wont to elect the bravest of the battle-field.

Pecúnia sémper *amplíssimo quóque, clarissimóque* contémpta est. — Money was always despised by all the greatest and most illustrious of men.

Múlti mortáles convenêre, máxime *próximi quique.* — Many flocked together, especially (all) the nearest neighbors.

Notíssimum quódque málum máxime tolerábile est. — The most familiar evil is always ‡ the easiest to bear.

Óptimus quisque máxime posteritáti sérvit. — The best man always serves posterity the most.

Miltiades máxime nitebâtur, ut *primo quóque témpore* § cástra fíerent. — Miltiades made special efforts to have the camp constructed at the earliest moment possible.

Máximae cuíque fortúnae mínime credéndum est. — The greatest prosperity is always least to be trusted.

C. The superlative is sometimes linked to another superlative of a separate clause, by means of *ut . . . . ita*, as . . . . so (the . . . . the).‖ E. g.

Ut quísquis óptime dícit, *ita máxime* dicéndi difficultátem pertiméscit. — The better any one speaks, the more he dreads the difficulty of speaking.

---

* The superlative of eminence alone may thus admit of a comparative.

† *Quisque* designates distributively every individual possessed of the same quality in its highest degree, and *quique* the several classes to which that quality is common.

‡ When the predicate contains an additional superlative, as in this instance, the *quisque* of the subject may be rendered by *always*. So *Optimum quidque rarissimum est*, The best things are always the rarest.

§ So also *Primo quoque die*, At the earliest possible day. And frequently in connection with an ordinal; as, *Quinto quoque anno*, In every fifth year. *Septimus quisque dies*, Every seventh day. *Decimum quemque militem*, Every tenth soldier.

‖ Here the superlative is rendered by the comparative, as will be perceived from the examples.

Út quisque ést vir óptimus, íta difficíllime ésse álios ímprobos suspicátur.	The better the man, the less easily will he suspect others of being bad.

D. The superlative often appears in connection with *quam, quantus, qui, ut qui,* [*] to denote that the object admits of comparison with the most eminent of its kind. E. g.

Tám súm mítis, quám qui leníssimus.	I am as mild as the most lenient man (that ever lived).
Tám grátum id míhi érit, quám quód gratíssimum.	It will be as acceptable to me as anything ever was.
Gratíssimum míhi féceris, si huic commendatióni méae tántum tribúeris, quántum cui tribuísti plúrimum.	You will oblige me greatly, if you will attach as much importance to this recommendation of mine, as you ever did to any.
Gráta éa rés, ut quae máxime senátui únquam, fúit.	That affair was as grateful, as any ever was to the senate.
Caésar sit pro praetóre eo júre, quó qui óptimo.	Cæsar can be proprætor with as good a right, as any one ever was.
Dómus celebrátur íta, út cúm máxime.	The house is as much frequented, as it ever was.
Máter múltos jám ánnos, et núnc cum máxime, fílium interféctum cúpit.	For many years already the mother has wished her son killed, and now more than ever.

E. The force of the superlative may be increased in several ways :—

1. By the particles *multo, longe* (= by far), *quam,* or *vel* (= even). E. g. *Multo maximum bellum,* By much the greatest war. *Longe humaníssimus,* By far the most humane. *Quam gratíssimus,* Extremely grateful. *Vel mínima,* Even the smallest things. *Quam brevíssime,* With the utmost possible brevity.

2. By *quam, quantus, qualis,* or *ut* in connection with one of the forms of *possum.* E. g.

Caésar quám aequíssimo lóco potest,[†] *cástra commúnit.*	Cæsar fortifies his camp in the most favorable locality he can (find).
Jugúrtha quám máximas pótest[†] *cópias ármat.*	Jugurtha equips the largest force he can.
Tántis ánimi corporísque dolóribus, quánti in hóminem máximi cádere possunt.	With as much suffering of mind and body as can possibly fall to the lot of man.
Sic Caésari té commendávi, ut	I have recommended you to Cæsar

---

* Here the indefinite *qui* = "any one."
† With *possum* in this construction the infinitive of the nearest verb is commonly understood, as here *communire, armáre.*

gravissime diligentissimêque pó-
tui.

in the most earnest and urgent
manner I could.

3. Sometimes (though rarely) by *maxime;* as, *Maxime gravissimum,*
By far the heaviest. *Hi sunt vel maxime humanissimi,* These are by
far the most humane.

4. *Quam* with the positive, or *quam* (*quantum*) *volo* or *possum,*
sometimes have superlative force. E. g. *quam late* (= *latissime*), far
and wide; *quam magnum* = *maximum; quam potero dilucide atque
perspicue,* as clearly and perspicuously as I can.

F. THE PERFECT TENSE OF "SUM."

INDICATIVE.

SINGULAR.		PLURAL.	
I have been	fúi	*We have been*	fúimŭs
Thou hast been	fúistĭ	*Ye have been*	fúistĭs
He has been,	fúĭt,	*They have been,*	fŭĕrunt *or* fŭĕrĕ.

SUBJUNCTIVE.

SINGULAR.		PLURAL.	
That I may have been	fŭĕrĭm	*That we may have been*	fŭĕrĭmŭs
That thou mayst have been	fŭĕrĭs	*That ye may have been*	fŭĕrĭtĭs
That he may have been,	fŭĕrĭt,	*That they may have been,*	fŭĕrĭnt.

In like manner are inflected all the compounds of *sum;* as, *abfui,*
I have been absent; *adfui* and *interfui,* I have been present; *potui,*
I have been able.

| *Ever, at any time.* | *Unquam.* |
| *Never.* | *Nunquam, nullo tempŏre.* |

Have you been at the market ?	Fuistine in fóro ?
I have been there.	Fúi.
Have I been there ?	Egón' ĭbi fúi ?
You have been there.	Fuísti.
You have not been there.	(Íbi) nôn fuísti.
Has your father been there ?	Fuítne páter túus íllic ?
He has not been there ?	Nôn fúit (íllic).
Have we been there ?	Án nôs íbi fúimus ?
Yes, ye have been there.	Sáne quídem, fuístis.
Have you been at the ball ?	Interfuistine saltatióni ?
I have been there.	Intérfui.
Have they been there ?	{ Núm ílli interfuérunt ? { Illíne interfuérunt ?
They have not been there.	Nôn interfuérunt.
Have you ever been at the play ?	Interfuistine únquam spectáculo ?
I have never been there.	Égo véro núnquam intérfui.
You have never been there.	Tù núnquam interfuísti.
He has never been there.	Ílle núnquam intérfuit.
Have you already been in the garden ?	Fuistine júm in hórtulo ?

I have not yet been there.	{ Nôndum fúi. { Égo íbi nôndum fúi.
You have not yet been there.	Tù íbi nôndum fuísti.
Nor have they ever been there.	Néque flli únquam íbi fuérunt.
Have you already been at my father's ?	Fuistíne jám ápud pátrem méam (cum pátre méo) ?
I have not yet been there ?	Égo ápud éum (cum éo) nôndum - fúi.
The play, spectacle.	Spectacŭlum, i, n.

Exercise 85.

Where have you been ? — I have been at the market. — Have you been at the ball ? — I have been there. — Have I been at the play ? — You have been there. — Hast thou been there ? — I have not been there. — Has your cousin ever been at the theatre ? — He has never been there. — Hast thou already been in the great square ? — I have never been there. — Do you intend to go thither ? — I intend to go thither — When will you go thither ? — I will go thither to-morrow. — At what o'clock ? — At twelve o'clock. — Has your son already been in my large garden ? — He has not yet been there. — Does he intend to see it ? — He does intend to see it. — When will he go thither ? — He will go thither to-day. — Does he intend to go to the ball this evening ? — He does intend to go thither. — Have you already been at the ball ? — I have not yet been there. — When do you intend to go thither ? — I intend to go thither to-morrow. — Have you already been in the Englishman's room ? — I have not yet been in it. — Have you been in my rooms ? — I have been there. — When have you been there ? — I have been there this morning. — Have I been in your room or in that (an in illo) of your friend ? — You have neither been in mine nor in that of my friend, but in that of the Italian.

Exercise 86.

Has the Dutchman been in our storehouses or in those (in íllis) of the English ? — He has neither been in ours nor in those of the English, but in those of the Italians. — Hast thou already been at the market ? — I have not yet been there, but I intend to go thither. — Has the son of our bailiff been there ? — He has been there. — When has he been there ? — He has been there to-day. — Does the son of our neighbor intend to go to the market ? — He does intend to go thither. — What does he wish to buy there ? — He wishes to buy some chickens, oxen, cheese, beer, and cider there. — Have you already been at my cousin's house ? — I have already been there. — Has your friend already been there ? — He has not yet been there. — Have we already been at our friends' ? — We have not yet been there. — Have our friends ever been at our house ? — They have never been there. — Have you ever been at the theatre ? — I have never been there. — Have you a mind to write a letter ? — I have a mind to write one. — To whom do you wish to write ? — I wish to write to my son. —

Has your father already been in the country ? — He has not yet been there, but he intends to go thither. — Does he intend to go thither to-day ? — He intends to go thither to-morrow. — At what o'clock will he depart ? — He will depart at half past six. — Does he intend to depart before he breakfasts ? — He intends to breakfast before he departs. — Have you been anywhere ? — I have been nowhere.

Lesson XLV. — PENSUM QUADRAGESIMUM QUINTUM.

OF THE PERFECT TENSE.

A. The perfect tense serves to represent an action or event as completed, either just now or at some indefinite past time. As,

Amāvi, { I have loved (just now), *or*
{ I loved (once, yesterday).

Scripsi, { I have written (and have now done writing), *or*
{ I wrote (at some past time).

1. With the former of these significations it is called the *perfect definite,* and corresponds to the same tense in English. With the latter, it is called the *perfect indefinite,* and corresponds to the simple form of the English imperfect.*

2. The perfect indefinite occurs most frequently as the tense of historical narration. E. g. *Cato, quoad* vixit, *virtutum laude* crēvit, Cato increased in reputation for virtue, as long as he lived. *Lepidus ad me heri vesperi litteras* misit, Lepidus sent me a letter last evening.

3. Examples of the perfect definite are : — *Filium unicum adolescentulum habeo. Ah! quid* dixi, *me habere! imo* habui, — I have an only son. Alas! What, did I say "I have one"? No, I have had one. Fuimus *Troes,* fuit *Ilium,* We Trojans have been, Ilium has existed (but is now no longer). *Ferus omnia Juppiter Argos* transtülit, Cruel Jupiter has transferred everything to Argos (and it is there now).

FORMATION OF THE PERFECT ACTIVE.

B. The terminations of the perfect tense for the respective conjugations are : 1. *āvi,* 2. *ŭi (ēvi),* 3. *i,* 4. *ĭvi (ĭi).* E. g.

---

* I. e. to the form *I loved, wrote,* &c., but not to *I was loving, writing,* which is the Latin Imperfect.

1. Amāvi, laborāvi, apportāvi, lāvi (= lavāvi).
2. Monŭi, habŭi, studŭi, — delēvi, complēvi.
3. Lēgi, scripsi, dilexi, attŭli, mīsi.
4. Audīvi, scīvi, īvi, prodĭi, sitīvi.

REMARKS.

1. The perfect tense contains the second root of the verb, which serves as the basis for the formation of several other parts. (Cf. Lesson XXVIII. C. 1-5).

2. The second root of the first, second, and fourth conjugations is formed from the first or general root (*am, mon, aud*), by adding, 1. *āv*, 2. *ēv* (*ŭ*),* 4. *īv* ; as *amāv, delēv* (*monŭ*), *audīv*.

3. The second root of the third conjugation is either the same as the first,† as *lēg, exŭ, bĭb*, or is formed by adding *s*,‡ as *scrips* (= scrib + s), *dix* (= dic + s), *dux* (= duc + s).

4. Some verbs of the second conjugation form their second root according to the analogy of the third, and, *vice versa*, several of the third assume *ŭi*. E. g. *augeo* — *auxi, fulgeo* — *fulsi, video* — *vīdi ;* § *alo* — *alŭi, colo* — *colŭi, pōno* — *pŏsŭi,* &c.

5. Many verbs form their second root irregularly ; as, 1. *Seco* — *secŭi, lavo* — *lāvi, veto* — *vetŭi,* &c. 2. *Jubeo* — *jussi, haereo* — *haesi, audeo* — *ausus sum,* &c. 3. *Arcesso* — *arcessīvi, cresco* — *crēvi, cupio* — *cupīvi, fĕro* — *tŭli, mitto* — *mīsi, nosco* — *nōvi, quaero* — *quaesīvi, sperno* — *sprēvi, uro* — *ussi, verro* (*everro*) — *verri,* &c. 4. *Aperio* — *aperŭi, farcio* — *farsi, salio* — *salŭi, sarcio* — *sarsi, venio* — *vēni,* &c. A list of these is given at the end of the Grammar.

6. A number of verbs reduplicate the initial consonant in the second root ; as, *do* — *dĕdi, sto* — *stĕti,* ‖ *curro* — *cucurri, disco* — *didici, posco* — *popŏsci, mordeo* — *momordi,* &c.

7. Compounds generally form the second root like their simple verbs ; as, *affero* (*adfero*) — *attŭli* (= ad + tuli), *conficio* — *confĕci, exaudio* — *exaudīvi,* &c.

---

* Most verbs of the second conjugation have *u*, but the original termination was *ev*, which by dropping *e* becomes *v* or *u*.

† Always the same when the root ends in a vowel; as, *minŭo* — *minŭi, acŭo,* — *acŭi, metŭo* — *metŭi,* &c.

‡ This *s*, preceded by *c, g, h,* or *qu*, gives rise to the compound consonant *x ;* as, *dico* — *dixi, figo* — *fixi, traho* — *traxi, coquo* — *coxi.*
When preceded by *b*, the latter is changed into *p* ; as *nubo* — *nupsi, scribo* — *scripsi,* &c.
When preceded by *d*, either *d* or *s* is dropped (most commonly the latter); as, *edo* — *ēdi, defendo* — *defendi ; claudo* — *clausi, lŭdo* — *lūsi.*
An *s* in the first root is frequently dropped in the second, and the root-vowel prolonged; as, *frango* — *frēgi, fundo* — *fūdi, vinco* — *vīci, relinquo* — *relīqui.*

§ The prolongation (and change) of the root-vowel is quite frequent; as, *căpio* — *cēpi, ago* — *ēgi, făcio* — *fēci, lĕgo* — *lēgi, vĕnio* — *vēni,* &c.

‖ *Sto* and *spondeo* drop the second *s: spopondi.* This reduplication includes the vowel following the consonant, which sometimes, however, is changed into *e ;* as *fallo* — *fefelli.*

8. The perfect subjunctive is formed from the perfect indicative, by changing *i* into *ĕrim*, as, *amāvi — amāvĕrim, monŭi — monŭerim*, &c.

INFLECTION OF THE PERFECT ACTIVE.

C. The following paradigms exhibit the inflection of the perfect, indicative and subjunctive : —

FIRST CONJUGATION.

INDICATIVE.	SUBJUNCTIVE.
Amāvi, *I loved, have loved.*	Amāvĕrim, *that I may have loved.*

SING.	ămāvī	SING.	ămāvĕrim
	ămāvistı		ămāvĕrís
	ămāvĭt,		ămāvĕrĭt,
PLUR.	ămāvīmŭs	PLUR.	ămāvĕrĭmŭs
	ămāvistĭs		ămāvĕrĭtis
	ămāvērunt *or* -re.*		ămāvĕrint.

SECOND CONJUGATION.

INDICATIVE.	SUBJUNCTIVE.
Monŭi, *I reminded, have reminded.*	Monŭerim, *that I may have reminded.*

SING.	mŏnŭī	SING.	mŏnŭĕrim
	mŏnŭistī		mŏnŭĕrís
	mŏnŭĭt,		mŏnŭĕrĭt,
PLUR.	mŏnŭĭmŭs	PLUR.	mŏnŭĕrĭmŭs
	mŏnŭistĭs		mŏnŭĕrĭtĭs
	mŏnŭērunt *or* -re.		mŏnŭĕrint.

THIRD CONJUGATION.

INDICATIVE.	SUBJUNCTIVE.
Lĕgi, *I read, have read.*	Lĕgĕrim, *that I may have read.*

SING.	lēgī	SING.	lēgĕrĭm
	lēgistī		lēgĕrís
	lēgĭt,		lēgĕrĭt,
PLUR.	lēgĭmŭs	PLUR.	lēgĕrĭmŭs
	lēgistĭs		lēgĕrĭtĭs
	lēgērunt *or* -re.		lēgĕrint.

FOURTH CONJUGATION.

INDICATIVE.	SUBJUNCTIVE.
Audīvi, *I heard, have heard.*	Audīvĕrim, *that I may have heard.*

SING.	audīvī	SING.	audīvĕrim
	audīvistī		audīvĕrís
	audīvĭt,		audīvĕrĭt,

---

* The form in *ērunt* is the more common of the two.

PLUR. audīvĭmŭs PLUR. audīvērĭmŭs
audīvistĭs audīvĕrĭtis
audīvērunt *or* -re. audīvĕrint.

So conjugate *apportāvi*, I have brought; *lāvi*, I have washed; *curāvi*, I have ordered ; — *vidi*, I have seen ; *vēni*, I have come; *habŭi*, I have had ; *secŭi*, I have cut ; *jussi*, I have commanded ; — *fēci*, I have made ; *refēci*, I have mended ; *misi*, I have sent ; *volŭi* and *nolŭi*, I have been willing, unwilling ; — *cupīvi*, I have desired ; *īvi (exīi, prodīi)*, * I have gone (out, forth) ; *quaesīvi*, I have sought, &c.

REMARKS.

In the tenses derived from the second root, the syllables *āvi, ēvi, īvi* are frequently contracted.

a.) In the first conjugation, *āvi* followed by an *s*, and *ave* followed by an *r*, are changed into *ā ;* as, *amāsti, amāstis, amāssem, amāsse*. for *amavisti, amavistis, amavissem, amavisse*, &c., and *amārunt, amārim, amāram, amāro*, instead of *amavērunt, amāvēram, amāvēro*, &c.

b.) The same takes place with *ēvi* of the second and third conjugations ; as, *complêsti, complêsse, nêsti, nêstis*, for *complevisti, complevisse, nevisti, nevistis*, and *delêram, consuêrunt, nêrunt*, instead of *delevēram, consuevērunt, nevērunt*. So *decrêssem, decrêsse, quiêssem siris*, for *decrevissem*, &c. The termination *ōvi* of *novi* and its compounds, and also of the compounds of *moveo*, suffers a similar contraction ; as, *nôrunt, nôsse, cognôram, commôssem*, instead of *novērunt, novisse*, &c.

c.) In the fourth conjugation *īvi* before *s* frequently experiences a similar change ; as, *audĭsti, audĭssem, audĭsse*, for *audivisti, audivissem, audivisse*, &c. But most verbs of this conjugation have a second form in *ii*, which sometimes occurs in poetry, and, when an *r* follows, also in prose ; as, *audĭit, impedĭit, abĭisse*, for *audivit, impedivit, abivisse*, and (more frequently) *audieram, quaesierat, definierat*, instead of *audiveram*, &c.

d.) The syllable *is*, when preceded by an *s* or *x*, is sometimes syncopated in the perfect tense of the third conjugation ; as, *dixti, surrexe, evasti, divisse*, for *dixisti, surrexisse, evasisti, divisisse*, &c. But this contraction is antiquated, and used sometimes only by the poets.

e.) Antiquated forms of the perfect subjunctive are those in *assim, essim*, and *sim* (for *averim, uerim, erim*), which frequently occur in Plautus and Terence. E. g. *imperassit, licessit, occisit*, instead of *imperaverit, licuerit, occiserit*. Among these forms are included *faxit, faxint* (for *fecerit, fecerint*),† and *ausim, ausit* (for *ausus sim, ausus sit*), which have remained in use among the later writers.

IIave you had my coat ? Habuistine méam tógam ?
I have had it. Hábui.

---

* All the compos. of *eo* have *ii* rather than *īvi*.
† In invocations and wishes , as, *Faxit Deus*, God grant ! *Dii immortales faxint!*

No, indeed, I have not had it.	Nôn véro, égo éam nôn hábui.
Have I had it ?	{ Án égo éam hábui ? { Egón' éam hábui ?
Yes, you have had it.	Sáne quídem, éam habuísti.
Has he had any wine ?	Habuítne vínum ?
He has had a little.	Hábuit véro aliquántulum.
He has had none.	{ Núllum hábuit. { Nôn hábuit.
Have we had some books ?	Habuimúsne áliquot líbros ?
Yes, you have had some.	Sáne quídem, nonnúllos habuístis.
Have they had anything ?	Núm quíd habuérunt ?
They have had nothing.	Nihil habuérunt.
Has he been right or wrong ?	Útrum vére locûtus est, an errâvit ?
He has been correct.	Vére locûtus ést.
He has never been either right or wrong.	Ílle núnquam néque vére locûtus est, néque errâvit.
To take place.	{ *Lŏcum habēre.* { *Lŏcus est alicui rei.* { *Lŏcus datur alicui rei.*
Does the ball take place this evening ?	Datúrne (éstne) lócus saltatióni hódie vésperi ?
It does take place.	Dátur. Est.
When did the ball take place ?	{ Quándo fúit lócus saltatióni ? { Quô témpore dátus ést lócus salta- tióni ?
It took place yesterday.	Héri.
Yesterday.	Hĕri ; hesterno die.
The day before yesterday.	Nudíus tertíus.
The first time, the second time, the third time, &c.	Primum, itĕrum, tertium, quartum, &c. (*adverbs*).
The last time.	Postrēmum, ultīmum.
This time.	Nunc (*adv.*), hoc tempŏre.
Another time.	Alias (*adv.*), alio tempŏre.
Many times.	Saepíus (*adv. comp.*), sexcenties.
Several times.	{ Diversis temporĭbus. { Non uno tempore.
Time and again.	Iterum ac saepius, semel atque iterum.
How many times ?	Quotíes ? Quotíens ? (adv.)
So (as) many times.	Totíes, totíens. (adv.)
As many times (as often) .... as.	{ Quotíes .... totíes. { Totíes .... quotíes.
Once, twice, three times, four times, &c. (Cf. Lesson XXI. *F.*)	Sĕmel, bĭs, tĕr, quăter, quinquĭēs, sexīēs, &c.
Sometimes.	Intervlum, nonnunquam. (*adv.*)
Formerly, once.	Antĕhac, ōlĭm, quondam.

To be accustomed, wont.	Sŏlĕo, ĕre, sŏlĭtus sum (ALIQUID FACERE).
It is lawful, right.	Licĕt, licŭĭt, or lĭcĭtum est (ALICUI ALIQUID FACERE).

Are you accustomed to go to the market sometimes ?	Solêsne ire ínterdum in fórum ?
I am accustomed to go there sometimes.	Sóleo éo ire nonnúnquam.
Have you ever gone to the ball ?	Ivistíne únquam saltátum ?
I have gone there several times.	Égo véro ívi divérsis tempóribus.
I have gone there time and again.	Ívi véro sémel átque íterum (íterum ac saépius)
And I have never gone.	Égo aûtem núnquam ívi
Have I been wrong in buying books ?	Núm míhi líbros émere nôn lícuit ?
You have not been wrong in buying.	Ímmo véro tíbi quôsdam émere lícuit.

EXERCISE 87.

Have you had my glove ? — I have had it. — Have you had my pocket-handkerchief ? — I have not had it. — Hast thou had my umbrella ? — I have not had it. — Hast thou had my pretty knife ? — I have had it. — When hadst thou it ? — I had it yesterday. — Have I had thy gloves ? — You have had them. — Has your brother had my wooden hammer ? — He has had it. — Has he had my golden ribbon ? — He has not had it. — Have the English had my beautiful ship ? — They have had it. — Who has had my thread stockings ? — Your servants have had them. — Have we had the iron trunk of our good neighbor ? — We have had it. — Have we had his fine carriage ? — We have not had it. — Have we had the stone tables of the foreigners ? — We have not had them. — Have we had the wooden leg of the Irishman ? — We have not had it. — Has the American had my good work ? — He has had it. — Has he had my silver knife ? — He has not had it. — Has the young man had the first volume of my work ? — He has not had the first, but the second. — Has he had it ? — Yes, sir, he has had it — When has he had it ? — He has had it this morning. — Have you had sugar ? — I have had some. — Have I had good paper ? — You have had some. — Has the sailor had brandy ? — He has had some. — Have you had any ? — I have had none. — Have you had the headache ? — I have had the toothache. — Have you had anything good ? — I have had nothing bad. — Did the ball take place yesterday ? — It did take place. — When does the ball take place ? — It takes place this evening.

EXERCISE 88.

Has the German had good beer ? — He has had some. — Hast thou had large cakes ? — I have had some. — Has thy brother had any ? — He has had none. — Has the son of our gardener had flour ? — He has had some. — Have the Poles had good tobacco ? — They have had

P   21

some. — What tobacco have they had ? — They have had tobacco
for smoking, and snuff. — Have the English had as much sugar as tea ?
— They have had as much of the one as of the other. — Has the physician been right ? — He has been wrong. — Has the Dutchman been
right or wrong ? — He never has been either right or wrong ? — Have
I been wrong in buying honey ? — You have been wrong in buying
some. — What has your cousin had ? — He has had your boots and
shoes. — Has he had my good biscuits ? — He has not had them. —
What has the Spaniard had ? — He has had nothing. — Who has had
courage ? — The English have had some. — Have the English had
many friends ? — They have had many of them. — Have we had
many enemies ? — We have not had many of them. — Have we had
more friends than enemies ? — We have had more of the latter than
of the former. — Has your son had more wine than meat ? — He has
had more of the latter than of the former. — Has the Turk had more
pepper than corn ? — He has had more of the one than of the other.
— Has the painter had anything ? — He has had nothing.

EXERCISE 89.

How often have you read that book ? — I have read it twice. —
Have you ever heard this man ? — I have never heard him. — Have
you heard him sometimes ? — I have heard him sometimes. — Do you
sometimes go to the theatre ? — I go thither sometimes. — Has your
brother gone to the ball ? — He has (gone there). — Has he gone to
the ball as often as you ? — He has gone (thither) oftener than I. —
Do you sometimes go into the garden ? — I formerly went into it frequently. — Does your old cook ever go to the market ? — He goes there
frequently. — He went there the day before yesterday — Hast thou
gone to the ball oftener than thy brothers ? — I have gone thither
oftener than they. — Has your cousin often been at the play ? — He
has been there several times — Have you sometimes been hungry ?
I have often been hungry. — Has your valet often been thirsty ? —
He has never been either hungry or thirsty. — Have you gone to the
play early ? — I have gone thither late. — Have I gone to the ball as
early as you ? — You have gone thither earlier than I. — Has your
brother gone thither too late ? — He has gone thither too early. —
Have your brothers had anything ? — They have had nothing. —
Who has had my purse and my money ? — Your servant has had both.
— Has he had my stick and my hat ? — He has had both. — Hast
thou had my horse or that of my brother ? — I have had neither yours
nor that of your brother. — Have I had your note or that of the physician ? — You have had both — What has the physician had ? — He
has had nothing — Has anybody had my golden candlestick ? — Nobody has had it. — When hast thou been at the ball ? — I was (there)
last evening. — Hast thou found any one there ? — I have found no
one there.

Lesson XLVI.—PENSUM QUADRAGESIMUM SEXTUM.

OF THE PERFECT PASSIVE.

A. The perfect tense of the passive voice is composed of the perfect participle and *sum* or *fui.* Thus:—

INDICATIV	SUBJUNCTIVE.
Amātus sum *or* fui, *I have been loved,* or *I was loved.*	Amātus sim *or* fuĕrim, *that I may have been loved.*
SING. amātus sum *or* fui	SING. amātus sim *or* fuĕrim
amātus ĕs *or* fuisti	amātus sīs *or* fuĕris
amātus est *or* fuit,	amātus sīt *or* fuĕrit,
PLUR. amāti sŭmus *or* fuĭmus	PLUR. amāti sīmus *or* fuerĭmus
amāti estis *or* fuistis	amāti sītis *or* fuerĭtis
amāti sunt *or* fuĕrunt.*	amāti sint *or* fuĕrint.

So inflect *monĭtus sum,* I have been admonished; *lectus sum,* I have been read; *audĭtus sum,* I have been heard.   To these add *lacerātus sum,* I have been torn; *lautus sum,* I have been washed; *servātus sum,* I have been preserved; *laudātus sum,* I have been praised; *vituperātus sum,* I have been blamed; *ornātus sum,* I have been adorned; *doctus sum,* I have been taught; *habĭtus sum,* I have been held; *jussus sum,* I have been commanded;—*dilectus sum,* I have been cherished; *ductus sum,* I have been led; *fractus sum,* I have been broken; *missus sum,* I have been sent; *scriptus sum,* I have been written; *sublātus sum,* I have been taken away; *erudĭtus sum,* I have been instructed; *munĭtus sum,* I have been defended; *punĭtus sum,* I have been punished; *vestītus sum,* I have been clothed.

REMARKS.

1. The perfect participle employed in the formation of this tense is derived from the supine in *um,* which is usually termed the *third* root of the verb.   (Cf. Lesson XXIV. *C.* Rem. 1.)

2. The third root of the first, second, and fourth conjugations is derived from the first or general root (*am, mon, aud*) by annexing, 1. *āt,* 2. *ĭt (ĕt),* 4. *ĭt;* as, amātum, monĭtum (delētum), audītum.

3. The third root of the third conjugation is formed by annexing *t* to the general root; as, *dictum, exūtum, lectum.*   This *t* of the third root, like the *s* of the second (p. 237, note ‡), gives rise to several modifications of the consonants preceding it.   Thus:—

a.) When the first root ends in *g, h,* or *qu,* these letters are changed into *c;* as, *rego — rectum, traho — tractum, coquo — coctum.*

---

* So if the subject is feminine, Sing. *amāta sum, ĕs, est;* Plur. *amātae sŭmus, estis, sunt;* and when neuter, Sing. *amātum est;* Plur. *amāta sunt.*

b.) *B* is changed into *p*; as, *scrībo* — *scriptum, nubo* — *nuptum.*

c.) Sometimes the root is changed before the addition of *t*; as, *colo* — *cultum, frango* — *fractum, gero* — *gestum, rumpo* — *ruptum, sperno* — *sprētum, sterno* — *strātum, uro* — *ustum, vinco* — *victum.*

d.) When the first root ends in *d* or *t*, the third adds *s* instead of *t*, and those letters are either dropped or converted into *s*; as, *edo* — *ēsum, defendo* — *defensum, lūdo* — *lūsum, discedo* — *discessum.*

e.) A number of other verbs add likewise *s* and modify the root; as, *excello* — *excelsum, fallo* — *falsum, pello* — *pulsum, premo* — *pressum, spargo* — *sparsum, verro* — *versum.*

f.) Some verbs in *sco* drop *sc* before the *t* of the third root; as, *cresco* — *crētum, nosco* — *nōtum, quiesco* — *quiētum, pasco* — *pastum.*

g.) A number of verbs form their third root in *ŭt* or *ĭt*, as, *bibo* — *bibĭtum, vomo* — *vomĭtum, pōno* — *posĭtum, arcesso* — *arcessĭtum, cupio* — *cupĭtum, quaero* — *quaesĭtum,* &c.

4. The reduplication (p. 237, Rem. 6) does not extend to the third root. E. g. *do* — *dătum, stō* — *stătum, curro* — *cursum, mordeo* — *morsum,* &c.

5. Verbs which are irregular in the second root are generally likewise so in the third; as, *seco* — *sectum, lavo* — *lavātum* (but *lautus* or *lōtus*), *fero* — *latum, aperio* — *apertum, mitto* — *missum, salio* — *salsum, venio* — *ventum,* &c.

6. Inceptive verbs in *sco* generally want the third root, and so many others. For these, and other irregularities of verbs, the student may consult the list of irregular verbs at the end of the book, or his lexicon.

Have you been loved?	Ésne (fuistīne) amâtus?
I have been loved.	Amâtus sum.
Has he been hated?	Fuítne in ódio?
He was not hated.	In ódio nôn fúit.
Has she been praised?	{ Écquid est laudâta? { Éstne laudâta?
Yes, truly, she has been praised.	Sáne quídem, laudâta est (fúit).
No, she has been blamed	Ímmo véro vituperâta est.
Has any one been punished?	{ Écquis ést punîtus? { Númquis est poénã afféctus?
No one has been punished.	{ Némo punîtus ést. { Némo quísquam poénã afféctus est.
Who has been rewarded?	Quís est praémio ornâtus?
The young man has been rewarded.	Adolescéntulus praémio ornâtus est.
Have we been despised?	Núm nôs contémpti súmus?
We have not been despised.	Nòn súmus
Have they (*fem.*) been reprehended?	Án íllae reprehénsae súnt?
They have been reprehended.	Véro quídem, reprehénsae súnt.
Have ye been sent?	{ Éstis míssi? { Núm éstis míssi?
We have not been sent.	Míssi nôn súmus.

PERFECT OF DEPONENT VERBS.

B. The perfect tense of deponent verbs is formed like that of the passive voice (cf. *A.*).   Thus: —

INDICATIVE.	SUBJUNCTIVE.
Hortātus sum *or* fui, *I have exhorted, I exhorted.*	Hortātus sim *or* fuerim, *that I may have exhorted.*

SING. hortātus sum *or* fui   SING. hortātus sim *or* fuĕrim
    hortātus ĕs *or* fuisti   hortātus sīs *or* fuĕris
    hortātus est *or* fuit,   hortātus sit *or* fuĕrit,

PLUR. hortāti sŭmus *or* fuĭmus   PLUR. hortāti sīmus *or* fuĕrĭmus
    hortāti estis *or* fuistis   hortāti sītis *or* fuĕrĭtis
    hortāti sunt *or* fuērunt.   hortāti sint *or* fuerint.

So *verĭtus sum* or *fui*, I have feared; *locūtus sum* or *fui*, I have spoken; *blandītus sum* or *fui*, I have flattered.   To these add *arbĭtrātus sum*, I have thought; *comitātus sum*, I have escorted; *morātus sum*, I have delayed; — *merĭtus sum*, I have earned; *miserĭtus sum*, I have pitied; *tutŭtus sum*, I have defended; — *lapsus sum*, I have fallen; *oblītus sum*, I have forgotten; *profectus sum*, I have departed; *secŭtus sum*, I have followed; — *expertus sum*, I have experienced; *largītus sum*, I have lavished, &c.   (Cf. Lesson XXXV.)

Have you ever spoken Latin?	*Locutūsne és únquam Latíne?*
I have never spoken it.	*Núnquam locútus sum.*
Has he been accustomed to write letters?	Solitúsne est scríbere epístolas?
He has been accustomed (to do so).	Sáne quídem, sólitus est.
Who have obtained the preference?	Quís principâtum consecûtus est?
Our friend (has obtained it).	Nóster amícus.
We have obtained it ourselves.	Nôsmet ípsi principâtum consecúti súmus.
Whom have they flattered?	Cui * blandíti súnt?
They have flattered no one.	Blandíti súnt némini.
Has he departed (for a journey)?	Núm est proféctus?
He has not yet left.	Nôndum proféctus ést.
Has she remained at home?	Moratáne est dómi?
Yes, she has (remained).	Véro, morâta est.
How much money has he lavished?	Quántum pecúniae largítus est ílle?
He has lavished more than was proper.	Largítus ést plûs (ámplius) aéquo.
Have you spent more money than I?	Largitúsne és majôrem pecúniam quám égo?

---

* *Blandīri* ALICUI is the usual construction.
21*

No, I have (on the contrary) spent less.	Ímmo véro minôrem largítus súm.
The king.	Rex, rēgis, *m*.
The successor.	Successor, ōris,* *m*.
The lawyer, barrister, counsellor.	Patrōnus (i, *m*.) causārum ; causídicus, i, *m*. ; jurisconsultus, i, *m*.
The office, employment.	Mūnus, ěris, *n*.
Learned.	Doctus, erudītus, a, um.
To succeed (one in office).	Succēdo, ěre, cessi, cessum (IN ALICUJUS LOCUM, REGNO).
To grow sick, to be taken ill.	{ Aegresco, ěre, ——, ——.†
	{ Fīo (fiěri, factus sum) aegrōtus.
To fall sick.	Incído (ěre, cídi, cāsum) in morbum.
To recover one's health, to grow well.	{ Convalesco, ěre, lŭi, ——.
	{ Fīo (fiěri, factus sum) sānus.
What has become of him ?	{ *Quid ex éo factum est ?*
	{ *Quid éo (de éo) fáctum ést ?*
He has become a doctor, a lawyer, a king.	Fáctus ést médicus, patrônus causârum, réx.
He has turned soldier.	Fáctus ést miles.
He has enlisted.	Relâtus ‡ est inter mílites.
Have you become a lawyer ?	Factúsne és considícus ?
No, I have become a merchant.	Nôn véro, fáctus súm mercâtor.
What becomes of children ? ·	Quíd fit ex líberis ?
Children become men.	{ Líberi fiunt homines adúlti.
	{ Fíunt ex líberis hómines adúlti.
Has he fallen sick ?	Incidítne in mórbum ?
He has fallen sick.	Véro quídem, incidit.
Have you recovered your health ?	{ Factúsne és sânus ?
	{ Convaluistíne ex mórbo ?
I have not recovered.	{ Nôn factus sum.
	{ Nôn conválui.
Whom has he succeeded (in office) ?	{ Cújus in lócum succéssit ?
	{ Cújus múneris fáctus est succéssor ?
He has succeeded the king (to the throne).	{ In lócum rêgis succéssit.
	{ Fáctus est succéssor rêgis.

EXERCISE 90.

Why has that child been praised ? — It has been praised because it has studied well. — Hast thou ever been praised ? — I have often been praised. — Why has that other child been punished ? — It has been punished because it has been naughty and idle. — Has this child been rewarded ? — It has been rewarded, because it has worked well. — When was that man punished ? — He was punished day before

---

* This word always requires the genitive of the office.
† Compare A. Rem. 6.
‡ From *refero, -erre, -tŭli, -lătum.*

yesterday. — Why have we been esteemed ? — Because we have been studious and obedient. — Why have these people been hated ? — Because they have been disobedient. — By whom has the room been swept ? — It has been swept by your servant. — How many times has it been swept ? — It has been swept twice. — Has your book been read as often as mine ? — It has been read oftener than yours. — Why has that book been burnt ? — Because it was a worthless one. — Have you been commanded to write ? — I have not been commanded to write, but to speak. — Whither has the young man been sent ? — He has been sent into the country. — By whom have you been instructed ? — I have been instructed by my parents and masters. — Has the book been torn by any one ? — It has been torn by our children. — Have our shirts been washed ? — They have not yet been washed. — When were our glasses broken ? — They were broken yesterday. — Have you been punished as severely (*tam serēre*) as I ? — I have been punished more severely than you. — By whom were these letters written ? — They were written by our enemies. — Has our friend been loved by his masters ? — He has been loved and praised by them, because he was studious and good ; but his brother has been despised by his, because he was naughty and idle.

EXERCISE 91.

What has become of your friend ? — He has become a lawyer. — What has become of your cousin ? — He has enlisted. — Was your uncle taken ill ? — He was taken ill, and I became his successor in his office. — Why did this man not work ? — He could not work, because he was taken ill. — Has he recovered ? — He has recovered. — What has become of him ? — He has turned a merchant. — What has become of his children ? — His children have become men. — What has become of your son ? — He has become a great man. — Has he become learned ? — He has become learned. — What has become of my book ? — I do not know (*Haud scio*) what has become of it. — Have you torn it ? — I have not torn it. — What has become of our neighbor ? — I do not know what has become of him. — When did your father set out ? — He set out yesterday. — Have our friends already set out ? — They have not yet set out. — With whom have you spoken ? — I have spoken with my neighbor. — Has any one spoken to those men ? — No one has spoken to them. — Whose money have they squandered ? — They have squandered their own. — Has any one exhorted you ? — My master has exhorted me. — Has your brother obtained the preference ? — He has not obtained it. — Have you flattered any one ? — I never flatter any one. — Do our enemies flatter us ? — They do flatter us. — Has your father remained at home ? — He has remained. — Did he remain at home yesterday ? — He did not remain at home. — Have you been accustomed to go to the theatre ? — I have not been accustomed to go. — Whom has your brother succeeded in office ? — He has become the successor of his father.

Lesson XLVII. — PENSUM QUADRAGESIMUM SEPTIMUM.

OF THE SUPINES.

A. The supine in *um* always implies a purpose (*to, in order to, for the purpose of*), and is chiefly used after verbs of motion, such as *eo, abeo, venio, mitto, missus sum, do,* &c. As,

Éo cúbitum, saltâtum, venâtum, êsum.	I go to sleep, to dance, to hunt, to eat.
Ábeo exulâtum, pátriam defén- sum, pâcem petítum.	I go off into exile, to defend my country, to sue for peace.
Vénio quéstum, sciscitâtum, gra- tulâtum.	I come to complain, to inquire, to congratulate.
Rédeo spectâtum, obsecrâtum, hiemâtum.	I return to see, to beseech, to win- ter.
Míssus sum bellâtum, cónsúltum.	I have been sent to wage war, to consult.
Dô álicui áliquam núptum.	I give some one in marriage.

B. RULE. — Supines in *um* have an active sense, and govern the same cases as their verbs.* E. g.

Divitíacus Rômam ad senâtum *vénit, auxílium postulâtum.*	Divitiacus came to Rome to the senate, in order to ask for aid.
Venérunt questum injúrias, ét ex foédere *rês repetítum.*	They came to complain of injuries, and to demand restitution ac- cording to the treaty.
Nôn égo Graiis *servítum mátribus* íbo.	I shall not go to serve Grecian matrons.
Hánnibal invíctus *pátriam defen- sum* revocâtus est.	Hannibal was recalled unconquered to defend his country.
Cóctum égo, nôn *vapulâtum* con- dúctus súm.	I was employed to cook, not to be flogged.
Míssus ést *sciscitâtum,* quíbus précibus suppliciísque déos póssent placâre.	He was sent to inquire by what prayers or offerings they might appease the gods.

REMARKS.

1. The verb *ire* with the supine in *um* is sometimes equivalent to the English *I will, I am about;* as, *Cur te is perdítum!* Why will you

---

* The supines in *um* and *u* are, in point of form, nouns of the fourth declen- sion, the former in the accusative, the latter in the ablative or dative (when *u = ui*). Their construction, however, shows them to be parts of the verb.

make yourself unhappy? *Fuĕre cives*, qui *seque remque publicam* perditum irent, There were citizens, who were engaged in ruining both
themselves and the republic.   But *ire* with the supine is frequently
nothing more than a circumlocution for the same tense of the verb;
as, *ultum ire = ulcisci*, to revenge; *raptum eunt = eripiunt*, they plunder; *perditum eamus = perdamus*, we may ruin.

2. The supine in *um* retains its active signification with a passive
verb.   E. g. *Contumeliam mihi per hujusce petulantiam factum itur*,
They are insulting me with the petulance of this man.

3. In connection with the passive infinitive *iri*, the supine in *um*
serves to form the future infinitive passive; as, *amatum iri*, to be about
to be loved; *auditum iri*,* to be about to be heard, &c.   (Cf. Lesson
XLVIII. *B*.)

4. Many verbs want the supine in *um*.   In these cases (and often
also where the supine exists), the purpose implied in the verb of
motion may be indicated by various other constructions; as, *Venio
spectătum, ad spectandum, spectandi causā, spectaturus, ut spectem*, or
spectāre, I come to see, for the sake of seeing, about to see, &c.   In
general, the use of the supine is not extensive, and the best writers
more frequently prefer the gerund with *ad* or. *causā*, or the future
participle in *urus*.   (Cf. Lesson XXX. *D*.)

C. The supine in *u* is used in a passive sense after
fas, nefas, opus, and after adjectives signifying *good* or
bad, pleasant or *unpleasant, worthy* or *unworthy, easy* or
difficult, and the like.   E. g.

Si hóc *fàs* est *díctu.*	If it is right to say so.
Néfas est *dictu.*	It is impiety to say so.
Íta *dictu ópus* est.	Thus we must say.
Honéstum, dígnum, túrpe, mirá-bile est *dictu.*	It is honorable, worthy, disgraceful, wonderful to tell *or* to be told.
Fácile, difficile, mélius, óptimum ést *fáctu.*†	It is easy, difficult, better, best, to do *or* to be done.
Quid ést tám *jucúndum cógnitu* atque *audítu*, quam sapiéntibus senténtiis gravibúsque vérbis ornâta orá:io ?	Is there anything so delightful to know and to hear as a discourse replete with sage sentiments and weighty arguments ?
Sápiens *vitátu*, quídque *petitu* sit *mélius*, caúsas réddet tíbi.	The philosopher will render you an account of what it is best to avoid, and what best to seek.
Hernici nîhil úsquam *dictu dí-gnum* aúsi súnt.	The Hernici never achieved any-thing worth mentioning anywhere.

---

* The passive infinitive *iri* in this connection is used *impersonally.*
† So likewise *dulce auditu*, sweet to hear; *mollissimum tactu*, of the softest
touch; *facile inrentu*, easy to find, *or* to be found; *speciosa dictu*, plausible to
be said; *fœdum inceptu*, foul to be undertaken, &c.

REMARKS.

1. The supine in *u* does not govern any case, and is hence put with the passive voice. It is commonly rendered like the infinitive passive, but frequently better translated actively. The supines thus employed are not numerous. The principal are *dictu, auditu, cognĭtu, factu, inventu, memorātu*.

2. The adjectives most frequently found in connection with this supine are *bonus, parcus, magnus, dulcis, gravis, levis, fidus, durus, deformis, speciosus, dignus, indignus, proclivis, facilis, difficilis, mirabilis,* and others in *lis;* also *rārus, necessarius, acerbus, vehemens, turpis, foedus,* &c.

3. The supine in *u* sometimes (though rarely) occurs with a verb; as, *Pudet dictu,* It is shameful to be said. *Primus cubĭtu surgat, postrēmus cubĭtum eat,* Let him (the steward) be the first to rise and the last to go to bed. *Priusquam ego obsonātu redeo,* Before I return from the purchase of food.*

4. Instead of the supine in *u,* especially after *facilis* and *difficilis,* the following constructions frequently occur : —

a.) The infinitive present; as, *Facile est* vincere *non repugnantes,* It is easy to conquer where there is no resistance. *Id dicere obscoenum est,* It is obscene to say so.

b.) The gerund with *ad;* as, *Facillimus ad concoquendum,* The easiest to cook. *Jucundum ad audiendum,* Delightful to hear *or* to be heard.

c.) The passive voice and the adjectives *facile, difficile,* &c. as adverbs. E. g. *Non* facile dijudicatur amor verus et fictus, Real love and feigned are not easily distinguished.

d.) Sometimes the present participle, and more, rarely a supine in *um;* as, *Decemviri* colloquentibus erant *difficiles,* The decemviri were difficult of access. *Optimum factum,* Best to do.

e.) Quite frequently a verbal noun in the case required by the adjective ; as, *Justae causae* facilis est defensio, The defense of a just cause is an easy one. *Difficilis est animi, quid aut qualis sit,* intelligentia (= *Difficile est* intellectu, quid, &c.), It is difficult to understand the nature of the mind. So *jucunda potui* (for *potu*), Delightful to drink. *Facilis divisui,* Easy to divide. *Erant rari adĭtūs,* They were rarely to be seen (rare of access). *Cognitione dignum,* Worth knowing.

	INF.	PERF.	SUPINE.†
To do — done.	Agĕre	— ēgi,	actum.
To make (do) — made.	Facĕre	— fēci,	factum.
To make (manufacture) — made.	Conficĕre	— confēci,	confectum.
To take off — taken off.	Exuĕre	— exŭi,	exūtum.

---

* In these cases the supine appears really as the ablative of a verbal substantive. But here the verbals in *io* are by far more common; e. g. *a frumentatione redire,* to return from a foraging expedition.

† The forms *actum, factum,* &c. may either be regarded as the supine "to act," "to do," or as the neuter of the perfect participle "acted," "done," &c.

To pull off — pulled off.	Detrahĕre — detraxi, detractum.
To say — said.	Dicĕre — dixi, dictum.
To speak — spoken.	Loqui — locūtus sum.
To converse with — conversed with.	Collŏqui — collocūtus sum.
To dare — dared.	Audēre — ausus sum.
To cut — cut.	Secāre — secŭi, sectum.
To mow — mowed.	Mētĕre — messŭi, messum.
To burn — burnt.	{ Combūrĕre — combussi, combustum.
	{ Concremāre — āvi, ātum.
To wash — washed.	Lavāre — lāvi, lavātum (lautus, lōtus).
To pick up — picked up.	Tollĕre — sustŭli, sublātum.
To preserve — preserved.	{ Servāre — āvi, ātum.
	{ Sepōnĕre — posŭi, posĭtum.
To tear — torn.	Lacerāre — āvi, ātum.

What have you done?	Quid fecísti (egísti)?
I have done nothing.	Ego níhil féci.
Has the tailor made my coat?	Confecítne sártor méam tógam?
He has made it.	Confécit véro.
He has not yet made it.	Éam nóndum confēcit.
Have you taken off your clothes?	Exuistíne te véstibus?
I have taken them off.	Sic est, éxui.
Have they taken off their boots?	Detraxerúntne sibi cáligas pédibus?
They have not taken them off.	Nòn detraxérunt.
Have we taken off our hats?	Núm nôs cápita nudávimus?
You have not taken off your hats.	Vôs cápita nòn nudavístis.
Has he told you that?	Dixítne tíbi hoc?
He has told me.	Díxit véro.
Who has told him that?	Quís hoc (íllud) éi díxit?
I have told him myself.	Egómet ípse.
Are you the brother of my friend?	Ésne tû fráter amíci méi?
I am.	Súm véro.
With which man have you spoken?	Cum quô hómine locûtus es?
I have spoken with that man.	Collocûtus súm cum hómine íllo.
Have you spoken to your friend?	Locutúsne és amíco túo (ad amícum túum)?
I have spoken to him.	Locûtus sum (éi, ad éum).
Which gloves have you picked up?	Quae digitábula sustulistí?
I have picked up yours.	(Sústuli) túa.
Have you preserved my books?	Servavistíne (servastíne) líbros méos?
I have not preserved them.	(Éos) nòn servávi.
Which books have you burnt?	Quôs líbros combussísti?
I have burnt no books.	{ Núllos (combússi).
	{ Ego nòn úllos líbros combússi.

Have you torn any shirts ?	Lacerâsti áliqua indúsia ?
I have torn some.	Lecerávi nonnúlla.
Has he torn any ?	Núm quae laceràvit ?
He has torn none.	{ Nôn laceràvit. { Núlla laceràvit.
What have ye washed ?	Quid lavístis ?
We have washed our white hand- kerchiefs.	Muccínia nóstra cándida lávimus.
What have they cut ?	Quíd secuérunt ?
They have cut our canes.	Secuérunt bácula nóstra.

EXERCISE 92.

Have you anything to do ? — I have nothing to do. — What has
your brother to do ? — He has to write letters. — What hast thou
done ? — I have done nothing. — Have I done anything ? — You have
torn my clothes. — What have your children done ? — They have
torn their beautiful books. — What have we done ? — You have done
nothing ; but your brothers have burnt my fine chairs. — Has the
tailor already made your coat ? — He has not yet made it. — Has your
shoemaker already made your boots ? — He has already made them.
— Have you sometimes made a hat ? — I have never made one. —
Hast thou already made thy purse ? — I have not yet made it. —
Have our neighbors ever made books ? — They made some formerly.
— How many coats has your tailor made ? — He has made thirty or
forty of them. — Has he made good or bad coats ? — He has made
(both) good and bad (ones). — Has our father taken his hat off ? —
He has taken it off. — Have your brothers taken their coats off ? —
They have taken them off. — Has the physician taken his stockings
or his shoes off ? — He has taken off neither the one nor the other. —
What has he taken away ? — He has taken away nothing, but he has
taken off his large hat. — Who has told you that ? — My servant has
told it to me. — What has your cousin told you ? — He has told me
nothing. — Who has told it to your neighbor ? — The English have
told it to him. — Are you the brother of that youth ? — I am. — Is
that boy your son ? — He is. — How many children have you ? — I
have but two. — Has the bailiff gone to the market ? — He has not
gone thither. — Is he ill ? — He is. — Am I ill ? — You are not. —
Are you as tall as I ? — I am. — Are your friends as rich as they say ?
— They are. — Art thou as fatigued as thy brother ? — I am more
(so) than he.

EXERCISE 93.

Did you come to complain ? — I did not come to complain ; I came
to inquire and to congratulate. — Were they sent to see ? — They
were sent to see and to congratulate. — Did he return (*Rediritne*) to
make war ? — No, he returned to sue for peace. — Have you spoken
to my father ? — I have spoken to him. — When did you speak to
him ? — I spoke to him the day before yesterday. — Have you sometimes spoken with the Turk ? — I have never spoken with him. —
How many times have you spoken to the captain ? — I have spoken

to him six times. — Has the nobleman ever spoken with you? — He
has never spoken with me. — Have you often spoken with his son? —
I have often spoken with him. — Have you spoken with him oftener
than we? — I have not spoken with him so often as you (have). —
To which son of the nobleman have you spoken? — I have spoken to
the youngest (minǐmus natu). — To which men has your brother spoken? — He has spoken to these. — What has your gardener's son cut?
— He has cut trees. — Has he cut (messuǐtne) corn? — He has cut
some. — Has he cut as much hay as corn? — He has cut as much of
the one as of the other. — Have you picked up my knife? — I have
picked it up. — What have you picked up? — We have picked up
nothing. — Have you burnt anything? — We have burnt nothing. —
Hast thou burnt my fine ribbons? — I have not burnt them. — Which
books has the Greek burnt? — He has burnt his own. — Which ships
have the Spaniards burnt? — They have burnt no ships. — Have you
burnt paper? — I have not burnt any. — Has the physician burnt
notes? — He has burnt none. — Have you had the courage to burn
my hat? — I have had the courage to burn it. — When did you burn
it? — I burnt it yesterday. — Where have you burnt it? — I have
burnt it in my room. — Who has torn your shirt? — The ugly boy of
our neighbor has torn it. — Has any one torn your books. — Nobody
has torn them. — Is it right to do so? — It is wrong. — Is it wonderful
to be told? — It is very wonderful (permirabile). — What is best to
be done? — It is best to depart (set out). — Is there any so delightful to know and to hear as the Latin tongue? — There is nothing
more delightful (jucundius). — What has he achieved? — It is not
worth mentioning what he has achieved.

Lesson XLVIII. — PENSUM DUODEQUINQUA-
GESIMUM.

OF THE INFINITIVE MOOD.

A. The infinitive mood expresses the action of the
verb in an indefinite or general manner, but at the same
time represents it either as completed or uncompleted,
i. e. as present, past, or future.

Hence the infinitive of Latin verbs has three tenses: the
present, perfect, and *future.* For each of these the active and
the passive voices both have separate forms. They are: —

1. The present infinitive active, derived from the first root of the
verb; as, amāre, monēre, lĕgĕre, audīre, to love, admonish, read, hear.*

---

* Compare Lesson XXIV. *B. C.*

2. The present infinitive passive, likewise derived from the first root; as, amāri, monēri, legi, audīri, to be loved, admonished, read, heard.*

3. The perfect infinitive active, formed from the second root by adding *isse*; as, amāvisse (amāsse),† monūisse, lēgisse audivisse (audisse), to have loved, admonished, read, heard.

4. The perfect infinitive passive, formed by combining *esse* or *fuisse* with the perfect participle; as, amātum (am, um)‡ esse or fuisse, to have been loved, &c.

5. The future infinitive active, formed by adding *esse* to the future participle active; as, amātūrum (am, um)§ esse, to be about to love, &c.

6. The future infinitive passive, formed by adding the passive infinitive of *ire* to the supine in *um*; as, amātum īri, to be about to be loved, &c.

B.   The following paradigms exhibit all the forms of the infinitive mood, both active and passive.

FIRST CONJUGATION.

INFINITIVE ACTIVE.	INFINITIVE PASSIVE.
PRES. amāre, *to love.*	amāri, *to be loved.*
PERF. amāvisse (amāsse), *to have loved.*	amātum esse *or* fuisse, *to have been loved.*
FUT. amātūrum esse, *to be about to love.*	amātum īri, *to be about to be loved.*

SECOND CONJUGATION.

PRES. monēre, *to remind.*	monēri, *to be reminded.*
PERF. monūisse, *to have reminded.*	monĭtum esse *or* fuisse, *to have been reminded.*
FUT. monĭtūrum esse, *to be about to remind.*	monĭtum īri, *to be about to be reminded.*

THIRD CONJUGATION.

PRES. lĕgĕre, *to read.*	lēgi, *to be read.*
PERF. lēgisse, *to have read.*	lectum esse *or* fuisse, *to have been read.*
FUT. lectūrum esse, *to be about to read.*	lectum īri, *to be about to be read.*

FOURTH CONJUGATION.

PRES. audīre, *to hear*	audīri, *to be heard.*
PERF. audīvisse (audisse), *to have heard.*	audītum esse *or* fuisse, *to have been heard.*
FUT. audītūrum esse, *to be about to hear.*	audītum īri, *to be about to be heard.*

---

* Compare Lesson XXXIII. *B.*   † See page 239, Remarks.
‡ And when it occurs in the nominative, amātus (a, um) esse or fuisse, &c.
§ And in the nominative amatūrus (a, um) esse, &c.

REMARKS.

1. Instead of the future infinitive active or passive, the periphrastic forms *fore*,* *ut*, or *futūrum esse*, *ut*, with the subjunctive, are often employed, especially when the verb has no supine or participle in *Prus*. E. g. *Spēro fore* (or futūrum esse), ut *renias*, for *Spēro te venturum esse*, I hope that you will come. *Credo fore ut epistola scribātur*, instead of *Credo epistolam scriptum iri*, I think that the letter will be written. So also in the past tenses: *Sperābam fore, ut ventres*, I hoped that you might come. *Credēbam fore, ut epistola scriberētur*, I thought that the letter would be written. And of an act completed at some future time: *Spero fore, ut vēnēris* (perf. subj.), I hope that you will have come. *Sperābam fore, ut vēnisses*, I hoped that you might have come. *Credo (Credēbam) epistolam scriptam fōre*, I think (thought) that the letter will be (would be) written.

2. Neuter verbs (unless they are used impersonally) have generally the infinitives of the active voice only. Many of this class want the supine and future participle, and have consequently *fore ut*. E. g.

Īre,	īvisse,	Itūrum esse.
Vĕnīre,	vēnisse,	ventūrum esse.
Esse,	fŭisse,	fŭtūrum esse.
Posse,	pŏtŭisse,	*fore, ut possim.*
Velle,	vŏlŭisse,	*fore, ut velim*, &c.

	Inf.	Perf.	Supine.
To drink — drink.	Bibĕre — bibi,		— .
To carry — carried.	{ Ferre — tŭli,		lātum.
	{ Portāre — āvi,		ātum.
To bring — brought.	{ Afferre — attŭli, allātum.		
	{ Apportāre — āvi, ātum.		
To send — sent.	Mittĕre — misi, missum.		
To write — written.	Scribĕre — scripsi, scriptum.		
To learn — learnt.	Discĕre — dĭdĭci, —— .		
To see — seen.	Vidēre — vīdi, visum.		
To give — given.	Dăre — dĕdi, dătum.		
To lend — lent.	{ Commodāre — āvi, ātum.		
	{ Credĕre — credĭdi, credĭtum.		
To go — gone.	Īre — īvi, ĭtum.		
To come — come.	Vĕnīre — vēni, ventum.		
To know (to be acquainted with) — known.	{ Nôsse — nōvi, nōtum.		
	{ Cognoscĕre — cognōvi, cognĭtum.		

Did you drink some of my wine?	Bibistĭne de vīno mĕo ?
I did not drink (any of it).	Nôn bibi.
Has he brought me the book ?	Apportavĭtne (attulĭtne) mĭhi lĭbrum ?

---

* This is the present infinitive of the obsolete *fŭo*, I am; but generally = *futurum esse*. The only remaining forms of *fŭo* in actual use are the imperf. subj. *fŏrem, fŏres, fŏret*, —— , —— , *fŏrent*.

He has brought it.	Apportâvit (áttŭlit).
Did they send us letters?	{ Miscrúntne nóbis lítteras? { Dederúntne lítteras ad nòs?
They have sent none.	{ Nôn misérunt. { Dedérunt núllas.
Did we write notes?	Scripsimúsne schédŭlas?
We have written some.	Scrípsimus véro nonnúllas.
Have you seen the man?	Vidistísne hominem?
We have not seen him.	(Éum) nòn vídimus.
Have you seen my book?	Án vidístis líbrum méum?
Yes, we have seen it.	Véro quídem, vídimus.
Where have you seen it?	Úbĭnam éum vidístis?
(We have seen it) in your room.	(Vídimus éum) in cubículo túo.
Have you become acquainted with (do you know) those people?	Nostine (congnovistĭne) hómines íllos?
I have become acquainted with them.	Sáne quídem, égo éos nóvi (cognóvi).
Have you known these men?	Notine tibi fuérunt hómines ílli?
I have not known them.	Nòn fuérunt.
Do you learn to write?	Discísne scríbere?
Yes, I am learning it.	Ita est, dísco.
I am learning the art of writing.	Égo ártem scribendi edísco.
Have you learnt to read Latin?	Didicistíne légere Latíne (lítteras Latínas)?
I have learnt it.	Dídici.
Of whom?	Apud quem (a quô)?
Of my master.	Apud magístrum méum (a magístro méo).
When did you lend me that umbrella?	Quándo míhi umbráculum íllud commodavísti?
(I lent it to you) day before yesterday.	Núdius tertius.
Did the man come to your father?	Ivítne hómo ad pátrem túum?
He did come.	Ívit véro.
Did your brother go out into the fields?	Exiítne fratérculus túus in ágros?
He did go out.	Éxiit.
At what time did you come into the city?	Quô témpore venístis in úrbem?
(We came) yesterday evening.	(Vénimus) héri vésperi.
When did they come home?	Quándo advenérunt (ílli) dómum súam?
They came this morning.	Advenérunt hódie mâne.
Where have you seen my cousin?	Úbi (quô lóco) consobrinum méum vidísti (conspéxísti)?
I have seen him in the theatre.	Égo éum in theátro vídi (conspéxi).

To get, order (anything to be done). See page 170.	{ *Jubēre — jussi, jussum.* { *Curāre — āvi, ātum.*

To get anything mended.	{ Aliquid reparāri jubēre. { Aliquid reficiendum curāre.
To get anything washed.	{ Aliquid lavāri jubēre. { Aliquid abluendum curāre.
To get anything made.	{ Aliquid confĭci jubēre. { Aliquid conficiendum curāre.
Are you getting a coat made ?	Jubēsne tógam cónfĭci ? Curâsne tíbi tógam conficiéndam ?
I am getting one made.	Júbeo véro ûnam cónfĭci. Cúro ûnam conficiéndam.
I have ordered (got) one made.	Jússi ûnam cónfĭci. Égo ûnam conficiéndam curávi.
Has your brother had his shirt washed ?	Curavítne frâter túus indúsium súum lavándum ?
He has (had it done).	Curâvit id faciéndum.
Have you ordered your stockings to be washed ?	Jussistíne tû tibiália túa lavári ?
I have ordered them to be washed.	Jússi (éa lavári).
Have you had your shoes mended ?	Curavistísne cálceos véstros reficiéndos ?
We have not had them mended.	Reficiéndos éos nôn curávimus.
The cravat.	*Focāle, is, n.
To bind (a book).	Compingo, ĕre, pēgi, pactum.
Have you sometimes had cravats mended ?	Curávistine ínterdum focália reficiénda ?
I have had some mended sometimes.	Curávi véro ínterdum nonnúlla reficiénda.
Have you ordered your book to be bound ?	Jussistíne líbrum túum compingi ?
I have ordered it to be bound.	Sáne quídem, jússi éum compíngi.
By whom have you had your books bound ?	Cui líbros túos compingendos credidísti ?
I have had them bound by our neighbor, the binder.	Égo éos vicíno nóstro, bibliopégo, compingendos crédidi.
The bookbinder.	{ *Bibliopegus, i, m. { *Librōrum compactor, ōris, m.

EXERCISE 94.

Have you drunk wine ? — I have drunk some. — Have you drunk much of it ? — I have drunk but little of it. — Hast thou drunk some beer ? — I have drunk some. — Has thy brother drunk much good cider ? — He has not drunk much of it, but enough. — When did you drink any wine ? — I drank some yesterday and to-day. — Has the servant carried the letter ? — He has carried it. — Where has he carried it to ? — He has carried it to your friend. — Have you brought us some apples ? — We have brought you some. — How many apples have you brought us ? — We have brought you twenty-five of them. — When did you bring them ? — I brought them this morning. — At

Q   22 *

what o'clock ? — At a quarter to eight. — Have you sent your little
boy to the market ? — I have sent him thither. — When did you send
him thither ? — This evening. — Have you written to your father ? —
I have written to him. — Has he answered you ? — He has not yet answered me. — Have you ever written to the physician ? — I have never
written to him. — Has he sometimes written to you ? — He has often
written to me. — What has he written to you ? — He has written to
me something. — Have your friends ever written to you ? — They
have often written to me. — How many times have they written to
you ? — They have written to me more than thirty times. — Have
you ever never seen my son ? — I have never seen him. — Has he ever seen
you ? — He has often seen me. — Hast thou ever seen any Greeks ?
— I have often seen some. — Have you already seen a Syrian ? — I
have already seen one. — Where have you seen one ? — At the theatre. — Have you given the book to my brother ? — I have given it
to him. — Have you given money to the merchant ? — I have given
some to him. — How much have you given to him ? — I have given
to him fifteen crowns. — Have you given gold ribbons to our good
neighbors' children ? — I have given some to them. — Will you give
some bread to the poor (man) ? — I have already given some to him.
— Wilt thou give me some wine ? — I have already given you some.
— When didst thou give me some ? — I gave you some formerly. —
Wilt thou give me some now ? — I cannot give you any.

EXERCISE 95.

Has the American lent you money ? — He has lent me some. —
Has he often lent you some ? — He has lent me some sometimes. —
When did he lend you any ? — He lent me some formerly. — Has the
Italian ever lent you money ? — He has never lent me any. — Is he
poor ? — He is not poor ; he is richer than you. — Will you lend me
a crown ? — I will lend you two of them. — Has your boy come to
mine ? — He has come to him. — When ? — This morning. — At what
time ? — Early. — Has he come earlier than I ? — At what o'clock
did you come ? — I came at half past five. — He has come earlier
than you. — Where did your brother go to ? — He went to the ball.
— When did he go thither ? — He went thither the day before yesterday. — Has the ball taken place ? — It has taken place. — Has it
taken place late ? — It has taken place early. — At what o'clock ? —
At midnight. — Does your brother learn to write ? — He does learn
it. — Does he already know how to read ? — He does not know how
yet. — Have you ever learnt German ? — I learnt it formerly, but I
do not know it. — Has your father ever learnt French ? — He has
never learnt it. — Does he learn it at present ? — He does learn it.
— Do you know the Englishman whom I know ? — I do not know
the one whom you know ; but I know another. — Does your friend
know the same nobleman whom I know ? — He does not know the
same ; but he knows others. — Have you known the same men whom
I have known. — I have not known the same ; but I have known
others. — Have you ever had your coat mended ? — I have sometimes

had it mended. — Hast thou already had thy boots mended ? — I have
not yet had them mended. — Has your cousin sometimes had his
stockings mended ? — He has several times had them mended. — Hast
thou had thy hat or thy shoe mended ? — I have neither had the one
nor the other mended. — Have you had my cravats or my shirts
washed ? — I have neither had the one nor the other washed. — What
stockings have you had washed ? — I have had the thread stockings
washed. — Has your father had a table made ? — He has had one
made. — Have you had anything made ? — I have had nothing made.

Lesson XLIX. — PENSUM UNDEQUINQUAGE-
SIMUM.

OF PARTICIPLES.

A. Of the four participles of the Latin verb, the present active
and the future passive are formed from the first root of the verb, and
the future active and perfect passive from the third. (Cf. Lesson
XXVIII. *B.* 8, 9, and *D.* 1, 2.) The terminations of these participles
for the respective conjugations are : —

PRES. ACT. 1. *ans,* 2. *ens,* 3. *ens (ĭens),* 4. *ĭens.*
FUT. ACT.   1. *ātūrus,* 2. *ĭtūrus,* 3. *tūrus,* 4. *ĭtūrus.*
PERF. PASS. 1. *ātus,* 2. *ĭtus,* 3. *tus,* * 4. *ĭtus.*
FUT. PASS. 1. *andus,* 2. *endus,* 3. *endus (ĭendus),* 4. *ĭendus.*

B. The following paradigms exhibit the participles
of the several conjugations in regular order : —

FIRST CONJUGATION.

ACTIVE.		PASSIVE.	
PRES.	ămans, *loving.*	PERF.	ămātus, a, um, *loved.*
FUT.	ămātūrus, a, um, *about to love.*	FUT.	ămandus, a, um, *to be loved.*

SECOND CONJUGATION.

PRES.	mŏnens, *reminding.*	PERF.	mŏnĭtus, a, um, *reminded.*
FUT.	mŏnĭtūrus, a, um, *about to remind.*	FUT.	mŏnendus, a, um, *to be reminded.*

THIRD CONJUGATION.

PRES.	lĕgens, *reading.*	PERF.	lectus, a, um, *read.*
FUT.	lectūrus, a, um, *about to read.*	FUT.	lĕgendus, a, um, *to be read.*

* On the irregularities of the third root of the second and third conjugations,
see Lesson XLVI. *A.* Rem. 1 – 6.

PRES. căpĭens, *taking.*   PERF. captus, a, um, *taken.*
FUT. captūrus, a, um, *about*   FUT. căpĭendus, a, um, *to be*
     to take.   *taken.*

FOURTH CONJUGATION.

PRES. audĭens, *hearing.*   PERF. audītus, a, um, *heard.*
FUT. audītūrus, a, um, *about* FUT. audĭendus, a, um, *to be*
     to hear.   *heard.*

C. Deponent verbs generally have all the participles. Of these the future in *dus* is passive, like that of other verbs, but the perfect participle in *tus* has commonly an active sense. E. g.

PRES.   hortans, vĕrens, sĕquens, blandiens, *exhorting, fear-ing, following, flattering.*

PERF.   hortātus, verĭtus, secūtus, blandītus, *having exhort-ed, feared, followed, flattered.*

FUT. ACT. hortatūrus, verĭtūrus, sectūrus, blandītūrus, *about to exhort, fear, follow, flatter.*

FUT. PASS. hortandus, verendus, sequendus, blandĭendus, *to be exhorted, feared, followed, flattered.*

REMARKS.

1. The present participle in *ns* is declined like an adjective of one termination (cf. page 21), and the participles in *us, a, um,* like *bonus.*

2. Participles sometimes drop the distinction of time and assume the character of adjectives or nouns. E. g. *amans,* loving (in love), or a lover; *doctus,* learned; *nātus,* a son. When employed as adjectives, they become susceptible of comparison. (Cf. Lesson XLI. *C.* and *F.*)

3. Neuter verbs generally have only the participles of the active voice. Of some, however, the future passive participle in *dum* is used impersonally.* Others again have also a perfect participle, which sometimes has a passive and sometimes an active sense.

4. The perfect participle of deponent verbs is generally active. The following sometimes occur also in the passive sense: *adeptus, comitātus, commentātus, complexus, confessus, contestātus* and *detestātus, populātus* and *depopulātus, dimensus* and *emensus, effātus, ementītus, emerĭtus, expertus* and *inexpertus, execrātus, interpretātus, medĭtātus, metātus, moderātus, opinātus, pactus, partītus, perfunctus, periclĭtā-tus, stipulātus, testātus.* E. g. *Depopulatus agrum,* Having devastated the field. *Depopulātum agrum,* The devastated field. *Partītus exercĭ-tum,* Having divided the army. *Partīto exercĭtu,* The army having been divided.

5. The following perfect participles, though from active verbs, are also employed in an active sense: *juratus,* having sworn; *pransus,*

---

* Compare page 118, note *.

having taken lunch; *coenātus*, having dined; *pōtus*, having drunk. To these add *ausus, gavīsus, solĭtus, fīsus, confīsus; exōsus, perōsus,* and *pertaesus.*

6. The English perfect participle active, of which Latin verbs generally are destitute, is commonly rendered either by a separate clause, or by the ablative of the passive participle. E. g. "When he had exterminated the kings," is either *Quum reges exterminasset,* or passive, *Regĭbus exterminātis,* The kings having been exterminated. The latter is called the *Ablative Absolute,* on which see Lesson LXXIII.

7. The genitive plural of participles in *rus* rarely occurs, except that of *futūrus.*

8. The present participle of the verb *sum* is wanting, the obsolete *ens* occurring only in the compounds *absens, praesens,* and *potens.* The present participle of *eo,* I go, is *iens,* gen. *euntis.*

CONJUGATIO PERIPHRASTICA.

D. The participles in *rus* and *dus,* with the auxiliary *sum,* give each of them rise to a new conjugation, called the *conjugatio periphrastica.* In this connection the participle in *rus* denotes an *intention,* and that in *dus, necessity* or *propriety.* (Cf. Lesson XXV. *C. D.*) E. g.

1. Amātūrus sum, *I am about to love (on the point of loving).**

INDICATIVE.	SUBJUNCTIVE.
PRES. amatūrus sum	amatūrus sim
IMP. amatūrus ĕram	amatūrus essem
PERF. amatūrus fui	amatūrus fuĕrim
PLUP. amatūrus fuĕram	amatūrus fuissem.
FUT. amatūrus ĕro.†	

INFINITIVE.

PRES. amatūrum esse.   PERF. amatūrum fuisse.

2. Amandus sum, *I am to be loved,* or *must be loved.*‡

INDICATIVE.		SUBJUNCTIVE.
PRES.	amandus sum	amandus sim
IMP.	amandus ĕram	amandus essem
PERF.	amandus fui	amandus fuĕrim
PLUP.	amandus fuĕram	amandus fuissem.
FUT.	amandus ĕro	
FUT. PERF. amandus fuĕro.		

INFINITIVE.

PRES. amandum esse.   PERF. amandum fuisse.

---

* And so in the remaining tenses, INDIC. *I was, have been, had been, shall be, about to love.* SUBJ. *that I may be, might be, may have been, might have been, about to love.*

† The Future Perfect *amatus fuĕro* does not occur.

‡ And so in the remaining tenses: — IND. *I was to be loved, I shall have to be loved,* &c., always with the agent in the dative. E. g. *tibi, hominibus, nemini,* by you, by men, by no one. See Lesson XXV. *C. D.*

OF THE USE OF PARTICIPLES.

E. Participles as such do not express any absolute determination of time, and can only be said to be present, past, or future, with reference to the time of the action denoted by the verb of the sentence in which they stand. Hence the verb with which they are connected may itself be either present, past, or future.

Participles have the agreement of adjectives. The noun with which they are in concord may be either in the nominative, as the subject of the sentence, or in one of the oblique cases governed by another word.

Participles govern the same cases as their verbs. E. g.

Híc adolescéntŭlus ést (érat, érit) jússis túis *obédiens.*

This youth is (was, will be) obedient to your commands.

Abitúrae congregántur (congregabántur, congregabúntur) in lóco cérto.

When about to leave (just before leaving) they collect (did collect, will collect) together in a particular place.

Caèsar hóstem *profligâtum* perséquitur (persecûtus est, persequêtur).

Caesar pursues (has pursued, will pursue) the routed enemy.

Caèsar póntem in Arári *faciéndum* cûrat (curâvit, curâbit).

Caesar orders (did order, will order) a bridge to be constructed over the Arar.

Léx est récta rátio, *imperans* honésta, *próhibens* contrária.

The law is plain reason, commanding what is just, and prohibiting the contrary.

Jácet córpus *dormiéntis,* ut *mórtui.*

The body of one sleeping (asleep) is like that of a dead man.

Proditiônis *insimulâtus,* ad ómnia crímina respóndit.

Accused of treason, he replied to all the charges brought against him.

Brundúsium vénimus, *úsi* túâ felicitâte navigándi

Having had your own good luck on our voyage, we arrived at Brundusium.

Mágna párs hóminum est, quae *navigatúra* de tempestâte nôn cógitat.

There are many men, who never think of the weather, when they are about to sail.

Magna pars peccatôrum tóllitur, si *peccatúris* testis assístat.

A great many offences are prevented, if (where) there is a witness near those (who are) about committing them.

Équidem beátos púto, quíbus Deôrum múnere dátum est, aut fácere *scribénda,* aut scríbere *loquénda.*

I consider those happy, to whom it is vouchsafed either to achieve things destined to be recorded, or to record events destined to be repeated.

F. Participles are frequently employed instead of subordinate clauses introduced by a relative pronoun, or by one of the conjunctions *while, when, if, because, although,* &c.   E. g.

Pláto *scribens* mórtuus est.

Plato died *while* (in the act of) writing.

Dionýsius, Syracúsis *expúlsus,* Corinthi púeros docébat.

Dionysius, *after* having been expelled from Syracuse, was engaged in teaching at Corinth.

Tibérius, *trajectúrus* Rhênum, commeâtum ómnem transmisit.

Tiberius, when about crossing the Rhine, sent over all his supplies.

Sunt divítiae cértae, in quácúnque sórtis humánae levitâte *permansúrae.*

There are certain riches, *which will remain* in every vicissitude of human fortune.

Pisístratus primus Homéri líbros, *confúsos* ántea, sic disposuisse dícitur, ut nunc habêmus.

Pisistratus is said to have first arranged the poems of Homer, *which were confused* before, in the order in which we have them now.

Níhil affírmo, *dúbitans* plerúmque et míhi ípse *diffídens.*

I do not positively affirm anything, *since* I am myself uncertain and distrustful of myself.

Ut óculus, sic ánimus, sê *non videns,* ália cérnit.

Although the mind, like the eye, *does not see* itself, it yet perceives other things.'

Sócratis mórti illacrimáre sóleo, Platônem *légens.*

I always weep over the death of Socrates, *as often as* (*whenever*) I read Plato.

Epicúrus *non erubéscens* voluptátes perséquitur ómnes nominátim.

Epicurus enumerates the entire catalogue of pleasures *without blushing.* *

REMARKS.

1. Participles employed adjectively modify merely the noun, and not the entire sentence. E. g. *Terra sitiens,* The thirsting earth. *Bene tolerata paupertas,* Poverty well borne. *Metus magni mali impendentis,* The fear of a great impending evil. *Poenae meritae remisso,* The remission of a merited punishment.

2. The perfect and future passive participles often supply the place of a verbal substantive. E. g. *Hac litterae recitátae,* The reading of this letter. *Ab urbe condítā,* Since the founding of the city. *Post Christum nátum,* After the birth of Christ. *Propter Africam delētam,* On account of the destruction of Africa   *Consilium urbis delendae,* The design for the destruction of the city.

---

* So also *non loquens,* without speaking, &c. But the English *without* (with verb) is also expressed by the ablative of the perfect participle; as, *non expectato auxilio,* without expecting any help, &c.

3. After verbs of *seeing, hearing,* or *representing,* the present participle may stand, as in English, instead of the infinitive. E. g. *Socratem audio dicentem,* I hear Socrates say. *Catonem vĭdi in bibliothĕcā sedentem,* I saw Cato sitting in the library. *Xenophon facit Socratem disputantem,* Xenophon represents Socrates as maintaining.

4. After *habeo, teneo, possideo,* and similar verbs, and also after *volo, nolo, cupio, facio, oportet, do, reddo,* and *curo,* the perfect participle is used to designate a past event of which the result or consequences are still remaining. E. g. *Cognĭtum habeo,* I (have learnt and still) know. *Clausum teneo,* I keep shut. *Me excusātum volo,* I wish myself excused. *Perfidiam perspectam habebat,* He perceived the perfidy. *Exercĭtum coactum habēbat,* He kept the army subjected. *Missos faciant honores,* Let them resign their claim to places of trust or honor. *Inventum tibi curābo,* I'll see him found for you.

5. The participle in *rus* is used by the later writers of the language (instead of the supine in *um*), after verbs of motion, to denote the purpose. E. g. *Catilīna ad exercitum proficiscitur, signa* illatūrus *urbi,* Catiline goes to the army in order to invade the city. (Cf. Lesson XXX. *D. Obs.*) The present participle is sometimes put in the same sense; as, *Canes alium rogantes regem misĕre ad Jovem,* The dogs sent to Jupiter to ask for another king.

6. An intended effect or purpose is also indicated by the future participle in *dus,* after *curāre* (to order or get anything done), and also after *dāre, tradĕre, mittĕre, concedĕre, permittĕre, accipĕre,* and *suscipĕre, locāre, conducĕre,* and similar verbs. E. g. *Conon muros dirū-tos Athenārum reficiendos curāvit,* Conon ordered the demolished walls of Athens to be repaired. *Vīta data est utenda,* Life is given us to be enjoyed. *Fabius saucios milĭtes curandos dividit patribus,* Fabius distributes the wounded soldiers to be provided for by the senators. *Aedem Castŏris P. Junius habuit tuendam,* P. Junius had the temple of Castor to guard. *Patriam vel diripiendam vel inflammandam reliquĭmus,* We have left our country either to be plundered or destroyed by fire.

EXERCISE 96.

Are you about to love? — I am about to love. — Are they going to read (*lecturus*)? — They are not going to read; they are going to write (*scripturus*). — Are we going to learn (*disciturus*) Latin? — We are going to learn it. — Were you about to read the book which I have lent you? — I was about to read it. — Were they about opening (*apertūrus*) the window? — They were on the point of opening it. — Is he about to sell (going to sell, *vendĭturus*) his books? — He is not going to sell them. — Am I about going (*iturus*) to the theatre? — You are not going. — Was he going to give (*daturus*) you money? — He was about to give me some. — Was the physician about to come (*venturus*)? — He was on the point of coming. — Must you be loved (*amandus*)? — I must be loved. — By whom (*cui*) is your little boy to be loved? — He must be loved by his parents and teachers. — Must the letter be read (*legendus*)? — It must be read. — By whom?

— It must be read by his friends and neighbors. — Must the fire be lighted ? — It is not to be lighted (*accendendus*) : it is to be extinguished. — Must you set out on a journey * ? — I must set out. — When was he obliged to set out ? — He was obliged to set out this morning. — Must you go (*eundum*) into the garden ? — I am not obliged to go there. — Must we breakfast (*jentandum*) now ? — We are not to breakfast yet. — What is to be done by us ? — We must speak Latin, and write letters to our friends.

EXERCISE 97.

Have you seen any one writing ? — I have seen my father writing and reading by the fire. — Did they hear us speaking (*loquentes*) ? — They did not hear us. — Where have you seen our friend ? — I have seen him standing (*stantem*) by the window. — Where was your little brother last evening ? — He was in his room, reading (*legens*) the book which you gave him. — Is our servant in the field ? — No, he is in the garden cutting (*secans*) trees. — Does he keep the window open (*apertam*) ? — No, he keeps it shut. — Do you wish to be excused? — I do wish to be excused. — Will you resign your claim (*missos facere*) to posts of honor ? — I cannot resign it. — Do you not perceive the treachery (*perfidiam*) ? — I do perceive it. — Did he give you the letter to read (to be read = *legendus*) ? — He did give it (to me). — To whom did you give the shirts to be washed ? — I have given them to my servant. — Did they lend us the books to be torn (*discindendus*) ? — No ; on the contrary, they have lent them to us to be read and remembered (*memoriâ tenendos*). — Will you send me your gloves to mend (to be mended) ? — I am unwilling to send them. — Has the tailor received coats to mend ? — He has received coats and shirts to mend (*reficienda*). — Where have you left your hat to be repaired ? — I have left it with (*apud*) the hatter. — Is the stranger coming to our house ? — He is coming in order to bring you (*tibi allaturus*) the tobacco you have bought of him. — Did that happen (*evēnit*) before (*ante*) or after the building of the city? — It happened after (*post*). — Did Socrates live (*vixitne Socrates*) after the birth of Christ ? — No, he lived before it. — Was your brother rewarded ? — No ; on the contrary, he suffered (*affectus est*) a merited punishment. — Do you see the sailors coming ? — I do not see them coming, but going away (*abeuntes*). — Where did you find your gloves ? — I found them lying on the table. — Did you find your neighbor sitting by the fire ? — No, I found him walking (*ambulantem*) in his garden.

---

* *Profciscendumne tibi est ?* And so the rest, according to Lesson XXV. *D.*

Lesson L. — PENSUM QUINQUAGESIMUM.

OF THE IMPERFECT TENSE.

A. The imperfect tense represents an action or state as incomplete, and going on at some past time. As,

Amābam,	{ I was loving (was engaged in loving). { I loved, did love.*
Scribēbam,	{ I was writing (was occupied with writing). { I wrote, did write.
Amābar,	{ I was (being) loved. { I was the object of continued love.
Litterae scribēbantur,	{ A letter was being written. { Some one was engaged in writing a letter.

B. The imperfect tense always involves a reference (either direct or indirect) to the time of another past action or event, which was either simultaneous with or antecedent to it. Hence, in narration, it frequently exchanges with the perfect indefinite, which, as the leading tense, then indicates the principal event, while the imperfect serves to point out the accessory circumstances connected with it. In its grammatical construction, however, the imperfect may either stand as the leading verb of an independent sentence, or subordinate in clauses introduced by a conjunction or a relative. It is thus used, —

I. With direct reference to another past action or event simultaneous with it. E. g.

Quúm Caésar in Gálliam *vénit,* altérius factiônis príncipes *érant* Aédui, altérius Sequáni.	When Cæsar arrived in Gaul, the Ædui *were* the leaders of the one party, and the Sequani of the other.
Quâ tempestâte Carthaginiénses pleraêque Áfricae *imperitábant* Cyrenénses quôque mágni atque opulénti *fuêre.*	At the time when the Carthaginians *were ruling* nearly all Africa, the Cyrenians were also a great and opulent people.
Cimon celériter ad principâtum *pervênit. Habêbat†* enim sátis eloquéntiae, súmmam liberalitâtem, mágnam prudéntiam.	Cimon rapidly advanced to the highest office of the state. For *he had* sufficient eloquence, the highest degree of liberality, and great sagacity.

---

* The Latin imperfect always implies duration or continuance of action (in the indicative at least), and has consequently the sense of the English *I was loving.* Sometimes, however, it is convenient to render it like the perfect indefinite: *I loved, did love.*

† The imperfect here denotes a *permanent* quality or characteristic, in opposition to the momentary event indicated by the perfect *pervenit.*

Aéqui sê in óppida *recepérunt* murísque sê *tenébant.*

The Æqui retreated into their towns, and kept themselves within their walls.

Caésar Alésiam circumvallâre *instituit.* *Érat* óppidum in cólle súmmo, cújus rádices dúo duábus ex pártibus flúmina *subluébant.* Ante íd óppidum planíties *patébat;* réliquis ex ómnibus pártibus cólles óppidum *cingebant.**

Cæsar began to invest Alesia. The town was situated on the top of a hill, whose base was washed on two sides by two rivers. In front of this town a plain extended; on all the remaining sides the town was surrounded by hills.

II. To denote frequently repeated past action, as exhibited either in individual habits, or in manners, customs, and usages. E. g.

L. Cássius idéntidem in caúsis quaérere *solébat,* cuí bóno fuísset.

L. Cassius, in hearing causes, was accustomed to inquire frequently for whose advantage it had been.

Dicébat mélius, quam scrípsit, Horténsius.

Hortensius was wont to speak better than he wrote.

Majóres nóstri libértis nôn múlto sécus ác sérvis *imperábant.*

Our ancestors were accustomed to command their freedmen very nearly like slaves.

Ánseres Rómae públice *alebántur* in Capitólio.

It was customary at Rome to support geese at public expense in the Capitol.

Sócrates *dicébat* (== dícere *solébat*), ómnes in éo, quód scírent, sátis ésse eloquéntes.

Socrates was accustomed to say, that all men were eloquent enough in what they knew.

III. To denote an event, in which the narrator participated as an eyewitness. E. g.

Úno díe séx proéliis fáctis .... ad duôrum míllium número ex Pompejánis cecidísse *reperiebímus.*†

Six battles having been fought in one day, we found that nearly two thousand of Pompey's party had been killed.

Eôdem fére témpore póns in Ibéro própe efféctus *nuntiabátur,* et in Sícöri vádum *reperiebátur.*

About the same time it was reported (to us) that a bridge over the Ebro was nearly completed, and a ford over the Segre found.

REMARKS.

1. The imperfect sometimes expresses merely a *conatus,* i. e. an attempt, effort, or intention. E. g. *Consúles* sedábant *tumultus, sedan-*

---

* The imperfect (*erat, subluebant,* &c.) of this example denotes *permanent situation,* in opposition to the comparatively momentary event indicated by the perfect *instituit* So the *tenebant* of the preceding example.
† The language of Cæsar, who was himself engaged in the events described.

do interdum movēbant, The consuls were attempting to quell the insurrection, but in doing so they sometimes only excited it. *Cato pro
lege, quae* abrogabātur, *ita disseruit*, Cato spoke in favor of the law,
which it was attempted to abolish, in the following manner.

2. The imperfect is sometimes used to represent an action or condition as past, though still existing at the time of the narrator. E. g.
*Manus etiam data est elephantis, quia propter magnitudīnem corpŏris
difficĭles adītus* habēbant *ad cibos*, Elephants were furnished with a
trunk, because, owing to the hugeness of their structure, they had (at
the time they were thus furnished) a difficult access to their food.

3. In epistolary correspondence, the Romans frequently employ
the imperfect or the perfect where in English we put the present.
E. g. *Haec* scribēbam *mediā nocte*, I wrote (= I write) this at midnight.
Novi nihil nunc erat *apud nos.   Quae ad eam diem, quum haec* scribēbam, *audiverāmus, inanis rumor* videbatur, — There is at present nothing new with us. What we had (have) heard up to the day I wrote
(write), appeared (appears) to be an empty rumor.

4. Instead of the imperfect indicative, the historians frequently use
the *present infinitive*, in order to impart animation to the narrative.
E. g. *Neque post id locorum Jugurthae dies aut nox ulla quieta fuere;
neque loco neque mortali cuiquam aut tempori satis* credēre; *cives,
hostes juxta* metuēre; circumspectare *omnia et omni metu* pavescēre;
alio atque alio loco saēpe contra decus regium noctu requiescēre, &c.
Subsequently to that time Jugurtha had not a single quiet day or
night ; nor did he exactly trust any place or occasion, or any of his
fellow-men : he dreaded citizens and enemies alike ; he suspected
everything, and trembled under the influence of every species of apprehension, &c.   This is called the *Infinitīvus Historĭcus.*

5. The above remarks concerning the use of the imperfect apply
to the indicative alone. On the sense of the imperfect subjunctive,
see *D*. and *E*. of this Lesson.

FORMATION OF THE IMPERFECT TENSES ACTIVE.

C. The imperfect indicative active is formed from the root
of the indicative present (*am, mon, leg, aud*), by adding the terminations, 1. *ābam*, 2. *ĭbam*, 3. *ēbam* (*ĭēbam*), 4. *ĭēbam ;* and
the imperfect subjunctive from the present infinitive, by adding
m. E. g.

1. { IND. amābam, lavābam, apportābam, dăbam.
     { SUBJ. amārem, lavārem, apportārem, dărem.

2. { IND. mŏnēbam, habēbam, studēbam, egēbam.
     { SUBJ. monērem, habērem, studērem, egērem.

3. { IND. legēbam, scribēbam, mittēbam, faciēbam.
     { SUBJ. legērem, scribērem, mittērem, facĕrem.

4. { IND. audiēbam, sciēbam, sitiēbam, esuriēbam.
     { SUBJ. audirem, scirem, sitīrem, esurīrem.

INFLECTION OF THE IMPERFECT ACTIVE.

D. The inflection of the imperfect active is exhibited by the following paradigms:—

FIRST CONJUGATION.

INDICATIVE.	SUBJUNCTIVE.
Amābam, *I was loving.*	Amārem, *that I might, could, would, should love.*

	SING. ămābăm		SING. ămārĕm
	ămābās		ămārĕs
	ămābăt,		ămārĕt,
PLUR.	ămābāmŭs	PLUR.	ămārēmŭs
	ămābātĭs		ămārētĭs
	ămābant.		ămārĕnt.

SECOND CONJUGATION.

INDICATIVE.	SUBJUNCTIVE.
Mŏnēbam, *I was reminding.*	Mŏnērem, *that I might, could, would, should remind.*

	SING. mŏnēbăm		SING. mŏnērĕm
	mŏnēbās		mŏnērĕs
	mŏnēbăt,		mŏnērĕt,
PLUR.	mŏnēbāmŭs	PLUR.	mŏnērēmŭs
	mŏnēbātĭs		mŏnērētĭs
	mŏnēbant.		mŏnērent.

THIRD CONJUGATION.

INDICATIVE.	SUBJUNCTIVE.
(1.) Lĕgēbam, *I was reading.*	Lĕgĕrem, *that I might, could, would, should read.*

	SING. lĕgēbăm		SING. lĕgĕrem
	lĕgēbās		lĕgĕrēs
	lĕgēbăt,		lĕgĕrĕt,
PLUR.	lĕgēbāmŭs	PLUR.	lĕgĕrēmŭs
	lĕgēbātĭs		lĕgĕrētĭs
	lĕgēbant.		lĕgĕrent.

(2.)	Făcĭēbam, *I was doing.*	Făcĕrem, *that I might, could, would, should do.*

	SING. făcĭēbăm		SING. făcĕrĕm
	făcĭēbās		făcĕrēs
	făcĭēbăt,		făcĕrĕt,
PLUR.	făcĭēbāmŭs	PLUR.	făcĕrēmŭs
	făcĭēbātĭs		făcĕrētĭs
	făcĭēbant.		făcĕrent.

23*

FOURTH CONJUGATION.

INDICATIVE.	SUBJUNCTIVE.
Audiēbam, *I was hearing.*	Audīrem, *that I might, could, would, should hear.*

SING.	audiēbăm	SING.	audīrĕm
	audiēbās		audīrēs
	audiēbăt,		audīrĕt,
PLUR.	audiēbămŭs	PLUR.	audīrēmŭs
	audiēbātĭs		audīrētĭs
	audiēbant.		audīrent.

So conjugate, — 1. *Apportābam*, I was bringing; *curābam*, I was ordering; *dăbam*, I was giving; *lavābam*, I was washing; *secābam*, I was cutting. 2. *Audēbam*, I was daring; *egēbam*, I was needing; *habēbam*, I was having; *jubēbam*, I was commanding; *vidēbam*, I was seeing. 3. *Arcessēbam*, I was calling (fetching); *convalescēbam*, I was getting better; *dūigēbam*, I was cherishing; *frangēbam*, I was breaking; *mittēbam*, I was sending; *ponēbam*, I was placing; *scribēbam*, I was writing; — *capiēbam*, I was taking; *cupiēbam*, I was desiring; *fugiēbam*, I was fleeing. 4. *Aperiēbam*, I was opening; *esuriēbam*, I was desirous of eating; *saliēbam*, I was salting; *veniēbam*, I was coming, &c.

E. The following are more or less irregular in the formation of the imperfect:—

1. Ĕram, *I was.* — Essem, *that I might be.*

IND.   S. ĕrăm, ĕrās, ĕrăt; P. ĕrāmŭs, ĕrātĭs, ĕrant.
SUBJ.   S. essem, essēs, essĕt; P. essēmŭs, essētĭs, essent.

2. Potĕram, *I was able.* — Possem, *that I might be able.*

IND.   S. pŏtĕrăm, pŏtĕrās, pŏtĕrăt; P. pŏtĕrāmŭs, pŏtĕrātĭs, pŏtĕrant.
SUBJ.   S. possĕm, possēs, possĕt; P. possēmŭs, possētĭs, possent.

So the remaining compounds of *sum*, viz.: *adĕram* — *adessem* and *interĕram* — *interessem*, I was present; *prodĕram* — *prodessem* (from *prŏsum*), I was conducing; *praeĕrat* — *praeessem*, I was presiding over; *superĕram* — *superessem*, I was left, &c.

3. Ibam, *I was going.* — Irem, *that I might go.*

IND.   S. ībăm, ībās, ībăt; P. ībāmŭs, ībātĭs, ībant.
SUBJ.   S. īrĕm, īrēs, īrĕt; P. īrēmŭs, īrētĭs, īrent.

So all the compounds of *eo*, viz.: *adĭbam* — *adīrem*, I was approaching; *antĕĭbam* — *antĕīrem*, I was going before; *inĭbam* — *inīrem*, I was going in; *praeterĭbam* — *praeterīrem*, I was going by; *subĭbam* — *subīrem*, I was undergoing; *transĭbam* — *transīrem*, I was going beyond. The compound *ambio* has *ambĭbam* or *ambiēbam*.

4. Vŏlēbam, *I was willing.* — Vellem, *that I might be willing.*

IND   S. vŏlēbăm, vŏlēbās, vŏlēbăt; P. vŏlēbāmŭs, vŏlēbātĭs, vŏlēbant.

IND.   S. vellĕm, vellĕs, vellĕt; P. vellēmŭs, vellētĭs, vellent.

So the compounds of *volo: malēbam — mallem,* I was preferring, and *nōlēbam — nollem,* I was unwilling.

5. Fĕrēbam, *I was bearing.* — Ferrem, *that I might bear.*

IND.   S. fĕrēbăm, fĕrēbās, fĕrēbăt; P. fĕrēbāmŭs, fĕrēbātĭs, fĕrēbant.

SUBJ. S. ferrĕm, ferrēs, ferrĕt; P. ferrēmŭs, ferrētis, ferrent.

In like manner the compounds of *fĕro: affĕrēbăm — affĕrrĕm,* I was bringing; *aufĕrēbăm — auferrĕm,* I was carrying off, &c.

6. Fīēbam, *I was becoming.* — Fīĕrem, *that I might become.*

IND.   S. fīēbăm, fīēbās, fīēbăt; P. fīēbāmŭs, fīēbātĭs, fīēbant.

SUBJ. S. fīĕrĕm, fīĕrēs, fīĕrĕt; P. fīĕrēmŭs, fīĕrētĭs, fīĕrent.

So also the compounds of *fīo,* viz.: *calefīēbam — calefīĕrem,* I was (being) warmed; *frigefīēbam — frigefīĕrem,* I was made cold; *labefīēbam — labefīĕrem,* I was shaken, &c. (Compare Lesson XXXIII. F. Remark.)

7. Edēbam, *I was eating.* — Edĕrem, *that I might eat.*

IND.   S. ĕdēbam, ĕdēbās, ĕdēbat; P. ĕdēbāmŭs, ĕdēbātĭs, ĕdēbant.

SUBJ. S. ĕdĕrēm or *essem,* ĕdĕrēs or *esses,* ĕdĕrĕt or *esset;* P. ĕdĕrēmŭs or *essēmŭs,* ĕdĕrētĭs or *essētĭs,* ĕdĕrent or *essent.*

8. The imperfect of *queo,* I can, and *nequeo,* I cannot, resembles that of a compound of *eo.* Thus, *quĭbam — quĭrem; nequĭbam — nequĭrem.* Of *āĭo,* I say, the indicative only occurs, *āĭēbam, as, at,* &c. *Inquam,* I say, has only *inquĭēbam (inquĭbam)* and *inquĭēbant.*

9. The preteritives *ōdi,* I hate; *memĭni,* I remember; *nōvi,* I know (am acquainted with); and *consuēvi,* I am accustomed, having a present signification in the perfect, employ the pluperfect in the sense of the imperfect. Thus,

> Odĕram — odissem,* *I was hating.*
> Memĭnĕram — meminissem, *I was remembering.*
> Novĕram — novissem, *I knew (was acquainted with).*
> Consuēvĕram — consuēvissem, *I was accustomed.*

Was I loving?   Egóne amâbam?
You were not loving.   Nôn amábas.
What did he bring us?   Quíd nóbis apportâbat?

---

* The pluperfect is inflected like the imperfect of *sum.* Thus IND. *odĕram, ăs, at; ămus, ātis, ant.* SUBJ. *odissem, ĕs, et; ēmus, ētis, ent.* So the rest.

He was bringing us wine, bread, and meat.	Apportábat nóbis vinum, pánem, et cárnem.
Were ye opening the window?	Aperiebatísne fenéstram?
We were opening it.	Aperiebâmus.
Were they sending us anything?	Númquid nóbis mittébant?
They were sending (you) nothing (whatever).	(Vóbis) níhil quídquam mittébant.
When, while (conjunction).	*Quum, cum* (c. Ind. and Subj.).
Do you listen when (while) I speak?	Auscultâsne, quúm égo lóquor?
Does he stay at home when his father goes out?	Tenétne se dómi, quúm páter éjus in públicum pródit?
He does stay at home.	Ténet sê vêro dómi.
Did you write when (while) I was reading?	Scripsistíne (éo témpore), quúm égo legêbam?
I was writing when you were reading (when you read).	Égo véro scribêbam, quúm tû legísti (légeres).

F. Obs. The conjunction *quum* or *cum*, denoting a relation of time (in the sense *eo tempore, quum*, or *tum, quum*), is commonly followed by the indicative; but when the verb is in the imperfect or pluperfect, it may also stand in the subjunctive.

Did he stay at home when you went out?	Tenuítne sê dómi, quúm tû in públicum prodíbas (prodíres*)?
He did remain at home.	Tenêbat sê dómi.
Did they study when they were at Leipsic?	Dederúntne óperam lítteris, quúm Lípsiae† dégerent (degébant)?
They did study.	Dedêrunt.
What was he doing when you returned home?	Quíd faciêbat, quúm dómum revertísti?
He was playing.	Ludêbat.
Were you at Berlin when I was there?	Erâsne Berolíni eôdem témpore, quum et égo íbi éram (éssem)?
I was not there then.	Égo íbi éo témpore nôn fúi.
Was our friend sleepy when he came home?	Cupidúsne sómni érat amícus nóster, quúm domum vênit (véneret)?
He was sleepy.	(Sómni cúpidus) nôn érat.
What did your brother intend to do?	Quíd fácere fráter túus cogitâbat?
He was intending to go into the country.	Rûs íre cogitâbat.

---

* But the imperfect subjunctive thus employed does not express *duration* or *continuance* of an action or state (as does the indicative), but a mere statement of what has occurred (like the perfect indefinite). Compare *B*. Rem. 5, and also *E*.

† On the genitives *Lipsiae, Berolini, Lutetiae*, &c., see Lesson LVI. *B*.

Were they hearing what we said?	Núm éa, quae díximus, audiébant?
They were not hearing (them).	Nôn audiébant.
Where were those men going whom we saw yesterday?	Quô íbant víri ílli, quôs héri vídimus?
They were going into the garden.	Íbant in hórtos.
Was he accustomed to write better than he spoke? (Cf. B. II.)	Scribebátne mélius quám locûtus est?
He did not write as well.	Scribêbat nôn aéque béne.
What was Socrates wont to say?	Quíd dícere solêbat Sócrates?
He was wont to say that we should know ourselves.	Dicêbat, nôs debêre nôsmet ípsos cognóscere.
Did our ancestors speak Latin?	Núm majóres nostri Latíne loquebántur (lóqui solébant)?
No, they spoke English and German.	Nôn véro; Ánglice et Germánice loquebántur.
Did you come in order to see?	Venistíne, ut vidéres?

G. Obs. When the perfect indefinite is followed by a clause introduced by the conjunction *ut*, or by a relative, the verb of that clause stands in the imperfect subjunctive.*

I did come in order to see.	Égo véro véni, ut vidêrem.
Had he anything to eat?	Habuítne, quod éderet (ésset)?
He had nothing either to eat or to drink?	Nôn habuit, quód éderet aut bíberet.
The boy fell from the roof, so as to break his leg.	Púer de técto décidit, ut crûs frángeret.†

EXERCISE 98.

Was he reading? — He was reading. — At what time? — He was reading this morning, between (*inter*) seven and eight o'clock. — Were you writing when I came home? — I was writing a letter to my brother. — Was he studying when I went out? — He was not studying when you went out, but when you were at the theatre. — Were you working while I was playing? — No, I was playing while you were working. — When was he writing the letter? — He was (engaged in) writing it at midnight. — Was he getting better when you saw him? — He was not getting (any) better. — Where were you, when I was calling the physician? — I was in my garden. — Were you opening the window when I was passing (*praeteribam*)? — I was opening it. — Were the children breaking our glasses? — They were not breaking them. — What did you do when I was going home? — I was reading the book which our friend has lent me. — What did your brother say when you entered his room? — He said nothing. —

* Not by the *perfect* subjunctive, which is generally used only with reference to an action just completed (with the perfect *definite*).

† The perfect *fregerit* would convert this into a statement of what has just occurred: — "The boy *has* (just now) *fallen* from the roof, so that he *has broken* his leg."

R

Were you present at the ball? — I was not present. — Was the boy
diligent? — He was both diligent and well behaved. — Was he able
to walk out this morning? — He was not able. — Were you at home
when I received my money? — I was not at home. — Did he desire
to see his father? — He was desiring to see him very much (*valde*).
— Was the coffee (being) warmed? — It was not being warmed. —
Was he willing to learn Latin? — He was unwilling to do so. — Who
was eating? — Our neighbor was eating and drinking. — Did he come
to see you? — He came in order to see me, and to give me a new
book. — Had you anything to write to your friend, when you were in
the country? — I had many things to write to him. — Have you nothing to eat this morning? — I have nothing. — Were they accustomed
to write as well as they spoke? — They were accustomed to write
better. — Did you speak French when you were in Paris (*Lutetiae*)?
— I spoke French and Latin.

Lesson LI. — PENSUM UNUM ET QUINOUAGE-SIMUM.

OF THE IMPERFECT PASSIVE AND DEPONENT.

A. The imperfect tense of the passive voice is formed
from the active, by changing *m* into *r*. E. g.

1. { IND. amābar, lavābar, apportābar, dūbar.
   { SUBJ. amārer, lavārer, apportārer, dūrer.

2. { IND. monēbar, habēbar, jubēbar, delēbar.
   { SUBJ. monērer, habērer, jubērer, delērer.

3. { IND. legēbar, scribēbar, mittēbar, capiēbar.
   { SUBJ. legērer, scriberer, mittĕrer, capĕrer.

4. { IND. audiēbar, aperiēbar, erudiēbar, puniēbar.
   { SUBJ. audirer, aperirer, erudirer, punirer.

B. The inflection of the imperfect passive is exhibited by the following paradigms: —

FIRST CONJUGATION.

INDICATIVE.	SUBJUNCTIVE.
Amābar, *I was loved.*	Amārer, *that I might be loved.*
SING. ămūbăr	SING. ămārĕr
ămābărĭs *or* -rĕ	ămārĕrĕ *or* -rĭs *
ămābātŭr,	ămārētŭr,

---

* Compare page 162, note *.

PLUR. ămābāmŭr

ămābāmĭnĭ

ămābantŭr.

PLUR. ămārēmŭr

ămārēmĭnĭ

ămārentur.

SECOND CONJUGATION.

INDICATIVE.

Monēbar, *I was reminded.*

SUBJUNCTIVE.

Monērer, *that I might be reminded.*

SING. mŏnēbăr

mŏnēbārĭs *or* -rĕ

mŏnēbātŭr,

PLUR. mŏnēbāmŭr

mŏnēbāmĭnĭ

mŏnēbantŭr.

SING. mŏnērĕr

mŏnērērĕ *or* -rĭs

mŏnērētŭr,

PLUR. mŏnērēmŭr

mŏnērēmĭnĭ

mŏnērentŭr.

THIRD CONJUGATION.

INDICATIVE.

(1.) Legēbar, *I was read.*

SUBJUNCTIVE.

Legĕrer, *that I might be read.*

SING. lĕgēbăr

lĕgēbārĭs *or* -rĕ

lĕgēbātŭr,

PLUR. lĕgēbāmŭr

lĕgēbāmĭnĭ

lĕgēbantŭr.

SING. lĕgĕrĕr

lĕgĕrērĕ *or* -rĭs

lĕgĕrētŭr,

PLUR. lĕgĕrēmŭr

lĕgĕrēmĭnĭ

lĕgĕrentŭr.

(2.) Capiēbar, *I was taken.*

Capĕrer, *that I might be taken.*

SING. căpiēbăr

căpiēbārĭs *or* -rĕ

căpiēbātŭr,

PLUR. căpiēbāmŭr

căpiēbāmĭnĭ

căpiēbantŭr.

SING. căpĕrĕr

căpĕrērĕ *or* -rĭs

căpĕrētŭr,

PLUR. căpĕrēmŭr

căpĕrēmĭnĭ

căpĕrentŭr.

FOURTH CONJUGATION.

INDICATIVE.

Audiēbar, *I was heard.*

SUBJUNCTIVE.

Audirer, *that I might be heard.*

SING. audiēbăr

audiēbārĭs *or* -rĕ

audiēbātŭr,

PLUR. audiēbāmŭr

audiēbāmĭnĭ

audiēbantŭr.

SING. audirĕr

audirērĕ *or* -rĭs

audirētŭr,

PLUR. audirēmŭr

audirēmĭnĭ

audirentŭr.

So conjugate, — 1. *Apportābar*, I was brought; *dăbar*, I was given; *lavābar*, I was washed; *secābar*, I was cut.   2. *Habēbar*, I was held (considered); *delēbar*, I was destroyed; *jubēbar*, I was commanded; *vidēbar*, I was seen (I seemed).   3. *Arcessēbar*, I was called; *dilĭgē-*

bar, I was cherished; *frangēbar,* I was broken; *mittēbar,* I was sent; *ponēbar,* I was put; *scribēbar,* I was written. 4. *Aperīebar,* I was opened; *erudīēbar,* I was instructed; *punīēbar,* I was punished, &c.

REMARK. — Of the irregular verbs given on pp. 270 and 271, *sum, possum, volo,* and their compounds, have no passive voice. Of *eo,* the third person singular *ībātur, īrētur* occurs impersonally.* *Fĕro* and its compounds have *fĕrēbar — ferrer* regularly. The compounds of *facio,* which change the radical *a* into *i,* have a regular imperfect; as, *interficīēbar — interfĭcĕrer,* while those which retain *a* generally take *fĭēbam — fĭērem;* as, *calefĭēbam — calefĭērem.* *Edo* has *edēbar — edĕrer* regularly, except in the third person singular subjunctive, where *essētur* may stand for *edĕrētur.*

Was *I* (being loved)?	Egóne amâbar?
You were not loved, but your brother.	Tû nôn amabâris, sed frâter túus.
Were you and he loved?	Án tû átque ílle amabámini?
We were not loved.	Nôn amabâmur.
Were they despised?	Écquid ílli despicátui habebántur?
They were despised.	Sáne quídem, habebántur.
Was the book (being) read?	Legebatúrne líber?
It was read.	Sic ést; legebâtur.
Did they give you the book to be read?	Dederúntne tíbi líbrum, ut legerê-tur?
No, they gave it to me to be torn.	Ímmo véro míhi éum dedérunt, ut lacerarêtur.
Was the bread brought to be eaten?	Apportatúisne ést pânis, ut ederêtur (essêtur)?
Did ye speak in order to be heard?	Estísne locúti, ut audirémini?
No, we spoke in order to be understood.	Nôn véro; locúti súmus, ut intelli-gerêmur.
Were they (being) killed?	Núm ílli interficiebántur?
They were (being) killed.	Nôn interficiebántur.
Was the coffee (being) warmed?	Calefiebátne coffêa?
It was done.	Fáctum ést véro.

IMPERFECT OF DEPONENT VERBS.

C. The imperfect of deponent verbs follows the analogy of the imperfect passive. Thus:—

INDICATIVE. SUBJUNCTIVE.
1st CONJ. Arbitrābar — arbitrārer, *I was thinking.*
Comitābar — comitārer, *I was escorting.*
Dominābar — dominārer, *I was ruling.*
Hortābar — hortārer, *I was exhorting.*
Morābar — morārer, *I was staying.*

---

* But the transitive compounds *adeo, anteo, ineo, praetereo, subeo,* and *transeo,* have a regular passive voice; as, *adībar — adīrer,* &c.

2d CONJ.   Fatēbar — fatērer, *I was confessing.*
Merēbar — merērer, *I was earning.*
Miserēbar — miserērer, *I was pitying.*
Tuēbar — tuērer, *I was defending.*
Verēbar — verērer, *I was fearing.*

3d CONJ.   Fungēbar — fungěrer, *I was performing.*
Labēbar — laběrer, *I was falling.*
Loquēbar — loquěrer, *I was speaking.*
Obliviscēbar — obliviscěrer, *I was forgetting.*
Sequēbar — sequěrer, *I was following.* ●

4th CONJ.   Blandiēbar — blandīrer, *I was flattering.*
Experiēbar — experīrer, *I was experiencing.*
Largiēbar — largīrer, *I was lavishing.*
Mentiēbar — mentīrer, *I was lying.*
Partiēbar — partīrer, *I was dividing.*

REMARK. — All these are inflected precisely like the examples furnished under *B*. The following phrases will illustrate them still further.

Whom were you exhorting?	Quém hortabâris?
I was exhorting my son.	Égo méum fīlium hortâbar.
Was he escorting his friend?	Núm ílle amícum súum comitabâtur?
He did not escort him.	Éum nôn comitabâtur.
Where were ye staying?	Úbi morabámini?
We were staying in Paris.	Morabâmur Lutétiae.
Were you earning (gaining) any good?	Merebarísne quídquam bóni?
No, I was acquiring less favor than hatred.	Ímmo véro mínus égo favôris quám ódii merébar.
Were we defending your brother?	Écquid nôs frâtrem túum tuebâmur?
Ye were defending him really.	Vôs éum tuebámini profécto.
When did they speak to the tailor?	Quô témpore cum sartôre colloquebántur?
They spoke to him last evening.	Loquebántur cum éo héri vésperi.
Did ye follow any one?	Núm quém (áliquem) sequebámini?
We did not follow any one.	Núllum (néminem) sequebâmur.
Were you flattering any one?	Écquid álicui (cuíquam) blandiebâris?
I was flattering no one.	Blandiêbar némini (núlli).
Were those men lying?	Núm víri ílli mentiebántur?
Not at all, they were not lying.	Nôn véro; mínime mentiebántur.
Did he come in order to talk with us?	Núm ílle vênit, út nobíscum loquerêtur?
No, he rather came to flatter us.	Ímmo véro vênit, ut nóbis blandirêtur.
Did he say when he would come?	Dixítne, quô témpore veníret?
He did say so.	Díxit véro.

24

At first, in the beginning.	Prīmum ; prīmo, a prīmo, in prīmo.
Afterwards, then.	Deinde, post, postea.
Hereupon, upon this.	Deinde, dein ; exinde, exin (adv.).
Did he say yes or no ?	Útrum díxit étiam an nôn ?
At first he said yes, afterwards no.	A prímo díxit étiam, post nôn.
At first he worked, but afterwards he played.	Prīmum laborâvit, deínde aûtem lûsit.
He came afterwards.	Vênit (advênit) póstea.
Upon this (then) he said.	Deínde (exínde) díxit.
Here is your book, and there your paper.	Híc ést líber túus, íllic chárta túa.
Now you must work.	Núnc ést tíbi laborándum.
To-day I do not go out.	Hódie égo in públicum nôn pródeo.
Yesterday my father departed.	Héri páter méus profectus est.

As soon as (conj.).	⎧ Simul ac (atque), simul ut. ⎨ Ubi, quum primum. ⎩ (With the Perf. Indic.)
I am accustomed to drink as soon as I have eaten.	Égo, símul atque édi, bíbere sóleo.
As soon as I have taken off my shoes, I take off my stockings.	Símul út mê excalceávi, tibiália détraho pédibus.
As soon as he heard this, he departed.	Quúm prímum haêc audívit, proféctus est.
What do you usually do after supper ?	Quid post cíbum vespertínum fácere sóles ?
Afterwards I sleep.	Deínde (póstea) dórmio.
To sleep.	Dormĭo, ĭre, ivi (ĭi), ĭtum.
To live ; to be alive.	⎧ Vīvo, ĕre, xi, ctum. ⎨ In vītā esse. Vītā frŭor (frŭi, frŭ- ⎩ ĭtus or fructus sum).
Is your father yet alive ?	⎧ Vivítne páter túus etiámnunc ? ⎨ Éstne páter túus in vítā etiám- ⎩ nunc ?
He is yet (still) alive.	⎧ Est in vítā etiámnunc. ⎨ Vítā frúitur etiámnunc.
He is no longer alive.	⎧ In vítā ést nôn jám. ⎨ Vítā frúitur nôn ámplius.
Is our cousin still sleeping (yet asleep) ?	Dormítne nóster consobrínus etiámnunc ?
He does still sleep.	Dórmit véro etiámnunc.
To give away.	⎧ Abaliēno, āre, āvi, ātum. ⎨ Dono (dat.) dăre (alicui aliquid).
To cut off.	⎧ Ampŭto, āre, āvi, ātum. ⎨ Abscīdo, ĕre, ĭdi, īsum. ⎩ Also, praecidĕre, desecāre, &c.

To cut off one's head.	Alicui cǎput amputāre. Cǎput abscīděre cervicibus alicū̆jus.
To cut one's throat.	Jugulāre alǐquem. Jugǔlum alicui praecīděre.
To cut off one's ears.	Abscīděre (praecīděre) alicui aures.
To cut one's (own) nails.	Resecāre (-sěcui, -sectum) ·ungues.
What (injury) have they done to him?	Quid injúriae éi intulérunt ?
They have cut off his ears.	Abscidérunt éi aúres.
Have they cropped the dog's ears ?	Praeciderúntne aúres cáni ?
They have cropped them.	Praecidérunt.
They have cut off his head.	Amputavérunt éi cáput.
They have cut his throat.	Praecidérunt éi júgulum.
Were you cutting your nails ?	Resecabásne tíbi úngues?
I was not cutting them.	Nòn resecábam.
Has he given away anything ?	Núm quíd abalienâvit? Núm aliquid dóno dédit ?
He has not given away anything.	Níhil abalienâvit. Dóno dédit níhil.
He has given away his coat.	Abalienâvit (dóno dédit) suam tógam.
To arrive.	Advěnio, íre, ēni, entum.
To go away, to go off (from a place).	Aběo, íre, ívi (íi), ítum. Discēdo, ěre, essi, essum. (AB ALIQUO, AB or EX ALIQUO LOCO.)
At length, at last.	Tandem, denǐque, postrēmo (adv.).
Without (prep.).	*Sine* (prep. cum abl.).
Without money, books, friends.	Sine pecúniā, lǐbris, amícis.
Without any danger.	Sine úllo perículo.
Without any doubt.	Sine úlla dubitatióne.
Without speaking.	Nihil dicens, tacens. Verbum non faciens.
Without saying a word.	Ne ûnum quídem vérbum fáciens.
Without having said a word.	Vérbo omníno núllo fácto.
He went away without saying a word.	Ábiit vérbum omníno ·núllum fáciens (vérbo núllo fácto).
Has he arrived at last ?	Advenítne tándem?
He has arrived.	Advênit véro.
He has not yet arrived.	Nóndum advênit.
Are they coming at last ?	Tandémne véniunt ?
They are coming.	Fáctum est.
Loud (adv.).	*Clārē* (adv.), *clārā vŏce*.
Does your master speak loud ?	Magistérne túus cláre lóquitur ?

He does speak loud.	Lóquitur véro cláre.
You must read louder.	Legéndum ést tíbi clárius (vôce claríôre).
In order to learn Latin, one must speak loud.	Sí quís Latíne edíscere vult, necesse est clárä vôce loquâtur.

EXERCISE 99.

Did you intend to learn English ? — I did intend to learn it, but I could not find a good master. — Did your brother intend to buy a carriage ? — He was intending to buy one, but he had no more money. — Why did you work ? — I worked in order to learn Latin. — Why did you love that man ? — I loved him because he loved me. — Have you already seen the son of the captain ? — I have already seen him. — Did he speak English ? — No, he spoke Latin and Greek. — Where were you at that time ? — I was in Italy. — Whom was the master exhorting ? — He was exhorting his scholars. — Were they not considered (*habebantur*) diligent ? — No, they were considered lazy and naughty. — Were you ordered (*juberi*) to go into the country. — I was not ordered to go there. — When was the letter (being) sent ? — It was sent yesterday. — Was the window (being) opened when we were passing ? — It was (being) opened. — Was the master heard when he spoke ? — He was heard, when he spoke loud. — Why was the boy punished ? — He was punished because he was negligent and bad. — Were you able to defend (*tuéri*) your friends ? — I was not able to defend them. — Were they accustomed to flatter you ? — They were accustomed to flatter me. — Did you come in order to flatter me ? — No, I came in order to talk to you. — Is your friend's brother still alive ? — He is still alive. — Are your parents still alive ? — They are no longer alive. — Was your brother still alive, when you were in Germany ? — He was no longer alive. — Were you yet asleep (sleeping), when I came this morning ? — I was asleep no longer. — Was your master accustomed to speak loud ? — He was. — Are you accustomed to speak loud, when you study Latin ? — I am not accustomed (to do so). — Has your cousin at last arrived ? — He has arrived at last. — Are you at last learning French ? — I am learning it at last. — What do you do after breakfast ? — As soon as I have breakfasted, I begin to write my letters. — I take off my clothes as soon as I have taken off my hat. — Do you drink as soon as you have eaten ? — I do. — What did they do after supper ? — They slept afterwards.

Lesson LII. — PENSUM ALTERUM ET QUINQUAGESIMUM.

OF THE USE OF THE INFINITIVE.

A. The infinitive may be regarded as a verbal substantive of the neuter gender singular number, and may as such stand either as the *subject* of a finite verb in the nominative, or as its *object* in the accusative.

REMARK. — The infinitive differs from regular verbal substantives, *a*) by admitting after it the case of the finite verb, and *b*) by indicating, at the same time, the completion or non-completion of the action denoted by the verb, i. e. by representing it as present, past, or future.

I. The infinitive is in the nominative, when it stands as the subject of an intransitive predicate.   E. g.

Béne *sentíre rectéque fácere* sátis ést ad béne beatéque vivéndum.	Good sentiments and correct conduct suffice to constitute a well-regulated and a happy life.
Hóc exitiósius érat quám Vespasiánum *sprevísse.*	This was more pernicious than to have despised Vespasian.
Apud Pérsas súmma laûs est *púlchre venári.*	Among the Persians, to excel in hunting is a matter of the highest praise.
Invidêre (= invidia) nôn cádit in sapiéntem.	Envy is below the character of a philosopher.
Ignóscere amíco humânum est.	To pardon one's friend is human.
Níhil est áliud, *béne et beáte vívere,* nísi *honéste et récte vívere.*	To live well and happily is tantamount to living honorably and correctly.

II. The infinitive stands as the object accusative after transitive or auxiliary verbs, and sometimes after prepositions.   E. g.

Víncere scis, Hánnibal, *victóriâ úti* néscis.	You know how to conquer, Hannibal, but not how to use your victory.
Cúpio té cónsulem *vidêre.*	I desire to see you consul.
Múltum ínterest ínter *dáre* et *accípere.*	There is a great difference between giving and receiving.
Quód crimen dicis, praeter *amâsse, méum?*	What charge have you to make, besides my having loved?
A Graécis Gálli úrbes moénibus *cíngere didicérunt.*	The Gauls learnt the art of surrounding their cities with walls from the Greeks.

24 *

Sólent díu cogitáre ómnes, qui mágna negótia vólunt ágere.

All who wish to accomplish great objects, are accustomed to deliberate long.

Súos quísque débet tuéri.

Every one is bound to defend his own (friends, &c.).

Sallústius státuit rès géstas pópuli Románi perscríbere.

Sallust resolved to write the exploits (history) of the Roman people.

Pompéium et hortári et oráre et monére . . . . nôn desístimus.

We do not cease to exhort and to beseech and to admonish Pompey.

Amícos néque ármis cógere, néque aúro paráre quéas ; offício et fide pariúntur.

You can neither make friends by force of arms, nor procure them with gold ; they are made by an obliging disposition and by fidelity.

OBSERVATIONS.

1. The verbs most commonly followed by the simple infinitive are those signifying, —

a.) WILLINGNESS or UNWILLINGNESS, DESIRE, and the like ; as, *volo, nolo, malo, cupio, studeo, opto,* &c.

b.) ABILITY or INABILITY, KNOWLEDGE or IGNORANCE ; as, *possum, queo, nequeo ; scio, nescio ; valeo ;* to which add *disco* and *debeo.*

c.) COURAGE or FEAR ; as, *audeo ; dubito, metuo, paveo, timeo, vereor.*

d.) HABIT or CUSTOM ; as, *assuesco, consuesco, insuesco, soleo.*

e.) To BEGIN, CONTINUE, CEASE, or REFRAIN ; as *coepi, incipio ; pergo, persevěro ; desino, desisto, intermitto, praetermitto ; recuso,* &c.

f.) PURPOSE or ENDEAVOR ; as, *curo, cogito, decerno, constituo, instituo, statuo, paro ; aggredior, conor, contendo, maturo, nitor, tendo, tento,* &c.

g.) Passive verbs signifying TO BE SAID, REPORTED, CONSIDERED, BELIEVED, &c. ; as, *audior, credor, dicor, existimor, feror, negor, nuntior, perhibeor, putor, trador,* &c. ; also *cogor, jubeor, videor.*

REMARK. — Many of the verbs here enumerated are also followed by the subjunctive, with one of the conjunctions *ut, ne, quo, quomInus,* &c. With some of them the latter construction is even the most common. (Cf. Lesson LIV.)

2. The infinitive is sometimes put after certain nouns, adjectives, and verbs, instead of an oblique case of the gerund. This construction occurs, —

a.) After nouns like *tempus, consilium, studium, animus, ars,* &c. (Cf. page 116.) E. g. *Tempus est majora* conari (= *conandi*), It is time to make greater attempts. *Consilium erat hiemando continuare*

(= *continuandi*) *bellum*, The design was to continue the war by going into winter quarters. *Fuerat animus Cheruscis* juvare (= *juvandi*) *Cattos*, The Cherusci had the intention of aiding the Catti.

b.) After the adjectives *parātus, insuētus, contentus,* and some others.* E. g. *Parātus audire,* Prepared to hear. *Vinci insuetus,* Unaccustomed to be conquered. *Contentus retinēre,* Content to retain.

c.) After the verbs *habēre, dăre,* and *ministrāre,* in expressions like *Nihil* habeo *ad te* scribĕre, I have nothing to write to you. *Ut* bibĕre *sibi jubēret* dari, That (something) should be given them to drink. *Ut Jŏvi* bibere *ministraret,* That he might give Jove to drink.

3. After the auxiliary verbs *volo, malo, nolo, cupio, incipio,* and others enumerated under *Obs.* 1, the noun or adjective of the predicate is in the nominative, when the quality denoted by it is regarded as already existing in the subject; but when the quality is not present, or missing, the infinitive following these verbs has a subject of its own in the accusative,† and the noun or adjective is likewise in the accusative. E. g. *Volo et esse et haberi gratus,* It is my wish both to be grateful and to be considered so. *Vos liberi esse non curatis?* Do you not care to be free? *Judĭcem me esse, non doctorem, volo,* I wish myself to be a judge, and not a teacher. *Ego me Phidiam esse mallem, quam vel optimum fabrum tignarium,* I would rather be a Phidias, than the best joiner in the world. *Timoleon maluit se diligi, quam metui,* Timoleon wanted himself to be loved rather than feared. *Gratum se videri studet,* He strives to have the appearance of being grateful.

4. In historical narration, the infinitive is sometimes used instead of the imperfect indicative. (Cf. Lesson L. B., Rem. 4.)

The coin.	*Nummus, i, m.*
The copper coin.	*Nummus cŭprĕus, i,* m.
The silver coin.	Nummus argentĕus, i, *m.*
The gold coin.	(Nummus) aurĕus *seu* aurĕŏlus, i, *m.*
The as (a copper coin).	As, *gen.* assis, *m.*
The sesterce (silver).	Sestertĭus, i, *m.*
The denarius (silver).	Denārĭus, i, *m.*
The aureus (gold).	Aurĕus, i, *m.*
The obole (Greek coin).	Obŏlus, i, *m.*
The drachma "	Drachma, ae, *f.*
The mina "	Mĭna, ae, *f.*
The talent‡ "	Talentum, i, *n.*
Roman, Greek, English money.	Pecūnĭa Romānōrum, Graecōrum, Anglōrum signo signāta.

---

* Chiefly in imitation of the Greeks; as, *Dignus eligi,* Worthy of being chosen. *Peritus obsequi,* Skilled in the art of yielding. *Utilis aspirare et adesse,* Useful to join and assist.

† Compare Lesson L. A.

‡ The *obolus — talentum* are Greek money, and the *as — aureus* Roman proper. On the full enumeration and value of these, see the Table of Coins in the Lexicon.

To contain, consist of.	Contĭneo, ēre, nŭi, tentum (ALI-QUID).
To be worth, to have the value of.	Effĭcĭor, i, -fectus sum (EX RE). Vāleo, ēre, ŭi, —— (ALIQUA RE).* Valōrem habēre (ALICUJUS REI).
To estimate, reckon.	Aestĭmo, āre, āvi, ātum.

An as is estimated the fourth part of a sesterce.

As quárta pars sestértii aestĭmátur.

The denarius contains four sestertii or sixteen asses.

Denárius quáttuor sestértios vel sédecim ásses cóntinet.

The aureus consists of twenty-five denarii, or one hundred sesterces.

Aúreus (númmus) effĭcitur ex quínque et vigínti denáriis vel céntum sestértiis.

A drachma has the value of six oboles.

Úna dráchma valōrem hábet sex obolōrum.

A hundred drachmas make a mina.

Céntum dráchmae mínam únam effĭciunt.

A talent contains sixty minas.

Taléntum válet sexagínta mínis.

How many groshes are there in a crown?

Ex quót gróssis effĭcitur thalērus?

Twenty-four.

Ex quáttuor et vigínti.

The grosh (modern).

Grossus, i, m.

To receive — received.

Accipĕre — accēpi, acceptum.

How much money have you received?

Quántam pecúniam accepisti?

I have received thirty talents of gold.

Accépi trigínta talénta aúri.

We have received a hundred sestertii.

Nôs céntum sestértios accépimus.

Have you received letters?
I have received some.

Écquid epístolas accepísti?
Accépi véro nonnúllas.

To promise.	*Promitto, ĕre, mīsi, missum.* *Polliceor, ēri, cĭtus sum.* (ALICUI ALIQUID *or* INFIN.)

Have I promised you anything?
You have promised me nothing.

Promisíne tíbi áliquid (quídquam)?
Tû míhi níhil réi promisísti (pollícitus és).

Do you promise to come to me?
I do promise it.

Pollicerísne tê ad mê ventúrum?
Sáne quídem, pollíceor.

Can he give us what he has promised?

Potéstne nóbis dáre quod promísit?

He can give you all that he has promised you.

Pótest vóbis dáre omnia, quae promísit.

To call.	Vŏco, āre, āvi, ātum (ALIQUEM). Arcesso, ĕre, īvi, ītum (ALIQUEM).

* Verbs of valuing are followed by the Ablative.

To wear out.	{ Dētĕro, ĕre, trīvi, trītum (ALIQUID). { Usū conterĕre, trīvi, trītum.
To spell.	Ordināre syllăbas litterārum.
How? In what way or manner?	*Quōmŏdo, quō pactō, quemadmŏdum, quī.*
Thus.	Sĭc, ĭtă (adv.).
In this manner.	Hōc mŏdo, ad hunc modum, hōc pacto.
Well.	Bĕne, rectē (*adv.*).
Badly.	Mălē, nēquīter (*adv.*).
So so, indifferently.	Sic sătis, mediocriter, utcunque.
Does he already know how to spell?	Scītne (didicītne) jám syllabas litterārum ordināre?
He does know how.	Scīt vēro. Dídicit.
How (in what manner) did you learn Latin?	Quemádmodum didicísti línguam Latīnam?
I have learnt it so.	Dídici éam hōc pácto.
How did I write my letters?	Quómodo scrípsi égo epístolas méas?
You have written them so so.	Scripsísti éas sic sátis.
Has she washed the shirt well?	Lāvītne illa indúsium béne?
She has washed it not badly.	Lâvit id nôn mále.
Whom do you call?	Quém vócas (cítas)?
I am calling my little brother.	Fratérculum méum vóco (cíto).
How (who) are you called?	Quómodo (quís) vocâris?
I am called a learner.	{ Vócor discípulus. { Aúdio discípulus.
Has he worn out his coat?	Detrivítne súam tógam?
To lie, to be placed.	{ Jăceo, ĕre, ŭi, ĭtum. { Posĭtum or situm esse. (IN or SUPER ALIQUA RE).
· *To lay place, put.*	{ Pōno, ĕre, pŏsŭi, pŏsĭtum. { Imp onĕre, reponĕre. † { Collŏco, āre, āvi, ātum. (ALIQUID IN or SUPER RE.)
To dry (*neuter*).	Siccesco, ĕre, ——, ——. •
To dry, make dry.	Sicco, āre, āvi, ātum.
To put out to dry.	Expōnĕre aliquid in sole siccandi causā (ut siccescat).
Where did you put the book?	Ŭbi (quô lóco) líbrum imposuísti?
I have placed it upon the table.	Impósui éum mensae (in mensam).‡
Where have they put my gloves?	Ŭbi posuérunt méa digitábula?

---

* An old ablative for *quô.*

† And various other compounds; as, *adponĕre,* to place near; *deponĕre,* to put down; *disponĕre,* to place apart; *exponĕre,* to spread out; *reponĕre,* *supponĕre,* to place under.

‡ The construction of *imponĕre* is ALICUI REI, IN REM, or IN RE.

They have placed them (in order) upon the chair.	Collocavérunt éa in séllä.
Where lies the book?	Úbi est pósitus líber?
It lies upon the table.	Pósitus est in (super) ménsä.
It has lain upon the table.	Pósitus érat in (super) ménsä.
Have you put wood upon the hearth?	Reposuistíne lígnum súper fóco?
I have put a little upon it.	Repósui véro aliquántulum.
Do you put out your coat to dry?	Exponísne túam tógam in sóle, ut siccéscat?
I do put it out.	Íta ést, expóno.
Have they put their stockings to dry?	Écquid in sóle exposuérunt tibiália súa, ut siccéscěrent?
They have not.	Nôn exposuérunt.

EXERCISE 100.

Hast thou promised anything? — I have promised nothing. — Do you give me what you have promised me? — I do give it to you. — Have you received much money? — I have received but little. — How much have you received of it? — I have received but one crown. — When have you received your letter? — I have received it to-day. — Hast thou received anything? — I have received nothing. — What have we received? — We have received long letters. — Do you promise me to come to the ball? — I do promise you to come to it. — Does your ball take place to-night? — It does take place. — How much money have you given to my son? — I have given him fifteen crowns. — Have you not promised him more? — I have given him what I have promised him. — Have our enemies received their money? — They have not received it. — Have you Roman money? — I have some. — What kind of money (*quid nummórum*) have you? — I have asses, sesterces, denarii, and aurei. — How many asses are there in a sesterce? — There are four. — What is the value of an aureus? — An aureus is worth a hundred sesterces. — Have you any German money? — I have crowns, florins, kreuzers, groshes, and deniers. — How many groshes are there in a florin? — A florin contains sixteen groshes, or sixty kreuzers. — Have you any oboles? — I have a few of them. — How many oboles are there in a drachma? — A drachma contains six oboles. — The silver mina (*mina argenti*) of the Greeks had the same value as the Roman denarius. — How many minas are there in a talent? — The talent contains sixty minas. — Will you lend your coat to me? — I will lend it to you; but it is worn out. — Are your shoes worn out? — They are not worn out. — Will you lend them to my brother? — I will lend them to him. — To whom have you lent your hat? — I have not lent it; I have given it to somebody. — To whom have you given it? — I have given it to a pauper.

EXERCISE 101.

Does your little brother already know how to spell? — He does know. — Does he spell well? — He does spell well. — How has your little boy spelt? — He has spelt so so. — How have your children written their letters? — They have written them badly. — Do you know Spanish? — I do know it. — Does your cousin speak Italian? — He speaks it well. — How do your friends speak? — They do not speak badly (*non male*). — Do they listen to what you tell them? — They do listen to it. — How hast thou learnt English? — I have learnt it in this manner. — Have you called me? — I have not called you, but your brother. — Is he come? — Not yet. — Where have you wet your clothes? — I have wet them in the country. — Will you put them to dry? — I will put them to dry. — Where have you put my hat? — I have put it upon the table. — Hast thou seen my book? — I have seen it. — Where is it? — It lies upon your brother's trunk. — Does my handkerchief lie upon the chair? — It does lie upon it. — When have you been in the country? — I was there the day before yesterday. — Have you found your father there? — I have found him there. — What has he said? — He has said nothing. — What have you been doing in the country? — I have been doing nothing there.

Lesson LIII. — PENSUM QUINQUAGESIMUM TERTIUM.

OF THE ACCUSATIVUS CUM INFINITIVO.

A. The infinitive may have a subject of its own in the accusative, but is then rendered into English by a separate clause introduced by the conjunction " that." E. g.

Órpheum poêtam dócet Aristóteles núnquam *fuísse.*	Aristotle informs us, *that* the poet Orpheus never *existed.*
An nesciêbam vítae *brévem ésse* cúrsum, glóriae *sempitérnum?*	Or was I not aware, *that* the career of life *is* short, and that of glory eternal?
Spéro *nóstram amicítiam* nòn egêre téstibus.	I hope, *that* our friendship *does* not *stand in need of* any witnesses.
Egóne *mê audivísse* áliquid ét didicísse nòn gaúdeam?	May I not rejoice, *that I have heard and learnt* something?

B. The *accusativus cum infinitivo* may, like the simple infinitive, stand either as the subject of a finite verb in the nominative, or as its object in the accusative.

I. The accusative with the infinitive stands as the *subject* of a sentence, when the predicate is an impersonal verb, or the copula *est*, *fuit*, &c. with a noun or adjective.   E. g.

Légem brévem ésse opórtet, quô . | A law should be brief, so that it
facílius ab imperítis teneâtur. | may be more easily remembered by the uneducated.

Ómnibus bónis éxpedit sálvam ésse rempúblicam. | It is for the advantage of all good citizens, that the republic should be safe.

Fácinus ést, vincíri cívem Românum; scélus, verberári; prope parricídium, necári. | It is audacity to have a Roman citizen bound; * it is a crime to have him beaten; it is almost parricide to have him killed.

Témpus ést, nôs de íllâ perpétuâ jám, nôn de hâc exíguâ vítâ, cogitâre. | It is time that we should already think of that perpetual life, and not of this brief one.

Áliud ést iracúndum ésse, áliud irâtum. | It is one thing to be irascible, and another to be angry.

Necésse ést légem habéri in rêbus óptimis. | The law must be reckoned among our best possessions.

Victórem párcere víctis aêquum ést. | It is just that the conqueror should spare the conquered.

Cónstat profécto ad salûtem cívium invéntas ésse léges. | It is manifest, that the laws were invented solely for the safety of the citizens.

REMARKS.

1. The accusative, with the infinitive thus used as the subject of a sentence, is equivalent to a noun in the nominative case, and may sometimes be converted into one. E. g. *Salvam esse rempublicam = salus reipublicae. Legem brevem esse oportet = legum brevitas necessaria est,* &c.

2. The predicates most frequently employed in this construction are:— *apertum, consentaneum, aequum, justum, verisimile,* &c. *est,* it is manifest, proper, fair, just, probable (i. e. that such a thing should happen or be done);—*tempus, mos, facinus, fas,* &c. *est,* it is time, customary, a crime, right, &c.;— the impersonal verbs *apparet,* it is apparent; *constat,* it is agreed; *licet,* it is lawful; *oportet,* it behooves; *opus est,* there is need; *necesse est,* it is necessary;— or the third person singular of passive verbs, as *intelligitur,* it is understood; *perspicitur,* it is perceived, &c.

II. The *accusativus cum infinitivo* stands as the *object-accusative* after the following classes of verbs :—

1. As the object of a sensation, perception, or emotion, after verbs signifying *to see, hear, feel, perceive, understand, think,*

---

* Literally, " That a Roman citizen should be bound," &c. But in this construction it is often preferable to use the active infinitive in English: *to bind a Roman,* &c.

know, believe, hope, and the like,* and also those denoting *joy, sorrow, shame, anxiety,* and *wonder.* E. g.

Vúles nôs, si íta sít, *privári* spê beatióris vítae.	You see that, if that is so, we are deprived of the hope of a better life.
Séntit ánimus *sê* súã vi, nôn aliénã, *movéri.*	The mind feels that it is moved by its own energy, and not by an extraneous one.
Pompéios desedísse térrae mótū *audivimus.*	We have heard that Pompeii was destroyed by an earthquake.
Éum *tê ésse fínge,* quí égo súm.	Imagine yourself to be the person, which I am.
Égo *íllum periísse dúco,* cuí périit púdor.	I consider him lost, whose shame is gone.
Spérant, sê máximum frúctum *ésse captúros.*	They hope that they will get the greatest advantage.
Cónscius míhi *éram, níhil* a mê *commíssum ésse,* quód bóni cujúsquam offénderet ánimum.	I was conscious that nothing had been done by me to offend the mind of any honorable man.
Méum fáctum probári abs tê *triúmpho gaúdio.*	I triumph with joy that my deed is approved by you.
Dóleo, nôn mê túis lítteris *certiórem fíeri.*	I am sorry that I am not informed by your letter.
Mínime mirâmur, tê túis praecláris opéribus *laetári.*	We do not at all wonder that you exult in your distinguished deeds.

2. As the object of a volition, after verbs signifying *to wish, desire, resolve, permit, command, compel, prohibit,* or *prevent.* E. g.

Tíbi favêmus, *tê* túã *frui* virtúte *cupimus.*	We favor you, and desire you to enjoy your virtue.
Útrum córporis, án tíbi *málles víres* ingénii *dári ?*	Which would you prefer (to be given you), strength of body or of intellect ?
Rém ad árma *dedúci studêbat.*	It was his endeavor that the matter should be decided by force.
Postulábimus nóbis *íllud concédi.*	We will demand that that should be conceded to us.
Júbet nôs Pýthius Apóllo *nóscere* nôsmet ípsos.	Pythian Apollo commands us to know ourselves.
Germáni *vínum* ad sê omníno *importári* nôn *sínunt.*	The Germans do not allow, on any account, the importation of wine among them.
Aristóteles *vérsum* in oratiône *vétat ésse,* númerum *júbet.*	Aristotle prohibits the use of verse in a discourse, but commands the rhythm.

---

* As, for example, *audio, video, sentio, animadverto, cognosco, intelligo, percipio, disco, scio, duco, statuo, memini, recordor, obliviscor,* and in general all the *verba sensuum et affectuum.*

S   25

3. After *verba declarandi*, or those signifying *to say, write, report, confess, deny, pretend, promise, prove, convince,* &c.* E. g.

Thales Milesius *áquam díxit esse* inítium rêrum.	Thales, the Milesian, said that water was the first principle of things.
Heródotus *scribit* Croesi *fílium,* cum ésset ínfans, *locútum* (sc. *ésse*).	Herodotus writes that the son of Crœsus spoke when he was an infant.
Solon *sê fúrere simulávit.*	Solon pretended to be a madman.
Confíteor, mê abs tê *cupísse* laudári.	I confess that I desired to be praised by you.
Dicaeárchus *vúlt efficere, ánimos ésse* mortáles.	Dicæarchus wants to make out that souls are mortal.
Pollicêtur Piso, *sése* ad Caésarem *itúrum* (sc. *esse*).	Piso promises that he will go to Cæsar.
Mágnum sólem ésse philósophus *probábit,* quántus sit, mathemáticus.	The philosopher will prove that the sun is large, but the mathematician (will show) how large it is.
Isócratem Plato .... *laudári fêcit* a Sócrate.	Plato represents Isocrates as commended by Socrates.

C. The infinitive, either with or without a subject accusative, may stand as the *appositum* of a noun, adjective, or demonstrative pronoun. E. g.

Haêc benígnitas étiam réi públicae est útilis, *rédimi* e servitúdine *cáptos, locupletári tenuióres.*	This is also a bounty of advantage to the commonwealth: to redeem captives from servitude, and to enrich the poorer classes.
In cognitióne et sciéntiâ *excéllere, pulchrum* putámus.	We consider it honorable to excel in knowledge and learning.
Íllud sóleo mirári, nôn *me* tóties *accípere* túas lítteras, quóties a frátre méo afferántur.	I am accustomed to wonder at it (at this), that I should not hear as often from you, as I do from my brother.
Id injustíssimum ípsum est, justítiae mercêdem *quaérere.*	It is the highest degree of injustice to make a trade of justice.

D. In impassioned exclamations and interrogations the accusative with the infinitive sometimes stands independently as the object of the emotion or passion expressed by it. E. g.

Mêne incepto *desístere* víctum ?	Shall *I,* vanquished, desist from my purpose ?

---

* The principal verbs of this class are *dico, trado, prodo, scribo, refero, nuntio, confirmo, nego, ostendo, demonstro, perhibeo, polliceor, promitto, spondeo,* &c. To these add *facère,* "to represent," and *efficere,* "to make out or prove."

Mê nôn cum bónis *esse?*	I not among the good and patriotic!
Tûne hóc, *Átti, dicere,* táli prúdéntiâ praéditum?	You say this, Attius, a man of prudence like your own!
O spectáculum míserum atque acérbum! Ludíbrio *esse* urbis *glóriam* et pópuli Románi *nômen!*	O wretched and mortifying sight! The glory of the city, the name of the Roman people, an object of derision!

REMARKS.

1. After verbs of seeing and hearing, the present participle* or *ut* ("how"), with the subjunctive, is sometimes put instead of an infinitive, and the verbs of joy, sorrow, &c. are also followed by the subjunctive, with QUOD ("that" *or* "because").†

2. After verbs of seeing and hearing, the present infinitive may frequently be rendered into English by the present participle. E. g. *Mugire* (= *mugientem*) *vidêbis sub pedibus terram,* You will perceive the earth quaking beneath your feet. *Majores natu audivi dicere* (= *dicentes*), I have heard those older than myself say. *Incustodĭtam lente videt ĭre* (= *euntem*) *juvencam,* He sees the untended heifer walking slowly.

3. After one of the past tenses, the accusative with the *present* infinitive is equivalent to the English *imperfect,* and the accusative with the *perfect* infinitive to the English *pluperfect.* E. g. *Vĭdi te scrībere,* I saw that you were writing. *Vĭdi te scripsisse,* I saw that you had written. *Dixit Cajum laudāri,* He said that Cajus was (then) praised. *Dixit Cajum laudātum esse,* He said that Cajus had been praised.

4. The verb *memĭni,* "I remember," is commonly followed by the present infinitive, even when the act denoted by the latter is already completed. E. g. *Memini Pamphĭlum mihi narrare,* I remember Pamphilus telling me (that Pamphilus told me). *Memĭni Catōnem mecum disserrēre,* I remember Cato discussing the question with me (to have discussed, &c.). — But also by the perfect: *Meministis me ita distribuisse initio causam,* You remember that in the beginning I have made this distribution of my argument.

5. After the expressions *satis mihi est, satis habeo, contentus sum,* and also after *me juvat, me pudet, melius erit, volo caveo,* &c., the perfect infinitive is put to denote the result and estimate of a completed action, where the English idiom more commonly has the present. E. g. *Contenti simus, id unum dixisse,* Let us be content to have said (to say) this one thing. *Melius erit quiesse,* It will be better to have rested (= to rest). *Sunt qui nolint tetigisse,* There are those who are unwilling to have touched (= to touch). *Commisisse cavet,* He bewares to commit, &c.

6. The present infinitive is sometimes put instead of the future. E. g. *Nervii, quae imperarentur, facere* ‡ *dixerunt,* The Nervii said, that

---

* See Lesson XLIX. F. Rem. 3.   ‡ Instead of *se facturos* (*esse*).
† Cf. Lesson LIV. *H.*

they would do whatever they were commanded. *Cato affirmat, se rivo Pontinium non triumphare,** Cato affirms that, while he is alive, Pontinius shall not triumph.

7. The infinitive passive of neuter verbs may stand impersonally without a subject, precisely like the third person singular passive of that class of verbs. E. g. *His persuadēri non potĕrat,* They could not be persuaded. *Quum posses jam suspicari, tibi esse successum,* When you might already suspect that you had been supplanted.

8. When, instead of the future infinitive, the formula *futurum esse, ut,* or *fore, ut* † is employed, the perfect and imperfect subjunctive following the *ut* represent the future action as incomplete or going on, while the perfect and pluperfect represent it as completed. E. g. *Credo fore, ut scribas,* I think that you will write. *Credēbam fore, ut scrihĕres,* I thought that you would be writing. *Credo fore, ut scripsĕris,* I think you will have written. *Credebam fore, ut scripsisses,* I thought you would have written.

9. The majority of the *verba sentiendi et declarandi* (cf. *B.* II. 1 and 3), which in the active voice are followed by the *accusativus cum infinitivo,* are in the passive voice followed by the infinitive alone, with the subject accusative in the nominative. But when they are employed impersonally, the subject accusative remains as in the active. E. g. Active : *Dico te esse patrem patriae.* Passive : (*Tu*) *dicĕris esse pater patriae.* Pass. Impers : *Dicĭtur, te esse patrem patriae* (It is said, that you are the father of your country). Pass. Personal : *Numa Pythagŏrae audĭtor fuisse credĭtur* (Numa is supposed to have been a hearer of Pythagoras). Impers. : *Credĭtur,*‡ *Pythagorae audĭtōrem fuisse Numam* (It is supposed that, &c.).

10. When the infinitive, preceded by a subject-accusative, is followed by another accusative of the object, it is liable to give rise to an ambiguity, which may be avoided by converting the infinitive active into the passive. Thus the oracular *Aio, te Romānos vincĕre posse* (I say, that you can conquer the Romans, or that they can conquer you), loses its ambiguity in *Aio, te a Romanis vinci posse,* or *Aio, Romanos a te vinci posse.*

11. The infinitive *esse* is frequently left unexpressed, especially in the compound infinitives *amatum, amatūrum,* and *amandum esse.* (Cf. Lesson XLVIII. *A.* and *B.*) E. g. *Lycurgus auctorem* (sc. esse) *legum Apollinem Delphicum fingit,* Lycurgus makes Delphic Apollo the inventor of laws.

12. The pronominal subject accusatives *me, te, se, eum, nos, vos, eos,* and the indefinite *aliquem,* are frequently omitted when they can be readily understood from the context. E. g. *Ea, quae dicam, non de memetipso, sed de oratore dicĕre* (= *me dicĕre*) *putētis,* I wish you to

---

* *Non triumphaturum.*
† Compare Lesson XLVIII. *B.* Rem. 1.
‡ The verbs of this class thus used impersonally are comparatively few. The most conspicuous of them are *nuntiātur, tradĭtur, credĭtur, intelligĭtur; dicĭtur, narrātur, fertur, prodĭtur, memoratur, cernĭtur, vidētur.*

think, that what I have to say I do not say with reference to myself, but with reference to the orator. *Subduc cibum unum diem athletae, ferre non posse* (= *se* non posse) *clamābit*, Deprive an athlete of his usual food for a single day, and he will declare that he cannot endure it. *Negāto sane, si voles, pecuniam accepisse* (= *te* accepisse), Deny then, if you will, that you have received money. *Hos clam Xerxi remīsit, simulans ex vinculis publicis* effugisse (= *eos* effugisse), These he sent back to Xerxes, under the pretence that they had escaped from prison.

Exercise 102.

Is it just that I should write (for me to write) ? — It is just. — It is not proper that you do this. — It is manifest that he has written the letter. — Is it probable (*verisimile*) that he has sent us the book ? — It is not probable. — Is it time that we should leave (*abire*) ? — It is not yet time to leave ; it is time to breakfast. — Is it right for me to go to the ball ? — It is not right. — Was it a crime to have a Roman citizen bound ? — It was a most audacious (*audacissimum*) crime. — Is it apparent that he was wrong (*erravisse*) ? — It is not apparent. — It is agreed (*constat*) that you have been wrong, and I right. — Did it behoove you to work ? — It did not behoove me to work, but it behooved you to write. — Is it necessary for us to learn Latin ? — It is necessary. — Is it lawful for us to go the theatre ? — It is now lawful. — Is it understood that he has arrived (*advenisse*) ? — It is understood that he arrived the day before yesterday. — It is understood that he will arrive (*adventurum esse*) to-morrow. — Is it necessary for me to write ? — It is necessary, but your letter should be brief.

Exercise 103.

Do you see that I am writing ? — I do see (it). — Did he see that we were coming ? — He did not see it. — Did they hear that I was reading (me reading) ? — They did not hear you. — Does he hear that I have written to you ? — He does hear (it). — Do you wonder that I should exult in your deeds ? — I do not wonder at all. — Does he feel that he is mortal (*mortālis*) ? — He does feel it. — Does he hope that you will come ? — He hopes that I will remain at home. — Do you believe that he will read your book ? — I do not believe that he will read it. — Do you know that that is so (*rem ita se habere*) ? — I do not know it positively (*non certe*), but I believe it to be so. — Are you glad that he has recovered his health ? — I am very glad (of it). — I am sorry that he is ill. — Does he desire you to send him the book ? — He does not desire me to send the book, but the paper. — Do you wish me to go off (*abire*) into the country ? — No, I wish you to remain in the city (*in urbe*). — Does he command us to write ? — He does not command us to write, but to read the books which he has lent us. — Does he forbid you (*vetátne te*) to go to the theatre ? — He does not forbid me. — Do you command me to know myself ? — I do command (you). — Did he say that he was ill ? — He said that he was thirsty. — Do they write that we have arrived ? — They do not write (it). — Do you deny (*negásne*) that I am right ? — I do not wish

25*

to deny it. — Do you confess that you were wrong ? — I deny that I was wrong. — Did he pretend to be asleep (*se dormire*) ? — He did pretend (it). — Did he promise to come (*se venturum*) ? — He could not promise (it).

Lesson LIV. — PENSUM QUINQUAGESIMUM QUARTUM.

VERBS WITH THE INFINITIVE OR SUBJUNCTIVE.

A. Many Latin verbs admit of a double construction, being sometimes followed by the *accusativus cum infinitivo*, and sometimes by the subjunctive, with one of the conjunctions *ut* (*uti*), *ne*, or *quod*, &c. With some of these the subjunctive is the rule and the infinitive the exception; with others the reverse is true. The construction of these verbs is elucidated in the following rules : —

B. Of the verbs signifying willingness, desire, or permission, *vŏlo*, *nōlo*, *mālo*, *patĭor*, and *sĭno* are commonly followed by the accusative with the infinitive, and sometimes only by *ut ;* but *opto*, *concēdo*, and *permitto* may have either the infinitive or *ut.* Verbs of demanding or compelling (*posco*, *postŭlo*, *flagĭto*, and *cōgo*) are more frequently construed with *ut.* E. g.

Vŏlo, *úti* mihi *respóndeas* (*instead of* Vŏlo te mĭhi respondēre).	I wish you to reply to me.
Ópto, tê hóc fácere, *or ut* hóc *fá-cias.*	I desire you to do this.
Augústus dóminum *sê appellári ne* a líberis quídem *pássus est.*	Augustus did not suffer it, even from his children, to be called master.
Tribúni plêbis *póstulant, ut* sacro-sáncti *habeántur.*	The tribunes demand the privilege of being regarded sacrosanct.
Senâtus P. Léntulum, *ut se abdi-câret* praetúrā, *coêgit.*	The senate compelled Publius Len-tulus to resign his praetorship.

REMARK. — *Volo ut* and *malo ut* may thus be employed instead of the infinitive ; but *nōlo ut* is never said. The verb *recusāre*, to refuse, (the opposite of *concedo*,) may have either the infinitive or *ne*.

C. Verbs denoting a *resolve* or *endeavor* to accomplish or prevent anything, are followed by the subjunctive with *ut* or *ne*, when a new subject is introduced; but when the subject remains the same, they generally have the infinitive, and sometimes only *ut* or *ne*.

Verbs of this class are *statuo, constituo, decerno, tento, paro, meditor, curo, nitor, contendo,* and the expressions *consilium capio, in animum duco* or *animum induco.* But *operam do,* I endeavor; *id (hoc, illud) ago,* I aim at, strive; *nihil antiquius habeo* (or *duco*), *quam,* I have (consider) nothing more important than; and *video,* in the sense of *curo,* have commonly *ut* only. E. g.

Státuit ad tê lítteras dáre (or *ut* lítteras ad tê *dét*).	He resolves to write to you.
Státuit, *ut* fílius éjus tíbi respóndeat.	He resolves that his son shall reply to you.
Qui sapiéntes appellári vólunt, indúcant ánimum divítias, honóres, ópes contémnere.	Let those who wish to be called philosophers make up their minds to despise wealth, honors, and influence.
Ópera dánda est, *ut* vérbis utámur quám usitatíssimis et quám máxime áptis.	It should be our study to employ the most familiar and (at the same time) the most suitable terms.
Ómne ánimal sê ípsum díligit, ac símul út órtum est, *id ágit, ut* sê consérvet.	Every animal loves itself, and as soon as it is born aims at the preservation of itself.
Id studuísti, ísti fórmae *ut* móres consímiles fórent.	It has been your endeavor, that your character should be like your appearance.
Vuléndum ést ígitur, *ut* eâ liberalitâte utâmur, quae prôsit amícis, nóceat némini.	We must see to it, that the liberality we indulge in be such, as will be a benefit to our friends and an injury to no one.

D. Verbs of *requesting, exhorting, persuading,* and *commanding* generally have the subjunctive with *ut* or *ne;* but sometimes also the infinitive.

The most common of these verbs are *rogo, oro, precor, peto; moneo, admoneo, commoneo, hortor, adhortor, cohortor, exhortor; suadeo, persuadeo, impello, perpello, excito, incito, impero.* So also *nuntio, dico, scribo,* when they imply an order or command. E. g.

Tê et óro et *hórtor ut* díligens sis.	I beseech and exhort you to be diligent.
Tê íllud *admóneo, ut* quotídie *meditêre,* resistendum ésse iracúndiae.	I advise you to consider every day that passion must be resisted.
Móneo obtestórque, *uti* hôs, qui tíbi génere propínqui súnt, cúros hábeas.	I remind and conjure you to cherish those who are akin to you by birth.
Senâtus *imperâvit* decémviris, *ut* líbros Sibyllínos *inspícerent.*	The senate ordered the committee of ten to inspect the Sibylline records.
Caêsar Dolabéllae *dixit, ut* ad mê	Cæsar told Dolabella to write to

scríberet, *ut* in Itáliam quám primum *venìrem*.	me (requesting me) to come to Italy as soon as possible.
Themístocles *persuásit* pópulo, *ut* pecúniá públicä clássis céntum návium *aedificarêtur*.	Themistocles prevailed upon the people to construct a fleet of a hundred ships at the expense of the public treasury.

REMARKS.

1. With the verbs of this class, the longer construction with *ut* is preferred by the prosaists of the best period, but later writers have more frequently the briefer infinitive.

2. *Monĕo, admonĕo,* and *persuadĕo,* when they signify " to remind or to persuade that something *is so* " (and not " that something *should be done* ") have the Acc. cum Inf.

3. The verbs of *commanding* (i. e. *imperāre, mandāre, praescríbĕre, edícĕre, decernĕre,* &c.) that anything *should be done,* have generally *ut* according to the rule. The only exceptions are *jubĕo* and *vĕto,* which are commonly followed by the *accusatire with the infinitire* (either active or passive). E. g. *Jubeo te scríbere,* I command you to write. *Vetat eum abíre,* He tells him not to leave. *Librum lĕgi jussit,* He ordered the book to be read (i. e. that it should be read). *Vetuit castra munīri,* He prohibited that the camp should be fortified.*

E. Verbs signifying *to effect, cause,* or *bring about,* are regularly followed by the subjunctive with *ut* or *ne.*

Such are *facio, efficio, perficio, evinco, pervinco, impetro, assequor,* and *consequor.* E. g.

Fácito ut scíam.	Let me know.
Sol *éfficit, ut* ómnia *flóreant.*	The sun causes all things to flourish.
Epaminóndas *perfécit ut* auxílio sociôrum Lacedaemónii *priva-réntur.*	Epaminondas caused the Lacedæmonians to be deprived of the aid of the allies.
A sólo ímpetrat, *ut* aliénas árbores *álat.*	He prevails upon the soil to grow exotic trees.
Quâ in rê níhil áliud *assequêris,* nísi *ut* ab ómnibus audácia túa cognoscâtur.	By which you will gain nothing else, except that your audacity will be known by all.

REMARKS.

1. The expression *facere ut* is sometimes a mere circumlocution for the same tense of the verb following it. E. g. *Fēcit, ut dimitteret milĭtes,* instead of *dimĭsit milĭtes,* He dismissed his men.

2. *Fac,* in the sense of " imagine " or " suppose," and *efficĕre,* " to

---

* Yet *jubeo ut hoc facias* (or without the *ut:* — *jubeo tibi hoc facias*) and *veto ne hoc facias* likewise occur in harmony with the general rule.

make out" or " to prove," have the Acc. cum Inf.* But *efficĭtur,*
" it follows," has sometimes *ut ;* as, *Ex quo efficĭtur, ut,* From which
it follows that, &c. *Facĕre,* " to represent," is usually connected
with the present participle or the infinitive passive.†

F. Among the verbs regularly followed by the subjunctive
with *ut,* are a number of impersonal expressions. They are, —

1. Those signifying "it remains," " it follows "; as, *restat, relinquĭtur,
superest, reliquum (proxĭmum, prope, extrēmum, futūrum) est,* and *sequi-
tur.* To these may be added *accēdit ut,** " add to this, that."

2. Those signifying " it happens," " it comes to pass "; as, *accĭdit,
incĭdit, fit, fieri non potest, evēnit, usu vēnit, occurrit, contingit, est,* " it is
the case," and *esto,* " grant it, that."

Restat, ut his respóndeam.	It remains now for me to reply to these.
Si haec enuntiátio nôn vêra est, *séquitur, ut* fálsa sit.	If this proposition is not true, it follows that it is false.
Relinquĭtur, ut, si víncimur in Hispániā, quiescāmus.	If we are vanquished in Spain. the only thing left us is to keep quiet.
Fórte *evēnit, ut* in Privernāte essēmus.	It so happened that we were on the Privernan estate.
Fieri nôn pótest, *ut* quis Rómae sit, quum est Athénis.	It is not possible for any one to be at Rome when he is at Athens.
Quándo *fúit, ut,* quod lícet, nôn líceret?	When was it the case, that that which is lawful was unlawful?

REMARKS.

1. Like *reliquum est, ut,* we sometimes find other expressions with
ut. Such are *novum est, rarum, naturale, mĭrum, singulare, usitatum,
necesse est, ut ; verisimile, rerum, falsum est, ut ; aequum, rectum, utile
est, ut.* But the majority of these are more commonly construéd
with the infinitive. (Cf. Lesson LIII. *B.* I.)

2. *Mos* or *moris est,* and *consuetudo est,* " it is customary," " it usually happens," are often followed by *ut,* like *accidit,* &c.

3. *Contingit* not unfrequently occurs with the infinitive, sometimes
even with the dative of the predicate. E. g. *Mihi fratrique meo* desti-
nari praetoribus *contĭgit,* I and my brother happened to be chosen
praetors.

G. Verbs denoting *willingness, unwillingness,* or *permission,*
and also those of *asking, demanding, advising,* and *reminding,*
are sometimes followed by the subjunctive WITHOUT *ut* or *ne.*

Such are *volo, nolo, malo, permitto, licet ; oro, precor, quaeso, rogo,
peto, postulo ; suadeo, censeo, moneo, admoneo, hortor.* To these add
curo, decerno, jubeo, mando ; the imperatives *fac,* " see that," and
cave, " beware," and the impersonal *oportet* and *necesse est.*

---

* Compare page 290. † Compare page 290, note.

Vélim fieri *pósset*, ut, &c. — I wish it were possible that, &c.

Málo, te sápiens hóstis *métuat*, quám stúlti cíves *laúdent*. — I prefer an intelligent enemy fearing you to stupid citizens praising you.

Síne, tê *exórem*, mi páter. — Allow me to entreat you, my father.

A tê péto, mê abséntem *díligas* átque *deféndas*. — I ask of you to love and to defend me in my absence.

Póstulo, Áppi, ótiam átque ótiam *consíderes*. — I beseech you, Appius, to consider again and again.

Suádeo *vídeas*, tánquam si túa rès agátur. — I advise you to look, as if your own interests were at stake.

Hérus mê *jússit* Pámphylum hódie *observârem*. — My master commanded to watch Pamphylus to-day.

Fác scíam (= fácito *ut* scíam). — Pray let me know (inform me).

Cáve crédas. — Do not believe.

Frémant ómnes *lícet* — Every one is allowed to murmur.

Philosóphiae *sérvias oportet*, ut tíbi contíngat vêra libértas. — You should serve philosophy in order to acquire true liberty.

Vírtus voluptâtis áditus *interclúdat necésse est*. — Virtue necessarily prevents the access of pleasure.

H. Verbs signifying *joy, sorrow, surprise,* or *wonder* are followed either by the accusative with the infinitive, or by *quod* ("that" or "because") with the indicative or subjunctive.

Such verbs are *gaudeo, delector, doleo, succenseo, angor, poenĭtet; mĭror, admĭror, glorior, gratŭlor, gratĭas ago, queror, indĭgnor,* &c. E. g.

Gaúdeo, quód tê interpellávi. — I am glad that I have interrupted you.

Dolêbam, quód consórtem gloriósi labôris amíseram. — I was sorry to have lost the sharer of the glorious enterprise.

Mirári sê aiêbat, *quód* nôn ríderet harúspex. — He was accustomed to express his surprise, that the soothsayer did not laugh.

Tíbi ágo grátias, quód mê ómni moléstiâ *líberas*. — I thank you for liberating me from inconvenience of every kind.

Grátulor tíbi, *quód* ex provínciâ sálvum tê ad túos *recepísti*. — I congratulate you for having safely returned from the province to your friends.

Quéreris super hôc étiam, *quód* expectâta tíbi nôn míttam cármina. — You also complain of this, that I do not send you the expected poems.

REMARKS.

1. *Quod* is chiefly employed in connection with past tenses. *Quod* with the indicative denotes a *fact*, and with the subjunctive a *supposition* or the *opinion of another*.

2. *Quod* is also frequently employed instead of the Acc. cum Inf. after substantives, and after expressions like "it is pleasant" or "unpleasant," "it pleases" or "displeases," *magnum est*, *accēdit* (= "add to this"), &c. It is thus frequently preceded by one of the pronouns *hoc, id, illud*, and is often equivalent to the English "the fact or circumstance that." E. g. *Augēbat iras*, quod *soli Judaei non cessissent*, The *fact* (or *circumstance*) *that* the Jews alone had not surrendered, augmented the indignation. *Inter causas malorum nostrorum est*, quod *rivīmus ad exempla*, Among the causes of our miseries is *the fact that* we are living after the examples of others. *Quod victor victis pepercit, magnum est*, That the conqueror spared the conquered is great. *In Caesare mitis est clemensque natura.* Accēdit, quod *mirifice ingeniis excellentibus delectatur*, Cæsar is of a gentle and mild nature. Add to this, that (in addition to this) he takes the greatest delight in intellectual pre-eminence.

3. *Quod* is always put, instead of the Acc. cum Inf. or *ut*, in *explanatory* or *periphrastic clauses*, which (generally) refer to an oblique case of the demonstratives *hoc, id, illud*, or *istud*. E. g. Hoc uno *praestamus vel maxime feris*, quod *colloquīmur inter nos*, *et* quod *exprimēre dicendo sensa possūmus*, We excel the brutes chiefly in this, that we converse with each other, and are able to express our sensations in language. *Phocion non* in eo *solum offenderat*, quod *patriae male consulērat*, *sed etiam* quod *amicitiae fidem non praestiterat*, Phocion had not only given offence by the fact that he had mismanaged the interests of his country, but also because he had exhibited a want of faith in friendship.

4. *Quod* stands also in expressions like *adde, quod*, or *adde huc, quod* (add to this that, besides), and after *facere* in connection with an adverb like *bene, male*, &c. E. g. *Bene facis*, quod *me mones*, You do well to remind me. *Humaniter fecit*, quod *ad me venit*, He acted humanely by coming to me.

5. *Quod* stands with several different senses in constructions like the following : —

a.) At the beginning of a sentence, in the sense of "as to," "with respect to." E. g. Quod *scribis te velle scire, qui sit reipublicae status, summa dissentio est*, As regards your expressing a desire to know the state of the republic, (I have to report) the greatest dissension. Quod *mihi de nostro statu* gratulāris, *minime miramur te tuo opere laetāri*, As to your congratulating me on my present condition, I am not at all surprised that you rejoice in your own work.

b.) In the sense of "as far as." E. g. *Tu*, quod *potĕris, ut adhuc fecisti, nos consiliis juvābis*, Do you assist us, *as far as* you can, and as you have done heretofore, with your advice and influence. *Epicurus se unus*, quod *sciam, sapientem profiteri est ausus*, Epicurus is the only one, *as far as* I know, who has dared to profess himself a sage.

c.) Instead of *ex quo* or *quum*, "since." E. g. *Tertius dies est*, quod *audīvi*, &c., It is now three days *since* I have heard, &c. To these may be added *tantum quod*, "scarcely." E. g. Tantum quod *ex Arpinati venĕram, quum mihi litterae a te reddĭtae sunt*, I had but just returned from Arpinum, when a letter from you was handed to me.

EXERCISE 104.

Do you wish me to go to the theatre with you ? — I do not wish you, but your brother, to go with me. — Do you desire me to write to your father ? — I do wish that you would write to him. — Do you allow (*sinisne*) me to go to the ball ? — I do not allow you to go there. — Does he suffer (*patitur*) letters to be written by us ? — He does not suffer it. — Did they compel you to resign your office (*munĕre*) ? — They were not able to compel me (*me cogĕre*). — Did he urge (*flagitavitne*) you to go out with him ? — He did urge me. — Does he refuse to come to us ? — He does refuse. — Have you determined to learn Latin ? — I have not determined (to do so). — Has he resolved (*decrevitne*) to study French ? — He has resolved (to do so). — What is he aiming at (*Quid ágit*) ? — He is exerting himself (*Id agit ut*) to commit this book to memory. — Do you endeavor (*studésne*) to become diligent ? — I do strive to be diligent and good. — Must we see to it, that we love our neighbor ? — We must see to it by all means (*quam maxime*).

EXERCISE 105.

Do you ask me to remain at home ? — No; on the contrary, I beseech and exhort you to go out. — Did he exhort you to go into the country ? — No, he exhorted me to write a letter. — Do you advise me to resist passion (*ut iracundiae resistam*). — I do advise you. — I remind and conjure you to cherish those who love you. — Did he remind you that that was so (*rem ita se habuisse*) ? — He reminded and persuaded me (*mihi*) that that was really (*re vera*) so. — Did they order any one to be killed ? — They ordered the soldier to be killed. — Does he prohibit (*vetatne*) the reading of the book ? — He does, on the contrary, order it to be read. — Did your father write you to come home ? — He, on the contrary, wrote me to remain in the country. — Did you tell your servant to bring you the book ? — I did tell him. — Does your master command you to attend to your studies ? — He does command me. — Did you persuade him to read my book ? — I could not persuade him. — Can it be that I am wrong ? — It is not possible that you are wrong. — When was it the case that I was wrong ? — Allow me to entreat you to write. — Pray let me know when you are coming. — Do not believe that he is your friend. — Are you glad that I have written to your friend ? — I am delighted (*delector*) that you have done it. — Are you sorry that you have lost your book ? — I am very sorry that I have lost it. — Is he surprised that I did not bring the doctor ? — He is surprised that he does not come. — Do you thank me for having liberated you from trouble (*molestiâ*) ? — I do thank you with all my heart (*toto pectore*). — Do you congratulate me for having recovered ? — I do congratulate you. — Why does his master complain ? — He complains of this, that he is negligent and idle.

Lesson LV. — PENSUM QUINQUAGESIMUM QUINTUM.

OF IMPERSONAL VERBS.

A. Impersonal verbs are those which are used in the third person singular only, and without reference to any definite subject. They are in English commonly introduced by the pronoun *it.* E. g. *Tonat,* it thunders; *pluit,* it rains; *oportet,* it behooves.

REMARKS.

1. Impersonal verbs thus occur in all the conjugations, and in all the moods and tenses of complete verbs. E. g. 1. *Constat,* it is manifest; 2. *nocet,* it is hurtful; 3. *accidit,* it happens; 4. *convenit,* it is agreed upon. — *Constāre,* to be manifest; *tonŭit,* it thundered; *nocĕat,* let it be hurtful, &c.

2. The majority of the impersonal verbs of the Latin language are also used personally, but generally with a modified or different signification. Many again admit a subject of the neuter gender, such as an infinitive (either with or without a subject accusative) or a clause used substantively, and sometimes a pronoun of the neuter gender. (Cf. Lesson LII. *A.* 1; LIII. *B.*)

3. Impersonal verbs generally want the imperative, except *licet,* which has *licēto* (let it be lawful). The rest employ the present subjunctive imperatively; as, *Tonet,* Let it thunder! *Pudeat te,* Be ashamed of yourself!

4. The majority want also the participles, gerunds, and gerundives. The only exceptions are the following, of which some, however, have acquired the force of adjectives: — *decens,* becoming; *libens,* willing; *licens,* free, bold; *poenitens,* penitent; — *licitūrus, poenitūrus, pudĭtū-rus,* about to be lawful, to repent, to be ashamed; — *pigendus, puden-dus, poenitendus,* to be regretted, ashamed of, repented of. To these add the gerunds *poenitendi, pudendo, ad pigendum.*

B. Impersonal verbs may be divided into several classes. They are: —

I. Those serving to designate the ordinary phenomena of nature, or the state of the weather. As, —

PRESENT.	PERFECT.*	INFINITIVE.	
Dilūcŭlat,	dilūcŭlāvit,	dilūcŭlāre,	*it dawns.*
Fulgŭrat,	fulgŭrāvit,	fulgŭrāre,	*it lightens.*
Fulmĭnat,	fulmĭnāvit,	fulmĭnāre,	*it thunders.*
Gĕlat,	gĕlāvit,	gĕlāre,	*it freezes.*
Grandĭnat,	grandĭnāvit,	grandĭnāre,	*it hails.*

* Of some of these verbs the second root is not used.

26

PRESENT.	PERFECT.	INFINITIVE.	
Lapĭdat,	{ lapĭdāvit, lapĭdātum est, }	} lapĭdāre,	*it rains stones.*
Lucescit, Luciscit, Illucescit, }	luxit, illuxit,	(lucescĕre, { luciscĕre, (illucescĕre, }	*it grows light.*
Ningit,	ninxit,	ningĕre,	*it snows.*
Noctescit,	——,	noctescĕre,	*it grows dark.*
Plŭit,	{ plŭvit, plŭit, }	pluĕre,	*it rains.*
Regĕlat,	regĕlāvit, '	regĕlāre,	*it thaws.*
Rōrat,	rōrāvit,	rōrāre,	*it dews, dew falls.*
Tŏnat,	tŏnŭit,	tonāre,	*it thunders.*
Vesperascit, Advesperascit,	vesperāvit, advesperāvit,	vesperāre, advesperāre, }	*it becomes evening.*

REMARK. — These verbs sometimes (though rarely) occur in connection with a *personal* subject. E. g. *Jupiter tonat et fulgurat. Dies* or *coelum vesperascit. Lapides pluunt. Lapidibus pluit. Sanguinem pluit,* &c. But this use is chiefly confined to the third person, and rather the exception than the rule. It is consequently unnecessary to supply a personal subject (e. g. *Jupiter, Coelum,* &c.) to account for the ordinary construction of these verbs.

II. The following verbs, denoting *an affection of the mind, an obligation,* or *permission:* —

PRESENT.	PERFECT.	INFINITIVE.	
Mĭsĕret (me),	{ mĭsĕrŭit (*rarely*), { mĭsĕrĭtum est, (mĭsertum est, }	} mĭsĕrēre,	{ *it moves me to pity,* *I have pity.*
Pĭget (me),	{ pĭgŭit *or,* pĭgĭtum est, }	pĭgēre,	*it chagrins, irks.*
Poenĭtet (me),	poenĭtŭit,	poenĭtēre,	*it repents me, I repent.*
Pŭdet (me),	{ pŭdŭit, *or* pŭdĭtum est, }	pŭdēre,	{ *it shames me, I am* *ashamed.*
Taedet (me),	{ taedŭit (*rarely*), pertaesum est, }	taedēre,	*it wearies, disgusts.*
Oportet (me),	oportŭit,	oportēre,	*it behooves.*
Lĭbet (lŭbet),	{ lĭbŭit, *or* lĭbĭtum est, }	lĭbēre,	*it pleases.*
Lĭcet (mihi),	{ lĭcŭit, *or* lĭcĭtum est, }	lĭcēre,	*it is lawful, allowed.*
Dĕcet (me),	dĕcŭit,	dĕcēre,	*it becomes.*
Dēdĕcet (me),	dēdĕcŭit,	dēdĕcēre,	*it misbecomes.*
Lĭquet (mihi),	lĭcŭit,	lĭquēre,	*it is manifest.*

REMARKS.

1. The subject of the emotion denoted by some of the foregoing verbs is put in the accusative ; as, *Miseret me, te, illum,* It moves me,

you, him, to pity (i. e. I pity, you pity, &c.).　*Pudet nos, vos, illos,*
We, you, they are ashamed.　So also *oportet me, te, illum; decet (dedecet) nos, vos,* &c.　But *libet* and *licet* are followed by the dative
(*mihi, tibi,* &c.).

2. The verbs *libet, licet, decet, dedecet,* and *liquet* sometimes occur
in the third person plural, and assume a personal subject.

III. The third person singular of a number of complete verbs,
which is frequently employed impersonally, but in a sense more
or less different from the ordinary signification of these verbs.
Thus : —

PRESENT.	PERFECT.	INFINITIVE.	
Accĭdit,	accĭdit,	accĭdĕre,	
Contingit,	contĭgit,	contingĕre,	*it happens, occurs,*
Evĕnit,	evēnit,	evĕnīre,	*comes to pass.*
Fīt,	factum est,	fĭĕri,	
Attĭnet,	attĭnŭit,	attĭnēre,	*it belongs to, per-*
Pertĭnet,	pertĭnŭit,	pertĭnēre,	*tains.*
Accēdit,	accessit,	accēdĕre,	*there is to be added.*
Condūcit,	conduxit,	condūcĕre,	*it conduces.*
Constat,	constĭtit,	constāre,	*it is evident.*
Convĕnit,	convēnit,	convĕnīre,	*it is agreed on.*
Dēbet,	dēbŭit,	dēbēre,	*it ought.*
Displĭcet,	displĭcŭit, displĭcĭtum est,	displĭcēre,	*it displeases.*
Dŏlet,	dŏlŭit,	dŏlēre,	*it pains (grieves).*
Est (= licet),	fŭit,	esse,	*it is lawful, one may.*
Expĕdit,	expĕdīvit,	expĕdīre,	*it is expedient, ad-*
Prōdest,	prōfŭit,	prōdesse,	*vantageous.*
Fallit (me),	fĕfellit (me),	fallĕre,	
Fŭgit (me),	fūgit (me),	fūgĕre,	*it escapes my notice.*
Praetĕrit (me),	praetĕriit (me),	praetĕrīre,	
Incĭpit,	incēpit,	incĭpĕre,	*it begins.*
Interest,	interfŭit,	interesse,	*it concerns.*
Rēfert,	rētŭlit,	rēferre,	
Jŭvat,	jŭvit,	jŭvāre,	*it delights.*
Delectat,	delectāvit,	delectāre,	
Nŏcet,	nŏcŭit,	nŏcēre,	*it hurts.*
Obest,	obfŭit,	obesse,	
Pătet,	pătŭit,	pătēre,	*it is clear.*
Plăcet,	plăcŭit, plăcĭtum est,	plăcēre,	*it pleases.*
Praestat,	praestĭtit,	praestāre,	*it is preferable, bet-* *ter.*
Restat,	restĭtit,	restāre,	*it remains.*
Sŏlet,	sŏlĭtum est,	sŏlēre,	*it is usual.*
Assŏlet,	assŏlĭtum est,	assŏlēre,	
Stat,	stĕtit,	stāre,	*it is resolved.*
Succurrit,	succurrit,	succurrĕre,	*it suggests itself.*

PRESENT.	PERFECT.	INFINITIVE.	
Sufficit,	suffēcit,	sufficĕre,	*it suffices.*
Suppĕtit,	suppĕtivit,	suppĕtĕre,	*there is on hand (left).*
Văcat,	văcăvit,	văcăre,	*there is leisure ; it pleases.*

REMARK. — The subject of these verbs thus used impersonally can only be an infinitive (either with or without a subject accusative) or an entire clause, but sometimes also the nominative of a neuter pronoun. (Cf. Lessons LII., LIII., LIV.)

IV. The third person singular passive, especially of *intransitive* verbs denoting motion, and which otherwise do not admit of the passive voice. E. g.

Currĭtur, *there is running.*
Ītur, *there is going.*
Adĭtur, *there is approaching.*
Ventum est, *some one has come.*
Clamātur, *there is calling.*
Favētur, *there is favoring.*
Flētur, *there is weeping.*
Ridētur, *there is laughing.*
Bĭbĭtur, *there is drinking.*

Dīcĭtur, *it is said.*
Tradĭtur, *it is related.*
Scrībĭtur, *it is written.*
Pugnātur, *there is fighting.*
Peccātur, *there is sinning.*
Persuadētur, *there is persuading.*
Certātur, *it is contended.*
Sentītur, *it is perceived.*

REMARKS.

1. The agent, by which the activity denoted by these verbs is exercised, is either left indefinite, or expressed by the ablative with *a* or *ab* (e. g. *ab aliquo, a me, te, nobis, ab hominibus*, &c.). It is most frequently to be inferred from the context. Thus : *Ubi eo ventum est* (sc. *ab iis*), When they had come there. *His persuadēri non proterat* (sc. *ab aliquo*), They could not be persuaded (by any one). *Curritur ad praetorium* (sc. *a militĭbus*), There is a rush towards the general's tent (on the part of the soldiers). *Pugnātur omnibus locis,* There is a general battle.

2. Among the verbs employed impersonally we must include the neuter of the future passive participle with *est, erat, fuit, erit*, &c.; as, *amandum est*, there must be loving (some one must love, it is necessary to love) ; *scribendum fuit*, it was necessary to write ; *currendum erit*, it will be necessary to run. That this construction requires the dative of the agent (e. g. *alicui, mihi, tibi, hominibus*, &c.) is already known from Lesson XXV.

Does it thunder ?
It does thunder and lighten.
Does it not hail ?
It does hail.
Does it rain ?
It does not rain ; it snows.
Did it rain or snow ?
It rained very hard.
Is it growing light or dark ?

Tonátne ?
Íta ést, tónat átque fúlgurat.
Nónne grándinat ?
Grándinat véro.
Núm plúit ?
Nôn plúit; ningit.
Útrum plûvit án nínxit ?
Plûvit veheménter.
Lucescítne an advesperáscit ?

It is growing dark.	Vesperáscit.
Is it hailing out of doors?	Écquid fóris grándinat?
It is hailing hard.	Sic ést, válde grándinat.
Did it freeze last night?	Gelavítne nócte próximā?
It did not freeze.	Nôn gelâvit.
Is it foggy?	Éstne coêlum nebulôsum?
It is (foggy).	Est (nebulôsum).
Does the sun shine?	Lucétne sôl?
It does shine.	Lûcet.
We have (enjoy) sunshine.	Útimur sôlis lúmine.
The sun does not shine.	{ Sôl nôn lûcet. { Sôlis lúmine nôn útimur.
The sun is in (is blinding) my eyes.	{ Sôl míhi óculos nócet. { Lûmen sôlis míhi oculôrum áciem praestríngit.

The weather.	*Tempestas, ātis,* f. ; *coelum, i,* n.
Good, fine, bad, very bad weather.	Tempestas bŏna, serēna, mŭla, de- terrĭma.
The face, countenance.	Facĭes, ei, *f.;* ōs, ōris, *m.;* vultus, ūs, *m.*
The eyes; the eyesight.	Ocŭli, ōrum, *m.;* acies (ei, *f.*) ocu- lōrum.
The thunder.	Tonĭtrus, ūs, *m.*
The thunderbolt.	Fulmen, ĭnis, *n.*
The snow.	Nix, *gen.* nĭvis, *f.,* or pl. nĭves.
The hail.	Grando, ĭnis, *f.*
The fog, mist.	Nebŭla, ae, *f.*
The rain.	Plŭvĭa, ae, *f.;* imber, ris, *m.,* or pl. imbres.
The sunshine.	Lūmen sōlis, *or simply* sōl, sōl calĭ- dus.
The parasol.	Umbella, ae, *f.*
Foggy.	Nebulōsus, a, um.
Hard, violently.	Valde, vehementer (*adv.*).
To have (use, enjoy).	Ūtor, ūti, ūsus sum (ALIQUA RE, ALIQUO).
To shine.	Lūcĕo, ēre, luxi, ——.
To shine brightly.	{ Fulgĕo, ēre, fulsi, ——. { Splendĕo, ēre, ŭi, ——.
The wind.	Ventus, i, *m.*
To blow.	Flō, āre, āvi, ātum.
To cease (rest).	Quiesco, ēre, ēvi, ētum.
To rise.	Orior, īri, ortus sum.
Windy.	Ventōsus, a, um.
Stormy.	Nimbōsus, a, um; procellōsus, a, um.
Srong, vehement.	Vĕhĕmens, tis, *adj.*
Is it windy? Does the wind blow?	{ Éstne tempéstas ventôsa? { Flátne véntus?

T   26*

It is windy. The wind does blow.	Ést tempéstas ventôsa. Flát véro véntus.
Has the wind risen ?	Ortúsne ést véntus ?
No, it has ceased.	Ímmo véro quiêvit.
It is not stormy.	Coêlum nôn ést procellôsum.
It is very windy.	Tempéstas válde ventôsa ést. Válde flát véntus.

The spring.	Vēr, *gen.* vēris, *n.*
The autumn.	Auctumnus, i, *m.*
In the spring, summer, autumn, winter.	Vēre, aestāte, auctumno, hiĕme.
To travel.	*Ĭter,* or *ĭtĭnĕra facĕre ; peregrināri* (abroad).
To ride in a carriage.	Vĕhor, vĕhi, vectus sum. Invĕhi (CURRU, IN RHEDA).
To ride on horseback.	Vĕhi (invĕhi) equo. Equĭto, āre, āvi, ātum.
To ride up, away, around.	Advĕhi, abvĕhi, circumvĕhi.
To go (come, travel) on foot.	Pedĭbus *or* pĕdĕs* ire (vĕnire, Ĭter facĕre).
To travel (make a tour) on foot.	Iter pedestre facĕre *or* confĭcĕre.
To like, take pleasure in.	*Delector, āri, ātus sum* (ALIQUID FACĔRE).

Do you like riding in a carriage ?	Delectarisne ín véhi cúrru (in rhédā) ?
No, I prefer riding on horseback.	Nôn véro ; équo véhi málo.
Where did our friend ride to (on horseback) ?	Quô equitâvit amícus nóster ?
He has ridden into the forest.	Equitâvit in sílvam.
It is good (pleasant), bad (unpleasant) to do anything.	*Jucundum, injucundum est aliquid facĕre.*
Is it pleasant to go on foot.	Éstne jucúndum íre pédĭbus (pédes) ?
It is very pleasant.	Ést profécto perjucúndum.
Did he go on foot or in a carriage ?	Útrum ívit pédĭbus án curru vectus est ?
No, he went on horseback.	Ímmo véctus ést équo.

EXERCISE 106.

Are you going out to-day ? — I never go out when it is raining. — Did it rain yesterday ? — It did not rain. — Has it snowed ? — It has snowed. — Why do you not go to the market ? — I do not go there, because it snows. — Do you wish (to have) an umbrella ? — If (*si*)

---

* Pĕdĕs, -ĭtis, *m.*, one who goes on foot.

you have one. — Will you lend me an umbrella ? — I am not unwilling to lend you one. — What sort of weather is it ? — It thunders and lightens. — Does the sun shine ? — The sun does not
shine; it is foggy. — Do you hear the thunder ? — I do not hear it.
— How long (*quam diu*) did you hear the thunder ? — I heard it
until (*usque ad*) four o'clock in the morning. — Is it fine weather
now ? — It is not; the wind blows hard, and it thunders much. —
Does it rain ? — It does rain very fast. — Do you not go into the
country ? — How (*quo modo*) can I go into the country ? do you not
see how (*quam vehementer*) it lightens ? — Does it snow ? — It does
not snow, but it hails. — Did it hail yesterday ? — It did not hail, but
it thundered very much. — Have you a parasol ? — I have one. —
Will you lend it to me ? — I will lend it to you. — Have we sunshine ?
— We have; the sun is in my eyes. — Is it fine weather ? — It is very
bad weather; it is dark. — We have no sunshine. — How is the
weather to-day ? — The weather is very bad. — Is it windy ? — It is
very windy. — Was it stormy yesterday ? — It was stormy. — Why
did you not go into the country ? — I did not go because it was stormy.
— Do you go to the market this morning ? — I intend to go there, if
it is not (*si non est*) stormy. — Do you intend to breakfast with me
this morning ? — I intend breakfasting with you, if (*si*) I am hungry.

EXERCISE 107.

Does the Pole intend to drink some of this wine ? — He does intend
to drink some of it, if he is thirsty. — Do you like to go on foot when
you are travelling (*iter faciens*) ? — I do not like to travel on foot. —
Did you travel to Italy (*in Italiam*) on foot ? — I did not go on foot,
because the roads (*viae*) were too bad (*nimis lutulentae*). — Do you
like to ride in a carriage ? — I like to ride on horseback. — Has your
cousin ever gone on horseback ? — He has never gone on horseback.
— Did you ride on horseback the day before yesterday ? — I rode on
horseback to-day. — Does your brother ride on horseback as often as
you ? — He rides oftener than I. — Hast thou sometimes ridden on
horseback ? — I have never ridden on horseback. — Will you go (in
a carriage) into the country to-day ? — I will ride thither. — Do you
like travelling ? — I do not like (it). — Does your father like travelling in the winter ? — He does not like travelling (to travel) in the
winter; he likes travelling in the spring and summer. — Is it good
travelling (pleasant to travel) in the spring ? — It is good travelling
in the spring and autumn, but it is bad travelling in the winter and
in the summer. — Have you sometimes travelled in the winter ? — I
have often travelled both in the winter and in the summer. — Does
your brother travel often ? — He travels no longer; but he formerly
(*quondam*) travelled much. — When do you like to ride on horseback ?
— I like riding on horseback in the morning, after breakfast. — Is it
good travelling in the country ? — It is good travelling there. —
Whither are they running (*Quorsum curritur*) ? — They are running to the forum. — Have they (has any one) come (*ventumne est*)
into the house ? — They have not yet come. — Was there laughing

(*ridebaturne*) in the theatre? — There was laughing and shouting (*clamabâtur*) there. — Is it said that he has arrived (*eum advenisse*)? — No, it is said that   has remained in the country. — Is it pleasant to go on foot to-day? — It is not pleasant. — When did the wind rise? — It rose at four o'clock this morning.

Lesson LVI. — PENSUM QUINQUAGESIMUM SEXTUM.

CONSTRUCTION OF NAMES OF PLACES.

A. In answer to the question *Whither?* the name of the place is put in the Accusative with *in* or *ad;* but before the proper names of cities, these prepositions are commonly omitted. E. g.

In hórtos, in theátrum, ad lócum públicum, ad urbem íre.	To go into the garden, into the theatre, to the public square, towards the city.
In Itáliam, in Germániam, in Américam, Lésbum profícísci.	To set out for Italy, for Germany, for America, for Lesbus.
Rôman, Lutétiam, Londínum, Cartháginem, Athénas conténdere.	To be on one's way to Rome, to Paris, London, Carthage, Athens.

B. Rule. — In answer to the question *Where?* the name of the place is put in the Ablative with *in;* but if the place is a city, the name, when of the first or second declension and singular number, stands in the Genitive; and when of the third declension or plural number, in the Ablative without a preposition. E. g.

In hórtis, in theátro, in lóco público, in úrbe ésse.	To be in the garden, in the theatre, in the public square, in the city.
In Itáliä, in Germánia, in África demorári.	To stay in Italy, in Germany, in Africa.
Rómae, Lutétiae, Londíni, Berolíni, Lésbi vívĕre.	To live at Rome, in Paris, London, Berlin, on Lesbus.
Athénis, Syracúsis, Carthágine, Neápoli nátum ésse.	To be born at Athens, in Syracuse, Carthage, Naples.

C. In answer to the question *Whence?* the name of the place is put in the Ablative with *ex* or *ab*, but before the proper names of cities the preposition is commonly omitted. E. g.

Ex hórtis, ex theátro, a lóco público, ab úrbe venire.

To come out of the garden, out
of the theatre, from the public
square, from the city.

Ex Itáliā, ex Ásiā, ab África fú-
gere.

To flee out of Italy, out of Asia,
from Africa.

Rómā, Lutétiā, Athénis, Carthá-
gine expúlsum ésse.

To be banished from Rome, Paris,
Athens, Carthage.

REMARKS.

1. The names of cities sometimes occur with the prepositions *in*, *ex*,
or *ab*, and the names of countries without them.* E. g. *Ab Epheso
in Syriam profectus*, Having started from Ephesus for Syria. *Ab
Epidauro Piraeum advectus*, Conveyed from Epidaurus into the Pi-
ræus. But this is an exception to the general rule.

2. The preposition *ad* may stand before names of cities only in the
sense of "towards" or "in the vicinity of." E. g. *Iter dirigĕre* ad
Mutĭnam, To direct one's course towards Modena. *Tres viae sunt* ad
Mutĭnam, There are three roads to Modena. *Pugna* ad *Trebĭam*, The
battle of (== near) Trevi. *Istos libros lēgit* ad *Misēnum*, He read
these books near Misenum.

3. The names of countries rarely occur in the genitive, instead of
in the ablative with *in*. E. g. *Graeciae, Lucāniae* == in Graeciā, in
Lucaniā. *Romae Numidiaeque* == et Romae et in Numidiā.

4. If the name of the city has an *adjective* or an *appositum*
connected with it, then the Romans put

a.) In answer to the question *Whither?* and *Whence?* the accusative and ablative with and without the usual prepositions. E. g.
Doctas Athenas or *ad doctas Athenas*, To learned Athens. (*In*) *Carthagĭnem Novam*, To New Carthage. *Ipsā Samo*, From Samos itself.
De vitiferā Viennā, From vine-bearing Vienne.

b.) In answer to the question *Where?* the ablative with *in*, where
the genitive would otherwise be required, and the ablative without *in*
in all other cases. E. g. In *ipsā Alexandriā*, In Alexandria itself. In
Albā Helviā.† But without *in*:— *Athenis tuis*, In your Athens.
Carthagĭne Novā, in New Carthage.

c.) When one of the words *oppidum, urbs, locus*, &c. stands in apposition with the proper name of the town, it is commonly preceded
by the preposition; but in answer to the question *Where?* these

---

* The *in*, however, is regularly omitted in connections like the following:—
Terrā marique, "by land and by sea." and before *loco* and *locis*, when these
words occur in the sense of "state" or "situation"; as, *hoc loco, multis locis,
meliore loco*, &c. So likewise before *toto* or *totā*, "the entire or whole"; as
totā urbe, toto mari, totis campis, and never *in totā*, &c. *Hoc libro, primo libro*,
&c. are said when the entire book is meant; but *in hoc (primo*, &c.) *libro*, when
a particular passage is referred to.
† And never *Albae Helviae*; rather without *in*, simply *Albā Helviā* like the
Albā Longā of Virg. Aen. VI. v. 766. Hence also *In Nŏvo Eborāco*, or simply
Nŏvo Eborāco, and not *Nŏvi Eborāci*, New York, which is as unusual as the
Teani Apŭli of Cic. pro Cluent. 9.

words are always in the Ablative. E. g. *Tarquinios*, in urbem *Etruriae florentissimam*, To Tarquinii, the most flourishing city of Etruria. *Neapŏli*, in *celeberrĭmo oppĭdo*, At Naples, a most celebrated town. But *Antiochiae nātus est*, celebri *quondam* urbe *et copiosā*, He was born at Antioch, a city formerly celebrated and wealthy.

d.) If the word *urbs* or *oppidum* precedes the name of the city, the preposition is always put, and the proper name stands as *appositum* in the same case. E. g. *Ad urbem Romam ex oppido Thermis*, in *urbe Romā* (not *Romae*), *in oppido Adrumēto* (not *Adrumēti*).

5. The poets frequently answer the inquiry *Whither?* by the simple accusative, where in prose a preposition is required. E. g. *Italiam Lavīnaque vēnit litŏra* (sc. *in*), He came to Italy and the Lavinian coast. *Speluncam eandem* (sc. *in*) *deveniunt*, They come into the same cave. *Verba refers aures* (= ad aures) *non pervenientia nostras*, You utter words which do not reach our ears.

So likewise the question *Where?* by the ablative without *in*. E. g. *Silvisque agrisque viisque corpora foeda jacent*, The foul bodies lie scattered through the woods, and in the fields and on the ways. This poetical license is imitated by the prose writers of the silver age, who frequently omit the *in*; as, *medio agro, Gabinā viā, regione* for *in regione*, &c.

6. The construction of the names of cities is adopted, —

a.) By the names of the smaller islands, of which some have cities of the same name. E. g. *Rhodi, Cypri, Corcyrae*, in Rhodes, Cyprus, Corcyra. *Rhodum, Cyprum, Corcyram*, to Rhodes, Cyprus, Corcyra. Thus also, *Chersonesum redire*, To return into the Chersonesus. *Chersonesi habitāre*, To live in the Chersonesus. To these add *Delos, Samos, Lesbos*, and *Ithaca*. But the larger islands (e. g. *Britannia, Creta, Euboea, Sardinia*, and *Sicilia*) are commonly construed like names of countries.

b.) By *domus* and *rūs*, on the construction of which see page 132 and page 157.

c.) By the words *hŭmus, bellum* and *militĭa*, which, in answer to the question *Where?* stand in the genitive. Thus, *hŭmi*, on the ground.[*] But *belli* and *militiae* (in war, in the field) occur thus only in connection with *dŏmi*; e. g. *belli domique*, in war and at home; *domi militiaeque*, at home and in the field; *nec belli nec domi*, neither in the field nor at home. To these add *vicinĭae* for *in viciniā*, in the neighborhood; *foras* and *foris*, out of doors; the last of which, however, have assumed the character of adverbs.

Almost, nearly.	*Fĕrē, fĕrmē; prŏpe, prŏpĕmŏdum.* (Adverbs.)
About.	*Circĭter, circa; fermē.*
Scarcely, hardly.	*Vix, paene.* (Adverbs.)

---

[*] But in connection with a verb of motion, *in hŭmum*, never *hŭmum*, but rather *hŭmi* instead of *in humum. Humo* occurs in the sense of *from* the ground. So also *in bellum, ex bello.*

How old are you (What is your age)?	Quótum ánnum ágis ? Quót ánnos hábes ?
I am ten years old.	Décimum ánnum ágo. Décem ánnos hábeo.
How old is your brother?	Quótum ánnum ágit fratérculus túus ?
He is six years old.	Séxtum ánnum ágit. Ánnos séx hábet.
He is scarcely two years old.	Vix dúo annôrum nâtus est.
To be born.	Nascor, i, nâtus sum.
The year.	Annus, i, *m.*
Older, younger.	Major nâtu,* minor nâtu.
The oldest, youngest.	Maximus, minimus nâtu.
Are you older than your sister?	Ésne májor nátu quám soror túa (sorôre túâ) ?
Yes, I am much older.	Súm véro múlto májor nátu.
How old are you?	Quót ánnos nâtus és ? (Cf. Less. LVII. *A.* Rem. 2.)
I am almost twenty years old.	Viginti fere annos nâtus sum.
How old is your sister?	Quótum ánnum hábet sóror túa ?
She is about twelve years old.	Duódecim círciter ánnos hábet (nâtus est).
She is scarcely eight years old.	Vix ócto ánnos hábet. Ócto paéne ánnos nâta ést.
Of what age would you take me to be?	Quíd aetâtis tíbi vídeor ?
You seem to be about thirty.	Vidêris ésse annôrum círciter triginta.
To seem, appear.	Vídĕor, êri, vīsus sum.
The age (of life).	Aetas, âtis, *f.*
I am *over* twenty years old (*older* than twenty years).	Májor (quam) viginti ánnos nâtus sum. Májor (quam) annorum † viginti sum.
He is *under* thirty-three years old (*younger* than thirty-three years).	Mínor (quam) três et triginta ánnos nâtus ést. Mínor (quam) annôrum tríum et triginta ést.
To understand, comprehend, seize.	*Accipio, ĕre, cēpi, ceptum.* *Intelligo, ĕre, lexi, lectum.* *Comprehendo, ĕre, di, sum.* *Căpio, ĕre, cēpi, captum.‡*

---

* Lit. " greater by or with respect to birth." So also *grandior,* either with or without *natu.*

† This is literally *I am older than a man of twenty years.* Instead of the genitive, the ablative may also be put, with or without *quam.* E. g. *Major* (or *minor*) *quam decem annis,* Over (or under) ten years of age. *Major tribus annis,* Over three years old.

‡ *Accipere* is " to hear and understand," more or less perfectly; *intelligere*

Do you understand me (i. e. what I say)? — Núm intelligis, quid dícam? (Lesson XXX. C. 2.)

I do not understand you. — Nôn intélligo (comprehéndo), quid dícas.

Have you understood the man? — Intellexistíne, id quod díxit hómo?

Yes, I have understood him. — Sáne quídem, intélléxi.

Do you comprehend that man (i. e. his motives, &c.)? — Intelligísne ístum hóminem?

I comprehend him but little. — Párum (mínus) intélligo.

I hear you, but I do not understand you. — Accípio quídem éa quae dícis, sed mínus comprehéndo.

The noise. — Strepítus, ūs, m.

The wind. — Ventus, i, m.

To bark. — Latro, āre, āvi, ātum.

The barking. — Latrātus, us, m.; gannitio, ōnis, f.

To hear, perceive. — Audíre, percípere, excipére auribus (ALIQUID).

Do you perceive the noise of the wind? — Percipísne ventôrum strépitum?

I do perceive it. — Égo véro percípio.

Have you heard the barking of the dogs? — Audivistíne latrātum cánum?

I have heard it. — Audívi.

Have they heard what we have said? — Núm excepérunt, quae nôs díximus?

They have not heard them. — Nôn excepérunt.

Do you seize my opinion? — Capísne méam senténtiam?

I do seize it. — Cápio véro.

Whose dog is this? — Cújus ést cánis hícce?

It is the Englishman's. — Cánis ést Ángli.

To read. — Lĕgo, ĕre, lēgi, lectum.

To read through. — Perlĕgo, ĕre, lēgi, lectum.

To remain, stay. — { Mănĕo, ēre, nsi, nsum.
 Permănĕo, ēre, nsi, nsum.

To stay, abide. — { Mŏror, āri, ātus sum.
 Dēmorāri, commorāri.

To take. — { Sūmo, ĕre, mpsi, mptum.*
 Căpĭo, ĕre, cēpi, captum.
 Accípĭo, ĕre, cēpi, ceptum.

To beat, inflict blows upon. — { Verbĕro, āre, āvi, ātum.
 Percŭtĭo, ĕre, cussi, cussum.

To strike. — Fĕrĭo, ire, ——, ——.

To lose. — { Amitto, ĕre, amisi, amissum.
 Perdo, ĕre, dĭdi, dĭtum.

---

and *comprehendere*, " to understand or comprehend " anything said or done; *capere*, " to seize, take, comprehend clearly." All these have ALIQUID. — *Intelligere* ALIQUEM is to comprehend one's character, motives, style, meaning, &c., generally.

  * *Sūmere* = " to take up " anything from its place of rest; *capère*, " to lay hold of, grasp, seize "; *accipère*, " to take " something offered.

To lose at play.	Perdĕre aliquid ălĕā.*
To know (anything).	{ Scĭo, ire, ívi, ītum. { Didĭci (= *I know, have learnt*).
To take away.	{ Aufĕro, erre, abstŭli, ablātum. { Dēmo, ĕre, mpsi, mptum. { Tollo, ĕre, sustŭli, sublātum.

D. Obs. *Auferre aliquid* in general is " to carry away or off," either in a good or bad sense.† With *alicui* or *ab aliquo* it signifies " to take away from," or " to deprive of." *Demĕre aliquid alicui* or *de* (*ex, ab*) *aliquā re* = " to take away or to abstract from." *Tollĕre aliquid* or *aliquem*, " to remove out of the way," and sometimes secondarily " to destroy."

Has this man carried away anything ?	Núm hómo íste quídquam ábstulit ?
He has not carried away anything at all.	Nôn véro ; níhil quídquam ábstŭlit.
Have I taken away anything from you ?	Abstulíne tíbi aliquid ?
You have taken away my book.	Abstulísti véro míhi líbrum.
Has he taken away some of our bread ?	Dempsítne (ille) áliquid de pâne nóstrā ?
He has not taken any of it.	Níhil démpsit.
What has the servant taken away ?	Quíd sústŭlit sérvus ?
He has taken away the wine from the table.	Vínum de ménsā sústŭlit.
Did you order the table to be cleared off ?	Jussistíne ménsam tólli ?
I have not yet done it.	Nôndum jússi.
Will you take away these books?	Écquid vis tóllere hôs líbros ?
I will.	Nôn vólo.
Has he read through the book which you lent him ?	Perlegítne librum, quem éi commodâsti ?
Did he stay at his home, or at his father's ?	Suaêne dómì morâtus est, an in patérnā ?
He remained at his father's.	Permánsit in patérnā.
Did they take what you gave them ?	Núm accepérunt, quod éis dedísti ?
They were unwilling to take it.	Accípere noluérunt.
Who has beaten our dog ?	Quis cánem nóstrum verberâvit (percússit) ?
No one has beaten him.	Némo éum verberâvit.
Have you lost anything ?	Númquid amisístis ?
We have lost nothing.	Níhil amísimus.

---

* *Aleā*, lit. in the game of dice; here, by any game of chance generally.
† Also with persons; as, *Aufer te hinc*, Get yourself gone! *Aufer te domum*, Be off home!

How much money did he lose at play ?	Quántum pecúniae amícus túus áleā pérdidit ?
He has lost a large amount.	Pérdidit pecúniam grándem.
Is he not unhappy ?	Nónne est infélix ?
He is quite unhappy.	Ést ádmodum infélix.
Do you know Latin ?	*Scísne (didicistíne) sermónem Latí- num ?*
I do not know it yet.	*Nóndum dídĭci.*
Do you know as much as this man ?	Ésne tû aeque dóctus atque hícce hómo ?
I do not know as much.	Nôn aéque dóctus súm.
Did you know that ?	Fuítne hóc tíbi nôtum ?
I did not know it.	Nôn fúit.
How many books has your cous- in already read ?	Quam múltos líbros consobrínus túus jam perlêgit ?
He has already read five of them, and at present he is reading the sixth.	Perlêgit júm quínque, et nunc séx- tum légit.
Where did our friends remain ?	Úbi amíci nóstri commoráti súnt ?
They have remained at home.	Commoráti súnt dómi.
They have kept themselves at home.	Tenuérunt sê dómi.
Will (does it please) your father give me anything to do ?	Placétne pátri túo mandâre míhi áliquid faciéndum ?
He desires to give you something to do.	Cúpit véro tíbi quíddam faciéndum mandâre.

EXERCISE 108.

Will you lend my brother a book ? — I have lent him one already. — Will you lend him one more ? — I will lend him two more. — Have you given anything to the poor ? — I have given them money. — How much money has my cousin given you ? — He has given me only a little ; he has given me only two crowns. — How old is your brother ? — He is twenty years old. — Are you as old as he ? — I am not so old. — How old are you ? — I am hardly eighteen years old. — How old art thou ? — I am about twelve years old. — Am I younger than you ? — I do not know. — How old is our neighbor ? — He is not quite thirty years old. — Are our friends as young as we (*ejusdem aetātis nobiscum*) ? — They are older than we. — How old are they ? — The one (*alter*) is nineteen, and the other (*alter*) twenty years old. — Is your father as old as mine ? — He is older than yours. — Have you read my book ? — I have not quite read it yet. — Has your friend finished his book ? — He has almost finished it. — Do you understand me ? — I do understand you. — Does the Englishman understand us ? — He does understand us. — Do you understand what we are telling you ? — We do understand it. — Dost thou understand German ? — I do not understand it yet, but I am learning it. — Do we understand the English ? — We do not understand them. — Do the Germans un-

derstand us ? — They do understand us. — Do we understand them ?
— We hardly understand them. — Do you hear any noise ? — I hear
nothing. — Have you heard the roaring of the wind ? — I have heard
it. — What do you hear ? — I hear the barking of the dogs. — Whose
dog is this ? — It is the dog of the Scotchman.

EXERCISE 109.

Where is your brother ? — He is at London. — Was he not at Berlin ? — No, he was at Carthage. — Have you ever been at Syracuse ?
— I have never been at Syracuse, but at Rome. — Is our friend at
New York ? — No, he is at Athens. — Do you intend to set out for
Italy ? — I intend to set out for Rome and Athens. — Where is your
son studying ? — He is studying at Paris. — Has he returned (*Rever-
tátne*) from Asia ? — He has not yet returned. — Where did he come
from ? — He came from Paris to London. — And I came from Germany to America. — Have you lost your stick ? — I have not lost it.
— Has your servant lost my note ? — He has lost it. — Where have
you remained ? — I have remained at home. — Has your father lost
(at play) as much money as I ? — He has lost more of it than you. —
How much have I lost ? — You have hardly lost a crown. — Where
has thy brother remained ? — He has remained at home. — Have
your friends remained in the country ? — They have remained there.
— Do you know as much as the English physician ? — I do not know
as much as he. — Does the French physician know as much as you ?
— He knows more than I. — Does any one know more than the
French physicians ? — No one knows more than they. — Have your
brothers read my books ? — They have not quite read them. — How
many of them have they read ? — They have hardly read two of them.
Has the son of my gardener taken anything from you ? — He has
taken my books from me. — What hast thou taken from him ? — I
have taken nothing from him. — Has he taken money from you ? —
He has taken some from me. — How much money has he taken from
you ? — He has taken from me almost two crowns.

Lesson LVII. — PENSUM QUINQUAGESIMUM SEPTIMUM.

OF THE CONSTRUCTION OF TIME.

A. In answer to the question *How long ?* the noun
denoting the duration of time is put in the Accusative,
sometimes with the preposition *per*, " through." E. g.

Únum tántum *diem* vívĕre.	To live for one day only.
Dúas hebdómades, três ménses in úrbe demorári.	To stay in the city for two weeks, three months.
Três hóras, séx ménses, per trién-nium cum áliquo habitâre.	To live with any one three hours, six months, for three (entire) years.
Nóctes diêsque alicui assidêre.	To sit by one's side night and day.
Ánnum jám *tértium et vicésimum* régnat.	He is already reigning the twentieth year.
Múlta saécula víguit Pythagore-órum nômen.	The name of the Pythagoreans was in vogue for many centuries.
Úrbs Véji *décem aestátes himês-que contínuas* circumséssa est.	The city of Veji was besieged for ten successive summers and winters.

REMARKS.

1. Duration of time is sometimes also expressed by the Ablative. E. g. *Triginta annis vixisse,* To have lived for thirty years. *Quattu-ordecim annis exilium tolerāre,* To suffer exile for fourteen years. But this is rather an exception peculiar to writers of the silver age.

2. The question *How old?* is commonly answered by *nātus,* "born," with the accusative of the time elapsed since the birth of the individual in question. E. g. *Unum tantum mensem nātus est,* He is but one month old. *Decem annos nātus sum,* I am ten years old. On these expressions, compare page 311.

B. In answer to the question *When?* the point or period of time is expressed by the Ablative, *without* the preposition *in.* E. g.

Hôc díe, hôc ánno, hâc hórā, hâc hebdómade.	This day, this year, this hour, this week.
Vêre, aestâte, auctúmno, híeme.	In the spring, summer, autumn, winter.
Díe, nócte, vésperi (véspere).	By day, at night, in the evening.
Ánno post Chrístum nâtum *milé-simo octingésimo quadragésimo séptimo.*	In the year one thousand eight hundred and forty-seven after the birth of Christ.
Pýrrhi tempóribus jám Apóllo vérsus fácere desíerat.	In the times of Pyrrhus, Apollo had already ceased to make verses.
Timóleon proélia máxima *natáli díe súo* fêcit ómnia.	Timoleon won all his greatest victories on his birthday.

REMARKS.

1. *In* before the ablatives *anno, die, horā,* &c. rarely occurs. *In tempŏre* can only be said when *tempus* has the sense of "emergency"; as, *hoc in tempŏre,* in this emergency; *in tāli tempŏre,* under such circumstances. The English "betimes" ("in time," "in season") is in Latin either *tempŏre* or *in tempŏre.* In this sense the adverbial

tempori and *temperi* are also used, from which the comparative *temperius*, more seasonably, earlier.

2. The English " by day," " in the night," may also be expressed by *interdiu* and *noctu*, especially in connections like *die ac noctu* or *die noctûque*, by day and by night; *nocte et interdiu*, by night and by day.

3. Substantives which do not of themselves denote any division of time, but are still used to express that relation, are put in the ablative partly with *in*, but frequently without it. So *initio* and *principio*, in the beginning; (*in*) *comitiis*, at the time of the election; (*in*) *tumultu*, in an insurrection; (*in*) *bello*,* in the war; *ejus adventu* or *discessu*, at the time of his arrival or departure. So also *ludis* (without *in*) for *tempore ludorum*, at the time of the public games; and *Saturnalibus*, *gladiatöribus*, *Latînis* (sc. *ludis*), at the time of the Saturnalian, gladiatorial, and Latin exhibitions.

C.   The time *within which* anything is done is expressed by the Ablative, generally without *in*, and sometimes by the Accusative with *intra*.   E. g.

Úrbes Áfricae *ánnis* prope *quinquagínta* núllum Românum exércitum víderant.	The cities of Africa had not seen a Roman army in nearly fifty years.
Quáttuor tragoédias *séxdecim diêbus* absolvísti.	You have finished four tragedies in sixteen days.
Frétum Eurípi sépties *die* recíprocat.	He makes the sound of Eurīpus ebb seven times a day.
In† *hórā* saépe ducéntos vérsus dictâbat.	He frequently dictated two hundred verses in an hour.
Intra décimum diem, quam (== postquam) vénerat.	Within ten days after his arrival.

D.   The question *How long ago?* is answered by the Accusative or Ablative, with *abhinc*, " before this time," and sometimes by the Accusative with *ante* and the pronoun *hic*.   E. g.

Ábhinc díes três. ⎫ Ábhinc tríbus diébus. ⎬ *Ante hôs* três díes. ⎭	Three days ago. (Three days before this. *These* three days *ago*.)
Ábhinc ánnos séx	Six years ago.
Ábhinc vigínti hóras.	Twenty hours ago.
Ante hôs séx ménses.	These six months ago.

---

* But when *bello* has an adjective, or a noun in the genitive, connected with it, the *in* is never put. E. g. *bello Punico secundo*, in the second Punic war; *bello Latinörum*, in the war of the Latins. So *Senensi proelio*, *pugnā Cannensi*, without *in*. Thus also *in pueritiā*, in boyhood, but *pueritiā extremā*, towards the end of boyhood; *ineunte adolescentiā*, at the beginning of youth.

† The preposition *in* is sometimes put in answer to the question *How much or how often in a given time?* But even in this instance the ablative may stand without it.

REMARK. — The question *How long ago?* is sometimes also answered by the simple ablative ; e. g. *paucis his diebus*, a few days ago, within a few days before this time.

E. In answer to the questions *How long before?* and *How long after?* the time is expressed either by the Accusative or Ablative, with *ante*, "before," and *post*, "after." E. g.

Ante séx ménses. ⎫ Séx ménsibus ánte. ⎬	Six months before (any given event).
Post quínque diêbus. ⎫ Quínque diêbus post. ⎬	Five days after (that event).

NOTE. — The words *ante* and *post* are usually put *before* the Accusative and *after* the Ablative. But they may also stand *between* the numeral and noun. The numeral may be either a cardinal or an ordinal. Thus the English "Three days before," and "Ten years after," may be expressed as follows : —

ACCUSATIVE.	ABLATIVE.
Ante três díes.	Tribus diêbus ánte.
Ante tértuum díem.	Tértio díē ánte.
Três ante díes.	Tribus ante diêbus.
Tértium ante díem.	Tértio ante díē.
Post décem ánnos.	Décem ánnis post.
Post décimum ánnum.	Décimo ánno post.
Décem post ánnos.	Décem post ánnis.
Décimum post ánnum.	Décimo post ánno.

Fúbius *tértio ánno ante* cónsul fúerat.	Fabius had been consul three years before.
M. Vólscius Fíctor *ante aliquot ánnos* tribûnus plêbis fúerat.	A few years before that time Marcus Volscius Fictor had been tribune of the people.
Néque íta múlto post Seleûcus a Ptolemaéo dólo interféctus ést.	But a short time after that, Seleucus was treacherously killed by Ptolemæus.
Homêrus *ánnis múltis* fúit *ante* Rómulum.*	Homer lived many years before Romulus.
Cónsul fáctus est *ánnis post* Rómam cónditam *trecéntis duodenonagínta*.	He was made consul three hundred and eighty years after the founding of Rome.

REMARKS.

1. *Post* and *ante* are usually put *after* their ablatives, or *between* them, as above. Sometimes, however, they occupy the first place ;

---

* This and the next following examples show that *ante* and *post* may (as prepositions) be followed by an accusative, indicative of the time before or after which the event has taken place. When this is the case, the preposition usually comes *after* the words *diêbus, annis*, &c.

as, *ante annis octo, post paucis diebus.* So also *post aliquanto,* some time afterwards ; *post non multo,* shortly after ; *post paulo,* a little while after that ; *ante paulo,* a little while before ; instead of the more common *aliquanto post,* &c.

2. The word *ante* may also stand in the sense *abhinc,* "ago," "before the present time" (cf. *D.*), but not vice versa.

3. *Ante* and *post,* followed by *quam* with a verb, give rise to the same variety of expression. E. g. *Anno ipso, antequam natus est Ennius,* An entire year before Ennius was born. *Numa rex annis permultis* ante *fuit,* quam *Pythagoras,* Numa was king many years before the time of Pythagoras. *Non multo* post, quam *tu a me discessisti,* Shortly after you left me. *Nono anno* postquam *in Hispaniam venerat,* Nine years after his arrival in Spain. *Cimon* post annum quintum, quam *expulsus erat, in patriam revocatus est,* Cimon was recalled into his country five years after he had been expelled from it.*

4. After the ablative of time, and also after *pridie* and *postridie,* the words *ante* and *post* are sometimes omitted, especially before *quam.* Thus : *Quemadmodum tertio anno rapuēre* (sc. *ante*), As they had plundered three years before. *Anno trecentesimo altĕro,* quam (= postquam) *condĭta erat Roma,* Three hundred and two years after the founding of Rome. *Pridie* quam (= antequam) *occiderētur,* The day before he was killed. *Postridie ad me venit,* quam (= postquam) *expectāram,* He came to me the day after I had expected him.†

5. The point of time at which anything *begins* is expressed by the ablative, with *ab* or *ex.* Thus : *ab urbe condĭtā,* from the foundation of the city ; *ab adolescentiā,* from youth up ; *ex eo tempŏre,* from (since) that time ; *ex Metello consŭle* (= ex consulātu Metelli), since the time of Metellus's consulship.

6. Relations of time are also expressed by *ad* or *usque ad,* "until"; *in* (cum Acc.), "till"; *de,* "at," or "during"; and *sub,* which cum. Acc. = "towards," or "about," but cum. Abl. "at," "by," "during." E. g. *Ab horā octārā usque ad vesperam collocūti sumus,* We conversed from the eighth hour until evening. *De nocte surgĕre,* To rise during the night. *De multā nocte vigilāre,* To watch late at night. *Sub lūcem,* Towards daylight. *Sub luce,* By daylight. *Sub exitu anni,* At the close of the year. *Sub tempus edendi,* Towards (near) dinnertime.

To bite, to wound by biting.	*Mordĕo, ēre, mŏmordi, morsum.* *Morsu vulnĕrāre* (ALIQUEM).
Why? on what account?	*Cur? quamobrem? quapropter? quā de causā?*

---

* Thus the English "Two hours before (or after) he had died," may in Latin be expressed as follows : *Duabus horis* antequam (postquam) *decessĕrat* = Ante (post) *duas horas,* quam *decessĕrat* = Altĕrā horā antequam (postquam) *decessĕrat* = Ante (post) *altĕram hōram,* quam *decesserat.*

† Instead of *quam, ex quo* and *quum,* "since," may also be used, with *post* omitted ; e. g. *Triduo,* quum *has dabam litteras,* Three days after writing this. So also the mere ablative of the relative ; e. g. *Octo diebus,* quibus *has litteras dabam,* Eight days after the date of this.

What is the reason that ?	{ *Quid est, cur ?* (*cum. subj.*) { Quid (causae) est, quod ?
Why not ?	Cur non ? quin ?
Because.	{ *Quŏd, quĭa* (cum ind. and subj.). { *Quĭ, quippe qui* (cum subj.).
For the reason — that (= *because*).	{ *Ob eam causam* or *proptereă — quod.* { *Ideo, idcirco, propterea — quia.*
Why do you beat the dog ?	Quaprópter cánem vérbĕras ?
I beat him because he has bitten me.	{ Égo éum vérbero, quod me momór- dit. Égo éum concútio, quíppe qui mô mórsu vulneráverit.
Why do you not call for the doctor ?	Cúr nôn (quin) médicum arcéssis ?
I do not call for him, because I do not need him.	Éum nôn arcesso propteréa, quía éjus nôn indígeo.
Why do they not read my book ?	Cúr nôn líbrum méum légunt ?
They do not read it, because they cannot comprehend it.	{ Nôn legunt, quíppe qui eúm intellí- gere nôn póssint. Éum ob hóc nôn légunt, quía intel- lígere nôn póssunt.
Do you know the man who has lent me his cane ?	Novistíne hóminem, quí mĭhi bácu- lum súum commodâvit ?
I do know him.	Nóvi, véro.
Do you breakfast before you go out ?	Sumĭsne jentáculum priúsquam in públicum pródis ?
Does the tailor show you the coat which he is mending ?	Ostendítne tíbi sártor tógam, quam réficit ?
He does show it.	Sáne quídem, osténdit.
Do you see the man who is in the garden ?	Núm vídes hóminem, quí est ın hórtulo ?
I do not see him.	Éum nôn vídeo.
To wait, remain.	{ *Oppĕrĭor, ĭri, perĭtus* or *pertus sum.* { *Mănĕo, ēre, nsi, nsum.* { *Expecto, āre, ăvi, ātum.* { *Praestŏlor, āri, ātus sum.*
To wait for any one.	{ Opperĭri or manēre aliquem. { Praestolāri alicui.
To expect any one *or* anything.	Expectāre aliquem *or* alĭquid.
To wait for anything.	Opperĭri alĭquid.
Are you waiting for your letters ?	Opperirísne epístolas túas ?
I am waiting for them.	Égo véro (éas) oppérior.
Is he waiting for his brother ?	Manétne (opperitúrne) súam frâ- trem ?
Is the servant waiting for his master ?	Núm sérvus héro súo praestolâtur ?
He is not waiting for him.	(Éi) nôn praestolâtur.

Do you expect your friends ?	Écquid amícos túos expéctas ?
I do not expect them.	(Éos) nôn expécto.
What are they expecting ?	Quid expéctant ?
They are expecting the money which you owe them.	Quám íis débes pecúniam expéctant.
To owe.	Debeo, ēre, ŭi, ĭtum (ALICUI ALIQUID).
Do you owe any one anything?	Debêsne álicui áliquid ?
I owe not a penny to any one.	Égo númmum débeo némini.
How much do you owe me ?	Quántam míhi débes pecúniam ?
I owe you a hundred crowns.	Débeo tíbi céntum thaléros.
Do I owe as much as you ?	Debeône tántam pecúniam quántam tú ?
You owe more money than I do.	Majôrem tû débes pecúniam quám égo.
Did they owe us anything?	Núm nóbis quídquam debuérunt ?
They owed us nothing.	Nóbis níhil debuérunt.
I am indebted to you for many things.	Débeo tíbi múlta.
The master.	Hĕrus, i, m.
The shilling.	*Shillingus, i, m.
The pound.	Libra (ae, f.) pondo; *or simply* pondo (indecl.).
Five pounds of gold.	Auri quinque pondo.
To return, come back.	{ Redĕo, ĭre, ĭi (ivi), ĭtum. Revertor, i, rsus sum.* (ALIQUO, AD ALIQUEM).
From (any place).	De, a (ab), ex (Prep. cum Abl.).
Hence, from there.	{ Inde, illinc istinc (adv). De (a, ex) eō (illō) locō.
At what o'clock do you usually return from the market ?	Quâ hórā de fóro revérti sóles ?
I am accustomed to return thence at twelve.	Sóleo revérti íllinc hórā duodécimā.
Has he come back from home ?	Rediítne (revertítne) dómo ? †
He has not yet come back from there.	Nôndum inde revértit.
Does the servant return early thence ?	Revertitúrne sérvus íllinc béne mâne ?
He is wont to return thence at ten o'clock in the morning.	Revérti índe sólet hórā décimā mâne.
Did they return before noon ?	Reverterúntne ánte merídiem ?
They did return at eleven o'clock.	Revertérunt véro hórā undécimā.
At nine in the morning.	Nônā mănĕ (sc. hōră).

---

* This verb is generally *revertor* in the present; but in the perfect *reverti* (from the active *reverto*), more frequently than *reversus sum.*

† See Lesson LVI. C.

U

At eight in the evening. — Octāvā vespĕri (*sc.* hōrā).

Towards five o'clock in the morning (evening). — Sub hōram quintam māne (vespĕri).

Towards noon, evening. — Sub merīdĭem, sub vespĕram.

How long ? — *Quam dĭu ?*

Long, for a great while — Dĭu (Adv.) ; *longum tempus* ; *perdiu* (= very long).

Longer. — Longĭus, diutĭus.

Longer than a year. — Plūs (amplĭus) anno ; anno longĭus ; amplĭus annum.

During, for (throughout). — *Per ; inter ; super* (Prep. cum Acc.) ; *in* (cum Abl.).

During the summer. — Per aestātem.

For an entire year. — Per annum intĕgrum.

During (within) the few days. — In diēbus paucis.

During dinner-time (while at dinner). — Inter (super) coenam.

During play-time (while playing). — Inter ludendum.

For the space of two, three, four days. — Biduum, triduum, quatriduum (*Acc.*)

(For) three entire days. — Universum (totum) triduum (*Acc.*).

For three months. — Trēs menses.

During twenty days. — Dies viginti.

For many years. — Multos annos.

Now for the third year (already three years). — Tertium jam annum.

(Within) these twenty years. — His annis viginti.

Within the next three years. — Proximo triennio.

A minute. — *Hōrae sexagesima (*sc.* pars) ; momentum, i, *n.*

A day. — Dies, *m.* & *f.* (Lesson VIII. *B.*)

A year. — Annus, i, *m.*

A month. — Mensis, is, *m.*

The summer. — Aestas, ātis, *f.*

The winter. — Hiems, emis, *f.*

The age. — Aetas, ātis, *f.*

The century. — Saecŭlum, i, *n.*

Whole, entire. — Tōtus, a, um ; intĕger, gra, grum ; universus, a, um.

How long did you speak with the man ? — Quám dĭu cum hómine collocútus és ?

I spoke with him three hours. — Collocútus súm cum éo trēs hóras.

How long did your brother remain in the country ? — Quám dĭu fráter túus rûre permánsit ?

He stayed there the entire summer. — Permánsit ibi (per) aestātem íntegram.

Did you stay long in the city ?	Moratúsne es díu ın úrbe ?
I stayed there for a great while.	Morâtus sum íbi lóngum témpus.
How long do you wish to stay with us ?	Quám díu commorári vis nobíscum ?
I desire to remain with you an hour, a month, a year.	Cúpio vobíscum commorári ûnam hôram, ûnum ménsem, ánnum.

Exercise 110.

Why do you love that man ? — I love him because he is good. — Why does your neighbor beat his dog ? — Because it has bitten his little boy. — Why does our father love me ? — He loves you because you are good. — Do your friends love us ? — They love us because we are good. — Why do you bring me wine ? — I bring you some because you are thirsty. — Why does the hatter drink ? — He drinks because he is thirsty. — Do you see the sailor who is in the ship ? — I do not see the one who is in the ship, but the one who is in the square. — Do you read the books which my father has given you ? — I do read them. — Do you know the Italians whom we know ? — We do not know those whom you know, but we know others. — Do you buy the horse which we have seen ? — I do not buy that which we have seen, but another. — Do you seek what you have lost ? — I do seek it. — Do you find the man whom you have looked for ? — I do not find him. — Does the butcher kill the ox which he has bought in the market ? — He does kill it. — Do our cooks kill the chickens which they have bought ? — They do kill them. — Does the hatter mend the hat which I have sent him ? — He does mend it. — Does the shoemaker mend the boots which you have sent him ? — He does not mend them, because they are worn out. — Does your coat lie upon the chair ? — It does lie upon it. — Does it lie upon the chair upon which I placed it ? — No, it lies upon another. — Where is my hat ? — It is in the room in which you have been. — Do you wait for any one ? — I wait for no one. — Do you wait for the man whom I have seen this morning ? — I do wait for him. — Art thou waiting for thy book ? — I am waiting for it. — Do you expect your father this evening ? — I do expect him. — At what o'clock has he gone to the theatre ? — He has gone thither at seven o'clock. — At what o'clock does he return from there ? — He returns from there at eleven o'clock. — Has your bailiff returned from the market ? — He has not yet returned from it. — At what o'clock has your brother returned from the country ? — He has returned from there at ten o'clock in the evening.

Exercise 111.

At what o'clock hast thou come back from thy friend ? — I have come back from him at eleven o'clock in the morning. — Hast thou remained long with him ? — I have remained with him about an hour. — How long do you intend to remain at the ball ? — I intend to remain there a few minutes. — How long has the Englishman remained with you ? — He has remained with me for two hours. — Do you intend to remain long in the country ? — I intend to remain there dur-

ing the summer. — How long have your brothers remained in town
(*in urbe*) ? — They have remained there during the winter. — How
much do I owe you ? — You do not owe me much. — How much do
you owe your tailor ? — I only owe him fifty crowns. — How much
dost thou owe thy shoemaker ? — I owe him already seventy crowns.
— Do I owe you anything ? — You owe me nothing. — How much
does the Frenchman owe you ? — He owes me more than you. — Do
the English owe you as much as the Spaniards ? — Not quite so much.
— Do I owe you as much as my brother ? — You owe me more than
he. — Do our friends owe you as much as we ? — You owe me less
than they. — Why do you give money to the merchant ? — I give him
some because he has sold me handkerchiefs. — Why do you not drink ?
— I do not drink because I am not thirsty ? — Why do you pick up
this ribbon ? — I pick it up because I want it. — Why do you lend
this man money ? — I lent him some because he is in want of some. —
Why does your brother study ? — He studies because he desires to
learn Latin. — Are you thirsty ? — I am not thirsty, because (*quippe
qui*) I have drunk. — Has your cousin already drunk ? — Not yet; he
is not yet thirsty. — Does the servant show you the room which he is
sweeping ? — He does not show me that which he is sweeping now,
but that which he swept yesterday. — Do you breakfast before you
go out ? — I go out before I breakfast. — What does your brother do
before he writes his letters ? — He buys paper, ink (*atramentum*), and
pens, before he writes them.

Lesson LVIII. — PENSUM DUODESEXAGE-SIMUM.

SYNTAX OF THE ACCUSATIVE.

A. The accusative serves to designate the direct object of transitive verbs, active or deponent, and stands
in answer to the question *Whom?* or *What?* (Cf. Lesson XXIV. *G.*) E. g.

Fílius pátrem ámat.	The son loves the father.
Déus múndum aedificávit.	God created the world.
Miltíades Athénas totámque Graéciam *liberávit.*	Miltiades liberated Athens and entire Greece.
Glória virtútem *tánquam úmbra séquitur.*	Glory follows valor like a shade.

REMARKS.

1. When the verb is changed into the passive voice, the object-
accusative becomes the subject of the verb. E. g. *Pater a filio amâ-*

tur. — *Mundus a Deo aedificâtur.* — *Athenae totâque Graecia a Milti-ade liberâtae sunt.* This conversion into the passive voice may always take place without any material alteration of the sense.

2. In addition to the accusative of the immediate object, many active verbs admit of another noun in the Genitive, Dative, or Ablative. These verbs are then said to govern two cases. E. g. *Pater filio (dat.) librum dedit.* — *Me* civitātis morum *piget taedetque,* I am weary of, and disgusted with, the morals of the city. *Democrïtus* oculis *(abl.) se privavit,* Democritus deprived himself of his eyes. Cf. Lessons LXI., LXVII., LXXI.

3. The object of an active verb is frequently an infinitive, with or without a subject-accusative, or a clause introduced by a relative or one of the conjunctions *ut, ne, quo,* &c. (Cf. Lessons LII., LIII., LIV.) E. g. *Ennius deos esse censet,* Ennius is of opinion that the gods exist. *Ante senectütem curâvi, ut bene vivěrem,* Before old age, my aim was to lead a good life.

   4. The accusative after transitive verbs is sometimes entirely suppressed. This is the case, —

a.) When the object is designedly left indefinite, in order to render the act alone conspicuous. E. g. *Ego semper* amāvi, *et si quid faciam nunc quoque quaeris,* amo, I have always loved, and if you inquire what I am doing now, my answer is, "I love." *Non sine summo dolore* scribo, I write with the deepest sorrow. *Tarquinius Delphos* mittěre *statuit,* Tarquin resolves to send to Delphi.

b.) When it has already been expressed, and can easily be understood from the context. E. g. *Complexus Coriolanus suos dimisit,* sc. *eos,* Coriolanus, having embraced his family, dismissed them. *Et scribo aliquid et lego ; sed cum* lego, *ex comparatiöne sentio, quam male* scribam, I write and read something at the same time ; but when I read, I perceive from the comparison how badly I write. So frequently the pronouns *me, te, se, eum, nos,* &c.

c.) In certain technical expressions, such as *movēre,* sc. *castra,* to decamp ; *appellěre, conscenděre, solvěre,* sc. *navem,* to land, embark, set sail ; *ducěre,* sc. *exercïtum,* to march (an army) ; *merēre,* sc. *stipendia,* to serve as a soldier ; *obïre,* sc. *diem suprēmum,* to die ; *agěre,* sc. *vïtam,* to live. In the same manner the object-infinitive is often omitted ; as, *In Pompejānum statim cogito,* sc. *proficisci,* I contemplate going to my estate near Pompeii immediately. *Ut solet,* sc. *fiěri,* As it commonly happens.

   5. The verb itself is sometimes omitted. This occurs, —

a.) In expressions like *Quid multa !* (See page 154.) *Quid ! quod* . . . . for *quid dicam de eo, quod,* What shall I say to the fact that. *Quae cum dixisset Cotta, finem,* sc. *fecit,* When Cotta had said this, he concluded his speech. *Sus Minervam,* sc. *docet,* The dunce instructs the sage.

b.) After the formulas *nihil aliud (amplius* or *minus) quam,* "only," "nothing more or less than," "nothing but," where one of the tenses

28

of *facere* may be supplied. *Nihil aliud* (sc. *fēcit*) *quam bellum com-parāvit*, His only thought was the preparation of a war. *Illā nocte* nihil aliud (sc. factum est) *quam vigilātum in urbe*, That night there was nothing but watching in the city (i. e. every one kept awake).

c.) In a sentence left unfinished by *aposiopesis.** E. g. *Quos ego* .... Whom I will ....

6. A transitive verb with its object may frequently be converted into a single verb denoting the same thing. E. g. *opus facĕre* = *operāri; auxilium ferre* = *auxiliāri; lachrĭmas fundĕre* = *lachrimāri; navem agĕre* = *navigāre*, &c.

7. The accusative sometimes depends upon a verbal noun or adjective, as the case governed by the verbs from which they are derived. Such are, —

a.) A few verbal nouns in *tio;* as, *domum itio* or *reditio*, a going or returning home. *Quid tibi hanc* curatio est *rem?* What is this business to you? But this usage is confined to Plautus.

b.) Verbal adjectives in *bundus*. E. g. *Populabundus agros ad oppĭdum pervenit*, Pillaging the fields, he came into the vicinity of the city. *Mirabundi velut somnii vanam speciem*, As if wondering at the fleeting visions of a dream. Sometimes also those in *lus;* as, *Facta consultaque ejus aemŭlus erat.*

c.) The verbals *ōsus*, *exōsus*, and *perōsus*, "hating," "detesting," and *pertaesus*, "weary of," "disgusted with." E. g. *Quum exosus arma in otio agĕret*, When, from a dislike for war, he lived in retirement. *Pertaesus ignaviam suam*, Weary of his own want of energy.

B. A number of neuter verbs are sometimes followed by an object-accusative derived from the same root, and of a signification similar to their own.

Such are *cursum currĕre, dolōrem dolēre, furōrem furĕre, gaudium gaudēre, jusjurandum jurāre, insaniam insanire, pugnam* (or *proelium*) *pugnāre, risum ridēre, somnĭum somniāre, sapōrem sapĕre, vītam vivĕre.* In all these instances, however, the object-accusative has generally an adjective connected with it, or is otherwise modified. E. g.

Mīrum somniávi *sómnium.*	I had a singular dream.
Jurávi *veríssimum pulcherrimúm-que jusjurándum.*	I have sworn most conscientiously and honorably.
Síccius Dentâtus triumphâvit cum imperatóribus súis *triúm-phos nóvem.*	Siccius Dentatus, with his generals, was honored with nine triumphs.

REMARK. — Instead of a noun of the same root with the verb, one of kindred signification merely is often put. E. g. *Proelia pugnāre*, to

---

* A rhetorical figure employed in abrupt transitions, as in the example given. The more frequent grammatical omissions of verbs or objects (in all the preceding instances) are called *ellipsis.*

fight battles ; *aleam ludere*, to play at dice ; *saltare Turnum* or *Cyclopa*, to dance the Turnus or the Cyclops ; *Bacchanalia vivere*, to lead a Bacchanalian life ; *Olympia vincere* or *coronari*, to conquer, to be crowned at the Olympic games ; *judicium vincere*, to gain one's case.

C. Many verbs, though commonly neuter, are sometimes employed transitively in a different sense, and then admit an object in the accusative. Such are, —

1. A number of verbs expressive of emotions, as of joy, sorrow, fear, shame. E. g. *dolere, erubescere, flere, gaudere, gemere, horrere, lamentare, lacrimare, lugere, moerere, plorare, queri*, &c., which, when followed by ALIQUEM or ALIQUID, then signify "to be grieved or to rejoice *at*," "to lament or weep *over*." Thus : *Flere necem filii*, To weep over the death of a son. *Doleo casum luctumque tuum*, I am pained by your calamity and sorrow.

2. Certain verbs of sensation, such as *olere, redolere, sapere*, and *resipere*, when they signify "to smell of," "to taste after." E. g. *Olet unguenta*, He smells of ointment. *Piscis ipsum mare sapit*, The fish tastes as salt as the sea itself. *Redolet antiquitatem*. — So also *anhelare crudelitatem*, to breathe cruelty ; *sitire sanguinem*, to thirst after blood ; *sonare quiddam peregrinum*, to emit a strange sound.

3. A variety of others, of which the following are the most common : — *ambulare*, to walk, *act.* to walk upon ; *dormire*, to sleep, *act.* to spend in sleep ; *fastidire*, to be haughty, *act.* to disdain ; *festinare* and *properare*, to make haste, *act.* to hasten or accelerate ; *ludere*, to play (sport), *act.* to play a game, or to act ; *manere*, to remain, *act.* to wait for ; *navigare*, to sail, *act.* to navigate ; *ridere*, to laugh, *act.* to deride ; *vigilare*, to watch, *act.* to spend in watching ; *vivere*, to live, *act.* to live = to spend.

4. The poets also say *pallere, pavere, tremere, trepidare* ALIQUID, instead of *timere* ALIQUID, "to dread anything"; and *ardere, calere, tepere, perire, deperire* ALIQUAM, instead of *amare* ALIQUAM, "to be in love with one."

REMARK. — Many neuter verbs admit of the accusative of a pronoun or adjective (of the neuter gender), without ever occurring with that of a substantive. E. g. *Hoc laetor*, I am rejoiced at it. *Id tibi succenseo*, I am displeased with you on this account. *Hoc laboro, id operam do*, It is my endeavor or aim. *Hoc non dubito*, I have no doubt about it. *Illud tibi non assentior*, On this point I do not agree with you. *Unum omnes student*, They all are aiming at one thing. On these accusatives, compare Lesson LIX. *D.* Remark 2.

To live, reside (in any place).	*Habitare* or *Domicilium habere* (ALIQUO LOCO).
To inhabit.	*Incolo, ere, ui, cultum* (ALIQUAM TERRAM, URBEM).
To live on or near (a street, river).	*Accolere* (viam, flumen).

Where do you live?

Úbi hábĭtas?

I live in the Via Sacra, number fifty.

Domicílium hábeo in Vĭā Sácrā, número quinquagésimo.

What country did your father live in?

Quám térram páter túus incólŭit?

He lived between the Rhine and the Alps.

Incóluit inter Rhênum Alpêsque.

What street do you live on?

Quám víam áccŏlis?

I live on Frederick Street, number one hundred and twenty-five.

Áccŏlo víam Fredericânam, número centésimo vicésimo quinto.

> To live with or at the house of any one.

> Apud aliquem (in dŏmo alicújus) habitāre.

> To stay (as guest) with any one.

> In alicújus dŏmo (apud alíquem) deversāri.

Did you ever live in the country?

Habitavistine únquam rúri?

No, I always lived in the city.

Ímmo véro sémper in úrbe habitávi.

Do you live with your cousin?

Habitásne apud consobrínum (túum)?

I do not live with him, but with my father.

Apud pátrem, nôn apud íllum hábito.

Does your friend still live where I have lived?

Habitátne amícus túus étiam núnc eôdem lóci, ubi égo habitávi?

He lives no longer where you have lived; he lives now on the great square.

Quo loco tû habitavísti, nôn ámplius hábitat; áccolit véro hôc témpore cámpum mágnum.

The street.
The number.

Vía, ae, f.; vícus,* i, m.
Nŭmĕrŭs, i, m.

How long? Up to what time?

Quam dĭu? Quŏ usque?

Till, until (Prep.).

{ Ad, usque ad (cum Acc.).
{ In, usque in "

Until noon, evening, morning.

Usque ad merĭdiem, vespĕram, mānĕ (tempus matutīnum).

Till to-morrow.

Usque ad diem crastĭnum; in crastīnum.

Till the day after to-morrow.
Until late at night.
Till daylight.
Until this day.
Till the next day.

Usque ad diem perendĭnum.
Ad multam noctem.
Ad lūcem.
Usque ad hunc diem.
Usque ad diem postĕrum (sequentem).

Until this moment.
Until now, hitherto.
Up to that time.

Usque ad momentum praesens.
Adhuc, adhuc usque.
Ad id tempus; ad id locōrum.

---

* *Vīcus* is a street lined with houses.

Up to a certain time.	Ad tempus quoddam.
To this place, hither, thus far, as far as here.	*Hūcusque, hactĕnus* (Adv.) ; *ad hunc usque locum.*
To that place, as far as there, so far, thither.	Eo usque, istuc (illuc) usque ; ad illum usque locum.
The week.	*Hebdŏmas, ădis, f., or hebdŏmăda, ae, f.*
Sunday.	*Dies sōlis ; dies domĭnĭcus.
Monday.	*Dies lūnae.
Tuesday.	*Dies Martis.
Wednesday.	*Dies Mercūrii.
Thursday.	*Dies Jŏvis.
Friday.	*Dies Venĕris.
Saturday.	*Dies Saturni.
Does your friend still live with you ?	Núm amícus túus apud tê étiam núnc (hódie étiam) hábitat ?
No, he lives with me no longer.	Nôn véro ; apud mê nôn ámplius hábitat.
How long (till when) did he live with you ?	Quô úsque apud tê (dómi túae) habitâvit ?
He lived with me no longer than a year.	Habitâvit apud mê nôn ámplius ánnum.
How long were you at the ball ?	Quám díu interfuísti saltatióni ?
(I was there) until midnight.	Ad médiam nóctem. (Cf. Lesson XXXV. *B.*)
How long did you stay with my father ?	Quám díu (quô úsque) apud pátrem méum morátus és ?
I stayed with him till eleven at night.	Commorátus súm apud éum úsque ad undécimam nóctis.
Till, until (conj.).	*Dum, usque dum ; dōnec ; quoad* (cum Ind. & Subj.)
Until I return.	Dúm (dônec) rédeo *or* rédeam.
Until I bring you the book.	Dúm (quóad) tíbi librum áffero *or* áfferam.
Until my brother returns.	Dúm (dônec) frâter revértitur.
To be willing, to wish — been willing, wished.	Velle — vŏlŭi, ——.
To wish, desire — wished, desired.	⎰ Cupĕre — cupĭvi, cupĭtum. ⎱ Optāre — āvi, ātum.
To be able, can — been able, could.	⎰ Posse — pŏtŭi, ——. ⎱ Quire — ĭvi, ĭtum.
Has he been willing to go for the physician ?	Voluítne arcéssere médicum ?
He has not been willing to go for him.	Arcéssere éum nóluit.
Did he wish to go out this morning ?	Cupivítne hódie mâne in públicum prodíre ?
He did not wish (to go out).	Nôn cupívit.

28 *

Have they been willing to do this?	Núm hóc fácere voluérunt?
They have not been willing.	Nôn voluérunt (noluérunt).
Could the book be found?	Potuítne liber inveníri?
It could (be found).	Véro, pótuit.
It could not be found.	Reperíri nôn pótuit.
One, people, they, any one (the French on).	Quis, aliquis; homines.

D. Obs. General assertions, in which in English we employ the indefinite *one, people, they, some one,* &c., may in Latin be expressed in several ways: —

1. By the Passive Voice, either personally or impersonally; as, *Dicitur esse ventūrus,* or *Dicitur eum esse ventūrum,* They say that he will come, It is said that he will come.

2. By the third person plural of the active voice; as, *Dicunt eum esse mortuum,* They (people) say that he is dead.

3. By the first person plural; as, *Si cogitamus,* If we reflect (if one reflects).

4. By the second person singular; as, *Pulchrum est dicere, quod scias,* It is handsome to say what *one* knows (what you know).

5. By *quis* or *aliquis;* as, *Si quis dicat,* If any one should say.

6. By the impersonal *licet;* as, *Licet videre,* One can see (we may see).

7. By the neuter of the participle in *dus;* as, *In villam revertendum est,* It is necessary to return to the villa.

Have they brought my shoes?	Calceíne méi apportáti sunt?
They have not yet brought them.	Nôndum apportáti sunt.
What have they said?	Quid dixérunt?
They have said nothing.	Níhil dixérunt.
What have they done?	Quid fáctum est?
They have done nothing.	Níhil fáctum est.
What news do they bring? (What is there new?)	{ Quid nóvi affértur? { Quíd tándem nóvi?
They say nothing new. (There is nothing new.)	{ Níhil nóvi affertur. { Níhil nóvi est.
Is there anything new?	Núm quídnam nóvi?
Have you anything new?	Habêsne áliquid nóvi?
I have something new.	Hábeo véro quíddam nóvi.
I have nothing new to write you.	Nóvi, quód ad tê scríberem, níhil érat.
New.	*Nŏvus, a, um; rĕcens, tis.*
My new garment.	Véstis méa rĕcens *or* nóva.*
His new clothes.	Vestímenta súa (ejus) recentía (nŏva).

---

* *Recens,* not yet worn out, and *nova,* just made, or after the latest fashion.

My new friend.	Amīcus mĕus nŏvus.
The new soldiers.	Milĭtes nŏvi.
The new law.	Lex rĕcens ac nŏva.
The brush.	Pēnĭcillus *or* pēnĭcŭlus, i, *m.*
To brush.	*Penĭcillo extergĕre* or *detergĕre* (*-tersi, -tersum*).

Have you brushed my new coat?	Extersistĭne (penicĭllo) tŏgam mĕam nŏvam?
No, I have not yet brushed it.	Nôn ; égo éam nŏndum extérsi.
Will you not brush your hat?	Nónne pĭleum túum penículo detérgĕre vis?
I have no time to brush it.	Déest mihi tempus ad éum detergéndum.

EXERCISE 112.

Where do you live? — I live in the large street (*in plateā*). — Where does your father live? — He lives at his friend's house. — Where do your brothers live? — They live in the large street, number one hundred and twenty. — Dost thou live at thy cousin's? — I do live at his house. — Do you still live where you did live? — I live there still. — Does your friend still live where he did live? — He no longer lives where he did live. — Where does he live at present? — He lives in William Street (*in viā Wilhelmiānā*), number one hundred and fifteen. — Where is your brother? — He is in the garden. — Where is your cousin gone to? — He is gone into the garden. — Did you go to the play yesterday? — I did go thither. — Have you seen my friend? — I have seen him. — When did you see him? — I saw him this morning. — Where has he gone to? — I do not know. — Has the servant brushed my clothes? — He has brushed them. — Has he swept my room? — He has swept it. — How long did he remain here? — Till noon. — How long have you been writing? — I have been writing until midnight. — How long did I work? — You worked until four o'clock in the morning. — How long did my brother remain with you? — He remained with me until evening. — How long hast thou been working? — I have been working till now. — Hast thou still long to write? — I have to write till the day after to-morrow. — Has the physician still long to work? — He has to work till to-morrow. — Must I remain long here? — You must remain here till Sunday. — Must my brother remain long with you? — He must remain with us till Monday? — How long must I work? — You must work till the day after to-morrow. — Have you still long to speak? — I have still an hour to speak. — Did you speak long? — I spoke till the next day. — Have you remained long in my room? — I have remained in it till this moment. — Have you still long to live in this house? — I have still long to live in it. — How long have you still to live in it? — Till Sunday. — How many triumphs did Dentatus celebrate? — He celebrated nine. — What sort of a life does your father live (*vivĕre*)? — He lives a retired (*otiōsus*) and a tranquil (*tranquillus*) one. — Who was wont to dance the Turnus? — The Romans were wont to dance it.

EXERCISE 113.

Does your friend still live with you ? — He lives with me no longer. — How long has he lived with you ? — He has lived with me only a year. — How long did you remain at the ball ? — I remained there till midnight. — How long have you remained in the carriage ? — I have remained an hour in it. — Have you remained in the garden till now ? — I have remained there till now. — Has the captain come as far as here ? — He has come as far as here. — How far has the merchant come ? — He has come as far as the end of the road. — Has the Turk come as far as the end of the forest ? — He has come as far as there. — What do you do in the morning ? — I read. — And what do you do then ? — I breakfast and work. — Do you breakfast before you read ? — No, Sir, I read before I breakfast. — Dost thou play instead of working ? — I work instead of playing. — Does thy brother go to the play instead of going into the garden ? — He does not go to the play. — What do you do in the evening ? — I work. — What hast thou done this evening ? — I have brushed your clothes, and have gone to the theatre. — Didst thou remain long at the theatre ? — I remained there but a few minutes. — Are you willing to wait here ? — How long must I wait ? — You must wait till my father returns. — Has anybody come ? — Somebody has come. — What have they wanted ? — They have wanted to speak to you. — Have they not been willing to wait ? — They have not been willing to wait. — What do you say to that man ? — I tell him to wait. — Have you waited for me long ? — I have waited for you an hour. — Have you been able to read my letter ? — I have been able to read it. — Have you understood it ? — I have understood it. — Have you shown it to any one ? — I have shown it to no one. — Have they brought my clothes ? — They have not brought them yet. — Have they swept my room and brushed my clothes ? — They have not done it yet.

Lesson LIX. — PENSUM UNDESEXAGESIMUM.

ACCUSATIVE AFTER VERBS. — *Continued.*

A. Many neuter verbs, especially those denoting motion, become transitive by composition with one of the prepositions *ad, ante, circum, con, in, inter, ob, per, praeter, sub, subter, super, supra,* or *trans,* and take an object in the accusative.

Such are *īre, meāre, cedĕre, gradi, radĕre, currĕre, ambulāre, volāre, fluĕre, labi, scandĕre, salīre, vagāri, venīre,* &c. So also *loqui, latrāre, vigilāre,* and a few denoting rest or situation; as, *jacēre, stāre, sedēre,* &c. The following may serve as specimens : —

ACTIVE.		NEUTER.	
adīre,	*to approach,*	*from* īre,	*to go.*
alloqui,	*to address,*	" loqui,	*to speak.*
antegredi,	*to precede,*	" gradi,	*to walk.*
circumsedēre,	*to surround,*	" sedēre,	*to sit.*
increpāre,	*to chide,*	" crepāre,	*to clatter.*
irridēre,	*to deride,*	" ridēre,	*to laugh.*
interjacēre,	*to be situate between,*	" jacēre,	*to lie.*
obīre,	*to undergo,*	" īre,	*to go.*
obsidēre,	*to besiege,*	" sedēre,	*to sit.*
percurrĕre,	*to run (pass) through,*	" currĕre,	*to run.*
praefluĕre,	*to flow before,*	" fluĕre,	*to flow.*
praetervolāre,	*to hurry by,*	" volāre,	*to fly.*
subīre,	*to undergo,*	" īre,	*to go.*
subterlabi,	*to glide under,*	" labi,	*to glide.*
supereminēre,	*to overtop,*	" eminēre,	*to project.*
suprascandĕre,	*to climb over,*	" scandĕre,	*to climb.*
transcendĕre,	*to cross,*	" "	"
transvolāre,	*to fly (pass) over,*	" volāre,	*to fly.*

EXAMPLES.

Tĕ núnc *álloquor,* Africâne.	I address *you* now, Africanus.
Cáto *allatrâre* Scipiônis *magnitúdinem* sólitus érat.	Cato had been in the habit of detracting from Scipio's greatness.
Saguntum Carthaginiénses *circúmsedent.*	The Carthaginians are besieging Saguntum.
Ámnis *máre inflúxit.*	The river emptied into the sea.
Euphrátes *Babylóniam médiam pérmeat.*	The Euphrates flows through the heart of Babylonia.
Pópulus sólet nonnúmquam *dígnos praeterire.*	The people sometimes slight the meritorious.
Quî vénit híc flúctus, *fluctus* (Acc. pl.) *superéminet ómnes.*	The wave, which now approaches, overtops all others.
Núm túum nômen vel *Caúcasum transcéndere* pótuit, vel Gangem *transnatâre?*	Has your name passed beyond the Caucasus, or swum beyond the Ganges?

REMARKS.

1. Of the verbs above enumerated, those compounded with *circum, per, praeter, trans,* and *super* alone are regularly transitive, and occur also in the passive. The rest are only so when used in a secondary or figurative sense. E. g. *Circumsedēmur,* We are besieged. *Tamĕsis* transīri *potest,* The Thames can be passed. *Fossa transilĭtur,* The ditch is leaped over. *Societas inĭtur,* A society is formed. *Mors pro patriā obĭtur,* Death is suffered for the fatherland.

2. Those compounded with *ad, ante, in, inter, ob, prae, sub, super,* and *supra* may stand as transitive verbs, but they remain more com-

monly neuter, and are followed either by the dative (according to page 157, *G.*) or by the accusative, with the *preposition repeated.** E. g. *In spem libertatis ingredior*, I indulge the hope of liberty. *Ad me adire quosdam memini*, I remember certain persons coming to me. *Aqua subit in coelum*, The water rises into the atmosphere.

3. To the neuter verbs, which sometimes become transitive, must be added those compounded with the prepositions *a*, *ab*, *cum*, *e*, and *ex*. E. g. *Colloquium abnuĕre*, to decline an interview; *societatem coire*, to enter into association with; *edormire crapŭlam*, to sleep off the effects of drinking; *egredi veritătem*, to go beyond the limits of the truth; *convenire aliquem*, to meet any one (speak with one); *altitudĭnem excedĕre*, to exceed a certain height, &c.

4. *Transitive* verbs, compounded with the prepositions *ad*, *circum*, *praeter*, and *trans*, are sometimes followed by *two* accusatives, of which one depends upon the verb and the other on the preposition. E. g. *Corcyram pedĭtum mille secum advexērunt*, They brought along with them a thousand infantry to Corcyra. *Allobroges omnia sua praesidia circumduxit*, He led all his forces around the Allobroges. *Argesilaus Hellespontum copias trajēcit*, Agesilaus sent his troops across the Hellespont.

B. The impersonal verbs *poenĭtet, pĭget, pŭdet, taedet, mĭsĕret*, and *verĭtum est* are followed by the accusative of the person affected by the emotions denoted by them. E. g.

Poénĭtet mê (tê, éum).	I am (you are, he is) sorry.†
Pĭget mê (tê, éum).	I am (you are, he is) chagrined.
Pŭdet nôs (vôs, éos).	We (ye, they) are ashamed.
Taêdet nôs (vôs, éos).	We (you, they) are disgusted.
Mĭseret mê (tê, éum).	I (you) pity, he pities.
Vérĭtum est mê.	I have been afraid.

REMARK.—The object of the emotion denoted by these verbs stands in the genitive. E. g. *Sapientiam nunquam sui poenitet. — Me tui pudet. — Te aliōrum miseret.* (See Lesson LXVII. *C.*)

C. The impersonal verbs *jŭvat, delectat, fallit, fŭgit, praeterit, dĕcet, lătet*, and *oportet* are likewise followed by the accusative of the person. E. g.

Júvat *or* deléctat mê, tê, nôs.	It delights me, you, us (I am delighted, &c.).

---

* The preposition, however, is also frequently a different one; as, *in aedes accedĕre, ad urbem subire, ad aures praecedĕre.* Hence many of these verbs are susceptible of several different constructions; as, *subire jugum*, to submit to the yoke; *subire montem* or *ad montem*, to come up (to) the mountain; *subire in coelum*, to rise up into the atmosphere; *subire muro* or *murum*, to come up close to the wall.

† This may literally be rendered by *It moves me to regret, chagrin, shame, disgust, pity, fear.*

Fállit, fúgit, praéterit mê.

It escapes my memory or notice, I do not know.

Mê nôn fúgit, praéterit.

I know very well.

Néminem véstrum praéterit.

Every one of you is aware.

Tê hilári ánimo esse, válde mê júvat.

I am delighted that you are in good spirits.

Nôs, nísi mê *fállit*, jacébimus.

Unless I am mistaken, we shall fail.

Nôn *mê fúgit*, vétera exémpla pro fíctis fábulis jam habéri.

I know very well, that the examples of antiquity are now regarded as fictions.

Nôn *mê praéterit*, usum ésse óptimum dicéndi magístrum.

I am aware, that practice is the best teacher of oratory.

Quôs nôn *vérĭtum est* in voluptâte súmmum bónum pónĕre.

Who were not afraid to assert pleasure to be the highest good

REMARKS.

1. The impersonal verbs of this class differ from those of B by sometimes admitting a subject nominative, although never a personal one. E. g. Candida pax *homines*, trux *decet* ira *feras*, Gentle peace becomes men, ruthless ferocity wild beasts.

2. *Decet*, " it becomes," with its compounds, *condecet, dedecet, indecet*, and *oportet*, never occur with the accusative alone, but always with an infinitive or with the Acc. cum Inf., and *oportet* sometimes with the subjunctive. E. g. *Decet verecundum esse adolescentem*, It is proper for a young man to be respectful. *Oratorem simulāre non dedecet*, It is not improper for an orator to dissemble. *Eum oportet amnem quaerere sibi*, He must seek a river. *Me ipsum ames oportet, non mea*, You must love me, and not my possessions. *Suis te* oportet *illecebris ipsa virtus* trahat *ad verum decus*, Virtue herself must attract you with her own charms to real honor.

3. *Decet* and *latet* are sometimes construed with the dative, but only by the older writers. Thus, *Ita nobis decet*, Thus it becomes us. *Latet mihi*, I am ignorant of the fact.

D. After verbs, participles, and adjectives, the accusative is sometimes put instead of the ablative, to mark the relation expressed by the English *in, as to, with respect to.* E. g.

Équus mícat aúribus et *trémit* *ártus*.

The horse moves its ears and trembles in its limbs.

Pontíficem *praeíre* jússit *verba*.

He ordered the pontifex to say the words before him.*

Ingénium plácidâ *mollímur* ab *árte*.

Our mind is rendered pliable and soft by placid art.†

Vírgo *infícitur téneras* rubôre *génas*.

The maiden's tender cheeks are suffused with blushes.‡

---

* Lit. *to go before* (or *first*) *as to the words* to be pronounced.
† Lit. *We are rendered pliable as to our minds.*
‡ Lit. *The maiden is suffused as to her cheeks.*

Advérsum fémur **trágulā** gráviter *íctus* cécidit.	He fell, heavily wounded in the front of his thigh by a javelin.
Tácitā cúrā *ánimum incénsus.*	His mind inflamed with silent anxiety.
Núdae bráchia ac lacértos.	Bare as to their arms and shoulders.

REMARKS.

1. This construction is of Greek origin, and occurs chiefly in poetry. It is called *synecdoche*.

2. Among the accusatives thus representing other cases, and rendered by *in, for, of, as to, with respect to,* are included, —

a.) The following, which frequently occur in prose even : *magnam partem,* in a great measure, mostly ; *maximam partem,* for the most part ; *partim* (= *partem*), in part, partly ; *vicem* (= *vice*), instead of ; *id genus* (for *ejus genĕris*), of that kind ; *omne genus* (for *omnis generis*), of every kind ; *summum,* at the utmost ; *minĭmum,* at least ; *cetera,* in other respects ; *reliqua,* as for the rest.

b.) The neuter accusatives *hoc, id, illud, quid, quod, aliquid, nihil,* and *nonnihil,* in expressions like *hoc, id, illud aetatis* (= *hujus, ejus, illius aetatis*), of this, that age ; *id tempŏris* or *id locorum* (for *eo tempore*), at that time ; *id auctoritātis* (for *eā auctoritate*), of that authority. So, *Valde* id (= in eo) *laborandum est,* We must seriously aim at this. *Nihil ego te accusavi,* I have accused you in no respect. *Quod* (= *cujus*) *nos poeniteret,* Of which it might repent us. *A me consilium petis,* quid (= cujus) *tibi auctor sim,* You ask my advice as to what plan I would recommend to you. *Thebani* nihil *moti sunt, quanquam* nonnihil *succensebant Romanis,* The Thebans were moved *in no respect,* although they were *somewhat* displeased with the Romans.

To steal (pilfer, abstract from).	Fŭror, ări, ătus sum (Dep.). Clĕpo, ĕre, clepsi, cleptum. Surrĭpĭo, ĕre, ĭpŭi, eptum. (ALICUI ALIQUID or ALIQUID AB ALIQUO).
To commit a theft.	Furtum facĕre (alicujus rei ; alicui = on any one).

E. *Obs.* *Furări* is to steal deliberately and maliciously ; *clepĕre,* to take away clandestinely and meanly, to filch ; *surripĕre,* to take away secretly, or to abstract.

Has any one committed a theft on any one ?	Númquis fúrtum fēcit álicui ?
No one has stolen anything from any one.	Némo cuíquam fúrtum fēcit áliquod.
What have they stolen from us ?	Quíd a nóbis furáti súnt ?
They have stolen our hay.	Furáti súnt a nóbis fœnum.
Has any one stolen your hat ?	Écquid tíbi píleum clépsit áliquis ?
Some one has stolen it.	Clépsit éum véro áliquis.
What have they stolen from you ?	Quíd ést tíbi surréptum ?
They have stolen nothing from me.	Surréptum ést míhi níhil.

All.   *Omnis, e ; cunctus, a, um ; univer-*
sus, a, um.

F. Obs. Omnis signifies " all," " the whole of," and sometimes
" every." *Cunctus* generally appears only in connection with a collective noun, or in the plural, in the sense " all together," or as many
as there are of a certain class or number. *Universus* (= *unus* and
versus) is " all collectively," " the whole," " entire."

All his money.	Ómnis éjus (súa) pecúnia.
All this wine.	Ómne hócce vinum.
All these children.	Ómnes hi líberi.
All these good children.	Ómnes hi líberi bóni.
The entire people.	Cúnctus pópulus.
All the citizens (as a body).	Cúncti cíves.
The whole of the (the entire) family.	Família univérsa.
For three entire days.	Tríduum univérsum.
All as a mass, without exception.	Ómnes univérsi.
All men.	Ómnes hómines; univérsi (hómines).
Everything which; all that.	Ómne quód (quodcúnque); ómnia quae (quaecúnque).
All the good wine.	Ómne vinum bónum.
All the good water.	Ómnis áqua bóna.
All the good children.	Líberi bóni ómnes (cúncti, univérsi).

To dye, color.	{ *Tingo, ĕre, nxi, nctum.* { *Colōre inficĕre (fēci, fectum).*
To color, paint.	Cŏlōro, āre, āvi, ātum.
To get anything dyed.	{ Aliquid colōre aliquo inficiendum curāre. { Aliquid colōre aliquo tingi jubĕre.
Black — white.	{ Āter, atra, atrum — albus, a, um. { Nĭger, ra, rum — candĭdus, a, um.
Green — red.	Virĭdis, e — rūber, rubra, rubrum.
Yellow — gray.	Flāvus, a, um — cānus, a, um.
Brown — blue.	Fuscus, a, um — caerŭlĕus, a, um.
To dye anything black, white, green, &c.	Aliquid colōre atro, albo, virĭdi, &c. inficĕre.
What color do you wish to dye your coat ?	Quŏ colōre tógam túam inficere vis ?
I wish to dye it black.	Cúpio éum inficere colōre átro.
Do you dye your cloth green ?	Tingísne pánnum túum colōre vĭridi ?
No; I am dying it red.	Nôn véro; tíngo éum colōre rúbro.
Did he get his hat dyed blue ?	Curavítne píleum súum caerúleo colōre inficiendum ?
No; he has got it dyed white.	Ímmo véro éum colōre álbo tíngi jússit.

V   29

The color.	Cŏlor, ōris, *m*.
The dyer.	Tinctor, ōris, *m*.
The word.	Verbum, i, *n*.; vocabŭlum, i, *n*.
The speech.	Sermo, ōnis, *m*.
How is this word written?	Quómodo scríbitur hócce vocábulum?
It is written thus.	Scríbitur hôc pácto.
How is his name written?	Quómodo scríbitur nomen éjus?
It is written with a z.	Scríbitur lítterā z.
Germany.	Germānĭa; Alemannĭa, ae, *f*.
Holland.	{ Terra (ae, *f*.) Batāvōrum. { *Hollandĭa, ae, *f*.
England.	*Anglĭa, ae, *f*.; Britannia, ae, *f*.
Spain.	Hispānĭa, ae, *f*.
Italy.	Itălĭa, ae, *f*.
France.	*Francogallĭa, ae, *f*.
America.	*Amērĭca, ae, *f*.
The Old World.	*Orbis antiquus.
The New World.	*Orbis nŏvus.
The world.	Mundus, i, *m*.
The country, land.	Terra, ae, *f*.
The globe.	Orbis, is, *m*.; orbis terrārum.
The United States of America.	Civitātes Americae foederātae.
Switzerland.	Helvetĭa, ae, *f*.
Prussia.	*Borussĭa, ae, *f*.
Turkey.	*Turcĭa, ae, *f*.
Russia.	*Russĭa, ae, *f*.; Ruthēnia, ae, *f*.
London.	Londīnum, i, *n*.
Paris.	Lutētĭa, ae, *f*. (Parisii).
New York.	*Nŏvum Eborăcum, i, *n*.
Rome.	Rōma, ae, *f*.
As far as my brother's.	Úsque in dómum méi frátris.
As far as England, Switzerland, America.	Úsque in Ángliam, Helvétiam, Américam.
As far as London, Paris, New York.	Úsque* Londínum, Lutétiam, Eboracum Novum.
As far as the vicinity of Rome.	Úsque ad Rômam.
To travel; to make (undertake) a journey.	{ Ĭter făcĕre — fēci, factum. { Peregrinatĭōnes suscipĕre — suscēpi, susceptum.
To be on a journey, to be abroad.	{ Peregrinor, āri, ātus sum. { Peregrinātum abesse — abfŭi.
To set out; to travel towards a place.	{ Proficiscor, i, fectus sum. { Tendo, ĕre, tĕtendi, tensum. { Contendĕre (ALIQUO).

---

* The *ad* of *usque ad* is commonly omitted before the names of towns, unless it is intended to express mere approximation.

When do you intend to start for England ?	Quô témpore in Ángliam proficísci cógitas ?
I intend to start next summer.	Aestáte próximā proficísci cógito.
In what country is he abroad ?	Quā in térrā peregrinátur ?
He is travelling in Holland.	Peregrinátur in térrā Batavôrum.
How far did he travel ?	Quô úsque fêcit íter ?
He has travelled across the Atlantic as far as America.	Íter per máre Atlánticum fêcit úsque in Américam.
Whither are you bound ?	Quô téndis ?
I am travelling to my brother, to Italy, to London.	Téndo ad frâtrem, in Itáliam, Londīnum.

EXERCISE 114.

Have they stolen anything from you (has anything been stolen from you) ? — They have stolen all the good wine from me. — Have they stolen anything from your father ? — They have stolen all his good books from him. — Dost thou steal anything ? — I steal nothing. — Hast thou ever stolen anything ? — I have never stolen anything. — Have they stolen your apples from you ? — They have stolen them from me. — What have they stolen from me ? — They have stolen from you all the good books. — When did they steal the carriage from you ? — They stole it from me the day before yesterday. — Have they ever stolen anything from us ? — They have never stolen anything from us. — Has the carpenter drunk all the wine ? — He has drunk it. — Has your little boy torn all his books ? — He has torn them all. — Why has he torn them ? — Because he does not wish to study. — How much have you lost (at play) ? — I have lost all my money — Do you know where my father is ? — I do not know. — Have you not seen my book ? — I have not seen it. — Do you know how this word is written ? — It is written thus. — Do you dye anything ? — I dye my hat. — What color do you dye it ? — I dye it black. — What color do you dye your clothes ? — We dye them yellow. — Are you sorry ? — I am not sorry. — Is he chagrined ? — He is very much (valde) chagrined. — Are they not ashamed ? — They are ashamed and disgusted. — Are you delighted that your brother has come ? — I am very much delighted. — Do you know that your book has been stolen ? — It has not escaped my notice that it has been stolen. — Are you addressing me ? — I am not addressing you, but the stranger (who is) standing by your side.

EXERCISE 115.

Do you get your trunk dyed ? — I get it dyed. — What color do you get it dyed ? — I get it dyed green. — What color dost thou get thy thread stockings dyed ? — I get them dyed white. — Does your cousin get his handkerchief dyed ? — He does get it dyed. — Does he get it dyed red ? — He gets it dyed gray. — What color have your friends got their coats dyed ? — They have got them dyed green. — What color have the Italians had their carriages dyed ? — They have had them dyed blue. — What hat has the nobleman ? — He has two hats, a white one and a black one. — Have I a hat ? — You have sev-

eral. — Has your dyer already dyed your cravat? — He has dyed it.
— What color has he dyed it? — He has dyed it yellow. — Do you
travel sometimes? — I travel often. — Where do you intend to go to
this summer? — I intend to go to Germany — Do you not go to
Italy? — I do go thither. — Hast thou sometimes travelled? — I have
never travelled. — Have your friends the intention to go to Holland?
— They have the intention to go thither. — When do they intend to
depart? — They intend to depart the day after to-morrow. — Has
your brother already gone to Spain? — He has not yet gone thither.
— Have you travelled in Spain? — I have travelled there. — When
do you depart? — I depart to-morrow. — At what o'clock? — At five
o'clock in the morning. — Have you worn out all your boots? — I
have worn them all out. — What have the Turks done? — They have
burnt all our good ships. — Have you finished all your letters? — I
have finished them all. — How far have you travelled? — I have
travelled as far as Germany. — Has he travelled as far as Italy? —
He has travelled as far as America. — How far have the Spaniards
gone? — They have gone as far as London. — How far has this poor
man come? — He has come as far as here. — Has he come as far as
your house? — He has come as far as my father's.

Lesson LX. — PENSUM SEXAGESIMUM.

VERBS FOLLOWED BY TWO ACCUSATIVES.

A. The verb *docēre*, "to teach," with its compounds
edocēre and *dēdocēre*, and *celāre*, "to conceal," admit
of two accusatives, one designating the person and the
other the thing taught or concealed. E. g.

Quis *músicam* dócuit *Epaminon-dam?*	Who taught Epaminondas music?
Catilína *juventútem*, quam illéxe-rat *mála facinŏra* edocébat.	Catiline was instructing the young men, whom he seduced, in pernicious crimes.
Demócritus *Polyaênum geomé-triam* vóluit dedocḗre.	Democritus wanted to make Poly-ænus unlearn geometry.
Nôn *tê* celávi *sermônem* Áppii.	I have not concealed from you the language of Appius.
Antígonus *íter ómnes* célat.	Antigonus concealed his route from every one.

REMARKS.

1. These verbs occur frequently with one accusative only, and *do-cēre* sometimes without any case, like the English "to teach," "to

instruct." Thus: *docēre edocēre, celāre aliquem, aliquid* or *aliquem aliquid;* — *dedocēre aliquem,* or *aliquem aliquid.*

2. When *docēre* and *edocēre* signify "to inform," the thing is expressed by the ablative with *de.* E. g. *De itinere hostium senātum edocet,* He informed the senate of the enemy's route. *Sulla de his rebus docētur,* Sulla is informed of these things. So also *celāre aliquem de re.*

3. An infinitive may take the place of the accusative of the thing. E. g. *Dionysius* tondēre *filias suas docuit,* Dionysius taught his daughters to shave.

4. When the construction becomes passive, the accusative of the person is changed into the nominative, and that of the thing either remains or is changed into the ablative, with or without *de.* E. g. *Omnes militiae artes edoctus,* Schooled in all the arts of war. *Et Graecis doctus litteris et Latīnis,* Learned both in Greek and Latin literature. *Per legatos cuncta edoctus,* Informed of everything by his agents. *Hoc, id, illud celābar,* I was kept ignorant of that. *Non est profecto de illo veneno celāta mater,* The mother was surely not kept ignorant of that poison.

5. Other verbs signifying "to instruct" (such as *erudio, instruo, instituo,* and *informo*) do not admit an accusative of the thing, but have either the ablative or *in.* E. g. *His in rebus jam te usus ipse erudīvit,* In these things experience itself has already taught you. *Iphicrates exercĭtum* omni disciplinā militāri *erudīvit,* Iphicrates instructed the army in every military discipline.

B. Verbs signifying to inquire, to ask, or demand, likewise admit of two accusatives: one of the person, and the other of the thing.

Such verbs are *rogo, oro, exoro; posco, reposco, flagĭto; interrogo, exquĭro, consŭlo, percontor,* &c. E. g.

Méo jûre *tê hóc beneficium* rógo.	I ask you for this favor, as one to which I am entitled.
Núnquam *déos divítias* rogávi.	I have never asked the gods for riches.
Oratiónes mê dúas póstŭlas.	You are demanding two orations of me.
Pâcem tê ómnes póscimus.	We all ask (sue) you for peace.
Caêsar *Aéduos fruméntum* quotídie flagĭtābat.	Cæsar was dunning the Æbui every day for supplies of corn.
Íbo et cónsŭlam *hanc rem amícos.*	I will go and consult my friends about this thing.
Súnt, *quae tê* vólŭmus percontári.	There are matters, about which we wish to question (examine) you.

REMARKS.

1. Verbs of asking or demanding sometimes have also *aliquid ab aliquo,* and those of asking or inquiring *aliquem de aliquā re.* E. g.

29 *

Quid *acta tua vita*, quid *studia*, quid *artes* a te *flagĭtent*, *tu vidēbis*, See yourself, what your past.life, your studies and science demand of you. *Visne, ut* te eisdem de rebus *Latīne interrogem?* Do you wish me to ask you about the same things in Latin ? So also *te oro, te rogo, ut*, &c.

2. After *peto*, I ask (beseech), and *quaero*, I ask or inquire, the double accusative never occurs, but the construction of those verbs is *petĕre aliquid ab aliquo*, or *petĕre ab aliquo*, *ut* or *ne*, and *quaerĕre aliquid ab (de, ex) aliquo*. E. g. *Quod ne facias peto a te*, Which I beseech you not to do. *Eadem secreto ab aliis quaerit*, He makes the same inquiry secretly of others.

C. Verbs signifying to name or call, to esteem, consider, learn or find, to make, render, constitute, choose, and the like, are followed by two accusatives, of which one constitutes the object and the other a part of the predicate.

Such are *dīco, voco, appello, nomĭno, nuncupo*, I call, name, nominate ; — *duco, habeo, judĭco, existĭmo, puto, arbĭtror*, I hold, esteem, consider, think ; — *intellĭgo, agnosco, reperio, invenio*, I perceive, learn, find ; — *facio, reddo, creo, delĭgo, designo, declaro*, I make, render, create, choose, designate, declare ; — *me praebeo, me exhĭbeo, me praesto*, I show or prove myself, and others of similar import. E. g.

Íram béne Énnĭus inítĭum insániae díxit.
Ennius has correctly called anger the beginning of madness.

Quâs stéllas Graéci cométas, nóstri crinítas vócant.
The stars which the Greeks call comets, are called long-hairs among us.

Octávium súi Caésarem salutábant.
His adherents hailed Octavius as emperor.

Epaminóndas philosóphiae praeceptórem hábuit Lysim.
Epaminondas had Lysis as an instructor in philosophy.

Fúlmen sinístrum auspícium óptimum habêmus.
We consider thunder from the left as the most auspicious omen.

Sócrates totíus múndi sê íncolam et civem arbitrabátur.
Socrates considered himself an inhabitant and citizen of the entire world.

L. Muraênam cónsulem renuntiávi.
I announced Lucius Muraena as consul.

Ancum Márcium régem pópulus creávit.
The people created Ancus Marcius king.

Cicerónem univérsa cívitas cónsulem declarávit.
The entire state declared Cicero consul.

Caêsar Cavárium régem constitúerat.
Caesar had appointed Cavarius king.

Pompéius sê auctórem méae salútis exhíbuit.
Pompey has shown himself the author of my safety.

REMARKS.

1. In the passive construction of these verbs, the accusatives are both converted into nominatives, of which one stands as the subject, and the other as part of the predicate. E. g. Ira *bene ab Ennio* initium *insaniae dictum est.* — Octavius *a suis* Caesar *salutabātur.* — Ancus Marcius rex *a populo creatus est,* &c.   (Cf. Lesson XXXIV. *C.*)

2. An adjective or participle may supply the place of the second accusative. E. g. *Bene de me merĭtis* grātum me *praebeo*, I show myself grateful to those who have done me favors. *Scythārum gens* antiquissima *semper habita est,* The Scythian nation has always been considered the most ancient. So also the common expression *aliquem certiōrem facĕre,* to inform any one (of anything, *alicujus rei* or *de aliquā re*), in the passive *certior factus sum,* I am informed; and *reddĕre aliquem irātum, placĭdum, meliōrem,* to make any one angry, calm, better, &c.

➤ 3. Instead of a second accusative, the verbs *habēre* and *putāre*, "to consider," frequently have *pro* with an ablative, or *loco, numĕro* or *in numero* with the genitive. E. g. *Aliquem* pro amico, pro hoste *habēre,* To regard any one as a friend, as an enemy. *Aliquid* pro certo, pro nihĭlo *putāre* or *habēre,* To consider anything as certain, as of no account. *Aliquem* in numero *deorum habēre,* To consider one a divinity. *Aliquid beneficii* loco *numerāre,* To regard anything as a kindness. So also *ad,* " as ": *Trecentos armātos ad custodiam corpŏris habuit,* He had a body-guard of three hundred men.

4. The accusatives are sometimes connected by *esse.* E. g. *Patriae sanctiora jūra quam hospitii* esse *duxit,* He considered the rights of his country more sacred than those of hospitality.

D. THE ACCUSATIVE AFTER PARTICLES.

I. In exclamations the accusative is put after the interjections *o, heu, eheu, ecce, en, hem, pro, bĕne,* and frequently also without them. E. g.

Heu (eheu) mê mĭserum! or *Mê mĭserum!*	Alas! Wo is me!
O hŏminem fortunâtum!	O fortunate man!
Pŏpŭlum véro *praeclârum!*	O people truly great and noble!
Écce mê! En mĭserum hŏminem!	Here I am! Behold an unhappy man!
Pro deôrum atque hóminum *fĭdem!*	For heaven and mercy's sake!
Hem Dâvum tĭbi!	There's Davus now for you!
Et *béne nôs! béne tê!*	And our health! your health!*

REMARKS.

1. All these interjections may likewise be followed by the vocative.

---

* An expression used in drinking. Ovid. Fast. 2. 637.

Vae and *hei* are commonly put with the dative. E. g. *Vae mihi mísero!* Ah! wretched me! *Hei mihi!* Wo is me!

2. *En* and *ecce* are more frequently put with the nominative. E. g. *Ecce homo!* Behold the man! *Ecce tuae litterae!* Here is your letter! *En ego!* Here I am! But in comedy usually *ecce me, eccum* (= *ecce eum*), *eccos, eccillum, eccillam, eccistam.* (Cf. page 37, Rem. 2.)

II. The prepositions *ad, apud, ante, adversus* and *adversum, cis* and *citra, circa* and *circum, circĭter, contra, erga, extra, infra, inter, intra, juxta, ob, penes, per, pone, post, praeter, prope, propter, secundum, supra, trans, versus,* and *ultra,* are invariably followed by the accusative; *in* and *sub* only in answer to the question *Whither?*

REMARKS.

1. These prepositions generally precede words governed by them, except *versus,* which is commonly put after. E. g. *Brundusium versus,* Towards Brundusium. *Ad oceanum versus,* Towards the ocean.

2. *Super* and *subter* commonly take likewise the accusative, but sometimes also the ablative. (Cf. Lesson LXXII. D. Rem.) *Clam,* "without the knowledge of," has commonly the ablative, but sometimes also the accusative or genitive. E. g. *Clam vobis. Clam patrem atque omnes. Clam patris.*

Up, above; in the upper part, on the top (Rest).	{ Supra; sŭper (adv.). { In summo,* in superiŏri parte.
Up, upwards (Motion).	Sursum (adv.); ad summum.
Below, down, in the lower part (Rest).	{ Infra, subter (adv.). { In imo, in inferiŏri parte.
Down, downwards (Motion).	Deorsum (adv.); ad imum.
From above down.	{ Dēsŭper, superne (adv.). { De superiŏri lŏco.
From top to bottom.	A summo ad imum.
From the foot (bottom) to the top.	Ab imo ad summum.
On the top of the hill.	{ In súmmo cólle. { In superióri párte cóllis.
In the lower part (basement) of the house.	{ In imā dōmo. { In inferióri párte dómūs.
At the foot of the mountain.	Sub radícibus móntis.
To the top of the hill.	{ Ad summum collem. { In superiôrem partem collis.
Into the lower part of the house.	{ Ad imam dómum. { In inferiôrem pártem dómūs.
To be up, below.	{ Supra (in súmmo) ésse. { Infra (in imo) ésse.

---

* Generally *summo, a, o,* in agreement with the noun; as, *in summo monte, in summā arbŏre.* So also *imus, a, um.* (Cf. page 176.)

To go upwards, downward.	Súrsum, deórsum íre.
To come from above.	Désŭper, supérne veníre.

To go up, to ascend.	{ Ascendo,* ĕre, di, sum. Escendo, ĕre, di, sum. (MONTEM, IN, AD LOCUM).
To come down, to descend.	Descendĕre (ab, de, ex loco — in, ad locum).

To ascend (go up) a mountain.	Ascéndĕre móntem.
To mount a horse, to embark in a ship.	Ascéndĕre in équum, in nâvim.
To ascend (rise) to dignity, to honors.	Ascéndere gradum dignitâtis, ad honóres.
To get into a carriage, upon the mast.	Escéndĕre vehículum, in mâlum.
To descend from a more elevated region into the plains.	Ex superióribus lócis in planítiem descéndere.
To ascend, descend a river.	Advérso flúmine, secundo flúmine vehi.

Where is your father going to ?	Quô téndit páter túus ?
He is ascending the mountain.	Ascéndit (in) móntem.
Has the boy ascended the tree ?	Escendítne púer (in) árborem ?
He has ascended it.	Escéndit véro.
Does he not wish to come down ?	{ Nónne descéndere cúpit ? Nónne deórsum veníre vult ?
Yes, he does wish it.	Íta ést, cúpit.
Are you on the top of the house ?	Ésne in súmmâ dómo ?
No, I am in the basement.	Immo véro in ímâ súm.

On this side (Rest).	Cítra (Prep. et Adv.).
To this side (Motion).	Cis, citra (Prep. cum Acc.).
On that side, beyond (Rest).	Trans, ultra (Prep. et Adv.).
To that side, beyond (Motion).	Trans, ultra (Prep. cum Acc.).

To live (to be situate) on this, on the other side of the Rhine.	Cis, trans Rhênum incólĕre (situm esse).†
To come to this side of the river.	Cis (citra) flúmen veníre.
To go to that side (beyond, across) the hill.	Trans (ultra) cóllem abíre.
Is he on this side or on that ?	Útrum ést cítra án últra ?
He is beyond.	Últra est.
Hither, in this direction.	{ Hūc ; horsum (adv.). In hunc lŏcum.
Thither, in that direction.	Illuc ; illorsum, istorsum (adv.).

---

* Compounded of *ad* + *scando* (I climb). So *escendo* = *ex* + *scando ; descendo* = *de* + *scando*. The first and second of these verbs may be used either transitively with the accusative, or intransitively with the preposition *in*, *ad*, &c. The last of them (*descendere*) is always neuter.

† This is sometimes expressed by a compound of *cis ;* as *cisalpīnus, cisrhenānus, cismontānus*, living or situate on this side of the Alps, Rhine, mountain. And again *transalpīnus, transmarīnus*, &c.

The hill, the mountain.	Collis, is, *m.*; mons, tis, *m.*
The river, stream.	Amnis, is, *m.*; flūmen, ĭnis, *n.* Flŭvĭus, i, *m.*
The present, gift.	Dōnum, i, *n.*; mŭnus, ĕris, *n.* Mŭnuscŭlum, i, *n.*
The new-year's present.	Strēna, ae, *f.*
To make one a present of anything (To present one with anything).	*Dăre alicui aliquid dōno (munĕri).* * *Aliquem aliquā rĕ donāre.* *Alicui aliquid donāre.*
To receive something as a present from any one.	Dōno (munĕri) accipĕre aliquid ab aliquo.
To give back again, to return, restore.	Reddo, ĕre, dĭdi, dĭtum. Restĭtŭo, ĕre, ŭi, ūtum. (ALICUI ALIQUID).
Did he return you your book again?	Reddidĭtne (restituĭtne) tíbi líbrum túum?
He has returned it.	Réddidit véro. Restítuit.
From whom did your brother receive a new-year's present this year?	A quo accêpit hôcce ánno fráter túus strēnam?
He received one from his father.	Accêpit ûnam a pátre.
Did he ever make you a present?	Dedítne tíbi únquam áliquid dóno? Donavítne te únquam áliquā rĕ?.
He has already made many presents.	Dédit míhi jám multa múneri. Donâvit míhi vero jám múlta.
Will you return (restore) me my little presents?	Núm vis míhi munúscula méa restitúere?
I am not willing.	Nôn vólo. Nólo.
Have you already commenced your letter?	Fecistine jam inítium epístolae scribéndae?
I have not yet begun it.	Nóndum féci.
Must our presents be returned?	Númquid múnĕra nóstra restituénda súnt?
They are not to be returned.	Restituénda nôn súnt.
Must I ascend the hill?	Éstne míhi cóllis ascendéndus?
It must be ascended.	Ést véro ascendéndus.
Whence? Where from? Out of (an enclosed place).	*Unde? Ex (a) quō lŏco?* *Ex, e* (Prep. cum Abl.).
Where do you come from?	Únde vénis?
I come from the garden.	Vénio ex hórtulo.
Where did your brother come from this evening?	Únde (ex quō lóco) vênit fráter túus hódie vésperi?
He came from the theatre.	Vênit a theátro.
Where are those men coming from?	Únde hómines ílli véniunt?

---

* On this second dative ("for or as a present"), compare Lesson LXIII. *B.*

They have descended from the mountain.	Descendérunt de mónte.
To be worth.	{ *Vălĕo, ĕre, ŭi, ĭtum* (ALIQUO PRETIO). *Alicūjus prĕtĭi esse.*
To be worth so much, how (as) much, more, less.	*Tanti, quanti, plūris, minōris* (sc. *pretii*), *valēre.**
To be worth ten sesterces, two hundred pounds of gold.	Decem sestertiis, ducentis† pondo auri valēre.
To be worth much, very much, most, little, least, nothing.	Magno, permagno, plurĭmo, parvo, minĭmo, nihĭlo (*sc.* pretio) valēre.
How much may that horse be worth?	{ Quánti circiter prétii iste équus est? Quanti fortásse válet íste équus?
It is worth about a hundred crowns.	{ Céntum círciter thalērum est. Válet fortásse céntum thaléris.
This is worth more, less than that one.	Híc plūris, minóris válet quam ílle.
The one is not worth so much as the other.	Ílle (álter) nôn *tánti* válet, *quánti* álter.
How much is this thing worth?	{ Quánti prétii haêc rês êst? Quánti haêc rês válet?
This is not worth much.	{ Haêc rês párvi prétii est. Haêc rês párvo válet.
That is worth nothing.	{ Hóc nullius prétii est. Hóc níhĭlo válet.
You are not worth it.	Tánti nôn és.
To be better or *worth more* (*To excel*).	*Meliōrem* or *praefĕrendum esse.* *Praestāre, antecellere* (ALICUI).
Am I not as good as my brother?	Nónne égo tánti sum, quánti fráter méus?
You are better (worth more) than he.	Ímmo véro mélior (plūris) és.
I am not as good as you.	Tánti nôn súm égo, quánti tû.
This is preferable (better).	Hóc praêstat (preferéndum ést).
He excels all his fellow-students.	Commilitónĭbus suis ómnibus antecéllit.

EXERCISE 116.

Do you call me? — I do call you. — Where are you? — I am on the mountain; are you coming up? — I am not coming up. — Where are you? — I am at the foot of the mountain; will you come down? — I cannot come down. — Why can you not come down? — Because

---

* And so also *tantŭdem*, just so much; *quantĭvis* and *quantĭcunque*, whatever. But never *magni, parvi,* &c. (Cf. Lesson LXVII. *A.*)
† And so always the ablative, when the value is definitely given by a substantive, or by *magno, permagno,* &c. (Cf. Lesson LXXI. *A.*)

I have sore feet. — Where does your cousin live ? — He lives on this
side of the river. — Where is the mountain ? — It is on that side of
the river. — Where stands the house of our friend ? — It stands on
that side of the mountain. — Is the garden of your friend on this or
that side of the wood ? — It is on that side. — Is our storehouse not
on that side of the road ? — It is on this side. — Where have you been
this morning ? — I have been on the great mountain. — How many
times have you gone up the mountain ? — I have gone up three times.
— Is our father below or above ? — He is above. — Have the neighbor's boys given you your books back again ? — They have given
them to me back again. — When did they give them back again to
you ? — They gave them back again to me yesterday. — To whom
have you given your stick ? — I have given it to the nobleman. — To
whom have the noblemen given their gloves ? — They have given
them to Englishmen. — To which Englishmen have they given them ?
— To those whom you have seen this morning at my house. — To
which people do you give money ? — I give some to those to whom
you give some. — Do you give any one money ? — I give some to
those who want any. — Who has taught you music ? — No one ; I
have never learned music. — Did your brother conceal his purpose
(*consilium*) from you ? — He did not conceal it from me. — Did he
ask you for anything ? — He asked me for some money. — What did
the stranger question you about ? — He questioned me about the
way. — Whom did you have for a master ? — I had an Englishman
and a German for masters (*praeceptōres*).

EXERCISE 117.

Have you received presents ? — I have received some. — What
presents have you received ? — I have received fine presents. — Has
your little brother received a present ? — He has received several. —
From whom has he received any ? — He has received some from my
father and from yours. — Do you come out of the garden ? — I do not
come out of the garden, but out of the house. — Where are you going
to ? — I am going into the garden. — Whence comes the Irishman ?
— He comes from the garden. — Does he come from the same garden
from which you come ? — He does not come from the same. — From
which garden does he come ? — He comes from that of our old friend.
— Whence comes your boy ? — He comes from the play. — How
much is that carriage worth ? — It is worth five hundred crowns. — Is
this book worth as much as that ? — It is worth more. — How much
is my horse worth ? — It is worth as much as that of your friend. —
Are your horses worth as much as those of the French ? — They are
not worth so much. — How much is that knife worth ? — It is worth
nothing. — Is your servant as good as mine ? — He is better than
yours. — Are you as good as your brother ? — He is better than I. —
Art thou as good as thy cousin ? — I am as good as he. — Are we as
good as our neighbors ? — We are better than they ? — Is your umbrella as good as mine ? — It is not worth so much. — Why is it not
worth so much as mine ? — Because it is not so fine (*non aeque ele-*

gans) as yours. — Do you wish to sell your horse ? — I do wish to sell it. — How much is it worth ? — It is worth two hundred florins. — Do you wish to buy it ? — I have bought one already. — Does your father intend to buy a horse ? — He does intend to buy one, but not yours.

Lesson LXI. — PENSUM UNUM ET SEXAGESI-MUM.

SYNTAX OF THE DATIVE.

A. The dative is the case of the remote object, and serves to designate that *for* or *with respect to* which, or the person *for whose benefit* or *detriment** the agent acts, or that with reference to which it is possessed of certain attributes. Hence the predicate, with which the dative is connected, may be either a transitive verb, a neuter verb, an adjective, or an adverb.

B. The dative after transitive verbs denotes the person or object, with reference to which an action is performed, and stands in answer to the question *To whom?* or *For whom?* E. g.

Páter *fílio* líbrum *dédit.*	The father gave his son a book.
Dáte pánem *paupéribus.*	Give bread to the poor.
Pisístratus *síbi, nōn pátriae* Megarénses *vícit.*	Pisistratus conquered the Megarenses for his own benefit, and not for that of his country.
Tû túas inimicítias ut *reipúblicae donáres* tê vicísti.	By sacrificing your personal enmities to the common weal, you have won a conquest over yourself.
Hanníbalis bélla gésta múlti *memóriae prodidérunt.*	Many have left us records of the wars of Hannibal.
Zaleúcus et Charóndas léges *civitátibus súis conscripsérunt.*	Zaleucus and Charondas wrote laws for the benefit of their states.
Quántum *consuetúdini famaêque dándum sít,* id cúrent vívi.	As to the extent of the concessions we are expected to make to custom and to fame, let that be determined by the living.

REMARKS.

1. The accusative is often omitted, or its place supplied by an entire clause. E. g. *Tibi aras, tibi occas, tibi séris, tibi eidem métis,*

---

* In this sense it is commonly called the *Dativus commódi* vel *incommódi.*

You plough, harrow, and sow for yourself, and for your benefit you also reap. *Promitto* tibi, *tegŭlam illum in Italiā nullam relictūrum*, I assure you he will not leave a tile on a roof in Italy.

2. When the verb becomes passive, the dative remains as before. E. g. *Liber* filio *a patre dătus*, A book given by a father to his son. *Dator pānis* pauperĭbus, Let bread be given to the poor. *Megarenses a Pisistrato ipsi, non patriae victi sunt.*

C. The dative after neuter verbs represents the person with reference to whom, or for whose benefit, anything is done or exists. E. g.

Mĭhi quĭdem *esúrio*, nôn tĭbi.	I am hungry on my own account, and not on yours.
Nôn sôlum *nóbis* dívites *ésse* vólumus, sed *liberis, propínquis, amícis,* maximêque *reipúblicae.*	We desire to be rich, not only for our own benefit, but for that of our children, relations, and friends, and especially for that of the republic.
Cívitas Româna párum ôlim *vacábat liberálibus disciplínis.*	The Roman nation formerly had but little leisure for the liberal arts and sciences.
Plúres in Ásiā múlieres *síngulis víris* sólent *núbere.*	In Asia several women are accustomed to get married to one husband.
Néque *Caésari* sôlum sed étiam *amícis* éjus *ómnibus supplicábo.**	Nor will I supplicate Cæsar alone, but all his friends besides.

REMARKS.

1. The pronominal datives *mihi, tibi, sibi, nobis,* and *vobis* often imply merely a remote interest or curiosity on the part of the speaker. E. g. *Quid* mihi *Celsus agit?* What, pray, is Celsus after? *Quid* tibi *vis, insâne?* What do you want, insensate man? *Quid sibi velit, non intelligo,* I do not understand what he is after. *Quid ait tandem* nobis *Sannio?* What has Sannio to say for himself?

2. After the verbs *esse, fore, suppetĕre, deesse,* and *defĭt,* the dative denotes the person *in possession* or *in want of* the object designated by the nominative. E. g. *Sunt* mihi *libri,* I have books. *Est* homĭni cum Deo *similitudo,* Man has a resemblance to the Deity. *An nescis, longas* regĭbus *esse manus?* Or are you not aware, that kings have long hands? *Si cauda* mihi *foret,* If I had a tail. *Si vĭta* (mihi) *suppĕtet,* If I have life left (if life remains). *Lac* mihi *nŏvum non aestate, non frigŏre defĭt,* I have no lack of fresh milk either in summer or in winter. *Cui res non suppĕtat,* (ei) *verba non desint,* (The orator) who has a poor subject, should have words at his command.

---

* The verb *supplicâre = supplex esse.* The *nubĕre* of the preceding example properly signifies "to put on the veil," and with *alicui viro,* "to put on the marriage-veil *for* a man," i. e. to marry him.

DATIVE AFTER ADJECTIVES.

D. The dative stands after adjectives and adverbs as the end or object for or against which the quality denoted by them is represented as existing in the subject. E. g.

Cúnctis ésto benígnus, núllis blándus, paúcis familiâris, ómnibus aêquus.	You should be kind to every one, a flatterer of no one, intimate with few, just towards all men.
Públius dictátor léges secundíssímas plebi, adversas nobilitáti túlit.	Publius, the dictator, promulgated laws in favor of the people and opposed to the nobility.

The adjectives thus followed by the dative are quite numerous. They are those signifying, —

1. LIKE or UNLIKE, SIMILAR or DISSIMILAR : — *par, impar, dispar, aequâlis ; simîlis, assimîlis, consimîlis, dissimîlis, absimîlis, discŏlor.* E. g. *Canis lupo simîlis est,* The dog resembles the wolf. *Proxîmo rēgi dissimîlis,* Unlike the preceding king. *Ennio aequalis fuit Livius,* Livy was contemporary with Ennius.*

2. USEFUL or INJURIOUS : — *utîlis, bŏnus, saluber, salutâris, fructuŏsus ; inutîlis, noxîus, funestus, pestîfer, damnŏsus, perniciŏsus,* &c. E. g. *Salubrîor meliorque inŏpi, quam potenti,* More salutary, and better for poor than for rich men. *Ratio pestifēra multis, admodum paucis salutâris est,* Reason is destructive to many, and advantageous to few. *Universae Graeciae utîlis,†* Useful to entire Greece.

3. PLEASANT or UNPLEASANT : — *grātus, acceptus, dulcis, jucundus, laetus, suavis ; ingrātus, injucundus, molestus, grăvis, acerbus, tristis,* &c. E. g. *Scientiae suavitate nihil est hominîbus jucundius,* Nothing is more agreeable to men than the sweetness of knowledge. *Romŭlus multitudini gratior fuit, quam patrîbus,* Romulus was more acceptable to the masses than to the senate. *Verebâris, ne mihi gravis esses,* You were afraid of becoming troublesome to me.

4. INCLINED, FRIENDLY, DEAR, and their opposites AVERSE, HOSTILE : — *amîcus, benevŏlus, carus, familiâris, aequus, fîdus, fidēlis, propensus, propîtius, secundus ; adversus, aliēnus, inimîcus, contrârius, infensus,* &c. E. g. *Non fortūnae, sed hominibus amîcus,* Friendly (= a friend)‡ to men and not to fortune. *Uni aequus virtūti atque*

---

* The adjectives *simîlis, dissimîlis, par,* and *impar* are also followed by the genitive, especially when they denote similarity of character or intellect. E. g. *mei, tui, sui, nostri, vestri simîlis,* like me, you, &c., or my, your, &c. equal. *Dispar sui,* unlike itself. *Cujus paucos pares haec civitas tulit,* Like whom this state has produced but few. — *Aequalis,* in the sense of "contemporary," is more commonly followed by the genitive ; as, *ejus aequalis.* Also substantively with an adjective ; as, *meus aequalis.*

† But also *utîlis* or *inutîlis ad aliquid.* E. g. *Homo ad nullam rem utîlis,* a man fit for nothing.

‡ *Amîcus, inimîcus,* and *familiâris* are properly adjectives, and stand as such

ejus amīcis, Friendly to virtue alone, and to its friends. *Antonius Galliam sibi infestam inimicamque cognōvit,* Antonius learnt that Gaul was hostile to him. *Illi causae maxime est aliēnum,** It is entirely irrelevant to that case.

5. NEAR or ADJOINING : — *vicīnus, finitǐmus, confīnis, contermǐnus, proptǐor, proxǐmus.* E. g. *Proxǐmus sum egomet mihi,* I am my nearest neighbor. *Aethiopǐa Aegypto est contermǐna,* Æthiopia is conterminous with Egypt. *Mala sunt vicīna† bonis,* Adversity is next door neighbor to prosperity.

6. BELONGING TO ONE'S SELF or TO ANOTHER : — *affǐnis, cognātus, propinquus, proprius, peculiāris, commūnis, sacer; aliēnus, contrārius,* &c. E. g. Nobis propria *est mentis agitatio atque sollertia,* There is peculiar to us a certain agitation and sagacity of mind. Omni aetati *mors est commūnis,* Death is common to every age. Huic *affǐnes‡* scelěri *fuěrunt,* They were accomplices of this crime.

7. KNOWN or UNKNOWN : — *nōtus, certus, ignōtus, obscūrus, incertus, dubǐus, insolǐtus,* &c. E. g. Magis historǐcis *quam* vulgo *nōtus,* Known rather to the historians than to the vulgar. *Certius tibi est quam mihi,* It is a matter of greater certainty to you than to me. *Novum et* morǐbus *vetěrum insolǐtum,* New and unknown (unusual) to the manners of the ancients.

8. FIT or UNFIT, SUITABLE or UNSUITABLE : — *aptus, idoneus, accommodātus, commǒdus, necessārius, parātus, promptus, proclivis; — convenǐens, congruens, consentāneus, decōrus, honestus; turpis, foedus, indecōrus, absǒnus, absurdus.* E. g *Aptum esse consentaněumque* tempori et personae, To be fit and suitable for the occasion and person. Tibi *erunt parāta verba,* You will have words ready for you. Castris *idōneus locus,* A suitable site for a camp. *Congruens et conveniens decretis ejus,* Consistent with his avowed principles. *Ratiōni consentaneus,* In harmony with reason. *Absonum fidei,* At variance with credibility.§

9. EASY or DIFFICULT : — *facǐlis, expedǐtus, commǒdus; difficǐlis,*

---

in every degree of comparison; as, *Amicǐor libertāti quam suae dominationi.* — *Homo mihi amicissǐmus, mihi familiarissǐmus.* But they frequently occur as substantives with a genitive or an adjective. E. g. *Amǐcus patris.* — *Noster amǐcus.* So also the superlative *amicissǐmus* or *familiarissǐmus meus,* A very great or most intimate friend of mine. *Inimicissǐmus tuus,* Your mortal foe. *Amicissǐmus nostrorum homǐnum,* A warm friend of our men (our party).

* The construction of *aliēnus* is either *alicui rei, alicujus rei, re* or *a re.* Thus, *aliēnum nostrā amicitiā, a dignitate meā,* incompatible with our friendship, with my dignity. Several of these adjectives take also *erga, ad* or *in; as, benevǒlus, benignus erga aliquem; — propensus* ad or in *aliquem.*

† *Vicīnus* and *vicīna* are also used substantively, and then followed by the genitive or adjective; as, *vicīnus ejus, meus.*

‡ But *affǐnis* in this sense also has the genitive; as, *affǐnis hujus suspiciōnis, affǐnis rei capitālis.* So also *proprǐum oratōris,* peculiar to the orator; and *mea, tua propria,* peculiar to me, to you.

§ But also *ad natūram aptus* or *accommodātus; ad causam idōneus; parātus ad usum; promptus ad mortem, ad aliquem morbum proclivis; — convenǐens, congruens, consentaneus cum re; absǒnus, absurdus a re.*

ardŭus, invius. E. g. *Juvĕnis caecus,* contumeliae *opportūnus, facĭlis injuriae,* A blind youth, exposed to contumelies and to injuries. *Id si* tibi *erit commodum,* If that will be convenient to you. *Invia* virtūti *nulla est via,* No way is impassable to virtue.

10. VERBALS in *bĭlis,* and COMPOUNDS like *obnoxius, obvius, supplex, superstes,* &c.   E. g. *Mors* mihi *non est terribĭlis,* Death is not terrible to me.   E. g. *Obvium esse alicui,* To meet any one.   *Supplĭcem esse alicui,* To be a suppliant to (to supplicate) any one.   *Superstĭtem esse alicui,* To survive any one.*

To affirm, contend.	⎧ Affirmo, āre, āvi, ātum. ⎨ Contendo, ĕre, di, tum. ⎩ (CUM ACC. ET INFIN.)
To deny.	Nĕgo, āre, āvi, ātum.
What do you say?	Quid áis?
I say that you have my book.	Áio, tê tenêre méum líbrum.†
I say that I have not it.	Négo, mê tenêre líbrum túum.
I assure you, that I have it not.	⎰ Égo tíbi affírmo, mê éum nôn te- ⎱ nére.
Have you not had it?	Nónne éum tenuísti?
I have had it, but I have it no longer.	Ténui véro, sed (éum) téneo nôn ámplius.
Do you contend that you have been correct?	Contendísne, tê vére locûtum (esse)?
I say that I have not been correct.	Négo, mê vére locûtum.
I affirm that you have been wrong.	Affírmo, tê erravisse.
No more, no longer.	*Non jam* (or *jam non*). *Non amplius.*
Do you still love your brother?	Diligísne frâtrem étiam núnc?
I love him no longer.	Díligo éum nôn ámplius.
Where have you put the pen?	Ubi pénnam posuísti?
I have laid it upon the table.	Impósui éam ménsae (in ménsā).
Does it lie upon the table?	⎰ Sitáne ést super ménsā? ⎱ Inpositáne est ménsae?
It does lie upon it.	Síta est. Impósita est.
Is he still lying upon the ground?	Jacétne húmi étiam núnc?
He is lying there no longer.	⎰ Íbi nón jám jácet. ⎱ Jácet ibí nôn amplius.
Some, a little.	*Aliquantŭlum, paulŭlum, pauxíllum.*
Could you give me a little water?	Possísne míhi dáre aliquántulum áquae?
I can give you some.	Égo tibí aliquántulum dáre póssum.
It is necessary, I must.	*Necesse est, me oportet,* &c. (Cf. Lesson XXXIV. *D.*)

---

* Also *supplex* and *superstes alicujus,* which among the later writers is even more common than the dative.
† Compare page 290.

W   30 *

It was necessary, I was obliged.	Necesse fuit, me oportuit, &c.
Is it necessary (for some one) to go to the market?	Eundúmne est in fórum? Necesséne est íre in fórum?
It is necessary (for some one) to go there.	Eúndum ést véro. Necésse est.
What must one do in order to learn Latin?	Quid nôs faciâmus necésse ést, ut línguam Latínam ediscámus?
One must be very diligent.	Opórtet nôs símus imprímis diligéntes. Ópus est múltã indústriã et diligéntiã.
What must he do?	Quíd éum fácěre opórtet?
He must go for a book.	Necésse ést líbrum appórtet. Ópus ést éum apportâre líbrum.
What must I do?	Quíd fácere míhi ópus ést? Quíd opórtet fáciam?
You must sit still.	Ópus ést, út sédeas quiêtus. Necésse est tíbi sedêre quiéte.

To sit.	Sedĕo, ēre, sēdi, sessum.
Still, quiet.	Quiētus, a, um.
Silent, still.	Tacĭtus, a, um; sĭlens, tis
The livelihood, subsistence, competency.	Victus, ūs, m.; copia victūs; id, quod suppeditat ad victum cultumque.
To have enough to live on, to have a competency.	Habēre ad sumptum. Habēre unde aliquis vīvat. Non laborāre de victu cultūque.
Not to have enough to live on.	Deest alicui in sumptum. Vix habēre unde aliquis vivat.
Have you a (comfortable) subsistence?	Habêsne ad súmptum? Habêsne unde commóde vívas?
I have a comfortable one.	Égo de víctu cultûque nôn labóro.
I have not a competency	Déest mihi in súmptum.
I have scarcely anything to live upon.	Víx hábeo unde vívam.

To live.	Vīvo, ĕre, vixi, victum.
The expense.	Sumptŭs, ūs, m.
Beef.	Bubŭla,* ae, f.
Mutton.	Vervecina, ae, f.
Veal.	Vitūlina, ae, f.
Pork.	Porcina, ae, f.
Ham.	Perna, ae, f.
A piece of ham, &c.	Frustum pernae, &c.

---

* With bubŭla — porcīna, the word cáro, flesh, meat, is understood, and sometimes expressed.

What must I buy ?	Quid míhi eméndum est ? Quíd ópus est, ut émam ?
You must buy some beef.	Eménda ést tíbi búbula. Ópus est, ut émas búbulam
What must (should) I do ?	Quíd mê fácere opórtet ? Quid opórtet fáciam ?
You must (ought) to work.	Opórtet tê operári. Opórtet tû operêre.*
What ought we to have done ?	Quíd nôs fácere opórtuit ? Quíd nos fecĕrêmus opórtuit ? †
We ought to have attended to our studies.	Opórtuit nôs óperam dáre stúdiis.
What do you wish ?	Quid vis ? Quid cúpis ?
I want some money.	Ópus ést míhi pecúniă. Égeo pecúniă
Do you want much ?	Éstne tíbi ópus magnă.
I do want a large amount.	Ópus ést míhi véro cópiă magnă.
How much do you want (need) ?	Quantă éges ? Quántă ést tíbi ópus ?
I only want a crown.	Ópus est míhi non nísi ûnus thalê- rus. Úno tántum thaléro égeo.
Is that all you want ?	Nôn est tíbi ópus nísi hóc ?
That is all I want.	Nôn ést míhi ópus nísi hóc.
Do you not want more (money) ?	Nôn est tíbi ópus majôre (pecúniă) ?
I do not need any more.	Majôre nón indígeo.
What does he (want) need ?	Quíd (quă rê) índiget ?
He needs a new coat.	Tóga nóvă índiget.
Have you what you want ?	Habêsne quód tíbi ópus sit ?
I have what I want.	Hábeo véro, quód míhi ópus est ?
Have they what they want ?	Habéntne quód íis ópus ést ?
They have so.	Hábent véro.
Have you been obliged to work much to learn Latin ?	Fuítne tíbi mágni labôris,‡ sermó- nem Latínum edíscerĕ ?
I have been obliged to work very hard.	Fúit prórsus permágni labôris.

EXERCISE 118.

Were you yesterday at the physician's ? — I was at his house. — What does he say ? — He says that he cannot come. — Why does he not send his son ? — His son does not go out. — Why does he not go out ? — Because he is ill. — Hast thou had my purse ? — I tell you that I have not had it. — Hast thou seen it ? — I have seen it. — Where is it ? — It lies upon the chair. — Have you had my knife ? — I tell you that I have had it. — Where have you placed it ? — I have placed it upon the table. — Will you look for it ? — I have already

---

* See page 162, note.   † See page 273, G.
‡ Lit. " Was it a matter of great labor ? " &c. On this genitive compare Lesson LXVIII. B.

looked for it. — Have you found it ? — I have not found it. — Have
you looked for my gloves ? — I have looked for them, but I have not
found them. — Has your servant my hat ? — He has had it, but he
has it no longer. — Has he brushed it ? — He has brushed it. — Are
my books upon your table? — They are (lic) upon it. — Have you
any wine ? — I have but little, but I will give you what I have. —
Will you give me some water ? — I will give you some. — Have you
much wine ? — I have much. — Will you give me some ? — I will
give you some. — How much do I owe you ? — You owe me nothing.
— You are too kind. — Must I go for some wine ? — You must go for
some. — Shall I go to the ball ? — You must go thither. — When
must I go thither ? — You must go thither this evening ? — Must I
go for the carpenter ? — You must go for him. — Is it necessary to go
to the market ? — It is necessary to go thither — What must one do
in order to learn Russian ? — One must study much (*opus est multâ
diligentiâ*). — Must one study much to learn German ? — One must
study much. — What shall I do ? — You must buy a good book. —
What is he to do ? — He must sit still. — What are we to do ? — You
must work. — Must you work much, in order to learn the Arabic ? —
I must work much to learn it. — Does your brother not work ? — He
does not want to work. — Has he wherewithal to live ? — He has. —
Why must I go to the market ? — You must go thither to buy some
beef. — Why must I work ? — You must work in order to get a com-
petency. — What do you want, Sir ? — I want some cloth. — How
much is that hat worth? — It is worth three crowns. — Do you want
any stockings ? — I want some. — How much are those stockings
worth ? — They are worth twelve kreutzers. — Is that all you want ?
— That is all. — Do you not want shoes ? — I do not want any —
Dost thou want much money ? — I want much. — How much must
thou have ? — I must have six crowns. — How much does your brother want ? — He wants but six groshes. — Does he not want more ? —
He does not want more. — Does your cousin want more ? — He does
not want so much as I. — What do you want ? — I want money and
boots. — Have you now what you want ? — I have what I want. —
Has your brother what he wants ? — He has what he wants.

Lesson LXII. — PENSUM ALTERUM ET SEX-
AGESIMUM.

DATIVE AFTER VERBS. — *Continued.*

A. The dative also follows intransitive verbs signifying to benefit, favor, please, trust, and their opposites,
and those signifying to command, obey, serve, or resist,
to approach, menace, and to be angry.

Such are *prosum, auxilior, adminicŭlor, opitŭlor, patrocĭnor, subve-nio, succurro, medeor; noceo, obsum, officio, incommodo, insulto, insi-dĭor.* — *Faveŏ, gratifĭcor, indulgeŏ, ignosco, studeŏ, parco, adŭlor, blandĭor, lenocĭnor, palpo, assentĭor, assentor, respondeŏ; adversor, re-fragor, obsto, renĭtor, repugno, resisto, invideo, aemulor, obtrecto, convi-cĭor, maledico. Placeŏ, arrideŏ, displiceŏ.* — *Domĭnor, imperŏ; pareŏ, cēdo, ausculto, obedĭo, obsequor, obtemperŏ, morigeror* (= morem gero), *audiens sum, servio, inservio, ministro, famŭlor, ancillor, praestolor.* — *Credo, fĭdo, confĭdo, diffĭdo.* — *Immineŏ, propinquo, appropinquo, impendeo, occurro.* — *Minor, commĭnor, irascor, stomachor, succenseo.* The impersonal verbs *conducit, contingit, expedit, licet, placet,* &c. Examples : —

Ipsi pátriae condúcit, píos cíves habêre in paréntes.	It is advantageous to the state itself, to have its citizens respectful towards their parents.
Níhíl *Numantínis* víres córporis *auxiliátae* sunt.	Their physical strength was of no service to the Numantians.
Nôn lícet súi cómmodi caúsâ *no-cêre álteri.*	It is not lawful to injure another for the sake of personal advantage.
Éfficit hóc philosóphia : *medêtur ánimis.*	Philosophy produces this effect : it cures the mind.
Germáni ab párvulis *labóri* ac *duritiae stúdent.*	The Germans apply themselves to toil and hardships from their infancy.
Trebátium objurgávi, quod pá-rum *valetúdini párcêret.*	I chided Trebatius for sparing his health too little.
Álii *Sullánis,* álii *Cinnánis párti-bus favébant.*	Some favored Sulla's party, others that of Cinna.
Nímíum *ílli,* Menedéme, *indúlges*	You indulge him too much, Mene-demus.
Próbus *ínvidet némini.*	The honest man envies no one.
Aliórum *laúdi* átque *glóriae* máxi-me *invidéri* sólet.	The reputation and glory of others are generally the object of envy.
Némo altérius, qui *súae confídit,* virtúti ínvidet.	No one envies the excellence of another, who has any confidence in his own.
Múndus *Déo pâret,* et *huíc obé-diunt* mária terraéque.	The world is subject to God, and to him the seas and lands render obedience.
Stô expéctans, si quíd *míhi ímpe-rent.*	I stand waiting to see whether they have any commands for me.
Omníno *irásci amícis* nôn témere sóleo.	I am not accustomed to be rashly angry with my friends

REMARKS.

1. Some of these verbs sometimes occur with a transitive force. E. g. *Imperāre alicui aliquid,* To demand anything of any one; *cre-dĕre alicui aliquid,* to entrust anything to any one; *mināri* or *commi-*

nāri alicui aliquid, to menace any one with anything. But most of them are always neuter, and only admit of an impersonal construction in the passive. E. g. *Mihi parcĭtur, inridētur, obtrectātur*, I am spared, envied, traduced. *Tibi incommodātur, maledicĭtur*, You are incommoded, reviled.

2. *Jubĕo* is an exception to verbs of commanding, and occurs only with the Acc. cum Inf. (Lesson LIII. *B.* II. 2.) So *juvo* and *adjuvo*, " I aid, assist," always have *aliquem*, and not *alicui*, like *auxilior*, &c.

3. *Benedĭcere*, " to bless," generally has *alicui* (like maledicere), but sometimes *aliquem*. So *medicāri alicui* (like *medēri*), to heal, cure, but *medicari aliquid*, to prepare chemically. The construction of *invidēre* (to envy) is generally *alicui* or *alicui rei*, but may also be *alicui rem* or *aliquem aliquā re* (one on account of anything). E. g. *Honorem tibi invidet*, He envies you your honor.

4. A number of other verbs sometimes take the accusative or ablative instead of the dative. E. g. *Obtrectāre* (to produce) *alicui, alicui rei* or *rem*. *Auscultāre* (to listen to) and *praestolāri* (to wait for) *alicui* or *aliquem*. *Domināri* (to rule over) *alicui, in aliquem* or *in civitate*. *Fidĕre* and *confīdĕre* (to trust, confide) *alicui, alicui rei* or *aliquā re*. *Cēdo tibi, concēdo tibi*, "I yield, concede to you," are followed by an accusative or ablative of the thing; as, *cēdo tibi locum, cedo tibi agri possessione*; and *concēdo tibi libertātem, loco, de victoriā*, I concede to you your liberty, my place, the victory. *Res mihi convĕnit*, the thing suits or becomes me; but impersonally *convĕnit mihi tecum de aliquā re*, I agree with you about something.

5. Several verbs have either the accusative or dative, but with a difference of signification. E. g. *Caveo te*, I beware of you; *caveo tibi*, I am security for you; *caveo a te*, I take (require) security from you. *Consulo te*, I consult you, and *consulo tibi*, I provide for you. *Cupio* or *volo te*, I desire you, and *cupio* or *volo tibi* (or *tuā causā*), I wish for you (on your account). *Prospicio* and *provideo te*, I see you before, but *tibi*, I provide for you. *Tempero* and *moderor aliquid*, I arrange in proper order, and *mihi* or *rei*, I moderate.

B. Among the verbs followed by the dative are included those compounded with the adverbs *satis, bene,* and *male,* and with the prepositions *ad, ante, con, in, inter, ob, post, prae, sub,* and *super.* (Cf. Lesson XXXII. *G.*) Some of these verbs are transitive, and have also an accusative of the direct object; others are intransitive, and have the dative only. The following lists exhibit the most important of them : —

1. Transitive compounds, with the dative of the remote object.

Addo, *I add to.*	Adjĭcio, *I add to.*
Affĕro, *I bring to.*	Adjungo, *I join to.*
Affīgo, *I attach to.*	Admoveo, *I bring near to.*
Adhĭbeo, *I employ towards.*	Allīgo, *I tie to.*

Applico, *I attach to.*
Circumjicio, *I cast around.*
Compăro, *I provide for.*
Compōno, *I put together.*
Conféro, *I unite to.*
Conjungo, *I link to.*
Immisceo, *I mix with.*
Impōno, *I place upon.*
Imprimo, *I print upon.*
Inclūdo, *I include.*
Incido, *I cut into.*
Inféro, *I carry into.*
Ingéro, *I put or pour into.*
Injiceo, *I throw into.*

Insēro, *I implant.*
Inūro, *I brand, imprint upon.*
Interjicio, *I cast among.*
Interpōno, *I interpose.*
Objicio, *I throw before (to).*
Offundo, *I pour out to.*
Oppōno, *I place against.*
Posthăbeo, *I esteem less than.*
Postpōno, *I value less than.*
Praeféro, *I bear before; I prefer.*
Praeficio, *I set over.*
Praepōno, *I place before.*
Suppōno, *I place beneath.*
Substerno, *I spread under.*

2. Intransitive compounds, with the dative only.

Accēdo, *I draw near to.*
Acquiesco, *I acquiesce in.*
Adhaereo, *I adhere to.*
Allūdo, *I allude to.*
Annūo, *I assent to.*
Arrēpo, *I creep to.*
Assideo, *I sit near to.*
Aspiro, *I breathe upon.*
Antecello, *I excel, surpass.*
Collūdo, *I play with.*
Congrūo, *I agree with.*
Consentio, *I accord with.*
Consōno, *I harmonize with.*
Excello, *I excel.*
Incido, *I fall upon (into).*
Incumbo, }
Incūbo, } *I lie (sit) upon.*
Indormio, *I nod over.*

Inhaero, *I inhere in.*
Inhio, *I gape at.*
Immorior, *I die in (upon).*
Immoror, *I linger in.*
Innascor, *I am born in.*
Insisto, *I tread upon.*
Interjăceo, *I am situate between.*
Intervēnio, *I fall in with.*
Obrēpo, *I steal upon.*
Obstrēpo, *I make a noise at.*
Obversor, *I move before.*
Praemineo, *I surpass.*
Praestideo, *I preside over.*
Praevăleo, *I am stronger than.*
Succumbo, *I yield to.*
Supersto, *I stand upon.*
Supervivo, *I survive.*

3. To these add the compounds of *sum* : — *adesse*, to be present ; *inesse*, to be in ; *interesse*, to be among ; *praesse*, to be before (at the head of) ; *subesse*, to be beneath ; *superesse*, to remain over (left).

4. The compounds of *satis*, *bene*, and *male* are *satisdare*, *satisfacere* (*alicui*), to give one bail or satisfaction ; *maledicĕre*, *benedicĕre* (*alicui*), to praise or bless, to revile, asperse one ; *malefacere* (*alicui*), to injure one.

EXAMPLES.

Natûra *sénsibus* ratiônem *ad-junxit.*
    Nature has given us reason in addition to our senses.

Sthénius ést is, qui *nóbis assidet.*
    He who is sitting by our side is Sthenius.

Quís pótest iníquos *aéquis*, ímpios *religiósis anteférre ?*
    Who can prefer the unjust to the just, the impious to the religious?

Natûra vî ratiônis hóminem con-
   cíliat hómini.

Nature conciliates man to man by
   force of reason.

Párva *mágnis* saépe rectíssime
   conferúntur.

Small things are often correctly
   compared with great things.

Mágnus térror *íncidit* Pompéii
   exercítui.

Great terror befell the army of
   Pompey.

Cui sermóni nôs *intervénĭmus ?*

What conversation did we fall in
   with ?

Nôn cítius *adolescéntiae* senéctus,
   quám *puerítiae* adolescéntia
   obrêpit.

Old age steals no faster upon youth
   than youth does upon boyhood.

Hánnibal *Alexándro Mágno* nôn
   postponéndus est.

Hannibal cannot be put below
   Alexander the Great.

Déus ánimum *praefécit córpori.*

The Deity has put the mind over
   . the body.

Júdicis ést, *innocéntiae subve-*
   níre.

It is the duty of a judge to help
   (protect) innocence.

Néque *děésse,* néque *superésse*
   reipúblicae vólo.

I desire neither to be remiss towards the republic, nor to be
   above it.

Cui Géllius *benedíxit* únquam
   bóno ?

What patriotic man did Gellius
   ever speak well of ?

Satisfácěre ómnibus nôn póssum.

I am not able to satisfy every one.

Tû vérbis sólves núnquam, quód
   mi (= míhi) *malefécěris.*

You will never compensate with
   words the injuries you have
   done me.

REMARKS.

1. Many verbs compounded with prepositions, especially those with
ad, con, and *in,* are also followed by the case of the preposition, which
is frequently repeated. E. g. *Studium adhibēre* ad *disciplīnas,* To
apply one's self to the study of the sciences. *Consilia sua* mecum
communicāvit, He communicated his designs to me. In *omnium* animis *dei notionem impressit ipsa natūra,* Nature herself has imprinted
the idea of a divinity upon the minds of all.

2. Verbs compounded with the prepositions *ab, de,* or *ex,* are commonly followed by the ablative, but sometimes by the dative. E. g.
Alicui libertātem abjudicāre, to take away one's liberty ; *alicui impe-*
rium abrogāre, to deprive one of his command. *Alicui aliquid dero-*
gāre, detrahĕre, to derogate, to detract from. *Alicui virgĭnem despon-*
dēre, to betroth a maiden to any one. *Eripere alicui aliquid,* to snatch
away anything from any one. (Cf. Lesson LXXII. *E.*)

3. Many neuter verbs of motion, compounded with prepositions,
acquire an active sense, and admit an object in the accusative. (Cf.
Lesson LIX *A.* Rem. 1.)

To ask, demand (anything
   of any one).
{
  Posco, *ĕre, poposci, ——.*
  Postŭlo *āre, āvi, ātum.*
  Pĕto, *ĕre, īvi, ītum.*
    (ALIQUID AB ALIQUO.)

To ask, request (as a favor).	Rŏgo, āre, āvi, ātum. Ōro, āre, āvi, ātum. (ALIQUEM ALIQUID.)*

To ask (or demand) money of any one.
Pecúniam ab áliquo pétere (pósce-re, postuláre).

To ask (entreat) any one for money.
Áliquem pecúniam rogáre, oráre.

To beg money of any one
Áliquem pecúniam mendicáre.

To ask any to come (to write, to hear, &c.).
Pétĕre ab áliquo, *ut* véniat, *ut* scri-bat, *ut* aúdiat. (Cf. page 295.)

To entreat any one by letter to come.
Pétere prĕcibus per litteras ab áli-quo, *ut* véniat.

To request, beseech any one to come.
Rogáre, oráre áliquem, ut véniat.

I request you most earnestly to do so.
Id ut fácias, tĕ étiam átque étiam rógo.

I ask and beseech you most ear-nestly to help him.
Étiam atque étiam tê rógo atque óro, út éum júves.

What do you ask (want) of me?
{ Quíd a mê póstulas (pétis)?
 { Quíd mê fácere vis?

I do not ask (you for) anything.
Níhil póstulo.

Nor do I ask you for anything.
Néque égo abs tê quídquam póstu-lo (péto).

Did he ask (beg) you for (some) money?
Rogavítne tê pecúniam?

He did ask (me for some).
Rogâvit.

Did he beg some bread of us?
Mendicavítne pânem a nóbis?

He begged and entreated us for a little bread.
Nos aliquántulum pânis étiam at-que etiam rogâvit atque orâvit.

Do you ask (beg) him for some money?
Rogâsne éum pecúniam?

I ask (beg) him for some.
Rógo éum aliquántulum.

Do you ask me for anything?
{ Petísne áliquid a mê?
 { Rogâsne me áliquid?

I ask you for my book.
{ Péto a tê librum.
 { Rógo tê líbrum.

Do they ask us for the hat?
Núm píleum a nóbis póstulant?

They do not ask us for it.
Nôn póstulant.

To speak of any one or any-thing.
De aliquo seu aliquâ rĕ lŏqui, col-lŏqui.

Do they speak of this man.
Loquuntúrne hôc de víro?

They are speaking of him.
Loquúntur (de éo).

They do not speak of him.
(De éo) nôn loquúntur.

Do ye speak of my book?
Lóquiminine de líbro méo?

We do speak (of it).
Sîc ést. Lóquimur.

Do people speak of it?
Écquid de éo hómines loquúntur?

---

* On the government of these verbs see Lesson LX. *B.*

31

They speak much of it.	Loquúntur de éo múltum.
What do you say to it ?	Quid tû de éo cénses (júdicas) ?
I say that it is a good book.	Ego éum líbrum bónum ésse cénseo (júdico).
To judge, think (say).	{ Judíco, āre, āvi, ātum. Censeo, ēre, ŭi, ——. (ALIQUID DE ALIQUO.)
Is it your opinion that he was right ?	Censêsne, éum vére locûtum (ésse) ?
No, I think he was wrong.	Ímmo véro éum erravísse cénseo.
Content, satisfied.	*Contentus, a, um.*
To be contented (satisfied) with anything.	{ Aliquā rē contentum esse. In aliquā rē acquiescĕre (-ēvi, ētum).
To be content with any one.	Aliquem probāre, approbāre.
Are you satisfied with your new umbrella ?	Ésne umbráculo túo nóvo conténtus ?
I am contented with it.	Súm éo conténtus.
I am not (at all) satisfied with it.	Haúd súm éo conténtus.
Of what do they speak ?	Quā de rē loquúntur ?
They speak of peace, of war, of your book.	Loquúntur de pâce, de béllo, de líbro túo.
With what are you contented ?	{ Quā rē és contentus ? Quā in rē acquiéscis ?
I am contented with my new coat.	Conténtus sum tógā méā nóvā.
Are you satisfied with your master ?	Écquid magístrum túum próbas ?
I am quite satisfied with him.	Próbo véro éum válde.
Are ye satisfied with him ?	{ Satín' vóbis probâtur ? Núm vóbis satísfacit ?
Are you satisfied with this man ?	Satisfacítne tíbi hícce hómo ?
I am satisfied.	Síc ést ; míhi satísfacit.
To study — studied.	{ *Studēre, studŭi,* ——. *Opĕram dăre* (ALICUI REI).
To correct — corrected.	{ Emendāre — āvi, ātum (ALIQUID). Corrigĕre — rexi, rectum.
To ask, interrogate.	Interrŏgo, āre, āvi, ātum (ALIQUEM ALIQUID, DE ALIQUA RE).
To inquire (carefully and minutely).	{ Sciscitor, āri, ātus sum. Percunctor, āri, ātus sum.
Have you asked him about the play ?	Núm éum de spectáculo interrogavísti ?
I have not asked him.	Éum nôn interrogávi.
Did he inquire who I am ?	Sciscitatúsne est, quis sim ?
Do you inquire after the price of this book ?	Percunctarísne de prétio líbri ?

Does your brother study literature?	Dát fráter túus óperam lítteris? Sequitúrne fráter túus stúdium litterárum?
He does study it.	Óperam dát. Séquitur.
Do you study to become a doctor?	Núm óperam dás fíeri médicus?
To pay.	*Solvo, ĕre, i, sŏlūtum.* *Numĕro, āre, āvi, ātum.*
To pay any one (in general).	Alíquem solvĕre, alícui satisfacĕre.
To pay for anything.	Solvĕre (aliquid) pro aliquă rē.
To pay any one for anything.	Solvĕre alicui pretium rei.
To pay money to creditors.	Sólvĕre pecúnias creditóribus.
To pay a debt.	Aès aliênum (pecúniam débítam) sólvere vel dissólvere.
To be able to pay, solvent.	Ésse solvéndo (*Dat.*), ad solvendum.
I have paid him.	Égo éum sólvi (éi satisféci).
They have not yet paid for the book.	Pro líbro nóndum solvérunt.
How much have you paid for your horse?	Quántam pecúniam pro équo solvísti?
I have paid two hundred crowns for it.	(Sólvi pro éo) ducéntos thaléros.
Did he pay the tailor for the coat?	Númquid' sartóri prétium véstis sólvit?
He has not paid him (for it).	(Éi) nôn sólvit.
Do you pay the shoemaker for the shoes?	Solvísne sutóri prétium calceórum?
I do pay him.	Égo véro sólvo.
What did they pay you for the knives?	Quíd tíbi pro cúltris solvérunt?
They paid me a large sum for them.	Solvérunt míhi (pro íis) pecúniam grándem.
They have nothing for them.	Níhil pro íis solvérunt.
Have you paid for your book?	Solvistíne pro líbro túo?
I have paid (for it).	Sólvi.
I have not yet paid for it.	Égo pro éo nóndum sólvi.
Can you pay what you owe?	Potésne sólvere, quod débes (*or* débitum, débita)?
I cannot pay what I owe.	Sólvere débíta haúd possum.
Did we pay our debts?	Solvimúsne aès aliênum (débita nóstra)?
We have paid them entirely.	Id (éa) pláne (omníno) dissólvimus.
Entirely, wholly.	*Prorsus, omnino, plăne* (adv.).
Entirely or for the most part.	Omnino aut magnä ex parte.

The uncle.	Patrŭus, i. *m.*; avuncŭlus, i, *m.*
The wages, fee.	Merces, ēdis, *f.*; prētĭum opĕrae, i, *n.*
The honorarium ; salary.	*Honorārĭum, i, *n.*; salārĭum, i, *n.*
The lesson (to be learnt).	Pensum, i, *n.*; discenda, *n. pl.*
The exercise, task (to be written).	Pensum imperātum, i, *n.*; exercĭtĭum, i, *n.*
The exercise, practice, e.g. in writing, speaking, &c.	Exercitātio (ōnis, *f.*) scribendi, dicendi, &c.
To do (write) one's exercises.	Pensum imperātum absolvĕre (absolvi, absolūtum).
The lecture or lesson (given by the teacher).	Schŏla, ae, *f.*
To deliver a lecture on any subject.	Schŏlam habēre de aliquā rē.
To be present at the lectures of any one.	Schŏlis alicūjus interesse.
To attend or frequent lectures.	Doctóres auditionêsque obire (-ĭvi, Itum).
The teacher, preceptor.	Doctor, praeceptor, ōris, *m.*; magister, ri, *m.*
The scholar, pupil.	Discĭpŭlus, alumnus, i, *m.*
The gentlemen, lord, sir.	Domĭnus, i, *m.*; vir amplissĭmus, illustrissĭmus, &c. (*in addresses*, &c.)
Have you (written) your exercises ?	Absolvistĭne túa pénsa imperâta ?
I have not yet done them.	(Éa) nôndum absólvi.
To receive a present from any one.	{ Accipĕre aliquid ab aliquo in mūnēre. Dōnum ab aliquo accipĕre.

EXERCISE 119.

Have we what we want ? — We have not what we want. — What do we want ? — We want a fine house, a large garden, a beautiful carriage, pretty horses, several servants, and much money. — Is that all we want ? — That is all we want. — What must I do ? — You must write a letter. — To whom must I write ? — You must write to your friend. — Shall I go to the market ? — You may go there. — Will you tell your father that I am waiting for him here ? — I will tell him so. — What will you tell your father ? — I will tell him that you are waiting for him here. — What wilt thou say to my servant ? — I will say to him that you have finished your letter. — Have you paid (for) your table ? — I have paid (for) it. — Has your uncle paid for the book ? — He has paid for it. — Have I paid the tailor for the clothes ? — You have paid him for them. — Hast thou paid the merchant for the horse ? — I have not yet paid him for it. — Have we paid for our gloves ? — We have paid for them. — Has your cousin already paid for his boots ? — He has not yet paid for them. — Does my brother pay you what he owes you ? — He does pay it me. — Do you pay what you owe ? — I do pay what I owe. — Have you paid (with the dative) the baker ? — I have paid him. — Has your uncle paid the butcher for the meat ? — He has paid him for it. — Have you paid your servant his wages ? — I have paid them to him. — Has your master paid you your wages ? — He has paid them to me. — When did he pay them to you ? — He paid them to me the day before yesterday. — What do you ask this man for ? — I ask him for my book. — What does this boy beg of me ? — He begs of you some money. — Do you ask me for anything ? — I ask you for a crown. — Do you ask me for the bread ? — I ask you for it. — Do the poor beg money of you ? — They beg some of me. — Which man do you ask for money ? — I ask him for some whom you ask for some.

EXERCISE 120.

Whom have you asked for some sugar ? — I have asked the merchant for some. — Of whom have the poor begged some money ? — They have begged some of the noblemen. — Of which noblemen have they begged some ? — They have begged some of those whom you know. — Whom do you pay for the meat ? — I pay the butchers for it. — Whom does your brother pay for his boots ? — He pays the shoemaker for them. — Whom have we paid for the bread ? — We have paid our baker for it. — Of whom have they spoken ? — They have spoken of our friend. — Do men speak of my book ? — They do speak of it. — Of what do we speak ? — We speak of war (de bello). — Do you not speak of peace ? — We do not speak of it. — Are you content with your scholars ? — I am content with them. — How old are you ? — I am not quite ten years old. — Does your brother know Latin ? — He does not know it. — Why does he not know it ? — Because he has not learned it. — Why has he not learned it ? — Because he has not had time. — Is your father at home ? — No, he is gone to England. — Do you intend going to Italy this summer ? — I do intend going thither. — Have you the intention of staying there long ? — I have the intention of staying there during the summer. — How long does your brother remain at home ? — Till twelve o'clock. — Have you had your gloves dyed ? — I have had them dyed. — What have you had them dyed ? — I have had them dyed brown. — Will you tell your father that I have been here ? — I will tell him so. — Will you not wait until he comes back again ? — I cannot wait.

Lesson LXIII. — PENSUM SEXAGESIMUM TERTIUM.

DATIVE AFTER THE PARTICIPLE IN "DUS."

A. After the participle in *dus* the agent is commonly expressed by the dative.* E. g.

---

* Compare Lesson XXV. *D.*

Legéndus míhi saépius *ést* Cáto májor.	I must read Cato the elder oftenen.
Níhil *est hómini* tam *timéndum,* quam invídia.	Nothing is to be feared by men so much as envy.
Nôn *paránda nóbis* sólum, sed *fruénda* étiam sapiéntia *est.*	Wisdom should not only be acquired by us, but also enjoyed.
Récto tíbi invictóque moriéndum ést.	You must die firm and unconquered.
Ut *tíbi ambulándum* et *ungéndum,* sic *míhi dormiéndum est.*	As you must walk and anoint yourself, so I must sleep.

REMARKS.

1. Instead of the dative, the ablative with *a* or *ab* sometimes occurs, as after passive verbs. E. g. *Eros* a te *colendus est,* Eros must be worshipped by you. *Non majóres nostros* venerandos a nóbis *putátis?* Do you not think that our ancestors are to be venerated by us?

2. The dative is frequently omitted, and the agent left indefinite. E. g. *Graecis utendum erit litteris,* It will be necessary to use Greek letters. *Consensio omnīum gentīum lex natūrae putanda est,* The consent of all the races of men is to be considered the law of nature. *Orandum est* (sc. *nóbis),** *ut sit mens sana in corpore sāno,* We should pray for a healthy mind in a healthy body.

3. Passive verbs sometimes have the dative of the agent instead of the usual ablative with *a* or *ab.* E. g. *Audītus est* nobis (= a nobis) *Laeliae saepe sermo,* We have often heard the conversation of Lælius. Mihi (= a me) *consilium captum jam diu est,* The plan has been formed long ago by me. *Barbarus hīc ego sum, quia non intelligītur* ulli (= ab ullo), I am a barbarian here, since I am not understood by any one.

VERBS FOLLOWED BY TWO DATIVES.

B. The verbs *sum, forem, fīo, do, venio,* and a number of others, are sometimes followed by two datives, of which one designates the person and the other the end or object.

Such are *do, accipio, habeo, relinquo, delīgo, mitto, eo, venio,* and others of similar import. Also *duco, largior, tribuo,* and *verto.* E. g.

Hóc *ést míhi cúrae.*	I take care of this (It is my care, I attend to it).
Est tíbi honóri.	It is an honor to you.
Nobis ést *voluptáti.*	It is a pleasure to us.
Est arguménto.†	It serves as an argument.
Ámpla dómus *dedécori domino* saépe *fū.*	An ample mansion often becomes a dishonor to its master.

---

* The dative thus suppressed is generally *mihi, tibi, nobis, vobis, homínibus,* &c., and easily supplied from the context.
† See Remark 1.

Áttalus régnum súum *Románis* | Attalus gave his kingdom to the
dóno dédit. | Romans as a present.
Caésar quínque cohórtes *cástris* | Cæsar leaves five cohorts as a
praesídio relínquit. | guard for the camp.
Pausánias vênit *Átticis auxílio.* | Pausanias came to the assistance of
| the Athenians.

Vírtus sóla néque *dátur dóno,* | Virtue alone can neither be offered
néque *accípitur.* | nor received as a gift.
Nímia fidúcia *calamitáti* sólet *esse.* | Too much confidence is wont to be
| a source of calamity.

Incúmbite, ut et *vóbis honóri,* et | Exert yourselves, so that you may
amícis utilitáti et *reipúblicae* | be able to become an honor to
emoluménto esse possítis. | yourselves, useful to your friends,
| and a source of profit to the
| commonwealth.

REMARKS.

1. The dative of the person is frequently left indefinite, and that of the end or object alone expressed. E. g. *Hoc est honori, laudi,* This is an honor, laudable. *Vitam rustícam tu* probro *et* crimini *putas esse,* You consider rural life a reproach and crime (sc. to any one). So several of the above examples.

2. Datives of this description are very frequent. The most common are *dare aliquid muněri, dono, praemio ; — relinquěre aliquid custodiae, praesidio ; — aliquid est* or *putátur vitio, crimini, probro, opprobrio, laudi, salúti, utilitáti, emolumento ; — aliquid est curae, cordi, derisui, usui.* So also *caněre receptúi,* to sound the retreat ; *opponěre pignóri,* to pledge or pawn. In this connection the verb *sum* frequently has the sense of the English *it affords, serves, brings,* &c.

3. Instead of the dative of the end or object, the nominative or accusative may also be put, and sometimes the preposition *ad* or *in.* E. g. *Hoc argumentum, indicium est,* This is proof, an indication (evidence). *Dedit mihi aliquid donum* (for *dono*). *Exercitum* ad *praesidium* (for *praesidio*) *relíquit. Dare aliquid* in *dotem,* To give anything as a dowry. So also *pro argumento est.*

C. After expressions like *mihi est nōmen* or *cognōmen,* the name of the individual is either in the nominative or dative, but sometimes in the genitive. E. g.

Ést míhi nômen Bálbus, Bálbo,* | My name is Balbus.
or Balbi. |
Nómina his *Lacumo* atque *Aruns* | The names of these (sons) were
fuérunt. | Lacumo and Aruns.
Cuí póstea *Appio Claúdio* fúit | Whose name was afterwards Appi-
nômen. | us Claudius.

---

* The dative stands by *attraction* in the same sense as the pronoun *mihi* (*cui, altěri,* &c.).

Quôrum *álteri Capitóni* fúit co-gnômen.	One of whom was surnamed Capito.
Nômen *Mercúrii* mihi est.	My name is Mercury.

REMARK. — After the expressions *dare, addere, indĕre, dĭcĕre, pōnĕre, impōnĕre* or *tribuĕre alicui nomen* or *cognōmen*, the name is commonly in the dative, but may also stand in the accusative. E. g. *Dare alicui cognomen tardo ac* pingui, To surname (nickname) one "the slow and the dull." *Cui* Ascanium *parentes dixēre nomen*, Whom the parents called Ascanius. And in the passive : — *Quibus nōmen* histrionibus *indĭtum est*, Who have received the name of histrions. *Cui cognomen* superbo *ex morĭbus dătum*, Who was surnamed "the proud," from his manners.

D. The verbs *aspergo* and *inspergo, circumdo* and *circumfundo, dono* and *impertio, indŭo* and *exŭo*, are construed either with the dative of the person and the accusative of the thing (*alicui aliquid*), or with the accusative of the person and the ablative of the thing (*aliquem aliquā rē*). E. g.

Aspérgit *áram sánguine* (or *árae sánguinem*).	He besprinkles (stains) the altar with blood.
Déus *ánimum* circúmdedit *córpore* (or *córpus ánimo* circúmdedit).	The Deity surrounded the soul with a body.
Dóno *tíbi pecúniam* (or *tê pecúniā*).	I make you a present of money.
Teréntia *impértit tíbi múltam salútem*.	Terentia sends you greeting.
Plúrĭmā *salúte Parmenónem* impértit Gnátho.	Gnatho presents his best compliments to Parmeno.
Índuit (éxuit) *síbi véstem*.	He puts on (takes off) his dress.
Caêsar *hóstes ómnes ármis* éxüit.	Cæsar deprived all his enemies of their arms.

REMARKS.

1. So also *interclŭdĕre alicui aliquid* or *aliquem aliquā re* and *ab aliquā re*, to cut one off from anything ; and *interdīcĕre alicui aliquid* or *alicui* (but not *aliquem*) *aliquā re*. E. g. *Intercludit hostĭbus fugam, milĭtes intĭnĕre* or *ab exercĭtu*, He prevents the enemy's escape, prevents the march of the soldiers, cuts them off from the army. *Vitellius* accusatori aquā atque igne *interdixit*, Vitellius forbade the accuser the use of water and fire (i. e. exiled him).

2. In the passive the dative or ablative remain, and the accusative becomes the nominative. E. g. *Ara aspergĭtur sanguĭne* or *sanguis arae aspergĭtur*. — *Duabus quasi a natūrā indūti sumus personis*, We are by nature furnished as it were with two persons. *Doctrinis aetas puerĭlis impertīri debet*, The age of boyhood ought to be furnished with instruction. *Interdicāmur aquā et igni*, Let us be prohibited from the use of water and fire.

DATIVE AFTER PARTICLES.

E. The dative is also put after certain particles. Such are :—

1. Adverbs, especially those derived from adjectives which govern the dative. As *propĭus, proxĭme, comĭnus, obvĭam, praesto; convenienter, congruenter, constanter, amīce,* &c. E. g. *Propĭus Tiběri, quam Thermopȳlis,* Nearer to the Tiber than to Thermopylæ. *Quam proxĭme hostĭum castris,* As close to the enemy's camp as possible. *Obvĭam ire alicui,* To go to meet any one. *Convenienter natūrae vivĕre,* To live agreeably to nature. *Bene mihi, bene vobis, bene omnĭbus,* Health to me, to you, to all (in drinking).

2. The interjections *vae* and *hei,* and others. E. g. *Vae victis est! — Hei misěro mihi ! — Ecce tibi !* * — *Hem tibi talentum auri !* There is a talent of gold for you !

To eat, to take food.	$\begin{cases} \text{Ĕdo, ĕre, ēdi, ēsum.} \\ \text{Cĭbum sūmĕre (capĕre, capessĕre),} \\ \text{manducāre.} \end{cases}$

PRES. IND. SING. ĕdo, ĕdis *or* ēs, ĕdit *or* ēst ; †
　　　PLUR. ēdĭmus, ēdĭtis *or* ēstis, ĕdunt.

PRES. SUBJ. SING. ĕdam *or* ĕdim, ĕdas *or* ĕdis, ĕdat *or* ĕdit ;
　　　PLUR. ĕdāmus *or* ĕdimus, ĕdātis *or* ĕditis, ĕdant *or* ĕdint.

To eat or to consume anything as food (*trans.*).	Edĕre, manducāre aliquid.
To taste (anything as food or drink).	Gusto, āre, āvi, ātum (ALIQUID).
To feed or live upon.	Vescor, i, —— (CARNE, LACTE, &c.).
The breakfast.	Jentācŭlum, i, *n.*
The lunch.	Prandĭum, i, *n.*
The dinner.	Coena, ae, *f.*
The supper.	Cĭbus vespertīnus, i, *m.*
To breakfast.	Jento, āre, āvi, ātum.
To eat a lunch.	Prandĕo, ēre, prandi, pransum.
To dine.	Coeno, āre, āvi, ātum.
To sup.	Cĭbum vespertīnum sūmere.
At what time do you dine ?	Quótā (*sc.* hórā) coénas ?
I dine at five.	$\begin{cases} \text{Quíntā coéno.} \\ \text{Hórā quíntā coéno.} \end{cases}$
Have you already dined ?	Ecquid jám coenavísti ?
I have dined long ago.	Coenávi profécto jám dūdum.

---

* See page 344.

† Several other syncopated forms of this verb resemble those of *esse,* but have e long by nature. E. g. *edere* or *esse; editur* or *estur; ĕdĕrem* or *essem* (Imperf. Subj.); *ĕdis, ĕdĭte* or *es, ĕste* (Imperat.), &c. The tenses derived from the second and third roots are regular.

X

I have dined earlier than you.	Égo matúrius coenávi quám tû.
Will you take a lunch with me?	Visne prándium súmere apud mê (mêcum)?
I cannot: I have already eaten my lunch.	Nôn póssum; jám díu prándi.
Do you sup late?	Sumisne cíbum vespertinum séro?
I sup later than you.	Égo cíbum vespertinum súmo sérius quám tû.

Before me, you, him, us, &c.	*Ante mê, tê, éum, nôs, &c.*
After me, you, him, us, &c.	*Post mê, tê, éum, nôs, &c.*
Did you breakfast before your brother or after him?	Útrum jentavísti ante an post frátrem túum?
I breakfasted after him.	Post éum jentávi.
Do you wish to taste our wine?	Núm vis vínum nóstrum gustâre?
I do not wish to taste it.	Gustâre nôn cúpio.
On what do they live?	Quô cíbo vescúntur?
They live upon bread and milk.	Vescuntur pâne átque lácte.

To try, to make an attempt.	{ *Tento, âre, âvi, âtum.* { *Experior, íri, pertus sum.*
To try, endeavor (to do anything).	Conor, âri, âtus sum (ALIQUID FACERE).
Will you try (see) what you can do?	Visne tentâre (experíri), quíd póssis?
To try the fortunes of war.	Fortûnam belli tentâre *seu* experíri.
Does your brother try to write a letter?	{ Tentátne fráter túus epístolam scríbere (*or* ut epístolam scríbat)?
He is trying.	Téntat véro.
Are ye endeavoring to see?	Númquid spectâre conámini?
We are not endeavoring.	Nôn conâmur.
Will you try to do this?	Visne tentâre hóc fácere (út hóc fácias)?
I have already tried (endeavored) to do it.	Id fácere jám tentávi (conâtus sum).
You must try to do it better.	Tentándum est, ut rém mélius fácias.
Have you tried (i. e. tasted) this wine?	Gustavistíne ístud vinum?
I have tasted it.	Gustávi.
Whom are you looking for?	Quém quaêris?
I am looking for one of my brothers.	Únum ex méis frátribus (quaéro).
An uncle of mine.	*Únus ex* (de) *méis pátruis.*
A neighbor of ours.	*Únus ex* (de) *nóstris vicínis.*
A relation of yours.	Únus ex (de) túis cognátis.
(Some) one of his cousins.	Áliquis ex (de) éjus consobrínis.
(Some) one of their friends.	Áliquis ex (de) eôrum amícis.
A certain friend of ours.	Quídam ex nóstris amícis.

To inquire or look after some one.	Quaero, ĕre, quaesivi, quaesĭtum alĭquem.
To inquire after something.	Quaerĕre *seu* exquīrĕre alĭquid (de alĭquā rē).
Do they inquire after any one?	Quaerúntne álĭquem?
They are inquiring after one of our relations.	Quaérunt véro únum ex cognátis nóstris.
Whom are ye looking for?	Quém quaérĭtis?
We are looking for one of your friends.	Quaérimus álĭquem (quéndam) de familiáribus túis.
Are you looking for anything?	Quaerísne álĭquid?
I am inquiring for the way.	Quaéro (exquíro, rógo) víam (íter).
Does he try to see me?	{ Tentátne mê vidêre? { Écquid mê visêre téntat?
He is trying to see you.	Sáne, te vidêre (visêre) téntat.
The parents.	Parentes, um, *m. pl.*
The acquaintance.	Nōtus, i, *m.;* amícus, i, *m.*
A piece of bread.	Segméntum (frústum) pânis.
A glass of water.	Scýphus áquae.
A sheet of paper.	Plágŭla (ae, *f.*) chártae.
The piece, fragment, bit.	{ Fragmentum, i, *n.* (broken off). { Segmentum, i, *n.* (cut off). { Frustum, i, *n.* (bit).
The small piece, bit.	Frustŭlum, i, *n.* *
The little book.	Libellus, i, *m.*
The little house.	Domuncŭla, aedicŭla, ae, *f.*
The little heart.	Corcŭlum, i, *n.*
The little picture.	Imagiuncŭla, ae, *f.*
The little child, the baby.	Infantŭlus, i, *n.*
The little boy.	Puercŭlus, pupŭlus, i, *m.*
The suckling.	(Infans) lactens, tis, *m.*
The favorite, darling.	Deliciae, árum, *pl. f.;* amōres, um, † *pl. m.*
The apprentice.	Tiro, ōnis, *m.;* discípulus (artifĭcis), i, *m.*

EXERCISE 121.

Have you already dined? — Not yet. — At what o'clock do you dine? — I dine at six o'clock. — At whose house (*apud quem*) do you dine? — I dine at the house of a friend of mine. — With whom did you dine yesterday? — I dined with a relation of mine. — What have you eaten? — We have eaten good bread, beef, apples, and cakes. — What have you drunk? — We have drunk good wine, good beer, and good cider. — Where does your uncle dine to-day? — He dines with us. — At what o'clock does your father eat supper? — He eats supper at nine o'clock. — Do you eat supper earlier than he? — I eat

* On these diminutives compare page 89.
† On these *pluralia tantum* see page 70.

supper later than he. — At what o'clock do you breakfast ? — I breakfast at ten o'clock. — At what o'clock did you eat supper yesterday ?
— We ate supper late. — What did you eat ? — We ate only a little
meat and a small piece of bread. — When did your brother sup ? —
He supped after my father. — Where are you going to ? — I am going
to a relation of mine, in order to breakfast with him. — Do you dine
early ? — We dine late. — Art thou willing to hold my gloves ? — I
am willing to hold them. — Who has held your hat ? — My servant
has held it. — Will you try to speak ? — I will try. — Has your little
brother ever tried to do exercises ? — He has tried. — Have you ever
tried to make a hat ? — I have never tried to make one. — Have we
tasted that beer ? — We have not tasted it yet. — Which wine do you
wish to taste ? — I wish to taste that which you have tasted. — Have
the Poles tasted that brandy ? — They have tasted it. — Have they
drunk much of it ? — They have not drunk much of it. — Will you
taste this tobacco ? — I have tasted it already. — How do you find it ?
— I find it good. — Why do you not taste that cider ? — Because I
am not thirsty. — What is your name ? — My name is Charles (*Carŏ-
lus*). — What is the name of your father ? — His name is William
(*Wilhelmus*). — Is his name not Frederic (*Fredericus*) ? — No, it is
James (*Jacŏbus*). — Is this an honor to you ? — No, it is a disgrace.

EXERCISE 122.

Whom are you looking for ? — I am looking for the man who has
sold a horse to me. — Is your relation looking for any one ? — He is
looking for an acquaintance of his. — Are we looking for any one ? —
We are looking for a neighbor of ours. — Whom dost thou look for ?
— I look for a friend of ours. — Are you looking for a servant of
mine ? — No, I am looking for one of mine. — Have you tried to
speak to your uncle ? — I have tried to speak to him. — Have you
tried to see my father ? — I have tried to see him. — Have you been
able to see him ? — I have not been able to see him. — After whom
do you inquire ? — I inquire after your father. — After whom dost
thou inquire ? — I inquire after the tailor. — Does this man inquire
after any one ? — He inquires after you. — Do they inquire after
you ? — They do inquire after me. — Do they inquire after me ? —
They do not inquire after you, but after a friend of yours. — Do you
inquire after the physician ? — I do inquire after him. — What do
you ask me for ? — I ask you for some meat. — What does your little
brother ask me for ? — He asks you for some wine and some water.
— Do you ask me for a sheet of paper ? — I do ask you for one. —
How many sheets of paper does your friend ask for ? — He asks for
two. — Dost thou ask me for the little book ? — I do ask you for it. —
What has your cousin asked for ? — He has asked for a few apples
and a small piece of bread. — Has he not breakfasted yet ? — He has
breakfasted, but he is still hungry. — What does your uncle ask for ?
— He asks for a glass of wine. — What does the Pole ask for ? — He
asks for a small glass (*scyphŭlus*) of brandy. — Has he not already
drunk ? — He has already drunk, but he is still thirsty.

Lesson LXIV. — PENSUM SEXAGESIMUM QUARTUM.

SYNTAX OF THE GENITIVE.

A. A noun determining another noun is put in the genitive, in answer to the question *Whose ? Of whom ? Of what ?* E. g.

Dómus *Caésaris.* Árbores *silvá-rum. Belli* calámitas. Flúmi-na *néctaris.*	The house of Cæsar. The trees of the forests. The calamity of war. Rivers of nectar.
Ámor *virtútis.* Lectio *librórum.* Desidérium *ótii.* Spês *salútis.*	The love of virtue. The reading of books. The desire of ease. The hope of safety.
Cústos *virtútum ómnium* verecún-dia ést.	Reverence is the guardian of every virtue.
Singulórum facultátes et cópiae divítiae súnt *civitátis.*	The property and resources of in-dividuals constitute the wealth of the state.
Núma *divíni* aúctor *júris* fúit, Sérvius cónditor *ómnis* in civi-táte *discríminis ordínúmque.*	Numa was the institutor of divine law, Servius the founder of all the distinctions and orders in the state.
Víta *mórtuum* in memóriá *vivó-rum* est pósita.	The life of the dead depends upon the memory of the living.

REMARKS.

1. The genitive serves to express a variety of relations, such as origin or source, cause and effect, quantity, quality, measure, time, character, the whole of a given mass or number, the object of an activity, the material of which anything is made, &c.

2. The genitive thus depending on a noun may represent either the subject or the object of the activity or state implied in this relation, and is hence called either *subjective* or *objective.* Thus *pater amat* gives rise to the subjective *amor patris*, the father's love (towards the son); but (*pater*) *amat filium*, to the objective *amor filii*, the (father's) love of (i. e. towards) his son. So also *homínum facta*, the deeds of men, and *lux solis*, the light of the sun (subjective); but *remedium dolóris*, the remedy *against* pain; *taedium labóris*, disgust *for* labor.*
Sometimes, though rarely, both these genitives occur in the same con-struction; as, *Caesáris translátio pecuniárum*, Cæsar's transfer of the funds. *Attici mémor officii*, Mindful of the favor of Atticus. *Multa Theophrasti oratiónis ornamenta*, Many of the ornaments of Theo-

---

* The relation expressed by the subjective genitive is in English indicated by the possessive case, or by "of"; that of the objective by "of," "for," "towards," "against," and similar prepositions.

phrastus's style. *Inexplebĭlis* honōrum Marii *fames,* Marius's insatiable desire of honors.

3. Sometimes the context alone can determine whether a genitive is subjective or objective. Thus *metus regis* may be either the fear entertained by the king, or the fear of the king entertained by some one else. To prevent ambiguity, the Romans commonly put, instead of the objective genitive, the accusative or ablative, with one of the prepositions *in* or *erga,* towards ; *in* or *adversus,* against ; *cum,* with ; *ab* or *ex,* from, on the part of, &c. E. g. *Amor meus* erga *or* in *te,* My affection for (towards) you. *Metus ab hoste,* Fear from the enemy. *Odĭum* in *or* adversus *alĭquem,* Hatred against any one. *Amicĭtia* cum *alĭquo,* Friendship for any one. *Cura* de *republĭcā,* Anxiety for the commonwealth.

4. The objective genitive is sometimes a personal pronoun. E. g. *Accusator mei,* My accuser. *Commendatio tui,* The recommendation of you. *Ratio sui,* Regard for one's self. *Misericordia vestri,* Compassion on you. *Cura nostri,* Care for ourselves. But the subjective genitive is commonly represented by the possessive pronoun ; as, *liber meus, tuus, noster,** &c.

5. The genitive is sometimes put instead of an appositum. So frequently after *vox, nomen, verbum,* and *vocabulum ;* as, *Haec vox voluptātis,* This word "pleasure." *Appellatio domini, patris,* The appellation " master," " father." *Ex amōre nomen amicĭtiae ductum est,* The name of friendship is derived from love. *Triste est nomen ipsum carendi,* The very name of " want" is painful. Thus also *Arbor fĭci,* The fig-tree. *Promontorĭum Misēni,* The promontory Misenum.

6. An adjective sometimes supplies the place of the genitive. E. g. *Aliēna* (= *aliōrum*) *vita,* The life of others. *Venus Praxitelia* (= *Praxitĕlis*), The Venus of Praxiteles. *Hercules Xenophontĕus* (= *Xenophontis*), The Hercules delineated by Xenophon. *Vis hiemālis* (= *hiĕmis*), The severity of winter. *Hostīlis* (= *hostis*) *libĭdo,* The wantonness of the enemy.

7. The dative sometimes expresses a relation similar to that of the genitive, and stands in place of it. E. g. *Castris praefectus,* The commander of the camp. *Munĭmentum libertāti,* A bulwark of (to) liberty. *Legātus fratri,* The lieutenant of his brother. *Caput Latio,* the capital of Latium. *Ego* huic causae *patronus exstĭti,* I have come out as the defender of this cause. *Natŭrā tu* illi *pater es, consilĭis ego,* You are his father by nature, and I by advice.

8. The noun on which the genitive depends is sometimes omitted. This takes place, —

---

* Yet this rule is sometimes reversed, the possessive pronoun being put instead of the genitive, and the latter for the former. E. g. *Origo sui* (= *sua*), His origin. *Conspectus vestri* (= vester) *venerabĭlis,* Your venerable aspect. And on the other hand, *invidĭa, fidŭcĭa tua* (for *tui*), Envy towards, confidence in you. *Injŭriae meae* (for *mei*), Injuries done to me. So always *meā, tuā, suā, nostrā, vestrā causā* (never *mei causā,* like *homĭnis causā*), For my (your, &c.) sake, on my account.

a.) When it has already been expressed, and can easily be supplied from the context. E. g. *Julius quaestor Albucii fuerat, ut tu Verris,* Julius had been quæstor to Albucius, as you to Verres. *Animi linea-menta sunt pulchriora, quam corpŏris,* The features of the mind are fairer than *those* of the body. *In portum, qui Menelai vocātur,* Into the port which is called the port of Menelaus.

b.) When it is one of the words *aedes, homo, civis, servus, libertus, uxor, filius, filia, discipŭlus, sententia,* or the ablative *causā.* E. g. *Ad Vestae, Jovis Statōris* (sc. *aedem*), To the temple of Vesta, of Jupiter Stator. *Verania Pisōnis* (sc. *uxor*), Verania, the wife of Piso. *Hasdrūbal Gisgōnis* (sc. *filius*). *Caecilia Metelli* (sc. *filia*). *Hujus video Byrrhiam* (sc. *servum*). *Flaccus Claudii* (sc. *libertus*). *Vitan-dae suspiciōnis* (sc. *causā*), For the sake of avoiding suspicion. *Con-tra Philōnis* (sc. *sententiam*), Against the opinion of Philo.

THE GENITIVE OF QUALITY AND MEASURE.

B. In connection with an adjective or numeral, the genitive frequently expresses the relations of property, quality, character, age, time, measure, or number. E. g.

Vír et *consĭlii mágni* et *virtûtis.*	A man of great judgment and virtue.
Óppidum *máximae auctoritâtis.*	A town of distinguished authority.
Púer *décem annôrum.*	A boy of ten years.
Fóssa *quíndecim pédum.*	A ditch of fifteen feet.
Clássis *septuagínta návium.*	A fleet of seventy ships.
Claúdius érat *somni brevíssimi,* sc. homo.	Claudius was a man of very little sleep.
De línguā Latínā *sécuri* es *ánimi.*	You are unconcerned about the Latin language.
Júvenis evâsit vére *indŏlis régiae.*	He turned out really a youth of royal disposition.
Classis *mille* et *ducentârum ná-vium longârum* fúit.	The fleet consisted of a thousand and two hundred galleys.

REMARKS.

1. The quality may also be expressed by the ablative with *praedĭ-tus, instructus,* or *ornātus* understood, and the extent of time or space by the accusative, with *nātus, lātus,* or *longus* expressed. E. g. *Vir summo ingenĭo* (sc. *praedĭtus*), A man of (endowed with) the highest genius. *Fossa quíndĕcim pedes lata,* A ditch fifteen feet wide. *Puer decem annos nātus,* A boy twelve years of age.

2. The accusatives *sĕcus, gĕnus, pondo,* and *libram* (or *pl. libras*), occur instead of the genitive in expressions like *liberi virĭle secus,* Male children. *Aliquid id genus* (= *ejus genĕris*), Something of that kind. *Aves omne genus* (= *omnis genĕris*), Birds of every species. *Corona aurĕa libram pondo,* A golden crown of a pound in weight.

Willingly (gladly, with fondness).	{ Căpĭdĕ, lĭbenter, lĭbenti anĭmo. { Lŭbens, tis; non invĭtus, a, um.
More willingly (eagerly, gladly).	Libentĭus, pŏtĭus; libentiōri anĭmo.
Very (or most) willingly, &c.	Libentissĭmē, libentissĭmo anĭmo.
Unwillingly, with reluctance.	{ Invīto anĭmo, grăvāte. { Invītus, a, um.
To do anything willingly (to like to do it).	Făcĕre áliquid libénter, libénti ánĭmo, lúbens, &c.
To like, take pleasure in anything.	{ Delector, āri, ātus sum. { Gaudĕo, ēre, gavīsus sum. { (ALIQUA RE.)
To love, to be fond of anything.	{ Amāre aliquid. { Appetĕre (-īvi, ītum) aliquid.
I like to see (look on).	{ Deléctor spectâre. { Júvat* mē spectâre.
I like to have (possess).	Deléctor (mē júvat) habêre (possidêre).
I like to study (am fond of my studies).	{ Gaúdeo stúdiis litterârum. { Égo lítteris studêre deléctor.
I like to eat, drink.	{ Júvat mē édere, bíbere. { Deléctor édere, bíbere.
I like to be called diligent.	Ámo vocári díligens.
Do you like (are you fond of) wine?	{ Delectarísne bíbere vinum? { Appetísne vinum?
I do like it. I am very fond of it.	Deléctor véro. Máxĭme áppeto.
Is he fond of fish?	{ Juvátne éum comédere písces? { Appetítne písces?
He is fond of them.	Júvat. Áppetit.
Do you like a large hat?	Núm píleo ámplo delectâris (gaúdes)?
No, I like a small (a tight) one.	Ímmo véro árcto gaúdeo(deléctor).
Do you like to hear my brother?	Écquid frâtrem méum aúdis libénti ánimo?
I do like to hear him.	Aúdio éum nôn invítus.
I do not like to hear him.	Égo éum invíto ánimo aúdio.
I am extremely fond of hearing him.	Aúdio éum libentíssime.
I am extremely anxious to see him.	Flágro cupiditâte éjus vidéndi.
Do they like to do it?	Faciúntne id (hoc) libénter?
They do not dislike to do it.	Id nôn invíti fáciunt.
Chicken.	(Căro) gallīnācĕa.
Fowl.	Altíles, f. pl. or altília, n. pl.

---

* An impersonal verb: "It pleases, delights me." Perfect: Jŭvit mĕ, tĕ, ĕum, &c.

Fish.	Pisces, ium (*pl. of* piscis, is, *m.*).
Pike.	Esōces, *pl. of* esox, ōcis, *m.*
Salmon.	Salmōnes, *pl. of* salmo, ōnis, *m.*
Trout.	*Truttae, *pl. of* trutta, ae, *f.*

Do you like (are you fond of) chicken, fowl, pike?	Delectarísne comédere gallináceam, altília, esóces?
I like all these things very well.	Éa ómnia máxime áppeto.
I do not like them.	Comédere nôn deléctor. Ómnia haêc nôn cómedo nísi invítus.

By heart; from memory.	*Memōrĭter* (Adv.) ; *ex memoriâ.*
To learn by heart, to commit to memory.	*Edisco, ĕre, edidĭci,* ——. *Memoriae mandāre,* or *committĕre* (ALIQUID).
To commit verbally, in part.	Ediscĕre aliquid ad verbum, per partes.
To know by heart.	Memoriâ tenēre, in memoriâ habēre (ALIQUID).

Have you learnt your exercises by heart?	Edidicistísne pénsa imperâta?
We have learnt them.	Edidícimus profécto.
We have faithfully committed them to memory.	Memóriae éa fidéliter mandávimus (commísimus).
Do you know them by heart?	Tenêsne éa memóriâ?
I do not know them.	Nôn téneo.
Do your scholars like to learn by heart?	Écquid discípuli túi memóriae committere delectántur?
They do not like it.	Nôn delectántur.
Does he learn his lesson by heart?	Ediscítne pénsum súum?
He does commit it word for word.	Edíscit véro ad vérbum.

How often? How many times?	*Quăm saepe? Quŏtĭes? Quŏtĭens?*
Six times a day, a month, a year.	*Sexĭes in die, in mense, in anno.*
Once, twice, three, four, five times a week. (Cf. page 317, note †.)	Sĕmĕl, bĭs, tĕr, quăter, quinquĭes in hebdomâde.
How many times do you eat a day?	Quótíes in díe cíbum súmere sóles?
I eat three times a day.	Égo tér in díe cíbum cápere sóleo.
Does he eat as often as I?	Edítne (êstne) tám saepe quam égo?
He eats oftener; he eats five times a day.	Saépius édit quám tû; cíbum sûmit quínquies in díe.
What time (of the day) do you go out?	Quò témpore in públicum próditis?

We go out early in the morning. | Pródimus in públicum prímā lûce mâne.

If (conjunction). | *Si* (cum Indic. & Subj.).

I intend to pay what I owe you, if I receive my money. | Égo quód tíbi débeo sólvere cógito, si pecúniam méam accípio.

Do you intend to buy wood? | Cogitâsne émere lígnum?

I do intend to buy some, if they pay me what they owe me. | Cógito véro aliquántum émere, si míhi pecúnias débitas sólvunt.

Do you reply, if (when) you are asked (questioned). | Respondêsne, si (cum) interrogâris?

I do reply. | Respóndeo.

The weather (= *sky, state of the weather*). | *Tempestas, ātis,* f.; *coelum, i,* n.; *coeli stấtus, ûs,* m.

Good, clear, favorable weather. | Tempestas bŏna, serēna, opportūna.

Bad, windy, unfavorable weather. | Tempestas măla, ventōsa, adversa.

Warm, cold, very cold weather. | Tempestas calĭda, frĭgĭda, perfrĭgĭda.

Severe, stormy, cloudy weather. | Tempestas vĕhĕmens, turbulenta, nebŭlōsa.

Dark, moist, dirty, rainy weather. | Tempestas turbĭda, humĭda, spurca, pluviŏsa.

Steady, excellent weather. | Tempestas certa, egregia.

A dry state of the atmosphere. | Sicca coeli quālĭtas; siccĭtas, ātis, f.

A fine, clear, serene sky (weather). | Sūdum coelum; coelum serēnum.

Changeable, inconstant weather. | Varĭum coelum; varietas coeli.

What sort of weather is it? How is the weather? | Quâlis tempéstas est? Quae est coéli quálĭtas?

It is fine weather at present. | Tempéstas núnc est bóna (seréna).

What sort of weather was it yesterday? | Quâlis érat tempéstas hestérna (héri)?

The weather was bad yesterday. | Málus érat coéli státus héri.

How is the weather to-day? | Quâlis est coéli státus hodiérnus?

It is fine, clear weather to-day. | Sūdum (serēnum) hódie est coélum.

It is neither very cold nor very warm to-day. | Tempéstas hodiérna néque perfrĭgĭda néque praecálida ést.

Is the weather damp (moist)? | Éstne coéli státus úvidus?

The weather is too dry. | Nímia ést siccĭtas. Coéli quálĭtas nímis sícca est.

Dark, obscure. | Tenebrĭcōsus, a, um. Coecus, a, um. Caligĭnōsus, a, um.

Obscure, dusky, gloomy.	Obscūrus, a, um. Subobscūrus, a, um.
Clear, light.	Clārus, a, um. Illustris, is, e.
Dry.	Siccus, a, um.

Is it gloomy in your room ?	Éstne cubículum túum obscúrum ?
It is somewhat gloomy in it.	Ést véro subobscúrum.
No, it is quite light in it.	Ímmo véro ádmodum ést clárum (illústre).
Is the night a dark one ?	Éstne nóx caliginôsa ?
Is it moonlight ?	Éstne lúmen lúnae ? Lucétne lûna ?
It is.	Est. Lûcet véro.
There is no moonlight to-night.	Nóx ést illûnis. Lûna sílet.
We have too much sun.	Nímis ést sôlis.
We have no rain.	Térra ést éxpers ímbrium.

To perceive (to notice, mark, see).	(*Ocŭlis*) percĭpĭo, ĕre, cēpi, ceptum. Cerno, ĕre, crēvi, crētum. Notāre. Vidēre. Observāre.

Have you perceived any one ?	Écquem (num quém) notavísti ?
I have perceived no one.	Núllum (néminem) notávi.
Do you perceive the soldiers who are going into the storehouse ?	Cernísne mílites íllos hórreum introeúntes (qui in horreum íněunt) ?
I perceive those who are going in.	Cérno véro éos, qui íntro éunt.
I see the child which plays (played).	Égo infántulum ludéntem vídeo.
I see the man who has my money.	Vídeo hóminem, qui pecúniam méam ténet.
I perceive him, who is coming.	Égo éum, qui vénit, percípio.
I see also him, who owes me money.	Vídeo et éum (éum quóque), qui míhi pecúniam débet.

The soldier.	Miles, ítis, *m.*
Also (likewise).	Quŏque (*put after the emphatic word*), et, etiam.

Exercise 123.

Do you perceive the man who is coming ? — I do not perceive him. — What do you perceive ? — I perceive a great mountain and a small house. — Do you not perceive the wood ? — I perceive it also. — Do you perceive the men who are going into the garden ? — I do not perceive those who are going into the garden, but those who are going to the market. — Do you see the man to whom I have lent money ? — I do not see the one to whom you have lent, but the one who has lent you some. — Have you perceived the house of my parents ? — I have perceived it. — Do you like a large hat ? — I do not like a large hat, but a large umbrella. — What do you like to do ? — I like to write. — Do you like to see those little boys ? — I do like to see them.

— Do you like beer ? — I like it. — Does your brother like cider ? — He does not like it. — What do the soldiers like ? — They like wine and water. — Dost thou like wine or water ? — I like both. — Do these children like to study ? — They like to study and to play. — Do you like to read and to write ? — I like to read and to write. — How many times do you eat a day ? — Four times. — How often do your children drink a day ? — They drink several times a day. — Do you drink as often as they ? — I drink oftener. — How many times a year does your cousin go to the ball ? — He goes thither twice a year. — Do you go thither as often as he ? — I never go thither. — Does your cook often go to the market ? — He goes thither every morning. — Do you often go to my uncle's ? — I go to him six times a year. — Do you like fowl ? — I do like fowl, but I do not like fish. — What do you like ? — I like a piece of bread and a glass of wine. — What fish does your brother like ? — He likes pike. — Do you learn by heart ? — I do not like learning by heart. — Do your pupils like to learn by heart ? — They like to study, but they do not like learning by heart. — How many exercises do they do a day ? — They only do two, but they do them well. — Do you like coffee or tea ? — I like both. — Do you read the letter which I have written to you ? — I do read it. — Do you understand it ? — I do understand it. — Do you understand the man who speaks to you ? — I do not understand him ? — Why do you not understand him ? — I do not understand him because he speaks too badly. — Have you received a letter ? — I have received one. — Will you answer it ? — I am going to answer it (*Rescriptūrus sum*).

EXERCISE 124.

Do you intend going to the theatre this evening ? — I do intend going thither, if you go. — Has your father the intention to buy that horse ? — He has the intention to buy it, if he receives his money. — Has your cousin the intention to go to England. — He has the intention to go thither, if they pay him what they owe him. — Do you intend going to the ball ? — I do intend going thither, if my friend goes. — Does your brother intend to study German ? — He does intend to study it, if he finds a good master. — How is the weather to-day ? — It is very fine weather. — Was it fine weather yesterday ? — It was bad weather yesterday. — How was the weather this morning ? — It was bad weather, but now it is fine weather. — Is it warm ? — It is very warm. — Is it not cold ? — It is not cold. — Is it warm or cold ? — It is neither warm nor cold. — Did you go to the country the day before yesterday ? — I did not go thither. — Why did you not go thither ? — I did not go thither, because it was bad weather. — Do you intend going into the country to-morrow ? — I do intend going thither, if the weather is fine. — Is it light in your room ? — It is not light in it. — Do you wish to work in mine ? — I do wish to work in it. — Is it light there ? — It is very light there. — Can you work in your small room. — I cannot work there. — Why can you not work there ? — I cannot work there because it is too dark. — Where is it too dark ? — In my small room. — Is it light in that hole ? — It is dark there. — Is it dry in the street? — It is damp there. — Is the weather damp? — The weather is not damp. — Is the weather dry? — It is too dry. — Is it moonlight? — It is not moonlight; it is very damp. — Why is the weather dry? — Because we have too much sun and no rain. — When do you go into the country? — I intend going thither to-morrow, if the weather is fine, and if we have no rain. — Of what does your uncle speak? — He speaks of the fine weather. — Do you speak of the rain? — We do speak of it. — Of what do those men speak? — They speak of fair and bad weather. — Do they not speak of the wind? — They do also speak of it. — Dost thou speak of my uncle? — I do not speak of him. — Of whom dost thou speak? — I speak of thee and thy parents. — Do you inquire after any one? — I inquire after your uncle; is he at home? — No, he is at his best friend's.

Lesson LXV. — PENSUM SEXAGESIMUM QUIN-TUM.

THE GENITIVE OF THE WHOLE.

A. Nouns denoting a measure or weight, and adjectives or pronouns of the neuter gender denoting a part, are followed by the genitive of the whole.

The principal words of this class are: —

1. Substantives denoting, — *a.*) Definite measure; as, *medimnum, modius, concha; amphora, congius; sextarius, hemina; jugĕrum* (of land); *punctum, vestigium* (of time). *b.*) Definite weight; as, *as, libra, pondo, uncia, mina, talentum. c.*) Quantity or number in general; as, *mensura, modus, vis, copia, multitudo, acervus, numĕrus, grex, globus,* &c., and negatively *nihil.*

2. The nominative and accusative of the neuter adjectives* *tantum, quantum, aliquantum, multum, plus, amplius, plurimum, parum, minus, minimum, nimium, dimidium, reliquum, aliud.*

3. The nominative and accusative of the neuter pronouns *hoc, id, illud, idem, quod, quid,* with their compounds *aliquid, quidquam, quiddam, quidquid,* &c.

4. The adverbs *sat, satis, abunde, affătim, părum, partim,* and *nimis.*

EXAMPLES.

Conon *pecūniae quinquagínta talénta* cívibus súis donâvit.	Conon made his fellow-citizens a present of fifty talents.
Caĉsar pópulo praeter *fruménti*	In addition to ten measures of corn

---

* Which in this construction are, however, always employed substantively.

dénos módios ac *tótidem ólei li-bras*, trecénos quóque nímmos viritim divísit.	and as many libras of oil, Cæsar also divided among the people three hundred sesterces to each.
In *júgere Leontíni ágri medímnum* fére *trítici* séritur.	At Leontini nearly a medimnum of wheat is usually sown on an acre of land.
Flúmina jám *láctis*, jám *flúmina néctaris* íbant.	Now streams of milk, now streams of nectar flowed.
Justítia *nihil* éxpetit *prétii*.	Justice seeks no reward.
Úndíque ad ínferos *tantúndem víae* ést.	The distance to the other world is the same from every place.
Románi ab sóle orto in *múltum diéi* stetére in ácie.	The Romans stood in battle array from sunrise till late in the day.
Gálli *hóc* síbi *solátii* proponébant.	The Gauls proposed this consolation to themselves.
Id tántum *hóstium*, quód ex ad-vérso érat, conspéxit.	He saw only so much of the enemy as was in front of him.
Tíbi *ídem consílii* dô, quód mi-hímet ípsi.	I give you the same advice as I do to myself.
Quid caúsae ést, cúr philósophos nôn légant?	What is the reason why they do not read the philosophers?

REMARKS.

1. After the neuter pronouns and adjectives *hoc, id, illud, aliquid, quid? quantum,* &c. the genitive is sometimes again a neuter adjective used substantively; as, *aliquid boni, quiddam mali, quid novi?* &c. This construction is, however, confined to adjectives of the second declension. Those of the third, and comparatives in *us,* generally remain adjectives in agreement with the pronoun; as, *aliquid turpe, memorabile;** melïus aliquid; quid gravïus?*

2. The genitives *gentïum, terrárum, loci,* and *locorum* after the ad-verbs *ubi, ubique, ubicunque, usquam, nusquam, unde, hic, huc, eo, eodem, quo, quocunque, quoquo, aliquo,* and *longe* serve to add empha-sis to the expression. E. g. *Ubi gentïum? Ubi terrárum?* Where in the world? *Aliquo terrárum,* Somewhere, in some place or another. *Quo loci* for *quo loco; eódem loci* for *eódem loco.* To these add the expressions of time, *ad id locórum,* up to that time; *adhuc locórum,* up to this time; *interéa loci,* meanwhile; *postéa loci,* afterwards.

3. The adverbs *huc, eo,* and *quo,* in the sense of "degree" or "ex-tent," are also put with a genitive. E. g. *Huc arrogantiae,* To this degree of arrogance. *Eo insolentiae,* To that extent of insolence. *Quo amentiae?* To what degree (extent) of folly?

4. Other adverbs construed with the genitive are *pridie* and *pos-tridie,* and, among the later writers, *tum* or *tunc.* E. g. *Pridie ejus*

---

* But in connection with one of the second declension, sometimes also the genitive; as, *aliquid novi ac memorabilis; quidquam, non dico civilis, sed humani.* So, on the other hand, adjectives of the second declension are often in agree-ment with the pronoun; as, *aliquid bonum, novum,* equally correct.

diĕi, on the day before (that); *postridie ejus diei*, on the following day; * *tum (tunc) tempŏris*, at that time, then.

5. Neuter adjectives in general, both singular and plural, are often employed substantively with a genitive by the poets and the prose-writers of a later date.† E. g. *Ad summum montis*, To the top of the mountain. *Relĭquum noctis*, The rest of the night. *Medium* and *se-rum diĕi*, The middle of, late in, the day. *In medio aedĭum*, In the midst of the house. *Extrēmo aestātis*, In the latter part of the sum-mer. *Summa (= summae partes) pectŏris*, The upper parts of the chest. *Cujusque artis difficilima*, The most difficult parts of every art. *In occultis reconditisque templi*, In the secret recesses of the temple. *Subĭta belli*, The surprises of war. *Incerta casuum*, The uncertainties of chance. *Infrequentissĭma urbis*, The most unfrequented parts of the city.

6. When the adverbs of quantity *sat, satis, abunde, affātim, pắrum, partim,* and *nĭmis* are followed by the genitive, they may be regarded as substantives of the neuter gender. E. g. *Satis honorum, satis su-perque vitae erat*, There were honors enough, there was life enough, and even more than enough. *Potentiae gloriaeque abunde*, An abun-dance of power and glory. *Affatim est homĭnum*, There is a sufficiency of men. *Lepōris pắrum*, But little wit. *Nĭmis insidiārum*, Too many stratagems. *Eōrum* partim *in pompā,* partim *in acie illustres esse volu-ērunt*, Some of them wished to distinguish themselves by their display, and others on the battle-field.

7. The demonstratives *id* and *tantum* are sometimes omitted when *quod* or *quantum* follows. E. g. *Medĭco* mercēdis quantum‡ *poscet, promitti jubēto*, Let the doctor be promised as large a fee as he de-mands. *Romānus exercĭtus,* quod *inter Palatĭnum Capitolinumque collem* campi§ *est, complēverat,* The Roman army had filled the space included between the Palatine and Capitoline hills.

8. The genitive also occurs before the preposition *tĕnus,* "up to," and sometimes after interjections. E. g. *Pectŏris tenus,* Up to the chest. *O mihi nuntii beati!* O blessed harbinger to me! *Foedĕris* heu *tacĭti!* Alas for the tacit alliance!

GENITIVE AFTER PARTITIVES.

B. Partitives, including nouns, adjectives, pronouns, numerals, and adverbs, denoting a number, division, or part of a plurality, are followed by the genitive plural of the whole.

The partitives susceptible of this construction are,—

---

* But more frequently with the accusative: as, *pridie* or *postridis eum diem.*
† By Cicero and Cæsar rarely except in the plural. By Livy and Tacitus frequently in both numbers.
‡ *Tantum mercēdis, quantum.*
§ For *id campi,* quod.

1. Substantives denoting a certain number of countable objects, such as *centuria, legio, cohors, manipŭlus;* also *pars, decĭma* or *decŭma, nihil,* &c.

2. The pronouns *uter, alter, neuter, uterque alteruter, alius, sŏlus, nullus, nēmo, ille, hic, quis, qui,* and their compounds *quicunque, quisquis, aliquis,* &c. So also *multi, plurĭmi, plerique. pauci, quot, quotcunque, quotus, quotus quisque, aliquot, tot, cetĕri,* and *reliqui.*

3. Comparatives and superlatives, inclusive of a few adjectives of superlative signification, like *unus* (the only one), *medius, princeps.*

4. Numerals, both cardinal and ordinal. Examples of all these are : —

Sérvius Túllius *équĭtum duódĕcim* scrípsit *centúrias.*
Servius Tullius enrolled twelve squadrons of horse.

Nihil ómnium rêrum mélius, quám ómnis múndus administrâtur.
Of all things nothing is better regulated than the entire universe.

Píscium fémĭnae majóres quám máres sunt.
Female fishes are larger than the males.

Promulgavêre lêgem, ut *cónsulum álter* ex plêbe crearêtur.
They promulgated a law, that one of the consuls should be chosen from among the people.

Animálium ália ratiônis expértia súnt, *ália* ratiône uténtia.
Some animals are destitute of reason, and others endowed with it.

Utérque nóstrum ad súum stúdium libéllos evolvêbat.
Both of us were unfolding manuscripts for our respective studies.

Cum *núllo hóstium* únquam congréssus ést.
He never fought with any of his enemies.

Némo mortálium ómnibus hóris sápit.
No man is wise at all times.

Múltae, céterae istârum árbŏrum.
Many, the rest of these trees.

Par *cuilibet superiôrum regum.*
Equal to any one of the preceding kings.

Quótus quisque philosophôrum ?
How many among the philosophers ?

Néque *stultôrum quisquam* beâtus, néque *sapiéntium* nôn beâtus.
Not a single fool was ever a happy man, nor a wise man not happy.

Príor hôrum in proélio cécidit.
The former of these fell on the battle-field.

Májor Nerônum. *Senióres* Pátrum.
The elder of the Neros. The senior senators.

Gallôrum ómnium fortíssimi súnt Bélgae.
The bravest of all the Gauls are the Belgae.

Aristídes *únus ómnium* justíssimus fuísse tráditur.
Aristides is said to have been the most just of all (his contemporaries).

Quórum quáttuor cónsŭles, *dúo* dictátor ac magíster équĭtum fuérunt.
Of whom four were consuls, and two dictator and lieutenant-dictator.

REMARKS.

1. The genitive singular of a collective may take the place of the genitive plural. E. g. *Cetĕri nostri ordĭnis*, The rest of our order. *Prīmus Romāni genĕris*, The first of the Roman nation. *Totīus injustiliae nulla*, Of all the instances of injustice, none, &c.

2. Poets (and sometimes other writers) extend this construction to adjectives of the positive degree, and to substantives denoting a part of a genus. E. g. *Nigrae lanārum*, Black wool. *Vetĕres Romanorum ducum*, The older Roman generals. *Degenĕres canum*, Dogs of degenerate breed. *Pennatōrum animalĭum bŭbo et ōtus*, Of the winged animals the owl and the horn-owl. — So also the perfect participle: *Delecti equĭtum*, The select of the horsemen. *Expedīti milĭtum*, The light-armed portion of the army. — To these add *omnes* and *cuncti*, when they are used in the sense of *singŭli*. E. g. *Omnes Tarquinii genĕris*, Every one of the family of Tarquin. *Cunctae provinciārum*, All of the provinces.

3. The partitive (pronoun or adjective) commonly takes the gender of its genitive (as in all the above examples), but sometimes also that of another noun expressed or implied in its connection. E. g. *Indus omnĭum flumĭnum maxĭmus*, The Indus the largest of all rivers. *Hordĕum frugum omnĭum molissimum* est*, Barley is the softest of all grain. (*Ego*), *qui plurĭma mala omnĭum Graecōrum in domum tuam intŭli*, I who of all the Greeks have done your house the greatest injury.

4. An adverb may take the place of the partitive. E. g. *Caesar omnĭum fere oratōrum Latīne loquĭtur elegantissime*, Caesar speaks the most elegant Latin of nearly all the orators. *Gallus maxime omnĭum nobilĭum Graecis litteris studŭit*, Of all the Roman nobles Gallus paid most attention to the literature of Greece.

5. The noun denoting the whole is sometimes put in the same case with the partitive. E. g. *Duae filiae* (= *duarum filiārum*) *harum, altĕra occīsa, altera capta est*, Of their two daughters, the one was killed and the other taken prisoner. This is done chiefly by poets and historians.

6. Instead of the genitive, the prepositions *ex, de, inter, in*, and *ante* are sometimes used, especially after superlatives, numerals, and *unus*. E. g. *Acerrĭmus ex omnĭbus nostris sensĭbus*, The acutest of all our senses. *Unus ex* (or *de*) *multis*, One out of many. *Acerrĭmus inter recusantes*, The most violent among those refusing. *Sapientissĭmus in septem*, The wisest among the seven (sages of Greece). *Ex quibus* (sc. *filiis*) *relĭquit duos*, Of which (i. e. number of sons) she has left two.

7. When the partitive denotes the *entire number* referred to, it stands in the same case with its noun. E. g. (Nos) *trecenti conjurāvĭmus*, Three hundred of us have conspired. *Numerāte, quot ipsi sitis*,

---

* Superlatives thus frequently prefer the gender of the noun in agreement with them.

Count how many there are of you in all. Nostri (*poss. pron.*) septu-
aginta *cecidērunt*, Our men, seventy in number, fell. *Neque* hi *admŏ-
dum sunt* multi, Nor does the (entire) number of these amount to
many. (Cf. Lesson XVIII. *G.*)

· 8. When the pronouns and adjectives above enumerated as partitives do not denote parts of a whole, they stand adjectively in agreement with their nouns.* E. g. *Alter consul, doctissĭmus Rŏmānus,
multi, pauci, aliquot homĭnes, tot annos, quot habet*, &c. In this respect
the English is generally a safe guide.

To speak of anything to any one.	De alĭquā rē lŏqui (*sermōnem ha-bēre, verba facĕre) cum aliquo (ad aliquem).*
Do you see the man, of whom I have spoken to you ?	Vidêsne hóminem, *de quô* égo tê-cum locûtus sum ?
I do not see the paper, of which you speak.	Égo chártam, *de quâ* lóquĕris, nôn vídeo.
I have purchased the horse, of which you have spoken to me.	Égo équum, *de quô* mêcum sermô-nem habuísti, pecúniā comparávi.
Has your father the books, of which I am speaking ?	Habetne páter túus líbros, *de quibus* lóquor ?
I see the boy whose brother has killed my dog ?	Vidêsne púĕrum, *cújus* fráter cánem méum necávit ?
I see the child, whose father set out yesterday.	Vídeo infántem, cújus páter héri proféctus est.
I see the man, whose dog you have killed.	Vídeo hómĭnem, cújus cánem ne-cavísti.
Do you see the people, whose horse I have bought ?	Vidêsne hómines, *quôrum* équum égo émi.
I have seen the merchants, whose shop you have taken.	Vídi mercatóres, *quôrum* tabérnam conduxísti.
To take (hire, rent).	Condūco, *ĕre, duxi, ductum.*
To burn down (to be de-stroyed by fire).	⎰ *Deflagro, āre, āvi, ātum.* ⎱ *Igni absumĕre. Flammā delēri.*
Do you wish to take (rent) my house ?	Vísne méas aédes condúcĕre ?
I do not wish to take it.	Nólo éas condúcĕre.
Do you see the man, whose house (home) is burnt down ?	Vidêsne hóminem, cújus domus deflagrâvit (igni absúmpta *or* delêta est) ?
I do see him.	Vídeo.
I have had a talk with the man, whose library has been burned.	Égo cum hómine, cújus bibliothêca flámmis delêta est, collóquium hábui.
Have you read the book, which I have lent you.	Legistíne líbrum, quém tíbi commo-dávi ?

---

* Except *uterque*, which is always *horum, illorum, quorum uterque*. But also
quod utrunque exemplum, both of which examples.

I have read it.

Fáctum est.

Have you the paper which you want (need)?

Habêsne chártam, quae tíbi ópus est?

I have that which I want (need).

Hábeo quae míhi ópus est.

I have what I want (need).

Hábeo quód míhi ópus est.   •

Which book have you?

Quém líbrum hábes?

I have that which I want.

Éam, quae míhi ópus est.

Which nails has the man?

Quôs clávos hómo hábet?

He has those which he needs.

Éos, quíbus índiget (quī éi ópus súnt).

Which gloves has he?

Quae digitábúla hábet?

He has those of his brother.

Digitábúla frâtris hábet.

I see the children to whom you gave apples.

Video líberos, quíbus mâla dedísti.

Of which men do you speak.

De quíbus homínibus lóquěris?

I speak of those whose children have been assiduous.

Lóquor de íis, quôrum líběri diligéntes fuérunt.

Towards (to).

Versus (prep.).

Towards the south.

Ad merídiem vérsus.

Towards Italy.

In Itáliam vérsus.

Towards Dresden, Rome.

Drésdam, Rômam vérsus.*

The way to Berlin.

Vía, (íter) Berolínum (vérsus).

The way from Berlin to Dresden.

Vía (íter) a Berolíno Drésdam versus (or ad Dresdam).

To take the way (to direct one's course towards).

{ Íter álíquo movêre (môvi, môtum). Cúrsum súum álíquo dirigĕre (rexi, rectum). }

To enter upon (to take) a way (road).

Víam or íter intire or ingrĕdi.

Which way has he taken?

Quórsum íter môvit (cúrsum súum diréxit).

He has taken the way to Leip-sic.

{ Íter môvit Lípsiam vérsus. Cúrsum súum Lípsiam diréxit. }

Which way will you take?

{ Quórsum íter movêre vis? Quám víam intire vis? }

I will take (enter upon) this way.

Égo hánc intire (íngredi) cogíto.

And I that one.

Et égo íllam.

So that.

Ut (conj. with the subj.).

I have lost my money, so that I cannot pay you.

Pecúniam méam pérdidi, ut tíbi sólvere non póssim (nôn quéam).

He is sick, so that he cannot go out.

Aegrôtus est, ut in públicum prodíre nôn póssit.

He was also eloquent, so that no one excelled him in eloquence.

Fúit et disértus, ut némo éi pâr ésset eloquéntiā.

So (to such an extent or degree) — that.

Ita (sic, tam, ĕo, adĕo, usque ĕo) — ut (with the subj.).

---

* Compare Lesson LVI. B. and C.

| He loved him so much, that he was commonly regarded as his son. | Éum *sic* dilígébat, *ut* is éjus vúlgo haberétur fílius. |
| Was he so stupid as to consider that life? | Adeóne érat stúltus, *ut* íllam vítam ésse arbitrarétur? |

For (conjunct.).	*Nam; enim* (with the indic.).
I cannot pay you; for I have no money.	Égo tíbi débitum sólvere néqueo. *Nam* pecúniā cáreo.
He cannot come to your house; for he has no time.	Dómum túam veníre nòn pótest. Nam ótium éi déest.
Advice is difficult, I see; for I am alone.	Vídeo difficile ésse consílium. Súm *enim* * sólus.

| *Or* (disjunctive conj.). | *Aut, věl, -vě.* |
| *Either — or.* | { *Aut — aut.* *Věl — věl.* *Sive — sive.* |

C. Obs. The disjunctive *aut* implies essential difference, and a mutual exclusion of things. *Vel* and the enclitic *ve*, a mere verbal difference. E. g.

Am I slave to you, or you to me?	Tíbi égo, *aut* tū míhi sérvus súm?
Enough of our affairs, or (and) even too much.	De nóstris rêbus sátis, *vel* étiam nímium múlta.
I maintain that things which can be seen or touched are real.	Ésse éa díco, quae cérni tang*ive* póssunt.
Either no one was ever a wise man, or if any one, Cato was.	*Aut* némo, *aut*, si quisquam, Cáto sápiens fúit.
Every body is either water, or air, or fire, or earth, or some mixture of these, or a part of them.	Ómne córpus *aut* áqua, *aut* áër, *aut* ignis, *aut* térra ést, *aut* áliquid, quód ést concrêtum ex hís, *aut* ex áliquā párte eôrum.
The poets were recognized or received by the Romans at a comparatively late period.†	Sérius a Románis poétae *vel* cógnīti *vel* recépti sunt.
The laws of the Cretans, which either Jove or Minos established, inured their youth to hardships.	Crêtum léges, quas *sive* Júpiter, *sive* Mínos sánxit,‡ labóribus erúdiunt juventûtem.

---

* *Enim* rarely stands in the first of the clause; *nam*, on the other hand, always.

† I. e. It was comparatively late before the Romans *either* recognized (knew) or received poets among them. Here *vel* is used, because the notion of recognizing and receiving do not exclude or contradict each other.

‡ *Sive — sive* express complete indifference, and are hence often rendered by *whether — or*. "Whether Jove or Minos, no matter which of the two," or "Either Jove or Minos, as you may choose to have it."

EXERCISE 125.

Did your cousin learn German? — He was taken ill, so that he could not learn it. — Has your brother learnt it? — He had not a good master, so that he could not learn it. — Do you go to the ball this evening? — I have sore feet, so that I cannot go to it. — Did you understand that Englishman? — I do not know English, so that I could not understand him. — Have you bought that horse? — I had no money, so that I could not buy it. — Do you go into the country on foot? — I have no carriage, so that I must go thither on foot. — Have you seen the man from whom I received a present? — I have not seen him. — Have you seen the fine horse of which I spoke to you? — I have seen it. — Has your uncle seen the books of which you spoke to him? — He has seen them. — Hast thou seen the man whose children have been punished? — I have not seen him. — To whom were you speaking when you were in the theatre? — I was speaking to the man whose brother has killed my fine dog. — Have you seen the little boy whose father has become a lawyer? — I have seen him. — Whom have you seen at the ball? — I have seen the people there whose horses and those whose carriage you bought. — Whom do you see now? — I see the man whose servant has broken my looking-glass. — Have you heard the man whose friend has lent me money? — I have not heard him. — Whom have you heard? — I have heard the French captain whose son is my friend. — Hast thou brushed the coat of which I spoke to you? — I have not yet brushed it. — Have you received the money which you were wanting? — I have received it. — Have I the paper of which I have need? — You have it. — Has your brother the books which he was wanting? — He has them. — Have you spoken to the merchants whose shop we have taken? — We have spoken to them. — Have you spoken to the physician whose son has studied German? — I have spoken to him. — Hast thou seen the poor people whose houses have been burnt? — I have seen them. — Have you read the books which we lent to you? — We have read them. — What do you say of them? — We say that they are very fine. — Have your children what they want? — They have what they want.

EXERCISE 126.

Of which man do you speak? — I speak of the one whose brother has turned soldier. — Of which children did you speak? — I spoke of those whose parents are learned. — Which book have you read? — I have read that of which I spoke to you yesterday. — Which paper has your cousin? — He has that of which he has need — Which fishes has he eaten? — He has eaten those which you do not like. — Of which books are you in want? — I am in want of those of which you have spoken to me. — Are you not in want of those which I am reading? — I am not in want of them. — Is any one in want of the coats of which my tailor has spoken to me? — No one is in want of them. — Do you see the children to whom I have given cakes? — I do not see them. — To which children must one give cakes? — One must give

33 *

some to those who learn well, and who are obedient and good. — To whom do you give to eat and to drink? — To those who are hungry and thirsty. — Which way has he taken? — He has taken the way to Vienna (*Vindobonam*). — Where did you reside when I was at Berlin? — I resided at Munich (*Monaci*). — Where was your father when you were at Bâle (*Basiliae*)? — He was at Strasburg (*Argentorati*). — Were you in Spain when I was there? — I was not there at that time; I was in Italy. — At what time did you breakfast when you were in Germany? — I breakfasted when my father breakfasted. — Can the physician come to-day? — He cannot come, for he is himself sick. — Is it true that every man is either good or bad? — It is true. — This lesson must either be written or learnt by heart. — We should never praise those who are (either, *vel*) bad or idle. — Did he come to your house last evening? — He had the headache, so that he could not come.

Lesson LXVI. — PENSUM SEXAGESIMUM SEXTUM.

OF THE GENITIVE AFTER ADJECTIVES.

A. Many adjectives, especially those signifying an affection or activity of the mind, such as desire or disgust, knowledge or ignorance, and many of those denoting likeness, equality, community, property, plenty, and their opposites, are followed by the genitive of the object. E. g.

Graéculi súnt *contentiónis cupidióres*, quam *veritátis.*

The paltry imitators of the Greeks are fonder of contention than of the truth.

Graecárum litterárum Cáto *perstudiósus* fúit.

Cato was very much devoted to the study of Greek literature.

Cónscia méns *récti* fámae mendácia rídet.

A mind conscious of rectitude laughs at the false reports of fame.

Cáto et *reipúblicae perítus* et *júris consúltus* fúit.

Cato was experienced in public affairs and learned in the law.

Ómnes *immémórem benfícii* odérunt.

Every one hates the man who is forgetful of benefits received.

Cýri et *Alexándri símilis* ésse vóluit.

He wished to be like Cyrus and Alexander.

Víri própria est máxime fortitúdo.

Courage is pre-eminently characteristic of man.

Memória *communis* est *multárum ártium.*

Memory is common to many arts.

Gálli súnt hómines *insuéti labôris*. | The Gauls are men unaccustomed to labor.
Útinam tê, fráter, nôn sôlum *vítae*, sed étiam *dignitâtis méae supérstitem* reliquissem! | Would that I had left you, my brother, a survivor not only of my life, but also of my rank!
Reférta quóndam Itália *Pythagoreórum* fúit. | Italy was formerly full of Pythagoreans.
Ínops senâtus *auxílii humáni* ad déos pópulum ac vôta vértit. | Destitute of human help, the senate directed the people and its prayers to the gods.

The adjectives thus followed by the genitive are those signifying, —

1. DESIRE or DISGUST : — *avĭdus, cupĭdus, studiōsus, fastidiōsus.* So also *aemŭlus, amīcus, inimīcus, invĭdus,* which sometimes, however, have the dative.* E. g. *Cupĭdus, avĭdus contentiōnis,* Fond of contention. *Amīcus, inimīcus veritātis,* Friendly, hostile towards the truth. *Aemŭlus, invĭdus laudis,* Emulous, envious of praise. *Litterārum Latinārum fastidiōsus,* Averse to Latin literature.

2. KNOWLEDGE, SKILL, or IGNORANCE : — *consciŭs, gnārus, certus, consultus, perītus, mĕmor, provĭdus, prudens;* — *insciŭs, nesciŭs, ignārus, imperītus, imprudens, rŭdis, immĕmor.* E. g. *Ejus rei conscius, gnārus, certĭor,* Conscious of, acquainted with, informed of, that thing. *Consilii certior factus,* Informed of the design. *Jūris consultus, prudens* or *perītus,* Learned, skilled, experienced in the law. *Mĕmor, immĕmor beneficii,* Mindful, forgetful of kindness. *Imprudens legis,* Ignorant of the law. *Imperītus belli,* Unskilled in warfare. *Rudis artĭum,* Ignorant of the arts.†

3. LIKENESS or UNLIKENESS of mind, disposition, or character‡: — *simŭlis, consimŭlis, dissimĭlis, aequalis, par, dispar; proprius, publĭcus, sacer, affĭnis, commūnis, socĭus, vicīnus, aliēnus, insuētus;* to which add *superstes* and *supplex.* (All these also with the dative.) — E. g. *Simŭlis homĭnis,* Like man (in character). *Dissimilis Alexandri,* Unlike Alexander. *Par, dispar alicūjus,* Equal, unequal to any one. *Aequalis tempŏrum illorum,* Contemporary with those times. *Proprium Romani genĕris,* Peculiar to the Roman nation. *Insŭla eorum dcōrum sacra,* An island sacred to those gods. *Commūnis utriusque nostrum,* Common to both of us. *Affĭnis alicūjus culpae,* An accomplice to some crime. *Aliēnum suae dignitātis,* Foreign to his dignity. *Superstes aliōrum,* Surviving others. *Supplex Dei,* Supplicating God.

4. PLENTY or WANT : — *plēnus, refertus, fertĭlis, inops, inānis, jejū*

---

* Compare page 351.

† *Perītus consultus* and *rŭdis* also occur with the ablative. E. g. *Omni genĕre litterārum perītus,* Familiar with every kind of literature. *Jureperitus* or con*sultus* instead of *juris perītus,* &c. The adjective *conscius* may have either the genitive or dative of the thing, but the person is always in the dative. E. g. *conscius facinŏris* or *facinŏri,* privy to a crime; but ALICUI *conscium esse facinŏris,* to be in the secret of a crime with any one. SIBI *conscium esse alicūjus rei,* to be conscious of anything.

‡ Compare page 351.

nus; compos, particeps, expers, exheres; potens, impotens, consors, princeps, many of which are also construed with the ablative.* E. g. *Plēnus metus,* Full of fear. *Referta negotiatōrum,* Full of merchants. *Fertĭlis frūgum hominumque,* Abounding in produce and in men. *Inops auxĭlii,* Destitute of help. *Virtūtis, mentis compos,* Possessed of virtue, master of one's intellect. *Ratiōnis particeps, expers,* A partaker of reason, destitute of it. *Paternōrum bonōrum exheres,* Disinherited of one's patrimony. *Sui potens,* Master of one's self. *Consors imperii,* Sharing command. *Eloquentiae princeps,* The first in eloquence.

REMARKS.

1. Poets, and their imitators in prose, extend this construction to many other adjectives, especially to those denoting an affection of the mind. E. g. *Ambiguus consilii, auxius* futūri, *benignus* vini, *certus* scelĕris, *dubius* viae, *impiger* militiae, *integer* vitae, *interrĭtus* leti, *incautus* futūri, *incertus* sententiae, *laetus* labōris, *modĭcus* voluptātum, *pervicax* irae, *piger* perĭculi, *secūrus* futūri, *segnis* occasiōnum, *socors* futūri, *timĭdus* lūcis, &c., in all of which the genitive stands instead of the more usual ablative or accusative, with *de, in,* or *ad.* So after adjectives generally, the genitive is sometimes employed (by the same class of authors) instead of the ablative, to express the relation " with respect to," " in regard to," " in "; as, *Diversus morum,* Different in respect to manners. *Integer vitae,* Irreproachable in life.

2. The genitive *anĭmi* frequently serves as a sort of complement to adjectives of every kind, especially in the prose of a later date. E. g. *aeger, anxĭus anĭmi,* sick, anxious in mind; *atrox, caecus anĭmi,* of a ferocious, blind mind; *confusus, incertus anĭmi,* &c.

3. Some of the adjectives enumerated under this rule occur also with prepositions. E. g. *Prudens, rudis* in *jure civĭli. — Rudis* ad *pedestria bella. — Mihi* in *publĭcā re socius, in privātis omnĭbus conscius esse soles.*

GENITIVE AFTER PARTICIPLES IN " NS."

B. Participles in *ns* sometimes assume the character of adjectives, and then take the genitive instead of the case of their verbs.

The participles most frequently thus employed are *amans, appĕtens, colens, fugiens, intelligens, metuens, negligens, observans, retĭnens, tolĕrans, patĭens* and *impatĭens, tempĕrans* and *intempĕrans,* &c.

Examples are: *Amans patriae,* Attached to one's country. *Amantissĭmus fratris,* Most affectionate towards his brother. *Religiōnis colens, neglĭgens, contemnens,* An observer, neglecter, contemner of religion. *Patiens* or *impatiens inedĭae, frigŏris,* Capable or incapable

---

* *Potens, impotens, consors,* and *princeps* never occur with the ablative; *compos, particeps, expers, exheres,* rarely. Of the rest (*refertus, plenus,* &c.), some have the ablative even more frequently than the genitive. E. g. *Insŭla referta divitiis,* an island abounding in wealth.

of enduring hunger, cold. *Appetens laudis,* Eager for praise. *Sui despiciens,* Despising one's self. *Deōrum metuens,* Fearing the gods. *Sitiens virtūtis,* Thirsting after virtue. *Imminentium intelligens,* Aware of coming events. *Omnium rērum abundans,* Abounding in all things. *Insolens belli,* Unaccustomed to warfare.

Quís fámulus *amántior dómini,* quam cánis ?	Is there any servant more attached to his master than the dog ?
Súmus natúrā *appetentíssimi honestátis.*	We are by nature covetous of honor.
Virtûtem ob éam rém laudárunt, quod *effíciens* ésset *voluptátis.*	They lauded virtue merely because they considered it productive of pleasure.
Éques Românus est, *súi negótii* béne *gérens.*	He is a Roman knight, who manages his business well.

REMARKS.

1. Participles in *ns,* when used as such, are followed by the case of the verb to which they belong.* E. g. *patiens frigus, labōrem,* (actually) enduring cold, hardship; but *patiens frigŏris, labōris,* capable of enduring cold, hardship. (As participles proper, they denote a transient condition with reference to some particular time; as adjectives, a permanent capacity or quality.)

2. Verbals in *ax* likewise govern the genitive. E. g. Capax *imperii,* Capable of command. *Justitiae* tenax, Tenacious of justice. *Terra* ferax *arbŏrum,* A land abounding in trees. *Tempus* edax *rerum,* Time, the destroyer of things. *Vir cibi vinique capacissĭmus,* A man capable of holding a large quantity of food and wine. So also a few participles in *tus,* as *completus, consultus ;* but these have already been included among the adjectives of *A.*

To run.	{ *Curro, ĕre, cŭcurri, cursum.* { *Cursu tendĕre* (ALIQUO).
To run up (to), down, out, through, forth, &c.	Accurrĕre, dēcurrĕrc, excurrĕre, percurrĕre, prōcurrĕre, &c.
To run away (flee).	{ Aufūgĭo, ĕre, fūgi, ——. { Profūgĭo, ĕre, fūgi, ——.
Behind.	Post, pōne (*Prep. cum Acc.*).
Behind the door.	Post (pōne) fŏres.
Behind the stove.	Post (pōne) fornācem.
Behind the ear.	Post (secundum)† aurem.
Behind one's back.	Post tergum, post, &c.
To stand behind the door.	Pone fores assistĕre.
To run behind the house.	Post aedes currĕre.
Where is he running to ?	Quô cúrrit ? Quórsum cúrsu téndit ?
He is running behind the stove.	(Téndit, cúrrit) post (pone) fornācem.

---

* Cf. Lesson LXIX. *E.*
† *Secundum* == "close behind," "next to."

Where did they run to?	Quórsum cucurrérunt (cúrsu contendérunt)?
They ran behind the house into the woods.	Cucurrérunt pone aédes in sílvam.
Did they run away behind (towards) the trees?	Núm pone versus árbores aufugiébant?
They did not run away.	Nôn aufugiébant.
Where was he sitting?	Úbi sedêbat (considêbat)?
He was sitting behind the stove.	Sedêbat post (ad) fornâcem.

The stove.	Fornax, ācis, f.; camīnus, i, m.
The fireplace.	Fŏcus, i, m.
The oven.	Furnus, i, m.
The blow, knock.	Ictus, ūs, m.; verber, ĕris, n.; plāga, ae, f.
The push; the kick.	Pulsus, ūs, m.; ictus calcis seu pĕdis.
The stab.	Ictus, ūs, m.; plāga, ae, f.
The sting.	Punctum, i, n.
The blow with a stick.	Ictus bacŭli or fustis.
The stab with a knife.	Ictus cultri (cultelli).
The fisticuff.	Pugni ictus; cŏlăphus, i, m.
The sword stab.	Ictus gladii or ensis.
The sword.	Gladĭus, i, m.; ensis, is, m.
The broadsword, spade.	Spātha, ae, f.
The sabre.	Acinăces, is, m.
The point of a sword.	Mucro, ōnis, m.
To draw the sword.	{ Ensem (e vagīnā) edūcĕre. Gladium stringĕre (strinxi, strictum).
To sheath (put up) the sword.	Gladium (ensem) in vagīnam recondĕre (-condĭdi, condĭtum).
To be begirt with a sword, spade, sabre, &c.	Gladio, ense, spāthā, acinăce succinctum esse.
To push (any one with anything).	{ Offendo, ĕre, di, sum. Fŏdĭo, ĕre, fŏdi, fossum. (ALIQUEM ALIQUA RE.)
To push, shove (any one out of doors, &c.).	{ Trūdo, ĕre, si, sum. Prōtrudĕre (ALIQUEM FORAS, &c.).
To strike.	{ Fĕrĭo, īre, ——, ——. Percŭtĭo, ĕre, ussi, ussum. Pulso, āre, āvi, ātum.
To beat.	{ Caedo, ĕre, cecīdi, caesum. Verbĕro, āre, āvi, ātum.
To give one a beating.	Alĭquem verberāre, pulsāre, or verbĕrĭbus caedĕre.
To castigate, punish one with a lashing.	{ Alĭquem verbĕrĭbus castigāre. Verbĕrĭbus in alĭquem animadvertĕre (-ti, -sum).

To give one a blow, inflict a blow upon one.	Plāgam alicui inferre *or* inflīgere (-xi, ctum).
To give one a blow with the fist.	Alicui pugnum *or* colaphum, impingĕre (-pēgi, pactum).
To strike one into the face.	Alicui alapam ducĕre.
To strike one with fisticuffs.	Aliquem pugnis caedĕre (colaphis pulsāre).
To beat one with a stick.	Aliquem fusti verberāre.
To beat one with lashes (whip one).	Aliquem verberĭbus pulsāre (percutĕre).
To beat one to death.	Aliquem usque ad mortem mulcāre.
To be beaten, punished with a beating.	⎧ Vapŭlo, āre, āvi, ātum.* ⎨ Tergo plector. ⎩ Pulsāri et verberāri.
To wound one with a sword-cut.	Gladĭo aliquem caesim vulnerāre.
To wound one with a sword-stab.	⎰ Gladĭo aliquem punctim vulnerāre. ⎱ Gladii ictu aliquem vulnerāre.
To stab one.	Ictum alicūjus corpŏri infīgĕre (-fixi, -fixum).
To stab one to one's heart.	Alicūjus pectus ictu confodĕre).
To give one a kick.	⎰ Pēdis verbĕre aliquem ferire. ⎱ Calce aliquem percutĕre (castigāre).

Did you give this man a blow?	Inflixistine (intulistine) hómini ísti plāgam?
I did give him one.	Sáne quídem; égo éi únam inflíxi (íntŭli).
Did that boy strike his fellow with the flat of the hand?	Duxitne púer ílle condiscípulo súo álapam?
No, he struck him with the fist.	Nôn véro; impêgit éi cólăphum.
He gave each of them ten fisticuffs.	Impêgit éis dénos cólăphos.
Did they punish *him* with stripes?	⎧ Eúmne verbérĭbus castigábant? ⎨ In eúmne animadvertébant verbérĭbus?
He did punish him (It is he that was punished).	Éum. In éum.
What was beaten?	Quís vapulâvit (verberâtus est)?
The soldier was beaten with a stick.	Verberâtus est míles fústi.
Was he beaten hard?	Pulsatúsne est acérbe?
Yes, he was beaten to death.	Verberâtus est véro úsque ad mórtem.
Were you wounded with the point of the sword?	Vulnerabarísne gládio púnctim?
No; I was wounded with the edge.	Nón véro; vulnerâbar caêsim.

---

* On *vapŭlo*, see Lesson XXXIII. *A.* Rem. 3.

Did they kick him ?	Percusserúntne éum cálce (pédis verbéribus) ?
They did not kick him.	Nôn percussérunt.
The (military) officer.	Praefectus militāris.
The firelock.	*Tēlum (i, n.) ignífĕrum.
The gun.	*Sclopētum, i, n.
The rifle.	*Bombarda, ae, f.
The cannon.	*Tormentum (i, n.) bellĭcum.
The pistol.	{ *Sclopētum minōris modi. *Sclopētus minor.
The powder.	*Pulvis (-ĕris, m.) pȳrĭus.
The ball, bullet.	*Glans, -dis, f.
The cannon-ball.	*Glŏbus (i, m.) tormentis missus.
The shot; the report of a firelock.	Ictus, ūs, m.; frŭgor (ōris, m.) tēli ignífĕri.
The shot of a gun, pistol, cannon, &c.	Ictus sclopēti, sclopēti minōris, tormenti, &c.
The thunder-clap.	Fulmĭnis ictus, or simply fulmen, ĭnis, n.
To load a gun.	Pulvĕrem cum glande in sclopētum indĕre (dĭdi, dĭtum).
To load a cannon.	Pulvĕrum cum glŏbo in tormentum indĕre.
To shoot, fire (with fire-arms).	{ Emittĕre ictum tēlo ignífĕro. Sonum edĕre (insonāre) tēlo igni-fĕro.
To shoot with a gun.	{ Glandes e sclopēto mittĕre. Plumbum mittere.
To shoot with a pistol (for pleasure).	Sonum edĕre (insonāre) sclopēto minoris modi.
To fire with cannons.	Tēla tormentis mittĕre.
To shoot or discharge arrows.	Sagittas mittĕre.
To shoot at (some one or something).	Peto, ĕre, ĭvi, ĭtum (ALIQUEM seu ALIQUID TELO).
To fire at some one or something.	Tēlo ignífĕro petĕre alĭquem seu alĭquid.
To hurl a number of weapons (missiles) at one.	Tēla conjecĕre (-jēci, -jectum) in alĭquem.
Are you firing at any one ?	Petísne alĭquem télo ignífĕro ?
I am firing at a bird.	Véro, vólucrem péto.
How many times did he fire at that bird ?	Quóties íllum vólŭcrem sclopéto petivit ?
He fired at it several times.	Petívit éum plúribus tempóribus.
How many times did the boy fire ?	Quóties sónum púer édidit télo ignífero ?

He has fired twice with a pistol.	Sónum bís édidit sclopéto minôris modi.
He has fired five times with a gun.	Sónum édidit (insónuit) quínquies sclopéto.
Did you shoot with a gun?	Mittebâsne glándes e sclopéto?
No, I fired with a cannon.	Ímmo véro téla mittêbam torménto.
Did you ever shoot with arrows?	Misistíne únquam sagíttas?
I have shot with them several times.	Mísi véro divérsis tempóribus.
They have discharged all their missiles on him.	Téla in éum ómnia conjecérunt.
Do you hear the report of a gun?	Audísne fragôrem sclopéti?
No; but I hear the report of a cannon.	Nôn véro; aúdio aûtem fragôrem torménti béllici.
Did ye hear the report of thunder?	Audivistísne fragôrem fúlmlnis?
It is so; we heard a thunder-clap.	Íta est; fúlmen (fúlminis íctum) audívimus.
What are they doing?	Quíd águnt?
They are bombarding the city with cannons.	Úrbem torméntis béllicis vérberant.
Why are you pushing him?	Cúr éum offéndis (fódis)?
I push him because he has pushed me.	Égo éum ob éam rém offendo (fódio), quód mé offendit (fódit).
Did you push him out of doors?	Trudistíne éum fóras?
I did not push him out.	(Éum) nôn protrúsi.

EXERCISE 127.

Do you intend buying a carriage? — I cannot buy one, for I have not yet received my money. — Must I go to the theatre? — You must not go thither, for it is very bad weather. — Why do you not go to my brother? — I cannot go to him, for I cannot yet pay him what I owe him. — Why does this officer give this man a stab with his sword? — He gives him a stab with his sword, because the man has given him a blow with the fist. — Which of these two pupils begins to speak? — The one who is studious begins to speak. — What does the other do, who is not so? — He also begins to speak, but he is neither able to write nor to read. — Does he not listen to what you tell him? — He does not listen to it, if I do not give him a beating. — What does he do when you speak to him? — He sits behind the oven without saying a word. — Where does that dog run to? — It runs behind the house. — What did it do when you gave it a beating? — It barked, and ran behind the oven. — Why does your uncle kick that poor (miser) dog? — Because it has bitten his little boy. — Why has your servant run away? — I gave him a beating, so that he has run away. — Why do those children not work? — Their master has given them blows with the fist, so that they will not work. — Why has he given them blows with the fist? — Because they have been disobedient. —

34

Have you fired a gun ? — I have fired three times. — At whom did you fire ? — I fired at a bird which sat on a tree. — Have you fired a gun at that man ? — I have fired a pistol at him. — Why have you fired a pistol at him ? — Because he gave me a stab with his sword. — Are you fond of contention ? — I am not fond of it. — I am very much devoted to the study of Latin literature. — Why does your brother not work ? — Because he is not accustomed (*insuetus*) to labor. — Do you wish to be like that man ? — I do not wish to be like him. — Was Cyrus the equal (*par*) of Alexander ? — He was not his equal. — Is your father skilled in the law (*jūris perītus*) ? — He is not skilled in it. — Is the city full of (*referta*) strangers ? — It is full of them. — Who was the first in eloquence among the Romans (*quis Romanorum*) ? — Cicero was the first. — Are you attached to your country ? — I am very much attached to it. — Can you endure hunger and cold ? — I cannot endure (them). — Is he eager for praise ? — He is excessively eager (*appententissimus*) for it. — What does it behoove us to be ? — It behooves us to be thirsting after knowledge (*intelligentia*) and virtue.

Lesson LXVII. — PENSUM SEXAGESIMUM SEPTIMUM.

OF THE GENITIVE AFTER VERBS.

A. After verbs of valuing or esteeming, and also after those of buying and selling, hiring and letting, the indefinite price or value is expressed by the genitive.

Such verbs are *aestĭmo, facĭo, pendo, dūco, pŭto, habĕo; aestĭmor, fĭo, pendor,* and *sum ; — emo, mercor, vendo, venĕo, licĕo, taxo; stăre, constăre,* &c.

The genitives representing the indefinite price or value are, — *a*) Substantives like *nihĭli,* " (for) nothing"; *flocci, nauci, pĭli, pensi, teruncii, assis,* " for a trifle," " a mere song." *b*) The neuter adjectives *magni,* highly; *permagni,* very highly; *plūris,* more highly; *plurĭmi,* very highly, or the most; *parvi,* but little (of little account); *minōris,* less; *minĭmi,* very little *or* least; and so *tanti, tantĭdem, quanti, quantĭvis, quanticunque,* so much, just so much, as much, &c. Sometimes with *prĕtii* expressed. Examples are : —

Cómmii régis auctóritas *mágni* habebâtur.	The authority of King Commius was held in high esteem.
Nûlla vis aúri et argénti *plûris,* quam vírtus *aestimánda* ést.	No amount of gold or silver should be estimated higher than virtue.
Súmmum bónum *plúrimi aesti-mándum est.*	We must (should) attach the highest value to the summum bonum.

Právi hómines súa *párvi péndere*,
aliêna cúpĕre sólent.

Bad men are accustomed to under-
value their own possessions and
to covet those of others.

Nóli spectâre, *quánti* hómo *sit ;*
párvi énim *prétii ést*, qui jam
nihili sit.

Never mind how much the man is
worth, for he is worth but little
who is already worthless.

Émit Cánius hórtos *tánti, quánti*
Pýthius vóluit.

Canius has bought the garden for
the price which Pythius demanded.

Véndo méum fruméntum non
plúris, quam cétĕri.

I sell my grain no higher than
others.

Tánti quódque málum *est, quánti*
íllud taxávimus.

Every misfortune is of as much
account as we have rated that.

Núlla péstis humáno génĕri *plúris stétit*, quám íra.

No pest has cost the human family
more than resentment.

De Drúsi hórtis *quánti licuísse*
tû scribis.

With reference to Drusus's garden
you write, how much it was offered for.

Égo a méis mê amári et *mágni
péndi* póstülo.

I want myself to be loved and esteemed by my friends.

REMARKS.

1. The *definite* value or price after the above verbs is expressed by
a substantive in the ablative; as, *aestimāre aliquid pecuniā, tribus
denāriis ; vendere aliquid quinquaginta talentis,* &c.   (Cf. Lesson
LXXI. *A.*)

2. To the genitives of the price or value add *hújus, boni,* and *aequi
bonîque* in expressions like *Rem* hujus *non facǐo,* I do not care *that* * for
it.   *Rem* boni *facǐo,* or *rem* aequi bonîque *facio* (or *consŭlo*), I consider it just and proper, I acquiesce in it (let it be so).

3. The verbs *coeno* and *habǐto* likewise occur with the genitive of
the price.   E. g. *Quanti habǐtas?* What do you pay for your lodgings ?   *Tantǐne coenas, quanti habǐtas?* Do you pay as much for your
dinner as you do for your lodgings ?

4. *Aestimāre* also admits the ablatives *magno, permagno, plurǐmo,
parvo, minǐmo,* and *nihǐlo* ; and after the verbs of *buying* and *selling,*
these six ablatives are *always* put instead of their respective genitives.
Pro nihǐlo may stand instead of *nihǐli* after *putāre, ducĕre,* and *esse.*
E. g. *Aliquid* magni or magno (nihili, nihǐlo *or* nihil) *aestimāre ;* —
emere or *vendĕre aliquid* magno, parvo, plurǐmo, minǐmo (pretio) ; —
aliquid pro nǐhǐlo *ducĕre, putāre,* to consider anything of no account.

5. The price or value may also be expressed by an adverb; as *cāre,
bĕne, māle, grātis,* &c.   E. g. *Hoc mǐhi gratis* (= nihilo) *constat,* This
costs me nothing.   *Aves pingues* care *venĕunt,* Fat birds fetch a high
price.

B.   Verbs of reminding, remembering, and forgetting

---

* I. e. A straw, rush.   This was accompanied by a gesture on the stage.

are followed by the genitive of the person, and by the genitive or accusative of the object, remembered or forgotten.

Such verbs are *monĕo, admŏnĕo, commonĕo, commonefacĭo, alĭquem;* *
— *memĭni, reminiscor, recordor, obliviscor.*

Médicus rēgem módo *mâtris sororúmque*, módo· *tántae victóriae appropinquántis admonêre* nôn déstitit.	The physician did not cease to remind the king, now of his mother and sisters, now of the magnitude of the approaching victory.
Mílites hortâtus ést, ut *reminisceréntur pristínae virtûtis súae*, nêve *mulĭĕrum liberúmque oblivisceréntur.*	He exhorted his soldiers to remember their prowess exhibited on former occasions, nor to forget their wives and children.
Grammáticos *officii súi commonêmus.*	We remind the philologians of their duty.
Discípŭlos *íd ûnum móneo*, ut praeceptóres súos nôn mínus, quam ípsa stúdia áment.	I remind learners of one thing only, which is, that they should love their teachers as they do their studies.
Somno ánimus *mémĭnit praeterĭtórum*, praeséntia cernit, futûra praévĭdet.	In sleep the mind recalls the past, beholds things present, and foresees the future.
Vivórum mémini, nec támen Epi-cúri lícet *oblivísci.*	I mention living authorities; nevertheless, Epicurus must not be forgotten.
Bóni súnt cíves, qui pátriae *benefícia meminérunt.*	They are good citizens, who are mindful of the benefits of their country.
Hómines ínterdum *rês praeclaríssimas obliviscúntur.*	Men sometimes forget the most remarkable things.
Núnquam líberos méos adspício, quin Plancii *mérĭtum* in mê recórder.	I never look at my children but what I call to mind my obligations to Plancus.

REMARKS.

1. Neuter pronouns and adjectives (e. g. *hoc, id, illud, quod, quid, quae, multa*, &c.) are invariably in the accusative after all the above verbs. E. g. Id *unum te admonĕo*, I remind you of this one thing. *Multa admonēmur*, We are reminded of many things. But the accusative of substantives occurs only after verbs of reminding or forgetting; as, *beneficĭa, mandāta tua memĭni* or *oblītus sum.*

2. *Memĭni* (in the sense of "I think of," or "I make mention "), *recordor*, and *moneo*, with its compounds, also take the ablative with *de*. E. g. *De homĭne importunissĭmo ne meminisse quidem volo*, I do not even wish to mention the importunate man. *De Herŏde et de*

---

* Verbs of reminding have thus also an accusative of the person reminded. (Lesson LX. *C.*)

Mettio meminĕro, I will bear in mind Herod and Mettius. *Velim scīre, quid* de te *recordēre*, I should like to know what you recollect with reference to yourself. *Terentiam moneātis de testamento*, Remind Terentia of the will.

3. The accusative of the *person* (reminded of, remembered or forgotten) rarely occurs, except after *memĭni*, when used in the sense of "I still remember or recollect" (a person seen or known before). E. g. *Antipăter*, quem *tu probe meministi*, Antipater, of whom you have an honorable recollection. *Cinnam memĭni, vīdi Sullam*, I remember Cinna, I have seen Sulla. But *memento mei, nostri*, Remember me, us.

4. In this construction is included the expression *vĕnit mihi in mentem* (*aliquid* or *alicūjus rĕi*), "something occurs to me." Thus, *Vĕnit mihi* Platōnis in *mentem.* — *Tibi* tuārum virtūtum *venīat in mentem.* But also, Res *mihi in mentem veniēbat.* — Omnia *mihi in mentem venērunt.*

C. The impersonal verbs *poenĭtet, pĭget, pŭdet, taedet, misĕret, verĭtum est, misĕrētur,* and *miserescit* are followed by the genitive of the object by which the emotion is excited, and by the accusative of the person affected.[*] E. g.

Sapiéntiam† núnquam *sui poénĭtet.*	Wisdom never repents of itself.
Mé civitâtis *mórum piget taedétque.*	I am wearied and disgusted with the morals of the state.
Súnt hómines, *quôs libídinis infamiaéque súae* néque *pudeat,* néque *taédeat.*	There are men who are neither ashamed nor disgusted by their own licentiousness and disgrace.
Núnquam *Átticum suscépti negótii pertaésum ést.*	Atticus never grows weary of an undertaking once begun.
Misĕret té aliórum, túi nec *miseret,* nec *pudet.*	You pity others, but for yourself you have neither compassion nor shame.
Cave *té frâtrum,* pro frâtris salûte *obsecrántium, misereâtur.*	Beware of being moved to pity by the brothers beseeching you for the safety of their brother.
Ínopis núnc *té miseréscat méi.*	Let my poverty now move you to pity.
Nihílne *té pópuli verêtur,* qui vociferâre in víâ ?	Are you not afraid of the people, for vociferating in the street ?

REMARKS.

1. The personal verbs *miserĕor* and *miseresco,* "I pity," adopt the construction of *misĕret;* but *miserāri* and *commiserāri* are followed by the accusative. E. g. *Nihil nostri miserēre!* Have you no compassion

---

[*] Compare page 334.   † Wisdom is here personified.

Z   34*

for us? *Miserescĭte regis*, Pity the king. *Commiserătus est* fortūnam *Graeciae*, He commiserated the fate of Greece.

2. The accusative of neuter pronouns may stand instead of the genitive. E. g. *Sapientis est proprĭum, nihil*, quod (= cujus) *poenĭtēre possit, facere*, It is characteristic of a wise man to do nothing which he may have to repent of.

3. The object of the emotion may also be an infinitive, or a clause introduced by *quod*. E. g. *Me non pŭdet* fatēri *nescire, quod nesciam*, I am not ashamed to confess, that I am ignorant of what I do not know. *Quintum poenĭtet*, quod *anĭmum tuum offendit*, Quintus is sorry that he has offended you. *Non poenĭtet me vixisse*, I do not regret having lived.

4. The genitive after *pŭdet* sometimes signifies "*before* any one," and the accusative (*me, te*, &c.) is often omitted. E. g. *Me tui, mi pāter, pudet*, I am ashamed before you, my father. *Pudet deōrum homĭnumque*, It is a shame in the eyes of gods and men. *Nonne te hujus templi, non urbis, non vĭtae, non lūcis pudet?* Are you not ashamed *before* this temple? &c.

5. These impersonal verbs sometimes (though rarely) occur personally (i. e. in the plural, and with a subject nominative). E. g. *Non te haec* (nom.) *pudent?*

To forget.	*Obliviscor, i, oblĭtus sum* (ALICUJUS, ALICUJUS REI or ALIQUID).
You forget — he forgets.	Obliviscĕris — obliviscĭtur.
Ye forget — they forget.	Obliviscĭmĭni — obliviscuntur.
Is he forgetting me, thee, us, them?	Écquid méi, túi, nostri, illōrum oblivíscitur?
He is not forgetting thee, me, us, them.	Túi, méi, nóstri, illōrum nôn oblivíscitur.
Are you forgetting anything?	Obliviscerísne áliquid (alicújus rei)?
I am forgetting my pen, my paper, my book.	Oblivíscor véro méam pénnam, chártam, librum (*or* méae pennae, chartae, líbri).
Has he forgotten to bring you the book?	Oblĭtúsne ést tíbi líbrum apportâre?
He has forgotten to bring it to me.	Véro; éum míhi apportâre oblĭtus ést.
Have you forgotten that he has arrived?	Oblĭtúsne és, éum advenísse?
I have not forgotten it.	Nôn oblĭtus súm.
Can you forget that day?	Potésne oblivísci diéi illíus?
I can never forget it.	Égo éjus núnquam oblivísci póssum.
Must the offences be forgotten?	Obliviscendúmne est offensârum?
They are to be forgotten entirely.	Obliviscéndum est prórsus.
Has he forgotten what I have told him?	Oblĭtúsne ést, quód (quae) éi díxi?

He has by no means forgotten it.	Nòn véro; mínime oblítus est.
You have forgotten to write to me.	Lítteras ad mê dáre oblítus és.
You are forgetting to speak to him.	Cólloqui cum éo oblivísceris.
To belong to (any one).	{ *Est alíquid alicújus.* { *Est meus, tuus, ejus, &c.*
Does this horse belong to your brother?	Éstne híc équus fràtris túi?
It does belong to him.	Ést éjus.
To whom does that table belong?	Cújus ést ílla ménsa?
It belongs to us, to you, to them.	Nostra, vestra, illôrum (ménsa) est.
To whom do these gloves belong?	Cújus sunt haec digitábula?
They belong to me, to you, to him.	Méa, túa, éjus (illius) súnt.
They belong to the captains.	Centuriônum (digitábula) súnt.
Whose book is this?	Cújus est híc líber?
It is mine.	Méus ést.
Whose shoes are these?	Cújus súnt hi cálcei?
They are ours.	Nóstri súnt.
To fit (suit, become).	{ *Aptum (am, um) esse.* { *Bĕne convenìre (-vēni, -ventum).* { (ALICUI, ALICUI REI, AD ALI- { QUID.)
These shoes fit very well.	Hi cálcei ad pédes (pédibus) ádmodum ápti súnt (ad pédes óptime convéniunt).
Do these boots fit those men?	Aptaêne súnt illis víris ístae cáligae?
They do not fit them.	Nôn áptae súnt. Iis nôn béne convéniunt.
Does this garment fit me?	Vestísne haec mihi ápta est (béne cónvenit)?
It fits (suits) you very well.	{ Tíbi ut quae optíssima est. { Tíbi quám óptime cónvenit.
How does this hat sit?	Quómodo híc píleus sédet?
It sits very well.	Ádmodum béne sédet.
It becomes you very well.	Tè quám óptime décet.
See, whether this dress becomes me.	Contémpla, satín' haec mê véstis déceat.
To suit, please (any one).	{ Convenìre alicui. { Placēre (-cui, -cìtum) alicui. { Probāri alicui.
Does that cloth suit (please) your brother?	Convenítne (placétne) frátri túo íste pánnus?
It does suit him.	Plácet. Probâtur.
Do these boots suit (please) your friends?	Écquid hae cáligae amícis túis plácent (convéniunt)?

They do suit them.	Plácent. Probántur.
They do not suit them.	{ (íis) mínus plácent. { Nôn probántur (íis).
Does it suit you to do this?	Convenítne tíbi hóc fácere?
It does suit me to do it.	Íd fácere míhi cónvenit.
To become (*morally*). *It becomes, is morally proper.*	{ Děcet, decuit, decēre (Impers.). { (ALIQUEM FACERE ALIQUID). Est alicujus, est meum, tuum, &c. { (ALIQUID FACERE).
Does it become you to do this?	{ Decétne tê hóc fácere? { Tuúmne ést hóc ágere?
It does not become me to do it.	Íd fácere mê nôn décet (mê dé- decet).
Did it become him to write?	{ Eúmne scríbere decêbat (décuit)? { Ejúsne érat scríbere?
It did become him.	Decêbat. Érat éjus.
Does it become you to go on foot?	Decétne tê (tuúmne est) íre pé- dibus?
It does not become me.	Mê nôn décet. Méum nôn ést.
It does not become an orator to be angry.	Oratôrem irásci mínime décet.
It is proper, just.	*Pǎr est, justum est* (ALIQUEM FA- CERE ALIQUID).
Is it proper for him to say so?	Éstne pâr (jústum), éum hóc dí- cere?
It is proper, just.	Pâr est. Jústum est.
It is not proper.	Pâr nôn est. Néfas est.
To please, to be one's pleas- ure (*It pleases*).	{ Lǐbet, libǐtum est, libēre. { Collibet, collibǐtum est, &c. { Plǎcet, placuit, placēre. { (ALICUI FACĔRE ALIQUID.)
Does it please your brother to accompany us?	Libétne (collibétne) frátri túo séqui (comitári) nôs?
Does it suit your brother to go along with us?	Convenítne frátri túo nobíscum únā símul íre?
It does not please him to go with you.	Éi nôn plácet (líbet) vobíscum únā íre.
It does not suit him to go with you.	Símul (únā) vobíscum íre éi nòn cónvenit.
Did it please him to write to you?	Collibitúmne (placitúmne) ést éi litteras dáre ad tê?
It did please him.	Collíbitum est.
What is your pleasure?	Quid tíbi cóllibet?
What do you wish?	Quid vis (ímperas)?
I wish you to bring me the book?	Vólo, tê míhi apportâre líbrum.
Do you want anything?	Núm quíd vis? Núm quid ím- peras?

Do you want anything else? | Núm quíd céterum vis?
As you please. | Ut plácet. Ut júbes.
But concerning the republic, it does not please me to write any more. | Sed de repúblicā nôn míhi líbet plûra scríbere.

To please (to like). | { Plăceo, ēre, ŭi, ĭtum.
Prŏbor, āri, ātus sum.
Arrĭdĕo, ēre, ĭsi, ĭsum (ALICUI). }

Does this book please you (do you like this book)? | Probatúrne (placétne) tíbi hícce líber?
I like it very much. | Pérplacet. Válde míhi probátur.
I dislike it extremely (it displeases me very much). | { Veheménter míhi dísplicet.
Ab éo abhórreo. }
Do you dislike these books? | Núm líbri ílli tíbi dísplicent?
They do not displease me (I do not dislike them). | Míhi nôn dísplicent (nôn improbántur).
I do not like them very well. | { Mínus míhi probántur.
Mínus míhi árrident. }
How do you like it here (i. e. this place)? | Quómodo híc lócus tíbi plácet (probâtur)?
I like it very well. | Híc lócus míhi arridet (míhi válde plácet, probâtur).
I like this place extremely. | Híc lócus míhi praeter ómnes arrídet.
It is my delight. | Ést in delíciis méis.

To displease (to dislike). | { Displĭceo, ēre, ŭi, ĭtum.
Improbor, āri, ātus sum. }

Ready money, cash. | Pecunia praesens seu numerāta.
To pay down (cash). | Sólvere pecúniam praesentem (numerâtam).
To buy anything for cash. | Émĕre aliquid pecúniā numerātā (die oculátā).
To sell anything for cash. | Véndere aliquid pecúniā praesenti (díe oculátā).
On credit. | Pecúniā nôn praesénti seu numerátā. Díe caécā.
To buy, sell anything on credit. | Émere, véndere aliquid pecúniā nôn praesénti seu díe caécā.
Do you wish to buy on credit? | Vísne émere pecúniā nôn praesénti (die caécā)?
No, I wish to buy for cash. | Ímmo véro pecúniā numerātā émere cúpio.
I prefer to buy for cash. | Díe oculátā émere málo.
Does it suit you to sell me on credit? | Convenítne tíbi véndere míhi pecúniā nôn praesénti (díe caécā)?
It does not suit me. | Nôn cónvenit.
To succeed, prosper, turn out well (of things). | { Cēdo, ĕre, cessi, cessum.
Procēdĕre. Succēdĕre. }

To succeed (in an attempt, of persons).	*Procēdit, -cessit, -cedĕre.* *Contingit, contĭgit, contingĕre.* (MIHI, UT .... SUBJ.)
The thing succeeds well, is very successful.	Éa rès cêdit (procêdit, succêdit) béne, próspere, felíciter, faúste.
My undertaking succeeded, was successful.	Incéptum mihi béne céssit, procés-sit, succéssit.
My designs were not succeeding very well.	Consília mihi mínus (párum) cedé-bant (procēdébant succēdébant).
Do you succeed in learning Latin?	Procedítne tibi, ut línguam Lati-nam díscas? Procedísne in línguā Latínā?
I do succeed (in it).	Procêdit véro felíciter. Procêdo véro próspere.
I do not succeed in learning it.	Míhi nòn contíngit, ut éam edí-scam. Párum (minus) procédo.
Did those men succeed in selling their horses?	Contigítne víris íllis, ut équos súos vénderent?
They did not succeed.	Nòn cóntigit.
If my attempts should succeed.	Si incéptis succéderet.* Si incépta mihi succéderent.
He succeeded in liberating his country from slavery.	Huic cóntigit, ut pátriam ex servi-tûte in libertâtem vindicâret.
There is. There are.	*Est. Sunt.*
He is here, present, at hand.	*Ádest. Ad mánum est.*
There are here, present, at hand.	*Ádsunt. Ad mánum sunt.*
Is there any wine?	Éstne (adéstne) vínum?
There is some.	Ést. Ádest. Ad mánum est ali-quántulum.
There is none.	Nòn est. Núllum ádest.
Are there any apples?	Adsúntne mâla?
There are some.	Sunt (ádsunt) áliquot.
There are none.	Nòn sunt. Núlla ádsunt.
Are there any men (here)?	Adsúntne hómines?
There are some.	Ádsunt nonnúlli.
Is any one present?	Adéstne áliquis (quísquam)?
There is no one.	Némo ádest.
Was there any one here?	Adfuítne áliquis?
There was some one here.	Ádfuit véro nòn némo.
Were there many there?	Aderántne múlti (hómines)?
There were a great many there.	Áderant permúlti. Áderat vis (cópia, multitúdo) má-gna.
Are there men who will not study?	Súntne hómines, qui lítteris stu-dêre nólunt (nólint)?

---

* On the personal and impersonal use of these verbs, compare Lesson LV. *B.* III.

There are many who will neither work nor study.	Permúlti súnt, quí néve laboráre néve lítteris studére vólunt (vélint).
There are those whom it delights to cultivate the arts and sciences.	Súnt quos ártes studiáque cólere júvat.
There are many who are fond of being engaged in the liberal arts and sciences.	Múlti súnt, quí in ártibus ingénuis versári delectántur.
To keep, retain.	{ *Tĕnĕo, ēre, ŭi, ntum.* { *Retĭnĕo, ēre, ŭi, ntum.*
To clean, cleanse.	{ *Mundo, āre, āvi, ātum.* { *Mundum facĕre, emundāre.*
Directly, immediately.	*Stătim, e vestĭgĭo, actūtum.*
This instant.	E vestigio, hōc in vestigio tempŏris, confestim.
Clean.	Mundus, a, um.
The inkstand.	*Atramentārĭum, i, n.
Instantly, in a moment, suddenly.	Puncto (momento) tempŏris; extemplo.
Will you keep the horse?	Vísne retinére équum?
I will (keep it)	Vólo.
I do not desire to keep it.	Retinére éum nôn cúpio.
You must not keep my money.	{ Pecúnia méa tíbi nôn retinénda est. { Pecúniam méam tenére té nôn opórtet.
Will you clean my inkstand?	Vísne mihi emundáre atramentárium?
I will clean it.	Fácere nôn nólo.

EXERCISE 128.

Have you brought me the book which you promised me? — I have forgotten it. — Has your uncle brought you the handkerchiefs which he promised you? — He has forgotten to bring me them. — Have you already written to your friend? — I have not yet had time to write to him. — Have you forgotten to write to your parents? — I have not forgotten to write to them. — To whom does this house belong? — It belongs to the English captain whose son has written a letter to us. — Does this money belong to thee? — It does belong to me. — From whom hast thou received it? — I have received it from the men whose children you have seen. — To whom do those woods belong? — They belong to the king. — Whose horses are those? — They are ours. — Have you told your brother that I am waiting for him here? — I have forgotten to tell him so. — Is that your son? — He is not mine; he is my friend's. — Where is yours? — He is at Dresden. — Does this cloth suit you? — It does not suit me; have you no other? — I have some other, but it is dearer than this. — Will you show it to me? — I will show it to you. — Do these boots suit your uncle? — They do not suit him, because they are too dear (*nĭmis carus*). — Are these

the boots of which you have spoken to us ? — They are the same. —
Does it suit you to go with us ? — It does not suit me. — Does it become you to go to the market ? — It does become me to go thither. —
Did you go on foot into the country ? — It does not become me to go
on foot, so that I went thither in a carriage.

EXERCISE 129.

What is your pleasure, Sir ? — I am inquiring after your father. —
Is he at home ? — No, Sir, he is gone out. — What is your pleasure ?
— I tell you that he is gone out. — Will you wait till he comes back
again ? — I have no time to wait. — Does this merchant sell on credit ?
— He does sell on credit. — Does it suit you to buy for cash ? — It
does not suit me. — Where have you bought these pretty knives ? —
I have bought them at the merchant's whose shop you saw yesterday.
— Has he sold them to you on credit ? — He has sold them to me for
cash. — Do you often buy for cash ? — Not so often as you. — Have
you forgotten anything here ? — I have forgotten nothing. — Does it
suit you to learn this by heart ? — I have not a good memory, so that
it does not suit me to learn by heart. — Have you succeeded in writing a letter ? — I have succeeded in it. — Have those merchants succeeded in selling their horses ? — They have not succeeded therein.
— Have you tried to clean my inkstand ? — I have tried, but have
not succeeded in it. — Do your children succeed in learning the English ? — They do succeed in it. — Is there any wine in this cask ? —
There is some in it. — Is there any brandy in this glass ? — There is
none in it. — Is wine or water in it ? — There is (*inest*) neither wine
nor water in it. — What is there in it ? — There is vinegar in it. —
Are there any men in your room ? — There are some there. — Is
there any one in the storehouse ? — There is no one there. — Were
there many people in the theatre ? — There were many there. — Are
there many children that will not play ? — There are many that will
not study, but few that will not play. — Hast thou cleaned my trunk ?
— I have tried to do it, but I have not succeeded. — Do you intend
buying an umbrella ? — I intend buying one, if the merchant sells it
me on credit. — Do you intend keeping mine ? — I intend giving it
back again to you, if I buy one.

Lesson LXVIII. — PENSUM DUODESEPTUAGE-
SIMUM.

GENITIVE AFTER VERBS. — *Continued.*

A. After verbs of accusing, convicting, condemning,
acquitting, and the like, the name of the crime is put in
the genitive.

Such verbs are *arguĕre, coarguĕre, insimŭlāre, increpāre, increpĭtāre, urgēre,* to charge (accuse) ; — *accusāre, incusāre, agĕre, deferre ; arcessĕre, postulāre,* to accuse, arraign ; summon ; — *interrogāre,* to call to an account ; — *se alligāre, se adstringĕre,* to become guilty of ; — *tenēri, obstringi, obligāri,* to be guilty of ; — *convincĕre, captāre,* to convict ; — *judicāre, damnāre, condemnāre,* to condemn ; — *absolvĕre, solvĕre, liberāre, purgāre,* to acquit, absolve.   E. g.

Cícero Vérrem *avarítiae nímiae coárgŭit.*	Cicero charged Verres with excessive avarice.
Cannénsem quísquam exércitum *fŭgae* aut *pavóris insimŭlāre* pótest ?	Can any one accuse the army, which fought at Canna, of flight or cowardice ?
Gálba étiam *saevítiae* pópŭlum *incrépŭit* edícto.	Galba, in an edict, reproved the people for cruelty even.
Miltíades *accusâtus est prodĭtiônis.*	Miltiades was accused of treason.
Qui áltĕrum *incûsat próbri,* éum ípsum sê intuéri opórtet.	He who charges another with dishonor should look into his own breast.
Caêsar Dolabéllam *repetundârum * postŭlâvit.*	Caesar arraigned Dolabella on the charge of extortion.
Fúrti se *obligâvit.*	He was guilty of theft.
Themístocles ábsens *prodĭtiônis* est *damnâtus.*	Themistocles, in his absence, was condemned for treason.
Júdex éum *injuriârum absólvit.*	The judge acquitted him of the charge of personal injury.
Senâtus néc *liberâvit éjus cúlpae* rêgem, néque *árgŭit.*	The senate neither absolved the king from that charge, nor accused him of it.

REMARKS.

1. The genitive of the crime may be explained by *crimĭne* or *nomĭne* † understood. These ablatives are sometimes actually put. E. g. *Ne absens* invidiae crimĭne *accusarêtur.* — Nomĭne scelēris conjurationisque *damnati sunt.*

2. Genitives of the crime are *peccâti, maleficii, scelēris, caedis, fŭrti, veneficii, parricĭdii, peculâtûs, falsi, injuriârum, repetundârum, prodĭtiōnis, majestâtis ;* — *probri, avarítiae, audaciae, temerĭtātis, ignaviae, impietātis,* and others.

3. Instead of the genitive, the ablative with *de* or *in* is sometimes put. E. g. De pecuniis repetundis *accusatus est.* — Rosclum de luxuriâ *purgâvit.* — In crimĭne incendii *convicti sunt.* — In manifesto peccâto *tenebâtur.* So also : Inter sicarios *damnâtus est,* He was condemned as an assassin.

4. The punishment or fine to which any one is condemned, is likewise expressed by the genitive ; more rarely by the ablative. ‡   Thus

---

* Sc. *pecuniârum,* of money to be reclaimed, i. e. extorted.
† On the charge or accusation of, under the title of.
‡ But always the ablative when a *definite* sum is named. E. g. *Quindecim millĭbus gravis aeris est damnātus.*

mortis, capĭtis, multae, pecūniae, quadrupli, octupli, or *morte, capĭte, multā, pecuniā damnāri.* Sometimes also by *ad* or *in ;* as, *ad poenam, ad bestĭas, ad metalla, in metallum, in expensas damnāri.* E. g. *Miltiades* capĭtis *absolūtus,** pecuniā *multatus est.* — Tertiā parte *agri damnati sunt.* — *Multos* ad metalla, aut ad bestias *damnāvit.* The poets put also the dative ; as, *morti damnātus.*

5. The construction of the above verbs extends to several adjectives; as *reus, compertus, noxĭus, innoxĭus, insons, manifestus,* &c. E. g. *Reus est injuriārum,* He is accused of trespass. *Manifestus rērum capitalĭum,* Clearly convicted of a capital offence. *Noxĭus conjuratiōnis,* Guilty of conspiracy. *Sacrilegii compertus,* Found guilty of sacrilege.

B. After *esse* and *fĭĕrī* the genitive often stands elliptically, *res, negotĭum, mŭnus, officĭum, proprĭum,* or some other word signifying *part, business, duty, office, property,* &c., being understood. E. g.

Néque hóc *tánti labóris est, quánti* vidétur (sc. *esse*).

Nor is this *a matter* of as much difficulty as it seems to be.

Ést júdicis, nôn quid ípse vélit, sed quíd léx et relígio côgat, cogitáre.

It is *the business (duty)* of a judge to consider, not that which he himself may desire, but what the law and religion enforce.

Est adolescéntis, majóres nútu veréri.

It *belongs to* a young man to respect those older than himself.

Hóc *doctóris intelligéntis est,* vidére, quô férat natûra súa quémque.

It is *the part* of an intelligent instructor, to examine the natural aptitude of every one.

Tárdi ingénii est, rívŭlos consectári, fóntes rêrum nôn vidére.

It is *the sign (characteristic)* of a dull head, to follow the course of things, and not to see their causes.

Cujúsvis homĭnis est errâre ; nullius, nísi insipiéntis, in errôre perseverâre.

Every man *is liable* to err, but none but a fool will persevere in error.

Ars eârum rérum ·ést, quae sciúntur.

Science *relates to* those things which are the objects of cognition.

Petulántia magis est adolescéntium, quam sénum.

Petulance is characteristic rather of young than of old men.

Ómnia, quae *mulieris fuérunt, víri* fiunt.

Everything, which *belonged to* the woman, becomes the property of the husband.

Thébae *pópŭli Románi* jûre bélli fáctae súnt.

Thebes became the property of the Romans by right of war.

---

* "Released from capital punishment." Thus also *capĭtis accusâre* or *arcessĕre,* to arraign one on a capital charge; *capĭtis* or *capĭte anquirere, damnâre, condemnâre,* to doom or condemn one to death. A similar idiom is *votĭ* or *votôrum damnāri,* to have one's wish fulfilled or granted (*lit.* to be condemned to redeem one's vow).

Jám mê *Pompéii* tótum *ésse* scis. You know that I am already entirely for Pompey.

Família pecuniáque *agnatôrum gentiliúmque ésto.* The slaves and money shall become the property of the relations and members of the *gens*.

REMARKS.

1. The ellipsis of *negotĭum*, &c., which is commonly assumed to explain this construction, is sometimes expressed. E. g. *Non hôrum tempŏrum* negotium *est.* — *Sapientis est* proprium.* — *Id judĭcis, vĭri, praeceptôris* mŭnus *est.* — Officĭum *libĕri esse homĭnis puto.* In all of which examples the omission of these words would leave the sense unaltered.

2. The genitive of the personal pronoun is never put, but instead of it the neuter of the corresponding possessive. Hence *meum, tuum, suum, nostrum, vestrum est,* and not *mei, tui,* &c. *est.* E. g. *Non est mentĭri* meum, Lying is not my business (not characteristic of me). *Est tuum, vidĕre, quid agĭtur,* It is your part (it belongs to you) to see what is at stake. *Fuit* meum *jam pridem patriam lugĕre,* It was long ago my lot to mourn over my country.†

3. This rule extends also to verbs of *esteeming, believing,* and to passives of *appearing, seeming,* &c., generally with *esse* understood. E. g. *Tutelae nostrae duxĭmus,* sc. *esse,* We considered it a matter subject to our intervention. *Duri homĭnis vidĕtur,* sc. *esse,* It seems to betray a cruel man. *Tempŏri cĕdĕre, semper sapientis est habĭtum,* To yield to circumstances has always been considered characteristic of a prudent man.

4. When the genitive has a gerundive connected with it, *esse* stands in the sense of "to contribute or conduce to." E. g. *Regĭum imperĭum initĭo* conservandae libertātis *atque* augendae rei publicae *fuit,* At first the royal government contributed to the preservation of liberty, and to the advancement of the common weal.

5. In this construction are included the expressions *moris est* (= *est in more, est in more posĭtum*), or *consuetudĭnis est,* It is a characteristic feature of the manners and customs (e. g. of the Greeks, &c.); *est opĕrae* (= *est opĕrae prĕtĭum*), it is worth while, &c.; instead of which *mos est, consuetudo est* (e. g. *Gallorum, Graecōrum*), may also be employed.

C. The impersonal verbs *interest* and *rēfert* are followed by the genitive of the person interested or concerned, but where a personal pronoun is required, by the possessives *meā, tuā, suā, nostrā, vestrā,* and *cūjā.*‡ E. g.

---

* Compare page 352, note ‡.
† So also other adjectives in place of the genitive. E. g. *Hoc patrĭum* (= *patris*) *est.* — *Et agĕre et pâti fortĭa* Romanum *est,* &c.
‡ With these ablatives *causâ* or *rê* may be supplied. According to some grammarians, these pronouns are neut. acc. pl. with *commŏda* understood. The quantity of the final *a,* however, and the testimony of Priscian, decide in favor of the ablative.

Mágni *ínterest Cicerónis, vél meá* pótius, vel mehércle *utriúsque.*	It is a matter of great importance * to Cicero, or rather to me, or, by Hercules, to both of us.
Quís ést hódie, *cújus intersit,* istam légem manére ?	Who is there to-day (== now) that is at all concerned in the permanence of this law ?
Véstra, júdices, hóc máxime *ínterest.*	This is a matter of the highest importance to you, judges.
Nòn adscrípsi, quód *tuá* níhil *referébat.*	I have not added what does not concern you.
Humanitátis plúrímum *réfert.*	It is a matter of the highest moment to humanity.

REMARKS.

1. The *degree* of importance is expressed either by genitives like *magni, permagni, parvi, plúris, tanti,* and *quanti,* &c., or by adverbs or neuter accusatives used adverbially ; as, *multum, plus, magis, maxíme, parum, paulum, mínus, miníme, valde, magnópěre, nihil,* &c. The genitive of the person is often omitted. É. g. Magni refert, *hic quod velit,* It is a question of great consequence what this man wants. *Quod* permagni interest, *pro necessario habétur,* That which is of great importance is often deemed a matter of necessity. *Hoc non* plúris réfert, *quam si imbrem in cribrum geras,* This is of no more consequence than if you were to pour water into a sieve.

2. The *matter* or *thing* of consequence or importance is expressed, *a*) by the infinitive (with or without a subject accusative) ; *b*) by a clause introduced by *ut* (*uti*), *ne,* or an interrogative (*qui, qualis, quam,* &c.) ; and *c*) sometimes by the neuter pronouns *hoc illud,* &c. ; but never by a substantive. É. g. *Interest omnìum recte* facere, It concerns all to do right. *Quid nostrá refert,* victum esse *Antonìum?* What do we care for the defeat of Antonius ? *Reipublícae interest,* uti *salvus esset,* It is important to the commonwealth that he should be safe. *Non refert,* quam multos *libros, sed* quam bonos *habéas,* It matters not how many books you have, but how good they are.

3. In the sense of " it profits, it conduces to," these verbs also take the dative or the accusative with *ad.* E. g. Cui rei *id te assimuláre retúlit?* What advantage was it to you to pretend that ? *Magni* ad honōrem nostrum *interest,* It contributes greatly to oùr honor.

To cast, throw.	{ *Jǎcìo, ěre, jěci, jactum.* { *Jacto, āre, āvi, ātum.* { *Mítto, ěre, mǐsi, missum.*
To cast or throw at, upon, in, forth, &c.	Adjǐcěre, conjǐcěre, injǐcěre, projǐcěre, &c.
To throw stones at some one.	Lapídes mittěre *or* conjǐcěre in aliquem. Petěre alíquem lapídìbus.

---

* *Interest* == " it concerns, it imports, it is of importance to." *Réfert* == " it concerns, serves, profits, is the interest of."

To cast an eye upon some one or something.	Oc̆ŭlos in aliquem *or* aliquid conjic̆ĕre.
To cast one into prison (chains).	{ Alíquem in carcĕrem conjicĕre. { Dāre aliquem in vincŭla.
To throw the blame upon some one.	Culpam in aliquem conjicĕre *or* conferre.
To throw (prostrate) one's self at the feet of some one.	Projicĕre (sternĕre)* se ad pŏdes alicūjus.

Have you thrown a stone into the river?	Injecistine lápidem in flûmen?
I have thrown one in.	Injéci véro ûnum aliquem.
Does he throw the blame upon me?	Núm cúlpam in mê cónjicit (cónfert)?
He does not throw it upon you.	Nôn in tê cónjicit (cónfert).
Did you cast an eye upon that book?	Conjecistine óculos íllum in líbrum?
I did (cast an eye upon it).	Conjéci proféc̆to.
Was he casting a glance at the paper?	Adjiciebátne óculos ad chártam (*or* chártae)?
He was not.	Nôn adjiciêbat.
Were they throwing stones at you?	Númquid lápides in tê jactábant (conjiciébant)?
They were not.	Nôn jactábant.
Did he throw himself at the feet of the king?	Projecítne (prostravítne), sê ad pédes rêgis?
He did not prostrate himself.	Sê nôn prostrâvit.
Was he thrown into prison?	{ Conjectúsne est in cárcĕrem? { Datúsne est in víncŭla?
He was.	Fáctum est.
Where does the stone lie now?	Úbi núnc jácet lápis?
It lies in the river.	In flúmine.
Where did the book lie?	Úbi jácuit líber?
It was lying on the table.	Jacêbat super ménsam (in ménsâ).

To draw, pull.	{ Trắho, ĕre, xi, ctum. { Dūco, ĕre, xi, ctum.
To drag; to seize (hurry off).	{ Trắho, ĕre, xi, ctum. { Rắpio, ĕre, pŭi, ptum.
To draw the wagon.	Currum trăhĕre (*or when slowly or gently*, dūcĕre).
To draw the sword.	Gladīum (e vaginâ) edūcĕre *or* distringĕre.
To drag one into the street.	Extrăhĕre aliquem in publĭcum.
To drag one into servitude.	Abstrăhĕre aliquem in servitūdĭnem.
To drag one to punishment, to death.	Rắpĕre aliquem ad supplicĭum, ad mortem.
To hurry one off into prison, chains.	Abrĭpĕre aliquem in carcĕrem, in vincŭla.

---

* *Sterno, ĕre, strǔci, strǔtum.*

35 *

Where did they drag him to?	Quô éum rapuérunt?
They dragged (hurried) him into prison.	Abripuérunt éum in cárcĕrem (in víncula).
Did they not drag (hurry) him into slavery?	Nónne éum in servitúdĭnem abstraxérunt?
They did.	Fáctum ést véro.
Does the *horse* draw the carriage?	Equúsne tráhit (dûcit) cúrrum?
The horse does it.	·Équus.

The pain (of body or mind).	Dŏlor, ōris, *m.*
The evil, ill.	Mălum, i, *n.*
The trouble, inconvenience.	Molestĭa, ae. *f.*
The injury (injustice).	Injūria, ae, *f.*
The detriment, loss.	Detrimentum, damnum, i, *n.*
The loss.	Jactūra, ae, *f.*
To pain (bodily or mentally — of things).	Dŏlet, dŏlŭit, dŏlēre (MIHI ALIQUID).
To cause pain, to hurt (of things).	{ Dŏlōrĕm făcĕre or effĭcĕre alĭcui (bodily). { Dŏlōrem afferre alĭcui (mentally).
To pain, hurt one (of persons).	{ Alĭcui dolōrem făcĕre *or* effĭcĕre (*mentally and physically*). { Aegre făcĕre alĭcui (*mentally*).
To injure (hurt) one.	{ Injūriam alĭcui inferre. { Nŏcĕo, ēre, cŭi, cĭtum (ALICUI).
To offer violence to one.	{ Violāre alĭquem. { Alĭcui vĭm afferre.
To offer violence to one's self.	Vĭm (mănus) sĭbi inferre.
To molest any one.	Alĭcui molestĭam exhibēre.
To injure one's interest, (cause injury or loss).	Damnum (detrimentum) alĭcui inferre (afferre).
To be a loss or injury to one.	Damno *or* detrimento (*dat.*) esse alĭcui.
To suffer or sustain loss by anything.	Damnum (jactūram) facĕre alĭquā rē.

Does this pain you?	Dolétne tĭbi hóc?
It does pain me.	Dólet mĭhi profécto.
That pains (grieves) me very much.	{ Íd mĭhi mágnum dolôrem áffert. { Dólet mihi magnópere.
Does anything pain you?	Facítne (efficítne) tĭbi aliquid dolôrem?
My finger pains me.	Dolôrem mĭhi éfficit dígitus.
It pains me, when I am whipped.	Míhi dólet, quum égo vápŭlo.
My feet and head pain me.	Dólent míhi pédes átque cáput.
Have you hurt any one?	Núm cuiquam álĭquid dolôrĕs fecísti (effecísti)?
I have hurt no one.	Égo dolôrem féci némini.

Has he hurt your feelings?

{ Aegrēne tíbi fēcit?
Attulítne tíbi dolôrem?

He has not only hurt my feelings, but my person even.

Is míhi nòn sólum dolôrem, sed vím étiam áttūlit.

Has any one injured you?

Númquis tíbi nócŭit (injúriam íntuht)?

No one (has injured me).

Némo.

Were they molesting any one?

Éccui moléstias exhibébant?

They were molesting no one

Némini (núlli).

Was that a loss to you?

Fúĭtne tíbi íllud dámno (detriménto)?

Yes, I sustained a heavy loss by it.

Égo véro dámnum éo fécĭ mágnum.

Have I ever done you any harm (injury)?

Egóne tíbi únquam quídquam injúriae íntuli?

No, on the contrary, you have done me good.

Ímmo véro míhi beneficia tribuísti.

No, on the contrary

Immo, immo vēro, immo potĭus, immo enĭm vēro.

To do one good, to show one kindness.

{ *Benefĭcĭa alĭcui dăre* or *tribuĕre (-bŭi, būtum).*
Benefĭcĭĭs aliquem affĭcĕre or *ornāre.*

To overload me with benefits or kindness.

Benefĭcĭis alíquem cumulāre.

To show one civilities, attentions.

{ Offĭcĭa alĭcui tribuĕre.
Offĭcĭa in alĭquem conferre.

On the contrary, you have shown me nothing but civilities.

Ímmo énim véro míhi nòn nísi offícia tribuísti.

You have on the contrary overloaded me with many and great benefits.

Ímmo pótius mê múltis et mágnis beneffíciis cumulâsti.

It is a pity.

Doléndum ést.

His death is to be lamented.

Mórs éjus dolénda ést.

It is a pity, that he is not alive.

Doléndum ést, quód nòn in vítā est.

It is a pity, they did not come sooner.

Doléndum ést, quód nòn matúrius venérunt.

To be useful (to any one).

{ *Utĭlem (e) esse (ALICUI).*
Usŭi esse (ALICUI).

To be wholesome, good for one's health, to do one good.

{ *Prŏdest, prŏfŭit, prŏdesse.*
Condūcit, conduxit, condūcĕre.
Salutārem (salūti) esse.
(All with ALICUI.)

Does this do you good?

{ Conducítne tíbi hóc?
Estne tíbi hóc salúti?

It does do me good.

Condúcit.   Salúti ést profécto.

This is excellent for me (does me much good).

Hóc míhi máxime condúcit.

What is the servant doing with his broom?

Quíd scópis súis fácit (incéptat) sérvus?

He sweeps the room with it.	Púrgat (iis) cubículum.
What do you wish to make out of this wood ?	Quíd hôc ex lígno fácere vís ?
I wish to make nothing at all out of it.	Égo ex éo níhil quídquam fácere cúpio.
Have they done anything with him ?	Númquid de éo (éi) fecérunt ?
They have done nothing.	Níhil fecérunt.
To pass by or *before (any one* or *any place).*	Praeteríre, transíre (ALIQUEM, ALI-QUEM LÓCUM).
To walk by *or* before.	Praetergrédior, di, gressus sum.
To ride by *or* before.	Praetervĕhor, i, vectus sum (ALI-QUEM, ALIQUEM LOCUM).
When did you pass by my house.	Quándo dómum méam praeteri-vísti ?
I passed it on the day before yesterday.	Praetervi éam núdius tértius.
What place were they passing ?	Quém lócum praeteríbant ?
They were passing by the public square of the city.	Praeteríbant (transíbant) lócum úr-bis públicum.
Was it my brother whom you passed ?	Fratrémne méum praeteríbas ?
It was your brother.	Véro, frâtrem túum.
Who is passing by us ?	Quís nôs praéterit ?
Our tailor with his son is pass-ing us.	Sártor nóster cum fílio nôs praetér-eunt.
Who is driving by the theatre ? (It is) the doctor.	Quís theátrum praetervéhitur ? Médicus.
To throw away.	*Abjĭcio, ĕre, jēci, jectum.*
To lavish, squander.	{ *Effundo, ĕre, fūdi, fūsum.* *Dilapĭdo, āre, āvi, ātum.*
Did they throw away anything ?	Abjiciebántne áliquid ?
They threw away all their arms and weapons.	Abjiciébant véro árma atque têla súa ómnia.
How much money has he squan-dered ?	Quántam pecúniam dilapidâvit ílle ?
He has squandered his entire fortune.	Facultátes súas ómnes profûdit.
I have thrown away (lost) an entire hour.	Pérdidi tótam hôram.

EXERCISE 130.

How many times have you shot at that bird ? — I have shot at it twice. — Have you killed it ? — I have killed it at the second shot. — Have you killed that bird at the first shot ? — I have killed it at the fourth. — Do you shoot at the birds which you (see) upon the houses, or at those which you see in the gardens ? — I shoot neither at those which I (see) upon the houses, nor at those which I see in the gar-dens, but at those which I perceive upon the trees. — How many

times have the enemies fired at us ? — They have fired at us several
times. — Have they killed any one? — They have killed no one. —
. Have you a wish to shoot at that bird ? — I have a desire to shoot at
it. — Why do you not shoot at those birds ? — I cannot, for I have no
powder. — How many birds have you shot at ? — I have shot at all
that I have perceived, but I have killed none, for my powder was not
good. — Have you cast an eye upon that man ? — I have cast an eye
upon him. — Has your uncle seen you ? — I have passed by the side
of him, and he has not seen me, for he has sore eyes. — Has that man
hurt you? — No, sir, he has not hurt me. — What must one do in
order to be loved ? — One must do good to those that have done us
harm. — Have we ever done you harm ? — No, you have on the
contrary done us good. — Do you do harm to any one? — I do no
one any harm. — Why have you hurt these children? — I have not
hurt them. — Have I hurt you ? — You have not hurt me, but your
children (have). — What have they done to you? — They dragged
me into your garden in order to beat me. — Have they beaten you ?
— They have not beaten me, for I ran away. — Is it your brother
who has hurt my son? — No, sir, it is not my brother, for he has
never hurt any one. — Have you drunk of that wine? — I have
drunk of it, and it has done me good. — What have you done with
my book ? — I have placed it on the table. — Where does it lie now ?
— It lies upon the table. — Where are my gloves ? — They are lying
upon the chair. — Where is my stick ? — It has been thrown into the
river. — Who has thrown it into it ? — Was he accused of any crime ?
He was not accused of a crime, but of avarice. — Are they guilty
(*obligantne se*) of treason ? — They are guilty of treason and impiety.
— Did the judge absolve them from guilt (*culpae*) ? — He did not
absolve them. — Did the book become yours (*tuus*) ? — No, it became
(*factus est*) the property of my brother. — Is it important to you,
that I should write (*me littĕras dare*) to your friend ? — It is a matter
of the highest importance to humanity, that you should write to him. —
Who is liable (*cujus*) *est* to err ? — Every man is liable to err. — Is
it my duty to do what is right? — It is the duty of every man to do
what is right.

Lesson LXIX. — PENSUM UNDESEPTUAGESI-
MUM.

SYNTAX OF THE ABLATIVE.

A. The ablative serves to express a variety of relations, of which
the most important are those of CAUSE, CONDITION, MODALITY,
QUALITY, PLACE, TIME, DIFFERENCE, and NUMBER. All these
relations are in English indicated by means of prepositions, such as

2 A

by, with, from, of, on account of, with respect to. The Ablative of Time has already been considered in Lesson LVII., that of Place in Lesson LVI., and the Ablative after Comparatives in Lesson XLIII., q. v.

THE ABLATIVE OF CAUSE.

B. After verbs passive and neuter, and sometimes also after transitive verbs and adjectives, the ablative serves to indicate the cause, occasion, ground, or reason of the action or state expressed by them.* E. g.

Mári súpero inferóque Itália ínsulae módo *cíngitur.*	Italy is bounded by the upper and the lower sea, like an island.
Quaê dómus tam stábilis est, quae nôn *ódiis atque dissídiis* fúnditus póssit *evérti?*	What house is there so firm, that could not be destroyed to its very foundation by hatred and dissension ?
Etesiârum *flátū* nímii *temperántur* calóres.	The spells of excessive heat are moderated by the Etesian winds.
Darius *senectûte* díem *óbiit* suprêmum.	Darius died from the effects of old age.
Delícto dolêre, correctiône gaudêre nôs opórtet.	We should be sorry, for the fault and rejoice at its correction.
Concórdiā rês párvae *créscunt, discórdiā* máximae *dilabúntur.*	By concord small things increase and prosper, but by discord the greatest are reduced to ruin.
Múltis in rêbus *negligéntiā†* pléctimur.	We suffer punishment for negligence in many things.
Miltíades aêger érat *vulnéribus,* quae, &c.	Miltiades was sick from the wounds, which, &c.
Minturnénses Márium *féssum inédiā fluctibúsque* recreárunt.	The Minturnenses reinvigorated Marius, who had been exhausted by fasting and the effects of the sea.
Si *frúctibus* et *emoluméntis‡* amicítias *colêmus.*	If we will cultivate friendship on account of its advantages and emoluments, &c.
In cúlpā súnt, quî offícia désērunt *mollúiā* ánimi.	They are culpable, who neglect their duties from want of firmness.
Divérsis duóbus vítiis, avarítiā et luxúriā, cívitas Româna *laborábat.§*	The Roman state suffered from two opposite vices, from avarice and luxury.

---

* These relations are in English expressed by the prepositions *by, from, of, on account of, for.*

† = *propter negligentiam.*

‡ = *propter fructus et emolumenta,* or *fructǔum et emolumentōrum gratiā.* See note 5.

§ Compare note 2.

REMARKS.

1. After passive verbs, the impersonal cause alone stands in the ablative without a preposition, and the personal agent requires the preposition *a* or *ab*. (Cf. page 165.)

2. The adjectives and neuter verbs, thus followed by the ablative of the cause, are generally resolvable into a passive verb akin to them in sense. E. g. *Fessus longā standi morā,* Weary (i. e. having been *made* weary) from long standing. *Interiit fame == consumptus est fame,* He died of hunger. *Gaudeo tuo honōre == delector tuo honōre,* I rejoice in your honor. *Expectatio rumore crēvit == aucta est rumōre,* The expectation increased with the report.

3. In many of the above-mentioned cases the cause or occasion may also be expressed by prepositions; as by *ob, propter,* and *per* with the accusative, or by *ab, de, ex,* and *prae* with the ablative. E. g. *Ob merĭta sua carus,* Beloved on account of his merit. *Propter metum, prae lacrĭmis non scribĕre possum,* I am unable to write from fear, on account of the tears I shed. *Per valetudĭnem id bellum exsequi nequierat,* He had been unable to finish that war, on account of his health.* *Ex intestinis, ex pedibus laborare,* To suffer from the diarrhœa, from the gout.

4. The accusative *vicem,* "on account of," often occurs in connection with a genitive, or the possessives *meam, tuam,* &c., instead of the ablative *vice.* E. g. *Tuam vicem doleo,* I am grieved on your account. *Maestus non suam vicem, sed propter ipsum periclitantĭum fratrum* (sc. *vicem*), Sad not on his own account, but on account of his brothers in danger on his account.

5. After *transitive* verbs the cause, ground, or reason is sometimes expressed by the ablative alone,† but more commonly by *propter* with the accusative, or by *causā, gratiā, ergō,* or *nomĭne,* with the genitive. E. g. *Multi ex urbe* amicitiae causā (== *propter amicitiam*) *Caesārem secūti erant,* Many from the city had followed Cæsar out of friendship. *Coronā aureā donatus est* virtūtis ergō benevolentiaeque, He was presented with a crown of gold on account of his valor and benevolence.

6. When the cause is an intention or purpose, it is expressed by *hac mente, hoc consilio, ut* . . . ., and the motive by *amōre, irā, odio, laetĭtiā,* &c., in connection with some participles like *ductus, adductus, incensus, incitatus, mōtus,* &c. E. g. *irā incensus,* from feelings of revenge; *inopiā adductus,* induced by want; *coactus metu,* driven by fear. *Classem* ea mente *comparāvit,* ut *Italiam peteret,* He raised a fleet with the intention of invading Italy.

THE ABLATIVE OF THE MEANS OR INSTRUMENT.

C. After verbs of every kind, the ablative serves to indicate the *means* or *instrument* by or with which anything is effected or realized.

---

* *Per* and *propter* may also have an accusative of the person. E. g. *Si per me licuisset,* If I had given permission. *Propter quos vivit,* Through whom he lives. But the mere ablative of the person never occurs in any of these relations.

† As in the two examples preceding the last under the rule, page 418.

The corresponding English prepositions are *with*, *by*, *by means of*, *through*. E. g.

Lycúrgus léges súas *auctoritáte* Apóllinis Délphici *confirmávit.*	Lycurgus established his laws by the authority of Delphic Apollo.
Córnǐbus taúri, ápri *déntǐbus*, *mórsu* leónes sě *tutántur.*	Bulls defend themselves with their horns, boars with their tusks, lions with their jaws.
Benevoléntiam cívium *blandítǐis* collígere túrpe est.	It is disgraceful to solicit the favor of the people by means of flattery.
Natúram *expéllas fúrcā*, tamen úsque recúrret.	You may drive out nature with a pitchfork, yet it will incessantly return again.
Británni interióres *lácte* et *cárne vívunt.*	The Britons of the interior live on milk and flesh.
Hannibal Sagúntum *vi expugnávit.*	Hannibal took Saguntum by force.
Injúria *fít* duóbus módis, aut *vi*, aut *fraúde.*	Injustice is done in two ways, either by violence or fraud.

REMARKS.

1. The ablative is rarely employed, when the means or instrument has reference to a *person*, but generally either *per* with the accusative, or the periphrasis *alicujus operā, beneficio, consilio, culpā*, &c. E. g. Per te *salvus sum*, I am safe through your instrumentality. *Detrimenta* per homǐnes eloquentissǐmos *importáta*, Evils introduced by the most eloquent men. *Quorum* operā (= per quos) *plebem concitátam existǐmábant*, By whom they supposed the people to have been roused. *Equǐtem Romanum* beneficio tuo *conservávi*, I have saved a Roman knight through your kindness. *Cujus* indicio (= per quos) haec *cognověrant*, Through whom they had become informed of this.

2. *Per* with the accusative is often put instead of the ablative of the means, especially when reference is had to external circumstances. E. g. Per vim *ei bona eripuit*, He robbed him of his property by main force (by forcible measures). Per litteras *aliquem certiorem facěre*, To inform any one by letter. Per simulationem *amicitiae me perdidě-runt*, They have ruined me under the pretence of friendship. But the material instrument is always expressed by the ablative. E. g. *Vulnerăre aliquem gladio, cultro, sagittis*, To wound any one with the sword, with a knife, with arrows.

To spend, consume (time in anything).	*Ago, ěre, ēgi, actum.* *Consūmo, ěre, mpsi, mptum.* *Contěro, ěre, trivi, trìtum.* (TEMPUS (in) ALIQUĀ RĒ).
To devote time to anything.	Tempus pōněre in aliquā rě.
To spend imperceptibly, to beguile time with anything.	Fallo, ěre, féfelli, falsum (TEMPUS ALIQUĀ RĒ).
What do you spend your time in ?	Quā in rě témpus consûmis (cónteris) ?

I spend my time in studying (in studies).	Témpus in stúdiis litterârum cóntero (consúmo).
How has he spent his life?	Quómodo vítam (aetâtem) súam consúmpsit?
He has spent his life in perpetual travelling.	Aetâtem súam in perpétuâ peregrinatióne consúmpsit.
He has spent his life uselessly in idleness and feasting.	Vítam in ótio et convíviis absúmpsit.
He was in the habit of spending entire days by the fireside.	Tótos díes júxta fócum átque ígnem agêbat (= ágêre solêbat).
He was in the habit of wearing out entire nights in reading and writing.	Tótas nóctes legéndo et scribéndo conterêbat (= contérêre solêbat).
Is he spending a pleasant life?	Agítne vítam jucúnde (hílâre)?
On the contrary, he is having a hard life of it.	Ímmo pótius párce ac dúriter ágit vítam.
How did he spend the night?	Quómodo contrívit (consúmpsit) nóctem?
He was beguiling the hours with pleasant conversation.	Hóras fallêbat jucúndis sermónibus.
He has spent the livelong night in banqueting.	Feféllit spatiôsam nóctem convíviis.
Where did he spend his vacation?	Úbi (quô lóco) férias súas exigêbat?
He spent them in the country, in the city, at home.	Exigêbat éas rúri, in úrbe, dómi.
Does it behoove us to spend this day pleasantly?	Oportétne nôs húnc díem hílâre consumâmus?
By all means.	Máxime opórtet.
The vacation.	Feríae, ârum, *f.*
Travelling.	Peregrinátio, ônis, *f.*
The banquet.	Convívium, i, *n.*
To miss anything.	{ *Amittêre rem aliquam.* *Deerrâre aliquâ re.*
To miss (not find) any one.	{ *Alíquem non inveníre.* *Ab alíquo deerrare* or *aberrâre* (on the road).
To miss one's aim.	{ Propôsitum non assêqui (-cútus sum). Fine excídêre (-cídi, ——).
To miss one's turn.	{ Ordínem non servâre. Súis partíbus deesse.
Has the blow missed?	Deeravítne íctus?
It has missed.	Fáctum est.
Are you missing your way?	Deerrâsne itínere?
I am not missing it.	Nôn deérro.
I have missed (not found) him.	Éum nôn invéni.
You have missed your turn.	{ Ordínem non servâsti. Defuísti túis pártibus.
He has missed his aim.	Fíne éxcidit.

The turn (part, rôle).

Ordo, ĭnis, *m.* ; partes, ĭum, *f. pl.* ; vĭcis, *gen. f.*

In turn, in order.

Ex ordĭne, ordĭne, per ordĭnem.

It is my, thy, his, our, &c. turn.

{ Órdo mê, tê, éum, nôs vócat.
{ Méae, túae, éjus, nóstrae pártes súnt.

To take one's turn.

{ Ex ordĭne (per ordĭnem) aliquid agĕre.

To fail, neglect (to do any-thing).

{ *Praetermitto, ĕre, mĭsi, missum.*
{ *Nĕgligo, ĕre, lexi, lectum.*
{ (ALIQUID FACERE).

The merchant has failed to send me the money due (me).

Mercâtor mĭhi pecúniam débĭtam míttere praetermísit.

You have failed to come to me this morning.

Veníre ad mê hódie mâne neglex-ísti.

You have neglected to perform your duties and obligations.

Offícia túa et múnera obíre praeter-misísti.

Am I neglecting any one ?

Núm égo quénquam négligo ?

To hear anything of (con-cerning) any one.

Alĭquid de aliquo audīre, accĭpĕre.

To hear anything from any one

Alĭquid ab (ex) alĭquo audīre, acci-pĕre, cognoscĕre (-nŏvi, nĭtum).

To receive news from (con-cerning) any one.

Nuntium accĭpĕre ab (de) aliquo.

Have you heard from your friend ?

Accepistíne núntium ab amíco túo ?

I have heard.

Accépi.

Have you heard (learnt) any-thing new ?

Núm quídquam nóvi cognovísti ?

I have heard nothing at all.

Níhil quídquam audívi (accépi).

Of whom have you heard (news) ?

De quô cognovísti (núntium acce-písti) ?

I have heard from my father.

Núntium accépi a pátre.

I hear (learn) that your brother has arrived.

Accípio (aúdio, dísco), túum frâ-trem advenísse.

To assure (one of any-thing).

{ *Confirmo, āre, āvi, ātum.*
{ *Affirmāre* (ALICUI, ALIQUID).

To persuade.

Persuădĕo, ĕre, si, sum (ALICUI DE ALIQUA RE).

I assure you sacredly of this.

Hóc tíbi sáncte affírmo.

I wish you to be persuaded of this.

Hâc de rê tíbi persuadéri vélim.

I assure you (be assured).

{ Persuádeas tíbi vólo (vélim).
{ Persuâsum tíbi sit.

I assure you of my assistance (in your plans).

Persuádeas tíbi vélim, mê túis con-sĭliis non defutúrum.

Did he assure you of his assist-ance ?

Voluítne tíbi persuadéri, sê túis consíliis nôn defutûrum ?

To happen, occur, take place (generally).

{ *Fīo, fĭĕri, factus sum.*
{ *Evĕnio, īre, vēni, ventum.*

To happen to one (to meet with).	{ Accĭdo, ĕre, cĭdi, ——. Contingo, ĕre, tĭgi, tactum. 　(MIHI, TIBI, SIBI — ALICUI.)
A most serious calamity has hap-'pened.	{ Fácta ést (áccidit) calámitas gra-víssima. Rês péssimae accidérunt.
He has met with a great misfortune.	{ Áccidit éi málum péssimum. Mágnam in calamitâtem íncidit.
I have met with a most serious injustice.	Fácta ést míhi injúria gravíssima.
I have (meet with) the good fortune.	Contíngit míhi felícitas.
The good fortune; happiness.	Fortûna secunda; casus secundus; felicĭtas, âtis, *f.*
The bad fortune, misfortune; calamity.	Fortûna adversa; málum, i, *n.;* ca-lamĭtas, âtis, *f.*
To meet (any one by chance).	{ *Occurro, ĕre, ri, sum.* *Obvĭam venĭre* (ALICUI).
Did you meet with any one?	{ Occurristĭne álicui? Venistĭne álicui óbviam?
I have met with your brother.	Óbviam véni frâtri túo.
I met a large number of men.	Óbviam veniêbam multitúdini hó-minum.
To be, to exist, to be found.	Esse, inveniri, reperíri.
There, in that place.	Ibi, illic; ibĭdem (*adv.*).
Not even.	Nĕ — quĭdem.
Not even a book.	Nĕ líber quĭdem.
Not even one (not a single one).	Nĕ únus quĭdem.
Not even once.	Nĕ sémel quĭdem.
Not even the people.	Nĕ pópulus quĭdem.
The village.	Vicus, pâgus, i, *m.*
Are there many horses in this village?	{ Súntne (inveniuntúrne) múlti équi hôc in víco? Estne (invenitúrne) cópia equôrum hôc in víco?
There are a good many (here).	Inveniúntur (súnt) véro múlti (per-múlti).
There is not a single good horse (to be found) there.	Nĕ únum quĭdem équum bónum íbidem invénias.
Is there much wine this year?	Éstne hôc ánno cópia víni?
There is an abundance of it.	Ést éjus véro cópia mágna.
There are no apples this year.	Pôma hôc ánno núlla sunt (reperi-úntur).
Are there many learned men in France?	Inveniuntúrne múlti dócti in Fran-cogálliâ?
There are a great many there.	Inveniúntur (reperiúntur) íbi per-múlti.
To be of use (good, useful).	*Utĭlem* or *bónum esse* (alicui rei, ad rem) *usŭi esse ad rem.*

Of what use is that ?	Cui úsüi est hóc ?
It is good to eat.	Úsüi est ad vescéndum.
It is useful against bodily pain.	Útile ést contra dolóres córporis.
It is of no use (worth nothing).	Níhili est. Nullíus prétii est.
This is of no use (entirely useless).	Hóc núlli úsui ést (pláne inútile est).
What is this man good for ?	Quám ad rém útilis (idóneus) est hícce ?
He is not fit for anything.	Útilis (idóneus) ést ad núllam rém.
He is a good-for-nothing fellow.	{ Hómo ést nequíssimus. { Hómo níhili est.
Are there any faults in his little book ?	Reperiuntúrne vítia in éjus libéllo ?
There are none in it.	Reperiúntur núlla.
Is the stuff, which you have bought, good ?	Estne téxtum, quód emísti, bónum ?
No, it is good for nothing.	Nōa véro ; inútile est (nullíus prétii est).
The fault, defect.	Vitíum, i, n.
The material, stuff.	Textum, i, n. ; pannus, i, m.

EXERCISE 131.

I do not see my gloves ; where are they ? — They are lying in the river. — Who has thrown them into it ? — Your servant, because they were no longer good for anything. — What have you done with your money ? — I have bought a house with it. — What has the joiner done with that wood ? — He has made a table and two chairs of it. — What has the tailor done with the cloth which you gave him ? — He has made clothes of it for (Dative) your children and mine. — What has the baker done with the flour which you sold him ? — He has made bread of it for you and me. — Have the horses been found ? — They have been found. — Where have they been found ? — They have been found behind the wood, on this side of the river. — Have you been seen by anybody ? — I have been seen by nobody. — Have you passed by anybody ? — I passed by the side of you, and you did not see me. — Has any one passed by the side of you ? — No one has passed by the side of me. — By what is the field surrounded (cingítur) ? — It is surrounded by trees. — Of what disease (morbus) did he die (mortuus est) ? — He did not die of any disease, but from old age. — Have they been punished for negligence ? — They have been punished. — Is your brother sick from the wounds he has received ? — No, he is sick from the headache. — Do you cut your meat with a knife ? — I cut it with a knife and fork. — Were you injured by violence or by fraud ? — I was injured both by violence and by fraud.

EXERCISE 132.

Do you expect any one ? — I do expect my cousin, the officer. — Have you not seen him ? — I have seen him this morning ; he has passed before my house. — What does this young man wait for ? —

He waits for money. — Art thou waiting for anything? — I am waiting for my book. — Is this young man waiting for his money? — He
is waiting for it. — Has the king passed (in the carriage) here? —
He has not passed here, but before the theatre. — Has he not passed
before the new fountain? — He has passed there; but I have not
seen him. — What do you spend your time in? — I spend my time in
studying. — What does your brother spend his time in? — He spends
his time in reading and playing. — Does this man spend his time in
working? — He is a good-for-nothing fellow; he spends his time in
drinking and playing. — What did you spend your time in, when you
were at Berlin? — When I was at Berlin, I spent my time in studying, and riding on horseback. — What do your children spend their
time in? — They spend their time in learning. — Can you pay me
what you owe me? — I cannot pay it to you, for our bailiff has failed
to bring me my money. — Why have you breakfasted without me? —
You failed to come at nine o'clock, so that we have breakfasted without you. — Has the merchant brought you the stuff which you bought
at his house? — He has failed to bring it to me. — Has he sold it to
you on credit? — He has sold it to me, on the contrary, for cash. —
Do you know those men? — I do not know them; but I think that
they are good-for-nothing fellows, for they spend their time in playing.
— Why did you fail to come to my father this morning? — The tailor
did not bring me the coat which he promised me, so that I could not
go to him.

Lesson LXX. — PENSUM SEPTUAGESIMUM.

THE ABLATIVE OF MODE OR MANNER.

A. A substantive, denoting the *mode* or *manner* in
which anything is done, is put in the ablative with *cum* ;
but when it has an adjective or adjective pronoun connected with it, the preposition may be omitted. E. g.

Lítterae *cum cúrā diligentiâque* scríptae.	A letter written with care and diligence.
Cum dignitāte pótius cádere, quam *cum ignomíniā* servíre nôs opórtet.	We should rather fall with honor, than serve with dishonor.
Cum írā níhil récte fíeri pótest.	Nothing can be done properly with anger.
Cum clamóre in fórum cúrritur.	There is a rush towards the forum with clamors.
Cum siléntio audíti súnt.	They were heard in silence.
Ípse *mágnā cum cúrā et diligéntiā* scrípsit.	He himself has written with great care and diligence.

36*

Id *aéquo ánimo* nôn féret cívitas.	The state will not submit to that patiently.
Sídĕra cúrsus súos confíciunt *máximā celeritâte.*	The stars perform their revolutions with the utmost celerity.
Cum máximā offensióne Pátrum consulátū ábiit.	He resigned his consulship to the great dissatisfaction of the senate.
Déos sémper *púrā, íntegrā, incorruptā* et *ménte* et *vôce* venerêmur.	Let us always venerate the gods with pure, entire, uncorrupted heart and voice.

REMARKS.

1. The ablative of manner has adverbial force, and may often be resolved into an adverb. E. g. *cum curā,* i. e. *diligenter ; cum silentio,* i. e. *tacite, clam ; cum fídę,* i. e. *fideliter ; cum voluptâte,* i. e. *libenter ; cum bonā gratiā,* i. e. *benigne,* &c.

2. In certain expressions the ablative of nouns appears also without *cum,* even though no adjective is added. E. g. *Alíquid* sponte, voluntāte, jure, injuriā *facére,* To do anything of one's own accord, willingly, justly, unjustly. *Aliquid recte et* ordíne, modo et ratione, ratione et ordíne *facére,* To do anything properly, and in order, &c. *Lege agere,* To proceed according to the law. *Silentio praeteríre,* To pass over in silence. And so always without "cum": — *hoc modo, quo modo, eodem animo, eādem ratione,* &c.

3. *Cum* with the ablative also denotes that which is *simultaneous* or *concomitant.* E. g. *Cum occasu solis copias educére,* To lead out cne's forces at sunset. *Cum nuntio exíre,* To go out as soon as the message arrived. *Cum exercítu, cum copiis, cum militibus,* &c. *iter facere,* To march with one's army, forces, soldiers, &c. *Romam cum febri veni,* I came to Rome with a fever. But also *without* "cum"; as, *Egressus omnibus copiis,* Having marched forth with all the forces. *Ingenti exercítu ab urbe profectus,* Having left the city with a large army. *Duumvir* decem navíbus *vēnit,* The duumvir came with ten ships, &c. *Castra* clamore *invadunt,* They invade the camp with a clamor.*

B. After nouns, adjectives, and verbs, the ablative often expresses the relations indicated by the English *with respect to, by, in,* or *in point of.* E. g.

Natiône Medus est.	With respect to his nationality he is a Mede.
Hamílcar cognómíne Bárcas.	Hamilcar surnamed Barcas.
Dómo Carthaginiénses súnt.	They are Carthaginians (inhabitants of Carthage).
Paúci (céntum, mílle) nímero homínes.	But few (a hundred, thousand) men in number.

---

* The participles *junctus* and *conjunctus* sometimes thus appear *without* "cum." E. g. *Bellum* miserrimā fugā *junctum,* A war attended with a most wretched flight. *Nefaria libido* dedecóre, scelére *conjuncta,* Nefarious licentiousness connected with dishonor, with crime, &c.

Grándis nátu,* aetáte provéctus est.*	He is of full age, advanced in life.
Quiéti, alácres ánimo súmus.†	We are calm, cheerful in mind (= of a calm, cheerful mind).
Mémbris ómnibus cáptus ac *débílis* est.	He is nerveless and feeble in every limb.
Scélére pär est *ílli, indústriá inférior.*	He is equal to him in crime, inferior to him in industry.
Agesiláus fúit *claúdus* áltero péde.	Agesilaus was lame in one of his feet.
Sócrates lónge *lepóre* et *humanitáte* ómnibus *praéstitit.*	Socrates was far superior to every one in point of wit and humanity.
Péricles et Themístocles *grándes* érant *vérbis, crébri senténtiis, comprehensióne* rêrum *bréves.*	Pericles and Themistocles were grand in the use of words, abounding in apothegms, and brief in the comprehension of things.
Nôn sôlum *commóveor ánimo,* sed étiam *tóto córpóre perhorrésco.*	I am not only troubled in mind, but I shiver with horror in every limb.

REMARKS.

1. This ablative serves to restrict, limit, or define more particularly the words with which it is connected, and occurs in a great variety of expressions. E. g. *meá sententiá, meá opinióne, meo judicio,* in my opinion or judgment ; *re,* in reality, in fact ; *nomíne,* in (or by) name ; *genére,* by birth ; *domo,* by residence ; *eloquentiá,* in eloquence, &c.

2. Instead of this ablative of limitation or more particular definition, the poets and their imitators sometimes employ the accusative. E. g. *Fractus* membra (= membris) *labore,* Disabled in his limbs from labor. Humeros (= *humeris) oleo perfusis,* Anointed as to his shoulders with oil. *Víte* caput (= *capíte) tegitur,* He is covered as to his head with vine-leaves. *Tremit* artus (= *artíbus),* He trembles in his limbs. Os humerosque *deo símílis,* In countenance and shoulders like a divinity ‡ So also in ordinary prose even, *id tempóris* for *eo tempóre ; id aetális* for *eá aetate ; cetera* and *reliqua* for *ceteris* and *reliquis rebus,* &c. On this accusative compare Lesson XLVIII. *D.*

THE ABLATIVE OF QUALITY.

C. A noun and an adjective denoting a quality, character, or condition are put in the ablative with

---

* So also *major, mínor nátu ;* and *maxímus, minímus nátu.*

† This differs very little from the genitive or ablative of quality: — *quiéti, alacris aními* sumus ; *quiéto, alacri anímo* sumus.

‡ So passive verbs of *clothing* and *divesting* frequently have an accusative of the thing put on or taken off, instead of the more regular ablative. E. g. *Induor vestem* (= *veste*), I am (being) clothed in a garment. *Indúitur fáciem vultumque Dianae,* He puts on the form and countenance of Diana. *Inútile ferrum cingítur,* He begirds himself with the useless sword. *Puèri laevo suspensi locúlos tabulamque lacerto,* Boys with their little box of counters and their writing-tablet suspended from their left shoulder.

some tense of *esse, existĕre,* or *invenīri,* expressed or understood. E. g.

Agesilâus *statúrā fúit húmĭli et córpŏre exíguo.*	Agesilaus was of low stature and of a small body.
Rês *est insígni infámiā.*	It is an affair of signal disgrace.
Murêna *mediócri ingénio,* sed *mágno stúdio* rêrum vétĕrum, múltae indústriae et mágni labôris *fúit.*	Murena was a man of but moderate talent, but of great zeal for antiquities, of much industry and great perseverance.
Theophrástus aúctor est, ébur fóssĭle *cándido* et *nígro colóre inveníri.*	Theophrastus informs us, that fossil ivory is found of a white and black color.
In recentiôre Académiā *éxstĭtit divína quâdam celeritâte* ingénii Carnéades.	In the later academy Carneades shone as a man of almost a divine quickness of intellect.
Mágno timóre sum : sed béne sperámus.	I am in great fear, but we hope for the best.

So also without *esse :* —

Fúit quidam, *súmmo ingénio* vir, Zéno.[*]	There was a certain Zeno, a man of the highest order of intellect.
Pompéium, *praestantíssimā virtûte* vírum *(acc.).*	Pompey, a man of the most distinguished virtue.
Ést spelúnca quaêdam, *infinĭtā altitúdĭne.*	There is a certain cave of immense dimensions.
Diffĭcili tránsĭtu flûmen, *rípĭsque praerúptis.*	A river, difficult to cross, and of rugged banks.

REMARKS.

1. The ablative of quality may be explained by *instructus, praedĭtus, ornâtus,* "furnished, endowed, adorned with." (Cf. Lessons LXXI. *B.* and LXXII. *B.*)

2. This ablative differs upon the whole but little from the genitive of quality,[†] except that the latter expresses rather natural than acquired qualities, while the former is applied to both. The genitive of quality, moreover, seldom occurs in the plural, and comprises also determinations of measure which are never indicated by the ablative. Sometimes the genitive and ablative both occur in the same construction, as in the example, *Murĕna mediocri ingénio,* &c.

How long ?	{ *Quam longum (tempus) ?* [‡] { *Quăm dǐu ? Quăm dúdum ?*
Long, a long time.	Dǐu, longum tempus.
Very long.	Perdǐu, longíssime.
For a long time, a great while (past).	Jam dǐu, jam pridem.

---

[*] These examples may be explained by a relative with *est, fúit,* &c., or by the hypothecial *ens* (" being "). E. g. *Zeno,* qui vir erat *summo ingenio. Spelunca,* ens or quae est *infinitā altitudĭne,* &c.

[†] Compare Lesson LVII. *A.*   [‡] See Lesson LVII. *A.*

For some time (past).	Jam dúdum.
Longer (than, I, you, we, &c.).	Longíus, díutíus (quam égo, tû, nôs).
How long is it since?	{ Quám lóngum ést, ex quô? { Quám díu ést, quúm (or *ex quô*, sc. témpore)?
It is (already) long since.	{ Jám lóngum ést, ex quô. { Jám díu ést, quúm (ex quô).
It is now some time since.	Jám dúdum ést, ex quô (or quum).
It is not long since.	Nôn lóngum (haûd díu, haûd dúdum) ést, ex quô.
Is it long since you have breakfasted?	{ Estne jam lóngum, ex quô jentavísti? { Estne jam díu, quum jentavísti?
It is not long since I have breakfasted.	Haûd lóngum est, ex quô (quúm) jentávi.
It is some time since I have breakfasted.	Jám dúdum ést, ex quô (quúm) jentávi.
It is a great while since I breakfasted.	Jám pérdiu ést, ex quô témpore jentávi.
It is an hour since I have breakfasted.	Tóta jám hôra est, ex quô jentávi.
I breakfasted an hour ago.	Jentáculum súmpsi abhinc hôram (únā hórā ábhinc).
Two hours ago (within two hours).	{ Ábhinc dúas hóras. { Duábus hóris ábhinc
Three years ago (within three years).	{ Abhinc três ánnos. { Tribus ánnis ábhinc.*
An hour and a half ago.	{ Ábhinc sesquihôram. { Sesquihórā ábhinc.
Two hours and a half ago.	{ Dúas abhinc hóras et dimídiam. { Duábus hóris ábhinc et dimídiā.
Is it long since you saw him?	{ Estne témpus lóngum, ex quô éum vidísti? { Estne jam díu, cum éum nôn vídes?
It is a great while.	{ Témpus jám ést lóngum. { Jám pérdiu est.
How long is it since you saw him?	{ Quámdiu ést, ex quô éum vidísti? { Quám longum est témpus, cum eum non vidísti?
I saw him a year ago (within a year).	Égo éum vídi ábhinc ánnum (únō ánnō abhinc).
Is it long since you are living in this country?	{ Éstne jam lóngum témpus, ex quô hâc in térra dégis?
Have you lived long in this country?	Degísne jám díu hâc in térrā?

---

* See Lesson LVII. *D.*

I have lived here for three years.	Ánnus jám ést tértius, ex quô (quúm) híc dégo.
I have lived at Rome these three years.	{ Très ánni súnt, ex quô Rómae hábito. { Tértius jám ánnus ést, ex quô (quúm) Rómae hábito.
He has lived in America these twenty years.	{ Vigínti ánni sunt, ex quô in Américâ íncolit. { Vicésimus jám ánnus est, cum in Américâ íncolit.
How long is it since he was here?	Quám díu est, ex quo témpore áderat?
He was here a fortnight ago.	Áderat (ádfuit) hâc regiône ábhinc quíndecim díes.
It is but a year since you were in these parts.	Nôn ámplius ánno est (ánnus tántum est), ex quô hâc regiône áderas.
It is more than a year since.	*Ámplius jam ánno (ánnum) est, ex quô* or *quúm.*
It is scarcely six months since.	Víx séx ménses súnt, ex quô or quúm (cum).
It is nearly three years since.	{ Três própe ánni súnt, ex quô or quum. { Tértius própe ánnus ést, ex quô or cum.
It is now almost a year since.	Jám fére ánnus ést, ex quô or cum.
Almost, nearly.	Prope, fére, paene (*adv.*).
Scarcely.	Vix (*adv.*).
A few hours ago.	{ Ábhinc áliquot hóras. { Áliquot bóris ábhinc.
Half an hour ago.	{ Ábhinc semihôram. { Dimídiâ hórâ ábhinc.
A quarter of an hour ago.	{ Ábhinc quadrántem hórae. { Quadránte hórae ábhinc.
I have been living in this region these ten years.	Décem jám ánni súnt, ex quô hâc regiône hábito.
How long have you had the horse?	Quámdiu (quám lóngum témpus) équum habuísti?
I have had it nearly these five years.	Quíntus paéne ánnus ést, ex quô éum hábeo.
It is now a year since I have seen him.	Ûnus, jam est ánnus, cum éum nôn vídi.
It is more than a year since you have seen your brother.	Ámplius ánno (ánnum) est, ex quô frâtrem túum nôn vidísti.
How often have you heard him?	Quám saépe éum audivísti?
I have heard him more than twenty times.	Égo éum saépius quam vícies audívi.
I have seen them more than a hundred times.	Vídi éum saépius quam cénties.

How long? since what time?	*Ex quô témpore? Ex quô? Quam díu?*
Since childhood.	A puerítiâ, a púero.
Since the memory of man.	Post hóminum memóriam.
From time indefinite.	Infiníto ex témpore.
How long has he been dead?	Ex quô témpore (quám díu) mórtuus est?
He has been dead this great while.	Mórtuus ést jám díu (jám prídem).
He has been dead (for) these ten years.	Mórtuus ést jám décem ánnos (decénnium).
These three days (for three days).	Três díes.
This month (for a month).	Únum ménsem.
These two years.	Dúos ánnos, biénnium.
How long is it since you are here?	Quám lóngum témpus ést, cúm hic ádes?
It is three days since I am here.	{ Tértius jám dies ést, cum ádsum. { Três díes ádsum.
I am here since yesterday.	Ádsum ex hestérno díe.
How long is it since he is at home?	Ex quô témpore dómi est?
Since this morning.	Ex mâne hodiérno.
This long time.	Ex lóngo témpore (longíssime).
It is already a month since he is here.	Únus jám est ménsis, cum hic ést (ádest).
To cost.	{ *Stŏ, stāre, stĕti, stătum.* { *Consto, āre, stĭti, stătum.* (ALICUI ALIQUÂ RĒ.)
How much does this book cost you?	Quánti* hic líber tíbi stát?
It costs me three dollars and a half.	Stát míhi tríbus thaléris et dimídio.
It costs me five shillings and a quarter.	Cónstitit míhi quínque shillíngis et quadránte.
Did it cost you any more than mine?	Stetítne tíbi plúris, quám móus?
It cost me as much as yours did you.	Cónstitit míhi tánti, quánti tíbi túus.
It cost me a high price, not much, nothing.	Cónstitit míhi mágno, párvo, níhilo (sc. prétio).†
To purchase, buy.	{ *Ĕmo, ĕre, ēmi, emptum.* { *Coĕmĕre* (several things together). { *Compăro, āre, āvi, ātum.*
What have you purchased to-day?	Quíd emísti (comparásti) hódie?

---

* On this genitive of the price, see Lesson LXVII. *A.*
† On the ablative of the price, see Lesson LXXI. *A.*

I have purchased three pairs of shoes and two pairs of boots.	Égo tría pária calceórum et dúo pária caligârum coëmi (comparávi).
Did you purchase anything yesterday?	Comparavistíne áliquid hestérno díe?
I brought three quires of paper and a picture.	Égo três scápos chártae cum túbula pícta coëmi (comparávi).
The pound (weight).	Libra, ae, *f.*; libra pondo, *or simply* pondo (*indecl.*).
The half-pound.	Selibra, ae, *f.*; selibra pondo.
The dozen.	Duŏdĕcim (*as numeral*).
The foot (measure).	Pēs, *gen.* pĕdis, *m.*
The inch.	Dĭgĭtus, i, *m.*
The quire (of paper).	Scápus, i, *m.* (chartae).
The regiment (of soldiers).	{ *Lĕgĭo, ōnis, *f.* (*of foot*). *Turma, ae, *f.* (*of horse*).
The ring.	Anŭlus, i, *m.*
The picture.	Tabŭla picta, ae, *f.*; imāgo (-ĭnis) picta; pictūra, ae, *f.*
The small picture.	Tabella picta, ae, *f.*
The pair.	{ Pār, *gen.* păris, *n.* Bĭni, ae, a.
A pair of doves.	Pâr columbârum.
A pair of gloves.	{ Pâr digitabulôrum. Bína digitábŭla.
Two pairs of gloves.	Dúo pária digitabŭlôrum.
A noble pair of brothers.	Pâr nóbĭle frâtrum.
A pair of oxen, horses.	Júgum bóum, equôrum.
A pound of sugar.	(Líbra) póndo sácchări.
Five pounds of sugar.	Quínque póndo sácchări.
A bowl consisting of five pounds of gold.	Pátĕra ex quínque aúri póndo.
How many pounds of meat did you buy?	Quám múlta comparásti pondo cárnis?
I have bought (purchased) ten pounds of meat, five pounds of tobacco, and twenty quires of paper.	Égo cárnis póndo décem, tábáci póndo quínque, chártae scápos vigínti comparávi.
I have bought two dozen pens.	Égo bís duodénas pénnas coëmi.
I gave them each a dozen books.	Dédi éis duodénos líbros.

EXERCISE 133.

Have you ever been in this village? — I have been there several times. — Are there good horses in it? — There is not a single one in it. — Have you ever been in that country? — I have been there once. — Are there many learned men there? — There are many there, but they spend their time in reading? — Are there many studious children in that village? — There are some, but there are also others who will not study. — Are the peasants of this village able to read

and write ? — Some are able to read, others to write and not to read,
and many both to read and to write ; there are a few who are
neither able to read nor to write. — Have you done the exercises ? —
We have done them. — Are there any faults in them ? — There are
no faults in them, for we have been very assiduous. — Has your
friend many children ? — He has only one, but he is a good-for-
nothing fellow, for he will not study. — In what does he spend his
time ? — He spends his time in playing and running. — Why does
his father not punish him ? — He has not the courage to punish him.
— What have you done with the stuff which you bought ? — I have
thrown it away, for it was good for nothing. — How has your son
written his letter ? — He has written it with great care and diligence.
— He has written it with extreme negligence (*negligentissime*). —
Have you heard your little brother spell ? — I have heard him pa-
tiently and in silence. — Is your friend an Englishman ? — No, he is
a Frenchman by birth. — Are you an American by birth ? — No, I am
a German. — Are they Romans ? — No, they are Russians. — How
many are there of them ? — They are a hundred in number. — Are
they equal to us in industry ? — They are not our equals. — Do they
not excel us in humanity ? — They do not excel us. — We are not
inferior to them in diligence. — Is our friend a man of much talent
(*ingenio*) ? — He is a man of high talent and of the most distinguished
virtue. — They are men of low stature, of small talent, and of no virtue.

EXERCISE 134.

Have you been long in Paris ? — These four years. — Has your
brother been long in London ? — He has been there these ten years.
— Is it long since you dined ? — It is long since I dined, but not
long since I supped. — How long is it since you supped ? — It is
two hours and a half. — Is it long since you received a letter from
your father ? — It is not long since I received one. — How long is it
since you received a letter from your friend who is in Germany ? —
It is three months since I received one. — Is it long since you spoke
to the man whose son has lent you money ? — It is not long since I
spoke to him. — Is it long since you saw your parents ? — It is a great
while since I saw them. — Has the son of my friend been living long
in your house ? — He has been living there a fortnight. — How long
have you had these books ? — I have had them these three months. —
How long is it since your cousin set out ? — It is more than a month
since he set out. — What is become of the man who spoke English so
well ? — I do not know what is become of him, for it is a great while
since I saw him. — Is it long since you heard of the officer who gave
your friend a stab with his sword ? — It is more than a year since I
heard of him. — How long have you been learning German ? — I
have been learning it only these three months. — Are you already
able to speak it ? — You see that I am beginning to speak it. — Have
the children of the French noblemen been learning it long ? — They
have been learning it these five years, and they do not yet begin to
speak. — Why can they not speak it ? — They cannot speak it, be-

2 B　　　37

cause they are learning it badly (*male*). — How long is it since these children drank ? — They drank a quarter of an hour ago. — How long has your friend been in Spain ? — He has been there this month. — When did you meet my brother ? — I met him a fortnight (*quattuordecim dies*) ago. — Are there many soldiers in your country ? — There is a regiment of three thousand men there. — How long have I kept your cousin's money ? — You have kept it almost a year.

Lesson LXXI. — PENSUM UNUM ET SEPTUAGESIMUM.

THE ABLATIVE AFTER VERBS.

A. After verbs of buying, selling, valuing, estimating, and the like, the noun denoting the price or value is put in the ablative. E. g.

Spém *praétio* nôn *émo.*	I do not purchase hope with money.
Viginti taléntis ûnam oratiônem Isócrates *véndidit.*	Isocrates sold one of his orations for twenty talents.
Lis éjus *aestimâtur céntum taléntis.*	His fine was estimated at a hundred talents.
Quínta cívium clássis *úndĕcim millĭbus* assium *censebâtur.*	The fifth class of citizens was rated at eleven thousand asses each.
Scrúpŭlum aúri *valêbat sestértiis vicénis.*	A scruple of gold was worth twenty sesterces.
Múlto sánguine et *vulnéribus* Poénis victória *stétit.*	The victory cost the Carthaginians much blood and many wounds.
Quód nôn ópus ést, *asse* cârum est.	What one does not need is (too) dear for a penny.
Mágnos hómines *virtûte metimur,* non *fortûnâ.*	We measure great men by their moral worth, and not by their fortune.
Haêc rê, nôn *vérbis ponderántur.*	These things are judged of from the reality, and not from words.
Quód réctum est, nec *magnitúdine aestimâtur,* nec *número,* nec *témpore.*	That which is morally right is estimated neither by size, nor by number, nor by time.

REMARKS.

1. Verbs of buying and selling are also followed by the ablatives *magno, permagno, plurĭmo, parvo, minĭmo* (sc. *pretio*), but other verbs of this class more commonly take the genitives *magni, permagni,* &c. (Cf. Lesson LXVII. *A.*)

2. The ablative of price occurs in connection with many other verbs, besides those of buying and selling. E. g. *Triginta milĭbus* (*sestertium*),

habítat, He pays thirty thousand sesterces for a house (lodgings). *Docet talento*, He charges a talent for his instruction. *Vix drachmis est obsonátus decem*, He purchased provisions for scarcely ten drachmas. *Parvo aere meréo*, I serve for small pay. *Lavor quadrante*, I am washed (I bathe) for a quadrans. So *est* in the sense of "it is worth"; as, *Sal in Italiá est sextante*, In Italy salt is worth (sells for) a sextans.

B. Verbs of plenty or want, and corresponding transitive verbs, signifying to fill, endue, enrich, or to deprive, and the like, are followed by the ablative.

Verbs of plenty and want are *abundo, affluo, circumfluo, floreo, redundo, scateo, vigeo ; careo, egeo, indigeo, vaco,* &c.

Verbs of filling, enduing, depriving, &c. are *compleo, expleo* and *impleo, cumŭlo, imbŭo, refercio, satio* and *exsatio, satŭro, stipo* and *constipo; afficio, dono, remuneror, locupleto, orno, augeo ; — privo, spolio, orbo, fraudo* and *defraudo, nudo, exŭo,* &c. E. g.

Abundárunt sémper *aúro* régna Ásiae.	The kingdoms of Asia always abounded in gold.
Antiochía *eruditíssimis homínibus, liberalíssimísque studiis* affluébat.	The city of Antioch abounded in learned men and liberal pursuits of the highest order.
Régno caRébat Tarquinius, quum régno ésset expulsus.	Tarquin was without royal authority when he had been expelled from his realm.
Múlier *abúndat audáciá, consílio* et *ratióne defícitur.*	Woman has an abundance of audacity, but is deficient in deliberation and method.
Vacâre cúlpá mágnum est solátium.	To be free from guilt is a great consolation.
Déus *bónis ómnibus* * *explêvit* múndum.	God has filled the world with good things of every kind.
Témplum Junônis *egrégiis pictúris locupletâre* voluérunt.	They wanted to enrich the temple of Juno with choice paintings.
Natûra Germániam *decorâvit* altissimórum hóminum *exercútibus.*	Nature has adorned Germania with armies of the tallest men.
Demócritus dícitur *óculis* se *privásse.*	Democritus is said to have deprived himself of his eyes.
Consílio et *auctoritâte* nôn módo nôn *orbári,* sed étiam *augéri* senéctus sólet.	Old age is commonly not only not deprived of counsel and authority, but even advanced in it.

REMARKS.

1. The verbs *egeo, indigeo, compleo,* and *impleo* sometimes take the genitive instead of the ablative. E. g. *Aliquem temeritatis implêre,* To

---

* After verbs of filling, and others of this class, the ablative may also be put as the means or instrument. Cf. Lesson LXIX. C.

fill any one with temerity. *Complētus jam* mercatōrum *carcer est,* The prison is already full of merchants.*

2. To this construction belong *afficĕre* and *remunerāri,* in expressions like *afficĕre aliquem beneficio, honore, praemīo,* to bestow a kindness, an honor, a reward upon any one; *afficĕre aliquem ignominiā, injuriā, poenā, morte,* to inflict a dishonor, an injury, punishment, death upon any one; *remunerāri aliquem praemio,* to requite any one with a reward.

8. To this rule may also be referred the adjectives *orbus,* helpless, bereaved; *vacuus,* empty; and *refertus,* full, replete. E. g. *Orbus libĕris,* Bereaved of children. *Māre portŭbus orbum,* A sea without ports. *Vacŭae vites fructu,* Vines without fruit. *Insŭla referta divitiis,* An island full of riches.†

4. *Opus est,* "there is need," is either used impersonally with the ablative, or personally (as *opus est, opus sunt*) with the nominative. The person is then always in the dative. E. g. *Opus est mihi libris. — Multa tibi opus sunt. — Dux nobis et auctor opus est. — Auctoritāte tuā nobis opus est, et consilio.* — The thing needed is sometimes also expressed by the genitive, by an infinitive or supine in *u,* or by the ablative of a perfect participle. E. g. *Tempŏris opus est,* There is need of time. *Quid opus est plūra* (sc. proferre)? What need is there of saying more? *Nunc opus est te animo* valēre, Now you must be strong in mind. *Longius, quam quod* scitu *opus est,* Farther than is necessary to know. *Hoc* facto, maturato *opus est,* This must be done, hastened. To these add *Mihi opus est,* ut *lavem,* It is necessary that I should wash.‡

5. The construction of *usus est,* "it is necessary," is the same as that of *opus est.* E. g. *Nunc* manĭbus rapĭdis *usus est. — An cuiquam* est usus *homini, se* ut *cruciet?* Does any man need tormenting himself?

C. Verbs signifying to remove, to expel, to deter, to free, and others denoting separation, difference, or distance, are frequently followed by the ablative, without the prepositions *ab, de,* or *ex.*

The principal verbs of this class are *pello, depello* and *expello, ejicio, abterreo* and *deterreo, moveo, amoveo, demoveo, removeo: abeo, exeo, cedo, decedo, discedo, desisto, evado, abstineo: libero, expedio, solvo, exsolvo, exonero,* and *levo: — alieno* and *abalieno, distingo, discerno, secerno, differo, discrepo, dissideo, disto, abhorreo,* &c. E. g.

Censóres ómnes, quôs (*de*) senátu movérunt.	All the censors, whom they have removed from the senate.
Ne opífices quídem sê (*ab*) ártibus súis removérunt.	Not even the artisans withdrew from their trades.

---

* On *egeo* and *indigeo* compare page 113.
† But also *mare vacuum ab hostibus. — Referta Gallia negociatōrum,* according to Lesson LXVI. *A.*
‡ Compare pages 183 and 288.

Apud Germános quemcúnque mortálium *arcêre* (*a*) *técto* néfas habêtur.	Among the Germans it was considered wrong to drive away any human being from a roof.
Pópulus Atheniénsis Phociônem *pátriā pépūlit*.	The Athenian people expelled Phocion from his country.
Úsu úrbis prohibêre peregrínos inhumánum est.	It is inhuman to prevent strangers from the use of the city.
Brútus civitâtem *domináūu régio liberâvit*.	Brutus delivered the country from royal domination.
Pétiit Fláccus, ut *légibus solverêtur*.	Flaccus petitioned to be released from the laws.
Exónera civitâtem *váno* fórsitan *métu*.	Release the state from perhaps a groundless apprehension.
Levámur superstitióne, liberâmur mórtis metu.	We are relieved from superstition, we are delivered from the fear of death.
Sól ex aéquo *métā distâbat utrâque*.	The sun was equally distant from the east and west.

REMARKS.

1. The verbs *exsolvěre*, *exonerāre*, and *levāre* are always followed by the ablative, while *liberāre*, *expedīre*, *solvěre*, and the adjective *liber*, may have either *aliquā re* or *ab aliquā re*.

2. The verbs *alienāre*, *abalienāre*, *distinguěre*, &c. commonly have *ab*, and the ablative only among the poets. But *differre*, *discrepāre*, &c., and the adjective *diversus*, sometimes have the dative instead of *ab*.

3. The verb *separāre* commonly takes *ab*. The construction of *prohibēre* and *defendēre* is *aliquem re*, *ab re* or *ab aliquo*. That of *interdicěre*, *alicui aliquā re*, as in the formula *alicui aquā et igni interdicěre*, to banish one.

4. In imitation of the Greeks, the poets sometimes put the genitive instead of the ablative after verbs and adjectives of separation. E. g. *Me omnium jam laborum lěvas*, You release me now from all my labors. *Liber laborum*, Free from labors. *Purus scelěris*, Pure from guilt.

The host, inn-keeper.	Hospes, ĭtis, *m.* ; caupo, ōnis, *m.*
The property, fortune.	Facultātes, *f. pl.* ; bŏna, ōrum, *n.* ; rēs familiāris.
The patrimony.	Patrimōnium, i, *n.*
The entire, whole: all.	Tŏtus, a, um. Intĕger, gra, grum. Omnis, is, e.
To spend, expend.	Expendo, ĕre, di, sum.
To draw and spend (out of the public treasury).	Erŏgo, āre, āvi, ātum. Deprōmo, ĕre, mpsi, mptum.
To squander.	Diffundo, ĕre, fūdi, fūsum. Dilapĭdo, āre, āvi, ātum.
To spend, consume (in eating, &c.).	Comĕdo, ĕre, ēdi, ēsum. Consūmo, ĕre, mpsi, mptum. Conficĭo, ĕre, fēci, fectum.

37 *

How much have you spent to-day? | Quántam pecúniam hódie expendísti?
I have spent only ten dollars. | Décem tántum thaléros expéndi.
Have I spent more money than you? | Egóne majórem pecúniam expéndi quam tû?
You have, on the contrary, spent less than I. | Immo pótius minórem, quám égo, expendísti.
How much am I to pay? (What expense have I made?) | Quántum (pécuniae) comédi? Quíd súmptūs féci? Quántum tíbi débeo?
You have spent nearly a hundred dollars. | Ad céntum thaléros consumpsísti.
How much has he spent at the inn? | Quíd pecúniae confēcit (quid sumptus fēcit) apud hóspĭtem?
He has spent nearly all the money he has. | Pecúnias súas fére ómnes consúmpsit et confēcit.
Has he much property (large means)? | Tenétne facultátes mágnas?
He has nothing more, for he has squandered his entire patrimony. | Nôn ámplius; nám patrimónium súum íntegrum dilapidávit.
Did he squander what he had? | Profudítne súum?
He has squandered both his own and other people's money. | Profūdit véro et súum et aliêna.

Just now. | *Mŏdo, commŏdum; proxime (adv.); recens, tis, adj.*

The infant just born. | Infans módo nâtus (récens a nátu).
The stranger just arrived. | Récens ádvěna.
The men, who have just arrived. | Hómines, quí módo (próxime) advenérunt.
He just now writes. | Módo scríbit.
Have you just come? | Ádvenis módo?
He has just written. | Scrípsit módo.
I have just now seen your brother. | Égo frâtrem túum módo vidébam.
What countryman are you? | *Cújas (cujâtis) és?*
I am an American, an Englishman, a Russian. | Americânus, Ánglus, Rússus sum.
Where do you come from? | Únde vénis?
I am from London, Rome, Leipsic, Paris. | Vénio Londíno, Rómā, Lípsiā, Lutétiā Parisiórum. (Cf. Lesson LVI. *C.*)
I am a Londoner, Roman, from Leipsic, a Parisian. | Dómo Londinénsis, Románus, Lipsiénsis, Parisiénsis súin. (Cf. page 195.)

From Sparta. | Spartānus, i, *m.* (a, ae, *f.*).
From Athens. | Atheniensis, is, *m.* & *f.*
From Venice. | Venētus, i, *m.*
From Dresden. | *Dresdensis, is, *m.* & *f.*
From Berlin. | *Berolinensis, is, *m.* & *f.*

From Vienna.	*Vindobonensis, is, *m.* & *f.*
From New York.	*Neo-Eboracensis, is, *m.* & *f.*
From Cambridge.	*Cantabrigiensis, is, *m.* & *f.*
Are you from Athens?	Núm dómo Atheniénsis és?
No, I am from Venice (a Venetian).	Nôn véro; égo Venêtus súm.
To serve (any one).	Servio, íre, ívi (íi), ítum (ALICUI).
To wait upon, attend on one.	{ Ministráre alicui. { Apparēre alicui (*officially*).
To attend one professionally.	Opěram dăre (adesse) alícui.
To be in one's service.	{ In famulătu esse apud alíquem. { In ministěrío alicújus esse. { Servíre apud alíquem.
Was he in your service?	{ Erátne in ministério túo (in famulátu apud tê)?
He was in my service twenty years.	Érat apud mê in famulátu vigínti ánnos.
Does he serve (attend on you) well (promptly)?	Ministrátne tíbi béne (paráte)?
He does serve me very well.	Minístrat míhi véro ádmodum béne (paráte).
Did the doctor attend you to-day?	Deditne tíbi óperam hódie médicus?
No, he has neglected to attend me to-day.	Non; óperam míhi dáre hódie praetermísit.
To spoil, damage, corrupt.	{ Perdo, ěro, dídi, dítum. { Corrumpo, ěre, rūpi, ruptum. { Vitlo, āre, āvi, ātum.
To soil.	Inquíno, āre, āvi, ātum.
He has soiled his handkerchief.	Muccínium súum inquināvit.
Has any one spoiled your hat?	Écquis (númquis) píleum túum pérdidit?
No one (has spoiled it).	Némo.
Is your dress spoiled?	Vestísne túa vitiáta ést?
My dress is not spoiled, but my book is.	Nôn véstis méa, sed líber vitiátus est.
Is the sugar spoiled (damaged)?	Éstne sáccharum vitiátum (corrúptum)?
It is It is not.	Ést profécto. Nôn est.
To dress, clothe.	{ Vestes paráre alicui. { Vestio, íre, ívi, ítum.
To dress, fit, become (any one)	{ Convenīre (alícui). { Decēre (aliquem). { Dignum esse (aliquo).
Most beautifully, charmingly. Admirably.	Pulcherrime, optime. Mirifíce.
This coat fits you very well.	Haêc tóga tíbi óptime cónvenit.
How does this hat fit (become) me?	Quómodo míhi sédet (cónvenit) hícce píleus?
It fits you charmingly, admirably.	Sédet tíbi pulchérrime, mirifíce.

It does not become you very well. | Tíbi mínus cónvĕnit.

It misbecomes you. | { Tê nôn est dígnus.
{ Tê dédĕcet.

That garment becomes him admirably. | Véstis ílla éum décet mirífice (éo digníssima est).

Does the father clothe his children? | { Vestítne páter líberos súos?
{ Parátne páter véstes líberis?

He does clothe them. | Véstit.   Párat.

Does your father clothe you? | Patérne tíbi véstes nóvas párat?
He does. | Páter.

God himself is said to clothe the needy. | Déus ípse egénos vestíre dícitur.

How was the boy clothed? | Quemádmodum érat púer vestítus?
He was dressed in green. | Indútus érat véste víridi.

The girl was dressed in blue. | Puélla indúta érat véste caerúleā.

To be dressed in. | Indútum (am, um) esse (veste alíquā).

How large, of what size? | { Quam magnus, a, um?
{ Quantus, a, um?

How high? | { Quam altus (celsus), a, um?
{ Cújus magnitúdínis?

How deep? | { Quam altus, a, um?
{ Quam profundus, a, um?
{ Cújus profunditātis?

How high is his house? | Cújus altitúdínis est éjus dómus?

It is about thirty feet high. | { Álta ést círciter *trigínta pédes* (acc.).
{ Est pédum círciter trigínta.   (Cf. Lesson LXIV. B.)

D. Obs. In answer to the questions, *How far? How long* (*high, deep, wide, thick*)? the noun denoting the extent of space is generally put in the accusative without a preposition, but sometimes in the ablative.*

How deep is the well? | Quám áltus (profúndus) púteus ést?
It is twenty feet deep. | Altus (profúndus) ést vigínti pédes.

He had two ditches made, fifteen feet deep. Behind these he constructed a rampart of twelve feet. | Dúas fóssas *quíndĕcim pédes* látas perdúxit.   Post éas vállum duódecim pédum exstrúxit.

We have not gone a foot beyond. | *Pédem* nôn egréssi súmus.

The plain of Marathon is about ten thousand paces (ten miles) from Athens. | Cámpus Márathon ab Athénis círciter *mília* pássŭum *décem* ábest.

The army was about a three days' journey from the river Tenais. | Exércitus trídui *itínĕre* ábfŭit ab ámne Ténäi.

He encamped three miles from the city. | *Tría mília* pássuum ab úrbe cástra pósuit.

---

* This construction is consequently the same as that of Time, in answer to *How long?* on which compare Lesson LVII. *A.*

He established himself about six miles from Cæsar's camp.	Mílibus pássuum *sex* a Caésăris cástris consêdit.
True.	Vērus, a, um.
True virtue, friendship, religion.	Vêra vírtus, amicítia, religĭo.
A true and sincere (genuine) friend.	Vêrus et sincêrus amĭcus.
A true scholar.	Vír vére dóctus.
Is it true?	Verúmne est? Éstne vêrum?
It is true. It is so.	Vêrum est. Rês íta (sic) sê hăbet.
Is it not so?	Nónne? Áin' tû?
I do not deny it. I grant it.	Nôn négo. Concédo.
Is it true that his house has been burnt?	Verúmne ést, dómum éjus deflagrâtam ésse?
Is it true that he has lost his house by fire?	Éstne vêrum, éum dómum súam vi flammârum amisísse?
It is really so.	Rês prórsus íta sê hábet.
It is not true. It is false.	{ Nôn vêrum est. { Fálsum est.
Is it not true that you are squandering your patrimony?	Nónne vêrum est, tê patrimónium dilapidâre?
I do not deny that it is so.	Rém íta sê habêre nôn négo. (Lesson LIII. *B.* 3.)
As sure as I live, I know it to be so.	Íta vivam, ut scío, rém sic sê habêre.
As sure as I live, I do not know whether it is so.	Nê vivam, si scío, án vêrum sít (íta sê hábeat).
The philosopher.	Philŏsŏphus, i, *m.*
The key.	Clāvis, is, *f.*
The lock (bolt).	Claustrum, i, *n.*
The door.	Ostĭum, i. *n.*
The locksmith.	Fäber (ri, *m.*) claustrārĭus.
The saddle.	{ Sella equārĭa, ae, *f.* { *Ephippĭum, i, *n.*
The saddler.	Ephippĭōrum artĭfex (ĭcis, *m.*).
Has he a comfortable income?	Habétne, únde cómmode vivat?
He has. He has not.	Hábet. Nôn hábet.
How large is his income?	Quántus est éi rédĭtus pecúniae?
He has an annual income of a thousand aurei.	Annŭa hábet mílle aureôrum.
He has fifty crowns per month to live upon.	Rédĭtum ménstruum hábet quinquagínta thalêrum.
May I offer you (do you choose) some of this (dish)?	Vísne (optûsne) aliquántulum de hôc (cíbo)?
I should like some of it.	Ópto véro aliquántulum.
I do not like it.	Míhi nôn líbet.
It does not agree with me.	Míhi nôn pródest.
That will not do for me.	Hóc míhi nôn úsui est.
The income (of money, &c.).	Redĭtus, ūs, *m.* (redĭtus pecúniae).
The annual income (pension, &c.).	Annŭum, i, *n.*, or *pl.* annua, ōrum.

Annual.	Annuus, a, um.
Monthly.	Menstrūus, a, um.
To board (with any one).	{ Ālor, ăli, alītus* sum (ab aliquo). { Alicujus victu ūtor, ūti, ūsus sum.
Did you board with him ?	{ Alebarisne ab illo ? { Usúsne és éjus víctu ?
I did board with him.	Alêbar. Ûsus sum.

EXERCISE 135.

Who is the man who has just spoken to ycu ? — He is a learned man. — What has the shoemaker just brought ? — He has brought the boots and shoes which he has made us. — Who are the men that have just arrived ? — They are philosophers. — Of what country are they ? — They are from London. — Who is the man who has just started ? — He is an Englishman who has squandered away all his fortune in France. — What countryman are you ? — I am a Spaniard, and my friend is an Italian. — Wilt thou go for the locksmith ? — Why must I go for the locksmith ? — He must make me a key, for I have lost the one belonging to my room. — Where did your uncle dine yesterday ? — He dined at the inn-keeper's. — How much did he spend ? — He spent three florins. — How much has he a month to live upon ? — He has two hundred florins a month to live upon. — Must I go for the saddler ? — You must go for him, for he must mend the saddle. — Have you seen any one at the market ? — I have seen a good many people there. — How were they dressed ? — Some were dressed in blue, some in green, some in yellow, and several in red. — How much (*quanti*) did you buy your horse for ? — I bought it for twenty pounds of gold. — Did he sell his house for a high price (*magno*) ? — He sold it for a very high price (*permagno*) ; he sold it for ten thousand talents. — Did your books cost you as much as mine ? — They cost me just as much (*tantidem*) ; they cost me a thousand aurei. — How much do your lodgings cost you ? — They cost me ten dollars (crowns) per month. — How much do you pay for instruction (*quanti docēris*) ? — I pay fifty crowns for it. — How much is corn worth in this region (*regio*) ? — A medimnus of corn is worth only half a dollar in this region.

EXERCISE 136.

Who are those men ? — The one who is dressed in gray is my neighbor, and the one with the black coat the physician, whose son has given my neighbor a blow with a stick. — Who is the man with the green coat ? — He is one of my relations. — Are you from Berlin ? — No, I am from Dresden. — How much money have your children spent to-day ? — They have spent but little ; they have spent but one florin. — Does that man serve you well ? — He does serve me well ; but he spends too much. — Are you willing to take this servant ? — I am willing to take him if he will serve me. — Can I

---

* From *alo, ĕre, alŭi, alĭtum* or *altum,* to nourish, support.

take this servant? — You can take him, for he has served me very
well. — How long is it since he (first) served you? — It is but two
months since. — Has he served you long? — He has served me (for)
six years. — How much did you give him a year? — I gave him a
hundred crowns. — Did he board with you? — He did board with
me. — What did you give him to eat? — I gave him whatever I ate.
Were you pleased with him? — I was much pleased with him. — Is
he free from (*vacatne*) guilt? — He is entirely (*prorsus*) free from it.
— Does this country abound in gold? — It does not abound (in it).
Has he filled his glass with wine? — He has filled it with pure wine
(*mērum*). — Does he adorn his house with pictures? — He is adorn-
ing it. — Will you release us from fear (*metu*)? — I cannot release
you (from it). — Were they expelled (*expulsus*) from their country?
— They were not expelled.

Lesson LXXII.—PENSUM ALTERUM ET SEP-
TUAGESIMUM.

ABLATIVE AFTER VERBS AND ADJECTIVES.

A. The deponent verbs *ūtor, frŭor, fungor, potŏr,*
vescor, dignor, laetor, glorĭor, nītor, and the compounds
abūtor, perfrŭor, defungor, and *perfungor* are generally
followed by the ablative. E. g.

Nâvis óptime cúrsum cónficit éa, quae *scientíssimo gubernatóre útitur.*	That ship makes the best passage which has the most skilful helmsman.
Íd ést cujúsque próprium, *quô* quísque *frúitur* átque *útitur.*	The property of every one is that which he enjoys and uses.
Qui adipísci vêram glóriam vo-let, justítiae *fungâtur officiis.*	Let him, who desires to acquire real distinction, attend to the re-quirements of justice.
Defúncti béllo Púnico, Rómáni árma Macedóniae intulérunt.	Released from the Punic war, the Romans directed their arms against Macedonia.
Éadem perícŭla, *quíbus nos per-fíncti súmus.*	The same dangers which we have undergone.
Ímpediméntis castrísque nóstri *potíti súnt.*	Our soldiers made themselves mas-ters of the baggage and the camp.
Helvétiis persuâsit, perfácile esse, totíus Gálliae *império potíri.*	He persuaded the Helvetii, that it was very easy to get possession of entire Gaul.
Númídae plerúmque *lácte* et *fe-rínâ cárne vescebántur.*	The Numidians subsisted princi-pally upon milk and the flesh of wild beasts.

Ómne, *quô vescúntur* hómines,
pénus est.

Everything, which men live upon,
is food (provisions).

Haûd équidem *táli* mê *dígnor ho-*
nôre.

I do not consider myself worthy of
such an honor.

Núllā rê tám *laetári* sóleo, quam
meôrum officiôrum *consciéntia.*

There is nothing in which I am
wont to take so much delight, as
in the consciousness of my duties.

Núllā rê níti décet sapiéntem,
nísi *virtûte* animíque *consci-*
éntia.

The philosopher ought to rely on
nothing, except on virtue and
the consciousness of intellect.

REMARKS.

1. The verbs *útor, frûor, fungor, potior,* and *vescor* sometimes also
occur with the accusative. E. g. Rem *medici utuntur.* — Argentum
abútor. — *Frui* ingenĭum. — Militāre munus *fungens.* — *Potiri* admi-
nistrationem *regni.* — Absinthium *vescuntur.*

2. *Potior* also governs the genitive; as, *potiri rērum, imperii, domi-
natiōnis,* to obtain the chief command. The construction of *glorior* is
either RE, DE RE, or IN RE; that of *nitor* and *innitor,* RE, IN RE, AD or
IN REM. E. g. In virtūte *jure gloriāmur,* We justly seek our honor in
virtue. *Pompeii* in vitā *nitebātur salus civitatis,* The salvation of the
state depended upon the life of Pompey. Ad immortalitatem *gloriae
nitĭtur,* He is striving after an immortality of glory.

3. *Fido* and *confido* either take the ablative, like *nitor,* or the dative. E. g. *Nemo alterīus, qui suae confĭdit,* virtūti *invidet,* No one
envies the virtue of another, who has any confidence in his own.
Nemo potest fortūnae stabilitate *confĭdĕre,* No one can rely upon the
stability of fortune. — *Stāre,* "to abide by," has either the ablative or
in ; as, *Stant sententiā,* They abide by their opinion. *Stāre in fĭde,*
To remain true, faithful.

B. The preceding rule includes the adjectives *dignus, in-*
dignus, frētus, aliēnus, praedĭtus, and *contentus,* which are likewise followed by the ablative. E. g.

Nâtus súm ad agéndum sémper
áliquid *dignum víro.*

I am born for the constant performance of something worthy of
the character of man.

Excelléntium cívium vírtus *imi-*
tatiône, nôn *invídiā digna* ést.

The virtue of eminent citizens deserves imitation, and not envy.

Quam múlti *lûce indígni* súnt, et
tâmen díes óritur.

How many are unworthy of the
light of day, and yet it rises!

Haêc ad tê scrípsi libérius, *frêtus*
consciéntiā officii méi.

I have written you this somewhat
frankly, relying on my consciousness of duty.

Díi súnt benéfĭci, néque hoc *ali-*
ênum dúcunt *majestâte suā.*

The gods are beneficent, nor do
they consider this attribute at
variance with their majesty.

Epicûrus confirmat, déos *mém-*
bris humánis ésse *praedĭtos.*

Epicurus asserts, that the gods are
possessed of human limbs.

Mens est *praeédĭta mótu sempĭ-térno*.	The mind is endued with eternal motion.
Párvo est natûra *conténta*.	Nature is content with little.
Quod cuique témpŏris ad vivén-dum dátur, *eo* débet ésse *con-téntus*.	Every one ought to be contented with the space of time given him to live in.

REMARKS.

1. *Aliēnus*, in the sense of " averse *or* hostile to," has commonly either *ab* or the dative ; but in the sense of " unsuitable, incompati-ble," it has either the ablative or *ab*, and sometimes the genitive. E. g. *Homo aliēnus a litteris*, A man averse (or a stranger) to letters. *Am-bitioni aliēnus*, Averse to ambition. *Aliēnum a vitā meā*, Foreign to (inconsistent with) my life. *Aliārum rērum aliēna*, Not reconcilable with other things, unexampled.

2. *Dignus* sometimes (though rarely) occurs with the genitive. When connected with a verb, it takes either the infinitive, or the sub-junctive with *qui*. E. g. *Dignus salūtis.* — *Dignus, qui impĕret*, Worthy to command. *Horatius fere solus legi dignus*, Horace almost the only one worth reading. So also *contentus scripsisse*, satisfied to have written.

C. The participles *nātus, prognātus, genĭtus, sătus, edĭtus*, and *ortus* are sometimes followed by the ablative without the preposition *ex* or *a*.

Such ablatives are generally *lŏco, genĕre, stirpe, familiā, parentĭbus*, frequently in connection with an adjective.

Vir *sŭmmo lóco nâtus*.	A man of high rank by birth.
Virgĭnes *hónesto órtae lóco*.	Maidens of respectable descent.
Adolescéntes *amplíssimā família náti*.	Young men of illustrious descent.
Árchias *nâtus* est *lóco nóbili*.	Archias was of noble origin.
Húnc *Faúno* et *nýmphā génĭtum* accépĭmus.	The tradition is, that he was engen-dered by Faunus and a nymph.
Non *sángŭĭne humáno*, sed *stírpe dirĭnā sátus*.	Not begotten of human blood, but of divine pedigree.
Quâlis tíbi ílle vidêtur, *Tántalo prognâtus, Pelŏpe nâtus?*	What sort of a man do you con-sider that descendant of Tanta-lus, the son of Pelops ?

REMARK. — When connected with an adjective, this ablative may be regarded as that of *quality*, and always stands without a preposition. But when no adjective is added, the prepositions *ex* or *a* are frequent-ly employed. E. g. *Natus ex Penelopā.* — *Belgae ab Germanis orti*, &c.

THE ABLATIVE AFTER PREPOSITIONS.

D. The ablative is also governed by the prepositions *a, ab (abs), absque, clam, coram, cum, de, e, ex, in, prae, pro, sine, sub, subter*, and *tĕnus*. (Cf. Lesson XCIV.)

38

REMARK. — *In* and *sub* take the ablative only in answer to the question *Where?* *Super* only when it stands for *de,* "with respect to," "with reference to." *Subter* is more commonly construed with the accusative.

E. Verbs compounded with the prepositions *a, de,* or *ex* are followed by the ablative in a local sense, sometimes with the preposition repeated.* E. g.

Tù *éā* mê *abésse úrbe* miráris, in quā súmmum sit ódium hóminum ?

Do you wonder at my being absent from a city, in which the hatred of men is carried to the utmost extremes ?

Decédĕre província praêtor jussus ést.

The prætor was ordered to leave the province.

Ad éos, qui *vítā excessérunt,* revertâmur.

Let us now return to those who are already dead.

Amicítia *núllo lóco exclúdĭtur.*

Friendship is excluded from no place.

Némĭnem *a congréssu méo* jánĭtor méus *abstérrŭit.*

My porter never deterred any one from meeting me.

Ut *ex his regiónibus* Barbarôrum praesídia *depélleret.*

That he might expel the troops of the Barbarians from these regions.

Rês e *memóriā, de mánĭbus* elabúntur.

Things slip out of our memory, away from our hands.

REMARK. — The majority of these convey the idea of separation, and are consequently already included in Lesson LXXI. *C.*

F. Verbs of placing, putting, standing, sitting, and some others, are commonly followed by the ablative with *in,* but verbs of motion in general by the accusative with *in.*

Such verbs are *pōno, lŏco, collŏco, statŭo, constitŭo, consĭdo, habeo, duco, numĕro, defĭgo, mergo, incĭdo, insculpo, inscrĭbo,* &c. Verbs of motion : *eo, venio, advenio, advento,* and many others. E. g.

Pláto ratiônem *in cápĭte,* vélut *in árce* pósuit; íram *in péctŏre* locâvit.

Plato has put the reason in the head, as in a citadel, and passion in the heart.

Cónon núnquam *in hórtis súis* custôdem impósuit.

Conon never set a watch over his garden.

Stéllas *in* deôrum *nŭmero* reposuérunt.

They put the stars among the number of the gods.

Dólor *in máximis mális* dúcĭtur.

Pain is čonsidered one of the greatest of evils.

Áves quaêdam sê *in mári* mérgunt.

Some birds dive into the sea.

Legáti *in vúltu* rêgis defixérunt ócŭlos.

The ambassadors fixed their eyes upon the countenance of the king.

---

* This preposition, however, is not always the same, but one of kindred signification, as in Example 6.

Decémviri léges *in duódecim tá-*   The decemviri wrote the laws upon
  búlis scripsérunt.   twelve tables.
In Itáliam, in província advénit.   He arrived in Italy, in the prov-
                                        ince.
Proféctus ést Rômam, Délphos.*   He has gone to Rome, to Delphi.

REMARK. — *Impōnĕre, insculpĕre, inscrĭbĕre, inserĕre*, are also followed by the dative (*aliquid alicui rei*, according to Lesson LXII. *B.*),
and most of the above verbs frequently have *in rem* or *re* simply, instead of the *in re* of the rule. E. g. *imponere aliquid in rem ; insculpĕre aliquid aliquâ re*, &c.

To pity, *commiserate.*	*Mĭsĕror, āri, ătus sum.* *Commĭsĕrāri* (ALIQUEM, ALIQUID). *Mĕ mĭsĕrĕt (mĭserŭit, miserĭtum est)* ALICUJUS.†
To lament, mourn or weep over.	*Dēplōro, āre, āvi, ātum.* *Dĕflĕo, ēre, ēvi, ētum.* (ALIQUEM, ALIQUID.)
With all one's heart.	Ex anĭmo, tōto pectŏre (anĭmo).
Do you pity me, him, us, them?	Commiserarísne mê, íllum, nôs, éos? Miserétne te méi, illíus, nostri, eô- rum?
I do pity thee (him, you, them) with all my heart.	Égo véro tê (íllum, vôs, éos) ex áni- mo commíseror. Mê véro túi (illíus, véstri, eôrum) míseret tóto péctore.
Do ye commiserate this man ?	Miseramínine húnc hóminem ?
We commiserate him very much.	Commiserâmur éum vehémenter.
I have pitied your misfortunes.	Mê misérĭtum ést tuârum fortuná- rum.
I have lamented over lost hope.	Deplorávi spem pérdĭtam.
I have wept over his untimely death.	Deflévi mórtem éjus praematûram.
To confide or *trust in* (or *rely on* any one or thing).	*Fīdo, ĕre, fīsus sum.* *Confīdĕre* (ALICUI, ALICUI REI). *Frētum (am) esse* (ALIQUO, ALI- QUA RE).
To trust with, *intrust, commit* (anything to any one).	*Crēdo, ĕre, dĭdi, dĭtum.* *Concrēdĕre, committĕre, mandāre.* (ALICUI ALIQUID.)
To confide (commit) anything to the care of any one).	Comíttĕre (permíttĕre) áliquid fí- dĕi alicújus. Trādĕre áliquid in alicújus fídem.
To intrust one's plans, one's se- crets, to one.	Consílĭa, occúlta súa álicui crédĕre.
To commit (unbosom) one's self to one.	Sê (ánimum súum) álicui crédĕre.

---

* On these accusatives with and without *in*, compare Lesson LVI. *A.*
† On the government of this verb, see Lesson LXVII. *C.*

To intrust one's self to the protection of one.	In alicújus fídem sê trádere, permíttere.
To give one's self up to one.	Sê dáre (dédêre) álicui.
To give one's self up entirely to one.	Tótum sê dédere álicui.
Did he intrust you with anything?	Credidítne (commisítne) tíbi áliquid?
He intrusted his money to me.	Crédidit (commisit) míhi pecúnias súas.
He has deposited his money with me (for safe-keeping).	{ Pecúnias súas apud mê depósuit. Pecúnias súas míhi mandâvit (demandâvit).
What have you intrusted (committed) to his protection?	Quíd in éjus fídem tradidísti?
I have intrusted my only son to his protection.	Fídëi éjus fílium méum únicum commísi.
I have intrusted all my sons to the care of one master.	Égo fílios méos ómnes uníus magístri cúrae demandávi.
He trusted him with all his plans and secrets.	Credébat éi consília átque occúlta súa ómnia.
He has unbosomed himself to me.	Sê (ánimum súum) míhi crédidit.
He has surrendered himself entirely to me.	Tótum sê míhi dédidit.
Do you confide in me, him, us, them?	Confidísne míhi, éi, nóbis, íllis? ⬩
Do you rely on me, him, us, them?	Fretúsne és mê, éo, nóbis, íllis?
I do trust, rely on.	Confído. Frêtus sum.
The plan.	Consílium, i, n.
The secret.	Res secrēta, occulta, arcāna, f. sing.
Secrets.	Occulta, arcāna, secrēta, ōrum, n. pl.
The mystery.	Mystērium, i, n.
To keep anything secret.	Aliquid tácītum (occultum) tēnēre, or hăbēre.
To keep still (silent) about anything.	Rětícěo, ēre, cŭi (ALIQUID, DE ALIQUA RE).
To conceal (anything from any one).	Cēlo, āre, āvi, ātum (ALIQUEM ALIQUID,* DE ALIQUA RE).
To publish, divulge.	Pălăm făcěre aliquid.
Did he conceal the mystery from you?	Celavítne tê mystérium?
No, on the contrary, he communicated it to me.	Ímmo pótius íd mêcum communicâvit.
Did you keep the matter secret?	{ Tenuistíne rém occúltam? Reticuistíne rém (de rê)?
No, I imprudently divulged it.	Nòn véro; rém pálam féci égo inconsiderâtus.
To offer.	{ Offéro, ferre, obtŭli, oblātum. Deférre (ALICUI ALIQUID).

---

* Cf. Lesson LX. A.

To offer (promise) one's services to one.

Álicui ópĕram súam offérre *or* pollicéri.

To offer one's self to one.

Sê (semetípsum) álicui offérre.

Did he offer you his services (assistance)?

Obtulítne (pollicitúsne ést) tíbi óperam súam?

He has offered himself to me.

Ís semetípsum míhi óbtulit.

I offer and promise you all in my power.

Quídquid póssum, tíbi pollíceor ac défero.

The gods have offered (granted) you all you desired.

Díi tíbi omnia optáta detulérunt.

He offered him all his influence for the accomplishment of this end.

Ómnem éi súam auctoritátem ad hôc negótium conficiéndum détúlit.

Did he offer (proffer) us his help in the matter?

Núm óperam súam ad rém proféssus ést?

He has offered us his services of his own accord.

Óperam súam nóbis últro óbtulit (pollícitus est).

Voluntarily, of one's own accord.

Ultro (adv.), *suā (tuā, &c.) sponte, sponte et ultro.*

Unwillingly.

Invítus, a, um.

Did he leave unwillingly?

Discessítne invítus?

No, he left of his own accord.

Nôn véro; súā spónte et últro discéssit.

The Roman citizen.

Cīvis Romānus.

The American citizen.

Cīvis Americānus.

The citizen (inhabitant) of London, Paris, New York.

Incŏla (ae, *m.*) Londíni, Lutĕtiae, Eborāci Nŏvi.

The Hamburg merchant.

Mercātor Hamburgensis.

The Strasburg beer.

Cervisia Argentoratensis.

The student of Leipsic, Paris, Cambridge.

Cīvis academlae Lipsiensis, Parisiensis, Cantabrigiensis.

The inhabitant of a city.

Oppidānus, i, *m.*

The inhabitant of the country.

Rustĭcus, rusticānus, i, *m.*

To take care of, to be careful of anything.

{ *Curāre* or *sibi curae* (dat.) *habĕre aliquid.*
Ratiōnem alicūjus rĕi habĕre.
Respĭcĕre (spexi, spectum) aliquid.

Does he take care of his clothes?

{ Curátne véstem súam?
Habétne síbi cúrae véstem?

He does take care of them.

Cûrat. Hábet.

Do you take care of your hat?

Habêsne tíbi cûrae píleum?

I do not.

Nôn hábeo.

Do ye take care of your health?

{ Curatísne valetúdinem?
Habetísne ratiónem valetúdinis?

We do take care of our health and property both.

Hebêmus véro ratiónem et valetúdinis et réi familiâris.

Did he regard his own interest?

Núm cómmoda súa ipsius respiciêbat?

2 C   38 *

He regarded his own advantage less than that of others.	Súa ipsíus cómmoda mínus, quam aliêna respiciêbat.
To take care of, provide for, attend to.	Curâre (ALIQUEM ALIQUID). Providêre or consûlĕre (ŭi, tum) (ALICUI).
Will you take care of my horse?	Vísne méum équum curâre ? Vísne méo équo providêre ?
I will (am not unwilling).	Vólo. Providêre éi nôn nólo.
He is providing for his life and health in the best possible manner.	Vítae súae salutíque quam óptime cónsŭlit et próvĭdet.

Exercise 137.

How long has your brother been absent from the city ? — He has been absent these twelve months. — Has he been ordered to leave his country (*patriâ*) ? — He has been ordered. — Are there many philosophers in your country ? — There are as many there as in yours. — How does this hat fit me ? — It fits you very well. — How does this hat fit your brother ? — It fits him admirably. — Is your brother as tall as you ? — He is taller than I, but I am older than he. — How high is this man ? — He is five feet four inches high. — How high is the house of our landlord ? — It is sixty feet high. — Is your well deep ? — Yes, sir, for it is fifty feet deep. — How long have those men been in your father's service ? — They have been in his service already more than three years ? — Has your cousin been long at Paris ? — He has been there nearly six years. — Who has spoiled my knife ? — Nobody has spoiled it, for it was spoiled when we were in want of it. — Is it true that your uncle has arrived ? — I assure you that he has arrived. — Is it true that he has assured you of his assistance ? — I assure you that it is true. — Is it true that the six thousand men, whom we were expecting, have arrived ? — I have heard so. — Will you dine with us ? — I cannot dine with you, for I have just eaten. — Do you throw away your hat ? — I do not throw it away, for it fits me admirably. — Does your friend sell his coat ? — He does not sell it, for it fits him most beautifully. — There are many learned men in Berlin, are there not (*nonne*) ? asked Cuvier a man from Berlin. Not as many as when you were there, answered the man from Berlin.

Exercise 138.

Why do you pity that man ? — I pity him, because he has trusted a merchant of Hamburg with his money, and the man will not return it to him. — Do you trust this citizen with anything ? — I do not trust him with anything. — Has he already kept anything from you ? — I have never trusted him with anything, so that he has never kept anything from me. — Will you trust my father with your money ? — I will trust him with it. — What secret has my son intrusted you with ? — I cannot intrust you with that with which he has intrusted me, for he has desired me to keep it secret. — Whom do you intrust with your secrets ? — I intrust nobody with them, so that nobody knows them. — Has your brother been rewarded ? —`He has, on the contrary, been punished ; but I beg you to keep it secret, for no one knows it. — What has happened to him ? — I will tell you what has happened to him, if you promise me to keep it secret. — Do you promise me to keep it secret ? — I promise you, for I pity him with all my heart. — Do you consider (*ducisne*) that at variance (*aliēnum*) with your dignity (*dignitas*) ? — I do not consider (it so). — Does he attend to (*fungiturne*) the duties of justice ? — He does attend to them. — Have you experienced (*perfunctus*) the same dangers which I have experienced ? — I have not experienced the same. — What do they live upon ? — They live upon fish and milk. — Who has taken possession (*poteri*) of the baggage ? — The soldiers have made themselves masters of it. — What do you rejoice in (*laetari*) ? — I rejoice in the consciousness of virtue. — Is his virtue worthy of imitation ? — It is not worthy of it.

Lesson LXXIII. — PENSUM SEPTUAGESIMUM TERTIUM.

OF THE ABLATIVE ABSOLUTE.

A.   A noun and a participle in the ablative are often put independently of the rest of the proposition in which they occur, and serve as an abridged form of a clause introduced by the conjunctions *quum, dum, si, quod, quamquam, quamvis,* &c. Thus, *Sole oriente* (== *quum sol oritur*), The sun rising, i. e. when the sun rises. *Servio Tullio regnante* (== *dum Servius Tullius regnabat*), Servius Tullius reigning, i. e. while he was reigning, during his reign.* *Sole orto* (== *quum sol ortus esset*), The sun having risen, i. e. *when* (*after*) it had risen. *Cyro mortuo* (== *quum Cyrus mortuus esset*), Cyrus being dead, i. e. *when* he was dead, *after* his death. This construction is called the *Ablative Absolute*. It most commonly designates the time or concomitant of an action or event, but frequently also a CAUSE, REASON, CONDITION, or CONCESSION.

B. When the ablative absolute indicates the *Time* of an action or event, it is rendered into English by *when, while, during, after.* E. g.

Crástĭno díe, *oriénte sôle*, redíte in púgnam.	To-morrow, when the sun rises, return to the encounter.

---

* In this construction the present participle always refers to the time of the action denoted by the verb of the sentence, which may be either present, past, or future. The perfect participle indicates an action or event anterior to that expressed by the verb. (Compare Lesson XLIX. *E.*)

Jóve tonánte, cum pópulo agi nôn est fâs.

When Jove thunders, it is not right to address the people.

Quaéritur, útrum múndus *térrā stánte* circúmĕat, an *múndo stánte* térra vertâtur.

The question is, whether the heavens revolve while the earth stands still, or whether the earth turns and the heavens stand still.

Sólon et Pisístrătus *Sérvio Túllio regnánte* viguérunt.

Solon and Pisistratus flourished during the reign of Servius Tullius.

Vidêmus áquam spumâre, *igni subjécto*.

We observe that water foams whenever fire is put under it.

Diṍne interfécto, Dionýsius rúrsus Syracusârum potítus est.

After the murder of Dion, Dionysius again took possession of Syracuse.

Régĭbus exáctis, cónsüles creáti súnt.

After the expulsion of the kings, consuls were created.

REMARKS.

1. The noun entering into the construction of the ablative absolute always denotes a different person or object from those contained in the sentence; but pronouns sometimes constitute an exception to this rule. E. g. *Ego percussörem meum securum ambulāre patiar* me sollicĭto? Shall I allow my murderer to walk secure, while I am anxious? *Galliam Italiamque tentari* se absente *nolēbat*, He was not willing that Italy should be invaded in his absence. *Inviso sĕmel* princĭpe *seu bene seu male facta* (sc. *eum*) *premunt*, When a prince is once hated, then all his actions, whether good or bad, are construed against him.

2. The participle of the ablative absolute is generally either the present or the perfect. Instances of the future active are less frequent, and the future passive rarely occurs. E. g. *Rex apum nisi* migratūro agmĭne *foras non procēdit*, The king of the bees never comes out, unless the hive is about to migrate. *Itūro in Armeniam* majore filio, The elder son being about to go into Armenia. *Tanquam non* transitūris *in Asiam* Romanis, As if the Romans were not on the point of passing into Asia. *Quis est, qui*, nullis officii praeceptis tradendis, *philosophum se audeat dicere?* Will any one dare to call himself a philosopher, without having moral precepts to impart?

3. The perfect passive participle of the ablative absolute may frequently be rendered by the perfect active participle, which, in Latin, does not exist except in deponent verbs. E. g. *Pompeius*, captis Hierosolymis, *victor ex illo fano nihil tetĭgit*, Pompey, *having taken* Jerusalem (lit. Jerusalem *having been taken*), did not touch anything out of that temple.*

---

* The ablative absolute, in instances like this, manifestly arises from the want of a perfect active participle in Latin. The construction of deponent participles, on the other hand, is precisely like the English. E. g. *Hostes, hanc adepti victoriam* (= *hāc victoriā adeptā*), *in perpetuum se fore victores confidebant*, The enemy, *after* having won this victory, was confident of remaining victorious perpetually. (Compare Lesson XLIX. A. Rem. 4.)

4. When the perfect participle of deponent verbs is used in a passive sense,* it may stand in the ablative absolute, like that of transitive verbs. So likewise when the deponent is a neuter verb. E. g. *Partitis copiis*, The forces having been divided. *Periculo perfuncto*, The danger being overcome. *Adeptá libertáte*, Liberty having been obtained. *Profecto ex Italiá Valerio*, Valerius having left Italy. *Sole orto*, The sun having risen, &c.

C. When the ablative absolute denotes a *cause, condition,* or *concession*, it is rendered by the English *since, because, in consequence of, if, although*. E. g.

Ártes ínnumerábiles repértae súnt, *docénte natúrá*.	The arts are innumerable, since nature teaches them.
Ánxur brévi recéptum est, *negléctis die festo custódiis* úrbis.	Anxur was retaken in a short time, the watch of the city having been neglected on the day of a festival.
Flamínium Caélius *religióne neglectá* cecidísse apud Trasiménum scribit.	Cælius writes that Flaminius fell near Trasimenum in consequence of having neglected† the usual religious rites.
Natúrá reluctánte, írrïtus lábor ést.	Effort is fruitless, if nature opposes.
Quae pótest ésse jucúnditas vítae, *subláüis amicítiis?*	What pleasure can life possess, if friendship is banished from it ?
Quaénam sollicitúdo vexáret ímpios, *subláto suppliciórum métü?*	What anxiety would harass the wicked, if the fear of punishment were removed ?
Pérdïtis rébus ómnïbus, támen ípsa vírtus sé sustentáre pótest.	Though everything be lost, yet virtue is all-sufficient to sustain herself.
Propósïtá invídiá, poéná, mórte, qui níhïlo sécius rempúblicam deféndit, is vír vére putándus ést.	He who, in spite of odium, punishment, or death before him,‡ nevertheless defends the common interest, must be considered really a man.

REMARK.—The ablative absolute thus employed is sometimes linked to the preceding clause by one of the conjunctions *ut, velut, tanquam, etsi, quamquam,* or *quamvis*. E. g. Velut Diis *quoque simul cum patriá* relictis, As if the gods had been relinquished together with their country. Tanquam *non* transitúris *in Asiam* Románis, As if the Romans were not on the point of passing into Asia. Quamvis capïte *defectionis* subláto, Although the chief of the revolt had been removed.

D. The ablative absolute frequently consists merely of a

---

* A list of such participles is given in Lesson XLIX. *A*. Rem. 4.
† I. e. *because* he had neglected.
‡ I. e. *although* hatred, punishment, or death be placed before him.

noun in apposition with another noun, or of a noun and an adjective, with the participle of *esse* understood.* E. g.

Natúrā dúce, errári núllo pácto pótest.	Where nature guides, it is impossible to err.
Béllum Gállicum *C. Caésare imperatóre* gestum ést.	The Gallic war was carried on *under* the command of Cæsar.
Nâtus ést Augústus *M. Tullio Cicaróne et António consúlibus*.	Augustus was born during the consulship of M. Tullius Cicero and Antony.
Ascánius Creúsā mâtre, *Íllio incólūmi*, nâtus ést.	Ascanius was born of Creusa, when Troy was still uninjured.
Románi, *Hannĭbále vívo*, núnquam sê sine insídiis futúros existimábant.	The Romans thought that they never would be exempt from snares while Hannibal was alive.
Caésăre ignáro magíster équïtum constitûtus ést.	He was made master of horse without the knowledge of Cæsar.
Lúpus *mágno consectántium tumúltū* evâsit.	The wolf escaped amid the great commotion of those in pursuit of him.
Secúndis rébus súis vólet étiam móri.	He will even desire to die, though in prosperity.

·REMARKS.

1. The substantives, which most commonly thus take the place of the participle in the ablative absolute are:—*a*) Certain nouns denoting the action of a verb; as *adjūtor, adjutrix, auctor, comes, dux, interpres, judex, magister, magistrix, praeceptor, praeceptrix, testis*,† &c. *b*) The names of certain offices or dignities, such as *consul, imperātor, praetor, rex, domĭnus, magistrātus*, &c. E. g. *Eo adjutōre*, With his assistance. *Licinio quōdam auctōre*, At the instigation of a certain Licinius. *Se duce*, Under his own conduct. *Me rege*, With me for a king. *His magistratĭbus*, Under the administration of these consuls. So also, *Puĕro Cicerōne*, When Cicero was a boy. *Nobis puĕris*, When I was one.

2. Additional examples of adjectives are:— *Deo propitio*, If God is propitious. *Invĭtā Minervā*, Against the will of Minerva, i. e. with bad success. *Sereno coelo*, The sky being clear. *Iis invĭtis*, They being unwilling (i. e. against their will). *Tacĭtis nobis*, When (while) we are silent. *Illis consciis*, They being accessories,‡ &c.

3. This construction is sometimes represented by an adjective alone.

---

* Such a participle does not exist in Latin, but is usually supplied in English. E. g. *Natúrā dúce*, nature *being* our guide; *Caesáre imperatóre*, Cæsar *being* commander; *Íllio incólūmi*, Illium *being* yet safe, &c.

† Substantives of this class may frequently be resolved into a participle; as, *Eo adjutōre*, i. e. *adjuvante*. — *Natúrā dúce*, i. e. *ducente*. — *Fortunā comite*, i. e. *comitante*. — *Polybio judĭce*, i. e. *judicante*, &c.

‡ But sometimes these ablatives absolute may also be referred to the ablative of mode or manner. E. g. *Bono gubernatore*, The pilot being good, i. e. with a good pilot. *Probo navigio*, With a proper vessel (ship).

E. g. Serēno *per totum diem*, The sky being serene all day long. Tranquillo *pervectus Chalcĭdem*, Conveyed to Chalcis while the sea was calm.*

E. The ablative absolute is sometimes represented by the perfect participle alone, its subject being an entire clause. E. g.

Caêsar temeritâtem mĭlĭtum reprehéndit, *expósĭto quid inĭquĭtas lóci pósset.*	Cæsar, after having explained what the disadvantage of the ground might lead to, reprehended the rashness of his soldiers.
Alexánder, *audĭto Darêum appropinquâre cum exércĭtu,* óbviam ĭre constĭtŭit.	Alexander, having heard that Darius was approaching with an army, resolved to meet him.
Excépto quod nón sĭmul ésses, cétĕra laêtus.	Happy in every respect, except that you were not present.
Hánnibal, *cógnĭto insĭdias sĭbi parári,* fŭgā salûtem quaesĭvit.	Hannibal, having learned that plots were on foot against him, sought his safety in flight.

REMARKS.

1. The participles thus employed are but few. The principal one *audĭto, cognĭto, comperto, edĭcto, explorāto, despĕrāto, nuntiāto.* All these are passive, " it being heard, learned, found," &c.; but are generally rendered by the perfect active : " Cæsar *having* heard, learnt, found, given orders," &c.

2. An adjective sometimes supplies the place of this participle absolute. E. g. *Multi*, incerto (= quum incertum esset) *prae tenebris quid peterent aut vitārent, foede interiērunt,* Many, uncertain,† on account of the darkness of the night, what to seek or to avoid, perished disgracefully.

3. The participle absolute sometimes, though rarely, occurs without any subject whatever. E. g. *In cujus amnis transgressu,* multum certato, *pervicit Bardanes,* In passing which river, Bardanes conquered after a severe engagement. *Quum,* nondum palam facto, *viri mortuique promiscue complorarentur,* When, the matter being yet unpublished, the living and the dead were bewailed indiscriminately.‡

Every (one), each.	Quisque, quaeque, quodque or quidque, gen. cujusque.
Any (one) you please.	Quivis, quaevis, quodvis or quidvis, gen. cujusvis. Quilĭbet, quaelĭbet, quodlibet or quidlibet, gen. cujuslibet.

---

* These may be resolved into *Quum coelum serēnum, mare tranquillum fuisset.*
† Lit. " It being uncertain (a matter of uncertainty and doubt)."
‡ In these examples *multum certato* and *palam facto* stand impersonally.

Every one, everybody.	Unusquisque, *gen.* uniuscujusque. Singŭli (*each individually*). Nēmo (nullus) nôn, ūnus quilĭbet. Omnes.
Every man.	Omnis homo, omnes.
Every child.	Omnis infans.
Everything.	Omnia, ium, *n. pl.*, nihil nôn.
Every month, year.	Singŭlis mensĭbus, annis. In singulos menses, annos. Quot mensĭbus, annis.
All the world.	Omnes homĭnes.
Every one knows.	Némo nôn scît. Ómnes sciunt.
Every one sees.	Némo nôn videt. Némo est, quin (*but what*) vídeat.
It is in the mouth of every one (of all).	Hóc in ôre ómnium ést.
He knows (can do) everything.	Ílle ómnia pótest. Níhil nôn pótest.
I have seen everything.	Égo ómnia vídi. Níhil est, quod nôn vídĕrim.
Let every one keep what has fallen to his lot.	Quod cuíque óbtigit, id quísque té- nĕat.
A man's mind is the man himself.	Méns cujúsque, is est quísque.
I give him any name I please.	Dô nômen quódlibet ílli.
At all times (at any time you please).	Quibúslibet tempórĭbus.
I myself, as well as any one of you.	Égo nôn mínus, quám vestrum quí- vis.
A pleasure tour to Corinth is not everybody's privilege.	Nôn cuívis hómini cóntingit, adíre Corínthum.
It belongs to a great judge to decide what every one should render to every one (i. e. to his neighbor).	Mágni est júdĭcis statuĕre, quid quémque cuíque praestâre dé- bĕat.
He is fit for anything (everything).	Idóneus est árti cuilibet. Ómnium horârum hómo ést.
Every one, who ; everything which (whoever, whatever; whosoever, whatsoever).	Quisquis, quaequae, quodquod or quidquid, gen. cûjuscûjus. Quicumque, quaecumque, quodcum- que or quidcumque, gen. cûjus- cumque. (Cf. Lesson XII. *C.*)
Whoever (whosoever) he is (may be).	Quísquis ílle ést. Quicúmque ís ést.*
Whoever you are (may be).	Quísquis és.
However that may be.	Quóquo módo rês sê hábet (hábeat).
Whatever there is of gain (= all the gain).	Quodcúmque lúcri ést.

---

* *Quisquis* and *quicumque* are generally put with the indicative in Latin.

Whatever benefit (= all the benefit).	Quídquid benefícii.
Whatsoever we (may) write (all that we write).	Ómnia, quaecúmque scríbimus.
In whatsoever place one may be.	Quocúmque* in lóco quísquis ést.
He can do whatsoever (anything) he pleases.	Quodcúmque vélit, lícet fácere.

The whole, entire.	{ Intĕger, gra, grum. { Tŏtus, a, um, gen. totíus. { Universus, a, um.
The full (entire, complete).	Plēnus, a, um.
The entire (unbroken).	Solĭdus, a, um.
A whole (entire) year.	Ánnus intĕger.
A whole number.	Númĕrus íntĕger (plēnus).
A full (and entire) year.	Plēnus ánnus atque íntĕger.
Full (complete) liberty, joy.	Libertas sólĭda; gaúdium sólĭdum.
The whole (entire) city.	{ Univérsa cívĭtas. { Univérsĭtas úrbis.
The entire society.	Univérsa socíetas.
His entire property.	Facultátes súas (éjus) ómnes.
The whole of his patrimony.	Patrimónĭum súum (éjus) íntegrum.
The whole (of this) world.	Múndus híc tótus (ómnis).
The universe.	Univérsĭtas rêrum.
For three entire years.	{ Tótos três ánnos. { Três ípsos ánnos. { Tótum triénnĭum.
An entire boar, ox.	Sólĭdus áper, bôs.
The walk, promenade (act).	Ambulātĭo, deambulātĭo, ōnis, f.; spatĭum, i, n.
The short walk.	Ambulatiuncŭla, ae, f.
The walk, promenade (ground).	Ambulācrum, i, n.; spatium, ambulātĭo.
To take a walk.	Ambulatiōnem confícere.
To be on the walk (promenade).	In ambulácro ésse.
The concert.	{ *Concentus, ūs, m. { *Symphōnia, ae, f.
To go to the concert.	Concentum obíre (ívi, ítum).
To be (present) at a concert.	Concéntui (symphóniae) adésse.
To give a concert.	Concéntum édĕre (dĭdi, dĭtum).
The concert-room.	*Odēum, i, n.
Has he gone to the concert?	Obivítne concéntum?
Were there many at the concert?	Aderántne múlti (hómines) concéntui?
There was a large crowd there.	Ádĕrat véro vis hóminum mágna.
Did you find many out walking?	Invenistíne múltos in ambulácro (ambulántes)?

---

* So also sometimes separately cum quibus erat cumque; qua re cumque.

I found but a few.	Invéni nôn nísi paúcos.
To cut, wound.	*Secāre, vulnerāre.*
To cut off.	{ *Abscĭdo, ĕre, scĭdi, scīsum.* *Ampŭto, āre, āvi, ātum.*
To cut into (make an incision).	Incido, ĕre, cīdi, cīsum (ALIQUID).
Entirely.	Omnino, prorsus, plāne.
He has cut off his finger.	Dígitum éjus amputāvit.
He has had his finger cut off (amputated).	Is dígitum súum amputándum curāvit.
Have you cut (wounded) his finger?	Écquid dígitum éjus vulnerásti?
I have not cut (wounded) his finger, but his foot.	Égo nôn dígitum, sed pédem éjus vulnerávi.
He has cut my leg.	Crûs méum sécuit (incídit).
Alone (all alone).	{ *Sŏlus, a, um,* gen. *sŏlīus.* *Ūnus, a, um,* gen. *ūnīus.* *Ūnus sŏlus.*
To bring (carry) along.	(Sēcum) afferre, apportāre (ALIQUID ALICUI or AD ALIQUEM).
To bring (lead) along.	{ Sēcum dūcĕre (duxi, ductum). Sēcum addūcĕre, dedūcĕre. (ALIQUEM AD ALIQUEM.)
To bring along (by conveyance).	Advĕho, ĕre, vexi, vectum (ALIQUID AD ALIQUEM).
Have you come quite alone?	Venistíne ûnus sôlus?
No, I have brought all my friends with me.	Nôn véro; amícos méos ómnes mêcum dedúxi.
He has brought all his men along.	Ómnes súos sêcum addúxit.
Does he bring anything new with him?	Affértne sêcum áliquid nóvi?
He brings nothing.	Níhil áffert.
They have brought us some grain along.	Fruméntum nóbis sêcum advexérunt.
Did you bring your brother along?	Duxistíne têcum frâtrem?
I have brought him.	Dúxi.
To fall.	*Cado, ĕre, cĕcĭdi, cāsum.*
To fall gliding, to slip.	*Lābor, lābi, lapsus sum.*
To fall down, out, in.	Dēcĭdĕre, excĭdĕre, incĭdĕre (-cĭdi, -cāsum).
To slip down, out, in.	Dēlābi, ēlābi, illābi.
To let fall, drop (inadvertently) *anything out one's hands.*	{ *Excĭdit mĭhi aliquid mănu* or *de mănĭbus.* *Dēlābĭtur mihi aliquid de mănĭbus.*

To drop (from negligence).	Amittĕre alĭquid de mănu (*or* mănĭbus).
To drop (intentionally).	Dimittĕre alĭquid de mănĭbus.
Has he fallen?	Cecidĭtne? Lapsúsne est?
Yes, he has fallen into the well.	Íncĭdit véro in púteum.
He has fallen from the horse.	{ Lápsus ést ex équo. { Ex équo décĭdit.
The fruit falls from the trees.	Pôma ex arbórĭbus cádunt, decĭdunt.
Has he dropped anything?	Amisĭtne álĭquid de mánibus?
Yes, he has dropped his pen.	Dimĭsit véro pénnam de mánibus.
He has dropped his ring.	Éxcidit éi ánulus de mánu.
The ring dropped of its own accord from my finger.	Ánulus mĭhi suá spónte de dígito delápsus est.
You have dropped your gloves.	Excidérunt tíbi de mánu digitábula.
She is dropping her handkerchief.	Muccínium éi de mánibus delábitur.
Near, close by. *Near (not far from).*	Ápŭd, *juxta, prope* (Prep. c. Acc.). Nŏn *longe, haud* procŭl (alĭquo lŏco, ab alĭquo lŏco).
Near me, you, him.	Juxta mê, tê, íllum.
Near the fire, by the fire.	{ Ad (apud, juxta) fócum. { Apud (prope) carbónes.
Near (not far from) his castle.	Non lónge (haud prócul) ab éjus castéllo.
Near that spot.	{ Prope íllum lócum. { Prope ab íllo lóco.
What are you doing by the fire?	Quíd ágis apud carbónes?
I am engaged in writing and thinking.	In scribéndo et cogitándo occupátus sum.
Where do you live?	Úbi hábitas?
I live close by the castle.	Juxta (prope) castéllum hábito.
He lived not far from the king's residence.	Habitábat non lónge a dómo régiá.
He fell not far from the river.	Cécidit haûd prócul (a) flúvio.
The groom.	Stabulárĭus, i, *m.*; agáso, ŏnis, *m.*
Did you tell the groom to bring me the horse?	Dixistíne stabulário, ut addúcerct mĭhi équum?
I have told him.	Fáctumst (= fáctum est).
I have ordered him to do so.	Jússi éum fácere hóc.
To prevent, hinder.	{ Impĕdĭo, ĭre, ĭvi (ĭi), ĭtum (ALIQUEM (AB) ALIQUA RE). { Retardo, áre, ávi, átum (ALIQUEM IN ALIQUA RE).
To hinder (prevent) any one from sleeping, writing.	{ Impedĭre álĭquem quómĭnus (*or* ne) dórmiat, scríbat. { Retardáre álĭquem a dormiéndo, scribéndo (*or* ad dormiéndum, scribéndum).

Does he prevent you from reading?	Retardátne tê a legéndo (ad legéndum)?
	Impedítne te, quóminus (or ne) légas?
He does prevent me.	Retárdat. Ímpedit.
Or did I prevent you from sleeping?	An égo tê ad dormiéndum retardávi?
	An égo tê impedívi, quóminus dormíres?
You have not prevented me.	Mê nôn retardásti (impedísti).
Was he hindering him from flight?	Impediebátne (retardabátne) éum a fúgä?
He was not.	Nôn impediêbat.

EXERCISE 139.

Whom do you pity? — I pity your friend. — Why do you pity him? — I pity him because he is ill. — Do the merchants of Berlin pity anybody? — They pity nobody. — Do you offer me anything? — I offer you a gold ring. — What has my father offered you? — He has offered me a fine book. — To whom do you offer those fine horses? — I offer them to the French officer. — Do you offer that fine carriage to my uncle? — I do offer it to him. — Dost thou offer thy pretty little dog to these good children? — I do offer it to them, for I love them with all my heart. — What have the citizens of Strasburg offered you? — They have offered me good beer and salt meat. — To whom do you offer money? — I offer some to those Parisian citizens, who have assured me of their assistance. — Will you take care of my clothes? — I will take care of them. — Wilt thou take care of my hat? — I will take care of it. — Are you taking care of the book which I lent you? — I am taking care of it. — Will this man take care of my horse? — He will take care of it. — Who will take care of my servant? — The landlord will take care of him. — Does your servant take care of your horses? — He does take care of them. — Is he taking care of your clothes? — He is taking care of them, for he brushes them every morning. — Have you ever drunk Strasburg beer? — I have never drunk any. — Is it long since you ate Leipsic bread? — It is almost three years since I ate any. — Does he think himself (ducitne se) out of danger (sine periculo)? — He never can consider himself out of danger while his enemy is alive (his enemy being alive). — Is the republic safe (salvus)? — How can it be safe under the administration of consuls like these (his magistratibus)?

EXERCISE 140.

Have you hurt my brother-in-law? — I have not hurt him; but he has cut my finger. — What has he cut your finger with? — With the knife which you had lent him. — Why have you given that boy a blow with your fist? — Because he hindered me from sleeping. — Has anybody hindered you from writing? — Nobody has hindered me from writing; but I have hindered somebody from hurting your cousin. — Has your father arrived ? — Everybody says that he has arrived; but I have not seen him yet. — Has the physician hurt your son ? — He has hurt him, for he has cut his finger. — Have they cut off this man's leg ? — They have cut it off entirely. — Are you pleased with your servant ? — I am much pleased with him, for he is fit for anything. — What does he know ? — He knows everything. — Can he ride on horseback ? — He can. — Has your brother returned at last from Germany ? — He has returned thence, and has brought you a fine horse. — Has he told his groom to bring it to me ? — He has told him to bring it to you. — What do you think of that horse ? — I think that it is a fine and good one, and (I) beg you to lead it into the stable. — In what did you spend your time yesterday ? — I went to the public walk, and afterwards to the concert. — Were there many people in the public walk ? — There were many people there. — When did your brother return home ? — He returned at sunrise. — When was Augustus born ? — He was born during the consulship of Cicero. — Do you desire to learn Latin ? — I am not unwilling to learn, with you for a guide and instructor. — Having heard (*audito*) that our friend was about to arrive, I immediately resolved to go to meet him. — Why were these men punished ? — They were punished on account of neglected duties (*officiis neglectis*).

Lesson LXXIV. — PENSUM SEPTUAGESIMUM QUARTUM.

OF THE PLUPERFECT TENSE.

A. The pluperfect tense serves to represent a past action as entirely completed with reference to another past action just commencing or going on. It sustains the same relation to the imperfect, as the perfect does to the present. E. g.

Irrŭĕrant Dănăi, et téctum ómne tenébant.	The Greeks had forced their way in, and were in possession of the entire house.
Pausánĭas eódem lóco sepúltus ést, úbi vítam *posŭĕrat*.	Pausanias was buried in the very spot on which he had lost his life.
Quum dómum *intrâsset*, díxit amíco súo.	When he had entered the house, he said to his friend.
Cum vêr ésse *coépĕrat*, dábat sê labóri átque itinéribus.	After the commencement of spring he was wont to enter upon his labors and his journeys.

REMARK. — The Romans always observe the distinction indicated by the pluperfect, and put this tense even where the English idiom substitutes the perfect. E. g. " When he arrived (i. e. *had arrived*) in the city, he perceived," *Quum in urbem advenisset, animadvertit.* " When he saw (i. e *had seen*) the boy, he exclaimed," *Quum puĕrum conspexisset, exclamāvit.*

B. FORMATION OF THE PLUPERFECT TENSE.

1. The pluperfect active is formed from the perfect by changing the final *i* into, Indic. *ĕram*, Subj. *issem.* As,—

    1. Amāvi — amāvĕram, amavissem, *I had loved.*
    2. Monŭi — monuĕram, monŭissem, *I had reminded.*
    8. Lēgi — lēgĕram, legissem, *I had read.*
    4. Audīvi — audīvĕram, audīvissem, *I had heard.**

2. The pluperfect passive is formed from the perfect participle, by adding, Indic. *ĕram* or *fuĕram*, Subj. *essem* or *fuissem.* As,—

INDIC. Amātus, monĭtus, lectus, audītus ĕram *or* fuĕram, *I had been loved, reminded, read, heard.*
SUBJ. Amātus, monĭtus, lectus, audītus essem *or* fuissem, *that I might have been loved, reminded, read, heard.*

3. The pluperfect of deponent verbs is formed like that of the passive voice. As, —

INDIC. Hortātus, verītus, secūtus, blandītus ĕram *or* fuĕram, *I had exhorted, feared, followed, flattered.*
SUBJ. Hortātus, verītus, secūtus, blandītus essem *or* fuissem, *that I might have exhorted, feared, followed, flattered.*

INFLECTION OF THE PLUPERFECT ACTIVE.

C. The inflection of the pluperfect active is exhibited by the following paradigms: —

INDICATIVE.	SUBJUNCTIVE.
Amāvĕram, *I had loved.*	Amāvissem, *that I might have loved.*
SING. ămāvĕrăm	SING. ămāvissĕm
ămāvĕrās	ămāvissēs
ămāvĕrăt,	ămāvissĕt,
PLUR. ămāvĕrāmŭs	PLUR. ămāvissēmŭs
ămāvĕrātĭs	ămāvissētĭs
ămāvĕrant.	ămāvissent.

---

* SUBJ. *that I might have loved, reminded, read, heard.*

So conjugate *monuĕram* — *monŭissem*, *lēgĕram* — *lēgissem*, *audivĕram* — *audivissem*. To these add *apportāvĕram*, I had brought; *laborāvĕram*, I had labored; *lāvĕram*, I had washed; *dĕdĕram*, I had given; *stĕtĕram*, I had stood; — *habuĕram*, I had had; *studuĕram*, I had studied; *jussĕram*, I had commanded; *secuĕram*, I had cut; *vidĕram*, I had seen; — *attŭlĕram*, I had brought; *dilexĕram*, I had cherished; *misĕram*, I had sent; *arcessivĕram*, I had called; *cupivĕram*, I had desired; *quaesivĕram*, I had sought; *ussĕram*, I had burned; — *aperuĕram*, I had opened; *ivĕram*, I had gone; *scivĕram*, I had known; *sitivĕram*, I had been thirsty; *vēnĕram*, I had come; — *voluĕram*, I had wished; *noluĕram*, I had been unwilling.

The verb *sum* has regularly *fuĕram* — *fuissem*. And so its compounds, *abfuĕram* — *abfuissem*; *adfuĕram* — *adfuissem*; *interfuĕram* *interfuissem*; *profuĕram* — *profuissem*, &c.

REMARKS.

1. Verbs of the fourth conjugation (and generally those whose perfect ends in *ivi*) frequently reject the *v* before the final *ĕram* of the pluperfect indicative; as, *audiĕram*, *prodiĕram*, *quaesiĕram*,* &c., and *ivissem* is sometimes contracted into *issem*; as, *audissem*, *prodissem*, *quaesissem*, for *audivissem*, &c. (Compare page 239, Remarks.)

2. *Odĕram*, I hated; *meminĕram*, I remembered; *novĕram*, I knew, was acquainted with; *consuēvĕram*, I was wont, have the force of the imperfect, as *odi*, *memini*, &c. that of the present.

Had I loved?	Egón' amávĕram?
By no means; you had not loved.	Mínime géntium; nôn amávĕras.
Had we given you a book?	Núm nôs tíbi líbrum dédĕrâmus?
You had not given me one.	Nôn dederâtis.
Had he stood by the fire?	Stetĕrátne apud carbónes?
He did. He had stood there.	{ Fáctumst (= factum est). { Stétĕrat.
Had you called the physician?	Arcessivĕrâsne médicum?
Yes, I had called him.	Sáne, éum arcessívĕram.
Had they seen *our* friend?	Nostrúmne amicum vídĕrant?
They had not seen ours, but their own?	Nôn nóstrum, sed suúmmet vídĕrant.
When I had found the letter.	Quum lítteras inveníssem.
If we had studied our lesson, would you not have rewarded us?	Si pénso imperáto óperam dedissêmus, nónne nôs praémiis affecísses?
I should have done so.	Fáctum ésset.
What did he say when he entered your house?	Quíd díxit, quum dómum túam intrâsset (= intravísset)?
He wished me a good morning.	Mê sálvum ésse jússit.

---

* These, however, may be referred to the secondary form in *ii*, as *audii*, *prodii*, &c.

THE PLUPERFECT PASSIVE.

D. The Pluperfect Passive is thus inflected:—

<table>
<tr><td>INDICATIVE.</td><td>SUBJUNCTIVE.</td></tr>
<tr><td>Amātus ĕram or fuĕram, I had been loved.</td><td>Amātus essem or fuissem, that I might have been loved.</td></tr>
</table>

SING. amātus ĕram *or* fuĕrăm   SING. amātus essĕm *or* fuissĕm
     amātus ĕrās *or* fuĕrās   amātus essēs *or* fuissēs
     amātus ĕrăt *or* fuĕrăt,   amātus essĕt *or* fuissĕt,

PLUR. amātī ĕrāmŭs *or* fuĕrā-   PLUR. amāti essēmŭs *or* fuissē-
     mŭs   mŭs
     amāti ĕrātis *or* fuĕrātĭs   amāti essētis *or* fuissētĭs
     amāti ĕrant *or* fuĕrant.*   amāti essent *or* fuissent.

So conjugate *monĭtus, lectus, audĭtus ĕram* or *fuĕram*, I had been reminded, read, heard ; SUBJ. *monĭtus, lectus, audĭtus essem* or *fuissem*, that I might have been reminded, read, heard.　To these add *allātus, dătus, dilectus, habĭtus, jussus, missus, quaesītus, ustus ĕram* or *fuĕram*, I had been brought, given, cherished, considered, commanded, sent, sought, burned ; and SUBJ. —— *essem* or *fuissem*, that I might have been brought, given, cherished, &c.

Had you been admonished?	Erāsne (fuĕrāsne) mŏnĭtus ?
I had been admonished.	Fáctumst. Mónitus éram (fúeram).
Had the philosopher been heard ?	Auditúsne érat sápiens ?
He had not been heard.	Audītus nôn érat.
Had you been sent ?	Núm vôs míssi erātis (fuerātis) ?
We had not been sent.	Nôs nôn míssi erāmus (fuerāmus).
Had a ribbon been given you ?	Datáne tibi fúĕrat taénia ?
None had been given me.	Dáta nôn fúerat.
Had the letters been read ?	Erántne epístolae léctae ?
They had been read.	Fáctum est.　Érant.
If the book had been read.	Si líber léctus ésset (fuísset).
When the letter had been delivered.	Quum lítterae tráditae éssent (fuíssent).
Would that we had been sent !	Útĭnam nôs míssi essêmus (fuissêmus) !
Because they had not been chosen.	Quód nôn delécti éssent (fuíssent).

PLUPERFECT OF DEPONENT VERBS.

E. The pluperfect of deponent verbs is inflected like that of the passive voice.　Thus :—

---

* When the subject is feminine, then: *amāta ĕram* or *fuĕram*, Plur. *amātae erāmus* or *fuĕrĭmus*; SUBJ. Sing. *amāta essem* or *fuissem*, Plur. *amātae essēmus* or *fuissēmus.* When it is neuter: *amātum ĕrat* or *fuĕral*, Plur. *amāta erant* or *fuĕrant*; SUBJ. Sing. *amātum esset* or *fuisset*, Plur. *amāta essent* or *fuissent.*

INDICATIVE.	SUBJUNCTIVE.

Hortātus ĕram or fuĕram, *I had exhorted.*   Hortātus essem or fuissem, *that I might have exhorted.*

SING. hortātus ĕrăm or fuĕrăm
    hortātus ĕrās or fuĕrās
    hortātus ĕrăt or fuĕrat,
PLUR. hortāti ĕrāmus or fuĕrāmŭs
    hortāti ĕrātis or fuĕrātĭs
    hortāti ĕrant or fuĕrant.*

SING. hortātus essĕm or fuissĕm
    hortātus essēs or fuissēs
    hortātus essĕt or fuisset,
PLUR. hortāti essēmus or fuissēmŭs
    hortāti essētĭs or fuissētĭs
    hortāti essent or fuissent.

So conjugate *verĭtus, secŭtus, blandĭtus ĕram* or *fuĕram,* I had feared, followed, flattered; SUBJ. *verĭtus, secŭtus, blandĭtus essem* or *fuissem,* that I might have feared, followed, flattered. To these add *arbitrātus, comitātus, morātus, locūtus, oblĭtus, profectus, largĭtus, expertus ĕram* or *fuĕram,* I had thought, escorted, delayed, spoken, forgotten, departed, squandered, experienced; and SUBJ. —— *essem* or *fuissem,* that I might have thought, &c.

Had you escorted any one?	Comitatúsne éras áliquem?
I had escorted no one.	Égo néminem comitátus éram.
Had they not lavished their money?	Pecúnias súas nônne largíti érant?
It is, as you say.	Íta ést, ut dícis.
Had he flattered you?	Tíbine blandítus érat?
He had certainly not.	Nôn hércle véro.
Had we left when you arrived?	An tê adveniénte profécti erâmus?
It is clearly so.	Íta pláne.
Would you have remained at home if he had left?	Écquid tê dómi tenuísses, si proféctus ósset ílle?
I should certainly have done so.	Íta enímvéro.
After having read the book (= When I had read the book, The book having been read).	Quúm librum perlegíssem. Postquam (ut) librum perlégi. Libro perlécto.
After having cut the bread, (when he had cut, &c).	Quum pánem secuísset. Póstquam (úbi) pánem sécuit. Pâne in frusta dissécto.
After having eaten (when we had eaten).	Cum manducavissêmus. Póstquam (úbi, ut, símul ac) manducávimus.
After (when) you had cut yourself (after having cut yourself).	Quum tê cúltro vulneravísses. Postquam (ubi, ut) tê cúltro vulneravísti. (Tú) cúltro vulnerâtus.
After dressing yourselves (when you had dressed yourselves).	Quum vóbis véstem induissêtis. Postquam (ubi, ut) vóbis véstem induístis. (Vôs) véste indúti.

* And when the subject is feminine: *amāta — amātae;* when neuter: *amātum — amāta.*   2 D

After withdrawing from the fire (when he had withdrawn, &c.).	{ Quum a fóco discessísset. { Póstquam (úbi, út) a fóco discéssit.
After (when) thou hadst shaved.	{ Quum tíbi bárbam totondísses. { Postquam (ubi, ut) bárbam totondísti. { Barbā tuā tonsā.
After (when) he had warmed hïmself.	{ Quum córpus calefecísset (refovísset). { Postquam (ubi) córpus calefēcit (refōvit). { Córpore éjus calefácto (refóto).
When I had read the newspaper, I breakfasted.	{ Quum ácta pública legíssem (áctis públicis léctis), jentáculum súmpsi.
As soon as I had dressed myself, I went out.	{ Símul ac míhi véstem índui (= véste or véstem indûtus), in públicum prodívi.
When he had read the letter, he said.	Lítteris recitátis (léctis), díxit.
When he had cut the bread, he cut the meat.	Quum pânem secuísset, cárnem sécuit.
What did he do when he had eaten?	Quid êgit (fēcit) ílle, quum manducavísset?
He went to bed.	Ívit cúbĭtum.
Before I set out.	{ Ántequam (priúsquam) profíscar; { or simply *profectúrus*.

F. Obs. Antequam and piusquam, when they relate to a future action or event, are commonly followed by the present subjunctive.

Before I depart, I wish to see my children once more.	Priúsquam proficíscar, líberos méos íterum nûnc vidêre cúpio.
The storm threatens, before it rises.	Tempestas minâtur, ántequam súrgat.
The newspaper.	Acta diurna or publĭca, *n. pl.*
The accident	Câsus, us, *m.*
The death.	Mors, tis, *f.*
To go to sleep.	Cubĭtum ire.
To rise, get up.	(E lecto) surgo, ĕre, surrexi, surrectum.
To die.	{ Morĭor, íri, mortŭus sum. { Diem suum (*or* suprēmum) obire { (*or simply* obíre).
To be afflicted or grieved at (anything).	{ Dolĕo, ĕre, ŭi, ĭtum (ALIQUA RE or QUOD). { Aliquid est mihi dolōri.
Are you afflicted at the death of our friend?	Dolêsne amíci nóstri mórte?
I am very much afflicted at it.	{ Dóleo véro veheménter. { Ést míhi prórsus permágno dolóri.

At what is your father afflicted ?	Quam ob rem vír óptimus, páter túus, in dolôre ést ?
He is afflicted because he has lost his dearest friend.	Dolôre afféctus est, quod hóminem sui amicíssimum pérdidit.
To complain of some one or something.	Quĕror, i, questus sum. Conquĕri (ALIQUEM, DE ALIQUO, REM, DE RE, QUOD, &c.)
To wonder, to be astonished or surprised at.	Mĭror, āri, ātus sum. Demirāri (ALIQUEM, REM, Acc. cum Inf. or QUOD).*
Whom do you complain of ?	Quém (de quô) quérĕris ?
I complain of my friend.	Ego amicum méum (de amíco méo) quéror).
Of what does your brother complain ?	Quíd (quâ de rê) quérĭtur fráter túus ?
He complains of your not sending the book.	Quérĭtur super hóc, quod nôn míttas líbrum.
They complained of their brother.	Frâtrem súum conquerebántur.
Let them not complain of having been deserted.	Ne querántur, sê relíctos ésse.
He complained of the injustice of his adversaries.	De injúriis adversariôrum quéstus est.
We have no right to complain of everything that afflicts us.	Nôn ómnia, quae dolêmus, eôdem jûre quéri póssŭmus.
At what are you surprised ?	Quid mirâris ?
I am surprised that you have arrived.	Mĭror tê advenísse (quod advenísti).
I wonder what may have been the cause.	Mĭror, quid caúsae fúĕrit.
I am surprised that you should have despised this.	Mĭror, tê haec sprevísse.
We wondered why you should prefer the Stoics to us.	Admiráti súmus, quid esset, cur nóbis Stóicos anteférres.
I was surprised that you should have written with your own hand.	Admirâtus (mirâtus) súm, quód túâ mánû scripsísses.
Do you wonder at what I have done ?	Demirarísne fáctum méum ?
I do wonder at it.	Prórsus demíror.
Your fortune (lot) is to be pitied.	Fortûna túa querénda ést.
To be glad.	Gaudeo, ēre, gavīsus sum. Laetor, āri, ātus sum. (RE, DE RE, IN RE, Acc. cum Inf. or QUOD).
To be sorry.	Dŏlēre (RE, Acc. cum Inf. or QUOD). Dŏlet, pĭget, poenĭtet, misĕret (ME ALICUJUS REI, HOMINIS).†

---

* Compare Lesson LIV. *H.*
† On the construction of these verbs, see pages 289 and 298.

I am glad of it.   Gaúdeo hóc.   Hóc est míhi jucúndum.   Óptíme ést.

I am sorry for it.   { Moléstum ést.   Mále dícis.
{ Dóleo, quód íta est.

I am glad to see you.   Núnc tê conspício líbens.

I never was more rejoiced to see any one.   Níhil vídi quídquam laétius.

I am sorry for your misfortune.   Dóleo túum casum.

I am sorry for you.   Míséret mê túi.

Are you sorry for this injustice ?   Pígetne tê hújus injúriae ?

I am sorry for it.   Píget mê véro.

Were you grieved at the death of your friend ?   { Dolebásne, cum amícum túum mórtuum conspícéres ?

I was grieved in my inmost soul.   Dolébam ex íntímis sénsíbus.

I am glad to hear that your father is well.   { Patris túi valetúdínem cognóscére gaúdeo.
{ Gaúdeo, mê de valetúdine pátris túi certiórem fíéri.

To hear (learn, understand).   { Comperio, íre, péri, pertum.
{ Cognoscére (ALIQUID).
{ Certiórem fíéri (DE ALIQUĀ RE).

To pronounce.   { Enuncio, áre, ávi, átum.
{ Efféro, ferre, extúli, elátum.

Can the boy pronounce these words ?   Potéstne púer vérba haêc enunciáre (efférre) ?

He cannot do it yet.   Nôndum pótest.

Did he pronounce the letters correctly ?   Rectêne líttéras enunciávit ?

No, he pronounced them very badly.   Ímmo pérpéram enunciávit.

Could the Austrian pronounce my name ?   Potuístne Austríácus nômen méum efférre ?

He could not.   Nôn pótuit.

There are several words which are pronounced alike in the same cases.   Plúra sunt vérba, quae simílíter iísdem cásíbus efferúntur.

Dear.   Cárus, a, um.

Grateful, acceptable.   Grátus, acceptus, jucundus, a, um.

Sad, sorrowful.   Tristis, is, e ; moestus, a, um.

Disagreeable.   Injucundus, ingrátus, a, um.

The prince.   Princeps, cípis, m.

The count.   Cómes, ítis, m.

The baron.   Báro, ónis, m.

The Saxon.   Saxo, ónis, m.

The Prussian.   Borussus (Prussus), i, m.

The Austrian.   Austríácus, i, m.

The Christian.   Christiánus, i, m.

The Jew.   Judaeus, i, m.

The negro, Moor.	Hŏmo nĭger, *gen.* nigri, *m.*; Aethĭ-ops, ŏpis, *m.*
The Indian.	Indus, i, *m.*
The Aborigines.	Autochthŏnes, um, *pl. m.*

EXERCISE 141.

What did you do when you had finished your letter? — I went to my brother, who took me to the theatre, where I found one of my friends whom I had not seen for many years. — What did you do when you had breakfasted this morning? — When I had read the letter of the Polish count, I went out to see the theatre of the prince, which I had not seen before. — What did your father do after getting up this morning? — He breakfasted and went out. — What did your friend do after he had read the paper. — He went to the baron. — Did he cut the meat after he had cut the bread? — He cut the bread after he had cut the meat. — When do you set out? — I set out to-morrow; but before I leave, I wish to see my friends once more. — What did your children do when they had breakfasted? — They went out with their dear preceptor. — Where did your uncle go after he had dined? — He went nowhere; he stayed at home and wrote his letters. — What are you accustomed to dó when you have supped? — I usually go to bed. — At what o'clock did you rise this morning? — I rose at five o'clock. — What did your cousin do, when he (had) heard of the death of his friend? — He was much (*valde*) afflicted, and went to bed without saying a word (*non verbum faciens*). — Did you read before you breakfasted? — I read when I had breakfasted. — Did you go to bed when you had eaten supper? — When I had eaten supper, I wrote my letters, and then went to bed. — Are you afflicted at the death of your relation? — I am much afflicted at it. — When did your friend die? — He died last month. — Of what do you complain? — I complain of your boy. — Why do you complain of him? — Because he has killed the pretty dog, which I had received from one of my friends. — Of what has your uncle complained? — He has complained of what you have done. — Has he complained of the letter which I wrote to him? — He has complained of it.

Lesson LXXV. — PENSUM SEPTUAGESIMUM QUINTUM.

OF THE REFLEXIVE PRONOUNS.

A. When, in one and the same sentence, a subject of the third person becomes itself the object of the verb, or otherwise a member of the predicate, its person (whether singular or plural) is expressed by the personal reflexives *sui, sibi, se,* and its property by the possessive reflexive *suus, a, um.*

40

Ípse sê quísque dílĭgit, quód *per sê sĭbi quisque* * cârus ést.

Every one cherishes himself, because every one is naturally dear to himself.

Themistocles domicílium Magnésiae *sĭbi* constítŭit.

Themistocles fixed his abode at Magnesia.

Justítia propter *sêse* colénda ést.

Justice should be cultivated on its own account.

Lénto grádŭ ad vindíctam *súĭ* divĭna procêdit íra.

Divine indignation advances slowly (with slow step) to its own defence.

Étiam *férae sĭbi* injécto terrôre mórtis horréscunt.

Wild beasts even shrink with horror when subjected to the fear of death.

Súum quĭsque ingénium nóscat.

Every one should make himself acquainted with his own abilities.

Vérres sôlus cum *súā* cohórte relínquitur.

Verres alone is left with his cohort.

Béllum est, *súa* vítia nôsse.†

It is proper to know one's own faults.

Béstiis *hómĭnes* úti ad utilitâtem *súam* póssunt sĭne injúriä.

Men may use animals for their own convenience, without any injustice.

REMARK. — The reflexives can thus be put only when the subject remains the same. If another sentence with a new subject, or a new subject representing one, is added, then the demonstrative *is* takes the place of *sui*, &c., and the genitives *ejus, eorum*, that of *suus*. E. g. *Tiberius Gracchus* ejusque *frater occisi sunt*,‡ Tiberius Gracchus and his brother were killed. *Hannibal quamdiu in Italiā fuit, nemo ei in acie restĭtit, nemo adversus* eum *in campo castra posuit*, As long as Hannibal was in Italy, no one opposed him on the battle-ground, no one pitched a tent against him in the field. *Athenienses urbem* suam *aede Minervae ornavêrunt*, eorumque *magnificentiam mirata est posterĭtas*, The Athenians adorned their city with the temple of Minerva, and posterity has admired their magnificence.

B. The reflexives *sui, sibi, se*, and *suus, a, um*, belong to an oblique case of the same sentence, when they determine the subject-nominative itself, or when from a difference of person or number, or from the sense of the predicate, they cannot be referred to the nominative.

Hannibălem súĭ cíves e civitâte ejecérunt.

Hannibal was banished by his own countrymen.

Caesărem súa natûra mitiôrem fácit.

His natural disposition makes Cæsar more humane.

---

* When *quisque* is thus connected with the reflexive, the latter commonly precedes; as, *se quisque, sibi quisque, suum cuique*, &c.

† I. e. *aliquem nôsse*, "that one should know his own faults."

‡ This may be resolved into *Tiberius Gracchus occisus est*, ejusque frater *occisus est*. So also, *Antigonus et* hujus *filius Demetrius*, &c.

Súi cuíque móres fíngunt fortû- nam.	Every man's lot in life is shaped by his own character.
Récte díci pótest sciéntiam súam cujúsque ártis ésse.	Every art may correctly be said to have a science of its own.
Consérva túis súos.	Preserve the lives and happiness of those dear to your friends.
Apíbus frúctum restítuo súum.	I return (restore) their produce to the bees.
Volaterrános in súâ possessióne retinêbam.	I kept the Volaterrani in the pos- session of their own.
Rátio et orátio concíliat inter sê hómines.	Reason and language conciliate men among themselves.
Justítia súum cuíque tríbuit.	Justice gives (to) every one his own.
Cónsúles hóstem in súâ sêde in Álgido invéniunt.	The consuls found the enemy in his own residence at Algidum.
Múlta súnt civíbus inter sê com- múnia.	Citizens have many things in com- mon with each other.
Quíd est áliud, áliis súa erípĕre, áliis dáre aliêna ?	What else is giving to others what is not one's own, but robbing others of their own ?

REMARK. — When a new sentence is added, or a word representing one, the demonstrative *is* becomes necessary, as in *A*. Rem.　E. g. *Omitto* Isocratem *discipulosque* ejus,* I omit Isocrates and his disciples. Alexander *moriens anŭlum* suum *dedĕrat* Perdiccae ; *ex quo omnes conjecerant*, eum *regnum* ei *commendasse*, *quoad liberi* ejus *in suam tu- tēlam pervenissent*, The dying Alexander had given his ring to Perdiccas, from which every one had conjectured that he had commended the gov- ernment of his empire to his charge, until his children might become of age.

C.　In dependent clauses, in which the language, thoughts, sentiments, or purpose of the leading subject are expressed, the reflexives *sui, sibi, se,* and *suus* refer to that subject, and not to the one contained in the dependent clause.

Such clauses are introduced by the Acc. cum Inf., by interrogatives, relatives, and conjunctions, especially by *ut, ne, quo, qui, si,* &c.　E. g.

Némo ést orâtor, *qui sê* Demo- sthenis símilem ésse nôlit.	No one is an orator who is unwill- ing to be like Demosthenes.
Homêrum Colophónii *civem ésse* dícunt *súum,* Smyrnaéi véro *súum ésse* confírmant.	The inhabitants of Colophon say, that Homer is their citizen, but those of Smyrna prove him to be theirs.
Méus mê orâvit *fílius, ut túam* sorôrem póscerem uxôrem *sibi.*	My son has charged me to demand your sister in marriage for him.
Paêtus ómnes líbros, *quós* frâter *súus* reliquísset, míhi donâvit.	Paetus has made me a present of all the books which his brother had left him.

* This may be resolved into *Omitto Isocratem, discipulosque ejus omitto.*

Quíd ést amâre, nísi vélle bónis álíquem áffici quam máxímis, *etiámsi* ad *sê* níhil ex his ré-děat ?	What is love, but a desire that another might enjoy the highest possible good, even though no advantage to one's self should result from it ?

D. If in this construction the person of the speaker comes in collision with another subject nominative, the sense of the predicate must determine to which of the two the reflexive refers. E. g.

Agríppa Átticum orâbat, ut *sê sibi suísque** reservâret.	Agrippa besought Atticus to save himself for himself and his friends.
Scýthae petébant ab Alexándro, ut rêgis *súi* filiam matrimónio *sibi*† júngeret.	The Scythians besought Alexander to unite himself in marriage to the daughter of their king.
Quód *sibi* Caêsar denuntiâret, *se* Aeduôrum injúrias nôn neglectûrum; némínem *sêcum* sine *súá*‡ pernície contendísse.	With respect to Cæsar's message to him, that he (i. e. Cæsar) would not overlook the injuries of the Aedui, (Ariovistus replied,) that no one had ever contended with him, except for his own destruction.

REMARKS.

1. The reflexive is always put when a given person is to be contrasted with another, or its property with that of another (i. e. *himself*, *his own*, as opposed to *alius*, *aliénus*). It is thus often put, even where we might expect the weaker demonstrative *is, ejus*, —

a.) When the oblique case, to which it relates, can easily be inferred from what has gone before. E. g. *Ei sunt nâti fílă gemíni duo, ita formâ simíli pueri, uti mater* sua (*for* eōrum) *non internosse posset*, sc. *eos*, He had two twin boys, so like each other, that *their own* mother could not distinguish them. *Placetne a Carthaginiensibus captivos nostros, reddítis* suis (sc. *iis*), *recuperâri ?* Is it your pleasure to recover our captives from the Carthaginians, after returning (to them) their own ?

b.) When the construction admits of it, and the connection requires a more emphatic indication of the subject. E. g. *Cimon incídit in eandem invidiam, quam pater suus* (= *ejus*), Cimon incurred the same odium which his father had incurred. *Non a te ēmit rex, sed prius quam tu suum sibi vendĕres, ipse possēdit*, The king has not purchased of you, but has himself possessed it, before you could sell his own to him.

---

* In this sentence *se*, *sibi*, and *suis* all refer to the new subject *Atticus*.
† Here *sui* belongs to *Scythae*, and *sibi* to *Alexándro*.
‡ *Sibi* and *secum* refer to the speaker Ariovistus (expressed in a preceding sentence), *se* to Cæsar, and *suâ* to *némínem*.

2. *Is* and *ejus*, on the other hand, are employed where no such opposition of persons or property is intended, but where the subject is merely pointed out (i. e. the English *him*, *his*). They are thus put, —

a.) With reference to an oblique case of the *same sentence*, sometimes merely to prevent ambiguity. E. g. *Pisōnem nostrum merito ejus amo plurĭmum*, I love Piso dearly, as he deserves. *Achaei Macedōnum regem suspicātum habēbant pro ejus crudelitāte*, The Achæans suspected the king of the Macedonians on account of his cruelty. *Oratio principis per quaestōrem ejus audīta est*, The speech of the prince was heard by his quæstor.

b.) In *dependent* clauses, when a noun different from the subject is referred to; frequently also instead of the more emphatic *se*. E. g. *Judaei jussi a Caesāre, effigiem ejus in templo locāre, arma potius sumsēre*, When the Jews were commanded by Cæsar to place his image in their temple, they preferred to resort to arms. *A Curiōne mihi nuntiātum est, eum ad me venīre,** A message was sent me by Curio, that he was coming to me.

3. Instead of *is* and *ejus* the intensive *ipse* and *ipsius* are often used, especially when it becomes necessary to distinguish subjects different from those represented by *is* or *sui*. E. g. *Aedui contendunt, ut ipsis summa imperii transdātur*, The Ædui beg that the chief command might be transferred to themselves. *Parvi de eo, quod ipsis supererat, aliis gratificāri volunt*, Children wish to gratify others with what they themselves do not want. *Caesar milĭtes suos incusāvit : cur de suā virtūte, aut de ipsius diligentiā desperārent*, Cæsar blamed his soldiers (by asking them), why they despaired of *their own* valor or *his* personal assiduity.

Far, distant.	{ *Longus, longinquus, a, um* (adj.). { *Longe, procul* (adv.).
A long way or journey.	Longa via ; longum iter.
From afar.	Prŏcul, e longinquo, eminus (*adv.*).
How far ?	Quam longe ? Quousque ?
To be far or *distant from any place.*	Longe or prŏcul ab aliquo loco abesse.
To be far apart.	Multum distāre.
To be equally far apart.	Parĭbus intervallis distāre.
To be equally far.	Tantundem viae esse.
To be farther.	Longius esse *or* abesse.
How far is it from here to the city ?	Quám lónge ést hínc in úrbem ?
It is very far.	Perlónge ést.
It is not far.	Nôn est lónge (lóngŭle).
It is ten miles.	Lónge est mília pássuum décem.
Is it far from here to Berlin ?	Éstne lónge hínc Berolínum ?
It is not far.	Haûd lónge ést.
How many miles is it ?	Quót mília pássuum súnt ?

---

* Instead of *Curio mihi nuntiāvit, se ad me venīre.*

40 *

It is twenty miles.

Vigínti círciter mília pássuum súnt.

How many miles is it from Boston to New York?

Quót mília pássuum a Bostóniä ábest Nóvum Eborâcum?

It is about two hundred and fifty miles.

Abest (dístat) mília pássuum círciter ducénta et quinquagínta.

It is nearly a hundred miles from Berlin to Vienna.

Vindobóna a Berolíno círciter mília pássuum céntum úbest.

How far did the boy go?

Quám lónge ívit púer?

He went three steps.

Ívit lónge três pássus.

He went about far and wide.

Perambulâvit lónge latêque.

He said, that he had been two hundred miles from the city.

Díxit, sê ab úrbe abfuísse mília passuum ducénta.

Did he advance too far?

Éstne progréssus nímis lónge (*or* lóngius)?

Not as far as you.

Nôn tám lónge, quám tû.

How far has your brother advanced in his studies?

Quoúsque fráter túus in doctrínä procéssit?

He has not advanced very far.

Haûd perlónge procéssit.

The distance.

Distantia, ae, *f.;* intervallum, i, *n.*

The mile.

Mille passuum (*pl.* milia passuum), miliärium, i, *n.*

The step, pace.

Passus, ūs, *m.*

To prefer, like better.

{ Málo, malle, malui (cum Inf.).
Anteponére, anteferre, praeferre (REM REI).
Aliquid libentius (*potius*) facére, quam. }

Do you like to write better than to speak?

{ Mavísne scríbere quam lóqui?
Scribísne libéntius quam lóqueris? }

I like to speak better than to write.

{ Málo (pótius) lóqui quam scríbere.
Égo libéntius lóquor quam scríbo. }

Does he like to play better than to study?

{ Ludítne libéntius quam óperam dát stúdiis?
Mavúltne lúdere (pótius) quám óperam dáre stúdiis? }

He likes to do both.

Utrúmque libénti ánimo fácere sólet.

Do you like bread better than cheese?

Mavísne édere pânem quam cáseum?

I like both, neither equally well.

Égo utrúmque, neútrum páriter ámo.

Do you like tea as well as coffee?

Bibísne thêam aéque libénter quam coffêam?

I like coffee better.

Málo coffêam.

He likes beer better than wine.

Cervísiam libéntius quam vínum bíbit.

I prefer beef to veal.

{ Égo búbulam vitulínae anteféro, antepóno, &c.
Égo búbulam vitulínä potiórem hábeo. }

I prefer reading to writing. | Praeópto légere pótius quam scríbere.

The calf. | Vitŭlus, i, *m.*; vitŭla, ae, *f.*
Quick, fast. | Celerŭter, cŭto, festinanter (adv.).
Slow, slowly. | Tarde, lente (adv.).
Do you learn as fast as I? | Discĭsne tam celériter, quám égo?
I learn faster than you. | Égo cítius (facílius) disco, quam tú.
He eats faster, slower than I. | Mandŭcat cítius, léntius, quam égo.
I do not understand you, because you speak too fast. | Vérba túa nōn intélligo, proptérea, quód nimis celériter (celérius) lóquĕris.

He arrived sooner than was expected. | Advĕnit celérius opinióne.
Can you answer slowly? | Potésne respondére lénte?
I can. | Póssum.
Does he sail as slowly as I? | Navigátne tám tárde quam égo?
He sails slower. | Tárdius návigat.
I trust that you will be strong soon. | Confĭdo, cíto tĕ fírmum fóre.

Advance slowly! | { Procĕde lénte !
{ Festína lénte !

Cheap. | { ADJ. Vĭlis, parvi prĕtii; non magno parābĭlis.
{ ADV. Parvo prĕtio, aere pauco; parvo sumptu.

Dear. | { ADJ. Cārus, a, um; magni prĕtii.
{ ADV. Cāre, magno (prĕtio).

Does the merchant sell as dear as I? | Vendĭtne mercātor tám cáre, quam égo?
He does not sell as dear. | Mínus cáre véndit.
He sells dearer than you. | Cárius véndit quám tú.
Did you buy the horse cheap? | Emistíne équumvĭli (párvo prétio)?
I have bought it quite cheap. | Égo éum aĕre pauĭo émi.
He has bought the book at the lowest possible price. | Líbrum quám mínimo prétio ĕmit.
I have bought my hat cheaper than you yours. | Pĭleum méum égo minôris ĕmi, quám túum tú.
This man sells everything so dear, that no one can buy anything of him. | Híc vír ómnia *tam* cáre véndĕre sólet, *ut* némo ab éo quídquam émere póssit.*
I do not know what you wish to say. | Haŭd scío (néscio), quíd tíbi vélis.
You speak so fast, that I cannot understand you. | *Tam* celériter lóqueris, *ut* intelligere non póssim.
I assure you that he wishes to speak with you. | Affírmo tíbi, éum tēcum colloquéndi cúpĭdum ésse.

---

* *Ut* preceded by *tam, talis, tantus,* &c., requires the subjunctive. (Cf. Lesson LXXXVIII. A. 1.)

| Be so good as to speak a little slower. | Sis tam benígnus, ut aliquánto léntius loquâris. |
| Will you be kind enough to give me the book ? | Vísne ésse tam benígnus, ut míhi líbrum dês ? |

EXERCISE 142.

How far is it from Paris to London ? — It is nearly a hundred miles from Paris to London. — Is it far from here to Hamburg ? — It is far. — Is it far from here to Vienna ? — It is almost a hundred and forty miles from here to Vienna. — Is it farther from Berlin to Dresden than from Leipzic to Berlin ? — It is farther from Berlin to Dresden than from Leipzic to Berlin. — How far is it from Paris to Berlin ? — It is almost a hundred and thirty miles from here to Berlin. — Do you intend to go to Berlin soon ? — I do intend to go thither soon. — Why do you wish to go this time ? — In order to buy good books and a good horse there; and to see my good friends. — Is it long since you were there ? — It is nearly two years since I was there. — Do you not go to Vienna this year ? — I do not go thither, for it is too far from here to Vienna. — Is it long since you saw your Hamburg friend ? — I saw him but a fortnight ago. — Do your scholars like to learn by heart ? — They do not like to learn by heart; they like reading and writing better than learning by heart. — Do you like beer better than cider ? — I like cider better than beer. — Does your brother like to play ? — He likes to study better than to play. — Do you like meat better than bread ? — I like the latter better than the former. — Do you like to drink better than to eat ? — I like to eat better than to drink; but my uncle likes to drink better than to eat. — Does your brother-in-law like meat better than fish ? — He likes fish better than meat. — Do you like to write better than to speak ? — I like to do both. — Do you like fowl better than fish ? — Do you like good honey better than sugar ? — I like neither.

EXERCISE 143.

Does your father like coffee better than tea ? — He likes neither. — What do you drink in the morning ? — I drink a glass of water with a little sugar; my father drinks good coffee, my younger brother good tea, and my brother-in-law a glass of good wine. — Can you understand me ? — No, sir, for you speak too fast. — Will you be kind enough not to speak so fast ? — I will not speak so fast if you will listen to me. — Can you understand what my brother tells you ? — He speaks so fast that I cannot understand him. — Can your pupils understand you ? — They understand me when I speak slowly; for in order to be understood one must speak slowly. — Why do you not buy anything of that merchant ? — I had a mind to buy several dozen of handkerchiefs, some cravats, and a white hat of him; but he sells so dear, that I cannot buy anything of him. — Will you take me to another ? — I will take you to the son of the one whom you bought of last year. — Does he sell as dear as this (one) ? — He sells cheaper. — Do you like going to the theatre better than going to the concert ?

— I do like going to the concert as well as going to the theatre; but I do not like going to the public walk, for there are too many people there. — Do your children like learning Italian better than Spanish? — They do not like to learn either; they only like to learn German. — Do they like to speak better than to write? — They like to do neither. — Do you like mutton? — I like beef better than mutton. — Do your children like cake better than bread? — They like both. — Has he read all the books which he bought? — He bought so many of them, that he cannot read them all. — Do you wish to write some letters? — I have written so many of them, that I cannot write any more.

Lesson LXXVI. — PENSUM SEPTUAGESIMUM SEXTUM.

REFLEXIVE VERBS.

A. Reflexive verbs are those of which the action terminates in the agent himself.

Verbs of a reflexive sense in Latin are, —

1. Transitive and neuter verbs in connection with the accusative or dative of the reflexive pronouns *me, te, se, nos, vos, se, mihi, tibi, sibi, nobis, vobis, sibi.* E. g. *Se amare,* to love one's self; *sibi nocēre,* to hurt one's self; *sese fugae mandare,* to betake one's self to flight, &c.

2. A number of passive and deponent verbs, which exhibit more or less of a reflexive sense. E. g. *crucior,* I am tormented, I torment myself; *proficiscor,* I get myself under way; *laetor,* I rejoice; *vehor,* I ride, &c.

3. The impersonal verbs *me taedet, piget, pudet, poenitet, miseret,* It moves me to disgust, chagrin, shame, regret, pity, &c.

B. The following passive and deponent verbs may be regarded as reflexive: —

> Crucior, *I torment myself (I am tormented).*
> Delector, *I am delighted.*
> Fallor, *I deceive myself (I am deceived).*
> Fĕror, *I am impelled.*
> Grăvor, *I hesitate.*
> Inclinor, *I am inclined.*
> Lavor, *I wash myself, I bathe.*
> Laetor, *I rejoice.*
> Movĕor, } *I am moved, excited.*
> Commovĕor, }
> Mūtor, *I change, am changed.*
> Pascor, *I support myself by, I feed upon.*

Proficiscor, *I get myself under way.*
Vĕhor, *I am conveyed, I ride.*
Vescor, *I live upon, eat.*

To disguise one's self.	{ Aliēnam formam capĕre. Larvam sibi aptāre. Mentīri.
To represent to one's self (to imagine, suppose).	{ Propōnĕre sibi (aliquid). Cogitatione sibi fingĕre. Anĭmo concipĕre aliquid.
To rejoice.	{ Laetor, āri, ātus sum. Gaudeo, ēre, gavīsus sum. (RE, DE RE, IN RE, QUOD).
To be ashamed.	Pŭdet (ēre, pudŭit) me, te, eum. (ALICUJUS REI).
To flatter any one.	Blandīri alicui; adulāri aliquem.
To flatter one's self.	{ Sibi ipsi blandiri. Spem habēre *or* in spe esse (cum Acc. et Inf.).
To fear, to feel afraid of.	{ Tĭmeo, ēre, ŭi, ——. Metuo, ĕre, ŭi, ——. Vereor, ēri, verĭtus sum. (ALIQUEM, REM, NE, UT, &c.)
To look back or behind one's self.	Respĭcio, ĕre, spexi, spectum (AD ALIQUEM, REM).

Dost thou see thyself?	Vidēsne tē?
I do not see myself.	Ego mē nōn vídeo.
Have you cut yourselves?	Vulneravistísne vōs cúltro?
We have cut ourselves.	Véro, nōs vulnerávimus.
Do we flatter ourselves?	Númquid nóbis ípsi blandĭmur?
We do not.	Nōn blandĭmur.
Does he not disguise himself?	Nónne síbi lárvam áptat?
He does do it.	Fáctum est.
Of whom are you afraid?	Quém métuis (tímes)?
I am not afraid of any one.	Néminem métuo.
I am not afraid of him.	Ego éum nōn tímeo.
We must fear (reverence) the deity.	Déum nōs vereāmur opórtet.
I am afraid of hurting myself.	Tímeo, *ne* mĭhi nóceam.
He is afraid of cutting his finger.	Métuit, *ne* síbi dígitum *vúlneret.*
We were afraid that you would not come.	Metúimus, *ne non* (or *ut*) * veníres.
You were afraid that I would not write.	Timébas, *ut* scríbĕrem.
We are not afraid.	Sine timōre súmus.

---

* After verbs of fearing, "that" or "lest" is expressed by *ne,* and "that not" by *ne non* or *ut.* The verb must be in the subjunctive. (See Lesson LXXXVIII. *A.* III.)

To pass away the time (in anything).	Tempus (otium) tradūcĕre, consumĕre, or tĕrĕre (ALIQUĀ RE).
To enjoy something, to amuse one's self with anything.	Tempus or hōras fallĕre (fefelli, falsum) aliquā re.
The pastime, diversion.	Lūdus, i, m.; oblectatio, ōnis, f.; oblectamentum, i, n.
In what do you amuse yourself?	Quâ rê témpus fállis? Quâ rê taédium témpŏris mínŭis?
I amuse myself in reading, in conversation.	Hóras fállo legendo, sermónibus.
He diverts him with playing, with writing.	Témpus (ótium) fállit ludéndo, scribéndo.
They amused themselves in banqueting and feasting.	Ótium convíviis commissationibúsque inter sê terébant.
Each, each one; every, every one.	*Quisque, unusquisque; omnes, nemo non.*
Each one of you.	Quisque or unusquisque vestrum.
Each of you two.	Quisque or uterque vestrum.
Every one spends his time as he pleases.	Témpus súum quísque térit, ut síbi pláceat.
Every one amuses himself in the best way he can.	Ótium súum quísque fállit quam óptime pótest.
Everybody speaks of it.	Ómnes de rê loquúntur. In ôre ómnium est.
Every one knows.	Némo est, qui nésciat.
Everybody thinks.	Némo ést; quin (= qui nôn) exístimet.
Every man is liable to err.	Némo nôn érrat. Humânum est errâre.
I have nothing to amuse myself with.	Non hábeo, quô fállam témpus.
It is for amusement, for pastime.	Ést ad témpus falléndum. Ést ánimi caúsâ.
The taste.	Gustus (gustātus), ûs, m.; sensus, ûs, m.; judicium, i, n.
A man of taste, of none.	Homo elegans, inelegans.
To have taste.	Esse intelligentem; esse praedītum sapōre.
To have no taste.	Esse inelegantem, nôn sapōre.
To mistake, to be mistaken.	Erro, āre, āvi, ātum. Fallor, i, falsus sum.
To soil, stain.	Inquīno, āre, āvi, ātum. Macŭlo, āre, āvi, ātum.
To deceive, cheat.	Fallo, ĕre, fefelli, falsum. Decipio, ĕre, cēpi, ceptum.
To cheat, defraud any one of anything.	Fraudāre or defraudāre aliquem aliquā re or rem.

To believe.	{ *Crēdo, ĕre, dĭdi, dĭtum.* *Arbĭtror, āri, atus sum.* *Pŭto, āre, āvi, ātum.*
To believe anything *or* any one.	{ Alicui rei *or* alicui crēdĕre. Alicui *or* alicui rei fĭdem habēre *or* tribuĕre.
To believe in dreams.	Somniis credĕre *or* fidem tribuĕre.
To believe in ghosts.	Credĕre de umbris.
To believe one's eyes rather than one's ears.	Ocŭlis magis quam auribus credĕre.
To believe in God.	Deum esse credĕre ; Deum putāre.
The God.	Dĕus, i, *m. ;* nūmen, ĭnis, *n.*
To utter a falsehood, to lie.	{ Mentior, īri, ītus sum. Mendacium dicĕre.
The liar, the story-teller.	Mendax, ācis, *m.* & *f.*
Do you believe that man ?	Credísne (tribuísne fidem) ílli hó- mini ?
I do not believe him.	Nôn crédo. Fidem non tríbuo.
Do you believe what I am telling you ?	Putâsne vêrum, quod tíbi díco ?
I do believe it.	Púto.
Am I mistaken ?	Egóne fállor ?
You are not mistaken.	Nôn fállĕris.
Did he cheat you out of any- thing ?	Fraudavítne tê aliquā rê ?
He has cheated me out of my pay.	Véro, mê honorário fraudâvit.
Do you believe that he has soiled your book ?	Credisne éum líbrum túum inqui- navísse ?
I do not believe it.	Mínimi crédo.
Is he a man of taste ?	Praeditúsne est sapôre ?
He is not (a man of taste).	Nôn sápit. Hómo élegans nôn ést.
Every man has his taste.	{ Súum cuíque judícium est. De gústibus nôn disputándum est.
My taste is (= I like) to study and to ride on horseback.	Égo óperam lítteris dáre atque equitâre deléctor.
To rejoice at anything.	*Gaudēre, laetāri aliquā re, de* or *in aliquā re.*
I rejoice at your happiness.	Gaúdeo tuā felicitâte.
At what does your uncle rejoice ?	Quā rê pátruus túus laetâtur ?
He is delighted and rejoiced at my recovery.	Gaúdet vehementérque laetâtur valetúdĭne meā confirmátā.
I am greatly rejoiced at your diligence and industry.	Mágnae laetítiae míhi est diligéntia túa et indústria.
To go to bed.	*Cubĭtum ĭre ; dāre se somno ; con- ferre se in lectum.*
To get up, rise.	(*E lecto*) *surgo, ĕre, surrexi, sur- rectum.*
The bed.	Lectus, lectŭlus, i, *m.*
Sunrise.	Ortus sōlis, sol oriens, prima lux.

Sunset.	Occasus sōlis, sol occĭdens.
Early (in the morning).	Bĕne māne, matutīne, matūre.
Late (at night).	Sero, tarde; multā nocte.
At midnight.	Mediā nocte.
At a quarter past eleven.	Círciter quadrántem hórae post undécimam.
Do you rise early ?	{ Surgísne béne māne ? { Solêsne béne māne e lécto súrgere ?
I rise at sunrise.	{ Égo sóle oriénte súrgere sóleo. { E lécto súrgo cum ortu sôlis.
At what time do you go to bed ?	Quā hórā tê dās sómno (tê in léctum cónfers) ?
I usually go to bed at midnight.	Égo médiā nócte cúbitum íre sóleo.
He goes to bed at sunset.	Léctŭlum sê cónfert cum occásu sôlis.
At what time did you go to bed last night ?	Quô témpore sómno tê dedísti héri vésperi ?
I went to bed at ten.	In léctum me contŭli hórā décimā.
Díd he rise earlier than you.	Surrexítne matúrius quam tû ?
No, he rose later.	Ímmo véro tárdius surréxit.
The hair (of the head).	*Pĭlus, i,* m.; or pl. *pĭli; crīnes,* pl.
To cut one's hair.	{ Pĭlos recĭdere (cidi, cĭsum). { Pĭlos tondēre (totondi, tonsum).
To pull out any one's hair.	Alicui pĭlos evellēre (velli, vulsum).
He is pulling out his hair.	Pĭlos síbi evéllit.
He has cut his hair.	Pĭlos síbi recĭdit (totóndit).
I have had my hair cut.	{ Égo míhi pĭlos recidéndos curávi. { Pĭli míhi tónsi sunt.
Nothing but.	{ *Nĭhil praeter* (cum Acc.). { *Non nisi.*
He drinks nothing but water.	Níhil praeter áquam bíbet (bíbere sólet).
He has nothing but enemies.	{ Néminem nísi sibi inimícum hábet. { Praeter inimícos hábet néminem.
I saw no one but him.	Praeter íllum vídi néminem.
To run away, flee.	{ Aufugĭo, ĕre, fugi. { Profugĕre (ALIQUO).
Are you afraid to remain ?	Timêsne manêre ?
I am not afraid.	Nôn tímeo.
Is he afraid to write to you ?	Timétne (metuítne) lítteras dáre ad tê ?
He is not afraid.	Nôn tímet.

EXERCISE 144.

Have you written long or short letters ? — I have written (both) long and short ones. — Have you many apples ? — I have so many of them that I do not know which to eat. — Do you wish to give anything to these children ? — They have studied so badly, that I do not

2 E   41

wish to give them anything. — What dost thou rejoice at ? — I rejoice
at the good fortune that has happened to you. — What do your children rejoice at ? — They rejoice at seeing you. — Do you rejoice at
the happiness of my father ? — I do rejoice at it. — Do you flatter my
brother ? — I do not flatter him. — Does this master flatter his pupils ?
— He does not flatter them. — Is he pleased with them ? — He is
much pleased (*contentus*) with them when they learn well; but he is
not pleased with them when they do not learn well. — Do you flatter
me ? — I do not flatter you, for I love you. — Do you see yourself in
that looking-glass ? — I do see myself in it. — Why do you not remain
near the fire ? — Because I am afraid of burning myself. — Does this
man make his fire ? — Do you fear those ugly men ? — I do not fear
them, for they hurt nobody. — Why do those children run away ? —
They run away, because they are afraid of you. — Do you run away
from your enemies ? — I do not run away from them, for I do not fear
them. — Can you write a Latin letter without an error ? — I can write
one. — Does any one correct your letters ? — No one corrects them.
— How many letters have you already written ? — I have already
written a dozen. — Have you hurt yourself ? — I have not hurt myself. — Who has hurt himself ? — My brother has hurt himself; for he
has cut his finger. — Is he still ill ? — He is better. — I rejoice to
hear that he is no longer ill; for I love him, and I pitied him from
my heart. — Why does your cousin pull out his hair ? — Because he
cannot pay what he owes. — Have you cut your hair ? — I have not
cut it myself, but I have had it cut.

EXERCISE 145.

In what do your children amuse themselves ? — They amuse themselves in studying, writing, and playing. — In what do you amuse
yourself ? — I amuse myself in the best way I can, for I read good
books, and I write to my friends. — Every man has his taste; what is
yours ? — I like to study, to read a good book, to go to the concert,
and the public walk, and to ride on horseback. — Has that physician
done any harm to your child ? — He has cut his finger, but he has
not done him any harm. — Why do you listen to that man ? — I listen to him, but I do not believe him; for I know that he is a story-
teller. — Why does your cousin not brush his hat ? — He does not
brush it, because he is afraid of soiling his fingers. — What does my
neighbor tell you ? — He tells me that you wish to buy his horse; but
I know that he is mistaken, for you have no money to buy it. — What
do they say at the market ? — They say that the enemy is beaten. —
Do you believe it ? — I do believe it, because every one says so. —
Do you go to bed early ? — I go to bed late; for I cannot sleep, if I
go to bed early. — At what o'clock did you go to bed yesterday ? —
Yesterday I went to bed at a quarter past eleven. — At what o'clock
do your children go to bed ? — They go to bed at sunset. — Do they
rise early ? — They rise at sunrise. — At what o'clock did you rise
to-day ? — To-day I rose late; for I went to bed late last evening. —
Does your son rise late ? — He must rise early, for he never goes to
bed late. — What does he do when he gets up ? — He studies and
then breakfasts.

Lesson LXXVII. — PENSUM SEPTUAGESIMUM SEPTIMUM.

OF THE GENDER OF SUBSTANTIVES.

A. Gender originally depends upon the signification of words, and is in so far called *natural gender* or *sex.*

1. In substantives denoting *living beings*, i. e. men or animals, the natural gender is either *masculine* or *feminine*, according to the sex. *Inanimate* objects do not properly admit of any distinction of sex, and are hence said to be of the *neuter gender*.

2. The Latin language, however, attributes life to *many inanimate objects*, and extends the distinction of sex to them, i. e. represents them likewise as *masculine* or *feminine*. E. g. *hic mons, haec arbor.*

3. When the gender of a substantive is not already determined by its signification, it is indicated by its form (or termination). This is called the *grammatical gender*, and is either *masculine, feminine*, or *neuter*. E. g. *hic liber, haec mensa, hoc umbracŭlum.*

NATURAL GENDER.

B. The natural gender of substantives denoting living beings (i. e. men or animals) coincides with the sex of the individual designated. Hence, names and appellations of male beings are masculine, and those of females feminine. E. g. *Caesar, Cleopatra, vir, mulĭer, păter, māter.*

REMARKS.

1. Patrials and gentiles of the plural number are considered masculine; as, *Romāni, Carthaginienses*, &c. So also *lemŭres*, ghosts, and *mānes*, departed spirits.

2. The names of women are feminine, even where the termination is neuter. E. g. *mea Glycerium, tua Phanium.*

3. The only exception to this law are certain secondary appellations of men, which retain their original grammatical gender as determined by their form. Such are: FEM. *copiae*, military forces; *deliciae*, favorite, darling; *opĕrae*, operatives; *vigiliae, excubiae*, watch, sentinels. NEUT. *auxilia*, auxiliary troops; *servitia*, servants; *mancipĭum*, a slave; *acroāma*, a jester.*

C. The natural gender of living beings of the same species is indicated in three different ways: —

I. There is a separate word for each gender. E. g. *vir* —

---

* But *optio*, a lieutenant, is masculine, though derived from *optio*, f., choice.

mulĭer, păter — mãter, frăter — sŏror, patrŭus — amĭta, ma-rĭtus — uxor, taurus — vacca. Instances of this kind are comparatively few.

II. The noun is of the same root, but has a separate termination for each gender. E. g. *fīlĭus — fīlĭa, amīcus — amīca, magister — magistra, servus — serva, praeceptor — praeceptrix, lŭpus — lŭpa.*

REMARK. — Substantives thus admitting of two terminations are called *mobilia*, and are most commonly of the first and second declensions (MASC. *er* or *us*, FEM. *a*). Mobilia of the third declension form their feminines in *a, trix, ĭna, issa,* and *is ;* as, *caupo — caupōna,* innkeeper, hostess; *lēno — lēna,* pander, procuress; *lĕo — lĕaena,* lion, lioness; *tibīcen — tibīcĭna,* flute-player (male and female); *cantor — cantrix,* singer; *rex — regīna,* king, queen; *gallus — gallīna,* cock, hen; *Threx — Threĭssa* (or *Thressa*), a Thracian (man and woman); *nĕpos — neptis,* grandson, granddaughter.

III. One and the same noun is indifferently applied to both sexes, without any change of termination, and the gender is determined by the context (i. e. by the adjective in agreement with it, &c.) ; as, *hic* or *haec cīvis,* this citizen (male or female); *hic* or *haec hēres,* this heir (man or woman). Nouns of this class are said to be of the *common gender* (or *communia*).* Such are

1. The following names of persons : —

Antistes, *priest* (or *-ess*).	Incŏla, *inhabitant.*
Artĭfex, *artist.*	Index, *informer.*
Auctor, *author.*	Judex, *judge.*
Augur, *augur.*	Martyr, *witness.*
Civis, *citizen.*	Miles, *soldier.*
Comes, *companion.*	Munĭceps, *burgess.*
Conjux, *spouse.*	Parens, *parent.*
Custos, *keeper.*	Praesul, *chief priest.*
Dux, *leader.*	Sacerdos, *priest* (or *-ess*).
Exul, *exile.*	Satelles, *attendant.*
Haeres, *heir.*	Testis, *witness.*
Hospes, *guest.*	Vates, *prophet* (or *-ess*).
Hostis, *enemy.*	Vindex, *avenger.*

Among these are included adjectives of one termination used substantively ; as, *adolescens, affĭnis, juvĕnis, patruēlis, princeps,* &c.

2. Many names of animals ; as,

Anser, *goslin* or *goose.*	Cănis, *dog* or *bĭtch.*
Bōs, *ox* or *cow.*	Elephantus, *elephant.*

---

* Names of *inanimate* objects, which are sometimes of one gender and sometimes of another, are said to be of the *doubtful* gender ; as, *fīnis,* m. & f.

Grūs, *crane.*	Perdix, *partridge.*
Lĕpus, *hare.*	Serpens, *snake.*
Līmax, *snail.*	Sūs, *swine.*
Mūs, *mouse.*	Thynnus, *tunny-fish.*
Ovis, *sheep* or *ram.*	Vespertilio, *bat.*

REMARKS.

1. Some nouns of the common gender are *mobilia* at the same time. E. g. *antistes — antistīta, cliens — clienta, hospes — hospīta.*

2. From the nouns of the common gender we must distinguish, —

a) Masculine appellations of entire classes of persons in the plural, including also the other sex. E. g. *hi lĭbĕri,* children; *filii,* sons and daughters; *frātres,* brothers and sisters; *rēges,* the royal family; *parentes,* parents.

b) Epicoena, or those which, though including both sexes, are always of the same grammatical gender (i. e. always either masculine or feminine). Such are: MASC. *corvus,* the raven; *milvus,* the kite; *passer,* the swallow; *turdus,* the thrush. FEM. *alauda,* the lark; *aquila,* the eagle; *felis,* the cat; *rana,* the frog; *vulpes,* the fox,* &c.

3. The *communia* and *mobilia* occur most frequently as masculine nouns; as, *hic amīcus, equus, canis, civis,* &c. Exceptions are *sus, grus, serpens, limax* and *perdix,* which are more commonly feminine.

4. Among the general names of animals, *animans,* in the sense of "rational animal," or "man," is masculine, and when applied to other animals, feminine or neuter. *Quadrūpes* is generally feminine, sometimes neuter or masculine. *Ales* and *volucris,* "bird," is commonly feminine (always so in the plural); sometimes, however, masculine.

GENDER OF NAMES OF INANIMATE OBJECTS.

D. Besides the substantives which designate living beings, there are many others whose grammatical gender is likewise determined by their signification (cf. *A.* 2.) Such are : —

I. MASCULINES. — The names of the winds and months, and generally also those of rivers and mountains, are masculine.† E. g.

Aquĭlo, Auster, Bŏrēas, Etēsiae, Nŏtus.	The north wind, south wind, north-east wind, the Etesian winds, south wind.
Januārĭus, Aprīlis, Julĭus, November.	January, April, July, November.
Euphrātes, Ister, Tamĕsis, Tigris.	The Euphrates, the Danube, the Thames, the Tigris.
Āthos, Ēryx, Hĕlĭcon, Pangaeus.	Mount Athos, Eryx, Helicon, Pangæus.

---

* When it becomes important to distinguish sex, it is customary to add *mas* or *masculus* and *femina;* as, *felis mas, vulpes mascŭla, porcus femina.*

† Because the generic terms *ventus, mensis, fluvius* (*amnis*), and *mons* are of that gender.

41 *

EXCEPTIONS.

1. Of the names of rivers, *Albula, Allia, Duria, Matrŏna, Sagra, Sura, Styx,* and *Lethe* are feminine; *Elăver, Jader, Muthul,* and others of barbarous origin, neuter.

2. Of the names of mountains, *Aetna, Alpis, Calpe, Carambis, Cyllene, Ida, Oeta, Rhodŏpe,* are feminine; and *Pelion* and *Soracte,* neuter.

II. FEMININES. — The names of countries, islands, cities, trees and plants are generally feminine.* E. g.

Aegyptus, Gallia, Persis, Trōas.	Egypt, Gaul, Persia, Troas.
Dēlos, Rhŏdus, Salămis, Sicilia.	The island of Delos, Rhodes, Salamis, Sicily.
Carthāgo, Corinthus, Pўlos, Rōma, Troezen.	The city of Carthage, Corinth, Pylos, Rome, Troezen.
Abies, pirus, quercus, papўrus, rŏsa.	The fir-tree, pear-tree, the oak, the papyrus, the rose.

EXCEPTIONS.

1. Of the names of countries and islands, *Pontus, Hellespontus, Bospŏrus, Isthmus,* and *Sason* (island) are masculine. Those in *um,* and plurals in *a,* are neuter; as, *Latium, Samnium, Bactra,* &c. So the islands *Dianium* and *Delta.*

2. Of the names of cities, those in *ūs, untis,* plurals in *i,* and some of those in *us, i,* in *o* and *on,* are masculine; as, *Selinus, Delphi, Canōpus, Croto, Marathon,* &c. Those in *um, on, e, ur,* and plurals in *a,* are neuter; as, *Tarentum, Illion, Praeneste, Tibur, Arbēla,* &c. So are also a number of indeclinable barbarous names; as, *Gadir, Hispal, Nepet,* &c.

3. Of the names of trees and plants, *oleaster, pinaster, styrax; acanthus, asparagus, asphodĕlus, calamus, carduus, hellebŏrus, intŭbus, juncus, rhamnus,* and *scirpus* are masculine; *amarăcus, cytisus, lapathus, raphanus, rubus, spinus, larix, vepres,* and *sentis,* common. All of the second declension ending in *um,* and those of the third in *er,* are neuter; as, *balsămum, ligustrum; acer, papāver, piper, siser, tuber, robur,* &c.

III. NEUTERS. — The gender of all substantives denoting inanimate objects, and not included in Case I. or II. of this rule, is not determined by their *signification,* but by their *termination.* (Cf. Lesson LXXVIII. *A.*) Among these, however, there are several classes of words which are invariably NEUTER. Such are, —

1. All indeclinable nouns, whether singular or plural. E. g. *fas, nefas, nihil, cornu, gummi, Tempe, pondo.*† (Cf. page 61.)

2. All words and expressions used as substantives, without properly

---

* Because the generic terms *terra, insŭla, urbs, arbor,* are so.
† With the exception of indeclinable names of *persons;* as, *Adam, Ruth,* &c.

being such, and linked to an adjective or pronoun of the neuter gender. E. g. *A* longum; ultimum *vale; cras* hesternum; illud *nosce te
ipsum; scire* tuum; *pater* est dissyllabum (*A* long; the last farewell;
yesterday, which once was called "to-morrow"; the injunction,
"Know thyself"; thy knowledge; the word "father" is a dissyllable).

To take a walk.	{ *Spátíor, ári, átus sum.* { *Ambuláre, deambuláre.*
To go out to take a walk.	Ire *or* abíre deambulátum.
To take any one a walking.	Aliquem deambulátum ducĕre.
To take a drive out of the city.	Vehícŭlo extra urbem vectári.
To take a ride on horseback through the city, into the country.	Equo per urbem, rūs vectári.
To take a pleasure excursion into the country.	Excurrĕre rūs aními causā.
Do you wish to take a walk with me ?	Visne mêcum deambulátum íre ?
I am not willing to go with you.	Nólo têcum abíre.
I would rather take a drive out of the city with you.	Égo têcum vehícŭlo extra úrbem vectári málim.
Where was your master accustomed to walk ?	Quô lóco magíster túus spatiári solêbat ?
He was accustomed to walk in the garden every morning before breakfast.	Quotídie mâne ante jentáculum in hórtulo deambuláre solêbat.
Do you often walk ?	Ambulásne saépe ?
I take a walk every morning.	Égo véro quotídie mâne ambulátum ábeo.
Do you take your children a walking ?	Ducísne liberos túos ambulátum ?
I take them a walking every evening.	Dúco éos ambulátum quotídie vésperi.
He takes a walk every day.	Núllo nôn díe spatiátur.
Is he taking a drive or a ride ?	Útrum carpénto vectátur an équo ?
He is taking a drive.	Carpénto.
Where do you intend to go to-morrow morning ?	Quo íre crâs mâne cógitas ?
I intend to take an excursion into the country.	Excúrrere rûs cógito.
Do you wish to see your brother work ?	Cupísne vidêre frátrem túum operári ?
I do.	Cúpio.
When do you take a walk ?	Quô témpore ábis ambulátum ?
I take a walk whenever I have nothing to do at home.	Ambulátum égo íre sóleo, quandocúnque dómi níhil faciéndum invénio.
To teach.	*Dŏceo, ĕre, ŭi, doctum* (ALIQUEM ALIQUID).

To instruct (any one in anything). — Ĕrŭdĭo, īre, īvi, ītum. Institŭo, ĕre, ŭi, ūtum. (ALIQUEM ALIQUA RE).*

To give one lessons (in an art). — Trādo, ĕre, dĭdi, dĭtum (ALICUI ALIQUAM ARTEM).

To take lessons, to receive instruction (from any one). — Docēri, erudīri, instĭtui (AB ALI-QUO).

What does your master teach you? — Quíd tĕ magíster dócet?

He teaches me to read and to write. — Dócet mĕ légere et scríbere.

Did he teach you the Latin language? — Docuítne tĕ línguam Latínam?

He did teach me. — Dócuit.

Do you give lessons in dancing? — Tradísne tû ártem saltándi?

No, on the contrary, I give lessons in writing. — Ímmo pótius scríbéndi ártem trádo.

Who is instructing your little brother? — Quís fratérculum túum instítuit?

His master, the Englishman, is instructing him in the liberal arts. — Éjus magíster, Ánglus, éum ártibus liberálibus instítuit atque érudit.

He is taught grammar, the art of dancing. — Docêtur grammáticam, ártem saltándi.

Are you taking lessons in elocution? — Instituerísne árte dicéndi?

I am not taking any. — Non instítuor.

The instruction. — Institutio, ōnis, f.; disciplīna, ae, f.

The art, science. — Ars, gen. artis, f.

To dance. — Saltāre, saltatiōnem agĕre.

To reckon, cipher. — Ratiocināri; numĕros tractāre.

Ciphering (act of). — Ratiocinatio, ōnis, f.

Arithmetic. — Ars ratiocinandi, arithmetĭca, ae, f.

The Latin master. — Linguae Latīnae doctor seu magister.

The dancing-master. — Magíster saltandi.

The clergyman. — Clerĭcus, ecclesiastĭcus, i, m.

The scholar, savant. — (Vir) erudītus, doctus.

To remember, recollect. — Mĕmĭni, meminisse. Rĕcordor, āri, ātus sum. Reminiscor, i, ——.

To remember, recollect (any one). — Meminisse alicŭjus or aliquem.†

To remember or recollect anything. — Meminisse, recordāri or reminisci alicŭjus rei or rem.‡

---

* On the government of these verbs, see Lesson LX. A.

† On the construction of these verbs, compare Lesson LXVII. B.

‡ *Meminisse* is "to have still in one's memory," *reminisci*, "to recollect upon reflection what had already been supplanted in the memory," *recordāri*, "to remember or think of with interest and sympathy."

To remember (recollect) anything very well.	Commeminisse alicujus rei. Běne, praeclāre meminisse alicūjus rei.
Something occurs to me, comes to my mind.	Věnit mihi in mentem alicūjus rei or res.
Do you still remember that man?	Meministĭne íllum hóminem (illĭus hóminis)?
I still remember him very well.	Mémini éum béne.
Does he recollect his promise?	Rocordatúrne súa promíssa (suŏrum promissŏrum)?
He does not recollect them.	Éa (eŏrum) nŏn recordâtur (reminíscitur).
I remember my reading, seeing, hearing.	Mémini mê légere, vidêre, audĭre.
I remember having suffered the same.	Recórdor mê éadem perpéssum.
I wish to know, whether you remember anything concerning yourself?	Velim scíre, écquid de tê recordêre?
Remember me.	Memíneris méi. Fúcito, ut me memíneris.
Do you recollect that?	Reminiscerísne hóc?
I do not remember it.	Haud reminíscor.
I remember you.	Mémini tê or túi.
I remember them very well.	Praeclâre éos mémini.
He recollects us.	Nóstri reminíscitur.
I have remembered him.	Recordâtus súm (mémini) éjus.
One must love and praise one's friend.	Amícus súus cuíque amándus atque laudándus est.
Whom must we despise and punish?	Quém nôs dispiciâmus atque puniâmus opórtet?

EXERCISE 146.

Do you call me? — I do call you. — What is your pleasure? — You must rise, for it is already late. — What do you want me for? — I have lost all my money at play, and I come to beg you to lend me some. — What o'clock is it? — It is already a quarter past six, and you have slept long enough. — Is it long since you rose? — It is an hour and a half since I rose. — Do you often go a walking? — I go a walking when I have nothing to do at home. — Do you wish to take a walk? — I cannot take a walk, for I have too much to do. — Has your brother taken a ride on horseback? — He has taken an airing in a carriage. — Do your children often go a walking? — They go a walking every morning after breakfast. — Do you take a walk after dinner? — After dinner I drink tea, and then I take a walk. — Do you often take your children a walking? — I take them a walking every morning and every evening. — Can you go along with me? — I cannot go along with you, for I must take my little brother out a walking. — Where do you walk? — We walk in our uncle's garden

and fields. — Do you like walking? — I like walking better than eating and drinking. — Does your father like to take a ride on horseback? — He likes to take a ride in a carriage better than on horseback. — Must one love children who are not good? — One ought, on
the contrary, to punish and despise them. — Who has taught you to
read? — I have learnt it of (*ab* or *apud*) a French master. — Has he
also taught you to write? — He has taught me to read and to write.—
Who has taught your brother arithmetic? — A German master has
taught it him. — Do you wish to take a walk with us? — I cannot go
a walking, for I am waiting for my German master. — Does your
brother wish to take a walk? — He cannot, for he is taking lessons
in dancing.

EXERCISE 147.

Have you an English master? — We have one. — Does he also
give you lessons in Italian? — He does not know Italian; but we
have an Italian and Spanish master. — What has become of your
old writing-master? — He has taken orders (has become a clergyman). — What has become of the learned man whom I saw at your
house last winter? — He has set up for a merchant. — And what has
become of his son? — He has turned a soldier. — Do you still recollect my old dancing-master? — I do still recollect him; what has
become of him? — He is here, and you can see him if you like (*si
placet, si commŏdum est*). Hast thou a German master? — I have a
very good (one), for it is my father, who gives me lessons in German
and in English. — Does your father also know Polish? — He does
not know it yet, but he intends to learn it this summer. — Do you
remember your promise? — I do remember it. — What did you
promise me? — I promised to give you lessons in German; and I will
do it. — Will you begin this morning? — I will begin this evening, if
you please (*si tibi lĭbet* or *collĭbet*). — Do you recollect the man whose
son taught us dancing? — I no longer recollect him. — Do you still
recollect my brothers? — I do recollect them very well; for when I
was studying at Berlin, I saw them every day. — Does your uncle
still recollect me? — I assure you that he still recollects you. — Do
you speak German better than my cousin? — I do not speak it as
well as he, for he speaks it better than many Germans. — Which of
your pupils speaks it the best? — The one that was walking with me
yesterday speaks it the best of them all. — Is your uncle's house as
high as ours? — Yours is higher than my uncle's, but my cousin's is
the highest house that I have ever seen. — Has your friend as many
books as I? — You have more of them than he; but my brother has
more of them than both of you together. — Which of us has the most
money? — You have the most, for I have but thirty crowns, my friend
has but ten, and you have five hundred.

Lesson LXXVIII. — PENSUM DUODEOCTOGE-
SIMUM.

GENDER OF SUBSTANTIVES AS DETERMINED BY THEIR TERMINATION AND DECLENSION.

A. FIRST DECLENSION. — Substantives of the first declension ending in *ă* or *ē* are feminine, and those in *ās* and *ēs* masculine.

E. g. *Aula*, a hall; *stella*, a star; *aloë*, aloes; *epĭtŏme*, an abridgment; *tiăras*, a turban; *dynastes*, a ruler.

EXCEPTIONS are *dama*, m. & f., a doe, deer; *talpa*, f. & m., a mole; *Hadrĭa*, m., the Adriatic Sea; and *planetae*, m. pl., the planets. *Pandectae*, plural, is feminine, but the singular, *pandectes*, is masculine. *Manna*, in the sense of "grain" or "crumb," is regularly feminine, but the *manna* of the Israelites indeclinable neuter.

B. SECOND DECLENSION. — Of the nouns of the second declension, those ending in *ŭs* (*ŏs, ōs, ūs*) and *ĕr* are masculine, and those in *ŭm* and *ŏn* * neuter.

E. g. *anĭmus*, the mind; *scorpios*, a scorpion; *Athōs*, a mountain; *perĭplūs*, circumnavigation; *ager*, a field; — *antrum*, a cave; *colŏn*, the colon.

EXCEPTIONS.

1. Feminine are *alvus, carbăsus, colus, domus, humus,* and *vannus.* So also the Greek *arctus, apostrophus, dialectus, diametrus, diphthongus, exŏdus, methŏdus* (and other compounds of ἡ ὁδός), *lecγthus, miltus,* and *paragraphus.*

2. Common, but more frequently feminine, are *atŏmus*, an atom; *barbĭtus*, a lute; *fĭcus*, the fig; *grossus*, an unripe fig; *lōtus*, the lotus-flute; *phărus*, a lighthouse. Sometimes also *fasēlus*, a sort of boat, and *pampĭnus*, a vine-shoot. *Haec mālus* signifies the apple-tree, and *hic mālus*, the mast. *Hic epŏdus* is a shorter verse; *haec epŏdus*, an epode.

3. Neuters are *pelăgus*, the sea; *vīrus*, juice, poison; and *vulgus*, the vulgar.†

C. THIRD DECLENSION. — The third declension exhibits the greatest variety of terminations, and includes nouns of every gender.

I. Nouns of the third declension ending in *ŏ, ŏr, ōs, ĕr,* or *n* are MASCULINE.

---

* Those in *ŏs, ōs, ūs,* and *ŏn* are Greek nouns.
† But *vulgus* is sometimes also masculine.

E. g. *sermo*, speech; *honor*, honor; *flos*, a flower; *carcer*, a prison; *pecten*, a comb; *canon*, a rule, canon.

EXCEPTIONS.

1. Feminines in *o* are, — *a*) *caro, echo; Argo*, and those in *do* and *go*, except *ordo, cardo, ligo, harpăgo*, and *margo; b*) abstract and collective terms in *io;* as, *actio, lectio, portio, legio*, &c. *Pondo*, a pound, is an indeclinable neuter.

2. Of those in *or, arbor* is feminine. *Cor, marmor*, and *aequor* are neuter. *Ador* is commonly indeclinable.

3. Of those in *os, cos* and *dos* are feminine; *ŏs, ōris* and *ŏs, ossis* are neuter. So are also the Greek nouns *cetos, chaos, epos*, and *melos.*

4. Of those in *er, cadaver, iter, spinther, tūber, uber, ver*, and the plural *verbĕra* are neuter. *Linter* is more frequently feminine than masculine.

5. Of those in *n, aēdōn, halcўōn, sindōn*, and *icōn* are feminine. *Gluten, inguen, unguen, sanguen, carmen*, and others in *men*, are neuter.

II. Nouns of the third declension ending in *ās, ēs, ĭs, aus, ўs, x*, and *s* preceded by a consonant, are FEMININE.

E. g. *pietas*, piety; *rupes, is*, a rock; *quies, ētis*, rest; *iris*, the rainbow; *laus*, praise; *chelys*, a cithern; *pax*, peace; *hiems*, winter; *pars*, part.

EXCEPTIONS.

1. Of those in *as*, the name of the Roman pound, *as* (gen. *assis*) is masculine.* So are also Greek nouns in *as, antis;* as, *elephas*, &c. Neuter are *vas* (gen. *vasis*), *fas, nefas*, and Greek nouns in *as, ătis;* as, *erysipĕlas*, &c.

2. Nouns in *es, ĭtis*, and Greek nouns in *ēs, ĕtis*, are masculine ; as, *limes, limĭtis*, a cross-road ;† *lēbes, lebētis*, a caldron. So are also *acinăces, cōles, gausăpes, paries, pes*, and *praes* (surety). *Palumbes* is f. or m., and *ales*, m. or f. Neuters are *aes* and Greek nouns, as *cynosarges.*

3. Masculines in *is* are *amnis, assis, axis, caulis, collis, crinis, ensis, fustis, ignis, mensis, orbis, panis, piscis, sanguis, unguis, vomis*, and others. Common are *aqualis, clunis, corbis*, and (*pollen*) *pollĭnis.* More commonly masculine are *anguis, callis, canalis, canis, cinis, finis, funis, lapis, pedis, pulvis, scrobis* (*scrobs*), *tigris*, and *torquis;* more rarely *clunis, scobis* (*scobs*), and *volŭcris.*

4. Masculines in *x* are Greek nouns in *ax*, and many in *ex;* as, *thorax, judex, pontifex, rex*, &c. So also *calix, fornix, phoenix, saurix, varix; diox, esox, volvox, calyx, coccyx*, and *oryx.* Common are *imbrex, obex*, and *bombyx.* More frequently masculine are *grex, irpex, latex*, and *tradux.* More frequently feminine, *lodix, hystrix, perdix, natrix, sandyx*, and *calx* (the heel, and lime).

---

* Masculine are also all the parts of this weight; as, *sextans, quadrans, triens, quincunx, semis*, &c.
† But *merges, ĭtis*, "a sheaf," is feminine.

5. Of those ending in *s* preceded by a consonant, *dens, fons, mons, pons, chalybs,* and *hydrops* are masculine. So are the Greek names of animals; as, *gryps, epops,* &c. Common are *adeps, seps, lens, frons, forceps, scobs, stirps,* and *serpens.* Neuters are the philosophical terms *ens, accĭdens, antecēdens, consĕquens, anĭmans.*

III. Nouns of the third declension ending in *ă, ĕ, i, y,* or in *c, l, t, ăr, ŭr, ŭs,* are NEUTER.

E. g. *diadēma,* a crown; *sedĭle,* a seat; *hydromĕli,* mead; *mĭxy,* mushroom; *lac,* milk; *mel,* honey; *caput,* the head; *par,* a pair; *fulgur,* lightning; *corpus,* a body.

EXCEPTIONS. — Masculine are *sŏl, mugĭl, săl; furfur, turtur, vultur; lĕpus, mūs, tripūs,* and other compounds of πούς. Feminine are those in *us,* gen. *ŭdis* or *ūtis;* as, *palus, ŭdis; salus, ūtis;* to which add *tellus, ūris;* and *pecus, ŭdis.* The feminine of the common nouns *grus* and *sus* is the gender of the species.

D. FOURTH DECLENSION. — Nouns of the fourth declension ending in *ŭs* are masculine, those in *ū* neuter.

E. g. *fructus,* fruit; *cantus,* a song; *cornu,* a horn; *gĕlu,* ice.

EXCEPTIONS. — Feminine are *acus, manus, portĭcus, tribus,* and the plurals *Idus* and *Quinquātrus.* Common are *penus* and *specus.* The obsolete *genus* (for *genu*), *secus* (for *sexus,* m.), and *specus* occur as neuters only in the Nominative and Accusative.

E. FIFTH DECLENSION. — Substantives of the fifth declension are feminine.

E. g. *res,* a thing; *acies,* an edge; *spes,* hope; *fides,* faith.

EXCEPT *meridies,* which is masculine. On the gender of *dies,* m. & f., compare Lesson VIII. *B.*

To be cold, to feel cold.	Frīgeo, ēre, frixi, ——. Algeo, ēre, alsi, ——. Frīgus patior.
My feet, hands, are cold.	Frigeo pédibus, mánibus. Pédes, mánus mihi frigent.
To be warm, to feel warm, hot.	Căleo, ēre, ŭi, ——. Aestum sentio, aestuāre (to be hot).
The cold.	Frigus, ŏris, n.
The heat.	Aestus, ūs, m.

F. Obs. Calēre, "to be warm," is opposed to *frigēre,* "to be cold"; and *aestuāre,* "to feel warm, hot," to *algēre,* "to feel cold."

Are you cold?	Frigêsne (algêsne)?
I am very cold.	Véro, válde álgeo.
I am not at all cold.	Níhil frígŏris pátior.
Was your father cold?	Alsítne páter túus?

42

He was not cold.	Nôn álsit.
Is he warm ?	Calétne (aestuátne) ?
He is warm. (He feels warm, hot.)	Cálet. (Aéstŭat.)
Are they warm or cold ?	Útrum aéstuant án frígent ?
They are neither warm nor cold.	Néque aéstuant néque frigent
Who is (feels) cold ?	Quís álget ?
My brother is (feels) cold.	Fráter méus álget.
My hands are cold.	Mánus míhi frígent.
His ears are cold.	Aúres éi frígent.
My fingers are warm.	{ Dígiti míhi cálent.
	{ Cáleo dígitis.
Your boy felt warm.	Púer túus aéstuábat.
Who was cold (felt cold) ?	Quís fríxit (álsit) ?
The shoemaker was cold.	Sutor fríxit (álsit).
They instruct their youth in hunting, running, in suffering hunger, thirst, cold, and heat.	Erúdiunt juventútem venándo, curréndo, esuriéndo, sitiéndo, algéndo, aestuándo.

To make use of, to use.	{ *Ūtor, ūti, ūsus sum* (RE).*
	{ *Usitāri* (RE), *usurpāre* (REM).
Do you use my book ?	Uterísne méo líbro ?
I am using it.	Ūtor.
Has your father used it ?	Usúsne ést éo páter túus ?
He has not used it.	Nôn úsus ést.
May I use your horse for riding into the city ?	Licétne míhi équum túum usurpâre ad equitándum in úrbem ?
You may use it.	Lícet.
Did he use your books for reading ?	Usurpavítne túos líbros ad legéndum ?
He did not use them.	Non usurpâvit.
He has frequently used my ink, pen, and paper for writing.	Atraménto, pénnâ atque chártâ méis ad scribéndum usitabâtur.

To approach, draw near.	{ *Prope accēdo, ĕre, cessi, cessum* (REM, AD REM).
	{ *Appropinquāre* (REI, AD REM).
To withdraw, or go away from.	{ *Discēdo, ĕre, cessi, cessum* (RE, DE RE, EX LOCO).
	{ *Abire* (AB ALIQUO, A RE, EX LOCO).
Do you come to the fire ?	Accedísne ad fócum (ad carbónes) ?
I do come to it.	Accédo.
He has approached the fire.	Appropinquâvit fóco (ad fócum).
They have withdrawn from the fire.	De fóco discessérunt.
Why does that man go away from the fire ?	Quámobrem vír ílle a fóco discêdit (ábit) ?
He goes away from it because he is not cold.	De fóco discêdit proptérea, quod nôn álget.

---

* On the government of *ūtor*, see Lesson LXXII. *A.*

What do you recollect ?	Quid recordâris ?
I recollect nothing.	Níhil recórdor.

For what? Whereto? For what purpose?	Quo ? Quorsum ? (Ad) quid ? Ad quamnam rem ? Cuinam rei ?
What am I to do with so much money ?	Quô míhi tántam pecúniam ?
For what purpose do I engage in this discussion ?	Quórsum ígitur haêc dísputo ?
What do you want (need) money for ?	Quíd (cuínam réi) tíbi ópus ést pecúniā ?
I want it for buying a carriage.	Ópus ést míhi ad eméndam rhêdam.
What do you wish wine for ?	Ad quid vis vínum ?
(I want some) to drink, to sell.	Ad bibéndum, ad vendéndum.
What does this horse serve you for ?	Ad quíd (cui úsui) est tíbi hícce équus ?
I make use of it for riding.	Adhíbeo éum ad equitándum.
What use is it to philosophize about the matter ?	Quíd ópus ést in hôc philosophíri ?
Many things are not applied to the use for which they were intended.	Múlta nôn ad éum ûsum adhibéntur, cui destinâta súnt.
A quill does not subserve the purpose of a knife.	Cui úsui cúlter, éi nôn est pénna.
To employ, use (for a certain purpose).	Adhíbeo, êre, ŭi, ĭtum (ALIQUID AD REM).
To ride out.	Avĕhi or ēvĕhi equo. Equo vectãri extra urbem.
To drive out.	Carpento (vehicŭlo) vectãri *or* gestãri. Excurrĕre.

EXERCISE 148.

Which is the nearest way (*via proxima* or *brevissĭma*) to go to your uncle's castle ? — This way is shorter than the one we took yesterday ; but my father knows one which is the nearest of all. — Do you use my carriage ? — I do use it. — Has your father used my horse ? — He has used it. — What does this horse serve you for ? — It serves me to ride out upon. — Do you use the books which I lent you ? — I do use them. — May I (*licétne mihi*) use your knife ? — Thou mayest use it, but thou must not cut thyself. — May my brothers use your books ? — They may use them, but they must not tear them. — May we use your stone table ? — You may use it, but you must not spoil it. — For what purpose do your brothers want money ? — They want some to live upon. — What does this knife serve us for ? — It serves us to cut our bread, our meat, and our cheese with. — Is it cold to-day ? — It is very cold. — Will you draw near the fire ? — I cannot draw near it, for I am afraid of burning myself. — Why does your friend go away from the fire ? — He goes away from it because he is afraid of burning himself. — Art thou coming near the fire ? — I am

coming near it, because I am very cold. — Are thy hands cold ? —
My hands are not cold, but my feet are. — Do you go away from the
fire ? — I do go away from it. — Why do you go away from it ? —
Because I am not cold. — Are you cold or warm ? — I am neither
cold nor warm. — Why do your children approach the fire ? — They
approach it, because they are cold. — Is anybody cold ? — Somebody
is cold. — Who is cold ? — The little boy, whose father has lent you a
horse, is cold. — Why does he not warm himself ? — Because his father has no money to buy wood. — Will you tell him to come to me to
warm himself ? — I will tell him so. — Do you remember anything ?
— I remember nothing. — What does your uncle recollect ?   He recollects your promise. — What have I promised him ? — You have
promised him to go to Germany with him next winter. — I intend to
do so if it is not too cold. — Are your hands often cold ? — My hands
are scarcely ever (*nunquam fere*) cold, but my feet are often so. —
Why do you withdraw from the fire ? — I have been sitting near the
fire this hour and a half, so that I am no longer cold. — Does your
friend not like to sit near the fire ? — He likes, on the contrary, much
to sit near the fire, but only when he is cold. — May one approach
your uncle ? — One may approach him, for he excludes nobody
(*januā neminem próhibet*).

Lesson LXXIX. — PENSUM UNDEOCTOGESI-MUM.

DECLENSION OF GREEK NOUNS.

A. Many substantives of the Latin language are derived from the
Greek. They consist partly of general terms (or common nouns),
and partly of proper names of persons and places. These Greek
nouns generally retain more or less of their original inflection, but are
nevertheless referred to the first, second, and third declensions of
Latin nouns.

B. FIRST DECLENSION. — Greek nouns of the first declen-
sion end in $\bar{e}$ feminine, and in $\bar{a}s$, $\bar{e}s$ masculine. In the plural
they are inflected like Latin nouns, but in the singular they
deviate according to the following paradigms : —

Crambe, cabbage, *f.*; *Borĕas*, the north-wind, *m.*; *dynastes*, a ruler, *m.*

Nom.	crambē	Borĕās	dynastēs
Gen.	crambēs	Borĕae	dynastae
Dat.	crambae	Borĕae	dynastae
Acc.	crambēn	Borĕŭm *or* -ān	dynastēn
Voc.	crambē	Borĕā	dynastē
Abl.	crambē.	Borĕā.	dynastē.

Like *crambē*, decline *aloë*, aloes; *epitŏmē*, an abridgment; and the proper names *Circē, Danaë, Phoenĭcē*; — like *Boreas: tiăras*, a turban, and the proper names *Aenēas, Andreas, Midas, Perdiccas*; — like *dynastes: comētes*, the comet; *pyrĭtes*, a species of stone; *satrăpes*, a satrap; and the proper names *Anchĭses, Thersĭtes*, &c.

REMARKS.

1. The majority of these words are proper names. Many of them have a Greek and Latin termination at the same time. E. g. *musĭca* or *musĭce, Europa* or *Europe, Marsyas* or *Marsya, Sophistes* or *Sophista.**

2. The genitive *ēs* (from the nom. *ē*) belongs especially to proper names; as, *Arachnēs, Penelopēs*. So also *musĭcēs, rhetorĭcēs*. But with common nouns the genitive in *ae* is more frequent.

3. The accusative of those in *as* is sometimes *ăn* instead of the more common *am*: as, *Aeneăn, Pythagŏrăn*. So that of nouns in *e* and *es* is occasionally *am* instead of *en*; as, *Andromăcham, Anchisam*, &c.

4. The vocative of proper names and patronymics in *es* is sometimes (though rarely) *a* instead of *ē*; as, *Anchisā*. Sometimes also the Latin termination *ă*; as, *Atridă, Polydectă*.

5. The ablative of words in *e* and *es* is sometimes *a* instead of *ē*. E. g. *Semelā, Anchisā*.

6. Geographical names sometimes form their genitive plural in *ŏn* (instead of *ārum*); as, *Adulĭtŏn*. — Patronymics often have *um* instead of *ārum*; as, *Ausonĭdum, Dardanĭdum*.

7. Many nouns in *es*, especially those which were originally patronymics, pass over into the third declension; as, *Alcibiades, Euripĭdes, Miltiades* (gen. *is*), &c.

C. SECOND DECLENSION. — Greek nouns of the second declension end in *ŏs* or *ōs* masculine, and in *ŏn* neuter. They are thus declined: —

Scorpios, m., a scorpion; *Athōs*, m., Mount Athos; *symposĭon*, n., a banquet.

			SINGULAR.	PLURAL.
NOM.	scorpĭos	Athōs	symposĭon	symposĭa
GEN.	scorpĭi	Athō	symposĭi	symposĭŏn
DAT.	scorpĭo	Athō	symposĭo	symposĭis
ACC.	scorpĭon	Athōn *or* -ō	symposĭon	symposĭa
VOC.	scorpĭ	Athōs	symposĭon	symposĭa
ABL.	scorpĭo.	Athō.	symposĭo,	symposĭis.

So decline *barbĭtos*, a lute; *phasēlos*, the phasel (bean); and the proper names *Andros, Parŏs, Tĭtyŏs; Ceōs, Teōs; Ilĭon, Pelĭon*, &c.

---

* The older Roman authors, Cicero included, prefer the Latin form of the most current of these words. E. g. *grammatĭca, dialectĭca, rhetorĭca; Hecŭba, Sophista, Philoctĕta.* Yet Cicero has also *Archias, Epaminondas, Pythagoras, Perses*, and *Scythes*. The Greek forms *Europe, Helene, Penelope*, rather belong to poetry.

REMARKS.

1. Many of the Greek nouns become Latinized, and assume the regular terminations *us* and *um*. E. g. *camĭnus, cycnus; theatrum, antrum; Aeschylus, Codrus, Homĕrus*, &c. The Greek *ros* is often changed into *er;* as, *Alexander, Menander, Teucer*, instead of *Alexandros*, &c.

2. Among the poets the accusative is often *on*, even in words which have assumed the Latin *us;* as, *Menelaon, Noton*, instead of *Menelaum*, &c.

3. The genitive plural of these nouns is generally the Greek *ōn*, which sometimes occurs even in those otherwise inflected like Latin words. E. g. *Epodōn, Georgĭcōn, Satyrĭcōn*, &c. The genitive singular sometimes ends in *u*, and the nominative plural in *oe;* as, *Menandrū* (= *Menandri*); *Canephŏroe* (= *Canephŏri*).

4. Greek nouns in *ōs* generally retain this *ōs*, but sometimes change it into *ŭs;* as, *Athōs, Androgeōs*, or *Androgĕŭs, Tyndarĕŭs* (gen. *i* and the remaining cases regular). Sometimes they pass over into the third declension ; as, *Athōs, Androgeōs*, gen. *ōnis*.

5. Nouns, which in the original have *oos*, contracted *ŏus*, have in Latin sometimes *ŏus* and sometimes *ūs;* as, *Alcinŏus, Panthūs, periplŭs*. Hence the vocative *Panthū* of Virgil.

6. Nouns in *eus* are often inflected according to the second declension (as if they ended in the dissyllable *ĕus*); as, *Orpheus, i, o, um, eu, o*. But words of this class also belong to the third declension. (Cf. *D*.)

D. THIRD DECLENSION. — 1. Greek nouns of the third declension are all those ending in *ma, i, ān, ĭn, ōn, ēr, y, ȳn, yr, ys, eus, yx, inx, ynx*, and plurals in *ē*.

E. g. *poëma*, a poem ; *hydromĕli*, mead ; *Paeān*, Apollo ; *delphĭn*, a dolphin ; *agōn*, a contest ; *cratēr*, a basin ; *misy̆*, vitriol ; *Phorcȳn; martyr*, a witness ; *chlămys*, a cloak ; *Orpheus; calyx*, a cup ; *syrinx*, a reed ; *lynx*, a lynx ; *cetē*, pl., a sea-monster.

2. Greek nouns are also many of those ending in the Latin terminations *as, es, is, ōs, o*, and *ēn*.

E. g. *lampas*, a torch ; *Demosthenes; basis*, a pedestal ; *Minōs; rhinocerōs; echō; attagēn*, a woodcock.

3. The majority of these words follow the declension of those of Latin origin. E. g. *canōn, canŏnis; calyx, caly̆cis; chlamys, chlamy̆dis; poëma, poëmătis;* * *gigas, gigantis*, &c.

4. Many, however, retain their original terminations in some of the cases, especially among the poets. The following may serve as examples of their declension : —

---

* The dative and ablative plural of this word is more frequently *poëmatis* than *poëmatibus*.

Lampas, f., a torch; lamp.

	Singular.	Plural.
Nom.	lampas	lampădes
Gen.	{ lampădis / lampădos }	lampădum
Dat.	lampădi	lampadĭbus
Acc.	{ lampădem / lampăda }	{ lampădes / lampădas }
Voc.	lampas	lampădes
Abl.	lampăde,	lampadĭbus.

Heros, m., a hero.

	Singular.	Plural.
Nom.	heros	heröes
Gen.	heröis	heröum
Dat.	heröi	heröĭbus
Acc.	{ heröem / heröa }	{ heröes / heröas }
Voc.	heros	heröes
Abl.	heröe,	heröĭbus.

Chělys, f., a cithern.

	Singular.	Plural.
Nom.	chělys	chalÿes
Gen.	{ chelÿis / chelÿos }	chalÿum
Dat.	chelÿi	chalÿbus
Acc.	{ chelym / chelyn }	{ chalÿes / chalÿas }
Voc.	chely	chalÿes
Abl.	{ chelÿe / chely, }	chalÿbus.

Poësis, f., poetry.

	Singular.
Nom.	poësis
Gen.	{ poësis / poësëos }
Dat.	poësi
Acc.	{ poësim / poësin }
Voc.	poësi
Abl.	poësi.

Aër, m., the air.

aër	
aëris	
aëri	
aëra	
aër	
aëre.	

	Achilles, m.	Orphĕus, m.	Chremes, m.	Dido, f.
Nom.	Achilles	Orphĕus	Chremes	Dido
Gen.	{ Achillis / Achillĕos }	{ Orphĕos / Orphĕi or i }	{ Chremis / Chremētis }	{ Didūs / Didōnis }
Dat.	Achilli	Orphĕi or o	Chremi or ĕti	Dido or ōni
Acc.	{ Achillem or ōn / Achillĕa }	{ Orphĕa / Orphĕum }	{ Chremem or ēn / Chemētem or ta }	{ Dido / Didōnem }
Voc.	Achilles or e	Orpheu	Chremes or ē	Dido
Abl.	Achille or i.	Orpheo.*	Chreme or ēte.	Dido or ōne.

REMARKS.

1. The genitive in *os* belongs chiefly to roots in *d, y,* and *i;* as, *Pallădos, Tethÿos, basĕos, mathesĕos.* But it occurs far less frequently than the Greek accusative, and rather in poetry than in prose. With roots in *o* the *os* of the genitive becomes *ūs;* as, *Echūs, Clĭūs, Didūs, Sapphūs,* from *echo,* &c. A number of proper names in *es* form their genitive in *is* or *i;* as, *Demosthenis* or *i, Neoclis* or *i, Periclis* or *i,* from *Demosthenes,* &c. So also *Achilli, Ulyxi.*

2. The Greek accusative singular exhibits the terminations *a, in, yn, ĕn,* instead of the common Latin *em* or *im.*

a) The accusative in *a* occurs in the words *aër — aëra, aether — aethĕra,* and in proper names; as, *Pan — Pana,* &c. Some words have either *a* or *em;* as, *Babylona* or *Babylonem.*

b) The terminations *in, yn,* and *en* are often used by the poets, to

---

* Proper names in *eus* frequently pass over into the second declension.

avoid a hiatus; as, *basin, Halyn, Zeuxin*, instead of *basim, Halym*, &c.
Some nouns in *is, Idos* have *im* or *idem*, and feminines also *ida*: as,
Paris — *Parim* or *Parīdem; Doris* — *Dorim, Dorīdem*, or *Dorīda.*

c) The termination *ēn* belongs to nouns in *ēs*, as, *Aeschinēn,
Achillēn, Demosthenēn*, most of which also admit the Latin *em.*

3. The vocative singular of nouns in *s* differs from the nominative
as follows: — *a*) Those in *as, antis* have *ā*: as, *Pallā, Atlā, Calchā*,
from *Pallas*, &c   *b*) Those in *is* and *ys* have *i* and *y*, as, *Philli,
Tiphy*, from *Phillis, Tiphys*.   *c*) Those in *eus* have *eu*; as, *Orpheu*,
from *Orpheus*.   *d*) Those in *es* have *e*; as, *Achille, Socrate, Pylade.*

4. In the ablative singular roots in *i* generally have *i*; as, *basi, Ne-
apoli*; those in *id* have *ide*, and sometimes *i*; as, *Adonide, Paride;
Osiri*, from *Adonis, ĭdis*, &c.

5. The nominative plural of neuters in *os* is *ē*; as, *melos* — *melē;
epos* — *epē*. To which add the indeclinable plural *Tempē.*

6. The genitive plural in *ōn* occurs only in names of nations and
titles of books; as, *Chalybōn, metamorphoseōn libri.*

7. The termination *si* and *sin*, for the dative and ablative plural,
rarely occurs, and only in the poets; as, *Charĭsin, Lemniăsi*, from the
nominative *Charĭtes, Lemniădes.*

8. The accusative plural in *ăs* (instead of *ēs*) is often used in poetry,
sometimes also in prose; as, *phalangas, Macedŏnas, Allobrŏgas*, &c.

To shave, shave off (any one's beard).	*Rādo, ĕre, si, sum.* *Tondĕo, ēre, totondi, tonsum.* (ALICUJUS BARBAM).*
To shave one's self.	Barbam rādĕre *or* tondĕre; barbam pōnĕre.
To get shaved (by any one).	Rādi, tondēri (ab aliquo).
To get shaved commonly.	Tonsōri opĕram dăre.
To shave every day.	Faciem quotidie rasitāre.
When is your father in the habit of shaving?	Quô témpore bárbam abrádere só-let páter túus?
He shaves every morning, as soon as he gets out of bed.	Bárbam pônit quotídie mâne, simul ac súrgit.
Do you get shaved by the barber?	Tonderísne a tonsôre?
No, I am in the habit of shaving myself.	Nôn véro; égo ípse bárbam tondère consuévi.
The razor. The barber's shears.	Novacŭla, ae, *f.; *culter tonsōrius. Forfex, ĭcis, *f.*
To dress, put on clothes.	*Induĕre se *or* aliquem vestĭbus. Induĕre sibi *or* alicui vestes.*
To undress, put off clothes.	Exuĕre sibi *or* alicui vestes.

---

* *Radĕre* or *abradĕre* is "to shave with the *novacŭla* or razor," or "to
shave," in the modern sense; *tondĕre* is "to take off the beard with the *forfex*
or shears."

To wake, wake up (any one).	Expergefacio, ĕre, fēci, factum. Excito, āre, āvi, ātum. (ALIQUEM E SOMNO).
To awake (out of sleep).	Expergefio, fiĕri, factus sum. Expergiscor, i, experrectus sum. Somno solvor, solvi, solūtus sum.

Have you dressed yourself?   Induistine tibi véstes (tê véstibus)?

I have not yet dressed myself.   Nôndum índui.

Who has dressed the child?   Quis infánti véstes índuit?

Its mother has dressed it.   Máter éjus éi véstes induit.

When do you undress?   Quô témpore tíbi véstes éxuis?

I undress before I go to bed.   Véstes míhi éxuo, ante quam mê in léctum cónfĕro.

Have you waked up your brother this morning?   Expergefecistíne frâtrem túum hódie mâne?

I did not wake him up.   Éum nôn expergeféci.

At what time do you wake up in the morning?   Quô témpore mâne expergíscĕris?

I wake up at daybreak.   Égo prímâ lûce expergíscor.

Did I wake up earlier than you this morning?   Experrectúsne sum égo hódie mâne matúrius quám tû?

You woke up later than I.   Ímmo véro tárdius experréctus és.

Were you waked at eight?   Expergefactúsne és hórâ octávâ?

I was.   Fáctum est.

I wake up at seven every morning.   Égo quotídie mâne sómno solvor hórâ séptimâ.

Do not wake me up so early!   Ne mê tám béne mâne éxcites e sómno!

Stop making a noise, lest you wake me out of sleep!   Desíste tumultuári, ne mê expergefúcĕres!

To behave, conduct one's self.	*Gĕro, ĕre, gessi, gestum* (SE BENE, MALE, &c.).
To behave like, to show *or* prove one's self (a man, &c.).	Praebeo, ēre, ŭi, ĭtum. Praesto, āre, stĭti, stĭtum. (SE VERUM, PROBUM, &c.)
Towards.	Erga, in, adversus. (*Prep. c. Acc.*)
How does he behave (conduct himself)?	Quómodo sê gérit? Quâlem sê praébet?

He behaves well, respectably.   Béne, honéste sê gérit.

They behave badly, very badly, impudently.   Mále, pérperam, contumáciter sê gérunt.

Did the boy behave well towards his master?   Gessítne sê púer honéste érga praeceptôrem?

No, on the contrary, he behaved very badly.   Ímmo pótius pérperam sê géssit.

How did he behave to his fellow-scholars?   Quómodo sê gerêbat advérsus condiscípulos?

He did not behave any better.   Gerêbat sê nôn mélius.

He behaved too impudently.   Gerêbat sê contumácius.

He conducts himself like a citi-   Sê pro cíve gérit.
    zen.
He showed himself a man.   Praébuit sê vírum.
He has shown himself a scholar.   Praéstitit sê dóctum.

To come down, to descend.   *Descendĕre* (de *or* ex aliquo loco).
To ascend, mount, embark, &c.   *Ascendĕre* (locum, in *or* ad locum).

To alight, dismount from a   { Descendĕre ex equo.
    horse.   { Ex equo desilire (-silŭi *or* silii,
                    {   sultum).
To alight from a carriage.   { Descendĕre ex curru.
                     { Degrĕdi ad pĕdes.
To disembark.   Descendĕre *or* egrĕdi e nave.
To descend (sail down) the   Dēvĕhi nave per fluvium.
    river.
To come down the hill.   Descendĕre de colle.
To ascend the hill.   Ascendĕre collem, in collem.
To embark.   Ascendĕre navem, in navem.
To mount a horse.   Ascendĕre (in) equum.
To mount the rostrum.   Escendĕre in rostra.
    The dream.   Somnĭum, i, *n.*
    The beard.   Barba, ae, *f.*
A long, large beard.   Barba longa, promissa, magna.
A rough, grisly beard.   Barba horrída, hirsūta.
To have a strong beard.   Bĕne barbātum esse.
    The garret.   Tabulātum suprēmum ; coenacu-
                     lum, i, *n.*

Where is your brother ?   Úbi ést fráter túus ?
He is in the garret.   In coenáculo est.
Will you ask him to come down ? Vísne éum rogáre, ut descéndat ?
Who has ascended the walls ?   Quis muros ascéndit ?
The soldiers have ascended   Mílites éos scális ascendérunt.
    (scaled) them with ladders.
Did you ever go on board ship? Ascendistíne únquam in navem ?
I have never gone on board.   Núnquam ascéndi.
Do you not wish to get upon the Nónne in équum ascendĕre vis ?
    horse ?
It is so.   Ita ést.
You must ascend (rise) higher. Tê ad majôra ascéndĕre opórtet.
He can rise to the highest honors In súmmum lócum civitâtis ascén-
    of the state.   dere pótest.
Let us go down to our boats.   Descendâmus ad nóstras naviculas.
Did your cousin go down into   Núm patruêlis túus in púteum de-
    the well ?   scéndit ?
He did not do it.   Nôn fáctum ést.
What time was your father in the Quô tempôre ad fórum descendê-
    habit of going down to the   bat páter túus ?
    market ?
He usually went down there at   Descéndere solêbat hórā undécimā.
    eleven o'clock.

They dismounted.	Ex équis descendérunt.
The queen dismounted from her charger.	Ab équo regina desíluit.
From heaven descended the injunction, " Know thyself."	Ex coélo descéndit nósce té ípsum.

To be worth while.	{ *Esse opěrae pretǐum.* { *Est pretǐum.*
It is better.	*Mělǐus* or *satǐus est, praestat.*
Is it worth while to do this ?	Éstne ópěrae prétium hóc fácere ?
It is not worth while.	Nôn ést óperae prétium.
Is it worth while to write to him ?	Estne prétium dáre litteras ad éum ?
It is.	Est.
Is it better ?	Éstne mélius ? Satiúsne ést ? Praestátne ?
It is better.	Ést mélius, &c.
It is better to do this than that.	Mělius (sátius) ést fácere hóc, quam íllud.
It is better to stay here than to go a walking.	Praéstat híc manêre, quam ambulátum íre.

EXERCISE 149.

Have you shaved to-day ? — I have shaved. — Has your brother shaved? — He has not shaved himself, but has got shaved. — Do you shave often ? — I shave every morning, and sometimes also in the evening. — When do you shave in the evening ? — When I do not dine at home. — How many times a day does your father shave? — He shaves only once a day, but my brother has such a strong beard, that he is obliged to shave twice a day. — Does your uncle shave often ? — He shaves only every other day (*tertio quŏque die*) for his beard is not strong. — At what o'clock do you dress in the morning? — I dress as soon as I have breakfasted, and I breakfast every day at eight o'clock, or at a quarter past eight. — Does your neighbor dress before he breakfasts ? — He breakfasts before he dresses. — At what o'clock in the evening dost thou undress? — I undress as soon as I return from the theatre. — Dost thou go to the theatre every evening ? — I do not go every evening, for it is better to study than to go to the theatre. — At what o'clock dost thou undress when thou dost not go to the theatre ? — I then undress as soon as I have supped, and go to bed at ten o'clock. — Have you already dressed the child ? — I have not dressed it yet, for it is still asleep. — At what o'clock does it get up ? — It gets up as soon as it is waked. — Do you rise as early as I ? — I do not know at what o'clock you rise, but I rise as soon as I awake. — Will you tell my servant to wake me to-morrow at four o'clock ? — I will tell him. — Why have you risen so early ? — My children have made such a noise that they wakened me. — Have you slept well ? — I have not slept well, for you made too much noise. — At what o'clock must I wake you ? — To-morrow thou mayest wake me at six o'clock. — At what o'clock did the good captain awake ? — He awoke at a quarter past five in the morning.

EXERCISE 150.

When did this man go down into the well? — He went down into
it this morning. — Has he come up again? — He came up an hour
ago. — Where is your brother? — He is in his room. — Will you tell
him to come down? — I will tell him so; but he is not dressed yet. —
Is your friend still on the mountain? — He has already come down.
— Did you go down or up this river? — We went down it. — Has
your brother dined already? — He dined as soon as he had alighted
from his horse. — Is your uncle already asleep? — I believe that he
is asleep, for he went to bed as soon as he had alighted. — Did my
cousin speak to you before he started? — He spoke to me before he
got into the coach. — Have you seen my brother? — I saw him before I went on board the ship. — How did my child behave? — He
did behave very well. — How did my brother behave towards you?
He behaved very well towards me, for he behaves well towards everybody. — Is it worth while to write to that man? — It is not worth
while to write to him. — Is it worth while to alight in order to buy a
cake? — It is not worth while, for it is not long since we ate. — Is it
worth while to dismount from my horse in order to give something to
that poor man? — Yes, for he seems to want it; but you can give
him something without dismounting from your horse. — Is it better
to go to the theatre than to study? — It is better to do the latter
than the former. — Is it better to go to bed than to go a walking? —
It is better to do the latter than the former. — Is it better to get into
a coach than to go on board the ship? — It is not worth while to get
into a coach or to go on board the ship when one has no wish to
travel.

Lesson LXXX. — PENSUM OCTOGESIMUM.

DERIVATION OF ADJECTIVES.

A. Adjectives are either primitive or derivative; as, *bŏnus, mălus;
puerĭlis, amabĭlis.* Derivatives are formed from verbs (*verbals*), from
nouns (*denominatives*), from other adjectives, and sometimes from
adverbs (*adverbials*) and prepositions (*prepositionals*). All these are
subdivided into various classes, and characterized by peculiar terminations.

B. Adjectives derived from verbs end in *bundus, cundus,
ĭdus, ŭus, ĭlis, bĭlis, ax,* and *ŭlus.*

1. Those in *bundus* are formed chiefly from verbs of the first conjugation, and generally agree in sense with the present participle.
Sometimes, however, they convey the accessory notion of fulness or
abundance. E. g. *errabundus, populabundus,* wandering, pillaging

(from *errare, populāri*).   So also *hesitabundus, lacrīmabundus, mira-bundus*, full of hesitation, of tears, of wonder.   A few verbs in *cundus* have a similar sense; as, *rubicundus*, ruddy; *iracundus*, given to anger; *verecundus*, bashful, respectful.

2. Those in *tdus* are generally from intransitive verbs, and simply express the quality implied in the verb.   E. g. *calĭdus*, warm; *algĭdus*, cold; *rubĭdus*, red, reddish; *rapĭdus*, rapid (from *calēre, algēre, rubēre, rapēre*).   A few in *ŭus* have a similar signification; as, *assĭdŭus, con-grŭus, nocŭus* (from *assidēre, congruĕre, nocēre*).   But those in *ŭus* from transitive verbs have a passive sense; as, *conspicŭus*, visible; *in-dividŭus*, indivisible.

3. Those in *ĭlis* and *bĭlis* have a passive sense, and denote possibility or capacity.   E. g. *facĭlis*, easy (to be done); *fragĭlis*, fragile; *ama-bĭlis*, amiable; *delēbĭlis*, easy to destroy; *placabĭlis*, easily appeased. Some of them, however, are active; as, *horribĭlis, terribĭlis, fertĭlis*, &c.

4. Those in *ax* denote an inclination or propensity, frequently a vicious one.   E. g. *edax* and *vorax*, voracious; *furax*, thievish; *audax*, audacious; *rapax*, rapacious (from *edĕre, vorāre*, &c.).   The few in *ŭlus* are analogous; as, *bibŭlus*, given to drinking; *credŭlus*, credulous; *querŭlus*, querulous.

C.   The substantives from which derivative adjectives are formed are either *common nouns* or *proper names* of men and places.

I. Adjectives derived from common nouns end in *ĕus, ĭcus, ĭlis, ācĕus* or *icĭus, ālis, ātĭlis, ŭus, ĭnus (īnus), ārĭus, ōsus (nōsus), lentus, ĭvus, ernus, urnus, itĭmus, ster, ātus, ĭtus*, and *ūtus*.

1. The termination *ĕus* designates the material of which anything consists or is made, and sometimes also resemblance.   E. g. *aurĕus, ferrĕus, plumbĕus*, made of gold, iron, lead; *ignĕus, vitrĕus*, igneous, glassy.   Some of this class end either in *neus* or *nus*; as, *eburnĕus* or *eburnus*, of ivory; *quernĕus* or *quernus*, of oak.

2. Those in *ĭcus* and *ĭlis* signify "belonging or relating to," the for-mer in a general, the latter in a moral sense.   E. g. *aulĭcus, bellĭcus, rustĭcus*, relating to the court, to war, to the country; *puerĭlis, senĭlis, virĭlis*, belonging (peculiar) to the age of boyhood, old age, manhood. Sometimes both from the same noun; as, *civĭcus* and *civĭlis, hostĭcus* or *hostĭlis*.

3. The terminations *acĕus* and *icĭus* sometimes denote the material, and sometimes descent.   E. g. *chartacĕus, membranacĕus, cementicĭus*, made of paper, membrane, cement; *patrĭcius, tribunĭcius*, patrician, tribunitial.

4. Those in *ālis, āris*, and *atĭlis* are formed not only from nouns in *a*, but also from those of other terminations.   E. g. *ancorālis*, relating to an anchor; *convivālis*, convivial; *regālis*, royal, regal; *virginālis*,

43

virginal.* The termination *āris* is generally put when the letter *l* precedes; as, *consulāris, puellāris, vulgāris, Apollināris;* — *ātĭlis* conveys the sense of fitness; as, *aquātĭlis, volātĭlis.*

5. The termination *ĭus* belongs principally to substantives in *or;* as, *amatorĭus, censorĭus, imperatorĭus,* pertaining to love (or lovers), to the censor, to a commander. Sometimes also to other substantives; as, *regĭus, patrĭus,* royal, fatherly.

6. Adjectives in *ĭnus* are chiefly derived from names of animals, especially to denote the flesh of the same. E. g. *anatīnus, anserīnus, asinīnus, canīnus, equīnus, ferīnus, taurīnus,* of a duck, goose, ass, dog, horse, wild beast, bull.† Sometimes also from names of other beings; as, *masculīnus, feminīnus, divīnus, libertīnus.* Those in *ĭnus* are derived either from names of plants or minerals, or from words denoting time; as, *cedrīnus, fagīnus, adamantīnus,* of cedar, beech, adamant; *crastīnus, annotīnus, hornotīnus,* of to-morrow, of last year, of this year.

7. Those in *ārĭus* properly denote a trade or profession, sometimes also a more general relation. E. g. *carbonarĭus, coriarĭus, ostiarĭus, statuarĭus,* a collier, tanner, porter, statuary;‡ *aerarĭus, argentarĭus,* relating to copper, to silver (or money).

8. The terminations *ōsus* and *lentus* express fulness or abundance. E. g. *aerumnōsus, artificiōsus, tenebricōsus,* full of misfortune, of skill, of darkness; *corpulentus, fraudulentus, pulverulentus,* &c. Nouns of the fourth declension commonly have *uōsus;* as, *actuōsus,* full of action; *portuōsus, saltuōsus,* abounding in ports, in woods.

9. The terminations *ivus, ernus, urnus, ŭrnus,* and *ster* denote quality, manner, descent, time, place, &c. E. g. *furtivus, aestivus, natīvus,* secret, of the summer, native; *externus, maternus, paternus,* external, maternal, paternal; *diurnus, nocturnus, hibernus, vernus,* of the day, night, winter, spring; — *legitĭmus, maritĭmus,* legitimate, maritime; — *campester,* of the plain; *pedester,* pedestrian.

10. An extensive class of adjectives, ending in *ātus* (sometimes *ĭtus* or *ŭtus*), have the form and sense of the perfect participle, but are derived from nouns. E. g. *barbātus, dentātus, galeātus, falcātus,* furnished with a beard, with teeth, with a helmet, with scythes; *aurītus,* provided with ears; *pellĭtus,* covered with skins; *cornūtus,* horned; *nasūtus,* having a large (or acute) nose.

II. The adjectives derived from proper names may be divided into those formed from, — *a*) names of individuals; *b*) names of cities; *c*) names of nations; *d*) names of countries.

1. Adjectives derived from names of men end in *iānus, ānus, ĕus,* and *ĭnus;* as, *Caesariānus, Catoniānus, Ciceroniānus; Cinnānus, Sullānus; Caesarĕus, Herculĕus; Jugurthīnus, Plautīnus,* &c. The last

---

* So also from proper names; as, *Augustālis, Flaviālis, Trajanālis,* &c.

† When these adjectives denote the flesh of animals, the feminine is used with *caro* understood; as, *anserina, anatina, ferina, taurina,* &c.

‡ In this sense they stand substantively; but as adjectives proper they signify "relating to charcoal, leather, a door or doors, statuary."

of these terminations belongs more especially to derivative family names; as, *Paulinus, Rufinus, Agrippina, Plancina*, &c.

To these add the adjectives in *ēus, ius, ĭcus*, and *ĭdcus*, derived from Greek names of men. E. g. *Achillēus, Sophoclēus; Antiochius, Aristotelius; Homericus, Isocraticus; Archidcus.* Sometimes there are two of them (one in *ēus*, the other in *ĭcus*) from the same noun; as, *Philippēus* and *Philippicus, Pythagorēus* and *Pythagoricus.*

2. Adjectives derived from names of cities end in *ensis, inus, as,* and *ānus.* E. g. *Cannae — Canensis, Antiochia — Antiochensis; Florentia — Florentinus, Latium — Latinus; Arpinum — Arpinas, Privernum — Privernas; Roma — Romānus, Sparta — Spartānus.* To these add those in *ius* and *aeus* derived from Greek names of cities; as, *Corinthus — Corinthius, Ephesus — Ephesius; Larissa — Larissaeus, Smyrna — Smyrnaeus.*

3. Primitive names of nations give rise to adjectives in *icus* and *ius.* E. g. *Afer — Africus, Gallus — Gallicus, Scytha — Scythicus; Syrus — Syrius, Thrax — Thracius,* &c. Some of them are patrial substantives and adjectives at the same time; as, *Graecus, Etruscus, Sardus.*

4. The names of countries are generally themselves derivatives; as, *Gallia, Italia, Thracia* (from *Gallus, Italus, Thrax*). Some of these, however, give rise to adjectives in *ensis* and *ānus;* as, *Graeciensis, Hispaniensis; Africānus, Germanicānus,* &c. To these add two in *iācus: Aegyptiācus, Syriācus.*

D. Derivatives from other adjectives end in *ŭlus, ŏlus, cŭlus, ellus,* and *ānĕus.*

1. All of these except those in *ānĕus* are diminutives. E. g. *parvŭlus, primŭlus; paupercŭlus, levicŭlus; novellus, pulchellus;* some have even a double diminutive; as, *paucus — paulus* and *paulŭlus* (*pauxillus* and *pauxillŭlus*), *bonus — bellus, bellŭlus.*

2. Those in *ānĕus* are formed from adjectives in *us,* and denote similarity of quality. E. g. *rejectanĕus,* to be rejected; *collectaneus,* collected; *subitaneus,* sudden. And after the analogy of these, *consentaneus, praecidaneus, succidaneus.*

To hire, rent.	*Condūco, ĕre, duxi, ductum.* *Mercēde conducĕre* (ALIQUID AB ALIQUO).
To hire a house, a room.	*Domicilium,* conclāve (mercēde) *conducĕre.*
To live in a hired house.	*In condŭcto habitāre.*
The rent.	*Pretium conducti, pretium habitatiōnis.*
To let, rent.	*Locāre, elocāre* (ALICUI ALIQUID).
To part with any one or any thing.	*Demittĕre, missum facĕre, vendĕre aliquem or aliquid.*
To get rid of any one.	*Absolvĕre, dimittĕre aliquem.*

To get rid of anything.	Extrūdĕre (trūsi, trūsum) aliquid; vendĕre.
To get rid of debts.	Debĭta dissolvĕre.
Have you already hired a room?	Conduxistine jám conclắve?
Yes, I have hired one.	Véro, condúxi ûnum.
Does he live in a hired house?	Núm in condúcto hábitat?
He does not.	Nôn in condúcto hábitat.
Have they paid their rent?	Solverúntne prétium habitatiônis?
They have not yet paid it.	Nôndum solvérunt.
Have you a room to let?	Habêsne cubículum ad locándum?
I have none.	Nôn hábeo.
Do you intend to part with your horses?	Cogitâsne submovêre (véndere) équos?
I have already parted with them.	Égo éos jám pridem submóvi (véndidi).
He has parted with his carriage.	Piléntum síum dimisit (véndidit).
We have parted with our servant.	Sérvum nóstrum míssum fécimus.
Did you get rid of your damaged sugar?	Extrusistĭne sáccharum tíum depérditum?
I did get rid of it.	Extrúsi.
Did he get rid of his old horse?	Vendidítne équum súum vétulum?
He did not get rid of it.	Nôn véndidit.

To hope, expect.	*Sperāre, spem habēre, in spe esse.*
I hope.	Spéro, spês mê ténet.
As I hope.	Ut spéro, spéro.
To wait, tarry.	Exspectāre; spem pōnĕre (in aliquo *or* in aliquā re).

Do you expect (hope) to find him there?	Sperâsne, tê éum íbi invenire (inventûrum ésse)?
I do expect it.	Spéro. Spês mê ténet.
I hope that my father will come.	{ Spéro, pátrem ésse ventûrum. Spéro, fóre, ut páter véniat.
Our brother will come, I hope.	{ Fráter, ut spéro, véniet. Fráter, spéro, véniet.
I hope that our friendship will last for ever.	Spéro, aetérnam inter nôs amicítiam fóre.
I hope that I may meet you.	{ Spéro, fóre, ut égo tíbi óbviam véniam. Spéro, mê tíbi óbviam venire (ventûrum ésse).
Do you put your trust in God?	Ponísne spém in Déo?
I do.	Póno.
I hope no longer.	Spéro nôn ámplius.
You have no reason to hope.	Nôn ést, quód spéres.

To change.	*Muto, āre, āvi, ātum.*
To exchange, change.	*Commutāre, permutāre.*

To change, exchange one thing for another.	{ Mutāre *or* permutāre aliquid (cum) aliquā re. Commutāre aliquid cum aliquā re.
To exchange (mutually).	Res inter se mutāre *or* permutāre.
To change masters.	Dominos permutāre.
To exchange names.	Nomīna inter se permutāre.
To change one's clothes, one's hat, &c.	Mutāre vestem, pileum, &c.
To change one's horse.	{ Mutāre equum. Altĕri equo injici.
To change (draught-) horses.	Jumenta mutāre.
To change money.	Pecuniam (nummum) permutāre.
To exchange letters, to correspond with any one.	{ *Littĕras dăre et accipĕre.* *Litterārum commercio ūti.* *Per litteras cum aliquo colloqui or agĕre.*
To put on one's hat.	{ Pileum impōnĕre capĭti. Caput tegĕre (texi, tectum) pileo.
To put on linen.	Induĕre sibi lintea (se linteis).
To put on a cravat.	{ Induĕre collum focāli. Circumligāre collum focāli.
The linen.	Lintea, *n. pl.*
The cravat, neckcloth.	Focāle, is, *n. ;* pannus colāris.

Will you change your clothes?   Visne mutāre véstem?
I do not wish to change them.   Nólo mutāre.
Has he changed his linen, hat, cravat?   Mutavítne súa líntea, píleum, focále?
He has changed it.   Mutâvit.
Must I change my shirt?   Oportétne me mutáre indúsium?
It is proper that you should do so.   Opórtet tû hóc fácias.

Have they exchanged anything?   Commutaveríntne áliquid?
They have exchanged wine for oil, and oil for wine.   Commutavérunt vínum pro óleo et óleum pro víno.
They have exchanged a correct state of the republic for a false one.   Commutavérunt státum reipúblicae ex véro in fálsum.
They are bartering away honor and religion for money.   Fídem et religiônem pecúniā commútant.
Do you wish to change hats with me?   Vísne píleos mêcum permutáre?
I am not unwilling.   Nôn nólo.
They have exchanged gloves.   Digitábula inter sê permutavérunt.
Can you change me an aureus?   Potésne míhi permutáre aúreum?
I cannot.   Nôn póssum.
I have exchanged a florin for sixty kreutzers.   Égo florênum sexaginta kreútzeris permutávi.
The color has changed from black to white.   E nígro color éjus mutâtus ést in álbum.

43 *

Everything undergoes change.	Ómnia mutántur.
Has he changed his horse ?	{ Mutavítne équum ? { Injectúsne est álteri óquo ?
He has not changed it.	Nôn mutâvit.
Do you exchange letters (correspond) with your friend ?	Agísne (colloquerísne) per lítteras cum amíco túo ?
I do correspond with him.	Véro, ágo (cólloquor).
I correspond with all my friends.	Égo litterârum commercio cum amícis meís ómnibus útor.

To mix, mingle.	{ Misceo, ēre, miscŭi, mistum or mixtum. { Insĕro, ĕre, ŭi, rtum.
To mix or mingle among men.	Se immiscēre or inserĕre homínibus (dat.).
To mix, meddle with anything.	Se admiscēre or interponĕre alicui rei.
Not to meddle with, to refrain from anything.	Abesse or se abstinēre ab aliquâ re.
Does he meddle with your affairs ?	Admiscétne sê negótiis túis ?
He never meddles with other people's affairs.	Núnquam ílle sê negótiis aliénis admiscet (interpônit).
Have you mixed much among men ?	Immiscuistíne tê múltum homínibus ?
I have mixed much and often among them.	Íta ést, mê múltum ac saépe immíscui.
He mixes with the soldiers.	Míscet sê milítibus.

To recognize ; to acknowledge.	{ Recognosco, ĕre, nōvi, nĭtum. { Agnoscĕre (ALIQUEM, REM).
Do you recognize this man ?	Recognoscísne húnc hóminem ?
It is so long since I saw him, that I do not recollect him.	Túm díu est, ex quô éum nôn vídi, ut (éum) nôn recognóscam.
We ought to recognize God from his works.	Nôs Déum ex opéribus súis agnóscere opórtet.
I acknowledge my error.	Errôrem méum agnósco.

EXERCISE 151.

Have you already hired a room ? — I have already hired one. — Where have you hired it ? — I have hired it in William Street, number one hundred and fifty-one. — At whose house have you hired it ? — At the house of the man whose son has sold you a horse. — For · whom has your father hired a room ? — He has hired one for his son who has just arrived from Germany. — Did you at last get rid of that man ? — I did get rid of him. — Why has your father parted with his horses ? — Because he did not want them any more. — Have you discharged your servant ? — I have discharged him, because he served me no more well. — Why have you parted with your carriage ? — Because I do not travel any more. — Has your merchant succeeded

at last in getting rid of his damaged sugar ? — He has succeeded in
getting rid of it. — Has he sold it on credit ? — He was able to sell it
for cash, so that he did not sell it on credit. — Do you hope to arrive
early in Paris ? — I hope to arrive there at a quarter past eight, for
my father is waiting for me this evening. — For what have you exchanged your carriage which you no longer made use of ? — I have
exchanged it for a fine Arabian horse. — Do you wish to exchange
your book for mine ? — I cannot, for I want it to study German with.
Why do you take your hat off ? — I take it off, because I see my old
writing-master coming. — Do you put on another hat to go to the
market ? — I do not put on another to go to the market, but to go to
the great concert.

EXERCISE 152.

Why does your father put on other clothes ? — He is going to the
king, so that he must put on others. — Have you put on another hat
to go to the English captain ? — I have put on another, but I have
not put on another coat or other boots. — How many times a day
dost thou put on other clothes ? — I put on others to dine and to go
to the theatre. — Do you often put on a clean shirt (change your
shirt) ? — I put on a clean one every morning. — When does your
father put on a clean shirt ? — He puts it on when he goes to the
ball. — Does he put on a clean cravat (change his cravat) as often as
you ? — He puts one on oftener than I, for he does so six times a day.
— Did you often take fresh horses when you went to Vienna ? — I
took fresh ones every three hours. — Will you change me this gold
coin ? — I am going to change it for you; what money (*Quid nummórum*) do you wish for it ? — I wish to have crowns, florins, and
kreutzers. — Do you correspond with my friend ? — I do correspond
with him. — How long have you been corresponding with my brother ?
— I have been corresponding with him these six years almost. — Why
do you mix among those people ? — I mix among them in order to
know what they say of me. — Have you recognized your father ? —
I had not seen him for such a long time, that I did not recognize him.
— Do you still speak Latin ? — It is so long since I spoke it, that I
have nearly (*fere*) forgotten it all (*omnino*).

Lesson LXXXI. — PENSUM UNUM ET OCTO-GESIMUM.

OF THE FUTURE TENSE.

A. The future tense represents an action or event
that will take place hereafter. This action may be considered either as incomplete or going on at some time

to come (First or Simple Future), or as completed
(Future Perfect). E. g.

> Scríbam, *I shall write (shall be engaged in writing)*.
> Amábitur, *He will be loved (will be the object of love)*.
> Scrípsěro, *I shall have written.*
> Amâtus érit, *He will have been loved.*

B. FORMATION OF THE FIRST FUTURE.

1. The first future active is formed from the present indica-
tive by changing, 1. *o*, 2. *eo*, 3. *o* (*ĭo*), 4. *ĭo*, into, 1. *ābo*, 2. *ēbo*,
3. *am* (*ĭam*), 4. *ĭam.* As,

> 1. ămo — ămābo, *I shall or will love.*
> 2. mŏnĕo — mŏnēbo, *I shall or will remind.*
> 3. lĕgo — lĕgam, *I shall or will read.*
> (3.) cŭpio — căpĭam, *I shall or will take.*
> 4. audĭo — audĭam, *I shall or will hear.*

2. The first future passive is formed from the active, by
changing the final *m* into *r.* As,

> 1. amābo — amābor, *I shall or will be loved.*
> 2. mŏnēbo — monēbor, *I shall or will be reminded.*
> 3. lĕgam — lĕgar, *I shall or will be read.*
> (3.) cŭpĭam — căpĭar, *I shall or will be taken.*
> 4. audĭam — audĭar, *I shall or will be heard.*

3. The future of deponent verbs follows the analogy of the
passive. As,

> 1. hortor — hortābor, *I shall or will exhort.*
> 2. věrěor — věrēbor, *I shall or will fear.*
> 3. lŏquor — lŏquar, *I shall or will speak.*
> 4. blandĭor — blandĭar, *I shall or will flatter.*

REMARK. — The subjunctive mood wants both the future tenses.
On the manner of indicating future contingent action, see *F.*

INFLECTION OF THE FIRST FUTURE.

C. The following paradigms exhibit the inflection
of the first future, active and passive.

ACTIVE.	PASSIVE.
FIRST CONJUGATION.	
Amābo, *I shall or will love.*	Amābor, *I shall or will be loved.*
SING. ămābŏ	SING. ămābŏr
ămābĭs	ămăbĕrĭs *or* -rĕ
ămābĭt,	ămăbĭtŭr,

ACTIVE.	PASSIVE.
PLUR. ămābĭmŭs	PLUR. ămābĭmŭr
ămābĭtĭs	ămābĭmĭnĭ
ămābunt.	ămābuntur.

SECOND CONJUGATION.

Mŏnēbo, *I shall or will remind.*   Mŏnēbŏr, *I shall or will be reminded.*   •

SING. mŏnēbŏ	SING. mŏnēbŏr
mŏnēbĭs	mŏnēbērĭs *or* -rĕ
mŏnēbĭt,	mŏnĕbĭtŭr,
PLUR. mŏnēbĭmŭs	PLUR. mŏnēbĭmŭr
mŏnēbĭtĭs	mŏnēbĭmĭnĭ
mŏnēbunt.	mŏnēbuntŭr.

THIRD CONJUGATION.

Lĕgăm, *I shall or will read.*   Lĕgăr, *I shall or will be read.*

SING. lĕgăm	SING. lĕgăr
lĕgēs	lĕgērĭs *or* -rĕ
lĕgĕt,	lĕgētŭr,
PLUR. lĕgēmŭs	PLUR. lĕgēmŭr
lĕgētĭs	lĕgēmĭnĭ
lĕgent.	lĕgentŭr.

FOURTH CONJUGATION.

Audĭăm, *I shall or will hear.*   Audĭăr, *I shall or will be heard.*

SING. audĭăm	SING. audĭăr
audĭēs	audĭērĭs *or* -rĕ
audĭĕt,	audĭētŭr,
PLUR. audĭēmŭs	PLUR. audĭēmŭr
audĭētĭs	audĭēmĭnĭ
audĭent.	audĭentur.

So conjugate *apportăbo*, I shall bring; *curăbo*, I shall order; *dăbo*, I shall give; *laudăbo*, I shall praise; *lavăbo*, I shall wash; *regnăbo*, I shall rule; *secăbo*, I shall cut; *stăbo*, I shall stand; *vocăbo*, I shall call; — *audēbo*, I shall dare; *docēbo*, I shall teach; *gaudēbo*, I shall rejoice; *habēbo*, I shall have; *jubēbo*, I shall command; *studēbo*, I shall study; *tenēbo*, I shall hold; — *ăgam*, I shall act (do); *facĭam*, I shall make (do); *mittam*, I shall send; *pōnam*, I shall place (put); *scrĭbam*, I shall write; *sumam*, I shall take; — *aperĭam*, I shall open; *finĭam*, I shall finish; *punĭam*, I shall punish; *reperĭam*, I shall find; *sentĭam*, I shall feel; *venĭam*, I shall come; *invenĭam*, I shall find, &c.

To the above add the impersonal futures: *constăbit, fulgurăbit, gelăbit, grandinăbit, juvăbit, praestabit, restăbit;* — *apparēbit, attinēbit, debēbit, dolēbit, nocēbit, pertinēbit, placēbit, solēbit;* — *accĭdet, incipiet, lucescet, ninget, pluet, refĕret;* — *convenĭet, expedĭet,* &c. (Cf. Lesson LV.)

2 G

FUTURE OF DEPONENT VERBS.

D. The future of deponent verbs is inflected like that of the passive voice. Thus : —

Hortābor, *I shall or will exhort.*   Lŏquar, *I shall or will speak.*

SING. hortābŏr   SING. lŏquăr
.   hortābĕrĭs *or* -rĕ   lŏquĕrĭs *or* -rĕ
      hortābĭtŭr,   lŏquētŭr,
PLUR. hortābĭmŭr   PLUR. lŏquēmŭr
      hortābĭmĭnĭ   lŏquēmĭnĭ
      hortābuntŭr.   lŏquentŭr.

Verēbor, *I shall or will fear.*   Blandĭar, *I shall or will flatter.*

SING. verēbŏr   SING. blandĭăr
      verēbĕrĭs *or* -re   blandĭĕrĭs *or* -rĕ
      verēbĭtŭr,   blandĭētŭr,
PLUR. verēbĭmŭr   PLUR. blandĭēmŭr
      verēbĭmĭnĭ   blandĭēmĭnĭ
      verēbuntŭr.   blandĭentŭr.

So *arbitrābor*, I shall think; *comitābor*, I shall escort; *morābor*, I shall delay ; — *merēbor*, I shall earn; *miserēbor*, I shall pity ; *tuēbor*, I shall defend ; — *lābar*, I shall glide (fall); *obliviscar*, I shall forget; *proficiscar*, I shall depart; *sequar*, I shall follow ; — *experĭar*, I shall experience ; *largĭar*, I shall lavish, &c.

FUTURE OF IRREGULAR VERBS.

E. The future of *sum* is irregular ; *volo, fero, edo,* and *fio* follow the analogy of the third conjugation, *ĕo* and *quĕo* that of the fourth. E. g.

1. Ēro, *I shall or will be.*
     SING. ĕro, ĕrĭs, ĕrĭt ; PLUR. ĕrĭmus, ĕrĭtĭs, ĕrunt.
So *adĕro*, I shall be present ; *potĕro*, (from *possum*), I shall be able, and all the remaining compounds of *sum.*

2. Vŏlam, *I shall wish or be willing.* |
     SING. vŏlăm, vŏlēs, vŏlĕt ; PLUR. vŏlēmŭs, vŏlētĭs, vŏlent.
So *mālăm*, I shall prefer, and *nōlăm*, I shall be unwilling.

3. Fĕram, *I shall bear (carry),* ĕdam, *I shall eat,* and fīam, *I shall become,* are regularly inflected like *lĕgam.* So also their compounds ; as, *affĕram, comĕdam, calefĭam,* &c.

4. Ibo, *I shall or will go.*
     SING. ibo, ībis, ībit ; PLUR. ībĭmus, ībĭtĭs, ībunt.
So all its compounds ; as, *adĭbo, inĭbo, praeterĭbo, subĭbo, transĭbo,* &c. And in the passive impersonally *ĭbĭtur, inĭbĭtur,* &c.

5. The future of *queo* and *nequeo* is defective, *quibo, quibunt,* and *nequibunt* being the only persons in use.

Shall you love? ・ Amabísne? Num amábis?
I shall not love. Nôn amábo.
Will he have money? Habebítne pecúniam?
He will not have any. Nôn habêbit.
Shall you command him to Jubebísne éum abíre?
leave?
I shall command him. Jubébo.
Shall you send me the book? Mittêsne míhi líbrum?
I shall send it. Míttam.
Shall ye write letters? Scribetísne epístolas?
We shall write some. Véro, scribêmus nonnúllas.
Will they come or go away? Útrum ílli vénient an abíbunt?
They will come. Vénient.
Will he be contented? Erítne conténtus?
He will. Érit.
They will not be contented. Nôn érunt conténti.
Will it rain or snow to-day? Pluétne hódie an nínget?
Shall you exhort him to speak? Hortaberísne éum, ut vérba fáciat?
I shall exhort him. Hortâbor.
Will he defend us? Núm nôs tuébitur?
He will not defend us. Nôs nôn tuébitur.
Will they forget their duty? Obliviscentúrne offícia súa?
He will not forget them. Nôn obliviscéntur.
Shall ye squander any money? Númquid pecúniae largiémini?
We shall not squander any at all. Núllam omníno largiêmur.
Will we be loved? Amabimúrne? Nôsne amábimur?
You will not be loved. Nôn amabímini.
Will our books be read? Legentúrne líbri nóstri?
They will certainly be read. Legéntur síne úllâ dubitatiône.

FUTURE SUBJUNCTIVE.

F. Latin verbs have no special form for the future subjunctive. When, in dependent clauses, it becomes necessary to express future contingent action, the Romans proceed as follows: —

I. If the main clause contains a verb of the future tense, the present or imperfect subjunctive supplies the place of the first future subjunctive in the dependent clause. E. g.

Affírmo tíbi, si hóc beneficiam míhi *tríbuas*, mê magnópere *gavisúrum.*
If you will do me this favor, I assure you that I shall be greatly delighted.

Affirmábam tíbi, si íllud beneffícium míhi *tribúeres*, magnópere me gavisûrum.
I assured you that I should be greatly delighted, if you would do me that favor.

Affírmo tíbi, si hóc beneffícium míhi *tribuâtur*, me magnópere gavisûrum.
I assure you, that, if this favor is done me, I shall be greatly delighted.

Éum, ni *páreat* pátri, *habitûrum* infortúnium *ésse* díxit.

He said that he (i. e. the son) would be unfortunate, unless he obeyed his father.

Ex his quidam dixísse dícitur, *fôre, ut* brévi a Gállis Rôma *caperêtur.*

One of these is reported to have said, that Rome would in a short time be taken by the Gauls.

Tû si quíd fôrte ad mê scrípsĕris, *perficiam, ne* tê frústra scripsísse *arbitrêre.*

If you perchance shall write me, I will see that you shall not think that you have written to no purpose.

II. When no verb of the future tense precedes, and the construction still requires a future subjunctive, the participle in *rus*, with *sim* or *essem*, is employed. E. g.

Nôn dúbito, *quin reditûrus sit.*

I do not doubt but that he will return.

Nôn dubitâbam, *quin reditûrus ésset.*

I did not doubt but that he would return.

His de rêbus, quid *actûrus sis,* rescríbas míhi vélim.

I wish you to write to me, what you intend to do about these matters.

Nôn débes dubitâre, *quin sis futûrus,* qui ésse débes.

You should not doubt but that you will be what you ought to be.

Nôn dúbito, quin *futûrum sit, ut laudêtur.*

I do not doubt but he will be praised.

Múlti non dubitábant, *quin futûrum ésset, ut* Caesar a Pompéjo vincerêtur.

Many were convinced (did not doubt) that Cæsar would be conquered by Pompey.

Nescio, num *futûrum sit,* ut crâs hôc ípso témpore jam redíerit.

I do not know whether he will have returned to-morrow at this time.

The dust; the mud; the smoke.	*Pulvis, ĕris,* m.; *lŭtum, i,* n.; *fŭmus, i,* m.
Dusty.	Pulverulentus, a, um.
Muddy.	Lutōsus, lutulentus, a, um.
Smoky.	Fumōsus, a, um.
Is it dusty?	Ortúsne est púlvis?
It is dusty.	Órtus est.
It is very dusty.	Vis púlvĕris mágna est.
Is it muddy out of doors?	{ Écquid ést fóris lútum ? { Súntne víae lutósae ?
It is very muddy.	{ Súnt véro ádmodum lutósae. { Vis lúti permágna est.
Does it smoke ?	{ Ortúsne ést fúmus ? { Fumátne dómus ?
It is quite smoky (it smokes much).	Órta ést vis fúmi mágna.
It is too smoky (it smokes too much).	Ést nímis fúmi.

To go in or into (any place).	Intre, introïre, ingrĕdi (ingressus sum) (IN, AD LOCUM, LOCUM).
To enter.	Intrāre, introïre (LOCUM).
To sit.	Sĕdeo, ēre, sēdi, sessum (IN RE, AD REM).
To sit down, to take a seat.	Assido, ĕre, sēdi, sessum. Consido, ĕre, sēdi, sessum. Residēre, subsidĕre. (IN SELLA, HUMI, &c.)
To sit down by the side of any one.	Assidēre aliquem.
To be seated by the side of any one.	Assidēre alicui.
To sit still, keep one's seat.	Residēre, quiētum sedēre, non surgēre (surrexi, surrectum).
To be over, left.	Restāre, relinqui, reliquum esse.
To have left.	Reliquum habēre.
It remains (sc. that I should do this).	Réstat, réliquum est, ut hoc fáciam.
To fill.	Impleo, ēre, ēvi, ĕtum. Complēre, explēre, replēre. (ALIQUID ALIQUA RE.)
Shall you go in?	Ibísne íntro?
I shall not go in.	Nòn íbo.
I shall sit down upon this chair.	Ego hâc in séllā assídam.
Will you sit down by my side?	Vísne mê assídĕre?
Let me sit down upon the ground.	Considâmus húmo.
Will you please to sit down in the chair?	Placétne tíbi assídĕre in sellā?
No, I have no time to sit down.	Nôn, ótio ád assidendum cáreo.
Where is your scholar sitting?	Úbi sédet discípulus túus?
He is sitting over his books in school.	Assídet libris in schólā.
We sat down in the library.	In bibliothécā consédimus.
Will you sit down by the fire?	Vísne assídere apud carbónes?
No, I am not cold.	Nólo; nam nôn álgeo.
Will your boy come into the house?	Veniétne púer túus íntro?
He will (shall) come in immediately.	Sáne, vóniet íntro e vestígio.
Shall you go into the city with me?	Inibísne mêcum in úrbem?
I shall not go.	Nón iníbo.
How much money have you left?	Quanta tíbi pecunia réliqua est?
I have three florins left.	Reliqui sunt míhi três floréni.
I have but one florin left.	Únum tántum florēnum réliquum hábeo.

44

| If I pay him, I have but little left. | Si ílli débitum sólvam, réliquum nòn habébo nísi párum. |

G. Obs. The conjunction *si*, " if," and *nisi*, " if not," or " unless," is followed either by the indicative or subjunctive, according to the sense to be conveyed. (Cf. Lessons LXXXIV. and LXXXVI.)

If he comes, I shall speak to him.	Si véniet (vénit *or* véniat), cum éo cólloquar.
If the weather is fine to-morrow, I shall take a walk.	Si tempéstas crástína est (= érit) bóna, íbo ambulátum.
I shall pay you, if I receive my money.	Sólvam tíbi débita, si pecúnias méas accípiam.
If he addresses (speaks to) me, I shall answer him.	Si mê alloquêtur, respondébo.
If you will promise me to keep it secret, I shall tell it to you.	Si míhi pollicébĕris rém tacêre, técum communicábo.
I have spent all my money, so that I have none left.	Pecúniam méam ómnem expéndi, ut núlla relinquâtur.
Do you fill your goblet with wine ?	Implêsne póculum túum víno ?
I do fill it with pure wine.	Ímpleo íd méro.
Did he fill his purse with money?	Explevítne marsúpium súum pecúniã ?
He was not able to fill it.	Explêre nôn pótuit.
Shall you fill the bottle with wine?	Écquid lagênam implêbis víno ?
No, I shall fill it with pure water.	Ímmo pótius éam áquã púrã implébo.

EXERCISE 153.

Will your father go out to-day? — He will go out if it is fine weather. — Will your sister go out? — She will go out, if it is not windy. — Will you love my brother? — I shall love him with all my heart, if he is as good as you. — Will your parents go into the country to-morrow? — They will not go, for it is too dusty. — Shall we take a walk to-day? — We will not take a walk, for it is too muddy out of doors. — Do you see the castle of my relation behind yonder mountain? — I do see it. — Shall we go in? — We will go in, if you like. — Will you go into that room? — I shall not go into it, for it is smoky. — I wish you a good morning, madam. — Will you not come in? — Will you not sit down? — I will sit down upon that large chair. — Will you tell me what has become of your brother? — I will tell you. — Here is the chair upon which he sat often. — When did he die? — He died two years ago. — I am very much (*vehementer*) afflicted at it. — Hast thou spent all thy money? — I have not spent all. — How much hast thou left of it? — I have not much left of it; I have but one florin left. — How much money have thy sisters left? — They have but three crowns left. — Have you money enough

left to pay your tailor ? — I have enough of it left to pay him; but if
I pay him, I shall have but little left. — How much money will your
brothers have left ? — They will have a hundred crowns left. — Will
you speak to my uncle if you see him ? If I see him, I shall speak to
him. — Will you take a' walk to-morrow ? — If it is fine weather, I
shall take a walk; but if it is bad weather, I shall stay at home. —
Will you pay your shoemaker ? — I shall pay him, if I receive my
money to-morrow. — Why do you wish to go ? — If your father comes,
I shall not go; but if he does not come, I must go. — Why do you
not sit down ? — If you will stay with me, I will sit down; but if you
go, I shall go along with you. — Will you love my children ? — If they
are good and assiduous, I shall love them; but if they are idle and
naughty, I shall despise and punish them. — Am I right in speaking
thus ? — You are not wrong.

Lesson LXXXII. — PENSUM ALTERUM ET OCTOGESIMUM.

OF THE FUTURE PERFECT.

A. I. The future perfect of the active voice is formed from
the perfect indicative by changing *i* into *ĕro.*   E. g.

    1. amāvi — amāvĕro, *I shall have loved.*
    2. monŭi — monŭĕro, *I shall have reminded.*
    3. lēgi — lēgĕro, *I shall have read.*
    4. audīvi — audivĕro, *I shall have heard.*

II. The future perfect passive is compounded of the perfect
participle and *ĕro,* "I shall be."   E. g.

    1. amātus ĕro *or* fuĕro, *I shall have been loved.*
    2. monĭtus ĕro *or* fuĕro, *I shall have been reminded.*
    3. lectus ĕro *or* fuĕro, *I shall have been read.*
    4. audītus ĕro *or* fuĕro, *I shall have been heard.*

INFLECTION OF THE FUTURE PERFECT.

B. The inflection of the future perfect, active and
passive, is exhibited by the following paradigms : —

ACTIVE.	PASSIVE.
FIRST CONJUGATION.	
Amāvĕro, *I shall have loved.*	Amātus ĕro, *I shall have been loved.*
SING. amāvĕrŏ	SING. amātus ĕro *or* fuĕro
amāvĕrĭs	amātus ĕris *or* fuĕrĭs
amāvĕrĭt,	amātus ĕrit *or* fuĕrit,

ACTIVE.	PASSIVE.
PLUR. amāvĕrĭmŭs	PLUR. ămāti erimus *or* fuerĭmus
amāvĕrĭtĭs *	amāti erĭtis *or* fuerĭtis
amāvĕrint.	amāti ĕrunt *or* fuĕrint.

SECOND CONJUGATION.

Monuĕro, *I shall have reminded.*   Monĭtus ĕro, *I shall have been reminded.*

SING. monŭĕrŏ	SING. monĭtus ĕro *or* fuĕro
monŭĕrĭs	monĭtus ĕris *or* fuerĭs
monŭĕrĭt,	monĭtus ĕrit *or* fuĕrit,
PLUR. monŭĕrĭmŭs	PLUR. monĭti erimus *or* fuerĭmus
monŭĕrĭtĭs	monĭti erĭtis *or* fuerĭtis
monŭĕrint.	monĭti ĕrunt *or* fuĕrint.

THIRD CONJUGATION.

Lēgĕro, *I shall have read.*   Lectus ĕro, *I shall have been read.*

SING. lēgĕrŏ	SING. lectus ĕro *or* fuĕro
lēgĕrĭs	lectus ĕrit *or* fuerĭs
lēgĕrĭt,	lectus ĕrit *or* fuĕrit,
PLUR. lēgĕrĭmŭs	PLUR. lecti erimus *or* fuerĭmus
lēgĕrĭtĭs	lecti erĭtis *or* fuerĭtis
lēgĕrint.	lecti ĕrunt *or* fuĕrint.

FOURTH CONJUGATION.

Audīvĕro, *I shall have heard.* Audītus ĕro, *I shall have been heard.*

SING. audīvĕrŏ	SING. audītus ĕro *or* fuĕro
audīvĕrĭs	audītus ĕris *or* fuerĭs
audīvĕrĭt,	audītus ĕrit *or* fuĕrit,
PLUR. audīvĕrĭmŭs	PLUR. audīti erimus *or* fuerĭmus
audīvĕrĭtĭs	audīti erĭtis *or* fuerĭtis
audīvĕrint.	audīti ĕrunt *or* fuĕrint.

So conjugate *apportāvĕro,* I shall have brought; *curāvĕro,* I shall have ordered; *laudāvĕro,* I shall have praised; *vocāvĕro,* I shall have called; *dĕdĕro,* I shall have given; *secuĕro,* I shall have cut; *stĕtĕro,* I shall have stood; — *docuĕro,* I shall have taught; *habuĕro,* I shall have had; *jussĕro,* I shall have commanded; *tenuĕro,* I shall have held; *ēgĕro,* I shall have acted; *fēcĕro,* I shall have done (made); *misĕro,* I shall have sent; *posuĕro,* I shall have put; *scripsĕro,* I shall have written; *sumpsĕro,* I shall have taken; — *finīvĕro,* I shall have finished; *punīvĕro,* I shall have punished; *sitĭvĕro,* I shall have thirsted; *aperuĕro,* I shall have opened; *reperĕro,* I shall have found; *vēnĕro,* I shall have come, &c.

---

* The *i* of the *imus* and *itis* of this tense (as of the perfect subjunctive) is either long or short, perhaps more frequently long. The *is* of the second person singular is sometimes long.

To these add the irregular verbs *fuĕro*, I shall have been ; *potuĕro*, I shall have been able ; *voluĕro* (*noluĕro*, *maluĕro*), I shall have been willing (unwilling, more willing) ; *tulĕro*, I shall have carried ; *ivĕro* (*abivĕro*, *prodicĕro*, &c.), I shall have gone (gone away, gone out).

REMARK. — The future perfect active is liable to syncopation, like the perfect (cf. page 239). E. g. *amăro*, *delēro*, *consuĕro*, instead of *amāvĕro*, *delēvĕro*, *consuēvĕro*. That of the fourth conjugation is frequently derived from the secondary perfect in *ii*; as, *audiĕro*, *finiĕro*, *puniĕro*, *prodiĕro*, &c.

Will you have loved ?	Amaverísne ?
I shall have loved.	Véro, amávero.
If you and I shall have loved.	Si égo et tû amaverímus.
Will you have reminded ?	Núm vôs monuerítis ?
We will not have reminded.	Nôs nôn monuerímus.
Will they have read the book ?	Legeríntne líbrum ?
He will have read it.	Légerint.
Shall we have heard ?	Audiverimúsne ?
You will not have heard.	Nôn audiverítis.
Shall I have been loved ?	Egon' éro amâtus ?
You will not have been loved.	Nôn éris amâtus.
Shall we have been punished ?	Erimúsne puníti ?
You will not have been punished.	Puníti nôn éritis.
Will the letters have been written ?	Scriptaêne érunt epístolae ?
They will not have been written.	Nôn érunt scríptae.

FUTURE PERFECT OF DEPONENT VERBS.

C. The future perfect of deponent verbs is the same as that of the passive voice. E. g.

Hortātus ĕro, *I shall have ex-*   Blandītus ĕro, *I shall have flat-*
      horted.   *tered.*

SING. hortātus ĕro *or* fuĕro   SING. blandītus ĕro *or* fuĕro
         hortātus ĕris *or* fuerís   blandītus ĕris *or* fuerís
         hortātus ĕrit *or* fuĕrit,   blandītus ĕrit *or* fuĕrit,
PLUR. hortāti erímus *or* fuerímus   PLUR. blandīti erímus *or* fue-
                                                                    rímus

         hortāti erítis *or* fuerítis   blandīti erítis *or* fuerítis
         hortāti ĕrunt *or* fuĕrint.   blandīti ĕrunt *or* fuĕrint.

So, 2. *verĭtus ĕro*, I shall have feared ; 3. *locūtus ĕro*, I shall have spoken. To these add, according to the respective conjugations : *arbitrātus ĕro*, I shall have thought ; *comitātus ĕro*, I shall have escorted ; *morātus ĕro*, I shall have delayed ; — *merĭtus ĕro*, I shall have earned ; *miserĭtus ĕro*, I shall have pitied ; *tuĭtus ĕro*, I shall have defended ; *lapsus ĕro*, I shall have glided ; *oblĭtus ĕro*, I shall have forgotten ; *profectus ĕro*, I shall have departed ; *secūtus ĕro*, I shall have followed ; — *expertus ĕro*, I shall have experienced ; *largītus ĕro*, I shall have lavished.

44*

Will he have exhorted ?	Erítne hortâtus ?
He will not have exhorted.	Nôn érit hortâtus.
Will you have departed ?	Erísne proféctus ?
Yes, I shall have departed.	Véro, proféctus éro.
Shall we have flattered ?	Núm nôs blandíti érimus ?
You will not have flattered.	Blandíti nôn éritis.
Will they have forgotten their duties ?	Oblitíne érunt officiôrum suôrum ?
They will not have forgotten them.	(Eôrum) nôn óbliti érunt.

ON THE USE OF THE FUTURE PERFECT.

D. The future perfect declares that an action or event will be completed at or before the time of another future action or event. Hence it can only be used in connection with another future verb, with an imperative, or with a verb involving the notion of futurity. E. g.

Si in ómnibus ínnocens *fúero,* quid míhi inimicítiae *nocebunt ?*	If I am (shall have been) innocent in everything, what harm can enmity inflict on me ?
De Carthágine veréri nôn ánte *désinam,* quam íllam excísam *cognórěro.*	I shall not cease to be afraid of Carthage, until I shall have heard of its destruction.
Moráti mélius *érǐmus,* quum *didicerǐmus,* quae natûra desíderet.	We shall be better men, when we shall have learnt what nature requires of us.
Respondéto ad éa, quae de tê ípso *rogâro.*	Reply to what I ask (shall have asked) with reference to yourself.
Dâ míhi hóc, júm tíbi máximam partem defensiônis *praecíderis.*	Grant me this one point, and you will have cut off the best part of your defence.
Égo de venditiône víllae méae níhil *cógito,* nísi quid, quod mágis mê deléctet, *invénero.*	I do not (shall not) think of the sale of my villa, unless I shall have found something that can afford me greater pleasure.

REMARKS.

1. The distinction expressed by the future perfect is always observed in Latin, and is frequently put where the English idiom substitutes the first future, the present, or the perfect. E. g. *Ut sementem* fecĕris, *ita metes,* As you have (shall have) sown, so you will reap. *Si* invēnero, *tecum communicâbo,* If I find it (shall have found it), I will communicate it to you. And so frequently in conditional clauses, where the result is dependent on the previous fulfilment of a condition ; as, *si voluĕro, si potuĕro, si licuĕrit, si placuĕrit, si otium habuĕro,* where in English we commonly put the present or first future.

2. The future perfect is often elegantly put for the simple future,

in order to impart an air of rapidity or certainty to the event. E. g. *Ah, si pergis,* abiěro, If you proceed, I am off. *Quid inventum sit, paulo post* viděro, I shall see presently what has been found. Respiräro, *si te viděro,* I shall breathe again, if I have seen you. *Pergrātum mihi* fecěris, si *deděris operam, ut,* &c., You will oblige me very much, if you see to it that, &c. *Qui Antonium oppresserit, is hoc bellum teterrimum* confecěrit, He who puts down (shall first have put down) Antonius, will put an end to this destructive war.*

SUBJUNCTIVE OF THE FUTURE PERFECT.

E. The subjunctive of the future perfect, like that of the simple future, is wanting. (Cf. Lesson LXXXI. *F.*) Its place is supplied by the *perfect* and *pluperfect* subjunctive. E. g.

Affirmo tíbi, si hoc beneffcium míhi *tribuěris, mê* quamcúnque póssim grátiam tíbi *relatúrum.*	I assure you, that, if you shall have done me this favor, I shall render you all the thanks in my power.
Affirmábat míbi, si íllud beneffcium ípsi *tribuíssem, sê* quamcúnque pósset grátiam míhi *relatúrum.*	I assured you, that, if you should have done me that favor, I would render you all the thanks in my power.
Quís hóc nôn pérspicit, praecláre nobíscum *áctum íri,* si pópulus Romănus istíus uníus supplício *conténtus fúerit?*	Who does not see, that we shall fare nobly, if the Roman people shall have been contented by the punishment of this one individual.
De Rosciôrum audáciă túm *mê dictúrum* pollícitus súm, quum Erúcii crímina *diluíssem.*	I have promised to discourse on the audacity of the Roscii, as soon as I shall have refuted the charges preferred against Erucius.
I shall have written my letters before you return.	Epístolas méas, ántequam redíbis, scrípsero.
When I shall have paid for my horse, I shall have but ten florins left.	Quum équi prétium persólvero, décem tántum florénos réliquos habébo.
What will you do when you shall have dined?	Quíd fácies, quum coenávěris?
I shall go out.	In públicum prodíbo.
When I shall have spoken to your brother, I shall know what I have to do.	Quum ad frátrem túum locútus éro, tum scíam, quid mihi faciéndum sit.
Before (sooner). *Not until, not before.*	*Priusquam, antequam, antea quam.* *Non prius quam, non ante (antea) quam.*
Sooner (rather) than.	*Potius quam.*

---

* Thus frequently, when another clause already contains a future perfect, as in several of the examples given. — The future perfect *viděro* appears in the same sense in expressions like *mox, post, alias, alio loco* viděro, I shall see (or examine) presently, hereafter, elsewhere, in another place.

I shall not do it, before you tell me (shall have told me).   Íd nŏn príus fáciam, quam jússĕris.*

I shall not see him, until I go (shall have gone) thither.   Éum non vidébo, ántequam ílluc íero.

Did you see him before he left?   Vidistine éum, antequam discéssit?

I did see him.   Factum (est).

Outside of, out of, without.   *Extra* (Prep. cum Acc.).

Outside of the town, city.   Extra óppidum (úrbem).

The church stands outside the city.   Témplum extra úrbis múros sítum est.

I shall wait for you before the city gate.   Tê extra úrbis pórtam exspectábo.

The city gate.   Porta, ae, *f.* (*sc.* urbis, oppídi).

To go out.   { Exire, egrĕdi (e. g. per portam), fŏras ire.

To come out.   Exire, egrĕdi, prodire.

Seldom, rarely.   { Rāro, nŏn saepe; perrāro (*very rarely*).

To continue, proceed with.   { Pergo, ĕre, perrexi, perrectum (IN RE, FACERE REM). Persĕqui, continuāre (REM).

Will you continue as you began?   Visne pérgere, ut coepísti?

I will.   Vólo.

He continues (proceeds) with his speech, with his inquiry.   Perséquitur dicéndo, quaeréndo.

You must continue to speak loud.   Clárā vóce lóqui pérgas opórtet.

The appetite.   Cíbi appetentia *or* cupidītas (ātis, *f.*).

A keen appetite.   Edacĭtas, ātis, *f.*

A want of appetite.   Fastidĭum, i, *n.*

To have an appetite.   { Cíbum appetĕre. Alicui cíbi cupidītas est.

To have a good appetite.   Cíbum libenter sumĕre, libenter

To have no appetite.   Cíbum fastidire.   [coenāre.

Have you an appetite?   { Appetísne cíbum? Esne áppetens edúndi?

I have one.   Áppeto. Áppetens súm cíbi.

He had no appetite at all.   Cíbum fastidivit.

The narrative, tale.   Narratio, ōnis, *f.;* expositio, ōnis, *f.;* fabella, ae, *f.*

The shore (coast).   Litus, ŏris, *n.*

The bank, shore.   Ripa, ae, *f.*

On the bank, shore.   Juxta rīpam, ad (apud, juxta) lītus.

Is he still sitting under the tree by the sea-shore?   Residétne étiam núnc sub árbore juxta lítus?

He is sitting there no longer.   Résidet íbi nón ámplius.

The same.   Ídem, eădem, ídem.

The very same.   Idem ipse, is ipse, eadem ipsa, &c.

---

* Compare Lesson LXXXIX. A. VII.

One and the same.	*Ūnus et ĭdem.*
The same thing, things.	Ĭdem ; eădem.
Of the same kind.	Ejusdem genĕris.
Of the same color.	Ejusdem colōris.
To be the same (to make no dif-ference).	{ Nihil differre. { Nihil interesse.
It is all one (the same).	Nĭhil interest (dĭffert).
It is all one (makes no differ-ence) to me.	Méā nĭhil interest, refert. (Cf. page 411, *C.*)
It makes no difference, whether you go or stay.	Nĭhil interest, *utrum* ábeas *an* mo-rēris.
I am constantly obliged to hear the same thing.	Sémper ista audire eādem coáctus sum.
He is constantly driving at the same thing.	Úno ópere eándem incûdem díem noctémque túndit.
Such.	*Tālis, e ; hujusmŏdi, ejusmŏdi.*
Such a man, woman, child.	Tālis homo, mulĭer, infans, hŏmo hujusmŏdi, &c.
Such men deserve esteem.	Tāles hómines (hómines ejúsmŏdi) observántiā dígni sunt.
There is — there are.	{ Ibi (istic, illic) est — ibi sunt ; en, { ecce (cum Nom. or Acc.).
Here is — here are.	{ Hīc est, adest — hīc sunt, adsunt ; { en, ecce (cum Nom. or Acc.).
Here I am !	Ádsum. Écce mê !
Here he is.	Éccum* ádest. Én hic ést ĭlle.
Here is your letter.	Écce túae lítterae.
Here they are.	Éccos ádsunt. Én hic sunt ĭlli.
Here is my book.	Én tíbi líber méus.
Therefore, for that reason, on that account.	{ Eo, eā re, ob eam rem, ob eam { causam. { Ideo, idcirco, proptérĕa.
For which reason, on which ac-count.	Quocirca, quaproptĕr.
For the reason, that ; because.	{ Eo, quod ; ideo, quod ; proptérĕa, { quod.
Why do you complain ?	Quĭd est ĭgitur, cur querûre ?
This is the reason why I com-plain.	Haêc ést caûsa, cur (propter quam) quéror.
You see the reason why he left.	Quámobrem abíerit, caûsam vídes.
Here is the reason why he has changed his opinion.	En caûsa, cur senténtiam mutâvit.
Therefore I say so.	Éā de caûsā hóc díco.
I have cause for laugh-ing, weeping, &c.	{ *Est quod rídeam, fléam.* { *Est mĭhi caûsa ridéndi, flendi.*

---

* Compare pages 37, Rem. 2, and 344.

The father has no cause for weeping.	Nôn ést, quód páter fléat.
My sister's hands are cold.	{ Sóror méa álget mánibus. Frígent soróris méae mánus.
His feet are cold.	{ Álget pédibus. Pédes éjus frígent.
To hunt.	Venāri, in venatiōne esse.
To go a hunting.	Venātum īre.
To send back.	Remitto, ĕre, misi, missum.
To read again.	{ Relĕgo, ĕre, lēgi, lectum. Rursus, itĕrum legĕre.
Again (once more), a second time, anew.	Rursus (rursum), itĕrum, denŭo, de intĕgro.
The mistake, error.	Mendum, errātum, peccātum, vitium, i, n.
To make a mistake or mistakes (in anything).	{ Pecco, āre, āvi, ātum. Offendo, ĕre, di, sum. (IN ALIQUĀ RE.)
Full of errors.	Mendōsus, vitiōsus, a, um.
Free from errors.	Vitiis cărens, vitio pūrus, a, um.
To be free from mistakes or errors.	Vitiis carēre; sine vitiis esse.

EXERCISE 154.

When will you go to Italy ? — I shall go as soon as I have learnt Italian. — When will your brothers go to Germany ? — They will go thither as soon as they know German. — When will they learn it ? — They will learn it when they have found a good master. — How much money shall we have left when we have paid for our horse ? — When we have paid for it we shall have only a hundred crowns left. — Have you told my brother that I have been obliged to sell the carriage ? — I have told him so. — Have you written to the same man to whom my father wrote ? — I have not written to the same, but to another. — Have they already answered you ? — Not yet, but I hope to receive a letter next week — Have you ever seen such a person ? — I have never seen such a one. — Have you already seen our church ? — I have not seen it yet. — Where does it stand ? — It stands outside the town. — If you wish to see it, I will go with you in order to show it to you. — Who is there ? — It is I. — Who are those men ? They are foreigners who wish to speak to you. — Of what country are they ? — They are Americans. — Where have you been since I saw you ? — We sojourned long on the sea-shore, until a ship arrived, which brought us to France. — Will you continue your narrative ? — Scarcely had we arrived in France when we were taken to the king, who received us very well (nos benigne excēpit), and sent us back to our country. — Whom are you looking for ? — I am looking for my little brother. — If you wish to find him, you must go into the garden, for he is there. — The garden is large, and I shall not be able to find him, if you do not tell me in which part (quā in parte) of the garden he is. — He is sitting under the large tree under which we were sitting yesterday. — Now I shall find him.

EXERCISE 155.

Why do your children not live in France? — They wish to learn English, that is the reason why they live in England. — Why do you sit near the fire? — My hands and feet are cold, that is the reason why I sit near the fire. — What do the people live upon that live on the sea-shore? — They live upon fish alone. — Why will you not go a hunting any more? — I hunted yesterday the whole day, and I killed nothing but an ugly bird, that is the reason why I shall not go a hunting any more. — Why do you not eat? — I shall not eat before I have a good appetite. — Why does your brother eat so much? — He has a good appetite, that is the reason he eats so much. — If you have read the books which I lent you, why do you not return them to me? — I intend reading them once more, that is the reason why I have not yet returned them to you; but I shall return them to you as soon as I have read them a second time. — Why did you not bring me my clothes? — They were not made, therefore I did not bring them; but I bring them to you now; here they are. — You have learnt your lesson; why has your sister not learnt hers? — She has taken a walk with my mother, that is the reason why she has not learnt it; but she will learn it to-morrow. — When will you correct my exercises? — I will correct them when you bring me those of your sister. — Do you think you have made mistakes in them? — I do not know. — If you have made mistakes, you have not studied your lessons well; for the lessons must be learnt well, if you wish to have them free from errors. — It is all the same, if you do not correct them (for) me to-day, I shall not learn them before to-morrow (*ante diem crastĭnum non discam*). — You must make no mistakes in your exercises, for you have all you want to write them without any errors.

Lesson LXXXIII. — PENSUM OCTOGESIMUM TERTIUM.

OF THE CONSECUTIO TEMPORUM.

A. The tenses of the indicative mood may be connected with each other, according to the requirements of the speaker, and are subject to no limitation. E. g. *Ego, qui heri* ludēbam, *hodie* scribo, *cras mane autem, quum litteras ad te* dédĕro, *in urbem* proficiscar. But in dependent clauses, introduced by a conjunction or a pronoun, the tense of the subjunctive is always determined by that of the verb in the leading clause. This order or connection of tenses is called *consecutio tempŏrum*, and is subject to the following laws: —

I. The *Present*, the *Perfect Definite*, and the *Future Tenses*
of the leading clause, are followed by the *Present* or *Perfect
Subjunctive* in the dependent clause. E. g.

Vídeo (vídi, vidébo, vídĕro), *quíd ágas* or *quid égĕris.*	I see (have seen, shall see, shall have seen) what you are doing, *or* what you have done.
Dìc míhi, *quid ágat* or *quid égĕrit.*	Tell me what he is doing, *or* what he has done.
Rógo (rogávi, rogábo, rogávero), *ut scribas.*	I beg you (have begged, shall beg, shall have begged you) to write.
Hóc ídeo fácio (féci, fáciam, fécĕro), *ut intélligas.*	I do (have done, shall do, shall have done) this, in order that you may understand.
Némo íta caêcus ést (fúit, érit, fúĕrit), *ut nón intélligat* or *intelléxerit.*	No one is (has been, will be, will have been) so blind, as not to comprehend *or* to have comprehended.
Némo ést (fúit, érit, fúĕrit), *qui nón intélligat* or *intelléxerit.*	There is (has been, will be, will have been) no one, but what comprehends *or* has comprehended.
Némo ést, *qui nón intellectúrus sit.*	There is no one, but what will comprehend.

II. The *Imperfect*, the *Perfect Indefinite*, and the *Pluperfect*
of the leading clause, are followed by the *Imperfect* or *Pluperfect Subjunctive* in the dependent clause. E. g.

Vidébam (vídi, vídĕram), *quid ágeret* or *egísset.*	I was seeing (I saw, had seen), what he did, what he had done.
Rogàbam (rogávi, rogávĕram), *ut scribĕres.*	I begged (did beg, had begged) you to write.
Hóc ídeo faciêbam (féci, fécĕram), *ut intelligeres.*	I was doing (I did, had done) this, that you might understand.
Némo íta caêcus érat (fúit, fúĕrat), *ut nón intelligeret* or *intelléxisset.*	No one was (had been) so blind, as not to comprehend *or* to have comprehended.
Némo érat (fúit, fúerat), *qui nón intelligeret* or *intellexisset.*	There was (had been) no one, but what comprehended *or* had comprehended.
Némo érat, *qui nón intellectúrus ésset.*	There was no one, but what would comprehend.

NOTE. — The dependent clauses in which this construction occurs
are, — *a*) those containing an indirect question; *b*) those introduced
by *ut* or *ne* ; *c*) those introduced by a relative pronoun, or by one of
the relative conjunctions *quo, quin, quomìnus*, &c. The following
examples will illustrate this still further : —

Quaéritur, Corínthiis béllum indicámus, *an nón.*	The question is, whether we shall declare war against the Corinthians, *or* not.

Quaesívi, *écquis esset ventúrus.*

I inquired, whether any one was about to come.

Difficile díctu ést, *útrum hóstes mágis virtútem éjus pugnántes timuérint, an mansuetúdinem vícti dilézerint.*

It is difficult to say, whether his enemies dreaded his valor more in battle, than they cherished his clemency after being conquered.

Tê hórtor, *ut oratiónes méas studióse légas.*

I exhort you to read my orations carefully.

Óbsecro vôs, *ut diligénter attendátis.*

I beseech you to attend diligently.

Míhi opus est, *ut lávem.*

It is necessary for me to wash.

Equidem véllem, *ut aliquándo redíres.*

I could wish, that you might return at last.

In éo érat, *ut in múros eváderet míles.*

The soldier was on the point of escaping within the walls.

Mê óbsecras, *ne obliviscar* vigiláre.

You conjure me, not to forget to watch.

Timóleon orâvit ómnes, *ne id fácěrent.*

Timoleon requested them all, not to do that.

Decrêvit senâtus, *ut cónsul viděret, ne* quíd respública detriménti cáperet.

The senate decreed, that the consul should see that the republic sustained no injury.

Ex his delécti Délphos deliberâtam míssi súnt, *qui consulěrent* Apóllinem.

A select number of these were sent to Delphi, for the purpose of consulting Apollo.

Stúlti súmus, *qui* Drúsum cum Clódio conférre audeámus.

We are fools for venturing to compare Drusus with Clodius.

Tenéri nôn pótúi, *quin declarârem.*

I could not be prevented from declaring.

Níhil impědit, *quo mínus íd, quód* máxime *pláceat,* fácere possímus.

Nothing prevents us from being able to do what we like best.

REMARKS.

1. The tenses, which may thus enter into connection with each other, are called *similar* tenses. Similar are,—*a*) the *present,* the *perfect definite,* the *futures,* and the periphrastic tenses in *sim* and *fuěrim; b*) the *imperfect,* the *perfect indefinite,* the *pluperfect,* and the periphrastic tenses in *essem* and *fuissem.* Tenses, of which one belongs to the first, and the other to the second of these classes, are called *dissimilar;* as, the *present* and the *imperfect,* &c.

2. When, in historical narration, the present tense is used instead of the perfect indefinite, it is sometimes followed by the present and sometimes by the imperfect or pluperfect subjunctive. E. g. Scribit (= scripsit) *ad quosdam Melitenses, ut ea rasa perquirant,* He writes (wrote) to certain inhabitants of Malta, to inquire after those vases. *Nulli, quid scriptum esset, enunciat* (= enuntiàvit), He discloses (disclosed) to no one what had been written. *Ad propinquum suum scribit* (= scripsit), *ut iis, qui a Verre venissent, respondéret,* He writes to his relative to reply to those who had come from Verres.

3. The present indicative is followed by the imperfect subjunctive, when it is intended to convey the idea of duration in the past. E. g. *Hujus praecepti tanta vis, tanta sententia* est, ut *ea non homini cuipiam,* sed *Delphico deo* tribuerētur, The force and moral weight of this injunction *are* so great, that it *was* attributed not to any man, but to the Delphic deity. *Scitōte, oppidum esse in Sicilia nullum, quo in oppŭlo non isti delecta mulier ad libidinem* esset, Know, then, that there *is* not a town in Sicily in which this fellow *had not* an object of his lust.

4. The imperfect or pluperfect indicative may be followed by the perfect subjunctive, when the result of a past action is represented as extending into the present. E. g. Ardēbat *autem Hortensius cupidi-tāte dicendi sic, ut in nullo unquam flagrantius studium* vidĕrim, Hortensius was so fond of speaking, that (up to this time) I have never witnessed a more ardent passion in any one.

5. The perfect definite requires the imperfect subjunctive, whenever it is intended to represent the action as in operation, and not merely as a result. E. g. *Quoniam, quae subsidia novitātis* habēres, *et habēre* posses, exposui, *nunc de magnitudĭne petitiōnis dicam,* Having shown what resources you have, or can have, I will now speak of the importance of the demand. Adduxi *enim hominem, in quo satisfacere extĕris nationibus* possētis, I have produced a man, through whom you can satisfy the demands of foreign nations.

6. The imperfect and perfect indefinite are sometimes followed by the present subjunctive, to denote that the contents of the dependent clause are not limited to the time of the leading verb, but universally applicable. E. g. Nesciebat, *quid sit philosophia,* He did not know what philosophy is (i. e. was and still is). *Ad priores conditiones nihil* additum (est), *Africano praedicante, neque Romānis, si vincantur, animos minui, neque, si vincant, secundis rebus insolescere,* No additions were made to the former conditions, Africanus declaring, that the Romans neither lost their courage when conquered, nor ever grew insolent in their success when victorious.

7. When the verb of a subordinate clause depends upon an *infinitive,* its tense is determined as follows : —

a) The present infinitive is followed by the tense required by the verb, on which the infinitive depends. E. g. Incipĭte *deinde* mirāri, *cur pauci jam vestram* suscipiant *causam,* Begin then to wonder why so few now defend your cause. *Ipse* metuĕre incipies, *ne innocenti periculum* facessĕris, You will yourself begin to be afraid of having accused an innocent man. *Praedixĕrat his, ut parāti* essent facĕre, *quod ipsum* vidissent, He had directed them beforehand to be ready to do whatever they might see himself do.

b) The perfect infinitive is commonly followed by the imperfect or pluperfect subjunctive, but when it represents the perfect definite, sometimes also by the present or perfect. E. g. *Satis mihi multa verba* fecisse *videor, quare esset hoc bellum necessārium,* I think I have said enough to show why this war is necessary. *Nisi docet, ita se posse-disse, ut nec vi, nec clam, nec precario* possēderit, Unless he shows that he has taken possession in such a manner, as to have employed neither force nor secrecy nor entreaty.

8. Dissimilar tenses sometimes occur in the same construction, with different shades of signification. E. g. *Summâ difficultate rei frumentarii affecto exercitu .... usque eo, ut complures dies milites frumento caruerint, et extremam famem sustentârent, nulla tamen vox est ab iis audita*, Although the army labored under the greatest difficulty in procuring its necessary supplies, to such an extent, that for several days the soldiers *had no* corn and *were famishing*, yet *not* a word of discontent was heard from them.

To find one's self, to be (well or ill).	*Se habēre, valēre ; agĕre.*
How do you do ?	{ Quómŏdo tê hábes ? { Quómŏdo váles ?
I am very well.	Égo mê ádmŏdum bénc hábeo.
How was your cousin ?	Quómodo patruêlis tûus sê habêbat?
He was not very well.	{ Múle sê habêbat. { Párum valêbat.
Is your father well ?	Habétne se páter túus béne ?
No, he is in bad health.	{ Non ; mála conditiône ést. { Condítio éjus mála ést.
How goes it with him, her ?	Quíd ágitur cum éo, cum éâ ?
It goes badly with him.	Múle ágitur cum éo.
All is well with me.	Béne ágitur mêcum.
To stay, sojourn (in any place, with any one).	Morári, commorári, deversári, habitáre (ALIQUO LOCO, APUD ALIQUEM).
At present, now.	Nunc, in praesenti.
To censure, criticise, carp at (any one *or* anything).	{ Carpo, ĕre, carpsi, carptum (ALIQUEM). { Cavillári aliquem *or* aliquid ; — vellicáre aliquem.
To laugh at, deride, ridicule any one.	{ Illúdo, ĕre, lûsi, lûsum (REM, REI, ALIQUEM, IN ALIQUEM). { Deridêre aliquem ; — aliquem ludibrio habêre.
Did you stay long in Vienna ?	Moratúsne és díu Vindobónae ?
No, I stayed there only three days.	Immo três tántum díes morátus sum.
Where is your brother staying now ?	Úbi in praesónti deversátur fráter túus ?
He is staying in London at present.	Deversátur núnc Londíni.
How long did you remain with your uncle in New York ?	Quám díu ápud pátruum túum Nóvo in Eboráco commorabáris ?
I stayed with him for two years.	Commorábar apud éum per biénnium.
Did he censure (carp at) any one?	Carpebátne áliquem ?

He carped at no one.	Núllum carpêbat.
Why do you not deride this man a little?	Cur nôn ístum aliquantísper lúdis (illûdis)?
I have already laughed at him enough.	Éum jám lúsi jocóse sátis.
Are we derided by our accusers?	Illudimúrne ab accusatóribus?
We are not.	Nôn illúdimur.
Was he accustomed to make light of the precepts of his master?	Solebátne illúdĕre praecépta magistri?
He was not.	Fácere nôn solêbat.
You derided what I said.	Illúseras id, quod díxeram.

To gain, win.	$\left\{\begin{array}{l}\textit{Lucrum}\text{ or }\textit{quaestum facĕre}\text{ (EX RE).}\\ \textit{Lucrāri, lucrifacĕre}\text{ (REM).}\\ \text{Consĕqui, nancisci (nactus sum) \textsc{aliquid}.}\end{array}\right.$
To earn, get.	$\left\{\begin{array}{l}\text{Mereo, ēre, ŭi, ĭtum (REM).}\\ \text{Mereor, ēri, ĭtus sum.}\end{array}\right.$
To procure, get.	Parāre, comparāre (ALIQUID).
To earn one's bread, get one's living by.	Victum sibi parāre *or* quaeritāre (aliquā re faciendā).
How does he get his living?	Quà rê sibi víctum párat?
He supports himself poorly by working.	Víctum síbi aégre quéritat laborándo.
They supported themselves by writing.	Víctum síbi scribéndo quaeritavérunt.
Has your brother earned anything?	Meruítne frâter túus áliquid?
He has earned a large sum of money.	Grándem pecúniam méruit.
He has won immortality.	Immortalitâtem méruit (méritus ést).

To spill, pour out.	$\left\{\begin{array}{l}\textit{Effundo, ĕre, fūdi, fūsum.}\\ \textit{Profundĕre}\text{ (ALIQUID).}\end{array}\right.$
To stand, to be standing.	$\left\{\begin{array}{l}\text{Sto, stāre, stĕti, stātum esse (ALIQUO).}\end{array}\right.$
Ready.	Parātus, promptus, a, um (ad rem, in rem, re).
To make ready, to prepare.	Parāre, praeparāre (ALIQUID).
To prepare one's self, get one's self ready.	Se parāre (rei, ad rem).
To keep one's self ready.	Se tenēre parātum (ad rem).
What did he spill?	Quid effúdit?
He spilt wine upon the table.	Vinum super ménsam effúdit.
His father was shedding tears.	Páter éjus láchrimas profundêbat.
Our servant is spilling water under the table.	Fámulus nóster áquas sub mensas profúndit.
The Ganges empties into the Eastern Ocean.	Gánges se in Eôum océanum effúndit.

Is there any wine on the table ?	Éstne vinum super ménsam ?
There is none.	Nôn ést.
Is he preparing to speak ?	Parátne sê ad dicéndum ?
He is preparing.	Párat.
They prepared themselves for battle and for death.	Paravérunt se proélio et mórti.
Is he preparing war against any one ?	Parátne béllum álicui ?
He is preparing to command all Russia.	Párat imperâre ómni Rússiae.
Are you getting ready to set out ?	Parâsne proficísci ?
I am preparing to go into the woods.	Égo in silvam îre páro.
Is he ready to depart ?	Estne parâtus ad proficiscéndum ?
He is ready.	Parâtus est.
I am ready for every emergency, to undergo every danger.	Égo ad ómnem evéntum, ad ómnia perícula subeúnda parâtus sum.
To split, cleave.	{ *Findo, ĕre, fĭdi, fissum.* *Diffindĕre* (ALIQUID).
To pierce, transfix.	{ *Transfĭgo, ĕre, fixi, fixum.* *Transfŏdio, ĕre, fŏdi, fossum* (ALIQUEM, REM).
To break any one's heart.	{ Pectus *or* anĭmum alicujus vulnerâre, percutĕre.
To hang, suspend.	{ Suspendo, ĕre, di, sum (ALIQUID REI *or* DE RE).
To hang any one.	Affĭgĕre aliquem patibŭlo.
To hang one's self.	{ Suspendĕre aliquem arbŏri infelíci. Se suspendĕre, induĕre se in laqueam.
To hang, to be suspended.	{ Pendeo, ĕre, pependi, —— (AB, EX, IN, DE RE).
The thief.	Für, *gen.* füris, *m.*
The robber, highwayman.	Praedo, ōnis, *m.*, latro, ōnis, *m.*
The patient.	Aeger, *gen.* aegri, *m.*, agrŏtus, i, *m.*
Tolerably well.	Mediocríter, modice, sîc sátis.
It is rather late.	Séro, sérius ést.
He is rather severe.	Sevérior est.
She is rather tall.	Grandiúscula est.
It is rather far.	Longiúsculum est.
Was my hat hanging on the nail ?	Pendebátne de clávo píleus méus ?
It was hanging on it.	Sáne quídem, pendêbat.
Who has hung the basket on the tree.	Quís córbem suspéndit árbŏri (de árbore) ?
No one.	Némo.
The thief has been hanged.	Für est patíbulo affíxus (árbŏri infelíci suspénsus est).

45 *

I hang my coat on the nail.	Égo tógam méam clávo (de clavo) suspéndo.
You are breaking this man's heart.	Péctus hujúsce vúlneras.
The basket.	Corbis, is, *f.* & *m.*; *dim.* corbŭla, ae, *f.*

EXERCISE 156.

How is your father ? — Ho is only so so. — How is your patient ? — He is a little better to-day than yesterday. — Is it long since you saw your brothers ? — I saw them two days ago. — How were they ? — They were very well. — How art thou ? — I am tolerably well. — How long has your brother been learning German ? — He has been learning it only three months. — Does he already speak it ? — He already speaks, reads, and writes it better than your cousin, who has been learning it these five years. — Is it long since you heard of my uncle ? — It is hardly three months since I heard of him. — Where was he staying then ? — He was staying at Berlin, but now he is in London. — Do you like to speak to my uncle ? — I do like very much to speak to him, but I do not like him to laugh at me. — Why does he laugh at you ? — He laughs at me, because I speak badly. — Why has your brother no friends ? — He has none, because he criticises everybody. — What do you get your livelihood by ? — I get my livelihood by working. — Does your friend get his livelihood by writing ? — He gets it by speaking and writing. — Do these gentlemen get their livelihood by working ? — They do not get it by doing anything, for they are too idle to work. — Do you see what he has done ? — I do see it. — Did he know that you had arrived ? — He did not know it. — Have I advised you to write ? — You have not asked me. — Is any one so blind, as not to understand that ? — No one is so blind. — Did he exhort us to read his book ? — He did exhort us to read it diligently. — Was he on the point of (*in eo, ut*) escaping ? — He was not. — He could not be prevented from escaping (*evadĕre*). — Nothing could prevent him from escaping.

Lesson LXXXIV. — PENSUM OCTOGESIMUM QUARTUM.

OF THE INDICATIVE MOOD.

A. By the Indicative Mood the speaker asserts the action or state expressed by the verb as an absolute existence or a positive fact. Hence this mood is used, —

I. In leading and subordinate clauses, to denote that something really takes place, has taken place, or will take place hereafter. E. g.

Nihil *est* amabílius virtúte.	Nothing is worthier of esteem than virtue.
Ómnia *mutántur;* níhil *intěrit.*	Everything changes; nothing is lost.
Ut *vóles* mê ésse, íta *éro.*	I shall be what you desire me to be.
Éas léges, quâs Caêsar *recitâvit, pronuntiârit, túlit,* nôs everténdas *putábĭmus?*	Shall we imagine, that the laws, which Caesar has read, proclaimed, and enacted, are to be abolished?
Écce *bíbit* árcus; *plúet, crédo,* hódie.	Behold the rainbow drinks (draws up the water), I think it will rain to-day.
Quám nôn *ést* fácĭlis vírtus!	How easy the practice of virtue is!
Ut saêpe súmma ingénia in occúlto *látent!*	How often the most distinguished talents lie buried in obscurity!

II. In direct questions, i. e. in those which require an immediate answer. E. g.

Cújus híc líber *ést?* — Méus.	Whose book is this? — Mine.
Quis hómo *és?* — Égo sum Pámphilus.	Who are you? — I am Pamphilus.
Únde *dejéctus ést* Cínna? — Ex úrbe.	From what place was Cinna expelled? — Out of the city.
Quis Aristídem nôn mórtuum *díligit?* — Némo.	Who does not love Aristides, though dead? — No one.

REMARK. — In indirect questions, on the other hand, the verb is in the subjunctive. E. g. *Dic míhi, cujus híc liber* sit, Tell me whose book this is. *Nescio, quis homo sis,* I do not know who you are. (Cf. Lesson LXXXVII. *D.*)

III. In conditional clauses, when the case is asserted as a real, and not as a hypothetical or doubtful one. E. g.

Pôma ex arbórĭbus, *si* crúda *súnt,* vi *avellúntur; si* matûra et cócta, *décidunt.*	Unripe fruit is plucked from the trees by force; if ripe and mellow, it falls of its own accord.
Si quís oriénte Canícŭlä *nâtus ést,* in mári non *moriêtur.*	If any one is born when the dog-star rises, he will not die at sea.
Ísta vérĭtas, *etiámsi* jucúnda nôn *ést,* míhi támen grâta *ést.*	This truth, although it is not a pleasant one, is nevertheless agreeable to me.
Quî *póssum* putáre mê restitútum, *si distrahor* ab íis, per quôs restitútus súm?	How can I consider myself restored, if I am distracted by those through whom I was restored?
Núllä ália in civitâte, *nisi* in quâ pópuli potéstas súmma *est,* úllum domicílium *hábet* libértas.	Liberty can have no abode in any state, except where the power of the people is supreme.

Égo, *ni* púgna *restitúitur*, fortû-
nam cum ómnĭbus, infúmiam
sôlus *séntiam.*

Unless the contest is renewed, I
shall feel our misfortune in common with all, and the disgrace
alone.

REMARK. — When the condition expressed by *si* and *nisi* is not a
real, but merely a hypothetical one, the verb is in the subjunctive, on
which see Lesson LXXXVI.)

PECULIAR USE OF THE INDICATIVE.

B. The Romans sometimes use the indicative in constructions in which the English idiom requires the subjunctive.

I. With verbs and expressions denoting *ability, permission,
duty, necessity,* and the like, the present indicative is commonly
put instead of the imperfect subjunctive, and the imperfect, the
perfect indefinite, and the pluperfect indicative instead of the
pluperfect subjunctive.

Such verbs are *possum, licet, debeo, decet, oportet, necesse est ; longum, aequum, par, consentanĕum, satis, satius, melius, optĭmum est, erat,
fuit, fuĕrat,* and the like. So also the participle in *dus* with *sum, eram,*
&c. In all these cases the present is rendered by the English *might,
could, would,* or *should,* and the past tenses by *might, could, would,* or
should have. E. g.

Póssum pérsequi múlta oblecta-
ménta rêrum rusticûrum, sed
&c.

I *could* enumerate the many pleasures of agriculture, but, &c.

O quám *fácile érat* órbis impé-
rium occupâre !

O how easy it *would have* been to
obtain the command of the entire world !

Perturbatiónes animôrum *potĕram* égo mórbos appellâre ;
sed nôn conveniret ad ómnia.

I *might have* called the disorders of
the mind diseases, but the name
would not have been applicable
to all cases.

Oh, rêgem mê ésse *opórtuit.*

I *ought to have* been king.

Jéci fundaménta reipúblicae, sé-
rius omníno, quám *décuit.*

I have laid the foundation of the
republic, later doubtless, than I
should have done.

Líbĕros túos institĭere atque eru-
dîre *debuisti.*

You *ought to have* instructed and
educated your children.

Hóc fácere *debébas.*

You *should have* done this.

Lónge *utílius fúit,* angústias údI-
tus occupâre.

It would have been far better to
occupy the defile.

Haêc vía tíbi *érat ingrediénda.*

You should have entered upon this
road.

Nôn Ásiae nômen *objiciéndum*
Murénae *fúit,* ex quâ laûs fa-
míliae constitûta ést.

Murena *ought not to have been*
taunted with the name of Asia,
from which the glory of his
family is derived.

REMARKS.

1. In condititional sentences the historians sometimes likewise employ one of the past tenses of the indicative, instead of the more usual *pluperfect subjunctive*, to denote that something *would have taken place* under certain conditions. E. g. *Jam fames quam pestilentia tristior* erat (= fuisset), ni *annonae foret subventum*, The famine would have been a sadder calamity than the pestilence, unless additional supplies had been procured. *Temere fēcerat* (= fecisset) *Nerva, si adoptasset alium*, Nerva would have acted inconsiderately, if he had adopted another.

2. In like manner, the imperfect indicative sometimes (though less frequently) stands instead of the *imperfect* subjunctive, when the verb of the conditional clause is of the same tense. E. g. *Stultum* erat (= esset) *monēre, nisi fieret*, It would be folly to admonish, unless your advice were heeded. *Omnino supervacua* erat (= esset) *doctrīna, si natūra sufficeret*.

II. In general relative expressions, i. e. in those introduced by *quisquis, quotquot, quicunque, quantuscunque, quantuluscunque, utut, utcunque*, and other compounds of *cunque*, the verb is more commonly in the indicative than in the subjunctive. E. g.

Quídquid id ést.	Whatever that may be.
Quóquo módo rês sê hábet; or *Utcúnque sê hábet rês.*	However that may be.
Quicúnque is est.	Whoever he may be.
Quídquid habuit, quantumcúnque fúit, illud totum húbuit ex disciplínā.	Whatever property or greatness he possessed, he owed it all to his discipline and skill.
Quém sórs diêrum cúnque dábit, lúcro appône.	Mark as clear gain, whatever day your destiny may grant you.
Quídquid úl ést, tímeo Dánaos et dôna feréntes.	Whatever that may be, I dread the Greeks, even when they offer presents.
Hómines benévolos, qualescúnque súnt, gráve ést ínsequi contuméliā.	It is hard to pursue benevolent men of any description with insults.
Utcúnque sése rês hábet, túa ést cúlpa.	However that may be, the fault is yours.

REMARK.—The words above enumerated are sometimes also followed by the subjunctive, especially among the later Roman authors. E. g. *Quibuscunque verbis uti* velis, Whatever words you may wish to employ. *In quacunque parte sit titubatum*, In whatever part there may have been a failure.

III. In clauses introduced by *sive — sive*, the verb is generally likewise in the indicative. E. g.

Sive tacêbis, sive lóquêris, míhi perinde ést.	Whether you are silent, or whether you speak, it is all the same to me.

Sive vêrum *est, sive* fálsum, mîhi quídem íta renuntiâtum ést.

Whether it is true or false, it has been so reported to me.

Véniet témpus mórtis, et quídem celériter, et *síve retractâbis, sive properâbis*.

The time of death will come, and that quickly, whether you resist it or accelerate it.

REMARK.—Instances of the subjunctive also occur. E. g. *Nam* sive *illâ defensione uti* voluisses, sive *hâc, quâ utéris, condemnéris necesse est*, For, whether you had intended to use that defence or the one you are using now, you must be condemned.

To doubt, to be uncertain.	*Dubitâre, dubîum* or *in dubio esse.*
To doubt, question anything.	{ *Dubitâre de aliquâ re* or *aliquid.* { Rêm in dubium vocâre.
I doubt whether.	Dubíto, in dubio sum, *num* (with the subj.).
I doubt, whether .... or.	{ Dubíto, *utrum* .... *an* (with the { subj.).
I do not doubt, that (but that).	Nôn dubíto, *quin* (with the subj.).
Do you doubt that ?	{ Dubitâsne hóc ? { Vocâsne rém in dúbium ?
I do not doubt it.	{ Nôn dúbito. { Rém in dúbium nôn vóco.
It is not to be doubted.	Dubitâri nôn pótest.
What do you doubt ?	Quíd dúbitas ?
I doubt what that man has told me.	In dúbium vóco id, quod ílle mîhi narrâvit.
I doubt whether he has arrived.	Dúbito, num advénerit.
Who doubts that my father has left ?	Quís dúbitat, *quin* páter méus profectus sít ?
I do not doubt but that he will come.	{ Nôn dúbito, quin ventûrus sit. { Non dúbito, éum ventûrum esse.
He is sure that he will not come.	Nôn dúbitat, quin nôn ventûrus sit.
Who doubts that man is mortal ?	Quís dúbitat, hóminem mortâlem ésse ?
No one can question it.	Némo rém in dúbium vocâre possit.
It is doubtful whether the judges or the lawyers are to blame.	Dúbium ést, *utrum* júdices *án* jurisconsúlti vituperándi sint.
I am inclined to, perhaps, probably.	*Dubíto an, haud scio an, nescio an* (with the subj.).
I am inclined to give him the first place.	*Dúbito an* húnc prímum ómnium *pónam.*
A man of consummate wisdom, and *perhaps* the most distinguished of them all.	Vír sapientíssimus atque *haûd scio an* ómnium praestantíssimus.
It is perhaps enough.	*Haûd scio* (*néscio*) *an* sátis sít.
To agree or consent to a thing.	{ *Consentio, íre, sensi, sensum.* { *Convênit mihi* (CUM ALIQUO DE { ALIQUA RE).

To disagree, differ.	Discrepāre, dissentīre.
We agree.	{ Cónvěnit inter nôs. { Nôs convénimus.
Peace has been agreed upon.	Páx cónvěnit.
To admit, confess.	{ Fateor, ēri, fessus sum. { Confitēri (ALIQUID ALICUI).
To concede, grant.	Concēdo, ěre, cessi, cessum (ALI-CUI ALIQUID).
To agree, or to compose a difference.	{ Compōnere. In gratiam redire. { De controversiis transigěre (ēgi, actum).
To become reconciled to one.	Cum aliquo in gratiam redire.
To consent (to do anything).	Consentire, assentīri (FACERE, REM FIERI, UT FIAT).
Did you agree about the price ?	{ Convenítne tíbi eum éo de prétio ? { Convenítne tíbi prétium ?.
We did agree.	{ Convěnit míhi cum éo. { Convěnit prétium.
What did you agree upon ?	Quâ de rê consensístis inter vôs ?
We were agreed upon the safety of the republic.	De reipúblicae salûte consénsimus.
Did you agree in praising him ?	Vôs in íllo laudándo consensístis ?
We did not agree.	{ Nôn consénsimus. { Immo véro disénsimus.
The age of Homer is not agreed upon.	Super Homéri aetâte nôn consentĭtur.
Do you consent to my doing that ?	Consentísne, ut hóc fáciam ?
I do consent.	Nôn disséntio.
Do you confess (admit) that to be a fault ?	Faterísne íllud ésse vítium ?
I admit it.	Fáteor.
Do you confess your error ?	Confiteríane túum errôrem ?
I do confess it.	Confíteor.
How much did you pay for that hat ?	Quántam pecúniam ísto pro píleo solvísti ?
I paid three dollars for it.	Três thaléros.
At what price did he buy the horse ?	Quánti êmit ílle équum ?
He bought it *for* five hundred dollars.	(Émit éum) quingéntis thaléris.
Did they compose their difference ?	Transegerúntne de controvérsiis ?
They have composed it.	Composuérunt et transegérunt.
They have become reconciled.	In grátiam inter sê rediérunt.
He has become reconciled to me.	In grátiam mêcum rédiit.

---

* "For" with the price is not expressed, according to Lesson LXXI A.

To wear (clothes, a ring, &c.). { *Gěro, ěre, gessi, gestum.*
Gestāre (VESTEM, ANULUM, &c.).
Indŭtum esse veste, &c.

To wear a coat, a cloak.	Amictum esse togā, pallio.
To wear a sword.	Cinctum esse gladio.
Did he wear black or white clothes?	Útrum véstem gerêbat nígram an cándidam?
He wore white ones.	Cándidam gerêbat.
Had he boots or shoes on?	Caligísne an cálceis indûtus érat?
He had shoes on.	Indûtus érat cálceis.
He habitually wore a gem on his finger.	Gestábat gémmam dígito.

The custom, habit.   *Consuetudo,* ĭnis, f.; *mŏs,* gen. *mŏris,* m.

Against my custom.	Contra méam consuetúdǐnem.
It is against my custom.	Nôn est méae consuetúdinis.

It is customary. { Mós ést. Est môris (ut . . . .).
Consuetúdo obtǐnet (faciendi aliquid).

As is customary. { Ut est môris (consuetúdǐnis), ut sólet.

According to custom.	Pro (ex) consuetúdǐne, ex môre.

To observe, take notice of, perceive something.   *Vidēre, cernĕre, animadvertĕre, observāre, perspicĕre* (ALIQUID).

Do you perceive that?	Perspicísne hóc?
I do perceive it.	Véro, perspício.
Did you take notice of that?	Observastǐne (perspexistǐne) hóc?
I did not observe it.	Nôn observávi (perspéxi).
Did you notice what he did?	Animadvertistǐne, quod ílle fécĕrit?
I did notice it.	Animadvérti.

To expect, hope.   *Exspectāre, sperāre* (ALIQUID, ACC. cum INF.).

Do you expect to receive a letter from your uncle? { Exspectûsne lítteras a pátruo túo?
Sperâsne fóre, ut lítteras a pátruo accípias?

I do expect it.	Exspécto (spéro).
Did we expect it?	Núm nôs exspectávimus?
We did not expect it.	Nôn exspectávimus (mínime sperávimus).

To procure, get.   *Parāre, comparāre* (SIBI, ALICUI ALIQUID).

To acquire (procure).   *Acquīro, ěre, sīvi, sītum* (ALIQUID).

Can you get me some money?	Potésne míhi parâre pecúniam?
I cannot do it.	Fácere nôn póssum.
Has he been able to procure the necessaries of life?	Potuǐtne acquírĕre, quod ad vítae úsum pertíneat?
He has been able.	Pótuit.
I cannot get anything to eat.	Égo, quód édam, comparâre néqueo.
He has acquired wealth, honor, and influence.	Divítias, honóres, auctoritatemque acquisívit.

EXERCISE 157.

What have you gained that money by ? — I have gained it by working. — What have you done with your wine ? — I have spilt it on the table. — Where is yours ? — It is on the large table in my little room; but you must not drink any of it, for I must keep it for my father who is ill. — Are you ready to depart with me ? — I am so. — Why are you laughing at that man ? — I do not intend to laugh at him. — I beg of you not to do it, for you will break his heart if you laugh at him. — Why have they hanged that man ? — They have hanged him, because he has killed somebody. — Have they hanged the man who stole a horse (from) your brother ? — They have punished him, but they have not hanged him : they only hang highwaymen in our country. — Where have you found my coat ? — I found it in the blue room; it was hanging on a nail. — Will you hang my hat on the tree ? — I will hang it thereon ? — Do you doubt what I am telling you ? — I do not doubt it. — Do you doubt what that man has told you ? — I do doubt it, for he has often told me what was not true. — Why have you not kept your promise ? — I know no more what I promised you. — Did you not promise us to take us to the concert (on) Thursday ? — I confess that I promised you ; but the concert did not take place. — Does your brother confess his fault ? — He does confess it. — What does your uncle say to that letter ? — He says that it is written very well ; but he admits that he has been wrong in sending it to the captain. — Do you confess your fault now ? — I confess it to be a fault. — Have you at last bought the horse which you wished to buy ? — How could I buy the horse, if I am unable to procure money ? — Unless you pay me what you owe me, I shall not be able to go. — Ought I to have gone into the country yesterday ? — You ought to have done it. — You ought to have educated and instructed your son. — This letter ought to have been written by you. — O how easy it would have been to learn your lesson ! — It would have been far better to remain at home. — Do you know that man ? — Whoever he may be, I do not wish to know him. — However that may be, you have not done your duty (*officium tuum non servavisti*). — Whether you go or stay, it is all the same to me. — I shall have to write, whether I am sick or well.

Lesson LXXXV. — PENSUM OCTOGESIMUM QUINTUM.

OF THE FORM OF SENTENCES.

A. In respect to their form, sentences are either *absolute* or *conditioned, positive, negative,* or *interrogative.* (Cf. Lessons LXXXIV. and LXXXVI.)

46

I. A positive or affirmative proposition asserts the existence of a state in a given subject as present, past, or future by means of a finite verb only. Its force may be augmented by an adverb.

Adverbs of this class are called *adverbia asserendi*. The principal are *nae*, surely; *sāne, profecto*, really; *utique*, to be sure; *vēro*, in truth, truly; to which add the (generally) ironical *scilicet, videlicet, nimirum, nempe*, and *quippe*, of course, certainly, forsooth. E. g.

Nae illi veheménter *érrant*, si illam méam prístinam lenitâtem perpétuam spérant futûram.	They are certainly very much mistaken, if they expect that former lenity of mine to be perpetual.
Térra *profécto* múndi párs *ést*.	The earth is doubtless a part of the universe.
Éstne ípsus an nôn ést? — Ís ést, *cérte is ést*, is *ést profécto*.	Is it he himself or not? — It is he, certainly it is, it is the very man.
Íllud *scire útique* cúpio.	I desire to know that at all events.
Égo *véro* cúpio, tê ad mê veníre.	I certainly wish you to come to me.
Égo istíus pécŭdis consílio *scilicet* aut praesídio *úti* volébam?	Did I forsooth desire to use the advice or help of a beast like this?
Híc de nóstris vérbis érrat *vidélicet*.	He is manifestly mistaken about our language.
Demósthenes apud álios lóqui *vidélicet* didícerat, nôn múltum ípse sécum.	Demosthenes had learnt to speak with others, I suppose, not much by personal effort privately.
Nôn ómnia *nimirum* eídem díi dedêre.	The gods have certainly not granted everything to one man.
Quôs égo órno? — *Némpe* éos, qui ípsi súnt ornaménta réi públicae.	Whom do I honor? Those certainly who are themselves the ornaments of the republic.
Sòl Demócrito mágnus vidétur, *quippe* hómini erudíto, in geometriâque perfécto.	The sun seems large to Democritus, he being a learned man and perfect in geometry.

II. A negative sentence asserts the non-existence of a state in the subject, and is thus directly opposed to an affirmative one.

Negative sentences are formed by means of the adverbs *non*, not; *haud*, not at all; *minime*, by no means; *ne*, lest, that not. Also by *nemo, nullus, nihil, nunquam, nondum, nec, neque*, &c. To these add the negative verbs *nescio, nōlo, nēgo*, and *vēto*. E. g.

Nives in álto mári *nôn* cádunt.	Snow does not fall on the main sea.
Pausánias *haûd* íta mágnā mánu Graéciā fugâtus ést.	Pausanias was put to flight by not so very large a Grecian band.
Potéstis effícere, ut mále móriar: *ne* móriar, nôn potéstis.	You can make me die a cruel death, but you cannot prevent my dying.
Íta súm afflíctus, ut *némo* únquam.	I am so distressed as no one ever was before.

Nōn únquam álias ánte tántus térror senâtum invâsit.

Never at any time before did such a terror invade the senate.

Némo vír mágnus sine áliquo afflâtu divíno únquam fúit.

There never was a great man without a certain divine enthusiasm.

Epicûrus négat, úllum ésse témpus, quô sápiens nôn beâtus sit.

Epicurus denies that there is any time at which a wise man is not happy.

Flêtum duódĕcim tábŭlae in funéribus adhibéri vetuérunt.

The twelve tables prohibited the practice of wailing at funerals.

III. When two negations occur in the same sentence, the first or emphatic one generally destroys the second.

Such are *non nemo*, some one; *non nihil*, something; *non nunquam*, sometimes; *non nisi*, not except, i. e. only; *non ignoro*, I know very well; *non possum non loqui*, I cannot but speak. So also *nemo non*, every one; *nihil non*, everything; *nullus non*, each, every; *nunquam non*, always; *nusquam non*, everywhere. E. g.

Hóstis est in úrbe, in fóro; nôn némo étiam in íllo sacrário réi públicae, in ípsâ, ínquam, cúriâ nôn némo hóstis ést.

The enemy is in the city, in the forum; there is an enemy even in the sanctuary of the republic; in the senate-house itself, I say, there is an enemy.

Míhi líber ésse nôn vidêtur, qui nôn aliquándo nihil ágit.

He does not seem to me to be a free man, who is not sometimes disengaged from business.

Nōn súm néscius, quánto perículo vívam in tántâ multitúdine improbórum.

I am not unaware of the great danger in which I live, in the midst of such a multitude of rascals.

Nōn íi némini, sed nôn sémper úni parêre voluérunt.

It was not their wish to obey no one, but not perpetually the same individual.

Qui mórtem in mális pónit, nôn pótest éam nôn timêre.

He who considers death an evil cannot avoid fearing it.

Némo pótest nôn beatíssimus esse, qui in sê úno súa pónit ómnia.

No one can avoid being the happiest man in the world, who makes everything depend upon himself alone.

Atheniénses Alcibíadem nihil nôn effícere pósse ducébant.

The Athenians thought that Alcibiades could do everything.

Nihil ágĕre ánimus nôn pótest.

The mind cannot be inactive.

Alexándro núllius púgnae nôn secúnda fortûnâ fúit.

Alexander had fortune in his favor in every battle fought by him.

Diútius nescíre nôn póssum.

I can be ignorant no longer.

Núsquam ésse nôn póssunt.

They cannot be nowhere (= they must be somewhere).

INTERROGATIVE SENTENCES.

B. A sentence becomes interrogative, when the speaker asks another person for information, for instruction, or assent to his opinion. A sentence of this kind is complete only in connection with the answer.

I. If the inquiry is made merely for information, the emphatic
word is put at the beginning, and the expected answer is "yes"
or "no." If assent is required, then the answer to a positive
inquiry is "no," and to a negative one "yes." E. g.

Scis Áppium censôrem hic ostén-ta fácere ?	Do you know that Appius, the censor, is doing wonders here ?
Nŏn pátrem égo tê nóminem, úbi tû túam mê appélles fíliam ?	Shall I not call you father, when you call me your daughter ?
En únquam cuiquam contumeli-ósius audistis factam injúriam, quám haêc-ést míhi ?	Did ye ever hear of an injustice practised upon any one more insolently, than this is upon me ?
Quid ? Si tê rogávero áliquid, *nŏn* respondêbis ?	What ? If I have asked you anything, will you not reply ?
Infélix ést Fabrícius, quód rûs súum fódit ? — *Nŏn.*	Is Fabricius unhappy, because he digs his farm ? — No.
Nŏn vóbis vídeor cum áliquo de-clamatóre disputáre ? — *Étiam.*	Do I not seem to you to be disputing with some declaimer ? — Yes.

II. Questions requiring a more definite explanation or assent
are introduced by interrogative pronouns, adjectives, and adverbs.

Such are *quis, qui,* who ? *quid, quod,* what ? *quantus,* how great ?
quot, how many ? *quŏtus,* which, what (of a certain number) ? *quális,*
what kind of ? *quoties,* how many times ? *quam, ut,* how ? *quando,*
when ? *ubi,* where ? *quo,* whither ? *quâ,* which way ? *unde,* whence ?
To these add *cur,* why ? *quâre,* wherefore ? *qui,* or *quomŏdo,* how ?
quin, quidni, why not ? &c. E. g.

Quis hómo ést ? — Égo sum Pám-philus.	Who is the man ? — I am Pamphilus.
Qui státus, *quod* discrimen, *quae* fúerit in rê públicâ tempéstas ílla, *quis* néscit ?	Who does not know, what a state of things, what a danger, what a stormy time that was in the republic ?
Heus, *écquis* in vílâ ést ? *Écquis* hóc réclúdit ?	Holla ! Is there any one in the house ? Is any one opening the door ?
Quális est istôrum orátio ?	What is the character of the language used by these ?
Quális oratôris et *quánti* hóminis in dicéndo pútas ésse, históri-am scríbëre ?	What sort of an orator, and how great a man in the use of language, do you suppose it requires to write a history ?
Unde iste ámor tam improvísus ac tam repentínus ?	Whence this love of yours so unexpected and so sudden ?
Cur Africânum doméstici pariê-tes nôn texérunt ?	Why did his domestic walls not protect Africanus ?
Déus fálli *qui* potest ?	How can the Deity be deceived ?
Quin, quod ést feréndum, férs ?	Why do you not bear what has to be borne ?
Quidni póssim ?	Why should I not be able ?

III. Questions in Latin are frequently modified by particles; such as *ne*, perhaps? then? *nonne*, not? is it not so? *num*, *numne*, then? *an*, or perhaps? *anne, annon*, or not?

To *nonne* and *annon* the expected answer is always "yes"; to *num* and *an*, commonly "no." The enclitic *ne* is always subjoined to the emphatic word. When this word is the verb of the sentence, the answer may be "yes" or "no"; when another word, it is commonly "no." E. g.

Pergísne éam ártem illúdere, in quâ excéllis ípse?	Do you persist in deriding the very art in which you yourself excel?
Úbi aut quâlis sit túa méns? *Potésne* dícere?	Where or what is the nature of your mind? Can you tell?
Quám rém ágis? — *Egóne?* Argéntum cúdo, quód tíbi dém.	What are you driving at? — I? I am coining silver, to give to you.
Satisne est, nóbis vôs timéndos esse?	Is it not true, that you are to be feared by us?
Ain' tû? — *Mên'* rógas? — *Itáne* (sc. est)?	Do you really say so? — Do you ask *me*? — Is it so?
Quid nunc? Quâ spê aut quô consílio hûc ímus? Quid coéptas, Thráso? — *Egóne?*	What now? With what expectation or for what purpose do we come hither? What are you after, Thraso? — I?
Nónne animadvértis?	Do ye not perceive?
Num quídnam, inquam, nóvi?	Is there anything new, I say?
Num negâre aúdes?	Do you dare to deny it?
Númquid dúas habêtis pátrias?	Have you two native countries?
*Écquid** sentítis, in quánto contémtu vivâtis?	Do you perceive in what contempt you live?
Quid? Déum ípsum *númne* vidístī?	What? Hast thou beheld the Deity himself?
An quísquam pótest sine pert batióne méntis irâsci?	Can any one be angry without agitation of the mind?
An est úllum mâjus málum turpitúdine?	Is there any greater evil than dishonor?
Ánne est íntus Pámphilus?	Pamphilus is not in the house, is he?
An nón díxi ésse hóc futûrum?	Did I not say that this would be so?
An nón est ómnis métus sérvĭtus?	Is not fear of every kind servitude?

IV. Questions, to which a mere "yes" or "no" is expected, may be answered, —

1. By the repetition of the emphatic word of the question, with or without the addition of an intensive word.

2. "Yes," by *sane, etiam, vĕrum, vĕro, ita, ita est, ita enim vĕro.*

3. "No," by *non, non vĕro, minĭme, minĭme vĕro, nihil mĭnus.* E. g.

Éstne pópulus Collatínus ín suâ potestâte? — *Ést.*	Is the people of Collatia master of itself? — It is.

---

* After *numquid* and *ecquid* the answer is generally "no"; after *ecquid*, sometimes "yes."

Dâsne hóc nóbis ? — *Dó sîne.*

Tûne négas ? — *Négo hércle véro.*

Virtútes nárro. — Méas ? — Túas.

Ábiit Clítipho. — Sólus ? — *Só-lus.*

Nôn irâta és ? — *Nôn súm irâta.*

Éstne frâter íntus ? — *Nôn ést.*

Nôn exístimas, cádere in sapién-tem aegritúdinem ? — *Prórsus nôn árbitror.*

Haeccine túa dómus ést ? — *Íta,* inquam.

Fácies ? — *Vêrum.*

Vísne sermóni réliquo dêmus óperam sedéntes ? — *Sáne quí-dem.*

Cur nôn intróeo in nóstram dó-mum ? — Quid dómun vé-stram ? — *Íta enim véro.*

Dic mihi, cújum pécus ? an Moe-liboéi ? — *Nôn,* vérum Aegó-nis.

Nôn ópus est ? — *Nôn hércle véro.*

An tû hóc nôn crédis ? — *Míni-me véro.*

An Gállos existimâtis hic versári ánimo demísso útque húmili ? — *Nihil véro mínus.*

Do you concede this to us ? — I do.

Do you deny it ? — I verily deny it.

I report virtues.—Mine ?—Yours.

Clitipho has left. — Alone ? — Alone.

Are you not angry ? — I am not angry.

Is your brother in ? — He is not.

You do not suppose that a philos-opher can be affected by misfor-tune ? — I do not think it possi-ble.

Is *this* your house ? — It is.

Shall you do it ? — Yes.

Is it your wish that we attend to the rest of the discussion sitting ? — Certainly.

Why do I not go into *our* house ? — What, into your house ? — Ay, to be sure.

Tell me, whose flock this is ? that of Mœliboeus ? — No, but of Ægon.

It is *not* necessary ? — No, by my troth, no.

Or do you not believe this ? — By no means.

Do you think the Gauls remain here humble and submissive ? — Far from it.

REMARKS.

1. *Recte* and *optime* are either "yes" or "no," according to the nature of the question. *Scilicet,* "doubtless," "to be sure," affirms ironically. E. g. *Satin' salve ? dic mihi.* — *Recte,* Are you very well ? tell me. — I am. *Quid est ? — Nihil,* recte perge, What is it ? — Nothing. *Thucydidem,* inquit, *imitamur. — Optime,* We imitate Thu-cydides, he says. — Very well. *Ego tibi irascěrer ? tibi ego possem irasci ? — Scilicet !* I angry with you ? Could I be angry with you ? — Forsooth !

2. *Imo* or *immo* always corrects the preceding question, and either raises doubt or opposes something else to it (sometimes the very oppo-site). Hence it is sometimes "yes," "to be sure," and sometimes "no," "O no." E. g. *Credisne ? — Imo certe* (Ay, to be sure). — *Non patria praestat omnibus officiis ? — Immo vero* (certainly). — *Te-naxne est ? — Imo pertinax* (Nay, even pertinacious). — *Silebitne filius ?*

Immo vero (on the contrary) *obsecrabit patrem, ne faciat.* — *Dic, me orare, ut veniat.* — *Ad te?* — Imo *ad Philumenam* (No, but to Philumena).

3. If the answer is given with a noun, adjective, or pronoun, its case must be the one required by the verb of the question. E. g. *Cujus liber est?* — *Caesaris.* — *Mene vis?* — Te. *Quanti emisti?* — Parvo.

DISJUNCTIVE QUESTIONS.

C. I. An interrogative sentence may be composed of two or more members, in such a manner that one excludes the other. Such questions are called *disjunctive* or *double*, and are of two kinds, viz. : —

1. The second member is simply the negation of the first. E. g. Is ambition a virtue, *or none* (i. e. or is it not a virtue)?

2. The second member contains another question opposed to the first. E. g. Has he conquered, *or you* (i. e. or have you conquered)? If, in the answer to a double question, one of the cases is affirmed, the other is denied, and *vice versa*. E. g. It is not a virtue. He has conquered, and *not* you.

II. The particles employed in such disjunctive questions are as follows : —

1. The first member is either introduced by *utrum, num,* — *ne,* or stands without any particle.

2. The " or " of the second member is generally *an,* but when the first member is without a particle, the enclitic *ne* may take the place of *an.* When the question contains more than two members, the formula is *utrum, &c. . . . . an . . . . an, &c.*

3. The " or not " of the second member is *annon* (or *an non*), and more rarely *necne.*

The use of these particles gives rise to five different formulas for disjunctive questions. They are as follows : —

utrum,	utrumne	——	an,	anne,	annon.
num,	numquid	——	an,	annon.	
— ne		——	an,	annon.	
——		——	an,	annon.	
——		——	— ne,	necne.	

EXAMPLES.

Num tábulas hábet, *ánnon?*	Has he the pictures, or not?
Útrum ánimos sociórum ab rĕ públicā abalienábas, *án nón?*	Did you alienate the minds of our allies from the republic, or not?
Ísne est, quém quaéro, *ánnon?*	Is it he whom I am looking for, or not?
Súnt haĕc túa vérba, *nécne?*	Are these your words, or not?
Dícam huíc, *an nón* dícam?	Shall I tell him, or shall I not tell?

Útrum ígitur hâs córporis, an
Pythágorae tíbi mâlis víres ingénii dári ?

Which would you then rather have,
physical strength like this, or the
intellectual powers of Pythagoras ?

Útrum tándem perspicuísne dú-
bia aperiúntur, an dúbiis per-
spícua tollúntur ?

Are doubtful things elucidated by
those that are clear, or are the
clear corrected by the doubtful ?

Númquid dúas habêtis pátrias, an
ést ílla pátria commûnis ?

Have you two countries, or is that
your common country ?

Aristóteles ipséne érrat, an álios
vúlt errâre ?

Is Aristotle himself mistaken, or
does he wish others to be so ?

Récto itínere duxísti exércitum
ad hóstes, an per anfráctus
viârum ?

Did you march the army directly
against the enemy, or by a cir-
cuitous route ?

Útrum hóc tû párum commemi-
nísti, an égo nôn sátis intel-
léxi, an mutâsti senténtiam ?

Do you not recollect this very well,
or did I not sufficiently comprehend it, or have you changed
your opinion ?

Romámne vénio, an hic máneo,
an Arpinum fúgio ?

Shall I go to Rome, or remain here,
or flee to Arpinum ?

REMARKS.

1. *Utrum* indicates at the very outset that a second question is to
follow. In *direct* double questions beginning with *num*, the first member is expected to be denied, and the second affirmed. (Cf. Lesson
LXXXV. *B.* III.) In double questions otherwise introduced, either
member may be affirmed or denied.

2. The *ne* of the second member is almost entirely confined to *indirect* questions. E. g. *Sine sciam, captiva materne in castris tuis sim,* I
wish to know whether I am a captive or your mother in your camp.
Albus aterne fúeris, ignorat, He knows not whether you were white
or black. On the use of these particles in indirect disjunctive questions generally, see Lesson LXXXVII. *D.*

3. When "*or*" introduces no second question, but only another
word of the same question, it is expressed by *aut*. E. g. *Tibi ego aut
tu mihi servus es? — Voluptas melioremne efficit aut laudabiliorem
virum?*

4. If the second member of a double question is introduced by the
English "and not," the Romans put simply *non*. E. g. *Ergo histrio
hoc videbit in scena,* non *videbit vir sapiens in vita?* Will the actor
see this on the stage, *and* the philosopher *not* in life? *Hujus vos
animi* monumenta retinebis, *corpóris in Italia* nullum sepulcrum esse
patiemini? Will you retain the monuments of his genius, and not suffer
a sepulchre for his body in Italy?

The form, figure.	Forma, figura, ae, f. Species, ei, f.
The woman	Femina, ae, f.: mulier, ĕris, f.
The wife.	Conjux, ugis, f.; uxor, ōris, f.
The married woman.	Nupta, marita, ae, f.

The lady of the house, mistress.	Materfamilias, *f.;* hĕra, domĭna, ae, *f.*
The mother.	Māter, tris, *f.*
The daughter.	Filĭa, nāta, ae, *f.*
The girl.	Puella, ae, *f.*
The door.	Ostĭum, i, *n.;* janŭa, ae, *f.*
The bottle.	Lagēna, ae, *f.*
The phial.	Ampulla, ae, *f.*
The fork.	Furca, ae, *f.*
The spoon.	Cochlĕar, is, *n.*
The plate.	Catillus, i, *m.* (*pl.* catilla, *n.*); discus, i, *m.* (*large plate*).
The cup.	Pocillum ansātum (i, *n.*).
The saucer.	Scutella, ae, *f.*
The towel.	Mantēle, is, *n.;* mantēlium, i, *n.*
The napkin.	Mappa, mappŭla, ae, *f.*
The soup.	Juscŭlum, i, *n.*
The butter.	Butȳrum, i, *n.*
The dessert.	Mensa secunda (ae, *f.*); bellāria, ōrum, *n.*
To serve the dessert.	Mensam secundam apponĕre.
To eat (sip) soup.	Juscŭlum sorbēre (-būi).
To wipe.	{ Tergĕo, ēre, tersi, tersum. { Extergēre (ALIQUAM REM).
To speak through the nose.	De nāribus lŏqui.
The nose.	Nāsus, i, *m.;* nāres, ium, *f. pl.* (*nostrils*).
The silk.	Bombyx, ȳcis, *m.;* serĭca, ōrum, *n.*
Made of silk.	Serĭcus, bombycĭnus, a, um.
The silk stuff.	Serĭca, bombycīna, ōrum, *n.*
The silk stocking, cravat, &c.	Tibiāle serĭcum, focāle bombycīnum.
My good linen.	Lintea mĕa bŏna (*pl*).
His beautiful linen shirts.	Indusia ejus lintea pulchra.
The room (parlor).	Diaeta, ae, *f.*
The sleeping-room.	Cubicŭlum, i, *n.*
The closet, chamber.	Conclāve, is, *n.*
The wardrobe.	Conclāve vestiārĭum.
The dining-room.	Coenācŭlum, triclinĭum, i, *n.*
The front-room.	Cubicŭlum antĭcum.
The back-room.	Cubicŭlum postĭcum.
The study.	Musēum, i, *n.;* bibliothēca, ae, *f.*
To live in, occupy.	{ Habitāre (in) alĭquo lŏco. { Tenēre lŏcum.
To live in the front (or first part of the house).	Primum lŏcum aedĭum tenēre.
The sister.	Sŏror, ōris, *f.*
The young lady (virgin).	Virgo, ĭnis, *f.*
The tongue.	Lingua, ae, *f.*
The language.	Lingua, ae, *f.;* sermo, ōnis, *m.*

The street.	Vĭa, via publĭca (ae, *f.*); platĕa, ae, *f.* (*wide street*).
The city, town.	Urbs, *gen.* urbis, *f.*; oppĭdum, i, *n.*; civĭtas, ātis, *f.* (*inhabitants*).
The hand.	Mănus, ūs, *f.*
The right hand.	Dextra, ae, *f.*
The left hand.	Sinistra, laeva, ae, *f.*
The nut.	Nux, *gen.* nŭcis, *f.*
The father and his son or his daughter.	Păter et ĕjus fílius vel fília.
The mother with her son or daughter.	Mâter cum ĕjus fílio seu fília (nátā).
The child and its brother or its sister.	Infans ejúsque frâter sive sóror.
To take into one's hand.	In mănum sumĕre.
To hold in one's hand.	(In) mănū tenēre.
To write with one's own hand.	Mănū propriā scribĕre.
He thinks he will be praised.	Crédit, sê laudâtum íri.
I hope that I shall be loved.	Spéro, mê amâtum íri.

Exercise 158.

Are you not surprised at what my friend has done ? — I am much surprised at it. — At what is your son surprised ? — He is surprised at your courage. — Are you sorry for having written to my uncle ? — I am, on the contrary, glad of it. — At what art thou afflicted ? — I am not afflicted at the happiness of my enemy, but at the death of my friend. — How are your brothers ? — They have been very well for these few days. — Are you glad of it ? — I am glad to hear that they are well. — Are you a Saxon ? — No, I am a Prussian. — Do the Prussians like to learn French ? — They do like to learn it. — Do the Prussians speak German as well as the Saxons ? — The Saxons and the Prussians speak German well; but the Austrians do not pronounce it very well. — Which day of the week do the Turks celebrate (*agĕre* or *festum habēre*) ? — They celebrate Friday ; but the Christians celebrate Sunday, the Jews Saturday, and the negroes their birthday (*natalis*, sc. *dies*). — Has your sister my gold ribbon ? — She has it not. — Who has my large bottle ? — Your sister has it. — Do you sometimes see your mother ? — I see her often. — When did you see your sister ? — I saw her three months and a half ago. — Who has my fine nuts ? — Your good sister has them. — Has she also my silver forks ? — She has them not. — Why does your brother complain ? — He complains because his right hand aches. — Which bottle has your little sister broken ? — She broke the one which my mother bought yesterday. — Have you eaten of my soup or of my mother's ? — I have eaten neither of yours nor your mother's, but of that of my good sister. — Have you seen the woman that was with me this morning ? — I have not seen her. — Has your mother hurt herself. — She has not hurt herself. — Have you a sore nose ? — I have not a sore nose, but a sore hand. — Have you cut your finger ? — No, my lady, I have

cut my hand. — Will you give me a pen ? — I will give you one. —
Will you (have) this (one) or that (one) ? — I will (have) neither. —
Which (one) do you wish to have ? — I wish to have that which your
sister has. — Can you write with this pen ? — I can write with it. —
Shall you remain at home, or ride out or drive out ? — I shall remain
at home. — Has he washed his hands or his feet ? — He had done
both. — Has he learnt his lesson or not ? — He has learnt it. — He has
not learnt it. — You certainly are mistaken, if you suppose that you
will be praised, unless you are assiduous.

Lesson LXXXVI. — PENSUM OCTOGESIMUM SEXTUM.

OF THE SUBJUNCTIVE MOOD.

A. By the subjunctive mood the speaker does not absolutely
assert the existence of an action or state, but represents it as he
conceives it, as dependent upon other circumstances, and as possible only in consequence of them. Hence this mood serves to
express that which is contingent, conditional, or hypothetical;
or, in general, that which *may, can, might, could, would,* or *should*
be or be done.

The subjunctive is used more extensively in Latin than in English,
and is often put where the latter idiom requires or prefers the indicative It most commonly occurs in *subjoined* or dependent clauses, as
its name implies, but frequently also as the leading verb of an independent clause.

THE SUBJUNCTIVE IN HYPOTHETICAL PROPOSITIONS.

B. An hypothetical sentence is composed of two members, called
the *protasis* and *apodosis.* The former contains the *condition,* and is
commonly introduced by one of the conjunctions *si, nisi, etsi, etiamsi,*
or *tametsi :* the latter denotes the *inference* or *conclusion.* The subjunctive may occur in both these members of an hypothetical proposition, and represents an action or state as the *possible* consequence of
other circumstances; in other words, that something *would take place*
or *would have taken place, if* or *unless* something else *were so* or *had
been so.* In this use of the subjunctive (as *conditionālis*), the Latin
language makes an important distinction between the present and the
past tenses of that mood.

· I. In the protasis of a hypothetical proposition, the imperfect
and pluperfect subjunctive imply that the fact or reality *does*

not or *cannot* correspond with the supposition made, and in the apodosis that something *would be* or *would have been, if* the fact supposed *were* or *had been* a real one. E. g.

Si sémper óptima tenêre *possê-mus,* haûd sáne consílio múltum *egerêmus.*	If we were always able to keep what is best, we surely would not stand in need of much deliberation.
Nôn *póssem* vívere, *nísi* in lítteris *vivĕrem.*	I could not live, unless I lived in letters.
Si Neptûnus, quod Théseo promísĕrat, *nón fecísset,* Théseus fílio Hippólyto *nón orbátus ésset.*	If Neptune had not done what he had promised Theseus, Theseus would not have lost his son Hippolytus.
Aûrum et argéntum, aês, férrum frústra natûra divina *genuísset, nísi* éadem *docuísset,* quemádmodum ad eôrum vénas pervenirêtur.	Divine Nature would have produced gold and silver, brass, iron, to no purpose, unless she at the same time had taught us how to get at their veins.
Nec tû, *si* Atheniénsis *ésses,* clárus únquam *fuísses.*	Nor would you ever have been a distinguished man, if you had been an Athenian.
Id, *nísi* hic in túo régno *essêmus,* nôn *tulíssem.*	We would not have submitted to that, unless we were here in your kingdom.
Nôn, *si redísset* fílius, éi páter véniam *dáret?*	If the son had returned, would not his father give him leave?
Haêc, *si,* bís bina quót éssent, *didicísset,* cérte *nón díceret.*	If he knew how much twice two are, he would certainly not say this.

REMARKS.

1. The protasis and apodosis both generally contain either the imperfect or the pluperfect subjunctive. The imperfect, however, frequently takes the place of the pluperfect in one of the clauses, as in several of the preceding examples. When thus used, it serves to transfer a past action, partly at least, into the present time. E. g. *Quod certe non fecísset, si suum numĕrum nautârum naves* habêrent (= *habuíssent*), Which he would certainly not have done, if the ships *had had* (lit. *were then possessed of*) their usual complement of men. And in the apodosis: *Cimbri si statim infesto agmine urbem* petíssent, *grande discrimen* esset (= *fuísset*), If the Cimbri had at once invaded the city, there *would have been* a desperate struggle.

2. The mood of the verb in the apodosis is sometimes the indicative instead of the subjunctive. (Cf. Lesson LXXXIV. *A.* III.) E. g. *Quem hominem, si quā pudor in te* fuísset, *sine supplício dimíttere non* debuísti, If there had been any shame left in you, you ought not to have dismissed the man without punishment. *Quodsi Pompeius privátus esset hoc tempŏre, tamen* erat *mittendus,* Even if Pompey were at

this time a private man, it would still be necessary to send him. *Jamque castra exscindĕre* parabant (= *pararissent*), ni *Mucianus sextam legionem* opposuisset, And now they would have already begun to destroy the camp, unless Mucianus had opposed the sixth legion to them. *Praeclare* viceramus (= *vicissēmus*), nisi *Lepidus* recipisset *Antonium*, We would have won a signal victory, unless Lepidus has received Antony. This usage is confined chiefly to the pluperfect.

II. The present and perfect subjunctive in the protasis indicate that the reality either *does*, or at any rate *may*, *correspond* with the supposition made. The apodosis to such a clause then contains, either one of the same tenses of the subjunctive, or a tense of the indicative mood. E. g.

Memória *minuĭtur, nisi* éam *exérceas,* aut *si sis* natúrā tárdior.
: Your memory grows weaker, unless you exercise it, or if you by nature are somewhat slow of comprehension.

Aequabilitātem vítae servāre nôn *possis, si* aliórum virtûtem imĭtans *omĭttas* túam.
: You cannot preserve consistency of life, if while imitating the virtues of others you neglect your own.

Díes *defíciat, si velim* numerāre, quíbus bónis mále evénerit.
: The day would fail me, if I wished to enumerate the good men that have suffered evil.

Si injúriae nôn *sint,* haûd saépe auxílii *égeas.*
: If there were no injuries (inflicted), you would not often stand in need of help.

Si *exsistat* hódie ab ínfĕris Lycúrgus, *gaúdeat* murórum Spártae ruínis.
: If Lycurgus were to-day to rise from the dead, he might rejoice in the ruins of the walls of Sparta.

Sim imprúdens, si plûs *postŭlem,* quam hómini a rèrum natúrā tríbui pótest.
: I would be imprudent, if I demanded more than can be conceded to man from the nature of things.

Thucýdidis oratiónes égo laudāre sóleo ; imitāre néque *possim,* si *vélim,* nec *vélim* fortásse, si *póssim.*
: I am accustomed to praise the orations of Thucydides, but imitate them I neither could, if I would, nor would I perhaps, if I could.

Si *scieris* áspidem occúlte latēre úspiam, ímprobe *fécĕris,* nisi *monŭeris* álterum, ne assídĕat.
: If (for example) you should know of an asp lying concealed anywhere, you would do wrong, if you did not caution another not to sit down there.

Némo de nóbis únus excéllat ; sin quis *exstĭtĕrit,* álio in lóco et apud álios *sít.*
: Let no one of our number excel alone; but if any one has won distinction, let him be among others and in another place.

Si a corónā *relictus sim,* non *quéam* dícere.
: If I am deserted by my audience, I cannot speak.

47

REMARKS.

1. From the above examples it will be perceived, that in conditional clauses the present and perfect subjunctive may generally be rendered by the corresponding tenses of the indicative, from which they differ but little. Sometimes, however, it is better to translate them by the imperfect or pluperfect subjunctive. In Latin, however, the distinctions, already laid down, respecting the different tenses of the subjunctive, are never disregarded, and the present tenses (i. e. the present and perfect) always imply the reality or possibility of the fact supposed, while the past tenses (i. e. the imperfect and pluperfect) represent it as wanting or impossible. E. g. *Haec si tecum patria* loquàtur, *nonne impetrare* debeat? If your country should thus talk to you (an event which the speaker considers *possible*), ought it not to obtain what it requires of you? But, Si *universa provincia loqui* posset, *hâc vòce* uterètur, If the entire province could speak (an event which the speaker deems *impossible*), it would use this language towards you. And so in every instance of the kind.

2. When the clause introduced by *nisi, nisi forte,* or *nisi vero* stands as a correction of what has gone before, its verb is commonly in the indicative. E. g. *Nemo fere saltat sobrius*, nisi forte insanit, No one scarcely ever dances when he is sober, unless perchance he is insane. *Erat autem nihil novi, quod scribèrem*, nisi forte *hoc ad te* putas *pertinère*, I have nothing new to write you, unless perhaps you consider this of importance to you. — On the Indicative after *si, nisi,* &c., generally, see Lesson LXXXIV. *A.* III.

If, (conj.).	Si (cum IND. or SUBJ.).
If not, unless.	Nisi, ni : si non.
But if.	Sin, sin autem, si vero.
But if not.	Si non, si minus, si aliter.
If indeed.	Si quidem.
If (unless) perchance.	Si (nisi) forte.
If any one.	Si quis (or aliquis).
If anything.	Si quid (aliquid).
If at any time.	Si quando (aliquando).
If I had money.	{ Si mihi ésset pecúnia. { Si pecúniam habêrem.
If I saw him.	Si eum vidèrem.
If I were not.	Nisi égo éssem.
If he should do this.	Si hóc (or hóc si) fáceret (fáciat).
If any one should say this.	Si quis hoc dícat (díceret).
If perchance he were to lose his money.	Si pecúniam súam fórte pérdat (pérderet).
Were he at any time to beat his dog.	Si aliquándo cánem súam percutèret (percútiat).
If you were rich.	Si tû díves ésses.
If he is not ill, why does he send for the physician ?	Si aêger nôn ést, quid caúsae ést, cur médicum accéssat ?

Should you (= if you should) still receive my letter to-day, I beg you to call on me instantly.

Lítteras méas si hódie étiam *accípias*, a tê quaéso et péto, ut státim ad mê vénias.

Should he (= if he should) be hungry, something must be given him to eat.

Si esúriat, dándum est éi áliquid ad manducándum.

I should do it.

Fácĕrem.

He would have done it.

Fecísset.

We would go thither.

Nôs éo irêmus.

They would have gone thither.

Éo ivíssent.

They would have written to us.

Lítteras ad nôs dedíssent.

You would thank me once.

Grátias míhi aliquándo ágĕres (ágas).

I would buy this, if I had money. }

Émĕrem hoc, si pecúnia míhi ésset.

Si míhi ésset pecúnia, émĕrem hóc.

Had I money enough, I would pay for it.

Si pecúnia míhi sufficĕret, sólvĕrem pro hôc.

Had I money, I would give you some of it.

Si míhi ésset pecúnia, tíbi de éà dárem.

If I went thither, I should see him.

Si éo írem (éam), éum vidêrem (vídeam).

If I should give this to him, he would keep it.

Hóc, si éi dárem, tenêret.

If I should give that to him, he would not return it.

Ístud, si éi dárem, míhi nôn restitúĕret.

If you had come a little sooner, you would have met my brother.

Si aliquántulo matúrius venísses, frátrem méum convenísses.

If he knew what you have done, he would scold you.

Ílle si scíret fáctum túum, tíbi increpáret.

If there was any wood, he would make a fire.

Si lígnum adésset, ígnem accéndĕret.

If I had received my money, I would have bought a new pair of shoes.

Ego, si pecúniam míhi débitam accepíssem, nóvum calceórum pâr emíssem.

Would you learn Latin, if I learnt it?

Discĕrésne sermônem Latínum, si ego díscĕrem?

I would learn it, if you learnt it.

Díscĕrem, si tû díscĕres.

Would you have learnt English, if I had learnt it?

Didicissêsne Ánglice, si égo didicíssem?

I would have learnt it, if you had learnt it.

Dídicíssem, si tû didicísses.

Would you go to Germany, if I should go there with you?

Facĕrésne íter in Germániam, si égo têcum proficiscĕrer?

I should go there, if you would go with me.

Fácerem sáne, si tû mêcum proficiscerêris.

Would you have gone to Italy, if I had gone there?

Fecissêsne íter in Itáliam, si égo proféctus éssem?

I would have gone.

Véro, fecíssem.

Would you write a note, if I had written a letter?	Scriberêsne schédŭlam, si égo lîtteras scripsissem?
I should write a book, if you had written a letter.	Scríbĕrem égo líbrum, si tŭ líttĕras scripsísses.
Would you remain at home, if I went out?	Tenerêsne tê dómi, si égo in públicum prodírem?
I should remain at home.	Sáne, tenêrem mê dómi.
The (pair of) spectacles.	*Perspicíllum, i, n.
The old man.	Sĕnex, gen. sĕnis, m.
Optics.	Optĭcă, ĕs, f.
The optician.	Optĭcĕs gnārus.
The son-in-law.	Gĕner, ĕri, m.
The daughter-in-law.	Nŭrus, ūs, f.
The step.	Grădus, ūs, m. ; passus, ūs, m.
To make a step.	Grădum facĕre.
The progress.	Progressus, ūs, m. ; progessio, ōnis, f.
To make progress (in anything).	Procēdĕre. Progrĕdi. Profĭcĕre. Progressus facĕre. (IN ALIQUA RE.)
To progress in virtue.	{ Progressiōnem facĕre ad virtūtem. { Procēdĕre et progrĕdi in virtūte.
To make great progress.	Multum profĭcĕre (in aliquā re).
To make but little progress.	Pŭrum profĭcĕre.
Does he make progress in learning Latin?	Proficítne in línguā Latínā ediscéndā?
Really.	Vēre (adv.) ; rĕ verā, rĕ.
Once, at some future time.	Aliquando, olim (adv.).
I should like to know.	Scire vélim.
Would you have the goodness?	Velĭsne esse ĕā benignitâte (ut . . . .) ?
Would you be so good?	Velĭsne ésse tam benígnus (ut . . . .) ?
Would you do me the favor?	Velĭsne míhi dáre (tribúere) hoc ?
He might fall.	{ Cádat (cádĕret). { Fíeri potest, ut cádat.
He might do it.	Fácere hóc póssit.
To ask any one about anything.	Interrogāre aliquem aliquid *or* de aliquā re.
To keep one's bed.	Lecto tenēri, lecto affíxum esse.
Perhaps you are mistaken.	{ Nescio (dubito) an erres. { Fortasse erras.

EXERCISE 159.

Would you have money, if your father were here?—I should have some, if he were here.—Would you have been pleased, if I had had some books?—I should have been much pleased, if you had had some.—Would you have praised my little brother, if he had been good?—If he had been good, I should certainly not only have praised, but also loved, honored, and rewarded him. — Should we be praised, if we did our exercises? — If you did them without a fault, you would be praised and rewarded. — Would my brother not have been punished, if he had done his exercises? — He would not have been punished, if he had done them. — Would your sister have been praised, if she had not been skilful? — She would certainly not have been praised, if she had not been very skilful, and if she had not worked from morning until evening. — Would you give me something, if I were very good? — If you were very good, and if you worked well, I would give you a fine book. — Would you have written to your sister, if I had gone to Dresden? — I would have written and sent her something handsome, if you had gone thither. — Would you speak, if I listened to you? — I would speak, if you listened to me, and if you would answer me. — Would you have spoken to my mother, if you had seen her? — I would have spoken to her, and have begged of her to send you a handsome gold watch if I had seen her. — If the men should come, you would be obliged to give them something to drink. — If he could do this, he would do that. — A peasant having seen that old men used spectacles to read, went to an optician and asked for a pair. The peasant then took a book, and having opened it, said the spectacles were not good. The optician put another pair of the best which he could find in his shop upon his nose; but the peasant being still unable to read, the merchant said to him: "My friend, perhaps you cannot read at all?" "If I could," said the peasant, "I should not want your spectacles." — I have always flattered myself, my dear brother, that you loved me as much as I love you; but I now see, that I have been mistaken. I should like to know why you went a walking without me? — I have heard, my dear sister, that you are angry with me, because I went a walking without you. — I assure you that, had I known that you were not ill, I should have come for you; but I inquired at your physician's about your health, and he told me that you had been keeping your bed the last eight days.

Lesson LXXXVII. — PENSUM OCTOGESIMUM SEPTIMUM.

THE SUBJUNCTIVE IN INDEPENDENT PROPOSITIONS.

A. The present and perfect subjunctive are frequently used independently in a *potential* sense, and rendered by the English *may, can,* &c. In this construction the perfect is generally equivalent to the present. E. g.

Fórsitan *quaerátis.*	You may perhaps inquire.
Quis *dubitet?*	Who can doubt?

Vélim (nólim, málim) sic exísti-mes.	I wish you to (I do not wish you to, I would rather you would) think so.
Némo ístud tíbi concédat.	No one can concede this to you.
Fórsitan témere fécerim.	I may perhaps have acted rashly.
Hic quaérat quíspiam, cujúsnam causā tánta rêrum molítio fácta sit.	Here some one may inquire, on whose account so great exertions were made.
Íta facíllime sine invídiā laûdem inrénias et amícos páres.	You may thus easily win glory without any envy, and gain friends.
Fáveas tû hósti? bonôrum spém virtutémque debûttes? et te consulârem, aut senatôrem, aut dénique civem pútes?	Can you favor the enemy? Can you deject the hope and courage of the patriotic? and still consider yourself a man of consular rank, or a senator, or even a citizen?
At nôn históriā cessêrim Graécis, nec oppónĕre Thucýdidi Sal-lústium veírear.	But still I cannot surrender the palm in history to the Greeks, nor am I afraid to oppose Sallust to Thucydides.
Hóc sine dubitatiône confirmávĕ-rim, eloquéntiam rém ésse ómnium difficíllimam.	I can assert this without any hesitation, that eloquence is the most difficult of all things.

REMARKS.

1. The use of the present subjunctive instead of the perfect is an energetic expression, by which an unfinished action is represented as already completed. It is confined chiefly to the active form of verbs, but sometimes also occurs in the passive. E. g. *Ne illi quidem se no-bis merīto praetulĕrint gloriatique sint*, Not even they can justly call themselves better than us, and glory in it.

2. The *imperfect* subjunctive is rarely used in this potential sense, except where the idea of unreality or impossibility is to be conveyed. Thus of wishes to which no fulfilment is (or can be) expected: *Vellem*, I could wish; *nollem*, I should be unwilling; *mallem*, I should rather wish. To these add the second and third persons singular of *dico*, *pŭto*, *crĕdo*, *video*, *cerno*, and *discerno*, which frequently occur in a potential sense, instead of the *pluperfect* subjunctive. E. g. *Reos di-cĕres*, You would have called them guilty (i. e. if you had seen them). *Signum datum credĕres, ut vasa colligĕrent*, You would have supposed that a signal had been given to collect vases. *Haud facile discernĕres*, You could not have easily distinguished. *Quis unquam credĕret* (or *arbitrarētur*)? Who could ever have believed (*or* supposed)?

B. The present and perfect subjunctive are often used in independent clauses to express a wish, an asseveration, a request, command, or exhortation, and also a concession or permission. E. g.

With the subjunctive thus used, the English "not" is expressed by *ne*, and not by *non*. When a wish or request is conveyed, one of the verbs *velim*, *suadeo*, or *censeo* is often added.

Dĭ́i bĕ́ne vĕ́rtant !	May the gods grant success to it !
Dĭ́i *prohĭbĕant* a nŏ́bis ĭmpias mĕ́ntes !	May the gods defend us against impious minds !
Vŭ́leant cĭ́ves mĕ́i, vŭ́leant; sĭnt incŏ́lŭmes, sĭnt florĕ́ntes, sĭnt beŭ́ti !	Farewell to my fellow-citizens, farewell ! May they be safe, may they be prosperous, may they be happy !
Stĕt haĕ̆c ŭ́rbs praeclŭ́ra, mĭhĭque pŭ́tria carĭ́ssĭma !	Let this noble city remain unshaken, and my dearest fatherland !
Ne sŭ́lvus *sim*,* si ŭ́liter scrĭ́bo, ac sĕ́ntio.	Let me perish, if I write differently from what I think.
Vĕ́lim nĭhi *ignŏ́scas.*	I wish you to pardon (*or* excuse) me.
Quĭ́dquid vĕ́niat in mĕ́ntem, *scrĭbas vĕlim.*	I want you to write whatever comes into your mind.
Ĕ́ssĕdum ŭ́liquod *suŭ́deo* cŭ́pias.	I advise you to take some travelling conveyance.
Trĕ́vĭros *vĭtes, cĕ́nseo;* aŭ́dio capĭtŭ́les ĕ́sse.	I think you should avoid the Treviri; I hear that they are mortal against us.
Fŭ́cias. Relĭ́nquas. Ad nos vĕ́nias.	Do so. Relinquish. Come to see us.
Aŭ́diat, vĭdeat. Dĕ́sinant.	Let him hear, let him see. Let them cease.
Hŏ́c *ne* fĕ́ceris. Nĭhil ignŏ́vĕris.	Do not do this. Do not pardon anything.
Misericŏ́rdiă *ne commŏ́tus sis.*	Do not be moved by compassion.
Nĭ́hil incŏ́mmodo valetŭ́dĭnis tŭ́ae fĕ́cĕris.	Do not do anything to the detriment of your health.
Ĕ́mas, nŏn quŏ́d ŏ́pus ĕ́st, sed quŏ́d necĕ́sse ĕ́st.	Buy not what you want, but what is absolutely necessary.
Immĭtĕ́mus nŏ́stros Brŭ́tos, Camĭ́llos, Dĕ́cios; *anĕ̆mus* pŭ́triam, *pareŭ́mus* senŭ́tui, *consulĭmus* bŏ́nis.†	Let us imitate our Brutuses, our Camilli, our Decii; let us cherish our country, obey the senate, and provide for the patriotic.
Memĭnĕrĭmus ĕ́tiam advĕ́rsus ĭnfĭmos justĭ́tiam ĕ́sse servŭ́ndam.	Let us remember, that the requirements of justice must be observed towards the humblest even.
Ne desperĕ́mus; a lĕ́gibus nŏn recedŭ́mus.	Let us not despair; let us not swerve from the laws.

REMARKS.

1. The subjunctive instead of the imperative is especially frequent in the third person; as, *dicat, faciat, scribant,* let him say, let him do,

---

* So also *moriar, interenm, peream,* Let me die, perish (if that is so).
† In exhortations the subjunctive is commonly in the *plural.*

let them write. The second person thus used is commonly connected with a negative, and the perfect is put in the sense of the present; as, *ne dixeris, ne hoc feceritis*, do not say, do (ye) not do this. The subjunctive implies *a gentleness* of command, which is sometimes increased by the addition of words like *quaeso, oro,* I beseech you; *dum,* now, pray; and *sis* (= *si vis*), please. E. g. *Quaeso, parcas mihi,* I beg you to spare me. *Taceas (tace), sis,* Please be silent.

2. In prescriptions which relate to the past, the imperfect and pluperfect subjunctive are employed. E. g. *Pater ejus fortasse aliquando iniquior erat*; pateretur, His father was perhaps at times unjust; he was obliged to bear it. *Forsitan non nemo vir fortis dixerit,* restitisses, A brave man may say, perhaps, you ought to have resisted.

3. In exhortations *non* is sometimes used instead of *ne*. E. g. *Non* (for *ne*) *desperēmus,* Let us not despair.

C. The subjunctive is also used in doubtful questions, to which no positive answer is expected, and which imply the idea of the contrary.

These negative questions are commonly rendered by *can, shall, could,* &c. The subjunctive of this connection is called the *dubitative.*

Quid *fáciam?* Quô *éam?*	What can I do? Where can I go?
Quid *fácĕrem?* Quô *irem?*	What could I do? Where could I go?
Quid *fáciam? róger,* anne *rógem?*	What shall I do? Shall I ask or be asked?
Quém tê *appéllem?*	What shall I call you?
Quid *fáceret* áliud?	What else could he do?
Cur fortûnam *periclitarêtur?*	Why should he try his fortune?
Nam, quém *férret,* si paréntem nôn férret súum?	Who could he bear, if he could not bear his own parent?
Cum tempestâte *púgnem* periculóse pótius, quam ílli *obtémpe-rem* et *párēam?*	Shall I fight with the storm at my own peril, rather than yield to and obey it?
Apud exércitum mihi *fúeris,* ínquit, tót ánnos? fórum nôn *attígĕris? absfúeris* tamdiu?	You have been with the army, said he, for so many years? You have not come in contact with the forum? You have been absent so long?

REMARK. — In these questions the answer implied is commonly the opposite. E. g. *Quis possit,* Who can (could)? — No one. *Quis non possit?* Who could not? — Every one could. *Hoc non noceat?* This is not hurtful? — It is certainly so.

SUBJUNCTIVE IN INDIRECT QUESTIONS.

D. When a question is stated indirectly, or merely quoted, its verb is in the subjunctive.

A clause containing an indirect question is generally dependent upon another verb. The verbs on which an indirect question may depend are not only those of asking, but many others, especially those requiring the accusative with the infinitive. (Cf. Lesson LIII.)

All the words and particles used in direct questions may also introduce an indirect one. They are *quis, quid; qui, quae, quod; quot, quantus, quam, ubi, unde, quare, cur, uter, quo, quomodo; utrum, an, — ne, num.* (Cf. Lesson LXXXV. *B.* ii.)

When the question is double, it follows the construction of direct questions of the same class. (Cf. Lesson LXXXV.)

EXAMPLES.

Quaéritur, *quid faciendum sit.*	The question is, what is to be done.
Mórs ípsa *quid sit,* primum est vidéndum.	We must first see what death itself is.
Quális sit ánimus, ípse ánimus néscit.	The mind itself is ignorant of what mind is.
Dísce, *quid sit* vivĕre.	Learn what it is to live.
Quid quaêque nóx aut díes *férat,* incértum est.	It is uncertain what every night or day may bring.
Quaéritur, *cur* doctíssimi hómines de máximis rêbus *disséntiant.*	The question is, why the most learned differ on the most important points.
Diffícile díctu est, *quaênam* caû-sa *sit.*	It is difficult to say, what the reason is.
Nôn, *quantum* quísque *póssit,* sed *quánti* quísque *sit,* ponderándum est.	We are not to consider what any one can do, but what he is morally worth.
Nôn est, *cur* spês eôrum *infringâtur.*	There is no reason why their hope should be dejected.
Videâmus primum, deorúm*ne* providéntiâ múndus *regâtur.*	Let us see first, whether the world is governed by the providence of the gods.
Inter sê rogitábant, *num** quém plebéi cónsülis *poenitêret.*	They inquired of each other, whether any one was tired of the plebeian consul.
Antígonus nóndum statúerat, *conservâret* Eúmenem, *nec ne.*	Antigonus had not yet determined whether he would save Eumenes or not.
Delíbĕrat senâtus, captívos ab hóstibus *rédimat, an nôn.*	The senate is deliberating, whether to redeem the captives from the enemy, or not.
Ípse *qui sit, útrum sit, an nôn sit,* íd quóque néscit.	He himself does not know what he is, nor whether he is or is not.
Quód nescire málum est, agitê-mus, *utrúmne* divítiis hómines, *an sint* virtûte beáti.	Let us discuss what it is a misfortune not to know: whether men are made happy by riches, or by virtue.

---

* The particle *num* in indirect questions does not imply a negative answer, as in direct questions.   2 J

REMARKS.

1. When the question is regarded as direct, the indicative is some-times used, especially after imperatives like *dic*, *vide*. E. g. *Dic, quaeso*, num *te illa* terrent? Pray tell me, whether those things frighten you? *Quaerāmus*, ubi *maleficium* est (*for* sit), Let us in-quire where the mischief is. But instances like these are compara-tively rare.

2. The expressions *nescio quis*, *nescio quid*, in the sense of *aliquis* or *quidam*, *aliquid* or *quiddam*, are not linked to any particular mood of the verb. E. g. *Nescio quid* (= *paululum*) *turbatus esse mihi vidēris*, You seem to me to be somewhat agitated.

To propose.	{ *Ańimum indūcĕre* (ut . . . .). { *Cogitāre* (facĕre aliquid).
I have made up my mind to do this.	Stát mihi sententia (*or simply* stat mihi) fácere hóc.
I propose going on that journey.	Íter íllud fácere cógito.
I have made up my mind to leave here.	Stát mihi abíre hínc.
He proposes to write.	Ańimum indūcit scríbere *or* ut scríbat.
To endeavor, strive.	{ *Opĕram dăre* or *navāre*. { *Nŭti* or *enŭti* (*nĭsus sum*). { *Laborāre*, *contendĕre*. (All with UT . . . .)
To make great effort.	{ Omnĭbus virĭbus contendere. { Omnibus nervis connĭti.
To make a fruitless effort.	Opĕram et olĕum perdere; frustra nĭti.
I wish you would endeavor to do this.	Óperam dês vélim, ut hóc fácias.
I shall endeavor to accomplish it.	Id ut perficiam, enitar et contén-dam.
Take care of your health.	Da óperam, ut váleas.
I endeavor to succeed in it.	{ Rém éo perdúcere labóro. { Ego, ut rém próspere ágam, con-téndo.
To aspire after (any-thing).	{ *Nŭti, annŭti*, or *aspirāre* (AD REM). { *Pĕtĕrĕ* or *appĕtĕre* (REM).
To aspire after honors, riches, pleasure.	Petĕre honōres, divitias, voluptā-tem.
To aspire after praise, after one's money.	Ad laudem, ad alicujus pecuniam aspirāre.
The honor.	Honor, ōris, *m.*
Places of honor.	Honōres, munĕra honorifĭca.
For the sake of honor (hon-orary).	Honōris causā.
The riches.	Divitiae, ārum, *f.*

The title.	Appellatio, ōnis, *f.*; nōmen, Inis, *n.*; dignitas, ātis, *f.*
The reputation.	Existimatio, ōnis, *f.*; dignitas.
To be for (redound to) one's honor or reputation.	Honōri esse alicui.
To injure any one.	{ *Nocēre* (cǔi, cǐtum) *alicui.* { *Damnum inferre alicui.*
To be an injury to any one.	Damno *seu* detrimento esse alicui.
To plunge, precipitate.	Praecipitāre, dejicĕre (ALIQUEM DE LOCO, IN LOCUM).
To throw any one into the sea.	Dejicĕre aliquem in mǎre.
To plunge any one into a pit, into destruction, into misery.	Praecipitāre aliquem in fovĕam, in exitium, in mǎla (miserïas).
To tie, bind.	Ligāre; alligāre, deligāre, illigāre.
To tie a handkerchief a-round the neck.	Sudārium ligāre circum collum.
To tie the horse to the tree.	Equum ad arbŏrem alligāre.
To oblige (any one), *to lay one under obligations.*	{ *Alligāre* or *obligāre* (SIBI ALI-QUEM). { *Obstringo, ĕre, nxi, ctum.* { *Devincio, īre, vinxi, vinctum.* (SIBI ALIQUEM ALIQUĀ RE.)
To oblige any one by kind offices.	Obligāre *or* obstringĕre aliquem officiis.
To oblige any one greatly.	Pergrātum *seu* gratissimum facĕre alicui.
To lay one under perpetual obligations.	Aliquem sibi in perpetuum devin-cīre.
To render a service to any one.	Grātum facĕre alicui; officia alicui praestāre.
The obligation (duty).	Officium, i, *n.*
The use.	Usus, ūs, *m.*
You would oblige me very much, if you would do me this favor.	Gratissimum mǐhi fácies, hóc si beneficium mǐhi tríbuas.
If you would render me this service, you would lay me under lasting obligations.	Hóc si mǐhi offícium praéstes, mê tíbi in perpétuum devíncies.
Since you are happy, why, pray, do you complain?	Quóniam félix és, quíd, quaéso, quéréris?
I should not have complained of what he has done, if he had injured me alone; but in do-ing it, he plunged many fami-lies into misery.	Nihil de éo, quód fécerit, conqué-stus éssem, si mǐhi sóli nocuísset, sed hóc fáciens múltas famílias in mǎla praecipitâvit.
What do you wish to say with this (= what do you mean)?	{ Quídnam hóc dícis? { Quídnam hôc vis intélligi?
Since you have nothing to tell	Quóniam, quód éi núnties, nôn há-

him, why then do you wish to see him ?

bes, cur tàmen éum convenire vis ?

Who of them has made the best use of his money ?

Quis eórum pecúniä suä úsus est sapientíssime.

I should do it, if it were possible.

Fácerem hóc, si fíeri posset.

Were I in your place.

{ Si túo lóco essem.

If I were in your place.

{ Si égo éssem, qui tû és.

Had he (= if he had) the treasures of Crœsus.

Croési divítiae si míhi éssent.

That man would be happier, if he left off gambling.

Felícior ésset ílle, si míssam fácěret áleam.

He would have been happier, if he had left off gambling.

Felícior fuísset, si míssam fecísset áleam.

He would not have done it, had he (= if he had) foreseen the result.

Id nòn fecísset, si éxitum praevidisset.

I should think myself ungrateful, did I not (= if I did not) consider you as my benefactor.

Ingrátum mê putárem ésse, nísi tê míhi beneficiórum auctòrem judicárem.

The French would not have gained the battle, if they had not had superior forces.

Francogálli in proélio nôn vicíssent, ni hóstibus número superióres fuíssent.

I wish you would do this.

Vélim, ut hóc fácias.

I wish you would go there.

Vélim, ut ílluc éas.

I wish you had done it.

Véllem, ut illud fecísses.

I wish you had gone there.

Véllem, ut éo ivísses.

I should have wished to see him, had it been possible.

Conveníre éum voluíssem, si fíeri potuísset.

I should like to read, if I had only leisure.

Légěrem égo libentíssime, si módo míhi ótium ésset.

If I could, I would do it.

Fácerem hóc, si póssem.

If she were amiable, he would marry her.

Íllam, si amábilis ésset, uxôrem síbi súměret.

You would have been a philosopher, if you had observed silence.

Si tacuísses, philósophus fuísses.

Polite.

Urbänus; modestus; benignus, a, um.

Impolite.

Inurbänus, a, um.

Deaf.

Surdus, a, um.

Timid, bashful.

Timídus, a, um.

Carefully.

Cum curä ; accuräte, diligenter.

The occasion

Occasio, ŏnis, f.; locus, i, m.

Opportunity.

Opportunitas, potestas, ätis, f.

I have occasion, the opportunity for doing anything.

Est mihi occasio, potestas faciendi aliquid.

The insensibility.

Inhumanitas, immanitas, ätis, f.

The supplication, request.

Preces, pl.; flagitätio, ŏnis, f.

The career (in life).

Vitae curricŭlum.

To follow one's advice.　{ Sequi alicūjus consilium.
　　　　　　　　　　　　{ Alicūjus consilio temperāre.
To experience misery.　　In miseriā esse *or* versāri.

EXERCISE 160.

Well, does your sister make any progress? — She would make some, if she were as assiduous as you. — You flatter me. — Not at all; I assure you that I should be highly (*magnopere*) satisfied, if all my pupils worked like you. — Why do you not go out to-day? — I would go out if it were fine weather. — Shall I have the pleasure of seeing you to-morrow? — If you wish it, I will come. — Shall I still be here when you arrive? — Will you have occasion to go to town this evening? — I do not know, but I would go now if I had an opportunity. — You would not have so much pleasure, and you would not be so happy, if you had not friends and books. — Man would not experience so much misery in his career, and he would not be so unhappy, were he not so blind. — You would not have that insensibility towards the poor, and you would not be so deaf to their supplication, if you had been yourself in misery for some time. — You would not say that, if you knew me well. — Why has your sister not done her exercises? — She would have done them, if she had not been prevented. — If you worked more, and spoke oftener, you would speak better. — I assure you, sir, that I should learn better, if I had more time. — I do not complain of you, but of your sister. — You would have had no reason to complain of her, had she had time to do what you gave her to do. — What has my brother told you? — He has told me that he would be the happiest man in the world, if he knew the Latin language, the most beautiful of all languages. — I should like to know why I cannot speak as well as you. — I will tell you: you would speak quite as well as I, if you were not so bashful. But if you had studied your lessons more carefully, you would not be afraid to speak; for, in order to speak well, one must learn; and it is very natural, that (*necesse* or *par est, ut*) he who does not know well what he has learnt should be timid. — You would not be so timid as you are, if you were sure to make no mistakes. — There are some people who laugh when I speak. — Those are impolite people; you have only to laugh also, and they will no longer laugh at you. If you did as I (do), you would speak well. — You must study a little every day, and you will soon be no longer afraid to speak. — I will endeavor to follow your advice, for I have resolved to rise every morning at six o'clock, to study till ten o'clock, and go to bed early. — I wish your son would be more assiduous. — Let us be more diligent. — Let them listen to the advice of their friend, and not be deaf to the words of wisdom. — Let us imitate the best and wisest among men. — Do you know what that is? — I do not know what it is. — I do not know whether he will go out or remain at home. — Do you know whether he has finished his letter or not? — I do not know. — I beg you not to write. — Please be silent.

48

Lesson LXXXVIII.—PENSUM DUODENONA-GESIMUM.

THE SUBJUNCTIVE AFTER CONJUNCTIONS.

A. Dependent clauses denoting an intention, purpose, object, or result are put in the subjunctive. These clauses are commonly introduced by the conjunctions *ut, ne, quo, quin,* and *quominus.* The tense of the subjunctive is determined by that of the leading verb, according to Lesson LXXXIII.

I. *Ut* or *uti,* "that," "in order that," "so that," indicates the purpose, object, consequence, or effect of another action. When it expresses a result, it is commonly preceded by one of the words *sīc, ita, tam, tālis, tantus, ejusmŏdi,* &c. E. g.

Lêgum idcírco sérvi súmus, *ut* líberi ésse *possimus.*

We are therefore the servants of the law, that we may be able to be free.

Ésse opórtet *ut vīvas,* nôn vívěre, *ut ēdas.*

You should eat to live, and not live to eat.

Románi éum ab arátro abduxérunt, *ut* dictâtor ésset.

The Romans called him from the plough, that he might be dictator.

Pýlades quum sis, díces tê ésse Oréstem, *ut moriāre* pro amíco?

Since you are a Pylades, will you say that you are Orestes, in order to die for your friend?

Si ómnia fêcit, *ut sanâret,* perêgit médicus pártes súas.

If the doctor has done everything (he could) to cure, he has performed his duty.

Cum António *sīc* agēmus, *ut perspíciat,* tótum mê futûrum súum.

Let us treat with Antonius in such a manner, that he may see that I will be entirely in his favor.

Sicíliam Vérres *íta* vexâvit, ut éa restítui in prístinum státum núllo módo *póssit.*

Verres has harassed Sicily to such an extent, that it cannot by any means be restored to its former condition.

Ádeo aêqua postulâtis, *ut* últro vóbis *deferénda fúerint.*

Your demands are so reasonable, that it was necessary to accede to them voluntarily.

Pompéius *éā* ést virtûte ac fortúnā, *ut* éa *potúerit* sémper, quae némo praeter íllum.

Pompey's valor and success is such, that he has always been able to accomplish what no one else could.

Tālis ést órdo actiônum adhibéndus, *ut* in vítā ómnia *sínt* ápta inter se et conveniéntia.

We should observe such an order of our actions, that everything in life may be harmonious and consistent.

REMARKS.

1. The adverbs *ita, sic, tam* before the verbs and adjectives preceding *ut* are sometimes omitted, and the latter then is rendered by *so that*. (See examples on page 387.)

2. *Ut* is originally an adverb of manner and the correlative of *ita*, so — as. E. g. *Uti initium, sic finis est.* In this sense it is not followed by any particular mood, but has either the indicative or subjunctive, as the construction may require. When, in the sense of *as soon as*, it indicates a relation of time, it generally takes the indicative perfect. E. g. *Ut primum loqui posse coepi*, As soon as I could speak. — On *ut* with the sense of *would that* and *supposing that*, see Lesson LXXXIX.

II. *Ne* always implies a purpose or intended effect, and is equivalent to the English " lest," or " that not." E. g.

Cúra, *ne* dénúo in mórbum *incĭdas.*	See that you do not fall sick again.
Effício, *ne* cui molésti *sint.*	I see to it, that they do not become troublesome to any one.
Ne íd fieri *pósset*, obsidiône fiêbat.	The possibility of that was prevented by the blockade.
Timóleon orâvit ómnes, *ne* id *fácĕrent.*	Timoleon begged them all not to do that.
Mê óbsecras, *ne oblivĭscar* vigilâre.	You beseech me not to forget to watch.
Hortâtur éos, *ne* ánimo deffciant.	He exhorts them not to lose their courage.
Quod potuísti prohibêre, *ne fierel.*	Which you could have prevented from being done.

REMARKS.

1. *Ut non* is used instead of *ne*, when no intended effect, but a mere consequence, is to be expressed (in the sense of *so that not*), and also when the negation does not relate to the entire sentence, but only to a particular word of it. E. g. *Tum forte aegrotabam, ut ad nuptias tuas venire non possem*, I happened to be sick then, *so that* I could *not* come to your wedding. *Confer te ad Manlium, ut a me non ejectus ad alienos*, sed invitâtus *ad tuos isse videâris*, Go to Manlius, so that you may not have the appearance of having been cast out among strangers by me, but of having gone invited to your friends.

2. As a continuation of *ut* and *ne* in negative sentences the particle *neve* is used, which after *ne* stands in the sense of *aut ne*, " or lest," " or that not," and after *ut* in the sense of *et ne*, " and that not." E. g. *Legem tulit, ne quis ante actarum rerum accusarêtur* neve *multarêtur*, He enacted a law, that no one should be accused of past offences, nor (or) punished for them.✸

✸ Instead of *neve* preceded by *ut*, *neque* (or *nec*) is not unfrequently employed. E. g. *Persuadent, ut paterentur, nec ultima experiri vellent*, They exhort them to suffer it, *and not* to attempt to resort to extremes.

3. Instead of *ne*, the double conjunction *ut ne* is also used, especially in legal language. E. g. *Operam dant, ut judicia ne fiant*, They are endeavoring to prevent judgment. *Ut hic, qui intervĕnit, ne ignoret, quae res agatur*, That he who happens to come in may not be ignorant of what is going on.

III. After verbs denoting fear or apprehension, *ne* is equivalent to the English "that," or "lest," and *ut* or *ne non* to "that not." E. g.

Tímeo, *ne plúat.*	I am afraid that it will rain.
Tímeo, *ut plúat.*	I am afraid that it will not rain.
Tímeo, *ne nôn* * *plúat.*	
Véreor, *ut ápte dícam.*	I fear I do not speak correctly.
Véreor, *ut matúre vénias.*	I fear you will not come in proper time.
Métuo, *ne frústra labôrem suscéperis.*	I am afraid that you have worked in vain.
Timêbam, *ne evenírent* éa, quae accidérunt.	I was afraid that that would come to pass, which (actually) has occurred.
Veréndum est, *ne brévi témpore* fámes in úrbe *sít.*	It is to be feared that in a short time there will be a famine in the city.
Ómnes labóres tê excípere vídeo. Tímeo, *ut sustíneas.*	I perceive that you are undertaking the whole of the labor. I am afraid that you will not hold out.
Verêtur Hiémpsal, *ut* sátis fírmum *sit* (foêdus) et rítum.	Hiempsal was afraid that the compact would not be sufficiently firm and safe.
Verebámini, *ne nôn* id fácěrem, quód recepíssem sémel.	Ye were afraid that I would not perform what I had undertaken.
Metuêbat scílicet, *ne indicárent, ne* dolôrem férre nôn *póssent.*	He was afraid perhaps they might declare, that they would be unable to endure the pain.
Pávor céperat mílites, *ne mortíférum ésset* vúlnus Scipiônis.	The terror had invaded the soldiers, that Scipio's wound might be mortal.

REMARKS

1. This construction includes also substantives denoting fear, apprehension, or danger (as the *pavor* of the last example). So also the causative verbs *terrēre, conterrēre*, and *deterrēre.* To these add *carēre*, to beware, and *vidēre* and *observare*, in the sense of "to see, reflect, consider." E. g. *Cavendum est, ne assentatoribus patefaciámus aures*, We should guard against opening our ears to flatterers. *Videndum est, ne quis nervus laedátur*, We must see, that no nerve is hurt.†

---

* *Ne non* in this construction is equivalent to *ut.*
† In this sense, *Vide ne* = "See whether not *or* that," and *Vide ne non* =

2. When verbs of fearing do not imply a wish (that something might or might not take place), but merely an emotion of the mind, they take the infinitive. E. g. *Vereor dicere*, I am afraid to speak. *Metuit tangi*, He is afraid of being touched.

IV. *Quo* generally occurs only in connection with a comparative, and is equivalent to *ut eo*, "that," "so that," "in order that." *Non quo*, followed by *sed*, is equivalent to *non quod*, "not that," "not as if." E. g.

Áger nôn sémel arâtur, sed novâtur et iterâtur, *quó melióres* fétus póssit et *grandióres* édĕre.	The land is not ploughed once only, but a second and a third time, in order that it may produce better and larger crops.
Cohortârer vôs, *quô* ánimo *fortióre essétis.*	I should exhort you to be more resolute in mind.
Légem brévem ésse oportet, *quô faciliús* ab imperítis *teneâtur.*	A law should be brief, in order that it may be the more easily remembered by the simple.
Ad tê lítteras dédi, *nôn quó habérem* magnópĕre, quod scríbĕrem, *sed ut* lóquĕrer têcum absens.	I have written to you, not that I had anything particular to communicate, but in order that in my absence I might converse with you.

REMARKS.

1. *Quo* with the subjunctive always denotes a purpose. In the sense of *et eo*, "and by this means," and in the formula *quo — eo* or *hoc* (with comparatives), it has the indicative. E. g. Quo *plûres erant*, (hoc) *major caedes fuit*, The larger their number, the greater the massacre.

2. Instead of *non quo* in the sense given above, it is more common to say *non quod, non eo quod, non ideo quod, non quia*, and negatively *non quin*. E. g. Non quod *sola ornent*, sed quod *excellant*, Not that they are the only ornaments, but because they excel as such. Non quin *pari virtûte* et *voluntâte alii fuĕrint*, sed, &c., Not as if others were not his peers in virtue and resolution, but, &c.

V. *Quin* (= *qui* + *non*) is used after negative propositions, or after general questions involving a negation, and may generally be resolved either into *qui non* or into *ut non*.

1. In the sense of *qui* (*quae, quod*) *non*, it occurs principally after expressions like *nemo* (*nullus, nihil, vix, aegre*) *est, reperitur, quin*, &c., and after general questions introduced by *quis* or *quid*. E. g. *Quis est*, quin *intelligat?* Who is there (or is there any one), that does not comprehend? *Nemo rênit*, quin *videret*, No one came who did not see (without seeing).

___

" See whether or that *not.*" E. g. *Vide ne hoc tibi obsit*, See whether this does not hurt you. *Vide ne non satis sit*, See whether this is enough.

48 *

2. In the sense of *ut non* it occurs after expressions like *facere non possum, quin; fĭěri non potest, quin; nulla causa* or *nĭhil causae est, quin*, &c. E. g. *Facere non possum*, quin *mittam*, I cannot but send (cannot do otherwise than send). *Nulla causa est*, quin *hoc faciam*, There is no reason why I should not do this (I am authorized to do it).

3. It is moreover used, in the sense of the English *but that* or *that*, after verbs and expressions signifying doubt, distance, prevention, or omission, such as *non dubĭto, non est dubium, non ambigo, quin; non abest, nihil* (or *paucum, non procul, haud multum*) *abest, quin; non* (*vix, aegre*) *abstineo, quin; temperāre mihi* (or *tenēre me*) *non possum, quin; non impedĭo, non recuso, non* or *nĭhil praetermitto, quin*, &c. E. g. *Non dubĭto*, quin *profectus sit*, I do not doubt that he has left (his having left). *Nihil abest*, quin *misérrĭmus sim*, I lack nothing of being a most unhappy man.

4. Additional examples of all these constructions of *quin* are the following : —

Nĭhil ést, quin póssit depravári.	There is nothing but what can be corrupted.
Quís ést, quin cérnat, quánta vis sit in sénsibus ?	Who is there that does not perceive what a power there is in our senses ?
Nĭhil tám difficile ést, quin quaeréndo investigári *póssit*.	There is nothing so difficult that cannot be investigated by examination.
Nŭlla móra fŭit, quin decérnerent béllum.	There was no delay about their finishing the war.
Fácere nón pótui, quin tíbi senténtiam méam *declarárem*.	I could not refrain from declaring to you my opinion.
Nôn *dŭbĭto, quin* dómi *sit*.	I do not doubt but that he is at home.
Nŏn ést dŭbium, quin Helvétii plúrimum *póssint*.	There is no doubt but that the Helvetii are the most powerful and influential.
Haŭd mŭltum ábfŭit, quin ab exúltbus *interficerétur*.	He had a narrow escape from being murdered by the exiles.
Tenéri nón pótui, quin (hôc) tíbi *declarárem*.	I could not refrain from declaring this to you.
Impedíri nón pótest, quin progrediátur.	He cannot be prevented from advancing.
Nŏn póssumus, quin álii a nóbis disséntiant, recusáre.	We cannot refuse to allow others to dissent from us.
Dubitándum nón ést, quin núnquam *póssit* utílitas cum honestáte conténdere.	It is not to be doubted, that utility can never pretend to compete with honor.

REMARKS.

1. *Quin* in the sense of *qui, quae, quod non* commonly is used only for the nominative; and where it seems to stand for *quo non* or *cui non*, it may be resolved into *ut non*. Yet it is also found for *quod non*

acc. E. g. *Nego in Siciliâ quidquam fuisse*, quin (= quod non) *conquisierit*, I maintain that there was nothing in Sicily which he has not tried to rake together.

2. *Qui non* frequently occurs instead of *quin;* and so likewise *ut non*. E. g. *Quis est*, qui *hoc* non *sentiat?* Who is there that does not feel sensible of this? *Fieri non potest*, ut *eum tu in tuâ provinciâ* non *cognôris*, It is not possible that you should not have made his acquaintance in your own province.*

3. After *non dubito,* "I doubt not," the Acc. cum Inf. is sometimes put instead of *quin*. E. g. *Pompeius* non dubitat, ea, *quae de republicâ nunc sentiat, mihi valde* probari, Pompey doubts not but that his present sentiments with reference to the republic are acceptable to me. *Dubito* and *non dubito*, in the sense of "I hesitate," are commonly followed by the infinitive, but sometimes also by *quin*. E. g. *Non dubito respondêre*, I do not hesitate to reply. *Non dubitâri, id a te per litteras petere*, I did not hesitate (or scruple) to ask that of you by letter. *Dubitâtis, judices*, quin *hunc vindicetis*, Do you hesitate, judges, to defend this man?

4. The English "I doubt whether" is expressed by *dubito sitne, dubito num* or *numquid*, or in double sentences by *dubito sitne — an, dubito utrum — an*. But the expressions *dubito an, dubium est an*, have (like *nescio an*, page 538) the affirmative sense, "I am inclined to." E. g. *Dubitat an turpe non sit*, He is inclined to consider it no disgrace.

5. *Quin* in the sense of *why not?* has the indicative; sometimes also, with a similar force, the imperative or the first person plural of the subjunctive. E. g. *Quin conscendimus equos?* Why not mount our horses immediately? *Quin uno verbo dic*, Say it in one word! *Quin experiâmur*, Let us make the attempt at once!

VI. *Quômĭnus* (= *ut eo mĭnus*, "that not") is generally put only after verbs denoting prevention or hinderance, and which may likewise be followed by *ne*, or, where a negative precedes, by *quin*.

The principal verbs of this class are *defendêre, deterrêre, impedîre, intercedêre, obsistêre, obstâre, officêre, prohibêre, recusâre*. To these add *stat* or *fit per me, quômĭnus; non pugno, nihil moror, non contineo, quômĭnus,* and many others. E. g.: —

Aétas non *impedit, quô mĭnus* litterârum stúdia *teneâmus*, úsque ad últimum témpus senectûtis.	Age does not prevent us from adhering to the study of letters, even to the very end of our life.
Rêbus terrénis múlta extérna,	Many external circumstances can

---

* *Qui non* and *ut non*, instead of *quin*, are necessary when no negation precedes, or when *non* belongs not to the leading verb, but to some other word of the sentence. E. g. *Non adeo imperitus sum, ut nesciam*, I am not so ignorant as not to know (where *non* belongs to *imperitus*).

quóminus perficiántur, póssunt obsistere.

act as obstacles to the accomplishment of earthly things.

Quid óbstat, quóminus déns sit beátus?

What prevents God from being happy?

Epaminóndas nôn recusávit, quóminus légis poênam subiret.

Epaminondas did not refuse to submit to the penalty of the law.

Caêsar cognòvit, per Afránium stáre, quó minus proélio dimicárent.

Caesar was informed, that it was owing to Afranius, that they did not engage in battle.

Égo têcum in éo nôn pugnábo, quóminus, útrum vélis, éligas.

I will not oppose your choosing whichever of the two you please.

REMARKS.

1. After the verbs *impedio, deterreo, prohibeo,* and *recuso,* the infinitive is sometimes used instead of *quominus.* E. g. *Pudor impēdit exquirēre,* Shame prevents further inquiry. *Prohibentur exire,* They are prohibited from going out. *Quae facēre ipse recuso,* Which I myself refuse to do.

2. *Quo secius* may take the place of *quomĭnus.* E. g. *Impedimento est,* quo secius *lex ferātur,* It prevents the bill from passing.

The kitchen.	Culīna, ae, *f.*
The church.	Aedes, is, *f.*; templum, i, *n.*; ecclesia, ae, *f.* (*the assembly*).
Divine service.	Sacra publica, *n. pl.*
The school.	Schŏla, ae, *f.*; lūdus, i, *m.*
The high school.	Acadēmia, ae, *f.*: gymnasium, i, *n.*
The university.	Universitas litterārum.
The dancing-school.	Lūdus saltatōrius.
The fencing-school.	Lūdus pugnatōrius.
The play, comedy.	Comoedia, ae, *f.*; fabŭla, ae, *f.*
The drama.	Drāma, ătis, *n.*
The opera.	Drāma musicum.
The exchange.	Curia mercatōrum.
The bank.	Aerārium publicum.
To go to church.	{ In templum īre. { Sacra publica adire.
To be at church.	{ In templo esse. { Sacris publicis adesse.
To go to school.	{ In lūdum litterārum ire *or* itāre. { Schŏlam frequentāre.
To be at school.	In lūdo (schŏlā) esse.
To go to the play.	Īre spectātum comoediam (fabŭlam).
To be at the play.	Fabŭlae adesse.
To be fond of the play.	Libenter fabŭlam spectāre.
To act a play.	Fabŭlam agēre (dāre).
To go to the opera.	Drāma musicum auditum ire.
To be at the opera.	Drāmati musico adesse.
To go a fishing.	Piscātum ire, piscāri.

Fishing.	Piscātio, ōnis, *f.*: piscātus, ūs, *m.*
Where is the wife of the tailor?	Úbi est sartóris úxor?
She is in the kitchen.	In culínā ést.
Whose school did he go to?	Cújus schólam frequentábat?
He frequented the public school.	Schólam públicam frequentábat.
Will you go to the opera?	Vísne audítum íre dráma músicum?
I am not disinclined to go.	Audítum íre nōn nólo.
Were you at church this morning?	Adfuistíne hódie máne sácris públicis?
I was not present.	Nōn ádfui.
Are you fond of hunting?	Delectarísne venatiónibus?
I am not.	Nôn deléctor.

The entire day, all day.	Tōtum diem (*Acc.*)
The whole year.	Annum intĕgrum.
An entire week.	Hebdomădem ıntĕgram.
The whole morning.	Tòtum māne.
The whole evening.	Tòtum vespĕrum.
The whole night, all night.	Tòtam noctem.
Three entire days.	Tōtos trēs dies, trēs ipsos dies, tŏtum triduum.
Six entire months.	Tōtos sex menses.
The whole society.	Tōtus (universus) conventus *or* circŭlus.
This week.	Hăc hebdomăde.
This year.	Hōc anno.
Next week.	Hebdomăde proximā.
Last week.	Hebdomăde praeteritā *or* proxime elapsā.
The person (individual).	Persōna, ae, *f.*
The belly-ache.	Tormīna, ōrum, *n. pl.*
The stomach-ache.	Dòlor stomăchi.
The fruit.	Pōma, ōrum, *n.*
The peach.	Mālum Persĭcum.
The cherry.	Cerāsum, i, *n.*
The strawberry.	Frāgum, i, *n.*
The plum.	Prūnum, i, *n.*
The pear.	Pĭrum, i, *n.*
The potato.	Bulbus (i, *m.*) solāni.
Vegetables.	Olus, ĕris, *n.,* *or pl.* olĕra.
Pulse.	Legūmen, ĭnis, *n.*
Pastry.	{ Opus pistōrıum. { Crustŭla, ōrum, *n. pl.*
The tart.	Scriblīta, ae, *f.*
The dish.	Patīna, ae, *f.*; lanx, *gen.* lancis, *f.*
The small dish.	Patella, scutŭla, ae, *f.*
The table-cloth.	Mantēle, is, *n.*
The maid-servant.	Ancilla, ae, *f.*
The aunt.	Cognāta; amĭta (*paternal*); matertĕra (*maternal*), ae, *f.*

The cousin.	Amitīna; consobrina, ae, *f.*
The niece.	Fratris (*or* sorōris) filia.
The neighbor (female).	Vicina, ae, *f.*
The actor.	Histrio, ōnis, *m.* ; actor scenīcus.
The actress.	Scenīca, ae, *f.*
The countess.	*Comitissa, ae, *f.*
The country woman.	Rustīca, ae, *f.*
The cook.	Cŏqua, ae, *f.*
The foolish woman.	Stulta, inepta, ae, *f.*
The sister-in-law.	Affinis, is, *f.*; gloe, *gen.* glōris, *f.*
The merchandise, goods.	Merx, *gen.* mercis, *f.*; *pl.* merces.
The power, might.	Potentia, ae, *f.*; potestas, ātis, *f.*
The gazette, newspaper.	Acta publīca *or* diurna, ōrum, *n.*
The cold (in the head).	Gravēdo, ĭnis, *f.*
To have a cold.	Gravedĭne laborāre.
To take a cold.	Gravedĭne affĭci.
To have a cough.	Laborāre tussi.
To make one sick.	{ Morbum alicui afferre. { Aliquem valetudĭne tentāre.
This makes me sick.	{ Hóc mĭhi áffert morbum. { Hóc mē dolōre áfficit.
The cough.	Tussis, is, *f.* (*acc.* im).
Violent.	Grăvis, is, e.
Violently.	Valde, gravĭter.
All at once, suddenly.	Subĭto, repentino, derepentine (*adv.*).
At once, immediately.	Stătim, illĭco, e vestigio.

EXERCISE 161.

Where is your cousin? — He is in the kitchen. — Where is your mother? — She is at church. — Is your sister gone to school? — She is gone thither. — Does your mother often go to church? — She goes thither every morning and every evening. — She goes thither as soon as she gets up. — At what o'clock does she get up? — She gets up at sunrise. — Dost thou go to school to-day? — I do go thither. — What dost thou learn at school? — I learn to read, write, and speak there. — Where is your aunt? — She is gone to the play with my little sister. — Do your sisters go this evening to the opera? — No, madam, they go to the dancing-school? — Is your father gone a hunting? — He has not been able to go a hunting, for he has a cold. — Do you like to go a hunting? — I like to go a fishing better than a hunting. — Is your father still in the country? — Yes, madam, he is still there. — What does he do there? — He goes a hunting and a fishing there. — Did you hunt when you were in the country? — I hunted the whole day. — How long have you stayed with (*apud*) my mother. — I stayed with her the whole evening. — Is it long since you were at the castle? — I was there last week. — Did you find many people there? — I found only three persons there. — Who were those three persons? — They were the count, the countess, and their daughter. —

Are these girls as good as their brothers? — They are better than they. — Can your sisters speak German? — They cannot, but they are learning it. — Have you brought anything to your mother? — I brought her good fruits and a fine tart. — What has your niece brought you? — She has brought us good cherries, good strawberries, and good peaches. — Do you like peaches? — I do like them much. — How many peaches has your neighbor (fem.) given you? — She has given me more than twenty of them. — Have you eaten many cherries this year? — I have eaten many of them. — Were there many pears last year? — There were not many. — Have you read the newspaper to-day? — I have read it. — Is there anything new in it? — I have not read anything new in it. — Does he eat to live, or does he live to eat? — He lives to eat. — Why do you study Latin? — I study it, in order that I may read, speak, and write it. — Is he so bad, that he must be punished? — He is. — Did your father exhort you not to go to the play? — He begged and conjured me not to go there. — He was sick yesterday so that he could not come to the lesson (*ad scholam*). — Are you afraid that it will rain to-day? — I am rather afraid that it will not rain. — Is your brother afraid to speak Latin? — He is afraid; for he is as yet ignorant of the language. — He should be more diligent, in order that he may be able to speak more readily (*facilius*). — I give you this advice, not that I think you need it, but in order to encourage (*animum alicui addĕre*) you. — I cannot refrain from writing to you. — There is no doubt but that you are correct. — I do not doubt but that he will arrive to-morrow. — Can he prevent you from advancing? — He cannot prevent me. — He could refrain from weeping, when he heard that you were so unfortunate and unhappy. — What can prevent us from being happy? — Nothing can prevent us from being as happy as any one ever was.

Lesson LXXXIX. — PENSUM UNDENONAGE-SIMUM.

SUBJUNCTIVE AFTER CONJUNCTIONS. — *Continued.*

A. The subjunctive is put after various other particles, besides those already considered in the preceding Lesson.

I. After particles denoting a wish, such as *utĭnam, utĭnam ne, ut* or *utĭ, o* or *o si,* "O that," "would that," the verb is always in the subjunctive.

In this construction the present and perfect subjunctives are used of things considered as possible, the imperfect and pluperfect when the wish is regarded as a vain or impossible one. E. g.

Utĭnam hábeam!	*Utĭnam habú-* *erit!*	O that I may have! I wish that he may have had!

Útinam hâbêrem! Útinam habuísset!	Would that I had! O that he had had!
Útinam módo conâta effícere póssim!	May I but be able to accomplish my endeavors!
O míhi praetéritos réferat si Júppiter ánnos!	O that Jupiter may restore to me my past years!
Íllud útinam ne vére scríbĕrem!	Would to God that what I have written were no reality!
Útinam mínus vítae cúpidi fuissêmus!	O that we had been less desirous of preserving life!
Ut tê dú pérduint!	May the gods destroy you!

REMARK. — The particle is sometimes omitted. E. g. *Tecum ludĕre sicut ipsa possem!*

II. After the particles of comparison *quasi, quam si*, and after *tamquam, ut, velut, simílĭter ac, idem ac, aeque ac, perinde ac, proinde ac*, with or without *si*, and *ceu*, "as if," "just as if," the verb is always in the subjunctive. E. g.

Sed quíd égo his téstĭbus útor, *quasi* rês dúbia aut obscûra *sit?*	But why do I use witnesses like these, as if the case were a doubtful or an obscure one ?
Quaêstor ést fáctus, *quam si* ésset súmmo lóco nâtus.	He was made questor, as if he had been of the highest rank by birth.
Párvi prímo órtu sic jácent, *tánquam* omníno síne ánimo sínt.	Infants, when they are just born, lie as if they were entirely without life.
Crudelitâtem éjus, *vélut si* coram adésset, horrébant.	They shrunk from his cruelty, as if he were present before them.
Simíliter fácis, *ac si* mê róges.	You act just as if you were asking me.
Delêta est Aúsŏnum gens, *perínde ác si* internecívo béllo certásset.	The Ausonian nation has become extinct, as if it had engaged in internecine warfare.

III. The particles *non quod, non eo quod, non ideo quod*, and *non quia*, "not because," *non quo*, "not as if," and *non quin*, "not but that," are followed by the subjunctive, but the *sed quod* or *sed quia* of the subsequent clause requires the indicative. E. g.

Nôn idcírco quorúndam amicôrum ûsum dimisĕram, *quod* íis succénsĕrem, *sed quód* eôrum me suppudêbat.	I had given up the acquaintance of certain friends, not because I was angry with them, but because I was somewhat ashamed of them.
Nôn quô vérba únquam pótius, quám rês, *exercúerim, sed quia* assuévĕram militáribus ingéniis.	Not that I have ever dealt in words rather than in substance, but because I had become accustomed to military minds.

Crásso commendatiônem nôn súm pollícĭtus, *nôn quin éam* valitûram apud tê *arbitrârer*, *séd* (*quod*) míhi egêre commendatiône nôn *videbâtur*.

I did not promise Crassus any recommendation, not because I thought that it would have no effect with you, but because he did not seem to me to need any recommendation.

IV. The subjunctive is likewise put after the conjugations *dum, mŏdo* or *dummŏdo,* " provided," and *dum ne, mŏdo ne* or *dummŏdo ne,* " provided not." So also after *ut* and *ne,* when they signify "although," "although not," and after *nēdum* or *ne,* " not to say," " much less," " much more." E. g.

Neque, *dum* síbi régnum *parâret,* quídquam pónsi habêbat.

Nor did he have a regard for anything, provided he might win royal authority.

Cicero ómnia postpósuit, *dúmmŏdo* praecéptis pâtris parêret.

Cicero disregarded everything, provided he might obey the instructions of his father.

Dum ílle *ne sis,* quém égo ésse nólo, sis méâ caúsâ, qui lúbet.

So long as you are not what I do not wish to be, you may be what you please, for aught I care.

Ut désint víres, támen ést laudánda volúntas.

Although the strength be wanting, yet the wish is to be commended.

Vêrum *ut* hóc nôn *sit,* támen sérvet rempúblicam.

Though this be not so, it may nevertheless save the republic.

Ne sit súmmum málum dólor, málum cérte ést.

Although pain is not the greatest evil, it is still unquestionably an evil.

Núnquam suffêrre éjus súmptus quéat, *nêdum* tû *póssis.*

He never can defray his expenses, much less can you.

Vix in ípsis téctis frĭgus vitâtur, *nêdum* in mári et in vîâ *sit* fácile abésse ab injúriâ tempŏris.

The cold can scarcely be avoided in the houses themselves; much less easy it is to be exempt from the ill effects of the season at sea and on the roads.

Quíppe secúndae rês sapiéntium ánimos fâtigant; *ne* ílli corrúptis móribus victóriae *temperárent.*

Since prosperity tries the minds of the wise even, much less could they who are men of corrupt morals restrain themselves from an abuse of the victory.

V. *Quamvis* (*quantumvis, quantumlibet*), "however," and *licet,* "although," commonly take the subjunctive; but *utut,* "however," and *quamquam,* "although," have more frequently the indicative. E. g.

Lícet strénuum métum *pútes ésse,* velócior támen spês ést.

Although you may consider fear rapid in its operation, yet hope is quicker.

2 K   49

Quámvis *licet* Ménti delúbra et Virtúti et Fídei *consecrémus*, támen haêc in nóbis ípsis síta vidêmus.

Although it be true, that we dedicate shrines to the Intellect, to Virtue, and to Faith, we nevertheless perceive that they reside in ourselves.

Quód túrpe ést, íd, *quámvis occultétur*, támen honéstum fíeri núllo módo pótest.

That which is morally disgraceful, however it may be concealed, can never by any means become honorable.

Vítia méntis, *quantúmvis*, exígua *sínt*, in május excédunt.

The vices of the mind, however small they may be, increase and spread.

Útut haêc *sínt*, támen hóc fáciam.

However these things may be, I shall nevertheless do it.

Quámquam *excellébat* abstinéntiā, támen exsílio décem annórum multâtus ést.

Although he was noted for his moderation, he yet was punished with an exile of ten years.

REMARK. — Tacitus uses the subjunctive after *quamquam* as after *quamvis*. Cicero only occasionally. Later authors reverse the rule, and put *quamquam* with the subjunctive, and *quamvis* with the indicative.

VI. *Dum, donec,* and *quoad,* in the sense of " as long as," or " while," require the indicative; but when they signify " until," they may have either the indicative or subjunctive. E. g.

Aegróto *dum* ánima ést, spês ésse dícitur.

As long as the patient keeps up his spirits, there is said to be hope.

Cáto *quoad víxit*, virtûtum laûde crêvit.

Cato advanced in renown for virtue as long as he lived.

Delíbĕra hóc, *dum* égo rédeo.

Think this over until I return.

De comítiis, *donec* rédiit Marcéllus, siléntium fúit.

Respecting the election, there was nothing said until Marcellus returned.

Expectâte, *dum* cónsul aut dictâtor *fíat* Kaéso.

Wait, until Kaeso becomes consul or dictator.

Quoad perrént̂um *sít* éo, quo súmpta nâvis ést.

Until they may have arrived at the spot for which the ship was taken.

VII. *Antequam* and *priusquam* are commonly followed by the present subjunctive, when they imply a reference to the future, and by the imperfect or pluperfect subjunctive when they imply a causal connection between two past events. But when these conjunctions express merely a relation of time, the verb is in the indicative. E. g.

Tragoédi quotídie, *ántequam pronúntient*, vôcem sénsim éxcitant.

Tragic actors gradually tune their voice every day, before they begin to declaim.

Ante vidêmus fulguratiônem, *quam* sónum *audiâmus.*

We perceive the lightning before we hear its voice.

In ómnibus negótiis *príus, quam aggrediâre,* adhibénda est praeparátio díligens.

You should make diligent preparations in every transaction, before you set to work at it.

Caêsar ad Pompéii cástra pervênit *príus, quam* Pompéius sentíre *pósset.*

Cæsar arrived at Pompey's camp before Pompey could perceive it.

Saépe mágna índoles virtûtis, *priúsquam* réi públicae prodésse *potuísset,* exstíncta fúit.

It has often been the case, that a great natural capacity for virtue was lost, before it could become an advantage to the republic.

Dábo óperam, ut ístuc véniam *ante, quam* pláne ex túo ánimo *éffluo.*

I shall endeavor to come to your place, before I am entirely forgotten by you.

Mémbris útimur *príus, quam* didícimus,* cújus éa utilitátis caúsâ habeâmus.*

We use our limbs, before we have learnt the end for which we have them.

OF THE CONSTRUCTION OF "QUUM."

B. Quum or *cum* expresses either a relation of time, and is equivalent to *tum quum, eo tempore quum,* or *ex eo tempore quum,* "then when," "when," "while," "after," or "since"; or it denotes the relation of cause and effect, and is equivalent to the English "since," "although," "because." The former is called the *quum temporâle,* and is generally followed by the indicative, the latter the *quum causâle,* and is followed by the subjunctive.

I. The clause introduced by *quum temporale* may either be the leading or a subordinate one, and the verb may be in any tense of the indicative.

Fácile ómnes, *quum valêmus,* récta consília aegrótis dámus.

When we are well, we all of us can easily give advice to those who are sick.

Áger quum múltos ánnos *quiévit,* uberióres efférre frúctus sólet.

When land has been left fallow for many years, it usually yields more abundant crops.

Qui nôn deféndit injúriam, néque propúlsat a súis, *quum pótest,* injúste fácit.

He who does not repel injustice, nor protect his friends against it, when he can, acts unjustly.

Quúm haêc in Hispániâ *gerebántur,* comitiórum jám appetébat díes.

While these things were carried on in Spain, the day of the elections was approaching.

Vôs *túm* paruístis, *quum páruit* némo, qui nóluit.

You obeyed at a time when no one obeyed, that was not disposed to do so.

---

* In the last two of these examples, these conjunctions express merely a relation of time.

Quum inimíci nóstri veníre di-céntur, tum in Epirum íbo.	When our enemies will be reported as coming, then I shall go into Epirus.
Jám·vêr appetêbat, quum Hán-nibal ex hibérnis móvit.	Spring was already approaching, when Hannibal moved out of his winter-quarters.
Vix ánnus intercésserat, quum Sulpicius accusávit C. Norbá-num.	A year had scarcely elapsed when Sulpicius preferred an accusation against Norbanus.
Múlti ánni súnt, quum Fábius in aêre méo ést. *	It is many years since Fabius is my debtor.
Trigínta díes érant ípsi, quum hás dabam lítteras.	There were thirty entire days, since the date of this letter.

REMARK. — On the imperfect and pluperfect subjunctive after quum temporale, see III.

II. *Quum causále* is rendered by the English *since, because, although,* and is followed by the subjunctive. E. g.

Quae cum íta sínt.	Since these things are so.
Quum sciam, scírem.	Since I know, though I knew.
Quum intelléxerim, intellexíssem.	Since I have understood, had understood.
Socratis ingénium variósque ser-mónes immortalitáti scríptis súis trádidit Pláto, quum lít-teram Sócrates núllam reli-quísset.	Plato in his writings has bequeathed us an immortal record of the genius and various discourses of Socrates, though Socrates him-self had not left a syllable.
Dionýsius quum in commúnibus suggéstis consístere nôn audê-ret, concionári ex túrre áltá solêbat.	Dionysius was in the habit of ha-ranguing the people from a high tower, as he did not dare to stand upon the usual platforms.
Coélo seréno intérdiu obscuráta lúx ést, quum lûna sub órbem sólis subísset.	Daylight has sometimes been dark-ened, even under a clear sky, on account of the moon having passed beneath the orbit of the sun.
Druéntia, quum áquae vím vé-hat ingéntem, nôn támen ná-vium pátiens ést.	The (river) Durance, although it carries a large quantity of water, is yet unfit for navigation.
Égo mé saépe nóva vidéri dícere intélligo, quum pervétèra di-cam.	I know that I have often the ap-pearance of saying new things, when (i. e. although) I say some-thing that is quite old.
Phócion fúit perpétuô paûper, quum divitíssimus ésse póssct.	Phocion was perpetually poor, when (i. e. although) he might have been very rich.

III. In narration *quum* is commonly followed by the imper-fect and pluperfect subjunctive, though generally rendered by the English *when* or *after.* E. g.

---

* On this use of *quum*, compare Lesson LVII.

Zenōnem, *quúm* Athénis *éssem*, audiēbam frequénter.	I frequently heard Zeno's discourses, when I was at Athens.
Fúit témpus, *quum* rúra *cólérent* hómines, néque * úrbem *habé-rent.*	There was a time when men inhabited the country, and had no cities.
Íbi éum quúm Caêsar *vidísset,* níhil úspere, níhil acérbe díxit.	When Cæsar saw him there, he said nothing that was harsh, nothing that was bitter.
Thucýdides líbros súos túm scripsísse dícitur, quúm a repúblicā *remótus* atque in exsílium *púlsus ésset.*	Thucydides is said to have written his books after he had been removed from public life and driven into exile.

REMARKS.

1. The subjunctive sometimes stands after *quum* where we might expect the indicative. E. g. *Si tibi* tum, quum petēres *consulātum, affui,* If I assisted you at the time you were a candidate for the consulate, &c. But in most such cases there are generally other reasons for the subjunctive. E. g. *Qui dies est, quae nox,* quum *ego non ex istorum insidiis divino consilio* eripiar?† What day is there, what night, in which I was not saved from the wiles of these wretches, by a Divine Providence?

2. In Livy and Tacitus *quum* is sometimes also followed by the historical infinitive. E. g. *Nec multum erat progressa navis,* quum *dato signo* ruĕre *tectum loci,* Nor had the ship advanced far, when at the given signal the deck fell in.

To march.	{ *Ambulāre, incēdĕre.* { *Castra movēre, movēre.* { *Iter facĕre.*
To walk, to go on foot.	Incēdĕre, pedĭbus īre, ambulāre
To step.	Gradior, i, gressus sum.
To advance.	Prōgrĕdi, pergĕre.
To travel.	{ Proficisci, iter facĕre. { Tendĕre, contendĕre (AD LOCUM).
To travel abroad.	Peregrināri.
To travel through a place.	Transīre, iter facĕre per lŏcum.
To travel or pass by a place.	Alíquem locum praetergrŏdi, praetervĕhi, non attingĕre.
To go (leave for) abroad.	Abīre, discēdĕre, proficisci.
The traveller.	Peregrinātor, peregrīnus.
The wanderer (traveller on foot).	Viātor, ōris, *m.*
To travel a mile.	Mille passuum emetīri (emensus sum) *or* conficĕre.
To make a step.	Gradum *or* passum facĕre.
To take a step (i. e. measures).	Agĕre et moliri; consilium inīre.

---

* *Neque* here, as frequently, = *et non.*
† The subjunctive here depends upon the indefinite general question.

49 *

To enter on a journey.	Se dăre in viam; proficisci.
To make *or* deliver a speech.	Verba facĕre; oratiōnem habēre; dicĕre.
To transact business.	Rem gerĕre ;. negotiāri, mercatū-ram facĕre.
Business, a piece of business, an affair.	Negotium, i, *n.* ; rēs, rĕi, *f.* ; opus, ēris, *n.*
To be engaged in anything.	Occupātum esse aliquā rē.
To be at leisure.	Otiōsum esse, vacāre.
Where is the traveller going to?	Quô téndit viâtor?
He is going towards Vienna.	Vindobónam vérsus téndit.
Is the merchant occupied with business?	Occupatúsne est mercātor negó-tiis?
He is very much occupied (with it).	Ést véro occupatíssimus.
He is distracted with business.	Disténtus ést negótiis.
How many miles did he travel?	Quót mília pássuum eménsus est?
He has travelled twenty.	Vigínti.
Did the clergyman speak?	Fecítne vérba cléricus?
He did not.	Nôn fēcit.
Did I transact the business well?	Gessíne rém béne?
You have transacted it in the best possible manner.	Sáne, éam quam óptime gessísti.
Was the master at leisure?	Vacavítne praecéptor?
He was not at leisure.	Nôn vacâvit.
To salt, season with salt.	{ Salíre, sǎle condíre (REM). { Sălem aspergĕre (REI).
Salt meat.	Caro sǎle condīta.
Salt fish.	Salsamenta, ōrum, *n.*
Fresh meat.	Caro rĕcens (*gen.* carnis recentis).
The food, victuals.	Cíbus, i, *m.* ; esca, ae, *f.* ; cibaria, ōrum, *n.*
The dish, mess.	Cíbus, i, *m.* ; fercŭlum, i, *n.*
The milk.	Lac, *gen.* lactis, *n.*
The milk-food.	Cibus lactens; lactentia, ĭum, *n. pl.*
Milk soup.	Jūs lactens.
Salt meats.	Cibaria salsa, *n. pl.*
To partake of food, to eat.	Cibum capĕre *or* sūmĕre.
To attract.	{ Attrahĕre, traxi, tractum. { Ad se trahĕre (ALIQUID, ALI- QUEM.)
To allure, entice.	{ Allicĭo, ĕre, lexi, lectum. { Allectāre (ALIQUEM AD SE).
To excite, to delight.	Delectāre ; oblectāre.
To charm, enchant.	{ Rapio, ĕre, pŭi, ptum. { Permulceo, ĕre, si, sum.
To enrapture, ravish.	{ Admiratiōne afficĕre. { Suavissime afficĕre. { Voluptāte perfundĕre.

The beauty.   Pulchritūdo, ĭnis, *f.*
The harmony.   Harmonĭa, ae, *f.*; concentus, ūs, *m.*
The voice.   Vox, *gen.* vōcis, *f.*
The power, force.   Vis, *plur.* vīres, *f.*
The power, authority.   Potestas, ātis, *f.*
To have power (influence) over ony one.   Multum (*or* plurĭmum) apud alĭquem posse *or* valēre.
To occupy one's self with anything.   Versāri *or* occupāri in aliquā re.
To meddle with anything.   Se immiscēre (ŭi, mixtum *or* mistum) alicui rĕi.
To trouble one's head about anything.   Curāre rem; laborāre de re; se immiscēre rei.
The quarrel, contest.   Lis, *gen.* litis, *f.*; rixa, ae, *f.*
The commerce, traffic.   Mercatūra, ae, *f.*; negotia, ōrum, *n.*
I do not meddle with other people's business.   Ego mē aliénis negótiis nòn immísceo.
It is strange.   Mirábĭle díctu ést.
The art of painting.   Ars pingendi, ars pictōria.

Chemistry.   Chymĭca, ae, *f.*
The chemist.   Chymĭcus, i, *m.*
The art.   Ars, artis, *f.*
To look at some one.   Adspicĕre, adspectāre, intuēri alĭquem.

To concern (some one).
- Attingo, ĕre, tĭgi, tactum (ALI-QUEM).
- Pertinēre (AD ALIQUEM *or* REM).
- Spectāre ad rem.

What is that to me?
- Quíd ad mê?
- Quíd íd meā réfert *or* ínterest?

What is that to you?
- Quíd tíbi cum íllā rê?
- Quíd id tuā réfert?

I have nothing to do with that.
- Id níhil ad mê áttinet.
- Id meā níhil ínterest.

As far as I am concerned.   Quód ad mê áttinet.
This concerns (has reference to) you.
- Rês ad tê spéctat.
- De tê fábula narrâtur.

What has that to do with the matter?   Quid hóc ad rém?
I do not like to meddle with things that do not concern me.   Ego mē aliénis lítibus nòn nísi invítus immísceo.
Did the song of the maiden attract you?   Allexítne te cántus puéllae?
It truly enchanted me.   Immo mē suavíssime affēcit.
The magnet attracts iron.   Mágnes férrum ad sê állicit et tráhit.
Is he engaged in the art of painting?   Versatúrne in árte pingéndi?
No, he occupies himself with chemistry.   Nôn; in chýmicā versâtur.

The singing (song).	Cantus, *m.*
To repeat.	Repĕto, ĕre, ivi (ĭi), ĭtum. Iterāre, retractāre (ALIQUID).
The repetition.	Repetitio, iterātio, ōnis, *f.*
The beginning, commencement.	Initĭum; princĭpĭum, i, *n.*
The wisdom.	Sapĭentia, ae, *f.*
The study, application to letters.	Tractātio litterārum. Litterārum studia, ōrum, *n.*
The goddess.	Dĕa, dīva, ae, *f.*
The nightingale.	Luscinĭa, ae, *f.*
The Lord.	Domĭnus, Deus, i, *m.*
The Creator.	Creātor, auctor, ōris, *m.*
To create.	Creāre, efficĕre.
The creatiori.	Creātio, ōnis, *f.* (*act.*). Mundus, i, *m.*; rērum natūra (*effect*).
The heaven.	Coelum, i, *n.*
The earth.	Terra, ae, *f.*
The solitude.	Solitūdo, ĭnis, *f.*
The goodness.	Benignĭtas, humanĭtas, ātis, *f.*
The cleanliness.	Munditia, ae, *f.*, *or* mundities, ēi, *f.*
The uncleanliness.	Immunditia, ae, *f.*
The government.	Magistrātŭs, *us, m., or pl.* magistrātŭs; senātus, ūs, *m.*
Sensible, reasonable.	Sānus, prūdens, modestus.
For my, thy, our sake; on my, thine own account.	Meā, tuā, nostrā causā *or* gratiā.
On his, on the father's account.	Ejus causā, patris causā *or* gratiā.
Not only — but also.	Non mŏdo — sed (or rērum) etiam. Non tantum — sed etiam. Non sōlum — sed etiam.
Not only not — but not even.	Non modo (non) * —— sed ne .... quĭdem.
He was not only unlike the preceding king, but even more cruel than Romulus.	Nōn sōlum próximo régi dissímilis, sed ferócior étiam Rómulo fúit.
Such a man will never venture not only to do, but not even to think, anything that is not honorable.	Tālis vír nôn mŏdo fácere, sed ne cogitáre quídem quídquam audêbit, quod nôn honéstum sit.

---

* In this construction the first *non* is generally omitted, when both members of the sentence have a common predicate, as in the second of the following examples, where *audēbit* is the common verb, and *ne — quidem* equivalent to *etiam non.*

EXERCISE 162.

Will you dine with us to-day? — With much pleasure. — What have you for dinner? We have good soup, some fresh and salt meat, and some milk-food. — Do you like milk-food? — I like it better than all other food. — Are you ready to dine? — I am ready. — Do you intend to set out soon? — I intend setting out next week. — Do you travel alone? — No, madam, I travel with my uncle. — Do you travel on foot or in a carriage? — We travel in a carriage. — Did you meet any one in your last journey (*ultimo in itinĕre tuo ad*) to Berlin? — We met many wanderers. — What do you intend to spend your time in this summer? — I intend to take a short journey. — Did you walk much in your last journey? — I like very much to walk, but my uncle likes to go in a carriage. — Did he not wish to walk? — He wished to walk at first, but after having taken a few steps, he wished to get into the carriage, so that I did not walk much. — What have you been doing at school to-day? — We have been listening to our teacher, who made a long speech on the (*qui verba faciēbat multa de*) goodness of God. — What did he say? — After saying, "God is the creator of heaven and earth; the fear of the Lord is the beginning of all wisdom"; he said, "Repetition is the mother of studies, and a good memory is a great benefit of God." — Why did you not stay longer in Holland? — When I was there, the living was so dear that I had not money enough to stay there any longer. — What sort of weather was it when you were on the way to Vienna? — It was very bad weather; for it was stormy, and snowed, and rained very heavily. — May I have leisure to read through the book? — Would that I had an opportunity to do (*faciendi*) what you have done! — O that he had never written that letter! — You act as if you were sad; what is the matter with you (*quid tristis es*)?

EXERCISE 163.

What are you doing all the day in this garden? — I am walking in it. — What is there in it that attracts you? — The singing of the birds attracts me. — Are there any nightingales in it? — There are some in it, and the harmony of their singing enchants me. — What does your niece amuse herself with in her solitude? — She reads a good deal and writes letters to her mother. — What does your uncle amuse himself with in his solitude? — He employs himself in painting and chemistry. — Does he no longer do any business? — He no longer does any, for he is too old to do it. — Why does he meddle with your business? — He does not generally meddle with other people's business (*alienis negotiis se immiscēre non assŏlet*); but he meddles with mine, because he loves me. — Has your master made you repeat your lesson to-day? — He has made me repeat it. — Did you know it? — I did know it pretty well. — Have you also done some exercises? — I have done some, but what is that to you, I beg? — I do not generally meddle with things that do not concern me; but I love you so much (*tantŏpere*), that I concern myself much about what you are doing. — Does any one trouble his head about you? — No one troubles his head about me; for I am not worth the trouble. — Not only

for the sake of cleanliness, but also for the sake of health, prudent
people avoid (*vitāre*) uncleanliness, and wash themselves often.—
Shall you buy that horse?—I shall buy it, although it is not an
English one.—Though he is my cousin, he nevertheless does not
come to see me.—Although they are not rich, they are nevertheless
very benevolent.—I do not know, whether he is at home or not.—
The question is (*quaerĭtur*), whether he will do it or not.

Lesson XC.—PENSUM NONAGESIMUM.

SUBJUNCTIVE AFTER RELATIVES.

A. Relative pronouns and adverbs are followed by the subjunctive, when the clause introduced by them contains the *consequence* or
result, or the *cause, reason, purpose,* or *motive* of what has gone before.

B. When the relative is preceded by *is, hic, ille, tālis, tantus, ejusmŏdi, hujusmŏdi, adeo* or *tam*, so as to denote a consequence or result, its verb is in the subjunctive.

In this construction *qui* becomes equivalent to *ut ego, tu, ille,* &c.;—
cūjus to *ut mei, tui, sui, illīus, ējus;—cui* to *ut mihi, tibi, sibi, ei, illi,*
and so through all the cases. E. g.

Égo *is* súm, *qui* níhil únquam
meā pótius, quam meōrum cívium causā *fécĕrim.*

My character is such, that I have
never done anything on my own
account rather than on that of
my fellow-citizens.

Éa *ést* Romāna *géns, quae* vícta
quiéscĕre *nésciat.*

Such is the character of the Roman
race, that it cannot rest when
conquered.

Nōn tū *is és, qui,* qui sis, *néscias.*

You are not such a man as to be
ignorant of what you are.

Nōn égo súm *ille férreus, qui* frā-
tris moerōre nōn *móvĕar.*

I am not so heartless a man as not
to be moved by the sorrow of
my brother.

Innocéntia est afféctio *tālis* ánimi, *quae nóceat* némini.

Innocence is that disposition of the
mind which does nobody any
harm.

Est *hujŭsmŏdi* réus, *in quó* hómine níhil *sit,* praeter súmma
peccāta.

He is so guilty, that there is nothing in the man but the most cul-
pable offences.

In córpŏre si quíd *ejŭsmodi* est,
quod réliquo córpori *nóceat,*
úri secarīque pátimur.

If there is anything in our body of
such a character as to injure the
remaining parts of it, we suffer
it to be burnt or cut.

Núlla géns *tám féra*, némo ómnium *tám immānis* est, *cújus* méntem nôn *inbúerit* deôrum opínio.

There is no race so savage, no man so monstrous, whose mind is not imbued with the idea of a God.

REMARKS.

1. The demonstrative to which the relative refers is sometimes to be supplied. E. g. *Nunc dicis aliquid* (sc. ejusmodi), *quod ad rem* pertineat, Now you say something to the point.

2. This rule includes relative expressions containing a limitation or restriction. Such are, — *Quod sciam* or *intelligam*, As far as I know or understand. *Quod commodo tuo fiat*, So far as it can be done without inconvenience to you. *Quod sine alterĭus injuriā fiat* or *fieret*, As far as it can be done without injury to another. *Quod salvā fide possim*, So far as I can honorably.*

3. When a comparative precedes, the clause introduced by *quam qui* (*quam cujus*, *cui*, *quorum*, &c.) requires the subjunctive. E. g. *Major sum*, quam cui possit *fortūna nocēre*, I am superior to the injuries of fortune. *Majōra deliquērant*, quam quibus *ignosci* posset, They had been guilty of too grave offences to be pardoned.†

C. When the relative is preceded by an indefinite expression, positive or negative, or by an indefinite question involving a negation, its verb is in the subjunctive.

Such expressions are *est*, *sunt*, *existunt*, *inveniuntur*, *reperiuntur* (with *homĭnes* understood) ; — *nemo*, *nullus*, *nihil est* ; — *quis est?* *quid est?* *qui*, *quae*, *quod* (sc. *negotium*, &c.) *est?* *quantum est?* *quotusquisque est?* &c. E. g.

Súnt, qui dícant, cénseant.
There are those who say, those who suppose.

Súnt, qui díxerint, vídĕrint.
There are those who have heard, those who have seen.

Invéntus ést, qui flámmis impónĕret mánum.
There was one found who put his hand into the flames.

Fuérunt, qui dícĕrent.
There were those who said.

Ést áliquid, quod nôn *opórteat*, etiámsi licet.
There is something which does not behoove us, although not unlawful.

Múlti érunt, quibus récte lítteras dáre *póssis.*
There will be those whom you can properly trust with letters.

Némo ést orátor, *qui* sê Demósthenis símilem ésse *nólit.*
There is no orator who is unwilling to be like Demosthenes.

Nôn deĕrunt, quî Cássii et Brúti *meminerint.*
There will not be wanting those who remember Cassius and Brutus.

---

* So frequently with *quidem*; as, *Quos* quidem *aut invenĕrim aut legĕrim*, As far at least as I have been able to find or read. But *quantum* in this construction has the indicative; as, *Quantum possum*, As much as (as far as) I can.

† For the same reason *quam*, even without a relative, is sometimes followed by the subjunctive. E. g. *In his litteris longior fui*, quam *aut* vellem (instead of velle), *aut quam me putâvi fore.*

Helvétiis dómi *nihil erat, quó fá-mem tolerárent.*	The Helvetii had nothing at home, wherewith to still their hunger.
Quis ést, qui utília fúgiat ?	Who is there that seeks to avoid the useful ?
Quótus quísque est, qui voluptá-tem *néget ésse bónum ?*	How many are there among men, that deny pleasure to be a good ?
Plúres auctóres *invénio,* qui Ro-mános Horátios *vócent.*	I find several authors who call the Horatii Romans.
Núm ámplius quíd *desíderas, quod respóndeas ?*	There is nothing else that you desire to reply ?
Nihil habébam nóvi, *quód* post *accidísset,* quam *dedíssem* ad tê lítteras.	I have nothing new to communicate, that occurred after my writing this to you.

REMARKS.

1. This rule includes also the expressions *non est quod, nihil est quod* (*quare* or *cur*), "there is no ground or reason why"; and *est ut* (when it = *est cur*), "there is ground, reason." E. g. *Est quod gaudeas,* You have reason to rejoice. *Non est, quod te pudeat,* You need not be ashamed. *Nihil est, quod pertimescat,* He has no cause to dread. *Non est, cur eorum spes infringātur,* There is no reason why they should be dejected. *Ille* erat ut *odisset defensorem salūtis meae,* He had reason to hate the defender of my safety. Non est *igitur* ut *mirandum sit,* There is consequently nothing to be wondered at. Quid est, cur *virtus ipsa per se non* efficiat *beatos ?* What is the reason that virtue of herself does not make men happy ?

2. The subjunctive also follows *habeo quod, non habeo quod.* E. g. *Non habeo, quod dicam,* I have nothing to say. *Quid habes, quod reprehendas ?* What fault have you to find ? *Non habeo, qui* (= quâ re) *utar,* I have nothing to live on. *Quo se vertĕret, non habēbat,* He knew not where to turn to.†

3. When, in connection with the expressions *sunt qui,* a particular and determinate subject is expressed, the verb is in the indicative. E. g. *Sunt autem* bestiae quaedam, *in quibus* inest *aliquid simile virtūtis,* There are certain animals in which there is something that resembles virtue. But when the subject is merely a general one, such as *multi, pauci, nemo,* &c., or is entirely suppressed, the subjunctive is the common construction, and the indicative in these cases is generally employed by poets only.

D. When the relative clause denotes the *purpose, object,* or *motive* of what has gone before, it may be resolved into a clause with *ut,* and the verb is in the subjunctive.

---

* This rule extends to the active verbs *habeo, reperio, invenio, nanciscor, desidero, quaero,* and *relinquo,* after all of which the relative may take the subjunctive. Cf. note 2.

† But this last example more properly belongs to Lesson LXXXVII. *D.* So likewise, *Non habeo* quid *dicam,* I know not what to say. *Quid faceret, non habēbat,* He knew not what to do. These are indirect questions.

The relative is then either *qui* in the sense of *ut is*, or *quo*, "in order that" (before a comparative), or *quā*, *ubi*, *unde*, "where," "whence," in the sense of "in order that there, or thence."

The verbs on which such clauses depend are especially those of choosing, ordering, devoting, sending, coming, going, and receiving. E. g.

Lítterae posteritátis caúsā repértae súnt, *quae* subsídio oblivióni ésse *póssent.*	Letters were invented for the benefit of posterity, as a protection against oblivion.
Dolabélla vénĕrat ípse, *qui ésset* in consílio, et prímus senténtiam *díceret.*	Dolabella had appeared in person, so that he might take a part in the deliberation, and gave his opinion first.
Súnt múlti, qui erípiunt áliis, *quód* áliis *largiántur.*	There are many who rob some of that which they wish to lavish upon others.
Cohortárer vôs, *quô* ánimo *fortiôre essêtis.*	I should exhort you to be more resolute.
Darius póntem fēcit in Ístro flúmĭne, *quâ* cópias *tradúcĕret.*	Darius constructed a bridge over the Danube, over which he might lead his forces.
Themístocli Artaxérxes Lampsacum úrbem donárat, *unde* vinum *súmeret.*	Artaxerxes made Themistocles a present of the city of Lampsacum, from which he might get his wine.

E. When the clause introduced by the relative contains the ground or reason of what has gone before, the verb is in the subjunctive.

The relative is then either *qui*, rendered by "that," "because," or "since," or *quippe qui, ut qui, utpote qui,* "as one who," "inasmuch as he," &c. E. g.

Mágna ést Pélŏpis cúlpa, *qui* nôn *erudíĕrit* fílium, nec *docíĕrit,* quátĕnus ésset quídque curándum.	The great fault of Pelops is, that he did not educate his son, nor teach him to what extent to carry everything.
Áctio malúĭmus íter fácerĕ pédibus, *qui* incómmŏde *navigassémus.*	We preferred to start from Actium on foot, *because* we had had a bad passage at sea.
Sôlis cándor illústrior ést, *quíppe qui* in imménso múndo tam lónge latēque *collúceat.*	The light of the sun is brighter (than any other), inasmuch as it shines so far and wide in the immensity of the universe.
Súnt hómines natúrā curiósi, *ut qui* sermúncŭlis étiam fabéllísque *ducántur.*	Men are naturally curious, since they are influenced even by idle talk and fables.
A Catilínā Antónius nôn procul ábĕrat, *utpote qui* in fúgā *scquerêtur.*	Antonius was not far from Catiline as he pursued him in his flight.

50

O fortunâte adoléscens, *qui* túae virtûtis Homêrum praecônem *invénĕris !*	O lucky young man, for having found a Homer to proclaim thy valor!
Mê infelîcem, *qui* per tót ánnos tê vidêre nôn *potuĕrim !* *	How unfortunate I am, that I have not been able to see you for so many years!

F. After the adjectives *dignus, indignus, aptus,* and *idoneus,* the question *for what ?* is answered by the relative with the subjunctive, and sometimes by a simple infinitive. E. g.

Dígnus, indígnus est, *qui amêtur.*	He is worthy, unworthy of being loved.
Idóneus est, *qui ímperet.*	He is competent to command.
Qui modéste paret, vidêtur, *qui* aliquándo *impĕret, dígnus* ésse.	He who modestly obeys seems to be worthy of commanding at some future time.
Liviánae fâbulae nôn sátis *dígnae* sunt, *quae* itĕrum *legántur.*	The dramas of Livy are scarcely worth reading a second time.
(Méntem) sôlam censébant *idóneam* (ésse), *cui crederêtur.*	They held that the intellect alone was fit to be relied upon.
Núlla videbâtur *áptior* persôna, *quae* de aetâte *loquerêtur.*	There seemed to be no person better qualified to discourse on old age.
Lyricôrum Horátius fére sôlus *légi dígnus* ést.	Of the lyrical poets Horace is almost the only one worth reading.
Utérque óptimus érat, *dignúsque* álter *éligi* álter *éligere.*	They both were men of the first order; and worthy the one to be chosen, and the other to choose.

G. In narration, the imperfect and pluperfect subjunctive are sometimes put after relative pronouns and adverbs, when a repeated action is spoken of. E. g.

Elephánti tûtum ab hóstibus, *quacúmque incéderent,* ágmen praebébant.	The elephants formed a safe protection against the enemy, wherever they might march.
Domitiânus, *quóties* ótium *ésset,* áleâ sê oblectâbat.	Domitian amused himself with dice-playing, whenever he was at leisure.
Sócrates *quam* sê *cúnque* in pártem *dedísset,* ómnium fácile fúit prínceps.	Socrates was confessedly the first in everything to which he had applied himself.
Néc quísquam Pýrrhum, *quâ tulísset* impĕtum, sustinêre váluit.	Nor could any one stand against Pyrrhus, where he had charged upon the enemy.

REMARK. — The subjunctive is thus sometimes put after *quum,*

---

* In this and the preceding example, the student should notice the *person* of the verb, which adapts itself to that of the antecedent of the relative.

" when "; *ubi* and *ut*, in the sense of " as soon as," and after *si*. E. g.
Id ubi dixisset, *hastam in fines eorum emittebat*, When (or as soon as)
he had said that, he sent the javelin within their limits.   But in all
the cases of this rule, the indicative is even more frequently used than
the subjunctive.

To die of a disease.	*Morĭor (mori, mortuus sum) aliquo morbo.*
The small-pox.	Variŏlae, ārum, *pl.*
The fever.	Febris, is, *f.*
The intermittent, tertian, quartan, continual fever.	Febris remittens, tertiāna, quartā-na, quotidiāna.
To get the fever.	In febrim incĭdĕre (incĭdi, incā-sum).
To have the fever.	Febri laborāre, febrim habēre.
An attack of fever; a fit.	Accessus febris; mōtus febriculō-sus.
The fever comes on.	Febris accēdit.
The fever stops.	Febris decēdit.
The apoplexy.	Apoplexia, ae, *f.*
To be struck with apoplexy.	Corripĭor (i, reptus sum) apo-plexiā.
To open (active).	{ *Aperio, ĭre, erŭi, ertum.* { *Patefacio, ĕre, fēci, factum.*
To unlock, unbolt.	{ Reclūdo, ĕre, si, sum. { Rĕsĕro, āre, āvi, ātum.
To open, be open (*neut.*).	{ Aperĭor, īri, ertus sum. { Reclūdi, reserāri.
To stand or lie open.	Patĕo, ēre, patŭi, ——.
To close, shut (act.).	{ *Claudo, ĕre, si, sum.* { *Obsĕro, āre, āvi, ātum.*
To cover (shut).	Operio, ĭre, ŭi, rtum.
To shut, close (*neut.*).	Claudi, obserāri ; operīri.
To sell well, readily (*of goods*).	{ Vendibĭlem (*or* -bĭle) ēsse. { Emptōres facĭle invenīre.
Of what disease did your sister die ?	Quô mórbo mórtua est sóror túa ?
She died of the small-pox.	Mórtua ést varíŏlis.
Did you ever get the fever ?	Incidistíne únquam in fébrim ?
Yes, I had the tertian fever once.	Sáne ; in fébrim tertiánam quón-dam incĭdi.
Was the old man struck with apoplexy ?	Correptúsne est sénex apopléxiā ?
He was struck.	Corréptus ést.
Did the wine sell well last year ?	Invenítne vínum fácile emptóres ánno próxime elápso ?
I do not know how it sold.	Haûd scío, quómodo vendĕrētur.
Will you shut the door ?	Vísne óstium claúdĕre ?
No, I will open it (wide).	Immo íd pótius patefácere málo.

Has he already locked (bolted) the door? | Observavítne jam óstium?

He has not yet bolted it. | Nôndum obserâvit.

The key opens the door (fits the lock). | Clávis óstium áperit.

The door opens easily. | Óstium fäcile aperitur.

The door does not shut. | Fóres híant.

The window shuts well. | Fenéstra ex tóto claûsa ést.

The window does not shut easily. | Fenéstra nôn fäcile operitur.

The door of the temple stood open. | Jánua témpli patêbat.

Nature opened the way. | Natûra íter patefēcit.

They opened their ears to flatterers. | Aúres súas assentatóribus patefecérunt.

Letters can either be lost, or opened, or intercepted. | Lítterae aut interire, aut aperíri, aut intércipi póssunt.

From afar, afar off. | *E longinquo; procul; emĭnus.*

Summer clothes. | Vestes aestívae.

To conceive, comprehend. | { Comprehendo, ĕre, dî, sum.
{ Mente complector (i, plexus sum).

That is not said. | Hóc nôn dícitur.

That cannot be comprehended. | { Hóc comprehéndi nôn pótest.
{ Hóc in intelligéntiam nôn cádit.

It is evident, manifest, clear. | { Est plānum, evidens, manifestum,
{   in aperto.
(Constat, lûcet, líquet.*

According to the circumstances of the case. | *Pro rĕ, pro rĕ nátâ.*

According to circumstances. | Ex tempŏre, pro tempŏre.

Under these circumstances. | His rêbus; quae cum íta sínt.

To proceed according to circumstances. | Ex rĕ consŭlĕre (ûi, tum).

According as, as. | *Pro eo ut, prout* (cum Indic.).

As the circumstances admitted. | Próut facultātes homǐnis ferēbant.

As the case may demand. | Próut rês póstŭlat.

As far as the difficulty of the case admitted. | Pro éo ut difficúltas témporis túlit.

As far as I can. | Quántum in mê sítum est. Ut pótĕro.

According as I deserve. | Pro éo ut mérĕor.

It depends upon circumstances. | Hóc ex rê et ex témpore péndet.

Everything depends upon you alone. | In tê úno pósita súnt ómnia.

It all depends on this. | { Hóc cáput réi est.
{ Ómnia húc rédĕunt.

To put, place, lay, set. | *Pōnĕre, locāre, statuĕre* (ALIQUID IN ALIQUO LOCO).

---

* On the construction of these expressions, see Lesson LIII. *B.* Rem. 2.

To put anything before the fire.	Appōnĕre *or* propōnĕre aliquid igni (ad ignem).
To put, or place upon.	{ Impōnĕre aliquem *or* aliquid in rem. Collocāre aliquid in re.
To put anything in its proper place.	Aliquid suo loco pōnĕre.
To put (seat) the boy upon the horse.	Impōnĕre puĕrum in equum.
To set the glass upon the table.	Scyphum in mensā statuĕre (ŭi, ūtum).
To put back anything to its place.	Aliquid suo loco repōnĕre.
To stick, fix, insert.	{ *Infĭgo, ĕre, fixi, fixum.* *Insĕro, ĕre, serŭi, sertum.* (ALIQUID REI *or* IN REM.)
To insert the thread into the needle.	Inserĕre filum in acum.
To put the ring on the finger.	Anŭlum digĭto inserĕre.
The javelin sticks fast in the gate.	Hasta infigitur portae.
Do not put the glass upon the table; for it will break.	Ne scyphum in mensā státuas. Nam frangêtur.
To be angry (at some one).	{ *Irascor, i, irātus sum.* *Succenseo, ĕre, ŭi, sum.* *Irātum esse* (ALICUI).
To be angry (about anything).	*Grarĭter* or *moleste ferre* (ALIQUID).
To pretend to be angry with any one.	Se simulāre alicui irātum.
What are you angry about?	Quid succénses (irásceris)?
I am angry with you, for having carried away my book.	Tibi succénseo, quod míhi líbrum abstulísti.
He has done nothing for you to be angry about.	Níhil fêcit, quod succénseas.
I am angry that he did not come.	Irâtus súm, éum nôn venísse (*or* quod nôn vênit).*
Are you sorry for having done it?	{ Poenitétne tê fácti? Poenitétne tê hóc fecísse?
I am sorry for it.	{ Id mê poénitet. Dólet míhi váldc.
I do not regret having lived.	Nôn poénitet mê vixísse.
Are the women handsome?	Súntne mulieres formósae?
They are so.	Súnt véro.
They are well-bred and handsome.	Et béne morátae et formósae súnt.
What countrywomăn is she?	{ Cújus ést ílla? Únde vênit?
She is from France.	{ Dómo Francogálla ést. Ex Francogálliã vênit.

---

* On the government of these verbs, see Lesson LIV. *II.*

2 L   50 *

What sort of a pen have you lost ?	Quâlem pénnam (quid pénnae) amisísti ?
A gold one.	Aúrĕam.
What sort of pens has your sister made ?	Quáles pénnas fídit sóror túa ?
Good ones.	Bónas.
To cut a pen.	Pennam *or* calămum findĕre (fídi, fissum).
To mend a pen.	Pennam *or* calămum temperāre.
To put pen to paper.	Calămum sumĕre ; se ad scribendum conferre.
Happy.	Fēlix, ícis ; beātus, a, um.
Unhappy, miserable.	Infēlix, ícis ; míser, a, um.
Polite, courteous.	Urbānus, benignus, modestus, a, um.
Impolite, uncivil.	Inurbānus, a, um ; rustĭcus, a, um.

EXERCISE 164.

Of what illness did your sister die ? — She died of the fever. — How is your brother ? — My brother is no longer living. He died three months ago. — I am surprised at it, for he was very well last summer when I was in the country. — Of what did he die ? — He died of apoplexy. — How is the mother of your friend ? — She is not well ; she had an attack of ague the day before yesterday, and this morning the fever has returned. — Has she the intermitting fever ? — I do not know, but she often has cold fits. — What has become of the woman whom I saw at your mother's ? — She died this morning of apoplexy. — Did the wine sell well last year ? — It did not sell very well ; but it will sell better next year, for there will be a great deal of it, and it will not be dear. — Why do you open the door ? — Do you not see how it smokes here ? — I do not see it ; but you must open the window instead of opening the door. — The window does not open easily ; that is the reason why I open the door. — When will you shut it ? — I will shut it as soon as there is no more smoke. — Why do you not put those beautiful glasses on the small table (*mensŭla*) ? — If I put them upon that little table they will break. — Did you often go a fishing when you were in that country ? — We often went a fishing and a hunting. — If you will go with us into the country, you will see the castle of my father. — You are very polite, sir ; but I have seen that castle already. — Are you such a man, as to be capable of doing that (*hoc facĕre possis*) ? — I am by no means so heartless ; nor are you such a man as not to know who I am. — Such is our character, that we cannot be contented with anything but liberty. — Are there any who affirm that this is not true ? — There are none. — Is there any one who does not understand ? — There is no one. — There were many who said that you were mistaken. — Had your brother anything new to write to you ? — He had many things to write to me. — Are you not fortunate for having found such a book ? — I am as happy as any man in the world (for it). — Did he begin to write this morning ? — He could not begin, because he had no ink. —

Is your brother competent (*idoneus*) to teach ? — He is not competent to teach, but to write. — Is he worthy to command ? — He is as worthy as any one. — Did your teacher often go out walking ? — He took a walk as often as he was at leisure. — Has my son been diligent ? — He was confessedly the first in everything to which he applied himself.

Lesson XCI. — PENSUM UNUM ET NONA-GESIMUM.

OF THE SUBJUNCTIVE IN INTERJECTED CLAUSES.

A. Interjected clauses, in which the language or thoughts of the person spoken of are conveyed, or which are essential to the definition of what has gone before, have a verb in the subjunctive.

Clauses of this kind always occur in sentences, which are themselves dependent upon another proposition ; e. g. in the construction of the Acc. cum Inf., or in sentences dependent on a conjunction, &c. They are commonly introduced either by a relative (pronoun or adverb), or by a conjunction. E. g.

Tháles, qui sapientíssimus in séptem fúit, hómines existimáre dixit oportêre, *ómnia, quae cerneréntur*, deôrum *ésse plêna*.	Thales, who was the wisest of the seven sages, said that men ought to consider all things *beheld by our senses* as full of divinities.
Caesar hortátus est mílites, *ne éa, quae accidissent, gráviter férrent.*	Cæsar exhorted his soldiers not to be chagrined *at what had `happened.*

REMARK. — Sentences, in which the language or sentiments of another (or of one's self) are stated *indirectly*, are said to be in the *oratio obliqua*, in contradistinction to the *oratio directa*, in which they are quoted as they were uttered. Thus the above clauses stated in the *oratio directa* are : " *Omnia*, quae cernuntur, *deôrum plêna* sunt." — " *Ne ea*, quae accidêrunt, ferte *graviter* " (Do not be chagrined at what has happened).* Thus also in English : *I wrote him, " I shall come to-morrow" (oratio directa)*; and : *I wrote him that I would come to-morrow (oratio obliqua)*. And in the third person : *He said, " I have conquered"*; and indirectly : *He said that he had conquered.* — The following rules will elucidate these cases more fully.

B. When an interjected clause occurs in the construction of the *accusativus cum infinitīvo*, either as an expression of the

---

* The student will notice here the change of mood and tense in the direct statement: *quae accidêrunt* instead of *quae accidissent*; *quae cernuntur* instead of *quae cernerentur*, and the imperative *ne — ferte* instead of *ne — ferentur*.

language or sentiments of the person spoken of, or otherwise as an essential part of that which is advanced in the statement, the verb of that clause is in the subjunctive. E. g.

Môs est Athénis, *laudári* in conciône *éos*, qui *sint* in proéliis *interfécti*.	It is customary at Athens to deliver public eulogies on those who have fallen in battle.
Sócrates dícere solêbat, *omnes in eo, quod scírent*, sátis *ésse eloquéntes*.	Socrates was in the habit of saying, that all men were eloquent enough in what they knew.
Eléus Híppias, quum Olýmpiam venísset, gloriâtus est, *nihil esse úllâ* in árte rêrum ómnium, *quód ípse nesciret;* nec sôlum hâs ártes, *quibus liberáles* doctrínae atque ingénuae *contineréntur;* sed ánulum, *quem habêret*, pállium, *quó amíctus*, sóccos, *quibus indútus ésset, sê súâ mánu confecísse.*	Hippias of Elis, having come to Olympia, boasted, that there was nothing in any one of all the arts, which he himself did not understand; and that these arts were not only those, in which the liberal sciences were contained, but that he himself had manufactured with his own hand the ring which he wore, the cloak which he had on, and the shoes that were on his feet.
Príncipes Aeduôrum, nôn *dubitâre sê*, dicébant, *quîn*, si Helvétios *superávẽrint* Románi, únâ cum réliquâ Gálliâ Aéduis libertâtem *sint ereptúri.*	The leaders of the Aedui said, that they had no doubt but that, if the Romans conquered the Helvetii, they would deprive the Aedii, together with all the rest of Gaul, of their liberties.

REMARKS.

1. When the interjected clause is an addition of the speaker or writer himself, and not the language or sentiments of the subject spoken of, the verb is in the indicative. E. g. *Cave tibi amicos esse crēdas,* quos vicisti, Beware of regarding those whom you have conquered as your friends.

2. If the interjected relative clause is merely explanatory of a fact, or a circumlocution for a noun or adjective, its verb is sometimes in the indicative. E. g. *Caesar per exploratōres certior factus est, ex eâ parte vici,* quam *Gallis* concessěrat, *omnes noctu discessisse,* Cæsar was informed by his scouts, that during the night all had left that section of the village which he had conceded to the Gauls. *Nam sic habetōte, magistratĭbus* iisque, qui praesunt, *rempublicam continēri,* For these shall be your sentiments, that the republic is maintained by its magistrates and by those who are at the head of it.

C. When the interjected clause occurs in a sentence introduced by a conjunction, as an essential part of the purpose, request, precept, command, or supposition of the same, the verb of that clause is in the subjunctive. E. g.

Úbii orábant, *ut* síbi Caêsar auxílium *férret;* vel, *si* id fácere
prohiberêtur, exércĭtum módo
Rhênum *transportáret.*

The Ubii besought Cæsar to come
to their assistance, or, if he was
prevented from doing so, to bring
at least his army across the Rhine.

Réx imperâvit, *ut, quae* béllo
ópus *éssent,* pararéntur.

The king ordered such preparations to be made, as might be necessary for the war.

Éo simus ánimo, *ut* níhil in mális
ducámus, quóol sít vel a déo
immortáli vel a natúrā *constitútum.*

Let us be so disposed, as to consider nothing an evil, that may
have been appointed either by
the immortal God or by nature.

REMARKS.

1. When the subjunctive clause introduced by *ut* does not denote a
purpose, command, &c., but merely a result or definition (as after
tam, ita, talis,* &c.), the verb of the interjected clause is in the indicative. E. g. *Eloquendi vis effĭcit, ut ea,* quae ignorāmus, *discĕre, et ea,*
quae scimus, *alios docēre possĭmus,* The power of speech enables us to
learn the things we are ignorant of, and to teach others what we know.
Asia tam opĭma est et fertilis, ut multitudĭne earum rērum, quae exportantur, *facile omnĭbus terris antecellat,* Asia is so rich and fertile, that
in the multiplicity of exportable products it easily excels all other
countries.

2. The verb of the interjected clause is sometimes in the indicative,
when the speaker adds it on his own account. E. g. *Xerxem litteris
certiōrem fēci, id agi, ut pons,* quem in Hellesponto fecĕrat, *dissolverētur,* I informed Xerxes by letter, that a plan was on foot to destroy
the bridge which he had constructed over the Hellespont.

D. Dependent clauses generally, introduced by relatives or
conjunctions, take a verb in the subjunctive, when they convey
the sentiments of the person or party spoken of, and not of the
speaker himself. E. g.

Énnius nôn cénset, lugéndam
ésse mórtem, *quam* immortálitas *consequátur.*

Ennius does not think that death
is to be regretted, which (in his
opinion) is followed by immortality.

Sócrates accusâtus est, *quod corrúmpĕret* juventûtem et nóvas
superstitiónes *inchíceret.*

Socrates was impeached, because
(as his enemies alleged) he corrupted the youth, and introduced
new superstitions.

Nóctu ambulâbat in público Themístocles, *quod sómnum* cápere
nôn *pósset.*

Themistocles was in the habit of
walking abroad at night, because
(he said that) he could not get
any sleep.

Plínius májor períre ómne témpus arbitrabâtur, *quod* stúdiis
nôn *impertirétur.*

Pliny the elder considered all the
time lost which (he said) was not
devoted to his studies.

---

* Compare Lesson LXXXVIIL

| Aristídes nónne ob éam caûsam expúlsus est pátriâ, *quod* praeter módum jústus *ésset?* | Was not Aristides expelled from his country, because (it was alleged) that he was too just? |

REMARKS.

1. In all the above examples the writer himself does not indorse or positively affirm the opinion advanced in the dependent clause ; if he did, the verb would be in the indicative.

2. On the use of the reflexives *se, sui, sibi,* and *suus* in this construction, see Lesson LXXV. *C.*

3. Instead of the subjunctive of the verb itself, the expressions *quod dicĕret, quod arbitrarētur,* " because he said," " because he thought," are sometimes put, and the verb is made dependent upon these. E. g. *Ab Atheniensibus, locum sepulturae intra urbem ut dārent, impetrāre non potui,* quod *religione se impediri* dicĕrent,* I could not prevail upon the Athenians to grant me a burial-place within the limits of the city, because they said that they were prevented from doing so by religious scruples.

The utility, use.	*Utilĭtas, ātis* f.; *ūsus, ūs,* m.
The advantage.	*Commŏdum, emolumentum, lucrum, i,* m.
To be of use.	Utilitātem *or* ūsum afferre (ALICUI).· Usŭi esse, prodesse, condūcĕre (ALICUI).
To be of great use.	Magnam utilitātem afferre; vakle *or* plurĭmum prodesse; magnae utilitāti esse (ALICUI).
To be of little use.	Párum utilitātis afferre ; parvae esse utilitāti; párum (non multum) prodesse (ALICUI).
To be of no use.	Nihil prodesse (ALICUI) ; longe abesse (AB ALIQUO).
To profit by, derive profit from anything.	Utilitātem, fructum, commŏdum capĕre *or* percipĕre ex aliquâ re.
To turn anything to one's advantage or profit.	Aliquâ rê úti ; aliquid in rem suam convertĕre ; lucri facĕre aliquid.
To turn everything to one's own profit.	Omnia ad suam utilitātem referre.
To look to one's own advantage.	Commŏdis suis consulĕre *or* servíre.
To benefit (be useful) to any one.	Alicújus commodis consulĕre *or* servire.
Of what use is this?	Cui úsúi ést hóc ? Quid réfert? Quid pródest?

* Instead of the *quod religione se impedirētur* of the rule, or the *quod religione se impediri dicēbant,* when the speaker himself is the authority for the truth of the assertion. This construction, although grammatically incorrect, is not uncommon.

That is of no use.
: Hóc est núlli úsui.
: Hóc nihil pródest.

It is of use to me; it is to my advantage.
: Hóc míhi pródest (míhi útile est).
: Est e rê méā; est in rém méam.

It is for the advantage of the state.
: Hóc ést e rê públicā.

Of use, of advantage.
: Ex úsu, e rē, in rem (alicūjus).

Useful; advantageous.
: Utĭlis; salutāris; fructuōsus.

Useless; of no use.
: Inūtĭlis; sine utilitāte; carens fructu.

It is well, right, fair, just, proper (to do anything).
: Aequum, pār, jus, fas est (ALIQUID FACERE).

It is not well, unjust, wrong (to (do anything).
: Injustum, inīquum, nĕfas est (ALIQUID FACERE).

I consider it proper, right, fair.
: Aequum esse censeo (e. g. te hoc facĕre, &c.).

Is it right to do this?
: Aequímne ést fácere hóc?

It is not right; it is wrong.
: Nôn aêquum est; néfas est.

Is it useful to write much?
: Éstne útile (prodéstne) múltum scríbere?

It is very useful, of great use.
: Ést sáne máxime útile.
: Plúrimum pródest.

Did he derive much advantage from his books?
: Cepítne multum frúctum ex líbris súis?

He derived not much from them.
: Ímmo éi nôn múltum profuérunt.

Is it for your advantage?
: Estne e rê túā?

It is not; it is for my father.
: Nôn est; est e rê pátris.

What is your name?
: Quód ést tíbi nômen?
: Quînam vocâris?

My name is Charles.
: Ést míhi nômen Carólus (Caróli, Carólo).*
: Appéllor Carólus.

What do you call this (how is this called) in Latin?
: Quíd ést (dícitur, vocâtur) hóc Latíne?

What does this signify in French?
: Quid ést (sónat, signíficat) hóc Francogállice?

This signifies *parler* in French.
: Hóc Francogállice *parler* ést (sónat, signíficat).

It is not easy to tell.
: Nôn fácile est díctu.

Do they call him king, philosopher, Frederic?
: Appellíntne éum rĕgem, philósophum, Frédéricum?

They do.
: Fáctum.

To name, call.
: Nomināre, appellāre, vocāre, dicĕre.

To give one a name.
: Nōmen alicui dăre (indĕre, imponĕre).

The name, appellation (of a person or object).
: Nōmen†; appellatio; vocabŭlum.

---

* Compàre page 367.

† The *nomen* is properly the middle of the three names of a free Roman citi-

The name of emperor.	Nōmen imperatōris.
Called William; William by name.	{ Qui dícitur (vocàtur) Guiliélmus. Nómine Guiliélmus.
William.	Wilhelmus (Guilielmus), i, m.
Francis.	Franciscus, i, m.
James.	Jacōbus, i, m.
Elizabeth.	Elisabētha, ae, f.
Eleanor.	Leonōra, ae, f.
Wilhelmine.	Wilhelmīna, ae, f.
Schiller.	Schillĕrus, i, m.
Goethe.	Goethĭus, i, m.*
Euripides.	Euripĭdes, is, m.
Plato.	Plato, ōnis, m.
George the Third.	Georgĭus Tertĭus.
Henry the Fourth.	Henrīcus Quartus.
Charles the Great.	Carōlus Magnus.
Louis the Fourteenth.	Ludovicus Quartus Decĭmus.
To speak a language.	Aliquā linguā lŏqui or ūti.
Fluently, with facility.	Expedite, facĭle; profluente celeritāte.
He speaks Latin fluently.	{ Linguā Latīnā facĭle lóquitur. Línguae Latínae perītus est.
Charles the Fifth spoke several European languages fluently.	Carōlus Quíntus linguārum Eurōpénsium plúribus profluénte celeritāte utebâtur (loquebâtur).
Have you ever heard such a thing?	Audivistine únquam tále quid?
Never.	Núnquam.
I have never seen or heard such a thing.	Núnquam égo áliquid tále neque vídi neque audívi.
Such a thing.	Aliquid tále, tále quid.
The army.	Exercĭtus, ūs, m.
The camp.	Castra, ōrum, n.
Europe. — European.	Eurōpa, ae, f. — Eurōpensis, e; Eurōpaeus, a, um.
The works (of an author).	Opĕra; scripta, ōrum, n.
Sooner — than.	*Prius (citius, ante) — quam.*
Rather — than.	*Prius (potius, citius) — quam.*
He arrived sooner than.	Cítius, quám égo, advênit.
I will rather pay him than go thither.	Débitum éi sólvere pótius, quam éo ire, málo.
I will rather burn the coat than wear it.	Combûram pótius, quam gestâbo, véstem.
Rather than squander my money, I will throw it into the river.	In flúvium conjícere praeópto, quam dilapidâre pecúniam.

zen, who had a *praenōmen, nōmen,* and *cognōmen* (family name). Sometimes, however, it stands generally for any one of these names.

* Modern proper names are either indeclinable without any change (e. g. Schiller, Goethe), or they assume analogous Latin terminations.

Sure, certain.	*Certus, explorātus, a, um.*
To be sure of a thing.	{ Rem explorātam habēre. .Certo *or* pro certo scire. Explorātum mihi est.
Are you quite sure of it ?	Satín' hóc tíbi explorātum 'st ?
I am sure of it.	{ Explorātum hábeo. Pro cérto scío hóc.
I am sure that he has arrived.	Hóc cérto scío, éum advenísse.
To repair (or go) to any place.	*Se conferre aliquo.* *Ire, proficisci aliquo.*
To withdraw, retire anywhere.	Concēdĕre aliquo.
I went to my room.	Égo mĕ in conclāve méum cóntuli.
He repaired to that town.	Úrbem in íllam sĕ cóntŭlit.
He repaired to his army.	Ad exércitum súum proféctus ést.
I repaired to that place.	In lócum íllum proféctus súm.
He retired into the country to live.	Rûs habitātum concéssit.
Go where you please.	I, quô tíbi collibeat.
To go to any one, to meet any one.	{ Accēdĕre, se conferre ad aliquem. Adire, convenire aliquem.

Exercise 165.

When did you see my father's castle ? — I saw it when I was travelling last year. It is one of the finest castles that I have ever seen; it is seen far off. — How is that said ? — That is not said. That cannot be comprehended. — Cannot everything be expressed in your language ? — Everything can be expressed, but not as in yours. — Will you rise early to-morrow ? — It will depend upon circumstances; if I go to bed early, I shall rise early, but if I go to bed late, I shall rise late. — Will you love my children ? — If they are good, I shall love them. — Will you dine with us to-morrow ? — If you will get ready (*si vis apparāre*) the food I like, I shall dine with you. — Have you already read the letter which you received this morning ? — I have not opened it yet. — When will you read it ? — I shall read it as soon as I have time. — Of what use is that ? — It is of no use. — Why have you picked it up ? — I have picked it up, in order to show it to you. — Can you tell me what it is ? — I cannot tell you, for I do not know; but I shall ask my brother, who will tell you. — Where have you found it ? — I have found it on the bank of the river, near the wood. — Did you perceive it from afar ? — I did not want to perceive it from afar, for I passed by the side of the river. — Have you ever seen such a thing ? — Never. — Is it useful to speak much ? — If one wishes to learn a foreign language, it is useful to speak a great deal. — Is it as useful to write as to speak ? — It is more useful to speak than to write; but in order to learn a foreign language, one must do both. — Is it useful to write all that one says ? — That is useless. — Does your uncle walk often ? — He walks every morning before breakfast, because (he says) it is wholesome (*salutare*). — Why was he expelled from the academy ? — He was expelled from it, be-

51

cause (it was alleged that) he was sick. — What did he boast of ? — He boasted that he had not only learnt all the lessons which are contained in this book, but that he himself had with his own hand written all the exercises, belonging to every one of them. — What did your master command you to do ? — He commanded me to bring him the book which he had lent me.

EXERCISE 166.

Where did you take this book from ? — I took it out of the room of your friend (fem.). — Is it right to take the books of other people ? — It is not right, I know; but I wanted it, and I hope that your friend will not be displeased; for I will return it to her as soon as I have read it. — What is your name ? — My name is William. — What is your sister's name ? — Her name is Eleanor. — Why does Charles complain of his sister ? — Because she has taken his pens. — Of whom do those children complain ? — Francis complains of Eleanor, and Eleanor of Francis. — Who is right ? — They are both wrong; for Eleanor wishes to take Francis's books and Francis Eleanor's. — To whom have you lent Schiller's works ? — I have lent the first volume to William and the second to Elizabeth. — How is that said in French ? — That is not said in French. — How is that said in German ? — It is said thus. — Has the tailor already brought you your new coat ? — He has brought it to me, but it does not fit me well. — Will he make you another ? — He must make me another; for rather than wear it, I will give it away. — Will you use that horse ? — I shall not use it. — Why will you not use it ? — Because it does not suit me. — Will you pay for it ? — I will rather pay for it than use it. — To whom do those fine books belong ? — They belong to William. — Who has given them to him ? — His good father. — Will he read them ? — He will tear them rather than read them. — Are you sure that he will not read them ? — I am sure of it, for he has told me so.

Lesson XCII. — PENSUM ALTERUM ET NONA-GESIMUM.

OF THE IMPERATIVE MOOD.

A. The imperative of Latin verbs has two forms, called the imperative *present* and the imperative *future*. Both of these serve to express *a command*, sometimes also *a wish*, *an advice* or *exhortation*, that something should be done. But the imperative present requires the immediate performance of an injunction, whereas the future implies that something should be done in connection with (i. e. in consequence of, after, or simultaneously with) some other act. E. g. PRES. *Discēde !* Leave (be off) !

Discēdīte! Leave ye! FUT. *Quum legĕris, tum discedǔto!* Leave, after you have read!

NOTE.—The second action, on which the imperative future depends, is not always expressed, but may generally be supplied from the context.—Compare *F. II.*

B. FORMATION OF THE IMPERATIVE.

1. The imperative present active is formed from the present infinitive, by dropping the termination *"re."* As,—

    1. amāre — ămā, *love thou.*
    2. monēre — mŏnē, *remind thou.*
    3. legĕre — lĕgĕ, *read thou.*
    (3.) capĕre — căpĕ, *take thou.*
    4. audīre — audī, *hear thou.*

2. The imperative present passive has the same form as the present infinitive active in all the conjugations. As,—

    1. amāre, *be thou loved.*
    2. monēre, *be thou reminded.*
    3. legĕre, *be thou read.*
    (3.) capĕre, *be thou taken.*
    4. audīre, *be thou heard.*

3. The imperative future active is formed from the present by changing, 1. *ā*, 2. *ē*, 3. *ĕ*, 4. *ī*, into, 1. *āto*, 2. *ēto*, 3. *ĭto*, 4. *īto*, and the passive, by adding *r* to these terminations of the active As,—

    1. amā — amāto, amātor, *thou shalt love, be loved.*
    2. monē — monēto, monētor, *thou shalt remind, be reminded.*
    3. legĕ — legĭto, legĭtor, *thou shalt read, be read.*
    (3.) capĕ — capĭto, capĭtor, *thou shalt take, be taken.*
    4. audī — audīto, audītor, *thou shalt hear, be heard.*

INFLECTION OF THE IMPERATIVE.

C. The following paradigms exhibit the inflection of the imperative, active and passive.

FIRST CONJUGATION.

ACTIVE.	PASSIVE.
Present.	*Present.*
S. amā, *love (thou).*	S. amāre, *be thou loved.*
P. amāte, *love ye.*	P. amāmĭnī, *be ye loved.*
Future.	*Future.*
S. 2. amāto, *thou shalt love.*	S. 2. amātor, *thou shalt be loved.*
S. 3. amāto, *let him love.*	S. 3. amātor, *let him be loved.*
P. 2. amatōte, *ye shall love.*	P. 2. amāmĭnor, *ye shall be loved.*
P. 3. amanto, *let them love.*	P. 3. amantor, *let them be loved.*

SECOND CONJUGATION.

ACTIVE.	PASSIVE.
Present.	*Present.*
S. monē, *remind (thou).*	S. monēre, *be thou reminded.*
P. monēte, *remind ye.*	P. monēminī, *be ye reminded.*
Future.	*Future.*
S. 2. monēto, *thou shalt remind.*	S. 2. monētor, *thou shalt be reminded.*
S. 3. monēto, *let him remind.*	S. 3. monētor, *let him be reminded.*
P. 2. monetōte, *ye shall remind.*	P. 2. monēminor, *ye shall be reminded.*
P. 3. monento, *let them remind.*	P. 3. monentor, *let them be reminded.*

THIRD CONJUGATION.

Present.	*Present.*
S. legĕ, *read (thou).*	S. legĕre, *be thou read.*
P. legĭte, *read ye.*	P. legĭmĭnī, *be ye read.*
Future.	*Future.*
S. 2. legĭto, *thou shalt read.*	S. 2. legĭtor, *thou shalt be read.*
S. 3. legĭto, *let him read.*	S. 3. legĭtor, *let him be read.*
P. 2. legĭtōte, *ye shall read.*	P. 2. legĭmĭnor, *ye shall be read.*
P. 3. legunto, *let them read.*	P. 3. leguntor, *let them be read.*

FOURTH CONJUGATION.

Present.	*Present.*
S. audī, *hear (thou).*	S. audīre, *be thou heard.*
P. audīte, *hear ye.*	P. audīminī, *be ye heard.*
Future.	*Future.*
S. 2. audīto, *thou shalt hear.*	S. 2. audītor, *thou shalt be heard.*
S. 3. audīto, *let him hear.*	S. 3. audītor, *let him be heard.*
P. 2. audītōte, *ye shall hear.*	P. 2. audīmĭnor, *ye shall be heard.*
P. 3. audīunto, *let them hear.*	P. 3. audīuntor, *let them be heard.*

So conjugate *apportā*, bring; *dā*, give; *laudā*, praise; *regnā*, rule; — *audē*, dare; *gaudē*, rejoice; *habē*, have; *jubē*, command; *studē*, strive; — *age*, come on (stir); *mitte*, send; *pōne*, put; *scrĭbe*, write; *sūme*, take; — *apĕrī*, open; *punī*, punish; *repĕrī*, find; *sentī*, feel; *venī*, come.

IMPERATIVE OF DEPONENT VERBS.

D. The imperative of deponent verbs follows the analogy of the passive voice. Thus: —

FIRST CONJUGATION.
Present.

S.   hortāre, *exhort* (*thou*).
P.   hortāmĭnĭ, *exhort ye.*

Future.

S. 2. hortātor, *thou shalt exhort.*
S. 3. hortātor, *let him exhort.*
P. 2. hortāmĭnor, *ye shall exhort.* ·
P. 3. hortantor, *let them exhort.*

SECOND CONJUGATION.
Present.

S.   verēre, *fear (thou).*
P.   verēmĭnĭ, *fear ye.*

Future.

S. 2. verētor, *thou shalt fear.*
S. 3. verētor, *let him fear.*
P. 2. verēmĭnor, *ye shall fear.*
P. 3. verentor, *let them fear.*

THIRD CONJUGATION.
Present.

S.   loquĕre, *speak* (*thou*).
P.   loquimĭnĭ, *speak ye.*

Future.

S. 2. loquĭtor, *thou shalt speak.*
S. 3. loquĭtor, *let him speak.*
P. 2. loquimĭnor, *ye shall speak.*
P. 3. loquuntor, *let them speak.*

FOURTH CONJUGATION.
Present.

S.   blandīre, *flatter (thou).*
P.   blandīmĭnĭ, *flatter ye.*

Future.

S. 2. blandītor, *thou shalt flatter.*
S. 3. blandītor, *let him flatter.*
P. 2. blandimĭnor, *ye shall flatter.*
P. 3. blandĭuntor, *let them flatter.*

So inflect *comĭtāre*, escort; *morāre*, delay (stay); *laetāre*, rejoice; *recordāre*, remember; — *merēre*, earn; *miserēre*, pity; *tuēre*, defend; — *fruĕre*, enjoy; *morĕre*, die; *obliviscĕre*, forget; *ulciscĕre*, revenge; *utĕre*, use; — *experīre*, experience (try); *largīre*, spend; *opperīre*, wait for (expect); *ordīre*, begin; *partīre*, divide.

IMPERATIVE OF IRREGULAR VERBS.

E. Of the irregular verbs, *possum, volo, malo, queo, nequeo,* and *fio* want the imperative mood. That of the rest is as follows : —

1. Esse, *to be.* — PRES. ĕs — este, *be thou, be ye.* FUT. 2. esto — estōte, *thou shalt be, ye shall be ;* 3. esto — sunto, *let him be, let them be.*

So the compounds *abes, ades, dees,* &c. Some of which, however, like *possum*, do not admit of an imperative.

2. Edĕre, *to eat.* — PRES. ede *or* ēs — edĭte *or* este. FUT. 2. edĭto *or* esto — editōte *or* estōte ; 3. edĭto *or* esto — edunto.

So the compounds *adĕde, ambĕde, comĕde,* &c.

3. Ferre, *to bear.* — ACT. PRES. fĕr — ferte. FUT. 2. ferto — fertōte ; 3. ferto — ferunto. — PASS. PRES. ferre — ferimĭnĭ. FUT. 2. fertor — ferimĭnor ; 3. fertor — feruntor.

So also *affer, confer, perfer,* &c.

4. Nolle, *to be unwilling.* PRES. nōli — nolīte. FUT. 2. nolito — nolitōte ; 3. nolito — nolunto.

5. Ire, *to go.* — PRES. ĭ — ite. FUT. 2. ito — itōte ; 3. ito — eunto.

So the compounds *abi, exi, peri, prodi, redi,* &c.

6. Inquam, *I say.* — PRES. inque — inquĭte. FUT. inquĭto. — The rest is wanting. That of *aio*, I say, is *ai*, but obsolete.

51 *

7. Memĭni, *I remember*, has only the forms *memento — mementote*, remember thou, ye.

8. A few verbs occur in the imperative alone. They are *apăge*, away, begone! *ave*, hail! *salve*, hail (good morning, &c.); *vale*, farewell; and *cedo*, say, tell me, let see. The remaining forms of these are *avēte, avēto; salvēte, salvēto; valēte, valēto*.

REMARKS.

1. The verbs *dĭco, dŭco, facio*, and *fĕro* drop the final *e* of the imperative present singular, and have *dic, duc, fac, fer*. So also the compounds of those verbs; as, *educ, calefac, effer, perfer*, &c. The only exceptions are the compounds of *facio*, which change the radical *a* into *ĭ;* as, *confĭce, perfĭce*, &c. — Of the verb *scire*, it is customary to say *scĭto — scĭtōte* instead of *scī — scĭte*.

2. In an imperative clause, the English "not" is always *ne* instead of *non*, and the English "nor" *neve* instead of *neque*. E. g. *Ne crucia te*, Do not torment yourself. *Ne saevi tantopere*, Do not be so fierce. *Ne audēto accedĕre neve loquĭtor*, Let him not venture to approach nor speak.

3. Instead of the simple imperative, it is not uncommon to employ the formulas *cura* (or *curāto*) *ut, fac ut* (or *fac* without *ut*), with the present subjunctive. E. g. *Cura, ut quam primum venĭas*, Try to come as soon as you can. *Fac (ut) anĭmo forti magnōque sis*, Be brave (strive to be brave) and magnanimous. So also in prohibitions, *fac ne, cave ne* (or *cave* without *ne*), with the subjunctive, and *nōli* with the infinitive. E. g. *Fac ne venĭre praetermittas*, Do not fail to come. *Cave (ne) putes*, Do not suppose (Beware of supposing). *Nōli existimāre*, Do not think. *Nolĭtōte dubitāre*, Be unwilling to doubt.

4. Instead of the imperative, the Romans frequently employ certain tenses of the indicative and subjunctive. They are, —

a) The first future indicative; as, *Facies* (= *facĭto*), *ut sciam*, Let me know. *Sed valēbis* (= *vale*), *meaque negotia vidēbis* (= *vide*), But farewell, and attend to my interests. *Tu non cessābis* (= *ne cessa*) *nosque dilĭges* (= *dilĭge*), Do you not cease from your efforts, and preserve your regard for us.

b) The second person of the present subjunctive. E. g. *Quum te bene confirmāris, ad nos venias* (= *venĭto*), When you shall have properly established your health again, you must come to see us. *Tuā quod nihil refert, ne cures* (= *ne cura*), Do not meddle with things that do not concern you. *Quod boni datur*, fruāre (= *fruĕre*), *dum licet*, Enjoy the proffered good while it is lawful.

c) The third person of the present subjunctive. E. g. *Audiat*, Let him hear. *Videat*, Let him see. *Desĭnant furĕre*, Let them cease to rage. *Donis impii ne placare audeant deos*, The impious shall not dare to appease the gods with presents.*

---

* The subjunctive for this person is even more common than the imperative proper. Compare Lesson LXXXVII. B. Rem.

d) The second person of the perfect subjunctive, chiefly in negative commands with *ne*. E. g. *Hoc* ne fecĕris (= *ne facito*), You shall not do this. *Nihil* ignovĕris (= *ignoscito*), Do not pardon anything. *Misericordiā commōtus ne sis*, Do not be moved with compassion.

F. OF THE USE OF THE IMPERATIVE.

I. The imperative present and its equivalents (cf. *E.* Rem. 3, 4) are used in direct commands or prohibitions, addressed by the speaker himself, and on his own authority. E. g.

Sérva, óbsĕcro, haéc nóbis bóna.	Preserve these blessings unto us, I pray thee.
Justítiam *cole* et.pietâtem.	Cultivate justice and piety.
Subvenīte mísĕro; *ūe* óbviam injúriae.	Come ye to the rescue of an unhappy man; face the injustice.
Prócul, o prócul *éste*, totóque *absístīte* lúco!	Away! away! Keep off from the entire grove!
Nímium *ne crédle* colóri.	Do not trust beauty too much.
Quaéso, ánimum *ne despónde*.	Do not, I pray you, give up your courage.
Cúra, ut váleas.	Farewell!
Mágnum *fác* ánimum *hábeas* et spém bónam.	Keep up your courage and hope.
Fác, ne quíd áliud *cúres*, nísi út quám commodíssime convaléscas.	See that you attend to nothing else, except the most suitable recovery of your health.
Cáre, si me ámas, *exístimes*, mê abjecísse cûram reipúblicae.	Beware, I beseech you, of supposing that I have thrown aside the cares of public life.
Nóli tê *oblivísci* Cicerônem ésse.	Do not forget that you are Cicero.
Nolīte id *vélle*, quód fíeri nôn pótest.	Do not desire that which is impossible.
Tú níhil invítā *díces faciésve* Minervā.	Say or do nothing but what you are fit for.
Si cértum est fácĕre, *fácias*: vêrum *ne* post cúlpam *cónfĕras* in mê.	If you are determined to do it, do so; but do not afterwards cast the blame on me.
Ne quaéras; éfferant, quae sêcum hûc attulérunt.	Do not ask me; let them take away what they have brought here with them.
Quód dúbĭtas, *ne fécĕris*.	Do not perform what you are in doubt about.

II. The imperative future is used in indirect commands or prohibitions, especially in contracts, laws, and wills, but also as the form of a request, demand, advice, or moral precept. E. g.

Amicítia his légibus *ésto*: — *Excédito* úrbibus, ágris, vícis, ca-	There shall be peace on these conditions: let him evacuate the

stéllis cis Taûrum usque ad Tánäim ámnem.

cities, fields, villages, and forts on this side of the Taurus as far as the river Don.

Régio império dúo *súnto*, iique Cónsüles *appellántor*, milítiae súmmum jûs *habénto*, némini *parénto*; íllis sálus pópüli suprêma léx *ésto*.

There shall be two persons of royal authority, and they shall be called Consuls; they shall have the chief command in war, shall be obedient to no one; the welfare of the people shall be their highest law.

Ímpius *ne audéto* placâre dónis íram deôrum.

No impious man shall dare to appease the anger of the gods with presents.

Hóminem mórtuum in úrbe *ne sepelíto, néve úrito*.

Thou shalt bury or burn a dead man in the city.

Nôn sátis ést púlchra ésse poémäta; dúlcia *súnto*, et quocúnque vólunt, ánimum auditôris *agúnto*.

It is not enough that poems be beautiful; they must be sweet, and must carry the minds of the hearer wherever they list.

Coeléstia sémper *spectáto*, ílla humâna *contémnito*.

You should always observe celestial things, and despise the things of earth.

Quum valetúdini túae consuluéris, tum *consúlito* navigatióni.

When you shall have provided for your health, then provide for your voyage.

Ubi nôs lavérimus, si vóles, *laváto*.

You shall wash, if you choose, where we have washed.

Pýthio Apóllini .... dónum *mittitóte*, lascíviam a vóbis *prohibetóte*.

Send a gift to Pythian Apollo, guard against insolence.

Si quô híc gradiêtur, páriter *progredíminor*.

If this man advances anywhere, proceed ye at the same time.

Jácta álea *esto* (= Jácta *sit* álëa)!

Let the die be cast!

To obey, to render obedience.	{ *Pareo, ĕre, ŭi.* *Obedio, íre, ĭi, ĭtum.* *Obtemperāre* (ALICUI).
To obey any one.	Alicui parēre, obtemperāre.
To obey any one's commands.	{ Alicui parēre atque imperāta facĕre. Alicui dicto audientem esse.
To obey any one's precepts.	Alicujus praeceptis parēre *or* obedire.
To comfort, console any one.	{ Consolāri aliquem. Solatium alicui praebēre *or* afferre.
To offend any one.	{ Aliquem injuriā afficĕre. Aliquem offendĕre, laedĕre.
To borrow (anything of any one).	Mutuāri, mutŭum sūmĕre (ALIQUID AB ALIQUO).

To lend (anything to any one).	Mutŭum dăre, commodăre (ALICUI ALIQUID).
To lend money to any one (on interest).	Pecuniam alicui foenŏri dăre.
To borrow money (of any one).	Pecuniam mutuam sumere, pecuniam petĕre (AB ALIQUO).
The patience.	Patientia, ae, f.; aequus animus.
The impatience.	Impatientia morae or spĕi.
To have patience.	Patientiă ūti; aequo animo esse.
Have patience!	Aéquo sis animo!
Be patient (wait)!	Exspécta! Máne!
Be attentive! (pl.)	Atténdite! Adestôte ánimis!
Go thither!	I íllo! Íte illórsum!
Give it to me!	Dá míhi hóc!
Lend me the book!	Cómmŏda míhi líbrum!
Lend me some money!	Dá míhi mútuam pecúniam!
Be (ye) good.	Éste bóni.
Know (ye) it.	Scitôte hóc.
Obey your instructors and never give them any trouble.	Praeceptóribus véstris paretôte, nóque íis unquam moléstiam exhibetôte.
Pay what you owe, comfort the afflicted, and do good to those that have offended you.	Débita sólves, éos, qui aégri ánimi sint, consolábĕris, iísque, qui tê injúriis affécerint, benígne fácies.
Love God, and thy neighbor as thyself.	Déum áma, proximúmque túum támquam temetípsum.
Let us always love and practise virtue; and we shall be happy both in this life and in the next.	Virtûtem sémper colámus et exercitêmus; haêc quum fíunt, beáti érimus et in hâc et in íllă in vérâ vítâ.
Let us see which of us (two) can shoot the best.	Videâmus, úter nóstrum sciéntius míttat sagíttas.
Sadness.	Tristitia, moestitia, ae, f.
The creditor.	Creditor, ōris, m.
The watch.	Horologĭum portabĭle.
The snuffbox.	Pyxis, ĭdis, f.
To add.	{ Addo, ĕre, dĭdi, dĭtum. Adjicio, ĕre, jēci, jectum. (ALIQUID REI, AD REM.)
To build, construct.	{ Aedifĭco, āre, ăvi, ătum. Exstrŭo, ĕre, xi, ctum.
To embark, to go on board ship.	Conscendĕre navem (or simply conscendĕre).
I embark for Europe.	{ Conscendo, ut in Eurōpam transmittam. In Eurōpam conscendo.
To set sail.	{ Vélum in altum dăre. Solvĕre (i, solūtum), sc. navem.

2 M

To set sail for any place.	{ Vēla (navem, cursum) dirigĕre aliquo. Navigāre ad locum.
He is sailing for America.	Cúrsum in Américam dírigit.
To sail with full sails.	Plenissimis velis navigāre *or* vehi.
He embarked on the sixteenth of last month.	Nâvem conscéndit séxto décimo ménsis próximi.
He set sail on the third instant.	Vêla dédit tértio hújus ménsis.
I am out of danger.	In pórtu návigo.
Flee with thy utmost speed!	Remígio velôque fúge!
We must do our utmost to avoid that.	Rês rémis velisque fugiénda est.
To execute a commission.	*Mandātum exsĕqui* or *persĕqui (secūtus sum).*
To give one a commission.	{ Mandāre alicui aliquid. Alicui negotium dāre.
I have executed your commission.	Mandâtum túum fidéliter exocūtus sum.
To do (*or* fulfil) one's duty.	Officium facĕre. Officio fungi. Officio suo non deesse.
To neglect one's duty.	{ Officio suo deesse. Officium praetermittere *or* negligĕre.
To set one a task.	Pensum alicui praescribĕre *or* imperāre.
To do (*or* perform) one's task.	{ Opus suum facĕre (conficĕre). Pensum imperātum absolvĕre *or* peragĕre.
It is my duty.	{ Méum officiùm (*or* múnus) ést. Méum ést.
I deemed it my duty.	Méum ésse putávi.
This man always fulfils his duty.	Híc vír officium súum sémper exséquitur.
He never swerves from his duty.	Ab officio núnquam discêdit (recêdit).
Have you done your task?	Absolvistíne pénsum imperâtum?
Not yet.	Nôndum absólvi.
To rely or *depend upon something.*	{ *Fido, ĕre, fīsus sum.* *Confīdĕre* (ALICUI, REI *or* RE). *Nītor, i, nixus sum* (RE).
Relying *or* depending upon anything.	Frētus *or* nixus aliquā re.
I rely upon you.	{ Confído tíbi. In fíde tuā requiésco.
I rely upon your humanity.	In humanitâte túā caûsam méam repóno.
You may rely upon him.	{ Confídĕre éi póssis. In éjus fíde requiéscere tíbi lícet.
He relies upon it.	Confídit hôc.

You may depend upon it.   Ne dúbĭta. Fáctum púta.

To suffice, to be sufficient.   *Satis esse. Sufficĕre, fĕci, fectum.*
(AD REM, QUOD . . . .)

To be contented with something.   Contentum esse aliquā rē ; nihil ultra desiderāre.

It is sufficient for me.   Hóc míhi sátis ést (súffĭcit).

It is abundantly sufficient for me.   { Míhi abúnde ést.
   { Míhi abúnde suffĭcit.

Will this money be sufficient for that man ?   Sufficiétne úlli pecúnia haêc ?

It will.   Sufficiet. Sátis érit.

Has this sum been sufficient for him ?   Núm haec súmma éi suffĕcit ?

It was not.   Nôn suffĕcit.

He was contented with it.   { Fúit eā conténtus.
   { Níhil últra desiderábat.

He would be contented, if you only add a few imperials.   Conténtus ésset, si paúcos tántum áddĕres imperiáles.

Little wealth suffices for the wise.   Párvo (paúcis) sápiens conténtus ést.

That is to say (i. e.).   *Hoc est ; id est : scilĭcĕt, nempe.*

And so on, and so forth (&c.).   *Et cetĕra, cetĕra ; et sic de cetĕris.*

Say on, go on.   Áge ! Pérge !

Otherwise, differently.   Alíter, sĕcus (*followed by* ac, atque, quam).

In another manner.   Alio mŏdo, alíter.

Else, otherwise.   Alíter, aut ; aliŏqui.

If not.   Sin alíter, sin mínus.

What else ?   Quid áliud ? Quid praetérea ?

Have you anything else to say ?   Num quid praetérea tíbi dicéndum ést ?

If I knew that, I should behave differently.   Íd si scírem, mê áliā ratiône (úlio mŏdo) gérĕrem.

If I had known that, I should have behaved differently.   Id si cógnĭtum habuíssem, mê alíter gessíssem.

I cannot do it otherwise.   Aliā ratiône fácĕre hóc nôn póssum.

Mend, else you will be punished.   Resipísce, sin mínus, puniêris.

If you go, very well ; if not, I shall command you.   Si ábis, béne ést ; sin mínus, tíbi mandábo.

To mend, reform.   { *Resipisco, ĕre, pŭi (pīvi).*
   { *In meliŏrem frugem redire.*

A man polite towards every one.   Homo erga omnes humānus (officiōsus).

A father who loves his children most affectionately.   Păter filiōrum suōrum amantíssimus.

You have to learn the twentieth lesson, and to translate the exercises belonging to it.   Ediscéndum ést tíbi pénsum vicésimum, et verténda sunt Latíne ad id pertinéntia dictáta.

I have received with the greatest pleasure the letter which you addressed to me, dated the 6th instant.	Lítteras, quâs séxto hújus ménsis ad mê dedísti, cum maximâ voluptâte accépi.
I think he must have been sick, otherwise he would not look so pale.	Crédo éum aegrôtum fuísse, alióquin spéciem tam pállidam nòn praebêret.
To translate.	Vertĕre, convertĕre, reddĕre.*

EXERCISE 167.

Have you executed my commission ? — I have executed it. — Has your brother executed the commission which I gave him ? — He has executed it. — Would you execute a commission for me ? — I am under so many obligations to you, that I will always execute your commissions when it shall please you to give me any. — Ask the horse-dealer (*mango, ōnis*) whether he can let me have the horse at the price which I have offered him. — I am sure that he would be satisfied, if you would add a few florins more. — I will not add anything. If he can let me have it at that price, let him do so ; if not, let him keep it. — Good morning, my children ! Have you done your task ? — You well know that we always do it ; for we must be ill not to do it. — What do you give us to do to-day ? — I give you the ninety-third lesson to study, and the exercises belonging to it to do, — that is to say, the 168th and 169th. Endeavor to commit no errors. — Is this bread sufficient for you ? — It would be sufficient for me, if I was not very hungry. — When did your brother embark for America ? — He sailed on the thirtieth of last month. — Do you promise me to speak to your brother ? — I do promise you, you may depend upon it. — I rely upon you. — Will you work harder for next lesson than you have done for this ? — I will work harder. — May I (*licéne miki*) rely upon it ? — You may. — Have patience, my dear friend, and be not sad ; for sadness alters nothing (*nihil emendat*). — Be not afraid of your creditors ; be sure that they will do you no harm. — You must have patience : I will pay all that you have advanced me (*mutuum dedísti*). — Do not believe that I have forgotten it, for I think of it every day (*in animo verso quotidie*). — Do not believe that I have had your gold watch, or that Miss Wilhelmine has had your silver snuff box, for I saw both in the hands of your sister when you were at the concert. — What a beautiful inkstand you have there ! pray, lend it to me. — What do you wish to do with it ? — I wish to show it to my sister. — Take it, but take care of it, and do not break it. — Do not fear. — What do you want of my brother ? — I want to borrow some money of him. — Borrow some of somebody else. — If he will not lend me any, I will borrow some of somebody else. — You will do well. — Do not wish (for) what you cannot have, but be contented with what Providence (*providentia divina*) has given you, and

---

* Thus, *in Latinum convertĕre, Latine reddere, ex Graeco in Latinum sermónem convertere*, &c.

consider (*et repûta*) that there are many men who have not what you have. — Life being short, let us endeavor to make it as agreeable as possible. — Have you done your exercises ? — I could not do them, because my brother was not at home. — You must not get your exercises done by your brother, but you must do them yourself.

Lesson XCIII. — PENSUM NONAGESIMUM TERTIUM.

ADVERBS.

A. Adverbs are indeclinable particles, which serve to qualify verbs, nouns, adjectives, participles, and other adverbs. E. g.

Bêne, récte, egrégie dixisti.	You have spoken well, correctly, nobly.
Natûra ratiôque cávet, ne quíd hómo *indecore effeminatéque* fáciat.	Nature and reason enjoin that man should do nothing that is unbecoming or effeminate.
C. Flamínius, *cónsul itĕrum.*	C. Flaminius, a second time consul.
Nimis múlta. Válde mágnus. Máxime idóneus.	Too many things. Very great. Most competent.
In ódium adducéntur adversárii, si quod eórum *supérbe, crudéliter, malitiôse fáctum* proferétur.	Our adversaries will incur odium, if anything haughty, cruel, or malicious shall be alleged of them.
Nimis feróciter legátos nóstros increpant.	They are too ferocious in their clamors against our ambassadors.

B. Adverbs are divided into various classes, according to their signification. The principal relations expressed by them are those of space, time, quantity, quality, measure, number, degree, manner, &c.

I. Adverbs expressing determinations of space may be divided into those denoting, —

1. PLACE. E. g. *hic,* here ; *ibi, istic, illic,* there ; *ubi,* where (for a complete list of these see IV.) ; — *intus,* within ; *subtus,* below ; *alĩbi,* elsewhere ; — *intro,* in, into the house ; *retro,* backwards ; *porro,* farther ; *protĕnus,* forward ; *sursum,* upwards ; *rectá,* right on ; *ultro citrôque,* up and down ; — *desŭper,* down, from above ; *indĩdem,* from the same place ; *utrimque,* from both sides ; — *prope,* near ; *longe, procul,* far ; *passim,* here and there ; *praesto,* at hand ; — *uspĩam, usquam,* somewhere ; *nusquam,* nowhere.

2. QUANTITY, DIMENSION, or MEASURE. E. g. *multum*, much; *paulum*, little; *parum*, but little, too little; *nimis*, *nimium*, too much; *satis*, enough; — *longe*, long; *late*, wide; *alte*, high; *crasse*, thick; *arte*, tight; — *modice*, moderately; *largiter*, abundantly; *breviter*, shortly.

3. ORDER or RANK. E. g. *primo, secundo, tertio, quarto,* &c., in the first, second, third, fourth, &c. place;* *postremo,* in the last place; *deinceps,* one after another.

II. Adverbs expressing determinations of time may be divided into those denoting, —

1. TIME PROPER. E. g. *diu*, long; *paulisper, parumper,* for a little while; *usque,* incessantly; — *jam,* now; *nuper,* lately; *pridem,* long ago; *heri,* yesterday; *cras,* to-morrow; *olim,* once; *quondam,* at some time, once; *nondum,* not yet; *alias,* at another time; *ante, antea,* before; *post, postea,* afterwards; *interdum,* sometimes; *interim, interea,* meanwhile; *dudum,* long since; *unquam,* ever; *nunquam,* never, &c. To these add the correlatives of IV.

2. MULTITUDE or NUMBER. E. g. *saepe,* often; *quotidie,* daily; *identidem,* repeatedly; *deinde,* after that; *subinde,* directly after that; *denique,* finally, briefly; — *semel,* once; *bis,* twice; *ter, quater, quinques, sexies,* &c., three, four, five, six, &c. times. (On these numeral adverbs see Lesson XXI. E.)

3. ORDER or DIVISION. E. g. *primum, iterum, tertium, quartum, postremum,* for the first, second, third, fourth, last time; * — *dupliciter,* doubly; *bifariam,* in two parts, on two sides; *trifariam,* threefold, on three sides; *quadrifariam,* fourfold, on four sides; *multifariam, plurifariam, omnifariam,* on many, on several, on all sides; — *bipartito, tripartito, quadripartito,* in two, three, four parts, twofold, &c., &c.

III. Adverbs of quality may be subdivided into those denoting, —

1. QUALITY PROPER. E. g. *bene,* well; *male,* badly; *perperam,* incorrectly; *frustra,* in vain; *gratis,* for nothing; *sedulo,* busily; *subito,* suddenly; *tuto,* safely; *certo,* certainly; *raro,* seldom; *crebro,* frequently; *vulgo,* generally; *plerumque,* for the most part, &c.

2. MANNER. E. g. *facile,* easily; *docte,* learnedly; *eleganter,* elegantly; *gregatim,* in flocks; *feliciter,* happily; *prudenter,* prudently, &c.

3. LIMITATION or DEGREE. E. g. *prope, propemodum,* nearly; *paene,* almost; *fere, ferme,* almost, about; *praesertim,* particularly; *precipue,* especially; *saltem,* at least; *dumtaxat,* only; *vix,* scarcely; *quidem,* indeed, at least; *ne — quidem,* not even; *prorsus,* entirely; *omnino,* altogether, wholly.

4. COMPARISON or SIMILITUDE. E. g. *sicut,* as, just as; *perinde,* just as if; *aliter, secus,* otherwise; *aeque,* equally; — *divinitus,* from God, divinely; *humanitus,* after the manner of men (and others in *itus*); — *simul, una,* together.

5. ASSENT, AFFIRMATION, or NEGATION. E. g. *ita, etiam,* yes;

---

* And so on from all the ordinals.

non, no ; *haud*, not at all ; *nae*, surely ; *sane, profecto* (= *pro facto*), really, indeed ; *utique*, undoubtedly ; *vero*, truly, really ; *nimirum, scilicet, videlicet, nempe*, of course, certainly, forsooth, namely ; *quippe*, indeed, to wit ; *alioquin*, otherwise, if not ; *imo* (*immo*), nay, rather ; *nequaquam, haudquaquam*, by no means ; *neutiquam, minime*, not at all.

6. INTERROGATION. E. g. *num*, whether ? *an*, perhaps ? *-ne*, then ? *cur*, why ? *quin, quidni*, why not ?

7. POSSIBILITY, REALITY, NECESSITY. E. g. *forte*, by chance, perchance ; *forsan, fortan, forsitan, fortassis, fortasse*, perhaps ; *utinam*, would that ! *certo*, certainly ; *necesse*, necessarily.

IV. A number of adverbs are *correlative*, i. e. they have a certain mutual relation and correspondence of form and signification.

Correlatives correspond with each other as *demonstratives, relatives, interrogatives, indefinites*, and *generals*, and denote either a place, time, quality, or degree. The following is a list of the most important of them : —

DEMONST.	RELAT.	INTERR.	INDEF.	GENERAL.
hic, ibi, istic, illic	ubi	ubi ?	sicubi, necubi, alicubi	ubicunque, ubiubi
huc, eo, istuc, illuc	quo	quo ?	siquo, nequo, aliquo	quocunque, quoquo
hac, eā, istac, illac	quā	quā ?	siquā, nequā, aliquā	quacunque, quāquā.
hinc, inde, istinc, illinc	unde	unde ?	sicunde, necunde, alicunde	undecunque, undeunde
tum, tunc, dum, etiam- nunc, nunc	quum	quando ?	siquando, nequando, aliquando	quandoque, quandocunque
toties	quoties	quoties ?	aliquoties	quotiescunque
tam (dam, nam)	quam	quam ?	aliquam	quamquam
ita, sic	ut, uti	ut ?	———	utcunque, utut.

REMARKS.

1. The relation denoted by adverbs may frequently be expressed by cases with or without prepositions. E. g. *cum curā* = *diligenter*, carefully, with care ; *cum fide* = *fideliter*, faithfully ; *cum voluptate* = *libenter*, with pleasure ; *eo tempore* = *tum*, at that time, then ; *hoc loco* = *hic*, in this place, here, &c.

2. Adverbs of quality ending in *e* or *ter* (vide C. 1), and many of those in *o* (C. 6), are susceptible of comparison like adjectives. E. g. *docte, doctius, doctissime ; fortiter, fortius, fortissime ; tuto, tutius, tutissime*. (See Lesson XLII.) Among comparatives may be included a few diminutives ; as, *longe — longule*, somewhat far off ; *saepe — saepicule, saepiuscule*, somewhat often, oftener ; *melius — meliuscule*, a little better ; *primum — primule*, first, firstly.

DERIVATION OF ADVERBS.

C. Adverbs are either *primitive* or *derivative*, *simple* or *compound*.

Primitive adverbs are irregular in form, and have consequently no definite terminations. E. g. *jam, nunc, tum, bis, semel, vix, sic, non,* &c.

Derivative adverbs, on the other hand, assume regular terminations, such as *ē, ter, um, ĕ, ĭtus, tim, sim,* &c.

Derivatives are formed either from nouns, adjectives, pronouns, or participles. They are as follows : —

1. Adverbs in *ē* denote *a quality,* and are formed from adjectives and participles of the first and second declensions. Those in *ter* denote *manner,* and are formed from adjectives and participles of the third declension. E. g. *altē,* high; *latē,* wide; *longē,* long, far; *līberē,* freely; *doctē,* learnedly; *libenter,* willingly; *eleganter,* elegantly; *fideliter,* faithfully; *prudenter,* prudently, &c. Hence redundant adjectives give rise to adverbs of both these terminations. E. g. *hilārē* and *hilarĭter,* from *hilārus* and *hilāris ; — luculente, opulente, turbulente,* and *luculenter, opulenter, turbulenter,* from *luculentus* and *luculens,* &c. So also *humānē* and *humanĭter, firmē* and *firmĭter,** &c.

Irregular are *benĕ, malĕ* (with short *e*), and *omnīno,* from *bonus, malus,* and *omnis.*

2. Adverbs in *um* and *ĕ* are derived from neuter adjectives of the second and third declensions, without any change of form. E. g. *multum, paulum, parvum* (from *parvus*), *primum, secundum,* &c. ; — *impunĕ, sublimĕ, facilĕ, difficilĕ* (instead of the more common *facilĭter, difficilĭter*), &c. So those in *ă* from neuters plural ; as, *crebrā,* frequently ; *acerbā,* fiercely.

3. Adverbs in *ĭtus* convey the notion of *origin, source,* or *manner,* and are derived from nouns and adjectives. E. g. *fundĭtus, radicĭtus, stirpĭtus,* from the foundation, by the root, root and branch ; *divinĭtus,* from God, divinely ; *humanĭtus,* after the manner of men, human ; *antiquĭtus,* of old, anciently ; *penĭtus,* from or in the inmost part, inwardly.†

4. Adverbs in *tim* and *sim* denote the manner of a condition or state *distributively,* and are derived from supines, adjectives, and nouns. E. g. *conjunctim, incīsim, ordinātim, separātim, strictim,* conjointly, in short clauses, in regular order, separately, closely (briefly) ; — *gregātim,* in flocks ; *acervātim,* in heaps ; *furtim,* stealthily ; *virātim,*

---

* Only a few adjectives in *us, a, um* have thus a double adverb, like those which are redundant.

† So, after the analogy of these, *comĭnus,* close at hand ; *emĭnus,* from a distance ; *intus,* within ; *subtus,* below, from below ; to which add *extrinsĕcus, intrinsĕcus,* and *mordĭcus.*

man by man; *singulātim*, singly; *paulātim*, by degrees; *privatim*, privately. So also *stātim*, at once; *raptim*, rapidly; *cautim*, cautiously; *carptim*, by parts or bits; *caesim*, with the edge (opposed to *punctim*, with the point); *divisim*, separately; *sensim*, gradually, &c.

5. An extensive class of adverbs are accusatives (singular or plural) of nouns, pronouns, adjectives, and participles. E. g. *bifariam*, *omnifariam* (sc. *partem*), in two parts, on all sides; *partim* (= *partem*), partly, in part; *examussim*, exactly; *affatim*, abundantly :—*foras*, (= *fores*), out of doors (motion); *alias*, elsewhere ;—*versum* (or *-us*), towards, in that direction; *rursum* (or *-us*), again.* Pronominals are *hinc, istinc, illinc*, hence, thence; *huc, istuc, illuc*, hither, thither; *utrimque*, on both sides; *interim*, meanwhile; *quam*, how, how much; *quin, quidni*, why not? *nequidquam*, in vain, to no purpose.

6. Others again are ablatives (singular or plural) of nouns, pronouns, &c. E. g. *forte* (from *fors*), perchance, perhaps; *pridie* (from *pris — dies*), *postridie, perendie*, on the day before, the day after, the day after to-morrow; *heri*, yesterday; *luci*, by day; *temperi*, in time; *rite* (= *ritu*), properly; *frustrā*, in vain; *dextrā* (sc. *manū*), on the right hand; *laevā, sinistrā*, on the left; *certo*, with certainty; *crebro*, repeatedly; *oppido*, very, exceedingly; *merito*, deservedly, &c. Pronominal ablatives are *hīc, istic, illic*, here, there; *ibi*, there; *alibi*, elsewhere; *ubi*, where; *ubique*, everywhere; *utrobique*, on both sides; *qui*, how ?†

7. Adverbs derived from verbs are *dumtaxat* (= *dum* + *taxat*), merely, at least; *scilicet* (= *scire* + *licet*), it is plain, verily; and *videlicet* (= *vidēre* + *licet*), you can see, plainly. To these add *mordicus*, with the teeth, tooth and nail (from *mordeo*).

8. Many adverbs of the Latin language are compounds. These are formed, —

a) By the union of two adverbs, or of an adverb and another part of speech. E. g. *sicut, velut, tamquam*, as if; *quousque*, how far? *jamdudum*, long ago; — *alicubi*, elsewhere; *nequaquam*, by no means; — *undelibet*, from any place you please; *ubivis*, wherever you please; *adhuc*, thus far; *deinde*, thence, then; *necubi*, lest anywhere.

b) By the union of other parts of speech. E. g. *hodie*, to-day; *postridie*, the day after; *quomodo*, how; *denuo* (= *de novo*), again; *scilicet*, forsooth; *postea*, afterwards; *alioqui*, otherwise, &c.

Sweet.	{ *Dulcis, e* : *suāvis, e.* Adv. *dulcīter, suavīter.*
Mild, soft, gentle, placid.	{ *Lēnis, mītis, mollis, e* ; *placĭdus, a, um.* *Adv.* leniter, mollĭter ; placĭde.

---

* To these may be added *multum, tantum, solum, primum, secundum*, and all those enumerated in Case 2.

† Similar to these are the old datives of motion, *eo*, thither; *eodem*, to the same place; *hoc, isto, istoc, illo*, hither, thither; *quo*, whither; *aliquo*, somewhere; *alio*, in another direction.

Agreeable, grateful.	Grātus, jucundus, a, um; suávis. *Adv.* jucunde, suaviter.
Sweet wine, honey.	Vinum, mel dulce.
A sweet song; a sweet voice; sweet flowers.	Suávis cantus; suávis vox; suávae flōres.
A mild air, breeze.	Aër mollis; ventus lēnis; aura, ae, *f.*
A gentle zephyr.	Zephyrus (i, *m.*) mollis.
A soft (placid) sleep.	Somnus placīdus (suávis)
Sour, acid.	Acīdus; acerbus, a, um. Acidūlus (== sourish).
Nothing can make life more a- greeable than the society of and intercourse with our friends.	Vítae nóstrae suavitáti mélius con- súlere níhil póssit, quam úsus consuetudóque cum amícis nó- stris.
To cry, scream, shriek.	Clamāre; conclamāre (of several). Clamōrem edēre or tollēre. Vociferāri.
To raise a great clamor.	Altum clamōrem tollere. Maxīmā vōce clamāre (clamitāre).
To cry out for help.	Vocāre aliquem in auxilium.
To help, aid (any one in any- thing).	Juvo, āre, jūvi, jūtum. Adjurāre, opitulāri. (ALIQUEM IN ALIQUA RE.)
To help, succor (any one in dis- tress).	Succurrēre (curri, cursum). Subvenire, praesidio venire (ALI- CUI).
To assist one in doing anything.	Opĕram suam alicui commodāre *or* praebēre (AD REM, IN RE FA- CIENDA).
I will help you to do it.	Adjuvábo tê fácere hóc (hôc in faciéndo).
He assists me in writing.	Óperam súam míhi praébet in scri- béndo.
Shall I help you to work?	Adjuvabône te in laborándo (labo- ráre)?
To inquire after some one.	Quaerēre percontāri, sciscitāri de aliquo.
To reach, hand (anything to any one).	Porrigĕre, rexi, rectum. Praebēre, ŭi, itum. (ALICUI ALIQUID.)
To offer (proffer).	Offĕro, erre, obtúli, oblātum. Deferre (ALICUI ALIQUID).
Complaisant, pleasing.	Benignus, officiōsus, liberális, hu- mānus.
To be so good, as, . . .	Esse tam benignum, ut . . . .
Be so good as to hand me that plate.	Sis tám benignus, ut míhi scútulam íllam pórrigas.
Will you be so good as to come early in the morning?	Vis (visne) ésse tam benignus, ut béne máne vénias?

Do me the favor to write, as soon as you can.	Dâ mĭhi hóc, ut quam primum potes scrĭbas.
Please return as soon as you can.	Quam primum pótes rédeas quaéso.
Please hand me the book. .	Quaéso mĭhi dês lĭbrum.
Be pleased to spare me.	Quaéso, parcas mĭhi.
If you please.	Si tĭbi plácet; sis (= si vis).
As you please.	{ Prout tĭbi lĭbet. { Ex tuâ voluntâte.
I ask, beseech you (= *please*).	*A te quaeso, a te quaeso et peto, peto quaesoque* (UT, or SUBJ. without UT).
To knock at the door.	Pulsâre januam (fóres, ostium)
Somebody is knocking at the door.	Pulsántur fóres.
To come to pass, to occur, happen.	Evenio, ĭre, vēni, ventum.
To happen, to befall (any one).	{ Accĭdo, ĕre, ĭdi, ——. { Contingo, ĕre, tĭgi, tactum. (ALICUI ALIQUID; UT, NE.)
It came to pass, happened by chance, that, &c.	Fórte evênit, ut . . . .
It commonly happens, that, &c.	{ Plerúmque évĕnit, ut . . . . { Úsu venĭre sólet, ut . . . .
Did anything happen?	Accidítne áliquid? Numquid accĭdit?
Nothing (has happened).	Nĭhil.
A great misfortune has happened.	Áccĭdit (evênit) magna calámitas.
A misfortune has happened to him.	Áccidit éi málum.
I had a misfortune.	{ Áccidit mĭhi málum. { Accépi calamitâtem.
One misfortune happened after another.	Accidêbat áliud ex álio málo.
If anything serious should happen to me (to you, to him), what will you do?	Si mĭhi (tibi, éi) áliquid humánĭtus áccidat, quid fúcies?
If my life should be spared.	Si mĭhi vita contĭgĕrit.
We have now more leisure than we have had for a great while.	Tántum habêmus ótii, quántum jám díu nóbis nôn cóntigit.
Is any one knocking at the door?	Pulsátne áliquis óstium?
No one is knocking.	Némo púlsat.
To pour.	{ *Fundo, ĕre, fŭdi, fŭsum* (REM EX RE, IN REM).
To pour into.	Infundĕre (aliquid rei).
To pour away; to shed.	Effundĕre, profundere (*sc.* aquam, sanguinem).
To fill one's cup.	{ Pocŭlum alicui infundĕre. { Pocŭlum alicui temperâre, vĭno implêre.

To shed tears; to weep.	Lacrĭmas effundĕre. Lacrĭmāre, flēre.
With tears in one's eyes.	Lacrĭmans; ŏcŭlis lacrĭmantĭbus.
I cannot refrain from tears.	Lácrĭmas tenêre nōn póssum.
What are you pouring into the cup?	Quid fúndis in póculum?
Wine.	Vinum.
He was pouring grain into the sack.	Fruméntum sácco infundêbat.
Will you fill my glass?	Vĭsne mĭhi póculum temperáre (infúndere)?
Yes, I shall (will) fill it with pure wine.	Sáne, íd méro implébo.
I pour away the wine; for it is good for nothing.	Vinum effúndo. Nam nǐhili ést.
Who is crying?	Quĭs lácrĭmat?
The mother has been crying all day long.	Máter tótum diem lácrĭmas effúdit.
Full (of anything).	*Plēnus* (alicújus rei *or* re). *Replētus* (aliquā re).
Full, entire, whole.	Plēnus, intĕger, tōtus.
A full glass of wine.	Scýphus víni plênus. Ínteger scýphus víni.
A book full of errors.	Líber scátens vítiis.
To taste, to have a certain taste or relish.	Săpĭo, ĕre, ĭvi (ĭi). Alĭquo sapŏre esse.
To have a pleasant taste.	Jucunde săpĕre. Suāvi esse sapŏre.
To have a bitter taste.	Amāro esse sapŏre.
Not to taste well.	Voluptáte carēre.
To like, relish anything.	Libenter sūmĕre (edŭre, bibĕra) áliquid; appetĕre.
To dislike (the taste of) anything.	Aliquid fastidíre.
How does this wine taste? How do you like this wine?	Quómodo hóc vinum sápit?
I like it very well.	Jucundíssime (sápit). Suavíssimo est sapŏre.
It tastes bitter.	Amáro sapóre ést.
I never tasted any better.	Égo núnquam jucúndius bíbi.
He dislikes cheese.	Cáseum fástidit.
I have no relish for food or drink.	Cíbum potúmque fastídio.
He knows what is good.	Sápit éi palátum.
The lady, mistress.	Domĭna, hĕra, ae, *f.*
The means.	Facultátes, um, *f.*
To have the means, to be able to afford.	Habēre facultátes. Sunt mihi facultátes (AD ALIQUID PERFICIENDUM).

I have not the means (I cannot afford). — Facultátes mihi dēsunt.

Can you afford to buy a horse ? — Súntne tíbi facultátes ad équum comparándum ?

I cannot. — Nòn sunt.

I have the means to live. — Hábeo únde vívam.

He has not the means to live. — Nòn hábet únde vívat.

To laugh (at anything). — *Rídeo, ēre, rísi, rísum* (ALIQUID, DE RE).

To laugh at, deride any one. — Ridēre, deridēre, irridēre; risum habēre alíquem.

I am laughed at. — Rídeor. Rísui sum.

They are laughing at something. — Ridētur áliquid.

You are laughed at. — Ridēris.

Do you laugh at that ? — Ridēsne hóc ?

I do. — Rídeo.

What are you laughing at ? — Quid rídes ?

I am laughing at you. — Tē irrídeo.

To meet with, meet ; to find. — { *Offendo, ēre, di, sum.* / *Incído, ēre, di, ——.* / *Invenire, reperire.* }

To meet with any one (by chance). — Offendēre alíquem; incidēre in alíquem.

To find or catch any one in anything. — Deprehendēre alíquem in alíquâ re.

He was caught in theft. — In fúrto deprehénsus ést.

When have you met him ? — Úbi éum offendísti ?

I met him in the market. — In fóro in éum íncidi.

We met them going to church. — Offéndimus éos ad templum cúntes.

I do not know what to do. — Néscio, quod fáciam.

I do not know where to go. — Néscio, quô mê convértam.

He does not know what to answer. — Néscit (nôn hábet), quod respóndeat.

We do not know what to buy. — Nescímus (nôn habēmus), quod emámus.

To trust one. — { *Fído, ēre, físus sum.* / *Confídēre* (ALICUI). }

To confide, rely on any one. — { Fidúciam pōnēre in alíquo. / Frētum esse alíquo. }

To unbosom one's self to any one. — { Se tótum alicui committēre. / Omnia consilia alicui credēre. }

To distrust, mistrust any one. — Diffidēre alicui.

Do you trust this man ? — Confidísne huic hómini ?

I do not trust him. — Nôn confído.

He trusts me. — Míhi confídit.

We must not trust everybody. — Nôn cuivis confídēre lícet.

Let this be said in confidence ! — { Hóc tíbi sóli díctum púta ! / Hóc lápidi díxěrim ! }

A word with you in confidence.	Tríbus vérbis tê vólo.
As to, as for, with respect to.	*Quod attinet ad.*
As to me, you, him, the book.	Quód ad mê, ad tê, ad íllum, ad líbrum áttinet.
With respect to the book which you demand, I do not know what to write you.	Quod ad librum, quem póscis, átti- net, nôn hábeo quód tibi scríbam.
To speak Hungarian, Bohemian.	Hungaríce, Bohemíce lŏqui
The goose.	Anser, ĕris, *m.*
The devil.	*Diabŏlus, i, *m.**

EXERCISE 168.

Do your scholars learn their exercises by heart? — They will rath- er tear them than learn them by heart. — What does this man ask me for? — He asks you for the money which you owe him. — If he will repair to-morrow morning to my house, I will pay him what I owe him. — He will rather lose his money than repair thither. — Charles the Fifth, who spoke fluently several European languages, said that we should speak Spanish with the gods, Italian with our mistress (*ami- cŭla*), French with our friend, German with soldiers, English with geese, Hungarian with horses, and Bohemian with the Devil. — Why does the mother of our old servant shed tears? What has happened to her? — She sheds tears because the old clergyman, her friend, who was so very good to her (*qui ei tam multa beneficia tribuĕrat*), died a few days ago. — Of what illness did he die? — He was struck with apoplexy. — Have you helped your father to write his letters? — I have helped him. — Will you help me to work when we go to town? — I will help you to work, if you will help me to get a livelihood. — Have you inquired after the merchant who sells so cheap? — I have inquired after him; but nobody could tell me what has become of him. — Where did he live when you were here three years ago? — He lived then in Charles Street, No. 55. — How do you like this wine? — I like it very well; but it is a little sour. — Have you already re- ceived the works of Cæsar and Cicero? — I have received Cæsar's only; as for those of Cicero, I expect to receive them next week. — How does your sister like those apples? — She likes them very well; but she says that they are a little too sweet. — Will you have the goodness to pass that plate to me? — With much pleasure. — Do you wish me to pass these fishes to you? — I will thank you to pass them to me. — Shall I pass the bread to your sister? — You will oblige me by passing it to her. — How does your mother like our food? — She likes it very well; but she says that she has eaten enough. — What dost thou ask me for? — Will you be kind enough to give me a little bit of that mutton? — Will you pass me the bottle, if you please? — Have you not drunk enough? — Not yet; for I am still thirsty. — Shall I pour out some wine for you? — No, I like cider better. — Why do you not eat? — I do not know what to eat. — Who knocks at the door? — It is a foreigner. — Why does he cry? — He cries be- cause a great misfortune has happened to him. — What has happened to you? — Nothing has happened to me. — Where will you go to this evening? — I don't know where to go to. — Where will your brothers go to? — I do not know where they will go to; as for me, I shall go to the theatre. — Why do you go to town? — I go thither in order to purchase some books. — Will you go thither with me? — I will go with you; but I do not know what to do there. — Must I sell to that man on credit? — You may sell to him, but not on credit; you must not trust him, for he will not pay you. — Has he already deceived anybody? — He has already deceived several merchants who have trusted him. — Must I trust those ladies? — You may trust them; but as for me, I shall not trust them; for I have often been deceived by the women, and that is the reason why I say, we must not trust everybody. — Do those merchants trust you? — They do trust me, and I trust them. — Why do those people laugh at us? — They laugh at us because we speak badly. — What are you laughing at? — I am laughing at your hat.

Lesson XCIV. — PENSUM NONAGESIMUM QUARTUM.

PREPOSITIONS.

A. Prepositions are particles, placed before certain cases of nouns or pronouns, in order to point out their relation to some other word of the sentence.

Prepositions primarily express either motion or a certain direction towards or from a place or object, in answer to the questions *whither?* *whence?* or else rest or motion in a place or object, in answer to the question *where?*

These purely local determinations are, however, frequently transferred to other ideas, and prepositions also express *relations of time* and *causal relations*.

B. Some Latin prepositions govern the accusative, others the ablative. Several are followed by either, according to the sense to be conveyed.

I. The prepositions which govern the accusative are, —

ad, *to, towards; at, near.*
adversus, adversum, *towards, against.*
ante, *before.*
apud, *at, with, in, near.*
circa, circum, *around, about.*
circiter, *about, towards.*

cis, citra, *on this side.*
contra, *against, opposite.*
erga, *towards, in respect to.*
extra, *without, beyond.*
infra, *below.*
intra, *within.*
inter, *between, among.*

juxta, *near, close by.*
ob, *for, on account of.*
penes, *with, in the power of.*
per, *through, by, during.*
pone, *behind.*
post, *after, behind.*
praeter, *beyond, by, before, except.*

prope, *near, close by.*
propter, *near; on account of.*
secundum, *along, next to; according to.*
supra, *above, over, upon*
trans, *beyond, over.*
ultra, *beyond.*

II. The prepositions which govern the ablative are, —

a, ab, abs, *from, from the part of.*
absque, *without.*
coram, *before, in the presence of.*
cum, *with, together with, beside.*
de, *from, down from, concerning.*
e, ex, *out of, from, after, since.*

prae, *before, for, on account of.*
pro, *before, for; in the place of; in consideration of, according to.*
sine, *without.*
tenus, *as far as, up to (after its case).*

III. The prepositions, which sometimes govern the accusative, and sometimes the ablative, are, —

in, *in, into, towards, upon.*
sub, *under, near, towards.*

subter, *under, beneath.*
super, *upon, above.*

REMARKS.

1. Prepositions generally *precede* the cases governed by them, except *tenus*, which is placed after them.*

2. *A* is put before consonants only, *ab* before vowels and sometimes also before consonants. The same rule applies to *e* and *ex*. — *Abs* is seldom used except in composition and before words beginning with *c, t, q.* E. g. *abscindo, abstraho, absque.*

3. Compound prepositions either retain the case of the second component, or are converted into adverbs. E. g. *in ante diem*, until the day before; *ex ante diem*, from the day before; *ex adversum Athenas*, opposite to Athens. But adverbs are *circum circa*, all around; *desuper*, from above; *insuper*, above, besides; *praeter propter*, about, more or less; *protinus*, onward, further on.

4. *Prope* is the only preposition compared, and retains its case after the comparative and superlative. E. g. *propius urbem*, nearer the city; *proxime Italiam*, nearest to Italy. But the adverb *prope* is followed by the dative; as, *propius Tiberi*, nearer to the Tiber.

5. A number of the above prepositions are originally adverbs, and still used as such without a case. Such are *ante*, before, in front; *circum* or *circa*, around; *citra*, on this side; *contra*, on the opposite side; *extra*, on the outside; *intra*, within; *infra*, below; *juxta*, close by; *post* or *pone*, behind; *prope*, near. E. g. *Ante et post moveri*, To be moved forward and backward. *Ingredi ante, non retro*, To enter forward, and not backward. *Prope, propius accedere*, To approach near, nearer. *Ut supra, infra scripsi*, As I have shown above (i. e. before), below. *Juxta consistere*, To stand near.

---

* On the exceptions to this rule, see Lesson XCVII. B. VII.

6. Poets and later prose-writers employ also the adverbs *clam, palam, simul,* and *prŏcul* as prepositions with the ablative. E. g. *Clam vobis,* Without your knowledge. *Palam populo,* Before the eyes of the people. *Simul his,* Together with these. *Procul urbe,* Far from the city. *Procul dubio,* Without any doubt.

PREPOSITIONS IN COMPOSITION.

C. Prepositions are frequently compounded with other parts of speech, especially with verbs.

The regular prepositions thus employed are called *separable,* in contradistinction to others which occur in composition only, and are hence called *inseparable.* In composition, the final consonant of prepositions frequently is assimilated or otherwise modified. (Cf. Lesson XXVII. *A.* Rem. 2.)

Prepositions generally add their proper signification to that of the word to which they are prefixed. Not unfrequently, however, they impart other shades, and sometimes even a different sense, to the original word.

I. The separable prepositions used in composition are, —

1. The following, which also occur either as adverbs or with cases: *ad,* to, towards, at, near, by; *ante,* before; *circum,* around, about, all around; *post,* after, behind; *prae,* before, very (with adjectives); *praeter,* past, by, beyond, besides; *super,* above, over, left, remaining; *subter,* beneath, under, privately. E. g. *advenio,* I arrive; *adduco,* I fetch, adduce; *antepŏno,* I prefer; *circumduco,* I lead around; *posthabeo,* I esteem less; *praecēdo,* I go before; *praeclārus,* very celebrated; *praetervĕhor,* I ride by; *praeterquam,* besides; *superjacio,* I throw over or upon; *subterjacio,* I throw beneath. (Cf. Lessons LIX. *A.* and LXII. *B.*)

2. The following, which also occur separately, but with cases only: *a, ab, abs,* away, from, down, un-; *de,* away, from, off, down, entirely; *e, ex,* out, forth, upward, very, completely; *in,* in, on, at, into, against; *inter,* between, among; *ob,* towards, against, before, around; *per,* through, much, very, thoroughly; *pro,* before, forth, for; *sub,* under, from below, secretly, somewhat, rather; *trans,* beyond, over, across. E. g. *abeo,* I go away; *abjungo,* I unyoke; *abscīdo,* I cut off; *depello,* I drive down, away; *descendo,* I descend; *defungor,* I discharge, get rid of; *edormio,* I sleep away or out; *effĕro,* I carry forth or out; *exhaurio,* I draw out, exhaust; *ineo,* I go in (into); *inspicio,* I look into, inspect; *intercălo,* I interpose, insert between; *intersto,* I stand between or among; *oblendo,* I spread before or against; *obtāro,* I stop or close up; *occumbo,* I sink down, fall into; *perfĕro,* I carry through; *perficio,* I accomplish, carry to an end; *procēdo,* I go forth; *prodico,* I foretell; *proconsul,* a proconsul; *subeo,* I undergo; *surrīgo* (or *surgo*), I lift or raise up; *subrūfus,* somewhat red, reddish; *transcendo,* I pass over, I cross; *transversim,* across, crosswise; and many others,

3. The following, which are compounded with adjectives only :
cis, on this side ; *extra*, outside, beyond ; *intra*, within, on the inside ;
ultra, beyond, on the other side.   E. g. *cisalpīnus*, on this side of the
Alps, Cisalpine ; *extraordinārius*, extraordinary ; *intramurānus*, within
the walls; *ultramundānus*, ultramundane.

II. The inseparable prepositions, employed in composition
only, are, —

1. *Ambi* (*amb*, *an*), around, about, on both sides.   E. g. *ambifariam*,
double; *ambīgo*, I drive about; *amplector*, I embrace; *anquīro*, I send
after ; *anfractus*, a bend (in a road).

2. *Dis* (or *di*), asunder.   E. g. *discēdo*, I leave ; *dissipo*, I scatter,
disperse ; *dimitto*, I dismiss ; *dirīmo*, I part, separate.

3. *Re* (*red*), re-, again, back.   E. g. *redeo, revertor*, I return ; *reclūdo*, I unlock, unbolt ; *rejicio*, I reject ; *remitto*, I send back again.

4. *Se* (for *sine*), aside, apart.   E. g. *secēdo*, I step aside, retire ;
sedūco, I lead aside, astray ; *sepōno*, I lay aside or apart ; *secūrus*, secure, without care.

5. *Sus*, upward.   E. g. *suscipio*, I undertake ; *suscito*, I raise up,
I rouse ; *suspendo*, I hang up ; *sustineo*, I hold up, sustain.

6. To these may be added *ve*, which denotes a faulty excess or de-
ficiency (= *male*).   E. g. *vegrandis*, ill-grown, diminutive; *vecors*,
heartless ; *vesānus*, insane, frantic.   So also the negative prefixes *ne*
and *in*, in compounds like *nefas*, not right, wrong ; *inhumānus*, inhuman, ill-bred.

Who is here?	*Quis hic ést ? Quis ádest ?*
It is I.	*Ego súm.*
Is it you ?	Tûn' és ? Númquid tû és ?
It is not I.	Nôn égo súm.
Is it I ?	{ Númquid égo súm ? { Egóne súm ?
It is you.	Dixísti : tû és.
It is he, she.	Ís ést, éa 'ést.
It is they.	Ílì (íi, íllì) súnt.
Are they your brothers ?	Súntne íllì frâtres túi ?
They are.	Sunt.
Are these your books ?	Núm hì líbri túi súnt ?
They are not.	Nôn súnt.
Is this my father ?	Ést hícce páter méus ?
It is.	Est.
Is it he, or not ?	Ís ést, án nôn ést ?
Are you the man, pray ?	Quaéso, an tû ís és ?
I am the man.	Is súm enimvéro.
Are you the man who is called doctor ?	Ésne tû is, qui médïcus appellâris ?
You are the man who has hon-ored me most frequently.	Tû és ís, qui mê saepíssime ornâ-sti.

I am the same that I was as an infant, as a boy, and as a young man.

Égo ídem súm, qui et ínfans fúi, et púer, et adoléscens.

It will be agreeable to us at least, who love you.

Nóbis quídem, qui tê amâmus, érit grâtum.

Is it you who laugh?

Tûn' (ís) és, qui rídes?

It is you who have done this.

Tû és ís, qui hóc fecísti.

It is you, gentlemen, who have said that.

Vôs éstis íí, víri nóbiles, qui haêc dixístis.

It is I who speak.

Égo súm ís, qui lóquor.

Is it they who speak?

Númquid íí sunt, qui loquúntur?

I have done this, who was a companion.

Haêc ís féci, qui sodâlis éram.

I am towards him what you wish me to be.

Is in íllum súm, quém tû mê ésse vis.

Do you give me that advice?

Ídne éstis auctóres míhi?

We are not of the number of those who hold to no truth.

Nôn súmus íí, quíbus níhil vêrum videâtur.

Nor are you such a man as not to know who you are.

Néque tû ís és, qui, quía sís, néscias.

I and my brother are going to write letters.

Égo et frâter meus lítteras datûri súmus.

You and your sister were at church.

Tû et sóror túa sácris públicis adfuístis.

You and I have written this.

Égo et tû haêc scrípsimus.

Lycurgus, the Spartan legislator.

Lycúrgus, Spartanôrum lêgum sánctor.

Religion, that daughter of heaven, is the most faithful companion of men.

Coéloílla nâta, relígio, hóminum ést cómes fidelíssima.

The duty of a father, as the natural tutor of his children, is to provide for them.

Offícium pátris est, quíppe tutôris filiôrum naturâlis, salúti suôrum consúlêre.

This honor is due to my friend, who is a brave man.

Híc hónos amíco méo, víro egrégio, debêtur (tribuéndus ést).

I gave the father, the honest old man, the model of his family, that advice.

Dédi hóc consílii pátri, séni ílli probíssimo, familiaêque súae exemplári egrégio.

That happened under Constantine the Great, the first Christian emperor.

Evenérunt haêc sub Constantíno Mágno, Christianôrum íllo imperatôre prímo.

It concerns my friend, the Counsellor N.

Réfert (ínterest) familiâris méi, consilárii N.

I have been well acquainted with him, who was the father of his country.

Égo íllo, qui pátriae súae páter fuit, familiáriter úsus súm.

To thee, my dearest friend, I give this ring.

Tíbi, amíco míhi caríssimo, húnc égo ánulum tríbuo.

Of me, who am his nearest relation, he asks nothing.

A mê, qui propinquíssimâ éi cognatiône conjúnctus súm, níhil póstulat.

O philosophy, thou guide of our life, that leads us to virtue, delivers us from vice.

O vítae philosóphia dux, virtútis indagátrix, expultríxque vitiórum.

The duty; part.

Offícĭum, i, n. ; *partes, ium,* f. pl. ; *mūnus, ĕris,* n.

This is your duty, your part.

Túum hóc ést mûnus, túae pártes.

The companion.

{ Comes, ĭtis, *m. & f.* ; socius, i, *m.* ; socĭa, ae, *f.*

The guardian.

Tūtor, ōris, *m.*

The model.

Exemplum, i, *n*; exemplar, āris, *n.* ; specĭmen, ĭnis, *n.*

A model of a man.

Vir recti exempli.

A model of a woman.

Uxor singulāris exempli.

An example of moderation and prudence.

Temperantiae prudentiaeque specĭmen.

A model of every virtue.

Auctor (exemplar) omnĭum virtūtum.

The family.

Familia, ae, *f.*; dŏmus, ūs, *f.*

The people (nation).

Natio, ōnis, *f.* ; gĕnus, ĕris, *n.* ; popŭlus, i, *m.*

Honest.

Prŏbus, bŏnus, a, um.

True, faithful.

Fidēlis, fidēli animo.

A faithful servant.

Servus fidēlis domĭno.

Faithful children.

Filii pĭi (officii memŏres).

A true picture.

Pictūra veritāti sĭmilis.

To look like, to appear.

{ Aliquam (alicújus) specĭem habēre, praebēre or prae se ferre.
Aliquā specĭe esse.
Alicujus (or alicui) simĭlem esse.

To look white, black, red, pale.

Albo, nigrō, rubro, pallĭdo esse colōre.

To look well (healthy).

Plēnum et speciōsum et colorātum esse.

To look respectable (in dress, &c.).

{ Decōro habĭtu esse.
Formā esse honestā et liberāli.

How does he look?

{ Quáli est spécie ?
Quám fórmam prae sê fért ?

He looks gay, sad, contented.

Spéciem hĭlāris, trístis, conténtĭ praêbet.

He looks modest.

Modéstiam prae sê fért.

He looks like a girl.

Vírgĭnis ŏs habĭtúmque gérit.

You look terribly.

Terríbĭli es fácie.

He looks like a slave.

Apparet húnc sérvum ésse.

You look like a doctor.

Spéciem praéfers médĭci.

He has the appearance of an honest man.

Spéciem víri bóni prae sê fért.

You are more stupid than you look.

Praeter spéciem stúltus és.

This beer looks like water.

Cerevísia haêc áquae sĭmilis ést.

My (his, our) equals.	*Homĭnes mei (sui, nostri) genĕris* or *ordĭnis.* *Homĭnes meae (suae, nostrae) farīnae.* *Aequi et pāres mei (sui, nostri).*
One of our number.	Ûnus e nóbis.
He has not his equal.	Pàrem hábet néminem.
To resemble any one.	*Simĭlem (consimĭlem) esse alicui* or *alicūjus.*
To resemble one in features.	Fácie alicūjus simĭlem esse. Os vultumque alicujus reférre.
To resemble one in manners.	Mores alicūjus reférre.
Each other ; mutually.	*Alius alii* or *alium.* *Alter alteri* or *alterum.* *Inter se ; inter ipsos.* *Invĭcem ; mutŭo.*
They love each other.	Álter áltĕrum ámat. Inter sê ámant.
They chided each other.	Álius álium increpábant.
We love each other.	Amâmus inter nôs.
They assist each other.	Álter álterum ádjŭvat. Álius alii subsĭdium férunt.
They look at each other.	Inter sê aspiciébant.
They quarrel with each other.	Inter sê (invĭcem, mútuo) disséntiunt.
You struck each other.	Álter alterum verbéribus caecidístis.
Neither party could see the other.	Neútri álteros cernébant.
He resembles me.	Fácie mîhi símilis ést.
I resemble your brother.	Égo frátri túo símilis súm.
You resemble me.	Tû mîhi símilis és.
They resemble each other.	Inter se consímiles sunt.
We resemble each other.	Inter nôs consímiles súmus.
He resembles him, as one egg does the other.	Nòn óvum tám símile óvo, quám híc ílli ést.
The brother and the sister love each other.	Fráter et sóror inter sê ámant.
Are you pleased with each other ?	Estísne inter vôs conténti ?
We are so.	Súmus.
To drink to any one.	*Propĭnāre alicui.* *Provocāre aliquem bĭbendo* (or *ad bĭbendum*).
To drink anything to any one.	Propĭnāre (or praebibĕre) alicui aliquid. Pocŭlum alicui tradĕre.
To drink to any one's health.	Alicui salūtem propĭnāre.

53 *

I drink to your health.	Salûtem tíbi propíno.
He drank a cup to him.	Cálicem súam éi propinâvit.
He challenged him repeatedly to drink.	Crébris éum propinatiónibus lacessivit.
To make the acquaintance of any one.	Nosco, ĕre, nōvi, nōtum. Cognosco, ĕre, ōvi, ĭtum. (ALIQUEM.)
To have made any one's acquaintance; to know one.	Aliquem nosse, cognosse, vidisse.
To know any one very well, intimately.	Aliquem bene, probe, pulchre, optime, penítus nosse *or* cognosse.
To know each other.	Se inter se nosse.
To have (or enjoy) the acquaintance of any one.	Usus mihi et consuetúdo est (intercēdit) cum aliquo. Familiarítas mihi intercēdit cum alíquo.
I have made his acquaintance.	Égo éum cognóvi (vídi).
I was glad to make his acquaintance.	Perlibénter éum vídi, éum cognóvi.
They know each other.	Nóti sunt inter sê.
They know each other very well.	Notíssimi sunt inter sê.
He knows himself thoroughly.	Pénítus ípsum sê nôvit.
To know any one by sight.	Aliquem de facie nosse.
Not to know any one.	Aliquem non nosse (*or* ignorāre). Aliquis mihi est ignōtus.
Do you know him?	Novistíne éum?
I do not know him.	Éum ignóro. Ést míhi ignôtus.
I am intimately acquainted with him.	Familiáritas míhi cum éo intercēdit. Útor éo familiáriter.
He is an acquaintance of mine.	Nôtus est míhi.
He is an old acquaintance of mine.	Úsus míhi vétus et consuetúdo cum éo intercēdit.
He is not a friend, he is but an acquaintance.	Nôtus tántum, nôn amícus, est.
She is an acquaintance of mine.	Nôta est mihi.
The acquaintance (knowledge of each other).	Notitia; úsus, ûs, *m.* Consuetūdo, ĭnis, *f.*
Our acquaintance is quite recent.	Notítia ínter nôs nuper ádmŏdum ést.
Again, once more. *Since, seeing that, as.*	Itĕrum, denuo, rursus (adv.). Quoniam (conj. c. Ind. or Subj.).
Since you have not done your exercises well, you must do them again.	Quóniam pénsa túa pérperam absolvísti, absolvénda sunt tíbi itĕrum.
As he did not come, I sent for him.	Quóniam nôn vénerat, éum arcessívi.
As it is already night, go ye to your homes.	Vôs, quóniam jám nóx ést, in véstra técta discédíte.

EXERCISE 169.

Where have you become acquainted with that lady ? — I have become acquainted with her at the house of one of my relations. — Is
it thou, Charles, who hast soiled my book ? — It is not I, it is your
little sister who has soiled it. — Who has broken my fine inkstand?
— It is I who have broken it. — Is it you who have spoken of me ?—
It is we who have spoken of you, but we have said of you nothing but
good (*nihil nisi bonum*). — Why does your cousin ask me for money
and books ? — Because he is a fool; of me, who am his nearest relation and best friend, he asks nothing. — Why did you not come to
dinner ? — I have been hindered, but you have been able to dine
without me. — Do you think that we shall not dine, if you cannot
come ? — How long did you wait for me ? — We waited for you till
a quarter past seven, and as you did not come, we dined without you.
— Have you drunk my health ? — We have drunk yours and that of
your parents. — A certain man was very fond of wine, but he found
in it two bad qualities (*qualitātes*). "If I put water to it," said he,
" I spoil it, and if I do not put any to it, it spoils me." — How does
your uncle look ? — He looks very gay ; for he is much pleased with
his children. — Do his friends look as gay as he ? — They, on the
contrary, look sad, because they are discontented. — My uncle has
no money, and is very contented, and his friends, who have a great
deal of it, are scarcely ever so. — Do you like your sister ? — I like
her much, and as she is very complaisant towards me, I am so towards
her ; but how do you like yours ? — We love each other, because we
are pleased with each other. — Does your cousin resemble you ? —
He does resemble me. — Do your sisters resemble each other ? —
They do not resemble each other ; for the eldest is idle and naughty,
and the youngest assiduous and complaisant towards everybody. —
Who knocks at the door ? — It is I; will you open it ? — What do
you want ? — I come to ask you for the money which you owe me,
and the books which I lent you. — If you will have the goodness to
come to-morrow, I will return both to you. — Do you perceive yonder
house ? — I do perceive it, what house is it ? — It is an inn (*deversō-
rium*) ; if you like, we will go into it to drink a glass of wine ; for I
am very thirsty. — You are always thirsty when you see an inn. — If
we enter it, I shall drink your health. — Rather than go into an inn,
I will not drink. — When will you pay what you owe me ? — When
I have money ; it is useless to ask me for some to-day, for you know
very well that there is nothing to be had of him who has nothing. —
When do you think you will have money ? — I think I shall have
some next year. — Will you do what I shall tell you ? — I will do it,
if it is not too difficult. — Why do you laugh at me ? — I do not laugh
at you, but at your coat. — Does it not look like yours ? — It does not
look like it ; for mine is short and yours is too long, mine is black and
yours is green.

Lesson XCV. — PENSUM NONAGESIMUM QUIN-TUM.

CONJUNCTIONS.

A. Conjunctions are particles, which serve to des-ignate the relation between one predicate and another, and to effect the connection of sentences.

The relation of one predicate to another may be either equal or unequal. Hence there are two kinds of conjunctions, of which one connects *similar sentences*, or, when the repetition of the predicate is unnecessary, *similar parts* of a sentence, and the other *dissimilar sentences.* •

The connection of dissimilar sentences is either a possible, real, or necessary one.

I. The following classes of conjunctions connect similar sen-tences or parts of them : —

1. COPULATIVES, or those which join or unite : — *et, ac, atque, -que* (enclitic), and ; *et, etiam, quŏque,* also ; *nec, neque,* and not, nor.

2. DISJUNCTIVES, or those which separate or disjoin : — *aut, vel, -ve* (enclitic), *sive, seu,* or ; *aut — aut,* either — or ; *neve — neve, neu — neu,* neither — nor.

3. ADVERSATIVES, or those which indicate opposition : — *at, ast, vērum, vēro, enimvēro, autem, sed,* but, however ; *atqui,* but yet.

II. The conjunctions connecting dissimilar sentences are as follows : —

1. CONDITIONALS, or those which express a condition : — *si,* if ; *sin,* but if ; *ni, nisi,* if not, unless ; *modo, dummŏdo,* provided, so that ; *dunne, dummŏdo ne,* provided that not.

2. CAUSALS, or those which indicate a cause, ground, or reason : — *nam, namque, enim, etĕnim,* for ; *quia,* because ; *quod,* that, because ; *quando, quandoquĭdem, quoniam, quum* or *cum, siquĭdem,* since.

3. FINALS, or those denoting an object, end, or purpose : — *ut, uti,* that, in order that ; *quo,* that, that the (with comparatives) ; *ne,* that not, lest ; *neve, neu,* and that not, nor that ; *quomĭnus,* that not.

4. CONSECUTIVES, or those which denote a consequence : — *ut,* that, so that ; *ut non,* that not, so that not ; *quin,* that not, but what.

5. CONCESSIVES, or those which denote a concession : — *etsi, tam-etsi, etiamsi,* even though, although ; *quanquam, quamvis,* although, however ; and their corresponding adversatives, *tămen,* yet, still ; *attă-men, veruntămen,* yet, nevertheless.

6. ILLATIVES, or those which denote an inference or conclusion : — *ergo, igĭtur, itaque,* therefore ; *ideo, idcirco, proinde, propterĕa,* there-fore, on that account ; *quāre, quōcirca, quapropter,* wherefore, on which account.

7. Among conjunctions may also be included a number of particles denoting a relation of time, and others used in questions or comparisons.   Such are, —

a) The *temporal* conjunctions *quum, ut, ubi*, when; *quum primum, ut primum, simulac, simulatque* (or simply *simul*), as soon as; *postquam*, after; *antequam* and *priusquam*, before; *quando*, when, at what time; *dum, usque dum, donec*, and *quoad*, until.

b) The *interrogative* conjunctions *num, utrum, an*, and the enclitic *ne*.   To these may be added *ec* and *en* in words like *ecquid, ecquando*, and *en unquam*, and also *numquid*, when it stands for *num*.

c) The *comparative* conjunctions *ut* or *uti, sicut, velut, prout, praeut*, the poetical *ceu, quam, tamquam* (with or without *si*), *quasi, ut si, ac si, ac*, and *atque*, all of which are rendered by the English *as, just as, as if*.

OF THE USE OF CONJUNCTIONS.

B. Copulative, disjunctive, and adversative conjunctions generally connect the same cases of nouns, pronouns, and adjectives, the same moods of verbs, and particles belonging to the same word.   E. g.

Máter túa et sóror a mê dilígitur.	Your mother and sister are loved by me.
Cur tíbi *fásces ac secúres, et tántam vím* impérii *tantáque ornaménta dáta* cénses ?	Why do you suppose the fasces and the axes,* and such great power of office, with so many marks of honor, were given you ?
Éa ésse díco, quae *cérni tángíve* póssunt.	I maintain the existence of those things, which can be seen or touched.
Vive *díu ac felíciter.*	Live long and happily.
Nôn módo prínceps, *sed et sólus* béllum indíxit.	He was not only the principal man that declared the war, but even the only one.
Pétéres vel pótius rogáres, stupôrem hóminis *vel* dícam pécúdis vidête.	You might ask or rather entreat us; look at the stupidity of the man, or I should rather say of the brute.

REMARKS.

1. This rule extends also to comparative conjunctions, and to all such as introduce clauses which are not subordinate or dependent on the preceding sentence, but co-ordinate or in the same construction with it.

2. The words connected with these conjunctions need not always be in the same case or mood, provided they sustain the same relation

---

* These were the emblems of office of the Roman consuls, &c.

to the general construction of the sentence. E. g. Meã *et* patris *causâ.*
— Tuâ *non magis quam* reipublicae *refert.* — Veniëbat *quotidie*, et *frequentius etiam* venisset, *nisi*, &c.

3. The conjunction is often emphatically omitted. E. g. *Velim nolim*, Willing or unwilling. *Ire redire*, To go backward and forward. *Qui indicabantur, eos vocāri, custodīri, ad senātum addūci jussi*, Those who were indicated I ordered to be summoned, put into custody, (and) brought before the senate.

4. On the construction of the remaining conjunctions, which introduce subordinate or dependent clauses, compare Lessons LXXXVI.-LXXXIX.

DOUBLE CONJUNCTIONS.

C. Copulative and disjunctive conjunctions are frequently *doubled*, i. e. expressed in both members of the sentence, so as to connect them more emphatically. Such combinations are, —

et — et (ac, atque), et — -que, -que — et, -que — -que.*	*both — and, as well — as, at once — and.*
nec — nec, neque — neque, neque — nec, nec — neque.†	*neither — nor.*
et — nec (neque).	*both — and not.*
neque (nec) — et, nec (neque) — -que.	*not only not — but even (also).*
aut — aut, vel — vel.	*either — or.*
sive — sive, seu — seu.	*either — or, whether — or.*

EXAMPLES.

Tē *et* móneo *et* hórtor.	I (both) admonish and exhort you.
Et mári *et* térrâ.	Both by sea and by land.
Officia *et* servâta praetermissáque.	Duties both observed and omitted.
Militiaêque domíque.	Both abroad and at home.
Nôn póssum réliqua *nec* cogitâre *nec* scríbere.	The rest I can neither think of nor write.
Et rém agnóscit, *nec* hóminem ignôrat.	He not only knows the thing, but is besides not ignorant of the man.
Nec míror *et* gaúdeo.	I not only do not wonder, but rejoice.
Nec tû interfuísti, *et* égo íd égi.	Nor had you anything to do with the affair, but I did it.

---

* In poetry only.   † Rarely used.

Aut dísce *aut* discêde.	Either learn or leave (one of the two).
Vel imperatôre *vel* mílíte mê utí- mìni.	Use me either as your commander or as a soldier (as you please).
Sive cásu *sive* consílio deôrum.	Either by chance or by divine appointment (I know not which).*

D. Adverbs are sometimes doubled in the same way, and used to connect words or clauses like conjunctions. Such are, —

mŏdo — mŏdo, ⎱ nunc — nunc. ⎰	*now — now, now — then again, at one time — at another.*
partim — partim.	*partly — partly.*
simul — simul, ⎱ quá — quá. ⎰	*both — and, as well — as.*
tum — tum.	*both — and; at one time — at another.*
quum — tum.	*as — so especially; not only — but especially.*

EXAMPLES.

Módo hóc, *módo* íllud dicit.	He at one moment says one thing, and then again another.
Módo hûc, *módo* ílluc vólat.	He now flies hither, now thither.
Núnc síngulos provôcat, *núnc* ómnes íncrĕpat.	He sometimes challenges them individually, and sometimes provokes them as a mass.
Símul súi purgándi caúsâ, *símul* ut, si quid póssent, de indúciis impetrárent.	Both in order to excuse themselves, and that they might, if possible, obtain some concessions respecting an armistice.
Pártim mê amíci deseruérunt, *pártim* prodidérunt.	My friends have partly deserted and partly betrayed me.
Quâ dóminus, *quâ* advocáti síbilis conscíssi.	Both the master and the advocates were put down with hisses.
Tum Graéce *tum* Latíne.	Both Greek and Latin.
Fortûna *quum* in réliquis rêbus, *tum praecípue* in béllo, plúrimum pótest.	The power of fortune is supreme, as in other things, so more especially in war.

E. Two conjunctions of different classes are sometimes placed in correlation with each other, or a conjunction with an adverb. E. g.

etsi, tametsi, etiametsi, ut, quamquam, quamvis — tamen, attamen, veruntamen, nihilomínus. ⎰	*although — yet, nevertheless.*
non mŏdo, non sŏlum, non tantum — sed etiam, verum etiam. ⎰	*not only — but also.*
non dícam (*or* dico) — sed.	*I will not say — but only.*

---

* The student will notice here the distinction between the words *aut, vel,* and *sive.* Cf. page 388.

non mŏdo (non) — sed ne — quidem.	*not only not — but not even.*
non mŏdo — sed vix.	*not only not — but scarcely.*
non mĭnus — quam.	*no less — than ; as much — as.*
non magis — quam.	*no more — than ; as much — as.*

EXAMPLES.

Tamétsi vicísse débeo, *támen* de méo jûre decêdam.	Although I ought to have conquered, I will nevertheless surrender part of my right.
Ut désint víres, *támen* est laudánda volúntas.	Though the ability be wanting, yet the will is to be commended.
Túllus Hostílius *non sólum* próximo régi dissímilis, *sed* ferócior *étiam* Rómulo fúit.	Tullus Hostilius was not only unlike the preceding king, but even more warlike than Romulus.
Égo *nón mŏdo* tíbi *nón* iráscor, sed *ne* reprehéndo *quídem* fáctum túum.	I am not only not angry with you, but I do not even reprehend what you have done.
Vêrum haec génera virtûtum *nón sólum* * in móribus nóstris, *sed vix* jam in líbris reperiúntur.	But virtues of this description are not only not found in our practice, but scarcely now in books.
Quid est énim mínus *nón díco* oratóris, *sed* hóminis ?	For what is less becoming, I will not say to an orator, but to a man ?
Alexánder nôn dúcis *mágis quam* mílitis múnia exequebâtur.	Alexander was wont to perform the duties of a soldier, no less than those of a commander.

To get into a scrape.	{ *Jurgia cum aliquo inceptāre.* *Rixas in se conflāre.* *In angustum ventre.*
To bring or get one into a scrape.	{ *Aliquem jurgiis (or* rixis) implicāre or illaqueāre. *Ad incĭtas redigĕre.*
To be involved in a scrape.	Rixis implicāri *or* illigāri.
To get out of a scrape (any one, one's self).	Expedīre, extricāre (aliquem, se) angustiis.
The quarrel, scrape.	Jurgĭum, i, *n.* ; rixa, ae, *f.*
The snare.	Laquĕus, i, *m.*
Always, perpetually.	Semper, perpetuo.
I have got out of the scrape.	{ Mê expedívi. Sálvus evási.
He is getting into a scrape.	Ríxas in se cónflat.
He is in a bad scrape.	Ad íncitas redáctus ést.
That man perpetually gets into bad scrapes ; but he always helps himself out again.	Hómo ílle perpétuo fére júrgiis se ímplicat, semper támen sê rúrsus éxpĕdit.

---

* Instead of *non solum non.* Cf. page 584.

Between. | `Inter (Prep. cum Acc.).

There is a difference between. | Est (intercēdit) discrīmen inter ....

The appearance, form, aspect. | { Aspectus, visus, ūs, *m.;* species, ēi, *f.;* forma, ae, *f.*

The face, sight. | Os, ōris, *m.*
The mien, look. | Vultus, ūs, *m.*

The countenance, physiognomy. | { Oris habĭtus *or* lineamenta. { Ōs vultusque.

To have the appearance, to appear, seem. | Vídēor, ēri, visus sum.

To look, appear. | { Speciem aliquam habēre, praebēre *or* pre se ferre. { Aliquā specie *or* formā esse. Vidēri.

To look well (healthy). | { Vigōris speciem prae se ferre. { Valetudinem vultu prodēre.

To look sad. | Tristi esse vultu.
To look ugly. | Deformem habēre aspectum.

To look good. | { Vidēri esse bonum, benignum. { Speciem boni viri prae se ferre.

To look angry, contented, pleased. | Speciem irāti, contenti, hilāris prae se ferre.

To look pleased with one. | Arridēre alicui.
To look cross at one. | Torvis ocŭlis aliquem intuēri.
To receive one kindly. | Accipĕre (excipere) aliquem humanĭter, comĭter, benigne.

A good-looking man. | Vir formā honestā (specie insigni).
A bad-looking man. | Homo specie tenŭi.
Bad-looking people. | Homines specie tenŭi (*or* humili).

You look very well. | { Spéciem bónam praébes. { Vigōris spéciem pródis.

He looks angry | Vúltum irātum prae sê fért.
She appears to be angry. | Vidētur esse irāta.
They appear to be contented. | Conténti ésse vidéntur.
They look pleased. | Vúltu hĭlari atque laeto súnt.
When I go to see that man, instead of receiving me with pleasure, he looks displeased. | Cum ístum vísito, tántum ábest, ut benígne mê excípiat, ut tórvis ócŭlis mê intuéri sóleat.
The man whom you see appears desirous of approaching us. | Ílle, quém vídes, nôs adíre vélle vidétur.

To visit, to go to see some one; to pay one a visit. | { *Aliquem* visĕre (si, sum). { *Invisĕre, visitāre aliquem.* { *Ad aliquem ire visĕre (ire et visĕre).*

To visit one on business. | Aliquem adire *or* convenīre.
To frequent, visit (a place). | Obire, adire, frequentāre, celebrāre.

To visit a sick person. | { Aegrōtum visĕre (*or* visitāre). { Ad aegrum ire visĕre.

54

To frequent any' one's house.	Alicūjus dŏmum frequentāre *or* celebrāre.
To frequent a society.	Conventum (circŭlum) celebrāre.
The society; assembly.	Conventus, ūs, *m.*; circŭlus, i, *m.*
To be in society.	{ Circŭlos frequentāre. { Multum inter hŏmines esse.
We have society to-day.	Convéntus visitántium (salutántium) apud nŏs ést hŏdie.
To associate with some one.	{ Aliquo multum *or* familiariter ūti { (ūsus sum). { Est mihi cum aliquo consuetūdo { ·(familiarītas).
To imagine.	Opināri, putāre; in opiniōnem venire.
He imagines that you will not come.	In opiniōnem vênit, fŏre, ut nôn vénias.
Does he often visit you?	Venítne saépe ad tê visĕre?
He visits me every day.	Ímmo mê quotídie visĭtat.
Did you ever associate with that man?	Fuítne tíbi cum íllo únquam consuetúdo?
Yes, I have associated much with him.	Sáne; éo múltum et familiáriter ûsus súm.
Did you frequent society, when you were in the city?	Celebrabâsne convéntus (círculos), quum in úrbe éases?
I did frequent it.	Véro, celebrâbam.
He is perpetually in society (among men).	Perpétuo fére inter hómines est.
It is all over with me! I am undone!	Áctum ést de mê! Périi!
It is all over!	Áctum ést! Áctum jám de ísto ést!
It is too late to consult to-day about what was done yesterday.	Fáctum fíeri inféctum nôn pótest.
The spite, displeasure.	*Stomăchus*, i, m.; *molestia, ae,* f.
The grief, sorrow.	{ *Dŏlor, ōris,* m.; *aegritūdo, ĭnis,* f.; { *sollicĭtūdo, ĭnis,* f.
To vex, spite, irritate one.	{ Molestiam exhibēre alicui. { Stomachum alicui movēre. { Vexāre, irritāre alĭquem.
To hurt any one's feelings.	{ Aegre facĕre alicui. { Aliquem (*or* alicūjus animum) offendĕre (IN ALIQUA RE).
To wound any one's feelings.	Aliquem mordēre.
To hurt any one's honor.	Alicūjus existimatiōnem offendĕre.
To detract from any one's reputation.	De famâ alicūjus detrahĕre.
To feel hurt.	{ Dolēre, in maerōre esse. { Aegre *or* moleste ferre (aliquid).

This hurts my feelings.	{ Hóc míhi aégre ést. { Hóc mê mórdet.
You have vexed that man.	Moléstiam exhibuísti ílli.
You have hurt that man's feelings.	Vírum ístum offendísti.
You have detracted from his honor.	{ Existimatiônem éjus offendísti. { Dignitâtem éjus labefáctavisti.
You have wounded him with words.	Tû éum vôce vulneravísti.
I did not wish to offend you.	{ Tê offensum nólui. { Pâce tuâ díxerim.
He takes it ill that you did not come.	Aégre fert, tê nôn venísse.
You should never offend against any one's honor or liberty.	Níhil ex cujúsquam dignitâte, níhil ex libertâte decérpsěris.
To swim.	{ *Nŏ, nāre, nāvi, ——.* { *Nāto, āre, āvi, ātum.*
The art of swimming.	Ars nandi.
A good (fit) place for swimming.	Lŏcus ad nandum idonĕus (*or* opportūnus).
I know a good place for swimming.	Lócum ad nándum idóneum cógnitum hábeo.
To experience.	*Experĭor, īri, pertus* or *perītus sum.*
To suffer, endure.	{ *Patĭor, pati, passus sum.* { *Perpetĭor, i, pessus sum.* { *Perferre, tolerāre* (ALIQUID).
To feel (experience).	Sentio, ire, si, sum.
To suffer, experience pain.	Dolĕre, sentire dolôrem.
I have experienced (suffered) a great deal.	Múlta égo expértus súm.
I have experienced a great many misfortunes.	Mála égo permúlta perpéssus súm.
He endures and suffers everything easily.	Pérfert et pátitur ómnia fácile.
His sick mind can neither suffer nor endure these things.	Ánimus éjus aêger haêc néque páti, néque pérpeti pótest.
We can endure neither our vices nor their remedies.	Néc vítia nóstra, néc remédia páti póssumus.
I know this rather from experience than from instruction.	Hóc mágis experiéndo quam discéndo cognóvi.
I had the misfortune to fall.	Áccidit míhi, ut cádĕrem.
He had the misfortune to lose all his children.	Áccidit éi, ut líberos súos ómnes amítteret.
I feel a pain in my head, in my heart.	{ Dólet míhi cáput, pês. { Cápite, péde labóro.
To neglect,	{ *Nôn curāre* (ALIQUID). { *Neglĭgo, ĕre, lexi, lectum* (ALIQUID, { FACERE ALIQUID).

To miss (neglect).	Negligĕre, praetermittĕre (rem, opportunitātem, &c.).
To omit.	Omittĕre, praetermittĕre, praeter-ire (ALIQUID).
You have neglected your promise.	Promíssa túa neglexísti.
You have neglected to come to your lesson.	In schólam veníre neglexísti (praetermisísti).
He never neglects or omits anything.	Níhil únquam négligit, nec praetermíttit.
Did he neglect the opportunity of defending himself?	Númquid occasiônem súi defendéndi praetermísit?
So far from neglecting it, he has seized it eagerly.	Tántum ábest, ut praetermisêrit, ut avidíssime ampléxus sit.
To yield.	*Cĕdo, ĕre, cessi, cessum* (ALICUI DE RE).
To yield to any one.	Cēdĕre, mōrem gerĕre, obsĕqui alicui (aliquā re).
To yield, give up one's place.	Cēdĕre loco *or* ex loco.
To yield to something; to acquiesce in it.	Cēdĕre rei; se accommodāre rei; acquiescĕre (ēvi, ētum) re, in re.
To yield to necessity.	{ Necessitāti parēre (cēdĕre). Veniam dāre necessitāti.
To make a virtue of necessity.	Errōres in consilium vertĕre.
We must yield to necessity.	Cedéndum ést necessitáti.
Did his brother acquiesce in his fate?	Núm fráter éjus fortúnā súā acquiêvit?
He did not acquiesce; but he has resolved to yield to necessity.	Nôn acquiêvit; nihilómĭnus véniam necessitáti dáre státuit.
Did the copyist omit anything?	Omisítne transcríptor aliquid?
He has omitted only a few words.	Paûca tántum verba omísit (praetériit).

EXERCISE 170.

Is it right to laugh thus at everybody? — If I laugh at your coat, I do not laugh at everybody. — Does your son resemble any one? — He resembles no one. — Why do you not drink? — I do not know what to drink; for I like good wine, and yours looks like vinegar. — If you wish to have some other, I shall go down into the cellar (*doliarium*) to fetch you some. — You are too polite, sir; I shall drink no more to-day. — Have you known my father long? — I have known him long, for I made his acquaintance when I was yet at school (*quum scholam adhuc frequentābam*). — We often worked for one another, and we loved each other like brothers. — I believe it, for you resemble each other. — When I had not done my exercises, he did them for me, and when he had not done his, I did them for him. — Why does your father send for the physician? — He is ill, and as the physician does not come, he sends for him. — Is that man angry with you?

— I think he is angry with me, because I do not go to see him; but I do not like to go to his house: for when I go to him, instead of receiving me with pleasure, he looks displeased. — You must not believe that he is angry with you, for he is not so bad as he looks.   He is the best man in the world (*homo omnium praestantissimus*) ; but one must know him in order to appreciate him (*dĭlĭgĕre carumque habēre*). — There is a great difference between you and him ; you look pleased with all those who come to see you, and he looks cross at them. — Why do you associate (*utĕris*) with those people ? — I associate with them because they are useful to me. — If you continue to associate with them you will get into bad scrapes, for they have many enemies. — How does your cousin conduct himself? — He does not conduct himself very well ; for he is always getting into some bad scrape. — Do you not sometimes get into bad scrapes? — It is true that I sometimes get into them, but I always get out of them again. — Do you see those men who seem desirous of approaching us ? — I do see them, but I do not fear them ; for they hurt nobody. — We must go away, for I do not like to mix with people whom I do not know. — I beg of you not to be afraid of them, for I perceive my uncle among them. — Do you know a good place to swim in ? — I do know one. — Where is it ? — On that side of the river, behind the wood, near the high-road (*via publica*). — When shall we go to swim ? — This evening, if you like. — Will you wait for me before the city-gate ? — I shall wait for you there ; but I beg of you not to forget it. — You know that I never forget my promises. — Have you reminded your brother not to write to-day ? — I have both reminded and exhorted him. — Who has conquered (*pervĭcit*)? — Cæsar has conquered both by sea and by land. — He has not only conquered, but even triumphed (*trĭumphāre*). — Does he speak Latin ? — He speaks both Greek and Latin. — Can he write a letter ? — He not only cannot write a letter, but he can scarcely read one.

Lesson XCVI. — PENSUM NONAGESIMUM SEXTUM.

INTERJECTIONS.

A. Interjections are particles denoting natural sounds, expressive of certain emotions of the mind.

The nature of these emotions, and their degree of intensity, are indicated by the tone or force with which this natural utterance is effected. Interjections thus take the place of an entire sentence, in which the verb would express the emotion, and an adverb its degree of intensity.

B. Interjections are classified according to the character of the emotion expressed by them. They denote, —

1. DELIGHT; as, *io, iu,* oh! ah! *euax* or *evax, euoē* or *evoe,* hurrah! huzzah!

2. LAUGHTER; as, *ha ha, ha ha he,* ha! ha!

3. GRIEF, PAIN; as, *ah,* ah! alas! *au,* hold! stop! *hei, heu, eheu, hoi, vae,* alas! woe! *o, oh, proh,* oh! alas!

4. SURPRISE; as, *aha,* aha! *atat, attate,* strange! ha! *hem, ehem,* ho! lo! how? there! *hui,* ha! ho! away! *papae,* strange! indeed! *tatae,* strange! wonderful! *vah, hah!* zounds!

5. DERISION; as, *hem,* ha! there! bravo! *vah, vaha, iohia,* ha! bravo!

6. PRAISE, APPLAUSE; as, *euge, eugepae, heia,* well done!

7. ENCOURAGEMENT; as, *eia,* up! come! on! and the imperatives *age, agĕdum,* pl. *agĭte,* come on! come now!

8. CALLING; as, *heus, eho, ehodum,* ho! soho! hark you (ye)!

9. ANSWERING; as, *hem,** ehem,* well! very well!

10. IMPRECATION; as, *vae,* woe!

11. DIRECTING ATTENTION; as, *en, ecce,* lo! behold!

12. AVERSION; as, *apăge* (an imperative), begone! away! fie! tush!

13. SILENCING; as, *'st,* hush!

REMARKS.

1. A number of substantives, adjectives, adverbs, and verbs are sometimes used like interjections. Such are: *Pax,* peace! be still! *Malum, indignum, nefas, infandum, misĕrum, miserabĭle!* as expressions of disgust or impatient astonishment. *Macte,* pl. *macti,* bravely! prosper! *Nae profecto,* surely! certainly! So *apage,* begone! *cedo,* give here! fetch hither (and also, pray tell me!); *sis* (= *si vis*), hear! do you hear? *agesis, agedum, agitedum,* come on! well! *sōdes* (= *si audies*), do you hear? hark you! To these add *quaeso, precor, obsecro* (sc. *te* or *vos*), I pray, I beg, prithee! pray! and *amabo* (sc. *te* and = *si me amas*), I pray you! pray do!

2. Among interjections may also be included the invocations of the deities, which frequently appear intercalated between the regular parts of a sentence. Such are *mehercule, hercŭle, mehercle, hercle, mehercules, hercules,* by Hercules! so help me Hercules! *pro Juppiter, per Jovem,* by Jupiter! *pol, edepol,* by Pollux! *ecastor, mecastor,* by Castor! *medius fidius,* by my faith! so help me God! *pro deum fidem, per fidem,* by my faith! faith!† &c.

---

* Some interjections, like *hem! vah!* &c., are used to express several different emotions.

† The expressions *mecastor* and *mehercules* may be resolved into, *Ita me Castor* or *Hercules juvet,* So help me Castor or Hercules! and *mehercule* into, *Ita me Hercule* (vocative) *juves,* So help thou me, Hercules!

C. Interjections either stand alone, or are followed by the nominative, genitive, dative, accusative, or vocative.

With the nominative, *en, ecce, o* (cf. page 344).
With the accusative, *o, ah, heu, en, hem, pro, bene* (cf. page 343.)
With the dative, *vae, hei, heu, ecce* (cf. page 369).
With the genitive, *o, heu, proh,* &c. (cf. page 383, Rem. 8).
With the vocative, see *D.*

Sed ecce núntii, ecce lítterae !	Behold the messengers! See the letter !
En déxtra fidêsque !	There is our right hand and our plighted faith !
O fortunâta mórs, quae pro pátriã est potíssimum réddíta !	Happy the death incurred especially for one's fatherland !
En míserum hóminem !	Lo there a wretched man !
Eheu me míserum !	Wretch that I am!
O hóminem fortunâtum, quí ejús-modi núntios hábeat !	O lucky man, to have messengers like those !
Sed béne Messâlam ! súa quísque ad pócula dicat.	The health of Messala ! Let each one say so to his cup !
Hei (or *vae*) *misero míhi !*	Woe is me !
Vae ríctis esse !	Woe to the conquered !
O míhi núntii beáti (gen.) !	O blessed harbinger to me !
O patérni génŏris *oblíte* (voc.) !	O thou forgetful of thy ancestry !

OF THE USE OF THE VOCATIVE CASE.

D. The vocative case is the special form for calling or invoking the person or object addressed.

The vocative constitutes in itself an entire sentence, like an interjection, and frequently occurs in connection with one. But if the sentence in which the vocative occurs contains a finite verb or an imperative, these must agree with it in number and person. E. g.

O díi bóni ! quíd ést in hóminis vítã díu ?	Good gods ! What can be said to last in human life ?
Quae rês únquam, *pro sancte Júppiter !* nôn módo in hâc úrbe, sed in ómnibus térris ést gésta májor ?	What greater exploit, O holy Jupiter! was ever achieved, not only in this city, but in any land ?
Víncere *scis, Hánnibal;* victóriã úti *néscis !*	You know how to conquer, Hannibal, but not to use your victory !
Équo *ne crédíte, Teúcri !*	Do not trust the horse, Trojans !
Quinctíli Vâre, legiónes *rédde !*	Return the legions, Quinctilius Varus.
Úrbem, úrbem, *mî Rúfe, cóle* et in ístã lûce *víve !*	Keep to the city, my Rufus, to the city, and live in that sun of yours !
Rúfe, míhi frústra ac nequíd-quam *crédíte amíce !*	O Rufus, in vain and to no purpose called my friend !

| Primus *nâte* méo nómine *dícte* púer ! | O son, the first boy, called by my name ! |
| *Salve* prímus ómnium párens pátriae *appellâte;* primus in tógā triúmphum linguaêque laúream *mérite !* | Hail first of all called parent of thy country; the first, who in the toga earned a triumph and the wreath of eloquence ! |

REMARKS.

1. Participles sometimes occur alone in the vocative, but only in poetry. E. g. *Primâ* dicte *mihi, summâ* dicende *Camenâ,* (O thou) sung in my first ode, to be sung in my last! And the two last of the above examples.

2. Poets, in imitation of the Greeks, thus frequently put the vocative of participles and adjectives where we might expect the nominative. E. g. *Quo* moritūre *mis ?* Whither art thou hastening so precipitately, ready to perish? *Sic venias* hodierne! Thus may you come to-day! So the common expression : Macte *virtute esto !* Success to you! Go on and prosper!

3. The nominative, on the other hand, sometimes occurs instead of the vocative, especially in poetry. E. g. *Degěner o populus !* O degenerate people! *Salve, urbis* genius! Hail, genius of the city! *Jane, veni ; novus anne, veni !* Come Janus, come new year, come!

What a grief! What a joy!	Quî dólor ! Quód gaudium !
What a man !	Qui vír ! Quántus (quâlis) vír !
How well you have done !	Quam béne fecísti !
How wretched the man is!	Quam míser ést hómo !

E. Obs. In exclamations, the Latin *qui, quae, quod,* or *quid* corresponds to the English " what a!" or " what!" *Quomodo, ut* or *quam* (with verbs and adjectives), to the English "how!" Sentences of this kind may also be introduced by *quantus, qualus, quoties,* &c.

What men !	Qui hómines !
How many men !	Quid hóminum !
What a fine book !	Quam púlcher líber !
What fine weather !	
What good people they are !	Quam ílli súnt benévöli !
What a happiness !	Quánta felícitas !
How fortunate (how lucky) !	Quam félix ! Quam fortunâtus !
How good you are !	Quam bónus és !
How stupid she is!	Quam stúlta ést !
How rich this man is!	Quam díves íste ést !
How handsome that woman is !	Quam formôsa ést múlier ílla !
How kind you are to me !	Quám és erga mê benévölus !
How happy you are !	Quam félix és !
What an affliction to my mind !	Qui moêror afflígit ánimum méum !
What language, what precepts, what a knowledge of antiquity !	Qui sérmo, quae praecépta, quanta notítia antiquitâtis !
How many, how great, how incredible misfortunes he has undergone !	Quót, quántus, quam incredíbiles haúsit calamitates !

To what a friend I have intrusted my property !

Qualîne amíco méa commendávi
bóna !

How much is conveyed in so
few words !

Quam múlta quam paúcis !

How insignificant man is!

Quam níhil est tótus homúncio !

How really troublesome the affair is !

Quam véro molésta ést rês !

How minute you are in impart-
ing advice !

Quam níhil praetermíttis in con-
sílio dándo !

How changed !

Quántum mutâtus !

How much she wept on the bo-
som of her daughter !

Quántum in sínu fíliae flêvit !

How those who are fond of praise
are unwilling to accuse themselves !

Ut sê accusâre nólunt, qui cúpiunt
laudâri !

How blind I was not to see that
before !

Mê caêcum, qui haêc ántea nôn
vídërim !

How much I am indebted to you!

Quam múlta tíbi débeo !

How much I am obliged to you!

Quántum tíbi súm devínctus !

How many obligations I am under to you!

Quam múltis beneficii vínculis tíbi
sum devínctus !

See how the matter has changed!

Víde, quam convérsa rês ést !

You remember how popular the
law seemed.

Meminístis, quam populâris léx videbâtur.

Think of the shortness of life !

Víta quam sít brévis, cógita !

How valuable knowledge is !

Quánti est sápere !

To run up to or towards (any
one).

Accurro, ĕre, accurri (or *accucur-
ri*), *accursum* (AD ALIQUEM, IN
LOCUM).

To hasten up.

Approperâre, advolâre (AD ALI-
QUEM, IN LOCUM).

To run to the assistance of any
one.

In alicújus auxilium accurrere, approperâre, advolâre.

To save, preserve.

Servâre, conservâre.

To deliver, rescue.

Eripio, ĕre, pŭi, eptum (ALIQUEM
A RE, EX RE).

To liberate, free, save any one
from anything.

Liberâre aliquem ab aliquâ re.

To try to save one's self.

Salûtem petĕre ; salûti suae consu-
lĕre.

To wish any one safe.

Aliquem salvum esse vello.

To hasten, hurry.

Festînâre, properâre, maturâre
(REM, *or* NEUT.).

To plunder, rob.

{ Praedâri (IN GENERAL).
{ Pilâre, expilâre (ALIQUEM, REM).

Deliver us from misery !

Erípite nôs ex misériis !

Save me from danger, from death!

{ Éripe mê a perículo !
{ Sérva mê a mórte !

Hurry slowly !

Festína lénte !

He desires you to be safe.	Tê sálvum ésse vúlt.
They sought their safety in flight.	Salûtem súam fúgā petivérunt.
Many people had hastened up; but instead of extinguishing the fire, the wretches set themselves to plundering.	Múlti advolávěrant; flámmas véro pérditi nôn módo nôn extinxérunt, sed praedári étiam coéperant.
To begin, commence (anything).	{ Incipěre, coepisse, inchoäre (ALI-QUID). Initium facere (REI).
To set about something.	Aggredior, i, gressus sum (REM, AD REM, FACERE REM.)
I begin to work.	Incípio (coépi) laboráre.
He has commenced to write.	Inítium fěcit scribéndi.
He has set himself to writing.	Aggressus est ad scribéndum.
I am beginning to speak.	Dicěre aggrédior.
Have they been able to extinguish the fire?	Num extíngui potuérunt flámmae?
Have they succeeded in extinguishing the fire?	Contigítne fis, ut flámmas extínguerent?
They have not succeeded.	Non cóntigit.
To indicate, show.	Indicäre, ostenděre, significäre.
To quarrel (with any one, with each other).	Rixäri, jurgäre; altereäri; litigäre (CUM ALIQUO, INTER SE).
To chide, reprove (any one).	Objurgäre, reprehenděre (ALI-QUEM).
To scold one.	{ Increpäre aliquem. Aliquem asperiöribus verbis casti-gäre.
To dispute, contend about anything.	Certäre, disputäre, dimicäre, con-tenděre (CUM ALIQUO, INTER SE DE RE.
The quarrel, dispute.	Rixa, ae. f.; jurgium, i, n.; lis, li-tis, f.
Did your master ever scold you?	Núm tê magíster túus únquam in-crépuit?
Never.	Núnquam.
What are they quarrelling about?	Quám ob rém inter sê rixántur?
They are quarrelling about a slave.	De sérvo inter sê rixántur.
They are disputing about who shall go first.	Dísputant, quís eörum primus íre débeat.
By all means, obstinately.	{ Obstináto animo, pertinaciter, prae-fracte.
By every means in one's power, with might and main.	Omni vi; summā ope; manïbus pe-dïbusque.
To pursue (any one).	Persěqui, insěqui; consectäri, in-sectäri (ALIQUEM).

To follow (any one, or *neut.*).	Sĕqui, consĕqui (ALIQUEM).
To come next in order.	Sĕqui, excipĕre (rem).
The following words.	Haec verba.
It follows from this, that, &c.	Hínc séquitur (*or* conséquitur), ut ....
To lose one's wits.	{ Mente căpior (captus sum). { De mentis potestate exire. { Insānum fiëri.
The proverb.	Verbum, proverbium, adagium, i, *n.*
The difference.	Discrimen, ĭnis, *n. ;* differentia, ae, *f.*
There is a difference between.	{ Aliquid interest (*or* differt) inter .... { Est quod díffĕrat inter ....
What a difference !	Quántum difffert !
The officer.	Praefectus militāris.
The ass.	Asĭnus, i, *m.*
The hare.	Lĕpus, ŏris, *m.*
To accept anything from any one.	Accipĕre (cēpi, ceptum) aliquid ab aliquo.
To our disgrace.	*Cum ignominiā nostrā.*
To my misfortune (ill luck).	*Cum meā calamitāte (or pernicie).*

EXERCISE 171.

Ah, it is all over with me ! — But, bless me ! (*pro Juppiter !*) why do you cry thus ? — I have been robbed of my gold rings, my best clothes, and all my money : that is the reason why I cry. — Do not make so much noise, for it is we who have taken them all in order to teach you to take better care of your things (*tua*), and to shut the door of your room when you go out. — Why do you look so sad ? — I have experienced great misfortunes : after having lost all my money, I was beaten by bad-looking men ; and to my still greater ill-luck I hear that my good uncle, whom I love so much, has been struck with apoplexy. — You must not afflict yourself so much, for we must yield to necessity ; and you know well the proverb : " It is too late to consult to-day about what was done yesterday." — Can you not get rid of that man ? — I cannot get rid of him, for he will absolutely (*utĭque*) follow me. — He must have lost his wits. — What does he ask you for ? — He wishes to sell me a horse, which I do not want. — Whose houses are these ? — They are mine. — Do those pens belong to you ? — No, they belong to my sister. — Are those the pens with which she writes so well ? — They are the same. — Which is the man of whom you complain ? — It is he who wears a red coat. — " What is the difference between a watch and me ? " inquired a lady (of) a young officer. — " My lady," replied he, " a watch marks the hours, and near you one forgets them." — A Russian peasant, who had never seen asses, seeing several in Germany, said : " Lord (*mehercule*), what large hares there are in this country ! " — How many obligations I am under to you, my dear friend ! you have saved my life ! without you I had been lost. — Have those miserable men hurt you ? — They have beaten and robbed me; and when you ran to my assistance they were about to strip (*exuere*) and kill me. — I am happy to have delivered you from the hands of those robbers. — How good you are! — Will you go to your friend's to-night? — I shall perhaps go. — And will your sisters go? — They will perhaps. — Was you pleased at the concert yesterday? — I was not pleased there, for there was such a multitude of people there that one could hardly get in. — I bring you a pretty present with which you will be much pleased. — What is it? — It is a silk cravat. — Where is it? — I have it in. my pocket. — Does it please you? — It pleases me much, and I thank you for it with all my heart. — I hope that you will at last accept something of me. — What do you intend to give me? — I will not tell you yet, for if I do tell you, you will find no pleasure when I give it to you. — Why do those men quarrel? — They quarrel because they do not know what to do. — Have they succeeded in extinguishing the fire? — They have at last succeeded in it; but it is said that several houses have been burnt. — Have they not been able to save anything? — They have not been able to save anything; for, instead of extinguishing the fire, the wretches who had come up set themselves to plundering. — Why did our friend set out without me? — They waited for you till twelve o'clock, and seeing that you did not come, they left without you.

Lesson XCVII. — PENSUM NONAGESIMUM SEPTIMUM.

OF THE ORDER OF WORDS IN SENTENCES.

A. The order or succession of words in Latin sentences is determined by their degree of relative importance, which depends upon the intention of the speaker. The general principle of this order is, that *the most important word should occupy the first place*, and that those modifying, expanding, or defining it should *follow each other* in regular succession, according to their relative weight in the construction. This is called the *natural order*.

B. In unconnected sentences, the word which the speaker intends to make prominent is placed at the beginning. But words limiting or defining others are placed after them. E. g.

Rátio praéest, *appetítus* obtémperat.	Reason commands, desire obeys.
Hábet rês pública adolescéntes nobilíssimos, parátos defensóres.	The republic has noble young men, ready for its defence.
Sémper oratôrum eloquéntiae moderátrix fúit auditôrum prudéntia.	The intelligence of the audience has always been the regulator of the eloquence of orators.

Lacedaémone fúit honestíssimum domicílium senectútis.	At Lacedæmon there was the most honorable home for old age.
Béllum sociále. Senátus populusque *Románus.*	The social war. The senate and people of Rome.
D. Brútus *Imperátor, Cónsul designátus,* S. D.* Ciceroni.	D. Brutus commander, consul elect, to Cicero greeting.
Jûs *géntium.* Lex *natúrae.* Perítus *réi militáris.* Parátus *ad perículum.*	The law of nations. The law of nature. Skilled in military affairs. Ready for danger.
Divína natúra dédit *ágros, árs* humána aedificávit *úrbes.*	Divine nature gave us our lands, and human art has built our cities.

I, According to the natural order, the subject precedes the predicate. The oblique cases, and other words serving to expand the predicate, are commonly put before the verb, which then occupies the last place in the sentence.   E. g.

Cónsules núnquam *fúerant;* régibus *exáctis* creáti sunt.	There had never been any consuls; they were created after the expulsion of the kings.
Vídi Catónem in bibliothécá *sedéntem.*	I saw Cato sitting in the library.
Hábent opiniónem, Apóllinem mórbos *depéllĕre,* Jóvem impérium coeléstium *tenére,* Mártem bélla *régĕre.*	They believe that Apollo cures diseases, that Jupiter is the ruler of the gods, that Mars presides over battles.
Hóminem natúra nôn sôlum celeritáte méntis *ornávit,* sed étiam sénsus tánquam satéllites *attríbuit* ac núntios, figurámque córporis hábilem et áptam ingénio humáno *dédit.*	Nature has not only endowed man with quickness of intellect, but has also furnished him with the senses as its satellites and messengers, and given him a suitable bodily form, adapted to the human mind.

REMARK. — The copula *sum* is put either at the end or between the subject and the predicate. E. g. *Haec vita mors* est. — *Numa Pompilius rex* creátus est. — *Patres* fuĕre *auctóres.* — *Claudius* erat *somni brevissimi.* — *Facta dictis* sunt *exaequanda.*

II. An adjective denoting a quality is commonly put after its noun; but when that quality is represented as the leading or distinctive characteristic, it precedes it.

The same applies to the genitive, which may either follow the word limited by it, or, as the emphatic word, precede it.   E. g.

---

* I. e. *Salútem dicit,* Sends greeting. In superscriptions to letters, the name of the writer usually comes first. The abbreviation S. D. then either precedes or follows the person addressed, which is always in the dative. Thus equally correct: *Cicero Trebatio S. D.* Among the later writers, however, the order is reversed, and the person addressed is put first.

Vir *óptimus*. Cívis *bónus*. Poê- | A most excellent man. A good
na *merîta*. Díi *immortáles*. | citizen. Merited punishment.
Júppiter *Optimus Máximus*. | The immortal gods. Jupiter
  | the Supreme.

Magíster *équitum*. | The master of cavalry.
Curatóres *viârum.** | The inspectors of roads.
Ornaméntum *civitátis*. | The ornament of the state.
Auditor *Platônis*. | A hearer of Plato.
Bónus vir *or* cívis. *Súmma* res | A good man, citizen.† The whole
 pública.   *Tuum* consílium. | state. *Your* advice. The Athe-
 Atheniensis Demosthenes. | nian Demosthenes.
Senátûs consúltum.   *Persârum* | A decree of the senate. The king
 rex Daríus.   Eudóxus, *Platô-* | of the Persians, Darius. Eudox-
 nis auditor.   Miltíades, *Cimô-* | us, the hearer of Plato. Mil-
 nis fílius. | tiades, the son of Cimon.

REMARKS.

1. An adjective or noun limiting the meaning of two or more nouns is placed either before or after them. E. g. Nostro *incommŏdo detrimentaque doleámus*, Let us lament over our misfortune and loss. *Zeno non tam* rērum *inventor fuit, quam* verborum novórum, Zeno was not so much an inventor of new things, as of new words.

2. When an adjective is limited by other words, it is put first, and separated from its noun by the words thus limiting it. E. g. *Tua* erga me *benignitas*, Your kindness towards me. *Maxĭma* post hominum memoriam *classis*, The largest fleet since the memory of man. *Brevissimus* in Britanniam *trajectus*, The shortest crossing into Britannia.

III. A demonstrative pronoun before its noun directs the attention to the latter; but when placed after it, it merely points out its relation to the predicate. E. g.

Híc vir. *Haêc* ménsa. *Hóc* bá- | This man. This table. This staff.
 cŭlum.   *Ílla* princípia et *hi* | Those beginnings and this re-
 recéntes rêrum éxitus. | cent issue of things.
Haêc est méa et *hújus frâtris* | This is my proper country and
 meî germâna pátria. | that of this brother of mine.
Vírginem égo *hánc* sum ductûrus. | I am going to marry this virgin.
Caêdem hánc ípsam contra rem- | The senate has declared, that this
 públicam senâtus fúctam ésse | very carnage was made against
 decrêvit. | the republic.
Túmulus is ípse, in quô cóndĭta | The very hill on which the city
 úrbs est. | was built.

IV. *Quisque* is commonly put after *sibi, suus,* superlatives, or ordinals. E. g.

---

* In titles the genitive is thus commonly put last.
† I. e. one whose leading trait is goodness. *Vir bonus* is only in general opposed to *malus*.

Súa cuíque virtúti laûs própria debêtur.

Every virtue is entitled to its proper praise.

Súa cujúsque animántis natûra ést.

Every animal has its peculiar nature.

Mínime *sibi quísque* nôtus est, et difficíllime *de sê quísque* séntit.

Every one knows least of himself, and every one experiences the greatest difficulty in observing himself.

Epicuréos *doctíssimus quísque* contémnit.

The wisest men all despise the Epicureans.

Décimus quísque fústi necátur.

Every tenth man was beaten to death.

Óptimi quíque expetébant a mê doctrínam.

The best men have all sought instruction from me.

REMARK. — *Sibi* and *suus* before *quisque* thus acquire a distributive signification. When the distribution is already contained in other words of the sentence, *quisque* precedes the reflexive. E. g. *Quanti* quisque se *ipse facit, tanti fiat ab amicis.* — *Gallos Hannibal* . . . . *in civitates* quemque suas *dimisit.* — The same order is observed in *alius ullus*; e. g. *Neque* alia ulla *fuit causa.*

V. Adverbs before the words qualified by them denote that which is distinctive or characteristic; after them they merely limit or restrict their signification.

Béne fácta *mále* locâta *mále* fácta árbitror.

I consider ill-bestowed acts of kindness injuries.

Áccidit, ut réliquae (*sc.* náves) *fere* ómnes rejiceréntur.

It happened that nearly all the rest of the ships were driven back.

Flûmen Dûbis *paene* tótum óppidum cíngit.

The river Dubis surrounds nearly the entire town.

Història exíguo témpŏre absólvi *nôn pótest.*

History cannot be despatched in a short time.

Laélius *sémper fére* cum Scipiône solêbat rusticári.

Laelius generally was accustomed to rusticate with Scipio.

Lêgem *eísdem própe* vérbis in décimam tábulam conjecérunt.

They have expressed the law in nearly the same words in the twelfth table.

Quódsi Cnéus Itáliam relínquet, *fáciet* omníno *mále.*

But if Cneus will leave Italy, he will act very unwisely.

VI. The same applies to the oblique cases determining the predicate; before the verb they indicate the sense in which it is to be taken, after it they only specify or limit it (cf. I.). E. g.

Médici *ex quibusdam rébus et adveniéntes et crescéntes mórbos* intélligunt.

Physicians understand both approaching and growing diseases from certain symptoms.

Epódorix et Viridómărus, insi-

Epedorix and Viridomarus, having

muláti proditiônis *ab Romá-*   been accused of treason, were
nis indíctā caúsā interfécti   killed by the Romans without
súnt.   any trial.

Ingénia humâna *súnt ad suam*   Men are naturally too eloquent in
cuique levándam cúlpam nímio   palliating every one his own
plús facúnda.   guilt.

VII. Prepositions, as their name implies, are generally
placed before the cases governed by them. *Tĕnus* and *versus*
alone follow them. So also *cum* in *mēcum, tēcum, sēcum, nobiscum, vobiscum, quōcum, quibuscum.* E. g.

Ab hóste ótium fúit.	There was rest from the enemy.
Mánum *de tábulā !*	Hands off from the picture !
Germáni státim *e sómno* lavántur.	The Germans bathe immediately after sleep.
Víx súm *apud mê.*	I am scarcely in my senses.
Póst móntem sê occultâvit.	He concealed himself behind the mountain.
Antíochus *Taúro tenus* regnâre jússus ést.	Antiochus was commanded to rule as far as the Taurus.
A Pompéio dissidêbat, *quócum* junctíssime víxerat.	He was at variance with Pompey, with whom he had been on terms of intimacy.
Curándum ést, ut éos, *quibúscum* sermônem conferêmus, et ve-réri et dilígĕre videâmur.	We must endeavor to have the appearance of respecting and cherishing those with whom we engage in conversation.

REMARKS.

1. An adjective or relative pronoun is often emphatically put before the preposition, so that the latter stands between it and its noun.
E. g. *Magno* cum *metu.* — *Quā* in *urbe.* — *Hanc* ob *causam.* — *Quem*
ad *modum.* — *Nullā* in *re.*

2. Relatives, and sometimes also the demonstrative *hic*, are frequently put before their preposition, although no substantive follows.
E. g. *Socii putandi,* quos inter (= inter quos) *res communicāta est.* —
Res, causa, quā de (= de quā) *agĭtur.* So also : Hunc *adversus ;*
hunc *circum ;* hunc *juxta ;* quem *penes ;* quam *super ;* quem *ultra,* &c.*

3. Prepositions are sometimes separated from their cases, generally
by an attributive genitive or an adverb, sometimes also by some other
word. E. g. Post *vero Sullae* victoriam. — Post *autem Alexandri
Magni* mortem. — Propter *vel* gratiam, *vel* dignitatem. — *Honore
digni* cum *ignominiā* dignis *non sunt comparandi.* — In *suum cuique*
tribuendo.†

---

* Poets and later prose-writers extend this transposition to personal pronouns and to substantives. E. g. Se *erga ;* te *propter ;* me *penes ;* te *sine ;*
Scythas *inter ;* Misênum *apud* et Ravennam ; thalamo *sub* flumĭnis.
† Poets extend this liberty much further. E. g. Per *ego te* deos oro. — *Vis
animi pervicit et extra processit longe* flammantia moenia *mundi,* &c.

VIII. When two terms are opposed to or contrasted with each other, they are placed as near together as possible.

A word may thus be opposed to itself in a different form, or to one of kindred signification; as, *Manus manum lavat.* — *Aliis aliunde est periculum.** Or else two different terms may form an antithesis to each other; as, *Fragile* corpus animus *sempiternus movet.*

Húmines homínibus máxime útĭles ésse póssunt.	Men can become eminently serviceable to each other.
Arma ármis propulsántur.	Arms are repelled by arms.
Nihil ést únum úni tam símile, tam pâr, quam ómnes inter nosmetípsos súmus.	Nothing resembles another so closely as we all do each other.
Nóxii ámbo, álter in álterum caûsam cónfĕrunt.	Both mortal, they cast the blame upon each other.
Utérque utrique ést córdi.	They like each other.
Áliud áliis vidêtur óptimum.	One thing seems best to one, another to another.
Três frátres vidêre vídeor.	It seems to me as if I saw three brothers.
Quae mê *movérunt, movíssent* éadem tô profécto.	The same things which affected me would certainly have affected you.
Mortáli immortalitátem nôn árbitror contemnéndam.	I do not think that immortality should be despised by a mortal.
Rátio nóstra conséntit, púgnat orátio.	Our reason assents, but language opposes.
Est génus hóminum fallácium, *ad voluntátem* loquéntium ómnia, nihil *ad veritátem.*	There is a class of deceitful men, who always speak as others would have them, and never according to the truth.

REMARK. — This rule includes formulas like *Dii deaeque.* — *Dies noctesque.* — *Die ac nocte.* — *Domi bellique.* — *Domi militiaeque.* — *Terrā marique.* — *Ultro citroque,* &c.

C. I. In sentences containing two or more connected clauses, the connecting word generally occupies the first place in the clause introduced by it.

The connecting word may be either a relative, a demonstrative pronoun or adverb, or a conjunction. Sometimes also another word, and always the one which bears the closest relation to what has gone before.

If the connective refers to a particular word of the preceding clause (e. g. a relative to its antecedent), the latter stands as near to it as possible.

Correlatives (e. g. *tantus* — *quantus,* &c.) occupy the same relative position in their respective clauses.

---

* I. e. "To some there is danger from one quarter, to others from another."

The conjunctions usually put at the beginning of their clause are : *et, ac, atque; sed, at, verum; vel, aut; nam, namque,* and *etenim.* Generally also *itaque.* E. g.

Lóquimur *de íis amícis, quós* nóvit vita commûnis.	We speak of such friends as are known in ordinary life.
Cónsul, qui ûnus supérerat, móritur.	The only surviving consul dies.
Hánnibal *três exércitus máximos* comparâvit. *Ex his* ûnum in Áfricam misit.	Hannibal raised three very large armies. One of these he sent into Africa.
Tántum cuique tribuéndum, *quántum* ípse effícere póssis.	You should assign to another no more than what you can perform yourself.
Némo orâtor *tam múlta* scrípsit, *quam múlta* nóstra súnt.	No orator has written as much as my writings amount to.
Fúror in sapiéntem cádere pótest, non pótest insánia. *Sed* haec ália quaéstio ést.	The philosopher is susceptible of rage, but not of madness. But that is another question.
Nôn ést in pariétibus rês pública, *at* in áris et fócis.	The republic is not in the walls of our homes, but upon our hearths and altars.
Alcibíades ad ómnes rês áptus consilîque plênus. *Namque* imperâtor fûit súmmus mári et térrâ.	Alcibiades was fit for every kind of business, and full of sagacity; for he was the commander-in-chief by sea and land.
A tê péto, ne témere *náviges.* *Sólent naútae* festinâre quéstus súi caúsâ.	I ask of you not to be too rash about sailing. It is the custom of seafaring men to hurry for the sake of gain.
Pausánias nôn móres pátrios sólum, sed étiam *cúltum vestítúmque* mutâvit. *Apparátu* régio utebâtur, véste Médiâ ; *satéllites* Médi et Aegýptii sequebúntur; *epulabátur* môre Persárum .... *supérbe* respondêbat et crudéliter imperâbat. *Spártam* redíre nolêbat.	Pausanias changed not only the established customs of his country, but also his entire mode of life. He kept up the state of a king and wore a Persian dress. Medes and Egyptians constituted his retinue; he dined after the fashion of the Persians; his replies were haughty; his commands cruel. He was unwilling to return to Sparta.

II. The conjunctions *quoque, autem, vero, enim, quidem,* and the enclitics *que, ne,* and *ve,* always follow the emphatic word of the sentence. So frequently *etiam, igitur, tamen, ergo, deinde,* and *praeterea;* sometimes also *itaque* and *idcirco.*

These words then generally occupy the second or third place in the clause. When the copula *est* or a verb is the emphatic word, then *autem, enim, igitur,* and *ergo* often stand in the third, fourth, or fifth place. E. g.

Gýges a núllo videbâtur; *ípse autem* ómnia vidébat.

Gyges was not visible to any one. But he himself saw everything.

Quíd ést énim libértas ? Potéstas vivéndi, ut vélis.

For what is liberty ? The power of living as you please.

Sénsit in sê íri Brûtus. *Ávide ítaque* sê certámini óffert.

Brutus perceived that he was assailed. Hence he at once offered to engage in the contest.

Núlli ést ígitur natúrae obédiens aut subjéctus Déus.

God is therefore obedient or subject to no nature.

Huic hómini parcêtis ígitur, júdíces, cújus túnta peccáta sunt ?

Will you then spare this man, O judges, whose crimes are so great ?

Scímus músicen nóstris móribus abésse a príncipis personâ ; *saltâre véro* in vítio póni.

We know that, according to our manners, music is incompatible with the character of our prince, and that dancing is considered a vice in him.

Scíre velim, quíd cógites, *de totâque* rê quid exístimes.

I should like to know what your plans are, and what you think of the entire business.

Quíd sapiénte póssit ésse praestántius, quum utâtur tot, *tam variisque* virtútibus ?

What can be superior to the philosopher, when he enjoys so many and such a variety of virtues ?

Nóstra córpŏra vertúntur, *nec quód* fúimusve, sumúsve, crâs érimus.

Our bodies undergo perpetual change, nor will we be to-morrow what we have been or are at present.

III. In quotations, the formulas *inquam, aio, dico, nego, quaeso, obsecro, censeo, credo, spero, opinor, existimor,* and *arbitror* are placed after the emphatic words. So also the vocative. E. g.

Caêsar, prolápsus in egressu nâvis, *Téneo tê, ínquit, Africa !*

Cæsar, advancing from the ship, exclaimed: Africa, I have you !

Vírtus, vírtus, ínquam, Cáii Fánni, et conciliat amicítias, et consérvat.

Virtue, virtue, I say, Caius Fannius, is at once the conciliator and the preserver of friendships.

Víde, quaéso, satísne réctum sít, nôs in ístis lócis ésse.

Pray see whether it is exactly right, that we should be in places like these.

Áttica méa, óbsecro tê, quid ágit ?

Pray tell me, what is my Attica doing ?

In eásdem solitúdines tû ipse, árbitror, vénies, in quíbus nôs consedísse aúdies.

You will, I think, get into the same retirement, in which you will hear that we have settled down.

IV. Conjunctions, relatives, interrogatives, and interjections, which commonly occupy the first place of a clause, are sometimes supplanted by the emphatic word. E. g.

Némo ést, *tíbi qui* suadère, sapiéntius póssit te ípso.	There is no one that can give you better advice than you yourself.
Nòn quéo, *rétĕra úlla pópuli Románi gaúdia quánta* fúĕrint, judicâre.	I am unable to judge how great those former pleasures of the Roman people were.
Quid? *liberálitas gratuitáne* est, an mercenária?	What? Is liberality gratuitous or mercenary?
Sic profécto rês sê hábet, *núllum út* sít vítae témpus, in quô nôn déceat lepôrem humanitatémque versári.	It is really so, that there can be no time of life, in which pleasantry and urbanity cannot be indulged in.
Tú *quum* ípse tántum librôrum hábeas, quôs hic tándem requíris? — *Commentários quôsdam*, inquam, *Aristotelios*, quôs hic sciêbam ésse, *réni ut* aufér- rem, quôs légerem, dum éssem otiôsus.	As you yourself have so many books, which, pray, are you searching for here? — I came to take off certain commentaries of Aristotle, which I knew were here, in order that I might read them while I am at leisure.

REMARK. — So frequently *quod si, quod etsi, quod nisi, quod quoni-am, quod quia, quod quum*, &c. E. g. *Sunt qui dicant, a me in exsilium ejectum esse Catilinam. Quod ego si verbo assequi possem, istos ipsos ejicerem qui haec loquuntur.*

V. Words properly belonging together according to the natural arrangement, are frequently separated by others, to which the speaker attaches greater importance.

Words thus crowded out of the first place in the sentence are often emphatically put at the end. E. g.

Justítia est úna *ómnium* dómina et regina *virtútum*.	Justice is pre-eminently the queen and mistress of all the virtues.
Aédui *équites* ad Caésarem *ómnes* revertúntur.	The cavalry of the Aedui all return to Caesar.
In *hâc* súnt *ínsulâ* domicília Aegyptiôrum.	This island contains abodes of Egyptians.
Recépto Caêsar *Órĭcō*, núllâ interpósitâ mōrâ, Apollóniam proficíscitur.	After retaking Oricum, Caesar, without any delay, advances into Apollonia.
Címon *barbarôrum* úno concúrsu *máximam vím* prostrâvit.	Cimon defeated in one engagement a very large force of Barbarians.
Ínsula ést Mélita sátis *láto* ab Sicíliâ *mári, periculosôque* disjúncta.	The island of Malta is separated from Sicily by a tolerably deep and dangerous sea.
Sít hóc a princípio persuâsum cívibus, *dóminos* ésse ómnium rêrum *ac moderatóres* déos.	Let the citizens first of all be persuaded of this, that the gods are the masters and governors of all things.
Quis potiône *úti* aut cíbo dúlci diútius *pótest?*	Who can use drink or sweet food any longer?
Hánc perféctam philosóphiam	I have always considered that to

sémper judicávi, quae de máximis quaestiónibus *copióse pósset, ornatêque dicere.*

be perfect philosophy which can
discourse with copiousness and
elegance on questions of the
highest interest.

Hóc mélius, quám tû, fácere potest *némo.*

No one could do this better than
you can.

Hôc témpore dáta ést Euméni
Cappadócia.

At this time Cappadocia was given
to Eumenes.

Proptérea quód áliud íter habé-
rent *nullum.*

Because they had no other road.

Ómnes múndi pártes úndíque
médium lócum capesséntes ni-
túntur *aequáliter.*

All parts of the world tend from
every direction towards the cen-
tral spot with equal forces.

ARRANGEMENT OF SENTENCES AND CLAUSES.

D. Clauses which mutually determine each other follow an arrangement similar to that of the words composing them.

I. Periphrastic clauses, or such as represent a noun, adjective, or adverb, occupy precisely the place in which the word
for which they stand would be.

Clauses of this kind generally commence with a relative. But they
include also those containing an infinitive with a case, and participial
clauses.

Hómines imperíti facílius, *quod
stúlte díxeris,* reprehéndere,
quam, *quod sapiénter tacúeris.*
laudâre póssunt.

Ignorant men can more easily find
fault with a foolish remark of
yours, than they can praise the
wisdom of your silence.

Laudâre eloquéntiam, et, *quánta
vis sit éjus, exprómere, quan-
támque íis, qui sínt éam conse-
cúti, dignitâtem áfférat,* néque
propósitum nóbis est hôc lóco,
néque necessárium.

To praise eloquence, and to show
the greatness of its force, and the
dignity it bestows on those who
have followed it, is neither our
purpose in this place, nor is it
necessary.

Profécto stúdia níhil prósunt
perveniéndi áliquo, nísi íllud,
*quód éo, quô inténdas, férat de-
ducátque,* cognôris.

Your studies are of no avail in ar-
riving at any result, unless you
have become acquainted with
that which carries and guides
where you intend to go.

II. Relative clauses precede those of their antecedents when
they contain the leading idea of the proposition ; but when they
merely expand or explain, they follow them. The same applies to clauses containing a comparison or an indirect question.
E. g.

Nôn fecíssem hóminis paéne ín-
fimi mentiônem, nisi judicâ-
rem, *qui suspiciósius aut crimi-*
2 P

I should not even mention the
well-nigh lowest man, unless I
thought that I had never heard

nósius díceret, audivísse mê néminem.

any one that spoke more suspiciously and criminally.

Témpus ést hujúsmodi, ut, úbi quisque ést, íbi ésse mínime vélit.

The times are such now, that every one wishes to be least where he happens to be.

Fráter túus quánti mê fáciat sempérque fécerit, ésse hóminem, qui ignôrat, árbitror néminem.

I believe there is no one who does not know how much your brother thinks of me, and has always thought of me !

Quemáxlmŏdum côram qui ad nôs intempestíve ádeunt, molésti saépe súnt, síc epístolae offéndunt, nôn lóco rédditae.

As those who come into our presence at improper seasons are often troublesome, so letters are offensive to us, that are not delivered at the proper time.

Quô májor ést in ánimis praestántia et divínior, éo majôre índigent diligéntiâ.

The greater and diviner the superiority of intellect, the greater diligence it stands in need of.

Vérres íta sê géssit in his rêbus, quási réus núnquam ésset futúrus.

Verres has conducted himself in this business, as if he never were going to be impeached.

III. Clauses containing a determination of time or place, and those denoting a cause, condition, or concession, occupy the first place, when they contain the conditions necessary to produce the given result ; but if they merely limit or explain, they are put last. E. g.

Alexánder, quum interemísset Clitum, familiârem súum, vix a sê mánus abstínuit.

When Alexander had killed Clitus, his friend, he could scarcely refrain from violence to himself.

Cogitáre debébas, ubicúnque ésses, tê fóre ín éjus ipsíus, quém fúgis, potestâte.

You should have considered, that, wherever you might be, you would be in the power of the very man from whom you endeavor to escape.

Ut consuetúdinem dicéndi mutârem, éa caûsa míhi in Ásiam proficiscéndi fúit.

The cause of my going into Asia was, that I might change my manner of speaking.

Fábula étiam nonnúnquam, etsi ést incredíbilis, támen hómines cómmovet.

A fiction even sometimes affects men, although it be an incredible one.

Conténdi cum Clódio, quum égo públicam caûsam, ille súam deféncleret.

I fought with Clodius when I defended the cause of the public and his own.

Scipióni érat mágna glória propósita,* si Hannibalem in Áfricam retraxísset.

Scipio would have had great glory before him, if he could have drawn Hannibal back into Africa.

---

* On this *erat proposita*, compare Lesson LXXXIV. A. III.

IV. The union of several clauses, harmoniously joined together, so as to express a complete thought, is called a *period*.

Periods are divided into several kinds, according to the style of composition to which they belong. The principal are the *historical*, the *didactic*, the *epistolary*; and the *oratorical*. Of these the epistolary is characterized by the greatest ease, freedom from restraint, and naturalness, while the oratorical aims at the severest symmetry, euphony, and harmony of all its members. E. g.

De meā in tē voluntāte sic vélim júdices, mē, quibuscúnque rébus ópus ésse intélligam, quánquam vídeam, quī sim hôc témpore et quid póssim, óperā támen et consílio, stúdio quídem cérte, réi, fámae, salúti túae praésto futûrum.	With respect to my disposition towards you, I wish you to think, that although I am aware what I am at present, and how little I can do, I shall nevertheless be ready to defend your interest, your reputation, and your welfare with my assistance and advice, at any rate with my endeavors.

The witness.	*Testis, is,* m.
An important witness.	Testis grăvis.
The guest (host).	Hospes, ĭtis, *m.*
The intimate friend.	Necessārius, i, *m.*
The tub.	Labrum, i, *n.*
The bath.	Balneum, i, *n.*
To depart this life.	A vitā discēdĕre.
To recommend any one.	Aliquem commendāre (ALICUI).
To recommend any one earnestly.	Aliquem in majōrem mŏdum commendāre.
The recommendation.	Commendatio, ōnis, *f.*
To report anything to any one.	Alicui aliquid deferre.
It has been so reported to me.	Íta ad mē delâta rês est.
To hold, possess.	Possĭdeo, ēre, ēdi, essum.
To hold openly or publicly.	Publice possidēre (ALIQUID).
Under another name.	Aliēno nomĭne.
To esteem or think much of any one.	Aliquem magni facĕre.
To treat any one generously.	Aliquem liberalĭter tractāre.
To write more fully and more frequently.	Et plurĭbus verbis et saepius scribĕre.
To be affected by anything.	Affectum esse alīquā re.
I think I shall come to Rome.	In Rōmam mē ventûrum púto.
I suppose you are aware.	Tê scire arbĭtror.
See that you take proper care of.	Fác, ut cúres (*cum Acc.*).
Take care of your health.	Dà ópĕram, ut váleas.
Out of respect for me.	Honôris méae caúsā.
You will do me a very great favor.	Id míhi veheménter grâtum érit.
I most earnestly request you.	Tê veheménter étiam atque étiam rógo.
Adieu.	Vále.

EXERCISE 172. — (LETTERS.)

1. MARCUS TULLIUS CICERO TO * * * GREETING.*

I am deprived of an important witness of my high regard (*amōris summi*) for you, — of your father, of distinguished memory (*clarissimo vīro*), who with his honors (*laudibus*), and especially with a son like you (*tum vero te filio*), would have overcome the destiny of (us) all (*superasset omnium fortunam*), if he had been so fortunate as to see you before he departed this life. But I hope that our friendship does not stand in need of any witnesses. May the gods prosper (*fortunāre*) your patrimony! You will at any rate (*certe*) have me (as one), to whom you may be as dear and agreeable (*jucundus*) as you were to your father. Adieu.

2. M. T. CICERO TO * * * GREETING.

I hope you are very well (*si vales, bene est*) ; I am well. We have thus far no reliable information (*quidquam certi*) either (*neque*) concerning Cæsar's arrival or (*neque*) concerning the letter, which Philotinus is said to have. If there is anything certain (*si quid erit certi*), I shall let you know (*certiōrem facĕre*) immediately. See that you take good care of your health. Adieu.

3. M. T. CICERO TO * * * GREETING.

I think that we shall come to Tusculanum either by the Nones (*Nōnis*),† or on the day after (*postridie*). Let everything be (*ut sint*) ready (for us) there. Perhaps there will be several with us, and we shall, I think, remain there for some length of time (*diutius*). If the tub is not in the bath, let it be (put) there (*ut sit*). So also whatever else may be (*Item cetera, quae sunt*) necessary for life (*ad virtum*) and health. Adieu.

4. M. T. CICERO TO * * * GREETING.

I earnestly recommend to you Hippias, the son of Philoxenus, of Calacta (*Calactīnus*), my guest and intimate friend. His property (*bona*), as (*quemadmodum*) the matter has been reported to me, is publicly held under another name, contrary to the laws of the Calactini. If this is so, the case itself (*res ipsa*) ought to prevail on your sense of justice (*ab aequitate tuā . . . impetrāre debet*), that you should help (*subvenīre*) him. But however that may be, I ask of you to relieve him (*expedīre*) out of respect for me, and to render him such assistance (*tantumque ei commodes*), both in this matter and in other respects (*et in cetēris*), as (*quantum*) your honor (*fides*) and dignity will admit (*patietur*). You will do me a very great favor.

---

* For greeting put either S. D., i. e. *Salūtem dīcit*, or S. P. D., *Salūtem plurimam dīcit*. The name of the person addressed in the dative. E. g. *Planco, Trebatio, Metello, Curiōni, Terentiae suae*.

† The Romans called the fifth day of the month *Nōnae, ārum*. In March, May, July, and October, this was the seventh day. Consult Lexicon.

5. M. T. CICERO TO * * * GREETING.

I think you are aware how greatly I esteemed Caius Avianus Flaccus; and I had learned from himself (*ex ipso audieram*), (who was) a most excellent and agreeable (*gratus*) man, how generously he had been treated by you. The sons of this (man), worthy in every respect (*dignissimos*) of that father, and my intimate friends, whom I greatly cherish (*unice diligo*), I recommend to you as earnestly (*sic*) as I can recommend any one (*ut majore studio nullos commendāre possim*). Caius Avianus is in Sicily. Marcus is with us. My desire is (*te rogo*), that you should honor (*ornāre*) the merit (*dignitas*) of the one present with you (*illius praesentis*), and defend the interest (*rem*) of both (of them). You can do nothing in that province (that will be) more agreeable to me. I most earnestly request you to do so.

6. M. T. CICERO TO * * * GREETING.

I hope you are very well; I am well. If I had anything to write to you, I should do (so) in more words and more frequently. You see how matters stand at present (*nunc quae sint negotia*). As to how I am personally (*ego autem quomŏdo*) affected, you will be able to ascertain (*cognoscere*) from Leptas and Trebatius. See that you take proper care of (*Tu fac ut . . . cures*) your health and that of Tullia. Adieu.

7. M. T. CICERO TO * * * GREETING.

I have read your letter; from which I understand that Cæsar considers you very learned in the law. You have reason to rejoice, that you have come to those places where you might have the appearance (*ubi viderere*) of knowing something (*aliquid sapĕre*). But if (*quodsi*) you had also gone into Britannia, there certainly would have been no one in that great island more experienced (*peritior*) than you. And yet (*verum tamen*) I envy you somewhat (*subinvideo*), for having been called, of his own accord (*ultro*), by one to whom others cannot even aspire (*aspirare*), not on account of his pride, but on account of his occupation. But in that letter of yours you have written me nothing about your affairs, which, I assure you (*mehercule*), are no less an object of concern to me (*mihi non minori curae sunt*) than my own. I am very much afraid of your feeling cold in your winter-quarters (*in hibernis*); on which account I advise you to keep up (*utendum censeo*) a good fire (*camino luculento*). Mucius and Manilius are of the same opinion (*idem placebat* with the dat.), especially as you are but sparingly supplied with military cloaks (*qui sagis non abundares*). I hear however (*quamquam audio*) that you feel warm enough where you are (*istic*); on account of which intelligence (*quo quidem nuntio*) I was, I assure you, very much concerned about you (*de te timueram*). But you are more cautious in military affairs than in the law (*in advocationibus*), since you desired neither to swim in the ocean, (though) extremely fond (*studiosissimus homo*) of swimming, nor to see the esse-

56

darii,* (though the man), whom before we could not even cheat blind-
folded (*quem antea ne andabatam quidem† defraudare poteramus*). But
jesting aside (*jam satis jocati sumus*), you yourself know how earnestly (*diligenter*) I have written to Cæsar about you; how often (I have
done so), I (myself know). But I had already ceased to do so (*jam
intermiseram*), lest I might seem to distrust the disposition (*voluntas*)
of a man most generous and affectionate towards me. And yet (*sed
tamen*) I thought that it was necessary to remind the man (*esse hominem commonendum*) in the letter (dat.) which I sent him last. I
accordingly did so (*Id feci*). I wish you to inform me of the result
(*quid profecerim*); and, at the same time, of your entire condition (*de
toto statu tuo*) and of all your plans. For I am anxious (*cupio*) to
know what you are doing, what you expect, (and) how long you
suppose this absence of yours from us (*istum tuum discessum a nobis*)
will be (i. e. last). For I assure you, that it is one consolation to me,
which enables me to bear more easily (*quare facilius possim pati*)
your absentment from us (*te esse sine nobis*), if it is an advantage to
you (to be so); but if it is none, (then) nothing can exceed the folly
of both of us (*nihil duobus nobis est stultius*); of me, for not drawing
you to Rome; of you, for not flying hither (at once). . . . . Let me
know therefore (*quare* at the beginning of the sentence) about all
(these) matters, as soon as you can. I shall certainly help you (*ju-
vero*), either with my sympathy (*consolando*), or with advice, or with
substantial assistance (*re*).

---

* An *essedarius* was either a soldier or a gladiator, that fought from a war-
chariot or *essedum*.

† An *andabata* was a sort of gladiator, who wore a helmet without visors,
and thus fought like a blind man.

LATIN VERBS.

A. PARADIGMS TO THE REGULAR CONJUGATIONS OF LATIN
    VERBS.

B. ANOMALOUS VERBS.

C. DEFECTIVE VERBS.

D. VERBS IRREGULAR IN THE FORMATION OF THE PERFECT
    AND SUPINE.

        I. FIRST CONJUGATION.

        II. SECOND CONJUGATION.

        III. THIRD CONJUGATION.

        IV. FOURTH CONJUGATION.

E. DEPONENT VERBS.

F. INCHOATIVE VERBS.

A. PARADIGMS TO THE REGULAR CONJUGATIONS OF LATIN VERBS.

(To Lesson XXVIII. *A-E.*)

ACTIVE VOICE.

PRES.	INFIN.	PERF.	SUPINE.
1. Amo,	amāre,	amāvi,	amātum, *to love.*
2. Monĕo,	monēre,	monŭi,	monĭtum, *to admonish.*
3. Lĕgo,	lĕgĕre,	lēgi,	lectum, *to read.*
4. Audio,	audīre,	audīvi,	audītum, *to hear.*

INDICATIVE MOOD.	SUBJUNCTIVE MOOD.
PRESENT, *I love, admonish, read, hear.*	PRESENT, *that I may love, admonish, read, hear.*
1. S. ăm-o, ăs, at; P. āmus, ātis, ant.	
2. S. mŏn-ĕo, ĕs, et; P. ēmus, ētis, ent.	S. ăm-em, ĕs, et; P. ēmus, ētis, ent.
3. S. lĕg-o, ĭs, it; P. ĭmus, ĭtis, unt.	S. mŏn-ĕam, ĕās, ĕat; P. ĕāmus, ĕātis, ĕant.
4. S. aud-ĭo, ĭs, ĭt; P. ĭmus, ĭtis, iunt.	S. lĕg-am, ās, at; P. āmus, ātis, ant.
	S. aud-iam, iās, iat; P. iāmus, iātis, iant.
IMPERFECT, *I loved, admonished, read, heard.*	IMPERFECT, *that I might love, admonish, read, hear.*
1. S. ăm-ābam, ābās, ābat; P. abāmus, abātis, ābant.	S. ăm-ārem, ārēs, āret; P. ārēmus, ārētis, ārent.
2. S. mŏn-ēbam, ēbās, ēbat; P. ebāmus, ebātis, ēbant.	S. mon-ērem, ērēs, ēret; P. ērēmus, ērētis, ērent.
3. S. lĕg ēbam, ēbās, ēbat; P. ebāmus, ebātis, ēbant.	S. lĕg-ĕrem, ĕrēs, ĕret; P. ĕrēmus, ĕrētis, ĕrent.
4. S. aud-iēbam, iēbās, iēbat; P. iebāmus, iebātis, iēbant.	S. aud-irem, īrēs, īret; P. īrēmus, īrētis, īrent.
PERFECT, *I have loved, admonished, read, heard.*	PERFECT, *that I may have loved, admonished, read, heard.*
1. S. amāv- 2. monŭ- 3. lĕg- 4. audīv- } i, isti, it; P. ĭmus, istis, ērunt or ēre.	1. S. amāv- 2. monŭ- 3. lĕg- 4. audīv- } ĕrim, ĕris, ĕrit; P. erimus, erītis, ĕrint.
PLUPERFECT, *I had loved, admonished, read, heard.*	PLUPERFECT, *that I might have loved, admonished, read, heard.*
1. S. amāv- 2. monŭ- 3. lĕg- 4. audīv- } ĕram, ĕrās, ĕrat; P. erāmus, erātis, ĕrant.	1. S. amāv- 2. monŭ- 3. lĕg- 4. audīv- } issem, issēs, isset; P. issēmus, issētis, issent.

FUTURE TENSES INDICATIVE.

FUTURE I., *I shall love, admonish, read, hear.*

1. S. ăm-ābo, ābis, ābit; P. abīmus, abītis, ābunt.
2. S. mŏn-ēbo, ēbis, ēbit; P. ebīmus, ebītis, ēbunt.
3. S. lĕg-am, ĕs, et; P. ēmus, ētis, ent.
4. S. aud-iam, iēs, iet; P. iēmus, iētis, ient

FUTURE II., *I shall have loved, admonished, read, heard.*

1. S. amāv- 2. monŭ- }
3. lĕg- 4. audīv- } ĕro, ĕris, ĕrit; P. erimus, erītis, ĕrint.

ACTIVE VOICE. — *Continued.*

IMPERATIVE MOOD.

PRESENT.

1. S. ăm-ă; P. ăte, *love thou, love ye.*
2. S. mŏn-ĕ; P. ēte, *admonish thou, admonish ye.*
3. S. lĕg-ĕ; P. ĭte, *read thou, read ye.*
4. S. aud-ī; P. īte, *hear thou, hear ye.*

FUTURE.

1. S. ăm-āto, āto, *thou shalt, let him, love.*
   P. ăm-ātōte, anto, *ye shall, let them, love.*
2. S. mŏn-ēto, ēto, *thou shalt, let him, admonish.*
   P. mŏn-ētōte, ento, *ye shall, let them, admonish.*
3. S. lĕg-ĭto, ĭto, *thou shalt, let him, read.*
   P. lĕg-ĭtōte, unto, *ye shall, let them, read.*
4. S. aud-ĭto, ĭto, *thou shalt, let him, hear.*
   P. aud-ĭtōte, ĭunto, *ye shall, let them, hear.*

INFINITIVE MOOD.

PRESENT.	PERFECT.
1. ăm-āre, *to love.*	1. amāv-isse, *to have loved.*
2. mŏn-ēre, *to admonish.*	2. monŭ-isse, *to have admonished.*
3. lĕg-ĕre, *to read.*	3. lĕg-isse, *to have read.*
4. aud-īre, *to hear.*	4. audīv-isse, *to have heard.*

FUTURE.

1. amāt-ūrum esse, *to be about to love.*
2. monĭt-ūrum esse, *to be about to admonish.*
3. lect-ūrum esse, *to be about to read.*
4. audĭt-ūrum esse, *to be about to hear.*

PARTICIPLES.

PRESENT.

1. ăm-ans, *loving.*	3. lĕg-ens, *reading.*
2. mŏn-ens, *admonishing.*	4. aud-iens, *hearing.*

FUTURE.

1. amāt-ūrus, *about to love.*	3. lect-ūrus, *about to read.*
2. monĭt-ūrus, *about to admonish.*	4. audĭt-ūrus, *about to hear.*

GERUNDS.

1. am-andi, *of loving.*	3. lĕg-endi, *of reading.*
2. mŏn-endi, *of admonishing.*	4. aud-iendi, *of hearing.*

SUPINES.

1. amāt-um, *to love.*	3. lect-um, *to read.*
2. monĭt-um, *to admonish.*	4. audīt-um, *to hear.*

PASSIVE VOICE.

PRES.	INFIN.	PERFECT.	
1. Amor,	amāri,	amātus sum,	*to be loved.*
2. Monĕor,	monēri,	monitus sum,	*to be admonished.*
3. Lĕgor,	lĕgi,	lectus sum,	*to be read.*
4. Audior,	audīri,	auditus sum,	*to be heard.*

INDICATIVE MOOD.	SUBJUNCTIVE MOOD.
PRESENT, *I am loved, admonished, read, heard.*	PRESENT, *that I may be loved, admonished, read, heard.*
1. S. ăm-or, ūris *or* re, ātur; P. āmar, āmĭni, antur.	S. ăm-er, ēre *or* ris, ētur ; P. ēmur, ēmĭni, entur.
2. S. mŏn-ĕor, ēris *or* re, ētur; P. ēmur, ēmĭni, entur.	S. mŏn-ĕar, eāre *or* ris, ĕātur ; P. eāmur, eāmĭni, ĕantur.
3. S. lĕg-or, ĕris *or* re, ītur; P. ĭmur, ĭmĭni, untur.	S. lĕg-ar, āre *or* ris, ātur ; P. āmur, āmĭni, antur.
4. S. aud-ior, īris *or* re, ītur; P. ĭmur, ĭmĭni, iuntur.	S. aud-iar, iāre *or* ris, iātur; P. iāmur, iāmĭni, iantur.
IMPERFECT, *I was loved, admonished, read, heard.*	IMPERFECT, *that I might be loved, admonished, read, heard.*
1. S. ăm-ābar, ābāris *or* re, ābātur; P. ābāmur, ābāmĭni, ābantur.	S. ăm-ārer, ārēre *or* ris, ārētur ; P. ārēmur, ārēmĭni, ārentur.
2. S. mŏn-ēbar, ēbāris *or* re, ēbātur; P. ēbāmur, ēbāmĭni, ēbantur.	S. mŏn-ērer, ērēre *or* ris, ērētur ; P. ērēmur, ērēmĭni, ērentur.
3. S. lĕg-ēbar, ēbāris *or* re, ēbātur; P. ēbāmur, ēbāmĭni, ēbantur.	S. lĕg-ĕrer, ĕrēre *or* ris, ĕrētur ; P. ĕrēmur, ĕrēmĭni, ĕrentur.
4. S. aud-iēbar, iēbāris *or* re, iēbātur; P. iēbāmur, iēbāmĭni, iēbantur.	S. aud-irer, irēre *or* ris, irētur; P. irēmur, irēmĭni, irentur.
PERFECT, *I have been loved, admonished, read, heard.*	PERFECT, *that I may have been loved, admonished, read, heard.*
1. amātus, 2. monĭtus, 3. lectus, 4. audītus, { sum *or* fui, ĕs *or* fuisti, est *or* fuit, &c. (Cf. p. 248.)	1. amātus, 2. monĭtus, 3. lectus, 4. audītus, { sim *or* fuĕrim, sis *or* fuĕris, sit *or* fuĕrit, &c.
PLUPERFECT, *I had been loved, admonished, read, heard.*	PLUPERFECT, *that I might have been loved, admonished, read, heard.*
1. amātus, 2. monĭtus, 3. lectus, 4. audītus, { ĕram *or* fuĕram, ĕrās *or* fuĕrās, ĕrat *or* fuĕrat, &c. (Cf. p. 464.)	1. amātus, 2. monĭtus, 3. lectus, 4. audītus, { essem *or* fuissem, essēs *or* fuissēs, esset *or* fuisset, &c.

FUTURE TENSES INDICATIVE.

FUTURE I., *I shall be loved, admonished, read, heard.*

1. S. ăm-ābor, ābĕris *or* re, ābĭtur; P. ābĭmur, ābĭmĭni, ābuntur.
2. S. mŏn-ēbor, ēbĕris *or* re, ēbĭtur; P. ēbĭmur, ēbĭmĭni, ēbuntur.
3. S. lĕg-ar, ēris *or* re, ētur; P. ēmur, ēmĭni, entur.
4. S. aud-iar, iēris *or* re, iētur; P. iēmur, iēmĭni, ientar.

FUTURE II., *I shall have been loved, admonished, read, heard.*

1. amātus, 2. monĭtus, { ĕro *or* fuĕro, ĕris *or* fuĕris, ĕrit *or* fuĕrit, &c.
3. lectus, 4. audītus, { (Cf. p. 519.)

56 *

PASSIVE VOICE. — *Continued.*

IMPERATIVE MOOD.

PRESENT.

1. S. ăm-āre; P. āmĭnĭ, *be thou, be ye, loved.*
2. S. mŏn-ēre; P. ēmĭnĭ, *be thou, be ye, admonished.*
3. S. lĕg-ĕre; P. ĭmĭnĭ, *be thou, be ye, read.*
4. S. aud-īre; P. īmĭnĭ, *be thou, be ye, heard.*

FUTURE.

1. S. ăm-ātor, ātor, *thou shalt, let him, be loved.*
   P. ăm-āmĭnor, antor, *ye shall, let them, be loved.*
2. S. mŏn-ētor, ētor, *thou shalt, let him, be admonished.*
   P. mŏn-ēmĭnor, entor, *ye shall, let them, be admonished.*
3. S. lĕg-ĭtor, ĭtor, *thou shalt, let him, be read.*
   P. lĕg-ĭmĭnor, untor, *ye shall, let them, be read.*
4. S. aud-ītor, ītor, *thou shalt, let him, be heard.*
   P. aud-īmĭnor, īuntor, *ye shall, let them, be heard.*

INFINITIVE MOOD.

PRESENT.	PERFECT.
1. ăm-ārĭ, *to be loved.*	1. amāt-um esse, *to have been loved.*
2. mŏn-ērĭ, *to be admonished.*	2. monĭt-um esse, *to have been admonished.*
3. lĕg-ĭ, *to be read.*	3. lect-um esse, *to have been read.*
4. aud-īrĭ, *to be heard.*	4. audīt-um esse, *to have been heard.*

FUTURE.

1. amāt-um īrĭ, *to be about to be loved.*
2. monĭt-um īrĭ, *to be about to be admonished.*
3. lect-um īrĭ, *to be about to be read.*
4. audīt-um īrĭ, *to be about to be heard.*

PARTICIPLES.

PERFECT.

1. amāt-us, *loved.*	3. lect-us, *read.*
2. monĭt-us, *admonished.*	4. audīt-us, *heard.*

FUTURE.

1. am-andus, *to be loved.*	3. lĕg-endus, *to be read.*
2. mon-endus, *to be admonished.*	4. aud-iendus, *to be heard.*

SUPINES.

1. amāt-u, *to be loved.*	3. lect-u, *to be read.*
2. monĭt-u, *to be admonished.*	4. audīt-u, *to be heard.*

B. ANOMALOUS VERBS.

The anomalous verbs of the Latin language are *sum, possum, vŏlo, nōlo, mālo, ĕdo, fĕro, fĭo, eo, quĕo,* and *nequĕo.*

1. Sum, esse, fui, futūrus, *to be.*

INDICATIVE.	SUBJUNCTIVE.

PRESENT.

SING. sum, *I am*
 ĕs, *thou art*
 est, *he is,*
PLUR. sŭmus, *we are*
 estis, *ye are*
 sunt, *they are.*

SING. sim, *that I may be*
 sis, *that thou mayst be*
 sit, *that he may be,*
PLUR. sīmus, *that we may be*
 sitis, *that ye may be*
 sint,* *that they may be.*

IMPERFECT.

SING. ĕram, *I was*
 ĕrās, *thou wast*
 ĕrat, *he was,*
PLUR. ĕrāmus, *we were*
 ĕrātis, *ye were*
 ĕrant, *they were.*

SING. essem, *that I might be*
 essēs, *that thou mightst be*
 esset, *that he might be,*
PLUR. essēmus, *that we might be*
 essētis, *that ye might be*
 essent,† *that they might be.*

PERFECT.

SING. fŭi, *I have been*
 fuisti, *thou hast been*
 fuit, *he has been,*
PLUR. fuīmus, *we have been*
 fuistis, *ye have been*
 fuĕrunt (fuĕre), *they have been.*

SING. fuĕrim, *that I may have been*
 fuĕris, *that thou mayst have been*
 fuĕrit, *that he may have been,*
PLUR. fuerīmus, *that we may have been*
 fuerītis, *that ye may have been*
 fuĕrint, *that they may have been.*

PLUPERFECT.

SING. fuĕram, *I had been*
 fuĕrās, *thou hadst been*
 fuĕrat, *he had been,*
PLUR. fuerāmus, *we had been*
 fuerātis, *ye had been*
 fuĕrant, *they had been.*

SING. fuissem, *that I might have been*
 fuissēs, *that thou mightst have been*
 fuisset, *that he might have been,*
PLUR. fuissēmus, *that we might have been*
 fuissētis, *that ye might have been*
 fuissent, *that they might have been.*

FUTURE TENSES INDICATIVE.

FUTURE I.

SING. ĕro, *I shall be*
 ĕris, *thou wilt be*
 ĕrit, *he will be,*
PLUR. ĕrīmus, *we shall be,*
 ĕritis, *ye will be*
 ĕrunt, *they will be.*

FUTURE II.

SING. fuĕro, *I shall have been*
 fuĕris, *thou wilt have been*
 fuĕrit, *he will have been,*
PLUR. fuerīmus, *we shall have been*
 fuerītis, *ye will have been*
 fuĕrint, *they will have been.*

IMPERATIVE.

PRESENT. SING. ĕs, *be thou.* PLUR.   FUTURE. SING. esto, *thou shalt be;*
este, *be ye.*   esto, *let him be.* PLUR. estōte, *ye shall be;* sunto, *let them be.*

---

* Obsolete forms are *siem, sies, siet, sient,* and *fuam, fuas, fuat, fuant.*
† Another form for the imperfect subjunctive is *fŏrem, fŏres, fŏret,* &c.

INFINITIVE.

PRESENT. esse, *to be.* PERFECT. fuisse, *to have been.* FUTURE. futūrum (am, um) esse *or simply* fŏre, *to be about to be.*

PARTICIPLES.

PRESENT. (ens), *being.* FUTURE. futūrus, a, um, *about to be.*

REMARKS.

1. The participle *ens* is not used except as a substantive (the philosophical "being," "entity"), and in the compounds *absens* and *praesens.*

2. Like *sum* are conjugated the compounds *absum, adsum, desum, insum, intersum, obsum, praesum, subsum,* and *supersum.* The preposition *pro* of *prosum* becomes *prod* when an *e* follows; as, *prodes, prodest, prodĕram, prodĕro, prodes,* &c.

2. Possum, posse, potui, *I am able, I can.*

INDICATIVE.	SUBJUNCTIVE.

PRESENT.

S. possum. potĕs, potest;   S. possim, possis, possit;
P. possŭmus, potestis, possunt.   P. possĭmus, possĭtis, possint.

IMPERFECT.

S. potĕram, potĕras, potĕrat;   S. possem, posses, posset;
P. poterāmus, poterātis, potĕrant.   P. possēmus, possētis, possent.

PERFECT.

S. potŭi, potuisti, potŭit;   S. potuĕrim. potuĕris, potuĕrit;
P. potuĭmus, potuistis, potuērunt.   P. potuerĭmus, potueritis, potuĕrint.

PLUPERFECT.

S. potuĕram, potuĕras, potuĕrat;   S. potuissem, potuisses, potuisset;
P. potuerāmus, potuerātis, potuĕrant.   P. potuissēmus, potuissētis, potuissent.

FUTURE TENSES INDICATIVE.

FUTURE I.	FUTURE II.

S. potĕro, potĕris, potĕrit;   S. potuĕro, potuĕris, potuĕrit;
P. poterĭmus, poteritis, potĕrunt.   P. potuerĭmus, potueritis, potuĕrint.

IMPERATIVE (*wanting*).   INFINITIVE.

            PRES. posse. PERF. potuisse.

PARTICIPLE PRES. potens (*only used adjectively*).

3. Vŏlo, velle, volŭi, *I am willing, I wish.*
4. Nōlo, nolle, nolŭi, *I am unwilling.*
5. Mālo, malle, malŭi, *I would rather, I prefer.*

INDICATIVE MOOD.

PRESENT.

S. vŏlo, vis, vult;   nōlo, non vis, non vult;   mālo, māvis, māvult;
P. volŭmus, vultis, vŏlunt.   nōlŭmus, non vultis, nōlunt.   malŭmus, mavultis, mālunt.

IMPERFECT.

S. volēbam, as, at;   nolēbam, as, at;   malēbam, as, at;
P. volebāmus, &c.   nolebāmus, &c.   malebāmus, &c.

PERFECT.

S. volui, isti, it;	nolui, isti, it;	malui, isti, it;
P. voluimus, &c.	noluimus, &c.	maluimus, &c.

PLUPERFECT.

S. voluĕram, as, at;	noluĕram, as, at;	maluĕram, as, at;
P. voluerămus, &c.	noluerămus, &c.	maluerămus, &c.

FUTURE I.

S. vŏlam, ēs, et;	nōlam, ēs, et;	mālam, ēs, et;
P. volēmus, &c.	nolēmus, &c.	malēmus, &c.

FUTURE II.

S. voluĕro, is, it;	noluĕro, is, it;	maluĕro, is, it;
P. voluerimus, &c.	noluerimus, &c.	maluerimus, &c.

SUBJUNCTIVE MOOD.

PRESENT.

S. vĕlim, is, it;	nōlim, is, it;	mālim, is, it;
P. velimus, itis, int.	nolimus, itis, int.	malimus, itis, int.

IMPERFECT.

S. vellem, ēs, et;	nollem, ēs, et;	mallem, ēs, et;
P. vellēmus, &c.	nollēmus, &c.	mallēmus, &c.

PERFECT.

S. voluĕrim, is, it;	noluĕrim, is, it;	maluĕrim, is, it;
P. voluerimus, &c.	noluerimus, &c.	maluerimus, &c.

PLUPERFECT.

S. voluissem, ēs, et;	noluissem, es, et;	maluissem, es, et;
P. voluissēmus, &c.	noluissēmus, &c.	maluissēmus, &c.

IMPERATIVE MOOD.

(*Wanting.*)	nōli — nolīte	(*Wanting.*)
	nolīto — nolitōte	
	nolīto — nolunto.	

INFINITIVE MOOD.

PRES.	velle	nolle	malle
PERF	voluisse.	noluisse.	maluisse.

PARTICIPLE.

vŏlens.	nōlens.	(*Wanting.*)

GERUND.

volendi	nolendi.	(*Wanting.*)
volendo.		

6. **Edo, ĕre** *or* **esse, ēdi, ēsum,** *I eat.*

PRES. INDIC. S. edo, ĕdis *or* ēs, ĕdit *or* est; P. edĭmus, edĭtis *or* estis, ĕdunt.
IMPERF. SUBJ. S. edĕrem *or* essem, edĕres *or* esses, edĕret *or* esset; P. ederēmus *or* essēmus, ederētis *or* essētis, edĕrent *or* essent.
IMPERAT. PRES. S. ĕde *or* ēs; P. edĭte *or* este.
IMPERAT. FUT. S. edito *or* esto, edito *or* esto; P. editōte *or* estōte, edunto.
INFIN. edĕre *or* esse.   PASSIVE FORMS. edĭtur *or* estur ; — ederētur *or* essētur.

The remaining tenses of this verb are regular.
The compounds of *edo,* inflected like it, are *adĕdo, ambĕdo, comĕdo, exĕdo, perĕdo.*

7. Fĕro, ferre, tŭli, lātum, *I carry, bear.*

ACTIVE VOICE.	PASSIVE VOICE.

INDICATIVE.

PRES. S. fĕro, fers, fert;	S. fĕror, ferris *or* re, fertur;
P. ferĭmus, fertis, fĕrunt.	P. ferĭmur, ferimĭni, feruntur.
IMPERF. ferēbam, as, at, &c.	ferēbar, āris *or* re, ātur, &c.
PERF. tŭli, isti, it, &c.	lātus sum *or* fui, &c.
PLUPERF. tulĕram, as, at, &c.	lātus ĕram *or* fuĕram, &c.
FUT. I. fĕram, ēs, et, &c.	fĕrar, ēris *or* re, ētur, &c.
FUT. II. tulĕro, is, it, &c.	lātus ĕro *or* fuĕro.

SUBJUNCTIVE.

PRES. fĕram, ās, at, &c.	fĕrar, āre *or* ris, ātur, &c.
IMPERF. ferrem, ēs, et, &c.	ferrer, ēre *or* ris, ētur, &c.
PERF. tulĕrim, is, it, &c.	lātus sim *or* fuĕrim, &c.
PLUPERF. tulissem, es, et, &c.	lātus essem *or* fuissem, &c.

IMPERATIVE.

PRES. S. fer; P. ferte.	S. ferre; P. ferimĭni.
FUT. S. ferto, ferto; P. fertōte, fĕrunto.	S. fertor, fertor; P. ferimĭnor, fĕruntor.

INFINITIVE.

PRES. ferre. PERF. tulisse.	PRES. ferri. PERF. lātum esse *or*
FUT. latūrum esse.	fuisse. FUT. lātum iri.

PARTICIPLES.

PRES. ferens. FUT. latūrus.	PERF. lātus. FUT. ferendus.

GERUND.	SUPINES.
ferendi, do, dum, do.	lātum. — lātu.

So also the compounds *affĕro, antefĕro, aufĕro* (= *ab* + *fĕro*), *circumfĕro, confĕro, defĕro, diffĕro,* &c. — Instead of *sustŭli,* the proper perfect of *suffĕro,* the form *sustĭnŭi* (from *sustĭneo*) is commonly employed, and *sustŭli,* as well as the supine *sublātum,* are considered parts of the verb *tollo,* I pick up, take away.

8. Fĭo, fĭĕri, factus sum, *I become, am made.*

INDICATIVE.	SUBJUNCTIVE.

PRESENT.

S. fĭo, fĭs, fit;	S. fĭam, fĭas, fĭat;
P. fĭmus, fĭtis, fĭunt.	P. fĭāmus, fĭātis, fĭant.

IMPERFECT.

S. fĭēbam, as, at;	S. fĭĕrem, es, et;
P. fiebāmus, ātis, ant.	P. fierēmus, ētis, ent.

FUTURE.	INFINITIVE.
S. fĭam, es, et;	PRES. fĭĕri. PERF. factum esse.
P. fĭēmus, ētis, ent.	FUT. factum iri.

The remaining parts of this verb are from *facĕre.* Such are *factus, faciendus, factus sum, eram, ero,* &c.
Among the compounds of *fio* are the defective *infit,* he begins; *defit* (*defiunt, defiat, defĭĕri*), there is wanting, and *confit* (*confĭĕri*), there is made.

9. Eo, ire, ivi (ii), ĭtum, *I go.*

INDICATIVE.	SUBJUNCTIVE.

PRESENT.

S. ĕo, Is, it;	S. ĕam, eas, eat;
P. īmus, ītis, eunt.	P. eāmus, eātis, eant.

IMPERFECT.

S. Ibam, Ibas, Ibat;   S. Irem, Ires, Iret;
P. ibāmus, ibātis, Ibant.   P. irēmus, irētis, Irent.

PERFECT.

S. Ivi, ivisti, Ivit;   S. Ivěrim (iěrim), ivěris, &c.
P. ivimus, &c.   P. iverimus, &c.

PLUPERFECT.

S. Ivěram (iěram), as, at;   S. ivissem, ivisses, ivisset;
P. ivěrāmus, &c.   P. ivissēmus, &c.

FUTURE TENSES INDICATIVE.

FUTURE I.   FUTURE II.

S. Ibo, Ibis, Ibit;   S. Ivěro, ivěris, ivěrit;
P. Ibimus, Ibitis, Ibunt.   P. iverimus, &c.

IMPERATIVE.   INFINITIVE.

PRES. S. I — P. Ite.   PRES. Ire.
FUT. { S. Ito — P. itōte   PERF. ivisse *or* isse.
   { S. Ito — P. eunto.   FUT. itūrum (am, um), esse.

GERUND.   PARTICIPLES.

eundi, do, dum, do.   PRES. iens, *gen.* euntis.
     FUT. itūrus, a, um.

SUPINES.

ACT. Itum.   PASS. Itu.

So the compounds *abeo, adeo, coěo, exeo, ineo, intereo, pereo, praetereo, prodeo, redeo.* But all these have generally *ti* instead of *ivi* in the perfect; as, *abii, exii, perii, prodii,* &c. To these add *veneo* (= *venum* + *eo*), I am sold. *Ambio,* I go around, is the only compound regularly conjugated like *audio,* and has consequently *ambiēbam, ambiens, ambiendi,* &c.

The only passive forms of *eo* are the impersonal *itur* and *itum est.* But the compounds of *eo* which have acquired a transitive sense have a regular passive voice; as, *adeo, ineo, praetereo.*

A future in *eam, ies, iet, ient* (instead of *ibo, ibis,* &c.), occurs only in later authors, and is confined to the compounds.

10. Quěo, quīre, quīvi, quītum, *I can.*

11. Nequěo, nequīre, nequīvi (nequii), nequītum, *I cannot.*

PRESENT INDICATIVE.

S. quěo, quis, quit;   S. nequěo, nequis, nequit;
P. quimus, quitis, quěunt.   P. nequimus, nequitis, nequěunt.

IMPERFECT.

S. quibam, as, at;   S. nequibam, as, at;
P. quibāmus, &c.   P. nequibāmus, &c.

PERFECT.

S. quivi — quivit;   S. nequivi, nequisti, nequivit (nequiit);
P. — — quivěrunt.   P. — — nequivěrunt (nequiěrunt).

PLUPERFECT.

     S. — — nequiěrat.
     P. — — nequiěrant.

FUTURE.

S. quibo — —;   S. — — —
P. — — quibunt.   P. — — nequibunt.

PRESENT SUBJUNCTIVE.

S. quěam, quěas, quěat;   S. nequěam, nequěas, nequěat;
P. queāmus, queātis, quěant.   P. nequeāmus, &c.

IMPERFECT.

S. quĭrem — quĭret;
P. — — quĭrent.

S. nequĭrem — nequĭret;
P. nequirēmus — nequĭrent.

PERFECT.

S. — — quivĕrit.

S. nequivĕrim — nequĭĕrit;
P. — — nequĭĕrint.

PLUPERFECT.

S. — — —;
P. — — nequissent.

S. — — nequisset;
P. — — nequissent.

INFINITIVE.

PRES. quĭre. PERF. quivisse
(quisse).

PRES. nequĭre. PERF. nequivisse
(nequisse).

PARTICIPLE.

PRES. quiens, *gen.* queuntis.

PRES. nequiens, *gen.* nequeuntis.

These verbs are both conjugated like *eo*. Many of the forms, however, are seldom used, except those of the present. Nepos and Cæsar never employ any of them. Instead of *nequeo* Cicero frequently puts *non queo*.

Passive forms are *quitur, nequitur, quita est, nequitum est*, but these are rarely used, and only in connection with an infinitive passive. E. g. *Forma nosci non quita est*, The form could not be distinguished.

C. DEFECTIVE VERBS.

Defective verbs are those which occur only in certain forms and connections.

The principal verbs of this class are *aio* and *inquam*, I say; *fāri*, to speak; the præteritives *coepi*, I have begun; *memĭni*, I remember; *nŏvi*, I know; *odi*, I hate; the imperatives *apăge, ăve, salve*, and *vāle*. So also *cĕdo, quaeso*, and *fŏrem.* -

1. Aio, *I say.*

INDIC. PRES. āio, ăis, ăit; P. — — āiunt.
" IMPERF. aiēbam, as, at; P. aiebāmus, ātis, ant.
" PERFECT. — — āit.
SUBJ. PRES. — aias, aiat; P. — — aiant.
IMPER. ai (*obsolete*). PART. aiens (*only as adject.*).

Instead of the interrogative *aisne* the contracted *ain'* frequently occurs.

2. Inquam, *I say.*

INDIC. PRES. inquam, inquis, inquit; P. inquĭmus, inquĭtis, inquĭunt.
" IMPERF. inquiēbam, &c. P. inquiebāmus, &c.
" PERF. — inquisti, inquit; P. — inquistis, —.
" FUTURE. — inquies, inquiet; P. — — —.
SUBJ. PRES. — inquias, inquiat; P. — inquiātis, inquiant.
IMPERAT. S. inque, inquĭto; P. inquĭte.

The present *inquam* sometimes supplies the place of the first person perfect, which is wanting.

3. Fāri, *to speak, say.*

INDIC. PRES. — — fātur; P. — — fantur.
IMPERAT. fāre. PART. fātus, a, um. GER. fando.

So the compound forms *affāmur, affamĭni, affābar, effābor, effabĕris.* This verb rarely occurs except in poetry. The first person *for*, and the subj. *fer, fĕtur*, are never used.

4. Coepi, coepisse, coeptūrus, *I have begun*.
5. Memĭni, meminisse, ——, *I remember*.
6. Nōvi, novisse, ——, *I know*.
7. Ōdi, odisse, osūrus, *I hate*.

INDICATIVE PERFECT.

S. coepi	memĭni	nŏvi	ŏdĭ
coepisti,	meministĭ	novisti (nōsti)	-odisti
coepit,	meminit,	nŏvit,	ŏdit,
P. coepĭmus	meminĭmus	novĭmus	odimus
coepistis	meministis	novistis (nōstis)	odistis
coepērunt.	meminērunt.	novērunt (nōrunt).	odērunt.

PLUPERFECT.

coepĕram,	meminĕram,	novĕram (nōram),	odĕram,
as, at, &c.	as, at, &c.	as, at, &c.	as, at, &c.

FUTURE.

coepĕro,	meminĕro,	novĕro,	odĕro.
is, it, &c.	is, it, &c.	is, it, &c.	is, it, &c.

SUBJUNCTIVE PERFECT.

coepĕrim,	meminĕrim,	novĕrim (nōrim),	odĕrim,
is, it, &c.	is, it, &c.	is, it, &c.	is, it, &c.

PLUPERFECT.

coepissem,	meminissem,	novissem (nossem,	odissem,
es, et, &c.	es, et, &c.	es, et, &c.	es, et, &c.

IMPERATIVE.

(*Wanting.*)	S. memento,		(*Wanting.*)
	P. mementōte.		

INFINITIVE.

coepisse.	meminisse.	novisse.	odisse.

PARTICIPLES.

PERF. PASS. coeptus.	—	—	perūsus, exōsus (*active*).
FUT. ACT. coeptūrus.	—	—	osūrus.

Of the above verbs *memĭni, nŏri,* and *odî* have a present signification. Hence the pluperfect has the sense of the imperfect, and the second future that of the first.

Instead of *coepi* the passive *coeptus est* is also used, especially in connection with the infinitive passive. E. g. *Oppugnāri coeptum est oppidum,* The town began to be besieged.

8. Apāge, *away!* Ave, Salve, *hail.* Vale, *farewell.*

Apāge has sometimes an accusative after it ; as, *Apāge tĕ,* Away with you!
Salve also occurs in the present indic., *salveo. Vale* and *ave* are regular imperatives of the verbs *valeo,* I am well, and *aveo,* I am desirous, and are defective only in consequence of the change of signification.

All of these imperatives have also a plural and a future form; as,

S. ave. F. avēto. P. avēte.
S. salve. F. salvēto. P. salvēte.
S. vale. F. valēto. P. valēte.

FUTURE forms with the imperative force are *salvēbis, valēbis.*
INFINITIVES are *salvēre, valēre.*

9. Cĕdo, *give me,* or *say, tell.*

This verb may stand either as the singular or plural. Special plural forms are *cedĭte* and *cĕtte.* Its sense is similar to that of the French *tenez.*

10. Quaeso, *I pray, pray.*

This verb is most commonly interjected in the sentence, like the English "pray," "please." Its plural is *quaesŭmus.*

11. Fŏrem, *I might be.*

From the obsolete root *fŭo,* and contracted for *fŭĕrem.* It is otherwise regular, and the infinitive is *fŏre,* "to be about to be." (Cf. page 666.)

D. VERBS WHICH ARE IRREGULAR IN THE FORMATION OF THE PERFECT AND SUPINE.

Many Latin verbs are irregular in the formation of the second and third roots, which frequently assume the characteristics of another conjugation. These will be enumerated and examined in the following lists, according to their respective conjugations.

I. First Conjugation.

Regular verbs of the first conjugation end in *o, āre, āvi, ātum.* E. g.

>Ambŭlo, ambulāre, ambulāvi, ambulātum, *to walk.*
>Celo, celāre, celāvi, celātum, *to conceal.*
>Impĕro, imperāre, imperāvi, imperātum, *to command.*
>Vulnĕro, vulnerāre, vulnerāvi, vulnerātum, *to wound.*

Several verbs of the first conjugation follow the analogy of the second, and form their perfect in *ŭi* and the supine in *ĭtum.* A few more are otherwise irregular in these parts. They are:—

Crĕpo, āre, crepŭi, crepĭtum, *to ring, clatter, resound.*
Compounds are *concrepāre, discrepāre,* and *increpāre.*

Cŭbo, āre, cubŭi, cubĭtum, *to lie, recline.*
So the compounds *accŭbo, excŭbo, incŭbo, secŭbo,* and others. But the compos. of *cŭbo* which take an *m* before *b* are of the third conjugation (c. g. *discumbĕre*).—The regular perfects *cubāvi* and *incubāvi* also occur.

Dō, dāre, dĕdi, dătum, *to give.*
So *circumdăre, pessundăre, satisdăre,* and *venundăre.* But the remaining compos. belong to the third conjugation; as, *addĕre, condĕre, reddĕre,* &c.—Obsolete forms of the pres. subj. are *duim, duis, duit,* from the secondary *duo.*

Dŏmo, āre, domŭi, domĭtum, *to tame, curb.*
So the compos. *edŏmāre* and *perdŏmāre.*

Frĭco, āre, fricŭi, fricātum *or* frictum, *to rub.*
So the compos. *defricāre, infricāre, perfricāre,* and *refricāre.*

Jŭvo, āre, jūvi, jūtum, juvatūrus, *to assist, help.*
So also *adjuvāre, adjūvi, adjūtum, adjutūrus* or *adjuvatūrus.*

Lăvo, āre, lāvi, lavātum, lautum, *and* lōtum, *to wash.*
An infinitive *lavĕre* occurs in the older Latinity and in poetry.

Mĭco, āre, micŭi, ——, *to glitter, shine.*
So *emĭco, āre, emicŭi, emicātum.* But *dimĭco,* I contend, fight, has the regular perfect *dimĭcāvi.*

Nĕco, āre, āvi, ātum, *to kill,* is regular, but the
Compos. *enĕcāre* has *āvi, ātum* and *enecŭi, enectum.* The participle is commonly *enectus; internecāre* has *internecātus.*

Plĭco, āre, āvi *and* ŭi, ātum *and* ĭtum, *to fold.*

So the compos. *applicāre, complicāre, explicāre,* and *implicāre.* But *duplĭco, multiplĭco,* and *supplĭco,* which are derived from adjectives in *plex,* have regularly *āvi, ātum.*

Pōto, āre, āvi, potātum *and more commonly* pōtum, *to drink.*

The participle is *pōtus,* which is both passive, "drunk," and active, "having drunk." The compos. *appōtus* is active, " having drunk sufficiently"; and *epōtus,* passive, " emptied by drinking."

Sĕco, āre, sĕcui, sectum, secatū- rus, *to cut.*

Compos. *desecāre, dissecāre, perse- cāre.* But *praesecāre* and *resecāre* have *cātum* or *ctum* in the supine.

Sŏno, āre, sŏnŭi, sonĭtum, sonatū- rus, *to sound.*

So *consonāre, dissonāre, personāre, resonāre.*

Stō, stāre, stĕti, stătum, *to stand.*

So *antestāre, circumstāre, interstāre,* and *superstāre.* But the remaining

compounds have *ĭti* in the perfect; as, *adstāre, constāre,* perf. *adstĭti, con- stĭti;* so *exstāre, instāre, obstāre, per- stāre, praestāre,* and *restāre.* Some of these compounds want the supine. *Distāre* has neither perf. nor supine. *Praestāre* has (in later authors only) sup. *praestĭtum,* but very frequently *praestatūrus.*

Tŏno, āre, tonŭi, (tonĭtum,) *to thunder.*

So *attonāre* (part. *attonĭtus*), *into- nāre* (part. *intonātus*); but *circumto- nāre* wants the third root.

Vĕto, āre, vetŭi, vetĭtum, *to pro- hibit, forbid.*

☞ Among the irregularities of the first conjugation may be included the perfect participles of the verbs *coenāre* and *jurāre,* which are used in an active sense ; — *coenātus,* " having dined"; *jurātus,* " having sworn." So the compounds *conjurātus,* " having conspired," and *injurātus,* " one who has not sworn." Among later authors *conspirātus* is used actively like *conju- rātus,* and in the same sense.

II. Second Conjugation.

Regular verbs of the second conjugation end in *ĕo, ēre, ŭi, ĭtum.* E. g.

Dēbĕo, debēre, debŭi, debĭtum, *to owe.*
Hăbĕo, habēre, habŭi, habĭtum, *to have.*
Mĕrĕo, merēre, merŭi, merĭtum, *to earn.*
Tăcĕo, tacēre, tacŭi, tacĭtum, *to be silent.*

The verbs of the second conjugation, which deviate from the forms exhibited in these examples, may be divided into, —

1. Those which are irregular or defective in the formation of the perfect or supine roots, but yet remain within the limits of the conjugation.

2. Those which follow the analogy of the third conjugation in the formation of those parts.

3. Those which want the second and third roots entirely.

4. Semideponentia.

1. The verbs of the second conjugation which are irregular or defective in the second or third root, but still do not tran- scend the limits of the conjugation, are, —

a) Those which have *vi* instead of *vŭi,* or *ēvi* instead of *ŭi,* in the perfect.

Căvĕo, ēre, cāvi, cautum, *to beware.*
So *praecavēre.*

Connĭveo, ēre, nivi *and* nixi, ——, *to close the eyes, to wink.*

Deleo, ēre, delēvi, delētum, *to extinguish, destroy.*

Făveo, ēre, fāvi, fautum, *to favor.*

Ferveo, ēre, fervi *and* ferbŭi, ——, *to glow, to be hot.*

Obsolete are the forms *fervit, fervat, fervēre,* according to the third conj. The double perfect (in *vi* and *bŭi*) extends also to the inchoatives *defervescēre, effervescēre,* and *refervescēre.* But *confervescēre* has generally *conferbui.*

Flĕo, flēre, flēvi, flētum, *to weep.*

Fŏveo, fovēre, fōvi, fōtum, *to cherish.*

Mŏveo, ēre, mōvi, mōtum, *to move.*

So the compos. *amovēre, admovēre, commovēre, permovēre,* &c.

The root OL, *to grow,* gives rise to the compos. *abolĕo,* I abolish;

aboleso, I cease; *adoleo* and *adolesco,* I grow up; *exoleo* or *exolesco* and *obsolĕo* or *obsolesco,* I grow out of use; all of which have *ēvi* in the perfect.

The supine of *aboleo* is *abolĭtum.* The rest want this part entirely, but have given rise to the adjectives *adultus, exolētus,* and *obsolētus.*

Păveo, ēre, pāvi, ——, *to fear, tremble.*

From this the inchoative *expavesco, ēre, expāvi,* of which the perfect is especially frequent.

The root PLE, *to fill,* gives rise to the compos. *complĕo, explĕo,* and *implĕo,* I fill, fill up; all of which have *ēvi, ētum.*

Vŏveo, ēre, vōvi, vōtum, *to vow.*

So the compos. *devovēre,* to curse.

b) Those which have *tum* or *sum* instead of *ĭtum* in the supine.

Censeo, ēre, censui, censum, *to suppose, think.*

The participle *census* occurs with an active sense. So also *census sum,* from a deponent *censeor.* *Percenseo* wants the supine. *Accenseo* has *accensus; succenseo, successurus;* and *recenseo,* two supines *recensum* and *recensitum.*

Dŏceo, ēre, docŭi, doctum, *to teach.*

So the compos. *dedocēre, edocēre,* and *perdocēre.*

Misceo, ēre, miscŭi, mistum *or* mixtum, *to mix.*

The supine *mixtum* is the more common and correct. Compos. are *admiscēre, commiscēre, immiscēre, permiscēre.*

Tĕneo, ēre, tenŭi, (tentum,) *to hold.*

Compos. *abstĭnēre, attĭnēre, contĭnēre, detĭnēre, distĭnēre, retĭnēre,* and *sustĭnēre,* all of which have *tentum* in the supine. *Pertĭnēre* wants the supine, and the simple *tentum* rarely occurs.

Torreo, ēre, torrŭi, tostum, *to roast.*

c) Those which have *ŭi* in the perfect regularly, but no supine.

Arceo, ēre, arcŭi, *to drive away.*

But the compos. *coёrcēre* and *exercēre* have a supine in *ĭtum.*

Calleo, ēre, callŭi, *to be callous.*

Candeo, ēre, candŭi, *to shine, to glow.*

Egeo, ēre, egŭi, *to want, need.*

Compos. *indigēre.*

Emineo, ēre, eminŭi, *to project, rise aloft.*

Floreo, ēre, florŭi, *to bloom, flourish.*

Frondeo, ēre, frondŭi (*and* effrondŭi), *to have leaves.*

Horreo, ēre, horrŭi, *to shiver, shudder.*

So *abhorrēre* and a number of inchoatives.

Langueo, ēre, langŭi, *to languish.*

Lăteo, ēre, lătŭi, *to be concealed, to be hid.*

Compos. *interlatēre, perlatēre,* and *sublatēre.*

Mădeo, ēre, mădŭi, *to be wet.*

Nĭteo, ēre, nĭtŭi, *to shine.*

Compos. *enitēre, internitēre,* and *praenitēre.*

Oleo, ēre, olŭi, *to smell.*
  Compos. *obŏlēre, redŏlēre,* and *sub-ŏlēre.*
Palleo, ēre, pallŭi, *to be pale.*
Păteo, ēre, patŭi, *to stand open.*
Rĭgeo, ēre, rigŭi, *to be stiff.*
Rŭbeo, ēre, rubŭi, *to be red.*
Sĭleo, ēre, silŭi, *to be silent.*
Sorbeo, ēre, sorbui, *to sip.*
  The perfect *sorpsi* rarely occurs.
  Compos. are *absorbēre* and *exsorbēre.*
Sordeo, ēre, sordŭi, *to be filthy.*

Splendeo, ēre, splendŭi, *to shine.*
Stŭdeo, ēre, studŭi, *to strive.*
Stŭpeo, ēre, stupŭi, *to be aston-ished, amazed.*
Tĭmeo, ēre, timŭi, *to be afraid.*
Torpeo, ēre, torpŭi, *to be torpid.*
Tŭmeo, ēre, tumŭi, *to be tumid, to swell.*
Vĭgeo, ēre, vigŭi, *to be lively, strong.*
Vĭreo, ēre, virŭi, *to be green.*

REMARK. — Besides the verbs here enumerated, there are a number of others, derived from adjectives. But these occur more rarely in the form here presented, and are generally inchoatives. Cf. *F.*

2. The verbs of the second conjugation which form the per-fect and supine after the analogy of the third, are as follows : —

a) Those which have *i* in the perfect and *sum* in the supine.

Mordeo, ēre, momordi, morsum, *to bite.*
Pendeo, ēre, pependi, pensum, *to hang.*
  The compos. *dependeo* and *impendeo* lose the reduplication: *dependi, impen-di.*
Prandeo, ēre, prandi, pransum, *to dine.*
  The participle *pransus* has an active sense, "having dined."
Sĕdeo, ēre, sēdi, sessum, *to sit.*
  So the compos. *assidēre, circumse-dēre* or *circumsidēre, desidēre, insidēre, obsidēre, possidēre,* and *supersedēre.* But *dissidēre* and *praesidēre* want the supine.

Strīdeo, ēre, stridi, ——, *to hiss.*
  This verb wants the supine. In poetry the infinitive is often *strīdēre.*
Spondeo, ēre, spopondi, sponsum, *to vow, promise.*
  Compounds drop the reduplication; as, *despondeo, desponsi; respondeo, re-sponsi.*
Tondeo, ēre, totondi, tonsum, *to shave.*
  Compounds without reduplication are *attondeo, attondi; detondeo, deton-di.*
Vĭdeo, ēre, vīdi, visum, *to see.*
  So the compos. *invidēre, pervidēre, praevidēre,* and *providēre.*

b) Those which have *si* in the perfect and *sum* in the supine.

Ardeo, ēre, arsi, arsum, *to be on fire, to burn.*
Denseo, ēre, densi, densus (*ad-jective*), *to thicken.*
Haereo, ēre, haesi, haesum, *to ad-here, stick.*
  Compos. are *adhaerēre, cohaerēre, inhaerēre.*
Jubeo, ēre, jussi, jussum, *to com-mand, bid.*
Maneo, ēre, mansi, mansum, *to remain.*
  Compos. *permanēre, remanēre.*

Mulceo, ēre, mulsi, mulsum, *to soothe, caress.*
  Compos. *demulcēre* and *permulcēre.* The participle *permulctus* for *permul-sus* is doubtful.
Mulgeo, ēre, mulsi, mulsum, *to milk.*
  Comp. part. *emulsus.*
Rīdeo, ēre, rīsi, rīsum, *to laugh.*
  Compos. *arridēre, deridēre, irridēre, subridēre.*
Suadeo, ēre, suāsi, suāsum, *to ad-vise.*
  Compos. *dissuadēre, persuadēre.*

Tergeo, ēre, tersi, tersum, *to wipe.*
This verb is even more frequently of the third conj., *tergo, ĕre, si, sum.* But

the compos. *abstergēre, detergēre, extergēre,* are more commonly of the second.

c) Those which have *si* or *xi* in the perfect, and *tum* in the supine, or supine wanting.

Augeo, ēre, auxi, auctum, *to increase.*

Frigeo, ēre, frixi, ——, *to be cold.*

Indulgeo, ēre, indulsi, indultum, *to indulge.*

Lūceo, ēre, luxi, ——, *to shine.*

Lūgeo, ēre, luxi, ——, *to mourn.*

Torqueo, ēre, torsi, tortum, *to turn, twist.*
Compos. *contorquēre, distorquēre, extorquēre.*

d) Those which have *si* in the perfect, but no supine.

Algeo, ēre, alsi, *to be cold.*
The supine is wanting, but an adjective *alsus, a, um,* cool, cold, exists.

Fulgeo, ēre (*in poetry also* fulgĕre), fulsi, *to glitter.*

Turgeo, ēre, tursi (*rarely*), *to swell.*

Urgeo (urgueo), ēre, ursi, *to urge, impel.*

3. Those which have neither perfect nor supine.

Aveo, ēre, *to desire.* (Cf. p. 672.)
Calveo, ēre, *to be bald.*
Cāneo, ēre, *to be gray.*
Cieo, ciēre, *to move, rouse.*
    An obsolete form of this verb is *cio, cire.* Both have the common perfect *cīvi,* supine *cītum* (from *cieo*) and *cĭtum* (from *cio*). Compos. are *concieo, excieo, incieo, percieo.* Participles in use are *concītus, excītus,* moved, excited; but *excĭtus,* called out. So *incītus* and *percītus* in the sense of "to move"; but *accīre,* to call, has only *accītus.* From *cĭtum* the frequentative *cĭtāre,* and the compos. *excĭtāre, incĭtāre,* and *suscĭtāre.*

Flāveo, ēre, *to be yellow.*
Foeteo, ēre, *to stink.*
Hĕbeo, ēre, *to be dull.*
Hūmeo, ēre, *to be moist.*
Līveo, ēre, *to be livid.*
Mīneo, ēre, *to hang over.*
    Compos. *imminēre, prominēre.*
Moereo, ēre, *to mourn, to be sad.*
Polleo, ēre, *to have power.*
Renīdeo, ēre, *to shine; to smile.*
Scāteo, ēre (*sometimes* scatēre), *to swarm with.*
Squāleo, ēre, *to be filthy.*
Vĕgeo, ēre, *to be active.*

4. The following semideponentia. (Cf. page 161, Rem. 4.)

Audeo, ēre, ausus sum, *to dare, venture.*
    An obsolete perfect is *ausi,* from which the future subjunctive *ausim, ausis, ausit, ausint.* The poets use the participle *ausus* and *inausus* in a passive sense.

Gaudeo, ēre, gavisus sum (*Part. Fut.* gavisūrus), *to rejoice.*

Soleo, ēre, solitus sum, *to be accustomed.*
Compos. impers. *assŏlet.*

III. Third Conjugation.

The verbs of the third conjugation exhibit the greatest diversity in the formation of their perfect and supine. The regular formation of the perfect has already been explained on page 237, Rem. 3, notes † and ‡, and that of the supine on page 246, Rem. 3. For the sake of clearness on this point, we will here enumerate the different classes of regular verbs, arranged according to the termination of their first root, and then add to each class the verbs which deviate from the established rule.

1. Verbs which have a vowel or a *v* before the final *o* of the present, form their perfect in *i* and the supine in *tum*. E. g.

Acuo, ĕre, acŭi, acūtum, *to sharpen.*
Compos. *exacuĕre, peracuĕre,* and *praeacuĕre.*

Arguo, ĕre, argŭi, argūtum, *to accuse.*
Compos. *coarguĕre, redarguĕre.* The perf. part. is commonly *convictus.*

Congruo, ĕre, congrŭi, ——, *to agree.*
Supine wanting. So also *ingruĕre* (primitive root not in use).

Imbuo, ĕre, imbŭi, imbūtum, *to dip, steep.*

Induo, ĕre, indŭi, indūtum, *to put on.*
So also *exuĕre.*

Luo, ĕre, lŭi, lūtum (luitūrus), *to pay, atone for.*
From another *luo,* I wash, are derived the compos. *abluĕre, eluĕre, diluĕre,* and *polluĕre,* all of which have a supine in *lūtum.*

Metuo, ĕre, metŭi, ——, *to fear.*
The supine *metūtum* rarely occurs.

Minuo, ĕre, minŭi, minūtum, *to diminish.*
Compos. *comminuĕre, deminuĕre, diminuĕre,* and *imminuĕre.*

(Nuo, *to beckon,* is not used.)
Compos. *abnŭo, ĕre, abnŭi, abnutūrus,* to deny, refuse. Others are *annuĕre, innuĕre,* and *renuĕre,* all without supine.

Pluo, ĕre, plŭi, *generally impersonal* pluit, *it rains.*
Compos. *compluĕre, impluĕre,* and *perpluĕre,* commonly likewise impersonal and without supine.

Ruo, ĕre, rŭi, ruitūrus, *to fall.*
Compos. have supine in *rŭtum*; as, *diruĕre, obruĕre,* and *proruĕre.* But *corruĕre* and *irruĕre* want the supine.

Solvo, ĕre, solvi, solūtum, *to loosen, untie.*
Compos. *absolvĕre, dissolvĕre, exsolvĕre, persolvĕre.*

Spuo, ĕre, spŭi, spūtum, *to spit.*
Compos. *conspuĕre* and *despuĕre.*

Statuo, ĕre, statŭi, statūtum, *to place, establish.*
Compos. *constituĕre, destituĕre, instituĕre, restituĕre,* and *substituĕre.*

Sternuo, ĕre, sternŭi, ——, *to sneeze.*
From this the frequentative *sternutāre.*

Suo, ĕre, sŭi, sūtum, *to sew.*
Compos. *consuĕre, dissuĕre,* and *resuĕre.*

Tribuo, ĕre, tribŭi, tribūtum, *to bestow, impart.*
Compos. *attribuĕre, contribuĕre,* and *distribuĕre.*

Volvo, ĕre, volvi, volūtum, *to roll.*
Compos. *evolvĕre, involvĕre,* and *pervolvĕre.* Frequentative *volutāre.*

Irregular verbs of this class are, —

Căpĭo, ĕre, cēpi, captum, *to take.*
So *antecapĕre.* But other compounds change *ă* into *ĭ,* and the supine *a* into *e*; as, *accĭpĕre, excĭpĕre, decĭpĕre, percĭpĕre, praecĭpĕre, recĭpĕre, suscĭpĕre,* all of which have *ceptum* in the supine.

Cŭpĭo, ĕre, cupivi, cupītum, *to desire.*
An imperf. subj. *cupĭret* occurs. Compos. *discupĕre* and *percupĕre.*

Făcĭo, ĕre, fēci, factum, *to do, make.*
So *arefacĕre, calefacĕre, consuefacĕre, frigefacĕre, lubefacĕre, patefacĕre,*
satisfacĕre, and *tepefacĕre,* all of which have *fio, fĭeri, factus sum* in the passive. Other compounds change *a* into *i,* and have a passive in *icior,* supine in *ectum*; as, *afficio, afficior, affectum.* So also *conficĕre, deficĕre, interficĕre, officĕre, perficĕre, proficĕre,* and *reficĕre.*

Fluo, ĕre, fluxi, fluxum, *to flow.*
Compos. *affluĕre, confluĕre, effluĕre, interfluĕre.*

Fŏdĭo, ĕre, fōdi, fossum, *to dig.*
Compos. *confodĕre, effodĕre, perfodĕre, suffodĕre.*

Fŭgio, ĕre, fūgi, fugĭtum, *to flee*.
Compos. *aufŭgĕre, confŭgĕre, effŭgĕre*, and *perfŭgĕre*.

Jăcio, ĕre, jēci, jactum, *to throw*.
So *superjăcĕre*, which however has also *superjectum*. Other compounds change *á* into *i*, and in the supine into *e*; as, *abjĭcio, abjēci, abjectum*. So also *adjĭcĕre, dejĭcĕre, ejĭcĕre, injĭcĕre, objĭcĕre, rejĭcĕre, transjĭcĕre*, or *trajĭcĕre*.

(Lacio, *frequentat.* lactāre, *I allure*, obsolete.)
Compos. in use are *allĭcio. ĕre, allexi, allectum*, to allure; and so *illĭcĕre* and *pellĭcĕre*. But *elĭcio* has *elĭcui, elĭcĭtum*.

Pārio, ĕre, pepĕri, partum (*but* paritūrus), *to bring forth*.
An infinitive *parĭri* instead of *pări* occurs.

Quătio, ĕre, ——, quassum, *to shake*.

Compos. *concŭtio, ĕre, cŭssi, cŭssum*. So *discŭtio, excŭtio, incŭtio, percŭtio, repercŭtio*.

Răpio, ĕre, rapŭi, raptum, *to seize, rob*.
Compos. *arrĭpio, arrĭpŭi, arreptum*. So *abrĭpĕre, derĭpĕre, erĭpĕre, surrĭpĕre*.

Săpio, ĕre, sapivi *and* sapŭi, ——, *to taste; to be wise*.
So *resĭpĕre*, to smell after. But *desĭpĕre* has no perfect.

Spĕcĭo, ĕre, spexi, spectum, *to see*.
Compos. *aspĭcio, spexi, spectum*. So also *conspĭcĕre, despĭcĕre, dispĭcĕre, inspĭcĕre, perspĭcĕre, respĭcĕre*, and *suspĭcĕre*.

Strŭo, ĕre, struxi, structum, *to build*.
So *construĕre, exstruĕre, destruĕre*, and *instruĕre*.

Vivo, ĕre, vixi, victum, *to live*.

2. Verbs ending in *bo* or *po* form their perfect in *psi* and the supine in *ptum*. E. g.

Carpo, ĕre, carpsi, carptum, *to pluck*.
Compos. *concerpo, concerpsi. concerptum*. So *decerpĕre* and *discerpĕre*.

Glūbo, ĕre, glupsi, gluptum, *to peel*.

Nŭbo, ĕre, nupsi, nuptum, *to veil, to marry*.
Compos. *obnŭbĕre*.

Rēpo, ĕre, repsi, reptum, *to creep*.
Compos. *adrepĕre, irrepĕre, obrepĕre, prorepĕre*, and *subrepĕre*.

Scalpo, ĕre, scalpsi, scalptum, *to carve, engrave*.

Scribo, ĕre, scripsi, scriptum, *to write*.
So the compos. *adscribĕre, describĕre, inscribĕre*, and *praescribĕre*.

Sculpo, ĕre, sculpsi, sculptum, *to cut, sculpture*.
Compos. *exsculpĕre* and *insculpĕre*.

Serpo, ĕre, serpsi, serptum, *to creep*.
So *inserpĕre, proserpĕre*.

Irregular verbs of this class are, —

Accumbo, ĕre, cubŭi, cubĭtum, *to recline*.
So all the compounds of *cubăre*, which assume an *m*; as, *discumbĕre, incumbĕre, occumbĕre, procumbĕre*, and *succumbĕre*.

Bĭbo, ĕre, bĭbi, bĭbĭtum, *to drink*.
Compos. *ebibĕre, imbibĕre*.

Lambo, ĕre, lambi, lambĭtum, *to lick*.

Rumpo, ĕre, rūpi, ruptum, *to burst, break*.
Compos. *abrumpĕre, corrumpĕre, erumpĕre, interrumpĕre, irrumpĕre, perrumpĕre, prorumpĕre*.

Scăbo, ĕre, scabi, ——, *to scratch, rub*.

Strĕpo, ĕre, strepŭi, strepĭtum, *to rumble, rattle*.

3. Verbs ending in *do* or *to* form their perfect in *si* and the supine in *sum*. E. g.

Claudo, ĕre, clausi, clausum, *to shut*.

The compos. are derived from another form, *clūdo*; as, *concludĕre, excludĕre, includĕre, secludĕre*.

Divĭdo, ĕre, divisi, divisum, to divide.

Laedo, ĕre, laesi, laesum, to hurt, injure.

Compos. allīdĕre, collīdĕre, elīdĕre, illīdĕre.

Lūdo, ĕre, lūsi, lūsum, to play.

Compos. alludĕre, colludĕre, deludĕre, eludĕre, and illudĕre.

Plaudo, ĕre, plausi, plausum, to clap, beat.

So applaudĕre. The remaining compos. have ōdo, ōsi, ōsum; as, complodĕre, explodĕre, supplodĕre.

Rādo, ĕre, rāsi, rāsum, to scrape.

So abradĕre, circumradĕre, corrodĕre, deradĕre, and eradĕre.

Rōdo, ĕre, rōsi, rōsum, to gnaw.

Compos. abrodĕre, arrodĕre, circumrodĕre, derodĕre, and perrodĕre.

Trūdo, ĕre, trūsi, trūsum, to push.

Compos. detrudĕre, extrudĕre, protrudĕre.

Vādo, ĕre, ——, ——, to go, walk.

Perfect and supine wanting. But evādo, evāsi, evāsum. So also invadĕre and pervadĕre.

The irregular verbs of this class are, —

a) Those which form their perfect in di and the supine in sum. E. g.

Accendo, ĕre, accendi, accensum, to set on fire.

So incendĕre and succendĕre.

Cūdo, ĕre, cūdi, cūsum, to pound, forge.

Compos. excudĕre, procudĕre.

Defendo, ĕre, di, sum, to defend.

Edo, ĕre, ēdi, ēsum, to eat.

So exedĕre and comedĕre, ēdi, ēsum (but also comestus).

Fundo, ĕre, fūdi, fūsum, to pour.

Compos. are affundĕre, confundĕre, diffundĕre, effundĕre, infundĕre, offundĕre, and profundĕre.

Mando, ĕre, mansi, (rarely) mansum, to chew, masticate.

Offendo, ĕre, di, sum, to offend.

Prehendo (prendo), ĕre, di, sum, to lay hold of.

Compos. apprehendĕre, comprehendĕre, deprehendĕre, and reprehendĕre.

Scando, ĕre, di, sum, to climb.

So ascendĕre, conscendĕre, descendĕre, inscendĕre.

Strido (also strideo), ĕre, stridi, ——, to creak, grate.

b) Those which have reduplicated perfect. E. g.

Cădo, ĕre, cecĭdi, cāsum, to fall.

Compos. incĭdo, incĭdi, incāsum. So occidĕre and recidĕre. But the remaining compos. want the supine; as, accidĭt, concĭdo, decĭdo, and excĭdo.

Caedo, ĕre, cecidi, caesum, to cut.

Compos. abscīdo, abscĭdi, abscīsum. So concidĕre, decidĕre, excidĕre, incidĕre, occidĕre, praecidĕre, &c.

Condo, ĕre, condĭdi, condĭtum, to construct.

So the remaining compos. of dăre, except those mentioned on page 673; as, abdĕre, addĕre, dedĕre, edĕre, perdĕre, reddĕre, tradĕre, and vendĕre. But abscondĕre has generally perf. abscondi instead of abscondĭdi; and instead of the passive vendi, it is common to say venire.

Crēdo, ĕre, crēdidi, crēdĭtum, to believe.

So accrēdĕre, accredĭdi.

Pēdo, ĕre, pĕpēdi, pedĭtum, to break wind.

Pendo, ĕre, pependi, pensum, to weigh.

Compos. appendo, appendi, appensum. So likewise without reduplication dependĕre, expendĕre, impendĕre, perpendĕre, suspendĕre.

Tendo, ĕre, tŏtendi, tensum or tentum, to stretch.

Compos. extendo, extendi, extensum and extentum; and so with both supines detendĕre, ostendĕre, protendĕre, and retendĕre. The rest have supine in tum only; as, attendĕre, contendĕre, *dislendĕre, intendĕre, oblendĕre, prae-tendĕre,* and *subtendĕre.* (But more commonly *extentum, protentum,* and vice versa *ostensum.*)

Tundo, ĕre, tŭtŭdi, tunsum *and* tūsum, *to beat, strike.*

Compos. have only *tūsum,* and no reduplication; as, *contundo, contŭdi, contūsum.* So *extuudĕre, obtundĕre,* and *retundĕre.*

c) Those which have **ss** in the supine, or are otherwise irregular.

Cēdo, ĕre, cessi, cessum, *to give place, to retire.*
So the compos. *abscēdo, accēdo, antecēdo, concēdo, decēdo, discēdo, excēdo, incēdo, intercēdo, recēdo,* and *succēdo.*

Fīdo, ĕre, fīsus sum, *to trust.*
So *confīdĕre, diffīdĕre;* but these have sometimes perf. *confīdi, diffīdi,* instead of *confīsus sum,* &c.

Findo, ĕre, fĭdi, fissum, *to cleave, split.*
So *diffindĕre, diffĭdi.*

Frendo, ĕre, ——, fressum *and* frēsum, *to crush, grind.*
Instead of this also *frendĕre, frendŭi.*

Mēto, ĕre, messŭi, messum, *to reap.*
Compos. *demetĕre.* Instead of *messui* and *demessui* more commonly *messem fēci.*

Mitto, ĕre, mīsi, missum, *to send.*
So the compos. *admitto, amitto, committo, demitto, dimitto, emitto, inmitto, omitto, permitto, praetermitto, promitto, remitto,* and *submitto.*

Pando, ĕre, pandi, passum (*more rarely* pansum), *to lay open, set open.*
Expandĕre has *expansum* and *expassum;* but *dispandĕre,* only *dispansum.*

Pēto, ĕre, petīvi *or* petĭi, petītum, *to ask.*

Compos. are *appēto, compēto, expēto, oppēto,* and *repēto.*

Scindo, ĕre, scĭdi, scissum, *to split, to tear.*
Compos. *conscindo, conscĭdi, conscissum.* So also *discindĕre, interscindĕre, perscindĕre, proscindĕre,* and *rescindĕre.* But *abscindo* has only *abscindĕre, abscĭdi,* and *exscindo* only *exscindĕre.*

Sido, ĕre, sīdi *or* sēdi, sessum, *to take a seat, sit down.*
Perfect and supine commonly from *sĕdēre.* Compos. *consīdo, consēdi, consessum.* So *assīdĕre, desīdĕre, insīdĕre, residĕre,* and *subsīdĕre.*

Sisto, ĕre, stĭti (*obsolete*), stătum, *to put, set.*
But *sisto* in the sense of "to stand still" has *stĕti, stătum.* The compos. are all intransitive and have *stĭti, stĭtum;* as, *consisto, constĭti, constĭtum.* So *adsisto, desisto, existo, insisto, obsisto, persisto,* and *resisto.* *Circumsto* has either *circumstĭti* or *circumstĕti.*

Sterto, ĕre, stertŭi (*obsolete* sterti), ——, *to snore, snort.*

Verto, ĕre, ti, sum, *to turn.*
So the compos. *adverto, animadverto, averto, converto, everto, perverto,* and *subverto.* — *Divertĕre, praevertĕre,* and *revertĕre* are more frequently deponents in the present and imperfect.

4. Verbs ending in *go, co, cto, quo,* and *guo* form their perfect in *xi* and the supine in *ctum.* E. g.

Cingo, ĕre, cinxi, cinctum, *to gird, surround.*
Compos. *accingĕre* and *discingĕre.*

Cŏquo, ĕre, coxi, coctum, *to cook.*
So *concoquĕre* and *decoquĕre.*

Dico, ĕre, dixi, dictum, *to say.*
So the compos. *addico, contradico, edico, indico, interdico,* and *praedico.*

Dūco, ĕre, duxi, ductum, *to lead, conduct.*

So the compos. *abdūcĕre, addūcĕre, circumdūcĕre, condūcĕre,* and a number of others.

Fligo, ĕre, flixi, flictum, *to strike* (obsolete).
Compos. *affligĕre, configĕre, infligĕre.* But *profligāre* is of the first conjugation.

Frigo, ĕre, frixi, frictum (*rarely* frixum), *to roast.*

Jungo, ĕre, junxi, junctum, *to join together.*
So compos. *adjungo, conjungo, disjungo, sejungo,* and *subjungo.*

Lingo, ĕre, linxi, linctum, *to lick.*

Mungo, ĕre, munxi, munctum, *to blow the nose.*
Compos. *emungĕre.*

Plango, ĕre, planxi, planctum, *to strike; to lament.* ·

Rŏgo, ĕre, rexi, rectum, *to guide, direct.*
Compos. *arrigĕre, corrigĕre, dirigĕre, erigĕre, porrigĕre.* To these add *pergo* (for *perrigo*), *perrexi, perrectum,* and *surgo* (for *surrigo*), *surrexi, surrectum.* Compos. of *surgo* are *assurgo, consurgo, exsurgo,* and *insurgo.*

Stinguo, ĕre, ——, ——, *to extinguish* (rarely used).
Compos. in use are *extinguo* and *re-*

stinguo, which have regularly *inxi, inctum.* So also *distinguo* and *instinguo,* but from another root.

Sūgo, ĕre, suxi, suctum, *to suck.*

Tĕgo, ĕre, texi, tectum, *to cover.*
Compos. *contegĕre, detegĕre, obtegĕre, protegĕre,* and *retegĕre.*

Tingo (tinguo), ĕre, xi, ctum, *to dip in, moisten.*

Trăho, ĕre, traxi, tractum, *to draw.*
So compos. *attrăho, contrăho, detrăho, extrăho, pertrăho, protrăho, retrăho,* and *subtrăho.*

Ungo (or unguo), ĕre, unxi, unctum, *to anoint.*
Compos. *perungĕre* and *inungĕre.*

Vĕho, ĕre, vexi, vectum (*frequent.* vecto), *to carry, convey.*
So *advĕhĕre, invĕhĕre.* — The passive is *vĕhor, vĕhi, vectus sum,* to drive, ride. So *circumvĕhor, invĕhor, praetervĕhor.*

The irregular verbs of this class are, —

a) Those which reject the *n* before *ctum* in the supine, or assume *xum.*

Ango, ĕre, anxi, ——, *to choke.* (Supine wanting.)

Clango, ĕre, ——, ——, *to sound.*

Figo, ĕre, fixi, fixum, *to fix or fasten in.*
So *affigĕre, transfigĕre.*

Fingo, ĕre, finxi, fictum, *to form, fashion.*
Compos. *affingĕre, confingĕre, effingĕre,* and *refingĕre.*

Flecto, ĕre, flexi, flexum, *to bend.*
Compos. *inflectĕre.*

Mingo (or mejo), ĕre, minxi, mictum, *to make water.*

Necto, ĕre, nexi *or* nexŭi, nexum, *to tie, bind.*

Ningo, ĕre, ninxi, ——, *to snow* (commonly impers. ningit, &c.).

Pecto, ĕre, pexi, pexum, *to comb.*

Pingo, ĕre, pinxi, pictum, *to paint.*
Compos. *appingĕre, depingĕre,* and *expingĕre.*

Plecto, ĕre, ——, ——, (commonly only passive plector,) *to punish.*
Another *plecto,* to braid, is obsolete, but exists in the deponents *amplector* and *complector, plexus sum.*

Stringo, ĕre, strinxi, strictum, *to draw tight.*
Compos. *adstringĕre, constringĕre, distringĕre, obstringĕre,* and *perstringĕre.*

b) Those which do not change the characteristic consonant in the perfect.

Ăgo, ĕre, ēgi, actum, *to drive; to do.*
Compos. *cŏgo* (for *codgo*), *cŏĕgi, coactum.* So also *abigĕre, adigĕre, exigĕre, perdigĕre, redigĕre, subigĕre,* and *transigĕre.* — *Prodigĕre* wants the supine; *ambigĕre* and *satagĕre* have neither perfect nor supine.

Dēgo, ĕre, dēgi, ——, *to pass, spend* (vitam, *life, &c.*).

Frango, ĕre, frēgi, fractum, *to break.*
Compos. *confringĕre, effringĕre, perfringĕre,* and *refringĕre.*

Ico (or icio), ĕre, ici, ictum, *to strike; to make* (e. g. foedus, a treaty).

Lĕgo, ĕre, lēgi, lectum, *to read.*
So compos. *perlegĕre, praelegĕre,* and with *i* in the root *colligĕre, deligĕ-*

re, elĭgĕre, and *selĭgĕre.* But *dĭlĭgo, intellĭgo,* and *neglĭgo* have *lexi* in the perfect.

Linquo, ĕre, liqui, ——, *to leave.* (Poetical.)
Compos. *relinquo, relĭqui, relĭctum.*

So also *delinquĕre* and *derelinquĕre.*

Vinco, ĕre, vici, victum, *to conquer, vanquish.*
Compos. *convincĕre, devincĕre,* and *evincĕre.*

c) Those which reduplicate in the perfect.

Pango, ĕre, pepĭgi, pactum, *to make a compact.*
But *pango,* I set or fix in, has *panxi* or *pēgi, panctum.* The compos. *compingo, impingo* have *pēgi, pactum.* So also *oppango, oppēgi.* But *depango* and *repango* have no perfect.

Parco, ĕre, peperci, parsum, *to spare, save.*
The perfect *parsi* is obsolete, and

the supine *parcĭtum* uncertain. Compos. *comparcĕre.*

Pungo, ĕre, pupŭgi, punctum, *to stab.*
Compos. *compungo, punxi, punctum.* So *dispungĕre* and *interpungĕre.*

Tango, ĕre, tetĭgi, tactum, *to touch.*
Compos. *attingo, attĭgi, attactum.* So *contingo, contĭgi,* and the impersonals *contingit, contĭgit; obtingit, obtĭgit.*

d) Those which form their perfect in *si* and the supine in *sum.*

Mergo, ĕre, mersi, mersum, *to immerse, dip.*
So *demergĕre, emergĕre, immergĕre, submergĕre.*

Spargo, ĕre, sparsi, sparsum, *to scatter.*
Compos. *adspergĕre, conspergĕre, ex-*

spergĕre, and *respergĕre,* all with *spersi, spersum.*

Tergo, ĕre, tersi, tersum, *to wipe.*
But also *tergeo, ēre* (compare p. 677).

Vergo, ĕre, ——, ——, *to incline or turn.*

5. Verbs ending in *lo, mo, no,* and *ro* are mostly irregular.

The following in *mo* may be regarded as regular: —

Cŏmo, ĕre, compsi, comptum, *to adorn.*

Dēmo, ĕre, dempsi, demptum, *to take away.*

Prōmo, ĕre, prompsi, promptum, *to take out, to draw.*
So compos. *deprōmĕre, exprōmĕre.*

Sūmo, ĕre, sumpsi, sumptum, *to take.*
Compos. *absūmĕre, adsūmĕre, consūmĕre, desūmĕre.*

Temno, ĕre, ——, ——, *to despise.* (Poetical.)
Compos. *contemnĕre, contempsi, contemptum.*

The irregular verbs of this class are, —

a) Those which have *vi* in the perfect.

Cerno, ĕre, crēvi, crētum, *to sift.*
In the sense of " to see," the perfect and supine do not occur. Compos. *decerno, decrēvi, decrētum;* and so *discernĕre, excernĕre,* and *secernĕre.*

Lĭno, ĕre, lēvi (*or* līvi), lĭtum, *to smear on, daub on.*
So compos. *callĭno, illĭno, oblĭno* (part. *oblĭtus*), and *perlĭno.* Other compos. are of the fourth conj., as *allĭnire, circumlinire,* and *illinire.*

Sĕro, ĕre, sēvi, sătum, *to sow.*
But *sero,* I join, connect, has *serŭi, sertum.* The compos. *consĕro* and *in-*

sĕro have either *sēvi, sĭtum* or *serŭi, sertum,* according to the sense. *Desĕro, dissĕro,* and *exsĕro* have *serŭi, sertum* only.

Sĭno, ĕre, sĭvi, sĭtum, *to allow, permit.*
From this perhaps also *situs,* situate. Compos. *desĭno, desĭi, desĭtum.* Instead of perf. also *desitus est.*

Sperno, ĕre, sprēvi, sprētum, *to disdain.*

Sterno, ĕre, strāvi, strātum, *to prostrate.*

58

So compos. *consterno, insterno,* and *prosterno.*

So *conterěre.* But *attěro* has either *attrěvi* or *atterši.*

Těro, ěre, trīvi, trītum, *to rub.*

b) Those which reduplicate in the perfect.

Căno, ěre, cecĭni, cantum, *to sing, sound.*

Compos. *succĭno, succinši, succentum.* So also *occĭno* or *occăno.* But *accĭno, intercĭno,* and *recĭno* (or *recăno*) want the perf. and supine.

Curro, ěre, cucurri, cursum, *to run.*

The compos. *accurro, decurro, excurro, incurro, percurro,* and *praecur-*

ro have more frequently *curri* than *cucurri* in the perfect.

Fallo, ěre, fefelli, falsum, *to deceive.*

Compos. *refello, refelli* without supine.

Pello, ěre, pepŭli, pulsum, *to drive away.*

Compos. *appello, appŭli, appulsum.* So the rest, *compello, depello, expello, impello, perpello, propello,* and *repello.*

c) Those which follow the analogy of the second conjugation.

Alo, ěre, alŭi, alĭtum *or* altum, *to nourish.*

Altus in Cicero and Sallust, *alĭtus* in later writers.

Cello (*not in use*), *but*

Compos. *antecello, excello,* and *praecello,* I excel, perf. *cellŭi,* supine wanting. But *percello, percŭli, perculsum,* to strike down.

Cŏlo, ěre, colŭi, cultum, *to cultivate.*

So *excolěre, incolěre,* and *percolěre.*

Consŭlo, ěre, ŭi, ultum, *to consult.*

Gěmo, ěre, ŭi, ĭtum, *to sigh, groan.*

Compos. *congĕmo* or *congemisco, ingĕmo* or *ingemisco,* perf. *ŭi,* supine wanting.

Gigno, ěre, genŭi, genĭtum, *to beget, produce.*

Perf. and supine from the obsolete *geno.* So *ingigněre* and *progigněre.*

Mŏlo, ěre, ŭi, ĭtum, *to grind* (*in a mill*).

Occŭlo, ěre, ŭi, ultum, *to conceal, hide.*

Pōno, ěre, pŏsŭi, pŏsĭtum, *to lay, place.*

Obsolete perf. *posĭvi.* Compos. *antepōno, appōno, compōno, depōno, dispōno, expōno, oppōno, praepōno, postpōno,* and *sepōno.*

Trěmo, ěre, ŭi, ——, *to tremble.*

Compos. *contremĕre.*

Vŏmo, ěre, ŭi, ĭtum, *to vomit.*

Compos. *evomĕre, revomĕre.*

d) Those which are otherwise irregular in the perfect and supine.

Ěmo, ěre, ēmi, emptum, *to buy.*

Compos. *adĭmo, adēmi, ademtum.* So *coëmĕre, dirimĕre, eximĕre, interimĕre, perimĕre,* and *redimĕre.*

Fěro, ferre, tŭli, lātum, *to bear, carry.* (Cf. page 669.)

(Fŭro), fŭrěre, ——, ——, *to rage.*

Perf. and supine wanting. So also first person singular. For the perf. commonly *insanĭvi.*

Gěro, ěre, gessi, gestum, *to carry, bear; perform.*

Compos. *congĕrěre, dīgerěre,* and *ingerěre.*

Prěmo, ěre, pressi, pressum, *to press.*

Compos. *comprimĕre, deprimĕre, exprimĕre, opprimĕre,* and *supprimĕre.*

Psallo, ěre, psalli, ——, *to play on a stringed instrument.*

Quaero, ěre, quaesĭvi, quaesītum, *to inquire, to seek.*

So compos. *acquīro, conquīro, exquīro, inquīro, perquīro,* and *requīro.*

Ūro, ěre, ussi, ustum, *to burn.*

So *adūrěre, comburěre, exurěre,* and *inurěre.*

Vello, ĕre, velli or vulsi, vulsum, to pluck, pick.

So *avello, evello,* and *revello.* But *convello* and *divello* have only *velli* in the perfect.

Verro, ĕre, verri, versum, to sweep.

Compos. *everrĕre.*

6. Verbs in *so* and *xo* are,—

Depso, ĕre, depsŭi, depsĭtum *and* depstum, *to knead.*

Pinso, ĕre, pinsŭi or pinsi, pinsĭtum *or* pistum, *to pound, grind.*

Texo, ĕre, texŭi, textum, *to weave.*

Compos. are *attexo, contexo, obtexo, pertexo, praetexo,* and *retexo.*

Viso, ĕre, visi, ——, *to go to see, to visit.*

A supine *visum* is borrowed from *vidĕre.*

Some of this class follow the analogy of the fourth conjugation:—

Arcesso (*or* accerso), ĕre, arcessĭvi, arcessĭtum, *to send for.*

Capesso, ĕre, capessĭvi, capessĭtum, *to take up, lay hold of.*

Facesso, ĕre, facessĭvi, facessĭtum, *to perform, accomplish.*

Incesso, ĕre, incessĭvi (*or* incessi), ——, *to attack, assail.*

Lacesso, ĕre, lacessĭvi (*or* ĭi), lacessĭtum, *to provoke.*

7. Verbs in *sco* form their perfect and supine as follows:—

Compesco, ĕre, compescŭi, *to curb, restrain.*

Cresco, ĕre, crēvi, crētum, *to grow.*

So the compos. *concresco, decresco,* and *excresco.* But *accresco, incresco,* and *succresco* want the supine.

Disco, ĕre, didĭci, (discĭtūrus), *to learn.*

Compos. *addisco, addĭdĭci.* So also *ediscĕre* and *dediscĕre.*

Dispesco, ĕre, dispescŭi, ——, *to divide, separate.*

Glisco, ĕre, ——, ——, *to begin, spread.*

Hisco, ĕre, ——, ——, *to yawn; to mutter.*

Nosco (gnosco), ĕre, nōvi, nōtum, *to become acquainted with.*

So *ignosco* and *dignosco.* But *agnosco, cognosco,* and *recognosco* have supine *agnĭtum, cognĭtum,* and *recognĭtum.*

Pasco, ĕre, pāvi, pastum, *to pasture, feed.*

Posco, ĕre, poposci, ——, *to demand, ask.*

So *deposco, exposco,* both with *poposci,* and *reposco* without perfect.

Quiesco, ĕre, quiēvi, quiētum, *to rest.*

Compos. *acquiescĕre, conquiescĕre,* and *requiescĕre.*

Suesco, ĕre, suēvi, suētum, *to accustom one's self.*

Part. *suētus,* accustomed. Compos. *assuesco, consuesco, desuesco,* and *insuesco.*

IV. Fourth Conjugation.

Regular verbs of this conjugation form their perfect in *īvi* or *ĭi,* and the supine in *ītum.* E. g.

Audio, audīre, audīvi *or* audĭi, audītum, *to hear.*

Erŭdio, erudīre, erudīvi *or* erudĭi, erudītum, *to instruct.*

Mūnio, munīre, munīvi *or* munĭi, munītum, *to fortify.*

Vestio, vestīre, vestīvi *or* vestĭi, vestītum, *to clothe.*

Irregular in one or both of the characteristic parts are the following : —

Amicio, ĭre, icŭi *or* ixi, ictum, *to clothe, put on.*
The perf. *amicŭi, amixi,* and *amicĭvi* scarcely ever occurs.

Aperio, ĭre, aperŭi, apertum, *to open.*
So *operio* and *cooperio.* But *comperio* and *reperio* have *pĕri, pertum.*

Cio, ĭre, cīvi, cītum, *to move, excite.*
This is the old and regular form for *cieo, cĭvi, cĭtum,* on which see p. 677. 3.

Eo, ĭre, īvi, ĭtum, *to go.* (See page 669.)

Farcio, ĭre, farsi, fartum (farctum), *to stuff.*
Supine more rarely *farsum.* Compos. *confercio* and *refercio, fersi, fertum.* Others are *infercio* and *effercio.*

Ferio, ĭre, ——, ——, *to strike.*
In the perf. active *percussi,* and in the passive *ictus sum,* are commonly used.

Ferocio, ĭre, ——, ——, *to be insolent, wild.*

Fulcio, ĭre, fulsi, fultum, *to prop.*
The perfect of *fulcio* has the same form as that of *fulgeo.*

Haurio, ĭre, hausi, haustum, *to draw.*
Supine more rarely *hausum;* but frequently *hausūrus.*

Punio, ĭre, īvi *or* ĭi, ĭtum, *to punish.*

Regular, except that its passive forms sometimes occur in a deponent sense.

Quĕo, quīre, quīvi *or* quĭi, quĭtum, *to be able.* (Cf. page 670.)

Raucio, ĭre, rausi, rausum, *to be hoarse.*
Compos. *irraucio.*

Sălio, ĭre, salŭi *or* salĭi, saltum, *to spring, leap.*
Compos. *desilire, exsilire, insilire,* &c., generally perf. *silŭi,* rather than *silĭi* or *silĭvi.* But *salire,* to salt, is regular.

Sancio, ĭre, sanxi, sanctum *and* sancītum, *to ordain, appoint.*
Sancĭtus is generally participle, and *sanctus* adjective.

Sarcio, ĭre, sarsi, sartum, *to patch, mend.*
Compos. *resarcire.*

Sentio, ĭre, sensi, sensum, *to feel, think.*
So *consentire, dissentire,* and *praesentire.* But instead of *assentio,* commonly *assentior* deponent.

Sepelio, ĭre, īvi, sepultum, *to bury.*
Sepio, ĭre, sepsi, septum, *to hedge in.*
Vĕnio, ĭre, vēni, ventum, *to come.*
Compos. *advenire, convenire, invenire, obvenire,* and *pervenire.*

Vincio, ĭre, vinxi, vinctum, *to bind.*
So compos. *devincire.*

REMARK. — Desiderative verbs in *ūrio* generally have neither perfect nor supine ; as, *dormitūrio, ĭre,* I desire to sleep; *coenatūrio, ĭre,* I desire to dine. The only exceptions are *esŭrio, esurĭvi, esurĭtūrus,* I am hungry ; *nuptūrio, nupturĭvi,* I wish to get married, and *partūrio, parturĭvi,* I wish to bring forth.

E. DEPONENT VERBS.

I. Deponent verbs of the first conjugation are all regular, and conjugated like *hortor* (page 173, *A*). E. g.

Adversor, āri, ātus sum, *to oppose, resist.*
Arbitror, āri, ātus sum, *to suppose, think.*
Aspernor, āri, ātus sum, *to despise.*
Auxilior, āri, ātus sum, *to help.*
Calumnior, āri, ātus sum, *to calumniate.*

Crimĭnor, āri, ātus sum, *to accuse.*
Cunctor, āri, ātus sum, *to hesitate.*
Domĭnor, āri, ātus sum, *to rule.*
Epŭlor, āri, ātus sum, *to feast.*
Fenĕror, āri, ātus sum, *to lend on interest.*
Glorior, āri, ātus sum, *to boast.*
Hospĭtor, āri, ātus sum, *to be a guest.*

Imĭtor, āri, ātus sum, *to imitate.*
Jacŭlor, āri, ātus sum, *to throw.*
Lĭcĭtor, āri, ātus sum, *to bid.*
Luctor, āri, ātus sum, *to struggle.*
Medĭcor, āri, ātus sum, *to heal.*
Modĕror, āri, ātus sum, *to moderate.*
Negotĭor, āri, ātus sum, *to do business.*
Odōror, āri, ātus sum, *to smell.*
Oscŭlor, āri, ātus sum, *to kiss.*
Parasĭtor, āri, ātus sum, *to act the parasite.*
Philosŏphor, āri, ātus sum, *to philosophize.*
Proelĭor, āri, ātus sum, *to fight.*

Ratiocĭnor, āri, ātus sum, *to reason, compute.*
Rustĭcor, āri, ātus sum, *to rusticate.*
Sciscĭtor, āri, ātus sum, *to inquire into.*
Stipŭlor, āri, ātus sum, *to stipulate.*
Suspĭcor, āri, ātus sum, *to suspect.*
Testifĭcor, āri, ātus sum, *to witness, attest.*
Tūtor, āri, ātus sum, *to protect.*
Urĭnor, āri, ātus sum, *to dive.*
Vāgor, āri, ātus sum, *to ramble.*
Venĕror, āri, ātus sum, *to venerate.*
Vociferor, āri, ātus sum, *to vociferate.*

To the above might be added many others equally regular.

The following occur only in certain authors as deponent, and more commonly as active verbs: *communicor, commurmŭror, fluctuor, frutĭcor, lacrĭmor, luxurior, nictor,* and *relifĭcor.*

Cicero employs *adŭlor, arbĭtror, crimĭnor,* and *dignor* both as deponent and as passive verbs.

II. The deponent verbs of the second conjugation are, —

Fateor, ēri, fassus sum, *to confess.*
Compos. *confĭteor, confessus sum; profĭteor, professus sum.* But *diffĭteor* wants the participle.

Liceor, ēri, licĭtus sum, *to offer a bid.*
So compos. *pollĭcēri.*

Medeor, ēri, ——, *to heal.*
Participle commonly *medĭcātus* from *medĭcāri.*

Mereor, ēri, merĭtus sum, *to merit, earn.*
Compos. *commerēri, demerēri,* and *promerēri.*

Misereor, ēri, miserĭtus or misertus sum, *to pity.*
Frequently impersonally *miseretur* or *miseret me.*

Reor, rēri, ratus sum, *to suppose.*

Tueor, ēri, tuĭtus sum, *to guard, protect.*
An obsolete form of this is *tuor* of the third conjugation, from which the adjective *tutus.* Compos. are *contuēri* and *intuēri.*

Vereor, ēri, verĭtus sum, *to fear.*
Compos. *reverēri* and *subverēri.*

III. The deponent verbs of the third conjugation are, —

Apiscor, apisci, aptus sum, *to gain, acquire.* (Obsolete.)
Compos. *adipiscor, adeptus sum,* and *indipiscor, indeptus sum,* with the same sense.

Divertor, *to turn aside;* praevertor, *to outstrip;* and revertor, *to return.*
The perfect of these verbs is derived from the active form *verto;* hence commonly *reverti, reverteram,* &c., for *reversus sum.* The part. *reversus,* however, has an active sense, "having returned."

Expergiscor, expergisci, experrectus sum, *to awake.*
From this *expergefacere,* part. *ex-*
pergefactus. But the verb *expergēre,* part. *expergĭtus,* is obsolete.

Fruor, frui, fruĭtus *or* fructus sum, *to enjoy.*
Compos. *perfruor, perfructus sum.*

Fungor, fungi, functus sum, *to perform.*
Compos. *defungi, perfungi.*

Grădior, grădi, gressus sum, *to step, walk.*
Compos. *aggredior, aggrĕdi, aggressus sum.* So also *congrĕdi, digrĕdi, egrĕdi, ingrĕdi, progrĕdi,* and *regrĕdi.*

Invĕhor, invĕhi, invectus sum, *to inveigh against.*

Irascor, irasci, ——, *to be angry.*
(Inchoative.)
Irātus sum has the sense of the present, "I am angry." For the perf. *succensui* is used.

Lābor, lābi, lapsus sum, *to glide, slip, fall.*
Compos. *collābi, delābi, dilābi, prolābi,* and *relābi.*

Lŏquor, lŏqui, locūtus sum, *to speak.*
Compos. *allŏqui, collŏqui, elŏqui, interlŏqui, oblŏqui.*

Miniscor (*not used*).
From it the compos. *comminiscor, comminisci, commentus sum,* to devise, imagine ; and *reminiscor, reminisci,* with the perf. *recordātus sum,* to remember. — The part. *commentus* has a passive sense, " devised," " invented."

Mŏrior, mŏri, mortuus sum, *fut. part.* moritūrus, *to die.*
Obsolete infinitive *morīri.* Compos. *commori, demori,* and *emori.*

Nanciscor, nancisci, nactus sum, *to obtain.*
Part. sometimes written *nanctus.*

Nascor, nasci, nātus sum, *to be born.*
Original form *gnascor,* which still exists in *agnatus* and *cognatus.* Compos. *enascor, innascor,* and *renascor.*

Nītor, niti, nīsus *or* nixus sum, *to strive, to rely upon.*
Compos. *adnīti, connīti, enīti,* and *obnīti.*

Obliviscor, oblivisci, oblitus sum, *to forget.*

Paciscor, pacisci, pactus sum, *to bargain, stipulate.*
Compos. *compacisci* or *compecisci, depacisci* or *depecisci,* all with *pactus sum.*

Pascor, pasci, pastus sum, *to feed, graze.*

Patior, păti, passus sum, *to suffer.*
Compos. *perpetior, perpěti, perpessus sum.*

Plecto, plectĕre, *to plait, braid,* gives rise to the
Compos. *amplector* and *complector, complexus sum,* to embrace.

Proficiscor, proficisci, profectus sum, *to travel, to depart.*

Quĕror, quĕri, questus sum, *to complain.*
Compos. *conquĕri.*

Ringor, ringi, ——, *to show one's teeth ; to chafe.*

Sĕquor, sĕqui, secūtus sum, *to follow.*
Compos. *assĕqui, consĕqui, exsĕqui, insĕqui, obsĕqui, persĕqui, prosĕqui,* and *subsĕqui.*

Ulciscor, ulcisci, ultus sum, *to revenge, punish.*

Utor, ūti, ūsus sum, *to use, enjoy.*
Compos. *abūti, deūti.*

Vescor, vesci, ——, *to eat, feed upon.*
The place of a perfect is supplied by *ēdi.*

IV. The deponent verbs of the fourth conjugation are, —

Adsentior, adsentīri, adsensus sum, *to assent.*
Also active, in the same sense, *adsentio, adsensi, adsensum ;* but more commonly deponent.

Blandior, blandīri, blandītus sum, *to flatter.*

Experior, experīri, expertus sum, *to experience.*
But *comperior,* I learn, am informed, is only used in the present ; perf. *compěri* from *comperio.*

Largior, largīri, largītus sum, *to lavish.*
Compos. *delargior.*

Mentior, mentīri, mentītus sum, *to lie, to tell falsehoods.*

Metior, metīri, mensus sum, *to measure.*
Compos. *dimetīri, emetīri,* and *permetīri.*

Molior, molīri, molītus sum, *to labor, strive, toil.*
Compos. *amolīri* and *demolīri.*

Opperior, opperīri, oppertus *or* opperitus sum, *to wait for, expect.*

Ordior, ordīri, orsus sum, *to begin, commence.*

Compos. *exordīri* and *redordīri.*

Orior, oriri, ortus sum (*fut. part.* oritūrus), *to rise.*

The Pres. Indic. follows the third conjug. *orēris, oritur, orimur.* But imperfect either *orirer* or *orērer.* So the compos. *coorior* and *exorior.* But *adorior* has commonly *adoriris* and *adoritur,* instead of *adorēris* and *adorītur.* — The fut. part. *oriundus* has the peculiar sense "sprung or descended from."

Partior, partiri, partitus sum, *to divide.*

Compos. *dispertior, dispertītus sum.*

So also *impertior* or *impartior.* All these also active, *partio, dispertio,* and *impertio.*

Potior, potiri, potītus sum, *to take possession of.*

The Pres. and Imperf. Subj. sometimes follow the third conjugation, *potītur, potimur, poterētur, poterēmur.*

Punior, puniri, punītus sum, (*instead of the active* punio,) *to punish*

Sortior, sortiri, sortītus sum, *to draw lots.*

F. INCHOATIVE VERBS.

Inchoative verbs end in *sco,* and are formed either from nouns or adjectives, or from other verbs.

The verbs from which inchoatives are formed are commonly of the second conjugation, but the inchoatives themselves are invariably of the third.

The inchoatives derived from verbs generally have the perfect, and sometimes also the supine, of their primitives.

The inchoatives derived from nouns or adjectives either want the perfect entirely, or assume *ui,* like those derived from verbs.

The following lists exhibit the most important verbs of this class.

1. Inchoatives derived from verbs, with the perfect and supine of their primitives: —

Abolesco (*oleo*), ĕre, abolēvi, abolētum, *to be annihilated.*

Adolesco (*oleo*), ĕre, adolēvi, adultum, *to grow up.*

Coalesco (*alo*), ĕre, coalui, coalĭtum, *to coalesce.*

Concupisco (*cupio*), ĕre, concupĭvi, concupĭtum, *to desire.*

Convalesco (*valeo*), ĕre, convalui, convalĭtum, *to convalesce.*

Exardesco (*ardeo*), ĕre, exarsi, exarsum, *to grow hot, to become inflamed.*

Exolesco (*oleo*), ĕre, exolēvi, exolētum, *to grow out of use.*

Indolesco (*doleo*), ĕre, indolui, indolĭtum, *to feel pain.*

Inveterasco (*invetĕro*), ĕre, inveterāvi, ātum, *to grow old.*

Obdormisco (*dormio*), ĕre, obdormĭvi, ĭtum, *to fall asleep.* (*So also* edormisco, *to take one's fill of sleep.*)

Revivisco (*vivo*), ĕre, revixi, revictum, *to revive, come to life again.*

Scisco (*scio*), ĕre, scīvi, scītum, *to decree, ordain.*

2. Inchoatives derived from verbs, with the perfect of their primitives: —

Acesco (*aceo*), ĕre, acui, *to grow sour.* So also concesco *and* peracesco.

Albesco *and* exalbesco (*albeo*), ĕre, exalbui, *to grow white.*

Aresco (*areo*), ĕre, arui, *to become dry.*

Calesco (*caleo*), ĕre, calui, *to grow warm.*

Canesco (*caneo*), ĕre, canui, *to turn gray.*

Conticesco (*taceo*), ĕre, conticui, *to become silent.*

Contremisco (*tremo*), ĕre, contremui, *to begin to tremble.*

Defervesco (*ferveo*), ĕre, deferbui, *to cease fermenting.*

Delitesco (*lateo*), ĕre, delitui, *to be concealed.*

Effervesco (*ferveo*), ĕre, efferbui, *to begin to boil.*

Excandesco (*candeo*), ĕre, excandui, *to grow hot.*

Extimesco *and* pertimesco (*timeo*), ĕre, extimui, *to become frightened.*

Floresco *and* de- *or* effloresco (*floreo*), ĕre, efflorui, *to begin to blossom.*

Haeresco *and* ad- *or* inhaeresco (*haereo*), ĕre, inhaesi, *to adhere to, to inhere.*

Horresco *and* ex- *or* perhorresco (*horreo*), ĕre, exhorrui, *to be terrified.*

Ingemisco (*gemo*), ĕre, ingemui, *to begin to sigh.*

Intumesco (*tumeo*), ĕre, intumui, *to begin to swell.*

Irraucisco (*raucio*), ĕre, irrausi, *to grow hoarse.*

Languesco *and* e- *or* relanguesco (*langueo*), ĕre, elangui, *to become languid.*

Liquesco (*liqueo*), ĕre, licui, *to begin to melt.*

Madesco (*madeo*), ĕre, madui, *to become wet.*

Marcesco *and* com- *or* emarcesco (*marceo*). ĕre, emarcui, *to decay, wither.*

Occallesco (*calleo*), ĕre, occalui, *to become callous.*

Pallesco *and* expallesco (*palleo*), ĕre, pallui, *to turn pale.*

Putresco (*putreo*), ĕre, putrui, *to decay.*

Resipisco (*sapio*), ĕre, resipui, *to recover one's senses again.*

Rubesco *and* erubesco (*rubeo*), ĕre, erubui, *to become red, to redden.*

Senesco *and* consenesco (*seneo*), ĕre, consenui, *to grow old.*

Stupesco *and* obstupesco (*stupeo*), ĕre, obstupui, *to become astonished.*

Tabesco (*tabeo*), ĕre, tabui, *to wither ; pass away.*

Tepesco (*tepeo*), ĕre, tepui, *to become tepid.*

Viresco *and* con-, e-, *or* reviresco (*vireo*), virui, *to turn green.*

3. Inchoatives derived from nouns and adjectives, without a perfect : —

Aegresco (*aeger*), ĕre, *to fall sick.*

Ditesco (*dives*). ĕre, *to become rich.*

Dulcesco (*dulcis*), ĕre, *to turn sweet.*

Grandesco (*grandis*), ĕre, *to grow up.*

Gravesco *and* ingravesco (*gravis*), ĕre, *to become heavy ; to grow worse.*

Incurvesco (*curvus*), ĕre, *to become crooked.*

Integrasco (*integer*), ĕre, *to begin anew or afresh.*

Juvenesco (*juvenis*), ĕre, *to grow young again.*

Mitesco (*mitis*), ĕre, *to grow gentle.*

Mollesco (*mollis*), ĕre, *to become soft.*

Pinguesco (*pinguis*), ĕre, *to become fat.*

Plumesco (*pluma*), ĕre, *to become fledged.*

Puerasco *and* repuerasco (*puer*), ĕre, *to grow up to be a boy.*

Sterilesco (*sterilis*), ĕre, *to become sterile.*

Teneresco *and* tenerasco (*tener*), ĕre, *to become tender.*

4. Inchoatives derived from nouns or adjectives, with a perfect in *ui* : —

Crebresco *and* in- *or* percrebresco (*creber*). ĕre, crebrui, *to increase, to grow frequent.*

Duresco *and* obduresco (*durus*), ĕre, durui, *to grow hard.*

Evanesco (*vanus*), ĕre, evanui, *to vanish.*

Innotesco (*notus*), ĕre, innotui, *to become known.*

Macresco (*macer*), ĕre, macrui, *to become lean.*

Mansnesco (*mansuetus*), ĕre, mansuēvi, *to grow gentle.*

Maturesco (*maturus*), ĕre, maturui, *to become ripe.*

Nigresco (*niger*), ĕre, nigrui, *to turn black.*

Obmutesco (*mutus*), ĕre, obmutui, *to become dumb or mute.*

Obsurdesco (*surdus*), ĕre, obsurdui, *to become deaf.*

Recrudesco (*crudus*), ĕre, recrudui, *to break open afresh (of wounds).*

Vilesco *and* evilesco (*vilis*), ĕre, evilui, *to become low, of trifling value.*

INDEX.

N. B. The figures of this Index refer to the pages of the book; the letters or figures after the page-reference, to the divisions or remarks of the lesson contained on that page. The dash —— indicates the repetition of the word at the head of the article. The abbreviation *constr.* stands for *construction of*; *id.* for *the same page.*

aut — aut, 388 and 634.
autem, place of, 38, B.
avarus and avidus, with the genit., 391. 1.
ave, 606. 8.
-ax, verbals in, with the genit., 393, Rem. 2.

B.

bellum, construed like names of towns, 310, b, c.
bene te, 348, note.
benedicere, with the dat., 358, Rem. 3.
biduum, triduum, 322.
-bilis, adjectives in, 505; with the dat., 353. 10; with the supine in u, 250, Rem. 2.
boni facio or consulo, 399, Rem. 2.
bos, declined, 16, note ‖.
brevi, with tempore understood, 194, Rem. 3.
-bundus, verbal adjectives in, 504, B.

C.

C, sound of, 3, E. 1.
canere receptui, to sound a retreat, 367, Rem. 2.
capitis or capite damnare, 410, note.
Cardinal numbers, 73, B; list of, 76 – 78.
caro, omitted, 193, Rem. 3.
Cases of nouns, 7, K.
Cause, ablative of, 418; various other modes of expressing, 419, Rem. 1–6.
causa and gratia, with mea, tua, sua, 584; omitted, 375, b.
cave, form of imperative, 606, Rem. 3; with the subjunct. without ne, 297, G.
-ce and -cine, enclitic, 37, Rem. 1.
cedo, imperative, 672. 9.
celare, with two accus., 340, A.
ceu, with the subjunctive, 576, II.
Ch, sound of, 3, E. 2.
cio or cieo, 677. 3 and 686.
circumdare and circumfundere, constr., 368, D.
cis, citra, 345.
clam, adv. and prep., 625, Rem. 6.
Clauses, co-ordinate and subordinate, 149, E; arrangement of, 657, D.
coenare and habitare, with the genit., 399, Rem. 2.
coepi, conjugated, 672. 4.
Collective nouns, 88, E. 2; with a plural verb, 154, B.
collibet or collibitum est, 404.
com, for cum, in composition with verbs, 125, note 4.

commiserari, constr., 401, Rem. 1.
communis, with dative, 352. 6.
Comparative degree, 212, A. 3; formation of, 213, C; expressed by minus, magis, 212, B. 2, 3; by ante, prae, praeter, and supra, 227, Rem. 5; rendered emphatic by magis, minus, potius, id. Rem. 6.
Comparatives, inflected, 217, A; —— construction of: with the ablative, 224, A; with ablative omitted, 225, Rem. 1; with quam, 225, B; with quam omitted, 227, C; two comparatives connected by quam, 228, D; modified by adverbs, 229, F.
Comparison, of adjectives, 212–217; regular, 213, C; anomalous, 213, D; defective, 214, E; by aeque — ac, minus — quam, 212, B; by magis, maxime, 216, F; —— adjectives which admit of none, 216, G.
Comparison, of adverbs, regular, 220, A; anomalous, id. B; defective, id. C.
compertus, with the genitive, 410, Rem. 5.
complere, constr. 435, B, and Rem. 1.
complures, declined, 104, C; sense of, 107.
compos, with the genitive, 391. 4.
Compound, substantives, 60, D; verbs, 124–126; adverbs, 617. 8; —— subject, 148, D; predicate, id.; sentences, 149, D; words, how divided, 5, d.
conducit, with the dative, 356, A.
confidere, constr., 358, Rem. 4.
Conjugatio Periphrastica, 261, D.
Conjugation of verbs, 110, B; of regular verbs, 664–665; of anomalous verbs, 666–671; of defective verbs, 671–673; of impersonal verbs, 371; —— verbs of the four conjugations alphabetically arranged, 673–689.
Conjunctions, classified, 632–633; copulative, disjunctive, and adversative, how used, 633; double, 634, C; omitted, id. Rem. 3; in correlation with each other, 635, E; adverbs repeated like conjunctions, id. D; place of in sentences, 653, C, and 654, II.
conjunctus, with the ablat., 426, note.
conscius, constr., 391, note †.
Consecutio Temporum, 527–531.
consentaneum est, 288, Rem. 2.
consentire, constr., 359 and 538–539.
considere, constr., 446, F.
Consonants, sounds of, 2–3.
Constructio ad synesin, 168, Rem. 2.
Construction, of sentences, 147–150; of the comparative, 224–230; of the

THE END.

ERRATA.

Page	Line	
2	15	read "*fret*," instead of "*fre*."
40	16	read "Nom. ŭtĕr," instead of "Nom. ŭt."
89	12	read "puercŭlus," instead of "puerlŭlus."
97	27	read "I have them not," instead of "I have it not."
127	28	read "*nolo*," instead of "*volo*."
141	34	read "*comĕdim*" for "*commedim*," and in the line below, "*comĕdam*" for "*commedam*."
145	1	read "*occĭdĕre*," instead of "*accĭdĕre*."
167	20	read "*nŏvus*," instead of "*nōvus*."
220	36	read "Lesson XCIII," instead of "Lesson LXX."
246	16	read "*Quid éi*," instead of "*Quid éo*."
272	36	read "(*veniret,*)" instead of "(*vénĕret*.)"
292	22	read "not lawful," instead of "now lawful."
315	12	read "*Revertŭne*," instead of "*Revertáine*."
341	9	read "tondēre," instead of "tondĕre."
371	14	read "visĕre," and on the line below, "(visĕre)," instead of "visêre."
400	11	read "*prístĭnae*," instead of "*pristínae*."
532	15	read "nancisci," instead of "naucisci."
545	31	read "sine perturbatione."
576	41	read "succensêrem," instead of "succénserem."
578	26	read "has life in him," instead of "keeps up his spirits."
585	9	read "*in itinĕre vestro*," instead of "*itinĕre tuo*."
593	44	read "Cujas," instead of "Cujus."
629	23	read "They looked," instead of "They look."
644	56	read "Quot, quantas," instead of "Quot, quantus."
650	18	read "*detrimentŏque*," instead of "*detrimentaque*."